# DRUGS AND SOCIETY

## FOURTEENTH EDITION

### GLEN R. HANSON, PhD, DDS
*Vice Dean*
*Professor, Pharmacology*
*School of Dentistry*
*University of Utah*
*Salt Lake City, Utah*

### PETER J. VENTURELLI, PhD
*Professor Emeritus*
*Department of Sociology and Criminology*
*Valparaiso University*
*Valparaiso, Indiana*

### ANNETTE E. FLECKENSTEIN, PhD
*Professor*
*School of Dentistry*
*University of Utah*
*Salt Lake City, Utah*

JONES & BARTLETT
LEARNING

*World Headquarters*
Jones & Bartlett Learning
5 Wall Street
Burlington, MA 01803
978-443-5000
info@jblearning.com
www.jblearning.com

Jones & Bartlett Learning books and products are available through most bookstores and online booksellers. To contact Jones & Bartlett Learning directly, call 800-832-0034, fax 978-443-8000, or visit our website, www.jblearning.com.

Substantial discounts on bulk quantities of Jones & Bartlett Learning publications are available to corporations, professional associations, and other qualified organizations. For details and specific discount information, contact the special sales department at Jones & Bartlett Learning via the above contact information or send an email to specialsales@jblearning.com.

19794-5

**Production Credits**

VP, Product Management: Amanda Martin
Director of Product Management: Cathy L. Esperti
Content Strategist: Ashley Malone
Content Coordinator: Elena Sorrentino
Project Manager: Kristen Rogers
Project Specialist: Kelly Sylvester
Digital Project Specialist: Rachel DiMaggio
Director of Marketing: Andrea DeFronzo
VP, Manufacturing and Inventory Control: Therese Connell
Composition: Exela Technologies

Project Management: Exela Technologies
Cover Design: Briana Yates
Senior Media Development Editor: Troy Liston
Rights & Permissions Manager: John Rusk
Rights Specialist: Benjamin Roy
Cover Image (Title Page, Chapter Opener):
    © FOTOGRIN/Shutterstock; © RoyStudio.eu/Shutterstock
Printing and Binding: LSC Communications
Cover Printing: LSC Communications

**Library of Congress Cataloging-in-Publication Data**
Names: Hanson, Glen (Glen R.), author. | Venturelli, Peter J., author.
    | Fleckenstein, Annette E., author.
Title: Drugs and society / Glen R. Hanson, Peter J. Venturelli, Annette E. Fleckenstein.
Description: Fourteenth edition. | Burlington, MA : Jones & Bartlett
    Learning, [2022] | Includes bibliographical references and index.
Identifiers: LCCN 2020018522 | ISBN 9781284197853 (paperback)
Subjects: MESH: Substance-Related Disorders
Classification: LCC RC564 | NLM WM 270 | DDC 362.29—dc23
LC record available at https://lccn.loc.gov/2020018522

6048

Printed in the United States of America
24 23 22 21 20    10 9 8 7 6 5 4 3 2 1

# BRIEF CONTENTS

# CONTENTS

## CHAPTER 1

## Introduction to Drugs and Society   1

## CHAPTER 2

## Explaining Drug Use and Abuse   63

## CHAPTER 15

# Over-the-Counter, Prescription, and Herbal Drugs   493

## CHAPTER 16

# Drug Use in Subcultures of Special Populations   535

# FEATURES

© FOTOGRIN/Shutterstock.

## HERE AND NOW

## CASE IN POINT

## SIGNS AND SYMPTOMS

## HOLDING THE LINE

## POINT/COUNTERPOINT

## PRESCRIPTION FOR ABUSE

## FAMILY MATTERS

## DO GENES MATTER?

© FOTOGRIN/Shutterstock.

# PREFACE

This *Fourteenth Edition* continues a long tradition of providing the most accurate, recent, and accessible information on drug use, misuse, and abuse, available in a form that is ideally suited for students at all college levels in the medical, social, and psychological fields. Thus, this new version of *Drugs and Society* further enhances its reputation as one of the leading texts on drug use and abuse. The authors have integrated their mastery in the fields of drug abuse, pharmacology, and sociology by using their expertise and knowledge of teaching, research experiences, and drug prevention and treatment to create an edition that reflects the most important and current information relative to drug abuse issues available in a textbook. For example, this edition includes new information on important topics, such as:

1. The potential value of genetics in assessing risk, consequences, and even the possible treatment of drug use disorder or addiction;
2. Discussion of the abuse and extent of performance-enhancing drugs in athletic and sport activity;
3. Statistics of use and the impact of drugs of abuse;
4. The most recent findings concerning the extent of vaping;
5. The relentless escalation of prescription abuse and related overdose deaths by opioid analgesics and the increased fatality when mixing opioids and other drugs with sedative properties, such as valium-type medications;
6. The characteristics of alcohol use and abuse including major costs to society;
7. The pattern of methamphetamine resurgence use in the United States and its trafficking patterns from Mexico;
8. The recent connections between methamphetamine and heroin/opioid use;
9. The status of clinical trials for the use of hallucinogenic drugs such as Ecstasy (MDMA) to treat mental conditions such as posttraumatic stress disorder and the use of ketamine to treat depression;
10. Update on the problems associated with rapidly escalating drug costs in the United States and how to address these challenges;
11. Tobacco regulation by the Food and Drug Administration and the continued increase in the popularity of e-cigarettes; and

12. Recent changes in most state marijuana laws in the United States that legally redefine marijuana as medicine for neurological and mental health issues and as a legal drug for recreational marijuana use.

*Drugs and Society* is an exceptionally comprehensive text on drug use and abuse and drug-related problems, with current and updated references to substantiate and support the latest findings about drug use and abuse information. This text is also written on a personal level, and directly addresses the drug information that college and university students need from the sociological, psychological, and pharmacological perspectives, addressing both micro- and macro-level drug use and abuse information. Many chapters include excerpts from personal experiences with recreational drug users, habitual (often addicted) drug users, and former drug users. Students will find these personal accounts interesting and insightful. This particular approach has been inspired by instructors, students, and reviewers, resulting in a truly unique text that combines comprehensive presentation of the latest drug information with personal accounts.

*Drugs and Society* is a multiperspective text offering university students from other disciplines a better understanding of drug use and abuse. Students in nursing, physical education or kinesiology, and other social sciences such as psychology, sociology, criminology or criminal justice, social work, history, and economics will find that our text provides useful and timely perspectives and information to help them understand the following:

- Social, psychological, pharmacological, and biological explanations for why drug use and abuse occur
- The outcomes of drug use and abuse
- How to prevent and treat drug use and abuse
- How drugs and medications can be effectively used for therapeutic purposes

To achieve these goals, we have presented the most current, objective, and authoritative views on drug abuse in an easily understood manner. The fourteenth edition of *Drugs and Society* continues to teach students from different disciplines how to understand the complexity of drug use and abuse from pharmacological, neurobiological, psychological, and sociological perspectives.

## What Is New and Improved?

*Drugs and Society, Fourteenth Edition* includes updated statistics and current examples of the key principles being taught in this text and frequently uses the new DSM-5 as a source for updated information. The new coverage includes discussion of the following topics.

- The most recent information on developments in states that have or intend to legalize recreational and medical marijuana use, as well as coverage of the major differences between the three main strains of marijuana; namely, *Cannabis sativa, Cannabis indica,* and *Cannabis ruderalis.*
- The current status of prescription abuse, including opiate painkillers, stimulants (e.g., performance enhancers), and the central nervous system (CNS) sedative-hypnotics.
- Details on public advertising of prescription products and resulting consumer controversies.
- The most recent information on the personal and social consequences of use of methamphetamine and narcotic analgesics.
- The latest status of over-the-counter (OTC) stimulants and decongestants as well as abuse of OTC products and the efforts to switch more prescription drugs to OTC status.
- Updated data and major drug use findings of drug abuse by junior high, high school, college and university students, adolescents, young adults, middle-aged adults, and senior citizens.
- Coverage of current topics such as steroid abuse in major professional sports, OxyContin abuse, restrictions on pain pills, marijuana legalization for medical and recreational use, heroin potency, designer drugs, synthetic drugs (Spice and K2), and marijuana wax.
- How risk and protective factors directly affect drug abuse.
- The most recent information on alcohol and other drug use problems in preadolescent, adolescent, college, and noncollege populations.
- Recent information on "vaping."
- The most recent survey data from the National Household Survey on Drug Use and Health (NHSDUH), *Monitoring the Future* studies, the Centers for Disease Control and Prevention (CDC), the Center for Behavioral Health Statistics and Quality (CBHSQ), the Substance Abuse and Mental Health Services Administration (SAMHSA), the U.S. Department of Justice (USDOJ), the National Council on Alcoholism and Drug Dependence (NCADD), the Bureau of Justice Statistics (BJS), the National Institute on Drug Abuse (NIDA), and the World Health Organization (WHO).

## Chapter Breakdown

The multidisciplinary material in the text encompasses pharmacological, biomedical, sociological, and social-psychological perspectives.

**Chapter 1** provides a thorough overview of the historical and current dimensions of drug use (statistics and trends) and the most common currently abused licit (such as OTC and prescription drugs) and illicit types of drugs. Included are the latest findings regarding the abuse of stimulants (including Ritalin and Adderall), bath salts, prescription and performance-enhancing drugs, hallucinogens and psychedelics and other similar drugs, depressants, alcohol, nicotine, cannabis (marijuana and hashish), synthetic cannabinoids, designer drugs and synthetic drugs or synthetic opioids, anabolic steroids, inhalants and organic solvents, and narcotics and opiates.

**Chapter 2** comprehensively explains drug use and abuse and addiction from multidisciplinary theoretical standpoints, including the latest theoretical, biological, psychological, social-psychological, and sociological perspectives. This chapter also theoretically explains the use and abuse of illicit drugs.

**Chapter 3** discusses new drug development (both OTC and prescription) and how the law deals with drugs of abuse and individuals who abuse them.

**Chapter 4** helps students understand the basic biochemical operations of the nervous and endocrine systems and explains how psychoactive drugs and anabolic steroids alter such functions.

**Chapter 5** instructs students about the factors that determine how drugs affect the body. This chapter also details the physiological and psychological variables that determine how and why people respond to drugs used for therapeutic and recreational purposes.

**Chapters 6 through 14** focus on specific drug groups that are commonly abused in the United States. Those drugs that depress brain activity are discussed in the following chapters:

- **Chapter 6** Sedative-hypnotic agents
- **Chapters 7** Alcohol use from a pharmacological perspective
- **Chapter 8** Alcohol use from a social scientific and behavioral perspective
- **Chapter 9** Opioid narcotics

Drugs that stimulate brain activity are covered in the following chapters:

- **Chapter 10** Amphetamines, bath salts
- **Chapter 11** Nicotine

The last major category of substances of abuse is hallucinogens, also known as *psychedelics*, which generally alter and distort sensory perception. These substances are discussed in the following chapters:

- **Chapter 12** Hallucinogens, such as LSD, mescaline, Ecstasy, and PCP
- **Chapter 13** Marijuana, marijuana wax, and synthetic cannabinoids (Spice-related types of drugs)
- **Chapter 14** Inhalants

Although most drugs of abuse cause more than one effect (e.g., cocaine can be a stimulant and have some hallucinatory properties), the classification we have chosen for this text is frequently used by experts and pharmacologists in the drug abuse field and is based on the most likely drug effect. All of the chapters in this section are similarly organized. They discuss the following:

- the historical origins and evolution of the agents so students can better understand society's attitudes toward, and regulation of, these drugs;
- previous and current clinical uses of these drugs to help students appreciate distinctions between therapeutic use and abuse;
- patterns of abuse and distinctive features that contribute to each drug's abuse potential; and
- nonmedicinal and medicinal therapies for drug-related dependence, withdrawal, and abstinence.

**Chapter 15** explores the topic of drugs and drug therapy. Like illicit drugs, nonprescription, prescription, and herbal drugs can be misused if not understood. This chapter helps students appreciate the benefits of proper drug use as well as recognize that licit (legalized) drugs also can be problematic—and a problem that has been declared by many experts, politicians, and news media to be the greatest drug abuse issue in the United States. This chapter also discusses the recent surge in abuse of prescription drugs such as opioid painkillers, stimulants, and CNS depressants; the dramatic increase in overdose deaths caused by these substances; and how to mitigate these problems.

**Chapter 16** focuses on and examines drug use, drug dependence, and drug abuse in the following seven major drug-using subcultural populations: (1) athletes involved in sports; (2) women; (3) adolescents; (4) college students; (5) HIV and AIDS subpopulations; (6) a percentage of professional actors, actresses, and music celebrities; and (7) Internet users seeking and purchasing illicit drugs.

**Chapter 17** explains what is involved in prevention of drug use and abuse. This chapter focuses on the following topics: (1) major factors affecting an individual's use of drugs; (2) major types of drug abuse prevention programs; (3) major types of drug users who must be recognized before creating any effective prevention program; (4) the four levels of comprehensive prevention programs for drug use and abuse; (5) major family factors that can affect the use of drugs; (6) primary prevention programs in higher education; (7) four recent large-scale prevention programs; and (8) two additional prevention measures that may substitute for the attraction to drug use.

**Chapter 18** focuses on assessing addiction, the issue of comorbidity, and principles and forms of drug dependence treatment.

© FOTOGRIN/Shutterstock.

**DRUGS AND SOCIETY**

FOURTEENTH EDITION

GLEN R. HANSON
PETER J. VENTURELLI
ANNETTE E. FLECKENSTEIN

ACCESS CODE INSIDE

**NAVIGATE**
ADVANTAGE ACCESS

Besides including the most current information concerning drug use and abuse topics, each chapter includes updated and helpful learning aids for both students and instructors. Utilizing these feature boxes for classroom or blog discussions and debates or as individual reflective writing assignments can drive stronger comprehension and retention of core concepts while reinforcing critical-thinking skills.

## HOLDING THE LINE
### States Are Allowing Cannabis Buyers' Clubs

Despite federal drug laws prohibiting the cultivation, possession, use, and sale of marijuana, 33 states plus the District of Columbia have recently enacted the legalization of recreational and medical marijuana. The 33 states are Alaska, Arizona, Arkansas, California, Colorado, Connecticut, Delaware, Florida, Hawaii, Illinois, Louisiana, Maine, Maryland, Massachusetts, Michigan, Minnesota, Missouri, Montana, Nevada, New Hampshire, New Jersey, New Mexico, New York, North Dakota, Ohio, Oklahoma, Oregon, Pennsylvania, Rhode Island, Utah, Vermont, Washington, and West Virginia (ProCon.org, 2019). Out of 325,719,178 of U.S. population as of March 17, 2018 (ProCon.org, 2019), the estimated number of medical marijuana users would be 2,132,777 (ProCon.org, 2019).

Why should medically ill patients, those afflicted with AIDS and associated wasting, lack of appetite, nausea, arthritis, hepatitis C, migraines, multiple sclerosis, muscle spasms, chronic pain, glaucoma, and other illnesses (such as posttraumatic stress disorder, depression, or bipolar disorder) or those suffering the deleterious effects of chemotherapy or radiation not be able to legally purchase marijuana if they find relief from the effects of their illnesses? The first cannabis buyers' club began in 1996 when the voting citizens of Marin County, California, passed "Proposition 215, which authorized the use of medical marijuana . . . for those who have a doctor's recommendation" (Nolde, 2002). The main problem facing this club in Marin County, and all the other cannabis buyers' clubs throughout the United States, is that although these 23 states and DC have legalized such enterprises, they continue to violate federal drug laws, causing a conflict between federal and state law. At times, the clubs can be ordered closed by a superior court judge, resulting in federal agents raiding the clubs, confiscating the marijuana, and arresting the owners and operators of these establishments.

To date, this cyclical pattern of raids and arrests by federal officials continues to sporadically occur because of this rift between state and federal laws. The clubs are either for-profit or nonprofit organizations whose sole intent is to distribute marijuana for medicinal purposes when prescribed by a licensed physician. Many of the buyers (known as *patients*) report relief and satisfaction from their use of marijuana. For example, a man named Clay Shinn, 46, was diagnosed with AIDS in 1992. At the time of his interview, he had been going to the Marin Alliance's Cannabis Buyers' Club for five years. "It's made a major difference in my life," he said. After taking his [AIDS] medication morning, afternoon, and evening, he said, "I was always getting nauseated.... I could set my watch by it. I hate it. God, it's awful. Now I don't barf anymore" (Nolde, 2002). Another interviewee, who is an arthritic, HIV-positive cabaret performer, said, "After I leave here . . . I won't feel my pain" (Goldberg, 1996). Another man, the club's director, reiterated that, "'You have to be sick or dying'. . . If you are, with a doctor's note to prove that you have AIDS or cancer or another condition with symptoms that marijuana is known to alleviate, Mr. Peron [the club's director] is willing to sell some relief" (Goldberg, 1996). Finally, Dennis Peron, the founder of the San Francisco Buyers' Club, stated, "We have over 400 senior citizens that come here for arthritis, glaucoma, pain, etc. We have an old woman trapped in her wheelchair, day in and day out. Marijuana makes her feel a little bit better. I don't require a letter of diagnosis for people 65 or older—things wear out—or for people who are blind or deaf, as they say it helps their other senses" (Fuhrman, 1995).

What are your views regarding the prescribed use of marijuana, especially when these clubs or cooperatives provide seriously ill patients with a safe and reliable source of medical cannabis information and patient support? What about buying clubs for recreational use of marijuana—are your views similar to buying clubs selling marijuana only for medicinal purposes? Would you support a cannabis buyers' club or cooperative in your community that sells medical marijuana and recreational marijuana? What are your views regarding federal laws that prohibit such establishments while states pass laws allowing these establishments to legally operate? How do you think this current problem of the illegality on the federal level should be resolved? Finally, how do you think this dilemma will be resolved in your lifetime?

Data from Nolde, H. (2002, July 1). Medical pot war rages on. *Marin Independent Journal*. Retrieved from http://cannabisnews.com/news/13/thread13278.shtml; Fuhrman, R. A. (1995). Cannabis buyers' club flourishes in 'Frisco." San Francisco, CA: Cannabis Buyers' Club; Goldberg, C. (1996, February 26). Marijuana club helps those in pain. *The New York Times*. Retrieved from http://query.nytimes.com/gst/fullpage.html?res=9C06E6DF1139F936A1575 1C0A960958260&sec=&spon=&pagewanted=all; ProCon.org. (2013). How many people in the United State use medical marijuana? Santa Monica, CA: Author. Retrieved from http://medicalmarijuana.procon.org/view.answers.php?questionID=001199; ProCon.org. (2018, May 17). Number of legal medical marijuana patients. Santa Monica, CA: Author; ProCon.org. (2019, July 24). Legal medical marijuana states and DC. Santa Monica, CA: Author.

• **Holding the Line:** Vignettes that help readers assess efforts to deal with drug-related problems.

## ► CASE IN POINT
### Specific Signs of Marijuana Use

This excerpt, from the author's files, illustrates labeling theory:

After my mom found out, she never brought it up again. I thought the incident was over—dead, gone, and buried. Well . . . it wasn't over at all. My mom and dad must have agreed that I couldn't be trusted anymore. I'm sure she was regularly going through my stuff in my room to see if I was still smoking dope. Even my grandparents acted strangely whenever the news on television would report about the latest drug bust in Chicago. Several times that I can't ever forget were when we were together and I could hear the news broadcast on TV from my room about some drug bust. There they all were whispering about me. My grandma asking if I "quitta the dope." One night, I overheard my mother reassure my dad and grandmother that I no longer was using dope. You can't believe how embarrassed I was that my own family was still thinking that I was a dope fiend. They thought I was addicted to pot like a junkie is addicted to heroin! I can tell you that I would never lay such a guilt trip on my kids if I ever have kids. I remember that for [two] years after the time I was honest enough to tell my mom that I had tried pot, they would always whisper about me, give me the third degree whenever I returned late from a date, and go through my room looking for dope. They acted as if I was hooked on drugs. I remember that for

a while back then I would always think that if they think of me as a drug addict, I might as well get high whenever my friends "toke up." They should have taken me at my word instead of sneaking around my personal belongings. I should have left syringes lying around my room!

Approximately 17 years after this interview was conducted, this author was able to revisit the same interviewee, who at the time of this second interview was 37 years of age. After showing him the preceding excerpt, he commented,

You know, Professor, while today marijuana use is no longer such a big deal, I can still tell you that it took years to finally convince my family that I was not a "big time drug user." Though my grandma is now dead, I can still remember how she would look at me when I would tell her that I just smoke it once in a while. I knew she never believed that I was just an occasional user by the look on her face, when she would ask ". . . and last night when you went out, did you smoke the dope again?" My mom, who is now living with my sister, still mentions how I went wild those days when I was drugging it up! Yes, I have to say it had a big impact on me when my own family believed I was a drug addict back then. I will never forget those looks from my family every time I would walk into the house on weekends when I would return from a night out with my friends.

Interview with a 20-year-old male college student at a private university in the Midwest, conducted by Peter Venturelli on November 19, 1993. Second interview with same interviewee male, 37 years of age, June 2010.

• **Case in Point:** Examples of relevant clinical or social issues that arise from the use of each major type of drug.

## HERE AND NOW
### Spice and K2: Past and Current Usage Rates

Spice, also known as *herbal incense*, is dried, shredded plant material treated with a cannabinoid analog. Although labels on spice products will list the ingredients as "natural" psychoactive plant products, chemical analyses show that their active ingredients are primarily synthetic cannabinoids added to the plant material. These synthetic analogs function similarly to the active ingredient in marijuana, Δ9-THC (SAMHSA, 2014a).

*K2* and *Spice* are two names for a more recently created psychoactive designer drug whose dried, leafy, natural herbs are sprayed with a psychoactive chemical; it is then smoked so the user can experience euphoric effects. In 2011, prior to the Synthetic Drug Abuse Prevention Act being signed into law, one in nine U.S. high school seniors reported having used synthetic marijuana. In 2012, a large sample survey found that annual prevalence was 11.4%, ranking synthetic marijuana as the second most widely used class of illicit drug after marijuana among 12th graders (Johnston et al., 2016). In 2018, synthetic marijuana use significantly dropped. Annual use in 2018 among 8th graders was 1.6%, 10th graders 2.9%, and 12th graders 3.5% (NIDA, 2018c).

Eighth, 10th, and 12th graders were asked if they associated a great risk with trying synthetic marijuana once or twice; the results showed that there was quite a low level of perceived risk (only 23% and 25%, respectively, thought there was great risk in using once or twice).

Another study at a large public university in Georgia between November 2011 and March 2012 found that the highest level of use was among male students largely identifying with the lesbian, gay, bisexual, and transgender (LGBT) community. This was the first known study to obtain a detailed profile of users of any type of synthetic cannabinoid. Findings indicated the following:

1. The average age of first use was 18 years.
2. The percentage ever using synthetic cannabinoids was twice as high for males as for females (19% vs. 9%).
3. Heavier users were more likely to identify themselves as LGBT; significantly less usage was found in students identifying themselves as heterosexual.

Earlier findings are that "[e]fforts at the federal and state levels to close down the sale of these substances appear to be having an effect" (Johnston et al., 2016. Overall, beginning in 2015 through 2018, use of synthetic marijuana cannabinoids, (K2 and Spice) have statistically decreased for 8th, 10th, 12th graders and college students).

Data from Johnston, L. D., O'Malley, P. M., Bachman, J. G., & Schulenberg, J. E. (2013). Monitoring the future national results on drug use: 2012 overview, key findings on adolescent drug use. Ann Arbor, MI: Institute for Social Research, The University of Michigan; Center for Substance Abuse Research (CESAR). (2013, 20 May). Study finds that 14% of undergraduate students at a Southeastern University report synthetic cannabinoid use; users more likely to be male and identify as LGBT CESAR FAX. Retrieved from http://www.cesar.umd.edu; Johnston, L. D., O'Malley, P. M. & Miech, R. A., Bachman, J. G., & Schulenberg, J. E. (2016, February). Monitoring the future national survey results on drug use, 1975-2015: Overview, key findings on adolescent drug use. Ann Arbor, MI: Institute for Social Research, The University of Michigan; National Institute on Drug Abuse (NIDA). (2018c): Synthetic cannabinoids (K2/Spice). Bethesda, MD: Author. Retrieved from https://www.drugabusedgnuse.gov/publications/drugfacts/synthetic-cannabinoids-k2spice

• **Here and Now:** Current events that illustrate the personal and social consequences of drug abuse.

## FAMILY MATTERS
### Addiction Genes

Is it true that addiction related to drug abuse can be associated with a person's genetics? It is well known that genetic variants are likely associated with diseases such as Alzheimer's and Parkinson's. In fact, many Americans are spitting into test tubes and sending their saliva samples to laboratories to assess their risk of developing these neurological and other genetics-related pathologies. What if we could do the same thing for drug addiction—spit into a container and send it off in a mailer and within a few weeks get a report that would tell us the likelihood that sometime during our life we would experience drug addiction? While genetic research does tell us that various aspects of substance abuse have been linked to more than 100 different abnormal gene expressions, the potential of so many drug abuse–related genes suggests that addiction is a complicated behavioral manifestation, which likely means it will be extremely difficult to develop a simple saliva test to reliably warn us of drug addiction vulnerability. So, what is the value of these findings confirming the connection between some abnormal genes and drug addiction? The following are conclusions that we can draw because of the research establishing linkage between addiction and variant gene expression:

• Because genes are associated with the expression of biological elements such as proteins, genetic research demonstrates that the addiction process has organic bases like many other pathological conditions and as such suggests it should be viewed as the consequence of a disease process and not a moral failure. For example, proteins related to abnormal dopamine (neurotransmitter) receptors, abnormal alcohol metabolic products, nausea-producing tobacco by-products and abnormal serotonin uptake transporters are just a few of the variant genes found to be connected with drug abuse problems.

• The identification of so many genetic factors potentially linked to addiction suggests there is no single element required for every expression of addiction, but that addiction is likely caused by a complicated interplay of biology with environment. This has been confirmed by findings that genetics only contribute to ~50% of addiction vulnerability while the balance is associated with experience.

• Even if a person was found to have one of the abnormal genes linked to addiction, this does not mean that problems with drugs are inevitable, but it could suggest that such a person should take greater care to avoid environments or drug consumption that would encourage drug abuse.

• Identification of genes linked to addiction may provide leads for developing effective treatment or prevention strategies. For example, if expression of a specific dopamine receptor was associated with developing addiction, then perhaps medications that block this receptor would have therapeutic value to prevent or treat the related addiction condition.

• The role of genes in the expression of addiction helps us understand the basis for the familial clustering of this drug-related condition. However, it should be remembered as previously mentioned that this does not mean that everyone in the family is destined to have drug problems. It does suggest, however, that everyone in such a family needs to be cautious around these drugs. In addition, these family members should particularly emphasize an antidrug culture in the home.

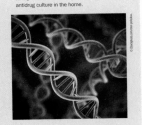

May, H. (2017, Winter). Genes and addiction. Continuum. Salt Lake City, UT: University of Utah. Retrieved from https://continuum.utah.edu/features/genes-and-addiction

• **Family Matters:** Examples of how genetics and heredity contribute to drug abuse and its issues.

## PRESCRIPTION FOR ABUSE
### *How to Spice Things Up*

"Mr. Happy," "Scooby Snax," and "Kronic" are street names referring to drugs that in 2018 were linked to 160 cases of severe bleeding and four deaths in central Illinois. These drug products also go by the more familiar terms of *Spice* and *K2*. Such names represent a large group of chemicals sometimes classified as "synthetic (made in chemistry lab) cannabinoids (i.e., related to marijuana ingredients)." These substances for the most part were originally produced by legitimate research chemists studying the natural cannabinoid system and their chemistry was published in legitimate scientific journals. Once the knowledge of the synthetic chemistry of these substances became public, illicit drug manufacturers used the information to create hundreds of their own adulterated products for sale on the black market. Drugs like Spice and K2 have been called "synthetic marijuana" or "fake weed" to suggest to the unwary buyer that their consumption will in some way mimic the effects caused by smoking marijuana. Because of the national trend throughout the United States to legalize the medical and/or recreational use of marijuana, the association with marijuana-related chemicals is thought to encourage the popularity of these illegal substances and the misconception that Spice, K2-like and related drugs are harmless and maybe even therapeutic. Nothing can be further from the truth. In fact, these designer synthetics often are much more powerful and toxic than THC (the natural ingredient in marijuana), and more potentially dangerous because much of their pharmacology and toxicology is unknown. An additional complication is the lack of consistency in the production of these cannabinoid rip-offs. Even though the packages are very colorful and appear to be high tech, there is no quality control or standardization; thus, there have been many reports of dangerous side effects such as hypertension, a racing heart, agitation, paranoia, psychosis, seizures and nausea and vomiting. When the Spice and K2 substances first appeared in the United States in 2008 they were sold over-the-counter in convenience stores, truck stops and smoke shops because the ingredients were basically unknown and not prohibited. After 2-4 years several states passed "designer" laws banning the sales of these synthetic cannabinoids. Despite this effort, prosecuting the sellers of these drugs was next to impossible because when one of these drugs was identified and outlawed, the store owner quickly replaced it with a substitute chemical with a minor structural change. This modified substance was technically legitimate until dangerous side effects were identified and reported to law enforcement.

It is estimated that ~4% of the population in the United States, mostly males, has tried Spice/K2 substances, many of which are laced with other unknown toxic chemicals. These products often consist of dried herbs that have been sprayed by the cannabinoid-related chemicals which are either rolled into joints or smoked in pipes like typical marijuana. Sometimes the designer chemicals are even added to foods or tea and consumed orally.

Watson, S. (2018, September). K2/Spice: What to know about these dangerous drugs. WebMD. Retrieved from www.webmd.com/mental-health/addiction/news/20180910/k2-spice-what-to-know-about-these-dangerous-drugs

• **Prescription for Abuse:** Current stories that illustrate the problems of prescription abuse and its consequences.

## ►POINT/COUNTERPOINT

### Who Should Know the Results of Your HIV Test If You Test Positive?

Most people would probably want to keep such results private, but would your opinion about HIV-positive people keeping their results confidential change in the following circumstances?

- You require first aid after a serious auto accident, and the emergency medical technician assisting is HIV positive.
- Your doctor is HIV positive.
- Your dentist is HIV positive.

the HIV-positive person, exposing an infected person to social ostracism and gossip and potentially creating fear and panic in others; and (4) potentially destroy a partner or marriage relationship if the significant other or spouse is notified.

Arguments for mandatory disclosure to others potentially affected by the results of this disease include (1) to protect domestic or marital partners, (2) to protect others from HIV-positive workers who could infect them (such as surgeons who are involved in invasive bodily care or procedures), and (3) to honor the public's right to know of the threat of contracting this terminal disease.

Currently, employers cannot legally terminate a

- **Point/Counterpoint:** Features that expose students to different perspectives on drug-related issues and encourage them to draw their own conclusions.

- **Key Terms:** Highlighted definitions of new terminology that are conveniently located on the same page as their discussion in the text.

## KEY TERMS

**addiction**
generally refers to the psychological attachment to a drug; addiction to "harder" drugs such as heroin results in both psychological and physical attachment to the chemical properties of the drug, with the resulting satisfaction (reward) derived from using the drug in question

**withdrawal symptoms**
psychological and physical symptoms that result when a drug is absent from the body; physical symptoms are generally present in cases of drug dependence to more addictive drugs such as heroin; physical and psychological symptoms of withdrawal include perspiration, nausea, boredom, anxiety, and muscle spasms

**drug(s)**
any substance that modifies (either by enhancing, inhibiting, or distorting) mind or body functioning

**licit drugs**
legalized drugs such as coffee, alcohol, and tobacco

**illicit drugs**
illegal drugs such as marijuana, cocaine, and LSD

**over-the-counter (OTC)**
legalized drugs sold without a prescription

## Learning Objectives

**On completing this chapter, you should be able to:**

> Explain how drug use is affected by biological, genetic, and pharmacological factors, as well as cultural, social, and contextual factors.
> Develop a basic understanding of drug use and abuse.
> Explain when drugs were first used and under what circumstances.
> Indicate how widespread drug use is and who potential drug abusers are.
> List four reasons why drugs are used.
> Rank in descending order, from most common to least, the most commonly used licit and illicit drugs.
> Name three types of drug users and explain how they differ.
> Describe how the mass media promotes drug use.
> Explain when drug use leads to abuse.
> List and explain the stages of drug dependence.
> List the major findings regarding drugs and crime.
> Describe employee assistance programs, and explain their role in resolving productivity problems.
> Explain the holistic self-awareness approach.

- **Learning Objectives:** Goals for learning are listed at the beginning of each chapter to help students identify the principal concepts being taught.

**LEARNING PORTFOLIO**

### Key Terms

| | |
|---|---|
| acute | 173 |
| additive interactions | 165 |
| antagonistic interactions | 165 |
| biotransformation | 173 |
| blood–brain barrier | 171 |
| chronic | 173 |
| cross-dependence | 179 |
| cross-tolerance | 179 |
| cumulative effect | 173 |
| dependence | 176 |
| dose-response | 163 |
| drug interaction | 165 |
| dysphoric | 182 |
| half-life | 173 |
| intramuscular (IM) | 170 |
| intravenous (IV) | 170 |
| margin of safety | 164 |
| mental set | 180 |
| metabolism | 173 |
| metabolites | 174 |
| pharmacokinetics | 168 |
| placebo effects | 180 |
| plateau effect | 172 |
| potency | 164 |
| psychological dependence | 180 |
| rebound effect | 179 |
| reverse tolerance | 178 |
| side effects | 162 |
| subcutaneous (SC) | 170 |
| synergism | 166 |
| teratogenic | 175 |
| threshold dose | 172 |
| tolerance | 164 |
| toxicity | 164 |
| vaping | 170 |
| withdrawal | 162 |

### Discussion Questions

1. How does the concept of drug "potency" apply to the therapeutic use and abuse of drugs?
2. How can drug interactions be both detrimental and beneficial? Give examples of each.
3. Why would a drug with a relatively narrow margin of safety be approved by the Food and Drug Administration for clinical use? Give an example.
4. What are possible explanations for the fact that you (for example) may require twice as much of a drug to get an effect as does your friend?
5. Why might the blood–brain barrier prevent a drug from having abuse potential?
6. Why would the consumption of a drug of abuse by a nursing mother be a problem for the infant? Give an example.
7. Why do you think vaping of nicotine and THC in marijuana have become so popular so quickly?
8. Contrary to your advice, a friend is going to spend $20 on methamphetamine. What significance will the pharmacokinetic concepts of threshold, half-life, cumulative effect, and biotransformation have on your friend's drug experience?
9. How would the factors of tolerance, physical dependence, rebound, and psychological dependence affect a chronic heroin user?
10. Why would the lack of physical dependence on LSD for some drug abusers make it less likely to cause addiction than cocaine, which does cause physical dependence?

### Summary

1. All drugs have intended and unintended effects. The unintended actions of drugs can include effects such as nausea, altered mental states, dependence, a variety of allergic responses, and changes in the cardiovascular system.
2. Many factors can affect the way an individual responds to a drug: dose, inherent toxicity, potency, and pharmacokinetic properties such as the rate of absorption into the body, the way it is distributed throughout the body, and the manner in which and rate at which it is metabolized and eliminated. The form of the drug as well as the manner in which it is administered can also affect the response to a drug.
3. Potency is determined by the amount of a drug necessary to cause a given effect. Toxicity is the ability of the drug to affect the body adversely. A drug that is highly toxic is particularly potent in terms of causing a harmful effect.

- **Discussion Questions:** Provocative and engaging questions at the end of each chapter encourage students to discuss, ponder, and critically analyze their own feelings and biases about the information presented in the book.

- **Summary:** Concise summaries found at the end of each chapter correlate with the learning objectives.

Because of these unique features, we believe that this edition of *Drugs and Society* is particularly "user friendly," has the most current and accurate information available in a textbook, and will encourage student motivation and learning.

# Resources to Accompany *Drugs and Society, Fourteenth Edition*

*Navigate Advantage Access for Drugs and Society, Fourteenth Edition* is a complete, interactive online courseware solution combining authoritative content with interactive tools, assessments, and grading functionality.

This online course combines a host of interactive activities to facilitate learning and allow students to check their progress using quizzes and assessments. Course setup is easy with the preplanned lessons and lecture outlines found within the platform. *Navigate* is flexible and allows instructors to customize content. Automatic grading saves time and provides on-demand analysis of how students are progressing in the course, allowing the instructor to tailor the teaching based on student needs. Other tools such as a built-in calendar, system email, and a robust grade book are also available within *Navigate*.

With *Navigate Advantage Access*, students can immediately evaluate their understanding of important concepts and objectives by easily toggling between textbook narrative, activities, and assessments. This enables them to process, synthesize, and retain course concepts in less time through rich media content.

*Navigate Advantage Access for Drugs and Society, Fourteenth Edition* includes the following:

- An interactive, animated eBook with personalization tools such as highlighting, bookmarking, and notes
- Student resources, including a full study guide separated by chapter, a course glossary, slides in PowerPoint format, discussion questions, and more!

# ACKNOWLEDGMENTS

The many improvements that make this the best edition of the *Drugs and Society* series could not have occurred without the hard work and dedication of numerous people.

We are indebted to the many reviewers who evaluated the manuscript at different stages of development. Much of the manuscript was reviewed and greatly improved by comments and suggestions from the following:

- Christina H. Lesyk, LMSW, SUNY Canton
- Grace Lartey
- Dr. Holly Nevarez, California State University, Chico
- Ellen Lee, RN, MS, EdD, CHES, California State University, Fullerton
- Kathy Finley, MS, School of Public Health, Bloomington
- Michelle F. Papania, Florida Atlantic University
- Zuzana Bic, DrPH, MUDr. (MD)
- Fidencio Mercado, MS, LPC, LCDC, The University of Texas Rio Grande Valley
- Dian L. Williams, PhD, RN, Rutgers University

The authors would like to express once again their gratitude for the comments and suggestions of users and reviewers of previous editions of *Drugs and Society*.

At their respective institutions, each of the authors would like to thank a multitude of people too numerous to list individually, but who have given them invaluable assistance.

Dr. Fleckenstein gratefully acknowledges the support of her family in her participation in the preparation of this revised text. Also appreciated is the support of her colleagues at the University of Utah School of Dentistry.

At Valparaiso University, Professor Venturelli is grateful to Ashleigh Rios, a former student of his. Ashleigh assisted him with her suggestions, carefully (and sometimes painfully) searching for the latest statistical information for nearly all of his updated tables. He is grateful that in a few weeks, Ashleigh will assist him in revising the test bank that will accompany this text edition. Professor Venturelli would also like to gratefully acknowledge all of the interviewees (students and working people) who were interviewed for hours on end regarding their information, opinions, and personal use and experiences (past and present) with drugs. Even though the final copy of the revised chapters remains the author's responsibility, this edition has been substantially enhanced by all of their efforts, loyalties, and the dedicated assistance of others, including Cathy Esperti and Ashley Malone at Jones & Bartlett Learning. Working with these and countless other professionals and dedicated staff members at Jones & Bartlett Learning has been instructive, productive, and very rewarding.

Dr. Hanson is particularly indebted to his wife, Margaret, for her loving encouragement. Without her patience and support this endeavor would not have been possible. She reminds him that what is truly important in this world is service to our family and to each other. Also appreciated is the support of his children and his colleagues at the University of Utah School of Dentistry, School of Medicine, and College of Pharmacy.

© FOTOGRIN/Shutterstock.

Dr. Glen R. Hanson is the vice dean of the School of Dentistry and a professor of pharmacology in the School of Dentistry at the University of Utah. He is also the Senior Advisor for the Mountain Plains PTTC (Prevention Technology Transfer Center), which is supported by the Substance Abuse Mental Health Service Administration of the Department of Heath and Human Services. During his approximately 30 years in academics, he has received more than $30 million from the National Institute on Drug Abuse (NIDA), affiliated with the National Institutes of Health (NIH), to research the neurobiology of drug abuse, and he has authored more than 240 scientific papers and 50 book chapters on the subject. Dr. Hanson has lectured on drug abuse topics throughout the world. He served as the director of the Division of Neuroscience and Behavioral Research at NIDA, after which he became NIDA's acting director from 2001 to 2003. Dr. Hanson works with scientists, public officials, policy makers, and the general public to more effectively deal with problems of drug abuse addiction.

Dr. Peter J. Venturelli has been the coauthor of this text since the second edition of *Drugs and Society* in 1988. In addition to revising this text every two years, the experiences and qualifications of Dr. Venturelli in academia and professional life include publishing research in drug and ethnic anthologies and scholarly journals, authoring approximately 60 conference papers at national professional sociological meetings, serving in elected and administrative positions in professional sociological and drug research associations, receiving research grants involving drug use and ethnicity, authoring the latest drug research, serving as a board member at the Baldwin Research Institute (alcohol and drug retreats), and teaching undergraduate and graduate students for the past 32 years.

Dr. Annette E. Fleckenstein has been a coauthor of *Drugs and Society* since its seventh edition and is a professor and assistant dean in the School of Dentistry at the University of Utah. She has researched the neurobiology of substance abuse for more than 20 years, lectured on topics related to substance abuse throughout the United States and abroad, and authored more than 110 scientific papers and book chapters on this and related subjects. Dr. Fleckenstein has been a NIDA-funded researcher for more than 20 years and has a long history of lecturing to undergraduate, graduate, and professional students.

CHAPTER **1**

# Introduction to Drugs and Society

## Did You Know?

▶ The popular use of legal drugs, particularly alcohol and tobacco, have caused far more deaths, sickness, violent crimes, economic loss, and other social problems than the use of all illegal drugs combined.

▶ The effect a drug has depends on multiple factors: (1) the ingredients of the drug and its effect on the body, (2) the traditional use of the drug, (3) individual motivation, and (4) the social and physical surroundings in which the drug is taken.

▶ The first attempts to regulate drugs were made as long ago as 2240 BC.

▶ After marijuana, illicit prescription drugs are now the second leading drug of abuse.

▶ Drug abuse is an "equal-opportunity affliction." This means that drug consumption is found across all income levels, social classes, genders, races, ethnicities, lifestyles, and age groups.

▶ Among racial and ethnic groups in the United States, past-month illicit drug use is highest among African Americans and whites and lowest among Asians.

▶ Approximately 70% of drug users in the United States are employed (18 years or older) either full time or part time, and 76% of full- or part-time employees are heavy drinkers.

▶ In major industry categories, past-month illicit drug use was highest in accommodations and food services; arts, entertainment, and recreation; and management; the highest amount of heavy alcohol use was found in the mining, construction, and accommodations and food services industries.

▶ Approximately 60% of individuals arrested for most types of crimes test positive for illegal drugs at the time of their arrest.

## Learning Objectives

**On completing this chapter, you should be able to:**

❯ Explain how drug use is affected by biological, genetic, and pharmacological factors, as well as cultural, social, and contextual factors.

❯ Develop a basic understanding of drug use and abuse.

❯ Explain when drugs were first used and under what circumstances.

❯ Indicate how widespread drug use is and who potential drug abusers are.

❯ List four reasons why drugs are used.

❯ Rank in descending order, from most common to least, the most commonly used licit and illicit drugs.

❯ Name three types of drug users and explain how they differ.

❯ Describe how the mass media promotes drug use.

❯ Explain when drug use leads to abuse.

❯ List and explain the stages of drug dependence.

❯ List the major findings regarding drugs and crime.

❯ Describe employee assistance programs, and explain their role in resolving productivity problems.

❯ Explain the holistic self-awareness approach.

## Introduction

Each year, at an accelerating rate, social change driven by technology affects not only us individually but also our families, communities, cities, nation, and the world. It can certainly be said that technology is one of the primary forces driving change in our society and societies worldwide at an unprecedented and relentless speed, affecting our daily living.

As an example of technological change, let us look at the transformation of the landline telephone into cellular phone technology. In all likelihood, your great-grandparents had a single black stationary rotary type of landline phone at home to communicate with friends and family living at a distance, and they shared telephone lines with other families. Your grandparents experienced newer styles of the same telephone, with one or two other telephones installed in other rooms in their apartments and homes. While growing up, your parents had the same landline type of telephone, but it came in an array of colors and was more stylized, and the standard was multiple extensions of this phone throughout their home in bedrooms, hallways, or kitchens. Today, your available technology may still include a landline phone,[1] with additional features such as voice mail, call waiting, call forwarding, and call blocking, to name a few of many other standard feature options available with landline phones.

An outgrowth of the landline phone and the military radiophone, the cell phone is the gadget most of us carry today without any sense of technological awe. With more than 7 billion worldwide subscribers (Nair, 2015), the cell phone and its recent cousin, the smartphone, named as such because it includes additional software functions resembling a computer, are portable warehouses of technological services that connect to a cellular network. Current cell phones can include an array of accessories and services beyond making phone calls, including caller identification; voice messaging; voice memos; an alarm clock; a stopwatch; calendars; appointment scheduling; current times and temperatures in different cities around the world; a calculator; video games; text messaging (or SMS); a camera with photo albums; Internet service; email; infrared; Bluetooth; an MP3 player; storage for downloaded music, movies, or podcasts; geographic positioning system (GPS) features; radio broadcasts; maps; stock market quotes; weather; reminders; Skype or FaceTime; and Google Maps, to name a few "basic" applications. As of 2019, more than 2 million apps are available for download offering an array of information, accessories, and services. The completely portable cell phone with its keypad or touchscreen did not exist for the general public until 1973. Further, newer generations of cell phones will include unimaginable new applications, accessories, and services.

Consider another example. More than likely, your great-grandparents wrote letters on manual typewriters (or by hand). Your grandparents wrote letters on electric typewriters, whereas your parents started writing letters on electric typewriters and then had to change to computers. Today, you often communicate with family members and friends by email, text messaging, Facebook, Facebook Messenger, WhatsApp, Instagram, Twitter, Google+, Skype, and Dropbox. Although many of the electronic devices in your life may seem normal, a visit to a science and technology museum can offer many surprises and, more than likely, an appreciation for how things were and how much they have changed.

These examples illustrate how technology is in a continuous state of development and how it affects our day-to-day lives. In a sense, the technology we use today will be replaced tomorrow, as newer and more advanced forms of innovation give birth to new technology and software.

What does this have to do with drug use and abuse? Just as electronics continually evolve, drugs follow similar paths of evolution. Today, thousands of new drugs are available that are used either legally or illegally. These drugs are used for medicinal purposes, recreational purposes, and to achieve effects that do not include maintaining health. Some people in society use drugs to cope with pressures emanating from social change. Others use and eventually abuse drugs to cope with, delay, or postpone reality. For some, illicit drug use becomes a primary method for instant recreation, a way to avoid anxieties, or a substitute to fulfill human desires and pleasures.

Despite the extensive amount of available information regarding the dangers of drug use and an increasing number of laws prohibiting nonmedical drug use, many people today continue to abuse legal and illegal types of drugs.

---

[1]Landline phones continue to disappear from U.S. households; approximately 42.8% of American homes had landline phones as of December 2017 (Burke, 2019).

## Drug Use

Anyone can become dependent on and addicted to a drug. The desire to use a drug before drug dependence and addiction occur is both seductive and indiscriminate of its users. Most people do not realize that drug use causes at least four major simultaneous changes:

1. The social psychological basis of an attraction to a drug can be explained as feeling rewarded or satisfied because social pressures can appear to have become postponed, momentarily rectified, or neutralized and perceived as nonproblematic.
2. Pharmacologically, the nonmedical use of most drugs alters body chemistry largely by interfering with homeostatic functioning. Drugs *enhance, depress, accelerate, or distort* the perception of reality.
3. Using a drug may satisfy an inborn or genetically programmed need or desire. Psychoactive drugs interfere with the way neurons send, receive, and process signals via neurotransmitters.

Many argue that our "reality" would become perilous and unpredictable if people were legally free to dabble in their drugs of choice. Many do not realize, however, that even legal drugs can be used to alter our perception of reality, can become severely addicting, and can destroy our social relationships with loved ones. Before delving into more specific information, we begin by posing key questions related to drug use that will be discussed in this chapter:

- What constitutes a drug?
- What drugs are commonly abused?
- What are designer drugs?
- How widespread is drug abuse?
- What is the extent and frequency of drug use in our society?
- What are the current statistics and trends of drug use?
- What types of drug users exist?
- How does the media influence drug use?
- What attracts people to drug use?
- When does drug use lead to drug dependence?
- When does the final stage of drug addiction occur?
- What are the costs of drug addiction to society?
- What is gained by learning about the complexity of drug use and abuse?

## Dimensions of Drug Use

To determine the perception of drug use in our country, we asked several of the many people we interviewed for this text, "What do you think of the extent and the amount of drug use in our society?" The following are four of the more typical responses:

I think it is a huge problem, especially when you think about the fact that there are so many people doing drugs. Even in my own family, my sister's kids have had drug problems. My niece became addicted to cocaine, nearly died one night from overdosing, had to leave college for a year and go into rehab. I cannot emphasize enough how this was one of the most beautiful (physically and mentally sharp) and polite nieces I ever had. The rest of the family had no idea why she left school last year. Then, just last week, my sister tearfully announced during a Christmas gathering that Cindee was heavily into drugs while attending her second year of college. We were all shocked by this information. Now, just think how many other kids are addicted to such junk while the people who really care and love them do not have a clue. If the kids are having to deal with this, just stop and think how many other people in other jobs and professions are battling or have caved into their drugs of choice.

How many workers are there on a daily basis doing jobs that require safety and are "high" on drugs? This is a scary thought. Just think of a surgeon on drugs, or an airline pilot. Yes, we have big monster problems with controlling drug use. *(From Venturelli's research files, female dietician in Chicago, age 43, February 9, 2003)*

A second response to the same question:

I use drugs, mainly weed and alcohol, and at least once a month I have a night of enjoying coke with several friends. As long as I am not a burden on my family, I think drug use is a personal choice. Locking up people for their drug use is a violation of my rights as a human being. For many years now, our government has not been able to stop recreational drug use, this is despite the millions that have been arrested, and countless numbers of other drug users incarcerated. What's the point of all this? If after so many years of trying to enforce drug laws has met with failure, we need to take a long hard look at the small percentage of people like me who are fully employed, have families, pay our taxes regularly and outside of drug use, are fully functioning adults. The funny thing is that the two drugs [referring to alcohol and tobacco] that are legalized are far worse or at least as debilitating as the drugs that are legally prohibitive [sic]. Drug use is a personal choice and unless you are causing problems for other people, it should remain a personal choice. If I am using drugs on a particular night at home either by myself or with friends and we are not outside causing problems, we should not be in violation of any drug law or laws. Substances to get high have been around for hundreds and probably thousands of years, these substances that some of us like should not be any concern to others. Even my pet cat loves his catnip and appears to get a high from it; should I prohibit this little pleasure? I let him occasionally have it even if, for example, my neighbor thinks catnip is affecting the normal nature of my cat. How about if I get a rise from snorting or smoking one of the herbs in my kitchen cabinet? Whose business is it if I like to use herbs in this manner? Maybe we should also outlaw catnip and herbs? Again, drug use for whatever purpose is a personal decision and all the laws against the use of drugs are not going to stop me from using drugs. *(From Venturelli's research files, male residing in a Midwestern town, age 27, May 6, 2010)*

A third response to the same question:

My drug use? Whose business is it anyway? As long as I don't affect your life when I do drugs, what business is it but my own? We come into the world alone and leave this world alone. I don't bother anyone else about whether or not so and so uses drugs, unless of course, their drug use puts me in jeopardy (like a bus driver or pilot high on drugs). On certain days when things are slow, I even get a little high on cocaine while trading stocks. These are the same clients who I have had for years and who really trust my advice. Ask my clients whether they are happy with my investment advice. I handle accounts with millions of dollars for corporations and even the board of education! Never was my judgment impaired or adversely affected because of too much coke. In fact, I know that I work even better under a little buzz. Now, I know this stuff has the potential to become addictive, but I don't

let it. I know how to use it and when to lay off for a few weeks. *(From Venturelli's research files, male investment broker working in a major metropolitan city in California, age 48, June 2, 2000)*

A fourth response to the same question, from an interviewee who recently moved from Indiana to Colorado:

Well, things are changing regarding drug use purely for recreational purposes. I am referring to marijuana of course. In Colorado, marijuana is now legalized. I also think this is the way it should be not only in Colorado but also throughout the country. I can now actually see how state after state will eventually legalize marijuana. There will be holdout states, like usually deep southern states, but it's just a matter of time. I think it was Oakland, California, where by taxing the sale of marijuana, the city was collecting a nice amount of tax revenues from marijuana sales. If I am not in error, it was reported as millions of dollars they were collecting. Now, don't you think this alone will attract other cities and states to legalize and tax this drug in order to gain tax revenues, especially when state and city tax revenues are in dire need to increase revenue coming in? It won't be the spread of liberalism that will legalize marijuana; it will be common business sense that will get rid of the ridiculous laws outlawing marijuana use and sales. I have always smoked pot and nothing has ever stopped me. On top of this add the millions who feel the same way. If you don't want to use this drug to relax like others may use alcohol that is fine but leave the users alone and stop making law violators! It is still illegal and you [referring to this interviewer] and I know that all these laws and the millions upon millions spent on trying to stop marijuana drug users have not worked, so why keep this up? Again, why prohibit something that given its history cannot be stopped? *(From Venturelli's research files, male attorney, currently practicing law and residing in the state of Colorado, age 33, January 2, 2013)*

These four interviews reflect vastly contrasting views and attitudes about drug use. The first interview shows the most contrast from the second, third, and fourth interviews. The second, third, and fourth interviews show a similarity of views about drug use, largely from an insider's (user's) perspective, which indicate a strong determination and belief that drug use should not be legally controlled and should be left to the discretion of users. Although much about these viewpoints can certainly be debated, an interesting finding is that such vastly different views about drug use are not only evident, but also, more importantly, often divide drug users and nonusers. From a more social psychological standpoint, drug users or sympathizers of drug use are often considered **insiders** with regard to their drug use, whereas nonusers or those who are against drug use are **outsiders**. These two classifications result in decidedly different sets of values and attitudes about drug usage. Such great differences of opinion and views about drugs and drug use often result from the following sources: (1) prior socialization experiences, such as family upbringing, relations with siblings, and types of peer-group associations; (2) the amount of exposure to drug use and drug users; (3) the age of initial exposure to drug use; and (4) whether an attitude change has occurred regarding the acceptance or rejection of using drugs. Keep in mind that this text views the following four principal factors as affecting how a drug user experiences a drug:

1. *Biological, genetic, and pharmacological factors.* Substance abuse and addiction involve biological and genetic factors. The pharmacology of drug use focuses on how the ingredients of a particular drug affect the body and the nervous system and, in turn, a person's experience with a particular drug.
2. *Cultural factors.* Society's views of drug use, as determined by custom and tradition, affect our initial approach to and use of a particular drug.
3. *Social factors.* The motivation for taking a particular drug is affected by needs such as diminishing physical pain; curing an illness; providing relaxation; relieving stress or anxiety; trying to escape reality; self-medicating; heightening awareness; wanting to distort and change visual, auditory, or sensory inputs; or strengthening confidence. Included in the category of social factors is the belief that attitudes about drug use develop from the values and attitudes of other drug users; the norms in their communities, subcultures, peer groups, and families; and the drug user's personal experiences with using drugs. (These are also known as *influencing social factors.*)
4. *Contextual factors.* Specific contexts define and determine personal dispositions toward drug use as demonstrated by moods and attitudes about such activity. Specifically, these factors encompass the drug-taking social behavior that develops from the physical surroundings where the drug is used. For example, drug use may be perceived as more acceptable at fraternity parties, while socializing with drug-using friends, outdoors in a secluded area with other drug users, in private homes, secretly at work, or at music concerts.

Paying attention to the cultural, social, and contextual factors of drug use leads us to explore the sociology and psychology of drug use. Equally important are the biological, genetic, and pharmacological factors and consequences that directly focus on why and how drugs may be appealing and how they affect the body—primarily the central nervous system and brain functions.

Although substances that affect both mind and body functioning are commonly called *drugs*, researchers in the field of drug or substance abuse use a more precise term: **psychoactive drugs (substances)**. Why the preference for using this term as opposed to *drugs*? Because the term *psychoactive drugs* is more precise regarding *how* drugs affect the body. This term focuses on how drugs affect the **central nervous system (CNS)**, the part of the nervous system composed of the spinal cord and brain that is responsible for integrating sensory information and responding accordingly. In particular, the term encompasses how psychoactive drugs alter mood, consciousness, thought processes, perception, or behavior. Psychoactive drugs can be used to

## KEY TERMS

**insiders**
people on the inside; those who approve of or use drugs or both

**outsiders**
people on the outside; those who do not approve of or do not use drugs

**psychoactive drugs (substances)**
drug compounds (substances) that affect the central nervous system and alter consciousness or perceptions

**central nervous system (CNS)**
part of the nervous system composed of the spinal cord and brain that is responsible for integrating sensory information and responding accordingly

treat physical, psychological, or mental illness. In addition, with continued use, our bodies can tolerate increasingly larger doses of drugs, often resulting in the need for progressively greater amounts to achieve the same level of effect. For many substances, a user is at risk of moving from occasional to regular use or from moderate to heavy use, ultimately culminating in chronic use. A chronic user may then risk **addiction** a mostly psychological attachment defined as "a complex condition, a brain disease that is manifested by compulsive substance use despite harmful consequences . . ." (APA, 2019) and experiences **withdrawal symptoms** that are psychological or physical in nature whenever the drug is not consumed.

Generally speaking, any substance that modifies the nervous system and state of consciousness is a **drug**. Such modifications include one or more of the following: enhancement, inhibition, or distortion of the body that affects patterns of behavior and social functioning. Psychoactive drugs are classified as either **licit** (legal) or **illicit** (illegal). (See **Table 1.1** for a sample list of slang terms used by drug users.) For example, coffee, tea, cocoa, alcohol, tobacco, and **over-the-counter (OTC)** drugs are licit. When licit drugs are used in moderation, they often go unnoticed and are often

Examples of illicit drugs that can become costly once drug dependence occurs.

© Comstock Images/Getty Images.

socially acceptable. Marijuana, cocaine, crack, and all of the hallucinogenic types of drugs are examples of illicit drugs. With the exception of marijuana—which some states allow for medical use and small amounts for personal use—federal law continues to prohibit the possession and use of all of these drugs.

Researchers have made some interesting findings about legal and illegal drug use:

- The use of legal substances such as alcohol and tobacco is much more common than the use of illegal drugs such as marijuana, cocaine, heroin, and hallucinogens (psychedelics). Other legal drugs such as depressants and stimulants, although less popular than alcohol and tobacco, are still more widely used than heroin and LSD.
- The popular use of licit drugs, particularly alcohol and tobacco, has caused far more deaths, sickness, violent crime, economic loss, and other social problems than the combined use of all illicit drugs. (See **Figure 1.1** for an illustrated comparison.)

Cigarette smoking and exposure to tobacco smoke led to at least 480,000 premature deaths annually in the United States (includes deaths from secondhand smoke: 278,544 deaths annually among men and 201,773 deaths annually among women). More than 88,000 U.S. deaths are caused by excessive alcohol consumption each year (direct and indirect causes of death include drunk driving, cirrhosis of the liver, falls, cancer, and stroke). The popular use of licit drugs, particularly alcohol and tobacco, has caused far more death, sickness, violent crime, economic loss, and other social problems than the combined use of all illicit drugs. The annual overdose death rate for the 12-month period

## KEY TERMS

**addiction**

generally refers to the psychological attachment to a drug; addiction to "harder" drugs such as heroin results in both psychological and physical attachment to the chemical properties of the drug, with the resulting satisfaction (reward) derived from using the drug in question

**withdrawal symptoms**

psychological and physical symptoms that result when a drug is absent from the body; physical symptoms are generally present in cases of drug dependence to more addictive drugs such as heroin; physical and psychological symptoms of withdrawal include perspiration, nausea, boredom, anxiety, and muscle spasms

**drug(s)**

any substance that modifies (either by enhancing, inhibiting, or distorting) mind or body functioning

**licit drugs**

legalized drugs such as coffee, alcohol, and tobacco

**illicit drugs**

illegal drugs such as marijuana, cocaine, and LSD

**over-the-counter (OTC)**

legalized drugs sold without a prescription

**TABLE 1.1** A Sampling of 73,000 Slang Terms Relating to Drugs, Drug Use, and the Drug Trade

| Slang Term | What It Means | Slang Term | What It Means |
|---|---|---|---|
| 24-7 | Crack cocaine | Blunt | Marijuana or cocaine inside a cigar |
| 80 | OxyContin pill | Boost and shoot | Steal to support a drug habit |
| 714s | Methaqualone | Brain ticklers | Amphetamines |
| 3750 | Marijuana and crack rolled in a joint | Brown bombers | LSD |
| Abolic | Veterinary steroids | Brown sugar | Heroin |
| A-bomb | Marijuana cigarette with heroin or opium | Buddha | Potent marijuana spiked with opium |
| AC/DC | Codeine cough syrup | Bull dog | Heroin |
| Acid, acid cube | LSD, sugar cube with LSD | Bundle | Heroin |
| Acid freak | Heavy user of LSD | Ditch weed | Inferior quality marijuana |
| Adam | Methylenedioxymethamphetamine (MDMA) | Dr. Feelgood | Heroin |
| Air blast | Inhalants | Easy lay | Gamma hydroxybutyrate (GHB) |
| All star | User of multiple drugs | Fantasy | GHB |
| Amped | High on amphetamines | Flower flipping | Ecstasy (MDMA) mixed with mushrooms |
| Angel dust | PCP | Forget-me-drug | Rohypnol |
| Author | Doctor who writes illegal prescriptions | Fries | Crack cocaine |
| Baby habit | Occasional use of drugs | Garbage rock | Crack cocaine |
| Balloon | Heroin supplier; a penny balloon that contains narcotics | Hit the hay | Smoke weed |
| Bam | Amphetamine; depressants | Hippie crack | Inhalants |
| Barbies | Depressants | Hot ice | Smokable methamphetamine |
| Battery acid | LSD | Huff, huffing | Inhalants, to sniff an inhalant |
| Batu | Smokable methamphetamine | Ice cream habit | Occasional use of a drug |
| Beam me up, Scottie | Crack dipped in PCP | Idiot pills | Depressants |
| Beanies | Methamphetamine | Kiddie dope | Prescription drugs |
| Beast | Heroin, LSD | Lemonade | Heroin; poor quality drugs |
| Belladonna | PCP | Lunch money drug | Rohypnol |
| Bender | Drug party | Magic mushroom | Psilocybin or psilocin |
| Biker's coffee | Methamphetamine and coffee | Monkey dust | PCP |
| Bin Laden | Heroin (after 9/11) | Moon gas | Inhalants |
| Black beauties | Amphetamines, depressants | Mother's little helper | Depressants |
| Blasted | Under the influence of drugs | Nose candy | Cocaine |

(continues)

**TABLE 1.1** A Sampling of 73,000 Slang Terms Relating to Drugs, Drug Use, and the Drug Trade (*continued*)

| Slang Term | What It Means | Slang Term | What It Means |
|---|---|---|---|
| Blow your mind | Getting high on hallucinogens | Paper boy | Heroin peddler |
| Pepsi habit | Occasional use of drugs | Tornado | Crack cocaine |
| Pony | Crack cocaine | Totally spent | Hangover after MDMA |
| Ringer | Good hit of crack, to hear bells | Water-water | Marijuana cigarettes dipped in embalming fluid or laced with PCP |
| Shot | To inject a drug, an amount of coke | West Coast | Ritalin (ADHD drug) |
| Soda | Injectable cocaine | Working man's cocaine | Methamphetamine |
| Special "K" | Ketamine | Zig Zag man | Marijuana rolling papers |
| Strawberry | LSD; female who trades sex for crack or money to buy crack | Zombie | PCP; heavy user of drugs |
| The devil | Crack cocaine | Zoom | Marijuana laced with PCP |

Reproduced from Office of National Drug Control Policy (ONDCP). (2016). *Street terms: Drugs and the drug trade*. Washington, DC: Author. Retrieved from http://www.streetlightpublications.net/misc/ondcp.htm

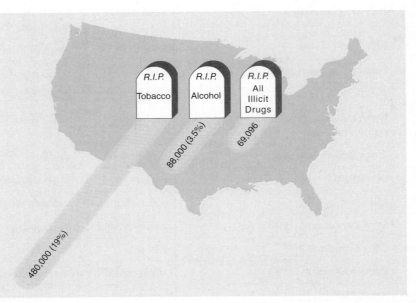

**FIGURE 1.1** Cigarette smoking and exposure to tobacco smoke led to at least 480,000 premature deaths annually in the United States (includes deaths from secondhand smoke (278,544 deaths annually among men and 201,773 deaths annually among women). More than 88,000 U.S. deaths are caused by excessive alcohol consumption each year (direct and indirect causes of death include drunk driving, cirrhosis of the liver, falls, cancer, and stroke). The popular use of licit drugs, particularly alcohol and tobacco, has caused far more deaths, sickness, violent crimes, economic loss, and other social problems than the combined use of all illicit drugs. The annual overdose death rate for the 12-month period ending November 2018 was 69,096, which was a drop from 72,300 in 2017. "The drug overdose death numbers include deaths due to natural and semi-synthetic opioids, synthetic opioids other than methadone (fentanyl and its analogs), methadone, methamphetamines and other stimulants, cocaine, and benzodiazepines" (Cato Institute, 2019). Drug licit and illicit overdose deaths rose from 16,849 in 1999 to 69,096, in 2018. "[T]he sharpest increase occurred among deaths related to fentanyl and fentanyl analogs (other synthetic narcotics) with more than 28,400 overdose deaths" (NIDA, 2019a).

Data from Mokdad, A. H., Marks, J. S., Stroup, D. F., & Gerberding, J. L. (2004, March 10). Actual causes of death in the United States, 2000. *Journal of the American Medical Association (JAMA)*, 291, 1238–1245; Centers for Disease Control and Prevention (CDC). (2019, November 15). Fast facts. Atlanta, GA: U.S. Department of Health and Human Services. Retrieved from https://www.cdc.gov/tobacco/data_statistics/fact_sheets/fast_facts/index.htm; Centers for Disease Control and Prevention (CDC). (2018a, January 3). Fact sheets—Alcohol use and your health. Atlanta, GA: U.S. Department of Health and Human Services. Retrieved from https://www.cdc.gov/alcohol/fact-sheets/alcohol-use.htm; Singer, J. A. (2019, June 26). CDC provisional drug death numbers show slight improvement. Credit harm reduction. Washington, DC: CATO Institute. Retrieved from https://www.cato.org/blog/cdc-provisional-drug-death-numbers-show-slight-improvement-credit-harm-reduction; National Institute on Drug Abuse (NIDA). (2019a). Overdose death rates. Bethesda, MD: National Institutes of Health. Retrieved from https://www.drugabuse.gov/related-topics/trends-statistics/overdose-death-rates

ending November 2018 was 69,096, which was a drop from 72,300 in 2017. "The drug overdose death numbers include deaths due to natural and semi-synthetic opioids, synthetic opioids other than methadone (fentanyl and its analogs), methadone, methamphetamines and other stimulants, cocaine, and benzodiazepines" (Singer, 2019). Licit and illicit drug overdose deaths rose from 16,849 in 1999 to 69,096 in 2018. "[T]he sharpest increase occurred among deaths related to fentanyl and fentanyl analogs (other synthetic narcotics) with more than 28,400 overdose deaths" (NIDA, 2019a). (Data from CDC, 2018a, 2019; Mokdad, Marks, Stroup, & Gerberding, 2004; NIDA, 2019a; Singer, 2019.)

Societal reaction to various drugs changes with time and place. Today, opium is an illegal drug and widely condemned as a *pan-pathogen* (a cause of all ills). In the 18th and 19th centuries, however, it was a legal drug and was popularly praised as a panacea (a cure for all ills). Alcohol use was widespread in the United States in the early 1800s, became illegal during the 1920s, was legalized a second time in the 1930s, and has been widely used ever since. Cigarette smoking is legal in all countries today. In the 17th century, it was illegal in most countries, and smokers were sometimes harshly punished. For example, in Russia, smokers could lose their noses; in Hindustan (India), they could lose their lips; and in China, they could lose their heads (Thio, 1983, 1995, 2000). Today, new emphasis in the United States on the public health hazards from cigarettes again is leading some people to consider new measures to restrict or even outlaw tobacco smoking.

**Table 1.2** introduces some of the terminology you will encounter throughout this text. It is important that you understand how the definitions vary.

**TABLE 1.2** Commonly Used Terms

| Term | Description |
| --- | --- |
| Gateway drugs | The word *gateway* suggests a path or entryway leading to an entrance. Gateway is a theory that the early use of alcohol, tobacco products, and marijuana (the most heavily used illicit type of drug) leads to the use of more powerfully addictive drugs such as cocaine, heroin, and highly addictive prescription medicines. |
| Medicines | Compounds generally prescribed by a physician that treat, prevent, or alleviate the symptoms of disease. (These can also include over-the-counter [OTC] drugs purchased at pharmacies.) |
| Prescription medicines | Drugs that are prescribed by a physician. Common examples include antibiotics, antidepressants, and drugs prescribed to relieve pain, induce stimulation, or induce relaxation. These drugs are taken under a physician's recommendation because they are more potent than OTC drugs. In the United States, on a yearly basis, physicians write approximately 4.0 billion prescriptions (Henry J. Kaiser Family Foundation, 2015), with sales totaling $374 billion in 2015 ("U.S. Prescription Drug Spending," 2015). |
| Over-the-counter (OTC) | OTC drugs can be purchased at will without seeking medical advice or a prescription. Examples include aspirin, laxatives, diet pills, cough suppressants, and sore throat medicines. Approximately 1,000 active ingredients are used in the more than 100,000 OTC products available in the marketplace today (Consumer Healthcare Products Association [CHPA], 2012), and it is estimated that there are more than 300,000 marketed OTC drug products (U.S. Food and Drug Administration 2015). In 2010, $23 billion were spent in the United States on OTC medicines* (CHPA, 2012). |
| Drug misuse | The unintentional or inappropriate use of prescribed or OTC drugs. Misuse includes but is not limited to (I) taking more drugs than prescribed; (2) using OTC or psychoactive drugs in excess without medical supervision; (3) mixing drugs with alcohol or other drugs, often to accentuate euphoric effects or simply not caring about the effects of mixing drugs; (4) using old medicines to self-treat new symptoms of an illness or ailment; (5) discontinuing certain prescribed drugs at will or against a physician's recommendation; and (6) administering prescription drugs to family members or friends without medical approval and supervision. |
| Drug abuse | Also known as *chemical or substance abuse*. The willful misuse of either licit or illicit drugs for recreation, perceived necessity, or convenience. Drug abuse differs from drug use in that drug use is taking or using drugs, whereas drug abuse is a more intense and often willful misuse of drugs, often to the point of becoming addicted. |

*(continues)*

**TABLE 1.2** Commonly Used Terms (*continued*)

| Term | Description |
|---|---|
| Drug addiction | Drug addiction involves noncasual or nonrecreational drug use. A frequent symptom is intense psychological preoccupation with obtaining and consuming drugs. Most often psychological and—in some cases, depending on the drug—physiological symptoms of withdrawal are manifested when the craving for the drug is not satisfied. Today, more emphasis is placed on the psychological craving (mental attachment) to the drug than on the more physiologically based withdrawal symptoms of addiction. |

*This amount excludes OTC sales by Walmart and does not include vitamins, minerals, and nutritional supplements.

Data from Fischer, M. A., Stedman, M. R., Lii, J., Vogeli, C., Shrank, W. H., Brookhart, M. A., & Weissman, J. S. (2010 April). Primary medication non-adherence: Analysis of 195,930 electronic prescriptions. *Journal of General Internal Medicine, 25*, 284–290; The Henry J. Kaiser Family Foundation. (2010). *Prescription drug trends*. Retrieved from http://www.kff.org/rxdrugs/3057.cfm. Accessed January 12, 2013; Consumer Healthcare Products Association (CHPA). (2019). *OTC retail sales—1964–2011*. Washington, DC: Author; U.S. Food and Drug Administration. (2015). *Drug applications for over-the-counter (OTC) drugs*. Retrieved from http://www.fda.gov/drugs/developmentapprovalprocess/howdrugsaredevelopedandapproved/approvalapplications/over-the-counterdrugs/default.htm; Consumer Healthcare Products Association (CHPA). (2012). *The value of OTC medicine to the United States*. Washington, DC: Booz & Co. Retrieved from http://www.yourhealthathand.org/images/uploads/The_Value_of_OTC_Medicine_to_the_United_States_BoozCo.pdf

# Major Types of Commonly Abused Drugs

The six types of major drugs in use are (1) prescription drugs, (2) over-the-counter drugs, (3) recreational drugs (e.g., coffee, tea, alcohol, tobacco, and chocolate), (4) illicit drugs, (5) herbal preparations (generally derived from plants), and (6) commercial drugs (paints, glues, pesticides, and household cleaning products).

To begin, we now briefly examine the major drugs of use and often abuse. The drugs examined next are prescription drugs, performance-enhancing drugs, stimulants, bath salts, hallucinogens (psychedelics) and other similar compounds, depressants, alcohol, nicotine, cannabis (marijuana and hashish), synthetic cannabis (Spice and K2), anabolic steroids, inhalants and organic solvents, narcotics and opiates, and designer drugs, synthetic drugs, and synthetic opioids. A brief overview of each follows.

## ▮ Prescription and Performance-Enhancing Drugs

The term *nonmedical use* of prescription drugs also refers to these categories of misuse. The three classes of medication most commonly misused are:

**KEY TERM**

**psychotherapeutic drugs**
drugs that are used to treat mental disorders such as depression, schizophrenia, and manic–depressive disorders

1. *opioids*, which are usually prescribed to treat pain;
2. *central nervous system* (CNS) *depressants*, which include tranquilizers, sedatives, and hypnotics, and are used to treat anxiety and sleep disorders; and
3. *stimulants*, which are most often prescribed to treat attention-deficit hyperactivity disorder (ADHD)

Many national studies and published reports indicate that the intentional abuse of prescription drugs such as pain relievers, tranquilizers, stimulants, and sedatives to get high is a growing concern—particularly among teens—in the United States. **Psychotherapeutic drugs** are drugs that are used to treat mental disorders such as depression, schizophrenia, and manic–depressive disorders. These drugs warrant special attention given that they now make up a significantly larger part of the overall U.S. drug problem than they did 10 to 15 years ago. In part this is because the use increased for many prescription drugs over that period and because the use of many street drugs has declined substantially since the middle to late 1990s. It seems likely that young people are less concerned about the dangers of using these prescription drugs outside of a medical regimen because they are widely used for legitimate purposes. (Indeed, the low levels of perceived risk for sedatives and amphetamines observed among 12th graders illustrate this point.) Also, prescription psychotherapeutic drugs are now being advertised directly to the consumer, which implies that they are both widely used and safe to use (Johnston, O'Malley, Miech, Bachman, & Schulenberg, 2016; SAMHSA, 2019c).

In the United States, young people and adults frequently abuse prescription drugs; the only illicit drug that is abused more frequently is marijuana (SAMHSA. 2019a). In 2017, "an estimated 18 million people (more than 6% of those aged 12 and older) have misused prescription drugs such as prescription opioids, CNS depressants, and stimulants at least once in the past year" (NIDA, 2018a).

Misuse of prescription drugs is highest among young adults ages 18 to 25, with 14.4% reporting nonmedical use in the past year. Among youth ages 12 to 17, 4.9% reported past-year nonmedical use of prescription medications (Miech et al., 2017). After alcohol, marijuana, and tobacco, prescription drugs (taken nonmedically) are among the most commonly used drugs by 12th graders. NIDA's *Monitoring the Future* survey of substance use and attitudes in teens found that about 6% of high school seniors reported past-year nonmedical use of the prescription stimulant Adderall® in 2017, and 2% reported misusing the opioid pain reliever Vicodin (NIDA, 2018a). Regarding older adults, "more than 80% of older patients (ages 57 to 85 years) use at least one prescription medication on a daily basis, with more than 50% taking more than five medications or supplements daily" (NIDA, 2018a).

Three categories of prescription drugs that are currently abused are narcotics, depressants, and stimulants. Narcotics (e.g., OxyContin, Vicodin, Percocet) include analgesics or **opioids** that are generally prescribed for physical pain. Abuse occurs when they are used nonmedically because of their euphoric and numbing effects. Depressants (e.g., Xanax, Valium, Librium) are generally used to treat anxiety and sleep disorders. These drugs are abused because of their sedating properties. Stimulants (e.g., Ritalin, Dexedrine, Meridia) are used to treat attention-deficit disorder (ADD), attention-deficit hyperactivity disorder (ADHD), and asthma. These drugs are abused because of their euphoric effects and energizing potential.

The two drugs in the stimulants category most often abused are Ritalin (methylphenidate hydrochloride) and Adderall (amphetamine). These prescription drugs are legitimately prescribed for ADHD, ADD, and narcolepsy (a sleep disorder) (Center for Substance Abuse Research [CESAR], 2003). When used nonmedically, they are taken orally as tablets or the tablets are crushed into a powder and snorted (a far more popular method). Students often illegally purchase these tablets for $5 each from other students who have a legal prescription for the medication.

I feel like Dr. Pill. All these brothers [fraternity brothers] are always looking for me at parties so that I can sell them a few tabs. What the heck, I make extra money selling Ritalin, enough to buy essentials like beer and cigarettes. *(From Venturelli's research files, male undergraduate student at a Midwestern university, age 20, December 9, 2004)*

And,

Funny how when I go back to the frat house during homecoming there are other undergrads who have taken over my business and continue to sell their prescribed Ritalin mostly for partying. *(A second interview with the same former student, age 26, now employed in real estate, October 2, 2010)*

These drugs often are used in conjunction with alcohol or marijuana to enhance the high or to stay awake to increase comprehension and remain focused while reading or studying for an exam (CESAR, 2003). Both prescription drugs (Ritalin and Adderall) are readily available and can be easily obtained by teenagers, who may abuse these drugs to experience a variety of desired effects. Increasingly, younger adolescents are obtaining prescription drugs from classmates, friends, and family members or are stealing the drugs from school medicine dispensaries and from other people who have legitimate prescriptions.

Ritalin, Adderall, and other stimulant abusers tend to be late middle school, high school, and college students. Other findings regarding teen abuse of stimulants Ritalin and Adderall include the following (Partnership for Drug-Free Kids, 2016):

- One in eight teens (about 2.7 million) report having misused or abused Ritalin or Adderall at least once in their lifetime.
- Around 1.9 million teens (9%) report having misused or abused Ritalin or Adderall in the past year.
- One in four teens (26%) believe that prescription drugs can be used as a study aid.
- Almost one-third of parents (29%) say they believe that ADHD medication can improve a child's academic or testing performance, even if the teen does not have ADHD.
- One in six parents (16%) believe that using prescription drugs to get high is safer than using street drugs.

**KEY TERM**

**opioids**
drugs derived from opium

- More than half of teens (56%) indicate that it is easy to get prescription drugs from their parents' medicine cabinet. In fact, about half of parents (49%) say anyone can access their medicine cabinet.

In addition, the Partnership for Drug-Free Kids and MetLife Foundation (2013) note that Hispanic and African American teens are more likely to report misusing or abusing prescription drugs compared to their white counterparts, with 27% of Hispanics, 29% of African Americans, and 20% of Caucasians reporting use.

With regard to college students using Adderall, the findings include the following (Muir Wood, 2016):

- Full-time college students were twice as likely as non–full-time college students to abuse Adderall.
- About 6.4% of college students admitted to unauthorized Adderall use in 2006–2007.
- College students who abused Adderall were three times as likely to abuse marijuana, eight times as likely to abuse prescription tranquilizers, and five times as likely to abuse prescription painkillers.
- Cocaine use is more common among college students who use Adderall, and students who use both drugs face an increased risk of heart attack, heart problems, and stroke.

## ▪ Stimulants

Some stimulants can be considered to be **gateway drugs** (see definition in Table 1.2); these substances act on the CNS by increasing alertness, excitation, euphoria, pulse rate, and blood pressure. Insomnia and loss of appetite are common outcomes. The user initially experiences pleasant effects, such as a sense of increased energy and a state of euphoria or being "high." In addition, users feel restless and talkative and have trouble sleeping. High doses used over the long term can produce personality changes. Some of the psychological risks associated with chronic stimulant use include violent, erratic, or paranoid behavior.

### KEY TERMS

**gateway drugs**
alcohol, tobacco, and marijuana—types of drugs that when used excessively may lead to using other and more addictive drugs such as cocaine, heroin, or crack

**Drug Enforcement Administration (DEA)**
the principal federal agency responsible for enforcing U.S. drug laws

Other effects can include confusion, anxiety, and depression and loss of interest in sex or food. *Major stimulants* include amphetamines, cocaine and crack, methamphetamine (meth), and methylphenidate (Ritalin). *Minor stimulants* include, cocoa, theophylline, theobromine, sugar, caffeine, and nicotine (the most addictive minor stimulant).

## ▪ Synthetic Cathinones (Bath Salts)

Synthetic cathinones, also commonly known as *bath salts*, are human-made stimulants chemically related to cathinone, a substance found in the khat plant. Khat is a shrub grown in East Africa and southern Arabia, where some people chew its leaves for their mild stimulant effects. Human-made versions of cathinone can be much stronger than the natural product and, in some cases, extremely dangerous (NIDA, 2018b).

Synthetic cathinones are marketed as cheap substitutes for other stimulants such as methamphetamine and cocaine, and methylenedioxymethamphetamine (MDMA), which is sold as Molly, often contain synthetic cathinones instead (NIDA, 2018b).

The usual method of taking this drug is sniffing or snorting, but it can also be taken orally, smoked, or mixed with a solution and then injected into a vein. According to Dr. Mark Ryan, director of the Louisiana Poison Center, bath salts are "the worst drug" he has seen in his 20 years there, noting that "with LSD, you might see pink elephants, but with this drug, you see demons, aliens, extreme paranoia, heart attacks, and superhuman strength like Superman. . . . If you had a reaction, it was a bad reaction" (Vargas-Cooper, 2012, p. 60). Other reactions include "very severe paranoia, suicidal thoughts, agitation, combative/violent behavior, confusion, hallucination/psychosis, increased heart rate, hypertension, chest pain, death or serious injury. The speed of onset is 15 minutes, while the length of the high from these drugs is 4–6 hours" (Partnership at DrugFree.Org, 2013). In October 2011, these synthetic stimulants were listed as Schedule I substances under the Controlled Substances Act. The **Drug Enforcement Administration (DEA)** classifies illicit drugs under Schedules I through V, largely depending on their abuse potential. Synthetic stimulants are classified as Schedule I drugs, meaning that they have a high potential for abuse.

## ▪ Hallucinogens, Psychedelics, and Other Similar Drugs

Whether synthetic or grown naturally, hallucinogens and psychedelic drugs produce intense alterations of perceptions, thoughts, and feelings. They

Packets of bath salts sold in head shops.

most certainly influence the complex inner workings of the human mind, causing users to refer to these drugs as *psychedelics* (because they cause hallucinations or distortion of reality and thinking). In addition to amplifying states of mind, hallucinogens induce a reality that is reported to be qualitatively different from that of ordinary consciousness. For example, while the user is under their influence, these drugs can affect the senses of taste, smell, hearing, and vision. Tolerance to hallucinogens builds rapidly, which means that increasing amounts of this drug are needed for similar effects. Hallucinogens include LSD, mescaline, **MDMA** (Ecstasy), phencyclidine (PCP), psilocybin or "magic mushrooms," ketamine, and the more potent (hybrid) varieties of marijuana, hashish, and opium that are smoked.

## Depressants

These drugs depress the CNS. If taken in high enough quantities, they produce insensibility or stupor. Depressants are also taken for some of the same reasons as hallucinogens, such as to relieve boredom, stress, or anxiety. In addition, the effects of both opioids (drugs that are derived from opium) and morphine derivatives appeal to many people who are struggling with emotional problems and looking for physical and emotional relief, and in some cases to induce sleep. Depressants include alcohol (ethanol), opiates (such as heroin and morphine), sedatives, barbiturates, benzodiazepines (such as diazepam [Valium]), and methaqualone (Quaalude).

### ALCOHOL

Known as a gateway drug, **ethanol** is a colorless, volatile, and pungent liquid produced through the fermentation of grains, berries, or other fruits and vegetables. Alcohol is a depressant that mainly affects the CNS. Excessive amounts of alcohol often cause a progressive loss of inhibitions,

flushing and dizziness, loss of coordination, impaired motor skills, blurred vision, slurred speech, sudden mood swings, vomiting, irregular pulse, and memory impairment. Chronic heavy use may lead to high blood pressure, arrhythmia (irregular heartbeat), and cirrhosis (severe liver deterioration).

## Nicotine

Nicotine is also considered a gateway drug. It is a highly addictive, colorless, highly volatile liquid alkaloid found in all tobacco products, including cigarettes, chewing tobacco, pipe tobacco, and cigars. Because nicotine is so addictive and tobacco use is still socially acceptable under certain circumstances, smokers often start young and have an extremely difficult time quitting. Long-term use of tobacco products can lead to several different chronic respiratory ailments and cancers.

## Cannabis (Marijuana and Hashish)

Cannabis is the most widely used illicit drug[2] in the United States. Marijuana consists of the dried and crushed leaves, flowers, and seeds of the *Cannabis sativa* plant, which readily grows in many

---

[2]Federal law specifies that cannabis is an illicit drug, although 33 states have legalized this drug for medical purposes or for recreational use as of December 2019.

### KEY TERMS

**MDMA**
a type of illicit drug known as Ecstasy or Adam that has stimulant and hallucinogenic properties

**ethanol**
the chemical and pharmacological term for drinking alcohol; the psychoactive ingredient in alcoholic beverages; often called *grain alcohol*

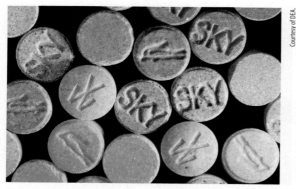

Courtesy of DEA.

Designer pills made from the illicit drug Ecstasy. This drug has some stimulant properties like amphetamines as well as hallucinogenic properties like LSD.

parts of the world. Delta-9-tetrahydrocannabinol (THC) is the primary psychoactive, mind-altering ingredient in marijuana that produces euphoria (often referred to as a "high"). Plant parts (mainly the leaves and buds of the plant) are usually dried, crushed, and smoked much like tobacco products. Other ways of ingesting marijuana include finely crushing the leaves and mixing them into the butter or oil that goes into making cookie or brownie batter and baking the batter. Another current derivative is **marijuana wax**, also known as *wax* or *ear wax, butter, honey oil, shatter, BHO* (which stands for "butane honey oil" or "butane hash oil"), and *dabs*. To date, this is one of the most powerful and the most potent (80% pure THC) types of marijuana on both the illegal and legal drug markets (in states where marijuana has either been decriminalized or medically sanctioned), with smoking or vaporizing this type of marijuana leading to a "quicker, stronger high" (Kimble,

### KEY TERMS

**marijuana wax**
a more recent, extremely potent cannabis product with approximately 80% THC levels made by using butane to extract the THC; the process produces a "waxy" residue that is smoked or vaporized and is highly hallucinogenic, often resulting in high levels of physical and mental impairment

**designer drugs**
new drugs that are developed by people intending to circumvent the illegality of a drug by modifying a drug into a new compound; Ecstasy is an example. Also known as *synthetic drugs* or *synthetic opioids*

**synthetic drugs or synthetic opioids**
see designer drugs

**structural analogs**
new molecular species created by modifying the basic molecular skeleton of a compound; structural analogs are structurally related to their parent compounds

2013). Finally, hashish is a cannabis derivative that contains the purest form of resin and also has extremely high amounts of THC.

### ▌ Designer Drugs, Synthetic Drugs, and Synthetic Opioids

In addition to the most commonly abused illicit drug categories just described, innovations in technology have produced new categories known as **designer drugs**, **synthetic drugs**, and **synthetic opioids**. These relatively new types of drugs are developed by people who seek to circumvent the illegality of a drug by modifying the drug into a new compound. Ecstasy is an example of a designer drug, synthetic drug, or synthetic opioid. Such drugs are created as **structural analogs** of substances already scheduled and legally prohibited under the Controlled Substances Act. Structural analogs are the drugs that result from altered chemical structures of already existing illicit drugs. Generally, these drugs are created by an underground chemist whose goal is to make a profit by creating compounds that mimic, change, or intensify the psychoactive effects of controlled substances. The number of designer drugs that are created and sold illegally is extremely large.

Anyone with knowledge of college-level chemistry can alter the chemical ingredients and produce new designer drugs, although it may be nearly impossible to predict their properties or effects except by trial and error. Currently, three major types of synthetic analog drugs are available through the illicit drug market: analogs of PCP; analogs of fentanyl and meperidine (both synthetic narcotic analgesics), such as Demerol or MPPP (also called MPTP or PEPAP); and analogs of amphetamine and methamphetamine (which have stimulant and hallucinogenic properties), such as MDMA, known as Ecstasy or Adam, which is widely used on college campuses as a euphoriant.

The production of these high-technology psychoactive substances is a sign of the new levels of risk and additional challenge to the criminal justice system. As the production and risk associated with the use of such substances increase, the need for a broader, better-informed view of drug use becomes even more important than in the past.

#### SYNTHETIC CANNABINOIDS: SPICE AND K2

Synthetic cannabinoids are human-made mind-altering chemicals that are either sprayed on dried, shredded plant material so they can be smoked or sold as liquids to be vaporized and inhaled in e-cigarettes and other devices. These products are also known as *herbal* or *liquid incense* (NIDA, 2018c).

Synthetic cannabinoids are substances that are designed to affect the body in a manner similar to marijuana but are not derived from the marijuana plant (Office of National Drug Control Policy [ONDCP] 2013b). They are most often smoked like marijuana. Street names for synthetic cannabis include *Spice, K2, Mr. Smiley, Red X Dawn*, and *Blaze*. "A package of K2, a synthetic marijuana, is a concoction of dried herbs sprayed with chemicals, used in the herbal blends that are sold in head shops on the Internet to a growing number of teens and young adults" (Caldwell, 2010). Many of the contents are listed as inactive on the product packaging (DEA. 2012). A retired organic chemistry researcher from Clemson University reports medical problems from synthetic cannabis use as

Courtesy of DEA.

K2 contains synthetic cannabinoids that affect the body in similar fashion as marijuana.

"overdoses, cases of addiction, and even suicide" (Caldwell, 2010).

K2 and Spice are generic trademarks that first went on sale in 2000, initially as legal herbs.

## HERE AND NOW

### Spice and K2: Past and Current Usage Rates

Spice, also known as *herbal incense*, is dried, shredded plant material treated with a cannabinoid analog. Although labels on spice products will list the ingredients as "natural" psychoactive plant products, chemical analyses show that their active ingredients are primarily synthetic cannabinoids added to the plant material. These synthetic analogs function similarly to the active ingredient in marijuana, Δ9-THC (SAMHSA, 2014a).

*K2* and *Spice* are two names for a more recently created psychoactive designer drug whose dried, leafy, natural herbs are sprayed with a psychoactive chemical; it is then smoked so the user can experience euphoric effects. In 2011, prior to the Synthetic Drug Abuse Prevention Act being signed into law, one in nine U.S. high school seniors reported having used synthetic marijuana. In 2012, a large sample survey found that annual prevalence was 11.4%, ranking synthetic marijuana as the second most widely used class of illicit drug after marijuana among 12th graders (Johnston et al., 2016). In 2018, synthetic marijuana use significantly dropped. Annual use in 2018 among 8th graders was 1.6%, 10th graders 2.9%, and 12th graders 3.5% (NIDA, 2018c).

Eighth, 10th, and 12th graders were asked if they associated a great risk with trying synthetic marijuana once or twice; the results showed that there was quite a low level of perceived risk (only 23% and 25%, respectively, thought there was great risk in using once or twice).

Another study at a large public university in Georgia between November 2011 and March 2012 found that the highest level of use was among male students largely identifying with the lesbian, gay, bisexual, and transgender (LGBT) community. This was the first known study to obtain a detailed profile of users of any type of synthetic cannabinoid. Findings indicated the following:

1. The average age of first use was 18 years.
2. The percentage ever using synthetic cannabinoids was twice as high for males as for females (19% vs. 9%).
3. Heavier users were more likely to identify themselves as LGBT; significantly less usage was found in students identifying themselves as heterosexual.

Earlier findings are that "[e]fforts at the federal and state levels to close down the sale of these substances appear to be having an effect" (Johnston et al., 2016. Overall, beginning in 2015 through 2018, use of synthetic marijuana cannabinoids, (K2 and Spice) have statistically decreased for 8th, 10th, 12th graders and college students).

Data from Johnston, L. D., O'Malley, P. M., Bachman, J. G., & Schulenberg, J. E. (2013). *Monitoring the Future National Results on Drug Use: 2012 Overview, key findings on adolescent drug use.* Ann Arbor, MI: Institute for Social Research, The University of Michigan; Center for Substance Abuse Research (CESAR). (2013, May 20). Study finds that 14% of undergraduate students at a Southeastern University report synthetic cannabinoid use; users more likely to be male and identify as LGBT. *CESAR FAX.* Retrieved from http://www.cesar.umd.edu; Johnston, L. D., O'Malley, P. M., & Miech, R. A., Bachman, J. G., & Schulenberg, J. E. (2016, February). *Monitoring the Future National Survey Results on Drug Use, 1975–2015: Overview, key findings on adolescent drug use.* Ann Arbor, MI: Institute for Social Research, University of Michigan; National Institute on Drug Abuse (NIDA). (2018c). *Synthetic cannabinoids (K2/Spice).* Bethesda, MD: Author. Retrieved from https://www.drugabusegabuse.gov/publications/drugfacts/synthetic-cannabinoids-k2spice

Several years later, it was discovered that they contained synthetic cannabinoids that affected the body in a similar fashion as marijuana (cannabis). In July 2012, federal law placed this drug under Schedule I, making it an illegal drug with the highest abuse potential. The illegality of this drug removed it from retail sales.

As mentioned, before 2012, Spice was sold as a legal herb-based alternative to cannabis. The ingredients list contained only herbs, with no cannabinoid constituents; however, the listed ingredients seemed suspiciously unlikely to produce the drug's reported effects. Street names and slang terms for K2 and Spice include *Spice, K2, Blaze, Red X Dawn, Bliss, Black Mamba, Bombay Blue, Fake Weed, Genie, Spice,* and *Zoh.*

Numerous organizations have now tested the chemicals used to produce the high in synthetic marijuana, that includes K2-Spice. "The five primary research chemicals that mimic THC, are JWH-018, JWH-073, JWH-200, CP-47,497, and cannabicyclohexanol" (The Partnership for a Drug Free New Jersey, n.d.).

The U.S. Army, U.S. Marines, U.S. Air Force, U.S. Coast Guard, and U.S. Navy have also outlawed this drug, and violators risk immediate expulsion from service and incarceration. (For information regarding the extent of Spice use, see "Here and Now: Spice and K2: Past and Current Usage Rates.")

Inhalants. These volatile chemicals, which include many common household substances, are often the most dangerous drug, per dose, a person can take. In addition, inhalants are most often used by young children.

Photographed by Kimberly Potvin.

## ▌ Anabolic Steroids

Steroids are a synthetic form of the male hormone testosterone. They are often used to increase muscle size and strength. Medically, steroids are used to increase body tissues, treat allergies, or reduce swelling. Steroids are available in either liquid or pill form. Athletes have a tendency to use and abuse these drugs because they can dramatically increase body mass and muscle tissue. Some side effects include heart disease, liver cancer, high blood pressure, septic shock, impotence, genital atrophy, manic episodes, depression, violence, and mood swings.

## ▌ Inhalants and Organic Solvents

Inhalants and organic solvents also are often considered gateway drugs and are extremely attractive to and popular among preteens and younger teenagers. Products used include gasoline, model airplane glue, and paint thinner. When inhaled, the vapors from these solvents can produce euphoric effects. Organic solvents can also refer to certain foods, herbs, and vitamins such as "herbal Ecstasy."

## ▌ Narcotics and Opiates

These drugs depress the CNS and, if taken in a high enough quantity, produce insensibility or stupor. Narcotics or opiates are highly addictive. Narcotics include heroin, opium, morphine, codeine, meperidine (often a substitute for morphine, also known as Demerol), Darvon, and Percodan.

# An Overview of Drugs in Society

Many people think that problems with drugs are unique to this era. In reality, drug use and abuse have always been part of nearly all—past and present—human societies. For example, the Grecian oracles of Delphi used drugs, Homer's Nestor's Cup induced sleep and provided freedom from care, and the mandrake root mentioned in Genesis, the first book of the Bible, produced a hallucinogenic effect. In Genesis 30:14–16, the mandrake is mentioned in association with bartering for lovemaking:

> In the time of wheat harvest Reuben went out, found some mandrakes in the open country, and brought them to his mother Leah. Then Rachel asked Leah for some of her son's mandrakes, but Leah said, "Is it so small a thing to have taken away my husband, that you should take my son's mandrakes as well?" However, Rachel said, "Very well, let him sleep

with you tonight in exchange for your son's mandrakes." So when Jacob came in from the country in the evening, Leah went out to meet him and said, "You are to sleep with me tonight; I have hired you with my son's mandrakes." That night he slept with her.

Ancient literature is filled with references to the use of mushrooms, datura, hemp, marijuana, opium poppies, and so on. Under the influence of some of these drugs, many people experienced extreme ecstasy or sheer terror. Some old pictures of demons and devils look very much like those described by modern drug users during so-called bummers, or bad trips. The belief that witches could fly may also have been drug induced because many natural preparations used in so-called witches' brews induced the sensation of dis-association from the body, as in flying or floating.

As far back as 2240 BC, attempts were made to regulate drug use. For instance, in that year, problem drinking was addressed in the Code of Hammurabi, where it was described as "a problem of men with too much leisure time and lazy dispositions." Nearly every culture has experienced drug abuse, and as found in the historical record, laws were enacted to control the use of certain types of drugs.

## ■ How Widespread Is Drug Abuse?

As previously mentioned, drug abuse today is more acute and widespread than in any previous age (see "Here and Now: Numbers of Past Month: Illicit Drug Users and Illicit Drug Use Among People Aged 12 or Older by Age Group"). The evidence for this development is how often large

Amanda Geiger never saw the drunk driver.

**Friends Don't Let Friends Drive Drunk.**

Courtesy of the Advertising Council.

Photo by Michael Mazzeo

U.S. Department of Transportation

Although the media is often credited with glamorizing dangerous drug use, many successful prevention campaigns have used TV, radio, and print media as outlets. Since the Advertising Council began its "Friends Don't Let Friends Drive Drunk" campaign, 79% of Americans have stopped an intoxicated friend from getting behind the wheel.

quantities of illicit drugs are seized in the United States and throughout the world. Media exposure about illicit drug use is more likely to occur today than in the past. On any given day, you can scan most major national and international newspapers and run across stories about illegal drug manufacture, storage and distribution, use or abuse, and convictions. Drug use is an **equal-opportunity affliction**. This means that no one is immune from the effects of using or abusing both licit and

**KEY TERM**

**equal-opportunity affliction**
refers to the use of drugs, stressing that drug use cuts across all members of society regardless of income, education, occupation, social class, or age

# HERE AND NOW

## Numbers of Past-Month Illicit Drug Users and Age Groups by People Aged 12 and Older, 2018

Among people aged 12 and older in 2018, an estimated 53.2 million people used illicit drugs in the preceding year (**Figure A**), meaning that they had used an illicit drug during the year before the survey interview. The 53.2 million people who used illicit drugs corresponds to 19.4% of the population or approximately one in five people 12 and older in the United States (SAMHSA, 2019a).

The most commonly used illicit drug in the preceding year was marijuana, which was used by

43.5 million people. The second most common type of illicit drug use in the United States was prescription pain relievers: an estimated 9.9 million people in the preceding year. The third most common type of illicit drug use was prescription tranquilizers or sedatives: 6.4 million people. The fourth most common type of illicit drug use was hallucinogens by an estimated 5.6 million people. The fifth most common type of illicit drug use was cocaine with 5.5 million people. The smaller numbers of other past-year users

(continues)

# HERE AND NOW

## Numbers of Past-Month Illicit Drug Users and Age Groups by People Aged 12 and Older, 2018 (*continued*)

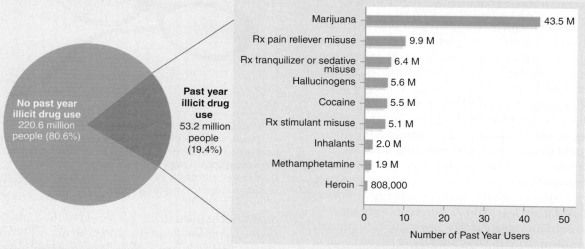

Rx = prescription.
Note: The estimated numbers of past year users of different illicit drugs are not mutually because people could have used more than one type of illicit drug use in the past year.

**FIGURE A**    Number of past month illicit drug users among persons aged 12 or older: 2018.

misusing prescription stimulants, inhalants, methamphetamine, and heroin is also shown in Figure A (SAMHSA, 2019b).

The age breakdown of past-year illicit users is as follows:

- *Aged 12–17*: Approximately 4.2 million adolescents aged 12 to 17 in 2018 were past-year illicit drug users, which corresponds to about one in six adolescents.

- *Aged 18 to 25*: Approximately two in five young adults aged 18 to 25 in 2018 (38.7%) were past-year users of illicit drugs. This percentage corresponds to about 13.2 million young adults who used illicit drugs in the past year.

- *Aged 26 or older*: In 2018, about one in six adults aged 26 or older (16.7%) were past-year users of illicit drugs, or about 35.9 million adults in this age group (SAMHSA, 2019a).

Data from Substance Abuse and Mental Health Administration (SAMHSA). (2019). *Key substance use and mental health indicators in the United States: Results from the 2018 National Survey on Drug Use and Health* (HHS Publication No. PEP19-5068, NSDUH Series H-54). Rockville, MD: Center for Behavioral Health Statistics and Quality (CBHSQ), Substance Abuse and Mental Health Services Administration (SAMHSA). Retrieved from https://www.samhsa.gov/data

illicit drugs. Research shows that drug consumption is found across the many different income, education, social class, occupation, race and ethnic, lifestyle, and age groups. To date, no one has proven immune from drug use or abuse.

Many of us, for example, are dismayed or surprised when we discover that certain individuals we admire—our family members (a mother, father, aunt, uncle, cousin, grandparent), close friends, workmates, celebrities, politicians, athletes, clergy, law enforcement personnel, physicians, academics, and even the seemingly upstanding man or woman next door—either admit to are accused of, need treatment for, or are arrested for licit or illicit drug use. We are also taken aback when we hear that cigarettes, alcohol, and marijuana abuse are commonplace in many public and private middle schools. Furthermore, most of us know of at least one (and many times more than one) close friend or family member who appears to secretly or not so secretly use drugs.

## ▮ Extent and Frequency of Drug Use in Society

Erich Goode (2012), a much-respected sociologist, lists the following four types of drug use.

1. *Legal instrumental use*: Taking prescribed drugs and OTC drugs to relieve or treat mental or physical symptoms.

2. *Legal recreational use*: Using such licit drugs as tobacco, alcohol, and caffeine to achieve a certain mental or psychic state.
3. *Illegal instrumental use*: Taking drugs without a prescription to accomplish a task or goal such as taking nonprescription amphetamines to drive through the night or relying excessively on barbiturates to get through the day.
4. *Illegal recreational use*: Taking illicit drugs for fun or pleasure to experience euphoria such as abusing prescribed methylphenidate (Ritalin) as a substitute for cocaine.

Why has the prevalence of licit and illicit drug use remained consistent since 1988? Why has this trend occurred when federal, state, and local government expenditures for fighting the drug war have been increasing at the same time? There are several possible answers, none of which offers a satisfactory response by itself. One perspective notes that practically all of us use drugs in some form, with what constitutes "drug use" being merely a matter of degree. A second explanation is that more varieties of both licit and illicit drugs are available today. One source estimated that approximately 80% of all currently marketed drugs were either unknown or unavailable 30 years ago (Critser, 1996). Regarding prescriptions, "the average number of prescriptions per person, annually, in 1993 was seven, and in 2005 it was 12 and in 2011, 13 prescriptions per person in the [United States]" (Critser, 2005, p. 23). Another source stated, "The retail sales of all OTC drugs that includes approximately 27 categories of drugs totaled over $35.2 billion in 2018" (CHPA, 2019). "In the United States, the rate of yearly prescription growth is projected to be 3.8% rate of inflation in the year 2020" (Bresnick, 2019).

By 2024, the total global prescription pharmaceutical market is projected to be at $1.2 trillion in sales. Similarly, other findings reflecting problems with prescription drug use are as follow (NIDA, 2014b):

- Fifty-two million people in the United States older than 12 have used prescription drugs nonmedically in their lifetime.
- Percentage of persons using at least one prescription drug in the past 30 days: 48.4% (2013–2016) (CDC, 2017a).
- Nearly 70% of Americans are on at least one prescription drug, and more than half take two.
- Approximately 6.1 million Americans have used prescription drugs nonmedically in the past month.

- Although the United States is just 5% of the world's population, it consumes 75% of the world's prescription drugs.
- With regards to obtaining prescription drugs, 54.2% reported obtaining them for free from a friend or relative, 18.1% from one doctor, and 16.6% buying or taking them from a friend or relative.

Such figures indicate that it may be more difficult to find people who do not use psychoactive drugs compared to individuals who do.

Further, a third category of drug sales has joined OTC and prescription drugs: herbal medicines, vitamins, minerals, enzymes, and other natural potions. According to Boyles (2009), "Out-of-pocket spending on herbal supplements, chiropractic visits, meditation, and other forms of complementary and alternative medicines (CAM) was estimated at $34 billion in a single year" and "Americans spend almost a third as much money out-of-pocket on herbal supplements and other alternative medicines as they do on prescription drugs." A more recent study found that "Americans will spend $21 billion on vitamins and herbal supplements in 2015. If protein powders are included, supplements are as big a market as all organic foods combined" (Scott, 2015). This is even though the U.S. Preventive Services Task Force does not recommend regular use of any multivitamins or herbs.

Other findings regarding these types of drugs include the following:

- More than four in five American adults (86%) take vitamins or supplements, according to a recent online survey conducted by the Harris Poll on behalf of the American Osteopathic Association (AOA, 2019).
- Americans will spend $21 billion on supplements in 2015.
- An estimated 75% of the world's population uses or has used some type of supplement, according to PharmacyTimes.com (Superior Supplement Manufacturing, 2019).
- "In the US alone, an estimated 54 million people over the age of 12 have used prescription drugs for nonmedical reasons in their lifetime" (Talbott Recovery, 2019).
- "Most abused prescription drugs fall under four categories, based on the number of people who misuse the drug: [p]ainkillers— 3.3 million users, [t]ranquilizers—2 million users [s]timulants—1.7 million users Sedatives—0.5 million users" (Talbott Recovery, 2019).

- The Food and Drug Administration (FDA) only spot tests 1% of the 65,000 dietary supplements on the market.

Drug use is so common that the average household in the United States owns about five drugs, of which two are prescription drugs and three are OTC drugs. Of the many prescriptions written by physicians, approximately one-third modify moods and behaviors in one way or another. A 2010 National Institute on Drug Abuse (NIDA, 2010) study and other research indicate that more than 60% of adults in the United States have, at some time in their lives, taken a psychoactive drug (one that affects mood or consciousness). More than one-third of adults have used or are using depressants or sedatives.

A third explanation is that "in the modern age, increased sophistication has brought with it techniques of drug production and distribution that have resulted in a worldwide epidemic of drug use" (Kusinitz, 1988, p. 149). In the 1980s and 1990s, for example, illicit drug cartels proliferated, and varieties of marijuana with ever-increasing potency infiltrated all urban and rural areas in the United States, as well as the world. Many of these varieties are crossbred with ultrasophisticated techniques and equipment available everywhere.

Finally, even coffee has undergone a technological revolution. Higher levels of caffeine content have become available worldwide. This trend has led to the phenomenal growth of the following: (1) franchise duplication of gourmet coffee bars in the United States (e.g., Starbucks, Peet's, Three Brothers Coffee); (2) sales of espresso and cappuccino coffeemakers for home use, with accompanying coffee grinders or coffee pods and capsules; and (3) sales of specialized coffees and teas through a multitude of email coffee and tea clubs.

Before 1990, it was difficult to purchase a cup of espresso or cappuccino in a typical restaurant (Meister, 2017); today, such types of coffees are widely available. Even at university unions and libraries, airports, shopping malls, and inner-city coffee shops, it is not unusual to see people lined up waiting to order and purchase their specially made and specially flavored coffee or tea. This is just one example of how caffeine (often seen as a benign drug) has evolved, with many new varieties of coffee beans from exotic islands and countries coming together with more sophisticated electronic equipment, with the result that the idea of simple brewing has been relegated to the past. The standard American "cup of coffee in the morning" has spilled into including coffee during the afternoon and evening. This is a small example of a much-tolerated drug maintaining its own impressive history of development, increased use, complexity in developing many more varieties, and added sophistication.

## ▮ Drug Use: Statistics, Trends, and Demographics

An incredible amount of money is spent each year on both licit and illicit chemicals that alter consciousness, awareness, or mood. The following are six categories of widely used licit and illicit types of psychoactive drugs:

1. *Social drugs.* Total costs, which includes costs to society, are approximately $249 billion on alcohol alone each year. The total economic cost of smoking is more than $300 billion a year, including nearly $170 billion in direct medical care for adults and more than $156 billion in lost productivity from premature death and exposure to secondhand smoke. In 2017, tobacco companies spent $9.36 billion marketing cigarettes and smokeless tobacco in the United States. This translates to more than $25 million each day, or more than $1 million every hour (CDC, 2017b). During 2012–2016, total U.S cigar unit sales grew by 29%, which was largely driven by increasing sales of cigarillos (CDC, 2017b).

2. *Prescription drugs.* In 2019, the total prescription drug revenue worldwide is expected to generate $844 billion U.S. in prescription drug revenue worldwide. Revenues are expected to reach nearly $1.2 trillion U.S. by 2024. There is an increasing growth especially in sales of so-called orphan drugs for the treatment of rare diseases (Mikulic, 2019). More than 131 million people—66% of all adults in the United States—use prescription drugs. Utilization is particularly high for older people and those with chronic conditions (Health Policy Institute, 2019).

3. *Over-the-counter (patent) drugs.* These products, including cough and cold items, external and internal analgesics, antacids, laxatives, antidiarrheal products, sleep aids, sedatives, and so on, had $35.2 billion in sales in 2018, with U.S. households spending an average of $338 per year on OTC products. Eighty-one percent of adults use OTC medicines as a first response to minor ailments (CHPA, 2019).

4. *Illicit drugs.* A report prepared by the RAND Corporation for the White House estimated that over a 10-year period, from 2000 to 2010,

an astonishing $1 trillion was spent on illicit drugs (Ferner, 2014). Pinpointing specific types of drugs, another source indicated that in 2016, Americans spent $145 billion on cannabis, cocaine, heroin, and methamphetamine, according to a new report (Midgette, 2019). Surveys of 8th, 10th, and 12th graders combined indicated that in 2017 and 2018, 34.4% and 33.9%, respectively had used an illicit drug during their lifetimes (Statista Inc., 2019).

5. *Nonmedical use and misuse of prescription-type drugs.* Prescription pain reliever misuse was the second most common form of illicit drug use in the United States in 2018, with 3.6% of the population misusing pain relievers. For people 12 and older and young adults 18 to 25, the percentages who misused prescription pain relievers in the preceding year were lower in 2018 than from 2015 to 2017. Similar decreases in pain reliever misuse were observed for adolescents 12 to 17 and adults 26 and older in 2018 compared with 2015 and 2016 but not when compared with 2017. Among people aged 12 and older in 2018 who misused pain relievers in the preceding year, the most common main reason for their last misuse of a pain reliever was to relieve physical pain (63.6%). More than half (51.3%) of people who misused pain relievers in the preceding year obtained the last pain reliever they misused from a friend or relative. The National Survey on Drug Use and Health (NSDUH) also allows an estimation of opioid misuse, which is defined as the use of heroin or the misuse of prescription pain relievers. In 2018, an estimated 10.3 million people 12 or older misused opioids in the preceding year, including 9.9 million prescription pain reliever misusers and 808,000 heroin users. Approximately 506,000 people misused prescription pain relievers and used heroin in the past year. The percentage of people aged 12 or older in 2018 who were past-year opioid misusers was lower than the percentages between 2015 and 2017, which was largely driven by declines in pain reliever misuse rather than by changes in heroin use. Finally, in 2018, the substances with the largest number of recent (i.e., past year) initiates of use or misuse were alcohol (4.9 million new users), marijuana (3.1 million new users), prescription pain relievers (1.9 million new misusers), and cigarettes (1.8 million new users) (SAMHSA, 2019a).

6. *Miscellaneous.* Finally, the amount spent on inhalants and other miscellaneous drugs,

such as nutmeg and morning glory seeds, cannot be estimated.

During 2016, an estimated 48,501,000 persons, or 18.0% of persons aged 12 and older, reported using illicit drugs or misusing prescription drugs in the preceding year (CDC, 2018b).

- By gender, the prevalence was 20.7% among males and 15.5% among females.
- By age, prevalence was highest among persons aged 18–25 (37.7%) and persons aged 26–34 (28.0%).
- By race and ethnicity, prevalence ranged from 9.2% among Asians to 23.6% among American Indians or Alaska Natives.

Regarding nationwide trends in the use of illicit drug use in 2018, the following findings are noteworthy:

- More than half of new illicit drug users begin with marijuana. Next most commonly used are prescription pain relievers followed by inhalants (which is most common among younger teens).
- After alcohol, marijuana has the highest rate of dependence or abuse among all drugs. Drug use is highest among people in their late teens and 20s. In 2013, 22.6% of those 18 to 20 reported using an illicit drug in the preceding month.
- In 2018, nearly one in five people 12 or older (19.4%) used an illicit drug in the preceding year, which is a higher percentage than in 2015 and 2016. The estimate of past-year illicit drug use for 2018 was driven primarily by marijuana use, with 43.5 million past-year marijuana users. The percentage of people 12 and older in 2018 who used marijuana in the past year (15.9%) was higher than the percentages in 2002 to 2017 (SAMHSA, 2019a).
- Prescription pain reliever misuse was the second most common form of illicit drug use in the United States in 2018, with 3.6% of the population misusing pain relievers. For people 12 and older and young adults 18 to 25, the percentages who misused prescription pain relievers in the preceding year were lower in 2018 than in 2015 to 2017 (SAMHSA, 2019a).
- Among people 12 and older in 2018 who misused pain relievers in the preceding year, the most common main reason for their last misuse of a pain reliever was to relieve physical pain (63.6%). More than half (51.3%) of people who misused pain relievers in the preceding year obtained the last pain reliever

they misused from a friend or relative (SAMHSA, 2019a).

- In 2018, an estimated 10.3 million people 12 and older misused opioids[3] in the previous year, including 9.9 million prescription pain reliever misusers and 808,000 heroin users. Approximately 506,000 people misused prescription pain relievers and used heroin in the preceding year (SAMHSA, 2019a).
- The percent of teens who reported past-month marijuana vaping rose from 2.6% to 3.9% of 8th graders, from 7.0% to 12.6% of 10th graders, and from 7.5% to 14.0% of 12th graders. This increase in past-month marijuana vaping in high school seniors is the second largest single-year increase ever measured in the 45-year history of the *Monitoring the Future* (MTF) survey (NIDA, 2019b).
- Cigarette smoking continued a downward trend and significantly fell among 12th graders reporting past-month use, daily use, or consumption of one-half pack or more per day.

- Significant five-year declines in cigarette smoking were reported by all grades and across all prevalence periods, including lifetime use (NIDA, 2019b).
- Past-month, past-year, and lifetime marijuana use remained steady among 8th, 10th, and 12th graders. Daily marijuana use, however, increased among 8th and 10th graders (NIDA, 2019b).
- Past-year prescription opioid misuse (reported in the survey as "narcotics other than heroin") continued a significant decline among 12th graders, with 2.7% reporting use in 2019 (NIDA, 2019b).
- In 2018, among full-time college students ages 19 to 22, 43% reported using marijuana sometime in the preceding 12 months and 25% reported using marijuana at least once in the previous 30 days. This represents the highest level of marijuana usage in the last 3.5 decades (Michigan News, 2019). Same-age high school graduates, ages 19–22, not attending college had similar rates of marijuana use (Michigan News, 2019).

[3]The National Survey on Drug Use and Health (NSDUH) defines opioid use as the misuse of prescription pain relievers or heroin.

**Table 1.3** shows that in regard to age groups, those 18 to 25 are by far the *heaviest* users and

**TABLE 1.3** Trend Data on the Prevalence of Illicit Drug Use: 2015–2018

|  | 2015 | 2016 | 2017 | 2018 |
|---|---|---|---|---|
| **Used in Past Month** |  |  |  |  |
| All ages 12+ | 10.1[a] | 10.6[a] | 11.2 | 11.7 |
| 12–17 | 8.8[a] | 7.9 | 7.9 | 8.0 |
| 18–25 | 22.3[a] | 23.2 | 24.2 | 23.9 |
| 26+ | 8.2[a] | 8.9[a] | 9.5[a] | 10.1 |
| **Used in Past Year** |  |  |  |  |
| All ages 12+ | 17.8[a] | 18.0[a] | 19.0 | 19.4 |
| 12–17 | 17.5 | 15.8 | 16.3 | 16.7 |
| 18–25 | 37.5 | 37.7 | 39.4 | 38.7 |
| 26+ | 14.6[a] | 15.0[a] | 16.1 | 16.7 |
| **Used in Lifetime (Ever Used)** |  |  |  |  |
| All ages 12+ | 48.8 | 48.5 | 49.5 | 49.2 |
| 12–17 | 25.3[a] | 23.0 | 23.9 | 23.9 |
| 18–25 | 57.5[a] | 56.3 | 57.0 | 55.6 |
| 26+ | 50.1 | 50.2 | 51.3 | 51.2 |

[a] Data difference between 2018 and this estimate significant at the 0.05 level. The rounding may make the estimates look identical.

Data from Substance Abuse and Mental Health Services Administration (SAMHSA). (2019b). *Results from the 2018 National Survey on Drug Use and Health: Detailed tables*. Rockville, MD: Author. Retrieved from https://www.samhsa.gov/data/sites/default/files/cbhsq -reports/NSDUHDetailedTabs2018R2/NSDUHDetTabsSect1pe2018.htm

# HERE AND NOW

## Sources of Prescription Drugs Misused by Youths

Although most people take prescription medications responsibly, in 2017 an estimated 18 million people (more than 6% of those aged 12 and older) misused such medications at least once in the preceding year. According to results from the 2017 National Survey on Drug Use and Health, an estimated 2 million Americans misused prescription pain relievers for the first time within the preceding year, which averages approximately 5,480 initiates per day. In addition, more than 1 million misused prescription stimulants, 1.5 million misused tranquilizers, and 271,000 misused sedatives for the first time (NIDA, 2018a).

In focusing on adolescents and young adults, the misuse of prescription drugs is highest among young adults 18 to 25, with 14.4% reporting nonmedical use in the previous year. Among youth 12 to 17, 4.9% reported past-year nonmedical use of prescription medications.

After alcohol, marijuana, and tobacco, prescription drugs (taken nonmedically) are among the most commonly used drugs by 12th graders. NIDA's *Monitoring the Future* survey of substance use and attitudes in teens found that about 6% of high school seniors reported past-year nonmedical use of the prescription stimulant Adderall in 2017, and 2% reported misusing the opioid pain reliever Vicodin (NIDA, 2018a).

Youths who misuse prescription medications are also more likely to report using other drugs. Multiple studies have revealed associations between prescription drug misuse and higher rates of cigarette smoking, heavy episodic drinking, and marijuana, cocaine, and other illicit drug use among adolescents, young adults, and college students in the United States. In the case of prescription opioids, receiving a legitimate prescription for these drugs during adolescence is also associated with a greater risk of future opioid misuse, particularly in young adults who have little to no history of drug use (NIDA, 2018a).

### Older Adults

Friends and family are the most common source of prescription drugs *misused** by youths in the United States, according to an analysis of data from NSDUH. Around one-half of youths who reported misusing prescription stimulants (50%), tranquilizers (47%), or sedatives (47%) in the past year said that they most recently obtained the medication for free from friends or family, as did one-third of those who reported the misuse of prescription opioids. The second most common source for obtaining stimulants, tranquilizers, and sedatives was purchasing from a friend or relative, drug dealer or stranger, or the Internet, and the second most common source for obtaining prescription opioids was acquiring them from a physician.

Another source (Keller, 2019) reported that teens get their prescription drugs from the following locations:

- medicine cabinets,
- a neighbor's house,
- Internet and online pharmacies,
- the dark web,
- a friend of a friend,
- at schools, and
- at parties.

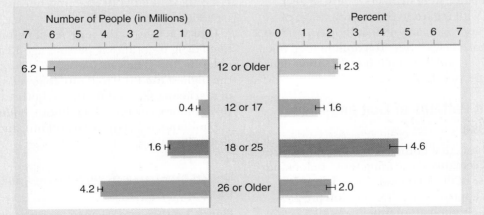

Past month prescription misuse of pain relievers, tranquilizers, stimulants, and sedatives by age group: 2016.

*(continues)*

# HERE AND NOW

## Sources of Prescription Drugs Misused by Youths (*continued*)

According to a University of Florida study, "[u]sing someone else's medication is the most common form of prescription stimulant misuse among adolescents," with researchers finding that 88% of teens who used the drugs nonmedically in the previous 30 days said "they had obtained the medications from someone else" (Keller, 2020a). Friends and family are the most common source of prescription drugs *misused** by youths in the United States, according to an analysis of data from NSDUH. Around one-half of youths who reported misusing prescription stimulants (50%), tranquilizers (47%), or sedatives (47%) in the previous year said that they most recently obtained the medication for free from friends or family, as did one-third of those who reported the misuse of prescription opioids. The second most common source for obtaining stimulants, tranquilizers, and sedatives was purchasing from a friend or relative, drug dealer or stranger, or the Internet; the second most common source for acquiring prescription opioids was from a physician (CESAR, 2009; Schepis & Krishnan-Sarin, 2009).

*Misuse* is defined as "taking a medication in a manner or dose other than prescribed; taking someone's else's prescription, even if for a legitimate medical complaint such as pain; or taking a medication to feel euphoria (i.e., to get high)" (NIDA, 2018a).

*Note:* Respondents also reported that prescription medicines were obtained "some other way" (stimulants, 5%; tranquilizers, 4%; sedatives, 12%; opioids, 7%). Data are from 36,992 adolescents aged 12 to 17 participating in the 2005 or 2006 National Survey on Drug Use and Health (or both). Of these youths, 8.3% reported any prescription drug misuse in the previous year, 7% reported opioid misuse, 2% reported tranquilizer misuse, 2% reported stimulant misuse, and 0.4% reported sedative misuse.

Reproduced from Center for Substance Abuse Research (CESAR). (2009). Friends and family are most common source of prescription drugs misused by youths. *CESAR FAX, 18*(32), using data from National Institute on Drug Abuse (NIDA). (2018a). Misuse of prescription drugs. Bethesda, MD: Author. Retrieved from https://www.drugabuse.gov/publications/misuse-prescription-drugs/overview; Schepis, T. S., & Krishnan-Sarin, S. (2009). Sources of prescriptions for misuse by adolescents: Differences in sex, ethnicity, and severity of misuse in a population-based study. *Journal of the American Academy of Child and Adolescent Psychiatry, 48*(8), 828–836; Substance Abuse and Mental Health Services Administration (SAMHSA). (2017). *Key substance use and mental health indicators in the United States: Results from the 2016 National Survey on Drug Use and Health*. Rockville, MD: Author. Retrieved from https://www.samhsa.gov/data/sites/default/files/NSDUH-FFR1-2016/NSDUH-FFR1-2016.htm

experimenters in terms of past-month, past-year, and lifetime users.

**Table 1.4** shows a more recent percentage of population and estimated number of alcohol, tobacco, and illicit drug users in the United States among persons aged 12 and older. In looking at *past-month usage*, an estimated 13.9 million Americans, or 51.1% of the total U.S. population age 12 and older, were drinkers. Statistics also reveal that with regard to past-month usage of cigarettes, approximately 46.9 million Americans (17.2%) smoked cigarettes, 31.9 million used illicit drugs (11.7%), and 27.6 million (8.4%) used marijuana in 2018 (see Table 1.4).

## ▪ Current Patterns of Licit and Illicit Drug Use

Table 1.4 shows that both licit and illicit drug use occurs and remains at alarming rates. In looking at *lifetime* use of illicit types of drugs, it is estimated that approximately 13.4 million people— approximately one-half of Americans 49.2% age 12 and older—have used illicit drugs during their lifetime (SAMHSA, 2019b).

**Figure 1.2** further shows that regarding lifetime use 80.8% of the U.S. population, used alcohol during sometime during their lifetime. Other lifetime drug uses and percentages of those using were cigarettes (55.7%); illicit drug use, which includes the misuse of prescription psychotherapeutics (49.2%); marijuana (45.3%); cocaine (14.7%); hallucinogens (15.8%); inhalants (9.1%); and heroin (1.9%) (see Figure 1.2).

**Figure 1.3** shows the number of past-month illicit drug users among persons age 12 and older in 2018. The category of *illicit drugs* shows the highest use (31.9 million), followed by use of marijuana (27.7 million), psychotherapeutics (5.4 million), cocaine (1.9 million), hallucinogens (1.6 million), inhalants (0.6 million), and heroin (0.4 million).

### NONMEDICAL USE OF PSYCHOTHERAPEUTIC DRUGS

**Figure 1.4** shows percentage of past month nonmedical use of psychotherapeutic drugs (pain relievers, tranquilizers, stimulants, and sedatives)

**TABLE 1.4** National Household Survey on Drug Abuse: 2018

Percentage of population and estimated number of alcohol, tobacco, and illicit drug users in the United States among persons aged 12 or older

| Substance | LIFETIME | | PAST MONTH* | |
|---|---|---|---|---|
| | Percentage | Number of Users (in Thousands) | Percentage | Number of Users (in Thousands) |
| Alcohol | 80.8 | 221,220 | 51.1 | 139,835 |
| Cigarettes | 55.7 | 152,480 | 17.2 | 46,956 |
| Any illicit drug† | 49.2 | 134,791 | 11.7 | 31,918 |
| Marijuana | 45.3 | 123,935 | 10.1 | 27,667 |
| Illicit drugs other than marijuana‡ | ¶nr | ¶nr | 3.2 | 8,855 |
| Smokeless tobacco | **15.6** | **42,599** | 2.9 | 7,972 |
| Nonmedical use of any psychotherapeutic§ | ¶nr | ¶nr | 2.0 | 5,424 |
| Pain Relievers | ¶nr | ¶nr | 1.0 | 2,852 |
| Cocaine | 14.7 | 40,194 | 0.7 | 1,949 |
| Crack | 3.4 | 9,177 | 0.2 | 436 |
| Tranquilizers | ¶nr | ¶nr | 0.6 | 1,799 |
| Hallucinogens | 15.8 | 43,255 | 0.6 | 1,630 |
| Ecstasy | 7.3 | 19,949 | 0.3 | 689 |
| LSD | 10.0 | 27,339 | 0.2 | 458 |
| PCP | 2.2 | 6,085 | 0.0 | 34 |
| Stimulants | ¶nr | ¶nr | 0.6 | 1,670 |
| Methamphetamine | 5.4 | 14892 | 0.4 | 1,001 |
| Inhalants | 9.1 | 24,783 | 0.2 | 612 |
| Heroin | 1.9 | 5,108 | 0.1 | 354 |
| Sedatives | §nr | §nr | 0.1 | 243 |

Note: The results obtained from this national survey were completed at 181,879 addresses, and 68,991 completed interviews were obtained. The survey was conducted from January 2018 through December 2018. Weighted response rates for household screening and for interviewing were 73.3% and 66.6%, respectively.

*Lifetime refers to ever used. This column shows the use of drugs from highest to lowest percentages as well as the number of persons using.

†Any illicit drugs, including the following: marijuana or hashish, cocaine (including crack), heroin, hallucinogens, inhalants, or prescription-type psychotherapeutics used nonmedically.

‡Illicit drugs other than marijuana include cocaine (including crack), heroin, hallucinogens, inhalant, or prescription-type psychotherapeutics used nonmedically.

§Nonmedical use of prescription-type psychotherapeutics includes the nonmedical use of pain relievers, tranquilizers, stimulants, or sedatives but does not include over-the-counter drugs.

¶nr = no report available

Data from Substance Abuse and Mental Health Services Administration (SAMHSA). (2019). *Results from the 2018 National Survey on Drug Use and Health: Detailed tables.* Rockville, MD: Center for Behavioral Health Statistics and Quality (CBHSQ), Substance Abuse and Mental Health Services Administration (SAMHSA).

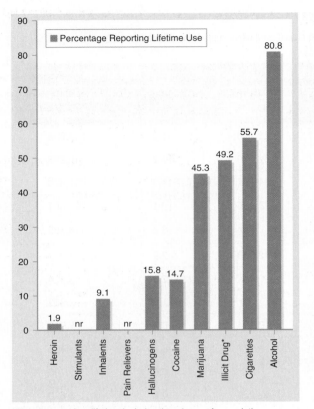

*Illicit drug use in a lifetime includes the misuse of prescription psychotherapeutics.

nr These percentages are not reported due to measurement issues.

**FIGURE 1.2**  Percentage of U.S. residents aged 12 or older reporting lifetime use of alcohol, tobacco, and illicit drugs: 2018.

Data from Substance Abuse and Mental Health Services Administration (SAMHSA). (2019). *Results from the 2018 National Survey on Drug Use and Health: Detailed tables*. Rockville, MD: Center for Behavioral Health Statistics and Quality (CBHSQ), Substance Abuse and Mental Health Services Administration (SAMHSA).

among four age groups—12 and older, 12 to 17, 18 to 25, and 26 and older—from 2015 through 2018; also see the Case in Point highlighting the number of painkiller prescriptions in each of the 50 states and the District of Columbia in 2012 (CDC, 2014). These groupings also include drugs that may be available as prescription medications but currently are much more likely to be manufactured and distributed illegally; one such drug is methamphetamine, which is included under stimulants. The latest major findings of nonmedical use of psychotherapeutic drugs in 2018 include the following (SAMHSA, 2019a):

- Prescription psychotherapeutic drugs consist of prescription stimulants, tranquilizers or sedatives (including benzodiazepines), and pain relievers. In NSDUH, misuse of prescription drugs is defined as use in any way not directed by a doctor, including use without a prescription of one's own, use in

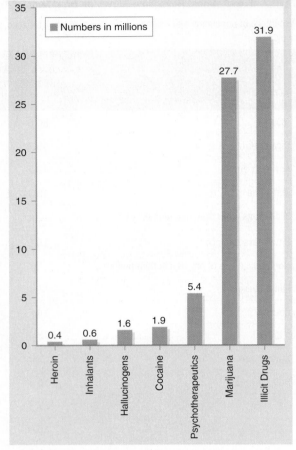

*Illicit drugs include marijuana/hashish, cocaine (including crack), heroin, hallucinogens, inhalants, or prescription-type psychotherapeutics used nonmedically.

**FIGURE 1.3**  Past-month use of selected illicit drugs among persons aged 12 or older, 2018. Illicit drugs include marijuana or hashish, cocaine (including crack), heroin, hallucinogens, inhalants, or prescription-type psychotherapeutics used nonmedically.

Data from Substance Abuse and Mental Health Services Administration (SAMHSA). (2019). *Results from the 2018 National Survey on Drug Use and Health: Detailed tables*. Rockville, MD: Center for Behavioral Health Statistics and Quality (CBHSQ), Substance Abuse and Mental Health Services Administration (SAMHSA). Retrieved from https://www.samhsa.gov/data/

greater amounts more often or longer than told to take a drug, or use in any other way not directed by a doctor. Misuse of over-the-counter drugs is not included (SAMHSA, 2019a).

- In 2018, an estimated 16.9 million Americans 12 and older misused prescription psychotherapeutic drugs at least once in the preceding year. This number of past-year prescription psychotherapeutic drug misusers corresponds to 6.2% of the population (SAMHSA, 2019a). Of the prescription drugs presented in this report, prescription pain relievers were the most commonly misused by people 12 and older (SAMHSA, 2019a).

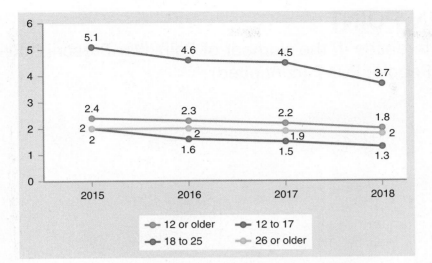

**FIGURE 1.4** Past-month nonmedical use of types of psychotherapeutic drugs among persons aged 12 or older: 2015–2018.

Reproduced from Center for Behavioral Health Statistics and Quality (CBHSQ). (2015). *Behavioral health trends in the United States: Results from the 2014 National Survey on Drug Use and Health* (HHS Publication No. SMA 15-4927, NSDUH Series H-50). Rockville, MD: Author; Substance Abuse and Mental Health Services Administration (SAMHSA). (2017). *Key substance use and mental health indicators in the United States: Results from the 2016 National Survey on Drug Use and Health* (HHS Publication No. SMA 17-5044, NSDUH Series H-52). Rockville, MD: Author; Substance Abuse and Mental Health Services Administration. (2019). *Key substance use and mental health indicators in the United States: Results from the 2018 National Survey on Drug Use and Health* (HHS Publication No. PEP19-5068, NSDUH Series H-54). Rockville, MD: Center for Behavioral Health Statistics and Quality (CBHSQ), Substance Abuse and Mental Health Services Administration (SAMHSA).

- The 16.9 million Americans in 2018 who had misused prescription psychotherapeutic drugs in the preceding year included 9.9 million who misused prescription pain relievers in that period, 5.1 million who misused prescription stimulants, and about 6.4 million who misused prescription tranquilizers or sedatives.

The estimate for the misuse of tranquilizers or sedatives includes 5.4 million who misused prescription benzodiazepines in the past year (SAMHSA, 2019a).

**Figure 1.5** shows past-month use of illicit drugs among persons 12 and older by age group in 2017

## ▶ CASE IN POINT

### State Differences in the Number of Painkiller Prescriptions per 100 People, 2017

The color-coded U.S. map (**Figure A**) shows the number of painkiller prescriptions per 100 people in each of the 50 states plus the District of Columbia in 2017 (CDC, 2017a). The major findings include the following:

- The overall national opioid prescribing rate declined from 2012 to 2017, and in 2017 the prescribing rate had fallen to the lowest in more than 10 years at 58.7 prescriptions per 100 persons (total of more than 191 million total opioid prescriptions) (CDC, 2017a).

- However, in 2017, prescribing rates continued to remain especially high in certain areas across the country.

- In 16% of U.S. counties, enough opioid prescriptions were dispensed for every person to have one (CDC, 2017a).

- Leading the country in highest pain prescriptions per 100 persons are Alabama, Arkansas, Mississippi, and Tennessee.

- The states with the lowest pain prescriptions per 100 persons were New York, Hawaii, and California, as well as the District of Columbia.

**Figure B** shows the total number and rate of opioid (painkiller) prescriptions dispensed in the United States between 2006 and 2017.

*(continues)*

► **CASE IN POINT**

## State Differences in the Number of Painkiller Prescriptions per 100 People, 2017 (*continued*)

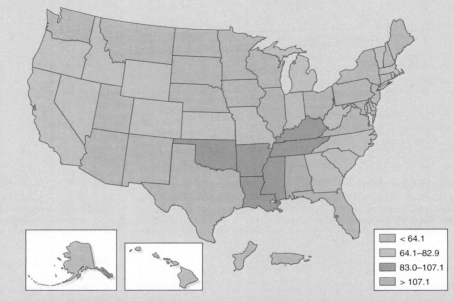

| | |
|---|---|
| ▨ | < 64.1 |
| ▨ | 64.1–82.9 |
| ▨ | 83.0–107.1 |
| ▨ | > 107.1 |

**FIGURE A**  This color-coded U.S. map shows the number of painkiller prescriptions per 100 people in each of the 50 states in 2017.

Reproduced from Centers for Disease Control and Prevention (CDC). (2017c). *U.S. state prescribing rates, 2017.* Atlanta, GA: Centers for Disease Control and Prevention. Retrieved from https:// www.cdc.gov/drugoverdose/maps/rxstate2017.html

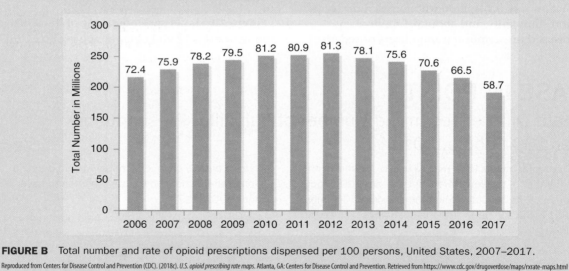

**FIGURE B**  Total number and rate of opioid prescriptions dispensed per 100 persons, United States, 2007–2017.

Reproduced from Centers for Disease Control and Prevention (CDC). (2018c). *U.S. opioid prescribing rate maps.* Atlanta, GA: Centers for Disease Control and Prevention. Retrieved from https://www.cdc.gov/drugoverdose/maps/rxrate-maps.html

and 2018. With regard to age patterns, the following trends are apparent:

- Rates of drug use show significant variation by age group.
- In comparing 2017 with 2018, past-month illicit drug use was similar across age groups.
- In comparing 2017 with 2018, excluding ages 18 to 25, across all other age groups

(12 or older, 12 to 17, and 26 or older), past-month illicit drug use increased slightly in 2018.

- The highest percentage of illicit drug use was among those 18 to 25 (24.2% in 2017 and 23.9% in 2018).
- Of the four age groups (12 or older, 12 to 17, 18 to 25, and 25 and older), those 12 to 17

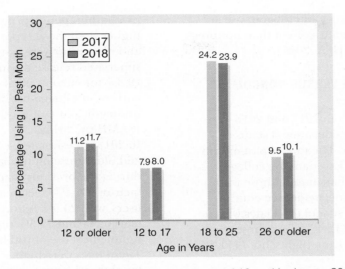

**FIGURE 1.5** Percentage of past-month illicit drug use among persons aged 12 or older, by age: 2017 and 2018.

had the lowest percentage of past-month illicit drug use.

### RACIAL AND ETHNIC DIFFERENCES

**Figure 1.6** shows average past-month illicit drug use among persons age 12 or older by race and ethnicity (black or African American, white, Hispanic or Latino, and Asian) for 2018. The figures in this chart reveal the following trends.

In 2018, the following were the major findings regarding illicit drug use by gender, education: college versus noncollege students, ethnicity and race, and criminal justice populations reported with earlier publishing dates.

### GENDER

- In 2018, as in preceding years, the rate of past-month illicit drug use among persons 12 and older was higher for males (14.0%) than for females (9.5%). Males were more likely than females to be current users of several different illicit drugs, including marijuana (12.3% vs. 8.0%), cocaine (1.0 vs. 0.4%), hallucinogens (0.8 vs. 0.4%), and crack (0.2% vs. 0.1%).

- In 2015, women continually have lower rates of substance use and substance use disorders (SUDs) than men. For example, past-year illicit drug dependence or abuse was 3.4% for men and 1.9% for women (SAMHSA, 2015).

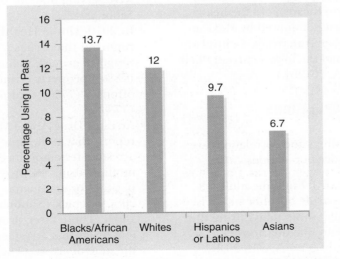

**FIGURE 1.6** Past-month illicit drug use among persons age 12 or older, by race or ethnicity: 2018.

- Rates of alcohol, drug, and tobacco use are lower among pregnant women than nonpregnant women (SAMHSA, 2015).

## EDUCATION: COLLEGE VERSUS NONCOLLEGE STUDENTS

- Illicit drug use rates in 2017 and 2018 were correlated with the educational status of adults 18 and older. The rate of past-month illicit drug use was lower among college graduates (9.2%) than among those with some college or associate degree education (12.4%), high school graduates with no further education (12.4%), and those who had not graduated from high school (11.4%) (SAMHSA, 2019b).
- Among full-time college students 18 to 22 in 2013, the rate of current illicit drug use was 9.4% for Asians, 19.7% for blacks, 21.5% for Hispanics, and 25.1% for whites.

## ETHNICITY AND RACE

- Past-month illicit drug use rates in 2018 were correlated with ethnicity and race for persons 12 and older. Illicit drug use from highest to lowest percentages having used illicit drugs: people having two or more races, 17.6%; blacks or African Americans, 13.7%; whites, 12.0%; Hispanic or Latino, 9.7%; and Asians, 6.7% (SAMHSA, 2019b).
- The current illicit drug use rate for blacks or African Americans, whites, Hispanics or Latinos, and Asians increased from 2017 to 2018. (Latest published findings in the breakdown of illicit drugs among Hispanic groups indicates that Puerto Ricans were the heaviest users of illicit drugs, followed by Mexican Americans and Cuban Americans. Central and South Americans had the lowest current illicit drug use [SAMHSA, 2019b].)

## CRIMINAL JUSTICE POPULATIONS AND ARRESTEES

Certain significant findings and correlations are unique to criminal justice populations:

- In 2013, an estimated 1.7 million adults 18 and older were on parole or other supervised release from prison at some time during the preceding year. About one-quarter (27.4%) were current illicit drug users, with 20.4% reporting current use of marijuana and 12.1% reporting current nonmedical use of psychotherapeutic drugs. These rates were higher than those reported by adults 18 and older who were not on parole or other supervised release during the preceding year (9.3% for current illicit drug use, 7.5% for current marijuana use, and 2.4% for current nonmedical use of psychotherapeutic drugs) (SAMHSA, 2014a).
- In 2013, an estimated 4.5 million adults 18 and older were on probation at some time during the previous year. More than one-quarter (31.4%) were current illicit drug users, with 23.5% reporting current use of marijuana and 12.3% reporting current nonmedical use of psychotherapeutic drugs. These rates were higher than those reported by adults who were not on probation during the preceding year (9.0% for current illicit drug use, 7.3% for current marijuana use, and 2.3% for current nonmedical use of psychotherapeutic drugs) (SAMHSA 2014a).
- "An estimated 56% of state prisoners, 45% of federal prisoners, and 64% of jail inmates have a mental health problem . . . at the time of the survey . . . conducted by the Urban Institute, . . . 49% of state prisoners, 40% of federal prisoners, and 60% of jail inmates had a symptom of a mental disorder, such as developmental and personality disorders, as well as clinical symptoms as specified in the *Diagnostic and Statistical Manual of Mental Disorders,* Fourth Edition (DSM-IV)" (KiDeuk, Becker-Cohen, & Serakos, 2015).
- In 2011, 197,050 sentenced prisoners were under federal jurisdiction. Of these, 94,600 were serving time for drug offenses (Carson & Sabol, 2012).
- In 2010, Home Health Testing (2010) reported that drugs were involved in a wide range of crimes, including violent crimes (78%), property crimes (83%), weapons offenses (77%), and parole violations (77%).
- Arrestee Drug Abuse Monitoring (ADAM) reports that at the time of arrest 40% of arrestees tested positive for the presence of multiple drugs. Approximately 40% tested positive for marijuana, 30% for cocaine, and 20% for crack (National Institute of Justice, 2009). These three drugs are the most prevalent drugs that arrestees test positive for at the time of arrest. (The 2013 ADAM II report provides a comparison of the results over the years; see ONDCP, 2013a.)

## ■ Types of Drug Users

Just as a diverse set of personality traits exists (e.g., introverts, extroverts, type A, obsessive–compulsive, and so on), drug users also vary according to their general approach or orientation, frequency of use, and types and amounts of the drugs they consume. Some are occasional or moderate users, whereas others display a much stronger attachment to drug use. In fact, some display such obsessive–compulsive behavior that they cannot let a morning, afternoon, or evening pass without using drugs. Some researchers have classified such variability in the frequency and extent of usage as fitting into three basic patterns: experimenters, compulsive users, and *floaters* or *chippers* (members of the last category drift between experimentation and compulsive use).

**Experimenters** begin using drugs largely because of peer pressure and curiosity, and they confine their use to recreational settings. Generally, they more often enjoy being with peers who also use drugs recreationally. Alcohol, tobacco, marijuana, prescription drugs, hallucinogens, and many of the major stimulants are the drugs they are most likely to use. They are usually able to set limits on when these drugs are taken (often preferred in social settings), and they are more likely to know the difference between light, moderate, and chronic use.

**Compulsive users**, in contrast, "devote considerable time and energy to getting high, talk incessantly (sometimes exclusively) about drug use . . . [and 'funny' or 'weird' experiences] . . . and become connoisseurs of street drugs" (Beschner, 1986, p. 7). For compulsive users, recreational fun is impossible without getting high. Other characteristics of these users include the need to escape or postpone personal problems, avoid stress and anxiety, and enjoy the sensation of the drug's euphoric effects. Often, they have difficulty assuming personal responsibility and suffer from low self-esteem. Many compulsive users are from dysfunctional families, have persistent problems with the law, or have serious psychological problems underlying their drug-taking behavior. Problems with personal and public identity, excessive confusion about their sexual identity and at times sexual orientation, boredom, family discord, childhood sexual or mental abuse, academic pressure, and chronic depression all contribute to the inability to cope with issues without drugs.

**Floaters or chippers** initially focus more on using other people's drugs without maintaining a steady supply of drugs. Nonetheless, floaters or chippers, like experimenters, are generally light to moderate drug users. Floaters or chippers feel a largely unconscious need to seek pleasure from using drugs and the desire to relieve moderate to serious psychological problems. Even though most are on a path to drug dependence, at this stage they may generally drift between or simultaneously intermix with other experimental drug-taking peers and chronic drug-using peers. In a sense, these types of drug users feel marginally attached to conventional society and often appear to conventional members of society as norm abiding, while masking their secret drug use. At this stage, floaters or chippers are not yet firmly attached to compulsive users often because they have not made the commitment to continually do drugs. (See "Signs & Symptoms: Who Is More Likely to Use Licit and Illicit Drugs?")

## ■ Drug Use: Mass and Electronic Media and Family Influences

Studies continually show that the majority of young drug users come from homes in which drugs are liberally used (Goode, 1999; National Association for Children of Alcoholics, 2005; SAMHSA, Office of Applied Studies 1996). Children from these homes constantly witness drug use at home, often on a daily basis. For instance, parents may consume large quantities of coffee to wake up in the morning and other forms of medication throughout the day: cigarettes with the morning coffee, pills for either treating or

## KEY TERMS

**experimenters**
first category of drug users, typified as being in the initial stages of drug use; these people often use drugs for recreational purposes

**compulsive users**
second category of drug users, typified by an insatiable attraction followed by a psychological dependence on drugs

**floaters or chippers**
third category of drug users; these users vacillate between the need for pleasure seeking and the desire to relieve moderate to serious psychological problems; this category of drug user has two major characteristics: (1) a general focus mostly on using other people's drugs (often without maintaining a personal supply of the drug) and (2) vacillation between the characteristics of chronic drug users and experimenter types

## SIGNS & SYMPTOMS
### Who Is More Likely to Use Licit and Illicit Drugs?

Many factors influence whether an adolescent tries drugs, including the availability of drugs within the neighborhood, community, and school and whether the adolescent's friends are using them. The family environment is also important: violence, physical or emotional abuse, mental illness, or drug use in the household increase the likelihood an adolescent will use drugs. Finally, an adolescent's inherited genetic vulnerability; personality traits such as poor impulse control or a high need for excitement; mental health conditions such as depression, anxiety, or ADHD; and beliefs such as drugs are "cool" or harmless make it more likely that an adolescent will use drugs (NIDA, 2014a).

According to the National Institute of Drug Abuse (2014a), adolescents experiment with drugs or continue taking them for several reasons, including the following:

- *To fit in*: Many teens use drugs "because others are doing it"—or they think others are doing it—and they fear not being accepted in a social circle that includes drug-using peers.

- *To feel good*: Abused drugs interact with the neurochemistry of the brain to produce feelings of pleasure. The intensity of this euphoria differs by the type of drug and how it is used.

- *To feel better*: Some adolescents suffer from depression, social anxiety, stress-related disorders, and physical pain. Using drugs may be an attempt to lessen these feelings of distress. Stress especially plays a significant role in starting and continuing drug use as well as returning to drug use (relapsing) for those recovering from an addiction.

- *To do better*: Ours is a highly competitive society in which the pressure to perform athletically and academically can be intense. Some adolescents may turn to certain drugs like illegal or prescription

stimulants because they think those substances will enhance or improve their performance.

- *To experiment*: Adolescents are often motivated to seek new experiences, particularly those they perceive as thrilling or daring.

In addition, adolescents' years can also be preoccupied with the need to explore. They can be preoccupied with using alcohol or other drugs to do the following (DEA, 2018):

- *relieve boredom,*
- *feel good,*
- *forget their troubles and relax,*
- *satisfy their curiosity,*
- *ease their pain,*
- *feel grown up,*
- *show their independence, and*
- *belong to a specific group.*

Finally, when attempting to determine who among drug users has a greater likelihood of becoming addicted, one research finding reports, "As with many other conditions and diseases, vulnerability to addiction differs from person to person. Your genes, mental health, family and social environment all play a role in addiction" (Helpguide.org, n.d.). The following risk factors increase a person's vulnerability to addiction (Helpguide.org, n.d.):

- family history of addiction;
- abuse, neglect, or other traumatic experiences;
- mental disorders such as depression and anxiety;
- early use of drugs; and
- method of administration (smoking or injecting a drug may increase its addictive potential).

Data from National Institute of Drug Abuse (NIDA). (2014c). *Principles of adolescent substance use disorder treatment: A research-based guide.* Bethesda, MD: Author. Retrieved from https://www.drugabuse.gov/sites/default/files/podata_1_17_14.pdf; Helpguide. (n.d.). *Drug abuse and addiction.* Helpguide.org. Retrieved from http://www.helpguide.org/articles/addiction/drug-abuse-and-addiction.htm; Drug Enforcement Administration (DEA). (2018). *Why do teens use drugs?* Washington, DC: U.S Government, Drug Enforcement Administration. Retrieved from https://www.getsmartaboutdrugs.gov/family/why-do-teens-use-drugs

relieving an upset stomach, vitamins for added nutrition, or aspirin for a headache. Finally, before going to bed, the grown-ups may take a few "nightcaps" or a sleeping pill to relax. The following is an interview related to the overuse of drugs:

Yeah, I always saw my mom smoking early in the morning while reading the newspaper

and slowly sipping nearly a full pot of coffee. She took prescription drugs for asthma, used an inhaler, and took aspirin for headaches. When she accused me of using drugs at concerts, I would pick up her pack of cigarettes and several prescription bottles and while she was raging on me, I would quietly wave all her drugs close up in front of her face. She would stop nagging within seconds and actually one time I think she wanted to laugh but turned away toward the sink and just started washing cups and saucers. The way I figure it, she has her drugs, and I have mine. She may not agree with my use of my drugs but then she is not better either. It's great to have a drug-using family ain't it? *(From Venturelli's research files, male college student, age 20, June 12, 2000)*

This next interview is an example of how "pill pilfering" can easily occur:

Yes, I came from a home with dozens of pharmacy prescriptions and with medicine cabinets crammed with over-the-counter drugs. In fact, my mom noticed that certain friends of mine were helping themselves to our medicine cabinet. At first, she told my dad that I was taking the pills. Finally, she had to remove most of the prescription medicines from the guest bathroom and hide them in her bedroom bathroom. This was about four years ago when I was in high school. She was right, several of my friends had a knack of lifting tabs from other homes when visiting friends. I know that one of my friends was into this when he told another friend of mine that our home had a nice variety of great drugs in the bathroom. Now, I know why my friends always had to go to the bathroom whenever they would stop by to see me. *(From Venturelli's research files, male attending a mid-size university in the Midwest, age 20, June 6, 2010)*

Some social scientists believe that everyday consumption of legal drugs—caffeine, prescription and OTC drugs, and alcohol—is fueled by the pace of modern lifestyles and greatly accelerated by the influence of today's increasingly sophisticated mass media.

If you look around your classroom building, the dormitories at your college, your college library, or your own home, evidence of mass media and electronic equipment can be found everywhere. Cultural knowledge and information are transmitted via media through electronic gadgets we simply "can't live without"—to the point that they help us define and shape our everyday reality. One recent survey reported that "digital peer pressure appears to have played a significant role in getting teens started on drugs and booze—something that was not the case before the era of social networking sites. Seventy-five percent of respondents said that seeing Facebook pictures of their peers partying with alcohol and marijuana encourages other teens to imitate them" (Huffington Post

2012, p. 1). In addition, "[c]ompared to teens who have not seen pictures on Facebook or other social networking sites of kids getting drunk, passed out, or using drugs, teens who have seen such pictures are: [f]our times likelier to have used marijuana, [m]ore than three times likelier to have used alcohol; and [a]lmost three times likelier to have used tobacco" (CASA Columbia, 2012, p. 3).

With regards to drug advertising, television remains the most influential medium. Today, most homes (82%) have more than one television (Nielsen Company, 2016). The Nielsen Company (2016) also reports that "in 2009 the average American home had 2.86 TV sets, which is roughly 18% higher than in 2000 (2.43 sets per home)." Just as the number of televisions in the average home has been increasing over the last 30 years, "[d]rug firms . . . [have been increasing] . . . their spending on television advertising to consumers seven-fold from 1996 to 2000" (CBS News, 2002). "Prescription drugs account for 10 percent of overall health spending in the United States, totaling $328 billion annually. (Also calculated as $450 billion when list prices and middle-man transactions are included. State and federal governments have focused on successfully managing these costs through a variety of approaches" (NCSL, 2020).

More recently,

According to an article in the *Journal of the American Medical Association*, between 1997 and 2016 spending for direct to consumer advertising for all types of healthcare service increased from $2 billion to $10 billion. Of this, $6 billion went toward ads for drugs. During this same time period, out of pocket costs for drugs went from $116.5 billion to $328.6 billion (after accounting for industry discounts and rebates). (*Williamsport Sun-Gazette*, 2020)

As an example,

[i]n 2014, two widely recognized erectile dysfunction drugs that have been on the market for more than a decade—Pfizer's Viagra and Eli Lilly's Cialis—ranked among the top five, . . . . Pfizer's advertising budget for its "little blue pill" has more than doubled in the past five years to $232 million, and the company notably started marketing directly to women. (Millman, 2015)

As another example, "Each year, the top 14 major alcohol marketers spent more than a $3.45 billion dollars on 'measured media' advertising, that is television, radio, print, online, direct mail and outdoor ads" (Federal Trade Commission, 2015). "The advertising budget for one beer—Budweiser—is more than the entire budget for research on alcoholism and alcohol abusers" (Kilbourne, 1989, p. 13). Other findings indicate that "Alcohol companies spent $4.9 billion on television advertising between 2001 and 2005. They spent 2.1% of this amount ($104 million) on 'responsibility advertisements'" (Center on Alcohol Marketing and Youth [CAMY], 2007). "For the entire period from 2001 to 2003, Anheuser-Busch spent 20 times more on product ads than on 'responsibility' ads and placed 30 times as many product ads as 'responsibility' ads" (CAMY, 2005).

Radio, newspapers, and magazines are also saturated with advertisements for OTC drugs that constantly offer relief from whatever illness you may have. There are pills for inducing sleep and for staying awake, as well as others for treating indigestion, headache, backache, tension, constipation, and the like. Using these medicinal compounds can significantly alter mood, level of consciousness, and physical discomfort.

# HERE AND NOW

## Abuse of Licit and Illicit Drugs by the Elderly

SAMHSA (2012a) reports the following regarding drug misuse and abuse by the elderly:

> Older adults are among those most vulnerable to medication misuse and abuse because they use more prescription and over-the-counter (OTC) medications than other age groups. They are likely to experience more problems with relatively small amounts of medications because of increased medication sensitivity as well as slower metabolism and elimination. Older adults are at high risk for medication misuse due to conditions like pain, sleep disorders [and] insomnia, and anxiety that commonly occur in this population. They are, therefore, more likely to receive prescriptions for psychoactive medications with misuse and abuse potential, such as opioid analgesics for pain and central nervous system depressants like benzodiazepines for sleep disorders and anxiety. Approximately 25% of older adults use prescription psychoactive medications that have a potential to be misused and abused. Older adults are more likely to use psychoactive medications for longer periods than younger adults. Longer periods of use increases the risk of misuse and abuse. In addition to concerns regarding misuse of medications alone, the combination of alcohol and medication misuse has been estimated to affect up to 19% of older Americans.

### Scope of the Problem: Drug Use and Abuse Among Older Adults

- "An estimated 4.8 million adults aged 50 and older have used an illicit drug in the past year.... The prevalence of illicit drug use was higher among adults aged 50 to 59 than those aged 60 and older) (Reardon, 2012).

- "Overall, alcohol was the most frequently reported primary substance of abuse for persons aged 50 or older. Opiates were the second most commonly reported primary substances of abuse, reported most frequently by individuals aged 50 to 59. These individuals also had the highest proportions of inpatient admissions for cocaine, marijuana, and stimulant abuse" (Bogunovic, 2012).

- Marijuana use was more common than nonmedical use of prescription-type drugs for adults aged 50 to 54 and those aged 55 to 59 (6.1% vs. 3.4% and 4.1% vs. 3.2%, respectively), but among those aged 65 or older nonmedical use of prescription-type drugs was more common than marijuana use (0.8% vs. 0.4%) (SAMHSA, 2009).

- Marijuana use was more common than nonmedical use of prescription-type drugs among males aged 50 or older (4.2% vs. 2.3%), but among females the rates of marijuana use and nonmedical use of prescription-type drugs were similar (1.7% and 1.9%) (SAMHSA, 2009).

- "Among adults aged 50 or older, the prevalence rates of any illicit drug use and marijuana use in the past year were higher among males than females" (Crabb, 2014).

- "Among adults aged 50 or older who used illicit drugs in the past year, 45.2% used only marijuana, 31.5% used only prescription-type drugs nonmedically, and 5.6% used only other illicit drugs (including cocaine, heroin, hallucinogens, or inhalants) with the remainder using other combinations of illicit drugs" (Crabb, 2014).

- "The number of Americans aged 50+ years is increasing as large numbers of baby boomers reach age 50 years or older, and this cohort uses more psychoactive drugs than older cohorts" (Li-Tzy & Blazer, 2011).

- Many Americans who are now young or middle-aged will carry their use and abuse of alcohol and other drugs with them into old age—and they will also live longer (SAMHSA, 2013).

- Older adults are more likely to take prescribed psychoactive medications for longer periods of time than younger adults and run an additional risk of becoming addicted to their prescribed medications (SAMHSA, 2013).

- Several factors have been associated with an increased risk of psychoactive prescription medication misuse and abuse among older adults:
  - female gender,
  - social isolation,
  - history of substance abuse, and
  - a mental health disorder, particularly depression.

- Older women are at higher risk because they are more likely to use psychoactive medications, especially benzodiazepines. This use may be associated with divorce, widowhood, lower income, poorer health status, depression, or anxiety (SAMHSA, 2012).

An example of elderly drug abuse includes the following:

Oh, I started with cigarettes when I was [14]. Then came the alcohol when I was [16], and now I am now 62 years old and still playing around with drugs. I have several friends who still smoke weed, but not too many around who continue like I do. I generally smoke cigarettes, weed (as they call it today), sometimes buy a little bag of coke and smoke that, too, and drink alcohol. I don't do the coke much because I like to smoke it, and it is tough on the heart. My drug using friends who are around my age don't really know about the coke use; they think I stopped this years ago. I still have days when I long for it, but I have enough of a hard time with the weed and the drinking. My children do not know how much I drink since I live alone, and they even think I have nothing to do with weed. So, I guess I am a closet user. At times I am sorry to continue with these unnecessary drugs, and it's even darn right embarrassing if anyone finds out. Even the cigarettes are a pain in the butt. I just need to get high every now and then, and I don't know why. I think it is something genetic since I want to quit all these drugs but simply do not do it. You asked if I think a lot of the elderly use drugs unnecessarily [drugs used without medical purposes]. Yes, there are many of us, especially the baby boomers who still smoke weed, but we kind of keep it secret. So, if the numbers of users my age are increasing, I would double the real number of users. As I said, many of us just keep it secret because we still work, have good jobs with a lot of responsibilities, and our kids would look down on us if they knew. You asked if I feel addicted to these drugs. Yes, I am addicted since I really don't want to quit everything, yet it is not good for my health and still keep using these drugs. Isn't this a classic example of addiction, which is to keep using drugs even though you know they are not good for you? If it's not addiction, what else would it be? *(From Venturelli's research files, male, age 62, April 22, 2011)*

Data from Reardon, C. (2012, January/February). The changing face of older adult substance abuse. *Social Work Today 12*, 8; Bogunovic, O. (2012, July 27). Substance abuse in aging and elderly adults. *Psychiatric Times*. Retrieved from http://www.psychiatrictimes.com/geriatric-psychiatry/substance-abuse-aging-and-elderly-adults; Substance Abuse and Mental Health Service Administration (SAMHSA). (2012c). *Older Americans Behavioral Health, Issue Brief 5: Prescription medication misuse and abuse among older adults.* Rockville, MD: Author. Retrieved from https://acl.gov/sites/default/files/programs/2016-11/Issue%20Brief%205%20Prescription%20Med%20Misuse%20Abuse.pdf; Office of Applied Studies (OAS). (2012). Illicit drug use among older adults. *The NSDUH* [National Survey on Drug Use and Health] *Report.* Rockville, MD: U.S. Department of Health and Human Services; Crabb, G. (2014, March 7). Illicit drug use among older adults. Naples, FL: Author. Retrieved from http://drgeorgecrabb.com/; Li-Tzy, W., & Blazer, D. G. (2011). Illicit and nonmedical drug use among older adults: A review. *Journal of Aging Health, 23*, 481–504; Substance Abuse and Mental Health Services Administration (SAMHSA). (2013). *Substance abuse among older adults.* Rockville, MD: Author.

Experts warn that such drug advertising is likely to increase.

In the early 1990s, the FDA lifted a two-year ban on consumer advertising of prescription drugs; since then, there has been an onslaught of new sales pitches. In their attempts to sell drugs, product advertisers use the authority of a physician or health expert or the seemingly sincere testimony of a product user. Viewers or listeners are strongly affected by testimonial advertising because these drug commercials can appear authentic and convincing.

The constant barrage of commercials, including many for OTC drugs, relays the message that taking drugs is an acceptable and normal response if you are experiencing restlessness or uncomfortable symptoms. As a result, television viewers, newspaper and magazine readers, and radio listeners are led to believe or unconsciously select the particular brand advertised when confronted with dozens upon dozens of drug choices for a particular ailment. In effect, this advertising reaffirms the belief that drugs are necessary when taken for a real or an imagined symptom.

# Drug Use and Drug Dependence

Why are so many people attracted to drugs and the effects of recreational drug use? Like the ancient Assyrians, who sucked on opium lozenges, and the Romans, who ate hashish sweets some 2,000 years ago, many users claim to be bored, in pain, frustrated, unable to enjoy life, or alienated. Such people turn to drugs in the hope of finding oblivion, peace, inner connections, outer connections (togetherness), or euphoria. The fact that many OTC drugs never really cure the ailment, especially if taken for social and psychological reasons, and the fact that frequent use of most drugs increases the risk of addiction, do not seem to be deterrents. People continue to take drugs for many reasons, including the following:

- searching for pleasure and using drugs to heighten good feelings;
- taking drugs to temporarily relieve stress or tension or provide a temporary escape for people with anxiety;
- taking drugs to temporarily forget one's problems and avoid or postpone worries;
- viewing certain drugs (such as alcohol, marijuana, and tobacco) as necessary to relax after a tension-filled day at work;
- taking drugs to fit in with peers, especially when peer pressure is strong during early and late adolescence;
- seeing drugs as a rite of passage;
- taking drugs to enhance religious or mystical experiences (few cultures teach children how to use specific drugs for this purpose);
- taking drugs to relieve pain and some symptoms of illness; and

- resuming drug use from teenage and young adult periods of life—for example, elderly baby boomers who may have used drugs in their youth.

It is important to understand why, historically, many people have been unsuccessful in eliminating their fascination with drugs. To understand, we must address questions dealing with (1) why people are attracted to drugs, (2) how experiences with the different types of drugs vary (here many attitudes are conveyed from the "inside"—the users themselves), (3) how each of the major drugs affects the body and the mind, (4) how patterns of use vary among different groups, and (5) what forms of treatment are available for the addicted.

## ▪ When Does Use Lead to Abuse?

Views about the use of drugs depend on one's perspective. For example, from a pharmacological perspective, if a patient is suffering severe pain because of injuries sustained from an automobile accident, high doses of a narcotic such as morphine or Demerol should be given to control discomfort. While someone is in pain, no reason exists not to take the drug. From a medical standpoint, once healing has occurred and pain has been relieved, drug use should cease. If the patient continues using the narcotic because it provides a sense of well-being, then he or she has become dependent to the point of addiction and the pattern of drug intake is then considered abuse. Thus, the amount of drug taken or the frequency of dosing does not necessarily determine abuse (even though individuals who abuse drugs usually consume increasingly higher doses). Most important is the motive for taking the drug, which is the principal factor in determining the presence of abuse.

Initial drug abuse symptoms include (1) excessive use, (2) constant preoccupation about the availability and supply of the drug, (3) denial in admitting the excessive use, and (4) reliance on the drug. All of these four factors frequently result in producing the initial symptoms of withdrawal whenever the user attempts to stop taking the drug. As a result, the user often begins to neglect other responsibilities or ambitions in favor of using the drug.

Even the legitimate use of a drug can be controversial. Often, physicians cannot decide even among themselves what constitutes legitimate use of a drug. For example, MDMA (Ecstasy) is currently prohibited for therapeutic use, but in 1985, when the Drug Enforcement Administration was deciding MDMA's status, some 35 to 200 physicians (mostly psychiatrists) were using the drug in their practice. These clinicians claimed that MDMA relaxed inhibitions and enhanced communication and was useful as a psychotherapeutic adjunct to assist in dealing with psychiatric patients (Levinthal, 1996; Schecter, 1989). From the perspective of these physicians, Ecstasy was a useful medicinal tool. However, the DEA did not agree and made Ecstasy a Schedule I drug. Schedule I excludes any legitimate, legal use of the drug in therapeutics; consequently, according to this ruling, anyone taking Ecstasy is guilty of drug abuse (Goode, 2012) and is violating drug laws.

If the problem of drug abuse is to be understood and solutions are to be found, identifying the causes of the abuse is most important. When a drug is being abused, it is not legitimately therapeutic; that is, it does not improve the user's physical or mental health. When drug use is not used for therapeutic purposes, what is the motive for taking the drug?

There are many possible answers to this question. Initially, most drug abusers perceive some psychological advantage when using these compounds. For many, the psychological lift is significant enough that they are willing to risk social exclusion, health problems, dramatic changes in personality, arrest, incarceration, and fines to have their drug. The psychological effects that these drugs cause may entail an array of diverse feelings. Different types of drugs have different psychological effects. The type of drug an individual selects to abuse may ultimately reflect his or her own mental state.

For example, people who experience chronic depression, feel intense job pressures, are unable to focus on accomplishing goals, or have a sense of inferiority may find that a stimulant such as cocaine or an amphetamine-type drug appears to provide immediate relief—a solution to a set of psychological frustrations. These drugs cause a spurt of energy, a feeling of euphoria, a sense of superiority, and imagined self-confidence. In contrast, people who experience nervousness and anxiety and want instant relief from the pressures of life may choose a depressant such as alcohol or barbiturates. These agents sedate, relax, provide relief, and even have some amnesiac properties, allowing users to suspend or forget their immediate pressing concerns or

problems. People who perceive themselves as creative or who have artistic talents may select hallucinogenic types of drugs to "expand" their minds, heighten their senses, and distort what appears to be a confining and sometimes monotonous nature of reality. As individuals come to rely more on drugs to inhibit, deny, accelerate, or distort their realities, they run the risk of becoming psychologically dependent on drugs.

Some people have argued that taking a particular drug to meet a psychological need, especially if a person is 21 years of age or older, is not especially different from taking a drug to cure an ailment. The belief here is that physical needs and psychological needs are really indistinguishable. In fact, several drug researchers and writers, including Szasz (1992) and Lenson (1995), believe that drug taking is a citizen's right and a personal matter involving individual decision making. They see drug taking as simply a personal choice to depart from or alter consciousness. Lenson states that taking drugs for recreational purposes is simply an additional form of diversity, a type of mental diversity that should exist with many other acceptable forms of diversity such as cultural, racial, religious, gender, and sexual orientation diversity. (For additional elaboration on these views, see Venturelli, 2000.) Obviously, this is a strikingly different and often extremely controversial point of view that can easily cause polemic and highly debatable perspectives!

## ■ Drug Dependence

This section introduces some underlying factors that lead to drug dependence. Our discussion emphasizes drug dependence instead of addiction because the term *addiction* is both controversial and relative, as evidenced with celebrities and rock and movie stars and their drug dependence, including some who have died from drug dependence. Stars such as Charlie Sheen, Mel Gibson, and Ben Affleck (alcoholism); John Belushi, Lindsay Lohan, and Robin Williams (alcoholism and cocaine); Robert Downey, Jr. (cocaine and heroin); Michael Jackson (prescription drugs); Philip Seymour Hoffman (illegal drug); Cory Monteith (illegal drug and alcohol); Chris Kelly (illegal drug); Whitney Houston (illegal drug); Amy Winehouse (alcohol); and Eminem (analgesic prescription drugs) are just a few examples.

Even when drug dependence becomes full-fledged, addiction remains debatable, with many experts unable to agree on one set of characteristics that constitutes addiction. Furthermore, the term *addiction* is viewed by some as a pejorative that adds to the labeling process.

The main characteristics necessary for drug dependence are as follows:

- Both physical and psychological factors precipitate drug dependence. Recently, closer attention has been focused on the mental (psychological) attachments than on the physical addiction to drug use as principally indicative of addiction—mostly, the craving aspect of wanting the drug for consumption.
- More specifically, *psychological dependence* refers to the need that a user may feel for continued use of a drug to experience its effects. *Physical dependence* refers to the need to continue taking the drug to avoid withdrawal symptoms that often include feelings of discomfort and illness.
- With repeated use, there is a tendency to become dependent on and addicted to most psychoactive drugs.
- Addiction to a drug sets in when the drug user has advanced within the dependence phase. (Having an addiction to a drug is simply an advanced stage of dependence.)
- Generally, the addiction process involves mental (psychological) and physical (physiological or biophysiological) dependence.

**Figure 1.7** shows that the process of addiction involves five separate phases: relief, increased use, preoccupation, dependency, and withdrawal. Initially, the **relief phase** refers to the relief experienced by using a drug, which allows a potential addict to escape one or more of the following feelings: boredom, loneliness, tension, fatigue, anger, or anxiety. The **increased use phase** involves taking greater quantities of

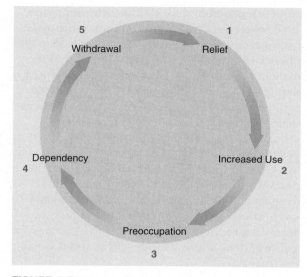

**FIGURE 1.7**   Stages of drug dependence.

the drug. The **preoccupation phase** consists of a continuous interest with and concern for the substance—that is, always having a supply of the drug—and taking the drug is perceived as "normal" behavior. The **dependency phase** is synonymous with addiction. In this phase, more of the drug is sought without regard for the presence of negative physical symptoms such as congested coughing or shortness of breath in cases of cigarette and marijuana addiction, blackouts from advanced alcohol abuse, and moderate to acute soreness and inflammation of nasal passages from snorting cocaine. The **withdrawal phase** involves such symptoms as itching, chills, tension, stomach pain, or depression from the nonuse of the addictive drug or an entire set of psychological concerns mainly involving an insatiable craving for the drug (Monroe, 1996).

## Noteworthy Costs of Substance Abuse

Many of the costs of drug abuse and addiction range from those for users to those for society. Consider, for example, the loss of an addicted person's connection with reality and the loss of responsible dedication to careers and professions, illnesses experienced by the addicted individual, marital strife, shortened lives, and so on. In addition, society pays a high price for drug abuse and addiction in the dollar costs of addiction to society, which can be enormous. Abuse of tobacco, alcohol, and illicit drugs costs our

**KEY TERMS**

**relief phase**
satisfaction derived from escaping negative feelings by using a drug

**increased use phase**
taking increasing quantities of a drug

**preoccupation phase**
constant concern with the supply of the drug

**dependency phase**
synonym for addiction

**withdrawal phase**
physical or psychological effects derived from not using a drug

nation more than $740 billion annually in costs related to crime, lost work productivity, and health care (NIDA, 2017).

## Narcotics and Heroin Usage

The **National Institute on Drug Abuse (NIDA)** has estimated that the typical narcotic habit costs the user approximately $150 a day to support his or her addiction. The precise dollar amount spent to support a narcotic addiction largely depends on the geographic location where the drug is procured and used, availability of the drug affecting the price, and numerous other factors. For example, a heroin addict, will spend "$150–200 per day in order to support his or her habit" (Heroin.net 2016), which adds up to $54,750 to $73,000 per year just to maintain the drug supply. It is impossible for most addicts to get this amount of money legally; therefore, many support their habits by resorting to criminal activity or by working as or for drug dealers.

As reported more recently,

The retail price of heroin varies by geographic region, but it generally costs about $5 to $10 for a "stamp bag," a waxed paper or plastic bag stamped by the dealer with a name or brand. These bags usually contain about one-tenth of a gram of heroin. . . . [Further] . . . [in] some cities, heroin can cost $15 to $20 a bag. . . . Heroin doesn't stay inexpensive for long, though. The illegal opioid is extremely addictive, and when addiction takes hold, an individual can easily spend $150 to $200 a day on the drug. At that rate, a heroin addiction could easily cost someone more than $53,000 a year. (Keller, 2020b)

Most crimes related to drugs involve theft of personal property—primarily burglary and shoplifting—and, less commonly, assault and robbery (often mugging). Estimates are that a heroin addict must steal three to five times the actual cost of the drugs to maintain the habit, which becomes an astronomical and impractical amount per year. Further, it is not unusual with crack and heroin use that a high proportion of hardcore addicts resort to pimping and prostitution (with no accurate figures available regarding the cost of drug-related prostitution), although some law enforcement officials have estimated that prostitutes take in a total of $10 billion to $20 billion per year. It has also been estimated that nearly three out of every four prostitutes in major cities have a serious drug dependency.

## Methamphetamine Usage

The misuse of methamphetamine—a potent and highly addictive stimulant—remains an extremely serious problem in the United States. In some areas of the country, it poses an even greater threat than opioids, and it is the drug that most contributes to violent crime. According to data from the 2017 National Survey on Drug Use and Health, more than 14.7 million people (5.4% of the population) have tried methamphetamine at least once. NSDUH also reports that almost 1.6 million people used methamphetamine in the year leading up to the survey, and it remains one of the most commonly misused stimulant drugs in the world (NIDA, 2019d).

The consequences of methamphetamine misuse are terrible for the individual—psychologically, medically, and socially. Using the drug can cause memory loss, aggression, psychotic behavior, damage to the cardiovascular system, malnutrition, and severe dental problems. Methamphetamine misuse has also been shown to contribute to increased transmission of infectious diseases such as hepatitis and HIV and AIDS (NIDA, 2019d).

Beyond its devastating effects on individual health, methamphetamine misuse threatens whole communities, causing new waves of crime, unemployment, child neglect or abuse, and other social ills. A 2009 report from the RAND Corporation noted that methamphetamine misuse cost the nation approximately $23.4 billion in 2005 (NIDA, 2019d).

In looking at the scope of methamphetamine misuse in the United States, we find that approximately 1.6 million people (0.6% of the population) reported using methamphetamine in the past year, and 774,000 (0.3%) reported using it in the past month, according to the 2017 NSDUH (NIDA, 2019c). The average age of new methamphetamine users in 2016 was 23.3 years old. An estimated 964,000 people

KEY TERM

**National Institute on Drug Abuse (NIDA)**
principal federal agency responsible for directing research related to drug use and abuse

aged 12 and older (about 0.4% of the population) had a methamphetamine use disorder in 2017—that is, they reported clinically significant impairment, including health problems, disability, and failure to meet responsibilities at work, school, or home as a result of their drug use. This number is significantly higher than the 684,000 people who reported having methamphetamine use disorder in 2016. The 2018 MTF survey of adolescent drug use and attitudes reported that about 0.5% of 8th, 10th, and 12th graders had used methamphetamine within the past year. Use of methamphetamine by adolescents has declined significantly since 1999, when this drug was first added to the survey (NIDA, 2019c).

Review of the use of this drug indicates that past-month methamphetamine use has been increasing. For example, in the yearly National Survey on Drug Use and Health there were 569,000 (0.2%) users in 2014 and 440,000 (0.2%) users in 2011 (CBHSQ, 2015; SAMHSA 2012).

The late 1990s brought significant concern regarding the nationwide increase in clandestine laboratories involved in synthesizing or processing this type of illicit drug. Such laboratories produced amphetamine-type drugs, heroin-type drugs, designer drugs, and LSD and processed other drugs of abuse such as cocaine and crack. The DEA reported that 390 laboratories were seized in 1993, a figure that increased to 967 in 1995. Another example of the phenomenal growth of methamphetamine laboratories was found in Missouri. From 1995 to 1997, seizures of such labs in Missouri increased by 535% (Steward & Sitarmiah, 1997). "In Dawson County in western Nebraska. . . . 'The percentage of meth-related crimes is through the roof' . . . as reiterated by an investigator with the county sheriff's office. . . . In the state as a whole, officials discovered 38 methamphetamine laboratories in 1999; last year [2001] they discovered 179" (Butterfield, 2002, p. A23). In 2012, the total number of meth clandestine laboratory incidents was 11,210 and included lab, dumpsite, chemicals, glass, and equipment incidents (USDOJ, 2013). Regarding seizures of this drug, one report states that "36,572 pounds: That's the amount of methamphetamine seized near the U.S.–Mexico border at U.S. Border Patrol stations and Customs and Border Protection ports of entry near the border from 2005 to 2011" (Chen, 2013). In 2015, the state

of Indiana had the highest number of clandestine methamphetamine lab incidents, resulting in 1,530 site seizures (Meth.IN.gov, 2015). The reasons for such dramatic increases and usage are related to the enormous profits and relatively low risk associated with these operations. As a rule, clandestine laboratories are fairly mobile and relatively crude (often operating in a kitchen, basement, or garage) and are run by individuals with only elementary chemical skills.

Another interesting discovery was that these laboratories were not always stationary in locations such as garages, barns, homes, apartments, and so on. Although these stationary labs predominated, especially in the production of methamphetamine, mobile labs also made an appearance:

> Cooking in cars and trucks helped producers in two ways: It eludes identification by law enforcement and motion helps the chemical reaction [of methamphetamine production]. Motels are a new production setting . . . [though fewer in number today]. Clandestine labs are also set up in federal parklands, where toxic by-products pose a danger to hikers and campers. (ONDCP 2002, p. 58)

To demonstrate how a drug such as methamphetamine affects society, in 2003, the following was reported:

> With portable meth labs popping up everywhere from motel bathrooms to the back seat of a Chevy, it was only a matter of time before they made their way onto campus. Last November, a custodian notified campus police at [University of Texas] about what appeared to be a lab set up in a music practice room in the [university's] Fine Arts Center. "We found beakers of red liquid, papers and other residue, and the room had this horrible odor. . . ."
>
> Students were on vacation, so the practice room, which had its windows blackened out, would have afforded the occupant a few days to cook. [One campus police official] . . . speculates that this is just the beginning: "Labs are popping up on campuses all over the country. It's just too easy now. You can get the recipe on the Internet. Still, how could someone be so brazen as to set up an operation next to the French horn section?" (Jellinek, 2003)

Because of a lack of training, inexperience, and the danger of experiencing the effects of methamphetamine while making the drug, the chemical "cooking" procedures are performed crudely, sometimes resulting in adulterants and impure products. Such contaminants can be highly toxic, causing severe harm or even death to the unsuspecting user as well as a greater likelihood of sudden explosion (Drug Strategies, 1995). Fortunately, when looking at all the illicit drugs produced by such underground laboratories, such outbreaks of physically harmful drugs do not occur often. Partial proof of this is found in the small number of news stories of deaths or poisonings from illicit drugs. Nevertheless, because profit drives these clandestine labs, which obviously have no government supervision, impurities or "cheap fillers" are always possible so that greater profits can be made. Here, caution is highly advisable in that drug purchasers do not have any guarantees when purchasing powerful illicit drugs.

## Overall Costs of Drug Addiction

Society continues paying a large sum even after users, addicts, and drug dealers are caught and sentenced because it takes from $75 to $1,500 per day to keep one person incarcerated. A post by the *Federal Register* (2015) reports, "The fee to cover the average cost of incarceration for Federal inmates in Fiscal Year 2014 was $30,619.85 ($83.89 per day)." More recent reports are that "[a]mong the 45 states that provided data (representing 1.29 million of the 1.33 million total people incarcerated in all 50 state prison systems), the total cost per inmate averaged $33,274 and ranged from a low of $14,780 in Alabama to a high of $69,355 in New York" (Vera Institute of Justice, 2020). Supporting programs such as methadone maintenance costs much less. New York officials estimate that methadone maintenance costs about $,3000 per year per patient. For non-hospital residential treatment, methadone costs average around $76.13 per day. With outpatient methadone programs, daily costs average around $17.78 per day (Methadone Centers, 2016), which is much less than the cost of incarceration.

A more long-term effect of drug abuse that has substantial impact on society is the medical and psychological care often required by addicts because of disease from their drug habits. Particularly noteworthy are the communicable diseases spread because of needle sharing within the drug-abusing population, such as hepatitis and HIV.

Also of great concern is drug abuse by women during pregnancy. Some psychoactive drugs can have profound, permanent effects on a developing fetus. The best documented is fetal alcohol syndrome, which can affect the offspring of alcoholic mothers. Cocaine and amphetamine-related drugs can also cause irreversible congenital changes when used during pregnancy. All too often, the affected offspring of addicted mothers become the responsibility of welfare organizations. In addition to the costs to society just mentioned, other costs of drug abuse include drug-related deaths, emergency room visits and hospital stays, and automobile fatalities.

## ■ Drugs, Crime, and Violence

There is a long-established close association between drug abuse and criminality. The beliefs (hypotheses) for this association range along a continuum between two opposing views: (1) Criminal behavior develops as a means to support addiction, and (2) criminality is inherently linked to the user's personality and occurs independently of drug use (Bureau of Justice Statistics [BJS], 2006; Common Sense for Drug Policy, 2020; Drug Strategies, 1995; McBride & McCoy, 2003). In other words, does drug addiction cause a person to engage in criminal behavior such as burglary, theft, and larceny to pay for the drug habit? Or does criminal behavior stem from an already existing criminal personality such that drugs are used as an adjunct to commit such acts? In other words, are drugs used in conjunction with crime to sedate and give the added confidence needed to commit daring law violations?

The answers to these questions have never been clear because findings that contradict one view in favor of the other continue to mount on both sides. Part of the reason for the controversy about the relationship between criminal activity and drug abuse is that studies have been conducted in different settings and cultures, employing different research methods and focusing on different addictive drugs. As a result, too many factors are involved to allow us to distinguish the cause from the result. We know that each type of drug has unique addictive potential and that interpretation of exactly when a deviant act is an offense (violation of law) varies. Furthermore, we know that people think differently while under the influence of drugs. Whether criminalistic behavior is *directly* caused by the drug use or whether prior socialization and peer influence work in concert to cause criminal behavior remains unclear. Certainly, we think it would be safe to believe that prior socialization, law-violating peers, and drugs are strong contributing factors for criminal behavior.

Although this controversy about the connection between drugs and crime continues to challenge our thinking, the following findings are also noteworthy.

- Drug abuse is implicated in at least three types of drug-related offenses: (1) offenses defined by drug possession or sales, (2) offenses directly related to drug abuse (e.g., stealing to get money for drugs), and (3) offenses related to a lifestyle that predisposes the drug abuser to engage in illegal activity—for example, through association with other offenders or with illicit markets (NIDA, 2014c).
- Individuals who use illicit drugs are more likely to commit crimes, and it is common for many offenses, including violent crimes, to be committed by individuals who had used drugs or alcohol before committing the crime, or who were using at the time of the offense (NIDA, 2014c).
- Of the estimated 1,654,282 drug law violations in the United States in 2018, 86.4% (1,429,300) were for possession of a controlled substance. Only 13.6% (224,982) were for sale or manufacture of a drug (Common Sense for Drug Policy, 2020).
- The United States ranks first in the world in the number of people incarcerated in federal and state correctional facilities. In 2014, 1,561,500 prisoners were under the jurisdiction of state and federal correctional authorities (BJS, 2015a). Almost half (48%) of the federal inmates were serving time for drug offenses (Carson & Sabol, 2012).
- The United States incarcerates more people for drug offenses than any other country (Natarajan, Petteruti, Walsh, & Ziedenberg, 2008; Sentencing Project, 2013).
- With an estimated 24.6 million Americans struggling with current (within 30 days of use) drug use or dependence (SAMHSA 2014a), the growth of the prison population continues to be driven largely by incarceration for drug offenses.
- In 2006, "17% of State and 18% of Federal prisoners committed their crime to obtain money for drugs" (Mumola & Karberg, 2007). Approximately one out of every six major

crimes are committed because of the offender's need to obtain money for drugs.
- An estimated 516,900 black males—37% of the sentenced male prison population—were in state or federal prison on December 31, 2014, on sentences of more than one year. White males made up an additional 32% of the male population (453,500 inmates), followed by Hispanic males (308,700 inmates, or 22%). White females in state or federal prison at yearend 2014 (53,100 prisoners) outnumbered black (22,600) and Hispanic females (17,800) combined (BJS, 2015b).
- Eighty percent of offenders abuse drugs or alcohol (National Council on Alcoholism and Drug Dependence [NCADD], 2015).
- Nearly 50% of jail and prison inmates are clinically addicted (NCADD, 2015).
- Approximately 60% of individuals arrested for most types of crimes tested positive for illegal drugs at arrest (NCADD, 2015).
- In 2011, 45% of arrestees tested positive for marijuana during their arrest, 41% for cocaine, 61% for opiates, and 61% for methamphetamine (ONDCP, 2012).
- The ADAM program reports that arrestees are tested for the presence of 10 drugs. The proportion of arrestees testing positive for any of the 10 drugs ranged from 63% in Atlanta to 83% in Chicago and Sacramento. Arrestees testing positive for multiple drugs in their system ranged from 12% in Atlanta to 50% in Sacramento (ONDCP, 2014).
- Marijuana remained the most commonly detected drug in urine testing, from 34% of ADAM II arrestees testing positive in Atlanta to 59% in Sacramento. Those who obtained marijuana in the prior 30 days reported little difficulty obtaining the drug, indicating an overall high availability of the drug in all sites (ONDCP, 2014).
- In federal prisons in 2015, the Bureau of Justice Statistics (2015b) reported that almost all (99.5%) drug offenders in federal prison were serving sentences for drug trafficking.
- Cocaine (powder or crack) was the primary drug type for more than half (54%) of drug offenders in federal prison.
- Race of drug offenders varied greatly by drug type. Blacks were 88% of crack cocaine offenders, Hispanics or Latinos were 54% of powder cocaine offenders, and whites were 48% of methamphetamine offenders (BJS, 2015b).

- More than one-third (35%) of drug offenders in federal prison at sentencing had either no or minimal criminal history (BJS, 2015b).
- Fifty-two percent of female jail inmates were found to be dependent on alcohol or drugs compared to 44% of male inmates (BJS, 2015b).
- Jail inmates between ages 25 and 44 had the highest rate of substance dependence or abuse (seven in 10 inmates). Those 55 and older had the lowest rate (nearly five in 10 inmates) (Karberg & James, 2002).
- More than 50% of drug or property offenders were dependent on or had abused a substance compared to more than 60% of violent and public-order offenders (Karberg & James 2002).
- Women and white inmates were more likely to have used drugs at the time of their offense (Karberg & James 2002).
- Thirty-two percent of state and 26.4% of federal prison inmates reported being under the influence of drugs at the time of their offense in 2004 (see **Table 1.5**). Approximately 44% were incarcerated for drug offenses in state prisons, and 32% were incarcerated in federal prisons. Of these, 46% in state prisons and 21% in federal prisons were arrested for possession. Forty-two percent were serving time in state prisons, and 34% were serving time in federal prisons for trafficking in drugs. One outcome of these findings is that one out of every four major crimes committed—violent, property, and drug offenses—involves an offender who is under the influence of drugs (Mumola & Karberg, 2007).
- Of the 1,561,231 arrests for drug law violations in 2014, 83.1% (1,297,384) were for possession of a controlled substance. Only 16.9% (263,848) were for the sale or manufacturing of a drug (DrugWarFacts, 2016).

In regard to the connection between drug use and crime, the following findings can be summarized: (1) Drug users in comparison to nondrug users are more likely to commit crimes, (2) a high percentage of arrestees are often under the influence of a drug while committing crimes, and (3) a high percentage of drug users arrested for drug use and violence are more likely to be under the influence of alcohol or stimulant types of drugs such as cocaine, crack, and methamphetamines.

**TABLE 1.5** Percentage of State and Federal Inmates Reporting Being Under the Influence of Drugs at the Time of Their Offense: 2004

| Offense | State (%) | Federal (%) |
|---|---|---|
| Total[a] | 32.1 | 26.4 |
| **Violent offenses** | 27.7 | 24.0 |
| Homicide | 27.3 | 16.8 |
| Sexual assault[b] | 17.4 | 13.8 |
| Robbery | 40.7 | 29.4 |
| Assault | 24.1 | 20.1 |
| **Property offenses** | 38.5 | 13.6 |
| Burglary | 41.1 | : |
| Larceny or theft | 40.1 | : |
| Motor vehicle theft | 38.7 | : |
| Fraud | 34.1 | 9.3 |
| **Drug offenses** | 43.6 | 32.3 |
| Possession | 46.0 | 20.9 |
| Trafficking | 42.3 | 33.8 |
| **Public order offenses**[c] | 25.4 | 18.7 |
| Weapons | 27.6 | 27.8 |
| Other public order | 24.6 | 8.0 |

[a]Includes offenses not shown.

[b]Includes rape and other sexual assault.

[c]Excluding DWI/DUI.

: Not calculated; too few cases to permit calculation.

Data from Mumola, C. J., & Karberg, J. C. (2007, January 19). *Drug use and dependence, State and Federal prisoners, 2004*. Washington, DC: U.S. Department of Justice (USDOJ), Office of Justice Programs (OJP), 1–12.

Drug-related crimes are undoubtedly overwhelming the U.S. judicial system. Table 1.5 shows the percentage of state and federal inmates reportedly under the influence of drugs at the time of their offenses in 2004. Approximately 29% of state and federal prisoners were under the influence of drugs for violent offenses (e.g., homicide, sexual assault, robbery, assault), 26% for property offenses (e.g., burglary, larceny or theft, motor vehicle theft, fraud), 38% for drug offenses (possession, trafficking), and 22% for public order offenses (e.g., weapons, other public-order offenses) (Mumola & Karberg, 2007). Furthermore, nearly 40% of the young people (often younger than 21) in adult correctional facilities reported drinking before committing a crime.

## DRUG CARTELS

**Drug cartels** are defined as large, highly sophisticated organizations composed of multiple drug-trafficking organizations (DTOs) and **drug cells** with specific assignments such as drug transportation, security and enforcement, or money laundering. (A drug cell is similar to a terrorist cell, consisting of only three to five members to ensure operational security. Members of adjacent drug cells usually do not know each other or the identity of their leadership.) Drug cartel command-and-control structures are based outside the United States; however, they produce, transport, and distribute illicit drugs domestically with the assistance of DTOs that are either a part of the cartel or in an alliance with it. Here are some reports of incidents in the world of drugs, violence, and crime:

> The United States–Mexico drug war strategy has led to the explosion of violence and criminal activity. The deep-rooted complicity between government officials and security forces on the one hand, and cartels on the other, means that the training, equipment, and firepower given in aid and sold to the Mexican government fuels violence on both sides.
>
> The lines blur. The cartels are not fighting the state for political power; they are seeking to protect a $40 billion drug-trafficking business that has been converted into a war for control of territory, a war against the people. (Carlsen, 2016)
>
> In recent years, . . . (notorious drug lord "El Chapo") . . . Guzmán extended the

operations of his Sinaloa cartel to an estimated 50 countries across Latin America, Africa, and Europe, even hooking up with one of the most notorious Italian mafias, the 'Ndrangheta. (Fausset & Wilkinson, 2014)

> In Mexico, [former] President Felipe Calderon may [have been] the constitutionally elected leader of the nation [in 2007], but in reality, drug cartels and warlords exercise de facto authority over much of the area. . . . Drug trafficking overwhelmingly is the prevailing social malady throughout the country, particularly along the border with the United States. In spite of lengthy declarations by government officials in Mexico City and Washington, and their insistence that important battles are being won against drug trafficking, criminal organizations like the Tijuana cartel continue to thrive, ruling over whole sections of the Mexican countryside like sectoral feudal lords. . . . The governor of the state of Nuevo Leon (bordering the United States), Natividad Gonzalez Paras, has declared that: "Unfortunately, the drug problem has escalated significantly in the past six to seven years. It is a national problem affecting most of the country's states. It is a dispute between cartels or organizations to control locations, cities, and routes."

In another news report:

> Once known merely as "mules" for Colombia's powerful cocaine cartels, today Mexico's narcotics traffickers are the kingpins of this hemisphere's drug trade, and the front line of the war on drugs has shifted from Colombia to America's back door.
>
> In August 2005, the *Christian Science Monitor* reported that according to senior U.S. officials, in the biggest reorganization since the 1980s, Mexican cartels had leveraged the profits from their delivery routes to wrest control from the Colombian producers. As a result, Mexican drug lords are in control of what the U.N. estimates is a $142 billion a year business in cocaine, heroin, marijuana, methamphetamine, and other illicit drugs.
>
> The new dominance of Mexican cartels has caused a spike in violence along the 2,000-mile U.S.–Mexico border where rival cartels

---

**KEY TERMS**

**drug cartels**
large, highly sophisticated organizations composed of multiple drug-trafficking organizations (DTOs) and cells with specific assignments, such as drug transportation, security/enforcement, or money laundering

**drug cells**
cells similar to terrorist cells and consisting of only three to five members to ensure operational security; members of adjacent drug cells usually do not know each other or the identity of their leadership

are warring against Mexican and U.S. authorities. Drugs are either flown from Colombia to Mexico in small planes, or, in the case of marijuana and methamphetamine, produced locally. Then, they're shipped into the U.S. by boat, private vehicles, or in commercial trucks crossing the border. . . .

The Sept. 26 edition of the *San Antonio Express-News* reported that a new method of intimidation is being utilized by Mexican drug cartels—beheadings. So far this year, at least 26 people have been decapitated in Mexico, with heads stuck on fences, dumped in trash piles, and even tossed onto a night-club dance floor. In the latter act of violence, which took place in early morning hours of Wednesday, Sept. 6, five heads were scattered on the dance floor of a bar in the state of Michoacan, notorious for drug trafficking. No arrests for the killings have been announced. (Worldpress, 2006)

And, in another news report:

The dead policeman is found propped against a tree off a dirt road on the outskirts of the city. He is dressed like a cartoon version of a Mexican cowboy wearing a blanket. The murder and symbolic mutilation of *policìa* has become almost routine in Caliacán, capital of the Mexican state of Sinaloa: Pablo Aispuro Ramìrez is one of 90 cops to be killed here this year. There is a note pinned to the body, a warning to anyone who dares to oppose the powerful drug lord who ordered the execution "I'm a copy-cowboy!" the note reads. "Ahoo-ya! There are going to be more soon." (Lawson, 2008, p. 76)

In addition,

The Tijuana-based Felix drug cartel and the Juarez-based Fuentes cartel began buying legitimate businesses in small towns in Los Angeles County in the early 1990s. . . . They purchased restaurants, used-car lots, auto-body shops and other small businesses. One of their purposes was to use these businesses for money-laundering operations. Once established in their community, these cartel-financed business owners ran for city council and other local offices. (Farah 2006, quoting an excerpt from In Mortal Danger by Tom Tancredo, a former U.S. Congressman, Colorado)

These news briefs are just a tiny sampling of the types of crimes and violence perpetrated by drug dealers. It is clear that production, merchandising, and distribution of illicit drugs have developed into a worldwide operation worth hundreds of billions of dollars (Goldstein, 2001). One publication states that the United Nations estimates that the global world drug trade is worth $320 billion annually (Stopthedrugwar. org, 2005). These enormous profits have attracted organized crime both in the United States and abroad—and all too frequently even corrupt law enforcement agencies (McShane, 1994). For the participants in such operations, drugs can mean incredible wealth and power. For example, dating back to 1992, Pablo Escobar was recognized as a drug kingpin and leader of the cocaine cartel in Colombia, and he was acknowledged as one of the world's richest men and Colombia's most powerful man (Wire Services, 1992). With his drug-related wealth, Escobar financed a private army to conduct a personal war against the government of Colombia (Associated Press, 1992). Until his death in 1993, he was a serious threat to his country's stability.

In December 1999, the notorious Juarez drug cartel was believed to be responsible for burying more than 100 bodies (including 22 Americans) in a mass grave at a ranch in Mexico. All of the deaths were believed to be drug related. According to a news story on this gruesome discovery, the alleged perpetrator, Vincente Carrillo Fuentes, is one among dozens of drug lords and lieutenants wanted by U.S. law enforcement agents (Associated Press, 1999). A more current drug lord, Ismael "el Mayo" Zambada, now in his early 70s, is "one of Mexico's most wanted drug lords, who has never been arrested despite a $5 million reward offered in the United States" (Campbell, 2010). This same news release indicated that the drug trade would not end until drug cartels are eliminated. Such occurrences, which are often reported by the mass media, indicate the existence of powerful and dangerous drug cartels that are responsible for the availability of illicit drugs around the world.

And, finally, more recent information involves another drug kingpin, "El Chapo" Guzmán:

Born in Badiraguato, Mexico, Joaquín Guzmán Loera (El Chapo) entered the drug trade as a teenager and founded the Sinaloa cartel in 1989, building it into an immensely profitable global drug-trafficking operation. Known for his violent actions and powerful influence, Guzmán established gangs—"Los Chachos," "Los Texas," "Los Lobos," and "Los Negros"— to protect his empire. Over the years, he has been accused of committing more than 1,000 murders throughout Mexico, including those of incompetent henchmen and rival bosses. . . .

On January 8, 2016, Mexican President Enrique Peña Nieto announced that Mexican authorities had recaptured Guzmán after a shootout in Los Mochis.

"Mission Accomplished," the President wrote. "We have him." (https://www.biography .com/crime-figure/el-chapo-joaquin-guzman -loera)

Drug-related violence takes its toll at all levels, as rival gangs fight to control their "turf" and associated drug operations. Innocent bystanders often become unsuspecting victims of the indiscriminate violence. For example, a Roman Catholic cardinal was killed on May 24, 1993, when a car he was a passenger in was inadvertently driven into the middle of a drug-related shootout between traffickers at the international airport in Guadalajara, Mexico. Five other innocent bystanders were killed in the incident (Associated Press, 1993). Finally, it was recently reported that, when spotted, the Mexican army engages in shooting at cartel members and likewise armed cartel members shoot back. When this occurs, mostly in border towns and cities in Mexico, innocent bystanders, many of them children, are often caught in the crossfire and are routinely killed (Del Bosque, 2010). On April 13, 2010, one report cites just such an incident. In Acapulco, Mexico, 24 people died, half of whom were innocent bystanders: "[T]he shootout broke out in the middle of the day in the center of the town as it was full of bystanders" (Associated Press, 2010, p. 38). In many other incidents, unsuspecting people have been injured or killed by drug users who, while under the influence of drugs, commit violent criminal acts.

## ▪ Drugs in the Workplace: A Persistent Affliction

"He was a good, solid worker, always on the job—until he suddenly backed his truck over a 4-inch gas line." If the line had ruptured, there would have been a serious explosion, according to the driver's employer. The accident raised a red flag: "under the company's standard policy, the employee was tested for drugs and alcohol. He was positive for both" (Edelson, 2000, p. 3).

Another tragic incident involving drug use occurred in Alvin, Texas, in December 2012, when "a 20-year-old man ran over two young boys, ages 11 and 12, in front of their father after having too much drink. Later, the driver was killed by gunshot, and the boys' father was charged" (Project Know, 2016).

Generally, once drug use becomes habitual, it enters the workplace because, second to the home and social environments, the work environment for full-time employees is the place where they spend the most time. The National Household Surveys, for example, found evidence of significant drug use among full-time workers, with approximately 7% to 9% drinking while working. In the surveys, 64.3% of full-time workers reported alcohol use within the past month (SAMHSA, 2012). Some 6.4% of full-time workers reported marijuana use within the past month. Part-time employees were slightly more likely to be past-month illicit drug users in comparison to full-time workers in 2010 (11.2 % vs. 8.4%) (SAMHSA 2012).

### WORKER SUBSTANCE ABUSE IN DIFFERENT INDUSTRIES

Substance use in the workplace negatively affects U.S. industry through lost productivity, workplace accidents and injuries, employee absenteeism, low morale, and increased illness. The loss to U.S. companies from employees' alcohol and drug use and related problems is estimated at billions of dollars a year. Research shows that the rate of substance use varies by occupation and industry (Larson, Eyeman, Foster, & Gfroerer, 2007). Studies also have indicated that employers vary in their treatment of substance use issues and that workplace-based employee assistance programs can be a valuable resource for obtaining help for substance-using workers (Delaney, Grube, & Ames, 1998; Reynolds & Lehman, 2003).

Regarding employment, highlights from SAMHSA (2014b) indicate the following:

### ILLICIT DRUG USE

- Current illicit drug use differed by employment status in 2013 and 2014. Among adults 18 and older, the numbers and percentage

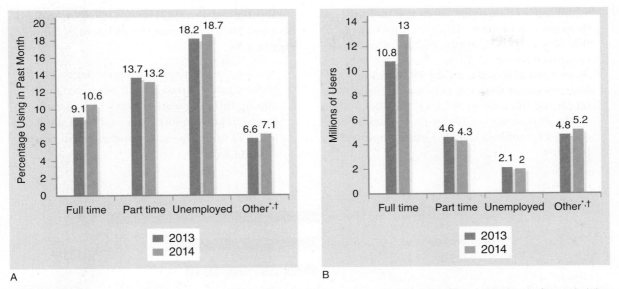

**FIGURE 1.8** Panel A shows the percentages of past-month illicit drug use among persons 18 and older by employment status in 2013 and 2014. Panel B shows the numbers in millions of past-month illicit drug users based on employment status.

*Difference between this estimate and the 2014 estimate is statistically significant at the .05 level.

†The Other employment category includes retired persons, disabled persons, homemakers, students, or other persons not in the labor force.

Reproduced from Center for Behavioral Health Statistics and Quality (CBHSQ). (2015). *Behavioral Health Trends in the United States: Results from the 2014 National Survey on Drug Use and Health* (HHS Publication No. (SMA) 15-4927, NSDUH Series H-50). Rockville, MD: Author.

of illicit drug use was higher for unemployed persons (2.1 million users—18.2%—in 2013 and 2 million—or 18.7%—in 2014) than for those who were employed full-time (10.8 million—or 9.1%—in 2013 and 13 million—10.6%—in 2014) or part time (4.6 million—13.7%—in 2013 and 4.3 million—13.2%—in 2014). The rate of other employment, which includes retired and disabled persons, homemakers, students, or other persons not in the labor force, was 4.8 million (6.6%) in 2013 and 5.2 million (7.1%) in 2014. These rates were all similar to the corresponding rates in 2012 (see **Figure 1.8**).

- Of the 22.4 million illicit drug users 18 and older in 2013, 15.4 million (68.9%) were employed either full- or part-time.

## ALCOHOL USE

- The rate of current alcohol usage in 2013 was 65.8% for full-time employed adults 18 and older, which was higher than the rate for unemployed adults (53.8%). The rates of binge drinking were similar for adults who were employed full-time and those who were unemployed (30.5% and 31.3%, respectively).

- Among adults in 2013, most binge and heavy alcohol users were employed. Among the 58.5 million adults who were binge drinkers, 44.5 million (76.1%) were employed either full- or part-time. Among the 16.2 million adults who were heavy drinkers, 12.4 million (76.0%) were employed.

## TOBACCO USE

- In 2013, current cigarette smoking was more common among unemployed adults 18 and older (40.1%) than among adults who were working full-time or part-time (22.8% and 23.4%, respectively).

- Use of smokeless tobacco in 2013 was higher among adults 18 and older who were employed full-time (4.8%) and those who were unemployed (4.9%) than among those who were employed part-time (2.2%) and those in the "other" employment category, which includes persons not in the labor force (1.9%).

## SUBSTANCE DEPENDENCE

- Rates of substance dependence or abuse were associated with current employment status in 2013. A higher percentage of unemployed adults aged 18 or older were classified with dependence or abuse (15.2%) than were full-time employed adults (9.5%) or part-time employed adults (9.3%).

- More than half of the adults 18 and older with substance dependence or abuse were employed full-time in 2013. Of the 20.3 million adults who were classified with dependence or abuse, 11.3 million (55.7%) were employed full-time.

Highlights from SAMHSA, Office of Applied Studies (2007), indicate the following (see **Figure 1.9**):

- Among the 19 major industry categories, the highest rates of past-month illicit drug use among full-time workers ages 18 to 64 were found in accommodations and food services (19.1%) and arts, entertainment, and recreation (13.7%).

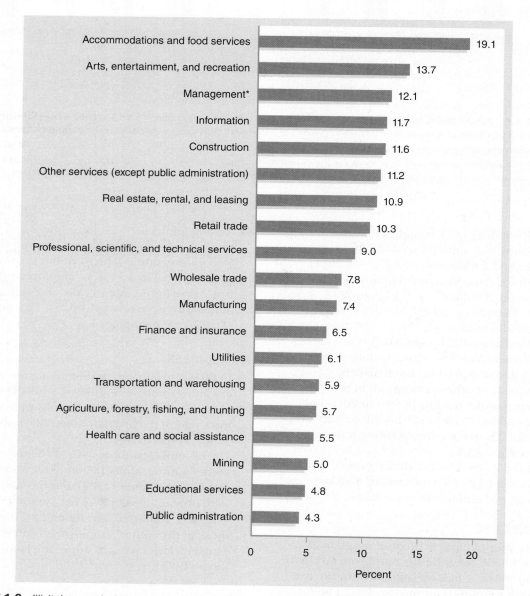

**FIGURE 1.9**   Illicit drug use by industry category: Past-month illicit drug use among full-time workers aged 18 to 64: 2011–2012, combined.

The full title of this category is "Management of companies and enterprises, administration, support, waste management, and remediation services."

Reproduced from Substance Abuse and Mental Health Services Administration (SAMHSA). (2012, March 24). *The National Survey on Drug Use and Health (NSDUH) Report: Worker substance use, by industry category.* Rockville, MD: Office of Applied Studies (OAS).

- The industry categories with the lowest rates of past-month illicit drug use were found in mining (5.0%), educational services (4.8%), and public administration (4.3%).
- The overall rate of past-month illicit drug use among full-time workers aged 18 to 64 was 8.6%. Rates of past-month illicit drug use ranged from 19.1% among workers in the accommodations and food services industry to 4.3% among workers in the public administration industry. These findings remained true even when controlling for gender and age differences across industries.
- The overall rate of past-year substance use disorder among full-time workers aged 18 to 64 was 9.5%. Rates of past-year substance use disorder ranged from 16.9% among workers in the accommodations and food services industry to 5.5% among workers in the educational services industry.
- Although the accommodations and food services industry group had the highest rate of past-year substance use disorder, this finding did not remain true after controlling for age and gender distributions. *This indicates that the high rate can be attributed to the demographic composition of the accommodation and food services industry.*

Although not shown in Figure 1.9, the following findings have also been reported (CBHSQ, 2013, unless otherwise noted):

- The overall rate of past-month heavy alcohol use among full-time workers 18 to 64 was 8.7%. Rates of past-month heavy alcohol use ranged from 17.5% among workers in the mining industry to 4.4% among workers in the health-care and social assistance industry.
- Workers in the mining (17.5%) and construction (16.5%) industries had the highest rates of past-month heavy alcohol use. For the workers in the construction industry, this finding remained true even when controlling for gender and age differences across industries. This indicates something unique about past-month heavy alcohol use for the construction industry that would remain even if the construction industry had the same gender and age distribution of any other industry. However, for the mining industry, this higher rate did not remain when controlling for age or gender differences. *This indicates that the high heavy alcohol use rate in the mining industry*

*can be attributed to the demographic composition of the mining industry.*

- Approximately 80% of large companies test for drug use, and approximately 60% of medium companies and 26% of small companies perform such testing. Of those companies that drug test, more than 90% use urine analysis, less than 20% use blood analysis, and less than 6% use hair analysis.
- Most companies that administer drug tests are testing for marijuana, cocaine, opiates, amphetamines, and PCP.
- Age is the most significant predictor of marijuana and cocaine use. Younger employees (18 to 24) are more likely to report drug use than older employees are (25 years or older).
- In general, unmarried workers report roughly twice as much illicit drug and heavy alcohol use as married workers. Among food-preparation workers, transportation drivers, and mechanics, and in industries such as construction and machinery (not electrical), the discrepancy between married and unmarried workers is especially notable.
- Workers who report having three or more jobs in the previous five years are twice as likely to be current or past-year illicit drug users as those who held two or fewer jobs over the same period (NCADD, 2016).
- Seventy percent of the estimated 14.8 million Americans who use illegal drugs are employed (NCADD, 2016).
- Marijuana is the most commonly used and abused illegal drug by employees, followed by cocaine, with prescription drug use steadily increasing (NCADD, 2016).
- Workers in occupations that affect public safety, including truck drivers, firefighters, and police officers, report the highest rate of participation in drug testing.
- "Among full-time workers, heavy drinkers and illicit drug users are more likely than those who do not drink heavily or use illicit drugs to have skipped work in the past month or have worked for three or more employers in the past year" (Robert Wood Johnson Foundation, 2001, p. 45).
- Most youths do not cease drug use when they begin working.

In summarizing this research on employees who abuse alcohol or other drugs, five major findings emerge: (1) These workers are three times more likely than the average employee to be late to work, (2) three times more likely to receive sickness benefits, (3) 16 times more likely to be absent from work, (4) five times more likely to be involved in on-the-job accidents (note that many of these hurt others, not themselves), and (5) five times more likely to file compensation claims.

# Employee Assistance Programs

Many industries have responded to drugs in the workplace by creating **drug testing** and **employee assistance programs (EAPs)**. Most often, drug testing generally involves urine screening, blood screening, or hair follicle analysis that is undertaken to identify which employees are using drugs and which employees may have current or potential drug problems. EAPs are employer-financed programs administered by a company or through an outside contractor. More than 400,000 EAPs have been established in the United States.

The following are some important findings regarding workplace substance use policies and programs among full-time workers:

- Full-time workers aged 18 to 64 who used illicit drugs in the past month were generally less likely than those who did not use illicit drugs in the previous month to work for an employer who had a written policy about employee use of alcohol and drugs. Similarly, full-time workers who drank heavily in the preceding month were less likely than those who did not drink heavily to have an employer that provided these workplace policies and programs (SAMHSA 2014b).
- Of employees ages 18 to 64 who had used an illicit drug in the past month, 32.1% worked for an employer who offered educational information about alcohol and drug use, 71% were aware of a written policy about drug and alcohol use in the workplace, and 45.4% worked for an employer who maintained an

EAP or other type of counseling program for employees who have an alcohol- or drug-related problem (SAMHSA, OAS 2007).

- Among full-time workers who used alcohol heavily in the preceding month, 37.2% worked for an employer who provided educational information about drug and alcohol use, 73.7% were aware of written policies about drug and alcohol use, and 51.1% had access to an EAP at their workplace (SAMHSA, OAS 2007).
- The most common EAP service that companies utilize is for job stress (87.9%), followed by substance abuse (84.1%), bereavement (83.4%), work–life balance (82.8%), and relationship counseling (82.2%); with slightly lower percentages mainly involving elder care, child care, or parenting issues (78.3%); family violence (75.2%); harassment (73.2%); and financial or legal services (72.6%) (Pyrillis, 2014).
- Approximately three-quarters of companies have an EAP (Pyrillis 2014).
- "U.S. enrollment in EAPs has increased by 285% since 2002, according to a 2011 survey by Open Minds, a market research firm based in Gettysburg, Pennsylvania. More than 97% of companies with more than 5000 employees have an EAP and continued growth is expected, according to the Employee Assistance Research Foundation" (Pyrillis, 2014).

EAP programs are designed to aid in identifying and resolving productivity problems associated with employees' emotional or physical concerns, such as those related to health, marital problems, family relationships, financial issues, and substance abuse. EAPs have also expanded their focus to combat employee abuse of OTC and prescription drugs in addition to illicit psychoactive substances. Overall, the programs attempt to formally reduce problems associated with impaired job performance.

Regarding drug testing today, the Society for Human Resource Management conducted an online survey taken by 454 randomly selected human resource managers from diverse organizations (U.S. Department of Labor, 2009). The following drug-testing practices were in effect:

- 84% of employers required new hires to pass drug screenings,
- 74% used drug screening when reasonable suspicion of drug use was determined,
- 58% of organizations used post-accident drug screening,

**KEY TERMS**

**drug testing**
urine, blood screening, or hair analysis used to identify those who may be using drugs

**employee assistance programs (EAPs)**
drug-assistance programs for drug-dependent employees

- 39% used random drug screening, and
- 14% used scheduled drug testing.

Further, 70% of those responding to this survey indicated that their organization has a written policy that addresses drug testing. From these survey results, we can see that the future for employee drug testing is bright. In all probability, if you have not already experienced such a screening, you will experience one at some point in your working life.

Today, drug testing can include the following types (U.S. Department of Labor 2016).

- *Urine*: Testing for drug metabolites in a person's urine.
- *Breath*: The breath-alcohol test is the most common test for finding out how much alcohol is currently in the blood.
- *Hair*: Analysis of hair provides a much longer "testing window," giving a more complete drug-use history going back as far as 90 days.
- **Oral fluids**: Saliva, or oral fluids, collected from the mouth also can be used to detect traces of drugs and alcohol. Oral fluids are easy to collect (a swab of the inner cheek is the most common method), harder to adulterate or substitute, and may be better at detecting specific substances, including marijuana, cocaine, and amphetamines or methamphetamines.
- **Sweat**: Another type of drug test consists of a skin patch that measures drugs in sweat. The patch, which looks like a large adhesive bandage, is applied to the skin and worn for some length of time. A gas-permeable membrane on the patch protects the tested area from dirt and other contaminants. Although relatively easy to administer, this method has not been widely used in workplaces and is more often used to maintain compliance with probation and parole.

The following drugs that are detectable differ in the length of time they are detectable (U.S. Department of Labor, 2016) as shown in the following.

- alcohol: 1 ounce for 1.5 hours
- amphetamines: 48 hours
- barbiturates: two to 10 days
- benzodiazepines: 2 to 3 weeks
- cocaine: 2 to 10 days
- heroin metabolites: less than 1 day
- morphine: 2 to 3 days
- LSD: 8 hours

- marijuana: casual use, 3 to 4 days; chronic use, several weeks
- methamphetamine: 2 to 3 days
- methadone: 2 to 3 days
- PCP: 1 week

# Venturing to a Higher Form of Consciousness: The Holistic Self-Awareness Approach to Drug Use

Whenever drug use leads to abuse, it rarely results from a single, isolated cause. Instead, it is often caused or preceded by multiple factors, which may include combinations of the following:

- hereditary (genetic) factors,
- psychological conditioning,
- peer-group pressures,
- inability to cope with the stress and anxiety of daily living,
- quality of role models,
- degree of attachment to a family structure,
- level of security with gender identity and sexual orientation,
- personality traits, and
- perceived ethnic and racial compatibility with society as a whole and socioeconomic status (social class).

As authors, we strongly endorse and advocate a **holistic self-awareness approach** that emphasizes a healthy balance among mind, body, and spirit. Health and wellness can be achieved only when these three domains of existence are free from any unnecessary use of psychoactive substances. The holistic philosophy is based on the idea that the mind has a powerful influence on

## KEY TERMS

**oral fluids**
oral fluid testing analyzes saliva samples for the presence of drugs of abuse and their metabolites

**sweat (perspiration)**
used for drug testing; a skin patch absorb sweats for analysis for the presence of cocaine, marijuana, opiates, amphetamine, methamphetamine, or PCP

**holistic self-awareness approach**
emphasizes that nonmedical and often recreational drug use interferes with the healthy balance of mind, body, and spirit

maintaining health. All three—mind, body, and spirit—work as a unified whole to promote health and wellness. Similarly, we are in agreement with holistic health advocates who emphasize the following viewpoint:

> Holistic Health is based on the law of nature that a whole is made up of interdependent parts. The earth is made up of systems, such as air, land, water, plants and animals. If life is to be sustained, they cannot be separated, for what is happening to one is also felt by all the other systems. In the same way, an individual is a whole made up of interdependent parts, which are the physical, mental, emotional, and spiritual. While one part is not working at its best, it impacts all the other parts of that person. . . . A common explanation is to view wellness as a continuum along a line. The line represents all possible degrees of health. The far left end of the line represents premature death. On the far right end is the highest possible level of wellness or maximum well-being. The center point of the line represents a lack of apparent disease. This places all levels of illness on the left half of the wellness continuum. The right half shows that even when no illness seems to be present, there is still a lot of room for improvement. . . . Holistic Health is an ongoing process. As a lifestyle, it includes a personal commitment to be moving toward the right end of the wellness continuum. No matter what their current status of health, people can improve their level of well-being. Even when there are temporary setbacks, movement is always headed toward wellness. (https://ahha.org/selfhelp-articles /holistic-health/)[4]

This passage embodies the essence of achieving a holistic self-awareness by presenting a unified blend of different perspectives that can add to

---

[4]Reproduced from Walter, 1999. Used with permission.

our awareness of what is at stake when the goal of drug use is for nonmedical purposes, such as using drugs for the sole purpose of achieving a high. Knowing about the holistic self-awareness perspective should expand people's often limited and narrow values and attitudes about drug use so that the information about and the use of drugs are viewed and understood from pharmacological, psychological, and sociological perspectives.

As previously mentioned, understanding drug use is important not only for comprehending our own health but also for understanding the following:

- why and how others can become attracted to drugs;
- how to detect drug use and abuse in others;
- what to do (remedies and solutions) when family members or friends abuse drugs;
- how to help and advise drug abusers about the pitfalls of substance use;
- what the best available educational, preventive, and treatment options are for victims of drug abuse; and
- what danger signals can arise when others you care about exceed normal or necessary drug usage.

Awareness and knowledge about drug use and abuse coupled with holistic health awareness can result in self-awareness, and self-awareness leads to self-understanding and self-assurance. Maintaining at least some belief in holistic self-awareness, either as a humanistic philosophy or adding this philosophy into a religious orientation you may already have, should increase your understanding of your own drug use practices as well as those of family members and close friends. By including at least some aspect of holistic self-awareness regarding the use of psychoactive substances, you will be better equipped to understand not only yourself but also others who may need advice and role modeling.

## LEARNING PORTFOLIO

## Discussion Questions

1. Give an example of a drug-using friend or family members and describe how the user may be affected by any three of the following: biological, genetic, pharmacological, cultural, social, and contextual factors responsible for abusing illicit drugs.

2. Discuss and debate whether the often-considered "benign" drug known as marijuana is or is not addictive. In your discussion or debate, consider the finding in Table 1.4 from SAMHSA (2019a) that for persons aged 12 or older, 45.3% of illicit drug users (123,935 million) used marijuana during their lifetime, and past-month users of this drug accounted for 10.1% of all illicit drug users (27,667 million). Explain how such high percentages and numbers of users of this "less addictive" drug is *harmless* or *harmful* to society?

3. What is the future of prescription drug abuse? For example, how much will it increase in the years to come? Do you think prescription drugs will ever become *the* drugs of choice for recreational or abusive use? Will prescription drug abuse ever surpass the use of marijuana? In addition, should parents be prosecuted for not guarding their legally prescribed drugs if their children are legally caught using prescription drugs?

4. In reviewing the ancient historical uses of drugs, how do you think drug use today is different from than in the past? Explain your answer.

5. Why do Americans use so many legal drugs (e.g., alcohol, tobacco, and OTC drugs)? What do you think is primarily responsible for such extensive nonmedical and recreational drug use?

6. Table 1.3 shows that the amount of illicit drug use for people aged 18 through 25 are consistently the highest percentages of illicit drug use for past-month, past-year, and lifetime (ever used) categories. Cite what you think are two main reasons why this age group continually uses illicit types of drugs despite laws against illicit drug use and other media messages and antidrug campaigns promoted by private organizations, state governments, the federal government, and efforts by law enforcement organizations against recreational drug use.

7. Because most casual and experimental drug users do not gravitate toward excessive drug use, should these two groups be left alone or perhaps be given legal warnings or fines? Overall, do you think recreational drug users should be punished by society?

8. Do the mass media promote drug use, or do they merely reflect our extensive use of drugs? Provide some evidence for your position.

## Key Terms

| | |
|---|---|
| addiction | 6 |
| central nervous system (CNS) | 5 |
| compulsive users | 31 |
| dependency phase | 38 |
| designer drugs | 14 |
| drug(s) | 6 |
| drug cartels | 44 |
| drug cells | 44 |
| Drug Enforcement Administration (DEA) | 12 |
| drug testing | 50 |
| employee assistance programs (EAPs) | 50 |
| equal-opportunity affliction | 17 |
| ethanol | 13 |
| experimenters | 31 |
| floaters or chippers | 31 |
| gateway drugs | 12 |
| holistic self-awareness approach | 51 |
| illicit drugs | 6 |
| increased use phase | 38 |
| insiders | 5 |
| licit drugs | 6 |
| marijuana wax | 14 |
| MDMA | 13 |
| National Institute on Drug Abuse (NIDA) | 39 |
| opioids | 11 |
| oral fluids | 51 |
| outsiders | 5 |
| over-the-counter (OTC) | 6 |
| preoccupation phase | 38 |
| psychoactive drugs (substances) | 5 |
| psychotherapeutic drugs | 10 |
| relief phase | 38 |
| structural analogs | 14 |
| sweat (perspiration) | 51 |
| synthetic drugs or synthetic opioids | 14 |
| withdrawal phase | 38 |
| withdrawal symptoms | 6 |

9. At what point do you think drug use leads to abuse? When do you think drug use does not lead to abuse?

10. What do you believe is the relationship between drug use and crime? Does drug use cause crime or is crime simply a manifestation of personality?

11. What principal factors are involved in the relationship between drugs and crime?

12. Should all employees be randomly tested for drug use? If not, which types of employees or occupations should always be randomly drug tested?

13. List and rank order at least three things you found especially interesting about drug use in this chapter.

14. Should all students and faculty be randomly drug tested at their schools and universities? Why or why not?

15. Do you think that the holistic self-awareness approach advocated by the authors regarding drug use is a viable one that can be used successfully for stopping drug use? Why or why not? What additional improvements if any can be made to strengthen this approach?

## Summary

1. Biological issues, genetic issues, pharmacological issues, and cultural, social, and contextual issues are the four principal factors responsible for determining how a drug user experiences drug use. Biological, genetic, and pharmacological factors take into account a particular drug's effects and how it affects the body. Cultural factors examine how society's views, determined by custom and tradition, effect and affect the use of a particular drug. Social factors include the specific reasons why a drug is taken and how drug use develops from factors such as family upbringing, peer-group alliances, subcultures, and communities. Contextual factors account for how drug use behavior develops from the physical surroundings in which the drug is taken.

2. Initial understanding of drug use includes the following key terms: *drug, gateway drugs, medicines and prescription medicines, over the counter* (OTC), *drug misuse, drug abuse,* and *drug addiction.*

3. Mentions of drug use date back to biblical times and ancient literature that goes back to 2240 BC. Under the influence of drugs, many people experienced feelings ranging from extreme ecstasy to sheer terror. At times, drugs were used to induce sleep and provide freedom from care.

4. Drug users are found in all occupations and professions, at all income and social class levels, and in all age groups. No one is immune to drug use. In summary, drug use is an equal-opportunity affliction.

5. According to sociologist Erich Goode (2012), drugs are used for four reasons: (a) legal instrumental use, (b) legal recreational use, (c) illegal instrumental use, and (d) illegal recreational use.

6. The most commonly used licit and illicit *past-month* use of drugs (rated from highest to lowest in the percentages [frequency] of use) are:
   - alcohol (51.1%)
   - cigarettes (17.2%)
   - any illicit drugs (11.7%)
   - marijuana (10.1%)
   - any illicit drugs other than marijuana (3.2%)
   - smokeless tobacco (2.9%)
   - nonmedical use of any psychotherapeutics (2.0%),
   - pain relievers (1.0%)
   - cocaine (0.7%)
   - tranquilizers (0.6%), hallucinogens (0.6%), stimulants (0.6%)
   - methamphetamine (0.4%)
   - inhalants (0.2%)
   - sedatives (0.1%), heroin (0.1%)

7. The three types of drug users are experimenters, compulsive users, and floaters or chippers. Experimenters try drugs because

of curiosity and peer pressure. Compulsive users use drugs on a full-time basis and continually desire to escape from or alter reality. Floaters or chippers vacillate between experimental drug use and chronic drug use.

8. The mass media tend to promote drug use through advertising. The constant barrage of OTC drug commercials relays the message that if you are experiencing some symptom, taking drugs is an acceptable option.

9. Drug use leads to abuse when the following occurs: (a) excessive use, (b) constant concern and preoccupation about the availability and supply of the drug, (c) refusal to admit excessive use, and (d) reliance on the drug.

10. The stages of drug dependence are *relief* from using the drug, *increased use* of the drug, *preoccupation* with the supply of the drug, *dependency* or addiction to the drug, and experiencing (either or both) physical or psychological *withdrawal* effects from not using the drug.

11. The following are the major findings of the connection between drugs and crime: (a) drug users are more likely to commit crimes, (b) arrestees are often under the influence of drugs while committing their crimes, and (c) drugs and violence often go hand in hand, especially when alcohol, cocaine, crack, methamphetamine, or other stimulant types of drugs are used.

12. Employee assistance programs (EAPs) are employer-financed programs administered by a company or through an outside contractor. More than 400,000 EAPs have been established in the United States They are designed to aid in identifying and resolving productivity problems associated with employees' emotional or physical concerns, such as those related to health, marriage, family, bereavement, finances, and substance abuse. Recently, EAPs have expanded their focus to combat employee abuse of OTC and prescription drugs as well as illicit psychoactive substances.

13. The holistic self-awareness philosophy is based on the idea that the mind, body, and spirit have a powerful influence on maintaining health. These three domains—mind, body, and spirit—work best when unobstructed by unnecessary drug use and when all three domains work in a unified manner to promote health and wellness.

# References

American Osteopathic Association (AOA). (2019, January 16). Poll finds 86% of Americans take vitamins or supplements yet only 21% have a confirmed nutritional deficiency. Chicago, IL: American Osteopathic Association. Retrieved from https://osteopathic.org/2019/01/16/poll-finds-86-of-americans-take-vitamins-or-supplements-yet-only-21-have-a-confirmed-nutritional-deficiency/

American Psychiatric Association (APA). (2013). *Diagnostic and statistical manual of mental disorders*, 5th edition (DSM-5). Washington, DC: Author.

American Psychiatric Association (APA). (2019). What is addiction. Washington, DC: Author. Retrieved from https://www.psychiatry.org/patients-families/addiction/what-is-addiction

Associated Press. (1992, August 17). Program to fight drug smuggling costs U.S. a lot, produces little. *Salt Lake Tribune, 244*, A-1.

Associated Press. (1993, May 25). Mexican cardinal, six others killed in cross-fire as drug battles erupt in Guadalajara. *Salt Lake Tribune, 246*, A-1.

Associated Press. (1999, December 5). Discovery of Mexican graves unlikely to slow flow of drugs. *The Times* [Munster, IN]: A-13.

Associated Press. (2010, March 14). Mexico: Drug war death toll worsens, 11 die in one shootout, 24 in a day in small-town gun battles. *Post Tribune* [Northwest IN]: *100*, 38.

Beschner, G. (1986). Understanding teenage drug use. In G. Beschner & A. Friedman (Eds.), *Teen drug use* (pp. 1–18). Lexington, MA: D.C. Heath.

Biography. (2020). Joaquin "El Chapo" Guzman Loera. Retrieved from http://www.biography.com/people/el-chapo-joaquin-guzman-loera

Birns, L., & Sánchez, A. (2007, April 23). The government and the drug lords: Who rules Mexico? Worldpress.org. Retrieved from http://www.worldpress.org/Americas/2763.cfm

Bogunovic, O. (2012, July 27). Substance abuse in aging and elderly adults. *Psychiatric Times.* Retrieved from http://www.psychiatrictimes.com/geriatric-psychiatry/substance-abuse-aging-and-elderly-adults

Boyles, S. (2009). Billions spent on alternative medicine in the U.S. WebMD. Retrieved from http://www.rxlist.com/script/main/art.asp?articlekey=104255#

Bresnick, J. (2019, February 25). Prescription drug prices set for 3.8% increase in 2020. Danvers, MA: Xtelligent Media, LLC.

Bureau of Justice Statistics (BJS). (2006). *Drugs and crime facts: Drug law violations.* Washington, DC: U.S. Department of Justice, Office of Justice Programs.

Bureau of Justice Statistics (BJS). (2015a) U.S. prison population declined one percent in 2014. [September 17]. Washington, DC: U.S. Department of Justice, Office of Justice Programs.

Bureau of Justice Statistics (BJS). (2015b). *Drug offenders in federal prison: Estimates of characteristics based on linked data* [October 27]. Washington, DC: U.S. Department of Justice, Office of Justice Programs.

Burke, K. (2019). How many people still use a landline phone in 2018? New research finds. Chattanooga, TN: Text Request. Retrieved from https://www.textre quest.com/blog/how-many-people-still-use-landline-phone/

Butterfield, F. (2002, February 11). As drug use drops in big cities, small towns confront upsurge. *The New York Times* [p. A23]. Retrieved from https://www.nytimes.com/2002/02/11/us/as-drug-use-drops-in-big-cities-small-towns-confront-upsurge.html

Caldwell, A. A. (2010, December). U.S. cracks down on fake pot. *Post-Tribune* [Merrillville, IN], *101*, 30.

Campbell, R. (2010, April). Mexican cartels cannot be defeated, drug lord says. Thomson Reuters. Retrieved from http://www.reuters.com/article/idUSTRE6331DZ 20100404

Carlsen, L. (2016, January 25). The opinion pages/letter: The drug war and Mexico. *The New York Times.* Retrieved from https://www.nytimes.com/2016/01/26/opinion/the-drug-war-and-mexico.html

Carson, E. A., & Sabol, W. J. (2012, December). *Prisoners in 2011.* NCJ239808. Washington, DC: U.S. Department of Justice, Bureau of Justice Statistics. Retrieved from http://bjs.ojp.usdoj.gov/content/pub/pdf/p11.pdf

CASA Columbia. (2012, August). *National survey of American attitudes on substance abuse XVII: Teens.* New York, NY: QEV Analytics. Retrieved from http://www.casacolumbia.org/upload/2012/20120822teensurvey.pdf

CBS News. (2002, February 13). Drug advertising skyrockets. CBS Worldwide. Retrieved from http://www.cbsnews.com/2100-204_162-329293.html

Center for Behavioral Health Statistics and Quality (CBHSQ) (2015). *Behavioral health trends in the United States: Results from the 2014 National Survey on Drug Use and Health* (HHS Publication No. SMA 15-4927, NSDUH Series H-50). Rockville, MD: Author.

Center for Substance Abuse Research (CESAR). (2003, December 1). Ritalin and Adderall abused by students as party drugs and study aids. *CESAR FAX.* Retrieved from http://www.cesar.umd.edu

Center for Substance Abuse Research (CESAR). (2009). Friends and family are most common source of prescription drugs misused by youths. *CESAR FAX, 18*(32).

Center for Substance Abuse Research (CESAR). (2013, May 20). Study finds that 14% of undergraduate students at a Southeastern university report synthetic cannabinoid use; users more likely to be male and identify as LGBT. *CESARFAX.* Retrieved from http://www.cesar.umd.edu

Center on Alcohol Marketing and Youth (CAMY). (2005, July 20). Alcohol industry "responsibility" advertising on television, 2001 to 2003. Washington, DC: Center on Alcohol Marketing and Youth. Retrieved from http://www.camy.org/_docs/resources/reports/archived-reports/alcohol-industry-responsibility-advertising-tv-01-03-full-report.pdf

Center on Alcohol Marketing and Youth (CAMY). (2007). *Drowned out: Alcohol industry's responsibility; advertising on television, 2001–2005.* Washington, DC: Center on Alcohol Marketing and Youth, 1–4.

Centers for Disease Control and Prevention (CDC). (2014). Vital signs: Opioid painkiller prescribing infographic. Retrieved from http://www.cdc.gov/vitalsigns/opioid-prescribing/infographic.html

Centers for Disease Control and Prevention (CDC). (2017a). Therapeutic drug use. Retrieved from https://www.cdc.gov/nchs/fastats/drug-use-therapeutic.htm

Centers for Disease Control and Prevention (CDC). (2017b). Economic trends in tobacco. Atlanta, GA: U.S. Department of Human Services. Retrieved from https://www.cdc.gov/tobacco/data_statistics/fact_sheets/economics/econ_facts/index.htm

Centers for Disease Control and Prevention (CDC). (2017c). *U.S. state prescribing rates, 2017.* Atlanta, GA: Centers for Disease Control and Prevention. Retrieved from https://www.cdc.gov/drugoverdose/maps/rxstate2017.html

Centers for Disease Control and Prevention (CDC). (2018a, January 3). Fact sheets—Alcohol use and your health. Atlanta, GA: U.S. Department of Health and Human Services. Retrieved from https://www.cdc.gov/alcohol/fact-sheets/alcohol-use.htm

Centers for Disease Control and Prevention (CDC). (2018b). *2018 annual surveillance report of drug-related risks and outcomes—United States.* Surveillance Special Report.

Atlanta, GA: Centers for Disease Control and Prevention and U.S. Department of Health and Human Services. Retrieved from https://www.cdc.gov/drugoverdose/pdf/pubs/2018-cdc-drug-surveillance-report.pdf

Centers for Disease Control and Prevention (CDC). (2018c). *U.S. opioid prescribing rate maps*. Atlanta, GA: Centers for Disease Control and Prevention. Retrieved from https://www.cdc.gov/drugoverdose/maps/rxrate-maps.html

Centers for Disease Control and Prevention (CDC). (2019, November 15). Fast facts. Atlanta, GA: U. S. Department of Health and Human Services. Retrieved from https://www.cdc.gov/tobacco/data_statistics/fact_sheets/fast_facts/index.htm

Chen, K. (2013, June 20). Meth seizures at U.S. ports of entry on the rise. Center for Investigative Reporting. Retrieved from http://cironline.org/blog/post/meth-seizures-us-ports-entry-rise-4739

Common Sense for Drug Policy. (2020). Drug war facts. Lancaster, PA: Author. Available https://www.drugwarfacts.org/node/3828

Consumer Healthcare Products Association (CHPA). (2012). *The value of OTC medicine to the United States*. Washington, DC: Booz & Co. Retrieved from http://www.yourhealthathand.org/images/uploads/The_Value_of_OTC_Medicine_to_the_United_States_BoozCo.pdf

Consumer Healthcare Products Association (CHPA). (2019). *OTC retail sales 1964–2018*. Retrieved from https://www.chpa.org/OTCRetailSales.aspx

Crabb, G. (2014, March 7). Illicit drug use among older adults. Naples, FL: Author. Retrieved from http://drgeorgecrabb.com/

Critser, G. (1996, June). Oh, how happy we will be: Pills, paradise, and the profits of the drug companies. *Harper's Magazine*, 39–48.

Critser, G. (2005). *Generation RX: How prescription drugs are altering American lives, minds and bodies*. Boston, MA: Houghton-Mifflin.

Delaney, W., Grube, J. W., & Ames, G. M. (1998). Predicting likelihood of seeking help through the employee-assistance program among salaried and union hourly employees. *Addiction, 93*, 399–410.

Del Bosque, M. (2010, January 5). Mexico's future in 2010, Calderon's failed drug war. *Texas Observer*, 1–2. Retrieved from http://www.texasobserver.org/lalinea/calderons-war-on-drugs-is-a-failure

Drug Enforcement Administration (DEA). (2012). *Drug fact sheet: K2 or Spice*. Washington, DC: U.S. Department of Justice. Retrieved from http://www.justice.gov/dea/pr/multimedia-library/publications/drug_of_abuse.pdf#page=62

Drug Enforcement Administration (DEA). (2018). Why do teens use drugs? Washington, DC: U.S Government, Drug Enforcement Administration. Retrieved from https://www.getsmartaboutdrugs.gov/family/why-do-teens-use-drugs

Drug Strategies. (1995). *Keeping score: What we are getting for our federal drug control dollars 1995*. Washington, DC: Author.

DrugWarFacts. (2016). Crime, arrests, and US law enforcement. Retrieved from http://www.drugwarfacts.org/cms/Crime#sthash.Hlaogs9z.fqvRrxej.dpbs

Edelson, E. (2000, February). Drug use in the workplace plummets. *Cannabis News*. Retrieved from http://cannabisnews.com/news/4/thread4627.shtml

Erowid Center. (2013). Spice product: Legal status. Erowid.org. Retrieved from http://www.erowid.org/chemicals/spice_product/spice_product_law.shtml

Fausset, R., & Wilkinson, T. (2014, February 22). "El Chapo" Guzman: Life of the cartel king of Sinaloa. *Los Angeles Times*. Retrieved from http://www.latimes.com/world/worldnow/la-fg-wn-guzman-arrest-20140222-story.html

Federal Register. (2015, March 9). Annual determination of average cost of incarceration. Washington, DC: Office of the Federal Register. Retrieved from https://www.federalregister.gov/articles/2015/03/09/2015-05437/annual-determination-of-average-cost-of-incarceration

Federal Trade Commission. (2015, March). *Self-regulation in the alcohol industry: Report of the Federal Trade Commission*. Washington, DC: Author. Retrieved from https://www.ftc.gov/system/files/documents/reports/self-regulation-alcohol-industry-report-federal-trade-commission/140320alcoholreport.pdf

Ferner, M. (2014, March 13). Americans spent about a trillion dollar on illegal drugs in the last decade. Huffington Post. Retrieved from http://www.huffingtonpost.com/2014/03/13/americans-trillion-dollars-drugs_n_4943601.html

Goldstein, A. (2001). *Addiction: From biology to drug policy*. New York, NY: Oxford University Press.

Goode, E. (1999). *Drugs in American society*, 5th ed. Boston, MA: McGraw-Hill.

Goode, E. (2012). *Drugs in American society*, 8th ed. New York, NY: McGraw-Hill.

Health Policy Institute. (2019). *Prescription drugs*. Washington, DC: Georgetown University and McCourt School of Public Policy.

Helpguide. (n.d.). Drug abuse and addiction. Helpguide.org. Retrieved from http://www.helpguide.org/articles/addiction/drug-abuse-and-addiction.htm

Henry J. Kaiser Family Foundation. (2016). Total number of retail prescription drugs filled at pharmacies. San Francisco, CA: Author. Retrieved from http://kff.org/other/state-indicator/total-retail-rx-drugs/?currentTimeframe=0&sortModel=%7B"colId":"Location","sort":"asc"%7D

Heroin.net. (2016). How much does heroin cost? Available http://heroin.net/about/how-much-does-heroin-cost/#the-street-cost-of-heroin

Home Health Testing. (2010). Facts about prison and drug use. Retrieved from http://www.homehealthtesting.com/blog/2010/06/facts-about-prison-and-drug-use/

Huffington Post. (2012, August 23). School drug use: Survey finds 17 percent of high school students drink, smoke, use drugs during the school day. Retrieved from http://www.huffingtonpost.com/2012/08/23/annual-survey-finds-17-pe_n_1824966.html

Jellinek, J. (2003, February 20). Musical meth lab uncovered. *Rolling Stone, 54.*

Johnston, L. D., O'Malley, P. M., Bachman, J. G., & Schulenberg, J. E. (2012). *Monitoring the Future: National Survey Results on Drug Use, 1975–2011, Volume I: Secondary school students.* Bethesda, MD: National Institute on Drug Abuse.

Johnston, L. D., O'Malley, P. M., Bachman, J. G., & Schulenberg, J. E. (2013). *Monitoring the Future National Results on Drug Use: 2012 Overview, key findings on adolescent drug use.* Ann Arbor, MI: Institute for Social Research, University of Michigan.

Johnston, L. D., O'Malley, P. M., Miech, R. A., Bachman, J. G., & Schulenberg, J. E. (2016, February). *Monitoring the Future National Survey Results on Drug Use, 1975–2015: Overview, key findings on adolescent drug use.* Ann Arbor, MI: Institute for Social Research, University of Michigan.

Karberg, J. C., & James, D. J. (2002). *Special report: Substance dependence, abuse, and treatment of jail inmates, 2002.* Washington, DC: U.S. Department of Justice, Office of Justice Programs, Bureau of Justice Statistics (BJS).

Keller, A. (2020a, March 2). How do teens get drugs. Orlando, FL: DrugRehab.com. Retrieved from https://www.drugrehab.com/teens/how-teens-get-drugs/

Keller, A. (2020b). How much does heroin cost? Orlando, FL: DrugRehab.com. Retrieved from https://www.drugrehab.com/addiction/drugs/heroin/how-much-does-heroin-cost/

KiDeuk, K., Becker-Cohen, M., & Serakos, M. (2015, March). *Research report: The procession and treatment of mentally ill persons in the criminal justice system.* Washington, DC: Urban Institute.

Kilbourne, J. (1989, June). Advertising addiction: The alcohol industry's hard sell. *Multinational Monitor,* pp. 13–16.

Kimble, J. (2013, October 22). Everything you need to know about marijuana wax. Atlanta, GA: Complex Media Inc. Retrieved from http://www.complex.com/pop-culture/2013/10/marijuana-wax-facts-info/

Kusinitz, M. (1988). Drug use around the world. In S. Snyder (Ed.), *Encyclopedia of psychoactive drugs,* Series 2. New York, NY: Chelsea House.

Larson, S. L., Eyeman, J., Foster, M. S., & Gfroerer, J. C. (2007). *Worker substance use and workplace policies and programs.* DHHS Publication No. SMA 07-4273, Analytic Series A-29. Rockville, MD: Substance Abuse and Mental Health Services Administration, Office of Applied Studies.

Lawson, G. (2008, November 13). The war next door: As drug cartels battle the government, Mexico descends into chaos. *Rolling Stone, 1065,* 74–81, 108–111.

Lenson, D. (1995). *On drugs.* Minneapolis, MN: University of Minnesota Press.

Levinthal, C. F. (1996). *Drugs, behavior, and modern society.* Boston, MA: Allyn & Bacon.

Li-Tzy, W., & Blazer, D. G. (2011). Illicit and nonmedical drug use among older adults: A review. *Journal of Aging Health, 23,* 481–504.

McBride, D. C., & McCoy, C. B. (2003). The drugs–crime relationship: An analytical framework. In L. K. Gaines & B. Kraska (Eds.), *Drugs, crime, and justice* (pp. 100–119). Prospect Heights, IL: Waveland Press.

McShane, L. (1994, April 18). Cops are crooks in N.Y.'s 30th Precinct. *Salt Lake Tribune, 238,* A-5.

Meister, E. (2017, October 19). A (very) brief history of NYC expresso. La Marzocco. Retrieved from https://home.lamarzoccousa.com/history-of-nyc-espresso/

Meth.IN.gov. (2015). Statistics. Retrieved from http://www.in.gov/meth/2330.htm

Methadone Centers. (2016, March 31). What is the typical methadone clinic cost? Retrieved from http://www.methadonecenters.com/typical-methadone-clinic-cost/

Michigan News. (2019). Marijuana use among US college students reached new 5-year high. Ann Arbor, MI: University of Michigan. Retrieved from https://news.umich.edu/marijuana-use-among-us-college-students-reaches-new-35-year-high/

Midgette, G. (2019, August 21). Americans send nearly 159 billion on illicit drugs each year. Thorofare, NJ: Healio Primary Care, Slack Inc. Retrieved from https://www.healio.com/primary-care/addiction/news/online/%7Babc172ec-c58b-44bf-8115-ce575294e7d3%7D/americans-spend-nearly-150-billion-on-illicit-drugs-each-year

Miech, R., Schulenberg, J., Johnston, L., Bachman, J., O'Malley, P., & Patrick, M. (2017). Monitoring the Future National Adolescent Drug Trends in 2017: Findings released. Ann Arbor, MI: Institute for Social Research, University of Michigan. Retrieved from http://www.monitoringthefuture.org//pressreleases/17drugpr.pdf

Mikulic, M. (2019, June 18). Projected worldwide total prescription drug revenue from 2018 to 2024. New York, NY: Statista Inc. Retrieved from https://www.statista.com /statistics/309387/global-total-prescription-drug-revenue -projection/

Mokdad, A. H., Marks, J. S., Stroup, D. F., & Gerberding, J. L. (2004, March 10). Actual causes of death in the United States, 2000. *Journal of the American Medical Association* (JAMA), *291*, 1238–1245.

Muir Wood. (2016). Teen Adderall abuse. Sonoma, CA: Muir Wood Adolescent and Family Services. Sonoma, CA: Author.

Mumola, C. J., & Karberg, J. C. (2007, January 19). *Drug use and dependence, State and Federal prisoners, 2004.* Washington, DC: U.S. Department of Justice. Retrieved from http://bjs.ojp.usdoj.gov/content/pub/pdf/dudsfp04.pdf

Nair, R. (2015, May 27). Internet & mobile phone users worldwide 2015: 50% populations on Internet. Dazeinfo. Retrieved from http://dazeinfo.com/2015/05/27 /internet-mobile-phone-users-worldwide-2000-2015 -report/

Natarajan, N., A. Petteruti, N. Walsh, & J. Ziedenberg. (2008, January). *Substance abuse treatment and public safety (a policy brief).* Washington, DC: Justice Policy Institute.

National Association for Children of Alcoholics. (2005). *Children of addicted parents: Important facts.* Rockville, MD: HopeNetworks.

National Conference of State Legislatures (NCSL). (2020). Costs and pricing: Overview. Author. Retrieved from https://www.ncsl.org/research/health/pharmaceuticals /costs-and-pricing.aspx

National Council on Alcoholism and Drug Dependence (NCADD). (2015, June 27). *Alcohol, drugs and crime.* New York, NY: Author.

National Council on Alcoholism and Drug Dependence, Inc. (NCADD). (2016). *Drugs and alcohol in the workplace.* New York, NY: Author.

National Institute of Justice. (2009). *Arrestee Drug Abuse Monitoring Program II (ADAM II), 2008 annual report.* Washington, DC: U.S. Department of Justice (DOJ), Office of National Drug Control Policy.

National Institute on Drug Abuse (NIDA). (2010). *Prescription medications.* Bethesda, MD: Author.

National Institute on Drug Abuse (NIDA). (2014a). Drug facts: High school and youth trends. December. Retrieved from https://www.drugabuse.gov/publications/drugfacts /high-school-youth-trends

National Institute on Drug Abuse (NIDA). (2014b). Popping pills: Prescription drug abuse in America. Bethesda, MD: Author.

National Institute of Drug Abuse (NIDA). (2014c). *Principles of adolescent substance use disorder treatment: A research-based guide.* Bethesda, MD: Author.

National Institute on Drug Abuse (NIDA). (2017). Trends and statistics. Bethesda, MD: Author.

National Institute on Drug Abuse (NIDA). (2018a). Misuse of prescription drugs. Bethesda, MD: Author. Retrieved from https://www.drugabuse.gov/publications/misuse -prescription-drugs/overview

National Institute on Drug Abuse (NIDA). (2018b). Synthetic cathinone's ("bath salts"). Bethesda, MD: Author. Retrieved from https://www.drugabuse.gov /publications/drugfacts/synthetic-cathinones-bath-salts

National Institute on Drug Abuse (NIDA). (2018c). *Synthetic cannabinoids (K2/Spice).* Bethesda, MD: Author. Retrieved from https://www.drugabuse.gov/publications/drugfacts /synthetic-cannabinoids-k2spice

National Institute on Drug Abuse (NIDA). (2019a). Overdose death rates. Bethesda, MD: National Institutes of Health. Retrieved from https://www.drugabuse.gov /related-topics/trends-statistics/overdose-death-rates

National Institute on Drug Abuse (NIDA). (2019b). Monitoring the Future Survey: High school and youth trends. Bethesda, MD: Author. Retrieved from https://www .drugabuse.gov/publications/drugfacts/monitoring -future-survey-high-school-youth-trends

National Institute on Drug Abuse (NIDA). (2019c). Methamphetamine: What is the scope of the methamphetamine misuse in the United States? Bethesda, MD: Author.

National Institute on Drug Abuse (NIDA). (2019d). Methamphetamine. Bethesda, MD: Author.

Nielsen Company. (2016). More than half the homes in the U.S. have three or more TVS. New York: Author. Retrieved from http://www.nielsen.com/us/en/insights /news/2009/more-than-half-the-homes-in-us-have -three-or-more-tvs.html

Office of Applied Studies (OAS). (2012). Illicit drug use among older adults. *The NSDUH* [National Survey on Drug Use and Health] *Report.* Rockville, MD: U.S. Department of Health and Human Services.

Office of National Drug Control Policy (ONDCP). (2002), *Pulse check: Trends in drug abuse.* Washington, DC: Author.

Office of National Drug Control Policy (ONDCP). (2012), *What America's users spend on illegal drugs, 2000–2006.* Washington, DC: Author.

Office of National Drug Control Policy (ONDCP). (2013a). *ADAM (Arrestee Drug Abuse Monitoring Program) II, 2012 Annual report, May.* Washington, DC: Author.

Office of National Drug Control Policy (ONDCP). (2013b). Synthetic drug (a.k.a. K2, Spice, bath salts, etc.).

Office of National Drug Control Policy (ONDCP). (2014, January). *ADAM II: 2013 Annual Report Arrestee Drug Abuse Monitoring Program II*. Washington, DC: Author.

Office of National Drug Control Policy (ONDCP). (2016). *Street terms: Drugs and the drug trade*. Washington, DC: Author. Retrieved from http://www.streetlightpublications.net/misc/ondcp.htm

Partnership at Drugfree.org. (2013). Drug guide: Bath salts. Retrieved from http://www.drugfree.org/drug-guide/bath-salts

Partnership for Drug-Free Kids. (2016). National study: Teen misuse and abuse of prescription drugs up 33 percent since 2008. New York: Author.

Partnership for Drug-Free Kids and MetLife Foundation. (2013). *The Partnership Attitude Tracking Study*. New York, NY: Partnership for Drug-Free Kids. Retrieved from http://www.drugfree.org/wp-content/uploads/2014/07/PATS-2013-FULL-REPORT.pdf

Partnership for Drug-Free New Jersey. (n.d.). K2 Spice. Millburn, NJ. Retrieved from http://drugfreenj.org/drug-encyclopedia/k2-spice/

Project Know. (2016). [Fifteen] of the most horrific drinking and driving accidents. Retrieved from http://www.projectknow.com/15-of-the-most-horrific-drinking-and-driving-accidents/

Pyrillis, R. (2014, June 5). Special report: EAPs: Devoid of data. Retrieved from https://www.workforce.com/news/special-report-eaps-devoid-of-data

Reardon, C. (2012, January/February). The changing face of older adult substance abuse. *Social Work Today, 12*, 8.

Reynolds, G. S., & Lehman, W. E. (2003). Levels of substance use and willingness to use the employee assistance program. *Journal of Behavioral Health Services and Research, 30*, 238–248.

Robert Wood Johnson Foundation. (2001, February). *Substance abuse: The nation's number one health problem*. Princeton, NJ: Author.

Schecter, M. (1989). Serotonergic-dopaminergic mediation of 3,4-methylenedioxy-methamphetamine (MDMA, Ecstasy). *Pharmacology, Biochemistry and Behavior, 31*, 817–824.

Schepis, T. S., & Krishnan-Sarin, S. (2009). Sources of prescriptions for misuse by adolescents: Differences in sex, ethnicity, and severity of misuse in a population-based study. *Journal of the American Academy of Child and Adolescent Psychiatry, 48*(8), 828–836.

Scott, C. (2015, March 9). Americans spend billions on vitamins and herbs that don't work. *Healthline News*. Retrieved from http://www.healthline.com/health-news/americans-spend-billions-on-vitamins-and-herbs-that-dont-work-031915

Sentencing Project. (2013, February 5). Drug policy news. Retrieved from http://www.sentencingproject.org/template/page.cfm?id=128

Singer, J. A. (2019, June 26). CDC provisional drug death numbers show slight improvement. Credit harm reduction. Washington, DC: CATO Institute. Retrieved from https://www.cato.org/blog/cdc-provisional-drug-death-numbers-show-slight-improvement-credit-harm-reduction

Statista Inc. (2019). Lifetime prevalence of use of any illicit drug for grades 8, 10 and 12 combined from 1991 to 2018. New York, NY: Author. Retrieved from https://www.statista.com/statistics/208420/us-lifetime-prevalence-drug-use-grades-8-10-12-since-1991/

Steward, P., & Sitarmiah, G. (1997, November 13). America's heartland grapples with rise of dangerous drug. *Christian Science Monitor, 1*, 18.

Stobbe, M. (2014, July 8). More U.S. households hanging up their landline phones. Associated Press. Retrieved from http://www.dailyfinance.com/2014/07/08/more-us-households-dump-landline-telephones/

Stopthedrugwar.org. (2005, July 1). Global: World drug trade worth $320 billion annually, UN says (pp. 1–2). Washington, DC: Author. Retrieved from https://stopthedrugwar.org/chronicle-old/393/320billion.shtml

Substance Abuse and Mental Health Services Administration (SAMHSA), Office of Applied Studies (OAS). (1996, July). *The relationship between family structure and adolescent substance use*. Rockville, MD: U.S. Department of Health and Human Services.

Substance Abuse and Mental Health Services Administration (SAMHSA), Office of Applied Studies (OAS). (2007). *The National Survey on Drug Use and Health (NSDUH) Report: Worker substance use, by industry category*. Rockville, MD: Author.

Substance Abuse and Mental Health Services Administration (SAMHSA), Office of Applied Studies (OAS). (2009). *Results from the 2008 National Survey on Drug Use and Health: National findings*. Rockville, MD: Author.

Substance Abuse and Mental Health Services Administration (SAMHSA). (2012a). *Results from the 2011 National Survey on Drug Use and Health: Summary of national findings*. Rockville, MD: Author.

Substance Abuse and Mental Health Services Administration (SAMHSA). (2012b). *The National Survey on Drug Use and Health (NSDUH) Report: Worker substance use, by industry category*. Rockville, MD: Author.

Substance Abuse and Mental Health Service Administration (SAMHSA). (2012c). *Older Americans Behavioral Health, Issue Brief 5: Prescription medication misuse and abuse among older adults*. Rockville, MD: Author.

Retrieved from https://acl.gov/sites/default/files/programs/2016-11/Issue%20Brief%205%20Prescription%20Med%20Misuse%20Abuse.pdf

Substance Abuse and Mental Health Service Administration (SAMHSA). (2012d).

Substance Abuse and Mental Health Services Administration (SAMHSA). (2013). *Substance abuse among older adults.* Rockville, MD: Author.

Substance Abuse and Mental Health Services Administration (SAMHSA). (2014a). *Results from the 2013 National Survey on Drug Use and Health: Summary of national findings.* Rockville, MD: Author.

Substance Abuse and Mental Health Services Administration (SAMHSA). (2014b). *The NSDUH Report: Workplace policies and programs concerning alcohol and drug use, August 7.* Rockville, MD: Author.

Substance Abuse and Mental Health Services Administration (SAMHSA). (2015). *Behavioral health barometer: United States.* Rockville, MD: Author. Retrieved from module-1-gender-matters.pptx

Substance Abuse and Mental Health Services Administration (SAMHSA). (2017). *Key substance use and mental health indicators in the United States: Results from the 2016 National Survey on Drug Use and Health.* Rockville, MD: Author. Retrieved from https://www.samhsa.gov/data/sites/default/files/NSDUH-FFR1-2016/NSDUH-FFR1-2016.htm

Substance Abuse and Mental Health Services Administration (SAMHSA). (2019a). *Key substance use and mental health indicators in the United States: Results from the 2018 National Survey on Drug Use and Health.* Rockville, MD: Author. Retrieved from https://www.samhsa.gov/data/sites/default/files/cbhsq-reports/NSDUHNationalFindingsReport2018/NSDUHNationalFindingsReport2018.pdf

Substance Abuse and Mental Health Services Administration (SAMHSA). (2019b). *Results from the 2018 National Survey on Drug Use and Health: Detailed tables.* Rockville, MD: Author. Retrieved from https://www.samhsa.gov/data/sites/default/files/cbhsq-reports/NSDUHDetailedTabs2018R2/NSDUHDetTabsSect1pe2018.htm

Substance Abuse and Mental Health Services Administration (SAMHSA). (2019c). *2018 National Survey on Drug Use and Health: Methodological summary and definitions.* Rockville, MD: Author. Retrieved from https://www.samhsa.gov/data/sites/default/files/cbhsq-reports/NSDUHDetailedTabs2018R2/NSDUHDetailedTabs2018.pdf

Superior Supplement Manufacturing. (2019). [Ten] surprising facts about supplements. Fountain Valley CA: Author.

Szasz, T. (1992). *Our right to drugs: The case for a free market.* Westport, CT: Praeger.

Talbott Recovery. (2019). 2018 prescription drug abuse statistics you need to know. Atlanta, GA: Author. Retrieved from https://talbottcampus.com/prescription-drug-abuse-statistics/

Tancredo. T. (2006). *In mortal danger: The battle for America's border and security.* Nashville, TN: Cumberland House Publishing.

Thio, A. (1983). *Deviant behavior,* 2nd ed. (pp. 332–333). Boston, MA: Houghton Mifflin.

Thio, A. (1995). *Deviant behavior,* 4th ed. New York, NY: Harper Collins College.

Thio, A. (2000). *Deviant behavior,* 6th ed. New York, NY: Pearson Education.

U.S. Department of Justice (USDOJ). (2013, January 27). Total of all meth clandestine laboratory incidents including labs, dumpsites, chem/glass/equipment. Washington, DC: Author.

U.S. Department of Justice (USDOJ). (2016, January 29). Multiple defendants in synthetic marijuana, bath salts distribution ring sentenced. Western District of Tennessee: U.S. Attorney's Office. Retrieved from https://www.justice.gov/usao-wdtn/pr/multiple-defendants-synthetic-marijuana-bath-salts-distribution-ring-sentenced

U.S. Department of Labor. (2009). *SHRM survey reveals majority of HR professionals' organizations drug test.* Washington, DC: Author.

U. S. Department of Labor. (2016), Drug-free workplace advisor: Workplace testing. Washington, DC: Author.

U.S. Food and Drug Administration. (2015). *Drug applications for over-the-counter (OTC) drugs.* Retrieved from http://www.fda.gov/drugs/developmentapprovalprocess/howdrugsaredevelopedandapproved/approvalapplications/over-the-counterdrugs/default.htm

U.S. Prescription Drug Spending Jumps to Record $374 Billion. (2015, April 14). *Chicago Tribune.* Retrieved from http://www.chicagotribune.com/business/ct-drug-spending-0415-biz-20150414-story.html

Vargas-Cooper, N. (2012, July–August). Bathlands. *Spin,* 58–64, 94.

Venturelli, P. J. (2000). Drugs in schools: Myths and reality. In W. Hinkle & S. Henry (Eds.), *Annals of the American Academy of Political and Social Science* (p. 567). Thousand Oaks, CA: Sage.

Vera Institute of Justice. (2020). Prison spending in 2015. In *Trends in Prison Population and Spending: 2010–2015.* Brooklyn, NY: Vera, 2020. Available https://www.vera.org/publications/price-of-prisons-2015-state-spending-trends/price-of-prisons-2015-state-spending-trends/price-of-prisons-2015-state-spending-trends-prison-spending

Walter, S. (1999). Holistic health. In N. Alison (Ed.), *The illustrated encyclopedia of body–mind disciplines* (pp. 1–2).

New York, NY: Rosen Publishing Group, Retrieved from http://ahha.org/rosen.htm

*Williamsport Sun-Gazette*. (2020, January 22). Televised drug advertisements. Opinion letters [Williamsport, PA]. Retrieved from https://www.sungazette.com/opinion/letters/2019/11/televised-drug-advertisements/

Wire Services. (1992, July 23). Cocaine kingpin escapes after bloody shootout. *Salt Lake Tribune, 244,* A-1.

Worldpress. (2006, November 2). Mexico: Drug cartels a growing threat. Retrieved from http://www.worldpress.org/Americas/2549.cfm#down

# Explaining Drug Use and Abuse

## Did You Know?

▶ Contrary to public perception, addiction is a complex disease.

▶ Most drugs of abuse include both physical and psychological addictions.

▶ Every culture has experienced problems with drug use or abuse. As far back as 2240 BC, Hammurabi, the Babylonian king and lawgiver, addressed the problems associated with excessive use of alcohol.

▶ Today, there are many more varieties of drugs, and many of these drugs are more potent than they were years ago.

▶ According to biological theories, drug abuse has an innate physical beginning stemming from physical characteristics that cause certain individuals either to experiment with or crave drugs to the point of abuse.

▶ Abuse of drugs by some people may represent an attempt to relieve underlying psychiatric disorders.

▶ No single theory can explain why most people use drugs.

▶ People who perceive themselves as drug users are more likely to develop serious drug abuse problems.

## Learning Objectives

**On completing this chapter, you should be able to:**

❯ List three to five major contributing factors responsible for addiction.

❯ List and briefly explain three models used to describe addiction.

❯ List six reasons why drug use or abuse is a more serious problem today than it was in the past.

❯ List and briefly describe the genetic and biophysiological theories that explain how drug use often leads to abuse.

❯ Explain how drugs of abuse act as positive reinforcers.

❯ Explain the major differences between substance use disorders and substance-induced disorders (addictive disorders).

❯ Understand how drug addiction can co-occur with various types of mental disorders.

❯ Briefly define and explain reinforcement or learning theory and some of its applications to drug use and abuse.

❯ Briefly explain sensation-seeking individuals and drug use.

❯ List and briefly describe the four sociological theories broadly known as social influence theories.

❯ Explain the link between drug use and other types of devious behaviors.

❯ List and describe three factors in the learning process that Howard Becker believes first-time users go through before they become attached to using illicit psychoactive drugs.

❯ Define the following concepts as they relate to drug use: *primary deviance, secondary deviance, master status,* and *retrospective interpretation.*

❯ Explain how Reckless's containment theory accounts for the roles of both internal and external controls regarding the attraction to drug use.

❯ Understand how making low-risk and high-risk drug choices directly affects drug use.

## Introduction

In this chapter, we focus on the major explanations of drug use and abuse. The questions we explore are: Why would anyone voluntarily consume drugs that are not medically needed or required? Why are some people particularly attracted to altering their minds with drugs? Why are others uneasy and uncomfortable with the euphoric effects of recreational drug use? Why do some people repeatedly subject their bodies and minds to the harmful effects of recreational and nonprescribed drug use and eventual addiction, stop their drug use, and then repeatedly relapse back to drug use? What logical reasons could explain such irrational behavior?

Following are four perspectives regarding drug use:

### ▮ First Perspective

I have had a long relationship with drug use. With the exception of one drug that I will never do again, I usually end up having a "romance" with drug use. I have tried and still like the use of weed, booze, and coke.... [referring to cocaine] Let's face it, I like the high feeling whenever I have time to myself and when I am off work. Weekends are best at least one night during my weekends off (*sic*). When I was younger I was worse and did a lot of drugs no matter what day of the week it was. How many times I would go to school high on weed! Many of my school friends knew I was high in school and only one teacher was ever suspicious about my drug use and he was a younger teacher who had heard from a friend of mine who was in the same English class. This guy had a blabbermouth even though he was a good friend. Today, I am 24 and still enjoy smoking weed every now and then. It has tapered off now that I am older, but whether it is alcohol or marijuana it is something I still like. My dad had problems with alcohol all his life and this is probably where my attraction and use of these two drugs comes from. I think a lot of it is inborn like it's genetic or something because I am the type that immediately likes the buzzed feeling. I don't try other drugs because I thoroughly enjoy what I do use and

know that there are other drugs out there I could easily like and want to continue using. I even like the buzz I get from some prescribed medicines whenever I am sick and they change my conscious state of mind. Yes, drugs and I get along well—always did. (*From Venturelli's research files, graduate student and part-time waiter in northwest Indiana, age 24, October 9, 2015)*

### ▮ Second Perspective

I grew up in a home with no alcohol present. I never saw my mom or dad drink alcohol. I think when they got married both of them had alcoholic parents. I never knew my grandparents since they died before I was born. My older brother remembers my grandfather since he lived until my brother was 7. He remembers that my grandfather would come over to visit and he was usually acting "weird." Later in life, he realized that my grandfather was probably drinking a lot and was probably under the influence. Anyway, before I was born my grandfather died of a stroke and my mom tells me that it was from drinking too much. He also had liver problems and my dad just recently told me his liver was shot from too much drinking. I tried bringing home a bottle of wine once and my mom and dad just watched me sip a glass without saying a word. They refused to have a drink with me and I recall how odd I felt doing this that when I look back on it, I was probably hurting their feelings. Anyway, I went away to college and during my first year, I started drinking a lot, got into all kinds of trouble with my college friends, law enforcement, my RA in a dorm I was living in, and the Dean of Students, and nearly flunked out of college that first year. After experiencing all these newfound problems, I decided that drinking alcohol was not for me. Besides, I was hurting my parents real bad when I was having these problems. Today at 31, I probably have a few drinks several times a year, but I am not really a drinker. One drink and I feel it right away. I can drink a sweet drink like a margarita, but many of my real close friends do not drink alcohol. I am just not around people who drink and actually, except for some college friends when I was attending Ball State who drank, I hardly ever had friends who drank. I had a girlfriend a few years ago but our relationship ended when I got tired of watching her drink while I waited to leave the bars at the end of the night. How drinkers want to keep drinking is very noticeable to a non-drinker. I also had an acquaintance at work who would call me several nights a week, and I had to listen to his incoherent conversations while he was drinking at home. I got tired of this, and one night I said that I prefer not to talk to him when he was drinking at home. Shortly after that conversation, he and his girlfriend moved away and I never heard from him again. What attracts people to drinking baffles me, and why they continue drinking when they have had plenty already is even more puzzling. I don't think they realize how stupid they act when intoxicated. Fuzzy thinking, uncoordinated, and [how] loud they become are other things I notice. Today, I am dealing with a stepson who is not only drinking at 16 but has also used other types of drugs and I can say that from dealing with his drug use, I am very much against the use of any drugs that are not necessary. *(From Venturelli's research files, male, age 31, May 18, 2010)*

## ▪ Third Perspective

When you ask about drug use, I literally draw a blank. This topic is really unknown to me. In my family, my grandparents on my dad's side were big-time drinkers. I think . . . my dad's experiences and especially . . . the car crash that killed my grandparents when they were in their 50s while coming home from a wedding after drinking heavily affected my dad very much. My mom comes from a Mormon family, so obviously she also does not drink any alcohol. My parents raised me and my three brothers without any examples or experiences regarding drug use. In my family, my wife and I hardly ever use any types of drugs—not even much of over-the-counter drugs. Occasionally, I will have a half a glass of wine several times a year, but I have to admit, I would rather be drinking water or freshly squeezed fruit juice. I just do not like the taste and the mild effect that such a small amount of alcohol has on me.

As you can imagine, I am very much against the use of any types of drugs, especially the illicit types of drugs. Drugs are addictive and people should not be doing or taking drugs. Taking drugs for fun does not have any real positive outcomes, and in the end, causes a lot of misery to families, and medical problems. I am quite certain that all of our family friends are nondrinkers and I know for certain that our best friends do not use any of the recreational types of drugs. You could say our lives are really drug free. Everything we do as a family is in the absence of drug use. *(From Venturelli's research files, male graduate university student, age 36, May 19, 2007)*

## ▪ Fourth Perspective

I am very much a party dog. I really like to party with my friends. I did get some friends in trouble a couple of times by supplying the alcohol and we had a raid by the police in La Porte at my house and got into a lot of trouble with my mom and dad. I just live for weekends when we get together getting high and laughing about all kinds of stupid stuff in the straight world. Last week I overdid it again, but this time had to go to the hospital for overdosing. I did Seconal, Xanax, Valium, and Librium, kept passing out and my friends took me to the emergency room where they had to pump my stomach. Will I do that again? Hopefully not because about a half hour later I would probably have been dead as the emergency doctor told me. My mom and dad found out and they warned me that the next time they will call the police. My dad is now convincing me to get help and will pay for it. I will try it but I am not giving up on the parties no matter what the rehab people say. I am only happy when I am buzzed and I think someday that will wear off when I am older. My older brother was the same way but not as bad as me and today he hardly drinks anymore, is married, and will soon have his first kid, so he had to give it up. I know I will do the same but for now this is my only time to have fun but I will do it more responsibly I guess. *(From Venturelli's research files, male, age 16, high school student, September 23, 2015)*

The preceding excerpts show extensive differences in values and attitudes regarding drug use.

The perspective of the first interviewee is that of a type of drug user who not only is strongly attracted to drug use but also markedly enjoys the drug experience of altering his consciousness. He includes the rationalized belief that his attraction to drugs has a biological basis. He also mentions that at a young age he was convincingly affected by his drug-using peers. The second interview shows how the emphasis on not using drugs in the interviewee's family was intergenerationally transmitted and persisted across two generations. After having some preliminary experiences with drug use, the interviewee in this second interview matures into a person shunning any recreational chemical alteration of his reality. The perspective of the third interviewee shows that if a person's early environment is drug free, then drug use is not an option. Finally, the perspective of the fourth interviewee represents a type of drug user who is largely unaware of the pitfalls of drug addiction and is recklessly involved with substance abuse. These four views represent a diverse range of motivations and reasons that influence people to either use or not use drugs.

Why such differences in drug use? In this chapter, we offer plausible substantive explanations why people use drugs recreationally and examine the underlying motivations regarding drug use. We will draw from major theoretical explanations to determine and explain probable causes *why* people recreationally use drugs and are prone to an excessive use of prescription and over-the-counter drugs that can easily lead to drug abuse and addiction.

To accomplish these goals, this chapter will explain the use and abuse of drugs from literally dozens of major biological, psychological, and sociological perspectives. Moreover, as we attempt to offer major theoretical and scientific explanations for drug use, you should develop an advanced understanding of the following:

- knowledge of the widespread use of drugs in the United States,
- awareness of drug use and abuse throughout the world,
- insight and understanding of why a certain percentage of people seek out nonmedical and recreational drug use,
- major social and psychological characteristics of drug users,

- how and why drugs are so seductive and irresistible,
- the physical and psychological processes and characteristics of addiction to alcohol and drug use, and
- knowledge of how alcohol and drug use creates profound changes in the brain.

## Drug Use: A Timeless Affliction

Historical records document drug use as far back as 2240 BC, when Hammurabi, the Babylonian king and lawgiver, addressed the problems associated with drinking alcohol. Even before then, the Sumerian people of Asia Minor, who created the cuneiform (wedge-shaped) alphabet, included references to a "joy plant" that dates from about 5000 BC. Experts indicate that the plant was an opium poppy used as a sedative (Escohotado & Symington 1999; International Network of People Who Use Drugs [INPUD], n.d.; O'Brien, Cohen, Evans, & Fine, 1992).

Virtually every culture has experienced problems with drug use or abuse. Today's drug use problems are part of a lengthy and rich tradition:

These [intoxicating] substances have formed a bond of union between men of opposite hemispheres, the uncivilized and the civilized; they have forced passages which, once open, proved of use for other purposes; they produced in ancient races characteristics which have endured to the present day, evidencing the marvelous degree of intercourse that existed between different peoples just as certainly and exactly as a chemist can judge the relations of two substances by their reactions. (Lewin, 1993, p. 3)

The quest for explaining drug use is more important than ever as the problem continues to evolve. There are many reasons why drug use and abuse are even more serious issues now than they were in the past:

- From 1960 to the present, drug use has become a widespread phenomenon.
- Today, drugs are much more potent than they were years ago. "For comparison, the national average of marijuana's THC [tetrahydrocannabinol] content in 1978 was 1.37%, in 1988 it was 3.59%, in 1998 4.43%, and in

2008 8.49%" (ProCon.Org, 2018). THC, or **tetrahydrocannabinol**—"marijuana's main psychoactive ingredient—in the marijuana samples rose from about 4% in 1995 to about 12 percent in 2014" (Blaszczak-Boxe, 2016, p. 1). The most recent finding indicates that "the average THC in Colorado weed is 18.7% (MarijuanaBreak Staff, n.d.). Finally, in 2017, *High Times* reported about "Godfather OG with a strain that had 34% THC" (MarijuanaBreak Staff, n.d.).

- The highest tested sample ever tested between 1975 and 2009 had 33.12% THC (domestic) and 37.20% THC (nondomestic). Another recent study indicated that the most potent strains of marijuana contain 25% THC (Hellerman, 2013).
- Whether they are legal or not, drugs are extremely popular. Their sales rack up many millions of dollars each year, and they have a major influence on many national economies.
- More so today than years ago, both licit and illicit drugs are introduced and experimented with by youths at a younger age. Older siblings, friends, and acquaintances often supply these drugs.
- Through the media, people in today's society are more affected by direct television and radio advertising, especially by drug companies that are "pushing" their newest drugs. Similarly, advertisements and sales promotions (coupons) for alcohol, coffee, tea, and vitamins are targeted to receptive consumer audiences, as identified through sophisticated market research.
- A good number of highly addictive drugs such as heroin and, to a lesser degree, cocaine are so potent that the potency alone kills its victims. Dealers find it financially advantageous to add fentanyl (a synthetic drug) to the mix of adulterants. Fentanyl is approximately 200,000 times more powerful than morphine. Another deadly adulterant added is carfentanil, which is used as a tranquilizing agent for elephants and other large mammals.
- Today, drug information is widely available. Literally thousands of websites provide information on drug usage, chat rooms are devoted to drug enthusiasts, and instructions on how to make drugs (mainly for recreational purposes) can be found on the Internet, and some can be purchased online.

On a daily basis, hundreds of thousands of spam emails are automatically sent regarding information on purchasing over-the-counter (OTC) drugs and prescription drugs without medical authorization (medical prescription). "Spam messages accounted for 57 percent of e-mail traffic in December 2018" (Statista, Inc., 2019). Approximately 19.9% of spam mail consists of medications and health-related goods and services.

- Drug use endangers the future of a society by harming its youth and potentially destroying the lives of many young men and women. When gateway drugs such as alcohol and tobacco are used at an early age, a strong probability exists that the use will progress to other drugs such as marijuana, cocaine, and amphetamines. Early drug use will likely lead to a lifelong habit, which usually has serious implications for the future.
- Drug use and especially drug dealing are becoming major factors in the growth of crime rates among the young. Membership in violent delinquent gangs is growing at an alarming rate. Violent shootings, drive-by killings, carjackings, and "wildings" occur frequently in cities (and increasingly in small towns).
- In 2013, a reported 68.9% of the estimated 22.4 million illicit drug users ages 18 or older were employed full- or part-time. Regarding alcohol, the same survey found that of adult binge drinkers, 79.3% (41.2 million people) were employed either full- or part-time. Of adult heavy drinkers, 76.1% (12.4 million people) were employed (Substance Abuse and Mental Health Services Administration [SAMHSA], 2019). Such startling findings regarding employment and drug use suggest not only decreased productivity but also increased absenteeism, job turnover, and medical costs as well as near accidents, serious accidents, and mistakes caused by workers.
- Another related problem is that drug use is especially serious today because we have become highly dependent on the expertise of others and highly dependent on technology.

**KEY TERM**

**tetrahydrocannabinol**
marijuana's main psychoactive ingredient

For example, the operation of sophisticated machines and electronic equipment requires that workers and professionals be free of the intoxicating effects of mind-altering drugs. Imagine the chilling fact that on a daily basis a certain percentage of pilots, surgeons, and heavy-equipment operators are under the influence of mind-altering drugs while working or that a certain percentage of school-bus drivers are under the effects of, say, marijuana or cocaine or both.

With remarkable and unsurpassed excellence in scientific, techn°logical, and electronic accomplishments, the United States would seem to be immune to drug use and abuse, which are widely considered irrational behaviors practiced by people with deep-seated psychological abnormalities. One might also think that drugs would be less alluring because of the statistically high proportion of accidents, crimes, domestic violence, relationship problems, and early deaths that result from the use and abuse of both licit and illicit drugs. Yet, as the latest drug-use figures show, knowing about these effects and outcomes does not deter drug use.

Considering these costs, what explains the continuing use and abuse of drugs? What could possibly sustain and feed the attraction to use mind-altering drugs? Why are drugs used when the negative consequences are so well documented and predictable?

In answering these questions, we need to list some basic reasons why people take drugs:

- People may be searching for pleasure that may appear to be out of reach without chemically altering the perception of reality.
- Drugs may relieve stress or tension or provide a temporary escape for people with excessive anxieties or severe depression.
- Peer pressure is a strong influence, especially for young people.
- In some cases, drugs may enhance religious or mystical experiences.
- Drugs are used to enhance recreational pursuits, such as the popular use of Ecstasy at raves and music festivals.
- Some users believe that illicit use of drugs can enhance their work performance—the use of cocaine by stockbrokers, office workers, and lawyers, for example.
- Drugs (primarily performance-enhancing drugs) can be used to improve athletic performance.

- Drugs can relieve pain and the symptoms of an illness.
- Drugs may offer a quick escape from worrisome and feared thoughts or experiences.

Although these reasons may indicate some underlying causes of excessive or abusive drug use, they also suggest that the variety and complexity of explanations and motivations are almost infinite. For any one individual, it is seldom clear when drug use shifts from casual drug use to abuse and addiction. When we consider the wide use of such licit drugs as alcohol, nicotine, and caffeine, we make the following discoveries:

1. More than 88% (241.6 million) of the U.S. population uses different types of illicit drugs on a monthly basis (SAMHSA, 2018);
2. nearly half (between 48% and 50% since 2011) have tried an illicit drug by the time they finish high school (Johnston et al., 2018); and
3. nearly half (45%) of 12th graders and one in 11 (9%) 8th graders in 2017 reported having been drunk at least once in their life (Johnston et al., 2018).

Further, some drugs can mimic many of the hundreds of moods people can experience. We can, therefore, begin to understand why the explanations for drug use and abuse are multiple and depend on both socialization experiences and biological differences. As a result of these two factors, which imply hundreds of variations, explanations for drug use cannot be forced into one or two theories.

Researchers have tackled the question of drug use and abuse from three major theoretical positions: biological, psychological, and sociological perspectives. Although the remainder of this chapter discusses these three major types of theoretical explanations, we first begin with a discussion of the motivation or "engine" responsible for the consistent attraction to recreational or nonmedical use of drugs—namely, addiction.

# The Origin and Nature of Addiction

Humans can develop intense relationships with drug compounds. Most people have chemically altered their mood at some point in their lives, if only by consuming a cup of coffee or a glass of white wine, and a majority do so occasionally. Yet for some individuals, drug compounds become the center of their lives, driving their behavior and determining their priorities, even to the point of catastrophic consequences to health and social well-being. Although the word *addiction* is an agreed-upon term referring to such behavior, little agreement exists as to the origin, nature, or boundaries of the concept of addiction. It has been classified as an exceptionally bad habit, a failure of morality, a symptom of other problems or a chronic disease in its own right.

Although public perception of drug abuse and addiction as a major social problem has waxed and waned since the turn of the 21st century, drug abuse and addiction to tobacco, alcohol, and illicit drugs has taken a toll on our nation, exacting more than $740 billion annually in costs related to crime, lost work productivity, and health care (NIDA, 2020).

For example, annual marijuana prevalence peaked among 12th graders in 1979 at 51%. Then use declined fairly steadily to 22% in 1992—a reduction of more than half. Use resurged in the 1990s, peaking in 1996 at 8th grade and in 1997 at 10th and 12th grades. Recent findings indicate that from 2013 through 2017 the percent of 12th graders who used in the last 12 months was at 38% (Johnston et al., 2018).

Alcohol and cigarettes also create problems when used by the youngest persons: Alcohol and cigarettes are the two major licit drugs included in the *Monitoring the Future Studies* surveys, though even these are legally prohibited for purchase by those the age of most of our respondents. Alcohol use is more widespread than use of illicit drugs. These two drugs are most widely used by today's teenagers. Despite recent declines, by the end of high school six out of every 10 students (59% after a significant 3% drop in 2018) have consumed more than just a few sips of alcohol at some time in their lives; and about a quarter (24%) have done so by 8th grade (Miech et al., 2019). In fact, nearly half (45%) of 12th graders and one in 11 (9%) 8th graders in 2017 reported having been drunk at least once in their life (Johnston et al., 2018).

Of greater concern than just any use of alcohol is its use to the point of intoxication: In 2018, more than two out of five 12th graders (43%), one-quarter of 10th graders (26%), and about one in 11 of all 8th graders (9.2%) said they had been drunk at least once in their lifetime. The levels of self-reported drunkenness during the 30 days immediately preceding the survey are high: 17.5%, 8.4%, and 2.1%, respectively, for grades 12, 10, and 8 (Miech et al., 2019).

**Binge drinking** consists of consuming five or more alcoholic drinks in a row and has also become a practice of great concern. In 2018, 13.8% of 12th graders, 8.7% of 10th graders, and 3.7% of 8th graders reported having engaged in binge drinking (Miech et al., 2019).

A more recent measure of consuming alcoholic beverages is **extreme binge drinking**, which consists of consuming 10 or more drinks in a row or 15 or more drinks in a row on a single occasion. Findings show that 4.6% of 12th graders were extreme binge drinkers, reporting having had 10 or more drinks in a row; 2.5% had 15 or more drinks in a row (Miech et al., 2019).

Further, the large numbers of 8th graders who have already begun using the so-called gateway drugs (tobacco, alcohol, inhalants, and marijuana) suggest that a substantial number are also at risk of proceeding further to such drugs as LSD, cocaine, amphetamines, and heroin. Government officials and researchers believe that *decreases* in perceived and believed harmfulness of using a drug are often leading indicators of future increases in actual use of that drug. "The authors of this study suggest that these trends may reflect '**generational forgetting**' of the dangers of these drugs, leaving the newer cohorts vulnerable to a resurgence of use" (Center for Substance Abuse Research [CESAR], 2007, p. 7; Knopf, 2017). From these major studies, it is apparent that both licit and illicit types of drugs continue to penetrate increasingly younger age groups.

## KEY TERMS

**binge drinking**
consuming five or more alcohol drinks in a row on a single occasion

**extreme binge drinking**
the consumption of 10 or more alcoholic drinks in a row or 15 or more drinks in a row on a single occasion

**generational forgetting**
when knowledge of adverse drug consequences experienced by a particular generation or population is lost by the younger cohort

## ▮ Defining Addiction

*Addiction* is described as a complex disease. In 1964, the World Health Organization (WHO) of the United Nations defined addiction as "a state of periodic or chronic intoxication detrimental to the individual and society, which is characterized by an overwhelming desire to continue taking the drug and to obtain it by any means" (World Health Organization Expert Committee on Addiction-Producing Drugs, 1964). Accordingly, addiction is characterized as chronic compulsive and at times uncontrollable drug craving, seeking, and use despite adverse physical or psychological consequences (National Institute on Drug Abuse [NIDA] 2018a). It is considered a brain disorder, because it involves functional changes to brain circuits involved in reward, stress, and self-control, and those changes may last a long time after a person has stopped taking drugs (NIDA, 2018a).

The word *addiction*, derived from the Latin verb *addicere*, refers to the process of binding to things. Today, the word largely refers to a chronic adherence to drugs. This can include both physical and psychological dependence. *Physical dependence* is the body's need to constantly have the drug or drugs; *psychological dependence* is the mental inability to stop using the drug or drugs.

The fifth edition of the *Diagnostic and Statistical Manual of Mental Disorders* (*DSM-5*), published by the American Psychiatric Association (APA, 2013), differentiates between **substance use disorders**[1] and **substance-induced disorders (addictive disorders)**. Substance-related and addictive disorders largely stem from activation of the

---

[1]In the DSM-5, substance abuse and substance dependence have been combined into a single condition called *substance-use disorder*.

reward pathways in the brain (which provide the pleasurable "high" feeling that a drug produces). In addition, those with

> lower levels of self control, which may reflect impairments of the brain inhibitory mechanisms, may be particularly predisposed to develop substance use disorders.... The following conditions may be classified as substance-induced: intoxication, withdrawal, and other substance [and] medication-induced mental disorders (psychotic disorder, bipolar and related disorder, depressive disorders, anxiety disorders, obsessive-compulsive and related disorders, sleep disorder, sexual dysfunctions, delirium, and neurocognitive disorders). (APA 2013, p. 481)

The diagnosis of substance use disorder (SUD) includes the following definitions:

- *Pharmacological*: The diagnosed individual may take the substance in larger amounts or over a longer period of time than originally intended.
- *Excessive time spent obtaining the substance*: The individual may spend an excessive amount of time obtaining or recovering from the drug(s) and its effects; in severe cases, nearly all of the individual's daily activities revolve around the substance.
- *Craving*: The user has an intense desire or urge for the drug (cannot think of anything other than securing and using the drug).
- *Social impairment*: The individual fails to fulfill major role obligations at work, school, or home despite having persistent or recurrent social or interpersonal problems caused by the effects of the substance; this includes withdrawal from personal or family obligations or hobbies and interests.
- *Risky use of the substance*: The individual may continue substance use despite knowing about a persistent or recurrent physical or psychological problem. He or she is unable to abstain from using the substance despite difficulties in using.
- *Tolerance*: The individual needs increased amounts or he or she will experience a diminished effect when using the same amount of the substance.
- *Withdrawal*: "Withdrawal . . . is a syndrome that occurs when blood or tissue concentrations of a substance decline in an individual who had maintained prolonged heavy use of substance" (APA, 2013, p. 484). (Often after developing withdrawal symptoms, "the

individual is likely to [resume consuming] the substance to relieve the symptoms . . . of withdrawal" [APA, 2013, p. 484].)

# ■ Models of Addiction

Various models have attempted to describe the essential nature of drug addiction. Newspaper accounts of "inebriety" in the 19th and early 20th centuries contain editorializing undertones that looked askance at the poor morals and life-style choices followed by the inebriate. This view has been termed the **moral model**, and although it may seem outdated from a modern scientific standpoint, it still characterizes an attitude among many traditional North Americans and members of many ethnic groups.

The prevailing concept or model of addiction in the United States is the **disease model**. Most proponents of this concept specify addiction to be a chronic and progressive disease over which the sufferer has no control. This model originated in part from research among members of Alcoholics Anonymous (AA) performed by E. M. Jellinek (1960), one of the founders of addiction studies. He observed a seemingly inevitable progression in his subjects, during which they made many failed attempts to stop drinking. This philosophy is currently espoused by the recovery fellowships of AA and Narcotics Anonymous (NA) and, to a large extent, the treatment field in general. It has even permeated the psychiatric and medical establishments' standard definitions of addiction. There are many variations under the broad rubric of the disease model, which has been bitterly debated. Viewpoints range from fierce adherence to equally fierce opposition, with intermediate views casting the disease concept as a convenient myth (Glaser, 2015; Smith, Milkman, & Sunderworth, 1985; Valentish, 2019).

Those who view addiction as another manifestation of something gone awry with the personality system adhere to the **characterological or personality predisposition model**. Every school of psychoanalytic, neopsychoanalytic, and psychodynamic psychotherapy has its specific "take" on the subject of addiction (Frosch, 1985). Tangentially, many addicts are also diagnosed with **personality disorders** (formerly known as *character disorders*), such as impulse-control disorders and sociopathy. Although few addicts are treated by **psychoanalysis** or psychoanalytic psychotherapy, a characterological type of model was a formative influence on the drug-free, addict-run "therapeutic community" model, which uses

harsh confrontation and time-extended, sleep-depriving group encounters. People who follow the therapeutic community model conclude that addicts must have withdrawn behind a **"double wall" of encapsulation** where they failed to grow, making such techniques necessary.

Others view addiction as a "career," a series of steps or phases with distinguishable characteristics. One career pattern of addiction includes six phases (Clinard & Meier, 2011; Waldorf, 1983):

1. Experimentation or initiation.
2. Escalation (increasing use).
3. Maintenance or "taking care of business" (optimistic use of drugs coupled with successful job performance).
4. Dysfunction or "going through changes" (problems with constant use and unsuccessful attempts to quit).
5. Recovery or "getting out of the life" (arriving at a successful view about quitting and receiving drug treatment).
6. Ex-addict (having successfully quit).

Finally, after examining countless theories that attempt to list or predict the stages of addiction to alcohol, tobacco, or illicit drug use, the

## KEY TERMS

**moral model**
belief that people abuse alcohol because they choose to do so

**disease model**
belief that people abuse alcohol because of some biologically caused condition

**characterological or personality predisposition model**
view of chemical dependency as a symptom of problems in the development or operation of the system of needs, motives, and attitudes within the individual

**personality disorders**
broad category of psychiatric disorders, formerly called *character disorders*, that includes the antisocial personality disorder, borderline personality disorder, schizoid personality disorder, and others; these serious, ongoing impairments are difficult to treat

**psychoanalysis**
theory of personality and method of psychotherapy originated by Sigmund Freud and focused on unconscious forces and conflicts and a series of psychosexual stages

**"double wall" of encapsulation**
adaptation to pain and avoidance of reality, in which the individual withdraws emotionally and further anesthetizes him- or herself by chemical means

following set of stages appears to be the most salient regarding addiction to drug use: (1) initial initiation and use of the drug, (2) patterned continuation into using the drug, (3) transition to drug abuse, (4) attempts at cessation (stopping the use), and (5) relapse (a return to abusive usage).

## ▌ Factors Contributing to Addiction

Many, perhaps millions, of individuals use or even occasionally abuse drugs without compromising their basic health, legal, and occupational status and social relationships. Why does a significant minority get caught up in abuse and addictive behavior? The answer stems from the fact that many factors—not a single factor—generally contribute to an individual becoming addicted (Sudhinaraset, Wigglesworth, & Takeuchi, 2016; Syvertsen, 2008). **Table 2.1** represents a compilation of factors identified as complicit in the origin or etiology of addiction and taken from the fields of psychology, sociology, and addiction studies.

In addition to the social and cultural factors listed in Table 2.1, other "cultural" risk factors for development of alcohol abuse include the following:

- drinking at times other than at meals;
- drinking alone;
- drinking as a reliever of stress or anxiety;
- patterns of solitary drinking (immediately drinking, smoking marijuana, or using other drugs after work, weekend drinking, late night drinking);
- drinking defined as a rite of passage into an adult role; and
- recent introduction of a chemical into a social group with insufficient time to develop informal social control over its use (Marshall, 1979).

Recall that the mix of risk factors differs for each person. It varies according to individual, peer, family, age, social, and cultural idiosyncrasies. Most addiction treatment professionals believe that it is difficult, if not impossible, to tease out these factors before treatment, when the user is still "talking to a chemical," or during early treatment, when the brain and body are still recuperating from the effects of long-term abuse. Once a stable sobriety is established, one can begin to address any underlying problems. An exception is the mentally ill chemical abuser, whose treatment requires special considerations from the outset.

In addition to the factors just listed, several age-dependent stressors and conflicts sometimes promote drug misuse. Risk factors that apply especially to adolescents include the following:

- peer norms favoring use;
- misperception of peer norms (users set the tone);
- power of age group (peer norms vs. other social influences);
- conflicts that generate anxiety or guilt, such as dependence versus independence, adult maturational tasks versus fear, and new types of roles versus familiar safe roles;
- teenage risk-taking and sense of omnipotence or invulnerability;
- use defined as a rite of passage into adulthood; and
- use perceived as cool, glamorous, sexy, facilitating intimacy, fun, and so on.

Risk factors that apply especially to middle-aged individuals include the following:

- loss of meaningful role or occupational identity because of retirement;
- loss, grief, or isolation from the loss of parents, divorce, or departure of children ("empty nest syndrome");
- loss of positive body image;
- dealing with a newly diagnosed illness (e.g., diabetes, heart problems, cancer); and
- disappointment when life's expectations are not met.

Even in each of these age groups a combination of factors is at play. The adolescent abuser might have risk factors that were primarily neurological vulnerabilities such as undiagnosed attention-deficit hyperactivity disorder. Alternatively, he or she may experience failure and rejection at school, disappointed parents, or be labeled odd, lazy, or unintelligent (Kelly & Ramundo, 2006).

In response to the information presented in Table 2.1, a student who was a recovering alcoholic commented, "You're an alcoholic because you drink!" He had a good point: The mere presence of one, two, or more risk factors does not create addiction. Drugs must be available, they must be used, and they must become a pattern of adaptation to any of the many painful, threatening, uncomfortable, or unwanted sensations or stimuli that occur in the presence of genetic,

**TABLE 2.1** Risk Factors for Addiction

| Risk Factor | Leading to This Effect |
| --- | --- |
| **Biologically Based Factors (Genetic, Neurological, Biochemical, and So On)** | |
| A less subjective feeling of intoxication | More use to achieve intoxication (warning signs of abuse absent) |
| Easier development of tolerance; liver enzymes adapt to increased use | Easier to reach the addictive level |
| Lack of resilience or fragility of higher (cerebral) brain functions | Easy deterioration of cerebral functioning, impaired judgment, and social deterioration |
| Difficulty in screening out unwanted or bothersome outside stimuli (low stimulus barrier) | Feeling overwhelmed or stressed |
| Tendency to amplify outside or internal stimuli (stimulus augmentation) | Feeling attacked or panicked; need to avoid emotion |
| Attention deficit hyperactivity disorder and other learning disabilities | Failure, low self-esteem, or isolation |
| Biologically based mood disorders (depression and bipolar disorders) | Need to self-medicate against loss of control or pain of depression; inability to calm down when manic or to sleep when agitated |
| **Psychosocial/Developmental "Personality" Factors** | |
| Low self-esteem | Need to block out pain; gravitation to outsider groups |
| Depression rooted in learned helplessness and passivity | Use of a stimulant as an antidepressant |
| Conflicts | Anxiety and guilt |
| Repressed and unresolved grief and rage | Chronic depression, anxiety, or pain |
| Posttraumatic stress syndrome (as in veterans and abuse victims) | Nightmares or panic attacks |
| **Social and Cultural Environment** | |
| Availability of drugs | Easy frequent use |
| Chemical-abusing parental model | Sanction; no conflict over use |
| Abusive, neglectful parents; other dysfunctional family patterns | Pervasive sense of abandonment, distrust, and pain; difficulty in maintaining attachments |
| Group norms favoring heavy use and abuse | Reinforced, hidden abusive behavior that can progress without interference |
| Misperception of peer norms | Belief that most people use or favor use or think it's cool to use |
| Severe or chronic stressors, as from noise, poverty, racism, or occupational stress | Need to alleviate or escape from stress via chemical means |
| Alienation factors: isolation, emptiness | Painful sense of aloneness, normlessness, rootlessness, boredom, monotony, or hopelessness |
| Difficult migration or acculturation with social disorganization, gender or generation gaps, or loss of role | Stress without buffering support system |

psychosocial, or environmental risk factors. Prevention workers often note the presence of multiple messages encouraging use: the medical use of minor tranquilizers to offset any type of psychic discomfort; the marketing of alcohol as sexy, glamorous, adult, and facilitative of social interaction; and so forth.

# The Vicious Cycle of Drug Addiction

*To stop drinking, study a drunkard when you are sober.*
—*Traditional Chinese proverb*

Drug addiction is a process, not a sudden occurrence. The body makes a series of physiological adaptations to the presence of alcohol and other drugs. For instance, brain cell tolerance and increased metabolic efficiency of the liver can develop, necessitating consumption of more of the chemical to achieve the desired effect. Physical dependence can also develop in which cell adaptations cause withdrawal syndromes to occur in the absence of the chemical.

Other factors can promote the cycle of addiction. For instance, drug abuse impairs cerebral functioning, including memory, judgment, behavioral organization, ability to plan, ability to solve problems, and motor coordination. Thus, poor decision making, impaired and deviant behavior, and overall dysfunction result in adverse social consequences such as accidents, loss of earning power and relationships, and impaired health. Such adverse social and health consequences cause pain, depression, and lowered self-esteem, which may result in further use of the drug as an emotional and physical anesthetic. The addict often adapts to this chronically painful situation by erecting a defense system of denial, minimization, and rationalization; the chemical blunting of reality may exacerbate this denial of reality. At this point, it is unlikely that the addict or developing addict will feel compelled to cease or cut back drug use on his or her own (Tarter, Alterman, & Edwards, 1983).

Family, friends, and colleagues often unwittingly "enable" the maintenance and progression of addiction. Examples include making excuses for addicts, literally and figuratively bailing them out, taking up the slack, denying and minimizing their problems, and otherwise making it possible for addicts to avoid facing the reality and consequences of what they are doing to themselves and others. Although these friends and family members may be motivated by simple naïveté, embarrassment, or misguided protectiveness, there are often hidden gains in taking up this role, known popularly as *codependency* (Beattie, 1987; Mental Health America, 2010). Varieties of cultural and organizational factors also operate in the workplace or school that allow denial of the existence or severity of abuse or dependency. This triad of personal denial, peer and kin denial and codependency, and institutional denial represents a formidable impediment to successful intervention and recovery (Drug Rehab.com 2018; Miller, 1995; Myers, 1990).

## ▪ Other Nondrug Addictions

The addictive disease model and the 12-step recovery model followed by AA and NA have appeared so successful for many addicts and their families and friends that other unwanted syndromes have been added to the list of "addictions." The degree to which the concept of addiction fits these syndromes varies. Gambling, for example, shows progressive worsening, loss of control, relief of tension from the activity, and continuance despite negative (often disastrous) consequences experienced by the addicted gambler. Recovering gamblers claim to experience a form of withdrawal. Gamblers Anonymous is a fellowship that has formed to assist its members. Clearly, gambling as an activity has much in common with chemical addictions, but it was debated as to whether it belonged in the category of addiction. However, for the first time in its publishing history, the most recent edition of the *Diagnostic and Statistical Manual of Mental Disorders,* the *DSM-5,* includes dependence on gambling as a mental disorder.

Many other groups have followed in the footsteps of Gamblers Anonymous, including those related to eating (Overeaters Anonymous) and sexual relationships (the Augustine Fellowship and Sex and Love Addicts Anonymous). In recent years, any excessive or unwanted behaviors—including excess shopping, hoarding, chocolate consumption, and even Internet use—have been labeled "addictions," which has led to satirical reporting in the press. Addiction professionals lament the overdefinition, which they believe trivializes the seriousness and suffering of those with rigorously defined addictions.

Like drug use, gambling can become addictive.

## Major Theoretical Explanations: Biological

Biological explanations have tended to use genetic theories and the disease model to explain drug addiction. The view that alcoholism is a sickness dates back to the early 19th century (Conrad & Schneider, 1980; Heitzeg, 1996). The disease perspective is upheld by Jellinek's (1960) view that alcoholism largely involves a loss of control over drinking and that the drinker experiences clearly distinguishable phases in his or her drinking patterns. For example, with alcoholism, the illness affects the abuser to the point of loss of control. Thus, the disease model views drug abuse as an illness in need of treatment or therapy.

According to biological theories, drug abuse has a beginning stemming from physical characteristics that cause certain individuals either to experiment with or crave drugs to the point of abusive use. **Genetic and biophysiological theories** explain addiction in terms of genetics, brain dysfunction, and biochemical patterns.

Biological explanations emphasize that the central nervous system's reward sensors in some people are more sensitive to drugs, making the drug experience more pleasant and more

rewarding for these individuals (Khantzian, 1998; Mathias, 1995; NIDA 2014, 2018a). In contrast, others find the effects of drugs of abuse extremely unpleasant, so these people are not likely to be attracted to these drugs (Farrar & Kearns, 1989; Grant, 2013; National Health Service [NHS], 2015; NIDA, 2018a).

Most experts acknowledge that biological factors play an essential role in drug abuse. These factors likely determine how the brain responds to these drugs and why such substances are addictive. By identifying the nature of the biological systems that contribute to drug abuse problems, improved prevention and treatment methods might be developed (Koob, 2000; Kuehn, 2010; NIDA, 2008b; NIDA, 2018).

All the major biological explanations related to drug abuse assume that these substances exert their **psychoactive effects** by altering brain chemistry or neuronal activity (in the basic functional cells of the brain). Specifically, the drugs of abuse interfere with the functioning of **neurotransmitters**—chemical messengers used for communication between brain regions.

The following sections detail three principal biological theories that help explain why some drugs are abused and why certain people are more likely to become addicted when using these substances.

### ■ Abused Drugs as Positive Reinforcers

Biological research has shown that stimulating some brain regions with an electrode causes highly pleasurable sensations. In fact, laboratory animals would rather self-administer stimulation to these brain areas than eat or engage in sex. It has been demonstrated that drugs of abuse also activate these same pleasure centers in the brain (NIDA, 2008b, 2018a; Weiss, 1999).

### KEY TERMS

**genetic and biophysiological theories**
explanations of addiction in terms of genetic brain dysfunction and biochemical patterns

**psychoactive effects**
how drug substances alter and affect the brain's mental functions

**neurotransmitters**
chemical messengers released by nervous (nerve) cells for communication with other cells

It is generally believed that most drugs with abuse potential enhance pleasure centers by causing the release of specific brain neurotransmitters such as **dopamine** (Bespalov Lebedev, Panchenko, & Zvartau, 1999; NIDA 2008b, 2018b). How do drugs work in the brain?

All drugs of abuse directly or indirectly target the brain's reward system by flooding the circuit with dopamine. Dopamine is a neurotransmitter present in regions of the brain that regulates movement, emotion, cognition, motivation, and feelings of pleasure. The overstimulation of this system, which rewards our natural behavior, produces the euphoric effects sought by people who abuse drugs and teaches them to repeat the behavior. (NIDA, 2008b, p. 17)

Drugs work on the brain by interfering with the way neurons send, receive, and process signals via neurotransmitters. Some drugs, such as marijuana and heroin, can activate neurons because their chemical structure mimics that of a natural neurotransmitter in the body. This allows the drugs to attach onto and activate the neurons. Although these drugs mimic the brain's own chemicals, they don't activate neurons in the same way as a natural neurotransmitter, and they lead to abnormal messages being sent through the network. (NIDA, 2018a, p.1)

Brain cells become accustomed to the presence of these neurotransmitters and crave them when they are absent, leading the person to seek more drugs (NIDA, 2008b; Spanagel & Weiss, 1999). In addition, it has been proposed that overstimulation of these brain regions by continual drug use "exhausts" these dopamine systems and leads to depression and an inability to experience normal pleasure (Volkow, 1999).

## ▮ Drug Abuse and Psychiatric Disorders

Biological explanations are thought to be responsible for the substantial overlap that exists between drug addiction and mental illness (NIDA 2007, 2018c) (see "Do Genes Matter? What

**KEY TERM**

**dopamine**
neurotransmitter present in regions of the brain that regulate movement, emotion, cognition, motivation, and feelings of pleasure; it mediates the rewarding aspects of most drugs of abuse

Is the Relationship between Addiction and Other Mental Disorders?").

Many individuals who develop substance-use disorders . . . are also diagnosed with mental disorders, and vice versa. Multiple national population surveys have found that about half of those who experience a mental illness during their lives will also experience a substance-use disorder and vice versa. Although there are fewer studies on comorbidity among youth, research suggests that adolescents with substance-use disorders also have high rates of co-occurring mental illness; [more than] 60 percent of adolescents in community-based substance-use disorder treatment programs also meet diagnostic criteria for another mental illness. (NIDA, 2018c, p. 1)

## ▮ Genetic Explanations

Why does one person become dependent on drugs while another, exposed to the same environment and experiences, does not?

—Schaffer Library of Drug Policy, 1994, p. 1

One biological theory receiving scrutiny suggests that inherited traits can predispose some individuals to drug addiction (Lemonick & Park, 2007; MacPherson, 2010; NIDA, 2016). Such theories have been supported by the observation that increased frequency of alcoholism and drug abuse exists among children of alcoholics and drug abusers (APA, 2000; NIDA, 2007; Uhl, Blum, Noble, & Smith, 1993; Uhl, Elmer, LaBuda, & Pickens, 2002). Using adoption records of some 3,000 individuals from Sweden, researchers Cloninger, Gohman, and Sigvardsson conducted one of the most extensive research studies examining genetics and alcoholism. They found that "children of alcoholic parents were likely to grow up to be alcoholics themselves, even in cases where the children were reared by nonalcoholic adoptive parents almost from birth" (Doweiko 2015, p. 37). Such studies estimate that drug vulnerability from genetic influences accounts for approximately 38% of all cases, with environmental and social factors accounting for the balance (Uhl et al., 1993). A more recent study found that "[f]amily studies that include identical twins, fraternal twins, adoptees, and siblings suggest that as much as half of a person's risk of becoming addicted to nicotine,

## DO GENES MATTER?

*What Is the Relationship Between Addiction and Other Mental Disorders?*

Some good evidence suggests that a comorbid relationship exists between addiction and other mental disorders (Center for Behavioral Health Statistics and Quality [CBHSQ] 2015; NIDA 2008a, 2010, 2018c, 2018d).

### What Is Comorbidity?

**Comorbidity** is a term used to describe two or more disorders or illnesses occurring in the same person. They can occur at the same time or one after the other. Comorbidity also implies interactions between the illnesses that can worsen the course of both.

### Is Drug Addiction a Mental Illness?

Yes, addiction changes the brain in fundamental ways, disturbing a person's normal hierarchy of needs and desires and substituting new priorities connected with procuring and using the drug. The resulting compulsive behaviors that weaken the ability to control impulses, despite the consequences, are similar to hallmarks of other mental illnesses.

### How Common Are Comorbid Drug Addiction and Other Mental Illnesses?

Many people who are addicted to drugs are also diagnosed with other mental disorders and vice versa. For example, compared with the general population, people addicted to drugs are roughly twice as likely to suffer from mood and anxiety disorders, with the reverse also true.[*]

### Why Do These Disorders Often Co-Occur?

Although drug use disorders commonly occur with other mental illnesses, this does not mean that one caused the other, even if one appeared first. In fact, establishing causality or even directionality (i.e., which came first) can be difficult. However, research suggests the following possibilities for their co-occurrence:

- Drug abuse may bring about symptoms of another mental illness. Increased risk of psychosis in some marijuana users suggests this possibility.

- Mental disorders can lead to drug abuse, possibly as a means of **self-medication**. Patients suffering from anxiety or depression may rely on alcohol, tobacco, or other drugs to temporarily alleviate their symptoms.

These disorders could also be caused by common risk factors, such as the following.

- *Overlapping genetic vulnerabilities*: Common genetic factors may make a person susceptible to both addiction and other mental disorders or to having a greater risk of a second disorder once the first appears.

- *Overlapping environmental triggers*: Stress, trauma (such as physical or sexual abuse), and early exposure to drugs are common factors that can lead to addiction and other mental illnesses.

- *Involvement of similar brain regions*: Brain systems that respond to reward and stress, for example, are affected by drugs of abuse and may show abnormalities in patients who have certain mental disorders.

- *Drug use disorders and other mental illnesses are developmental disorders*: This means they often begin in the teen years or even younger—periods

### KEY TERMS

**comorbidity**
two or more disorders or illnesses occurring in the same person; they can occur simultaneously or one after the other; also implies interactions between the illnesses that can worsen the course of both

**self-medication**
method of self-care in which an individual uses nonprescribed drugs to treat untreated and often undiagnosed medical ailments involving his or her psychological condition; self-prescribed drugs can include recreational drugs, psychoactive drugs, alcohol, and herbal products used to alleviate or diminish mental distress, stress and anxiety, mental illnesses, or psychological trauma

---

[*]Substance abuse and substance dependence are considered *substance use disorders*—a category under mental disorders—when they meet the diagnostic criteria delineated in the fifth edition of the *Diagnostic and Statistical Manual of Mental Disorders*. Drug dependence, as DSM-5 defines it, is synonymous with the term *addiction* (even though DSM-5 does not use the term *addiction*). Criteria for drug abuse hinge on the harmful consequences of repeated use but do not include compulsive use, tolerance, or withdrawal. Because the focus of this chapter is on comorbid drug use disorders and other mental illnesses, the terms *mental illness* and *mental disorders* will refer here to disorders other than drug use such as depression, schizophrenia, anxiety, and mania. The terms *dual diagnosis*, *mentally ill chemical abuser*, and *co-occurrence* are also used to refer to drug use disorders that are comorbid with other mental illnesses.

*(continues)*

## DO GENES MATTER? (*CONTINUED*)

when the brain experiences dramatic developmental changes. Early exposure to drugs of abuse may change the brain in ways that increase the risk for mental disorders. Also, early symptoms of a mental disorder may indicate an increased risk for later drug use.

### How Are These Comorbid Conditions Diagnosed and Treated?

The rate of comorbidity between drug use disorders and other mental illnesses calls for a comprehensive approach that identifies and evaluates both. Accordingly, anyone seeking help for either drug abuse or

addiction or another mental disorder should be checked for both and treated accordingly.

Several behavioral therapies have shown promise for treating comorbid conditions. These approaches can be designed to target patients according to specific factors such as age or marital status. Some therapies have proved more effective for adolescents, whereas others have shown greater effectiveness for adults; some therapies are designed for families and groups, others for individuals.

Although several medications exist for treating addiction and other mental illnesses, most have not been studied in patients with comorbidities. For

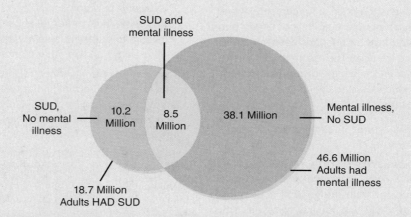

Past-year substance-use disorder (SUD) and mental illness among adults aged 18 or older: Numbers in millions, 2017.

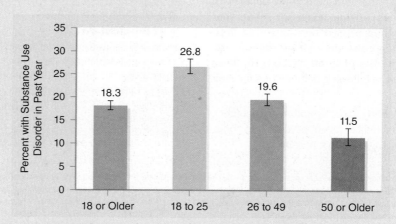

Past-year substance-use disorder among adults 18 or older with any mental illness in the past year, by age group: Percentages, 2017.

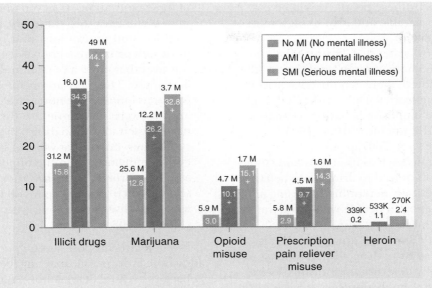

Levels of mental illness and the use of major drug substances among adults age 18 or older,* 2017.

Data from Center for Behavioral Health Statistics and Quality (CBHSQ). (2018). *2017 National Survey on Drug Use and Health: Detailed tables.* Rockville, MD: Substance Abuse and Mental Health Services Administration (SAMHSA).

example, individuals addicted to heroin, prescription pain medications, cigarettes, or alcohol can be treated with appropriate medications to ease withdrawal symptoms and drug craving; similarly, separate medications are available to help improve the symptoms of depression and anxiety. More research is needed, however, to better understand how such medications act when combined in individuals with comorbidities, or whether such medications can be dually effective for treating comorbid conditions.

................................................................................................................................................

Data from Center for Behavioral Health Statistics and Quality (CBHSQ). (2015). *2014 National Survey on Drug Use and Health: Detailed tables.* Rockville, MD: Substance Abuse and Mental Health Services Administration (SAMHSA); National Institute on Drug Abuse (NIDA). (2010). *Comorbidity: Addiction and other mental disorders* (pp. 1–2). Retrieved from https://www.drugabuse.gov/sites/default/files/rrcomorbidity.pdf; National Institute on Drug Abuse (NIDA). (2018a). *Understanding drug use and addiction.* Bethesda, MD: U.S. Department of Health and Human Services. Retrieved from https://www.drugabuse.gov/publications /drugfacts/understanding-drug-use-addiction; National Institute on Drug Abuse (NIDA). (2018c). *Common comorbidities with substance use disorders and mental illness.* Bethesda, MD: U.S. Department of Health and Human Services. Retrieved from https://www.drugabuse.gov/publications/research-reports /common-comorbidities-substance-use-disorders/part-1-connection-between-substance-use-disorders-mental-illness; National Institute on Drug Abuse (NIDA). (2018d). *Comorbidity: Substance use disorders and other mental illnesses.* Bethesda, MD: U.S. Department of Health and Human Services. Retrieved from https://www.drugabuse.gov/publications/drugfacts/comorbidity-substance-use-disorders-other-mental-illnesses

alcohol, or other drugs depends on his or her genetic makeup" (NIDA, 2016a).

Other studies attempting to identify the specific genes that may predispose the carrier to drug abuse problems have suggested that a brain target site (called a *receptor*) for dopamine is altered in a manner that increases the drug abuse vulnerability (Genetic Science Learning Center, 2015; Radowitz, 2003; Wyman, 1997). Studies that test for genetic factors in complex behaviors such as drug abuse are extremely difficult to conduct and interpret. It is sometimes impossible to design experiments that distinguish among genetic, social, environmental, and psychological influences in human populations. For example, inherited traits are known to be major contributors to psychiatric disorders such as schizophrenia and depression. Many people with one of these illnesses also have a substance abuse disorder (APA, 2013; SAMHSA, 2015). A high incidence of an abnormal gene in a cocaine-abusing population, for example, may not only be linked to drug abuse behavior but also be associated with depression or some other psychiatric disorder (Uhl et al., 2002; Uhl, Persico, & Smith, 1992).

Theoretically, genetic factors can directly or indirectly contribute to drug abuse vulnerability in several ways:

- Taking drugs of abuse, thus encouraging their use, may relieve psychiatric disorders that are genetically determined.
- In some people, reward centers of the brain may be genetically determined to be especially sensitive to addictive drugs; thus, the

use of drugs by these people would be particularly pleasurable and lead to high rates of addiction.

- Volkow (2016) states that "drug addiction is a disease of the human brain" and that in "the brains of addicts, there is reduced activity in the prefrontal cortex where rational thought can override impulsive behavior" (Elman & Borsook, 2016; Kuehn. 2010, p. 1905; Lemonick & Park, 2007, p. 43).
- Character traits such as insecurity and vulnerability that often lead to drug abuse behavior may be genetically determined, causing a high rate of addiction in people with those traits (Delva, 2019; Kuehn, 2010).
- Factors that determine how difficult it is to break away from drug addiction may be genetically determined, causing severe craving or extremely unpleasant withdrawal effects in some individuals. People with this predisposition are less likely to abandon their drug of abuse.

The genetic theories for explaining drug abuse may help us understand why drug addiction occurs in some but not all individuals. In addition, if genetic factors play a major role in drug abuse, genetic screening might be used to identify those people who are especially vulnerable to drug abuse problems and to help such individuals avoid exposure to these substances.

## Major Theoretical Explanations: Psychological

Psychological theories mostly deal with mental or emotional states, which are often associated with or exacerbated by social and environmental factors. Psychological explanations of addiction include one or more of the following: escape from reality, boredom (Burns, 1997), inability to cope with anxiety, destructive self-indulgence to the point of constantly desiring intoxicants, blind compliance with drug-abusing peers, self-destructiveness, and conscious and unconscious ignorance regarding the harmful effects of abusing drugs. Other authors write the following:

> [P]sychological theory explains that drug use and abuse begin because of the unconscious motivations within all of us. We are not aware

of these motivations, not even when they manifest themselves. So, there are unconscious conflicts and motivations that reside within us as well as our reactions to early events in our lives that move a person toward drug use and abuse. The motivations for drug use are within us, and we are not aware of them, nor are we aware that those are the reasons we have chosen to turn to drugs. In this case, the person may be weak or without self-esteem or even see themselves in the opposite manner, as all-important. Drug use then becomes a sort of crutch to make up for all that is wrong with their lives and wrong with their selves. (Moore, 2008, p. 1)

Psychologists propose several possible causes of addiction. First, people may engage in harmful behaviors because of an abnormality or *psychopathology* that manifests itself as mental illness. Second, people may learn unhealthy behavior in response to their environment. Third, people's thoughts and beliefs create their feelings. This, in turn, determines their behavior (Horvath, Misra, Epner, & Cooper, 2015).

Freud established early psychological theories that make up psychoanalytic psychology. He linked "primal addictions" with masturbation and postulated that all later addictions, including those involving alcohol and other drugs, were caused by ego impairments. Freud said that drugs compensate for insecurities that stem from parental inadequacies, which themselves may cause difficulty in adequately forming bonds of friendships. For example, Freud claimed that alcoholism is an expression of the death instinct, as are self-destruction, narcissism, and oral fixations.

> The . . . [psychoanalytic] . . . view suggests addiction is basically a disorder of self-regulation. For instance, individuals with histories of exposure to adverse childhood environments (e.g., physical and sexual abuse) tend to have diminished capacity to regulate negative emotions and cope effectively with stress. These individuals may be self-medicating anxiety and mood disorders. (Heshmat, 2019)

Although Freud's views represent interesting and mainly intuitive insights that are not often depicted in other theories, although his theoretical concerns are difficult to observe and test, and they do not generate enough concrete data for quantitative testing and verification.

## ■ Distinguishing Between Substance Abuse and Mental Disorders

The APA has established widely accepted categories of diagnosis for behavioral disorders, including substance use disorder (which includes substance abuse and substance dependence). As standardized diagnostic categories, the characteristics of mental disorders have been analyzed by professional committees over many years and today are summarized in the latest version of the DSM. In addition to categories for severe psychotic disorders and other more common mental disorders, experts in the field of psychiatry have established specific diagnostic criteria for various forms of substance abuse. All patterns of drug abuse that are described in this text have a counterpart description and classification in the DSM-5 for medical professionals. For example, the DSM-5 discusses the mental disorders resulting from the use or abuse of sedatives, hypnotics, or antianxiety drugs; alcohol; narcotics; amphetamine-like drugs; cocaine; caffeine; nicotine (tobacco); hallucinogens; phencyclidine; inhalants; and cannabis (marijuana). This manual of psychiatric diagnoses discusses in detail the mental disorders related to the drug use, the side effects of medications, and the consequences of toxic exposure to these substances (APA, 2013).

Because of the similarities between and the coexistence of substance-related mental disorders and primary psychiatric disorders, it is sometimes difficult to distinguish between the two. However, for proper treatment to be rendered, the designation and characteristics of a mental disorder and a psychiatric disorder should be differentiated. According to DSM-5 criteria, both substance abuse and substance dependence, together known as *substance use disorder*, can be identified by the occurrence and consequences of pharmacological factors, the amount of time spent obtaining the substance, craving, social impairment, risky use of the substance, and tolerance and withdrawal. (These categories were defined previously in this chapter.)

According to the National Alliance on Mental Illness, the relationship between substance abuse or dependency and mental illness is often termed **dual diagnosis**. Dual diagnosis is a broad diagnosis because it often assumes multiple causes. It can range from someone developing mild depression because of binge drinking to someone's symptoms of bipolar disorder becoming more severe when that person abuses heroin during periods of mania (National Alliance on Mental Illness [NAMI], 2015).

The following relationships are possible when mental illness and substance use occur simultaneously (NAMI, 2015):

- Drugs and alcohol can be a form of self-medication.
- Drugs and alcohol can worsen underlying mental illnesses.
- Drugs and alcohol can cause a person without mental illness to experience the onset of symptoms for the first time.
- Men are more likely than women to develop a co-occurring disorder.
- Individuals with lower socioeconomic status, military veterans, and people with more general medical illnesses are more likely to develop a co-occurring disorder.

According to the DSM-5, the following information can also help distinguish between substance-use disorder and primary mental disorders: (1) personal and family medical, psychiatric, and drug histories; (2) physical examinations; and (3) laboratory tests to assess physiological functions and determine the presence or absence of drugs. However, the possibility of a primary mental disorder should not be excluded just because the patient is using drugs—remember, many drug users use drugs to self-medicate their primary psychiatric problems (alcoholrehab.com, 2015a; NIDA, 2008a). Self-medicating is a method of self-care in which an individual uses nonprescribed drugs to treat untreated and often undiagnosed medical ailments involving a psychological condition.

The coexistence of underlying psychiatric problems in a drug user is suggested by the following circumstances: (1) the psychiatric problems do not match the usual drug effects (e.g., use of marijuana usually does not cause severe psychotic behavior), (2) the psychiatric disorder was present before the patient began abusing substances, and (3) the mental disorder persists for more than four weeks after substance use

KEY TERM

**dual diagnosis**
individual who is simultaneously manifesting a mental health disorder(s) and addiction to drug use at the same time (e.g., a drug addict experiencing depression or anxiety)

ends. The DSM-5 makes it clear that clarifying the relationship between mental disorders and substances of abuse is important for proper diagnosis, treatment, and understanding (APA, 2013; NIDA 2007, 2008a).

## ▪ The Relationship Between Personality and Drug Use

Since medieval times, personality theories of increasing sophistication have been used to classify long-term behavioral tendencies or traits that appear in individuals; these traits have long been considered to be influenced by biological or chemical factors. Although such classification systems have varied widely, nearly all have shared two commonly observed dimensions of personality: introversion and extroversion. Individuals who show a predominant tendency to turn their thoughts and feelings inward rather than to direct attention outward have been considered to show the trait of *introversion*. At the opposite extreme, a tendency to seek outward activity and share feelings with others has been called *extroversion*. Of course, every individual shows a mix of such traits in varying degrees and circumstances.

In some earlier research studies, introversion and extroversion patterns have been associated with levels of neural arousal in brain-stem circuits (alcoholrehab.com, 2015b; Apostolides, 1996; Carlson, 1990; Gray, 1987), and these forms of arousal are closely associated with effects caused by drug stimulants or depressants. "For example, people with introverted personalities, and who tend to have fewer positive feelings, or be attracted to rewards in life, are more likely to abuse drugs, according to the new review. In contrast, extroverted people who have more positive emotions are less likely to abuse drugs" (Rettner, 2014).

Drugs such as cocaine, alcohol, or Prozac all affect these processes and an individual's degree of extroversion. They can artificially correct an ineffective dopamine system and make someone feel more sociable or motivated to pursue a goal. Low levels of serotonin,

## KEY TERM

**social learning theory**
theory that emphasizes how an individual learns patterns of behavior from the attitudes of others, society, and peers

correlated with depression, may make people more responsive to dopamine and more susceptible to dopamine-stimulating drug use such as the use of cocaine, alcohol, amphetamine, opiates, and nicotine (Lang, 1996).

Such research hypothesizes that people whose systems produce high levels of sensitivity to neural arousal may find high-intensity external stimuli to be painful and may react by turning inward. With these extremely high levels of sensitivity, such people may experience neurotic levels of anxiety or panic disorders. At the other extreme, individuals whose systems provide them with the lowest levels of sensitivity to neural arousal may find that moderate stimuli are inadequate to produce responses. To reach moderate levels of arousal, they may turn outward to seek high-intensity external sources of stimulation (Eysenck & Eysenck, 1985; Gray, 1987; Rousar, Brooner, Regier, & Bigelow, 1995).

Because high- and low-arousal symptoms are easy to create by using stimulants, depressants, or hallucinogens, it is possible that these personality patterns of introversion or extroversion affect how a person reacts to substances. For people whose experience is predominantly introverted or extroverted, extremes of high or low sensitivity may lead them to seek counteracting substances that become important methods of bringing experience to a level that seems bearable.

## ▪ Theories Based on Learning Processes

How are drug use patterns learned? Regarding learning, operant conditioning explains how human beings acquire new patterns of behavior by the close association or pairing of one significant reinforcing stimulus with another less significant or neutral stimulus. Also known as **social learning theory** (Bandura, 1977; explained more fully in the "Social Learning Theory" section later in this chapter), this theory emphasizes that learned associations occur in the presence of other people using drugs coupled with other, often preconceived associations with the attitudes of society and friends about drug use (Gray & Bjorklund, 2014). In this method of learning, people form expectations and become used to certain behavior patterns. This specific process of learning is known as *conditioning*, and it explains why pleasurable activities may become intimately connected with other activities that are also pleasurable, neutral, or even unpleasant.

In addition, people can turn any new behavior into a recurrent and permanent one by the process of **habituation**—repeating certain patterns of behavior until they become established or habitual.

The basic process by which learning mechanisms can lead a person into drug use is also described in Bejerot's **addiction to pleasure theory** (Bejerot, 1965, 1972, 1975; Dixon, 2015; NIDA, 1980). This theory assumes that it is biologically normal to continue a pleasure stimulus once started. Several research findings support this theory, indicating that "a strong, biologically based need for stimulation appears to make sensation seeking young adults more vulnerable to drug abuse" (Mathias 1995, p. 1). Dixon (2015) and Khantzian (1998) also support this view. Another research finding complementing this theory states, "Certain areas of the brain, when stimulated, produce pleasurable feelings. Psychoactive substances are capable of acting on these brain mechanisms to produce these sensations. These pleasurable feelings become reinforcers that drive the continued use of the substances" (Gardner, 1992, p. 43). People at highest risk for drug use and addiction are those who maintain a constant preoccupation with getting high, seek new or novel thrills in their experiences, and are known to have a relentless desire to pursue physical stimulation or dangerous behaviors; these are classified as **sensation-seeking individuals** (Grabus, 2016; Zuckerman, 2000, 2007).

Drug use may also be reinforced when it is associated with receiving affection or approval in a social setting, such as within a peer-group relationship. Initially, the use of drugs may not be important or pleasurable to the individual, but eventually the affection and social rewards experienced when drugs are used become associated with the drug. Drug use and intimacy may then become perceived as highly worthwhile.

I don't know how to explain why but an attractive part of cocaine use is the instant feeling of intimacy with others who are also snorting this drug. You just don't want to leave the scene when the lines are cut on the glass surface and people are taking turns snorting coke. Even after I have had four or five lines and the conversation is very friendly and engaging, leaving the scene because someone is waiting for you at home or even if you have to meet with someone that night does not matter. Usually, everyone is feeling high, a lot of feelings of togetherness, and open to intimate conversation. I never saw anyone getting violent or anything like that, but I hear that it can happen especially if you have a grudge against someone before doing the coke. I think that coke just makes you more open and if you are an angry person then it will just bring it out in you. My experiences have been that everyone is just so friendly and everyone just pretends not to be overly anxious to do the next line. Actually, everyone is kind of pretending, because what they really want is more powder up their nose and an unending amount of time for talking the night away. *(From Venturelli's research files, male graduate student, residing in Chicago, age 26, May 18, 2000)*

Ten years later at age 36, the author was able to interview the same interviewee:

Back then I was a graduate student the last time you interviewed me. After I completed my master's degree I worked as a financial advisor and though I gave up regular use, on rare occasions I still have a hook up for cocaine and use it. It's a small amount on nearly a year basis. Why do I still dabble in it? The pleasures I had as a graduate student are still with me is my honest answer and it's still good but back then it was so often with so many memories of the good times. The last time I did snort cocaine was over a year ago and it's only when I visit a certain friend who also intermittently uses this drug. We just briefly revisit the past and it's all-good and everything but being 10 years older, I cannot get overinvolved with this drug as I used to 10 years ago. I have a lot more at stake regarding the clientele I have built up in addition to family responsibilities. My kids growing up would not be too happy if they knew their father uses drugs and my wife

**KEY TERMS**

**habituation**
repeating certain patterns of behavior until they become established or habitual

**addiction to pleasure theory**
theory that assumes it is biologically normal to continue a pleasure stimulus once begun

**sensation-seeking individuals**
types of people who characteristically are continually seeking new or novel thrills in their experiences

would be shocked that I still dabble in this. My wife is a schoolteacher and is fully engaged with teaching her students. For me it is like revisiting something in my past but when I meet up with my friend we do it and then leave it there for about a year or so. I think it's those prior experiences and good times that bring me to spend one or two nights a year to reuse this drug. *(From Venturelli's research files, financial advisor, age 36, July 2010)*

Keep in mind that the amount of a drug taken can affect the extent of sociability, as the following interview indicates:

Yes, I did read that quote [referring to the preceding quote] about how friendly everyone is while snorting lines. Well, I bet that person does not do too much coke—maybe it is like a weekend thing. What I am trying to say is that everyone is friendly at the beginning when snorting lines, but after doing a lot of snorting, people get real quiet—they sort of geek out. You see, too much of it at any one time makes you feel overloaded. It's like an amphetamine bombardment. In the beginning, it is like a "dusting" and people can become real friendly and talkative, but after doing it for an hour or so, it gets to you. Whenever I overdo it, and it is easy to do so, I become real quiet and several times even when I tried to change my mood by having sex, I could not even "get it up" so to speak. I usually do very well when I just have a little, but too much certainly can cause the sexual desire to peak, but the follow through is an entirely different matter. Too much just geeks you out after a while. *(From Venturelli's research files, male construction worker in Indiana, age 28, June 9, 2007)*

Through the conditioning process, a pleasurable experience such as drug taking may become associated with a comforting or soothing environment. When this happens, two different outcomes may result. First, the user may feel uncomfortable taking the drug in any other environment. Second, the user may become highly accustomed or habituated to the familiar environment as part

of the drug experience. The user may not experience the same level of rush or high in this environment and may respond by taking more drugs or seeking a different environment.

Finally, through this process of conditioning and habituation, a drug user becomes accustomed to unpleasant effects of drug use such as withdrawal symptoms. Such unpleasant effects and experiences may become habituated—neutralized or less severe in their impact—so that the user can continue taking drugs without feeling or experiencing the negative effects of the drug.

## ▮ Social Psychological Learning Theories

Other aspects of reinforcement or learning theory focus on how positive social influences by drug-using peers reinforce the attraction to drugs. Social interaction, peer camaraderie, social approval, and drug use work together as positive reinforcers to sustain drug use (Akers, 1992). Thus, if the effects of drug use become personally rewarding "or become reinforcing through conditioning, the chances of continuing to use are greater than for stopping" (Akers, 1992, p. 86; Galizio, 2005; Sutton & Barto, 2018). It is through learned expectations or association with others who reinforce drug use that individuals learn the pleasures of drug taking (Becker, 1963, 1967). Similarly, if drug use leads to poor and disruptive social interactions, drug use may cease.

Note that positive reinforcers such as peers, other friends and acquaintances, family members, and drug advertisements do not act alone to incite or sustain drug use. Learning theory, as defined here, also relies on some variable amounts of imitation and trial-and-error learning methods.

Finally, we must consider **differential reinforcement**, which is defined as the ratio between favorable and unfavorable reinforcers for sustaining drug use behavior. The use and eventual abuse of drugs can vary with certain favorable or unfavorable reinforcing experiences. The primary determining conditions are:

- the amount of exposure to drug-using peers versus non–drug-using peers,
- the general preference for drug use in a particular neighborhood or community,
- the age of initial use (younger adolescents are more greatly affected than are older adolescents), and
- the frequency of drug use among peers.

**KEY TERM**

**differential reinforcement**
ratio between reinforcers, both favorable and disfavorable, for sustaining drug use behavior

# Major Theoretical Explanations: Sociological

Sociological explanations for drug use share important commonalities with psychological explanations under social learning theories. The main features distinguishing psychological explanations from sociological explanations are that the former focus more on how the internal states of the drug user are affected by social relationships within families, peers, and other close and more distant relationships; sociological explanations focus on how factors external to the drug user affect drug use. Such outside forces include the types of families, adopted lifestyles of peer groups, and neighborhoods and communities in which avid drug users reside. The sociological perspective views the motivation for drug use as largely determined by the types and quality of bonds (attachment vs. detachment) that the drug user or potential drug user has with significant others and with the social environment in general. The degree of influence and involvement with external factors affecting the individual compared with the influence exerted by internal states distinguishes sociological from psychological analyses.

As previously stated, no one biological or psychological theory can adequately explain why most people use drugs. People differ from one another in terms of personality, motivational factors, upbringing, learned priority of values and attitudes, and problems faced. Because of these differences, many responses and reasons determine why people take drugs, which results in a plurality of theoretical explanations. Furthermore, the diverse perspectives of biology, psychology, and sociology offer their own explanations for drug use and abuse.

There are two sets of sociological theories: social influence and social structural. **Social influence theories** focus on microscopic explanations that concentrate on the roles played by significant others and their impact on an individual. **Structural influence theories** focus on macroscopic explanations of drug use and the assumption that the organizational structure of society has a major independent impact on an individual's use of drugs. The next sections examine these theories.

## ■ Social Influence Theories

The theories presented in this section are (1) social learning, (2) the role of significant others in socialization, (3) labeling, and (4) subculture theories. These theories share a common theme: An individual's motivation to seek drugs is caused by social influences or social pressures.

### SOCIAL LEARNING THEORY

Social learning theory explains drug use as learned behavior. Conventional learning occurs through imitation, trial and error, improvisation, rewarded behavior, and cognitive mental associations and processes (Akers & Sellers, 2008; Liska & Messner, 1999; Ritzer & Goodman, 2010; Ritzer & Stepnisky, 2017). Social learning theory focuses directly on how drug use and abuse are learned through interaction with other drug users. "[The] . . . motivations to use drugs are learned through associations with significant others in small, informal groups such as peer groups and families. It is in these intimate settings that individuals acquire attitudes regarding drugs and their use and observe the behavior of others" (Bahr & Hoffmann, 2016, p. 200).

This theory emphasizes the pervasive influence of *primary groups*—that is, groups that share a high amount of intimacy and spontaneity and whose members are emotionally entwined. Families and long-term friends are examples of primary groups. In contrast, secondary groups share segmented relationships in which interaction is based on prescribed roles. An example of a secondary group is the relationship between a customer and a salesclerk in a grocery store or relationships between employees scattered throughout a corporation. Social learning theory addresses a type of interaction that is highly specific. This type of interaction involves learning specific motives, techniques, and appropriate meanings that are commonly attached to a particular type of drug.

## KEY TERMS

**social influence theories**
sociological theories that view a person's day-to-day social relations as a primary cause for drug use

**structural influence theories**
theories that view the structural organization of a society, peer group, or subculture as directly responsible for drug use

The following are examples of first-time users learning drug-using techniques from their social circles:

The first time I tried smoking weed, nothing much happened. I always thought it was like smoking a cigarette. When the joint came around the first time, I refused it. The next time it came around, I noticed everyone was looking at me. So, I took the joint and started to inhale, then exhale. My friend sitting next to me said something to the effect, "Dude, hold it in; don't waste it. This is good weed and we don't have that much between us." Right after that, we did some "shotguns." This is where someone exhales directly into your mouth—lips to lips. My friend filled my lungs with his exhaled weed breath. After the first comment about holding it in, I started to watch how everyone was inhaling and realized that you really don't smoke weed like an ordinary cigarette; you have to hold in the smoke. *(From Venturelli's research files, male high school student in a small Midwestern town, age 16, February 15, 1997)*

I first started using drugs, mostly alcohol and pot, because my best friend in high school was using drugs. My best friend Tim [a pseudonym] learned from his older sister. Before I actually tried pot, Tim kept telling me how great it was to be high on dope; he said it was much better than beer. I was really nervous the first time I tried pot with Tim and another friend, even though I heard so much detail about it from Tim. The first time I tried it, it was a complete letdown. The second time (the next day, I think it was), I remember I was talking about a teacher we had and in the middle of the conversation, I remember how everything appeared different. I started feeling happy and while listening to Tim as he poked jokes about the teacher, I started to hear the background music more clearly than ever before. By the time the music ended and a new CD started, I knew I was high. *(From Venturelli's research files, male student at a private liberal arts college in the Midwest, age 22, February 15, 1997)*

First time I tried acid [LSD], I didn't know what to expect. Schwa [a pseudonym] told me it was a very different high from grass [marijuana]. After munching on one "square" [one dose of LSD]—after about 20 minutes—I looked at Schwa and he started laughing and said, "Feelin' the effects, Ki-ki?" I said, "Is this it? Is this what it feels like? I feel weird." With a devious grin . . . Schwa said, "Yep. We are now on the runway, ready to take off. Just wait a little while longer, it's going to get better and better. Fasten your seat belts!" *(From Venturelli's research files, male, age 33, May 6, 1996)*

Learning to perceive the effects of the drug is the second major outcome in the process of becoming a regular user. Here the ability to feel the authentic effects of the drug is being learned. The more experienced drug users in the group impart their knowledge to naïve first-time users. The coaching information they provide describes how to recognize the euphoric effects of the drug.

I was just curious after watching my roommate with his friends frequently passing around a joint and remember always saying "I'll pass on that" many times. One night I just tried it with my roommate late at night. I really did not know how to even smoke it, but my roommate made more coaching comments as I was taking hits. The first few puffs nothing happened, but after I took in two huge hits, and coughing as it nearly choked me, I started to feel different. I had kind of a mellow feeling. I was talking about something and in the middle of the conversation I started to focus on everything around me like I was in some kind of trance, not heavy, but my mind was in several places as I spoke. After a few moments, I said, "I feel different not like I drank alcohol but just feel different." My roommate smiled and said, "You like the feeling?" I said I did not know but there was nothing bad in my feelings about what I had just done. It was like a change in the way I was processing input coming in. I remember saying that I felt kind of like light-headed and relaxed. My roommate said something like "Welcome to the world of marijuana, Mr. Schaffer [pseudonym]!" We just both laughed. *(From Venturelli's research files, male attending a small, private liberal arts college in the Midwest, age 18, May 21, 2010)*

Another example of learning to perceive the effects:

One night several of us wanted to try weed so at my college dorm we went to see a friend of mine who always had plenty of weed so we could try some. Ron was a new friend who the day before agreed to let me and two of my guys on my dorm floor smoke some up. Two out of three of us had never smoked weed and it wasn't long before he lit up his little pipe and all four of us took in hits. We were passing it around and during the first few hits I did not feel anything at all and being a nonsmoker I watched my other friend who smokes cigarettes inhale the marijuana so I could also smoke it up. After two hits nothing was happening. However, after Ron got up to turn up the music playing on his computer and at that moment I was thinking that maybe nothing is going to happen. As I was thinking that maybe I was not inhaling it properly I suddenly started to feel different and within seconds the feelings were more intense. Definitely reality had gone through a change! At the same time I also felt a little freaked out because I did not know if others were having similar experiences. A few minutes later I finally blurted out "Hey, I am high on marijuana!" Suddenly everyone was amused and one friend of mine roared with laughter. As soon as I made this comment everyone became very animated and acted much sociable. I remember feeling like I was thinking on multiple levels—at times my mind was racing with many different thoughts. It was so different from an alcohol high. It definitely was more of a mental high than a body high. I started out being skeptical of the high and was hoping that the effect would weaken, but as everyone was enjoying themselves I changed my mind that the effects were positive and feeling this different was a new experience. I think other people experiencing the high helped knowing I was not alone and my other friends were in the same state of mind. In answering your question (asked by the interviewer) whether I used this drug in the days and weeks ahead I would have to say yes I did but I would only do it on weekends late at night with my roommate hours before going to sleep. No, I did not become attached to it because I am pretty busy with school and work and keep a busy schedule. I tried doing some homework one night while feeling the effects of weed but I ended up not competing much because getting high distracts me from any work I have to do and usually ended up doing nothing and just chilling out. With my heavy schedule of classes during this last semester and work schedule, I don't have any time during the week to waste away. Did I develop any kind of attachment to the pleasant feelings from a marijuana high? Not

really, maybe a very weak attachment because throughout the week I knew I would fall behind in not doing my homework. I came to the conclusion that although getting high was a lot of fun, I planned ahead when I would do the drug so that it did not interfere with other things that had to be completed. A good thing was that my roommate was a lot more hesitant in using this drug for fear of drug testing at his part-time job. In fact, most times I did this drug with another dorm student who was an avid user. I also think that if my roommate liked the drug more and was not so preoccupied with completing his degree in 3 instead of 4 years I would have used it much more often. *(From Venturelli's research files, male attending a private liberal arts college in the Midwest, age 22, November 2015)*

Once drug use has begun, continuing the behavior involves learning the following sequence: (1) identifying where and from whom the drug can be purchased, (2) maintaining steady contact with suppliers of the drug (i.e., drug dealers), (3) maintaining the secrecy of use from authority figures and casual non–drug-using acquaintances, (4) evaluating one's experiences with the drug as pleasurable, (5) using with more frequency, and (6) replacing non–drug-using friends with drug-using friends.

## ROLE OF SIGNIFICANT OTHERS

After a pattern of drug use has been established, the learning process plays a role in sustaining drug-taking behavior. Edwin Sutherland (1947) (see also Akers, 2009; Inderbitzin, Bates, & Gainey, 2013; Liska & Messner, 1999), a pioneering criminologist in sociology, believed that the mastery of criminal behavior depended on the frequency, duration, priority, and intensity of contact with others who are involved in similar behavior (Heitzeg, 1996; Venniro et al., 2018). This theory can also be applied to drug-taking behavior.

In applying Sutherland's principles of social learning, which he called *differential association theory*, the focus is on how other drug-using members of social groups reward criminal behavior and under what conditions this deviance is perceived as important and pleasurable.

Becker and Sutherland's theories explain why adolescents may use psychoactive drugs. Essentially, both theories say that the use of drugs is learned during intimate interaction with others who serve as a primary group. (See "Here and

This child is role-playing largely by imitating the habits of a significant other.

Now: Symptoms of Drug and Alcohol Abuse" for information on how the role of significant others can determine a child's disposition toward or away from illicit drug uses and "Here and Now: How Not to Encourage Your Teen to Use Drugs.")

Learning theory also explains how adults are taught the *motivation* for using a particular type of drug. This learning occurs through influences such as drug advertising, with its emphasis on testimonials by avid users, medical experts, and actors and actresses portraying physicians or nurses. Listeners, viewers, and readers who experience such commercials promoting a particular brand name of OTC drug are flooded with the necessary motives, preferred techniques, and appropriate attitudes for consuming drugs. When drug

advertisements and medical experts recommend particular drugs for specific ailments, in effect they are authoritatively persuading viewers, listeners, or readers that taking a drug will soothe or cure the medical problem presented (Joyce, 2018).

## ARE DRUG USERS MORE LIKELY TO BE DEVIOUS?

Social scientists—primarily sociologists and social psychologists—believe that many social development patterns are closely linked to drug use. Based on the age when an adolescent begins to consume alcohol and other drugs, predictions can be made about his or her sexual behavior, academic performance, and other behaviors such as lying, cheating, fighting, and using marijuana. Similar predictions can be made when the adolescent begins using marijuana. More recent studies (CBHSQ, 2015; CESAR, 2011) show a strong relationship between adolescent behavior problems and alcohol use.

**Figure 2.1** shows the percentages of adolescents (ages 12 to 17) using alcohol, cigarettes, marijuana, and other illicit drugs and engaging in various types of deviant behavior—namely, carrying a handgun, selling illegal drugs, stealing, and fighting. Highest to lowest percentages indicate the following (CBHSQ, 2015):

- 64.3% of adolescents using illicit drugs, 61.8% using marijuana, 42.6% using alcohol, and 34.5% using cigarettes sold illegal drugs.

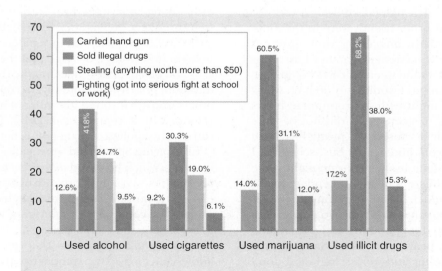

**FIGURE 2.1**  Percentages of delinquent behaviors in past year and past use of selected substances among persons aged 12 to 17 in Center for Behavioral Health Statistics and Quality (CBHSQ).

Data from Center for Behavioral Health Statistics and Quality (CBHSQ). (2018). *2017 National Survey on Drug Use and Health (NSDUH): Detailed tables*. Rockville, MD: Substance Abuse and Mental Health Services Administration (SAMHSA).

# HERE AND NOW
## How Not to Encourage Your Teen to Use Drugs

Parents may unwittingly encourage their teens to recreationally experiment with alcohol and other drugs. The following four factors may encourage teens to recreationally experiment with alcohol and other drugs of abuse.

1. *Being unclear or not voicing your opinion about drug use*: Before your child becomes affected by peer pressure, you should take a stance on drug use. Clearly indicate that experimentation with recreational drug use is not acceptable (Sack, 2013). Be certain to create an open atmosphere about your teen's opinions about drug use. If there is a family history of drug or alcohol problems, more concentrated—but not overbearing—discussions should be a primary goal.

2. *Not practicing what you preach*: Be a positive model for your child. "Children pay closer attention to what you do than what you say. Even fiercely independent teens are adversely affected by their parents, so if you drink excessively or use drugs, don't be surprised if your teen follows suit. Having a parent who uses drugs is a strong predictor of adolescent substance abuse" (Sack, 2013). Similarly, never provide alcohol or any other drugs to your teen and his or her friends in your home.

3. *Denying suspicions about your teen's probable drug use*: Bringing up these suspicions and discussing your suspicions with your teen can often be unpleasant. These suspicions frequently result from changes in your teen such as "moodiness, new friends, much less or much more energy, weight loss or gain, or inattention to personal hygiene" (Sack, 2013). Although at times adolescence is difficult to understand, remaining actively involved with your teen allows you as parent to witness firsthand beginnings in the use of drugs. At this time, denial may be more comfortable than voicing your suspicions, but denial can become deadly because drug use more than likely will advance to more dangerous levels.

4. *Waiting to get help*: The period of adolescence can be filled with challenges. "From moment to moment it can be difficult to know the right thing to do or say, but there are a few ways you can't go wrong. Spend lots of quality time with your teen and if something seems amiss, talk about it. For those occasions when talking doesn't get you anywhere, get help. Your teen's drug use isn't your fault, but you are a critical part of the solution" (Sack, 2013).

Data from Sack, D. (2013, March 4). 5 things parents do that may encourage teen substance abuse. Huffington Post. Retrieved from http://www.huffingtonpost.com/david-sack-md/teen-substance-abuse_b_2792838.html

---

- 40.8% of adolescents using illicit drugs, 35.1% using marijuana, 26.6% using alcohol, and 21.2% using cigarettes were involved in stealing.
- 16% of adolescents using illicit drugs, 13.9% using marijuana, 12.8% using alcohol, and 12.6% using cigarettes carried a handgun.
- 16.2% of adolescents using illicit drugs, 12.2% using marijuana, 9.9% using alcohol, and 9.1% using cigarettes engaged in physical fighting.

**Figure 2.2** shows varied amounts of drug (substance) use among Washington, D. C., public high school students aged 16 and older by academic performance. Specifically the use of marijuana, alcohol, and synthetic marijuana; smoking of little cigars (*cigarillos*) and using electronic vapor products within 30 days of being questioned steadily increases as grade performance decreases and the use of some drugs dramatically increases, with students having mostly D's and F's (see Figure 2.2).

Other notable findings from the 2017 District of Columbia Youth Risk Behavior Survey Surveillance Reports include the following:

- About one in 13 middle-school students report having had their first drink of alcohol, other than a few sips, at age eight or younger.
- Male and female high school students used marijuana at about the same rates, though males were more likely to be heavy users (40 or more times in the preceding 30 days).
- Lesbian, gay, and bisexual youths were disproportionately represented in youths who used alcohol, tobacco, and other drugs.
- Of students who reported drinking and driving, one in five did so frequently (on six or more occasions in the past 30 days).
- More than 15 percent of all high school students have used prescription pain medicine without a doctor's prescription or differently than how a doctor told them to use it.

# HERE AND NOW

## Symptoms of Drug and Alcohol Abuse

The following are profiles of children who are less likely and more likely, respectively, to use and abuse drugs.

### Less Likely to Use Drugs

- Child comes from an integrated functional family.
- Family has a clearly stated policy against drug use.
- Child has some amount of religious conviction.
- Child is an independent thinker and not easily swayed by peer pressure.
- Parents know the child's friends and the friends' parents.
- Child often invites friends into the house and their behavior is open, not secretive.
- Child is busy and productive and pursues many interests.
- Child has a good, secure feeling of self.
- Parents are comfortable with their own use of alcohol, drugs, and pills; set a good example in using these substances; and are comfortable in discussing their use.
- Parents set a good example in handling crises.
- Child maintains at least average grades and good working relationships with teachers.

### More Likely to Use Drugs

*Note:* A child will usually display more than one of the following symptoms when experimenting with drugs. Please remember that any number of the symptoms could also be the result of a physical impairment or disorder.

- Red, watery eyes; pupils larger or smaller than usual; blank stare;
- abrupt change in behavior (e.g., from highly active to passive, loss of interest in previously pursued activities such as sports or hobbies);
- diminished drive and ambition;
- moodiness;
- shortened attention span;
- impaired communication such as slurred speech or jumbled thinking;

- significant change in quality of schoolwork;
- deteriorating judgment and loss of short-term memory;
- distinct lessening of family closeness and warmth;
- suddenly popular with new friends who are older and unknown to family members;
- isolation from family members (hiding in bedroom or locking bedroom door);
- sneaking out of the house;
- secretive or suspicious behavior;
- sudden carelessness regarding appearance;
- inappropriate overreaction to even mild criticism;
- secretiveness about whereabouts and missing personal possessions;
- use of words that are odd and unfamiliar;
- secretiveness or desperation for money;
- rapid weight loss or appetite loss;
- "drifting off" beyond normal daydreaming;
- extreme behavioral changes such as hallucinations, violence, and unconsciousness that could indicate a dangerous situation close at hand and a need for fast medical attention;
- nonprescribed or unidentifiable pills;
- unfamiliar looking devices (e.g., smoking paraphernalia, pills, smaller plastic baggies or pipes, or other hidden paraphernalia in a child's or adolescent's bedroom);
- articles missing from the house (child could be stealing money or household articles to sell or trade for drugs);
- sudden appearance and possession of new items in the teen's bedroom—often electronic items—from money spent, bartered, or exchanged from drug dealing;
- unexplained need for money or contradictory explanations regarding the need for money; and
- making secretive phone calls or disappearing for long periods of time.

Data from L. A. W. Publications. (1985). *Let's all work to fight drug abuse* (p. 38). Addison, TX: C&L Printing; Drug Strategies. (1999). *Santa Barbara profile: Alcohol, tobacco, and other drugs.* Washington, DC: Drug Strategies; Liddle, H. (2001). *AAMFT consumer update: Adolescent substance abuse.* Alexandria, VA: American Association for Marriage and Family Therapy; Witmer, D. (2013). *Teen drug use warning signs.* About.com. Retrieved from http://parentingteens.about .com/cs/drugsofabuse/a/driug_abuse20.htm; Partnership for Drug-Free Kids. (2019). *Where families find answers.* New York, NY: Partnership to End Addiction. Retrieved from https://drugfree.org/article/look-for-warning-signs/. Accessed August 13, 2019.

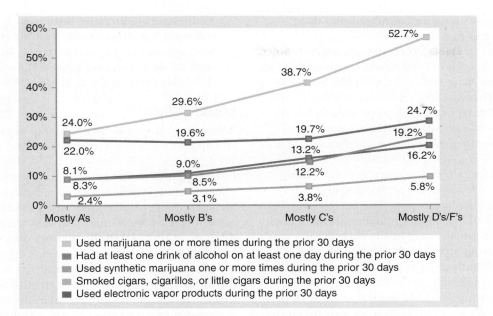

**FIGURE 2.2** Substance Use Among High School Students, by Academic Performance.

Data from Office of the State Superintendent of Education (OSSE). (2017). *District of Columbia youth risk behavior survey surveillance report (YRBS)*. Washington, DC: Author. Retrieved from https://osse.dc.gov/sites/default/files/dc/sites/osse
/publication/attachments/

- And, as Figure 2.2 shows that the use of marijuana, cigar, and electronic vapor products are all significantly associated with academic achievement among high schoolers.

Other studies show that early intense use of alcohol or marijuana presages less conventional behavior, greater susceptibility to peer influence, increased delinquency, and lower achievement in school. In general, drug abusers have 14 characteristics in common:

1. Drug use usually follows clear-cut developmental steps and sequences. Use of legal drugs such as alcohol and cigarettes almost always precedes use of illegal drugs.

2. Habitual use of marijuana is believed to cause an **amotivational syndrome** manifested by personality changes.[2] This change is characterized by apathy, lack of interest, and inability to accomplish or difficulty accomplishing goals. Past research also clearly shows that marijuana use is often responsible for attention and short-term

memory impairment and confusion (NIDA, 1996).

3. Immaturity, maladjustment, or insecurity usually precede the use of marijuana and other illicit drugs.

4. Those more likely to try illicit drugs, especially before age 12, usually have a history of poor school performance and classroom disobedience.

5. Delinquent or repetitive deviant types of behavior usually precede involvement with illicit drugs.

6. A set of values and attitudes that facilitates the development of deviant behavior exists before the person tries illicit drugs.

7. A social setting in which drug use is common, such as communities and neighborhoods in which peers use drugs indiscriminately, is likely to reinforce and increase the predisposition to drug use.

8. Drug-induced behaviors and drug-related attitudes of peers are usually among the

[2]Some argue that perhaps a general lack of ambition (lethargic behavior) may precede rather than result from marijuana use or that amotivational syndrome is present in some heavy marijuana users before the initial use of this drug; when the drug is used, the syndrome becomes more pronounced. In any case, some drug researchers believe that when marijuana is used steadily, it co-occurs with amotivational syndrome.

**KEY TERM**

**amotivational syndrome**
controversial syndrome whose proponents claim that heavy marijuana use causes a lack of motivation and reduced productivity

strongest predictors of subsequent drug involvement.

9. Children who feel their parents are distant from their emotional needs are more likely to become drug addicted (see "Here and Now: Does Divorce Affect Adolescent Drug Use?").

10. The younger the adolescent is when he/she begins to regularly use illicit drugs, the greater the probability of accelerated use and addiction to drug use later in life. Likewise, the older people are when they start using drugs, the lower the probability of accelerated use and addiction. The period of greatest risk of initiation and habitual use of illicit drugs is usually over by the early 20s.

11. The family structure has changed, with substantially more than half (58.6%) of all women (72 million) in the United States now working outside the home (U.S. Department of Labor, 2011). A higher divorce rate has led to many children being raised in single-parent households. How the lack of a stay-at-home parent or how membership in a single-family household affects the quality of childcare and nurturing is difficult to assess.

12. Mobility obstructs a sense of permanency, and it contributes to a lack of self-esteem. Often, when children are repeatedly moved from one location to another, their community becomes nothing more than a group of strangers. They may have little pride in their home or community and have no commitment to society.

13. Among minority members, a major factor involved in drug dependence is a feeling of powerlessness because of discrimination based on race, social standing, or other attributes. Groups subject to discrimination have a disproportionately high rate of unemployment and below-average incomes. In the United States, approximately 15.6 million children (21%) are reared in poverty (Landau, 2010). The adults they have as role models may be unemployed and experience feelings of powerlessness. Higher rates of delinquency and drug addiction occur in such settings.

14. Abusers who become highly involved in selling drugs begin by witnessing that drug trafficking is a lucrative business, especially in rundown neighborhoods. In some communities, selling drugs seems to be the only available route to real economic success (Jones, 1996; Shelden, Tracy, & Brown, 2001).

## LABELING THEORY

Although controversy continues over whether labeling is a theory or a perspective (Akers 1968, 1992; Heitzeg, 1996; Plummer, 1979), this text takes the position that labeling is a theory (Cheron 2001; Hewitt & Shulman, 2010; Liska & Messner, 1999), primarily because it explains something extremely important with respect to drug use. Although **labeling theory** does not fully explain *why* initial drug use occurs, it does detail the processes by which many people come to view themselves as socially deviant from others. Note that the terms *deviant* (in cases of individuals) and *deviance* (in cases of behavior) are sociologically defined as involving the violation of significant social norms held by conventional society. The terms are not used in a judgmental manner, nor are the individuals judged to be immoral or "sick"; instead, the terms refer to an absence of the patterns of behavior expected by conventional society.

Labeling theory says that other people whose opinions we value have a determining influence over our self-image (Best & Luckenbill, 1994; Goode, 2010; Liska & Messner, 1999). (For an example of how labeling theory applies to real-life situations, see "Case in Point: Specific Signs of Marijuana Use.")

Implied in this theory is the idea that we exert a limited amount of control over the image we portray. In contrast, members of society, especially those we consider to be significant others, have much greater influence and power in defining or redefining our self-image. The image we have of ourselves is vested in the people we admire and look to for guidance and advice. If these people come to define our actions as deviant, then their definition becomes incorporated as a "fact" of our reality.

We can summarize labeling theory by saying that the labels we use to describe people have a profound influence on their self-perceptions. For example, imagine a fictitious individual named Billy. Initially, Billy does not see himself as a compulsive drug user but as an occasional recreational drug user. Let us also assume that Billy is humorous, unpretentious, and outspoken about his drug use and likes to exaggerate the amount of marijuana he smokes on a daily basis.

### KEY TERM

**labeling theory**
theory emphasizing that other people's perceptions directly influence one's self-image

# HERE AND NOW
## Does Divorce Affect Adolescent Drug Use?

"When parents make a decision to divorce . . . , children are expected to cope with the decision. Except in cases involving abuse, it is rare that children will thrive during a divorce. The impact of divorce is that children will have problems and experience symptoms" (Brooks, 2019; Conner, 2011). One major symptom listed by Conner (see also Doherty & Needle, 1991; Kelly, 2000), a clinical psychologist, is drug or alcohol abuse. Further, as an example of how drug users may be affected by socialization, a study conducted by Needle (Needle, Su, & Doherty, 1990; see also Conner, 2011; NIDA, 1990; Siegel & Senna, 1994) found higher drug use among adolescents whose parents divorced (also see Heritage Foundation, 2016). According to the study, children who are adolescents when their parents' divorce exhibit more extensive drug use and experience more drug-related health, legal, and other problems than their peers (Heritage Foundation, 2016). This study linked the extent of teens' drug use to their age at the time of their parents' divorce. Teenagers whose parents divorce were found to use more drugs and experience more drug-related problems than two other groups of adolescents: those who were age 10 or younger when their parents divorced, and those whose parents remained married.

This study has important implications for drug abuse prevention efforts. Basically, it says not everyone is at the same risk for drug use. People at greater risk can be identified, and programs should be developed to meet their special needs.

In this research project, drug use among all adolescents increased over time. However, drug use was higher among adolescents whose parents had divorced when their children were either preteens or teenagers. Drug use was highest for those teens whose parents divorced during their children's adolescent years. Such families also reported more physical problems, family disputes, and arrests.

The research results showed that distinct gender differences existed in the way that divorce affected adolescent drug use, whether the divorce occurred during the offspring's childhood or in his or her adolescence. Males whose parents divorced reported more drug use and drug-related problems than females. Females whose caretaking parents remarried experienced increased drug use after the remarriage. By contrast, males whose caretaking parents remarried reported a decrease in drug-related problems following the remarriage.

The researchers caution that these findings may have limited applicability because most of the families studied were white and had middle- to high-income levels. Needle also notes that the results should not be interpreted as an argument in favor of the nuclear family. Overall, divorce affects adolescents in complex ways, and remarriage can influence drug-using behavior. When disruptions occur during adolescence, such turmoil can "trigger" a desire for extensive recreational licit and illicit drug use, often leading to drug abuse.

Data from Conner, M. G. (2011, August 24). *Children during divorce*. Retrieved from http://crisiscounseling.com/TraumaLoss/DivorceChildren.htm; Heritage Foundation. (2016). *Family and adolescent well-being*. Washington, DC: The Heritage Foundation. Retrieved from http://www.familyfacts.org/briefs/34/family-and-adolescent-well-being; Needle, R. H., Su, S. S., & Doherty, W. J. (1990). Divorce, remarriage, and adolescent substance use: A prospective longitudinal study. *Journal of Marriage and the Family, 52*, 157–159; National Institute on Drug Abuse (NIDA). (1990, Summer). Study finds higher use among adolescents whose parents divorce. *NIDA Notes, 5*, 10; Siegel, L. J., & Senna, J. J. (1994). *Juvenile delinquency: Theory, practice and law*. St. Paul, MN: West.

Slowly, Billy's friends begin to perceive him as a "real stoner." According to labeling theory, what happens to Billy? Because of being noticed when "high," his self-presentation and the comments he makes about the pleasures of drug use, his friends may begin to reinforce the exaggerated image of a drug user. At first, Billy may enjoy the reflected image of a "big-time" drug user, but after nearly all of his peers maintain a constant exaggerated image, his projected image may turn negative, especially when his friends show disrespect for his opinions. In this example, labeling theory predicts that Billy's perception

of himself will begin to mirror the consistent perception expressed by his accusers. If he is unsuccessful in eradicating the addict image or, in this example, the "stoner" image, Billy will reluctantly concur with the label that has been thrust on him. Or, to strive for a self-image as an occasional marijuana user, Billy may abandon his peers so that he can become acceptable once more in the eyes of other people.

An important originator of labeling theory is Edwin Lemert (Lemert, 1951; Liska & Messner, 1999; Williams & McShane, 1999), who distinguished between two types of deviance:

► **CASE IN POINT**

## Specific Signs of Marijuana Use

This excerpt, from the author's files, illustrates labeling theory:

> After my mom found out, she never brought it up again. I thought the incident was over—dead, gone, and buried. Well . . . it wasn't over at all. My mom and dad must have agreed that I couldn't be trusted anymore. I'm sure she was regularly going through my stuff in my room to see if I was still smoking dope. Even my grandparents acted strangely whenever the news on television would report about the latest drug bust in Chicago. Several times that I can't ever forget were when we were together and I could hear the news broadcast on TV from my room about some drug bust. There they all were whispering about me. My grandma asking if I "quitta the dope." One night, I overheard my mother reassure my dad and grandmother that I no longer was using dope. You can't believe how embarrassed I was that my own family was still thinking that I was a dope fiend. They thought I was addicted to pot like a junkie is addicted to heroin! I can tell you that I would never lay such a guilt trip on my kids if I ever have kids. I remember that for [two] years after the time I was honest enough to tell my mom that I had tried pot, they would always whisper about me, give me the third degree whenever I returned late from a date, and go through my room looking for dope. They acted as if I was hooked on drugs. I remember that for

> a while back then I would always think that if they think of me as a drug addict, I might as well get high whenever my friends "toke up." They should have taken me at my word instead of sneaking around my personal belongings. I should have left syringes lying around my room!

Approximately 17 years after this interview was conducted, this author was able to revisit the same interviewee, who at the time of this second interview was 37 years of age. After showing him the preceding excerpt, he commented,

> You know, Professor, while today marijuana use is no longer such a big deal, I can still tell you that it took years to finally convince my family that I was not a "big time drug user." Though my grandma is now dead, I can still remember how she would look at me when I would tell her that I just smoke it once in a while. I knew she never believed that I was just an occasional user by the look on her face, when she would ask ". . . and last night when you went out, did you smoke the dope again?" My mom, who is now living with her sister, still mentions how I went wild those days when I was drugging it up! Yes, I have to say it had a big impact on me when my own family believed I was a drug addict back then. I will never forget those looks from my family every time I would walk into the house on weekends when I would return from a night out with my friends.

Interview with a 20-year-old male college student at a private university in the Midwest, conducted by Peter Venturelli on November 19, 1993. Second interview with same interviewee male, 37 years of age, June 2010.

primary and secondary. **Primary deviance** is inconsequential deviance, which occurs without having a lasting impression on the perpetrator. Generally, most first-time violations of law, for

**primary deviance**
any type of initial deviant behavior in which the perpetrator does not identify with the deviance

**secondary deviance**
any type of deviant behavior in which the perpetrator identifies with the deviance

example, are primary deviations. Whether the suspected or accused individual has committed the deviant act does not matter. What matters is whether the individual identifies with the deviant behavior.

**Secondary deviance** develops when the individual begins to identify and perceive him- or herself as deviant. The moment this transition occurs, deviance shifts from being primary to secondary. Many adolescents casually experiment with drugs, but if they begin to perceive themselves as drug users, then this behavior is virtually impossible to eradicate. The same holds true with OTC drug abuse. The moment an individual believes that he or she feels better after using a particular drug, the greater the likelihood that he or she will consistently use the drug.

Howard Becker (1963) believed that certain negative status positions (such as alcoholic, mental patient, ex-felon, criminal, drug addict, and so on) are so powerful that they dominate others (Pontell, 1996; Williams & McShane, 1999). In the earlier example, if people who are important to Billy call him a "druggie," this name becomes a powerful label that takes precedence over any other status positions Billy may occupy. This label becomes Billy's **master status**—that he is a mindless "stoner." Even if Billy is also an above-average biology major, an excellent musician, and a dependable and caring person, such factors become secondary because his primary status has been recast as a "druggie." Furthermore, once a powerful label is attached, it becomes much easier for the individual to uphold the image dictated by members of society and simply act out the role expected by significant others. Master status labels distort an individual's public image because other people expect consistency in role performance.

Once a negative master status has been attached to an individual's public image, according to labeling theorist Edwin Schur, retrospective interpretation occurs. **Retrospective interpretation** is a form of "reconstitution of individual character or identity" (Schur, 1971, p. 52). It largely involves redefining a person's

image within a particular social stereotype, category, or group (see cartoon as an illustration). In the eyes of his peers, Billy is now an emotional, intelligent, yet weird or "freaky" stoner.

Finally, William I. Thomas's (1923) contribution to labeling theory can be summarized in the following theorem: "If men define situations as real, they are real in their consequences" (p. 19). Thus, in applying this dictum by Thomas to drug use, when someone is perceived as a drug user, the perception becomes the reality of that person's character and, in turn, shapes his or her self-perception.

## SUBCULTURE THEORY

**Subculture theory** speaks to the role of peer pressure and the behavior resulting from peer group influences. In all groups, there are certain members who are more popular and respected and, as a result, exert more social influence than other peer members. Often, these more socially endowed members are group leaders, task leaders, or emotional leaders who possess greater ability to influence others. Drug use that results from peer pressure demonstrates the extent to which these more popular and respected leaders can influence and pressure others to initially use or abuse drugs. The following four excerpts from interviews illustrate subculture theory:

I started using drugs at a young age. I was [eight] years old when my friend Linda and I would smoke cigarettes while my mom and dad were running the bar business. I would take a pack of cigarettes from my dad's tavern and we would go into a little clubhouse we built out of plywood and we would smoke one cigarette after another hidden in that little clubhouse my older brother built for me. It was not long before I would also sneak in

Courtesy of Alex Silvestri.

This cartoon illustrates the reflective process in retrospective interpretation that often occurs in daily conversations when we think that our unspoken thoughts are undetectable and hidden. In reality, however, these innermost thoughts are clearly conveyed through body language and nonverbal gestures.

**KEY TERMS**

**master status**
major status position in the eyes of others that clearly identifies an individual—for example, doctor, professor, alcoholic, heroin addict

**retrospective interpretation**
social psychological process of redefining a person in light of a major status position—for example, homosexual, physician, professor, alcoholic, convicted felon, or mental patient

**subculture theory**
explains drug use as a peer-generated activity

some liquor along with cigarettes and Linda and I would get buzzed on the alcohol and cigarettes and we would giggle and laugh while we were sitting in this little hutlike place and we thought we were having so much fun. My mom and dad never checked on us while we were in the hut and if I was wanted by my mom or dad they would call out my name from the back entrance door of the back kitchen and I either yelled back I am here or at times I would stroll in—really check-in quickly—and they would be busy with the business never suspecting anything was wrong. We did this a few times a week and it was like a secret we both kept away from our parents. I always saw everyone was drinking and smoking in my dad's bar so why not do the same with my friend Linda? A few years later, I did the same thing with my two male friends when I would stop by their parents' apartments during the weekdays when their parents were at work. I was always the kid who had the cigarettes and we would go for walks down a nearby alley and I would supply the smokes. Now that I think about this we were lucky we never got caught with our secret behavior. *(From Venturelli's research files, male office worker, residing in Chicago, age 47, July 12, 2015)*

A second account:

I first started messing around with alcohol in high school. In order to be part of the crowd, we would sneak out during lunchtime at school and get "high." About [six] months after we started drinking, we moved on to other drugs. . . . Everyone in high school belongs to a clique, and my clique was heavy into drugs. We had a lot of fun being high throughout the day. We would party constantly. Basically, in college, it's the same thing. *(From Venturelli's research files, male student at a small, religiously affiliated private liberal arts college in the Southeast, age 19, February 9, 1985)*

A third account:

I remember Henri was from Holland, and he never tried coke. One night all three of us were at Joe's apartment and Joe had a hefty amount of coke that he brought out from his bedroom. We started snorting it and when it was Henri's turn he said, "I never did this and maybe I shouldn't do it now." Paul, who was also a good friend of Henri, said "Come on

Henri, it won't do that much to you." Henri looked at each of us and shot back with "Okay, I will try it once." Well, that night Henri had about as much coke as the two of us had. It was all okay until Henri suddenly got sick and vomited a good number of times. We spent a good part of the night taking care of Henri making sure he did not pass out and made sure to get him back to his apartment and call it a night. Henri was just not used to the coke and we probably let him have too much being his first time. *(From Venturelli's research files, all three mentioned were seniors at a liberal arts college in Chicago, August 18, 2009)*

The fourth interview illustrates how friendship, coupled with subtle and not-so-subtle peer pressure, influences the novice drug enthusiast:

My roommate in college during my first year was a big drug user. He drank alcohol, smoked cigarettes, vaped, used marijuana and at times cocaine mostly on weekends. Here I was with him in the same room and all ever did was drink with high school friends. My roommate's neighborhood friends would come to visit him often from Chicago and it was not long before I got to know several of his close friends who introduced me to other drugs that at first try, I liked the feelings from these drugs. Other friends of his also warmed up to me as they witnessed my first experiences with drugs and our friendships got better as I got to know them. It was nice to have drug using friends I thought back then during my first year. *(From Venturelli's research files, investment fund manager, male, age 29, April 2019)*

In sociology, charismatic type leaders—defined as leaders with distinction in the eyes of others—are viewed as possessing status and power. In drug-using peer groups, such experienced drug users have power over inexperienced drug users. Members of peer groups are often persuaded to experiment with drugs if the more popular members say, "Come on, try some, it's great" or "Trust me, you'll really get off on this, come on, just try it." In groups where drugs are consumed, the extent of peer influence coupled with the art of persuasion and camaraderie or friendship are powerfully persuasive and cause the spread of drug use.

A further extension of subculture theory is the *social and cultural support perspective*. This perspective explains drug use and abuse in peer groups as resulting from an attempt by peers to solve problems collectively. In the neoclassic book *Delinquent Boys: The Culture of the Gang* (1955), Cohen pioneered a study that for the first time showed that delinquent behavior is a collective attempt to gain social status and prestige within the peer group (Liska & Messner, 1999; Siegel & Senna 1994; Williams & McShane, 1999). Members of certain peer groups are unable to achieve respect within the larger society. Such status-conscious youths find that being able to commit delinquent acts and yet evade law enforcement officials is admirable in the eyes of their delinquent peers. In effect, Cohen believed, delinquent behavior is a subcultural solution for overcoming feelings of status frustration and low self-esteem largely determined by lower-class status.

Although Cohen's emphasis is on explaining juvenile delinquency, his notion that delinquent behavior is a subcultural solution can easily be applied to drug use and abuse primarily in members of lower-class peer groups. Underlying drug use and abuse in delinquent gangs, for example, results from sharing common feelings of alienation and low self-esteem and a collective feeling of escaping from a society that appears uncaring, noninclusive, distant, hostile and discriminatory.

Consider the current upsurge in violent gang memberships. In such groups, drug dealing is a profitable venture, and drug use serves as a collective response to alienation and estrangement from conventional middle-class society. The hope of sudden monetary gain from drug dealing is perceived as a quick ticket into the middle class. In cases of violent minority gang members, the alienation results from racism, poverty, effects of migration and acculturation, and effects of minority status in a white, male-dominated society such as the United States (Glick & Moore, 1990; Moore, 1978, 1993; Sanders, 1994; Thornberry, 2001).

### ■ Structural Influence Theories

Structural influence theories focus on how elements in the *organization* of a society, group, or subculture affect the motivation and resulting drug use behavior that is for nonmedical—most often recreational—use. The belief is that no single factor in the society, the group, or the subculture produces the attraction to drug use but rather that the organization itself or the lack of organization largely causes this behavior to occur.

Social disorganization and social strain theories (Bahr & Hoffmann, 2016; Liska & Messner, 1999; Werner & Henry, 1995) identify the different types of social change that are disruptive and explain how, in a general sense, people are adversely affected by rapid social change. Social disorganization theory asks, "What in the larger structure and organization of the social order causes people to deviate?" Social strain theory offers an explanation regarding what causes some people to break away from social conformity. For example, this theory suggests that an inability to achieve sought-after goals, such as earnestly working hard yet being unable to meet financial obligations, compels some people out of shear frustration to deviate in achieving financial stability. One outcome viewed as a solution can result in drug dealing to achieve economic sustainability.

Overall, social disorganization theory describes a situation in which, because of rapid social change, previously conforming and affiliated individuals do not find themselves integrated into a community's social, commercial, religious, and economic institutions. When this type of alienation occurs, community members may, despite the fact that their parents served as role models of social conformity, find themselves increasingly disconnected from conventional living, resulting in a lack of effective attachment to the social order. As a result, these disconnected or *disaffiliated* people may, for example, be easily led into deviant behavior such as drug dealing or drug use as an attractive quick-fix solution to their financial problems.

An essential factor for effective and sustainable socialization is trusting, longer-term relationships within a relatively stable environment. As will be discussed later in this chapter, when major identity development and personality transformations occur during the teen years, some stability and trusting relationships in the immediate environment are crucial. Today, however, most Westernized societies (including the United States) are experiencing rapid social and technological development and social changes that result in more destabilizing and disorienting factors (Gergen, 2000; Ritzer, 1999, 2011).

Even though on the surface most people in society adapt to continually evolving social and technological social changes, on a cognitive level many people find themselves overwhelmed with the continual frantic pressure to keep up on a daily basis. The drive to keep up with social and technological innovation is more demanding today than ever before (Gergen, 2000). The

An example of feeling stressed and experiencing strain from an overly demanding society.

constant need to keep pace with change and the increasing multiplicity of realities and ever more contradictory realities produced by such change often appear barely controllable and increasingly chaotic. People who are less skillful in coping with the rapid pace caused by social and technological changes have difficulty in successfully maintaining a stable self-identity. For example, consider the large number of people who need psychological counseling and therapy because they find themselves unable to cope with personal, family, and work-related problems and conflicts. In one study, "an estimated 26.2% of Americans ages 18 and older—about one in four adults—suffer from a diagnosable mental disorder in a given year" (Kessler et al., 2005, p. 617). The following interview shows how such confusion and lack of control can easily lead to drug use:

*Interviewee:* The world is really much more complicated today than it was when I was growing up. Everything has a tendency to be in a perpetual state of flux.

*Interviewer:* Can you explain what you mean by the continual state of flux?

*Interviewee:* No one agrees with anything anymore. There are all these very divergent opinions. Just look at gay marriage for example. If my parents were alive today, I keep thinking what would my parents say about all this disagreement regarding marriage between two people? You know there was a time when marriage was always between a man and woman—not today. I know my parents never had to mentally deal with all these contrasting opinions. Even in their days I am sure they had contradictory ways of doing things but those other ways were never mainstream. I just think we are always on the cusp of total disagreements about things and ways of doing things.

*Interviewer:* How do you think people today cope with all this change?

*Interviewee:* Good and interesting question. Everything that was considered normal in the past is now up for grabs! People who never had a voice have a voice today. This is both good and bad.

*Interviewer:* Can you explain what you mean by good and bad?

*Interviewee:* Well, it's good for individuals to be liberated but I think it's bad for social agreement and social organization. It's like everything is being deconstructed. Sometimes I think about all these contradictory perspectives and honestly, I resolve my uncertainty by taking time out breaks by altering my reality. I do this by getting together with friends and we drink at least one night per week so we can get high laugh, sit back, and relax. In reality, I really think we cope with all this perceived mental turmoil by drinking in order to forget (really anesthetizing) or to suspend all the tension and turmoil in our daily lives. I also think with a good number of drug users the good feelings associated with their drug use is the ability to have time in order to cast out mental tension and conflict. I think as we "progress" as a society, drug use will only get worse because it becomes a great alternative coping mechanism for increasing numbers of people. *(From Venturelli's research files, male, Ph.D. graduate student attending a prominent university in Chicago, age 29, January 7, 2016)*

Similarly, an interview illustrates how a work environment can affect drug use:

I had one summer job once where it was so busy and crazy that a group of us workers would go out on breaks just to get high. We worked the night shift and our "high breaks" were between 2:00 and 5:00 in the morning. *(From Venturelli's research files, female first-year college student, age 20, July 28, 1996)*

## CURRENT SOCIAL CHANGE IN MOST SOCIETIES

Does social change per se cause people to use and abuse drugs? In response to this question, social change—defined as any measurable change caused by technological advancement that disrupts cultural values and attitudes about everyday life—does not by itself cause widespread drug use. In most cases, social change materialistically advances a culture by profoundly affecting the manner in which things are accomplished. At the same time, rapid social change disrupts day-to-day behavior anchored by custom and tradition, which has a tendency to fragment such conventional social groups as families, neighborhoods, and communities. By **conventional behavior**, we mean behavior that is largely dictated by custom and tradition that is continually being impacted by the rapidity of social change.

Examples of social change include the number of youth subcultures that proliferated during the 1960s (e.g., beatniks, mods, bikers, hippies) (Yinger, 1982) and other more recent lifestyles and subcultures such as rappers, punk rockers, potheads, Goths, street artists, skinheads, Satanists, gangstas, hipsters, and rave enthusiasts (Wooden, 1995). Furthermore, two other subcultures—teenagers and the elderly—have become increasingly independent and, in some subgroups, alienated from other age groups in society (see **Figure 2.3**).

Simply stated, today's social, economic, religious, and political institutions no longer clearly dominate and effectively dictate, embrace, influence, and lead people as they did in the past. Consequently, people are free to explore different means of expression and a vast array of recreational pursuits. For many, this liberating experience leads to attractive and novel outcomes; for others, this freedom from conventional societal norms and attitudes creates a type of alienation that can lead to drug use and abuse as self-medication.

The following two excerpts, gathered from interviews, illustrate social disorganization and strain theories:

> Honest to God, I know things occur much faster than they did 20 years ago. Change is happening faster and occurs more often. What helps is doing some drugs at night at home. I either drink alcohol or do lines of coke. Two different highs but I like them both. This is about the only recreation I have except for the TV at night, after working all darn day nonstop writing letters, answering phone calls, attending meetings, having to go on-site for inspections, and many other things I do each day. *(From Venturelli's research files, male home security systems manager, age 29, Chicago, Illinois, June 23, 2000)*

### KEY TERM

**conventional behavior**
behavior largely dictated by custom and tradition, which is often disrupted by the forces of rapid technological change

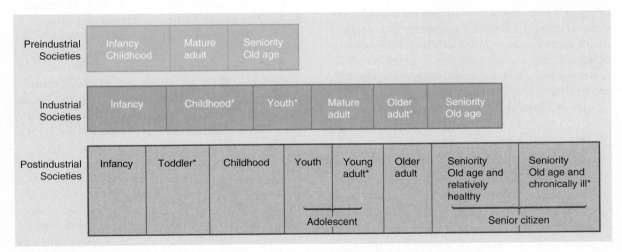

**FIGURE 2.3** Levels of technological development and resulting subcultures.

*Represents a newly developed and separate stage of identification and expression that impedes from the prior era.

Second interview:

Just as CNN flashes one news item after another at rapid speed, my life is similar. Most work days are so crammed with trying to constantly keep up, maintain my house and all that property upkeep demands, take care of the kids when my wife works nights, help clean the house, cook meals for all of us (since I am better at cooking than my wife), and dozens of other demands, that when the kids are finally asleep my wife and I try to relax with some combination of alcohol and weed. (We had to give up the coke because the kids are getting older and we don't mind if they find out we drink and smoke dope but the other stuff is out of the question. We don't want them to ever know we did coke.) Plus, those nights of staying up late when doing coke is too much for me now at this age. Really, the only time we can relax is when the kids are asleep and we can have a few drinks before going to bed. I keep hoping things will slow down, but it seems to either remain at the same frenzied pace or even get worse each year. *(From Venturelli's research files, male residing in a Midwestern town, age 31, February 10, 2010)*

Currently, there is a lack of reliable quantitative (statistical) evidence clearly proving that unprecedented rapid social change per se directly causes drug use. However, in looking at the impact of rapid social change and how it causes disaffiliation with established traditional social order, social disorganization theory may provide a better explanation for the formation and development of subcultural groups that use and often abuse illicit drugs as a response to the chaos created by rapid social change. Examples include the increasing use of methamphetamines in blue-collar subcultures, cocaine use in professional middle- and upper-middle-class occupational groups, crack use by disenfranchised and poor minority groups, opiates by Hispanic or Latina women (SAMHSA,

2009, 2018), and heroin use by middle- and upper-middle-class youth subcultures.

Figure 2.3 illustrates how the number of life-cycle stages increases, depending on a society's level of technological development. Overall, it implies that, as societies advance from preindustrial to industrial to our current postindustrial type of society, new subcultures emerge at an increasing rate of development (see Fischer, 1976, for similar thinking). In contrast to industrial and postindustrial societies, preindustrial societies do not have as many separate and distinct periods and cycles of social development. What is shown in Figure 2.3 and implied here is that the greater the number of distinct life cycles, the greater the fragmentation between the members of different stages of development. Generation gaps (conflicting sets of values and attitudes between age cohorts) cause much ignorance and lack of insight between age-group subcultures. This often leads to separation and fragmentation across age groups who develop and live within distinct lifestyle patterns, increasing the likelihood of conflict.

## CONTROL THEORY

The final major structural influence theory, **control theory**, emphasizes influences outside the self as the primary cause for deviating to drug use or abuse. Control theory places importance on positive socialization. **Socialization** is the process by which individuals learn and internalize the attitudes, values, and behaviors needed to participate in conventional society. Generally, control theorists believe that human beings can easily become deviant if left without the social controls imposed by family, social groups, and organizations. Thus, control theory advocates emphasize the necessity of maintaining bonds to family, school, peer groups, and other social, political, and religious organizations (Liska & Messner, 1999; Thio, 2010). In the 1950s and 1960s, criminologist Walter C. Reckless (1961; see also Liska & Messner, 1999; Siegel & Senna, 1994) developed the containment theory. According to this theory, the socialization process creates strong or weak internal and external control systems. The degree of self-control, high or low frustration tolerance, positive or negative self-perception, successful or unsuccessful goal achievement, and either resistance or adherence to deviant behavior determine internal control. Environmental pressures such as social conditions may limit the accomplishment of goal-striving behavior; such conditions include

**KEY TERMS**

**control theory**
theory that emphasizes that people left without bonds to other groups (peers, family, social groups) generally have a tendency to deviate from upheld values and attitudes

**socialization**
growth and development process responsible for learning how to become a responsible, functioning human being

poverty, minority group status, inferior education, and lack of employment.

The external or outer control system consists of effective or ineffective supervision and discipline, consistent or inconsistent moral training, and positive or negative acceptance, identity, and self-worth. Many believe that latchkey or unsupervised children have a higher risk of becoming delinquent because of nonexistent or inconsistent supervision and a lack of moral guidance experienced by latchkey or unsupervised children. Oftentimes, drug-addicted parents socialize children who develop delinquent tendencies because such parents are more likely to be inconsistent with discipline and adherence to disciplinary rules as a result of their drug addiction.

In applying control theory to the use or abuse of drugs, if an individual has a weak external social control system largely composed of a social environment lacking conformity to conventional and lawful behavior, then the internal control system, largely composed of coherent internal values and attitudes prohibiting drug use, must compensate for the external acceptance of drug use. Similarly, if an individual's external social control system prohibits drug use, his or her internal control system will not be seriously challenged. If, however, either the internal or the external control system is contradictory (weak internal vs. strong external), or the worst-case scenario in which both internal and external controls are weak, drug abuse is more likely to become an outcome.

**Table 2.2** shows the likelihood of drug use resulting from either strong or weak internal and external control systems. It indicates that if both internal and external controls are strong, then the use and abuse of drugs are less likely to occur. Travis Hirschi (1971), a much-respected sociologist and social control theorist, believes that delinquent behavior tends to occur when people lack (1) attachment to others, (2) commitment

to goals, (3) involvement in conventional activity, and (4) belief in a common value system (Liska & Messner, 1999; Thio, 2010). If a child or an adolescent is not bonded or circumscribed into a family setting or school curriculum and is not in alliance with nondelinquent peers, then the drift into delinquent behavior is inevitable.

We can apply Hirschi's theories to drug use as follows:

- Drug users are less likely than nonusers to be closely attached to conventional parents.
- Scholastically successful students are less likely to use drugs.
- Drug users are less likely to participate in social clubs and organizations and engage in team sport activities.
- Drug users are highly likely to have friends whose activities are congruent with their own attitudes. Drug users tend to associate with other drug users (similar to delinquents associating with other delinquents). Likewise, non–drug-using adolescents generally associate with non–drug-using adolescents.

The following excerpt illustrates how control theory works:

I was 15 when my mother confronted me with drug use. I nearly died. We have always been very close and she really cried when she found my "dugout" [paraphernalia that holds a quantity of marijuana] and a "one hitter" [a tubular device for smoking very small quantities of this drug] in her car. My fear was that she would inquire about my drug use with our next-door neighbors, whose children were my best friends. The neighbor residing on the left of our house was one of my high school teachers who knew me from the day I was born. The neighbor on the right side of our house was our church pastor. For a while after she confronted me, I just sneaked around more whenever I wanted to get high. After a few months, I became so paranoid of how my mother kept looking at me when I would come in at night that I eventually stopped smoking weed. Our family is very close and the town I live in (at that time the population was 400) was filled with gossip. I could not handle the pressure, so I quit. *(From Venturelli's research files, female postal worker residing in a small Midwestern Indiana town, age 22, February 9, 1997)*

In conclusion, control theory represents how conformity with supportive groups may prevent

**TABLE 2.2** Likelihood of Drug Use

| Individual Internal Control | External Social Control | |
| --- | --- | --- |
| | Strong | Weak or Nonexistent |
| Strong | Least likely (almost never) | Less likely (probably never) |
| Weak | More likely (probably will) | Most likely (almost certain) |

deviance. It suggests that social control is both formally and informally prescribed by family, school, and peer-group expectations. In addition, individuals who are not equipped with an internal system of self-control reflecting the values and beliefs of conventional society or who feel personally alienated from major social institutions are more likely to deviate without feeling guilty for their actions, often because parental or peer pressure results in a suspension or modification of internal beliefs.

# Danger Signals of Drug Abuse

How does one know when the use of drugs moves beyond normal use? Many people are prescribed drugs that affect their moods. Using these drugs as prescribed can be important for both physical and emotional health. Sometimes, however, it may be difficult to decide when the use of drugs to handle stress or anxiety becomes inappropriate. It is important that an individual's use of drugs does not result in either dependency or addiction. The following are some danger signals that can help you evaluate your drug use behavior:

1. Do people who are close to you often ask about your drug use? Have they noticed any changes in your moods or behavior?
2. Do you become defensive when a friend or relative mentions your drug or alcohol use?
3. Do you believe you cannot have fun without alcohol or other drugs?
4. Do you frequently get into trouble with the law, school officials, family, friends, or significant others because of your alcohol or other drug use?
5. Are you sometimes embarrassed or frightened by your behavior under the influence of drugs or alcohol?
6. Have you ever switched to a new doctor because your regular physician would not prescribe the drug you wanted?
7. When you are under pressure or feel anxious, do you automatically take a sedative, a drink, or both?

8. Do you turn to drugs after becoming upset, after confrontations or arguments, or to relieve uncomfortable feelings?
9. Do you take drugs more often than prescribed or for purposes other than those recommended by your doctor?
10. Do you take prescription drugs that have not been prescribed by a physician?
11. Do you often combine drugs and alcohol to heighten their effects?
12. Do you drink or take drugs regularly to help you sleep or even to relax?
13. Do you take an illicit or nonprescribed drug to get going in the morning?
14. Do you find it necessary or nearly impossible to not use alcohol or other drugs to have sex?
15. Do you find yourself not wanting to be around friends who do not use drugs or drink on a regular basis?
16. Have you ever seriously confronted the thought that you may have a drug addiction problem?
17. Do you make promises to yourself or others that you will stop getting drunk or using drugs?
18. Do you drink or use drugs alone?
19. Do you mentally highlight the days when you do not drink alcohol and think it is an accomplishment?

A higher number of "yes" answers indicate a greater likelihood that you are abusing alcohol or drugs. Many places offer help at the local level, such as programs in your community listed in the phone book or online under "Drug Abuse Help" or "Drug Counseling," including SMART Recovery at www.smartrecovery.org, Saint Jude Retreats at www.soberforever.net, or the National Council on Alcoholism and Drug Dependence (NCADD) at http://ncaddms.org/. Other resources include community crisis centers, telephone hotlines, and the National Mental Health Association. Getting through the first step in seeking help is often difficult. Once this is accomplished, many other positive things usually follow.

### ∎ Low-Risk and High-Risk Drug Choices

Some very real risks are associated with recreational drug use. Low-risk and high-risk drug choices refer to two major levels of alcohol and other drug use. **Low-risk drug choices** refer to values and attitudes that keep the use of alcohol

**KEY TERM**

**low-risk drug choices**
developing values and attitudes that lead to controlling the use of alcohol and drugs

and other drugs in control. **High-risk drug choices** refer to values and attitudes that lead to using drugs habitually and addictively, resulting in emotional, psychological, and physical health problems. Low-risk choices include abstinence from all drugs or remaining in control of the quantity and frequency of drugs use.

Low-risk choices require self-monitoring your consumption of alcohol and other drugs to reduce your risk of an alcohol and other drug-related problem. Both "low risk" and "high risk" are appropriate descriptive concepts that allow us to focus on the health and safety issues involved in drug use and refer to developing and maintaining completely different values and attitudes in your approach to alcohol and other drugs.

This chapter described numerous factors influencing drug use, theoretical explanations, and reasons why people start using or abusing drugs. A good number of theories were covered that attempt to explain initial and habitual use. Some people can easily become addicted to alcohol and other drugs because of inherited characteristics, personality, mental instability or illness, and vulnerability to current situations. Others who have more resistance to alcohol and drug addiction may have stronger convictions and abilities to cope with different situations.

## MAINTAINING A LOW-RISK APPROACH

To minimize the risk of alcohol- and drug-related problems, we suggest you remain aware of the following:

- Investigate your family drug history. Does anyone in your family have a history of alcohol or drug abuse? How many members of your family who have alcohol or drug problems are blood relatives? In other words, are you more likely to become dependent on alcohol or drugs because of the possibility of inherited genes or because of the values and attitudes to which you are exposed?
- Do you particularly enjoy the effects of alcohol and other drugs? Do you spend a lot of time thinking about how "good" it feels to be high?
- Does it seem as if the only time you really have fun is when you are using alcohol and other drugs?
- Keep in mind the following accepted findings.
  - *Body size:* A small person typically becomes more impaired by drug use than a larger person does.

- *Gender:* Women typically become more impaired than men of the same size, especially with regard to alcohol use but with other types of drugs as well.
- *Other drugs:* Taking a combination of drugs generally increases the risk of impairment and, in some combinations, accidental death.
- *Fatigue or illness:* Fatigue and illness increase the risk for alcohol and drug impairment.
- *Mindset:* As you set out to drink or use other drugs, are you expecting heavy use of alcohol or heavy involvement with drugs to the point of inebriation or severe distortion of reality as the evening's outcome? More important, what view do you have regarding moderate versus heavy use of drugs?
- *Empty stomach:* Taking drugs on an empty stomach increases their effects.

Also keep in mind that most excessive drug use comes with the following risks:

- It is against all school policies.
- It is unlawful behavior (risky with the law).
- Excessive alcohol and other drug use usually leads not only to public attention but also to criminal justice attention (police and the courts). Jail time or prison, fines, costly forced rehabilitation programs, and community service work are possible outcomes that affect life goals and plans.
- The defense costs involved in even simple drug possession charges are often $4,000 to $8,000 (often beyond an individual's ability to pay for such legal services).
- A criminal record is a public record and can be acquired or suddenly come to the attention of school officials (especially loan officers or government loan personnel), credit bureaus, as well as any other community members.

We leave you with this question: *Are excessive drug use and the resulting drug dependence still worth such risks?* This question is critical, especially when we know that the more often drugs are consumed, the greater the potential not only for drug dependence and addiction but also for damage to health, personal well-being, family and interpersonal relationships, and community respect.

### KEY TERM

**high-risk drug choices**
developing values and attitudes that lead to using drugs both habitually and addictively

# LEARNING PORTFOLIO

## Key Terms

## Discussion Questions

1. Define the terms *addiction, tolerance, dependence,* and *withdrawal.*
2. Describe and contrast the disease and characterological (personality predisposition) models of addiction.
3. List and briefly discuss several major biological, social, and cultural factors that may be responsible for addiction to drugs.
4. In addition to better cultivation techniques, cite several other possible reasons why the potency (THC levels) of the average marijuana joint has substantially increased since the 1960s.
5. Given that more than approximately 88% of the U.S. population are daily drug users in some form, do you think we need to reexamine our strict drug laws, which may be punishing a sizable number of drug users in our society who stubbornly want to use their drugs of choice?
6. Is there any way to combine the biological and sociological explanations for why people use drugs so that the two perspectives do not conflict? (Sketch out a synthesis between these two sets of theoretical explanations.)
7. Describe the relationship between mental illness and drug abuse.
8. Is the relationship between drug abuse and mental illness important? Why or why not?
9. Do you accept the behavioristic view that one school of psychology offers for explaining why people come to abuse drugs? (In a general sense, this view primarily states that when behavior is rewarded, people repeat behaviors that are rewarded.) Explain your answer in terms of how this occurs with drug users and drug abusers.
10. In reviewing psychological and sociological theories, which theory do you think best explains drug use? Defend your answer.
11. Does differential association theory take into account non–drug-using individuals whose socialization environment was drug infested? Explain your answer.
12. Are drug users socialized differently? Defend your answer. If you think this is true, *how* are they socialized differently?
13. Can divorce be blamed for adolescent drug use? Why or why not? If so, to what extent?
14. To what extent do you think rapid social change is a major cause of drug use and abuse? Cite three examples of how the speed of change in today's society may explain current drug use.
15. Is making low-risk choices regarding drug use a more effective approach for eliminating or moderating drug use rather than advocating "Just say no"?

# Summary

1. Chemical dependence has been a major social problem throughout U.S. history.

2. People define chemical addiction in many ways. The essential feature is a chronic attachment to drug use despite significant negative outcomes and consequences.

3. The major models of addiction are the *moral model*, the *disease model*, and the *characterological* or *personality predisposition model*.

4. Transitional periods such as adolescence and middle age are associated with unique sets of risk factors.

5. Drug dependence that advances to addiction generally occurs in stages affecting a minority of drug users who become caught up in vicious cycles that worsen their situation, causing psychological and biological abnormalities as they increase their drug usage. Although not inevitable, drug use has a general tendency to advance to severe drug dependence, which is also known as *addiction*.

6. Drug use is more serious today than in the past because (a) it has increased dramatically since 1960, (b) today's illicit drugs are more potent than in the past, (c) media often present drug use as rewarding, (d) drug use physically harms members of society, and (e) drug use and drug dealing by violent gangs continue to increase at alarming rates.

7. Genetic and biophysiological theories explain addiction in terms of genes, psychiatric disorders, reward centers in the brain, character traits, brain dysfunction, and biochemical patterns.

8. Drugs of abuse interfere with the functioning of neurotransmitters, which are chemical messengers used for communication between brain regions. Drugs with abuse potential enhance the pleasure centers by causing the release of a specific brain neurotransmitter such as dopamine, which acts as a positive reinforcer.

9. The American Psychiatric Association classifies severe drug dependence as *substance use disorder*. Drug abuse can cause mental conditions that mimic major psychiatric illnesses such as schizophrenia, severe anxiety disorders, and suicidal depression.

10. Four genetic factors can contribute to drug abuse: (a) Many genetically determined psychiatric disorders are relieved by drugs of abuse, which, in turn, encourage their use; (b) high rates of addiction result from people who are genetically sensitive to addictive drugs; (c) such character traits as insecurity and vulnerability, which often have a biological basis, can lead to drug abuse behavior; and (d) the inability to break away from a particular type of drug addiction may in part be genetically determined, especially when severe craving or unpleasant withdrawal effects dominate.

11. Introversion and extroversion patterns have been associated with levels of neural arousal in brainstem circuits. These forms of arousal are closely associated with effects caused by drug stimulants or depressants.

12. Reinforcement or learning theory says that the motivation to use or abuse drugs stems from how the "highs" from alcohol and other drugs reduce anxiety, tension, and stress. Positive social rewards and influences by drug-using peers also promote drug use.

13. Social influence theories include social learning, the role of significant others, labeling, and subculture theories. Social learning theory explains drug use as a form of learned behavior. Significant others play a role in the learning process involved in drug use or abuse. Labeling theory says that other people we consider important can influence whether drug use becomes an option for us. If key people we admire or fear come to define our actions as deviant, then the definition becomes a "fact" in our reality. Subculture theories trace original drug experimentation, use, and abuse to peer pressure and influence.

14. Many consistencies in socialization patterns are found among drug abusers, ranging from immaturity, maladjustment, and insecurity to exposure and belief that a life with drug use is appealing and that selling drugs is a lucrative business.

15. Sociologist Howard Becker believes that first-time drug users become attached to drugs because of three factors: (a) they learn the techniques of how to use the drug, (b) they learn to perceive the pleasurable effects of drugs, and (c) they learn to enjoy the drug experience.

16. Primary deviance is when deviant behavior is initially tried, yet the perpetrator does not identify with the deviant behavior; hence, it is viewed as inconsequential deviant behavior. Secondary deviance is when the perpetrator identifies with the deviant behavior (i.e., "Yes, I am a drug user because I like to do drugs.")

17. Both internal and external social control should prevail concerning drug use. Internal control deals with internal psychic and internalized social attitudes. External social control is exemplified by living in a neighborhood and community in which drug use and abuse are severely criticized or not tolerated as a means to seek pleasure or avoid stress and anxiety.

18. Low-risk and high-risk drug use choices refer to the process of developing values and attitudes toward alcohol and other drugs. Low-risk drug choices encompass values and attitudes leading to a controlled use of alcohol and drugs—from total abstinence to moderate use. High-risk choices encompass values and attitudes leading to using drugs both habitually and addictively.

# References

Akers, R. L. (1968, June). Problems in the sociology of deviance: Social definition and behavior. *Social Forces, 6,* 455–465.

Akers, R. L. (1992). *Drugs, alcohol, and society: Social structure, process, and policy.* Belmont, CA: Wadsworth.

Akers, R. L. (2009). *Social learning and social structure: A general theory of crime and deviance.* New Brunswick, NJ: Transaction.

Akers, R. L., & Sellers, C. S. (2008). *Criminological theories: Introduction, evaluation, and application.* New York: Oxford University Press, 2008.

alcoholrehab.com. (2015a). Introversion and addiction. Drug and Alcohol Rehab Asia (DARA Thailand). Retrieved from http://alcoholrehab.com/addiction-articles/introversion-and-addiction/

alcoholrehab.com. (2015b). Self-medication and substance abuse. Drug and Alcohol Rehab Asia (DARA Thailand). Retrieved from http://alcoholrehab.com/drug-addiction/self-medication-substance-abuse/

American Psychiatric Association (APA). (2000). Substance-related disorders. In *Diagnostic and Statistical Manual of Mental Disorders (DSM-IV-TR),* 4th ed. revised (pp. 191–295). Washington, DC: American Psychiatric Association.

American Psychiatric Association (APA). (2013). Substance-related and addictive disorders. In *Diagnostic and Statistical Manual of Mental Disorders (DSM-5),* 5th ed. (pp. 481–589). Washington, DC: American Psychiatric Association.

Apostolides, M. (1996). Special report: The addiction revolution: Old habits get new choices. *Psychology Today, 29,* 33–43, 75–76.

Bahr, S. J., & Hoffmann, J. P. (2016). Social scientific theories of drug use, abuse, and addiction. In H. H. Brownstein *(Ed.), The handbook of drugs and society* (pp. 197–217). West Sussex, UK: John Wiley & Sons.

Bandura, A. (1977). *Social learning theory.* Englewood Cliffs, NJ: Prentice Hall.

Beattie, M. (1987). *Codependent no more.* San Francisco, CA: Harper.

Becker, H. S. (1963). *Outsiders: Studies in the sociology of deviance.* New York, NY: Free Press.

Becker, H. S. (1967). History, culture, and subjective experience: An exploration of the social basis of drug-induced experiences. *Journal of Health and Social Behavior, 8,* 163–176.

Bejerot, N. (1965). Current problems of drug addiction." *Lakartidingen* (Sweden) *62*(50), 4231–4238.

Bejerot, N. (1972). *Addiction: An artificially induced drive.* Springfield, IL: Thomas.

Bejerot, N. (1975). The biological and social character of drug dependence. In K. P. Kisker, J. E. Meyer, C. Muller, & E. Stromogrew *(Eds.), Psychiatrie der Gegenwart, Forschung und Praxis,* 2nd ed. (Vol. 3, pp. 488–518). Berlin, Germany: Springer-Verlag.

Bespalov, A., Lebedev, A., Panchenko, G., & Zvartau, E. (1999). Effects of abused drugs on thresholds and breaking points of intracranial self-stimulation in rats. *European*

*Neuropsychopharmacology: Journal of the European College of Neuropharmacology, 9,* 377–383.

Best, J., & Luckenbill, D. F. (1994). *Organizing deviance,* 2nd ed. Englewood Cliffs, NJ: Prentice Hall.

Blaszczak-Boxe, A. (2016, February 8). Potent pot: Marijuana is stronger now than it was 20 years ago. *LiveScience.* Retrieved from http://www.livescience.com/53644-marijuana-is-stronger-now-than-20-years-ago.html

Brooks, R. (2019, November 19). The psychological effects of divorce on children. *Attorney at Law Magazine.* Retrieved from https://attorneyatlawmagazine.com/psychological-effects-divorce-children

Burns, D. B. (1997). The web of caring: An approach to accountability in alcohol policy. In *Designing alcohol and other drug prevention programs in higher education.* Newton, MA: Higher Education Center for Alcohol and Other Drug Prevention.

*Capitol Times.* (1999). Seven in 10 drug users work full-time. Retrieved from http://www.mapinc.org/drugnews/v99/n983/a01.html

Carlson, N. (1990). *Psychology: The science of behavior* (3rd ed.). Boston, MA: Allyn & Bacon.

Center for Behavioral Health Statistics and Quality (CBHSQ). (2015). *2014 National Survey on Drug Use and Health: Detailed tables.* Rockville, MD: Substance Abuse and Mental Health Services Administration (SAMHSA).

Center for Substance Abuse Research (CESAR). (2007, April 23). Eighth graders' perceived harmfulness of Ecstasy, LSD, and inhalant use continues to decrease; Suggests vulnerability to resurgence of use. Retrieved from http://www.cesar.umd.edu/cesar/cesarfax/vol16/16-16.pdf

Center for Substance Abuse Research (CESAR). (2011, September). District youth in brief: Early alcohol use. is early alcohol among DC public high school students associated with other risky behaviors? Retrieved from http://www.cesar.umd.edu/cesar/pubs/20110901%20DC%20YinB%203-8.pdf

Cheron, J. M. (2001). *Symbolic interactionism: An introduction, an interpretation, an integration,* 7th ed. Upper Saddle River, NJ: Prentice Hall.

Clinard, M. B., & Meier, R. F. (2011). *Sociology of deviant behavior,* 14th ed. Belmont, CA: Wadsworth Cengage Learning.

Cohen, A. K. (1955). *Delinquent boys: The culture of the gang.* Glencoe, IL: Free Press.

Conner, M. G. (2011, August 24). *Children during divorce.* Retrieved from http://crisiscounseling.com/TraumaLoss/DivorceChildren.htm

Conrad, P., & Schneider, J. W. (1980). *Deviance and medicalization.* St. Louis, MO: Mosby.

Delva, S. (2019). The 3 most common causes of insecurity in recovery. Delray Beach, FL: Palm Partners Drug Rehab Center. Retrieved from https://www.palmpartners.com/the-3-most-common-causes-of-insecurity-in-recovery/

Dixon, P. (2015). *Addicted to pleasure: Nature of drug addiction.* London, UK: Global Change, Ltd. Retrieved from http://www.globalchange.com/truth-about-drugs-chapter-3.htm

Doherty, W. J., & Needle, R. H. (1991). Psychological adjustment and substance use among adolescent before and after a parental divorce. *Child Development, 62,* 328–337.

Doweiko, H. E. (2015). *Concepts of chemical dependency,* 9th ed. Belmont, CA: Brooks/Cole Cengage Learning.

Drug Rehab.com. Why Do Alcoholics Lie and Blame Others?" Orlando, Florida: Advanced Recovery Systems, 2018. Retrieved from https://www.drugrehab.com/about-us/

Drug Strategies. (1999). *Santa Barbara profile: Alcohol, tobacco, and other drugs.* Washington, DC: Drug Strategies.

Elman, I., & D. Borsook. (2016). Common brain mechanisms of chronic pain and addiction. *Neuron, 89,* 11–36. Retrieved from https://www.sciencedirect.com/science/article/pii/S0896627315010338

Escohotado, A., & Symington, K. (1999). *A brief history of drugs: From the Stone Age to the Stoned Age.* Rochester, VT.

Eysenck, H. J., & Eysenck, M. W. (1985). *Personality and individual differences: A natural science approach.* New York, NY: Plenum Press.

Farrar, H., & Kearns, G. (1989). Cocaine: Clinical pharmacology and toxicology. *Journal of Pediatrics, 115,* 665–675.

Fischer, C. S. (1976). *The urban experience.* New York, NY: Harcourt Brace Jovanovich.

Frosch, W. A. (1985). An analytic overview of the addictions. In H. Milman & H. Shaffer *(Eds.), The addictions: Multidisciplinary perspectives and treatments* (pp. 160–173). Lexington, MA: Lexington Books/D.C. Heath.

Galizio, B. A. (2005). Positive and negative reinforcement: Should the distinction be preserved? Behavior Analyst, *28,* 85–98.

Gardner, E. L. (1992). Brain reward mechanisms. In J. H. Lowinson, P. Ruiz, R. B. Millman, & J. G. Langrod *(Eds.), Substance abuse: A comprehensive textbook,* 2nd ed. (pp. 60–69). Baltimore, MD: Lippincott Williams & Wilkins.

Genetic Science Learning Center. (2015, December 1). Genes affect your risk for addiction. *Learn Genetics.* Retrieved from http://learn.genetics.utah.edu/content/addiction/genes/

Gergen, K. (2000). *The saturated self: Dilemmas of identity in contemporary life.* New York, NY: Basic Books.

Glaser, G. (2015, April). The irrationality of Alcoholics Anonymous. *The Atlantic.* Retrieved from https://www.theatlantic.com/magazine/archive/2015/04/the-irrationality-of-alcoholics-anonymous/386255/

Glick, R., & Moore, J. (Eds.). (1990). *Drugs in Hispanic communities*. New Brunswick, NJ: Rutgers University Press.

Goode, E. (2010). *Deviant behavior*, 9th ed. Upper Saddle River, NJ: Prentice Hall.

Grabus, S. (2016). Sensation seeking promotes initiation, impulsivity promotes escalation of substance use. Bethesda, MD: National Institute on Drug Abuse.

Grant, K. L. (2013, February 26). 9 things nobody tells you about recreational drug use in your youth. *Elephant Journal*. Retrieved from http://www.elephantjournal.com/2013/02/9-things-nobody-tells-you-about-recreational-drug-use-in-your-youth/

Gray, J. A. (1987). *The psychology of fear and stress*, 2nd ed. Cambridge, UK: Cambridge University Press.

Gray, P., & Bjorklund, D. F. (2014). *Psychology*, 7th ed. London, UK: Worth.

Heitzeg, N. A. (1996). *Deviance: Rulemakers and rulebreakers*. Minneapolis, MN: West.

Hellerman, C. (2013, August 9). Is super weed, super bad? CNN.com. Retrieved from http://www.cnn.com/2013/08/09/health/weed-potency-levels/

Heshmat, S. (2019). A psychodynamic way of understanding addiction. *Psychology Today*. Retrieved from https://www.psychologytoday.com/us/blog/science-choice/201410/psychodynamic-way-understanding-addiction

Hewitt, J. P., & Shulman, D. (2010). *Self and society: A symbolic interactionist social psychology*, 11th ed. Boston, MA: Allyn & Bacon.

Hirschi, T. (1971). *Causes of delinquency*, 2nd ed. Los Angeles, CA: University of California Press.

Hogue, A & Liddle, H. A. (2009, May 1). Family-based treatment for adolescent substance abuse: Controlled trials and new horizons in services research. *Journal of Family Therapy 31*: 126–154. Retrieved from https://www.ncbi.nlm.nih.gov/pmc/articles/PMC2989619/

Horvath, A. T, Misra, K., Epner, A. K., & Cooper, G. M. (2015). Psychological causes of addiction. Retrieved from https://www.cascadementalhealth.org/poc/view_doc.php?type=doc&id=58686&cn=1409

Inderbitzin, M., Bates, K., & Gainey, R. (2013). *Deviance and social control: A sociological perspective*. Thousand Oaks, CA: Sage.

International Network of People Who Use Drugs (INPUD). (n.d.). INPUD's International diaries: Timeline of events in the history of drugs. Retrieved from https://inpud.wordpress.com/timeline-of-events-in-the-history-of-drugs/

Jellinek, E. M. (1960). *The disease concept of alcoholism*. Highland Park, NJ: Hillhouse Press, 1960.

Johnston, L. D., Miech, R. A., O'Malley, P. M., Bachman, J. G., Schulenberg, J. E., & Patrick, M. E. (2018). *Monitoring the Future: National survey results on drug use: 1975–2017: Overview, key findings on adolescent drug use*. Ann Arbor, MI: Institute for Social Research, University of Michigan.

Jones, J. (1996). *Hep-cats, narcs, and pipe dreams: A history of America's romance with illegal drugs*. Baltimore, MD: Johns Hopkins University Press.

Joyce, M. (2018, May 23). Consumer drug ads: The harms that come with pitching lifestyle over information. HealthNewsReview.org. Retrieved from https://www.healthnewsreview.org/2018/05/direct-to-consumer-tv-drug-ads/

Kelly, K. B. (2000, August). Children's adjustment in conflicted marriage and divorce: A decade review of research. *Journal of the American Academy of Child and Adolescent Psychiatry, 39*, 963–973.

Kelly, K., & Ramundo, P. (2006). *You mean I'm not lazy, stupid, and crazy?!* New York: Scribner.

Kessler, R. C., Chiu, W. T., Demler, O., & Walters, E. E. (2005). Prevalence, severity, and comorbidity of twelve-month DSM-IV disorders in the National Comorbidity Survey Replication (NCS-R). *Archives of General Psychiatry, 62*, 617–627.

Khantzian, E. J. (1998, June). Addiction as a brain disease. *American Journal of Psychiatry, 155*, 711–713.

Koob, G. (2000, October). Drug addiction. *Neurobiology of Disease, 7*(5), 543–545.

Knopf, A. (2017, December 18). Lloyd Johnston on MTF, survey he led for 42 years. *The Brown University Child and Adolescent Behavior Letter* (CABL). Retrieved from https://onlinelibrary.wiley.com/doi/abs/10.1002/cbl.30266

Kuehn, B. M. (2010, May 19). Integrated care key for patients with both addiction and mental illness. *Journal of the American Medical Association, 303*, 1905–1907.

Landau, E. (2010). Children's quality of life declining, says report. CNN.com. Retrieved from http://www.cnn.com/2010/HEALTH/06/08/children.wellbeing/index.html

Lang, S. (1996, October 11). Dopamine linked to a personality trait and happiness. *Cornell University Science News*. Retrieved from http://news.cornell.edu/stories/1996/10/dopamine-linked-personality-trait-and-happiness

L. A. W. Publications. (1985). *Let's all work to fight drug abuse*. Addison, TX: C&L Printing.

Lemert, E. M. (1951). *Social psychology: A systematic approach to the theory of sociopathic behavior*. New York, NY: McGraw-Hill.

Lemonick, M. D., & Park, A. (2007, July 14). The science of addiction. *Time*, pp. 42–48.

Lewin, L. (1993). Phantasica. In R. Rudgley (Ed.), *Essential substances: A cultural history of intoxicants in society*. New York, NY: Kodansha International.

Liska, A. E., & Messner, S. F. (1999). *Perspectives on crime and deviance.* Upper Saddle River, NJ: Prentice Hall.

MacPherson, K. (2010, August 28). It takes a rat to show how drugs alter brains. *Star Ledger [Newark, NJ],* pp. 1–2. Retrieved from http://www.nj.com/specialprojects /index.ssf?/specialprojects/addicts/addicts0826.html

MarijuanaBreak Staff. (n.d.). Average THC content over the years: 50 year look at cannabis potency. Parsippany, NJ: Author.

Marshall, M. (1979). Conclusions. In M. Marshall *(Ed.), Beliefs, behavior, and alcoholic beverages: A cross-cultural survey* (pp. 451–457). Ann Arbor, MI: University of Michigan Press.

Mathias, R. (1995, July–August). Novelty seekers and drug abusers tap same brain reward system, animal studies show. *NIDA Notes* 10(4), 1–5.

McCance-Katz, E. F. (2018). PowerPoint presentation: The National Survey on Drug Use and Health: 2017. Rockville, MD: SAMHSA.

Mental Health America. (2010). Co-dependency. Retrieved from http://www.nmha.org/go/codependency

Miech, R. A., Johnston, L. D., O'Malley, P. M., Bachman, J. G., Schulenberg, J. E., & Patrick, M. E. (2019). *Monitoring the Future national survey results on drug use, 1975–2018: Vol. I, Secondary school students.* Ann Arbor, MI: Institute for Social Research, University of Michigan.

Miller, N. S. (1995). *Addiction psychiatry: Current diagnosis and treatment.* New York: Wiley.

Moore, J. (1978). *Homeboys: Gangs, drugs and prison in the barrios of Los Angeles.* Philadelphia, PA: Temple University Press.

Moore, J. (1993). Gangs, drugs, and violence. In S. Cummings & D. J. Monti *(Eds.), Gangs: The origins and impact of contemporary youth gangs in the United States* (pp. 27–46). Albany, NY: State University of New York Press.

Moore, J. (2008, October 22). Psychological theory of drug abuse. *Yahoo Health,* pp. 1–2.

Myers, P. L. (1990). Sources and configurations of institutional denial. *Employee Assistance Quarterly, 5*(B), 43–54.

National Alliance on Mental Illness (NAMI). (2015). Dual diagnosis. Retrieved from https://www.nami.org/Learn -More/Mental-Health-Conditions/Related-Conditions /Dual-Diagnosis

National Health Service (NHS). (n.d.). Drugs and the brain. Retrieved from http://www.nhs.uk/Livewell /drugs/Pages/Dodrugsdamagebrain.aspx

National Institute on Drug Abuse (NIDA). *Theories on drug abuse: Selected contemporary perspectives.* NIDA Research Monograph Series. U.S. Department of Health and Human Services. Rockville, MD: U.S. Government Printing Office, 1980.

National Institute on Drug Abuse (NIDA). (1990, Summer). Study finds higher use among adolescents whose parents divorce. *NIDA Notes, 5,* 10.

National Institute on Drug Abuse (NIDA). (1996, February 20). Attention and memory impaired in heavy users of marijuana. Rockville, MD: Office of the National Institute on Drug Abuse.

National Institute on Drug Abuse (NIDA). (2007, February). Addiction and co-occurring mental disorders. *NIDA Notes, 21,* 3.

National Institute on Drug Abuse (NIDA). (2008a). *Comorbidity: Addiction and other mental illnesses.* Research Report Series. Bethesda, MD: U.S. Department of Health and Human Services.

National Institute on Drug Abuse (NIDA). (2008b). *Drugs, brains, and behavior: The science of addiction.* Bethesda, MD: National Institutes of Health, U.S. Department of Health and Human Services.

National Institute on Drug Abuse (NIDA). (2010). *Comorbidity: Addiction and other mental disorders.* Retrieved from https://www.drugabuse.gov/sites/default/files /rrcomorbidity.pdf

National Institute on Drug Abuse (NIDA). (2014, July). Drugs, brains, and behavior: The science of addiction. Bethesda, MD: NIH and NIDA. Retrieved from https://www .drugabuse.gov/publications/drugs-brains-behavior -science-addiction/drugs-brain

National Institute on Drug Abuse (NIDA). (2016a). Genetics and epigenetics of addiction. (February). Bethesda, MD: Author. Retrieved from https://www.drugabuse.gov /publications/drugfacts/genetics-epigenetics-addiction

National Institute on Drug Abuse (NIDA). 2016b). What are some ways that cocaine changes the brain? (May). Bethesda, MD: Author. Retrieved from https://www .drugabuse.gov/publications/cocaine/what-are-some -ways-cocaine-changes-brain

National Institute on Drug Abuse (NIDA). (2018a). *Understanding drug use and addiction.* Bethesda, MD: U.S. Department of Health and Human Services. Retrieved from https://www.drugabuse.gov/publications/drugfacts /understanding-drug-use-addiction

National Institute on Drug Abuse (NIDA). (2018b). Drugs, brains, and behavior: The science of addiction. Bethesda, MD: U.S. Department of Health and Human Services. Retrieved from https://www.drugabuse.gov/publications /drugs-brains-behavior-science-addiction/preface

National Institute on Drug Abuse (NIDA). (2018c). *Common comorbidities with substance use disorders and mental illness.* Bethesda, MD: U.S. Department of Health and Human Services. Retrieved from https://www .drugabuse.gov/publications/research-reports/common

-comorbidities-substance-use-disorders/part-1-connection
-between-substance-use-disorders-mental-illness

National Institute on Drug Abuse (NIDA). (2018d). *Comorbidity: Substance use disorders and other mental illnesses.* Bethesda, MD: U.S. Department of Health and Human Services. Retrieved from https://www.drugabuse.gov/publications/drugfacts/comorbidity-substance-use-disorders-other-mental-illnesses

National Institute on Drug Abuse (NIDA). (2020). Trends and statistics. Bethesda, MD: U.S. Department of Health and Human Services. Retrieved from https://www.drugabuse.gov/related-topics/trends-statistics

Needle, R. H., Su, S. S., & Doherty, W. J. (1990). Divorce, remarriage, and adolescent substance use: A prospective longitudinal study. *Journal of Marriage and the Family, 52,* 157–159.

O'Brien, R., Cohen, S., Evans, G., & Fine, J. (1992). *The encyclopedia of drug abuse,* 2nd ed. New York, NY: Facts on File.

Office of the State Superintendent of Education (OSSE). (2017). *District of Columbia youth risk behavior survey surveillance report (YRBS).* Washington, DC: Author. Retrieved from https://osse.dc.gov/sites/default/files/dc/sites/osse/publication/attachments/

Plummer, K. (1979). Misunderstanding labeling perspectives. In D. Downes & P. Rock *(Eds.), Deviant interpretations* (pp. 85–121). London, UK: Robertson.

Pontell, H. N. (1996). *Social deviance,* 2nd ed. Upper Saddle River, NJ: Prentice Hall.

ProCon.org. (2018, April 5). Is medical marijuana an effective treatment for servere/chronic pain? Chicago, IL: Author.

Radowitz, J. V. (2003, June 18). Smoking and drug abuse traits linked to genes. *The Independent.* London, UK: Independent Digital.

Reckless, W. C. (1961). A new theory of delinquency. *Federal Probation, 25,* 42–46.

Rettner, R. (2014). How personality increases risk of drug abuse. Live Science. Retrieved from https://www.livescience.com/44851-personality-substance-use-disorder-risk.html

Ritzer, G. *Enchanting a disenchanted world: Revolutionizing the means of consumption.* Thousand Oaks, CA: Pine Forge Press, 1999.

Ritzer, G. (2011). *The McDonaldization of society,* 6th ed. Thousand Oaks, CA: Pine Forge Press.

Ritzer, G., & Goodman, D. (2010). *Sociological theory,* 8th ed. New York, NY: McGraw-Hill Higher Education.

Ritzer, G., & Stepnisky, J. (2017). *Contemporary sociological theory and its classical roots,* 5th ed. Thousand Oaks, CA: Sage Publications.

Rousar, E., Brooner, K., Regier, M. W., & Bigelow, G. E. (1995). Psychiatric distress in antisocial drug abusers: Relation to other personality disorders. *Drug and Alcohol Dependence, 34,* 149–154.

Rudgley, R. (1993). *Essential substances: A cultural history of intoxicants in society.* New York, NY: Kodansha International.

Sack, D. (2013, March 4). 5 things parents do that may encourage teen substance abuse. Huffington Post. Retrieved from http://www.huffingtonpost.com/david-sack-md/teen-substance-abuse_b_2792838.html

Sanders, W. B. (1994). *Gangbangs and drive-bys: Grounded culture and juvenile gang violence.* New York, NY: Aldine De Gruyter.

Schaffer Library of Drug Policy. (1994, October 18). *Technologies for understanding and preventing substance abuse and addiction. Chapter 3: Biology and pharmacology.* Retrieved from http://www.druglibrary.org/schaffer/library/studies/ota/ch3.htm

Schur, E. M. (1971). *Labeling deviant behavior.* New York, NY: Harper & Row.

Shelden, R. G., Tracy, S. K., & Brown, W. B. (2001). *Youth gangs in American society,* 2nd ed. Belmont, CA: Wadsworth/Thomson Learning.

Siegel, L. J., & Senna, J. J. (1994). *Juvenile delinquency: Theory, practice and law.* St. Paul, MN: West.

Smith, D., Milkman, E., & Sunderworth, S. (1985). Addictive disease: Concept and controversy. In H. Milkman & H. J. Shaffer *(Eds.), Addictions: Multidisciplinary perspectives and treatments* (pp. 145–159). Lexington, MA: Lexington Books/D.C. Heath.

Spanagel, R.,, & Weiss, F. (1999). The dopamine hypothesis of reward: Past and current status. *Trends in Neuroscience, 22,* 521–527.

Statista, Inc. (2019). Global spam volume as percentage of total e-mail traffic from January 2014 to December 2018, by month. New York, NY: Author. Retrieved from https://www.statista.com/statistics/420391/spam-email-traffic-share/

Substance Abuse and Mental Health Services Administration (SAMHSA). (2009). *Substance abuse treatment: Addressing the specific needs of women.* Rockville, MD: U.S. Department of Health and Human Services.

Substance Abuse and Mental Health Services Administration (SAMHSA). (2015, October 27). *Substance abuse disorders.* Rockville, MD: U.S. Department of Health and Human Services. Retrieved from http://www.samhsa.gov/disorders/substance-use

Substance Abuse and Mental Health Services Administration (SAMHSA). (2018). *Key substance use and mental health indicators in the United States: Results from the 2017 National Survey on Drug Use and Health.* Rockville, MD: CBHSQ and SAMHSA. Retrieved from https://www.samhsa.gov/data/

Substance Abuse and Mental Health Services Administration (SAMHSA). (2019). Assess your workplace. Rockville, MD: U.S. Department of Health and Human Services. Retrieved from https://www.samhsa.gov/workplace /toolkit/assess-workplace

Sudhinaraset, M., Wigglesworth, C., & Takeuchi, D. T. (2016). Social and cultural contexts of alcohol use: Influences in a social-ecological framework. *Alcohol Research, 38,* 35–45.

Sutherland, E. (1947). *Principles of criminology,* 4th ed. Philadelphia, PA: Lippincott.

Sutton, R. S., & Barto, A. G. (2018). *Reinforcement learning,* 2nd ed. Cambridge, MA: MIT Press.

Syvertsen, J. L. (2008). Some considerations on the disease concept of addiction. In J. Inciardi & K. McElrath (Eds.), *The American drug scene: An anthology* (pp. 16–26). New York, NY: Oxford University Press.

Tarter, R. E., Alterman, A., & Edwards, K. L. (1983). Alcoholic denial: A biopsychosociological interpretation. *Journal of Studies on Alcohol, 45,* 214–218.

Thio, A. (2010). *Deviant behavior,* 10th ed. Boston, MA: Allyn & Bacon.

Thomas, W. I., & Thomas, D. S. *The child in America.* New York, NY: Knopf.

Thornberry, T. P. (2001). Risk factors for gang membership. In J. Miller, C. L. Maxson, & M. W. Klein (Eds.), *The modern gang reader,* 2nd ed. (pp. 200, 213–234). Los Angeles, CA: Roxbury.

Uhl, G., Blum, K., Noble, E., & Smith, S. (1993). Substance abuse vulnerability and D-2 receptor genes. *Trends in Neurological Sciences, 16,* 83–88.

Uhl, G., Elmer, G. I., LaBuda, M. C., & Pickens, R. W. (2002). Genetic influences in drug abuse: Human substance abuse vulnerability and genetic influences. In K. Davis, D. Charney, J. T. Coyle, & C. Nemeroff (Eds.), *Neuropsychopharmacology—5th generation of progress* (pp. 345–367). Philadelphia, PA: Lippincott Williams & Wilkins.

Uhl, G., Persico, A., & Smith, S. (1992, February). Current excitement with D-2 dopamine receptor gene alleles in substance abuse. *Archives of General Psychiatry, 49,* 157–160.

U.S. Department of Labor. (2011). Quick stats on women workers, 2010. Washington, DC: U.S. Department of Labor. Retrieved from http://www.dol.gov/wb /factsheets/QS-womenwork2010.htm

Valentish, J. (2019, June 28). Why addiction isn't a disease but instead the result of "deep learning." Sydney, Australia: National Drug and Alcohol Research Centre. Retrieved from https://ndarc.med.unsw.edu.au/blog /why-addiction-isnt-disease-instead-result-deep-learning

Venniro, M, Zhang, M., Caprioli, D., Golden, A. A., Heins, C., Hoots, J. K., . . . , & Shaham, Y. (2018, October 15). *Study shows impact of social interactions on addictive behavior.* Rockville, MD: NIDA.

Volkow, N. D. (2016, February). Biography of Dr. Nora Volkow. Rockville, MD: NIDA. Retrieved from https://www .drugabuse.gov/about-nida/directors-page/biography -dr-nora-volkow

Waldorf, D. (1983). Natural recovery from opiate addiction: Some social psychological processes of untreated recovery. *Journal of Drug Issues, 13,* 237–280.

Weiss, F. (1999). Cocaine dependence and withdrawal— Neuroadaptive changes in brain reward and stress systems. Retrieved from http://archives.drugabuse.gov/meetings /CCB/Weiss.html

Werner, E., & Henry, S. (1995). *Criminological theory: An analysis of its underlying assumptions.* Fort Worth, TX: Harcourt Brace College.

Williams, F. P. III, & McShane, M. D. (1999). *Criminological theory,* 3rd ed. Upper Saddle River, NJ: Prentice Hall.

Witmer, D. (2013). *Teen drug use warning signs.* About.com. Retrieved from http://parentingteens.about.com/cs /drugsofabuse/a/driug_abuse20.htm

Wooden, W. S. (1995). *Renegade kids, suburban outlaws: From youth culture to delinquency.* Belmont, CA: Wadsworth/ Thomson Learning.

World Health Organization Expert Committee on Addiction-Producing Drugs. (1964). *World Health Organization Technical Report, 273,* 9–10.

Wyman, J. (1997, July–August). Promising advances toward understanding the genetic roots of addiction. *NIDA Notes, 12,* 1–5.

Yinger, M. J. (1982). *Countercultures: The promise and the peril of a world turned upside down.* New York, NY: Free Press.

Zuckerman, M. (2000, November 1). Are you a risk taker? What causes people to take risks? It's not just a behavior. It's a personality. *Psychology Today.* Retrieved from http://www .psychologytoday.com/articles/200011/are-you-risk-taker

Zuckerman, M. (2007). *Sensation seeking and risky behavior.* Washington, DC: American Psychological Association.

# CHAPTER 3

# Drug Use, Regulation, and the Law

© FOTOGRIN/Shutterstock.

## Did You Know?

▶ Some patent medicines sold at the turn of the 20th century contained opium and cocaine and were highly addictive.

▶ For fiscal year 2019, according to the United States Office of National Drug Control Policy, the budget of a National Drug Control Program Agency to reduce availability of illegal drugs in the United States or abroad, exceeded $5 billion.

## Learning Objectives

**On completing this chapter, you should be able to:**

❭ Identify the major criteria that determine how society regulates drugs.

❭ Explain the significance of the Pure Food and Drug Act of 1906 and why it was important in regulating drugs of abuse.

❭ Describe the changes in drug regulation that occurred because of the Kefauver–Harris Amendment of 1962.

❭ Identify and explain the stages of testing for an investigational new drug.

❭ Discuss the special provisions (exceptions) made by the Food and Drug Administration (FDA) for drug marketing.

❭ Outline the procedures used by the FDA to regulate nonprescription drugs.

❭ Outline the major approaches used to reduce substance abuse.

❭ Explain the main arguments for and against legalizing drugs.

❭ List the most common types of drug testing.

# Introduction

Society mandates that it maintains control over which drugs are permissible and which drugs are prohibited. Through legislation, we decide which drugs are licit or illicit. We decide which licit drugs are readily available over the counter (OTC) and which can be obtained by prescription only. Thus, drug laws prohibit indiscriminate use of what society defines as a drug. In this chapter, you will come to better understand how society attempts to control drug use and abuse. In particular, this chapter examines the development of drug regulations in the United States that apply to both the manufacture of drugs and control of their use. Although many people assume that the regulation of drug manufacturing and drug abuse lie at opposite ends of the spectrum, regulation of drug manufacturing and abuse actually evolved from similar processes.

# Cultural Attitudes About Drug Use

Currently, cultural attitudes in the United States regarding the use of drugs blend beliefs in individuals' right to live their lives as they desire with society's obligation to protect its members from the burdens imposed by uncontrolled behavior. The history of drug regulation consists of regulatory swings in response to attempts by government to balance these two factors while responding to public pressures and perceived public needs. For example, more than 100 years ago, most people expected the government to protect citizens' rights to produce and market new foods and substances; they did not expect or desire the government to regulate product quality or claims. Instead, the public relied on private morals and common sense to obtain quality and protection in an era of simple technology. Unfortunately, U.S. society had to learn by tragic experience that its trust was not well placed; many unscrupulous entrepreneurs were willing to risk the safety and welfare of the public in an effort to maximize profits and acquire wealth. In fact, many medicines of these earlier times were not merely ineffective but often dangerous.

Because of the advent of high technology and the rapid advancements society has made, we now rely on highly trained experts and government watchdog agencies for consumer information and protection. Out of this changing environment have evolved two major guidelines for controlling drug development and marketing:

1. Society has the right to protect itself from the damaging effects of drug use. This concept not only is closely aligned with the emotional and highly visible issues of drug abuse but also includes protection from other drug side effects. Thus, although we expect the government to protect society from drugs that can cause addiction, we also expect it to protect us from drugs that cause cancer, cardiovascular disease, or other threatening medical conditions.

2. Society has the right to demand that drugs approved for marketing be safe and effective to the general public. If drug manufacturers promise that their products will relieve pain, those drugs should be analgesics; if they promise that their products will relieve depression, those drugs should be antidepressants; if they promise that their products will relieve stuffy noses, those drugs should be decongestants.

The public, through the activities of regulatory agencies and statutory enactments, has attempted to require that drug manufacturers produce safe and effective pharmaceutical products. Closely linked to these efforts is the fact that society uses similar strategies to protect itself from the problems associated with the specific drug side effect of dependence or addiction, which is associated with drug abuse.

# The Road to Regulation and the FDA

In the late 1800s and early 1900s, sales of uncontrolled medicines flourished and became widespread. Many of these products were called *patent medicines*, which signified that the ingredients were secret, not that they were patented. The decline of patent medicines began, in part, as a consequence of the 1906 Pure Food and Drug Act. This legislation required manufacturers to indicate the amounts of 11 dangerous products, including alcohol, cocaine, heroin, and morphine, on the label of each product (Schwann, 2006). It became obvious at this time that many medicinal products on the market labeled "nonaddictive" were, in fact, potent drugs "in sheep's labeling" and could cause severe dependence. However, most government interests at the time centered on regulation of the food industry, not drugs.

The shortcomings in the Pure Food and Drug Act quickly became obvious. In particular, the law did not allow the government to stop the distribution of dangerous preparations. As one example, an extract of horsetail weed, Banbar, was marketed by a shirt salesman as an injection-free cure for diabetes. Although the FDA established in court that diabetics were dying while on this preparation even though insulin was available, the government lost its case because it could not meet the standard of establishing fraud (Meadows, 2006; Schwann, 2006). As another example, no federal statute prevented the sale of a dangerous diet preparation containing dinitrophenol, a product that accelerated metabolism and created serious side effects, including cataracts (Schwann, 2006). Further, in 1911, the U.S. Supreme Court ruled that this act did not prohibit false therapeutic claims but only misleading and false statements about the identity or ingredients of a drug (FDA, 2009a).

The Pure Food and Drug Act was modified, albeit not in a consumer-protective manner, by the Sherley Amendment in 1912. The distributor of a cancer "remedy" was indicted for falsely claiming on the label that the contents were effective. The case was decided in the U.S. Supreme Court in 1911. Justice Oliver Wendell Holmes, writing for the majority opinion, said that, based on the 1906 act, the company had not violated any law because legally all it was required to do was accurately state the contents and their strength and quality. The accuracy of the therapeutic claims made by drug manufacturers was not controlled. Congress took the hint and passed the Sherley Amendment to add to the existing law the requirement that labels should not contain "any statement . . . regarding the curative or therapeutic effect . . . which is false and fraudulent." However, the law required that the government prove fraud, which turned out to be difficult (and is still problematic). This amendment did not improve drug products but merely encouraged pharmaceutical companies to be vaguer in their advertisements (Temin, 1980).

It was not until a drug company unwittingly produced a toxic product that killed more than 100 people, many of them children, that the FDA was given control over drug safety in the 1938 Federal Food, Drug, and Cosmetic Act (FDA 2012a, 2018f; Hunter, Rosen, &

DeChristoforo, 1993). The bill had been debated for several years in Congress and showed no promise of passage. Then a pharmaceutical company decided to sell a liquid form of a sulfa drug (one of the first antibiotics) and found that the drug would dissolve well in a chemical solvent (diethylene glycol) that was comparable to antifreeze. The company marketed the antibiotic as Elixir Sulfanilamide without testing the solvent for toxicity. Under the 1906 Pure Food and Drug Act, the company could not be prosecuted for the toxicity of this form of drug or for not testing the formulation of the drug on animals first. It could only be prosecuted for mislabeling the product on the technicality that the term *elixir* refers to a solution in alcohol, not a solution in diethylene glycol. Again, it was apparent that the laws in place provided woefully inadequate protection for the public.

The 1938 act differed from the 1906 law in several ways. Companies had to file applications with the government for all new drugs showing that they were safe (not effective—just safe) for use as described. The drug label had to provide instructions regarding safe use of the drug. The act demanded that safe tolerances be set for unavoidable poisonous substances and authorized the establishment of standards of identity, quality, and fill-of-container for foods. In addition, the act eliminated a Sherley Amendment requirement to prove intent to defraud in drug-misbranding cases (FDA, 2018f).

Before passage of the 1938 act, an individual could go to a doctor and obtain a prescription for any nonnarcotic drug or go to the pharmacy directly if this person had already decided what was needed. The labeling requirement in the 1938 act allowed drug companies to create a class of drugs that could not be sold legally without a prescription. It has been suggested that the FDA's actions were motivated by the frequent public misuse of two classes of drugs developed before passage of the 1938 law: sulfa antibiotics and barbiturates. People often took too little of the antibiotics to cure an infection and too much of the barbiturates and became addicted.

The 1938 Food, Drug, and Cosmetic Act allowed the manufacturer to determine whether a drug was to be labeled prescription or nonprescription. The same product could be sold as prescription by one company and as OTC by another. After the Durham–Humphrey Amendment was passed in 1951, almost all new drugs were placed in the prescription-only class. The drugs that were patented and marketed after World War II included potent new antibiotics and phenothiazine tranquilizers such as Thorazine. Both the FDA and the drug firms thought these products were potentially too dangerous to sell OTC. The Durham–Humphrey Amendment established the criteria, which are still used today, for determining whether a drug should be classified as prescription or nonprescription (FDA, 2018f). Basically, if a drug does not fall into one of the following three categories, it is considered nonprescription:

- The drug is habit forming.
- The drug is not safe for self-medication because of its toxicity.
- The drug is a new compound that has not been shown to be completely safe.

In addition, the Durham–Humphrey Amendment required any drug that is potentially harmful or habit forming to be dispensed under the supervision of a healthcare practitioner as a prescription drug and must carry the statement, "Caution: Federal law prohibits dispensing without prescription" (FDA, 2009b).

In 1959, Senator Estes Kefauver initiated hearings over concerns about the enormous profit margins earned by drug companies because of the lack of competition in the market for new, patented drugs. Testimony by physicians revealed that an average doctor in clinical practice often was not able to evaluate accurately the efficacy of the drugs he or she prescribed. The 1938 law did not give the FDA authority to supervise clinical testing of drugs; consequently, the effectiveness of drugs being sold to the public was not being determined. Both the Kefauver and Harris Amendments put forth in Congress were intended to deal with this problem but showed no likely signs of becoming law until the thalidomide tragedy occurred.

During the Kefauver hearings, the FDA received an approval request for Kevadon, a brand of thalidomide that was to be marketed in the United States. **Thalidomide** had been used

© Wellcome Images/Custom Medical Stock Photo.

Characteristic limb deformities caused by thalidomide.

in Europe, Canada, and Africa to treat morning sickness in pregnant women. Despite ongoing pressure, medical officer Frances Kelsey refused to allow the request to be approved because of concerns regarding dangerous side effects involving those who used the drug repeatedly (FDA, 2012b). By 1962, the damaging effects of thalidomide on developing fetuses became known. There are approximately two 24-hour intervals early in pregnancy when thalidomide can alter the development of the arms and legs of an embryo. If a woman takes thalidomide on one or both of these days, the infant could be born with abnormally developed arms or legs or both, a condition called **phocomelia**, from the Greek words for "flippers," or "seal-shaped limbs." Even though Kevadon was never approved for marketing in the United States, the manufacturers had distributed more than 2 million tablets in the United States for investigational use—a type of use that the regulations of that period left largely unchecked. Once the damaging effects of thalidomide became known, the FDA attempted quickly to recover the drug from patients and providers. For her efforts, Kelsey received the President's Award for Distinguished Federal Civilian Service in 1962, the highest civilian honor available to a government employee (National Library of Medicine, 2015).

Although standard testing probably would not have detected the congenital effect of thalidomide and the tragedy would likely have occurred

## KEY TERMS

**thalidomide**
sedative drug that, when used during pregnancy, can cause severe developmental damage to a fetus

**phocomelia**
birth defect; impaired development of the arms, legs, or both

anyway, these debilitated infants prompted passage of the 1962 Kefauver and Harris Amendments. They strengthened the government's regulation of both the introduction of new drugs and the production and sale of existing drugs. The amendments required, for the first time, that drug manufacturers demonstrate the efficacy as well as the safety of their drug products. The FDA was empowered to retract approval of a drug that was already being marketed. In addition, the agency was permitted to regulate and evaluate drug testing by pharmaceutical companies and mandate standards of good drug-manufacturing policy.

### ■ The Rising Demand for Effectiveness in Medicinal Drugs

To evaluate the effectiveness of the more than 4,000 drug products that were introduced between 1938 and 1962, the FDA contracted with the National Research Council to perform the drug-efficacy study. This investigation started in 1966 and ran for three years. The council was asked to rate drugs as either effective or ineffective. Although the study was supposed to be based on scientific evidence, this information often was not available, which meant that conclusions sometimes relied on the clinical experience of the physicians on each panel; these judgments were not always based on reliable information.

A legal challenge resulted when the FDA took an "ineffective" drug off the market and the manufacturer sued. This action finally forced the FDA to define what constituted an adequate and well-controlled investigation. Adequate, documented clinical experience was no longer satisfactory proof that a drug was safe and effective. Each new drug application now had to include information about the drug's performance in patients compared with the experiences of a carefully defined control group. The drug could be compared with (1) a placebo, (2) another drug known to be active based on previous studies, (3) the established results of no treatment, or (4) historical data about the course of the illness without the use of the drug in question. In addition, a drug marketed before 1962 could no longer be grandfathered in. If the company could not prove the drug had the qualifications to pass the post-1962 tests for a new drug, it was considered a new, unapproved drug and could not legally be sold.

### ■ Regulating the Development of New Drugs

The amended federal Food, Drug, and Cosmetic Act in force today requires that all new drugs be registered with and approved by the FDA. Congress mandates the FDA to (1) ensure the rights and safety of human subjects during clinical testing of experimental drugs, (2) evaluate the safety and efficacy of new treatments based on test results and information from the sponsors (often health-related companies), and (3) compare potential benefits and risks to determine whether a new drug should be approved and marketed. Because of FDA regulations, all pharmaceutical companies must follow a series of steps when seeking permission to market a new drug (see **Figure 3.1**).

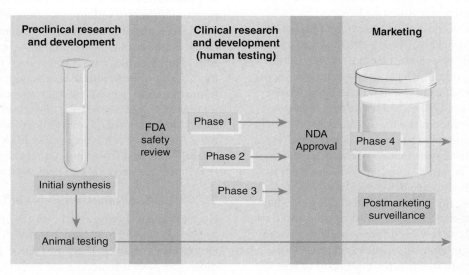

**FIGURE 3.1** Steps required by the FDA for reviewing a new drug.

## REGULATORY STEPS FOR NEW PRESCRIPTION DRUGS

### STEP 1: PRECLINICAL RESEARCH AND DEVELOPMENT

A chemical must be identified as having potential value in the treatment of a particular condition or disease. The company interested in marketing the chemical as a drug must run a series of tests on at least two or more animal species. Careful records must be kept of side effects, absorption, distribution, metabolism, excretion, and the dosages of the drug necessary to produce the various effects. Carcinogenic, mutagenic, and teratogenic variables are tested. The dose–response curve must be determined along with potency, and then the risk and benefit of the substance must be calculated. If the company still believes there is a market for the substance, it forwards the data to the FDA to obtain an investigational new drug (IND) number for further tests.

### STEP 2: CLINICAL RESEARCH AND DEVELOPMENT

Animal tests provide some information, but ultimately tests must be done on the species for which the potential drug is intended—that is, humans. These tests usually follow three phases.

Phase 1 is called the *initial clinical stage.* Small numbers of volunteers (usually 20 to 100), typically healthy people but sometimes patients, are recruited to establish drug safety and dosage ranges for effective treatment and to examine side effects. Medical students, paid college student volunteers, and other volunteers are often studied after obtaining informed consent. The data from Phase 1 clinical trials are collected, analyzed, and sent to the FDA for approval before the next phase of human subject testing can begin.

Phase 2 testing is called the *clinical pharmacological evaluation stage.* The effects of the drug are tested to eliminate investigator bias and to determine side effects and the effectiveness of the treatment. Because the safety of the new drug has not been thoroughly established, a few patients (perhaps 100 to 300 volunteers) with the medical problem the drug is intended to treat participate in these studies. Statistical evaluation of this information is carried out before proceeding with Phase 3 testing.

Phase 3 is the *extended clinical evaluation stage.* By this time, the pharmaceutical company has a good idea of both drug effectiveness and dangers. The drug can be offered safely to a wider group of participating clinics and physicians, who cooperate in the administration of the potential drug—when medically appropriate—to as many as thousands of volunteer patients who have given informed consent.

This stage makes the drug available on a wide experimental basis. Sometimes, by this point, the new drug has received some publicity, and people with the particular disease for which the drug was developed may actively seek out physicians licensed to experiment with it.

During Phase 3 testing, safety checks are made and any side effects that might show up as more people are exposed to the drug are noted. After the testing program concludes, careful analysis is made of the effectiveness, side effects, and recommended dosage. If there are sufficient data to demonstrate that the drug is safe and effective, the company submits a new drug application (NDA) as a formal request that the FDA consider approving the drug for marketing. The application usually comprises many thousands of pages of data and analysis, and the FDA must sift through it and decide whether the risks of using the drug justify its potential benefits. The FDA usually calls for additional tests before the drug is determined to be safe and effective and before granting permission to market it.

### STEP 3: PERMISSION TO MARKET

At this point, the FDA can allow the drug to be marketed under its patented name. According to a 2018 report, the cost of developing a new drug is estimated to be between $2 billion and $3 billion. The mean cost of clinical trials is estimated as $19 million (Johns Hopkins Bloomberg School of Public Health, 2018).

Once the drug is marketed, it continues to be closely scrutinized for adverse effects. This postmarketing surveillance is often referred to as Phase 4, and it is important because, in some cases, negative effects may not show up for a long time. For example, it was determined in 1970 that diethylstilbestrol (DES), when given to pregnant women to prevent miscarriage, causes an increased risk of a rare type of vaginal cancer in their daughters when these children enter their teens and young adult years. The FDA subsequently removed from the market the form of DES that had been used to treat pregnant women.

### EXCEPTIONS: SPECIAL DRUG-MARKETING LAWS

Concerns have been raised that the process used by the FDA to evaluate prospective drugs is laborious and excessively lengthy. Hence, an amendment was passed to accelerate the evaluation of urgently needed drugs. The so-called *fast-track rule* has been applied to the testing of certain drugs used for the treatment of rare cancers, acquired immunodeficiency syndrome (AIDS), and some other diseases. Fast tracking is a process designed to expedite the review of drugs to treat serious diseases and fill an unmet medical need. Filling an unmet medical need is defined as providing a therapy where none exists or providing one that may be potentially better than therapy available currently (FDA, 2018c).

According to the FDA,

> Determining whether a condition is serious is a matter of judgment, but generally is based on whether the drug will have an impact on such factors as survival, day-to-day functioning, or the likelihood that the condition, if left untreated, will progress from a less severe condition to a more serious one. AIDS, Alzheimer's, and cancer are obvious examples of serious conditions. However, diseases such as epilepsy, depression and diabetes are also considered to be serious conditions. (FDA, 2018c)

Many drugs that qualify for fast tracking also qualify for *priority review* by the FDA. A priority review designation "will direct overall attention and resources to the evaluation of applications for drugs that, if approved, would be significant improvements in the safety or effectiveness of the treatment, diagnosis, or prevention of serious conditions when compared to standard applications" (FDA, 2018g). Its goal is to reduce the time it takes for the FDA to review a new drug application, with a goal of completion in six months (compared to 10 months under standard review). Significant improvement may include (1) enhanced effectiveness in treatment, diagnosis, or prevention; (2) increased patient compliance that is predicted to lead to fewer serious adverse outcomes; (3) evidence of safety and effectiveness in a new subpopulation; or (4) substantial reduction or elimination of treatment-limiting drug reactions (FDA, 2018g).

The *breakthrough therapy* designation is designed to accelerate the review and development of agents that are intended to treat a serious condition. It requires clinical evidence indicating that the drug may provide significant improvement over existing therapy on one or more clinically significant endpoints. For purposes of breakthrough therapy designation, a "clinically significant endpoint generally refers to an endpoint that measures an effect on irreversible morbidity or mortality (IMM) or

on symptoms that represent serious consequences of the disease" (FDA, 2018b). The designation has several benefits, including eligibility for all fast-track designation features (FDA, 2018b, 2019b).

Of note, it is possible that drugs for serious conditions that fill an unmet medical can be approved based on a **surrogate endpoint** or **intermediate clinical endpoint**. This process is referred to as *accelerated approval* (FDA, 2018a).

Processes such as fast tracking, breakthrough designations, accelerated approval, and priority review have shortened review periods for drugs that treat serious conditions. As one example, the FDA reviewed Gleevec, a treatment for chronic myeloid leukemia, in 2.5 months (Motl, Miller, & Burns 2003).

Another special marketing law that has had considerable impact is the Orphan Drug Law. It allows drug companies to receive tax advantages if they develop drugs that are not especially profitable because they are useful in treating only small numbers of patients, such as those who suffer from rare diseases. A *rare disease* is defined as one that affects fewer than 200,000 people in the United States (FDA, 2018e). Fewer than 10 products supported by industry for rare diseases came to market between 1973 and 1983. Since its passage in 1984, more than 600 drugs and biological products for rare diseases have received approval for marketing (FDA, 2018d).

One additional attempt to accelerate the drug review is exemplified by the Prescription Drug User Fee Act of 1992. This law required drug manufacturers to pay fees to the FDA for the evaluation of NDAs. Congress required the FDA to use these fees to hire more reviewers so as to facilitate the review processes (FDA, 2015b).

## REGULATION OF NONPRESCRIPTION DRUGS

The Durham–Humphrey Amendment to the Food, Drug, and Cosmetic Act made a distinction between prescription and nonprescription

### KEY TERMS

**surrogate endpoint**
physical sign, laboratory measurement, radiographic image, or other measure that is expected to predict clinical benefit but is not itself a measure of clinical benefit

**intermediate clinical endpoint**
measure of a therapeutic effect that is considered reasonably likely to predict the clinical benefit of a drug, such as an effect on irreversible morbidity and mortality

(OTC) drugs and required the FDA to regulate OTC drug marketing. In 1972, the FDA initiated a program to evaluate the effectiveness and safety of the nonprescription drugs on the market and to ensure that they included appropriate labeling. Panels of drug experts that included physicians, pharmacologists, and pharmacists reviewed the so-called active ingredients in the OTC medications. Based on the recommendations of these panels, the active ingredients were placed in one of the following three categories:

1. Generally recognized as safe and effective for the claimed therapeutic indication
2. Not generally recognized as safe and effective or unacceptable indications
3. Insufficient data available to permit final classification

By 1981, the panels had made initial determinations about more than 700 ingredients in more than 300,000 OTC drug products and submitted more than 60 reports to the FDA.

In the second phase of the OTC drug review, the FDA evaluated the panels' findings and submitted a tentative adoption of the panels' recommendations (after revision, if necessary), following public comment and scrutiny. After some time and careful consideration of new information, the agency issued a final ruling and classification of the ingredients under consideration.

### ▌ The Effects of the OTC Review on Today's Medications

The review process for OTC ingredients has had a significant impact on the public's attitude about OTC products and their use (both good and bad) in self-medication. It was apparent from the review process that many OTC drug ingredients did not satisfy the requirements for safety and effectiveness. Consequently, it is almost certain that, future OTC medicines will contain fewer active ingredients but that these drugs will be safer and more effective than ever before.

In addition, with heightened public awareness, greater demand has been brought to bear on the FDA to make better drugs available to the public for self-medication. In response to these

pressures, the FDA has adopted a **switching policy** that allows the agency to review prescription drugs and evaluate their suitability as OTC products. According to the Consumer Healthcare Products Association, 700 drugs that would have required a prescription only 20 years ago have been switched to OTC status (FDA, 2016). The following criteria must be satisfied if a drug is to be switched to OTC status:

- The drug must have been marketed by prescription for at least three years.
- Use of the drug must have been relatively high during the time it was available as a prescription drug.
- Adverse drug reactions must not be alarming, and the frequency of side effects must not have increased during the time the drug was available to the public.

In general, this switching policy has been well received by the public. The medical community and the FDA are generally positive about OTC switches as well. Some concerns remain, however, that the wider access to more effective drug products will lead to increased abuse or misuse of OTC products. Hence, emphasis is placed on adequate labeling and education to ensure that consumers have sufficient information to use OTC products safely and effectively.

## The Regulation of Drug Advertising

Much of the public's knowledge and impressions about drugs come from advertisements. It is difficult to ascertain the amount of money currently spent by the pharmaceutical industry to promote its products. However, it has been estimated that spending on medical marketing increased from $17.7 to $29.9 billion from 1997 through 2016, "with direct-to-consumer advertising for prescription drugs and health services accounting for the most rapid growth, and pharmaceutical marketing to health professionals accounting for most promotional spending" (Schwartz & Woloshin, 2019).

The economics of prescription drugs are unique because a second party, the health professional, dictates what the consumer, the patient, will purchase. As a general rule, the FDA oversees most issues related to advertising of prescription drugs. In contrast, the Federal Trade Commission (FTC) regulates OTC advertising (FDA, 2015a).

KEY TERM

**switching policy**
FDA policy allowing the change of suitable prescription drugs to over-the-counter status

According to the FDA (2015c), physicians indicate that, for the most part, the advertisements for prescription drugs on television and radio have had both positive and negative effects on their patients and practices. The FDA has conducted surveys directed toward physicians to better understand how direct-to-consumer (DTC) prescription drug promotion affects the patient–doctor relationship, with the intent of informing the agency if advertising rules need to be changed to ensure better consumer understanding of the risks and benefits of prescription drugs. Highlights of the surveys include the following:

- Most physicians surveyed agreed that because their patient saw a DTC advertisement, he or she asked thoughtful questions. Approximately the same percentage of physicians thought the advertisements made their patients more aware of potential therapies.
- The physicians surveyed indicated that the advertisements did not convey information about risks and benefits equally well. In fact, 78% of physicians responded that their patients understand the possible *benefits* of the drug very well or somewhat well. In contrast, 40% of physicians indicated that their patients understand the possible *risks*. In addition, 65% responded that DTC advertisements confused patients.
- Approximately 75% of physicians surveyed indicated that DTC advertisements cause patients to think that a drug is more efficacious than it is, and many physicians felt some pressure to prescribe something when patients mentioned DTC advertisements.
- The physicians surveyed reported that patients understand that they need to consult a healthcare provider concerning appropriate treatments. Eighty-two percent responded either "very well" or "somewhat" when asked if they believe that their patients understand that only a physician can decide if a drug is appropriate for them.

A significant amount of prescription drug promotion is directed at health professionals. The approaches employed by manufacturers to encourage health professionals to prescribe their products include advertising in prestigious medical journals, direct mail advertising, and some radio and television advertising. Government advertising regulations control all printed and audio materials distributed by drug salespeople. Perhaps the most effective sales approach is when drug representatives personally visit health professionals; this tactic is harder to regulate.

Many people in and out of the medical community have questioned the ethics of drug advertising and marketing in the United States and are concerned about the negative impact that deceptive promotion has on target populations. One of the biggest problems in dealing with misleading or false advertising is defining such deception. Probably the best guideline for such a definition is summarized in the Wheeler–Lea Amendment to the FTC Act:

> The term *false advertisement* means an advertisement, other than labeling, which is misleading in a material respect; and in determining whether any advertisement is misleading, there shall be taken into account not only representations . . . but the extent to which the advertisement fails to reveal facts.

Tough questions are being asked as to how much control should be exerted over the pharmaceutical industry to protect the public without excessively infringing on the rights of these companies to promote their products. The solutions to these problems will not be simple. Nevertheless, efforts to keep drug advertisements accurate and informative are worthwhile and necessary if the public is expected to make rational decisions about drug use (see "Here and Now—Drug Advertising: What's in an Ad?").

## ■ Federal Regulation and Quality Assurance

No matter what policy is adopted by the FDA and other drug-regulating agencies, there will always be those who criticize their efforts and complain that they do not do enough or that they do too much. On the one hand, the FDA has been blamed for being excessively careful and requiring too much testing before new drugs are approved for marketing. On the other hand, when new drugs are released and cause serious side effects, the FDA is condemned for being ineffective in its control of drug marketing.

Note that federal regulations do not ensure drug safety or effectiveness for everyone. Too many individual variables alter the way individuals respond to drugs, making such universal assurances impossible. Federal agencies can only deal with general policies and make general decisions. For example, what if the FDA determines that a given drug is reasonably safe in 95% of

# HERE AND NOW

## Drug Advertising: What's in an Ad?

The FDA regulates the advertising of prescription drugs. Federal law does not bar drug companies from advertising any kind of prescription drug, even ones with the potential for severe injury, addiction, or withdrawal. The FDA cannot limit the amount of resources spent on prescription advertisements. It encourages pharmaceutical companies to use language that is clear and understandable to the general public.

According to the FDA, requirements of product claim advertisements include the following, but are not limited to:

- the generic and brand name of the drug,
- an FDA-approved use for the drug,
- a statement that a product is available by prescription only, and
- a "fair balance" description of the benefits and risks of the product

Data from Food and Drug Administration (FDA). (2019). Product claim ad (correct). Retrieved from https://www.fda.gov/drugs/drug-information-consumers/prescription-drug-advertising

the population and effective in 70%? Are these acceptable figures, or should a drug be safe in 99% and effective in 90% before it is deemed suitable for general marketing? What of the 5% or 1% of the population who will be adversely affected by this drug? What rights do they have to be protected?

There are no simple answers to these questions. Federal policies inevitably involve compromises that assume that the clinician who prescribes the drug or the patient who buys and consumes it (or both) will be able to identify when use of that drug is inappropriate or threatening. Unfortunately, sometimes drug prescribing and drug consuming are done carelessly and unnecessary side effects occur or the drug is ineffective.

It is always difficult to predict the future. Nevertheless, with the dramatic increase in new and better drugs becoming available to the public, it is not likely that federal or state agencies will diminish their role in regulating drug use. Now more than ever, the public demands safer and more effective drugs. This public attitude will likely translate into even greater involvement by regulatory agencies in issues of drug development, assessment, and marketing.

## Drug Abuse and the Law

The negative experiences described previously that Americans had at the turn of the 20th century with addicting substances such as opium led to the Harrison Act of 1914. It marked the first legitimate effort by the federal government to regulate and control the production, importation, sale, purchase, and distribution of addicting substances. The Harrison Act served as the foundation and reference for subsequent laws directed at regulating drug abuse issues.

Today, the Comprehensive Drug Abuse Prevention and Control Act of 1970 largely determines the ways in which law enforcement agencies deal with substance abuse. This act divided substances with abuse potential into categories based on the degree of their abuse potential and their clinical usefulness. The classifications, which are referred to as *schedules*, range from I to V. Schedule I substances have, in general, high abuse potential and no currently approved medicinal use; health professionals cannot prescribe them. Schedule II drugs also have high abuse potential but are approved for medical purposes and can be prescribed with restrictions. The distinctions among Schedule II through V substances reflect the likelihood of abuse occurring and the degree to which the drugs are controlled by governmental agencies. The least addictive and least regulated of the substances of abuse are classified as Schedule V drugs (see "Here and Now: Controlled Substance Schedules").

Several factors are considered when determining into which schedule a drug or other substance should be placed or whether a substance should be decontrolled or rescheduled (U.S. Department of Justice [USDOJ], 2017). Specific findings are not required for each factor. The factors include the following:

- The actual or relative abuse potential of the drug.

# HERE AND NOW

## Controlled Substance Schedules

Controlled substances classified as Schedule I, II, III, IV, or V drugs are described here.

### Schedule I

- Substances in this schedule have no currently accepted medical use in the United States, a lack of accepted safety for use under medical supervision, and a high potential for abuse.

- Examples of substances listed in Schedule I: heroin, lysergic acid diethylamide (LSD), marijuana (cannabis), peyote, methaqualone, and 3,4-methylenedioxymethamphetamine (Ecstasy).

### Schedule II/IIN

- Substances in this schedule have a high potential for abuse that may lead to severe psychological or physical dependence.

- Examples of Schedule II narcotics include hydromorphone (Dilaudid®), methadone (Dolophine®), meperidine (Demerol®), oxycodone (OxyContin®, Percocet®), and fentanyl (Sublimaze®, Duragesic®). Other Schedule II narcotics include morphine, opium, codeine, and hydrocodone. Examples of Schedule IIN stimulants include amphetamine (Dexedrine®, Adderall®), methamphetamine (Desoxyn®), and methylphenidate (Ritalin®). Other Schedule II substances include amobarbital, glutethimide, and pentobarbital.

### Schedule III/IIIN

- Substances in this schedule have a potential for abuse less than substances in Schedules I or II

and abuse may lead to moderate or low physical dependence or high psychological dependence.

- Examples of Schedule III narcotics include products containing not more than 90 milligrams of codeine per dosage unit (Tylenol with Codeine®), and buprenorphine (Suboxone®). Examples of Schedule IIIN nonnarcotics include benzphetamine (Didrex®), phendimetrazine, ketamine, and anabolic steroids such as Depo®-Testosterone.

### Schedule IV

- Substances in this schedule have a low potential for abuse relative to substances in Schedule III.

- Examples of Schedule IV substances include alprazolam (Xanax®), carisoprodol (Soma®), clonazepam (Klonopin®), clorazepate (Tranxene®), diazepam (Valium®), lorazepam (Ativan®), midazolam (Versed®), temazepam (Restoril®), and triazolam (Halcion®).

### Schedule V

- Substances in this schedule have a low potential for abuse relative to substances listed in Schedule IV and consist primarily of preparations containing limited quantities of certain narcotics.

- Examples of Schedule V substances include cough preparations containing not more than 200 milligrams of codeine per 100 milliliters or per 100 grams (Robitussin AC®, Phenergan with Codeine®), and ezogabine.

- Scientific evidence of the pharmacological effects of the drug.
- The state of current scientific knowledge regarding the substance. (This and the preceding factor are closely related. However, the preceding factor is primarily concerned with pharmacological effects, whereas this factor deals with all scientific knowledge with respect to the drug.)
- Its history and current pattern of abuse.
- What, if any, risk there is to the public health.
- The psychological or physiological dependence liability of the drug.
- The scope, duration, and significance of abuse.

- Whether the substance is an immediate precursor of a substance already controlled. The Controlled Substance Act allows inclusion of immediate precursors on this basis alone into the appropriate schedule and thus safeguards against possibilities of clandestine manufacture.

Penalties for illegal use or trafficking of these agents vary according to the agent's schedule, amount possessed, and number of previous drug-associated offenses (see **Table 3.1**).

The Controlled Substance Act made no provision for disposal of unwanted or unused prescription medications, except to relinquish these to law enforcement. This has led to the accumulation of unused drugs in homes and increased the likelihood of misuse and abuse.

The Secure and Responsible Drug Disposal Act was enacted to address this problem (see "Here and Now: Secure and Responsible Drug Disposal Act").

**TABLE 3.1** Federal Drug-Trafficking Penalties

| Drug/Schedule | Quantity | Penalties | Quantity | Penalties |
|---|---|---|---|---|
| Cocaine (Schedule II) | 500–4999 g mixture | **First Offense:** Not less than 5 years and not more than 40 years. If death or serious bodily injury, not less than 20 years or more than life. Fine of not more than $5 million if an individual, $25 million if not an individual.<br><br>**Second Offense:** Not less than 10 years and not more than life. If death or serious bodily injury, life imprisonment. Fine of not more than $8 million if an individual, $50 million if not an individual. | 5 kg or more mixture | **First Offense:** Not less than 10 years and not more than life. If death or serious bodily injury, not less than 20 years or more than life. Fine of not more than $10 million if an individual, $50 million if not an individual.<br><br>**Second Offense:** Not less than 20 years, and not more than life. If death or serious bodily injury, life imprisonment. Fine of not more than $20 million if an individual, $75 million if not an individual.<br><br>**2 or More Prior Offenses:** Life imprisonment. Fine of not more than $20 million if an individual, $75 million if not an individual. |
| Cocaine base (Schedule II) | 28–279 g mixture | | 280 g or more mixture | |
| Fentanyl (Schedule II) | 40–399 g mixture | | 400 g or more mixture | |
| Fentanyl analogue (Schedule I) | 10–99 g mixture | | 100 g or more mixture | |
| Heroin (Schedule I) | 100–999 g mixture | | 1 kg or more mixture | |
| LSD (Schedule I) | 1–9 g mixture | | 10 g or more mixture | |
| Methamphetamine (Schedule II) | 5–49 g pure or 50–499 g mixture | | 50 g or more pure or 500 g or more mixture | |
| PCP (Schedule II) | 10–99 g pure or 100–999 g mixture | | 100 g or more pure or 1 kg or more mixture | |

| Drug/Schedule | Quantity | Penalties |
|---|---|---|
| Other Schedule I and II drugs (and any drug product containing gamma hydroxybutyric acid) | Any amount | **First Offense:** Not more than 20 years. If death or serious bodily injury, not less than 20 years or more than life. Fine $1 million if an individual, $5 million if not an individual.<br><br>**Second Offense:** Not more than 30 years. If death or serious bodily injury, life imprisonment. Fine $2 million if an individual, $10 million if not an individual. |
| Flunitrazepam (Schedule IV) | 1 g | |
| Other Schedule III drugs | Any amount | **First Offense:** Not more than 10 years. If death or serious bodily injury, not more than 15 years. Fine not more than $500,000 if an individual, $2.5 million if not an individual.<br><br>**Second Offense:** Not more than 20 years. If death or serious injury, not more than 30 years. Fine not more than $1 million if an individual, $5 million if not an individual. |
| All other Schedule IV drugs | Any amount | **First Offense:** Not more than 5 years. Fine not more than $250,000 if an individual, $1 million if not an individual. |
| Flunitrazepam (Schedule IV) | Other than 1 g or more | **Second Offense:** Not more than 10 years. Fine not more than $500,000 if an individual, $2 million if other than an individual. |
| All Schedule V drugs | Any amount | **First Offense:** Not more than 1 year. Fine not more than $100,000 if an individual, $250,000 if not an individual.<br><br>**Second Offense:** Not more than 4 years. Fine not more than $200,000 if an individual, $500,000 if not an individual. |

| Drug | Quantity | First Offense | Second Offense |
|---|---|---|---|
| Marijuana (Schedule I) | 1000 kg or more mixture or 1000 or more marijuana plants | Not less than 10 years or more than life. If death or serious bodily injury, not less than 20 years, or more than life. Fine not more than $10 million if an individual, $50 million if other than an individual. | Not less than 20 years or more than life. If death or serious bodily injury, life imprisonment. Fine not more than $20 million if an individual, $75 million if other than an individual. |
| Marijuana (Schedule I) | 100–999 kg mixture or 100–999 marijuana plants | Not less than 5 years or more than 40 years. If death or serious bodily injury, not less than 20 years or more than life. Fine not more than $5 million if an individual, $25 million if other than an individual. | Not less than 10 years or more than life. If death or serious bodily injury, life imprisonment. Fine not more than $20 million if an individual, $75 million if other than an individual. |
| Marijuana (Schedule I) | More than 10 kg hashish, 50–99 kg mixture More than 1 kg of hashish oil; 50–99 marijuana plants | Not more than 20 years. If death or serious bodily injury, not less than 20 years or more than life. Fine $1 million if an individual, $5 million if other than an individual. | Not more than 30 years. If death or serious bodily injury, life imprisonment. Fine $2 million if an individual, $10 million if other than an individual. |
| Marijuana (Schedule I) | Less than 50 kg marijuana (but does not include 50 or more marijuana plants regardless of weight) | Not more than 5 yrs. Fine not more than $250,000, $1 million if other than individual | Not more than 10 yrs. Fine $500,000 if an individual, 2 million if other than individual |
| Hashish (Schedule I) | 10 kg or less | | |
| Hashish oil (Schedule I) | 1 kg or less | | |

U.S. Department of Justice (USDOJ). (2017). *Drugs of abuse: A DEA resource guide*. Retrieved from https://www.dea.gov/sites/default/files/drug_of_abuse.pdf

## ■ Drug Laws and Deterrence

As previously indicated, drug laws often do not serve as a satisfactory deterrent against the use of illicit drugs. People have used and abused drugs for thousands of years despite governmental restrictions. It is probable that they will continue to do so, even with stricter laws and greater support for law enforcement.

Nationwide, law enforcement made an estimated 10,554,985 arrests in 2017. Of these arrests, an estimated 1,632,921 arrests were for drug abuse violations. An estimated 990,678 were for driving under the influence (Federal Bureau of Investigation [FBI] 2018). This problem represents a tremendous cost to society in terms of damaged lives and family relationships; being arrested for a drug-related crime seriously jeopardizes a person's

# HERE AND NOW

## Secure and Responsible Drug Disposal Act

Prescription drug abuse is a major problem. According to the 2018 Substance Abuse and Mental Health Services Administration (SAMHSA, 2018) National Survey on Drug Use and Health, 6.2% of Americans age 12 or older had misused a psychotherapeutic in the year prior to the survey. Rates averaged across 2013 and 2014 indicated that more than 50% of those who misused prescription pain relievers age 12 or older got the prescription drugs they had most recently used from a friend or relative for free.

The Controlled Substances Act made no legal provisions for patients to rid themselves of unwanted pharmaceutical controlled substances except to give them to law enforcement. Pharmacies, physician offices, and hospitals were not permitted to accept the drugs. To combat this problem, President Barack Obama signed into law the 2010 Secure and Responsible Drug Disposal Act. This act authorized the Drug Enforcement Administration (DEA) to develop and implement regulations that outline methods to transfer unused or unwanted pharmaceutical controlled substances to authorized collectors for the purpose of disposal. The act also permitted long-term-care facilities to do the same on behalf of residents or former residents.

In 2014, the DEA implemented its final rule for the disposal of controlled substances. It authorizes certain DEA registrants (distributors, reverse distributors, manufacturers, retail pharmacies, narcotic treatment programs, and hospitals and clinics with on-site pharmacies) to amend their DEA registration to become authorized collectors. Law enforcement continues to have autonomy with respect to how these agencies collect pharmaceutical controlled substances, including holding take-back events.

U.S. Drug Enforcement Administration (DEA). (2014, September 8). *DEA releases new rules that create convenient but safe and secure prescription drug disposal options.* Washington, DC: DEA. Retrieved from https://www.dea.gov/press-releases/2014/09/08/dea-releases-new-rules-create-convenient-safe-and-secure-prescription; Substance Abuse and Mental Health Services Administration (SAMHSA). (2014). *Key substance use and mental health indicators in the United States: Results from the 2013 National Survey on Drug Use and Health* (NSDUH Series H-48, HHS Publication No. SMA 14-4863). Rockville, MD: SAMHSA. Retrieved from https://www.samhsa.gov/data/sites/default/files/NSDUHresultsPDFWHTML2013/Web/NSDUHresults2013.pdf; Substance Abuse and Mental Health Services Administration (SAMHSA). (2017). *The CBHSQ report: How people obtain the prescription pain relievers they misuse.* Retrieved from https://www.samhsa.gov/data/sites/default/files/report_2686/ShortReport-2686.html

opportunity to pursue a normal life. Drug taking is closely tied to societal problems, and it will remain a problem unless society provides more meaningful experiences to those who are most susceptible to drug abuse. Improved education and increased support should be given to preteens because that is the age when deviant behavior starts. In cases in which drug-education programs have been successful in involving students, the amount of drug taking and illegal activity seems to have decreased.

## ■ Factors in Controlling Drug Abuse

Three principal issues influence laws regarding drug abuse:

1. If a person abuses a drug, should he or she be treated as a criminal or as a sick person afflicted with a disease?
2. How is the user distinguished from the distributor of an illicit drug, and who should be more harshly punished—the person who creates the demand for the drug or the person who satisfies the demand?
3. Are the laws and associated penalties effective deterrents against drug use or abuse, and how is effectiveness determined?

In regard to the first issue, drug abuse may be considered both an illness and a crime. It can be a psychiatric disorder, an abnormal functional state in which a person is compelled (either physically or psychologically) to continue using the drug. It becomes a crime when the law, reflecting social opinion, makes abuse of the drug illegal. Health issues are clearly involved because uncontrolled abuse of almost any drug can lead to physical and psychological damage. Because the public must pay healthcare costs for societal damage, laws are created and penalties are implemented to prevent or correct drug abuse problems (see Table 3.1 on federal trafficking penalties).

Concerning the second issue, drug laws have always been more lenient on users than sellers of drugs of abuse. Actually, it is often hard to separate user from pusher because many drug abusers engage in both activities. Because huge profits are often involved, some people may not use the drugs they peddle and are only pushers; the law tries to deter use of drugs by concentrating on these persons but has questionable success. Organized crime is involved in major drug sales, and these "drug rings" have proved difficult to eliminate.

In regard to the third issue, considerable evidence indicates that U.S. criminal law has only limited success in deterring drug abuse. For example, during 2018, 11.7% of individuals aged 12 or older reported misusing a drug, an illicit drug, at least once in the past month (SAMSHA, 2019).

# Strategies for Preventing Drug Abuse

The U.S. government and the public became concerned about the increasing prevalence of drug use during the 1960s when demonstrations and nationwide protests against the Vietnam War proliferated as youth (mostly college students) rebelled against what they viewed as an unnecessary and unjust war. During the 1960s and early 1970s, for the first time, large numbers of middle- and upper-middle-class youth began using licit and illicit gateway drugs on a massive scale. In response, the government developed strategies for combating drug use and abuse. Important strategies it employed were **supply reduction**, **demand reduction**, and **inoculation**. More recently, the use of **drug courts** has become a major strategy.

## ■ Supply-Reduction Strategy

Early attempts at drug abuse prevention included both the Harrison Narcotic Act of 1914 and the 18th Amendment (Prohibition) to the U.S. Constitution. Both laws were intended to control the manufacture and distribution of classified drugs, with legislators anticipating that these restrictions would compel people to stop using drugs. The laws enforced supply reduction, which involves a lessening, restriction, or elimination of available drugs.

Supply-reduction drug-prevention policy attempts to curtail the supply of illegal drugs or their precursors and exerts greater control over other, more therapeutic drugs. Part of the supply-reduction policy includes **interdiction**, which includes decreasing the amounts of these agents that are carried across U.S. borders by using foreign crop eradication measures and agreements, by

imposing stiff penalties for drug trafficking, and by controlling alcoholic beverages through licensing.

The United States dedicates enormous resources to interdiction programs. For fiscal year 2019, the budget of the National Drug Control Program Agency to reduce availability of illegal drugs in the United States or abroad, by targeting the transportation link, which encompasses intercepting and ultimately disrupting shipments of illegal drugs and their precursors as well as the proceeds, exceeded 5 billion dollars (Office of National Drug Control Policy, 2019). Although seizures of large caches of illicit drugs are reported routinely in the national press, the evidence is mixed as to whether drugs are substantially less available. One can argue that as long as a strong demand for these psychoactive agents exists, demand will be satisfied if the price is right. Even if interdiction successfully reduces the supply of one drug of abuse, if demand persists, that drug is usually replaced by another drug with similar abuse potential.

## ■ Demand-Reduction Strategy

The demand reduction approach attempts to minimize the actual demand for drugs. Through programs and activities often aimed at youth, emphasis is placed on reformulating values, attitudes, skills, and behaviors conducive to resisting drug use. As part of this strategy, support for medical and group drug treatment programs for abusers is encouraged. Although this approach does not address the drug supply, it does attempt to curb and eventually eliminate the need to purchase drugs by reducing the buyer's demand.

**KEY TERMS**

**supply reduction**
drug-reduction policy aimed at reducing the supply of illegal drugs and controlling other therapeutic drugs

**demand reduction**
attempts to decrease individuals' tendencies to use drugs, often aimed at youth, with emphasis on reformulating values and behaviors

**inoculation**
method of abuse prevention that protects drug users by teaching them responsibility

**drug courts**
process that integrates substance abuse treatment, incentives, and sanctions and places nonviolent, drug-involved defendants in judicially supervised rehabilitation programs

**interdiction**
policy of cutting off or destroying supplies of illicit drugs

Drug abuse is a complex and highly individual problem, with many causes and aggravating factors. Even so, experience has shown that prevention and treatment are better strategies and, in the long run, less costly than interdiction or incarceration (Kreit, 2009). The following are some suggestions and strategies for how to reduce demand for drugs.

- The top priority of any prevention program, if it is to provide a long-term solution, must be reduction of drug demand by youth. Children must be the primary focus in any substance abuse program. Achieving success requires stabilizing defective family structures, implementing school programs that create an antidrug attitude, establishing a drug-free environment, and promoting resistance training to help youths avoid drug involvement. In addition, children should be encouraged to become involved in alternative activities that can substitute for drug-abusing activity. Potential drug abusers need to be convinced that substance abuse is personally and socially damaging and unacceptable.

- Education about drug abuse must be carefully designed and customized for the target population or group. For example, education based on scare tactics is not likely to dissuade adolescents from experimenting with drugs. Adolescents are at a stage of development when they feel invincible, and graphically depicting the potential health consequences of drug and alcohol abuse has little impact. A discussion about the nature of addiction and the addiction process is more likely to influence their attitudes. Adolescents need to understand why people use drugs to appreciate the behavior patterns in themselves. Other important topics that should be discussed are how drug abuse works and why it leads to dependence. To complement drug education, adolescents also should be taught coping strategies that include effective decision-making and problem-solving skills.

- Attitudes toward drug abuse and its consequence must be changed. The drug use patterns of many people, both young and old, are strongly influenced by their peers. If individuals believe that drug abuse is glamorous and contributes to acceptance by friends and associates, then the incidence of drug abuse will remain high. In contrast, if the prevailing message in society is that drug abuse is unhealthy and not socially acceptable, then the incidence will be much lower.

- Replacement therapy has been shown to be a useful approach to weaning the individual off of drugs of abuse. A common example of this strategy is the use of the narcotic methadone to treat the heroin addict. Use of methadone prevents the cravings and severe effects of withdrawal routinely associated with breaking the heroin habit. Unfortunately, many heroin addicts must be maintained on methadone indefinitely. Even though methadone is easier to control and is less disruptive than heroin, one drug addiction has been substituted for another, which draws criticism. Replacement therapy certainly is not the entire answer to all drug abuse problems, but it often can provide a window of opportunity for behavioral modification so that a long-term solution to the abuse problem is possible.

## ▌ Inoculation Strategy

The inoculation method of abuse prevention aims to protect drug users by teaching them responsibility. The emphasis is on being accountable, rational, and responsible about drug use and informing users about the effects of drugs on both mind and bodily function. Nonalcohol parties and responsible drinkers who use designated drivers are outcomes of applying inoculation strategy.

## ▌ Drug Courts

Drug courts are designed to deal with nonviolent, drug-abusing offenders. As of June 2015, more than 3,000 drug courts were in place in the United States. More than half target adults, including those who have been caught driving while intoxicated and a growing number of military veterans; others address juvenile, child welfare, and different case types (National Institute of Justice [NIJ] 2015). Drug courts integrate mandatory drug testing, substance abuse treatment, sanctions, and incentives in a judicially supervised setting. These courts hold offenders accountable for their actions and provide them with the support and tools necessary to rebuild their lives and become productive members of the community.

Recent statistics indicate that drug courts are effective. For example, the National Institute of Justice's Multisite Adult Drug Court Evaluation (National Criminal Justice Referral Service, 2017) found the following:

- Participants reported less drug use (56% vs. 76%) and were less likely to test positive (29% vs. 46%) than comparable offenders.
- Participants reported less criminal activity (40% vs. 53%) and had fewer rearrests (52% vs. 62%) than comparable offenders.
- Treatment investment costs were higher for participants, but less recidivism allowed drug courts to save an average of $5,680 to $6,208 per offender overall.

## Current and Future Drug Use

During the administrations of former Presidents Ronald Reagan and George H. W. Bush (1980–1992), the official policy of the U.S. federal government included a "get-tough" attitude about drug abuse. Slogans such as "Just Say No" and "War on Drugs" reflected the frustration of a public that had been victimized by escalating crime (many incidents were drug related); personally touched by drug tragedies in families, at work, or with associates and friends; and economically strained by dealing with the cost of the problem.

Much remains to be accomplished in the fight against substance abuse. During 2018, 3.2% of individuals ages 12 or older reported misusing an illicit drug other than marijuana in the previous month (SAMSHA, 2019). Fighting the War on Drugs is clearly difficult and complex. Despite substantial efforts, significant problems still exist and require the attention of politicians, clinicians, law enforcement agencies, families, counselors, and all concerned citizens.

### ■ Drug Legalization Debate

The persistence of the drug abuse problem and the high cost in dollars and frustration of waging the War on Drugs have energized the ongoing debate regarding legalizing the use of drugs of abuse. Proponents of legalization are no longer limited to libertarians and so-called academic intellectuals. Increasingly, this group includes representatives of a distressed law enforcement system. For example, some judges whose courts are swamped with drug cases and police officers who spend much of their on-duty time dealing with and arresting abusers have asserted that many of the drug laws are wasteful or ineffective.

Individuals and groups promoting the legalization of all substances of abuse commonly cite several arguments. For instance, proponents often contend that if drugs were legalized, violence and crime would become less frequent. These individuals point out that users often commit crimes to pay for illicit drugs. If these drugs were legal, then the tremendous profits associated with drugs because of their illegal status would disappear and, once gone, the black market and criminal activity associated with drugs would be eliminated. Furthermore, legalization would decrease law enforcement costs by eliminating the backlog of drug-related court cases and reduce populations in overcrowded prisons.

Conversely, opponents of drug legalization believe that legalization would lead to an increased availability of drugs that would, in turn, lead to increased use. They point out that the use of drugs—especially methamphetamine, phencyclidine (PCP), and cocaine—is often associated with violent criminal behavior. Numerous studies demonstrate the links among drugs, violence, and crime; the link between alcohol, a legal substance, and crime is also well documented. According to legalization opponents, drug use would merely increase the incidence of crime, even if the drugs were legally purchased. Accordingly, the economic (as well as social) cost to society would increase.

Legalization proponents claim that making illicit drugs licit would not cause more of these substances to be consumed, nor would addiction increase. They note that many individuals use drugs in moderation. Furthermore, many would choose not to use drugs, just as many abstain currently from tobacco and alcohol. Opponents contend that if drugs were made licit and more widely available, usage and addiction rates would increase. These individuals contend that legalizing drugs sends a message that drug use (like tobacco and alcohol) is acceptable and encourages drug use among individuals who currently do not use drugs.

Proponents claim that drug legalization would allow users the right to practice a diversity of consciousness. Just as diversity of race, ethnicity, sexual orientation, religion, and other varied lifestyles is allowed, legalization of drugs would permit individuals to alter their consciousness without legal repercussions as long as they do not harm or threaten the safety and security of others. Moreover, proponents argue that education, healthcare, road building, and a wide array of other worthwhile causes would benefit from the taxes that could be raised by legalizing and then taxing drugs. They argue that the United States has spent billions of dollars to control drug production, trafficking, and use with few, if any, positive results. They contend that the money spent on drug control should be shifted to other, more productive endeavors.

Opponents believe that health and societal costs would increase with drug legalization. It has been predicted that drug treatment costs; hospitalization for long-term, drug-related diseases; and treatment of the consequences of drug-associated family violence would further burden our already strapped healthcare system. Such a policy would increase costs to society because of greater medical and social problems resulting from greater availability and increased use of drugs. Two of the most frequently abused substances, alcohol and tobacco, are both legal and readily available today. These two substances arguably cause more medical, social, and personal problems than all the illicit drugs of abuse combined.

Although arguments for both sides warrant consideration, extreme policies are not likely to be implemented; instead, a compromise will most probably be adopted. For example, areas potentially ripe for compromise include the following (Kalant, 1992):

- *Selective legalization*: Eliminate harsh penalties for those drugs of abuse that are the safest and least likely to cause addiction.
- *Control of substances of abuse by prescription or through specially approved outlets*: Have the availability of the illegal drugs controlled by physicians and trained clinicians rather than by law enforcement agencies.
- *Discretionary enforcement of drug laws*: Allow greater discretion by judicial systems for prosecution and sentencing of those who violate

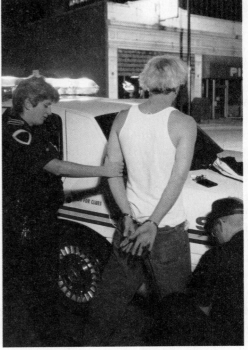

Substance abuse can lead to serious legal problems.

drug laws. Such decisions would be based on perceived criminal intent.

In conclusion, drug legalization remains a highly divisive issue in the United States. Although legalization would lessen the number of drug violators involved in the criminal justice system, the problems associated with legalizing current illicit drugs cause many members in our society to view this idea with disfavor. As previously stated, opponents of legalization argue that we already have substantial problems with licit drugs such as tobacco and alcohol. According to them, legalizing additional types of drugs would produce a substantial increase in the rate of addiction and in the social and psychological problems associated with drug use. Proponents favoring legalization assert that, despite the current drug laws and severe penalties for drug use, people continue to use illicit drugs.

## ■ Drug Testing

In response to the demand by society to stop the spread of drug abuse and its adverse consequences, drug testing has been implemented in some situations to detect drug users. The most common types of drug testing use breathalyzers and laboratory studies of urine, blood, and hair specimens. Urine and blood testing are preferred for detecting drug use. Hair-specimen testing must overcome technical problems, including complications from hair treatment (e.g., hair coloring) and environmental absorption, before hair can be used as a definitive proof of drug use.

The drugs of abuse most frequently tested for are marijuana, cocaine, amphetamines, narcotics, sedatives, and anabolic steroids. Drug testing is often mandatory in some professions in which public safety is a concern (such as airline pilots, railroad workers, law enforcement employees, and medical personnel) and for employees of some organizations and companies as part of general policy (such as the military, many federal agencies, and some private companies). Drug testing is also often mandatory for participants in sports at all levels—whether high school, college, international, or professional competition—to prevent unfair advantages that might result from the pharmacological effects of these drugs and to discourage the spread of drug abuse among athletes. Likewise, drug testing is used routinely by law enforcement agencies to assist in the prosecution of those believed to violate drug abuse laws. Finally, drug testing is used by health professionals to assess the success of drug abuse treatment—that is, to determine whether a dependent patient is diminishing his or her drug use or has experienced a relapse in drug abuse habits.

Drug testing to identify drug offenders is usually accomplished by analyzing body fluids (in particular urine), although other approaches (such as analysis of expired air for alcohol) are also used. To understand the accuracy of these tests, several factors should be considered:

- *Testing must be standardized and conducted efficiently.* To interpret testing results reliably, it is essential that fluid samples be collected, processed, and tested using standard procedures. Guidelines for proper testing procedures have been established by federal regulatory agencies as well as scientific organizations. Deviations from established protocols can result in false positives (tests that indicate a drug is present when none was used), false negatives (tests that are unable to detect a drug that is present), or inaccurate assessments of drug levels.
- *Sample collection and processing must be done accurately.* In many cases, drug testing can have punitive consequences (e.g., athletes cannot compete or employees are fired if results are positive). Consequently, drug users often attempt to outsmart the system. Some individuals have attempted to avoid submitting their own drug-containing urine for testing by filling specimen bottles with "clean" urine from artificial bladders hidden under clothing or in the vagina or by introducing "clean" urine into their own bladders just before collection. To confirm the legitimacy of the specimen, it often is necessary to have the urine collection witnessed directly by a trustworthy observer. To ensure that the fluid specimens are not tampered with, samples should be immediately coded and the movement of each sample from site to site during analysis should be documented and confirmed.
- *Just as it is important that testing identify individuals who are using drugs, it is also important that those who have not used drugs not be wrongfully accused.* To avoid false positives, all samples that test positive in screening (usually via fast and inexpensive procedures) should be analyzed again using more accurate, sensitive, and sophisticated analytical procedures to confirm the results.
- *Confounding factors that interfere with the accuracy of the testing can be inadvertently or deliberately present.* For example, excessive intake of fluid or use of diuretics increases the volume of urine formed and decreases the concentration of drugs, making them more difficult to detect.

The dramatic increase in drug testing since 1985 has caused some experts to question its value in dealing with drug abuse problems. Drug testing often is linked exclusively to punitive consequences, such as disqualification from athletic competition, loss of job, or even fines and imprisonment. Use of drug testing in such negative ways often does little to diminish the number of drug abusers or deal with their personal problems. However, drug-testing programs can have positive consequences by identifying drug users who require professional care. After being referred for drug rehabilitation, the offender can be monitored using drug testing to confirm the desired response to therapy. In addition, tests can identify individuals who put others in jeopardy because of their drug abuse habits when they perform tasks that are dangerously impaired by the effects of these drugs (e.g., airline pilots, train engineers, and truck drivers).

## ■ Pragmatic Drug Policies

Several principles for a pragmatic drug policy emerge from a review of past drug policies and an understanding of the drug-related frustrations of today. To create drug policies that work, the following suggestions are offered:

- Given the difficulties and high cost of efforts to prevent illicit drugs from reaching the market, it is logical to deemphasize interdiction and instead stress programs that reduce demand. To reduce demand, drug education and drug treatment must be top priorities.
- Government and society need to better understand the role played by law in their efforts to reduce drug addiction. Antidrug laws by themselves do not eliminate drug problems; indeed, they may even create significant social difficulties (e.g., as did the Prohibition laws banning all alcohol use). Used properly and selectively, however, laws can reinforce and communicate expected social behavior and values (e.g., laws against public drunkenness or against driving a vehicle under the influence of alcohol).
- Programs that employ public consensus should be implemented more effectively to campaign against drug abuse. For example, antismoking campaigns demonstrate the potential success that could be achieved by programs that alter drug abuse behavior. Similar approaches can be used to change public attitudes about drugs through education without making moral judgments and employing crusading tactics. Society needs to engage in more collaborative programs in which drug-using individuals and their families, communities, and helping agencies work together.

# LEARNING PORTFOLIO

## Discussion Questions

1. Describe the FDA approval process for assessing the safety and efficacy of a newly developed drug. What are advantages and disadvantages of this process?
2. Identify the principal legislative initiatives that mandate that drugs be proven safe or effective.
3. What are the principal advantages and disadvantages of switching products from prescription to OTC status?
4. What could account for the vast differences in attitudes and opinions regarding drug use and the law voiced by drug users and abusers and nonusers of drugs?
5. Would decriminalization of illicit drug use increase or decrease drug-related social problems? Justify your answer.
6. Compare and contrast supply reduction, demand reduction, and inoculation strategies for dealing with drug abuse.
7. List the principal arguments for and against legalizing drugs of abuse such as marijuana and cocaine.

## Key Terms

| | |
|---|---|
| demand reduction | 127 |
| drug courts | 127 |
| inoculation | 127 |
| interdiction | 127 |
| intermediate clinical endpoint | 119 |
| phocomelia | 116 |
| supply reduction | 127 |
| surrogate endpoint | 119 |
| switching policy | 120 |
| thalidomide | 116 |

## Summary

1. Societies have evolved to believe they have the right to protect themselves from the damaging impact of drug use and abuse. Consequently, governments, including that of the United States, have passed laws and implemented programs to prevent social damage from inappropriate drug use. In addition, such societies have come to expect that drugs are effective.
2. The 1906 Pure Food and Drug Act was not a strong law, but it required manufacturers to include on labels the amounts of alcohol, morphine, opium, cocaine, heroin, and marijuana extract in each product. It represented the first real attempt to make consumers aware of the active contents in the drug products they were consuming.
3. The 1938 Federal Food, Drug, and Cosmetic Act gave the FDA control over drug safety.
4. The 1951 Durham–Humphrey Amendment to the Food, Drug, and Cosmetic Act made a formal distinction between prescription and nonprescription drugs.
5. The Kefauver–Harris Amendment of 1962 required manufacturers to demonstrate both the efficacy and the safety of their products.
6. Drugs to be considered for marketing must first be tested for safety in animals. Following these initial tests, if the FDA favorably reviews the drug, it is given IND status. It then generally undergoes three phases of human clinical testing before receiving final FDA approval.

7.  In 1972, the FDA initiated a program to ensure that all OTC drugs were safe and effective. Panels were selected to evaluate the safety and effectiveness of OTC drug ingredients. Each ingredient was classified into a particular category: I, II, or III.

8.  The switching policy of the FDA allows the agency to review prescription drugs and evaluate their suitability as OTC products.

9.  Controversy exists as to how best to reduce substance abuse. A principal strategy used by governmental agencies to achieve this objective is interdiction; the majority of money used to fight drug abuse is spent on trying to stop and confiscate drug supplies. Experience has proved that interdiction is often ineffective. To reduce drug abuse, demand for these substances must be diminished. Youth must be a top priority in any substance abuse program. Finally, education should be used to change attitudes toward drug abuse and its consequences. Potential drug abusers need to be convinced that substance abuse is personally and socially damaging and unacceptable.

10. Major strategies for combating drug use and abuse are supply reduction, demand reduction, and inoculation. Supply reduction involves using drug laws to control the manufacture and distribution of classified drugs. Demand reduction aims to reduce the actual demand for drugs by working mainly with youth and teaching them to resist drugs. Inoculation aims to protect potential drug users by teaching them responsibility and explaining the effects of drugs on bodily and mental functioning.

11. Drug courts are designed to deal with nonviolent, drug-abusing offenders. They require substance abuse treatment and implement sanctions in a judicially supervised program. This emerging strategy has had positive social and economic impacts.

12. In response to the demand by society to stop the spread of drug abuse and its adverse consequences, drug testing has been implemented in some situations to detect drug users. Common drug testing uses breathalyzers and analysis of urine, blood, and hair specimens. Urine and blood testing are the preferred methods of testing for drug use. Hair-specimen testing must overcome several technical problems, including complications caused by hair treatment and environmental absorption, before it can be used as a definitive proof of drug use.

## References

Federal Bureau of Investigation (FBI). (2018), *Crime in the United States 2017*. Washington, DC: Author. Retrieved from https://ucr.fbi.gov/crime-in-the-u.s/2017/crime-in-the-u.s.-2017/topic-pages/persons-arrested

Food and Drug Administration (FDA). (2009a). This week in FDA history—May 29, 1911. Retrieved from http://wayback.archive-it.org/7993/20180126082025/https://www.fda.gov/AboutFDA/WhatWeDo/History/ThisWeek/ucm117785.htm

Food and Drug Administration (FDA). (2009b). This week in FDA history—Oct. 26, 1951. Retrieved from http://wayback.archive-it.org/7993/20180126082109/https://www.fda.gov/AboutFDA/WhatWeDo/History/ThisWeek/ucm117875.htm

Food and Drug Administration (FDA). (2012a). FDA history—Part II: 1938, Food, Drug, Cosmetic Act. Retrieved from https://www.fda.gov/about-fda/fdas-evolving-regulatory-powers/part-ii-1938-food-drug-cosmetic-act

Food and Drug Administration (FDA). (2012b). Kevauver-Harris amendments revolutionized drug development. Retrieved from https://www.fda.gov/consumers/consumer-updates/kefauver-harris-amendments-revolutionized-drug-development

Food and Drug Administration (FDA). (2015a). Prescription drug advertising: Questions and answers. Retrieved from https://www.fda.gov/drugs/prescription-drug-advertising/prescription-drug-advertising-questions-and-answers

Food and Drug Administration (FDA). (2015b). PDUFA legislation and background. Retrieved from: https://www.fda.gov/industry/prescription-drug-user-fee-amendments/pdufa-legislation-and-background

Food and Drug Administration (FDA). (2015c). The impact of direct-to-consumer advertising. Retrieved from https://www.fda.gov/drugs/drug-information-consumers/impact-direct-consumer-advertising

Food and Drug Administration (FDA). (2016). Now available without a prescription. Retrieved from https://www.fda.gov/drugs/drug-information-consumers/now-available-without-prescription

Food and Drug Administration (FDA). (2018a). Accelerated approval. Retrieved from http://www.fda.gov/ForPatients/Approvals/Fast/ucm405447.htm

Food and Drug Administration (FDA). (2018b). Breakthrough therapy. Retrieved from http://www.fda.gov/ForPatients/Approvals/Fast/ucm405397.htm

Food and Drug Administration (FDA). (2018c). Fast track. Retrieved from http://www.fda.gov/ForPatients/Approvals/Fast/ucm405399.htm

Food and Drug Administration (FDA). (2018d). Developing products for rare diseases & Conditions. Retrieved from https://www.fda.gov/industry/developing-products-rare-diseases-conditions

Food and Drug Administration (FDA). (2018e). FDA unveils plan to eliminate orphan designation backlog. Retrieved from https://www.fda.gov/news-events/press-announcements/fda-unveils-plan-eliminate-orphan-designation-backlog

Food and Drug Administration (FDA). (2018f). Milestones in U.S. food and drug law history. Retrieved from https://www.fda.gov/about-fda/fdas-evolving-regulatory-powers/milestones-us-food-and-drug-law-history

Food and Drug Administration (FDA). (2018g). Priority review. Retrieved from http://www.fda.gov/ForPatients/Approvals/Fast/ucm405405.htm

Food and Drug Administration (FDA). (2019a). Prescription drug advertising. Washington, DC: Author. Retrieved from https://www.fda.gov/drugs/drug-information-consumers/prescription-drug-advertising

Food and Drug Administration (FDA). (2019b). Frequently Asked Questions: Breakthrough Therapies. Retrievable: https://www.fda.gov/regulatory-information/food-and-drug-administration-safety-and-innovation-act-fdasia/frequently-asked-questions-breakthrough-therapies

Hunter, J. R., D. L. Rosen, and R. DeChristoforo. (1993, January). How FDA expedites evaluation of drugs. *Welcome Trends in Pharmacy,* pp. 2–9.

Johns Hopkins Bloomberg School of Public Health. (2018). Cost of clinical trials for new drug FDA approval are fraction of total tab. Retrieved from https://www.jhsph.edu/news/news-releases/2018/cost-of-clinical-trials-for-new-drug-FDA-approval-are-fraction-of-total-tab.html

Kalant, H. (1992). Formulating policies on the non-medical use of cocaine. In *Cocaine: Scientific and social dimensions* (Ciba Foundation Symposium), *166.* 261–276. New York: Wiley.

Kreit, A. (2009, March). *Toward a public health approach to drug policy.* Washington, DC: American Constitutional Society for Law and Policy.

Meadows, M. (2006). Promoting safe and effective drugs for 100 years. Washington, DC: FDA. Retrieved from https://www.fda.gov/files/about%20fda/published/Promoting-Safe-and-Effective-Drugs-for-100-Years.pdf.pdf

Motl, S., Miller, S. J., & Burns, P. (2003, February). Established by FDA to expedite patient access to medications. *American Journal of Health-System Pharmacy,* pp. 339–345. Retrieved from https://www.medscape.com/viewarticle/449551_6

National Criminal Justice Referral Service. (2017). Drug courts—Facts and figures. Retrieved from http://www.ncjrs.gov/spotlight/drug_courts/facts.html

National Institutes of Justice (NIJ). (2015). Overview of drug courts. Retrieved from http://www.nij.gov/topics/courts/drug-courts/Pages/welcome.aspx

National Library of Medicine. (2015). Dr. Francis Kathleen Oldham Kesley. Retrieved from https://www.nlm.nih.gov/changingthefaceofmedicine/physicians/biography_182.html

Office of National Drug Control Policy. (2019). National drug control budget FY 2020 funding highlights. Retrieved from https://www.whitehouse.gov/wp-content/uploads/2019/03/FY-20-Budget-Highlights.pdf

Schwann, J. P. (2006). FDA). How chemists pushed for consumer protection—The Food and Drugs Act of 1906. Washington, DC: FDA. Retrieved from https://www.fda.gov/files/about%20fda/published/How-Chemists-Pushed-for-Consumer-Protection-The-Food-and-Drugs-Act-of-1906.pdf

Schwartz, L. M., & Woloshin, S. (2019). Medical marketing in the United States, 1997—2016. *JAMA, 321*(1), 80–96.

Substance Abuse and Mental Health Services Administration (SAMHSA). (2014). Results from the 2013 National Survey on Drug Use and Health: Summary of national findings. Rockville, MD: SAMSHA. Retrieved from https://www.samhsa.gov/data/sites/default/files/NSDUHresultsPDFWHTML2013/Web/NSDUHresults2013.pdf

Substance Abuse and Mental Health Services Administration (SAMHSA). (2017). *The CBHSQ report: How people obtain the prescription pain relievers they misuse.* Rockville, MD: SAMSHA. Retrieved from https://www.samhsa.gov/data/sites/default/files/report_2686/ShortReport-2686.html

Substance Abuse and Mental Health Services Administration (SAMHSA). (2018). *Results from the 2017 National Survey on Drug Use and Health: Detailed Tables.* Rockville, MD.

Substance Abuse and Mental Health Services Administration (SAMHSA). (2019). *Key substance use and mental health indicators in the United States: Results from the 2018 National Survey on Drug Use and Health*

(HHS Publication No. PEP19-5068, NSDUH Series H-54). Rockville, MD: SAMHSA.

Temin, P. (1980). *Taking your medicine: Drug regulation in the United States.* Cambridge, MA: Harvard University Press.

U.S. Department of Justice (USDOJ). (2017). *Drugs of abuse: A DEA resource guide.* Retrieved from https://www.dea .gov/sites/default/files/drug_of_abuse.pdf

U.S. Drug Enforcement Administration (DEA). (n.d.) Controlled substance schedules. Retrieved from https://www .deadiversion.usdoj.gov/schedules/

U.S. Drug Enforcement Administration (DEA). (2014, September 8). *DEA releases new rules that create convenient but safe and secure prescription drug disposal options.* Washington, DC: DEA. Retrieved from https://www.dea .gov/press-releases/2014/09/08/dea-releases-new -rules-create-convenient-safe-and-secure-prescription

## CHAPTER 4

# Homeostatic Systems and Drugs

© FOTOGRIN/Shutterstock.

## Did You Know?

▶ The brain is composed of approximately 100 billion neurons that communicate with one another by releasing chemical messengers called *neurotransmitters*.

▶ Many drugs exert their effects by interacting with specialized protein regions in cell membranes called *receptors*.

▶ Some natural chemicals produced by the body have the same effect as narcotic drugs; these chemicals are called *endorphins*.

▶ The body produces a natural substance called *anandamide* that has effects similar to those produced by marijuana and drugs that are related to tetrahydro-cannabinol (THC).

▶ The illegal drug products known as *Spice* have ingredients that alter the cannabinoid systems of the brain.

▶ Drugs that affect the neurotransmitter dopamine usually alter perception of pleasure, mental state, and motor activity and can cause addictive behavior.

▶ The hypothalamus is the principal brain region for control of the endocrine system.

## Learning Objectives

**On completing this chapter, you should be able to:**

❯ Explain the similarities and differences between the nervous and endocrine systems.

❯ Describe how a neuron functions.

❯ Describe the role of receptors in mediating the effects of hormones, neurotransmitters, and drugs.

❯ Distinguish between receptor agonists and antagonists and describe how their effects relate to those of neurotransmitters.

❯ Describe the different features of the principal neurotransmitters associated with drug addiction.

❯ Outline the principal components of the central nervous system and explain their general functions.

❯ Identify which brain areas are most likely to be affected by drugs of abuse and how these effects contribute to drug dependence.

❯ Be familiar with the endorphin and cannabinoid nervous systems and their role in substance abuse and recent drug abuse problems (e.g., Spice).

❯ Distinguish between the sympathetic and parasympathetic nervous systems.

❯ Identify the principal components of the endocrine system.

❯ Explain how and why anabolic steroids are abused and the health impact attributed to abuse.

## Introduction

Why is your body susceptible to the influence of drugs, some natural products (e.g., herbs), and other substances? Part of the answer is that your body is constantly adjusting and responding to its environment in an effort to maintain internal stability and balance. This delicate process of dynamic adjustments—*homeostasis*—is necessary to optimize bodily functions and is essential for survival. These continual adjustments help maintain physiological and psychological balances and are mediated by the release of endogenous regulatory chemicals (such as neurotransmitters from neurons and **hormones** from glands). Many drugs, including substances that are abused, exert intended or unexpected effects by altering the activity of these regulatory substances, which changes the status and function of the **nervous system** or **endocrine system** and associated organs. For example, all drugs of abuse, including new so-called synthetic designer psychoactive substances, profoundly influence mental states by altering the chemical messages of the neurotransmitters in the brain, and some alter endocrine function by affecting the release and activity of hormones. By understanding the mechanisms of how drugs alter these body processes, we are able to distinguish drug benefits and risks and devise therapeutic strategies to deal with related biomedical problems.

This chapter is divided into two sections. The first section is a brief overview that introduces the basic concept of how the body is controlled by nervous systems and explains why drugs influence the elements of these systems. The second section is intended for readers who desire a more in-depth understanding of the anatomical, physiological, and biochemical basis of homeostatic functions. In this second section, the elements of the nervous system are discussed in greater detail, followed by an examination of its major divisions: the central, peripheral, and autonomic nervous systems (CNS, PNS, and ANS, respectively). The components and operation of the endocrine system also are discussed in specific relation to drugs. The use of anabolic steroids is presented as an example of drugs of abuse that have powerful effects on the endocrine system.

## Overview of Homeostasis and Drug Actions

The body continuously adjusts to both internal and external changes in the environment. To cope with these adjustments, the body systems include elaborate self-regulating mechanisms. The name given to this compensatory action is **homeostasis**, which refers to the maintenance of internal stability or equilibrium of the body and its functions. For example, homeostatic mechanisms control the response of the brain to changes in the physical, social, and psychological environments, as well as regulate physiological factors such as body temperature, metabolism, nutrient utilization, and organ functions. The two principal systems that help human beings maintain homeostasis are the nervous system (discussed in Section 1) and the endocrine system (described in Section 2). They are independent yet work together in a coordinated manner, and both are often influenced by common factors, such as drugs (Cherry, 2018).

## Section 1: Introduction to Nervous Systems

All nervous systems consist of specialized cells called **neurons** and **glia** (or non-neuronal cells). The glia are supporting cells and are critical for protecting and providing sustenance to the neurons. Although the glia are necessary for survival of the neurons and proper functioning of the

### KEY TERMS

**hormones**
chemical messengers released into the blood by glands

**nervous system**
relating to the brain, spinal cord, neurons, and their associated elements

**endocrine system**
relating to hormones, their functions, and sources

**homeostasis**
maintenance of internal stability; often biochemical in nature

**neurons**
specialized nerve cells that make up the nervous system and release neurotransmitters

**glia**
supporting cells that are critical for protecting and providing sustenance to the neurons

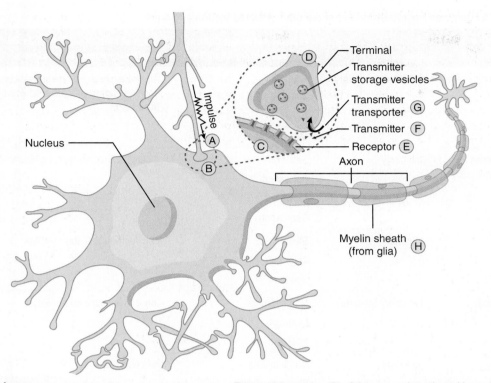

**FIGURE 4.1** The process of sending messages by neurons. The receiving region (B) of the neuron is activated by an incoming message (A) near the neuronal cell body. The neuron sends an electricity-like chemical impulse (C) down the axon to its terminal (D). The impulse causes the release of neurotransmitters (F) from their storage vesicles out of the terminal to transmit the message to the target. This is done when the neurotransmitter molecules activate the receptors on the membranes of the target cell (E). The activated receptors then cause a change to occur in intracellular functions of the target cell. The transmitters often are taken back up into the terminal by a transmitter transporter (G). Glial cells (glia) surround the neurons and their axons as a myelin sheath (H), providing insulation to enhance their abilities to send impulses and to support their other cellular functions.

nervous systems, they do not usually appear to be direct targets of the drugs of abuse this cell population and will not be discussed in detail here. Neurons are responsible for conducting the homeostatic functions of the brain and other parts of the nervous system by receiving and sending information. The transfer of messages by neurons includes electrochemical processes that involve the following elements (see **Figure 4.1**):

- Glia surround the neuron and its processes to support its ability to send chemical messages by insulating with myelin sheaths (H); they also provide nutrients for the neuron.
- The receiving region of the neuron (B) is affected by an electrochemical message (A) that either excites it (causing the neuron to send its own message) or inhibits it (preventing the neuron from sending a message).
- If the message is excitatory, a chemical impulse (A) (much like electricity) moves from the receiving region of the neuron, down its wirelike processes (called **axons**), to

the sending region (called the *terminal*) (D). When the electrochemical impulse reaches the terminal, chemical messengers called *neurotransmitters* (F) are released (for examples, see **Table 4.1**).

- The neurotransmitters travel extremely short distances and bind to specialized and specific receiving proteins called **receptors** on the outer membranes of their target cells (E).
- Activation of receptors by their associated neurotransmitters causes a change in the activity of the target cell. The target cells can

## KEY TERMS

**axon**
extension of the neuronal cell body along which electrochemical signals travel

**receptors**
special proteins in a membrane that are activated by natural substances or drugs to alter cell function

**TABLE 4.1** Common Neurotransmitters of the Brain Affected by Drugs of Abuse

| Neurotransmitter | Type of Effect | Examples of Major Central Nervous System Changes | Drugs of Abuse That Influence the Neurotransmitter (Drug Action) |
|---|---|---|---|
| Dopamine | Inhibitory–excitatory | Euphoria<br>Agitation<br>Paranoia<br>Motor changes | Amphetamines (e.g., methamphetamine), cocaine (activate), "bath salt" active ingredients |
| GABA (gamma-aminobutyric acid) | Inhibitory | Sedation<br>Relaxation<br>Drowsiness<br>Depression | Alcohol, diazepam-type, barbiturates (activate) |
| Serotonin | Inhibitory | Sleep<br>Relaxation<br>Sedation | LSD (activate), Ecstasy (MDMA) |
| Acetylcholine | Excitatory–inhibitory | Mild euphoria<br>Excitation<br>Insomnia | Tobacco, nicotine (stimulate) |
| Endorphins | Inhibitory | Mild euphoria<br>Blockage of pain<br>Slow respiration<br>Antistress | Narcotics (activate) |
| Anandamide | Inhibitory | Relaxation<br>Increased sense of well-being | Tetrahydrocannabinol (marijuana) (stimulate), Spice active ingredients |

be other neurons or cells that make up organs (such as the heart, lungs, kidneys, and so on), muscles, or glands.

Neurons are highly versatile and, depending on their functions, can send discrete excitatory or inhibitory messages to their target cells or organs. Neurons are distinguished by the types of chemical substances they release as neurotransmitters to send their messages. The neurotransmitters represent a wide variety of molecules that are classified according to their functional association as well as their ability to stimulate or inhibit the activity of target neurons, organs, muscles, and glands. They are discussed in greater detail in Section 2.

An example of a common neurotransmitter used by neurons in the brain to send messages is the substance dopamine. When released from neurons associated with the pleasure center in the brain, dopamine causes substantial euphoria by activating its receptor on target neurons ("Dopamine," n.d.). This effect is relevant to drugs of abuse because the addictive properties of these

substances (e.g., amphetamine or cocaine) relate to their ability to stimulate dopamine release from these neurons, and thus cause pleasant euphoric effects in the user (Brophy, 2018).

It is important to understand that many of the desired and undesired effects of psychoactive drugs (which alter the mental functions of the brain), such as the drugs of abuse, are due to their ability to alter the neurotransmitters associated with neurons. Some of the transmitter messenger systems most likely to be affected by drugs of abuse are listed in Table 4.1 and are discussed in greater detail in Section 2.

# Section 2: Comprehensive Explanation of Homeostatic Systems

For those desiring a more complete understanding of the consequences of drug effects on the homeostatic systems of the body, this section

## FAMILY MATTERS

### *Addiction Genes*

Is it true that addiction related to drug abuse can be associated with a person's genetics? It is well known that genetic variants are likely associated with diseases such as Alzheimer's and Parkinson's. In fact, many Americans are spitting into test tubes and sending their saliva samples to laboratories to assess their risk of developing these neurological and other genetics-related pathologies. What if we could do the same thing for drug addiction—spit into a container and send it off in a mailer and within a few weeks get a report that would tell us the likelihood that sometime during our life we would experience drug addiction? While genetic research does tell us that various aspects of substance abuse have been linked to more than 100 different abnormal gene expressions, the potential of so many drug abuse–related genes suggests that addiction is a complicated behavioral manifestation, which likely means it will be extremely difficult to develop a simple saliva test to reliably warn us of drug addiction vulnerability. So, what is the value of these findings confirming the connection between some abnormal genes and drug addiction? The following are conclusions that we can draw because of the research establishing linkage between addiction and variant gene expression:

- Because genes are associated with the expression of biological elements such as proteins, genetic research demonstrates that the addiction process has organic bases like many other pathological conditions and as such suggests it should be viewed as the consequence of a disease process and not a moral failure. For example, proteins related to abnormal dopamine (neurotransmitter) receptors, abnormal alcohol metabolic products, nausea-producing tobacco by-products and abnormal serotonin uptake transporters are just a few of the variant genes found to be connected with drug abuse problems.

- The identification of so many genetic factors potentially linked to addiction suggests there is no single element required for every expression of addiction, but that addiction is likely caused by a complicated interplay of biology with environment. This has been confirmed by findings that genetics only contribute to ~50% of addiction vulnerability while the balance is associated with experience.

- Even if a person was found to have one of the abnormal genes linked to addiction, this does not mean that problems with drugs are inevitable, but it could suggest that such a person should take greater care to avoid environments or drug consumption that would encourage drug abuse.

- Identification of genes linked to addiction may provide leads for developing effective treatment or prevention strategies. For example, if expression of a specific dopamine receptor was associated with developing addiction, then perhaps medications that block this receptor would have therapeutic value to prevent or treat the related addiction condition.

- The role of genes in the expression of addiction helps us understand the basis for the familial clustering of this drug-related condition. However, it should be remembered as previously mentioned that this does not mean that everyone in the family is destined to have drug problems. It does suggest, however, that everyone in such a family needs to be cautious around these drugs. In addition, these family members should particularly emphasize an antidrug culture in the home.

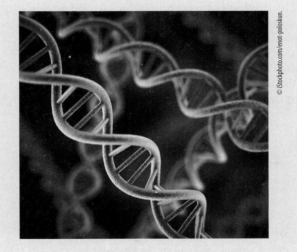

May, H. (2017, Winter). Genes and addiction. Continuum. Salt Lake City, UT: University of Utah. Retrieved from https://continuum.utah.edu/features/genes-and-addiction

provides an in-depth discussion of the anatomical and physiological nature and biological arrangements of the nervous and endocrine systems.

Because drugs of abuse are most likely to exert their psychoactive effects on neurons and their receptor targets, the nervous system is presented first and in greater depth, followed by a briefer description of endocrine function.

# ▌ The Building Blocks of the Nervous System

The nervous system is composed of the brain, spinal cord, and all the neurons that connect to other organs and tissues of the body. Nervous systems enable an organism to receive information about the internal and external environment and to make the appropriate responses essential to survival. Considerable money and scientific efforts are currently being dedicated to exploring the mechanisms whereby the nervous system functions and processes information, resulting in frequent exciting discoveries. Much of the exciting new knowledge about this system comes from the study of **genetics** (i.e., the study of cellular DNA and its functions) and **molecular biology** (i.e., the study of cellular functions and their regulation).

These disciplines include research tools that help us understand how genes regulate factors such as inheritability and the role of gene expression in determining risk factors for drug addiction that are passed from parents to offspring (Genetics Sciences Learning Center, n.d.; Jones & Comer, 2015) (see "Family Matters: Addiction Genes.").

## THE NEURON: THE BASIC STRUCTURAL UNIT OF THE NERVOUS SYSTEM

The fundamental building block of the nervous system is the nerve cell, or *neuron*. Each neuron in the CNS (brain and spinal cord) is in close proximity with other neurons, forming a complex network. The human brain contains about 100 billion neurons, each of which is composed of similar components but with different shapes,

sizes, and distinguishing neurochemistry. Neurons do not form a continuous cellular network. They always remain separate, never actually touching. The typical point of communication between one neuron and another is called a **synapse**. On average, each neuron in the brain makes about 2000 synaptic connections with neurons nearby and sometimes with those located many millimeters away in other brain regions. The gap (called the **synaptic cleft**) between neurons at a synapse may be only 0.00002 millimeters wide, but it is essential for proper functioning of the nervous system (see **Figure 4.2**).

The neuron has a cell body with a nucleus and receiving regions called **dendrites**, which are short, treelike branches that are influenced by information from the environment and surrounding neurons, such as that released by neurotransmitters.

The axon of a neuron is a threadlike extension that receives information from the dendrites near the cell body in the form of an electrochemical impulse; then, like an electrical wire, it transmits the impulse to the cell's terminal. Although most axons are less than 30 millimeters in length (i.e., about 1 inch), some may be quite long; for example, some axons extend from the spinal cord to the toes.

At the synapse, information is transmitted chemically to the next neuron, as shown in Figure 4.1. A similar synaptic arrangement also exists at sites of communication between neurons and target cells in organs, muscles, and glands; that is, neurotransmitters are released from the message-sending neurons and activate receptors located in the membranes of message-receiving target cells.

There are two types of synapses: excitatory and inhibitory. The *excitatory synapse* initiates an impulse in the receiving neuron when stimulated, thereby causing the release of neurotransmitters or increasing activity in the target cell. The *inhibitory synapse* diminishes the likelihood of an impulse in the receiving neuron or reduces the activity in other target cells. A receiving neuron or target cell may have thousands of synapses connecting it to other neurons and their excitatory or inhibitory information (see Figure 4.2A). The final cellular activity is a summation of these many excitatory and inhibitory synaptic signals and underscores the connectivity and complexity of these systems.

## THE NATURE OF DRUG RECEPTORS

Receptors are special proteins located in the membranes of receiving neurons and other target cells (see **Figure 4.3**). They help regulate the activity of

**KEY TERMS**

**genetics**
study of cellular DNA and its functions

**molecular biology**
study of cellular functions and their regulation

**synapse**
site of communication between a message-sending neuron and its message-receiving target cell

**synaptic cleft**
minute gap between the neuron and target cell, across which neurotransmitters travel

**dendrites**
short branches of neurons that receive transmitter signals

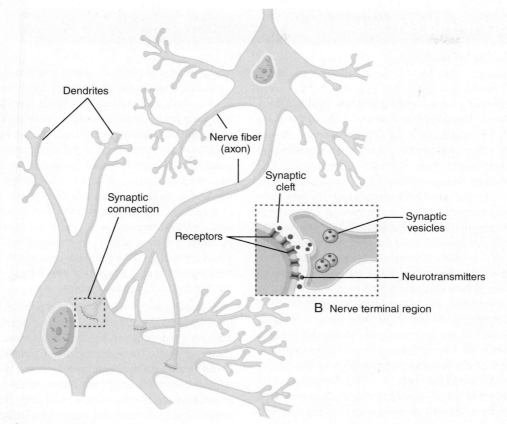

**FIGURE 4.2** (A) Each neuron may have many synaptic connections. They are designed to deliver short bursts of a chemical transmitter substance into the synaptic cleft, where the substance can act on the surface receptors of the receiving nerve cell membrane. Before release, molecules of the chemical neurotransmitter are stored in numerous vesicles, or sacs. (B) A close-up of the synaptic terminals, showing the synaptic vesicles. The gap between the synaptic terminal and the target membrane is the synaptic cleft.

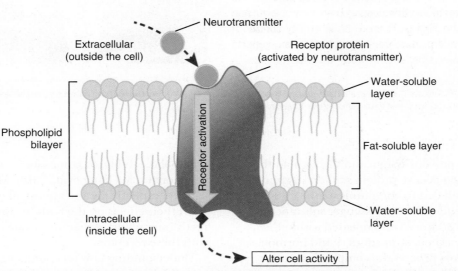

**FIGURE 4.3** Cell membranes consist of a bilayer of phospholipids. The water-soluble layers are pointed outward, and the fat-soluble layers are pointed toward each other. Large proteins, including receptors, float in the membrane. Some of these receptors are activated by neurotransmitters to alter the activity of the cell.

## PRESCRIPTION FOR ABUSE

!

### *How to Spice Things Up*

"Mr. Happy," "Scooby Snax," and "Kronic" are street names referring to drugs that in 2018 were linked to 160 cases of severe bleeding and four deaths in central Illinois. These drug products also go by the more familiar terms of *Spice and K2.* Such names represent a large group of chemicals sometimes classified as "synthetic (made in chemistry lab) cannabinoids (i.e., related to marijuana ingredients)." These substances for the most part were originally produced by legitimate research chemists studying the natural cannabinoid system and their chemistry was published in legitimate scientific journals. Once the knowledge of the synthetic chemistry of these substances became public, illicit drug manufacturers used the information to create hundreds of their own adulterated products for sale on the black market. Drugs like Spice and K2 have been called "synthetic marijuana" or "fake weed" to suggest to the unwary buyer that their consumption will in some way mimic the effects caused by smoking marijuana. Because of the national trend throughout the United States to legalize the medical and/or recreational use of marijuana, the association with marijuana-related chemicals is thought to encourage the popularity of these illegal substances and the misconception that Spice, K2-like and related drugs are harmless and maybe even therapeutic. Nothing can be further from the truth. In fact, these designer synthetics often are much more powerful and toxic than THC (the natural ingredient in marijuana), and more potentially dangerous because much of their pharmacology and toxicology is unknown. An additional complication is the lack of consistency in the production of these cannabinoid rip-offs. Even though the packages are very colorful and appear to be high tech, there is no quality control or standardization; thus, there have been many reports of dangerous side effects such as hypertension, a racing heart, agitation, paranoia, psychosis, seizures and nausea and vomiting. When the Spice and K2 substances first appeared in the United States in 2008 they were sold over-the-counter in convenience stores, truck stops and smoke shops because the ingredients were basically unknown and not prohibited. After 2-4 years several states passed "designer" laws banning the sales of these synthetic cannabinoids. Despite this effort, prosecuting the sellers of these drugs was next to impossible because when one of these drugs was identified and outlawed, the store owner quickly replaced it with a substitute chemical with a minor structural change. This modified substance was technically legitimate until dangerous side effects were identified and reported to law enforcement.

It is estimated that ~4% of the population in the United States, mostly males, has tried Spice/K2 substances, many of which are laced with other unknown toxic chemicals. These products often consist of dried herbs that have been sprayed by the cannabinoid-related chemicals which are either rolled into joints or smoked in pipes like typical marijuana. Sometimes the designer chemicals are even added to foods or tea and consumed orally.

Watson, S. (2018, September). K2/Spice: What to know about these dangerous drugs. WebMD. Retrieved from www.webmd.com/mental-health/addiction/news/20180910/k2-spice-what-to-know-about-these-dangerous-drugs

cells in the nervous system and throughout the body. These selective protein sites on specific cells act as transducers to communicate the messages caused by endogenous messenger substances (chemicals produced and released within the body) such as neurotransmitters and hormones. The receptors process the complex information each cell receives as it attempts to maintain metabolic stability, or homeostasis, and fulfill its functional role (Jiang et al., 2018). Many drugs used therapeutically and almost all drugs of abuse exert their effects on the body by directly or indirectly interacting (either to activate or antagonize) with these receptors.

Understanding how receptors interact with specific drugs has led to some interesting results.

For example, **opiate receptors** (sites of action by narcotic drugs such as heroin and morphine) are naturally present in animal and human brains (Valentino & Volkow, 2018). Why would human and animal brains have receptors for opiate narcotics, which are plant chemicals? Discovery of the opiate receptors suggested the existence of internal (endogenous) neurotransmitter substances in the body that normally act at these receptor sites and have effects like narcotic drugs such as codeine and morphine. This finding led to the identification of the body's own opiates, the **endorphins** (Valentino & Volkow, 2018 ). Another endogenous system that has been discovered because of specific receptor targets in the brain is the **cannabinoid system**. This is an example of novel CNS pathways identified and characterized because of our ability to study and understand genetics (Matsuda, 1997). These include pathways that are characterized by proteins activated by tetrahydrocannabinol (THC), the active ingredient in marijuana. These cannabinoid receptors are linked to functions associated with mood, reward, motivation, pain perception, decision making, and appetite (Zou & Kumar, 2018). Because of their involvement in such critical CNS functions, the cannabinoid receptors are more than just targets for marijuana. These cannabinoid receptors are activated by "designer" drugs, such as Spice, that can cause a marijuana-like effect. These drugs have been referred to as *false pot*, *legal weed*, or *new marijuana* (Watson, 2018) and likely can also be manipulated medically for legitimate therapeutic purposes. As with the endorphins, natural neurotransmitter substances have been discovered in the brain that selectively activate the cannabinoid receptors. These substances have a fatty-acid nature and include the substance **anandamide** and 2-arachidonoylglycerol (2-AG) (Zou & Kumar, 2018).

Specific receptors have also been found for the CNS depressant diazepam (Valium), which activates benzodiazepine receptors (Skolnick, 2012). Although less is known about the natural benzodiazepine system, it is likely that natural substances are also produced in the brain that mimic the effects of Valium and cause natural sedation and relaxation; however, as of yet, the definite identity of these Valium-like natural transmitters remains to be determined (Poisbeau, Gazzo, & Calvel, 2018).

Much remains unknown about how receptors respond to or interact with drugs. Through the use of molecular biology techniques, many of these receptors have been found to initiate a cascade of linked chemical reactions that can change intracellular environments to produce either activation or inactivation of cellular functions and metabolism (Jiang et al., 2018).

Receptors that have been isolated and identified are protein molecules; it is believed that the shape of the protein is essential in regulating a drug's interaction with a cell. If the drug is the proper shape and size and has a compatible electrical charge, then it may substitute for the endogenous messenger substance and activate the receptor protein by causing it to change its shape or conform. These molecular events have given us insight into why drug abuse occurs and how to prevent and treat addiction (Koob & Volkow, 2010).

## AGONISTIC AND ANTAGONISTIC EFFECTS ON DRUG RECEPTORS

A drug may have two different effects on a receptor when interaction occurs: **agonistic** or **antagonistic**. As shown in **Figure 4.4**, an agonistic drug interacts with the receptor and produces some type of cellular response, whereas an antagonistic drug interacts with the receptor but prevents that response.

An agonistic drug mimics the effect of a messenger substance (such as a neurotransmitter) that is naturally produced by the body and interacts with the receptor to cause some cellular change. For example, narcotic drugs are agonists that mimic the naturally occurring endorphins and activate opiate receptors; the THC in marijuana

## KEY TERMS

**opiate receptors**
receptors activated by opioid narcotic drugs such as heroin and morphine

**endorphins**
neurotransmitters that have narcotic-like effects

**cannabinoid system**
biological target of tetrahydrocannabinol in marijuana

**anandamide**
naturally occurring fatty-acid neurotransmitter that selectively activates cannabinoid receptors

**agonistic**
type of substance that activates a receptor

**antagonistic**
type of substance that blocks a receptor

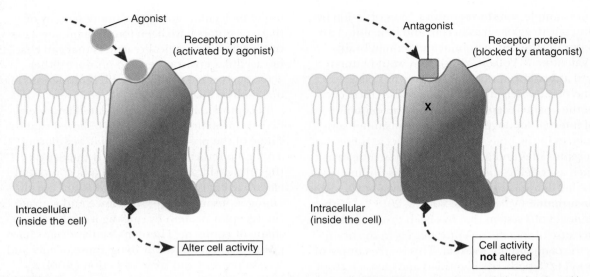

**FIGURE 4.4** Interaction of agonist and antagonist with membrane receptor. When this receptor is occupied and activated by an agonist, it can cause cellular changes. When blocked by an antagonist, the receptor cannot be activated.

is an agonist that activates cannabinoid receptors. An antagonist has the opposite effect: it inhibits the sequence of metabolic events that a natural substance or an agonist drug can stimulate, usually without initiating an effect itself. Thus, the drug naloxone (created to treat heroin overdoses) is an antagonist at the opiate receptors and blocks the effects of narcotic drugs such as heroin as well as the effects of the naturally occurring endorphins. In contrast, as of yet in the United States, there is no antagonist approved by the Food and Drug Administration (FDA) for the cannabinoid receptors. The drug Rimonabant (which was developed to suppress appetite) blocks the cannabinoid receptors; however, because of significant psychiatric side effects, this drug is not available in most countries for clinical use (Yadav & Murumkar, 2018). Other cannabinoid antagonists are being developed with the hope that they can be used clinically without serious side effects (Yadav & Murumkar, 2018).

## NEUROTRANSMITTERS: THE MESSENGERS

Many drugs affect the activity of neurotransmitters by altering their synthesis, storage, release, or deactivation (e.g., metabolism). By changing these processes, a drug may modify or block information transmitted by these neurochemical messengers. Thus, by altering the amount of neurotransmitters, such drugs can act indirectly, like agonists and antagonists, even though they do not directly change neurotransmitter receptors. They do influence the activity of these receptors by altering the amount of neurotransmitters available to naturally influence receptor function.

Experimental evidence shows that many different neurotransmitters exist, although much remains to be learned about their specific functions. These biochemical messengers are selectively released from specific neurons. Transmitters frequently altered by drugs of abuse include acetylcholine (ACh), norepinephrine, epinephrine, dopamine, serotonin, gamma-aminobutyric acid (GABA), the endorphins (peptides), and cannabinoids such as anandamide (fatty acids) (Gray & Nicoll, 2015). Because of the unique shapes and chemical features, each neurotransmitter affects only its specific receptors. Drugs can also affect these receptors if they are sufficiently similar in shape to the neurotransmitters. **Figure 4.5** summarizes some of the important features of the common neurotransmitters. Neurotransmitters are inactivated after they have done their job by diffusion away from their receptor target or by metabolism (by enzymes), or they are taken back up into the neuron by selective transporter proteins. If a deactivating enzyme or the reuptake is blocked by a drug, the effect of the transmitter may be prolonged or intensified.

## ACETYLCHOLINE

Large quantities of acetylcholine (ACh) are found in the brain. ACh is one of the major neurotransmitters in the autonomic portion of the PNS, which is discussed later in the chapter.

**Acetylcholine**
Chemical type: Choline product
Location: CNS—Basal ganglia, cortex, reticular activating
         system
         PNS—Neuromuscular junction, parasympathetic
         system
Action: Excitatory (nicotine receptor) and inhibitory
        (muscarinic receptor)

**Anandamide**
Chemical type: Fatty acid
Location: CNS—Cortex, cerebellum, limbic system
         Other—Immune system, pain regions,
         reproductive system
Action: Relaxation, analgesia, hunger

**Dopamine**
Chemical type: Catecholamine
Location: CNS—Basal ganglia, limbic system,
         hypothalamus
Action: Usually inhibitory

**Endorphins**
Chemical type: Peptide (small protein)
Location: CNS—Basal ganglia, hypothalamus, brain stem,
         spinal cord
         Other—Gut, cardiovascular system
Action: Inhibitory (narcotic-like effects)

**Epinephrine**
Chemical type: Catecholamine
Location: CNS—Minor
         PNS—Adrenal glands
Action: Usually excitatory

**GABA**
Chemical type: Amino acid
Location: CNS—Basal ganglia, limbic system, cortex
Action: Usually inhibitory

**Norepinephrine**
Chemical type: Catecholamine
Location: CNS—Limbic system, cortex, hypothalamus,
         reticular activating system, brain stem,
         spinal cord
         PNS—Sympathetic nervous system
Action: Usually inhibitory; some excitation

**Serotonin (5HT)**
Chemical type: Tryptophan-derivative
Location: CNS—Basal ganglia, limbic system, brain stem,
         spinal cord, cortex
         Other—Gut, platelets, cardiovascular
Action: Usually inhibitory

**FIGURE 4.5** Features of common neurotransmitters.

Neurons that respond to ACh are distributed throughout the brain. Depending on the region, ACh can have either excitatory or inhibitory effects. The receptors activated by ACh have been divided into two main subtypes based on the response to two drugs derived from plants: muscarine and nicotine. Muscarine (a substance in mushrooms that causes mushroom poisoning) and drugs that act in a similar manner activate **muscarinic** receptors.

Nicotine, whether experimentally administered or inhaled by smoking tobacco, stimulates **nicotinic** receptors.

### CATECHOLAMINES

**Catecholamines** include the neurotransmitter compounds norepinephrine, epinephrine, and dopamine, all of which have similar chemical structures. Neurons that synthesize catecholamines convert the amino acids (building blocks of proteins) phenylalanine or tyrosine to dopamine. In some neurons, dopamine is further converted to norepinephrine and finally to epinephrine (see **Figure 4.6**).

After release, most of the catecholamines are taken back up into the neurons that released them to be used over again; this process is called *reuptake*. An enzymatic breakdown system also metabolizes the catecholamines to inactive compounds. The reuptake process and the activity of metabolizing enzymes, especially monoamine oxidase (MAO), can be greatly affected by some drugs of abuse. If these deactivating enzymes or reuptake systems are blocked, the concentration of norepinephrine and dopamine may build up in the brain, significantly increasing the effect. Cocaine, for example, prevents the reuptake of norepinephrine and dopamine in the brain, resulting in continual stimulation of neuron catecholamine receptors.

### KEY TERMS

**muscarinic**
receptor type activated by acetylcholine (ACh); usually inhibitory

**nicotinic**
receptor type activated by acetylcholine (ACh); usually excitatory

**catecholamines**
class of biochemical compounds, including the transmitters norepinephrine, epinephrine, and dopamine

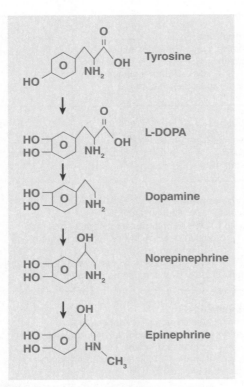

**FIGURE 4.6** Synthetic pathway for catecholamine neurotransmitters. The starting material is the amino acid tyrosine. By enzymatic action, the tyrosine becomes L-DOPA and is then converted to dopamine, followed by norepinephrine and finally epinephrine.

## NOREPINEPHRINE AND EPINEPHRINE

Although norepinephrine and epinephrine are structurally similar, their receptors are selective and do not respond with the same intensity to either transmitter or **sympathomimetic** drugs. Just as the receptors to ACh can be separated into muscarinic and nicotinic types, the norepinephrine and epinephrine receptors are classified into alpha and beta categories. Receiving cells may have alpha- or beta-type receptors, or both. Norepinephrine acts predominantly on alpha receptors and with less action on beta receptors.

The antagonistic (blocking) action of many drugs that act on these catecholamine receptors can be selective for alpha receptors, whereas others block only beta receptors. This distinction can be therapeutically useful. For example, beta

### KEY TERM

**sympathomimetic**
agents that mimic the effects of norepinephrine or epinephrine

receptors tend to stimulate the heart, whereas alpha receptors constrict blood vessels; thus, a drug that selectively affects beta receptors can be used to treat heart ailments without directly altering the state of the blood vessels (Farzam & Lakhar, 2019).

## DOPAMINE

Dopamine is a catecholamine transmitter that is particularly influenced by drugs of abuse (National Institute on Drug Abuse [NIDA], 2018a). Most if not all drugs that elevate mood have abuse potential or cause psychotic behaviors and alter the activity of dopamine in some way, particularly in brain regions associated with regulating mental states and reward systems. It is particularly important because of its role to cause us to repeat pleasurable activities (i.e., motivation). In addition, dopamine is an important transmitter in controlling movement and fine muscle activity as well as endocrine functions. Thus, because many drugs of abuse affect dopamine neurons, they can also alter all of these functions.

## SEROTONIN

Serotonin (5-hydroxytryptamine, or 5HT) is synthesized in neurons and elsewhere (e.g., in the gastrointestinal tract and platelet-type blood cells) from the dietary source of tryptophan. Tryptophan is an essential amino acid, meaning that human beings do not have the ability to synthesize it and must obtain it through their diet. Like the catecholamines, serotonin is degraded by the enzyme MAO; thus, drugs that alter this enzyme affect levels not only of catecholamines but also of serotonin.

Serotonin is also found in the upper brain stem, which connects the brain and the spinal cord (see **Figure 4.7**). Axons from serotonergic neurons are distributed throughout the entire CNS. Serotonin generally inhibits actions of its target neurons. One important role of the serotonergic neurons is to prevent overreaction to various stimuli. Consequently, a change in serotonergic systems can cause aggressiveness, excessive motor activity, exaggerated mood swings, insomnia, and abnormal sexual behavior. Serotonergic neurons also help regulate the release of hormones from the hypothalamus. Because many drugs of abuse affect serotonin systems, use of these drugs can interfere with these systems.

Alterations in serotonergic neurons, serotonin synthesis, and serotonin degradation have been

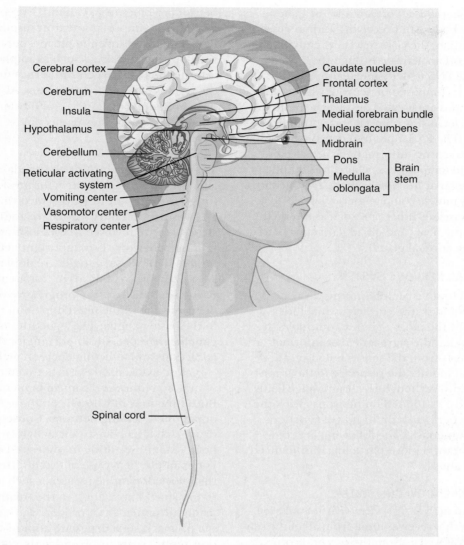

**FIGURE 4.7** Functional components of the central nervous system. The caudate nucleus is part of the basal ganglia and important for behavior selection and motor activity. Limbic structures include the hypothalamus, thalamus, medial forebrain bundle, and frontal lobe of the cerebrum; they are important for controlling emotions and other mental states. The insula has been identified as important for motivation.

proposed as factors in mental illness that also contribute to the side effects of many drugs of abuse. In support of this hypothesis is the fact that drugs such as psilocybin and lysergic acid diethylamide (LSD), which have serotonin-like chemical structures, are frequently abused because of their hallucinogenic properties and can cause psychotic effects (McIntosh, 2018).

### ■ Major Divisions of the Nervous System

The nervous system can be divided into two major components: the **central nervous system (CNS)** and the **peripheral nervous system (PNS)**. The CNS consists of the brain and spinal cord (see Figure 4.7), which receive information through the input nerves of the PNS. This sensory information allows the CNS to evaluate

### KEY TERMS

**central nervous system (CNS)**
one of the major divisions of the nervous system; composed of the brain and spinal cord

**peripheral nervous system (PNS)**
includes the neurons outside the CNS

the specific status of all organs and the general status of the body. After receiving and processing this information, the CNS reacts by regulating muscle and organ activity through the output nerves of the PNS (eMedicineHealth, 2015).

The PNS is composed of neurons whose cell bodies or axons are located outside the brain or spinal cord. It consists of input and output nerves to the CNS. The PNS input to the brain and spinal cord conveys sensory information such as pain, pressure, and temperature, whereas its output activities are separated into somatic types (control of voluntary muscles) and autonomic types (control of unconscious functions, such as essential organs like the heart and glandular activity such as that of the adrenal gland).

## THE CENTRAL NERVOUS SYSTEM

The human brain is an integrating (information-processing) and storage device with abilities unequaled by the most complex computers. It not only can handle a great deal of information simultaneously from the senses but also can evaluate and modify the response to the information rapidly. Although the brain weighs only three pounds, its 100 billion neurons give it the potential to perform a multitude of functions, often simultaneously. The following are some important brain regions particularly influenced by drugs of abuse.

### THE RETICULAR ACTIVATING SYSTEM

The reticular activating system (RAS) is an area of the brain that receives input from all of the sensory systems as well as from the cerebral cortex. The RAS is found at the junction of the spinal cord and the brain (see Figure 4.7). One of its major functions is to control the brain's state of arousal (sleep vs. awake).

Because of its complex, diffuse network structure, the RAS is highly susceptible to the effects of drugs. It is sensitive to the effects of LSD, potent stimulants such as cocaine and amphetamines, and CNS depressants such as alcohol and

benzodiazepines (e.g., Valium). Norepinephrine and ACh are important neurotransmitters in the RAS. High levels of epinephrine, norepinephrine, or stimulant drugs such as amphetamines activate the RAS. In contrast, drugs that block the actions of another transmitter, ACh, called **anticholinergic** drugs (e.g., antihistamines), suppress RAS activity, causing sleepiness.

### THE BASAL GANGLIA

The basal ganglia include the caudate nucleus and are the primary centers for involuntary and finely tuned motor functions involving, for example, posture and muscle tone. In addition, these structures are involved in establishing and maintaining behaviors. Two important neurotransmitters in the basal ganglia are dopamine and ACh. Damage to neurons in this area may cause Parkinson's disease, the progressive yet selective degeneration of the main dopaminergic neurons in the basal ganglia. The structures of the basal ganglia are especially important for developing addictions and affecting decision making.

A close association exists between control of motor abilities and control of mental states. Both functions rely heavily on the activity of dopamine-releasing neurons. Consequently, drugs that affect dopamine activity usually alter both systems, resulting in undesired side effects. For example, heavy use of tranquilizers (drugs that block dopamine receptors such as chlorpromazine [Thorazine]) in the treatment of psychotic patients can produce Parkinson-like symptoms. If such drugs are administered daily over several years, problems with motor functioning may become permanent. Drugs of abuse such as stimulants increase dopamine activity, causing enhanced motor activity as well as psychotic behavior.

### THE LIMBIC SYSTEM

The limbic system includes the hypothalamus and an assortment of linked brain regions located near it (see Figure 4.7). Besides the hypothalamus, the limbic structures include the thalamus, medial forebrain bundle, **nucleus accumbens**, and front portion of the cerebral cortex. Functions of the limbic and basal ganglia structures are inseparably linked; drugs that affect one system often affect the other as well.

The primary roles of limbic brain regions include regulating emotional activities (such as fear, rage, and anxiety), memory, modulation of

## KEY TERMS

**anticholinergic**
agents that antagonize the effects of acetylcholine

**nucleus accumbens**
part of the CNS limbic system and a critical brain region for reward systems

basic hypothalamic functions (such as endocrine activity), and activities such as mating, procreation, and caring for the young. In addition, reward centers are also believed to be associated with limbic structures, particularly in the nucleus accumbens. For this reason, it is almost certain that the mood-elevating effects of drugs of abuse are mediated by these limbic systems of the brain.

For example, studies have shown that laboratory animals given the option will self-administer most stimulant drugs of abuse (such as amphetamines and cocaine) through a cannula surgically placed into limbic structures (such as the medial forebrain bundle, nucleus accumbens, or frontal cerebral cortex). This self-administration is achieved by linking injection of the drug into the cannula with a lever press or other activity by the animal (Hanson et al., 2012). It is thought that the euphoria or intense "highs" associated with these drugs result from their effects on these brain regions. Some of the limbic system's principal transmitters include dopamine, norepinephrine, and serotonin; dopamine activation in the caudate nucleus and nucleus accumbens especially appears to be the primary reinforcement that accounts for the abuse liability of most drugs (NIDA, 2018a).

### THE CEREBRAL CORTEX

The unique features of the human cerebral cortex give human beings a special place among animals. The cortex is a layer of gray matter made up of nerves and supporting cells that almost completely surrounds the rest of the brain and lies immediately under the skull (see Figure 4.7). It is responsible for receiving sensory input, interpreting incoming information, and initiating voluntary motor behavior. Many psychoactive drugs, such as psychedelics, dramatically alter the perception of sensory information by the cortex and cause hallucinations that result in strange behavior.

A particularly critical part of the cortex is called the **frontal cortex**. This and associated cortical areas store memories, control complex behaviors, help process information, and play a role in decision making. Some psychoactive drugs disrupt the normal functioning of these areas, thereby interfering with an individual's ability to deal effectively and rationally with complex issues. Consequently, the behavior of persons addicted to drugs often appears bizarre and inappropriate; in extreme cases, it can lead to violence and criminal behavior (NIDA, 2018b).

### THE INSULA

The insula is a structure recently implicated in drug addiction. It is located deep in the brain, is connected with the pleasure pathways, and appears to be important for motivation. A recent finding determined that smokers who sustain an injury to their insula lose interest in using tobacco. This region has been associated with other addiction behaviors as well (Gilman et al., 2018).

### THE HYPOTHALAMUS

The hypothalamus (see **Figure 4.8**) is located near the base of the brain. It integrates information from many sources and serves as the CNS control center for the ANS and many vital support functions such as cardiovascular activity, hormone release, and temperature and appetite regulation (Kyrou & Tsigos, 2009). It also serves as the primary point of contact between the nervous and endocrine systems. Because the hypothalamus helps control the ANS, it is responsible for maintaining homeostasis in the body; thus, drugs that alter its function can have a major impact on systems that control homeostasis. The catecholamine transmitters are particularly important in regulating the function of the hypothalamus, and most drugs of abuse that alter the activity of norepinephrine and dopamine are likely to alter the activity of this brain structure as well (American Addiction Centers, 2018).

## ■ The Autonomic Nervous System

Although the cell bodies of the neurons of the **autonomic nervous system (ANS)** are located within the brain or spinal cord, their axons project outside of the CNS to involuntary muscles, organs, and glands; thus, the ANS is considered part of the PNS. The ANS is an integrative, or regulatory, system that does not require conscious control (i.e., you do not have to think about it to make it function). It is usually considered primarily a motor or output system. Several drugs that cannot enter the CNS because of the blood–brain barrier are able to affect the ANS only. The ANS is divided into two functional components: the

### KEY TERMS

**frontal cortex**
cortical region essential for information processing and decision making

**autonomic nervous system (ANS)**
controls the unconscious functions of the body

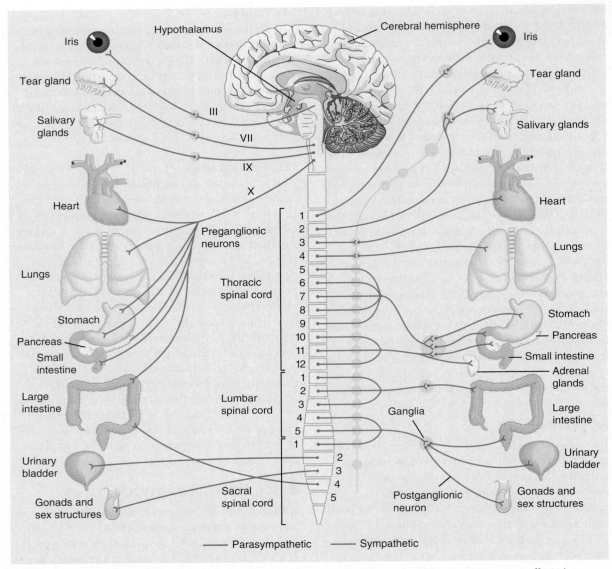

**FIGURE 4.8** Autonomic pathways of the parasympathetic and sympathetic nervous systems and the organs affected.

sympathetic and the parasympathetic nervous systems (Ernsberger & Rohrer, 2018). Both systems include neurons that project to most visceral organs and to smooth muscles, glands, and blood vessels (see Figure 4.8).

The two components of the ANS generally have opposite effects on an organ or its function. The way the heart works is a good example of sympathetic and parasympathetic control. Stimulation of the parasympathetic nervous system slows the heart rate, whereas stimulation of the sympathetic nerves accelerates it. These actions constitute a constant biological check and balance of regulatory system. Because the two parts of

the ANS work in opposite ways much of the time, they are considered physiological antagonists. These two systems control most of the internal organs, the circulatory system, and the secretory (glandular) system. The sympathetic system is normally active at all times; the degree of activity varies from moment to moment and from organ to organ. The parasympathetic nervous system is organized mainly for limited, focused activity and usually conserves and restores energy rather than expends it. For example, it slows the heart rate, lowers blood pressure, aids in absorption of nutrients, and is involved in emptying the urinary bladder. **Table 4.2** lists the structures and functions

**TABLE 4.2** Sympathetic and Parasympathetic Control

| Structure or Function | Sympathetic | Parasympathetic |
|---|---|---|
| Heart rate | Accelerates | Slows |
| Breathing rate | Accelerates | Slows |
| Stomach wall | Reduces motility | Increases motility |
| Skin blood vessels | Constricts | Dilates (vasomotor function) |
| Iris of eye | Constricts (pupil enlarges) | Dilates |
| Vomiting center | Stimulates | – |

of the sympathetic and parasympathetic nervous systems and their effects on one another.

The two branches of the ANS use two different neurotransmitters. The parasympathetic branch releases ACh at its synapses, whereas the sympathetic neurons release norepinephrine. An increase in epinephrine in the blood released from the adrenal glands (see the next section) or the administration of drugs that enhance norepinephrine activity causes the body to respond as if the sympathetic nervous system had been activated. As previously mentioned, such drugs are referred to as *sympathomimetics*. Thus, taking amphetamines (which enhance the sympathetic nervous system by releasing norepinephrine and epinephrine) raises blood pressure, speeds up heart rate, reduces motility of the stomach walls, and may cause the pupils of the eyes to enlarge; other so-called uppers such as cocaine have similar effects.

Drugs that affect ACh release, metabolism, or interaction with its respective receptor are referred to as *cholinergic* drugs. They can either mimic or antagonize the parasympathetic nervous system, according to their pharmacological action.

## ■ The Endocrine System

The endocrine system consists of glands, which are ductless (meaning that they secrete their chemical messengers, called hormones, directly into the bloodstream) (see **Figure 4.9**). These hormones are essential in regulating many vital functions, including metabolism, growth, tissue repair, and sexual behavior, to mention just a few. In contrast to neurotransmitters, hormones tend to have a slower onset, a longer duration of action, and a more generalized target. Although many tissues can produce and release hormones, three of the principal sources of these chemical messengers are the pituitary gland, the adrenal glands, and the sex glands.

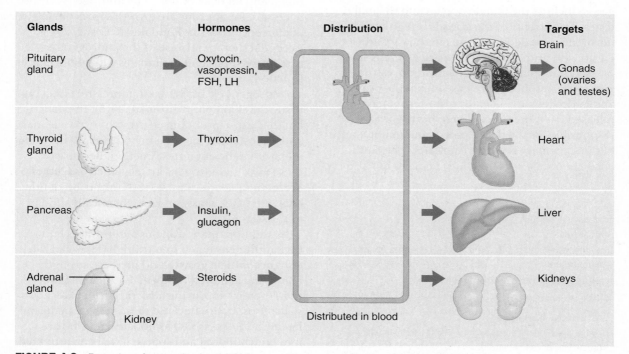

**FIGURE 4.9** Examples of some glands and their respective hormones in the endocrine system.

## ENDOCRINE GLANDS AND REGULATION

The pituitary gland is often referred to as the *master gland*. It controls many of the other glands that make up the endocrine system by releasing regulating factors and growth hormone. Besides controlling the brain functions already mentioned, the hypothalamus helps control the activity of the pituitary gland and thereby has a highly prominent effect on the endocrine system (Medlineplus, n.d.).

The adrenal glands are located near the kidneys and are divided into two parts: the outer surface, called the *cortex*, and the inner part, called the *medulla*. The adrenal medulla is actually a component of the sympathetic nervous system and releases adrenaline (another name for *epinephrine*) during sympathetic stimulation. Other important hormones released by the adrenal cortex are called *corticosteroids*, or just **steroids**. Steroids help the body respond appropriately to crises and stress. In addition, small amounts of male sex hormones (chemically related to the steroids) called **androgens** are released by the adrenal cortex. The androgens produce anabolic effects that increase the retention and synthesis of proteins, causing growth in the mass of tissues such as muscles and bones (Chrousos, 2015).

Sex glands are responsible for the secretion of male and female sex hormones that help regulate the development and activity of the respective reproductive systems. The organs known as *gonads* include the female ovaries and the male testes. The activity of the gonads is regulated by hormones released from the pituitary gland (see Figure 4.9) and, for the most part, remains suppressed until puberty. After activation, estrogens and progesterones are released from the ovaries, and androgens (principally testosterone) are released from the testes. These hormones are responsible for the development and maintenance of the secondary sex characteristics. They influence not only sex-related body features but also emotional states, suggesting that these sex hormones enter the brain and significantly affect the functioning of the limbic systems.

For the most part, drugs prescribed to treat endocrine problems are intended as replacement therapy. For example, diabetic patients suffer from a shortage of insulin produced by the pancreas, so therapy consists of insulin injections. Patients who suffer from dwarfism receive insufficient growth hormone from the pituitary gland; thus, growth hormone is administered to stimulate normal growth. Because some hormones can affect growth, muscle development, and behavior, they are sometimes abused to enhance athletic performance or bodybuilding and may be referred to as *performance enhancers*.

## THE ABUSE OF HORMONES: ANABOLIC STEROIDS

Androgens are the hormones most likely to be abused in the United States. In 2018, these drugs were self-administered by 1.4% of high school boys but less in corresponding girls in this country (Johnston et al., 2019). Testosterone, the primary natural androgen, is produced by the testes. Naturally produced androgens are essential for normal growth and development of male sex organs as well as secondary sex characteristics such as male hair patterns, voice changes, muscular development, and fat distribution. The androgens are also necessary for appropriate growth spurts during adolescence (Nassar, Raudales, & Leslie, 2018). Accepted therapeutic use of the androgens is usually for replacement in males with abnormally functioning testes.

Androgens clearly have an impressive effect on tissue development (Chrousos, 2015). In particular, they cause pronounced growth of muscle mass and a substantial increase in body weight in young men with deficient testes function. Because of these effects, androgens are classified as **anabolic steroids** (able to stimulate the conversion of nutrients into tissue mass) and are chemically similar to the steroids.

In addition, many athletes and trainers know that androgens taken in ultrahigh doses can enhance muscle growth and increase strength above that achieved by normal testicular function, thereby improving athletic performance (Chrousos, 2015). Because of this effect, male and female athletes, as well as nonathletes who are into bodybuilding and sports, have been attracted to these drugs in hopes of enlarging muscle

**KEY TERMS**

**steroids**
hormones related to the corticosteroids released from the adrenal cortex

**androgens**
male sex hormones

**anabolic steroids**
compounds chemically similar to steroids that stimulate production of tissue mass

# ▶ CASE IN POINT

## Is Winning Really Worth It?

Each year throughout the world, ~3,000 highly competitive athletes across almost every major sport test positive for so-called performance-enhancing drugs. These drugs come from various pharmacological categories such as natural and synthetic anabolic steroids (to train harder to build muscle mass and recover faster from difficult workouts), stimulants such as amphetamines (to increase alertness, endurance, and reflexes while decreasing the sense of fatigue), diuretics (to rapidly lose weight by increased urination and to mask other drugs in the urine tests), erythropoietin (to increase oxygen capacity of the blood in a process called *blood doping*), and growth hormones (to increase growth of body size and muscles). In many cases, athletes use multiple drugs for years in the belief that self-administering these substances would optimize their ability to perform at an enhanced level, giving them advantages over their competitors. Ultimately, the expectation is that these chemically dependent successes would earn for the athletes millions of dollars in sports contracts, product endorsements, and enhanced social prestige. Although the use of performance-enhancing drugs—called *doping*—is prohibited in almost every sport, under almost every circumstance, the intense temptation for many sports figures is to administer these substance to achieve financial and social success. Consequently, many of those associated with sports such as athletes, coaches, fans, and even country-sponsored programs believe that their strategies must include the use of banned substances by athletes despite the risk of detection or even worse, including dangerous medical and mental side effects. The following table shows a timeline of some of the most notable cases of athletes who were caught using illegal substances and the consequences.

Because the policy of banning most performance-enhancing drugs from use in athletics appears to have less than intended outcomes, there is controversy as to what should be done. The two recommended approaches include: (1) increasing the penalties for breaking drug use regulations and being less lenient in imposing "sentences" and (2) permitting the use of performance-enhancing drugs by all athletes under much more rigid regulation. Time will tell how our society decides to proceed to resolve this growing problem.

© Ivan Sekretarev/AP/Shutterstock.

| Year | Athlete | Competition | Drug Discovered | Consequences |
|------|---------|-------------|-----------------|--------------|
| 1981 | Ben Plucknett | Discus | Steroids | Stripped of world record and banned |
| 2005 | Jose Canseco | Baseball | Steroids | Implicates other baseball players |
| 2006 | Justin Gatlin | Sprinting | Steroid/growth hormone | Banned from competition |
| 2007–2010 | Barry Bonds, Roger Clemens, Mark McGwire | Baseball | Steroids | Embarrassed, no formal action |
| 2016–2018 | ~1,000 Russians | | Many different types | Banned many members of Russian Olympic team from 2016 Rio Olympics and 2018 South Korean Winter Olympics |

Khan, R. (2017, December 31). Doping in sports—Cheating or leveling the playing field? *Forbes*. Retrieved from https://www.forbes.com/sites/roomykhan /2017/12/31/doping-in-sports-cheating-or-leveling-of-the-playing-field/#6a3286db75ec. Accessed April 24, 2019; CNN. (2019). Performance enhancing drugs in sports fast facts. CNN Library. Retrieved from https://www.cnn.com/2013/06/06/us/performance-enhancing-drugs-in-sports-fast-facts/index.html. Accessed April 24, 2019.

size, improving their athletic performances, and enhancing their physiques despite their risks to both body and careers (see "Case in Point: Winning … But at What Cost?").

Several studies have suggested that anabolic hormones can have especially substantial negative effects. Athletic trainers and managers claim to see increases in severe injuries such as tears of muscles and ligaments because of aggravated trauma in overmuscled bodies exposed to these steroids (Druginfo, 2015). These drugs can also affect the limbic structures of the brain. Consequently, they may cause excitation and a sense of superior strength and performance in some users. These effects, coupled with increased aggressiveness, could encourage continual use of these drugs. Other CNS effects, however, may be disturbing to the user. Symptoms that may occur with extremely high doses include uncontrolled rage ("roid rage"), headaches, anxiety, insomnia, and perhaps paranoia (Chrousos, 2015). Because of concern about the abuse potential and side-effects profile of anabolic steroids, these drugs are controlled as Schedule III substances.

© wavebreakmedia/Shutterstock.

Anabolic steroids can cause pronounced growth of muscle mass.

## DESIGNER STEROIDS

In an attempt to circumvent the restriction on steroid use, some athletes have used the so-called designer steroid known as tetrahydro-gestrinone (THG). The FDA banned THG in products classified as nutritional supplements. Because of concerns that athletes were using THG to enhance performance, professional athletic organizations and the International Olympic Committee test athletes for this drug and disqualify them from competition if it is detected (Carmody, 2013).

# Conclusion

All psychoactive drugs affect brain activity by altering the ability of neurons to send and receive chemical messages. Consequently, drugs of abuse exert their addicting effects by stimulating or blocking the activity of CNS neurotransmitters or their receptors. Thus, to appreciate why these drugs are abused and the nature of their dependence, how neurons and their neurotransmitter systems function must be understood. In addition, many scientists believe that elucidating how substances of abuse affect nervous systems will help identify why some persons are at greater risk for abuse problems and will lead to new and more effective methods for preventing and treating drug addiction.

# LEARNING PORTFOLIO

## Discussion Questions

1. What are the similarities and differences between neurotransmitters and hormones?
2. Why is it important for the body to have chemical messengers (such as neurotransmitters) that can be quickly released and rapidly inactivated?
3. Why are receptors so important in understanding the effects of drugs of abuse?
4. What role do the opioid and cannabinoid systems play in drug abuse, and how can these neurosystems be used therapeutically?
5. What is the importance of the cannabinoid system with regard to recent "illegal" products known as Spice?
6. Why is it not surprising that drugs that affect the catecholamine transmitters also affect the endocrine system?
7. What are some mechanisms whereby a drug of abuse can increase the activity of dopamine transmitter systems in the brain?
8. How can knowing that the nucleus accumbens of the brain is important for motivation be used to treat drug addiction?
9. Why might a drug of abuse that damages the cerebral cortex make the user especially vulnerable to addiction?

## Summary

1. The nervous and endocrine systems help mediate internal and external responses to the body's surroundings. Both systems release chemical messengers to achieve their homeostatic functions. These messenger substances are called *neurotransmitters* and *hormones*, and they carry out their functions by binding to specific receptors throughout the CNS and other systems of the body. Many drugs exert their actions by influencing these chemical messengers either to mimic (agonists) or block (antagonists) their effects.
2. The neuron is the principal cell type in the nervous system. This specialized cell consists of dendrites, a cell body, and an axon. It communicates with other neurons and organs by releasing neurotransmitters that can either excite or inhibit at their target sites.
3. The chemical messengers from glands and neurons exert their effects by interacting with special protein regions in membranes called *receptors*. Because of their unique construction, receptors interact only with molecules that have specific shapes. Activation of receptors can alter the functions of the target system.
4. Endorphin (opioid) and cannabinoid systems were discovered because of drugs of abuse such as the opioid narcotics and

## Key Terms

marijuana, respectively. Besides being the target of drugs of abuse, these systems also have the potential to be pharmacologically manipulated to achieve therapeutic outcomes.

5. Agonists are substances or drugs that stimulate receptors. Antagonists are substances or drugs that bind to receptors and prevent them from being activated.

6. A variety of substances is used as neurotransmitters by neurons in the body. The classes of transmitters include the catecholamines, serotonin, acetylcholine, GABA, peptides, and cannabinoids. These transmitters are excitatory, inhibitory, or sometimes both, depending on which receptor is being activated. Many drugs selectively act to either enhance or antagonize these neurotransmitters and their activities.

7. The central nervous system consists of the brain and spinal cord. Regions within the brain help to regulate specific functions. The hypothalamus controls endocrine and basic body functions. The basal ganglia include the caudate nucleus and are primarily responsible for controlling motor activity and learned behaviors. The limbic system regulates mood and mental states and establishing behaviors and helps mediate the rewarding properties of drugs of abuse. The cerebral cortex helps interpret and process information, plays a role in decision making, and responds to input information.

8. The limbic system and its associated transmitters, especially dopamine and serotonin, are major sites of action for the drugs of abuse. Substances that increase the activity of dopamine cause a sense of well-being and euphoria, which encourages psychological dependence.

9. The autonomic nervous system is composed of the sympathetic and parasympathetic systems; neurons associated with these systems release noradrenaline and acetylcholine as their transmitters, respectively. These systems work in an antagonistic fashion to control unconscious, visceral functions such as breathing and cardiovascular activity. The parasympathetic nervous system usually helps conserve and restore energy in the body, whereas the sympathetic nervous system is continually active.

10. The endocrine system consists of glands that synthesize and release hormones into the blood. Distribution via blood circulation carries these chemical messengers throughout the body, where they act on specific receptors. Some of the principal structures include the pituitary, adrenals, and gonads (testes and ovaries).

11. Anabolic steroids are structurally related to the male hormone testosterone. They are often abused by both male and female athletes trying to build muscle mass and are referred to as *performance enhancers*. The continual use of high doses of anabolic steroids can cause annoying and dangerous side effects. The long-term effects of low, intermittent doses of these drugs have not been determined. Because of concerns voiced by most medical authorities, anabolic steroids have been classified as Schedule III substances.

# References

American Addiction Centers. (2018). Why is the endocrine system at risk from substance abuse. Brentwood, TN: .org/health-complications-addiction/endocrine-system

Carmody, T. (2013, January 17). Hacking your body: Lance Armstrong and the science of doping. The Verge. Retrieved from http://www.theverge.com/2013/1/17/3886424/programming-your-body-lance-armstrong-and-doping-technology

Cherry, K. (2018, November). The nervous system and and endocrine system. Very Well Mind. Retrieved from https://www.verywellmind.com/the-nervous-and-endocrine-systems-2794894

Chrousos, G. (2015). The gonadal hormones and inhibitors. In B. Katzung, S. Masters, & A. Trevor *(Eds.), Basic and clinical pharmacology*, 13th ed. (pp. 696–722). New York, NY: McGraw-Hill.

CNN. (2019). Performance enhancing drugs in sports fast facts. CNN Library. Retrieved from https://www.cnn.com/2013/06/06/us/performance-enhancing-drugs-in-sports-fast-facts/index.html

"Dopamine: The feel good hormone." (n.d.). Retrieved from https://images.app.goo.gl/dLmqiQ9Si5bW5xXe8

Druginfo. (2015). Steroids. Retrieved from www.druginfo.adf.org.au/fact-sheets/steroids

eMedicineHealth. (2015). Anatomy of the central nervous system. Retrieved from www.emedicinehealth.com /anatomy_of_the_central_nervous_system/article _em.htm

Ernsberger, U., & Rohrer, H. (2018, September 13). Sympathetic tales: Subdivisions of the autonomic nervous system and the impact of developmental studies. *Neural Development, 13*, 20. Retrieved from www.ncbi.nlm.nih .gov/pmc/articles/PMC6137933/

Farzam, K., & Lakhar, A. (2019, November 19). Adrenergic drugs. StatPearls. Retrieved from https://www.ncbi.nlm .nih.gov/pubmed/30480963

Genetics Sciences Learning Center. (n.d.). Genes affect your risk of addiction. Salt Lake City, UT: University of Utah, Genetic Science Learning Center. Retrieved from http:// learn.genetics.utah.edu/content/addiction/genes/

Gilman, J. M., Rodoman, M., Schuster, R. M., Pachos, G., Azzouz, N., Fava, M., & Evans, A. E. (2018). Anterior insula activation during inhibition to smoking cues. *Addictive Behavior Reports, 7*(1), 40–46.

Gray, J., & Nicoll, R. (2015), Introduction to the pharmacology of CNS drugs. In B. Katzung and A. Trevor *(Eds.), Basic and clinical pharmacology*, 13th ed. (pp. 362–368). New York, NY: McGraw-Hill.

Hanson, G. R., Hoonakker, A. J., Alburges, M. E., McFadden, L. M., Robson, C. M., & Frankel, P. S. (2012). Response of limbica neurotensin systems to methamphetamine self-administration. *Neuroscience, 203*, 99–107.

Jiang, H., A. López-Aguilar, L. Meng, Gao, Z., Liu, Y., Tian, X., . . . , & Wu, P. (2018, January 22). Modulating cell-surface receptor signaling and ion channel functions by in situ glycan editing. *Angewandte Chemie International, 57*(4), 967–971. Retrieved from https://www.ncbi.nlm .nih.gov/pubmed/29292859#

Johnston, L. D., Miech, R. A., O'Malley, P., Bachman, J. G., & Schulenberg, J. E. (2019, January). Use of Ecstasy, heroin, synthetic marijuana, alcohol, cigarettes declined among US teens in 2018. Ann Arbor, MI: University of Michigan News Service. Retrieved from http://www .monitoringthefuture.org/pubs/monographs/mtf -overview2018.pdf

Jones, J., & Comer, S. (2015, July 1). A review of pharmacogenetic studies of substance-related disorders. *Drug and Alcohol Dependence, 152*, 1–14. Retrieved from https:// www.ncbi.nlm.nih.gov/pubmed/25819021

Khan, R. (2017, December 31). Doping in sports—Cheating or leveling the playing field? *Forbes.* Retrieved from https://www.forbes.com/sites/roomykhan/2017 /12/31/doping-in-sports-cheating-or-leveling-of-the -playing-field/#6a3286db75ec

Koob, G. F., & Volkow, N. (2010). Neurocircuitry of addiction. *Neuropsychopharmacology, 35*, 217–238.

Kyrou, I., & Tsigos, C. (2009). Stress hormones: Physiological stress and regulation of metabolism. *Current Opinions in Pharmacology, 9*, 787–793.

Matsuda, L. (1997). Molecular aspects of cannabinoid receptors. *Critical Reviews in Neurobiology, 11*, 143–166.

May, H. (2017, Winter). Genes and addiction. Continuum. Salt Lake City, UT: University of Utah. Retrieved from https://continuum.utah.edu/features/genes-and -addiction

McIntosh, J. (2018). What is serotonin and what does it do? Medical News Today. Retrieved from www.medical newstoday.com/kc/serotonin-facts-232248

Medlineplus. (n.d.). Hormones. Bethesda, MD: U.S. National Library of Medicine. Retrieved from https:// medlineplus.gov/hormones.html

Nassar, G., Raudales, F., & Leslie, S. (2018). Physiology, testosterone. StatPearls. Retrieved from https://www.ncbi .nlm.nih.gov/books/NBK526128/

National Institute on Drug Abuse (NIDA). (2018a). Drug misuse and addiction. Bethesda, MD: National Institute on Drug Abuse. Retrieved from https://www.drugabuse .gov/publications/drugs-brains-behavior-science -addiction/drug-misuse-addiction

National Institute on Drug Abuse (NIDA). (2018b). Drugs, brain, and behavior: The science of addiction. Bethesda, MD: National Institute on Drug Abuse. Retrieved from https://www.drugabuse.gov/publications/drugs-brains -behavior-science-addiction/drugs-brain

Poisbeau, P., Gazzo, G., & Calvel, L. (2018). Anxiolytics targeting GABA-A receptors: Insights on etifoxine. *World Journal of Biological Psychiatry, 19*, S36–S45.

Skolnick, P. (2012). Anxioselective anxiolytics: On a quest for the Holy Grail. *Trends in Pharmacological Sciences, 33*, 611–620.

Valentino, R., & Volkow. N. (2018). Untangling the complexity of opioid receptor function. *Neuropsychopharmacology, 43*, 2514–2520.

Watson, S. (2018, September). K2/Spice: What to know about these dangerous drugs. WebMD. Retrieved from www.webmd.com/mental-health/addiction/news /20180910/k2-spice-what-to-know-about-these-dangerous -drugs

Yadav, M., & Murumker, P. (2018). Advances in patented CB1 antagonists for obesity. *Pharmaceutical Patent Analyst*, p. 7. https://www.future-science.com/doi/full/10.4155 /ppa-2018-0020

Zou, S., & Kumar, U. (2018). Cannabinoid receptors and the endocannabinoid system: Signaling and the function in the central nervous system. *International Journal of Molecular Sciences, 19*, 833–856.

## CHAPTER 5

# How and Why Drugs Work

© FOTOGRIN/Shutterstock.

## Did You Know?

▶ In the United States, 20% of total hospital costs result from medical care for health damage caused by substances of abuse.

▶ The same dose of a drug does not have the same effect on everyone.

▶ In excessive doses, almost any drug or substance can be toxic.

▶ Of strokes among young Americans, 65% are related to cigarette, cocaine, or amphetamine use.

▶ Many people who abuse cocaine also abuse alcohol to counter unpleasant side effects.

▶ Many of the overdose deaths caused by prescription drugs are the result of unanticipated drug interactions.

▶ Many drugs are unable to pass from the blood into the brain due to the blood–brain barrier.

▶ Gender affects responses to alcohol and tobacco.

▶ Hereditary factors may predispose some individuals to becoming psychologically dependent on drugs with abuse potential.

## Learning Objectives

**On completing this chapter, you should be able to:**

› Describe some of the common unintended drug effects.

› Explain why the same dose of a drug may affect individuals differently.

› Explain the difference between potency and toxicity.

› Describe the concept of a drug's margin of safety.

› Identify and give examples of additive, antagonistic, and potentiative (synergistic) drug interactions.

› Identify the pharmacokinetic factors that can influence the effects caused by drugs.

› Cite the physiological and pathological factors that influence drug effects.

› Explain the significance of the blood–brain barrier to psychoactive drugs.

› Define *threshold dose*, *plateau effect*, and *cumulative effect*.

› Describe how pharmacokinetics influences drug effects.

› Discuss the role of the liver in drug metabolism and the consequences of this process.

› Define *biotransformation*.

› Describe the relationships among drug tolerance, withdrawal, rebound, physical dependence, and psychological dependence and how they can affect drug abuse patterns.

› Discuss the significance of placebos in drug therapy and drug abuse.

› Describe drug craving, and explain its relationship to drug addiction and relapse.

## Introduction

A common belief is that drugs can solve most of life's serious physical, emotional, and medical problems. Although medications are essential to treatment for many diseases, excessive reliance on drugs causes unrealistic expectations that may lead to dangerous—even fatal—consequences. For example, drug addiction (frequently referred to as *substance* or *drug use disorder*) (American Psychiatric Association [APA], 2013) and dependence often follow from such unrealistic drug expectations. Obviously, not every person who uses drugs inappropriately becomes a drug addict, nor are patients who use drugs as prescribed by their doctor immune from becoming physically and mentally dependent on their prescribed medications. In fact, because of individual variability, it is difficult to predict accurately which drug users will or will not have drug problems such as addiction and dependence, although identifying persons with risk factors may make prevention strategies for drug abuse more effective.

In this chapter, we consider the factors that account for the variability of drug responses—that is, what determines how the body responds to drugs and why some drugs work but others do not. First, we review the general effects of drugs both intended and unintended. The correlation between the dose and response to a drug is addressed next, followed by a discussion of how drugs interact with one another. The section on pharmacokinetic factors considers how drugs are introduced into, distributed throughout, and eliminated from the body, along with physiological and pathological variables that modify how drugs affect the body. The final sections in the chapter consider concepts important to understanding drug abuse such as tolerance, physical versus psychological dependence, and addiction.

## The Intended and Unintended Effects of Drugs

When physicians prescribe drugs, their objective is usually to cure or relieve symptoms of a disease. Frequently, however, drugs cause unintended effects that neither the physician nor the patient expected. These are called **side effects**.

A response that is considered a side effect in one situation may actually be the therapeutic objective in another. For example, the antihistamines found in many over-the-counter (OTC) drugs have an intended main effect of relieving allergy symptoms, but they often cause annoying drowsiness as a side effect; in fact, for this reason their labels include warnings that they should not be used while driving a car. These antihistamines are also included in OTC sleep aids, in which their sedating action is the desired main effect.

Side effects can influence many body functions and occur in any organ (see **Figure 5.1**). The following are basic kinds of side effects that can result from drug use:

- nausea or vomiting;
- changes in mental alertness such as sedation or anxiety;
- dependence, which compels people to continue using a drug because they want to achieve a desired effect or because they fear unpleasant reactions, called **withdrawal**, that occur when use of the drug is discontinued;
- allergic reactions (hypersensitive reactions or sensitization), often experienced as rashes or breathing difficulty; and
- changes in cardiovascular activity altering the activity of the heart or blood pressure.

This short list of side effects demonstrates the types of risks involved whenever any drug (prescription, nonprescription, illicit, or even herbal product) is used. Consequently, before taking a drug, whether for therapeutic or recreational use, you should understand its potential problems and determine whether the benefits justify the risks. For example, it is important to know that morphine is effective for relieving severe pain, but it also depresses breathing and retards intestinal activity, causing constipation. Likewise, amphetamines can be used to suppress appetite for losing weight or to manage attention deficit hyperactivity disorder, but they also increase blood pressure and stimulate the heart and may interfere with sleep. Cocaine is a good local anesthetic, but it can be extremely addicting and can cause tremors or even seizures. The greater the danger associated with using a drug, the less likely that the benefits will warrant its use.

## KEY TERMS

**side effects**
unintended drug responses

**withdrawal**
unpleasant effects that occur when use of a drug is stopped

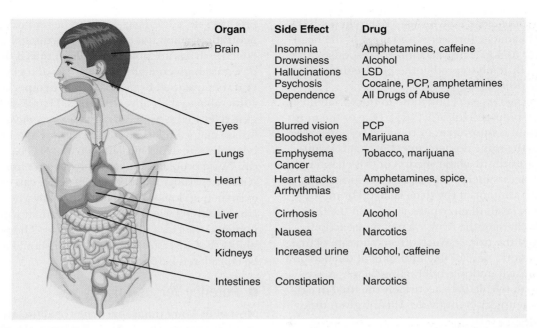

| Organ | Side Effect | Drug |
|---|---|---|
| Brain | Insomnia | Amphetamines, caffeine |
| | Drowsiness | Alcohol |
| | Hallucinations | LSD |
| | Psychosis | Cocaine, PCP, amphetamines |
| | Dependence | All Drugs of Abuse |
| Eyes | Blurred vision | PCP |
| | Bloodshot eyes | Marijuana |
| Lungs | Emphysema | Tobacco, marijuana |
| | Cancer | |
| Heart | Heart attacks | Amphetamines, spice, |
| | Arrhythmias | cocaine |
| Liver | Cirrhosis | Alcohol |
| Stomach | Nausea | Narcotics |
| Kidneys | Increased urine | Alcohol, caffeine |
| Intestines | Constipation | Narcotics |

**FIGURE 5.1** Common side effects with drugs of abuse. Almost every organ or system in the body can be negatively affected by the substances of abuse.

Adverse effects of drugs of abuse are particularly troublesome in the United States. Studies have suggested that almost a half-trillion dollars are spent each year in the United States because of medical care and premature deaths related to the use of addicting substances (Goplerud, Hodge, & Bessham, 2017).

# The Dose–Response Relationship of Therapeutics and Toxicity

All effects—both desired and unwanted—are related to the amount of drug administered. A small concentration of drug may have one effect, whereas a larger dose may create a greater effect or a different effect entirely. Because some correlation exists between the response to a drug and the quantity of the drug dose, it is possible to calculate **dose–response** curves (see **Figure 5.2**).

Once a dose–response curve for a drug has been determined in an individual, it can be used to predict how that person will respond to different doses of the drug. For example, the dose–response curve for user B in Figure 5.2 shows that 400 milligrams of ibuprofen will relieve only 50% of the user's headache. It is important to understand that not everyone responds the same way to a given dose of drug. Thus, in Figure 5.2, although 400 milligrams of ibuprofen gives 50%

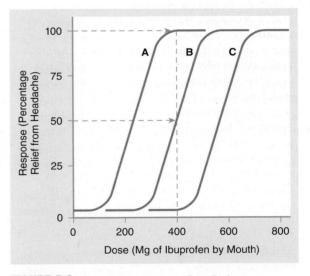

**FIGURE 5.2** Dose–response curve for relieving a headache with ibuprofen in three users. User A is the most sensitive and has 100% headache relief at a dose of 400 milligrams. User B is the next most sensitive and experiences 50% headache relief with a 400-milligram dose. The least sensitive is user C: With a 400-milligram dose, user C has no relief from a headache.

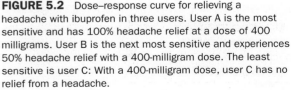

**KEY TERM**

**dose–response**
correlation between the amount of a drug given and its effects

relief from a headache for user B, it relieves 100% of the headache for user A and none of the headache for user C. This variability in response can make it difficult to predict the precise drug effect from a given dose.

Many factors can contribute to the variability in drug responses (Holford, 2015). One of the most important is **tolerance**, or reduced response over time to the same dosage, an effect that is examined carefully in a later section of this chapter. Other factors include the size of the individual, stomach contents if the drug is taken by mouth, different levels of enzymatic activity in the liver (which changes the drug via metabolic action), acidity of the urine (which affects the rate of drug elimination), time of day, and state of the person's health. Such multiple interacting factors make it difficult to calculate accurately the final drug effect for any given individual at any given time.

## ■ Margin of Safety

An important concept for developing new drugs for therapy, as well as for assessing the probability of serious side effects for drugs of abuse, is the **margin of safety**. The margin of safety is determined by the difference between the doses necessary to cause the intended (therapeutic or recreational) effects and the toxic unintended effects. The larger the margin of safety, the less likely that serious adverse side effects will occur when using the drug to treat medical problems or even when abusing it. Drugs with relatively narrow margins of safety, such as heroin or cocaine, have an extremely high rate of serious reactions in populations who abuse these substances.

There is no such thing as the perfect drug that goes right to the target in the body, has no toxicity,

**KEY TERMS**

**tolerance**
changes in the body that decrease response to a drug even though the dose remains the same

**margin of safety**
range in dose between the amount of drug necessary to cause a therapeutic effect and that needed to create a toxic effect

**potency**
amount of drug necessary to cause an effect

**toxicity**
capacity of one drug to damage or cause adverse effects in the body

produces no side effects, and can be removed or neutralized when not needed. Unfortunately, most effective drugs are potentially dangerous if the doses are high enough, if they are used recklessly, or if they are used by persons who are especially vulnerable to their adverse effects. Pharmacologists refer to the perfect drug as a *magic bullet*; so far, no magic bullets have been discovered. Even relatively safe drugs available on an OTC basis can cause problems for some prospective users. It is not surprising that all drugs of abuse can cause extremely serious side effects, especially when self-administered by users who are unfamiliar with the potential toxicities of these substances. The possibility that adverse effects will occur should always be considered before using any drug.

## ■ Potency Versus Toxicity

Most of us know that some drugs of abuse are more dangerous than others. For example, it is common knowledge that abuse of the narcotic drug heroin is more likely to be lethal than abuse of another narcotic drug, codeine. One important feature that makes heroin more dangerous than codeine is its high potency. **Potency** is a way of expressing how much of a drug is necessary to cause an effect, whether it be desired or toxic. The smaller the dose required to achieve a drug action, the greater the drug potency.

The concept of potency can also be used to describe a drug's ability to create a therapeutic effect. More potent medications require lower doses to be effective. Knowledge of a drug's potency is essential if it is to be used properly and safely.

**Toxicity** is the capacity of a drug to upset or even destroy normal body functions. Toxic compounds are often called *poisons*, although almost any compound—including sugar, table salt, aspirin, and vitamin A—can be toxic at sufficiently high doses. If a foreign chemical is introduced into the body, it may disrupt the body's normal functions. In many instances, the body can compensate for this disruption, perhaps by metabolizing and rapidly eliminating the chemical, and little effect is noted. Sometimes, however, the delicate balance is altered and the person becomes sick or even dies. If the body's functional balance is already under stress from disease, the introduction of a drug may have a much more serious effect than its use in a healthy person who can adjust to its toxicity.

A drug with high potency often is toxic even at low doses; therefore, the amount given must be carefully measured and the user closely monitored. If caution is not taken, serious damage to the body or death can occur. Very potent drugs that are abused, such as heroin-related drugs, are particularly dangerous because they are often consumed by unsuspecting users who are ignorant of the drug's extreme toxicity. Potency depends on many factors, such as the drug's absorption, its distribution in the body, individual metabolism, the form of excretion, the rate of elimination, and its activity at the site of action (Lange, 2015).

## Drug Interaction

A drug's effects can be dramatically altered when other drugs are also present in the body; this effect is known as **drug interaction** (Lange, 2015). A typical example of multiple drug use occurs when you treat your common cold. Because of your many cold-related symptoms, you may consume an assortment of pain relievers, antihistamines, decongestants, and anticough medications all at the same time.

Multiple drug use can create a serious medical problem because many drugs influence the actions of other drugs (Lange, 2015). Even physicians may be baffled by unusual effects when multiple drugs are consumed. Frequently, drug interactions are misdiagnosed as symptoms of a disease. Such errors in diagnosis can lead to inappropriate treatment and serious health consequences. Complications can arise that are dangerous, even fatal. The interacting substance may be another drug, or it may be some substance in the diet or in the environment such as a pesticide. Because approximately 20% of Americans take some type of herbal supplement, herbs are commonly interacting with both prescription and nonprescription drugs. For example, the herb Echinacea, which is often used to treat colds, can slow the metabolism of caffeine, leading to side effects such as jitters, headaches, and insomnia (Drugs.com, 2014). These interactions are not surprising given that some of the herbs contain drugs that occur naturally. Consequently, an herb that causes sedation such as melatonin almost certainly will enhance the depressing effects of either prescription or nonprescription sleep aids. Drug interaction is an area in which more research and public education are required (Drugs.com, 2014).

Depending on the effect on the body, drug interaction may be categorized into three types: additive, antagonistic (inhibitory), and potentiative (synergistic) (Lange, 2015).

### ■ Additive Effects

**Additive interactions** are the summation of effects of drugs taken concurrently. An example of an additive interaction results from using aspirin and acetaminophen (Tylenol) at the same time. The pain relief provided is equal to the sum of the two analgesics, which could be achieved by a comparable dose of either drug alone. Thus, if a 300-milligram tablet of Bayer aspirin were taken with a 300-milligram tablet of Tylenol, the relief would be the same as if two tablets of either Bayer aspirin or Tylenol were taken instead.

### ■ Antagonistic (Inhibitory) Effects

**Antagonistic interactions** occur when one drug cancels or blocks the effect of another drug. For example, if you take antihistamines to reduce nasal congestion, you may be able to antagonize some of the drowsiness often caused by these drugs by using a central nervous system (CNS) stimulant such as caffeine.

Often, drug abusers who use two drugs at the same time are trying to antagonize the unpleasant side effects of the first drug by administering the second. It has been reported that approximately 34% of the 500,000 emergency visits caused by cocaine consumption also involve the use of alcohol (DrugWise, n.d.; Fettiplace et al., 2015). The combined use of these two drugs may be a major factor in drug-related cardiovascular problems and death in emergency rooms (DrugWise, n.d.; Fettiplace et al., 2015). Nevertheless, it appears that some users may coadminister these drugs in an attempt to antagonize the disruptive effects of alcohol with the stimulant action of the cocaine.

**KEY TERMS**

**drug interaction**
when the presence of one drug alters the action of another drug

**additive interactions**
effects created when drugs are similar and actions are added together

**antagonistic interactions**
effects created when drugs cancel one another

## ■ Potentiative (Synergistic) Effects

The third type of drug interaction is known as *potentiation*, or **synergism**. Synergism occurs when the effect of a drug is enhanced by the presence of another drug or substance, whether synthetic or naturally occurring (Lange, 2015). A common example is the combination of alcohol and opioid analgesics such as oxycodone (e.g., OxyContin). It has been estimated that many of the people who die each year from prescription overdosing have alcohol and a prescribed CNS depressant in their system (America's Rehab Campuses, 2019). When such depressants are taken together, CNS functions become impaired and the person becomes groggy. A person in this state may forget that he or she has taken the pills and repeat the dose. The combination of these two depressants (or other depressants such as antihistamines) can interfere with the CNS to the point where vital functions such as breathing and heartbeat are severely impaired.

Although the mechanisms of interaction among CNS depressants are not entirely clear, these drugs likely enhance one another's direct effects on inhibitory chemical messengers in the brain. In addition, interference by alcohol with liver-metabolizing enzymes contributes to the synergism that arises with the combination of alcohol and some depressants such as barbiturates.

## ■ Dealing with Drug Interactions

Although many drug effects and interactions are not well understood, it is important to be aware of them. A growing body of evidence indicates that many of the drugs and substances we deliberately consume will interact and produce unexpected and sometimes dangerous effects (see **Table 5.1**). It is alarming to know that many of the foods we eat and some chemical pollutants also interfere with and modify drug actions. Pesticides, traces of hormones in meat and poultry, traces of metals in fish, nitrites and nitrates from fertilizers, and a wide range of chemicals—some of which are used as food additives—have been shown to interact with some drugs under certain conditions (Ryu, Kim, & Lee, 2018).

It is essential that the public be educated about the interactions most likely to occur with drugs

**KEY TERM**

**synergism**
ability of one drug to enhance the effect of another; also called *potentiation*

**TABLE 5.1**   Common Interactions with Substances of Abuse

| Drug | Combined with | Consequence of Interaction |
|---|---|---|
| **Sedatives** | | |
| Diazepam (Valium), triazolam (Halcion) | Alcohol, barbiturates | Increase sedation |
| **Stimulants** | | |
| Amphetamines, Ritalin | Insulin | Decrease insulin effect |
| | Antidepressants | Cause hypertension |
| **Narcotics** | | |
| Heroin, morphine | Valium | Increase sedation |
| | Anticoagulant | Increase bleeding |
| | Antidepressants | Cause sedation |
| | Amphetamines | Increase euphoria |
| **Tobacco** | | |
| Nicotine | Blood pressure medication | Elevate blood pressure |
| | Amphetamines, cocaine | Increase cardiovascular effects |
| **Alcohol** | | |
| | Cocaine | Produces cocaethylene, which enhances euphoria and toxicity |
| | Tylenol (acetaminophen) | Causes liver damage |

that are prescribed, self-administered legitimately (e.g., OTC drugs and herbal products), or taken recreationally (e.g., drugs of abuse) and that women are particularly vulnerable (see "Prescription for Abuse: Problems with Prescription Abuse in Women") (CDC, 2013). People need to be aware that OTC and herbal drugs are as likely to cause interaction problems as prescription drugs (Awortwe et al., 2018). For example, an OTC or herbal decongestant that contains mild CNS stimulants (e.g., pseudoephedrine) taken with potent CNS stimulants such as cocaine and

## PRESCRIPTION FOR ABUSE

### *Prescription Abuse Problems with Prescription Abuse In Women*

After her father died prematurely, Tina Orr felt she was also destined to die early. At age 35, Tina, like her father, went to an early grave because of a prescription overdose. Tina's sister described her as "the most amazing mother I'd ever met, incredibly kind and patient Her daughter was her whole world...she was so happy." However, as she struggled with worsening medical conditions, including obesity, problems with a growing prescription dependence became evident. Even though at one time she was receiving five different prescriptions, none seemed to solve her medical and emotional difficulties. Her sister says that just before her death Tina seemed to be upbeat planning to go back to school.

Problems with prescription overdoses are a particular problem for women and usually involve painkillers and drugs for mental illnesses. Some explanations for this problem is that women tend to have more chronic pain and emotional disorders for which they receive prescription painkiller drugs as well as antidepressants and antianxiety medications. They also tend to develop dependence on these medications faster than men, resulting in escalating use and

© Michal Kowalski/Shutterstock.

major withdrawal symptoms when trying to discontinue their drug use.

Because of these disturbing patterns of prescription overdoses in women, it is important that those who prescribe these medications discuss all the medications being used by their female patients (including OTC drug products). These women need to understand they should only use the prescription drugs as directed by a healthcare provider, store them in a secure place, not share their prescriptions with anyone else, and dispose of medications properly as soon as treatment is completed.

Centers for Disease Control and Prevention (CDC). (2013, July). Prescription painkiller overdoses: A growing epidemic, especially among women. Retrieved from http://www.cdc.gov/vitalsigns/prescriptionpainkilleroverdoses/index.html

amphetamines can cause interactions that fatally affect the heart and brain. If any question arises concerning the possibility of drug interaction, individuals should talk to their physician, pharmacist, or other healthcare providers.

Many drug abusers are multiple drug (*polydrug*) users with little concern for the dangerous interactions that might occur. It is common, for example, for drug abusers to combine multiple CNS depressants to enhance their effects, to combine a depressant with a stimulant to titrate a CNS effect (to determine the smallest amount that can be taken to achieve the desired "high"), or to experiment with a combination of stimulants, depressants, and hallucinogens just to see what happens. The effects of such haphazard drug mixing are impossible to predict, difficult to treat in emergency situations, and all too frequently fatal (see "Prescription for Abuse: Deadly Drug Mix").

## Pharmacokinetic Factors That Influence Drug Effects

Although it is difficult to predict precisely how any single individual will be affected by drug use, the following major questions represent different aspects of the body's response that should be considered when attempting to anticipate a drug's effects (Holford, 2015):

- How does the drug enter the body? (administration)
- How does the drug move from the site of administration into the body's system? (absorption)
- How does the drug move to various areas in the body? (distribution)

- How and where does the drug produce its effects? (activation)
- How is the drug inactivated, metabolized, and excreted from the body (biotransformation and elimination)?

These issues relate to the **pharmacokinetics** of a drug and are important considerations when predicting the body's response. They can impact the drug levels that are detected in the body when a drug test is conducted.

## ■ Forms and Methods of Taking Drugs

Drugs come in many forms. How a drug is formulated—solution, powder, capsule, or pill—influences the rate of passage into the bloodstream and consequently its efficacy. The means of introducing the drug into the body will also affect how quickly the drug enters the bloodstream and how it is distributed to the site of action, as well as how much will ultimately

### KEY TERM

**pharmacokinetics**
the study of factors that influence the distribution and concentration of drugs in the body

reach its target and exert an effect (Holford, 2015) (see **Figure 5.3**). The principal forms of drug administration are *oral ingestion*, *inhalation*, *injection*, and *topical application*.

### ORAL INGESTION

One of the most common and convenient ways of taking a drug is orally. This type of administration usually introduces the drug into the body by way of the stomach or intestines. Following oral administration, it is difficult to control the amount of drug that reaches the site of action, for three reasons:

1. The drug must enter the bloodstream after passing through the wall of the stomach or intestines without being destroyed or changed to an inactive form. From the blood, the drug must diffuse to the target area and remain there in sufficient concentration to have an effect.
2. Materials in the stomach or intestines such as food may interfere with the passage of some drugs through the gut lining and thus prevent drug action. For example, food in your stomach will diminish the effects of alcohol by altering its absorption.

| Method of Administration | Onset | Duration | Effect |
|---|---|---|---|
| **Smoking** | | | |
| *Cocaine* | Fast (~15 seconds) | Brief (10–15 minutes) | Potent and strong |
| *Heroin* | Fast (~20 seconds) | Short (1–2 hours) | Potent and strong |
| **Intravenous** | | | |
| *Cocaine* | Fast (20 seconds) | Short (30 minutes) | Potent and strong |
| *Heroin* | Fast (1–2 minutes) | Short (1–2 hours) | Potent and strong |
| **Snorting** | | | |
| *Cocaine* | Moderate (~10 minutes) | Short (45 minutes) | Less potent |
| *Heroin* | Moderate (~15 minutes) | Short (1–2 hours) | Less potent |
| **Oral** | | | |
| *Cocaine (coca leaf)* | Slow (30 minutes) | Moderate (~2–4 hours) | Minor |
| *Methadone* | Slow (30–60 minutes) | Long (24 hours) | Less euphoria/ used for treatment |
| **Vaping** | | | |
| *Marijuana* | Seconds | 10–15 minutes | Moderate |
| *Nicotine* | Seconds | 10–15 minutes | Moderate |

**FIGURE 5.3** Relationship between the method of drug administration and drug effects.

3. The liver might metabolize orally ingested drugs too rapidly and before they are able to exert an effect. The liver is the major detoxifying organ in the body, which means it removes chemicals and toxins from the blood and usually changes them into an inactive form that is easy for the body to excrete. This function is essential to survival, but it creates a problem for the pharmacologist in developing effective drugs or the physician prescribing the correct dose of a drug to treat a serious disease. The liver is especially problematic to oral administration because the substances absorbed from the digestive tract usually go to the liver before being distributed to other parts of the body and their site of action. For this reason, cocaine taken orally is not especially effective.

## PRESCRIPTION FOR ABUSE　❗

### Deadly Drug Mix

The death of another celebrity because of mixing drugs, including illicit and prescription drugs, as well as alcohol, has become an all-too-common occurrence. Usually there are many questions: Why did this happen? Could it have been avoided? How do we stop it from happening in the future? It seems almost incomprehensible that people who seem to have everything lose it all to a drug overdose, leaving their loved ones, as well as an adoring public, not understanding how it could happen. **Table A** lists some of the celebrities who lost their lives from 2009–2014 from intentional or accidental overdoses of drug combinations. This list does not include those overdosing on a single drug or those who overdosed but did not die.

**TABLE A** Celebrity Deaths Due to Intentional or Accidental Overdose of Drug Combinations: 2009–2014

| Name | Fame | Cause of Death | Drug Category | Year | Age at Death |
|------|------|----------------|---------------|------|--------------|
| Mac Miller | Rapper | Fentanyl, cocaine, alcohol | Prescription | 2018 | 26 |
| Tom Petty | Singer | Fentanyl and oxycodone | Prescription drugs | 2017 | 26 |
| Prince | Singer | Accidental fentanyl | Prescription drug | 2016 | 57 |
| Philip Seymour Hoffman | Actor | Heroin, cocaine, benzos, amphetamine | Prescription and illicit drugs | 2014 | 46 |
| Joan Rivers | Actress | Therapeutic complication with propofol sedation | Prescription drugs | 2014 | 81 |
| Cory Monteith | Actor | Toxic mix of heroin and alcohol | Illegal drugs and alcohol | 2013 | 31 |
| Chris Kelly | Rapper | Fatal overdose | Illegal drugs | 2013 | 34 |
| Whitney Houston | Singer | Prescription drugs and cocaine | Illegal and prescription drugs | 2012 | 48 |
| Michael Baze | Horse jockey | Cocaine and oxymorphone | Illegal and prescription drugs | 2011 | 28 |
| Derek Boogaard | Ice hockey player | Alcohol and oxycodone | Alcohol and prescription | 2011 | 28 |
| Erica Blasberg | Golfer | Multiple prescriptions | Prescription | 2010 | 25 |
| Michael Jackson | Singer and pop icon | Propofol and prescriptions | Prescriptions | 2009 | 50 |

Data from Drugs.com. (n.d.). Drug-related deaths—Notable celebrities. Retrieved from http://www.drugs.com/celebrity_deaths.html. Accessed May 23, 2019.

### INHALATION

Some drugs are administered by inhalation into the lungs through the mouth or nose. The lungs include large beds of capillaries, so chemicals capable of crossing membranes can enter the blood as rapidly as they can via intravenous injection and can be equally as dangerous (Holford, 2015). Ether, chloroform, and nitrous oxide anesthetics are examples of drugs that are therapeutically administered by inhalation. Nicotine, cocaine, methamphetamine, tetrahydrocannabinol (THC; active ingredient in marijuana), heroin, and products known as Spice are drugs of abuse that can be inhaled as smoke (de Havenon, Chin, Thomas, & Afra, 2011; Lisi, 2014; Mathias, 1997). One serious problem with inhalation is the potential for irritation to the mucous membrane lining of the lungs; another is that the drug may have to be continually inhaled to maintain the concentration necessary for an effect. Inhalation of illicit drugs of abuse is common to prevent contracting the human immunodeficiency virus (HIV), which can be transmitted by IV injection with contaminated needles (National Institute on Drug Abuse [NIDA], 2015).

In addition, some popular drugs can also be inhaled through **vaping** which is the act of inhaling and exhaling the flavored aerosol or vapor from electric devices such as e-cigarettes. This form of drug administration has rapidly become popular for nicotine and THC from marijuana (NIDA, 2018).

### INJECTION

Some drugs are given by **intravenous (IV)**, **intramuscular (IM)**, or **subcutaneous (SC)** injection. A major advantage of administering drugs by IV is the speed of action; the dosage is delivered rapidly and directly, and often less drug is needed because it reaches the site of action quickly. This method can be extremely dangerous if the dosage

Drugs can be introduced into the body using various methods, such as pills, capsules, oral liquids, topicals, or injections.

Electrical vaping devices are used to introduce flavored humidified vapor into the body containing drugs such as nicotine.

is calculated incorrectly, the drug effects are unknown, or the user is especially sensitive to the drug's adverse effects.

In addition, impurities in injected materials may irritate the vein; this issue is a particular problem in the drug-abusing population, in which needle sharing frequently occurs. The injection itself injures the vein by leaving a tiny point of scar tissue where the vein is punctured. If repeated injections are administered into the same area, the elasticity of the vein is gradually reduced, causing the vessel to collapse.

Intramuscular injection can damage the muscle directly if the drug preparation irritates the tissue or indirectly if the nerve controlling the muscle is damaged. If the nerve is destroyed, the muscle will degenerate (atrophy). A subcutaneous injection may damage the skin at the point of injection if a particularly irritating drug is administered. Another danger of drug injections arises when contaminated needles are shared by drug users. This danger has become a serious problem in

### KEY TERMS

**vaping**
the act of inhaling and exhaling drug-containing aerosol or vapor from electric devices

**intravenous (IV)**
drug injection into a vein

**intramuscular (IM)**
drug injection into a muscle

**subcutaneous (SC)**
drug injection beneath the skin

the spread of infectious diseases such as acquired immunodeficiency syndrome (AIDS), which is caused by HIV, and hepatitis. For example, in 2013, ~10% of the 47,000 diagnoses of HIV infection in the United States were the result of intravenous drug use (CDC, 2015).

### TOPICAL APPLICATION

Those drugs that readily pass through surface tissue such as the skin, the lining of the nose, and that under the tongue can be applied topically for systemic (whole-body) effects. Although many drugs do not appreciably diffuse across these tissue barriers into the circulation, there are notable exceptions. For example, a product to help quit smoking, a nicotine transdermal patch (Nicoderm), is placed on the skin; the drug passes through the skin and enters the body to prevent tobacco craving and withdrawal. In addition, several drugs of abuse such as heroin and cocaine can be "snorted" into the nose and rapidly absorbed into the body through the nasal lining (Dixon, n.d.).

## ■ Distribution of Drugs in the Body and Time–Response Relationships

Following administration (regardless of the mode), most drugs are distributed throughout the body in the blood. The circulatory system consists of many miles of arteries, veins, and capillaries and includes five to six liters of blood. Once a drug enters the bloodstream by passing through thin capillary walls, it is rapidly diluted and carried to organs and other body structures. It requires approximately one minute for the blood and the drugs it contains to circulate completely throughout the body.

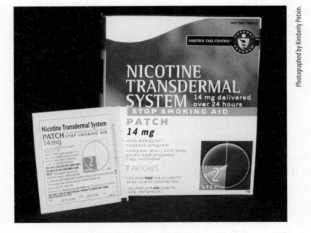

Transdermal nicotine patches are popular smoking-cessation aids.

### FACTORS AFFECTING DISTRIBUTION

Drugs have different patterns of distribution, depending on the following chemical properties (Le, 2019):

- their ability to pass across membranes and through tissues,
- their molecular size (large versus small molecules),
- their solubility properties (do they dissolve in water or in fatty [oily] solutions?), and
- their tendency to attach to proteins and tissues throughout the body.

These distribution-related factors are critical because they determine whether a drug can pass across tissue barriers in the body and reach its site of action. By preventing the movement of a drug into organs or across tissues, these barriers may interfere with drug activity and limit the therapeutic usefulness of a drug if it does not reach its site of action. Such barriers may also offer protection by preventing entry of a drug into a body structure where it can cause problems.

Blood is carried to the nerve cells of the brain in a vast network of thin-walled capillaries. Drugs that are soluble in fatty (oily) solutions are most likely to pass across these capillary membranes (known as the **blood–brain barrier**) into the brain tissue. Most psychoactive drugs, such as the drugs of abuse, are able to pass across the blood–brain barrier with little difficulty. However, many water-soluble drugs cannot pass through the fatty capillary wall; such drugs are not likely to cross this biological barrier and affect the brain. An interesting practical application of this pharmacokinetic principle is the use of "vaccines" to treat nicotine (Torrice, 2018), methamphetamine, or cocaine dependence. Like other vaccines, this approach stimulates the body to produce antibodies against a chemical target that is introduced into the body (often injected under the skin). Consequently, when specially formulated nicotine or cocaine (a chemical form that causes an immunoreaction) is injected into the body, it stimulates the production of reactive antibodies in the patient. These antibodies will then bind to nicotine or cocaine that is later consumed and has entered into the bloodstream. With the attached antibody,

### KEY TERM

**blood–brain barrier**
selective filtering between the cerebral blood vessels and the brain

the drug is too large to get across biological barriers such as the blood–brain barrier and often becomes pharmacologically inactive. This means that the antibodies prevent nicotine or cocaine from being rewarding or from having effects on the brain in general and help the addict to stop using the substance.

A second biological barrier, the placenta, prevents the transfer of certain molecules from the mother to the fetus. A principal factor that determines passage of substances across the placental barrier is molecular size. Large molecules do not usually cross the placental barrier, whereas small molecules do. Because most drugs are relatively small molecules, they usually cross from the maternal circulation into the fetal circulation; thus, most drugs (including drugs of abuse) taken by a woman during pregnancy enter and affect the fetus. This can cause a baby of a narcotic-using mother, for example, to experience severe withdrawal symptoms after birth (Tully, 2015). See "Case in Point: The Newborn Victims."

## REQUIRED DOSES FOR EFFECTS

Most drugs do not take effect until a certain amount has been administered and a crucial concentration has reached the site of action in the body. The smallest amount of a drug needed to elicit a response is called its **threshold dose**.

The effectiveness of some drugs may be calculated in a *linear* (straight-line) fashion—that is, the more drug taken, the more drug distributed throughout the body and the greater the effect. However, many drugs have a maximum possible effect regardless of dose; this is called the **plateau effect**. OTC medications in particular have a limit on their effects. For example, use of the

### KEY TERMS

**threshold dose**
minimum drug dose necessary to cause an effect

**plateau effect**
maximum drug effect regardless of dose

## ▶ CASE IN POINT
### The Newborn Victims

"**G**uilty, that's how I feel," Nicole said as she waited in a hospital conference room. No one could blame Nicole for her anguish and feelings of culpability as she watched her five-pound, five-day-old son intensely squirming in his white blanket; after all, it was her history of abusing opioid narcotics that caused her son's suffering. Although his discomfort and pain were obvious, Nicole could imagine how much worse her son would feel if he had not been given a dose of morphine to suppress his opiate cravings, high-pitched cry, and intense withdrawal symptoms. Without this morphine dose to mitigate his narcotic physical dependence, the newborn's body would have been writhing in agony, shaking, overcome with severe diarrhea, unable to eat, and completely miserable. Nicole knew that her son's body had become dependent on the methadone she was taking while he was in the womb. She remembered back 10 years when she was first prescribed a potent opioid painkiller to relieve pain associated with surgery to treat her obesity. In the years following, she gradually increased her dependence on these analgesics until she was downing up to a dozen of these pills at

a time. Although she avoided turning to heroin, she did spend all the money she could get her hands on to illegally obtain medications such as Vicodin and OxyContin to satisfy her narcotic habit. After several years, she finally sought professional help and began to receive legal daily doses of the potent narcotic methadone to replace her body's need for the narcotics. While methadone treatments made it possible for her to avoid the illegally obtained prescription painkillers, to avoid severe withdrawal during her pregnancy Nicole used methadone daily while her son was in utero. The consequence was that while Nicole's opioid-dependent body did not experience withdrawal, her son's developing body, much like his mother's, was physically dependent on these drugs by the time he was born. Also like his mother, now that he was born, he required daily narcotic treatment to prevent withdrawal from his mother's methadone.

In recent years, many hospitals claim there has been a flood of babies born dependent on drugs the mothers were using during their pregnancies. One doctor compared this trend to the spread of Ebola: "Nobody had it, and then all of a sudden everybody had it."

Data from Tully, M. (2015, June 1). Meet heroin's tiniest victims: Newborns. *USA Today*. Retrieved from https://www.desmoinesregister.com/story/news/2015/06/01/meet-heroins-tiniest-victims-newborns/28330491/http://www.USAtoday.com/story/news/nation-now/2015/06/01/heroin-babies-morphine-opiate-drugs/28299459/

nonprescription analgesic aspirin can effectively relieve your mild to moderate pain, but aspirin will not effectively treat your severe pains regardless of the dose taken. Other drugs may cause distinct or opposite effects, depending on the dose. For example, low doses of alcohol may appear to act like a stimulant, causing the drinker to be talkative and social, whereas high doses usually cause sedation, resulting in drowsiness and eventually sleep or even coma in extreme cases.

## TIME–RESPONSE FACTORS

An important factor that determines responses is the time that has elapsed between when a drug was administered and the onset of its effects. The delay in effect after administering a drug often relates to the time required for the drug to disseminate from the site of administration to the site of action. Consequently, the closer a drug is placed to the target area, the faster the onset of action.

The drug response is often classified as immediate, short term, or **acute**, referring to the response after a single dose. The response can also be **chronic**, or long term—a characteristic usually associated with repeated doses. The intensity and quality of a drug's acute effect may change considerably within a short period of time. For example, the main intoxicating effects of a large dose of alcohol generally peak in less than one hour and then gradually taper off. In addition, an initial stimulating effect by alcohol may later change to sedation and depression.

The effects of long-term or chronic use of some drugs can differ dramatically from the effects noted with their short-term or acute use. The administration of small doses may not produce any immediately apparent detrimental effect, but chronic use of the same drug (frequent use over a long time) may yield prolonged effects that do not become apparent until years later. Although for most people there are minimal effects caused by short-term use of small doses of tobacco, its chronic use has damaging effects on heart and lung functions (Jorenby, 2015). Because of these long-term consequences, research on tobacco and its effects often continues for years, making it difficult to unequivocally prove a correlation between specific diseases or health problems and use of this substance. Thus, the results of tobacco research are often disputed by tobacco manufacturers with vested financial interests in the substance and its public acceptance.

Another important time factor that influences drug responses is the interval between multiple administrations. If sufficient time for drug metabolism and elimination does not separate doses, a drug can accumulate within the body. This drug buildup due to relatively short dosing intervals is referred to as a **cumulative effect**. Because of the resulting high concentrations of drug in the body, unexpected prolonged drug effects or toxicity can occur when multiple doses are given within short intervals. This situation occurs with cocaine or methamphetamine addicts who repeatedly administer these stimulants during "binges" or "runs," increasing the likelihood of dangerous effects.

## ■ Inactivation and Elimination of Drugs from the Body

Immediately after drug administration, the body begins to eliminate the substance in various ways. The time required to remove half of the original amount of drug administered is called the **half-life** of the drug. The body eliminates the drug either directly without altering it chemically or (in most instances) after it has been metabolized (chemically altered) or modified. The process of changing the chemical or pharmacological properties of a drug by metabolism is called **biotransformation**. **Metabolism** usually makes it possible for the body to inactivate, detoxify, and excrete drugs and other chemicals, although metabolism can sometimes actually cause a drug such as heroin to become *more* active.

### KEY TERMS

**acute**
immediate or short-term effects after taking a single drug dose

**chronic**
long-term effects, usually after taking multiple drug doses

**cumulative effect**
buildup of a drug in the body after multiple doses taken at short intervals

**half-life**
time required for the body to eliminate or metabolize half of a drug dose

**biotransformation**
process of changing the chemical properties of a drug, usually by metabolism

**metabolism**
chemical alteration of drugs by body processes

The liver is the primary organ that metabolizes drugs in the body. This complex biochemical laboratory contains hundreds of enzymes that continuously synthesize, modify, and deactivate biochemical substances such as drugs. The healthy liver is also capable of metabolizing many of the chemicals that occur naturally in the body (such as hormones). These metabolizing enzymes are highly regulatable. Genetic variations in their structures can account for a wide variation in their activity, influencing onset, duration, and potency of drug effects, thereby affecting vulnerability to developing dependence and addiction (see "Family Matters: Genetics of Metabolic Enzymes and Alcoholism"). After the liver enzymes metabolize a drug (the resulting chemicals are called **metabolites**), the products usually pass into the urine or feces for final elimination. Drugs and their metabolites can appear in other places as well such as sweat, saliva, or expired air.

The kidneys are probably the next most important organs for drug elimination because they remove metabolites and foreign substances from the body. The kidneys constantly eliminate substances from the blood. The rate of excretion of some drugs by the kidneys can be altered by

making the urine more acidic or more alkaline. For example, nicotine and amphetamines can be cleared faster from the body by making the urine slightly more acidic, and salicylates and barbiturates can be cleared more rapidly by making it more alkaline. Such techniques are used in emergency rooms and can be useful in the treatment of drug overdosing. Changing urine acidity is also a technique used by drug abusers to accelerate elimination of substances from their body that would be identified by drug tests and result in disqualification from sports competition, loss of a job, or even termination of parole and a return to incarceration (Drug War Facts, 2016).

The body may eliminate small portions of drugs through perspiration and exhalation. Approximately 1% of consumed alcohol is eliminated in the breath and thus may be measured with a breathalyzer; this apparatus is used by police officers in evaluating suspected drunk drivers. Most people are aware that consumption of garlic will change body odor because garlic is excreted through perspiration. Some drugs are handled in the same way. The mammary glands are modified sweat glands, so it is not surprising that many drugs are concentrated and excreted in milk during lactation, including antibiotics, nicotine, barbiturates, caffeine, and alcohol. Excretion of drugs in a mother's milk can pose a particular concern during nursing because the excreted drugs can be consumed by and affect the infant (March of Dimes, 2015).

### KEY TERM

**metabolites**
chemical products of metabolism

## FAMILY MATTERS

### Genetics of Metabolic Enzymes and Alcoholism

It has been known for a long time that alcoholism frequently clusters in some families, and even to some extent in some races, suggesting that its expression is strongly influenced by heritability and gene expression. However, only because of recent sophisticated molecular biology techniques have we finally been able to identify some of the specific genes involved and how their expression influences the development of alcoholism. A particularly compelling discovery is the finding that liver enzymes known as alcohol dehydrogenases exist in several variant forms that are

determined by a person's genetics. One variant of this enzyme, known as ADH2, appears to be associated with decreased incidences of alcoholic liver cirrhosis. The protective properties of this gene expression likely relates to its ability to rapidly metabolize alcohol into acetaldehyde, which in turn causes facial flushing, nausea, headache, and drowsiness. It is thought that these adverse effects reduce alcohol consumption and the associated damage to the liver, especially in some Asian populations.

He, L., Deng, T., & Luo, H. (2015). Genetic polymorphism in alcohol dehydrogenase 2 (ADH2) gene and alcoholic liver cirrhosis risk. *International Journal of Clinical and Experimental Medicine, 8*, 7786–7793.

The breathalyzer takes advantage of the fact that alcohol is partially eliminated from the body in the breath.

# ■ Physiological Variables That Modify Drug Effects

As previously mentioned, individuals' responses to drugs vary greatly, even when the same doses are administered in the same manner. This variability can be especially troublesome when dealing with drugs that have a narrow margin of safety. Many of these variables reflect differences in the pharmacokinetic factors just discussed and are associated with diversity in body size, composition, or functions. They include the following factors (Lynch, 2019):

- *Age.* Changes in body size and makeup occur throughout the aging process from infancy to old age. Changes in the rates of drug absorption, biotransformation, and elimination also arise as a consequence of aging. As a general rule, young children and elderly people should be administered smaller drug doses (calculated as drug quantity per unit of body weight) because of their immature or compromised body processes.
- *Gender*: Variations in drug responses from gender usually relate to differences in body size, composition, or hormones (male vs. female types—e.g., androgens vs. estrogens). Most clinicians find many more similarities than differences between males and females relative to their responses to drugs, although there are clinically relevant differences in the effects of alcohol and tobacco on males and females.
- *Pregnancy*: During the course of pregnancy, unique factors must be considered when administering drugs. For example, the physiology of the mother changes as the fetus develops and puts additional stress on organ systems such as the heart, liver, and kidneys. This increased

demand can make the woman more susceptible to the toxicity of some drugs. In addition, as the fetus develops, it can be extremely vulnerable to drugs with **teratogenic** properties (which cause abnormal development). Consequently, it is usually advisable to avoid taking any drugs during pregnancy, if possible.

# ■ Pathological Variables That Modify Drug Effects

Individuals with diseases or compromised organ systems need to be particularly careful when taking drugs. Some diseases can damage or impair organs that are vital for appropriate and safe responses to drugs. For example, hepatitis (inflammation of and damage to the liver caused by a viral infection) interferes with the metabolism and disposal of many drugs, resulting in a longer duration of drug action and increased likelihood of side effects. Similar concerns are associated with kidney disease, which compromises renal activity and diminishes excretion capacity. Because many drugs affect the cardiovascular system (especially drugs of abuse such as stimulants, tobacco, and alcohol), patients with a history of cardiovascular disease (heart attack, stroke, hypertension, or abnormal heart rhythm) should be particularly cautious when using drugs. They should be aware of medicines that stimulate the cardiovascular system, especially those that are self-administered such as OTC decongestants and diet aids. These drugs should be either avoided or used only under the supervision of a physician.

# ■ Pharmacokinetics and Drug Testing

Drug testing has become an important part of the prevention, detection, and treatment of drug abuse. Many of the pharmacokinetic elements discussed in this section have important implications on drug testing and its ability to reliably determine which, how much, and when drugs have been abused. For example, how rapidly a drug gets into the blood or the urine after it is consumed, how long it stays in the body, and what its metabolites are can all profoundly influence drug-testing outcomes. However, even though we have come to rely a great deal on drug testing to evaluate employees,

**KEY TERM**

**teratogenic**
something that causes physical defects in a fetus

# HERE AND NOW
## Drug Test Results Can Be Flawed

We often rely on the outcomes of drug testing to make critical decisions about whom we should hire or fire, who has violated conditions of their parole and should go back to jail, which athlete has cheated and should be disqualified from competition, or how well a patient is responding to drug treatment. However, although results from drug testing can be an important tool, drug testing is far from perfect, and its flaws should be considered when basing important decisions on its outcomes. The following are facts and myths about this technology that should be remembered.

- *Fact*: The poppy seeds on a single bagel are sufficient to test positive for opioid narcotics such as Lortab or Vicodin.

- *Fiction*: Most standard drug tests screen for the opioid drug oxycodone (active ingredient in OxyContin), methadone, and the extremely potent opioid drug fentanyl. (Explanation: This is false because if these are drugs of interest, they must be specially requested to be included in the screening.)

- *Fact*: In 2009, about 150 million drug tests were conducted in the United States.

- *Fact*: Most physicians do not know what drugs are included in a "standard" drug test.

- *Fact*: About 5% to 10% of tested patients will have inaccurate results.

- *Fiction*: Passive inhalation of marijuana or cocaine accounts for 20% of the positives when testing for these substances. (Explanation: This is false because casual breathing of cocaine or marijuana smoke is insufficient to cause a positive outcome on standard drug tests.)

- *Fiction*: Methods to mask or falsify a drug test never work. (Explanation: Actually, efforts to mask a positive drug test appear to work about 50% of the time. Strategies such as adding bleach or household cleaner such as Drano to urine samples can mask drug detection.)

© Val Handumon/EPA/Landov.

Data from Fiore, K. (2010, May 23). APA: Drug test results often flawed. *MedPage Today*. Retrieved from http://www.medpagetoday.com/MeetingCoverage?APA/20253 and http://www.spancorp.com/?page_id=2383. Accessed May 30, 2019.

discourage athletes from cheating, and determine compliance in persons with a history of drug abuse problems, we should appreciate that this technology has significant drawbacks that should be considered if we are to accurately interpret its outcomes. To illustrate this point, see "Here and Now: Drug Test Results Can Be Flawed."

## Adaptive Processes and Drug Abuse

Your body systems are constantly changing so they can establish and maintain balance in their physiological and mental functions; such balance is necessary for optimal functioning of all organ systems, including the brain, heart, lungs, gastrointestinal tract, liver, and kidneys. Sometimes, drugs interfere with the activity of the body's

systems and compromise their normal workings. These drug-induced disruptions can be so severe that they can even cause death. For example, stimulants can dangerously increase the heart rate and blood pressure and cause heart attacks, whereas CNS depressants can diminish brain activity, resulting in unconsciousness and a loss of breathing reflexes.

To protect against potential harm, the organ systems of the body can adjust to disruption. Of particular relevance to drugs of abuse are the adaptive processes known as *tolerance* and **dependence** (both psychological and physical

**KEY TERM**

**dependence**
physiological and psychological changes or adaptations that occur in response to the frequent administration of a drug

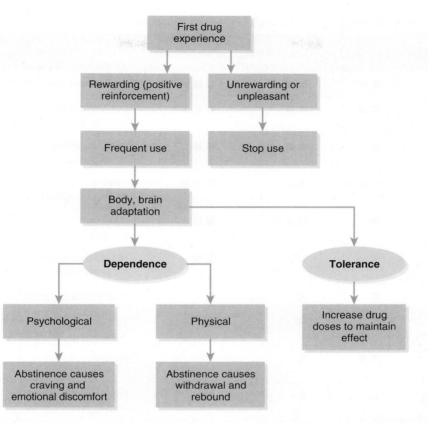

**FIGURE 5.4** The relationship and consequences of adaptive processes to drug abuse. The processes discussed in the text are highlighted in the figure.

types) and the related phenomenon of *withdrawal* (see **Figure 5.4**).

Tolerance and dependence are closely linked, most likely resulting from multiple drug exposures and thought to be caused by similar mechanisms. Tolerance occurs when the response to the same dose of a drug decreases with repeated use (Luscher, 2015). Increasing the dose can sometimes compensate for tolerance to a drug of abuse. For the most part, the adaptations that cause the tolerance phenomenon are also associated with altered physical and psychological states that lead to dependence. The user develops dependence in the sense that if the drug is no longer taken, the systems of the body become overcompensated and unbalanced, causing withdrawal. In general, withdrawal symptoms are opposite in nature to the direct effects of the drug that caused the dependence (Luscher, 2015).

Although tolerance, dependence, and withdrawal are all consequences of adaptation by the body and its systems, they are not inseparable processes. It is possible to become tolerant to a drug without developing dependence and vice versa (see **Table 5.2**). The following sections

provide greater detail about these adaptive drug responses, which are extremely important for many therapeutic drugs and almost all drugs of abuse (Luscher, 2015).

## ■ Tolerance to Drugs

The extent of tolerance and the rate at which it is acquired depend on the drug, the person using the drug, the dosage, and the frequency of administration. Some drug effects may be reduced more rapidly than others when drugs are used frequently. Tolerance to effects that are rewarding or reinforcing often causes users to increase the dosage. Sometimes abstinence from a drug can reduce tolerance, but with renewed use the tolerance can return quickly. It is important to remember that the body does not necessarily develop tolerance to all effects of a drug equally.

The exact mechanisms by which the body becomes tolerant to different drug effects are not completely understood but may be related to those mechanisms that cause dependence (Hussar 2014). Several processes have been suggested as

**TABLE 5.2** Tolerance, Dependence, and Withdrawal Properties of Common Drugs of Abuse

| Drug | Tolerance | Psychological Dependence | Physical Dependence | Withdrawal Symptoms (Include Rebound Effects) |
|---|---|---|---|---|
| Barbiturates | ■■ | ■■ | ■■■ | Restlessness, anxiety, vomiting, tremors, seizures |
| Alcohol | ■■ | ■■ | ■■■ | Cramps, delirium, vomiting, sweating, hallucinations, seizures |
| Benzodiazepines | ■ | ■■ | ■■ | Insomnia, restlessness, nausea, fatigue, twitching, seizures (rare) |
| Narcotics (heroin) | ■■■ | ■■ | ■■■ | Vomiting, sweating, cramps, diarrhea, depression, irritability, gooseflesh |
| Cocaine, amphetamines | ■* | ■■■ | ■■ | Depression, anxiety, drug craving, need for sleep ("crash"), anhedonia |
| Nicotine | ■ | ■■ | ■■ | Highly variable; craving, irritability, headache, increased appetite, abnormal sleep |
| Caffeine | ■ | ■ | ■ | Anxiety, lethargy, headache, fatigue |
| Marijuana | ■ | ■ | ■ | Irritability, restlessness, decreased appetite, weight loss, abnormal sleep |
| LSD (lysergic acid diethylamide) | ■■ | ■ | — | Minimal |
| PCP (phencyclidine) | ■ | ■ | ■ | Fear, tremors, some craving, problems with short-term memory |

■■■ Intense  ■■ Moderate  ■ Some  — Not significant

*Can sensitize.

candidates. Potent depressants such as barbiturates stimulate the body's production of metabolic enzymes, primarily in the liver, and cause drugs to be inactivated and eliminated faster. In addition, evidence suggests that a considerable degree of CNS tolerance to some drugs develops independently of changes in the rate of metabolism or excretion. This process reflects the adaptation of drug target sites in nervous tissues such as neurotransmitter receptors so that the effect produced by the same concentration of drug decreases over time.

Another type of drug response that can appear to be tolerance but is actually a learned adjustment is called *behavioral compensation*. Drug effects that are troubling may be compensated for or hidden by the drug user. Thus, alcoholics learn to speak and walk slowly to compensate for the slurred speech and stumbling gait that alcohol consumption usually causes. To an observer, it might appear as though the pharmacological effects of the drug are diminished, but they are

actually unchanged. Consequently, this type of adaptation is not a true form of tolerance.

### OTHER TOLERANCE-RELATED FACTORS

The tolerance process can affect drug responses in several ways. We have discussed the effect of tolerance that diminishes the action of drugs and causes the user to compensate by increasing the dose. The following are examples of two other ways that processes related to tolerance can influence drug responses.

### REVERSE TOLERANCE (SENSITIZATION)

Under some conditions, a response to a drug is elicited that is the opposite of tolerance. This effect is known as **reverse tolerance** or

### KEY TERM

**reverse tolerance**
enhanced response to a given drug dose; opposite of tolerance

*sensitization*. If you were sensitized, you would have the same response to a lower dose of a drug as you initially did to the original, higher dose. This condition seems to occur in users of morphine as well as amphetamines and cocaine (Addiction Blog, 2014).

Although the causes of reverse tolerance are still unclear, some researchers believe that its development depends on how often, how much, and in which setting the drug is consumed. It has been speculated that this heightened response to drugs of abuse may reflect adaptive changes in the nervous tissues (target site of these drugs). The reverse tolerance that occurs with cocaine use may be responsible for the psychotic effects or the seizures caused by its chronic use (Addiction Blog, 2014).

### CROSS-TOLERANCE

Development of tolerance to a drug sometimes can produce tolerance to other similar drugs. This phenomenon, known as **cross-tolerance**, may be the result of altered metabolism from chronic drug use. For example, a heavy drinker will usually exhibit tolerance to barbiturates, other depressants, and anesthetics because the alcohol has induced (stimulated) his or her liver metabolic enzymes to inactivate these other drugs more rapidly. Cross-tolerance might also occur among drugs that cause similar pharmacological actions. For example, if adaptations have occurred in nervous tissue that cause tolerance to one drug, such changes might produce tolerance to other similar drugs that exert their effects by interacting with that same nervous tissue site. This is common with all of the opioid narcotics, including both prescription (e.g., morphine) and illegal (e.g., heroin) drugs (Alcohorehab.com, 2015).

## ■ Drug Dependence

Drug dependence can be associated with either physiological or psychological adaptations. Physical dependence reflects changes in the way organs and systems in the body respond to a drug, whereas psychological dependence is caused by changes in attitudes and expectations. In both types of dependence, the individual experiences a need (either physical or emotional) for the drug to be present for the body or the mind to function normally.

### PHYSICAL DEPENDENCE

In general, the drugs that cause physical dependence also are associated with a drug withdrawal phenomenon called the **rebound effect**. This condition is also sometimes referred to as the *paradoxical effect* because the symptoms included in rebound phenomena are nearly opposite to the direct effects of the drug. For example, a person regularly consuming alcohol or benzodiazepines will be depressed physically while the drug is in the brain but during withdrawal may become irritable, hyperexcited, and nervous and generally show symptoms of extreme stimulation of the nervous system and perhaps even life-threatening seizures. These reactions constitute the rebound effect.

Physical dependence may develop with high-intensity use of such common drugs as alcohol, Xanax, narcotics, and other CNS depressants. However, with moderate, intermittent use of these drugs, most people do not become significantly physically dependent. Those who do become physically dependent often experience damaged social and personal skills and relationships and impaired brain and motor functions.

Withdrawal symptoms resulting from physical dependency can be mitigated by administering a sufficient quantity of the original drug or one with similar pharmacological activity. The latter case, in which different drugs can be used interchangeably to prevent withdrawal symptoms, is called **cross-dependence**. For example, benzodiazepines and other CNS depressants can be used to treat the abstinence syndrome experienced by the chronic alcoholic. Another example is the use of methadone, a long-acting narcotic, to treat withdrawal from heroin (Alcoholrehab.com, 2015). Such therapeutic strategies allow the substitution of safer and more easily managed drugs for dangerous drugs of abuse and play a major role in treating drug dependency.

## KEY TERMS

**cross-tolerance**
development of tolerance to one drug causes tolerance to related drugs

**rebound effect**
form of withdrawal; paradoxical effects that occur when a drug has been eliminated from the body

**cross-dependence**
dependence on a drug can be relieved by other similar drugs

## PSYCHOLOGICAL DEPENDENCE

**Psychological dependence** has been described as an intense desire to consume a drug that is linked to craving when the drug is not being used (World Health Organization, 2019). This sense of dependence usually causes repeated self-administration of the drug in a fashion described as abuse and can lead to substance use disorder. Such dependence may be found either independent of or associated with physical dependence. Psychological dependence does not produce the physical discomfort, rebound effects, or life-threatening consequences that can be associated with physical dependence. Even so, it does produce intense cravings and strong urges that frequently draw former drug abusers back to their habits of drug self-administration. In many instances, psychological aspects may be more significant than physical dependence in maintaining chronic drug use. Thus, the major problem with cocaine or nicotine dependence is not so much the physical aspect because withdrawal can be successfully achieved in a few weeks; rather, strong urges often cause a return to chronic use of these substances because of psychological dependence.

How does psychological dependence develop? If the first drug trial is rewarding, a few more rewarding trials will follow until drug use becomes a conditioned pattern of behavior. Continued positive psychological reinforcement with the drug leads in time to primary psychological dependence. Primary psychological dependence in turn may produce uncontrollable compulsive abuse of any psychoactive drug in certain susceptible people, leading to physical dependence. The degree of drug dependence is contingent on the nature of the psychoactive substance, the quantity used, the duration of use, and the characteristics of the person and his or her environment.

### KEY TERMS

**psychological dependence**
dependence that results because a drug produces pleasant mental effects

**mental set**
the collection of psychological and environmental factors that influence an individual's response to drugs

**placebo effects**
effects caused by suggestion and psychological factors independent of the pharmacological activity of a drug

Even strong psychological dependence on some psychoactive substances does not necessarily result in injury or social harm. For example, typical dosages of mild stimulants such as coffee usually do not induce serious physical, social, or emotional harm. Even though the effects on the CNS are barely detectable by a casual observer, strong psychological dependence on stimulants like tobacco and caffeine-containing beverages may develop; however, the fact that their dependence does not typically induce antisocial and destructive behavior distinguishes them from most forms of dependence-producing drugs.

## Psychological Factors

The general effect of most drugs is greatly influenced by a variety of psychological and environmental factors. Unique qualities of an individual's personality, his or her past history of drug and social experience, attitudes toward the drug, expectations of its effects, and motivation for use are extremely influential. These factors are often referred to collectively as the person's **mental set**. The setting, or total environment, in which a drug is taken may profoundly modify its effect.

The mental set and setting are particularly important in influencing the responses to psychoactive drugs (drugs that alter the functions of the brain). For example, ingestion of LSD, a commonly abused hallucinogen, can cause pleasant, even spiritual-like experiences in comfortable, congenial surroundings. In contrast, when the same amount of LSD is consumed in hostile, threatening surroundings, the effect can be frightening, taking on a nightmarish quality.

### ❚ The Placebo Effect

The psychological factors that influence responses to drugs independently of their pharmacological properties are known as **placebo effects**. The word *placebo* is derived from Latin and means "I shall please." The placebo effect is most likely to occur when an individual's mental set is susceptible to suggestion. A placebo drug is a pharmacologically inactive compound that the user thinks causes some therapeutic or physiological change. In some persons or in particular settings, a placebo substance may have surprisingly powerful consequences (Taylor, 2017). For example, a substantial component of most pain is perception. Consequently, placebos administered as pain relievers and promoted properly can provide dramatic relief. Therefore, in spite of what appears to be a drug effect, the placebo is not considered a pharmacological agent because it does not directly alter any body functions by its chemical nature.

The bulk of medical history may actually be a history of confidence in the cure—a history of placebo medicine—because many effective cures of the past have been shown to be without relevant pharmacological action, suggesting that their effects were psychologically mediated. In fact, even today, some people argue that placebo effects are a significant component of most drug therapy, particularly when using OTC medications or herbal products. It is important when testing new drugs for effectiveness that drug experiments be conducted in a manner that allows a distinction to be drawn between pharmacological and placebo effects. Such studies can usually be done by treating one group with the real drug and another group with a placebo that looks like the drug and then comparing the responses to both treatments.

# Addiction (Substance Use Disorder) and Abuse: The Significance of Dependence

The term *addiction* has many meanings. It is often used interchangeably with *dependence, drug abuse,* and *substance use disorder* (APA, 2013). The traditional model of the addiction-producing drug is based on opiate narcotics and requires the individual to develop tolerance and both physical and psychological dependence. This model often is not satisfactory because only a few commonly abused drugs fit all of these parameters. It is clearly inadequate for many drugs that can cause serious dependency problems but that produce little tolerance, even with extended use (see Table 5.2).

Because it is difficult to assess the contribution of physical and psychological factors to drug dependency, determining whether all psychoactive drugs truly cause drug addiction poses a challenge. To alleviate confusion, it has been suggested that the term *dependence* (either physical or psychological) or *substance use disorder* be used instead of *addiction*. However, because of its acceptance by the public, the term *addiction* is not likely to disappear from general use. In addition, addiction often implies compulsive behavior

(i.e., a need to have and use a drug despite negative consequences) that can be independent of physical dependence. This confusion is likely to continue until some consensus can be reached regarding how to best define this concept.

Some have speculated that the only means by which drug dependence and addiction can be eliminated from society is to prevent exposure to those drugs that have the potential to be abused. Because some drugs are such powerful, immediate reinforcers (i.e., they cause a rapid reward), it is feared that rapid dependence (psychological) will occur when anyone uses them. Although it may be true that most people, under certain conditions, could become dependent on some drug with abuse potential, in reality most people who have used psychoactive drugs do not develop significant psychological or physical dependence or addiction. For example, approximately 87% of those who use alcohol experience minimal personal injury and few negative social consequences. Of those who have used stimulants, depressants, or hallucinogens for illicit recreational purposes, only 10% to 20% become significantly dependent (Thomas, 2019). The following three sections discuss some possible reasons for this variability.

## ■ Hereditary Factors

The reasons why some people readily develop dependence on psychoactive drugs and others do not are not well understood. Of importance may be heredity, which predisposes some people to drug abuse (Learn.Genetics, 2015a) and the interaction of genetic vulnerability with high-risk environments (see "Family Matters: Family Addictions and Genetics"). For example, studies of identical and fraternal twins have revealed a greater similarity in the rate of alcoholism for identical twins than for fraternal twins if alcohol abuse begins before age 20 (Crane, 2019). Because identical twins have 100% of their genes in common and fraternal twins share significantly fewer of their genes, these results suggest that genetic factors can be important in determining the likelihood of alcohol dependence (O'Brien, 2006; Scott & Taylor, 2007). It is possible that similar genetic factors contribute to other types of drug dependence as well.

## ■ Drug Craving

Frequently, a person who becomes dependent develops a powerful, uncontrollable desire for drugs during or after withdrawal from heroin, cocaine, alcohol, nicotine, or other addicting substance. This desire for drugs is known as *craving*. Because researchers do not agree as to the nature of craving, there does not exist a universally recognized scientific definition or an accepted method to measure this psychological phenomenon; however, it is thought to be distinct from the phenomenon of withdrawal. Some drug abuse experts claim that craving is the principal cause of drug abuse and relapse after treatment; others believe that it is not a cause but a side effect of drugs that produce dependence. One definition is that drug cravings are to addicts what obsessions and compulsions are to obsessive–compulsive disorder. Craving is often assessed by (1) questioning patients about the intensity of their drug urges; (2) measuring physiological changes, such as increases in heart and breathing rates, sweating, and subtle changes in the tension of facial muscles; and (3) determining patients' tendency to relapse into drug-taking behavior (Sayette, 2016).

Evidence indicates that at least two levels of craving can exist. For example, cocaine users experience an acute craving when using the drug itself, but the ex-cocaine abuser can have

chronic cravings that are triggered by familiar environmental cues that elicit positive memories of cocaine's reinforcing effects.

Although it is not likely that craving itself causes drug addiction, it is generally believed that if pharmacological or psychological therapies could be devised that reduced or eliminated drug-craving treatment of drug dependence would be more successful. Thus, many researchers are attempting to identify medications or psychological strategies that interfere with the development and expression of the craving phenomenon.

## ■ Other Factors

If a drug causes a positive effect in the user's view, it is much more likely to be abused than if it causes an aversive experience (see Figure 5.4). Perhaps genetic factors influence the brain or personality so that some people find taking drugs an enjoyable experience (at least initially), whereas others find the effects unpleasant and uncomfortable (**dysphoric**) (Vergne & Anton, 2010). Other factors that could contribute significantly to drug use patterns include (1) peer pressure (especially in the initial drug experimentation); (2) home, school, and work environments; (3) feeling lonely or bullied; and (4) media influence (Bellum, 2013). An estimated 30% to 60% of drug abusers have some underlying psychiatric illness such as personality disorder, major depression, bipolar disorder, or schizophrenia (Dual Diagnosis, n.d.). In some

### KEY TERM

**dysphoric**
characterized by unpleasant mental effects; the opposite of euphoric

## FAMILY MATTERS

### *Family Addictions and Genetics*

Substance abuse, alcoholism, and associated trauma seem to have both genetic and environmental components, the interaction of which can have serious consequences. For example, alcoholism tends to run in families. Thus, children of alcoholics are at high risk of becoming alcohol users themselves because of their genetic vulnerability as well as because of the traumatic environments to which they are often exposed. Levels of conflict in families characterized by alcoholism are much higher than in families with

no alcoholism. The environment to which children with alcoholic parents are exposed may include a lack of communication, emotional and physical violence, isolation, and financial problems. At least half of all cases of child maltreatment are linked to a prevalence of substance abuse and alcoholism in the home. It has also been reported that children who receive prenatal exposure to drugs are two to three times more likely to be neglected or abused.

Data from Learn.Genetics. (2010). Genetics and addiction. Salt Lake City, UT: University of Utah, Genetic Science Learning Center. Retrieved from http://learn .genetics.utah.edu/content/addiction/genes/. Accessed November 18, 2015; About.com: Alcoholism. (2010). Genetics of alcoholism. The Recovery Place. Retrieved from http://alcoholism.about.com/od/genetics/Genetics_of_Alcoholism.htm. Accessed November 18, 2015.

cases, the drug user may be attempting to relieve symptoms associated with the mental disorder by self-medicating with the substance of abuse (Buckley & Brown, 2006; Purse, 2013).

Identifying all specific factors that influence the risk of drug abuse for each individual is difficult.

If such factors could be identified, treatment would be improved, and those at greatest risk for drug abuse could be identified and informed of their vulnerability. **Table 5.3** lists the prevalence, demographics, and clinical profiles of those who have been diagnosed with drug use disorder.

**TABLE 5.3** Epidemiology of Drug Use Disorder

To appreciate the magnitude and implications of drug use disorder (i.e., addiction or drug dependence), it is necessary to understand the prevalence, demographics, and clinical profiles of those diagnosed with this condition according to the American Psychiatric Association's (2013) *Diagnostic and Statistical Manual of Mental Disorders*, fifth edition (DSM-5). This table presents an epidemiological overview of drug use disorders to help the reader appreciate their overwhelming implications.

| Category | Incidence (%) | Category | Incidence (%) |
|---|---|---|---|
| **TOTAL** | | **Urbanicity, Lifetime** | |
| 12 month | 3.9 | Urban | 10.1 |
| Lifetime | 9.9 | Rural | 9.3 |
| Male lifetime | 12.3 | **Region, Lifetime** | |
| Female lifetime | 7.7 | Northeast | 10.8 |
| **Race or Ethnicity, Lifetime** | | Midwest | 10.0 |
| White | 10.8 | South | 8.4 |
| Black | 9.9 | West | 11.5 |
| Native American | 17.2 | **Disorder, Lifetime** | **Risk of Co-Occurrence (Normal Risk = 1)** |
| Asian/Pacific Islander | 4.2 | | |
| Hispanic | 7.2 | Alcohol use disorder | 4.0 |
| **Age (Years), Lifetime** | | Nicotine use disorder | 3.6 |
| 18–29 | 14.2 | Any mood disorder | 1.5 |
| 30–44 | 12.0 | Bipolar | 1.4 |
| 45–64 | 9.7 | Anxiety disorder | 1.3 |
| ≥65 | 2.0 | Posttraumatic stress disorder | 1.5 |
| **Education, Lifetime** | | Antisocial personality disorder | 2.0 |
| < High school | 10.2 | | |
| High school | 11.6 | **% Who Receive Treatment, Lifetime** | **Incidence** |
| Some college or higher | 9.1 | Total | 24.6 |
| **Family Income ($), Lifetime** | | Detoxification | 9.5 |
| 0–19,999 | 13.5 | Rehabilitation program | 12.5 |
| 20,000–34,999 | 10.5 | Physician or other healthcare professional provides | 11.4 |
| 35,000–69,999 | 9.6 | | |
| >70,000 | 7.2 | | |

Data from Grant et al., 2016.

# LEARNING PORTFOLIO

## Key Terms

## Discussion Questions

1. How does the concept of drug "potency" apply to the thera-peutic use and abuse of drugs?
2. How can drug interactions be both detrimental and benefi-cial? Give examples of each.
3. Why would a drug with a relatively narrow margin of safety be approved by the Food and Drug Administration for clinical use? Give an example.
4. What are possible explanations for the fact that you (for example) may require twice as much of a drug to get an effect as does your friend?
5. Why might the blood–brain barrier prevent a drug from hav-ing abuse potential?
6. Why would the consumption of a drug of abuse by a nursing mother be a problem for the infant? Give an example.
7. Why do you think vaping of nicotine and THC in marijuana have become so popular so quickly?
8. Contrary to your advice, a friend is going to spend $20 on methamphetamine. What significance will the pharmacoki-netic concepts of threshold, half-life, cumulative effect, and biotransformation have on your friend's drug experience?
9. How would the factors of tolerance, physical dependence, rebound, and psychological dependence affect a chronic heroin user?
10. Why would the lack of physical dependence on LSD for some drug abusers make it less likely to cause addiction than cocaine, which does cause physical dependence?

## Summary

1. All drugs have intended and unintended effects. The unin-tended actions of drugs can include effects such as nausea, altered mental states, dependence, a variety of allergic responses, and changes in the cardiovascular system.
2. Many factors can affect the way an individual responds to a drug: dose, inherent toxicity, potency, and pharma-cokinetic properties such as the rate of absorption into the body, the way it is distributed throughout the body, and the manner in which and rate at which it is metabo-lized and eliminated. The form of the drug as well as the manner in which it is administered can also affect the response to a drug.
3. Potency is determined by the amount of a drug necessary to cause a given effect. Toxicity is the ability of the drug to affect the body adversely. A drug that is highly toxic is particularly potent in terms of causing a harmful effect.

4. A drug's margin of safety relates to the difference in the drug doses that cause a therapeutic or a toxic effect. The bigger the difference, the greater the margin of safety.

5. Additive interactions occur when the effects of two drugs are combined; for example, the analgesic effects of aspirin plus acetaminophen are additive. Antagonistic effects occur when the effects of two drugs cancel; for example, the stimulant effects of caffeine tend to antagonize the drowsiness caused by antihistamines. Synergism (potentiation) occurs when one drug enhances the effect of another; for example, alcohol enhances the CNS depression caused by Valium.

6. Pharmacokinetic factors include absorption, distribution, biotransformation, and elimination of drugs. These factors can vary substantially between persons and have a significant impact on the outcome and interpretation of drug testing outcomes.

7. Many physiological and pathological factors can alter the response to drugs. For example, age, gender, and pregnancy are all factors that should be considered when making drug-related decisions. In addition, some diseases can alter the way in which the body responds to drugs. Medical conditions associated with the liver, kidneys, and cardiovascular system are of particular concern.

8. For psychoactive drugs to influence the brain and its actions, they must pass through the blood–brain barrier. Many of these drugs are fat soluble and able to pass through capillary walls from the blood into the brain.

9. The threshold dose is the minimum amount of a drug necessary to have an effect. The plateau effect is the maximum effect a drug can have, regardless of dose. The cumulative effect is the buildup of the drug in the body from multiple doses being taken within short intervals.

10. The liver is the primary organ for the metabolizing of drugs and many naturally occurring substances in the body such as hormones. By altering the molecular structure of drugs, the metabolism usually inactivates drugs and makes them easier to eliminate through the kidneys.

11. Biotransformation is the process that alters the molecular structure of a drug. Metabolism contributes to biotransformation.

12. Drug tolerance causes a decreased response to a given dose of a drug. It can be caused by increasing metabolism and elimination of the drug by the body or by a change in the systems or targets that are affected by the drug.

13. Physical dependence is characterized by the adaptive changes that occur in the body because of the continual presence of a drug. These changes, which are often chemical in nature, reduce the response to the drugs and cause tolerance. If drug use is halted after physical dependence has occurred, the body is overcompensated, causing a rebound response. Rebound effects are similar to the withdrawal that occurs because drug use is stopped for an extended period. Psychological dependence occurs because drug use is rewarding by causing euphoria, increased energy, and relaxation or because stopping drug use produces craving.

14. Suggestion can have a profound influence on a person's drug response. Health problems with significant psychological aspects are particularly susceptible to the effects of placebos. For example, because the intensity of pain is related to its perception, a placebo can substantially relieve pain discomfort. Other placebo responses may likewise result from the release of endogenous factors in the body.

15. A powerful, uncontrollable desire (craving) for drugs can occur with chronic use of some drugs of abuse. Although craving by itself may not be the principal cause of drug addiction, if it can be eliminated then treatment of substance abuse is more likely to be successful.

# References

Addiction Blog. (2014). Tolerance to cocaine. Retrieved from http://drug.addictionblog.org/tolerance-to-cocaine/

Alcoholrehab.com. (2015). Cross dependency and cross tolerance. Retrieved from http://alcoholrehab.com/drug-addiction/cross-dependency-cross-tolerance/

American Psychiatric Association (APA). 2013. *Diagnostic and statistical manual of mental disorders*, 5th ed. Washington, DC: Author.

America's Rehab Campuses. (2019, May). 25 shocking drug and alcohol abuse statistics. Retrieved from https://www.americasrehabcampuses.com/blog/25-shocking-drug-abuse-statistics/

Awortwe, C., Makiwane, M., Reuter, H., Mueller, C., Louw, J., & Rosendranz, B. (2018, April). Critical evaluation of causality assessments of herb-drug interactions in patients. *British Journal of Clinical Pharmacology, 84*(4), 679–693.

Bellum, S. (2013, October 17). Your environment may influence drug use. NIDA for Teens. Retrieved from https://teens.drugabuse.gov/blog/post/your-environment-may-influence-drug-use

Buckley, P., & E. Brown. (2006). Prevalence and consequences of dual diagnosis. *Journal of Clinical Psychiatry, 67*, e01.

Centers for Disease Control and Prevention (CDC). (2013, July). Prescription painkiller overdoses: A growing epidemic, especially among women. Retrieved from http://www.cdc.gov/vitalsigns/prescriptionpainkilleroverdoses/index.html

Centers for Disease Control and Prevention (CDC). (2015). HIV and injection drug use in the United States. Atlanta, GA: Author. Retrieved from http://www.cdc.gov/hiv/risk/idu.html

Crane, M. (2019). Genetics and addiction: Is alcoholism hereditary or genetic. American Addiction Centers. Retrieved from https://americanaddictioncenters.org/alcoholism-treatment/symptoms-and-signs/hereditary-or-genetic

de Havenon, A., Chin, B., Thomas, K., & Afra, P. (2011). The secret spice: An undetectable cause of seizure. *Neurohospitalist, 1*, 182–186.

Drugs.com. (n.d.). Drug-related deaths—Notable celebrities. Retrieved from http://www.drugs.com/celebrity_deaths.html

Drugs.com. (2014, December 19). 18 herbal supplements with risky drug interactions. Retrieved from https://www.drugs.com/slideshow/herb-drug-interactions-1069

Drug War Facts. (2016). Drug testing. Retrieved from http://www.drugwarfacts.org/cms/Drug_Testing#sthash.YDvgTUSi.dpbs

DrugWise. (n.d.). Drug interactions. Retrieved from http://www.drugwise.org.uk/drug-interactions/

Dual Diagnosis. (n.d.). The connection between mental illness and substance abuse. Retrieved from www.dualdiagnosis.org/mental-health-and-addiction/the-connection/

Fettiplace, M., Pickurk, A., Ripper, R., Kin, B., Kowal, K., Lis, K., Schwartz, D., Feinstein, D., Rubinstein, I., & Weinberg, G. (2015). Cardiac depression induced by cocaine or cocaethylene in alleviated by lipid emulsion more effectively than by sulfobutylether-b-cyclodextrin. *Academic Emergency Medicine, 22*, 508–517.

Fiore, K. (2010, May 23). APA: Drug test results often flawed. *MedPage Today*. Retrieved from http://www.medpagetoday.com/MeetingCoverage?APA/20253 and http://www.spancorp.com/?page_id=2383. Accessed May 30, 2019.

Goplerud, E., Hodge, S., & Bessham, R. A (2017). Substance use cost calculator for employers with an emphasis on prescription pain medication misused. *Journal of Occupational and Environmental Medicine, 59*, 1063–1071.

Grant, B., Saha, T., Ruan, W., Goldstein, R., Chou, S. P., Jung, J., Zhang, H., Smith, S. M., Pickering, R. P., Huang, B., & Hasin, D. S. (2016). Epidemiology of DSM-5 drug use disorder. *JAMA Psychiatry, 73*, 39–47.

He, L., Deng, T., & Luo, H. (2015). Genetic polymorphism in alcohol dehydrogenase 2 (ADH2) gene and alcoholic liver cirrhosis risk. *International Journal of Clinical and Experimental Medicine, 8*, 7786–7793.

Holford, N. (2015). Pharmacokinetics and pharmacodynamics: Rational dosing and the time course of drug action. In B. Katzung and A. Trevor (Eds.), *Basic and clinical pharmacology*, 13th ed., pp. 41–73. New York, NY: McGraw-Hill.

Jorenby, D. (2015). Tobacco. Merck manual professional version. Retrieved from http://www.merckmanuals.com/professional/SearchResults?query=tobacco

Le, J. (2019). Drug distribution to tissues. *Merck manual professional version*. Retrieved from www.merckmanuals.com/professional/clinical-pharmacology/pharmacokinetics/drug-distribution-to-tissues

Learn.Genetics. (2015a). Genes and addiction. Salt Lake City, UT: University of Utah, Genetic Science Learning Center. Retrieved from http://learn.genetics.utah.edu/content/addiction/genes/

Learn.Genetics. (2015b). Drugs of abuse. Salt Lake City, UT: University of Utah, Genetic Science Learning Center. Retrieved from http://learn.genetics.utah.edu/content/addiction/abuse/

Lisi, D. (2014, September). Designer drugs: Patients may be using synthetic cannabinoids more than you think. *Journal of Emergency Medical Services, 39*(9), 56–59.

Luscher, C. (2015). Drugs of abuse. In B. Katzung & A. Trevor (Eds.), *Basic and clinical pharmacology*, 13th ed. (pp. 552–566). New York, NY: McGraw-Hill.

Lynch, S. (2019). Overview of response to drugs. *Merck manual consumer version*. Retrieved from www.merckmanuals.com/home/drugs/factors-affecting-response-to-drugs/overview-of-response-to-drugs

March of Dimes. (2015, January). Keeping breast milk safe and healthy. Retrieved from http://www.marchofdimes.org/baby/keeping-breast-milk-safe-and-healthy.aspx

Mathias, R. (1997, March–April). Rate and duration of drug activity play major roles in drug abuse, addiction and treatment. *NIDA Notes, 12*, 8–11.

National Institute on Drug Abuse (NIDA). (2015). Drug facts: Inhalants. Retrieved from http://www.drugabuse.gov/publications/drugfacts/inhalants

National Institute on Drug Abuse (NIDA). (2018, December 17). Teens using vaping devices in record numbers. Retrieved from www.drugabuse.gov/news-events/news-releases/2018/12/teens-using-vaping-devices-in-record-numbers

O'Brien, C. (2006). Drug addiction and drug abuse. In L. Brunton, J. Lazo, & K. Parker, *The pharmacological basis of therapeutics*, 11th ed. (pp. 607–627). New York, NY: McGraw-Hill.

Purse, M. (2013). Living with bipolar disorder. Retrieved from http://bipolar.about.com/cs/dualdiag/a/0008_dual_diag.htm

Ryu, J., Kim, H., & Lee, S. (2018). Deep learning improves prediction of drug-drug and drug-food interactions. *Proceedings of the National Academy of Sciences, 115*, E4302–E4311.

Sayette, M. (2016). The role of craving in substance use disorder: Theoretical and methodological issues. *Annual Review of Clinical Psychology, 12*, 407–433

Scott, M., & Taylor, R. (2007). Health-related effects of genetic variations of alcohol-metabolizing enzymes in African Americans. *Alcohol Research and Health, 30*, 18–21.

Taylor, S. (2017, September 16). The power of placebos. *Psychology Today*. Retrieved from www.psychologytoday.com/us/blog/out-the-darkness/201709/the-power-placebo

Thomas, S. (2019). Addiction statistics. American Addiction Centers. Retrieved from https://americanaddictioncenters.org/rehab-guide/addiction-statistics

Torrice, M. (2018, February 19). Vaccines against addictive drugs push forward despite past failures. *Chemical & Engineering News, 96*(8), 18–21. Retrieved from https://cen.acs.org/articles/96/i8/Vaccines-against-addictive-drugs-push.html

Tully, M. (2015, June 1). Meet heroin's tiniest victims: Newborns. *USA Today*. Retrieved from http://www.USAtoday.com/story/news/nation-now/2015/06/01/heroin-babies-morphine-opiate-drugs/28299459/

Vergne, D. E., & Anton, F. (2010). Aripiprazole: A drug with a novel mechanism of action and possible efficacy for alcohol dependence. *CNS and Neurological Disorders—Drug Targets, 9*, 50–54.

World Health Organization. (2019). Management of substance abuse. Geneva, Switzerland: Author. Retrieved from www.who.int/substance_abuse/terminology/definition1/en/

## CHAPTER 6

# CNS Depressants: Sedative Hypnotics

© FOTOGRIN/Shutterstock.

## Did You Know?

▶ Alcohol temporarily relieves anxiety and stress because of its effects as a central nervous system (CNS) depressant.

▶ Benzodiazepines are by far the most frequently prescribed CNS depressants.

▶ Most people who are dependent on benzodiazepines obtain their drugs legally by prescription.

▶ Long-term users of Xanax can experience severe withdrawal symptoms if drug use is stopped abruptly.

▶ Although overdose deaths are rarely caused by benzodiazepines themselves, these drugs are often found in the bodies of those who are determined to have died from opioid narcotic consumption and likely contributed to the fatality.

▶ Our bodies probably produce a natural antianxiety substance that functions like drugs such as diazepam (Valium), triazolam (Halcion), and alprazolam (Xanax).

▶ The short-acting CNS depressants are the most likely to be abused.

▶ Gamma-hydroxybyrate (GHB) is a Schedule I "club drug" that occurs naturally in the body and can be easily synthesized by using information available on the Internet.

## Learning Objectives

**On completing this chapter, you should be able to:**

❯ Identify the primary drug groups used for CNS depressant effects.

❯ Explain the principal therapeutic uses of the CNS depressants and their relationship to drug dose.

❯ Explain why CNS depressant drugs are commonly abused.

❯ Identify the unique features of benzodiazepines.

❯ Understand how benzodiazepine dependence usually develops.

❯ Describe the differences in effects produced by short- versus long-acting CNS depressants.

❯ Describe the CNS depressant properties of antihistamines and compare their therapeutic usefulness to that of benzodiazepines.

❯ List the four principal types of people who abuse CNS depressants.

❯ Identify the basic principles in treating dependence on CNS depressants.

❯ Explain the unique properties of propofol as a potential drug of abuse.

❯ Explain why GHB is abused and how it relates to its analog compounds.

❯ Explain the role of detoxification in the treatment of dependency on CNS depressants.

## Introduction

Central nervous system (CNS) depressants are some of the most widely used and abused drugs in the United States. Why? When taken at low doses, they all produce a qualitatively similar "high" by their disinhibitory effects on the brain. In addition, they relieve stress and anxiety and even induce sleep—effects that appeal to many people, particularly those who are struggling with emotional problems and looking for a break, physically and mentally. CNS depressants also can cause a host of serious side effects, including problems with tolerance, dependence, and drug interactions. Ironically, many individuals who become dependent on depressants obtain them through legitimate means: a prescription given by a physician or other licensed healthcare provider. In fact, these drugs are second only to the narcotic medications as the most frequently abused group of prescription medications (National Institute on Drug Abuse [NIDA], 2018). Depressants also are available on the street, although this illicit source does not account for the bulk of the problem.

In this chapter, we briefly review the history of CNS depressants in terms of both development and use, and then we discuss the positive and negative effects these drugs can produce. Each major type of depressant drug is then reviewed in detail: benzodiazepines (Xanax- or Valium-like drugs),

barbiturates, and other minor categories. We move on to an examination of abuse patterns related to depressant drugs and discuss how drug dependence and withdrawal are treated. Finally, we conclude with a discussion of natural depressants.

## An Introduction to CNS Depressants

Why are CNS depressants problematic? First, in contrast to most other substances of abuse, CNS depressants are usually not obtained illicitly and self-administered but are prescribed under the direction of a physician. Second, use of CNS depressants can cause alarming—even dangerous—behavior if not monitored closely; most problems associated with these drugs occur because of inadequate professional supervision and chronic use. Third, several seemingly unrelated drug groups have some ability to cause CNS depression and all too frequently are the cause of death by drug overdoses (see "Case in Point: Even Celebrities Are Vulnerable) . When these drugs are combined, bizarre and dangerous interactions can result. Particularly problematic are combinations of alcohol or opioid narcotics with other CNS depressants. Finally, CNS depressants can cause disruptive personality changes that are unpredictable and sometimes extremely threatening.

► **CASE IN POINT**

### Even Celebrities Are Vulnerable

Movie star Heath Ledger had struggled with heroin abuse, but after treatment his opioid use disorder was thought to be under control. However, tragically, a year after attending rehab Ledger's body was discovered in his apartment (January 22, 2008). The autopsy report revealed significant amounts of six drugs, including two opioid narcotics and three benzodiazepine CNS depressants (i.e., diazepam, alprazolam, and temazepam). Although possibly accidental, it was concluded that death was the result of abuse of "prescription medicines," even though the level of each drug individually was not considered lethal. The synergistic combination of all of these CNS depressant drugs together was likely the cause of death, according to the medical examiner.

# ■ The History of CNS Depressants

Before the era of modern drugs, alcohol was the most common depressant used to ease tension, cause relaxation, and help forget problems. These effects undoubtedly accounted for the immense popularity of alcohol and help explain why this traditional depressant is the most commonly abused drug of all time.

Attempts to find CNS depressants other than alcohol that could be used to treat nervousness and anxiety began in the 1800s with the introduction of bromides. These drugs were popular until their toxicities became known. In the early 1900s, bromides were replaced by **barbiturates**. Like bromides, barbiturates were initially heralded as safe and effective depressants, but problems with tolerance, dependence, and lethal overdoses soon became evident. It was learned that the doses of barbiturates required to treat anxiety also could cause CNS depression, affecting respiration and impairing mental functions (Charney, Mihic, & Harris, 2006; Mandal, 2013). The margin of safety for barbiturates was too narrow, so research for safer CNS depressants began again.

Not until the 1950s were the first **benzodiazepines** marketed as substitutes for the dangerous barbiturates. Benzodiazepines were originally viewed as extremely safe and free from the problems of tolerance, dependence, and withdrawal that occurred with the other drugs in this category. Unfortunately, benzodiazepines have since been found to be less than ideal anti-anxiety drugs. Although relatively safe when used for short periods, long-term use can cause dependence and withdrawal problems much like those associated with their depressant predecessors (Fawcett, 2015). These problems have become a major concern of the medical community, as is discussed in greater detail later in the chapter.

Many of the people who become dependent on CNS depressants such as benzodiazepines began using the drugs under the supervision of a physician. Some clinicians routinely prescribe CNS depressants for patients with stress, anxiety, or apprehension without trying nonpharmacological approaches such as psychotherapy or counseling. This practice sends an undesirable and often detrimental message to patients—that is, CNS depressants are a simple solution to their complex, stressful problems. The following quote illustrates the danger of this practice:

> I am still, unfortunately, lost in "script addiction." . . . I have gone on-line asking for pills.

> I could really identify with the one posting about doctors who continue to write the 'scripts to increase/continue the patient "flow." This is exactly what is happening with me and my doctor. *(From America Online Alcohol and Drug Dependency and Recovery message board)*

During the 1970s and 1980s, there was an epidemic of prescriptions written for CNS depressants. For example, in 1973, 100 million prescriptions were written for benzodiazepines alone. Approximately twice as many women as men were taking these drugs at this time; a similar gender pattern continues today. During this period, many homemakers made CNS depressants a part of their household routine.

As the medical community became more aware of the problem, the use of depressants declined. Today, efforts are being made by pharmaceutical companies and scientists to find new classes of CNS depressants that can be used to relieve stress and anxiety without causing serious side effects such as dependence and withdrawal (Olfson, King, & Schoenbaum, 2015).

# ■ The Effects of CNS Depressants: Benefits and Risks

The CNS depressants are a diverse group of drugs that share an ability to reduce CNS activity and diminish the brain's level of awareness (Meštrovic, 2018). Besides the benzodiazepines, barbiturate-like drugs, and alcohol, depressant drugs include **antihistamines**, opioid narcotics such as heroin, and even marijuana-related substances for some people (Mayo Clinic Staff, 2019).

Depressants are usually classified according to the degree of their medical effects on the body. For instance, **sedatives** cause mild depression of

## KEY TERMS

**barbiturates**
potent CNS depressants, usually not preferred because of their narrow margin of safety

**benzodiazepines**
the most popular and safest CNS depressants in use today

**antihistamines**
drugs that often cause CNS depression and are used to treat allergies; often included in over-the-counter (OTC) sleep aids

**sedatives**
CNS depressants used to relieve anxiety, fear, and apprehension

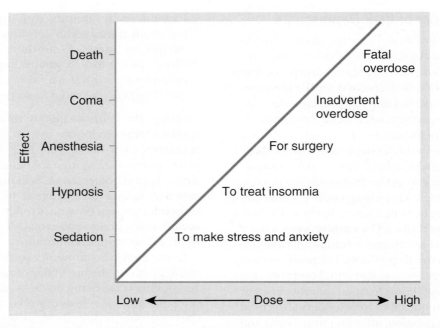

**FIGURE 6.1** Dose-dependent effects of CNS depressants. The therapeutic outcome may change according to the dose administered (e.g., a low dose of a CNS depressant can be effective to relieve the anxiety associated with stress, but a higher dose may cause drowsiness and be effective in the treatment of insomnia).

the CNS and relaxation. This drug effect is used to treat extreme anxiety and often is referred to as **anxiolytic**. Many sedatives also have musclerelaxing properties that enhance their relaxing effects.

Depressants also are used to promote sleep, for which they are frequently prescribed. Up to 9 million Americans have sleeping problems and take drugs like the benzodiazepines to help get a "good night's rest" (Ducharme, 2019). **Hypnotics** (from the Greek god of sleep, Hypnos) are CNS depressants that encourage sleep by inducing drowsiness. Often when depressants are used as hypnotics, they produce **amnesiac** effects as well. As already mentioned, the effects produced by depressants can be highly enticing and encourage inappropriate use.

## KEY TERMS

**anxiolytic**
drug that relieves anxiety

**hypnotic**
CNS depressant used to induce drowsiness and encourage sleep

**amnesiac**
causing the loss of memory

**anesthesia**
a state characterized by loss of sensation or consciousness

The effects of the CNS depressants tend to be dose dependent (see **Figure 6.1**). Thus, if you were to take a larger dose of a sedative, it might have a hypnotic effect. Often, the only difference between a sedative and a hypnotic effect is the dosage; consequently, the same drug may be used for both purposes by varying the dose. By increasing the dose still further, an anesthetic state can be reached. **Anesthesia**, a deep depression of the CNS, is used to achieve a controlled state of unconsciousness so that a patient can be treated, usually by surgery, in relative comfort and without memory of a traumatic experience. With the exception of benzodiazepines, if the dose of most of the depressants is increased much more, coma or death will ensue because the CNS becomes so depressed that vital centers controlling breathing and heart activity cease to function properly (Trevor & Way, 2015).

As a group, CNS depressant drugs used in a persistent fashion cause tolerance. Because of the diminished effect from tolerance, users of these drugs continually escalate their doses. Under such conditions, the depressants alter physical and psychological states, resulting in dependence. The dependence can be so severe that abrupt drug abstinence results in severe withdrawal that occasionally includes life-threatening seizures. Because of these dangerous pharmacological features, treatment of dependence on CNS depressants must proceed carefully (Trevor & Way, 2015)

## Types of CNS Depressants

All CNS depressants are not created equal. Some have wider margins of safety; others have a greater potential for nonmedicinal abuse. These differences are important when considering the therapeutic advantages of each type of CNS depressant. In addition, unique features of the different types of depressants make them useful for treatment of other medical problems. For example, some barbiturates and benzodiazepines are used to treat forms of epilepsy or acute seizure activity, whereas opioid narcotics are used to treat many types of pain. Some of these unique features will be dealt with in greater detail when the individual drug groups are discussed. The benzodiazepines, barbiturate-like drugs, antihistamines, and the naturally occurring gamma-hydroxybutyrate (GHB) are discussed in this chapter.

The unique features of the CNS depressants help determine the likelihood of their abuse. For example, abuse is more likely to occur with the fast-acting depressant agents than with those agents that have long-lasting effects. Currently, nonmedicinal use of these sedatives occurs in approximately 2% to 4% of the U.S. population.

CNS depressants can be used as hypnotics to initiate sleep.

This abuse is most likely from benzodiazepines such as Xanax and Valium (Olfson et al., 2015).

### ■ Benzodiazepines: Valium-Type Drugs

Benzodiazepines are widely used CNS depressants for anxiety and sleep (Olfson et al., 2015). Because of their wide margin of safety (death from overdose is rare), benzodiazepines have replaced barbiturate-like drugs for use as sedatives and hypnotics (NIDA, 2018). Benzodiazepines were originally referred to as *minor tranquilizers*, but this terminology erroneously implied that they had pharmacological properties similar to those of antipsychotic drugs (*major tranquilizers*) when they are actually quite different. Consequently, the term *minor tranquilizer* is usually avoided by clinicians.

The first true benzodiazepine, chlordiazepoxide (Librium), was developed for medical use and marketed around 1960. The extremely popular drug Valium came on the market about the same time (NIDA, 2018). In fact, Valium was so well received that it was the top-selling prescription drug in the United States from 1972 to 1978. Its popularity has since declined considerably, and it has been replaced by benzodiazepines such as alprazolam (Xanax) and lorazepam (Ativan) (Guina & Merrill, 2018).

Because of dependence problems, the benzodiazepines are now classified as Schedule IV drugs. In recent years, considerable concern has arisen that benzodiazepines are overprescribed. There is some speculation that these drugs can be used to replace opioid narcotics in treating pain. This would be inappropriate because the benzodiazepines are not analgesics. Clinicians are concerned about this overconfident and sometime inaccurate attitude toward benzodiazepines and their potential for dependence and other serious side effects (Trevor & Way, 2015), and they now warn patients against prolonged and unsupervised administration of these drugs (Chaterjee, 2019).

#### MEDICAL USES

Benzodiazepines are used for an array of therapeutic objectives, including the relief of anxiety, treatment of neurosis, relaxation of muscles, alleviation of lower back pain, treatment of some convulsive disorders, induction of sleep (hypnotic), relief from withdrawal symptoms associated with narcotic and alcohol dependence, and induction of amnesia, usually for preoperative administration (administered just before or during surgery or extremely uncomfortable medical procedures) (Nordqvist, 2019).

## MECHANISMS OF ACTION

In contrast to barbiturate-type drugs, which cause general depression of most neuronal activity, benzodiazepines selectively affect those neurons that have receptors for the neurotransmitter gamma-aminobutyric acid (GABA) (Greller, Traub, & Grayzel, 2019). GABA is an extremely important inhibitory transmitter in several regions of the brain, including the limbic system, the reticular activating system, and the motor cortex. In the presence of benzodiazepines, the inhibitory effects of GABA are increased. Depression of activity in these brain regions likely accounts for the ability of benzodiazepines to alter mood (a limbic function), cause drowsiness (a reticular activating system function), and relax muscles (a cortical function). The specific GABA-enhancing effect of these drugs explains the selective CNS depression caused by benzodiazepines.

Of considerable interest is the observation that these Valium-like drugs act on specific receptor sites that are linked to the GABA receptors in the CNS. As yet, no endogenous substance has been identified that naturally interacts with this so-called benzodiazepine site. It is probable, however, that natural molecules do exist that activate this same benzodiazepine receptor population and serve to reduce stress and anxiety by natural means (Trevor & Way, 2015). Because benzodiazepines have specific target receptors, it has been possible to develop a highly selective antagonist drug, flumazenil (Romazicon). This drug is used to treat benzodiazepine overdoses but must be used carefully because its administration can precipitate withdrawal in people taking benzodiazepines (Greller et al., 2019).

## TYPES OF BENZODIAZEPINES

Because benzodiazepines are so popular and thus profitable, several of these drugs are available by prescription. Currently, approximately 15 benzodiazepine compounds are available in the United States, and some 20 additional benzodiazepines are marketed in other countries (Greller et al., 2019).

Benzodiazepines are distinguished primarily by their duration of action (see **Table 6.1**). As a general rule, the short-acting drugs are used as

---

## PRESCRIPTION FOR ABUSE

### *Benzodiazepines: The Good and the Bad*

Jenn is a freelance book editor who has been using the benzodiazepine drug known as Valium for years. She describes this drug as essential for quickly managing her problems associated with extreme anxiety. She claims that Valium is the only thing that effectively relaxes her when she gets into the seat of a car; she nearly died in two car accidents as a teenager. She admits that when she takes Valium she "feels so much better—and can finally relax. Sometimes that makes all the difference in the world." She claims that benzodiazepines work almost immediately, in contrast to antidepressant drugs, which are also prescribed to relieve anxiety but require several weeks of treatment to achieve full efficacy. Benzodiazepines have also been shown to be effective in the treatment of insomnia, seizures, and alcohol withdrawal. However, these sedative hypnotic drugs are not without controversy. For example, most physicians will not prescribe benzodiazepines for more than a few weeks. With long-term treatment, the benzodiazepines cause the body to develop physical dependence, resulting in withdrawal if the drugs are discontinued "cold turkey." Long-term use often results in dose escalation and eventually can result in abuse and addiction. Short-term use can also adversely affect the user by interfering with cognition and decision making, as well as impairing reflexes and motor functions. Consequently, it is recommended that doctors manage their benzodiazepine-using patients carefully and avoid prescribing these drugs for long periods of time, especially in adults.

© Anchiy/Shutterstock.

Fawcett, K. (2015, February 19). Benzodiazepine: Helpful or harmful? *U.S. News & World Report Health*. Retrieved from http://health.usnews.com/health-news/patient-advice/articles/2015/02/19/benzodiazepines-helpful-or-harmful

**TABLE 6.1** Benzodiazepine and Nonbenzodiazepine Sedative-Hypnotic Properties

| Generic Name | Trade Name | Half-Life in Hours (Duration Group) | Metabolite Activity |
|---|---|---|---|
| **Benzodiazepines, Short-Acting** | | | |
| Alprazolam | Xanax | 6–27 (intermediate) | Inactive |
| Bromazepam | Lectopam | 8–20 (intermediate) | Inactive |
| Chlordiazepoxide | Librium | 5–30 (intermediate) | Active |
| Clobazam | Onfi | 36–42 (long) | Active |
| Clonazepam | Klonopin | 18–50 (long) | Inactive |
| Diazepam | Valium | 20–50 (long) | Active |
| Estazolam | Prosom | 10–24 (intermediate) | Inactive |
| Flunitrazepam | Rohypnol | 16–35 (intermediate) | Active |
| Flurazepam | Dalmane | 2–4 (short) | Active |
| Lorazepam | Ativan | 10–20 (intermediate) | Inactive |
| Midazolam | Versed | 1.5–3 (short) | Active |
| Oxazepam | Serax | 5–20 (short) | Inactive |
| Temazepam | Restoril | 3–19 (short) | Inactive |
| Triazolam | Halcion | 2–3 (short) | Inactive |
| **Nonbenzodiazepine Hypnotic** | | | |
| Eszopicione | Lunesta | 6–9 (short) | Active |
| Zolpidem | Ambien | 1.5–8.4 (short) | Inactive |

Benzodiazepine data from Greller, H., Traub, S., & Grayzel, J. (2019). Benzodiazepine poisoning and withdrawal. *UpToDate*. Retrieved from https://www.uptodate.com/contents/benzodiazepine-poisoning-and-withdrawal

hypnotics to treat insomnia, thus allowing the user to awake in the morning with few aftereffects (such as a hangover). The long-acting benzodiazepines tend to be prescribed as sedatives, giving prolonged relaxation and relief from persistent anxiety. Some of the long-acting drugs can exert a relaxing effect for as long as two to three days. One reason for the long action in some benzodiazepines is that they are converted by the liver into metabolites that are as active as the original drug (Guthrie & Bostwick, 2013). For example, Valium has been reported to have an approximate half-life of more than 100 hours and is converted by the liver into several active metabolites, including oxazepam (which itself is marketed as a therapeutic benzodiazepine).

## SIDE EFFECTS

Reported side effects of benzodiazepines include drowsiness, lightheadedness, lethargy, impairment of mental and physical activities, skin rashes, nausea, diminished libido, irregularities in the menstrual cycle, blood cell abnormalities, and increased sensitivity to alcohol and other CNS depressants (Guthrie & Bostwick, 2013; Trevor & Way, 2015). In contrast to barbiturate-type drugs, only extremely high doses of benzodiazepines have a significant impact on respiration when used alone. There are few verified instances of death resulting from overdose of benzodiazepines alone (Greller et al., 2019). Serious suppression of vital functions can occur, however, when these drugs are combined with other depressants, most often alcohol (Greller et al., 2019). In many overdose deaths involving opioid narcotic drugs, the co-use of benzodiazepines is also present.

Although their long-term effectiveness has been challenged, benzodiazepines are used 25% of the time to treat persistent disorders such as chronic insomnia or anxiety. Benzodiazepines have less effect on **REM sleep** (rapid eye movement, the restive phase) than do barbiturates. Consequently, sleep under the influence of benzodiazepines is more likely to be restful and satisfying. However, prolonged use of hypnotic doses of benzodiazepines may cause rebound increases in REM sleep and insomnia when the drug is stopped, especially if used for long periods of time (Guina & Merrill, 2018).

On rare occasions, benzodiazepines can have **paradoxical effects**, producing unusual responses such as nightmares, anxiety, irritability, sweating, and restlessness. Bizarre, uninhibited behavior—extreme agitation with hostility, paranoia, and rage—may occur as well.

Critics' complaints that Halcion causes unacceptable "amnesia, confusion, paranoia, hostility, and seizures" (Associated Press, 1994) prompted the Food and Drug Administration (FDA) to closely evaluate this benzodiazepine. Despite the fact that several other countries have banned Halcion, the FDA concluded that its benefits outweigh the reported risks but also noted, "In no way should this [the FDA's conclusion] suggest that Halcion is free of side effects. It has long been recognized and emphasized in Halcion's labeling that it is a potent drug that produces the same type of adverse effects as other CNS sedative hypnotic drugs" ("Sedatives/hypnotics/non-barbiturate," 2010, pp. 739–740). Although the FDA did not require that Halcion be withdrawn, it did negotiate changes in the labeling and package inserts with Halcion's manufacturer, Upjohn Pharmaceuticals. Halcion is currently only used to treat extremely severe short-term insomnia because of its fast action and short half-life; however, many clinicians refuse to use it at all because of its controversy (Drugs.com, 2019).

There is no obvious explanation for the strange benzodiazepine-induced behaviors. It is possible that, in some people, the drugs mask inhibitory centers of the brain and allow expression of antisocial behavior that is normally suppressed and controlled. Related concerns have also been made public about another highly

popular benzodiazepine, alprazolam (Xanax). In 1990, Xanax became the first drug approved for the treatment of panic disorder—repeated, intense attacks of anxiety that can make life unbearable (McEvoy, 2003). Reports that long-term use of Xanax can cause severe withdrawal effects and a stubborn dependency on the drug raised public concerns about the use of benzodiazepines in general. For example, how many people are severely dependent on these CNS depressants? What is the frequency of side effects such as memory impairment, serious mood swings, and cognitive problems? And how many patients using the benzodiazepines would be better served with nondrug psychotherapy (European Monitoring Centre for Drugs and Drug Addiction, 2015)? Clearly, use of the benzodiazepines to relieve acute stress or insomnia can be beneficial, but these drugs should be prescribed at the lowest dose possible and for the shortest time possible or withdrawal problems can result.

Of the benzodiazepines, Xanax is the most prescribed despite the fact that many prescribers consider it to have a high abuse liability with a severe withdrawal profile and a high association with visits to emergency rooms because of drug overdoses (Ait-Daoud, Hamby, Sharma, & Dievins, 2018). Two relatively new benzodiazepine-like CNS depressants approved for short-term treatment of insomnia are zolpidem (Ambien) and zalephon (Sonata). Both are classified as Schedule IV drugs. They have abuse potential, especially when used chronically and when they interact with other CNS depressants such as alcohol and narcotic analgesics. Recently, the FDA required warnings on these drugs against use in patients who experience complex sleep behavior with these substances (Food and Drug Administration [FDA], 2019).

## TOLERANCE, DEPENDENCE, WITHDRAWAL, AND ABUSE

As with most CNS depressants, frequent, chronic use of benzodiazepines can cause tolerance, dependence (both physical and psychological), and withdrawal (Greller et al., 2019). Such side effects are usually not as severe as those of most other depressants, and they occur only after using the drugs for prolonged periods (Greller et al., 2019).

Withdrawal can mimic the condition for which the benzodiazepine is given; for example,

## KEY TERMS

**REM sleep**
restive phase of sleep associated with dreaming

**paradoxical effects**
unexpected effects

withdrawal symptoms can include anxiety or insomnia (Drugs.com, 2015a). In such cases, a clinician may be fooled into thinking that the underlying emotional disorder is still present and may resume drug therapy without realizing that the patient has become drug dependent. This can happen after as little as one month of treatment. In situations in which users have consumed high doses of benzodiazepine over the long term, more severe, even life-threatening withdrawal symptoms may occur ("Sedatives/hypnotics/non-barbiturate," 2010); depression, panic, paranoia, and convulsions (Drugs.com, 2015b) have been reported (see **Table 6.2**). Severe withdrawal can often be avoided by gradually weaning the patient from the benzodiazepine (Guthrie & Bostwick, 2013). Long-term use of benzodiazepines (periods exceeding three to four months) to treat anxiety or sleep disorders has not been shown to be therapeutically useful for most patients (Guthrie & Bostwick, 2013). Even so, this approach is a common indiscriminate practice. As one user explains:

**TABLE 6.2** Abstinence Symptoms of Benzodiazepines: Withdrawal Timeline After Abruptly Stopping Benzodiazepine Use

Taking benzodiazepines more frequently, in higher doses, and with higher potency for longer periods of time or if shorter acting all increase the duration and intensity of benzodiazepine withdrawal.

| Duration of Abstinence (Days) | Symptoms |
| --- | --- |
| 1–4 days | Rebound anxiety, insomnia, sweating and nausea. These symptoms tend to start sooner with shorter-acting drugs. |
| 10–14 days | Withdrawal symptoms for short-acting drugs typically persist for 10–14 days before disappearing; in contrast, withdrawal symptoms for long-acting drugs peak at this time period and eventually disappear by 3–4 weeks. |
| >15 days | Persons severely dependent (i.e., used high doses for many months or even years) may experience recurring random episodes of protracted withdrawal symptoms (PAWS) months after quitting. |

Data from Fluyau, D., Revadigar, N., & Manobianco, B. E. (2018). Challenges of the pharmacological management of benzodiazepine withdrawal, dependence and decontamination. *Psychopharmacology, 8*, 147–168.

I sat in my general practitioner's office shaking and sweating, scared to death and weak. I've never felt worse. I told my doctor "everything hurts, and I can't sleep. I can't be awake. I can't move. I can't stop moving. I feel crazy." The doctor examined me and confessed he couldn't find any medical explanation. "Have you ever taken Klonopin (clonazepam) for panic?" Yes, I told him. I'd been taking it a few times a week for about a year. "When was the last time you took any?" About a week ago, I said. His jaw dropped. I was in the throes of serious benzo withdrawal, he told me. He was surprised that I was even standing. (Duberman, 2018)

It is extremely unusual to find nontherapeutic drug-seeking behavior in a patient who has been properly removed from benzodiazepines, unless that individual already has a history of drug abuse (Guthrie & Bostwick, 2013). Research has shown that when benzodiazepines are the primary drug of abuse, these CNS depressants are usually self-administered to prevent unpleasant withdrawal symptoms in dependent users. If benzodiazepine-dependent users are properly weaned from the drugs and withdrawal has dissipated, there is no evidence that craving for the benzodiazepines occurs because people usually do not consider the benzodiazepines particularly reinforcing. An exception to this conclusion appears to be former alcoholics. Many people with a history of alcoholism find the effects of benzodiazepines rewarding; consequently, more than 25% of previous alcoholics use benzodiazepines chronically (NIDA, 2018).

Benzodiazepines are commonly used as a secondary drug of abuse and combined with illicit drugs. For example, it is quite common to find heroin users who are dependent on benzodiazepines as well (NIDA, 2018).

Another frequent combination is the use of benzodiazepines with stimulants such as cocaine (Gorelick, 2015). Some addicts claim that this combination enhances the pleasant effects of the stimulant and reduces the "crashing" that occurs after using high doses. (More is said about benzodiazepine abuse later in this chapter.)

Note that benzodiazepines are occasionally used to make people vulnerable to the type of sexual assault referred to as a *date rape* (WebMD, 2018). The use of CNS depressants to commit these acts of violence is discussed in greater detail later in the chapter, but such assaults have

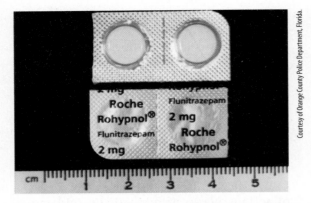

Courtesy of Orange County Police Department, Florida.

Rohypnol is a benzodiazepine outlawed in the United States.

sometimes involved the use of the **club drug** Rohypnol. Rohypnol (sometimes called *Rophie, Roche,* or *Forget Me*) is the proprietary name for flunitrazepam, a benzodiazepine. Rohypnol, which has been outlawed in the United States, comes as a tablet that can be dissolved in beverages without leaving an odor or taste and impairs short-term memory, making victims unable to recall details of the assault (WebMD, 2018). In 2018, 0.4% of high school seniors claimed to have used this drug (Johnston, 2018).

## ▌ Barbiturates

*Barbiturates* are barbituric acid derivatives that are used in medicine as sedatives and hypnotics. Barbituric acid was first synthesized by A. Bayer (of aspirin fame) in Germany in 1864. The reason that he chose the name *barbituric acid* is not known. Some have speculated that the compound was named after a girl named Barbara whom Bayer knew. Others think that Bayer celebrated his discovery on the Day of St. Barbara in a tavern that artillery officers frequented. (St. Barbara is the patron saint of artillery soldiers.)

The first barbiturate, barbital (Veronal), was used medically in 1903. Since then, more than 2,500 barbiturates have been synthesized; of these, about 50 were actually approved for human use. However, because of serious side effects, only a few are still prescribed for medical purposes. The names of the barbiturates traditionally end in *-al,* indicating a chemical relationship to barbital, the

first one synthesized. Historically, barbiturates have played an important role in therapeutics because of their effectiveness as sedative-hypnotic agents, which allowed them to be routinely used in the treatment of anxiety, agitation, and insomnia. However, because of their narrow margin of safety and their abuse liability, barbiturates have been largely replaced by safer drugs such as benzodiazepines. Despite the reduced therapeutic use of the barbiturates, 4.3% of high school seniors claimed to have recreationally used a barbiturate in 2018 (Johnston, 2018). Street names for barbiturates include *barbs, downers, Christmas trees, rainbows, sleepers,* and *yellow jackets* (Davis, 2018).

Uncontrolled use of barbiturates can cause a state of acute or chronic intoxication. Initially, there may be some loss of inhibition, euphoria, and behavioral stimulation—a pattern often seen with moderate consumption of alcohol. When taken to relieve extreme agitation or mental stress, barbiturates may cause delirium and produce other side effects that can include nausea, nervousness, rash, and diarrhea. The person intoxicated with barbiturates may have difficulty thinking and making judgments, may be emotionally unstable, may be uncoordinated and unsteady when walking, and may slur speech (not unlike the drunken state caused by alcohol).

When used for their hypnotic properties, barbiturates cause an unnatural sleep. The user awakens feeling tired, edgy, and quite unsatisfied, most likely because barbiturates markedly suppress the REM phase of sleep. (REM sleep is necessary for the refreshing renewal that usually accompanies a good sleep experience.) Because benzodiazepines suppress REM sleep (as do all CNS depressants) less severely than barbiturates, use of these agents as sleep aids is generally better tolerated.

Continued misuse of barbiturate drugs has a cumulative toxic effect on the CNS that is more life threatening than misuse of opiates. When taken in large doses or in combination with other CNS depressants, barbiturates may cause death from respiratory or cardiovascular depression. Because of this toxicity, barbiturates have been involved in many drug-related deaths, both accidental and suicidal. Repeated misuse induces severe tolerance of and physical dependence on these drugs. Discontinuing use of short-acting barbiturates in people who are using large doses can cause dangerous withdrawal effects such as life-threatening seizures. "Signs & Symptoms: Effects of Barbiturates and Other Depressants on the

**KEY TERM**

**club drug**
drug used at all-night raves, parties, dance clubs, and bars to enhance sensory experiences

Body and Mind" summarizes the range of effects of barbiturates and other depressants on the mind and body.

Concern about the abuse potential of barbiturates caused the federal government to include some of these depressants in the Controlled Substances Act. Consequently, the short-acting barbiturates such as pentobarbital and secobarbital are classified as Schedule II drugs, whereas the long-acting barbiturates such as phenobarbital are less rigidly controlled as Schedule IV drugs (Drug Enforcement Administration [DEA], 2016).

### EFFECTS AND MEDICAL USES

Barbiturates have many pharmacological actions. They depress the activity of nerves and skeletal, smooth, and cardiac muscles and affect the CNS in several ways, ranging from mild sedation to coma, depending on the dose. At sedative or hypnotic dosage levels, only the CNS is significantly affected. Higher anesthetic doses cause slight decreases in blood pressure, heart rate, and flow of urine. The metabolizing enzyme systems in the liver are important in inactivating barbiturates; thus, liver damage may result in exaggerated responses to barbiturate use (Trevor & Way, 2015).

Low doses of barbiturates relieve tension and anxiety, effects that give several barbiturates substantial abuse potential. The drawbacks of barbiturates are extensive and severe:

- They lack selectivity and safety.
- They have a substantial tendency to create tolerance, dependence, withdrawal, and abuse.
- They cause problems with drug interaction.

As a result, barbiturates have been replaced by benzodiazepines in most treatments, and only a few are still in medical use (Trevor & Way, 2015). Because of this decreased use, these drugs tend not to be readily available and are becoming less frequently abused in this country (Johnston, 2015). The long-acting phenobarbital is still frequently used for its CNS depressant activity to alleviate or prevent convulsions in some epileptic patients and seizures caused by strychnine, cocaine, and other stimulant drugs. Thiopental (Pentothal) and other ultrashort- and short-acting barbiturates are used as anesthesia for minor surgery and as preoperative anesthetics in preparation for major surgery (Davis, 2018).

### MECHANISM OF ACTION AND ELIMINATION

The precise mechanism of action for barbiturates is unclear. Like benzodiazepines, they likely interfere with activity in the reticular activating system, the limbic system, and the motor cortex. However, in contrast to benzodiazepines, barbiturates do

## SIGNS & SYMPTOMS

### Effects of Barbiturates and Other Depressants on the Body and Mind

| Dosage | Body | Mind |
| --- | --- | --- |
| Low dose | Drowsiness | Decreased anxiety, relaxation |
| | Trouble with coordination | Decreased ability to reason and solve problems |
| | Slurred speech | |
| | Dizziness | Difficulty in judging distance and time |
| | Staggering | |
| | Double vision | Amnesia |
| | Sleep | |
| | Depressed breathing | Brain damage |
| | Coma (unconscious and cannot be awakened) | |
| | Depressed blood pressure | |
| High dose | Death | |

not seem to act at a specific receptor site; they probably have a general effect that enhances the activity of the inhibitory transmitter GABA (Trevor & Way, 2015). Because benzodiazepines also increase GABA activity (albeit in a more selective manner), these two types of drugs have overlapping effects. Because the mechanisms whereby they exert their effects differ, it is not surprising that these two types of depressants also have different pharmacological features.

The fat solubility of barbiturates is another important factor in the duration of their effects (Trevor & Way, 2015). Barbiturates that are the most fat soluble move in and out of body tissues (such as the brain) rapidly and are likely to be shorter acting. Fat-soluble barbiturates also are more likely to be stored in fatty tissue; consequently, the fat content of the body can influence the effects on the user. Because women have a higher body-fat ratio than men, their reaction to barbiturates may be slightly different.

Withdrawal from barbiturates after dependence has developed causes hyperexcitability because of the rebound of depressed neural systems. Qualitatively (but not quantitatively), the withdrawal symptoms are similar for all sedative hypnotics, although they may vary in intensity and duration (Trevor & Way, 2015).

## ▌ Other CNS Depressants

Although benzodiazepines and barbiturates are the most frequently used substances for the specific purpose of producing CNS depressant effects, many other agents, representing an array of distinct chemical groups, can similarly reduce brain activity. Although the mechanisms of action might be different for some of these drugs, if any CNS depressants (including alcohol) are combined, they will interact synergistically and can suppress respiration in a life-threatening manner. Thus, avoid such mixtures if possible. Even some OTC products such as cold and allergy medications contain drugs with CNS depressant actions.

Some of these drugs have significant abuse potential, so they are restricted much like other CNS depressants. In this group of depressants, methaqualone is a Schedule II drug and chloral hydrate is a Schedule IV drug. Each classification is based on the drug's relative potential for physical and psychological dependence. Abuse of Schedule II drugs may lead to severe or moderate physical dependence or high psychological dependence. Schedule IV drugs are considered much less likely to cause either type of dependence (DEA, 2016).

### CHLORAL HYDRATE

Chloral hydrate (Noctec), or "knock-out drops," has the unsavory reputation of being a drug that is slipped into a person's drink to cause unconsciousness. In the late 1800s, the combination of chloral hydrate and alcohol was given the name Mickey Finn on the waterfront of the Barbary Coast of San Francisco when sailors were in short supply. An unsuspecting man would have a friendly drink and wake up as a crew member on an outbound freighter to China (Narconon, n.d.).

Chloral hydrate is a good hypnotic, but it has a narrow margin of safety. This compound is a stomach irritant, especially if given repeatedly and in fairly large doses. Addicts may take enormous doses of the drug; as with most CNS depressants, chronic, long-term use of high doses will cause tolerance and physical dependence (MedlinePlus, 2019).

### METHAQUALONE

Few drugs have become so popular so quickly as methaqualone. This barbiturate-like sedative hypnotic was introduced in India in the 1950s as an antimalarial agent. Its sedative properties, however, were soon discovered. It became available in the United States as Quaalude, Mequin, and Parest.

After several years of street abuse, methaqualone was classified as a Schedule II drug, and in 1984 it was reclassified to Schedule I (Drugs.com, 2015c). Since 1985, methaqualone has not been manufactured in the United States because of adverse publicity.

© MAErtek/ShutterStock, Inc.

Antihistamines are found in OTC medicines used to relieve cold and allergy symptoms.

Common side effects of methaqualone include fatigue, dizziness, anorexia, nausea, vomiting, diarrhea, sweating, dryness of the mouth, depersonalization, headache, and paresthesia of the extremities (a pins-and-needles feeling in the fingers and toes). Hangover is frequently reported.

## ANTIHISTAMINES

Antihistamines are drugs used in both nonprescription and prescription medicinal products. The most common uses for antihistamines are to relieve the symptoms associated with the common cold, allergies, and motion sickness. Although frequently overlooked, many antihistamines cause significant CNS depression and are used as both sedatives and hypnotics (Encyclopedia.com, 2006). For example, the agents hydroxyzine (Vistaril) and promethazine (Phenergan) are prescribed for their sedative effects, whereas diphenhydramine is commonly used as an OTC sleep (Olson, 2018).

The exact mechanism of CNS depression caused by these agents is not totally known but appears to relate to their blockage of acetylcholine receptors in the brain (they antagonize the muscarinic receptor types). This anticholinergic activity helps cause relaxation and sedation and can be viewed as a highly annoying side effect when these drugs are being used to treat allergies or other problems.

### THERAPEUTIC USEFULNESS AND SIDE EFFECTS

Antihistamines are viewed as relatively safe agents. Compared with other more powerful CNS depressants, antihistamines do not appear to cause significant physical or psychological dependence or addiction problems, although drugs with anticholinergic activity, such as the antihistamines, are sometimes abused, especially by children and teenagers (Reeves, Ladner, Perry, Burke, & Lazier, 2015). However, tolerance to antihistamine-induced sedation occurs quite rapidly. Reports of significant cases of withdrawal problems when use of antihistamines is stopped are rare. This situation may reflect the fact that these agents are used as antianxiety drugs for only minor problems and for short periods of time (often only for a single dose).

One significant problem with antihistamines is the variability of responses they produce. Different antihistamines work differently on different people. Usually, therapeutic doses cause decreased alertness, relaxation, slowed reaction time, and drowsiness. But it is not uncommon for some individuals to be affected in the opposite manner—that is, an antihistamine sometimes causes restlessness, agitation, and insomnia. There are even cases of seizures caused by toxic doses of antihistamine, particularly in children (Olson, 2018). Side effects of antihistamines related to their anticholinergic effects include dry mouth, constipation, and an inability to urinate. These factors probably help to discourage high-dose abuse of these drugs. However, OTC antihistamines are still sometimes taken for recreational purposes despite their unpleasant side effects (Olson, 2018).

Even though antihistamines are relatively safe in therapeutic doses, they can contribute to serious problems if combined with other CNS depressants. Many OTC cold, allergy, antimotion sickness, and sleep aid products contain antihistamines and should be avoided by patients using the potent CNS depressants or alcohol.

### NEW GENERATION OF SLEEP AIDS

In the past decade, several prescription products have been marketed for treating insomnia with the claim that they are less sedating and less likely to cause dependence than the traditional benzodiazepines and barbiturates. These heavily marketed medications include brand names such as Ambien, Lunesta, Rozerem, and Sonata. It is clear that although less sedating than the older sedative hypnotics, this new generation of sleep aids can cause next-day sedation and have resulted in some dependency, especially when used with other CNS depressants such as alcohol. In fact, the FDA recently required a "back-box" warning on these products to advise users of potential serious or life-threatening risks (Ducharme, 2019).

### PROPOFOL, AN ABUSED GENERAL ANESTHETIC

Propofol (Diprivan) was initially made available in 1986 and used intravenously for rapid sedation, analgesia, and general anesthesia in hospital or outpatient clinics. Its use for these purposes continues today. It has also been used off-label (i.e., not officially approved by the FDA) to relieve severe chronic or migraine headaches in pain clinics or for sleep induction in patients suffering from insomnia. Initially, propofol was thought to be free of abuse liability. However, although physical dependence is rare, because use of this drug can cause amnesia (sometimes referred to as the "Milk of Amnesia") and euphoria and relieve stress and pain, it has been abused and even involved in suicides and accidental deaths (Elements Behavioral Health, 2015), as was found to be the case in the highly publicized death of pop singer Michael Jackson (see "Case in Point: Misuse of Propofol Causes Death to Both Patients and Prescribers").

▶ # CASE IN POINT

## Misuse of Propofol Causes Death to Both Patients and Prescribers

Pop singer Michael Jackson died from an overdose of the potent general anesthetic propofol in June 2009. Because this drug is administered intravenously, legally it is only available to medical personnel in a clinical setting and should never be sent home with patients. In the case of Jackson, his personal physician had been making the drug available to help Jackson sleep and to deal with his anxiety prior to performances. Although the propofol-induced death of Jackson received considerable attention, abuse of this drug is much more likely to occur with the professionals who administer it such as healthcare workers, anesthesiologists, or nurse anesthetists than in the lay patient for whom the drug is prescribed. When abused, regardless of the background of the abuser, propofol can be an extremely dangerous drug with all-too-often deadly consequences.

© Richard Young/Shutterstock.

Data from Diaz, J., & Kaye, A. (2017). Death by Propofol. *Journal of the Louisiana State Medical Society, 369*, 28–32.

Recent abuse problems have particularly involved medical professionals such as doctors and nurses who have access to this anesthetic (Mitchell, 2018). Some doctors claim it has unique features and have referred to their experience with propofol as "dancing with the white rabbit." Part of its attraction is that it is still not an FDA-scheduled substance, it is easy to obtain, and its effects wear off in a matter of minutes (Elements Behavioral Health, 2015).

### GHB (GAMMA-HYDROXYBUTYRATE): THE NATURAL DEPRESSANT

GHB is a colorless, tasteless, and odorless substance found naturally in the body that results from the metabolism of the inhibitory neurotransmitter GABA. It was first synthesized nearly 30 years ago by a French researcher who intended to study the CNS effects of GABA (Bosch, Quednow, Seifritz, & Wetter, 2012). It was initially believed that GHB exerted its effects by enhancing CNS GABA systems, although this mechanism has been questioned (Schep, Knudsen, Slaughter, Vale, & Megarbane, 2012). Some evidence indicates that GHB is itself a neuromodulator, with its own receptor targets in the brain (Schep et al., 2012). Because of its CNS depressant effects, GHB has been used in Europe as an adjunct for general anesthesia, as a treatment for insomnia and narcolepsy (a daytime sleep disorder), and as a treatment for alcoholism

and alcohol withdrawal and narcotic dependence (Townsend, 2015). During the 1980s, GHB became available without a prescription in health-food stores and was used principally by body builders to stimulate the release of growth hormone with the intent to reduce fat and build muscle (Townsend, 2015). More recently, this substance became popular for recreational use because of its supposedly pleasant, alcohol-like, hangover-free high with aphrodisiac properties (Townsend, 2015). Because of its potential for abuse, access to GHB was restricted by the Drug Enforcement Administration in 2000 (DEA, 2013). In 2014, 1.0% of high school seniors were reported to have used GHB (Johnston, 2015). Because of its frequent use by young people at nightclubs and bars, GHB became known as a *club drug* (Sumnall, Woolfall, Edwards, Cole, & Beynon, 2008). Some of its common street names include *Easy Lay, G, Goop, Liquid Ecstasy, Liquid X,* and *Scoop* (Townsend. 2015).

GHB is generally taken orally after being mixed with a liquid or beverage. It has a rapid onset and, when large doses are consumed, can cause unconsciousness and coma in 15 to 40 minutes. These dangerous effects typically require emergency room treatment. Often, the recovery is also rapid, with persons regaining consciousness in two to four hours.

Because of concerns about GHB abuse and side effects, an advisory warning that this substance

GHB is often stored as a clear, colorless, odorless liquid.

is unsafe was first issued by the FDA in 1990. In 1997, the FDA released another warning that GHB was not approved for clinical use in the United States and was a potentially dangerous substance. Finally, because of the rising illicit use of GHB and resultant problems, this drug was made a Schedule I controlled substance by the DEA in March 2000 and is not frequently used in the United States today (Johnston, 2018).

Despite claims about its benign nature, statistical evidence suggests that in high doses GHB can be dangerous and even deadly (European College of Neuropsychopharmacology, 2018). However, there have recently been claims of a resurgence in the night-club scene, particularly in Europe (Palamar, 2018) Several documented deaths have been attributed to GHB overdoses. It also has been reported that GHB use can cause significant side effects such as hormonal problems, sleep abnormalities, drowsiness, nausea, vomiting, and changes in blood pressure (Townsend, 2015). Both users and clinicians seem to agree that GHB is most dangerous when combined with other drugs, especially other CNS depressants such as alcohol (Palamar, 2018).

Because GHB is illegal in the United States, it is currently available only through the underground "gray market" as a "bootleg" product manufactured by kitchen chemists and with suspicious quality and purity. The lack of reliability of these GHB-containing products and the highly variable responses of different people to this substance increase the likelihood of CNS problems when using this depressant (European College of Neuropsychopharmacology, 2018).

There is some debate as to whether the use of GHB can cause dependence and withdrawal. Some evidence suggests that chronic high-dose use of GHB may lead to prolonged abuse and a withdrawal syndrome consisting of insomnia, anxiety, and tremors that typically resolves in three to 12 days (Townsend, 2015). Another major concern with this substance is its use in cases of date rape. Because GHB can be stored as a clear, colorless, odorless liquid, it is easily added undetected to a beverage such as an alcoholic drink (WebMD, 2018). Its amnesiac and sedative properties disable users and make them vulnerable to sexual assault (National Institute on Drug Abuse [NIDA], 2015). Despite attempts to vigorously prosecute these cases, because the victims frequently are unable to recall details of the attack and the drug disappears so quickly from the bloodstream (its half-life is two to three hours), rape under the influence of GHB can be difficult to prove.

## Patterns of Abuse with CNS Depressants

The American Psychiatric Association (APA) considers dependence on CNS depressants to be a psychiatric disorder. According to its widely used *Diagnostic and Statistical Manual of Mental Disorders*, fifth edition (DSM-5; 2013), a substance dependence disorder can be diagnosed when symptoms such as the following occur within a 12-month period:

- The drugs are often taken in larger amounts or over a longer period of time than was intended.
- There is a persistent desire or unsuccessful efforts to cut down or control sedative, hypnotic, or anxiolytic use.
- A great deal of time is spent in activities necessary to obtain the sedative hypnotics or recovering from their effects.
- Important social, occupational, or recreational activities are given up or reduced because of sedative-hypnotic drug use.
- Sedative-hypnotic drug use recurs in situations in which it is physically hazardous (e.g., driving an automobile or operating machinery).
- Tolerance and withdrawal symptoms frequently occur.
- The person continues use of the substance despite recognizing that it causes social, occupational, legal, or medical problems

(see "Case in Point: Representative Patrick Kennedy Pleads for Help").

A review of the previous discussion about the properties of CNS depressants reveals that severe dependence on these drugs can satisfy all of these DSM-5 criteria; thus, according to the American Psychiatric Association, dependence on CNS depressants is classified as a form of mental illness.

The principal types of people who are most inclined to abuse CNS depressants include the following:

- Those who seek sedative effects to deal with emotional stress or try to escape from problems they are unable to face. Sometimes these individuals are able to persuade clinicians to administer depressants for their problems; at other times, they self-medicate with depressants that are obtained illegally.
- Those who seek the excitation that occurs, especially after some tolerance has developed. Instead of depression, they feel exhilaration and euphoria.
- Those who try to counteract the unpleasant effect or withdrawal associated with other drugs of abuse such as some stimulants, LSD, and other hallucinogens.
- Those who use sedatives in combination with other depressant drugs such as alcohol and heroin. Alcohol plus a sedative gives a faster high but can be dangerous because of the multiple depressant effects and synergistic

interaction. Heroin users often resort to barbiturates if their heroin supply is compromised.

As previously noted, depressants are commonly abused in combination with other drugs (Addiction Center, n.d.). In particular, opioid narcotic users take barbiturates, benzodiazepines, and other depressants to augment the effects of a weak batch of heroin or to counteract a rapidly shrinking supply. Chronic narcotic users also claim that depressants help to offset tolerance to opioids, thereby requiring less narcotic to achieve a satisfactory response by the user. It is not uncommon to see joint dependence on both narcotics and depressants.

Another common use of depressants is by alcoholics to soften the withdrawal from ethanol or to help create a state of intoxication without the telltale odor of alcohol. Interestingly, similar strategies are also used therapeutically to help detoxify the alcoholic. For example, long-acting barbiturates or benzodiazepines are often used to wean an alcohol-dependent person away from ethanol. Treatment with these depressants helps reduce the severity of withdrawal symptoms, making it easier and safer for alcoholics to eliminate their drug dependence.

Finally, as already mentioned, CNS depressants are used in conjunction with alcohol to commit sexual assaults. Because these drugs are sedating, remove inhibitions, and can induce a temporary

---

▶ **CASE IN POINT**

## Representative Patrick Kennedy Pleads for Help

On May 4, 2006, U.S. Representative Patrick Kennedy crashed his car into a Capitol barricade late at night. Fortunately, no one was seriously injured, but Kennedy agreed to plead guilty on a charge of driving under the influence of prescription drugs. The congressman already had a history of problems with CNS depressants such as sedative hypnotics and alcohol. Since leaving Congress in 2011, Kennedy has worked to change the perception of mental illness and addiction and has lobbied for the passage of congressional bills that require group health plans to offer benefits for mental health and drug dependence at the same level as for other medical conditions. Kennedy says these conditions are not moral issues or character flaws and should be treated with the same urgency as cancer and heart disease are treated.

© Steven Senne/AP/Shutterstock.

Data from Lightman, D. (2019). "Dreamers" with DUIs get the same break as a member of Congress. Impact 2020. Retrieved from https://www.mcclatchydc.com/news/policy/immigration/article230795314.html

state of amnesia, they are sometimes secretly added to an alcoholic beverage to incapacitate the intended victim of a date rape.

In general, those who chronically abuse the CNS depressants prefer (1) the short-acting barbiturates such as pentobarbital and secobarbital; (2) the barbiturate-like depressants such as glutethimide, methyprylon, and methaqualone; or (3) the faster-acting benzodiazepines such as diazepam (Valium), alprazolam (Xanax), or lorazepam (Ativan). Dependence on sedative-hypnotic agents can develop insidiously. Often, a long-term patient is treated for persistent insomnia or anxiety with daily exposures to a CNS depressant. When an attempt to withdraw the drug is made, the patient becomes agitated, unable to sleep, and severely anxious; a state of panic may be experienced when deprived of the drug. These signs are frequently mistaken for a resurgence of the medical condition being treated and are not recognized as part of a withdrawal syndrome of the CNS depressant. Consequently, the patient commonly resumes use of the CNS depressant, and the symptoms of withdrawal subside. Such conditions generally lead to a gradual increase in dosage as tolerance to the sedative-hypnotic develops. The patient becomes severely dependent on the depressant, both physically and psychologically, and the drug habit becomes an essential feature in the user's daily routines. Only after severe dependence has developed does the clinician often realize what has taken place. The next stage is the unpleasant task of trying to wean the patient from the drug (**detoxification**) with as little discomfort as possible.

The prevalence of abuse of illicit CNS depressants appeared to peak in the early 1980s for 12th graders. Illegal use of these drugs then decreased dramatically; however, abuse of these drugs has rebounded recently (see **Table 6.3**).

Finally, because of the frequent co-use of the sedatives like the benzodiazepine by persons abusing opioid narcotics, these drugs are often present in the blood of victims of narcotic overdose and thus contribute to the resulting deaths.

# Treatment for Withdrawal

All sedative hypnotics, including alcohol and benzodiazepines, can produce physical dependence and a barbiturate-like withdrawal syndrome if taken in sufficient dosage over a long period. Withdrawal symptoms include anxiety, tremors, nightmares, insomnia, anorexia, nausea, vomiting, seizures, delirium, and maniacal activity.

The duration and severity of withdrawal depend on the particular drug taken. With short-acting depressants such as pentobarbital, secobarbital, and methaqualone, withdrawal symptoms tend to have a faster onset of action and be more severe. They begin 12 to 24 hours after the last dose and peak in intensity between 24 and 72 hours later. Withdrawal from longer-acting depressants such as phenobarbital and diazepam develops more slowly and is less intense; symptoms peak on the fifth to eighth day (Harvard Medical School, 2018). It is not surprising that the approach to detoxifying a person who is dependent on a sedative hypnotic depends on the nature of the drug itself (i.e., to which category of depressants it belongs), the severity of the dependence, and the duration of action of the drug. The general objectives of detoxification are to eliminate drug dependence (both physical and psychological) in a safe manner while minimizing discomfort. Having achieved these objectives, it is hoped that the patient will be able to remain free of dependence on all CNS depressants. However, in reality detoxification is rarely sufficient by itself to ensure long-term abstinence from the drug (Harvard Medical School, 2018).

Often, the basic approach for treating severe dependence on sedative hypnotics is substitution with either pentobarbital or the longer-acting phenobarbital for the offending and usually

## KEY TERM

**detoxification**
elimination of a toxic substance such as a drug and its effects from the body

**TABLE 6.3** Annual Prevalence of Abuse of CNS Depressants for 12th Graders (Percentage per Year)

|  | 2001 | 2004 | 2007 | 2009 | 2012 | 2014 | 2018 |
|---|---|---|---|---|---|---|---|
| Any Illicit Drug | 41.4 | 38.8 | 35.8 | 36.5 | 39.7 | 38.7 | 38.8 |
| Sedatives (Including Benzodiazepines) | 6.9 | 7.3 | 6.2 | 6.3 | 5.3 | 4.7 | 3.9 |

Data from Johnston, L. (2018). *Monitoring the Future: Overview 2018*. Retrieved from http://www.monitoringthefuture.org/pubs/monographs/mtf-overview2018.pdf

shorter-acting CNS depressant. Once substitution has occurred, the long-acting barbiturate dose is gradually reduced. Using a substitute is necessary because abrupt withdrawal for a person who is physically dependent can be dangerous, causing life-threatening seizures. This substitution treatment uses the same rationale as the treatment of heroin withdrawal by methadone replacement. Detoxification also includes supportive nutritional measures such as vitamins, restoration of electrolyte balance, and prevention of dehydration. The patient must be watched closely during this time because he or she will be apprehensive, confused, and unable to make logical decisions (Ait-Daoud et al., 2018).

If the person is addicted to both alcohol and barbiturates, the phenobarbital dosage must be increased to compensate for the double withdrawal. Many benzodiazepine addicts who enter a hospital to be treated for withdrawal are also dependent on heroin and vice versa. In such cases, the sedative-hypnotic dependence should be addressed first because the associated withdrawal can be life threatening. Detoxification from any sedative hypnotic should take place under close medical supervision, typically in a hospital (Harvard Medical School, 2018).

Remember that eliminating physical dependence is not a cure. The problem of psychological dependence can be much more difficult to handle. If an individual is abusing a CNS depressant because of emotional instability, personal problems, or a highly stressful environment, eliminating physical dependence alone will not solve the problem, and drug dependence is likely to recur. These types of patients require intense psychological counseling and must be trained to deal with their difficulties in a more constructive

and positive fashion. Without such psychological support, benefits from detoxification will only be temporary, and therapy will ultimately fail.

## Natural Depressants

Some plants that contain naturally occurring CNS depressants are included in herbal products or made into herbal teas for relaxation or as treatment for sleep problems (Meštrović 2015). Probably the best known of this group is the kava kava plant (*Piper methysticum*). This plant belongs to the pepper family and grows on South Pacific islands (WebMD, 2019). Drinks and bars containing extracts from kava kava root are legally available in many health food stores, are especially popular in Polynesian populations, and are sometimes used in religious ceremonies. The extract is prepared from the part of the kava kava plant that grows beneath the surface of the ground. Small amounts of kava kava can produce euphoria and increased sociability, whereas larger doses cause substantial relaxation, lethargy, relaxed lower limbs, and eventually sleep (WebMD, 2019). Some users may experience visual and auditory hallucinations that can last one to two hours. Some users report that kava kava drinks can make the mouth numb, much like topical local anesthetics used by dentists. Rare cases have been reported of liver damage in frequent users (WebMD, 2019).

A second type of common herb that contains CNS depressants is the *Datura* family of plants. Although these botanicals are typically associated with hallucinogenic effects, in smaller amounts they sometimes can cause sedation and even induce sleep. Examples of these plants include *Datura inoxia* (devil's trumpet) and *Datura stramonium* (jimson weed or thornapple). The active ingredients in these plants are typically anticholinergic drugs such as atropine or scopolamine. In lower doses, these herbs, especially if they contain scopolamine, have been used to encourage sleep. In fact, the actions of the herbs are somewhat similar to the OTC antihistamine-containing sleep aids, which also work because of their anticholinergic actions. In higher doses, both atropine and scopolamine can cause hallucinogenic effects. The anticholinergic actions of these herbs can be quite annoying and include constipation, dry mouth, and blurred vision, just to mention a few (Encyclopedia.com, 2016).

© Alina555/iStockphoto.com.

Detoxification of patients is often done in groups to help provide support during this difficult time.

# LEARNING PORTFOLIO

## Discussion Questions

1. Why did benzodiazepine drugs replace barbiturates as the sedative-hypnotic drugs most prescribed by physicians?
2. Which features of CNS depressants give them abuse potential?
3. Why is long-term use of the benzodiazepines more likely than short-term use to cause dependence?
4. Why are some physicians careless when prescribing benzodiazepines for patients suffering from severe anxiety?
5. Currently, sleep aid products are available OTC. Should the FDA also allow sedatives to be sold without a prescription? Support your answer.
6. Are there any real advantages to using barbiturates as sedatives or hypnotics? Should the FDA remove them completely from the market?
7. What types of people are most likely to abuse CNS depressants? Suggest ways to help these people avoid abusing these drugs.
8. Should propofol be scheduled? If so, as what category?
9. What is the appeal of using GHB? Why is it used to commit sexual assaults?
10. What dangers are associated with treating individuals who are severely dependent on CNS depressants?
11. Why are CNS depressants often combined with alcohol or opioid narcotics and what are the consequences?
12. Why is detoxification by itself usually insufficient to achieve long-term therapeutic success when dealing with severe CNS depressant dependence?

## Summary

1. Several unrelated drug groups cause CNS depression, but only a few are actually used clinically for their depressant properties. The most frequently prescribed CNS depressants are benzodiazepines, which include drugs such as Valium, Ambien, and Xanax. Barbiturates once were popular, but their severe side effects mean they are no longer prescribed by most clinicians except to treat some seizures. Much like barbiturates, drugs such as chloral hydrate are little used today. Finally, some OTC and prescription antihistamines, such as diphenhydramine, hydroxyzine, and promethazine, are used for their CNS depressant effects.
2. The clinical value of CNS depressants is dose dependent. When used at low doses, these drugs relieve anxiety and promote relaxation (sedatives). When prescribed at higher doses, they can cause drowsiness and promote sleep (hypnotics). When administered at even higher doses, some of the

depressants cause anesthesia and are used for patient management during surgery.

3. The rapidly acting general anesthetic propofol has become well known because of its role in the accidental death of pop singer Michael Jackson. Although not currently included in the DEA's schedule, its abuse is becoming a problem with physicians and nurses who have access to it at work. Sometimes propofol is also used to relieve pain or help someone sleep.

4. Because CNS depressants can relieve anxiety and reduce stress, they are viewed as desirable by many people. If used frequently over long periods, however, they can cause tolerance that leads to dependence.

5. The principal reason that benzodiazepines have replaced barbiturates in the treatment of stress and insomnia is that benzodiazepines have a greater margin of safety and are less likely to alter sleep patterns. Benzodiazepines enhance the GABA transmitter system in the brain through a specific receptor, whereas the effects of barbiturates are less selective. Even though benzodiazepines are safer than barbiturates, dependence and significant withdrawal problems can result if the former drugs are used indiscriminately.

6. Benzodiazepine dependence often occurs in patients who suffer from stress or anxiety disorders and are under a physician's care. If the physician is not careful and the cause of the stress is not resolved, drug treatment can drag on for weeks or months. After prolonged benzodiazepine therapy, tolerance to the drug develops; when benzodiazepine use is stopped, withdrawal occurs, which itself causes agitation. A rebound response to the drug might resemble the effects of emotional stress (agitation), so use of benzodiazepine is continued. In this way, the patient becomes severely dependent.

7. The short-acting CNS depressants are preferred for treating insomnia. These drugs help the patient get to sleep and then are inactivated by the body; when the user awakens the next day, he or she is less likely to experience residual effects than with long-acting drugs. The short-acting depressants are also more likely to be abused because of their relatively rapid onset and intense effects. In contrast, the long-acting depressants are better suited to treating persistent problems such as anxiety and stress. The long-acting depressants are also used to help wean dependent people from their use of short-acting compounds such as alcohol.

8. Many antihistamines cause sedation and drowsiness because of their anticholinergic effects. Several of these agents are useful for short-term relief of anxiety and are available in OTC sleep aids. The effectiveness of these CNS depressants is usually less than that of benzodiazepines. Because of their anticholinergic actions, antihistamines can cause some annoying side effects. These agents are not likely to be used for long periods; thus, dependence or serious abuse usually does not develop.

9. The people most likely to abuse CNS depressants include individuals who (a) use drugs to relieve continual stress, (b) paradoxically feel euphoria and stimulation from depressants, (c) use depressants to counteract the unpleasant effects of other drugs of abuse such as stimulants, and (d) combine depressants with alcohol and heroin to potentiate the effects.

10. The basic approach for treating dependence on CNS depressants is to detoxify the individual in a safe manner while minimizing his or her discomfort. This state is achieved by substituting a long-acting barbiturate or benzodiazepine such as phenobarbital or Valium for the offending CNS depressant. The long-acting drug causes less severe withdrawal symptoms over a longer period of time. The dependent person is gradually weaned from the substitute drug until he or she is depressant free.

11. GHB is a naturally occurring substance related to the neurotransmitter GABA that has been used for its sedating, euphorigenic, and muscle-building properties. It

also has been used to debilitate victims during sexual assaults and date rapes. Because of concerns that this substance is frequently abused, GHB was classified as a Schedule I drug in 2000.

12. Some plants such as kava kava that contain naturally occurring CNS depressants are included in herbal teas for relaxation or treatment of insomnia.

# References

Advanced Recovery Systems. (2019). Which celebrities have battled with addiction? Retrieved from www.drugrehab.com/addiction/celebrities/

Ait-Daoud, N., Hamby, A., Sharma, S., & Dievins, D. (2018). A preview of alprazolam use, misuse and withdrawal. *Journal of Addiction Medicine, 12*, 4–10.

American Psychiatric Association (APA). (2013). *Diagnostic and statistical manual of mental disorders*, 5th edition. Washington, DC: Author.

Associated Press. (1994, July 27). Woman who used Halcion defense hangs self. *Salt Lake Tribune, 248*, D-3.

Bosch, O., Quednow, B., Seifritz, E., & Wetter, T. (2012). Reconsidering GHB: Orphan drug or new model antidepressant. *Journal of Psychopharmacology, 26*: 618–628.

Charney, D., Mihic, S., & Harris, R. (2006). Hypnotics and sedatives. In L. Brunton, J. Lazo, & K. Parker (Eds.), *The pharmacological basis of therapeutics*, 11th ed. (pp. 401–427). New York, NY: McGraw-Hill.

Chaterjee, R. (2019, January 25). Steep climb in benzodiazepine prescribing by primary care doctors. NPR. Retrieved from www.npr.org/sections/health-slots/2019/01/25/688287824/sleep-climb-in-benzodiazepine-prescribing-by-primary-care

Davis, K. (2018). Everything you need to know about barbiturates. Medical News Today. Retrieved from https://www.medicalnewstoday.com/articles/310066.php

Diaz, J., & Kaye, A. (2017). Death by Propofol. *Journal of the Louisiana State Medical Society, 369*, 28–32.

Drug Enforcement Administration (DEA). (2013). Gamma hydroxybutyric acid. Washington, DC: Author. Retrieved from http://www.deadiversion.usdoj.gov/drug_chem_info/ghb.pdf

Drug Enforcement Administration (DEA). (2016, August 29). Controlled substances: Alphabetical order. Retrieved from http://www.deadiversion.usdoj.gov/schedules/orangebook/c_cs_alpha.pdf

Drugs.com. (2015a). Benzodiazepines. Retrieved from http://www.drugs.com/drug-class/benzodiazepines.html

Drugs.com. (2015b). Sedative, hypnotic or anxiolytic drug use disorder. Retrieved from https://www.drugs.com/health-guide/sedative-hypnotic-or-anxiolytic-drug-use-disorder.html

Drugs.com. (2015c). Quaaludes. Retrieved from http://www.drugs.com/quaaludes.html

Drugs.com (2019). Halcion side effects. Retrieved from https://www.drugs.com/sfx/halcion-side-effects.html

Drugs.com. (2019, February). Triazolam. Retrieved from www.drugs.com/ppa/triazolam.html

Duberman, A. (2018). I had no idea I had "misused" Klonopin until I tried to stop taking it. Huffpost Personal. Retrieved from https://www.huffpost.com/entry/klonopin-withdrawal-experience_n_5bd8b01ae4b019a7ab57ddc3

Ducharme, J. (2019). Are sleeping pills safe? Here's what research says. *Time*. Retrieved from https://time.com/5584937/sleepingpills-safe/

Elements Behavioral Health. (2015, January 30). Why you should never abuse propofol. Retrieved from https://www.drugaddictiontreatment.com/types-of-addiction/prescription-drug-addiction/why-you-should-never-abuse-propofol/

Encyclopedia.com. (2006). Antihistamine. Retrieved from http://www.encyclopedia.com/topic/antihistamine.aspx

Encyclopedia.com. (2016). *Datura stramonium*. Retrieved from http://www.encyclopedia.com/topic/Jimson_weed.aspx

European College of Neuropsychopharmacology. (2018). Research shows club drug GHB associated with brain and cognitive changes. Medical Press. Retrieved from https://medicalxpress.com/news/2018-10-club-drug-ghb-brain-cognitive.html

European Monitoring Centre for Drugs and Drug Addiction Perspective on Drugs. (2015). The misuse of benzodiazepines among high-risk opioid users in Europe. Retrieved from http://www.drugsandalcohol.ie/24052/

Fawcett, K. (2015, February 19). Benzodiazepine: Helpful or harmful? *U.S. News & World Report Health*. Retrieved from http://health.usnews.com/health-news/patient-advice/articles/2015/02/19/benzodiazepines-helpful-or-harmful

Fluyau, D., Revadigar, N., & Manobianco, B. E. (2018). Challenges of the pharmacological management of benzodiazepine withdrawal, dependence and decontamination. *Psychopharmacology, 8*, 147–168.

Food and Drug Administration (FDA) (2019). Safety announcement. Drug Safety Communication. Retrieved from www.fda.gov/media/123819/download

Gorelick, D. (2015). Cocaine use disorder in adults: Epidemiology, pharmacology, clinical manifestations, medical consequences, and diagnosis. UpToDate. Retrieved from http://www.uptodate.com/contents/cocaine-use-disorder-in-adults-epidemiology-pharmacology-clinical-manifestations-medical-consequences-and-diagnosis

Greller, H., Traub, S., & Grayzel, J. (2019). Benzodiazepine poisoning and withdrawal. *UpToDate*. Retrieved from https://www.uptodate.com/contents/benzodiazepine-poisoning-and-withdrawal

Guina, J., & Merrill, B. (2018). Benzodiazepines I: Upping the care on Downers: The Evidence of risks, benefits and alternatives. *Journal of Clinical Medicine, 7,* 17.

Guthrie, S., & Bostwick, J. (2013). Anxiety disorders. In B. Alldredge (Ed.), *Applied therapeutics, The clinical use of drugs,* 10th ed. (pp. 1863–1869). Philadelphia, PA: Wolters Kluwer.

Harvard Medical School. (2018). Sedative, hypnotic or anxiolytic drug use disorder. Cambridge, MA: Harvard Health Publishing. Retrieved from www.health.harvard.edu/a_to_z/sedative-hypnotic-or-anxiolytic-drug-use-disorder-a-to-z

Johnston, L. (2018). *Monitoring the Future: Overview 2018.* Retrieved from http://www.monitoringthefuture.org/pubs/monographs/mtf-overview2018.pdf

Lightman, D. (2019). "Dreamers" with DUIs get the same break as a member of Congress. Impact 2020. Retrieved from https://www.mcclatchydc.com/news/policy/immigration/article230795314.html

Mandal, A. (2013, May 26). Barbiturate history. News Medical. Retrieved from http://www.news-medical.net/health/barbiturate-history.aspx

Mayo Clinic Staff. (2019). Marijuana. Mayo Clinic Patient Care and Health Information. Retrieved from www.mayoclinic.org/drugs-supplements-marijuana/art-20364974

McEvoy, G. (Ed.). (2003). *American Hospital Formulary Service drug information.* Bethesda, MD: American Society of Hospital Pharmacists.

MedlinePlus. (2019). Chloral hydrate. U.S. National Library of Medicine. Retrieved from https://medlineplus.gov/druginfo/meds/a682201.html

Meštrović, T. (2018). List of sedatives. News Medical. Retrieved from https://www.news-medical.net/health/List-of-Sedatives.aspx

Mitchell, J. (2018). Dr. Drew: "Star treatment" may have killed Tom Petty, Michael Jackson and Prince. *Clarion Ledger* [Jackson, MS]. Retrieved from https://www.clarionledger.com/story/news/2018/01/26/dr-drew-star-treatment-may-have-killed-tom-petty-michael-jackson-and-prince/1066653001/

Narconon. (n.d.). History of barbiturates. Retrieved from http://www.narconon.org/drug-information/barbiturates-history.html

National Institute on Drug Abuse (NIDA). (2015, December 1). Commonly abused drugs chart. Retrieved from https://www.drugabuse.gov/drugs-abuse/commonly-abused-drugs-charts

National Institute on Drug Abuse (NIDA). (2018). Benzodiazepines and opioids. Bethesda, MD: National Institute on Drug Abuse, National Institutes of Health. Retrieved from https://www.drugabuse.gov/drugs-abuse/opioids/benzodiazepines-opioids

Nordqvist, J. (2019, March). The benefits and risks of benzodiazepines. Medical News Today. Retrieved from https://www.medicalnewstoday.com/articles/262809.php

Olfson, M., M. King, & M. Schoenbaum. (2015). Benzodiazepine use in the United States. *JAMA Psychiatry, 72,* 136–142.

Olson, E. J. (2018). Is it OK to use OTC antihistamines to treat insomnia; I'd like to avoid prescription sleep aids. Rochester, MN: Mayo Clinic. Retrieved from www.mayoclinic.org/healthy-lifestyle/adult-health/expert-answers/sleeping-aids/faq-20058393

Palamar, J. (2018). The comeback and dangers of the drug GHB. The Conversation. Retrieved from https://theconversation.com/the-comeback-and-dangers-of-the-drug-ghb-90736

Reeves, R., Ladner, M., Perry, C., Burke, R., & Lazier, J. (2015). Abuse of medications that theoretically are without abuse potential. *Southern Medical Journal. 108,* 151–157.

Schep, L., Knudsen, K., Slaughter, R., Vale, J., & Megarbane, B. (2012). The clinical toxicology of gamma hydroxybutyrate, gamma butyrolactone and 1,4-butanediol. *Clinical Toxicology, 50,* 458–470.

Sedatives/hypnotics/non-barbiturate. (2010). In *Drug facts and comparisons,* 14th ed. (pp. 732–748). St. Louis, MO: Wolters Kluwer Health.

Sumnall, H., Woolfall, K., Edwards, S., Cole, J., & Beynon, C. (2008). Use, function, and subjective experiences of gamma-hydroxybutyrate (GHB). *Drugs and Alcohol Dependency, 92,* 286–290.

Townsend, C. (2015, October 19). The scary reason GHB is making a comeback. The Daily Beast. Retrieved from http://www.thedailybeast.com/articles/2015/10/19/the-scary-reason-ghb-is-making-a-comeback.html

Trevor, A., & Way, W. (2015). Sedative-hypnotic drugs. In B. Katzung (Ed.), *Basic and Clinical Pharmacology,* 13th ed. (pp. 369–383). New York, NY: McGraw-Hill Medical.

WebMD. (2018). Date-rape drugs (GHB, Rohypnol). Retrieved from www.webmd.com/mental-health/addiction/date-rape-drugs

WebMD. (2019). Kava. Retrieved from www.webmd.com/vitamins/ai/ingredientmono-872/Kava

# CHAPTER 7

# Alcohol: Pharmacological Effects

## Did You Know?

▶ Alcohol is the most consumed drug in the world.

▶ Ethanol leads all other substances of abuse in treatment admissions.

▶ Ethanol is the only alcohol used for human consumption; most of the other common alcohols are poisonous.

▶ Some wild animals and insects become drunk after seeking out and consuming alcohol-containing fermented fruit.

▶ Alcohol-related deaths outnumber deaths related to other drugs of abuse (except tobacco) by a margin of four to one.

▶ Women who abuse alcohol are more likely to suffer depression than male abusers.

▶ The lethal level of alcohol is between 0.4% and 0.6% by volume in the blood; the blood level most states consider to be illegal in someone driving is 0.08% but is as low as 0.05% in others.

▶ Consumption of alcohol by adolescents can cause persistent damage to their brain development.

▶ Among alcoholics, liver disorders account for approximately 10% to 15% of deaths.

▶ The Food and Drug Administration (FDA) has approved several medications for the treatment of alcohol dependence, although they are not universally effective.

▶ Fetal alcohol syndrome (FAS) is caused by alcohol consumption during pregnancy and is characterized by facial deformities, growth deficiencies, and mental retardation in the offspring.

▶ Addictions such as alcoholism are among the most inherited of the mental illnesses.

## Learning Objectives

**On completing this chapter, you should be able to:**

❭ Explain how common alcohol (ethanol) is a drug.

❭ Explain why people believe alcohol serves as a "social lubricant."

❭ Explain the pharmacokinetic properties of alcohol, and describe how they influence the effects of the drug.

❭ Explain the role of alcohol in polydrug abuse.

❭ Identify the possible physical effects of prolonged heavy ethanol consumption.

❭ Explain what alcohol dependence is and how it is treated.

❭ Explain the potential cardiovascular benefits and problems of moderate alcohol use and the dose-dependent nature of these effects.

❭ Describe fetal alcohol syndrome (FAS), its cause, and its effects.

❭ Explain how prolonged consumption of alcohol affects the brain and nervous system, liver, digestive system, blood, cardiovascular system, sexual organs, endocrine system, and kidneys and how it leads to mental disorders and damage to fetuses.

❭ Describe why use of alcohol by adolescents is particularly problematic and how this should influence the discussion about underage drinking.

❭ Explain why there is concern about how college students use alcohol, and discuss how to address this problem.

❭ Explain why malnutrition is so common among alcoholics.

# Introduction

This chapter focuses on how alcohol affects the body from a pharmacological perspective. Alcohol is the most widely consumed drug in the world, and for many it is as much a part of daily life as eating. Even so, most of those who use alcohol do not understand how it works or why it can change their personalities and behavior in bizarre and unpredictable ways, causing respectable and dependable people to engage in foolish and even dangerous behaviors (Gowin, 2010). In 2015, sales of alcoholic beverages in the United States totaled $266 billion (Morris, 2019). As a licit drug, alcohol is extensively promoted socially through advertising, exposing underage youth to 3.9 billion noncompliant alcohol promotional impressions from 2013 to 2015 (Johns Hopkins Bloomberg School of Public Health, 2015). More important, drinking is perceived as acceptable and even desirable. The popularity of this drug is clear; in 2018, 20% of high school seniors said they had been drunk (National Institute on Drug Abuse [NIDA], 2019). Binge drinking among teens is thought to be at epidemic levels, with about 13.8% of the high school seniors participating in episodes of extremely heavy alcohol use (NIDA, 2019). Although drinking by persons younger than 21 years is illegal, adolescents ages 12 to 20 drink 11% of all alcohol consumed in the United States, of which 90% is in the form of binge drinks (Centers for Disease Control and Prevention [CDC], 2015).

This chapter focuses on the many adverse effects of alcohol on the human body. Overall, it provides a foundation to understand the pharmacological nature of alcohol. Alcohol is widely consumed and leads all other addicting substances as a reason for treatment admissions (Grant et al., 2015) (see **Table 7.1**). Each year approximately 2 million people are admitted for treatment of substance dependence, and more than half of these receive treatment for alcoholism (Substance Abuse and Mental Health Services Administration [SAMHSA], 2009). We hope that such an

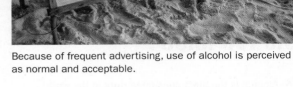

Because of frequent advertising, use of alcohol is perceived as normal and acceptable.

understanding of how this drug affects the various organ systems of the body will lead to more responsible use and less abuse of alcohol.

# The Nature and History of Alcohol

Alcohol has been part of human culture since the beginning of recorded history. The technology for alcohol production is ancient. Several basic ingredients and conditions are needed to produce this substance: sugar, water, yeast, and warm temperatures.

The process of making alcohol, called **fermentation**, is a natural one. It occurs in ripe fruit and berries and even in honey that bees leave in trees. These substances contain sugar and water and are found in warm climates, where yeast spores are transported through the air. Animals such as elephants, baboons, birds, wild pigs, and bees will seek out and eat fermented fruit. Elephants under the influence of alcohol have been observed bumping into one another and stumbling around. Intoxicated bees fly an unsteady beeline toward their hives. Birds eating fermented fruit become so uncoordinated that they cannot fly or, if they do, crash into windows or branches. In fact, fermented honey, called **mead**, may have been the first alcoholic beverage.

The Egyptians had breweries 6,000 years ago; they credited the god Osiris with introducing wine to humans. The ancient Greeks used large quantities of wine and credited a god, Bacchus (Dionysus), with introducing the drink. Today, we use the words *bacchanalia* and *dionysian* to refer to revelry and drunken events. The Hebrews were also heavy users of wine. The Bible mentions that Noah, just nine generations removed from Adam, made wine and became drunk.

## KEY TERMS

**fermentation**
biochemical process through which yeast converts sugar to alcohol

**mead**
alcoholic beverage made from fermented honey

**TABLE 7.1** Epidemiology of Alcohol Use Disorders (AUD)

Alcohol use disorder (AUD) ranks among the most prevalent mental disorders in the United States and throughout the world. The devastation caused by AUD on productivity, social, and personal functioning and financial and medical institutions is staggering. This table presents an epidemiological overview of AUD to help the reader appreciate its diversity and overwhelming implications.

| Category (lifetime, unless otherwise indicated) | Percent Incidence (of total unless otherwise indicated) | Category (lifetime, unless otherwise indicated) | Percent Incidence (of total unless otherwise indicated) |
| --- | --- | --- | --- |
| *12-Month Prevalence* | 13.9 | *Urbanicity* | |
| | | Urban | 29.2 |
| *Lifetime Prevalence* | | Rural | 28.6 |
| Total | 29.1 | *Region* | |
| Mild | 8.6 | Northeast | 28.8 |
| Severe | 13.9 | Midwest | 33.6 |
| *Lifetime Prevalence for Men* | 36 | South | 25.3 |
| *Lifetime Prevalence for Women* | 22.7 | West | 31.3 |
| *Lifetime Prevalence by Race and Ethnicity* | | *Who Receive Treatment* | |
| White | 32.6 | Total AUD | 19.8 |
| Native American | 43.4 | Mild AUD | 4.4 |
| Black | 22.0 | Moderate AUD | 8.7 |
| Asian | 15.0 | Severe | 34.7 |
| Hispanic | 22.9 | *Co-Incidence (Lifetime Category in Total AUD Patients)* | *Significant AOR (Adjusted Odds Ratio–Risk Compared to Normal [1])* |
| *Lifetime Prevalence by Age (Years)* | | Other drug use disorder | 4.1 |
| 18–29 | 37 | Nicotine use disorder | 3.1 |
| 30–44 | 34.4 | Bipolar disorder | 2.0 |
| 45–64 | 28.2 | Generalized anxiety disorder | 1.2 |
| ≥65 | 13.4 | | |
| *Education* | | Panic disorder | 1.3 |
| No High school | 22.3 | Persistent depression | 1.3 |
| High school | 28.4 | Antisocial personality disorder | 1.9 |
| Some college or higher | 30.8 | | |
| *Family Income ($)* | | Posttraumatic stress disorder | 1.3 |
| 0–19,999 | 28.9 | | |
| 20,000–34,999 | 27.9 | | |
| 35,000–69,999 | 29.0 | | |
| >70,000 | 30.0 | | |

Grant, B., Goldstein, R., Saha, T., Chou, S. P., Jung, J., Zhang, H., . . . & Hasin, D. S. (2015). Epidemiology of DSM-5 alcohol use disorder. *JAMA Psychiatry, 72*, 757–766.

Alcohol is produced by a single-celled microscopic organism, one of the yeasts, that breaks down sugar by a metabolic form of combustion, thereby releasing carbon dioxide and forming water and ethyl alcohol as waste products. Carbon dioxide creates the foam on a glass of beer and the fizz in champagne. Fermentation continues until the sugar supply is exhausted or the concentration of alcohol reaches the point at which it kills the yeast (12% to 14%). Thus, 12% to 14% is the natural limit of alcohol found in fermented wines or beers.

The **distillation** device, or *still*, was developed by Arabs around AD 800 and was introduced into medieval Europe around AD 1250. By boiling the fermented drink and gathering the condensed

# HERE AND NOW
## A Century of Alcohol

An overwhelming need to consume alcohol (known today as *alcoholism*) was first described in the literature by American physician Benjamin Rush in 1784, but the concept that excessive use of alcohol is a disease did not really evolve until the turn of the 20th century. This perspective was encouraged by the temperance movement of the late 19th century. Because of the ill effects of alcohol, temperance legally became Prohibition in 1919. Prohibition (which made alcohol illegal) was initially successful in reducing consumption, but consumption began to rebound in the late 1920s. However, it has been suggested that Prohibition was repealed in 1933 not because it failed to reduce alcohol use but because of shifting policy during the Great Depression that argued liquor manufacturing would create jobs and provide taxes on alcoholic beverages that could fund government programs.

The second half of the 20th century saw the emergence of the belief that genetics plays a major role in alcoholism. This concept suggests that some families and individuals are more vulnerable to alcohol addiction than others because of inherited traits. Researchers today are energetically moving forward to identify which genes might contribute to the development and expression of the addiction in an effort to improve prevention and treatment for alcoholism.

Dual Diagnosis. (2016). Disease theory of alcoholism. Retrieved from http://www.dualdiagnosis.org/alcohol-addiction/disease-theory-alcoholism/; Szalavitz, M. (2015). Genetics: No more addictive personality. *Nature, 522,* 548–549.

vapor in a pipe, a still increases the concentration of alcohol, potentially to 50% or higher. Because distillation made it easier for people to get drunk, it greatly intensified the problem of alcohol abuse. However, even before the invention of the still, alcoholic beverages were known to cause problems in heavy users that resulted in severe physical and psychological dependence. Toward the end of the 19th century, drug addicts (including those dependent on alcohol) were shunned as immoral and undesirable. It was in the 1930s when alcoholism started to be considered a medical condition requiring treatment (Dual Diagnosis, 2016). More recently, alcoholism has been officially termed as alcohol use disorder (AUD) by the American Psychiatric Association (APA, 2013) (see "Here and Now: A Century of Alcohol").

## Alcohol as a Drug

Alcohol (more precisely designated as *ethanol*) is a natural product of fermentation and considered by many to be the number-one abused drug (Thomas, 2019); this is based on findings such as the following:

**KEY TERM**

**distillation**
heating fermented mixtures of cereal grains or fruits in a still to evaporate and be trapped as purified alcohol

- 5.3% of the population 12 years of age or older have an alcohol disorder,
- more than 50% of American adults have had some history of problem drinking,
- 10% of U.S. children have grown up with a parent who has alcohol problems,
- alcohol is the third-leading cause of preventable death,
- 40% of U.S. hospital beds are used to treat conditions related to alcohol-associated problems,
- only one in five patients with alcohol use disorder receive treatment, and
- the relapse rate after treatment for alcohol disorder is ~40% to 60%.

Alcohol's impact on college students has been particularly disturbing, with reports stating that binge drinking among such individuals is commonplace (Bishop, 2012). This psychoactive substance depresses the central nervous system (CNS) while influencing almost every major organ system of the body (Kenna, 2013). Alcohol is also an addictive drug in that it may produce a physical and behavioral dependence (Kenna, 2013). Although tradition and attitude are important factors in determining the use patterns of this substance, the typical consumer rarely appreciates the diversity of pharmacological effects caused by alcohol, the drug. The pharmacological action of alcohol accounts for both its pleasurable and CNS effects as well as its hazards to health and public safety.

## ■ Alcohol as a Social Drug

Why is alcohol often perceived as an acceptable adjunct to such celebrations as parties, birthdays, weddings, and anniversaries, and as a way of relieving stress and anxiety? Social psychologists refer to the perception of alcohol as a **social lubricant**. This term implies that drinking is misconceived as safely promoting conviviality and social interaction and as an activity that bolsters confidence by repressing inhibitions and strengthening extroversion. Why do many people have to be reminded that alcohol is a drug like marijuana or cocaine and may have serious consequences for some people? The following reasons explain this misconception (DrugRehab.com, n.d.):

- The use of alcohol is legal.
- Individuals typically use alcohol before going out with friends to improve mood, reduce self-consciousness, and enhance social skills.
- Alcohol tends to improve social bonding.
- Alcohol improves empathy and friendliness, making the environment more comfortable.
- Alcohol reduces social fears or embarrassment in the presence of strangers or groups.
- Alcohol helps mitigate the effects of social anxiety disorders.

## ■ Impact of Alcohol

Although many people consider the effects of alcohol enjoyable and reassuring, the adverse pharmacological impacts of this drug are extensive. Its use causes approximately 14 million cases of alcoholism (severe alcohol dependence) at any one time; its effects are associated with more than 100,000 deaths each year in the United States (Buddy, 2019b); and it costs our society about $250 billion annually. These economic costs are broken down into the following categories:

- 72% due to workplace absenteeism, worker's compensations, Social Security disability, and unemployment expenses;
- 11% associated with healthcare expenses, including emergency care, hospitalization, treatment of alcohol use disorder, and the treatment of cirrhosis;
- 10% relates to criminal justice expenses; and
- 5% comes directly from motor vehicle crashes and associated insurance expenses.

The pharmacological effects of alcohol abuse cause severe dependence, which is classified as a psychiatric disorder according to the criteria provided by the American Psychiatric Association in its *Diagnostic and Statistical Manual of Mental Disorders*, fifth edition (*DSM-5*; APA, 2013). These effects also disrupt personal, family, social, and professional functioning and frequently result in multiple illnesses and accidents, violence, and crime (Hanson & Li, 2003). Alcohol consumed during pregnancy can lead to devastating damage to offspring and is a principal cause of mental retardation in newborns (Hanson & Li, 2003). After tobacco, alcohol is the leading cause of premature death in America. In the United States, approximately $207 billion is spent annually dealing with the social and health problems resulting from the pharmacological effects of alcohol. Of course, such estimates fall short in assessing the emotional upheaval and human suffering caused by this drug (Buddy, 2019b).

Despite all of the problems that alcohol causes, our free society has demanded access to this drug. At the same time, it is unthinkable to ignore its tremendous negative social impact. There are no simple answers to this dichotomy, yet clearly governmental and educational institutions could do more to protect members of society from the dangers associated with alcohol. The best weapons we have against the problems caused by alcohol are education, prevention, and treatment.

## ■ Alcohol and Crime

Although alcohol is considered to be a legal substance and can be consumed in public places by people 21 years of age or older without fear of being arrested, it is strongly associated with crime and other social problems. For example, the use of alcohol contributes to 40% of all violent crimes (e.g., murders, rapes, assaults, child abuse, and sexual abuse), and 37% of the approximately 2 million imprisoned offenders in the United States report that when arrested, they were under the influence of alcohol and most had blood alcohol levels of more than two to three times the legal limit. In fact, offenders of violent crimes are far more likely to have been using alcohol than any other drug. Alcohol is particularly implicated in violent acts when the attacker and victim are

**KEY TERM**

**social lubricant**
belief that drinking (misconceived as safe) represses inhibitions, strengthens extroversion, and leads to increased sociability

The use of alcoholic beverages is often associated with criminal behavior leading to incarceration.

Almost all violent crimes on college campuses involve the use of alcohol.

acquainted, accounting for two-thirds of such cases. In contrast, when the attacker and victim are strangers, alcohol is associated with only one-third of the cases (National Council on Alcoholism and Drug Dependence [NCADD], 2016).

More than 1 million people in the United States are arrested each year for driving under the influence (DUI) of alcohol. Because alcohol use impairs motor functions and diminishes decision making, nearly 40% of all traffic deaths are alcohol related. Most of the criminal acts caused by those influenced by alcohol include robbery, sexual assault, aggravated assault, intimate partner violence, child abuse, and homicide (Alcohol Rehab Guide, 2019; NCADD, 2016).

Use of alcohol is also prevalent in incidents of violence between college students. Each year more than 600,000 college students are assaulted by other students under alcohol's influence. In fact, almost 95% of all violent crimes on college campuses involve the use of alcohol by either the victim, the attacker, or both (NCADD, 2016).

Despite the fact that our prisons and jails are filled with inmates who are diagnosed as positive for drug or alcohol use dependency, fewer than

20% of these prisoners receive adequate treatment. This lack of treatment available to inmates accounts for the finding that around 95% of these former prisoners return to using alcohol or drugs after release from prison, with 70% going on to commit new crimes. It has been found time and again that treatment is the most effective strategy for breaking the criminal justice cycle for persons with alcohol problems. In the long run, effective treatment could save society considerable money and suffering (NCADD, 2016).

## ▮ Alcohol and Cancer

Although the impact of alcohol consumption on cancer has been somewhat controversial, there has been little dispute that heavy long-term regular use can contribute to cancers of the mouth, gastrointestinal tract, liver, and breast. However, the opinions on the effects of moderate drinking on cancer expression have been more equivocal. Even so, about 5% of cancers have been linked to alcohol and its consumption with an estimation of ~39,000 breast cancers in woman each year in the United States (Aubrey, 2018). It is not known exactly how alcohol use leads to cancer expression, but it is now evident that alcohol is one of the principal causes of preventable cancers; consequently, no health authority should recommend starting if you do not already drink.

## ▮ Alcopops

*Alcopops* are sugary, fruity, malt-based drinks merchandized in brightly colored packages that are attractive to adolescents. Some researchers claim that as many as 50% of drinkers 20 and younger have consumed alcopops, thus confirming their great appeal to teenagers. As many as 30% of those under age 18 claim alcopops as their favorite alcoholic drink. Their popularity exploded in the 1990s, growing at a rate of 2.5% per year until 2018 when the sales exceeded $1 billion. They attract young people because they resemble soft drinks and are thought to be relatively safe while offering a relatively cheap option for a consumer to get a mild buzz; however, some of these products can have alcohol contents that exceed that of wine (Chaudhuri, 2019). In fact, a recent study suggests that alcopops consumption causes disproportionate harm to teenage users (Alcohol Justice, 2015), who often do the following:

- drink more alcohol per day on more days each month,

- engage in binge drinking four times more often, and
- physically fight with others, receiving alcohol-related injuries that require medical attention.

Preferred brands include Smirnoff (Diageo) and Bacardi Malt Beverages (Bacardi). Despite concern about the consumption of alcopops by underage drinkers, the marketing of these products remains relatively uncontrolled, and the Federal Trade Commission has decided to allow the alcohol industry to regulate itself with little interference from the federal government (Chaudhuri, 2019).

## ■ Drinking and College Students

Alcohol consumption by college students and its negative consequences are clearly problems, leading to approximately 1,600 drinking-related deaths, 700,000 assaults, and 97,000 sexual assaults or date rapes per year (NIAAA, 2018b). About 58% of full-time students consume alcohol, and about 12% of students engaged in heavy binge drinking on five or more days during the preceding month (NIAAA, 2018a). All too often such alcohol consumption has tragic consequences (see

"Case in Point: Drinking and College Culture"). Despite these troubling findings associated with college students and alcohol, there is evidence from the 12th graders surveyed in the *Monitoring the Future* report of 2018 that the monthly heavy use of alcohol by adolescents entering the period of young adults actually decreased from 28.1% to 17.5 % from 2012 to 2018 (Johnston, 2019). It remains to be seen in the future if this will eventually result in decreased alcohol problems on U.S. college campuses. Despite the controversy as to the severity of college drinking and its future trends, everyone agrees that greater efforts should be made by colleges, government, and businesses to prevent alcohol-related deaths, injuries, and crimes (Bishop, 2012; Epstein, 2010).

## ■ Underage Drinking

Most alcohol use starts during the teen years. Youth who start drinking alcohol at an early age have a much greater likelihood of developing alcohol dependence when they become adults (Mayo Clinic, 2018). Possible explanations for this effect include (1) an altered expression of genes, which affects vulnerability to alcoholism (Dryden,

# ► CASE IN POINT

## Drinking and College Culture: A Tragic Mix

Heavy drinking is frequently assumed to be an integral part of the college experience, but it has also been found to be a highly reliable predictor of sexual assault in college. Evidence shows that women who admit they sometimes or often "overdrink" are twice as likely to be victims of attempted or completed sexual assaults as those who rarely or never drink. A county prosecutor in Michigan who has a large university under his jurisdiction tells people that alcohol is the "real date-rape drug."

Although the legal drinking age is 21, many students claim that alcohol is "liquid courage," and it "lubricates university social life" throughout the college experience, making it easier to meet and get sexually involved with other students. However, this combination can be explosive, especially for young college students exploring their sexuality in an environment with abundant beer and other alcoholic drinks. One of the many stories that can be told to illustrate this dangerous combination is that of a freshman at Boston University who attended

a fraternity party. After consuming a debilitating amount of alcohol, she vaguely remembers going upstairs with one of the fraternity members. She recalls waking up the next morning undressed and alone in a tiny room, sure that she had been raped. She also explains that she took a morning-after pill to prevent pregnancy and was tested for sexually transmitted disease; however, she was too frightened to report the incident to authorities. She recalls bumping into the man she was convinced raped her and how eye contact with him resulted in a panic attack.

Nearly 80% of college students claim that drinking less would effectively prevent sexual assaults. This claim is supported by another student who was sexually assaulted while under the influence. After expressing her regret for allowing herself to get into this situation, she stated, "I was too drunk to say no. But if I wasn't drunk, I wouldn't have gone upstairs [to the bedroom] at all. Nothing that happened that night would have happened if I'd been sober."

Data from Brown, E., Hendrix, S., & Svriuga, S. (2015, June 14). Drinking is central to college culture and to sexual assault. *Washington Post*. Retrieved from https://www.washingtonpost.com/local/education/beer-pong-body-shots-keg-stands-alcohol-central-to-college-and-assault/2015/06/14/7430e13c-04bb-11e5-a428-c984eb077d4e_story.html. Accessed June 2019.

# HERE AND NOW

## The Epidemic of Underage Drinking

As with most things, the way teenagers consume alcohol is different from the alcohol-consuming habits of adults. Teenagers are not inclined to sit around a table and slowly sip one or two glasses of wine with their meals or during a social gathering; instead, they drink quickly, cheaply, and completely to get drunk and drown their anxieties and frustrations with the sedative effects of ethanol. There are ever-increasing options to achieve this objective, including malt beverages, mixtures of alcohol plus supercaffeinated energy drinks, extremely sweet and fruity alcohol products merchandized in brightly colored packages, and even straight liquors. The alarming extent to which this occurs is underscored by the CDC report that 90% of all teen alcohol consumption is in the form of binge drinking and that about 200,000 adolescents end up in emergency rooms each year because of drinking problems. Even though we still have approximately 9 million underage drinkers in the United States, the good news is that from 2012 to 2018 underage drinking decreased by 22%.

Listfield, E. (2011, June 12). The underage drinking epidemic. *Parade Special Report*, pp. 6–8; Pager, T. (2015, June 11). Underaged drinking, binge boozing by minors is on the decline. *USA Today*. Retrieved from http://www.usatoday.com/story/news/2015/06/11/underage-binge-drinking/71021464/; Johnston, L. (2019). *Monitoring the Future 1975–2018*. Bethesda, MD: National Institute on Drug Abuse, National Institutes of Health. Retrieved from http://monitoringthefuture.org/pubs/monographs/mtf-overview2018.pdf

2009); and (2) interference with normal development of critical brain systems important for learning, memory, attention, information processing, and proper decision making (Reinberg, 2009; Trudeau, 2010). In addition, early drinkers are at increased vulnerability to the effects of other drugs as an adult such as nicotine in tobacco (American Public University, 2010). Findings such as these are especially disturbing in light of the facts that nearly 53% of students consume alcohol and 34% of them have been drunk before they graduate from high school (Johnston, 2019) and teenagers tend to consume alcohol in a binging fashion (Pager, 2015) (see "Here and Now: The Epidemic of Underage Drinking"). It is becoming apparent that heavy exposure to the toxic effects of alcohol during adolescence may have long-lasting and profound effects on young people, leading to mental health problems throughout their lives (Miller, 2019). For this reason, the American Academy of Pediatrics (Berchelmann, 2019) recommends that physicians discourage underage drinking by (1) screening their adolescent patients for alcohol use, (2) discussing the hazards of alcohol use with their teenage patients, (3) encouraging parents to be good role models for their children, and (4) supporting the continuation

© Peeradontax/Shutterstock.

Alcopops are colorful alcohol products promoted as an alternative to beer with considerable appeal to the underage drinkers.

of 21 as the minimum legal drinking age. Many experts believe that parents are key to preventing alcohol use by their children. They suggest that parents who send ambiguous messages to their kids about drinking or through their words and actions encourage this toxic teen behavior of alcohol consumption behavior (Dvorak, 2015) (see "Case in Point: Parents Must Say No").

## The Properties of Alcohol

Technically, alcohol is a chemical structure that has a hydroxyl group (–OH; one oxygen and one hydrogen atom) attached to a carbon atom. Of the many types of alcohol, several are important for our purposes. The first is **methyl alcohol** (*methanol*

**KEY TERM**

**methyl alcohol**
wood alcohol

# ► CASE IN POINT

## Parents Must Say No

Parents often throw parties for their teenage children and allow the beer to flow freely as teens socialize and shout over loud music. While it may be true that the adolescent and his or her friends will give hugs and high-fives to the "cool, progressive parents" who furnished the drinks and treat them as "real adults," the reality is that such parents have done their children and the friends a great disservice that could end tragically. An estimated 20% to 25% of parents supply alcohol to their teens, claiming that their teenagers are going to drink anyway, so they might as well drink at home under parental supervision. Other parents claim that drinking by adolescents is part of growing up and becoming an adult. "After all," they often claim, "I drank when I was a teenager and it didn't hurt me any." Research has overwhelmingly demonstrated that encouraging underage drinking actually is an extremely dangerous rite of passage for many teens. In fact, it has been determined that providing alcohol to underaged adolescents sends the dangerous message that parents condone drinking regardless of age. A common result of such a policy is that many of the teens who are attracted to these parties with alcohol are themselves heavy drinkers and are more than willing to train the other underaged adolescents how to become binge drinkers themselves, frequently exposing their developing brains to the hazards of toxic doses of alcohol. Experts say the solution to underage drinking is not for parents to be indulgent and enable the practice but to never provide alcohol or condone drinking. Parents must send a clear "Don't use" message because being a "cool parent" doesn't substitute for being a good parent.

© Anita Patterson Peppers/ShutterStock, Inc.

Weintraub, K. (2018, January 25). Study: Parents who give their teenagers alcohol are inviting trouble. *USA Today*. Retrieved from https://www.usatoday.com/story/news/2018/01/25/study-parents-who-give-their-teenagers-alcohol-inviting-trouble/1067481001/

or *wood alcohol*), which is made from wood products. Its metabolites are poisonous. Small amounts (4 milliliters) cause blindness by affecting the retina; larger amounts (80–150 milliliters) are usually fatal. Methyl alcohol is added to ethyl alcohol (*ethanol* or *grain alcohol*, the drinking type) that is intended for industrial use so people will not drink it. A similar mixture also is sometimes added to illegally manufactured ("bootleg") liquor.

Another type of poisonous alcohol, **ethylene glycol**, is used in antifreeze. A third type, **isopropyl alcohol**, is commonly used as rubbing alcohol and as an antiseptic (a solution for preventing the growth of microorganisms). These two types of alcohol are also poisonous if consumed.

Pure ethyl alcohol (ethanol) is recognized as an official drug in the U.S. Pharmacopoeia, although the various alcoholic beverages are not listed for medical use. Alcohol can be used as a solvent for other drugs or as a preservative. It is used to cleanse, disinfect, and harden the skin and to reduce sweating. A 70% alcohol solution is an effective bactericide. However, it should not be used on open wounds because it will dehydrate the injured tissue and worsen the damage. Alcohol may be deliberately injected in or near nerves to treat severe pain; it causes local anesthesia and deterioration of the nerve. In all alcoholic beverages—beer, wine, liqueurs or cordials, and distilled spirits—the psychoactive agent is the same, but the amount of ethanol varies (see **Table 7.2**). The amount of alcohol is expressed either as a percentage by volume or, in the older proof system, as a measurement based on the military assay method. To make certain that they were getting a high alcohol content in the liquor, the British military would place a

## KEY TERMS

**ethylene glycol**
alcohol used as antifreeze

**isopropyl alcohol**
rubbing alcohol; sometimes used as an antiseptic

**TABLE 7.2** The Concentration of Ethanol in Common Alcoholic Beverages

| Type of Beverage | Concentration of Ethanol (%) |
| --- | --- |
| U.S. beers | 4–6 |
| Wine coolers | 4–10 |
| Cocktails and dessert wines | 17–20 |
| Liqueurs | 22–50 |
| Distilled spirits | 40+ |

Different alcoholic beverages have a wide range of alcohol content.

sample on gunpowder and touch a spark to it. If the alcohol content exceeded 50%, it would burn and ignite the gunpowder. This test was "proof" that the sample was at least 50% alcohol. If the distilled spirits were "under proof," the water content would prevent the gunpowder from igniting. The percentage of alcohol volume is one-half the proof number. For example, 100-proof whiskey has a 50% alcohol content.

# The Physical Effects of Alcohol

How does alcohol affect the body? **Figure 7.1** illustrates how alcohol is absorbed into the body. After a drink, alcohol has direct contact with the mouth, esophagus, stomach, and intestines, acting as an irritant and an **anesthetic** (blocking sensitivity to pain). In addition, alcohol influences almost every organ system in the body after entering the bloodstream. Alcohol diffuses into the blood rapidly after consumption by passing through gastric and intestinal walls (the absorption process). Once the alcohol is in the small intestine, its absorption is largely independent of the presence of food; in the stomach, food retards absorption.

The effects of alcohol on the human body depend on the amount of alcohol in the blood, which is known as the **blood alcohol concentration (BAC)**. This concentration largely determines behavioral and physical responses to alcoholic beverages. Relative to behavior, the circumstances in which the drinking occurs, the

drinker's mood, and his or her attitude and previous experience with alcohol all contribute to the reaction to drinking. People demonstrate individual patterns of psychological functioning that may affect their reactions to alcohol as well. For instance, the time it takes to empty the stomach may be either reduced or accelerated as a result of anger, fear, stress, nausea, and the condition of the stomach tissues.

The blood alcohol level produced depends on the presence of food in the stomach, the rate of alcohol consumption, the concentration of the alcohol, and the drinker's body composition. Fatty foods, meat, and milk slow the absorption of alcohol, allowing more time for its metabolism and reducing the peak concentration in the blood. When alcoholic beverages are taken with a substantial meal, peak BACs may be as much as 50% lower than they would have been had the alcohol been consumed by itself. When large amounts of alcohol are consumed in a short period, the brain and other organs are exposed to higher peak concentrations. Generally, the more alcohol in the stomach, the greater the absorption rate. There is, however, a modifying effect of extremely strong drinks on the absorption rate. The absorption of drinks stronger than 100 proof is inhibited. This effect may be the result of its blocked passage into the small intestine or irritation of the lining of the stomach, causing mucus secretion, or both. (See "Here and Now: Half-Truths About Alcohol.")

Diluting an alcoholic beverage with water helps to slow absorption, but mixing with carbonated beverages increases the absorption rate. The carbonation causes the stomach to empty its contents into the small intestine more rapidly, causing a more rapid "high." The carbonation in champagne has the same effect.

**KEY TERMS**

**anesthetic**
drug that blocks sensitivity to pain

**blood alcohol concentration (BAC)**
concentration of alcohol found in the blood, often expressed as a percentage

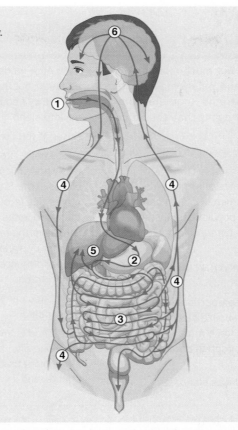

1. **Mouth**—Alcohol is consumed orally.

2. **Stomach**—Alcohol goes right into the stomach. A little of the alcohol passes through the wall of the stomach and into the bloodstream. Most of the alcohol continues down into the small intestine.

3. **Small intestine**—Alcohol goes from the stomach into the small intestine. Most of the alcohol is absorbed through the walls of the intestine and into the bloodstream.

4. **Bloodstream**—The bloodstream carries the alcohol to all parts of the body, such as the brain, heart, and liver.

5. **Liver**—As the bloodstream carries the alcohol around the body, it passes through the liver. The liver changes the alcohol to water, carbon dioxide, and energy. The process is called *oxidation*. The liver can oxidize only about one-half ounce of alcohol per hour. Thus, until the liver has time to oxidize all of the alcohol, the alcohol continues passing through all parts of the body, including the brain.

6. **Brain**—Alcohol goes to the brain almost as soon as it is consumed. It continues passing through the brain until the liver oxidizes all the alcohol into carbon dioxide, water, and energy.

**FIGURE 7.1**  How alcohol is absorbed in the body.

Data from Masters, S., & Trevor, A. (2015). The alcohols. In B. Katzung (Ed.), *Basic and clinical pharmacology*, 13th ed. (pp. 384–395). New York, NY: McGraw-Hill.

Once in the blood, distribution occurs as the alcohol uniformly diffuses throughout all tissues and fluids, including fetal circulation in pregnant women or the milk of a nursing mother (ScienceDaily, 2019). Because the brain has a large blood supply, its activity is quickly affected by a high alcohol concentration in the blood. Body composition—the amount of water available for the alcohol to be dissolved in—is a key factor in BAC and distribution. The greater the muscle mass, the lower the BAC that will result from a given amount of alcohol. This relationship arises because muscle has more fluid volume than does fat. For example, if two men each weigh 180 pounds but one man has substantially more lean mass than the other, the former will have a lower blood alcohol level after consuming four ounces of whiskey. The leaner man will show fewer effects. A woman of a weight equivalent to a man generally will have a higher blood alcohol level because women generally have a higher percentage of fat. Thus, they are affected more by identical drinks.

Alcoholic beverages contain almost no vitamins, minerals, protein, or fat—just large amounts of carbohydrates (Gramlich, Tandon, & Rahman, 2019). Alcohol cannot be used by most cells; it must be metabolized by an enzyme, **alcohol dehydrogenase**, which is found almost exclusively in the liver. Alcohol provides more calories per gram than does carbohydrate or protein and only slightly less than does pure fat. Because it can provide many calories, the drinker's appetite may be satisfied; as a result, he or she may not eat properly and end up with malnutrition (Gramlich et al., 2019). The tolerance that develops to alcohol is comparable to that observed with barbiturates. Some people have a higher tolerance for alcohol and can more easily disguise intoxication.

## KEY TERM

**alcohol dehydrogenase**
principal enzyme that metabolizes ethanol

# HERE AND NOW
## Half-Truths About Alcohol

Much is known about alcohol, but much more needs to be learned to effectively and safely manage its use. There are several half-truths that are commonly believed by the general public that should be addressed.

- *Belief*: If used in moderation, alcohol is healthy for everyone.
- *Fact*: Moderate drinking benefits only men older than 50 years of age and women who are post-menopausal. Even for these populations, the benefits appear to be minimal in persons who already have healthy lifestyles.
- *Belief*: Pound for pound, women hold their liquor as well as men.
- *Fact*: Because women have proportionally less body water and tend to metabolize alcohol more slowly than men, women become more intoxicated with comparable dose consumption per body weight.
- *Belief*: A drink before bed induces sleep.

- *Fact*: After moderate drinking, onset of sleep may be faster, but the sleep itself becomes restless, marked by frequent wakings and the inability to get back to sleep.
- *Belief*: If you don't feel drunk, it is okay to drive.
- *Fact*: People are typically unable to determine accurately how much alcohol is in their system. For most states in the United States, 0.08% to 0.1% (in some states this level is as low as 0.05%), alcohol in the blood is the legal threshold for driving (i.e., it is against the law to drive with this blood alcohol content or higher), but studies have shown that driving performance is significantly impaired at half this concentration.
- *Belief*: You can sober up by taking a shower or drinking caffeine.
- *Fact*: Time is the only thing that truly sobers up someone after consuming alcohol. Caffeine is a stimulant that does not neutralize the alcohol effects, and it can interfere with sleeping.

Data from Your health: Alcohol—The whole truth, seven half-truths about drinking, exposed. (1999, December). *Consumer Reports, 64,* 60–61; National Institute on Alcohol Abuse and Alcoholism (NIAAA). (2007). FAQs for the general public. Retrieved from http://www.niaaa.nih.gov/FAQs/General-English; Greenfield, S. (2002). Women and alcohol use disorders. *Harvard Review Psychiatry, 10,* 76–85; Beck, M. (2011, August 2). Testing the limits of tipsy. *Wall Street Journal.* Retrieved from https://www.wsj.com/articles/SB10001424053111903341404576482051743844220; Forever Recovery, A. (n.d.). 5 myths about alcohol abuse vs. the facts. Retrieved from aforeverrecovery.com/blog/information/5-myths-about-alcohol-abuse-vs-the-facts

## ▌ Alcohol and Tolerance

Repeated use of alcohol results in tolerance and reduces many of alcohol's pharmacological effects. As with other psychoactive drugs, tolerance to alcohol encourages increased consumption to regain its effects and can lead to severe physical and psychological dependence (Alcohol.org, 2019). Tolerance to alcohol is similar to that seen with CNS depressants such as the benzodiazepines. It consists of both an increase in the rate of alcohol metabolism (from the stimulation of metabolizing enzymes in the liver) and a reduced response by neurons and transmitter systems, particularly by increasing the activity of the inhibitory neurotransmitter, gamma-aminobutyric acid (GABA) to

## KEY TERM

**behavioral tolerance**
compensation for motor impairments through behavioral pattern modification by chronic alcohol users

this drug. Development of tolerance to alcohol is extremely variable; some users can consume large quantities of this drug with minor pharmacological effects. The tolerance-inducing changes caused by alcohol can also alter the body's response to other drugs (referred to as *cross-tolerance*) and can specifically reduce the effects of some other CNS depressants (Kenna, 2013).

Many chronic alcohol users learn to compensate for the motor impairments of this drug by modifying their patterns of behavior. These adjustments are referred to as **behavioral tolerance**. Examples of this adjustment include individuals altering and slowing their speech, walking more deliberately, or moving more cautiously to hide the fact that they have consumed debilitating quantities of alcohol.

## ▌ Alcohol Metabolism

Alcohol is principally inactivated by liver metabolism (Masters & Trevor, 2015). The liver metabolizes alcohol at a slow and constant rate and is unaffected by the amount ingested. Thus, if one can of beer is consumed each hour, the BAC will remain constant without resulting in intoxication. If more alcohol is consumed per hour, the BAC will rise proportionately because large amounts of alcohol that cannot be metabolized spill over into the bloodstream.

## ■ Polydrug Use

Alcohol is commonly consumed with other drugs such as tobacco (Kelly, Evens-Whipp, Chan, Tobourou, & Patton, 2015), prescription drugs (Kenna, 2013), and even illegal substances (Hedden et al., 2010); this mode of consumption is known as **polydrug use** (Kenna, 2013), and it occurs in about 64% of alcoholics (Hedden et al., 2010). Mixing alcohol with other types of drugs can intensify intoxication. This probably helps explain why marijuana users are more likely to combine their marijuana use with alcohol than with other drugs (Liquori, Gatto, & Jarrett, 2002; Peters & Hughes, 2010). In a recent report, approximately 64% of those seeking treatment for alcoholism also were diagnosed with another drug dependence (Hedden et al., 2010).

The reasons why individuals combine alcohol with other drugs of abuse are not always apparent. The following explanations have been proposed:

- Alcohol enhances the reinforcing properties of other CNS depressants.
- It decreases the amount of an expensive and difficult-to-get drug required to achieve the desired effect.
- It helps to diminish unpleasant side effects of other drugs of abuse such as the withdrawal caused by CNS stimulants.
- There is a common predisposition to use alcohol and other substances of abuse.

Clearly, coadministration of alcohol with other substances of abuse is a common practice that can be problematic and result in dangerous interactions (Addiction Center, 2016).

## ■ Short-Term Effects

The impact of alcohol on the CNS is most similar to that of sedative-hypnotic agents such as barbiturates. Alcohol depresses CNS activity at all doses (Masters & Trevor, 2015), producing definable results.

At low to moderate doses, **disinhibition** occurs; this loss of conditioned reflexes reflects a depression of inhibitory centers of the brain. The effects on behavior are variable and somewhat unpredictable. To a large extent, the social setting and mental state determine the individual's response to such alcohol consumption. For example, alcohol can cause one person to become euphoric, friendly, and talkative but prompt another to become aggressive and hostile. Low to moderate doses also interfere with motor activity, reflexes, and coordination. Often this impairment is not apparent to the affected person (D'Agostino, Wesley, Brown, & Fillmore, 2019).

In moderate quantities, alcohol slightly increases the heart rate; slightly dilates blood vessels in the arms, legs, and skin; and moderately lowers blood pressure. It stimulates appetite, increases production of gastric secretions, and markedly stimulates urine output. At higher doses, the social setting has little influence on the expression of depressive actions of the alcohol. The CNS depression incapacitates the individual, causing difficulty in walking, talking, and thinking. These doses tend to induce drowsiness and cause sleep. If large amounts of alcohol are consumed rapidly, severe depression of the brain system and motor control area of the brain occurs, producing incoordination, confusion, disorientation, stupor, anesthesia, coma, and even death (Villines, 2019).

The lethal level of alcohol is between 0.4% and 0.6% by volume in the blood (Masters & Trevor, 2015). Death is caused by severe depression of the respiration center in the brain stem, although the person usually passes out before drinking an amount capable of producing this effect. Although an alcoholic may metabolize the drug more rapidly than a light drinker, the toxicity level of alcohol stays about the same. In other words, it takes approximately the same concentration of alcohol in the body to kill a nondrinker as it does to kill someone who drinks on a regular basis. The amount of alcohol required for anesthesia is close to the toxic level, which is why it would not be a useful anesthetic. See "Signs & Symptoms: Psychological and Physical Effects of Various Blood Alcohol Concentration Levels" for a summary of the effects of various BAC levels.

## KEY TERMS

**polydrug use**
concurrent use of multiple drugs

**disinhibition**
loss of conditioned reflexes because of depression of the brain's inhibitory centers

# SIGNS & SYMPTOMS

## Psychological and Physical Effects of Various Blood Alcohol Concentration Levels

| Number of Drinks* | Blood Alcohol Concentration (%) | Psychological and Physical Effects |
|---|---|---|
| 1 | 0.02–0.03 | No overt effects, slight mood elevation. |
| 2 | 0.05–0.06 | Impairment begins. Feeling of relaxation, warmth; slight decrease in reaction time and in fine muscle coordination. |
| 3 | 0.08–0.09 | Balance, speech, vision, hearing slightly impaired; feelings of euphoria, increased confidence; loss of motor coordination. |
| 3–4 | 0.08 | Legal intoxication. |
| 4 | 0.11–0.12 | Coordination and balance becoming difficult; distinct impairment of mental faculties, judgment. |
| 5 | 0.14–0.15 | Major impairment of mental and physical control; slurred speech, blurred vision, lack of motor skills. |
| 7 | 0.20 | Loss of motor control—must have assistance in moving about; mental confusion. |
| 10 | 0.30 | Severe intoxication; minimum conscious control of mind and body. |
| 14 | 0.40 | Unconsciousness, threshold of coma. |
| 17 | 0.50 | Deep coma. |
| 20 | 0.60 | Death from respiratory failure. |

*Note:* For each hour elapsed since the last drink, subtract 0.015% blood alcohol concentration, or approximately one drink.

* One drink = one beer (4% alcohol, 12 oz.) or one highball (1 oz. whiskey).

Data from Ohio State Police Driver Information Seminars and the National Clearinghouse for Alcohol and Alcoholism Information, 5600 Fishers Lane, Rockville, MD, 85206; Evans, W. (2013, May 15). NTSB wants lower legal limit for blood alcohol. *Deseret News, 163,* A1.

As a general rule, it takes as many hours as the number of drinks consumed to sober up completely. Despite widely held beliefs, drinking black coffee, taking a cold shower, breathing pure oxygen, and so forth will not hasten the sobering process. Stimulants such as coffee may help keep the drunk person awake but will not improve judgment or motor reflexes to any significant extent.

## THE HANGOVER

A familiar consequence of overindulgence is fatigue combined with nausea, upset stomach, headache, sensitivity to sounds, and ill temper—the hangover. These symptoms are usually most severe many hours after drinking, when little or no alcohol remains in the body. No simple explanation exists for what causes the hangover. Theories include accumulation of acetaldehyde (a metabolite of ethanol), dehydration of the tissues, poisoning because of tissue deterioration, depletion of important enzyme systems needed to maintain routine functioning, an acute withdrawal (or rebound) response, and metabolism of the impurities in alcoholic beverages (Compound Interest, 2016).

The body loses fluid in two ways through alcohol's **diuretic** action, which sometimes results in dehydration: (1) The water content, such as in beer, increases the volume of urine; and (2) the alcohol depresses the center in the hypothalamus of the brain that controls release of a water-conservation hormone (antidiuretic hormone).

## KEY TERM

**diuretic**
drug or substance that increases the production of urine

With less of this hormone, urine volume is further increased. Thus, after drinking heavily, especially the highly concentrated forms of alcohol, the person is thirsty. However, this effect by itself does not explain the symptoms of a hangover.

The type of alcoholic beverage one drinks may influence the hangover that results. Some people are more sensitive to particular alcohol impurities than others. For example, some drinkers have no problem with white wine but an equal amount of some red wines gives them a hangover. Whiskey, scotch, and rum may cause worse hangovers than vodka or gin, given equal amounts of alcohol, because vodka and gin have fewer impurities. There is little evidence that mixing different types of drinks per se produces a more severe hangover. It is more likely that more than the usual amount of alcohol is consumed when various drinks are sampled.

A common treatment for a hangover is to take a drink of the same alcoholic beverage that caused the hangover. This practice is called "taking the hair of the dog that bit you" (from the old notion that the burnt hair of a dog is an antidote to its bite). This treatment might help the person who is physically dependent, in the same way that giving heroin to a heroin addict eases the withdrawal symptoms. The "hair of the dog" method may work by depressing the centers of the brain that interpret pain or by relieving a withdrawal response. In addition, it may affect the psychological factors involved in having a hangover; distraction or focusing attention on something else may ease the effects.

Another remedy is to take an analgesic compound such as an aspirin–caffeine combination after drinking. This treatment is based on the belief that aspirin helps control headache, and the caffeine may help counteract the depressant effect of the alcohol. In reality, these ingredients have no effect on the actual sobering-up process. In fact, products such as aspirin, caffeine, and Alka-Seltzer can irritate the stomach lining to the point where the person feels worse.

## ▪ Dependence

According to the World Health Organization (WHO), approximately 3.3 million deaths related to alcohol consumption occur each year around the world (WHO, 2018). It is estimated that 12.5 million men and women in the United States suffer from alcoholism. In this group, men are three times more likely than women

to develop significant dependence on this drug (WebMD, 2020).

In 2018, 36% of high school seniors drank alcohol and 20% consumed enough to become drunk (Johnston, 2019). Unfortunately, many people become so dependent on the psychological influences of alcohol that they become compulsive and continually consume it. These individuals can be severely handicapped because of their alcohol dependence and often become unable to function normally in society. People who have become addicted to this drug are called *alcoholics* and likely include many of the high school seniors who regularly drink heavily (Johnston, 2019). Because of the disinhibition, relaxation, and sense of well-being mediated by alcohol, some degree of psychological dependence often develops even in routine users, and the availability of alcoholic beverages at social gatherings becomes required.

Because of the physiological effects, physical dependence also results from the regular consumption of large quantities of alcohol. This consequence becomes apparent when ethanol use is abruptly interrupted and withdrawal symptoms result. The severity of the withdrawal can vary according to the length and intensity of the alcohol habit. The prototypic withdrawal patterns are as follows (Addictions and Recovery, 2019):

- anxiety, restlessness, irritability, and insomnia;
- headaches and dizziness;
- chest tightness, difficulty breathing, and rapid heartbeat;
- nausea, vomiting, diarrhea, and stomach cramps;
- muscle tension, tremors, and shakes; and
- sweating and tingling.

Recovery from alcohol dependence is a long-term process. Because of the severe withdrawal and the need for behavioral adjustments, most people relapse several times before achieving long-term abstinence. Even people who have not used alcohol for years may relapse under stressful circumstances, such as was apparently the case for well-known actor Phillip Seymour Hoffman, who died from a drug overdose in 2014 after two decades of sobriety. Despite the occasional tragic examples of relapse after long-term sobriety, for those who achieve five years of sobriety relapse is not all that common and is typically less than 15%, compared to 30% relapse rate for those who are abstinent for less than a year (Manejwala, 2014).

## MEDICATIONS FOR DEPENDENCE

Although alcohol dependence afflicts about 4% of the adult population, only 10% to 15% of these patients receive appropriate treatment. This is partially because of the misconception that alcoholism is best dealt with by "willpower" and medicine has no role. However, as we have discussed in this chapter, chronic alcohol use has numerous neurobiological consequences, so it makes sense that biological strategies based on medications can be helpful in treating persons severely dependent on alcohol. The following three medications currently are approved or are being considered by the FDA for adjunctive intervention (i.e., they should be used in combination with behavioral therapy) (Masters & Trevor, 2015; NIDA, 2018):

- The oldest drug approved for alcoholism treatment, disulfiram (Antabuse), has become less popular with many physicians because it makes users extremely sick and nauseous when they consume alcohol. It works by interfering with the metabolism of alcohol. It is easily avoided if the patient is anticipating drinking and is typically only helpful in the treatment of highly motivated alcoholics.
- Naltrexone (an opiate antagonist) relieves alcohol craving and helps to reduce relapse rates in alcohol-dependent patients. Although about 20% of this population have a positive response to naltrexone treatment, the other 80% are for the most part nonresponsive. One possible explanation for this is the existence of an opioid receptor variant in the responsive group that makes people vulnerable to the addicting effects of alcohol, which can be suppressed by naltrexone treatment. Thus, the lack of such a variant opioid gene in the majority of alcoholics could explain their lack of response to naltrexone (Falloon, 2010).
- The third drug, acamprosate (Campral), blocks the release of the exciting neurotransmitter glutamate, which reduces withdrawal in abstinent alcoholics.
- Finally, topiramate has been considered by the FDA for alcohol dependence treatment and is sometimes used "off-label" for this purpose. It is thought to work by increasing GABA inhibitory transmission and reducing glutamate stimulatory transmission, although the exact mechanism of action for alcohol treatment is not known.

Although these FDA-approved medications have significantly influenced strategies used to treat alcoholism, they are far from being universally effective. There continues to be considerable research as we try to discover even more effective medications for treating the problem of alcoholism. For optimal benefit, alcoholics need to be carefully subtyped (including features such as age, gender, duration of dependence, mental status, and even genetic makeup) and matched to the appropriate medication and behavioral therapy (Johnson, 2010).

## ■ Alcohol and Genetics

Large-scale studies of twins suggest that addictions such as alcoholism are among the most inherited types of mental illnesses. Consequently, because of our unique gene patterns, some of us get hooked on alcohol whereas others can party hard but afterward walk away without any need or desire to consume more alcohol. In general, it is believed that genetics account for 50% of a person's risk to develop alcoholism (Crane, 2019). Research has demonstrated that the specific genes that contribute to these inherited vulnerabilities can influence elements of alcohol intake such as excessive consumption, dampening of neuronal feedback that warns a person that he or she has consumed too much alcohol, or an enhanced sense of pleasure after drinking alcohol (Wallis, 2009).

Differences in the intensity of a hangover or the negative effects of drinking such as nausea or dizziness can also be influenced by genetics (see "Family Matters: Asian Glow") and are likely to affect frequency of use and the development of addiction to alcohol. Despite the prominent role of heritability in the expression of alcohol dependence, the environment is equally as important; if it is supportive and healthy, it can diminish the genetic influence and reduce the likelihood that alcoholism will be expressed even when a person's genetics increase the risk (Wallis, 2009).

# The Effects of Alcohol on Organ Systems and Bodily Functions

As previously mentioned, BAC depends on the size of the person, presence of food in the stomach, rate of drinking, amount of carbonation, and ratio of muscle mass to body fat. Furthermore, alcohol has pervasive effects on the major organs and fluids of the body (Thomas, n.d.). In fact, the effects of this substance on body functions

potentially can be so profound and destructive that alcoholism (severe addiction) is now considered a disease (MedlinePlus, 2019). The pervasive effects of alcohol on bodily organs are discussed in greater detail in the following sections and summarized in **Figure 7.2**.

## ■ Brain and Nervous System

Every part of the brain and nervous system is affected—and in extreme cases can be damaged—by alcohol (see Figure 7.2). An important finding demonstrates that even moderate consumption of alcohol can cause the shrinkage of brain volume. People who routinely drink more than 14 drinks per week lose approximately 1.6% of their brain size compared to nondrinkers. The greatest effect was observed in female heavy drinkers older than 70 years of age (Reinberg, 2007). In low to moderate doses, alcohol suppresses subcortical inhibitions of the cortical control centers, resulting in disinhibition. It also increases the release of endorphins, which likely contributes to the rewarding properties of alcohol; helps explain why naltrexone, an opioid receptor antagonist, is an effective treatment for some alcoholics; and may explain why some people have a higher risk of becoming an alcoholic.

In higher doses, it depresses the cerebellum, causing slurred speech and staggering gait. These doses also impair a person's ability to do tasks that require vigilance and rapid decision making. Often these people are unaware that their performance is impaired, making them potentially dangerous when engaging in activities such as driving a car (Masters & Trevor, 2015).

Extremely high doses depress the respiratory centers of the medulla, resulting in death. Furthermore, alcohol alters the production and functioning of transmitters such as dopamine, serotonin, GABA, and brain endorphins (Dekker, 2019). Recent findings suggest that even cannabinoid receptors—the targets of the active ingredients in marijuana—are affected by alcohol (Kenna, 2013). These neurochemical effects contribute to the fact that alcohol consumption can aggravate underlying psychiatric disorders such as depression and schizophrenia (Saisan, Smith, Robinson, & Segal, 2019).

Heavy drinking over many years may result in serious mental disorders and irreversible damage to the brain and peripheral nervous system, leading to permanently compromised mental function and memory and alterations in other brain systems (Sandoiu, 2019). In addition, abrupt cessation of alcohol consumption in the alcoholic

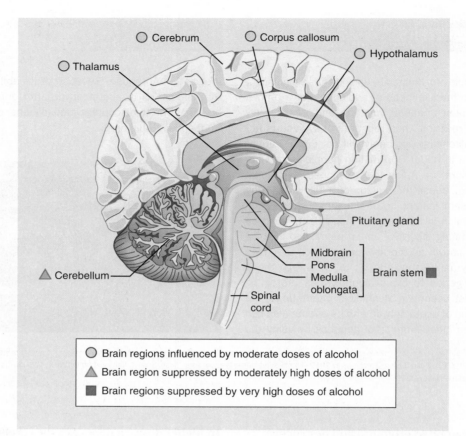

Cerebrum

Corpus callosum

Thalamus

Hypothalamus

Pituitary gland

Midbrain
Pons
Medulla
oblongata

Brain stem �

Cerebellum

Spinal
cord

○ Brain regions influenced by moderate doses of alcohol

▲ Brain region suppressed by moderately high doses of alcohol

■ Brain regions suppressed by very high doses of alcohol

**FIGURE 7.2** The principal control centers of the brain affected by alcohol consumption. Note that all areas of the brain are interconnected.

can result in serious withdrawal effects such as life-threatening seizures and require intensive emergency care (Lautieri, 2019).

## ▌ Liver

Alcoholism accounts for 60% to 80% of all liver-related deaths in high-income countries (Hydes, Gilmore, Sheron, & Gilmore, 2019). In the first stage, known as *alcoholic fatty liver*, liver cells

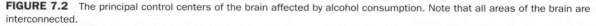

**hepatotoxic effect**
situation in which liver cells increase the production of fat, resulting in an enlarged liver

**alcoholic hepatitis**
second stage of alcohol-induced liver disease in which chronic inflammation occurs; reversible if alcoholic consumption ceases

**cirrhosis**
scarring of the liver and formation of fibrous tissues; results from alcohol abuse; irreversible

increase the production of fat, resulting in an enlarged liver. This direct toxic effect on liver tissue is known as the **hepatotoxic effect**. This effect is reversible and can disappear if alcohol use is stopped. Several days of drinking five or six alcoholic beverages each day produces fatty liver in males. For females, as few as two drinks of hard liquor per day several days in a row can produce the same condition. After several days of abstaining from alcohol, the liver returns to normal.

The second stage develops as the fat cells continue to multiply. Generally, irritation and swelling that result from continued alcohol intake cause **alcoholic hepatitis**. At this stage, chronic inflammation sets in and can be fatal. This second stage also is reversible if the intake of alcohol ceases.

Unlike stages 1 and 2, stage 3 is not reversible. Scars begin to form on the liver tissue during this stage. These scars are fibrous, and they cause hardening of the liver as functional tissue shrinks and deteriorates. This condition of the liver is known as **cirrhosis** and often is fatal.

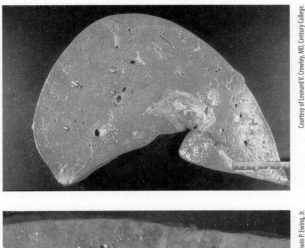

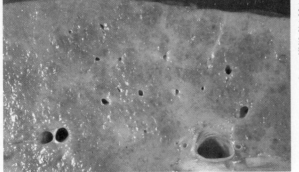

A normal liver (top) as it would be found in a healthy human body. An abnormal liver (bottom) that exhibits the effects of moderate to heavy alcohol consumption.

The liver damage caused by heavy alcohol consumption can cause problems when taking drugs that affect liver function. For example, the over-the-counter analgesic acetaminophen (Tylenol) can have a deleterious effect on the liver, especially when the function of this organ has already been compromised by alcohol (Masters & Trevor, 2015).

## ■ Digestive System

The digestive system consists of gastrointestinal structures involved in processing and digesting foods and liquids; it includes the mouth, pharynx, esophagus, stomach, and small and large intestines. As alcohol travels through the digestive system, it irritates tissue and can even damage the tissue lining as it causes acid imbalances, inflammation, and acute gastric distress. Often the result is gastritis (an inflamed stomach) and heartburn. The more frequently consumption takes place, the greater the irritation. One out of three heavy drinkers suffers from chronic gastritis. Furthermore, the heavy drinker has double the probability of developing cancer of the mouth

and esophagus because alcohol passes these two organs on the way to the stomach.

Prolonged heavy use of alcohol may cause ulcers, hiatal hernias, and cancers throughout the digestive tract. The likelihood of cancers in the mouth, throat, and stomach also dramatically increases (Promises, 2019). The pancreas is another organ associated with the digestive system that can be damaged by heavy alcohol consumption. Alcohol can cause pancreatitis, pancreatic cirrhosis, and alcoholic diabetes (Federico et al., 2015).

## ■ Blood

High concentrations of alcohol diminish the effective functioning of the hematopoietic (blood-building) system, decreasing production of red blood cells, white blood cells, and platelets. Problems with clotting and immunity to infection are not uncommon among alcohol abusers. Often, the result is lowered resistance to disease. Heavy drinking appears to affect the bone marrow, where various blood cells are formed. The suppression of the bone marrow can contribute to anemia, in which red blood cell production cannot keep pace with the need for those cells. Heavy drinkers are also likely to develop alcoholic bleeding disorders because they have too few platelets to form clots (Fleming, Mihic, & Harris, 2006; Masters & Trevor, 2015).

## ■ Cardiovascular System

The effects of ethanol on the cardiovascular system have been extensively studied, but much remains unknown. Ethanol causes dilation of blood vessels, especially in the skin. This effect accounts for the flushing and sensation of warmth associated with alcohol consumption.

The long-term effects of alcohol on the cardiovascular system are dose dependent. Some studies have suggested that regular light to moderate drinking (two or fewer glasses of wine per day) actually reduces the incidence of heart diseases such as heart attacks, strokes, and high blood pressure by 20% to 40% in some populations (Masters & Trevor, 2015), although the benefits have been challenged (Hartney, 2012). More recent studies have suggested that no amount of alcohol consumption is safe for overall health (Ducharme, 2019). The type of alcoholic beverage consumed does not appear to be important as to the coronary effect. Although the precise explanation for coronary actions is not known, it has been

Courtesy of Leonard V. Crowley, MD, Century College.

Courtesy of CDC/ Dr. Edwin P. Ewing, Jr.

suggested to be related to the effects of moderate alcohol doses in relieving stress and increasing the blood concentration of high-density lipoproteins (HDL) (Masters & Trevor, 2015). HDL is a molecular complex used to transport fat through the bloodstream, and its levels are negatively correlated with cardiovascular disease. In addition, moderate levels of alcohol decrease the formation of blood clots that can plug arteries and deprive tissues of essential oxygen and nutrients. The populations most likely to benefit from the protective properties of moderate levels of alcohol appear to be men older than 50 years of age and post-menopausal women. Moderate drinking on a daily average is approximately one drink (e.g., a glass of wine) for women and two drinks for men. However, note that some scientists argue that it is not the alcohol itself that protects against cardiovascular disease but the fact that moderate drinkers tend to live healthier lifestyles such as not smoking, eating good diets, and engaging in regular exercise (Rabin, 2009). These confounds need further study to determine if moderate consumption of alcohol is as healthy as suggested by earlier studies. Regardless of whether moderate drinking is healthy, drinking more than moderate amounts of alcohol can clearly result in increased health risks that more than offset the benefits (Ward, 2013).

Some of the confusion about alcohol's health influences may be result from the fact that the cardiovascular protective effect of moderate drinking is at least partially race specific. A report suggests that alcohol use that prevents cardiovascular disease in white men may actually increase heart disease in black men (Fuchs, 2004).

Because of the potential for developing addiction to alcohol and the increased health risk with heavy drinking, most health providers and researchers would not encourage a nondrinker to start to consume alcohol in an attempt to gain a health benefit. In addition, even in those populations most likely to benefit from moderate alcohol consumption, the benefit is likely to disappear in persons who already have healthy lifestyles that include low-fat diets, stress and weight-management techniques, and regular exercise. In general, most clinicians believe that alcohol use kills

more people (approximately 100,000 per year) than it saves, and those it kills tend to be younger (Hanson & Li, 2003; "Special Report," 1997; Ward, 2013).

Chronic intense use of alcohol changes the composition of heart muscle by replacing it with fat and fiber, resulting in a heart muscle that becomes enlarged and flabby. Congestive heart failure from **alcoholic cardiomyopathy** often occurs when heart muscle is replaced by fat and fiber. Other results of alcohol abuse that affect the heart are irregular heartbeat or arrhythmia, high blood pressure, and stroke. A common example of damage is "holiday heart," so called because people drinking heavily over a weekend turn up in the emergency room with a dangerously irregular heartbeat. Chronic excessive use of alcohol by people with arrhythmia causes congestive heart failure. Malnutrition and vitamin deficiencies associated with prolonged heavy drinking also contribute to cardiac abnormalities and other organ damage (Buddy, 2019a).

## ■ Sexual Organs

Although alcohol lowers social inhibition, its use interferes with sexual functioning. As Shakespeare said in *Macbeth*, alcohol "provokes desire, but it takes away the performance." Continued alcohol use causes prostatitis, which is an inflammation of the prostate gland. This condition directly interferes with a man's ability to maintain an adequate erection during sexual stimulation. Another frequent symptom of alcohol abuse is atrophy of the testicles, which results in lowered sperm count and diminished hormones in the blood (Dhawan & Sharma, 2002; Emanuele & Emanuele, 2010).

## ■ Endocrine System

Endocrine glands release hormones into the bloodstream. These hormones function as messengers that directly affect cell and tissue function throughout the body. Alcohol abuse alters endocrine functions by influencing the production and release of hormones and affects endocrine regulating systems in the hypothalamus, pituitary, and gonads. Because of alcohol abuse, levels of testosterone (the male sex hormone) may decline, resulting in sexual impotence, breast enlargement, and loss of body hair in men. Women experience menstrual delays, ovarian abnormalities, and infertility (Masters & Trevor, 2015).

KEY TERM

**alcoholic cardiomyopathy**
congestive heart failure resulting from the replacement of heart muscle with fat and fiber

## ■ Kidneys

Frequent abuse of alcohol can severely damage the kidneys. The resulting decrease in kidney function diminishes this organ's ability to process blood and properly form urine and can result in serious metabolic problems. Another consequence of impaired kidney function in alcoholics is that they tend to experience more urinary tract infections than do nondrinkers or moderate drinkers (National Kidney Foundation, 2015).

## ■ Mental Disorders and Damage to the Brain

Persons with mental disorders are significantly more likely to have an alcohol problem. This may be in part because heavy alcohol consumption compromises the functions of those parts of the brain that control emotions and social behavior (Saisan et al., 2019). For example, long-term heavy drinking can severely affect memory, judgment, and learning ability (Fleming et al., 2006). **Wernicke-Korsakoff's syndrome** is a characteristic psychotic condition caused by alcohol use and the associated nutritional and vitamin deficiencies. Patients who are brain damaged cannot remember recent events, and compensate for their memory loss with confabulation (making up fictitious events that even the patient accepts as fact) (Masters & Trevor, 2015).

Fetal alcohol syndrome is characterized by facial deformities, as well as growth deficiency and mental retardation.

## ■ The Fetus

In pregnant women, alcohol easily crosses the placenta and often damages the fetus in cases of moderate to excessive drinking. It can also cause spontaneous abortion because of its toxicity. Another tragic consequence of high alcohol consumption during pregnancy is **fetal alcohol syndrome (FAS)**, which is characterized by facial deformities, growth deficiency, mental retardation, and joint and limb abnormalities (Masters & Trevor, 2015). The growth deficiency occurs in embryonic development, and the child usually does not catch up after birth. The mild to moderate mental retardation does not appear to lessen with time, apparently because the growth impairment affects the functional development of the brain as well.

The severity of FAS appears to be dose related: The more the mother drinks, the more severe the fetal damage. A safe lower level of alcohol consumption has not been established for pregnant women (Masters & Trevor, 2015). Birth-weight decrements have been found at levels corresponding to about two drinks per day on average. Clinical studies have established that alcohol itself clearly causes the syndrome; it is not related to the effects of smoking, maternal age, parity (number of children a woman has borne), social class, or poor nutrition. Chronic maternal alcohol consumption is the leading cause of mental retardation and congenital defects in children (Masters & Trevor, 2015). Another study demonstrated that just a few episodes of heavy drinking by a pregnant woman increases the likelihood that the offspring will also abuse alcohol later in life (*Psychology Today*, 2007).

## ■ Gender Differences

Research has demonstrated important pharmacological differences in how males and females respond to the consumption of alcohol. For example, heavy alcohol use in women will cause accelerated damage to the brain, liver, heart,

## KEY TERMS

**Wernicke-Korsakoff's syndrome**
psychotic condition connected with heavy alcohol use and associated vitamin deficiencies

**fetal alcohol syndrome (FAS)**
condition affecting children born to alcohol-consuming mothers that is characterized by facial deformities, growth deficiency, and mental retardation

and muscles compared to male users. These differences persist even after adjusting for the quantity of alcohol according to the differences in gender size. The greater sensitivity of women to the effects of this drug may be the result of their tendency to metabolize alcohol more slowly than their male counterparts (NIDA, 2015), or it may be because a higher percentage of body fat in females leads to greater retention of the drug (Kenna, 2013; Leigh, 2007). In addition, problems associated with alcohol abuse might express differently in men and women, with females more likely to experience depression, whereas men are more likely to binge drink and engage in fighting (Norton, 2007). Other differences relate to their response to treatment. Gender differences in treatment outcomes likely reflect factors such as women's tendency to have a later onset of alcohol use and associated problems, a more positive family history, more marital disruption (Gomberg, 2003), and more associated psychiatric disorders such as depression, anxiety, and stress ("Female Drinkers and Drug Users," 2003; Kenny, Jones, & Barnett, 2015). Although the reasons for these differences are unclear, they must be considered as researchers and clinicians try to elucidate the causes, consequences, and most effective treatments for alcoholism.

## ▍ Malnutrition

As previously mentioned, malnutrition is a frequent and extremely serious consequence of severe alcoholism that tends to occur most often in less-affluent alcoholics. It has been suggested that malnutrition exaggerates the damage that alcohol causes to the body's organs, especially the liver. Malnutrition apparently expresses so frequently in this population because many alcoholics find it difficult to eat a balanced diet with adequate caloric intake. For example, heavy alcohol consumption often is associated with diets low in fruits and vegetables and high in calories from alcoholic beverages, added sugars, and unhealthy fats. Many alcoholics consume between 300 and 1,000 kilocalories per day (2,000 kilocalories per day is considered normal for an average adult male). In addition, most of the calories consumed by alcoholics come from alcohol, which contains seven kilocalories/gram (less than fat, which contains nine kilocalories/gram). The malnutrition problem is aggravated because alcohol's calories are empty; that is, alcohol does not contain other nutrients such as vitamins, minerals, protein, or fat. Because alcoholics may be deriving 50% or more of their usual caloric intake from alcoholic beverages, profound deficiencies in important nutrients result, leading to serious degeneration of health. In addition, the malnutrition problems may be further aggravated because of the damage done to the gastrointestinal tract by chronic exposure to the irritating effects of high doses of alcohol. This can damage the linings of both the stomach and intestines, thereby interfering with the proper absorption of essential nutrients from food (Buddy, 2019a; Thorley et al., 2015).

# LEARNING PORTFOLIO

## Discussion Questions

1. What evidence indicates that alcohol is a drug like marijuana, cocaine, or heroin?
2. Explain how alcohol is manufactured.
3. In the Western world, alcohol use has a long history. List and discuss some of these historical events, and describe how they affect present attitudes.
4. Explain how the effect of alcohol on brain function compares to that caused by other CNS depressants.
5. Explain how alcohol affects the mouth, stomach, small intestine, brain, liver, and bloodstream.
6. List at least five factors that affect the absorption rate of alcohol in the bloodstream.
7. Explain why alcohol is commonly consumed together with other drugs.
8. List three short-term effects of alcohol abuse.
9. Describe the symptoms and causes of a hangover.
10. What characterizes FAS?
11. How does gender affect responses to alcohol?
12. Why is malnutrition a common occurrence in alcoholics, and what are its consequences?

## Summary

1. Alcohol is considered a drug because it is a CNS depressant, and it affects both mental and physiological functioning.
2. Three types of poisonous alcohols are methyl alcohol, made from wood products; ethylene glycol, used as antifreeze; and isopropyl alcohol, used as an antiseptic. A fourth type, ethanol, is the alcohol used for drinking purposes.
3. The blood alcohol level produced depends on the presence of food in the stomach, the rate of alcohol consumption, the concentration of alcohol, and the drinker's body composition.
4. Alcohol depresses CNS activity at all doses. Low to moderate doses of alcohol interfere with motor activities, reflexes, and coordination. In moderate quantities, alcohol slightly increases heart rate; slightly dilates blood vessels in the arms, legs, and skin; and moderately lowers blood pressure. It stimulates appetite, increases production of gastric secretions, and at higher doses markedly stimulates urine output. The CNS depression incapacitates the individual, causing difficulty in walking, talking, and thinking.
5. Alcohol is commonly used in combination with other drugs (a) to enhance reinforcing properties, (b) to reduce the amount of expensive or hard-to-get drug required for an

## Key Terms

effect, (c) to reduce unpleasant side effects, or (d) because a predisposition for use of alcohol and other drugs exists.

6.  It is estimated that more than 50% of U.S. adults have had some history of problem drinking. Many of these persons can be so severely handicapped that they are unable to function normally in society. In the United States, only 20% of alcoholics receive appropriate treatment. In addition to important behavioral therapy, three medications have been approved by the FDA for adjunctive intervention for alcoholism: (a) disulfiram (Antabuse), which interferes with alcohol metabolism; (b) naltrexone (an opiate antagonist); and (c) acamprosate (Campral), which blocks the release of glutamate. Although these medications are quite useful in managing alcoholics, they are not universally effective.

7.  Some experts claim that moderate daily alcohol use can reduce cardiovascular diseases in men older than 50 years of age and in postmenopausal women, although recent findings do not support these conclusions.

8.  Long-term heavy alcohol use directly causes serious damage to nearly every organ and function of the body.

9.  Prolonged heavy drinking causes various types of muscle diseases and tremors. Heavy alcohol consumption causes irregular heartbeat. Heavy drinking over many years results in serious mental disorders and permanent, irreversible damage to the brain and peripheral nervous system. Memory, judgment, and learning ability can deteriorate severely.

10.  Women who are alcoholics or who drink heavily during pregnancy have a higher rate of spontaneous abortions. Infants born to drinking mothers have a high probability of suffering congenital defects such as FAS. These children have characteristic patterns of facial deformities, growth deficiency, joint and limb irregularities, and mental retardation.

11.  Alcohol has pervasive effects on the major organs and fluids of the body. Every part of the brain and nervous system is affected and can be damaged by alcohol. Among alcoholics, liver disorders include alcoholic fatty liver, alcoholic hepatitis, and cirrhosis. Alcohol also irritates tissue and damages the digestive system. Heavy use of alcohol seriously affects the blood, heart, sexual organs, endocrine system, and kidneys.

12.  Malnutrition is a common occurrence in severe alcoholism. It is the result of decreased caloric intake by alcoholics and the diminished consumption of essential nutrients because of the nutritional deficiency of alcoholic beverages and can lead to severe organ damage.

# References

Addiction Center. (2016, January 21). Polydrug use. Retrieved from http://www.addictioncenter.com/addiction/polydrug-use/

Addictions and Recovery. (2019). Alcohol abuse and alcoholism: Symptoms, withdrawal, treatment and recovery. Retrieved from https://www.addictionsandrecovery.org/alcohol-abuse-alcoholism.htm

Alcohol.org. (2019, July 15). Difference between alcohol tolerance vs. dependence, July 15. Retrieved from https://www.alcohol.org/effects/tolerance-vs-dependence/

Alcohol Justice. (2015, December). Alcopops: Sweet, cheap, and dangerous to youth. Retrieved from https://alcoholjustice.org/images/reports/AlcopopsReportFinalWeb.pdf

Alcohol Rehab Guide. (2019, May 15). Alcohol-related crimes. Newport Beach, CA: Northbound Treatment Services. Retrieved from https://www.alcoholrehabguide.org/alcohol/crimes/

American Psychiatric Association (APA). (2013). *Diagnostic and statistical manual of mental disorders*, 5th ed. Washington, DC: Author.

American Public University. (2010, March 7). Teenage smoking leads to increased susceptibility to alcohol withdrawal in adulthood. Retrieved from http://www.thaindian.com/newsportal/health/teenage-smoking-leads-to-increased-susceptibility-to-alcohol-withdrawal-in-adulthood_100330972.html

Aubrey, A. (2018, June 19). Drinking alcohol can raise cancer risk. How much is too much? NPR. Retrieved from https://www.npr.org/sections/thesalt/2018/06/19/621547571/drinking-alcohol-can-raise-cancer-risk-how-much-is-too-much

Beck, M. (2011, August 2). Testing the limits of tipsy. *Wall Street Journal.* Retrieved from https://www.wsj.com/articles/SB10001424053111903341404576482051743844220

Berchelmann, K. (2019). Why to have the alcohol talk early: A pediatrician-mom's perspective. Healthychildren.org. Retrieved from https://www.healthychildren.org/English/ages-stages/teen/substance-abuse/Pages/Why-to-Have-the-Alcohol-Talk-Early.aspx

Bishop, T. (2012, February 18). Huguely trial highlights alcohol abuse at colleges, universities. *Baltimore Sun.* Retrieved from http://articles.baltimoresun.com/2012-02-18/health/bs-md-student-drinking-20120216_1_binge-drinking-huguely-college-students

Brown, E., Hendrix, S., & Svriuga, S. (2015, June 14). Drinking is central to college culture and to sexual assault. *Washington Post.* Retrieved from https://www.washingtonpost.com/local/education/beer-pong-body-shots-keg-stands-alcohol-central-to-college-and-assault/2015/06/14/7430e13c-04bb-11e5-a428-c984eb077d4e_story.html

Buddy, T. (2019a). Alcohol's effect on nutrition. VeryWellMind. Retrieved from https://www.verywellmind.com/alcohols-effect-on-nutrition-3863403

Buddy, T. (2019b). Economic impact of alcohol abuse in the US. VeryWellMind. Retrieved from https://www.verywellmind.com/the-cost-of-excessive-alcohol-use-in-the-u-s-67482

Centers for Disease Control and Prevention (CDC). (2015). Facts sheet: Underaged drinking. Retrieved from http://www.cdc.gov/alcohol/fact-sheets/underage-drinking.htm

Chaudhuri, S. (2019, April 3). What health kick? Young Americans still thirst for alcopops. *Wall Street Journal.* Retrieved from https://www.wsj.com/articles/what-health-kick-young-americans-still-thirst-for-alcopops-11554296401

Compound Interest. (2016). The chemistry of a hangover. Retrieved from www.compoundchem.com/2016/01/01/hangover/

Crane, M. (2019). Genetics and addiction: Is alcoholism hereditary or genetic? American Addiction Centers. Retrieved from https://americanaddictioncenters.org/

D'Agostino, A. R., Wesley, M. J., Brown, J., & Fillmore, M. T. (2019). Effects of multisensory stop signals on alcohol-induced disinhibition in adults with ADHD. *Experimental and Clinical Psychopharmacology, 27*(3), 247–256. Retrieved from https://doi.org/10.1037/pha0000251

Dekker, A. (2019). What are the effects of alcohol on the brain?" *Scientific American.* Retrieved from https://www.scientificamerican.com/article/what-are-the-effects-of-a/

Dhawan, K., & Sharma, A. (2002). Prevention of chronic alcohol and nicotine-induced azospermia, sterility and decreased libido, by a novel tri-substituted benzoflavone moiety. *Life Science, 71,* 3059–3069.

DrugRehab.com. (n.d.). Social drinking. Advanced Recovery Systems. Retrieved from https://www.drugrehab.com/addiction/alcohol/social-situations/

Dryden, J. (2009, September 18). Young age at first drink may affect genes and risk for alcoholism. St. Louis, MO: Washington University. Retrieved from http://news.wustl.edu/news/Pages/14669.aspx

Dual Diagnosis. (2016). Disease theory of alcoholism. Retrieved from http://www.dualdiagnosis.org/alcohol-addiction/disease-theory-alcoholism/

Ducharme, J. (2018, August 24). A new study says any amount of drinking is bad for you. Here's what experts say. *Time.* Retrieved from https://time.com/5376552/how-much-alcohol-to-drink-study/

Dvorak, P. (2015, November 12). Parents who host teen drinking parties: Not cool, not smart, but they do it anyway. *Washington Post.* Retrieved from https://www.washingtonpost.com/local/parents-who-host-teen-drinking-parties-not-cool-not-smart-but-they-do-it-anyway/2015/11/12/a4a5a05e-8937-11e5-9a07-453018f9a0ec_story.html

Emanuele, M., & Emanuele, N. (2010). Alcohol and the male reproductive system. Bethesda, MD: National Institute on Alcohol Abuse and Alcoholism. Retrieved from https://pubs.niaaa.nih.gov/publications/arh25-4/282-287.htm

Epstein, J. (2010, June 4). Students aren't the only boozers. Inside Higher Ed. Retrieved from http://www.insidehighered.com/news/2010/06/04/acha

Evans, W. (2013, May 15). NTSB wants lower legal limit for blood alcohol. *Deseret News, 163,* A1.

Falloon, K. (2010, June 30). Naltrexone has mixed effects in alcoholics. Post-Gazette.com [Pittsburgh, PA]. Retrieved from http://post-gazette.com/pg/10181/1069113-114.stm

Federico, A., Cotticelli, G., Festi, D., Schiumerini, R., Addolorato, G., Ferrulli, A., . . . , Loguercio, C. (2015). The effects of alcohol on gastrointestinal tract, liver and pancreas; Evidence-based suggestions for clinical management. *European Review for Medical and Pharmacological Sciences, 19,* 1922–1940.

"Female drinkers and drug users tend to have more depressive disorders." (2003, March). *Women's Health Weekly,* p. 1.

Fleming, M., Mihic, S., & Harris, R. (2006). Ethanol. In L. Brunton, J. Lazo, & K. Parker *(Eds.), The pharmacological basis of therapeutics,* 11th ed. (pp. 591–606). New York, NY: McGraw-Hill.

Forever Recovery, A. (n.d.). 5 myths about alcohol abuse vs. the facts. Retrieved from aforeverrecovery.com/blog /information/5-myths-about-alcohol-abuse-vs-the-facts

Fuchs, F. (2004). Association between alcoholic beverage consumption and incidence of coronary heart disease in whites and blacks—The atherosclerosis risk in communities studies. *American Journal of Epidemiology, 160*, 466–474.

Gomberg, E. (2003). Treatment for alcohol-related problems: Special populations: Research opportunities. *Recent Developments in Alcoholism, 16*, 313–333.

Gowin, J. (2010, June 10). Your brain on alcohol: Is the conventional wisdom wrong about booze? *Psychology Today*. Retrieved from http://www.psychologytoday.com/blog /you-illuminated/201006/your-brain-alcohol

Gramlich, L., Tandon, P., & Rahman, A. (2019, June). Nutritional status in patients with sustained heavy alcohol use. UpToDate. Retrieved from https://www.uptodate.com /contents/nutritional-status-in-patients-with-sustained -heavy-alcohol-use

Grant, B., Goldstein, R., Saha, T., Chou, S. P., Jung, J., Zhang, H., . . . & Hasin, D. S. (2015). Epidemiology of DSM-5 alcohol use disorder. *JAMA Psychiatry, 72*, 757–766.

Greenfield, S. (2002). Women and alcohol use disorders. *Harvard Review Psychiatry, 10*, 76–85.

Hanson, G. R., & Li, T. K. (2003). Public health implications of excessive alcohol consumption. *Journal of the American Medical Association, 289*, 1031–1032.

Hedden, S. L., Martins, S. S., Malcolm, R. J., Floyd, L., Cavanaugh, C. E., & Latimer, W. W. (2010). Patterns of illegal drug use among an adult alcohol dependent population: Results from the national survey on drug use and health. *Drug and Alcohol Dependence, 106*, 119–125.

Hydes, T., Gilmore, W., Sheron, N., & Gilmore, I. (2019, February). Treating alcohol-related liver disease from a public health perspective. *Journal of Hepatology, 70*(2), 223–226.

Johns Hopkins Bloomberg School of Public Health. (2015). Center on Alcohol Marketing and Youth. Baltimore, MD: Author. Retrieved from http://camy.org/

Johnson, B. (2010). Medication treatment of different types of alcoholism. *American Journal of Psychiatry, 167*, 630–639.

Johnston, L. (2019). *Monitoring the Future 1975–2018*. Bethesda, MD: National Institute on Drug Abuse, National Institutes of Health. Retrieved from http://monitoring thefuture.org/pubs/monographs/mtf-overview2018.pdf

Kelly, A., Evens-Whipp, T., Chan, G., Tobourou, J., & Patton, G. (2015). A longitudinal study of the association of adolescent polydrug use, alcohol use, and high school non-completion. *Addiction, 110*, 627–635.

Kenna, G. (2013). Alcohol use disorders. In B. Aldredge (Ed.), *Applied therapeutics, Clinical use of drugs*, 10th ed. (pp. 2033–2054). Philadelphia, PA: Wolters Kluwer.

Kenny, S., Jones, R., & Barnett, N. (2015). Gender differences in the effect of depressive symptoms on prospective alcohol expectancies coping motives and alcohol outcomes in the first year of college. *Journal of Youth and Adolescence, 44*, 1884–1897. Retrieved from https://doi .org/10.1007/s10964-015-0311-3

Lautieri, A. (2019). Alcohol withdrawal symptoms, treatment and timeline. American Addiction Centers. Retrieved from https://americanaddictioncenters.org/withdrawal -timelines-treatments/alcohol

Lee, J. (2019). Asian flush research survey 2019—Finally some answers about Asian flush. Sunset. Retrieved from https://getsunset.com/blogs/news/asian-flush -research-survey-2019

Leigh, S. (2007, April 27). A woman's brain hit harder by alcohol abuse. Health Day. Retrieved from http://abcnews .go.com/Health/Healthday/story?id=4506743&page=1

Liquori, A., Gatto, C., & Jarrett, D. (2002). Separate and combined effects of marijuana and alcohol on mood, equilibrium and simulated driving. *Psychopharmacology, 163*, 399–405.

Listfield, E. (2011, June 12). The underage drinking epidemic. *Parade Special Report*, pp. 6–8.

Manejwala, O. (2014, February 13). How often do long-term sober alcoholics and addicts relapse? *Psychology Today*. Retrieved from https://www.psychologytoday.com /blog/craving/201402/how-often-do-long-term-sober -alcoholics-and-addicts-relapse

Masters, S., & Trevor, A. (2015). The alcohols. In B. Katzung (Ed.), *Basic and clinical pharmacology*, 13th ed. (pp. 384–395). New York, NY: McGraw-Hill.

Mayo Clinic. (2018). Alcohol use disorder. Mayo Clinic Patient Care and Health Information. Retrieved from https://www.mayoclinic.org/diseases-conditions /alcohol-use-disorder/symptoms-causes/syc-20369243

MedlinePlus. (2019). Alcoholism and alcohol abuse. Bethesda, MD: U.S. National Library of Medicine. Retrieved from https://medlineplus.gov/alcoholismandalcoholabuse .html

Miller, C. (2019). Mental health disorders and teen substance use. Child Mind Institute. Retrieved from https://childmind.org/article/mental-health-disorders -and-substance-use/

Morris, S. (2019). U.S. alcohol sales increased by 5.1% in 2018. The Drinks Business. Retrieved from https:// www.thedrinksbusiness.com/2019/01/us-alcohol-sales -increased-by-5-1-in-2018/

National Institute on Alcohol Abuse and Alcoholism (NIAAA). (2007). FAQs for the general public. Retrieved from http://www.niaaa.nih.gov/FAQs/General-English

National Institute on Alcohol Abuse and Alcoholism (NIAAA). (2018a). Alcohol facts and statistics. Retrieved from https://www.niaaa.nih.gov/alcohol-health/overview-alcohol-consumption/alcohol-facts-and-statistics

National Institute on Alcohol Abuse and Alcoholism (NIAAA). (2018b). Fall semester–A time for parents to discuss the risks for college drinking. Retrieved from https://www.niaaa.nih.gov/publications/brochures-and-fact-sheets/time-for-parents-discuss-risks-college-drinking

National Institute on Drug Abuse (NIDA). (2015, July). Sex and gender differences in substance use. Retrieved from https://www.drugabuse.gov/publications/research-reports/substance-use-in-women/sex-gender-differences-in-substance-use

National Institute on Drug Abuse (NIDA). (2018). Principles of drug addiction treatment: A research-based guide, 3rd ed. Retrieved from https://www.drugabuse.gov/publications/principles-drug-addiction-treatment-research-based-guide-third-edition/evidence-based-approaches-to-drug-addiction-treatment/pharmacotherapi-1

National Institute on Drug Abuse (NIDA). (2019). National survey results on drug use, 1975–2018. Retrieved from http://monitoringthefuture.org/pubs/monographs/mtf-overview2018.pdf

National Kidney Foundation. (2015). Alcohol and your kidneys. Retrieved from www.kidney.org/atoz/content/alcohol

Norton, A. (2007, April). Men and women show alcohol problems differently. Reuters Health. Retrieved from http://www.reuters.com/article/healthNews/id USLAU376770 20070423

Pager, T. (2015, June 11). Underaged drinking, binge boozing by minors is on the decline. *USA Today*. Retrieved from http://www.usatoday.com/story/news/2015/06/11/underage-binge-drinking/71021464/

Peters, E., & Hughes, J. (2010). Daily marijuana users with past alcohol problems increase alcohol consumption during marijuana abstinence. *Drug and Alcohol Dependence, 106*, 111–118.

Promises. (2019). 9 chilling effects of alcohol on the digestive system. Retrieved from https://www.promises.com/blog/long-term-effects-alcohol-intestines/

*Psychology Today*. (2007, May 1). Pregnant and under the influence. Retrieved from https://www.psychologytoday.com/articles/200304/pregnant-and-under-the-influence

Rabin, R. (2009, June 16). Alcohol's good for you? Some scientists doubt it. *The New York Times*. Retrieved from http://www.nytimes.com/2009/06/16/health/16alco.html

Reinberg, S. (2007). Drinking shrinks the brain. ABC News. Retrieved from http://abcnews.go.com/Health/Healthday/story?id=4506808&page=1

Reinberg, S. (2009, April 22). Binge drinking may damage teens' brains. ABC News. Retrieved from http://abcnews.go.com/Health/Healthday/story?id=7406188&page=1

Saisan, J., Smith, M., Robinson, L., & Segal, J. (2019, October). Substance abuse and mental health issues. HelpGuide. Retrieved from https://www.helpguide.org/articles/addictions/substance-abuse-and-mental-health.htm

Sandoiu, A. (2019). Alcohol use disorder: Brain damage may progress despite sobriety. Medical News Today. Retrieved from https://www.medicalnewstoday.com/articles/324901.php

ScienceDaily. (2019, April 30). Fetal alcohol spectrum disorder prevalence is very high in susceptible groups worldwide. Science News. Retrieved from https://www.sciencedaily.com/releases/2019/04/190430091840.htm

Special report: Alcohol: Weighing the benefits and risks for you. (1997, August). *UC Berkeley Wellness Letter, 13*, 4–5.

Substance Abuse and Mental Health Services Administration (SAMHSA). (2009). Treatment Episode Data Set (TEDS), 1999–2009. Retrieved from https://wwwdasis.samhsa.gov/dasis2/teds_pubs/2009_teds_rpt_natl.pdf

Szalavitz, M. (2015). Genetics: No more addictive personality. *Nature, 522*, 548–549.

Thomas, S. (n.d.). Alcohol and drug abuse statistics. American Addiction Centers. Retrieved from https://americanaddictioncenters.org/rehab-guide/addiction-statistics

Thomas, S. (2019). The effects of alcohol on the body. American Addiction Centers. Retrieved from https://americanaddictioncenters.org/alcoholism-treatment/body-effects

Thorley, H., Porter, K., Fleming, C., Jones, T., Kesten, J., Marques, E., Richards, A., & Savović, J. (2015, September 29). Interventions for preventing or treating malnutrition in problem drinkers. Who are homeless or vulnerably housed: Protocol for a systematic review. *Systematic Reviews, 4*, 131–140.

Trudeau, M. (2010, June 30). Teen drinking may cause irreversible brain damage. NPR. Retrieved from http://www.npr.org/templates/story/story.php?storyId=122765890

Villines, Z. (2019). What to know about alcohol and brain damage. Medical News Today. Retrieved from https://www.medicalnewstoday.com/articles/325644.php

Wallis, C. (2009, October 16). The genetics of addiction: Research shows how genes and the childhood experience pave the road to substance abuse. CNNMoney.com. Retrieved from http://money.cnn.com/2009/10/16/news/genes_addiction.fortune/index.htm

Ward, D. (2013, February 24). Even moderate drinking can boost risk of cancer. *Deseret News* [Salt Lake City, UT], *163*, A3.

WebMD. (2020). What is alcohol abuse? Retrieved from https://www.webmd.com/mental-health/addiction/what-is-alcohol-abuse#1

Weintraub, K. (2018, January 25). Study: Parents who give their teenagers alcohol are inviting trouble. *USA Today*. Retrieved from https://www.usatoday.com/story/news/2018/01/25/study-parents-who-give-their-teenagers-alcohol-inviting-trouble/1067481001/

World Health Organization (WHO). (2018). Alcohol. Media Center. Retrieved from http://www.who.int/mediacentre/factsheets/fs349/en/

Your health: Alcohol—The whole truth, seven half-truths about drinking, exposed. (1999, December). *Consumer Reports, 64*, 60–61.

# Alcohol: Behavioral Effects

## Did You Know?

▶ Seventy-seven percent of the U.S. population believes that, compared to all other drugs, alcohol creates the most family problems in our society.

▶ There were 139.8 million current drinkers (past month) of alcohol age 12 or older in 2018, including 67.1 million (48.0% of alcohol users) who were binge alcohol users and 16.6 million who were heavy alcohol users.

▶ Americans consumed twice as much alcohol in 1830 as they do now.

▶ Of all U.S. adult minority groups, Asian Americans have the highest rate of abstinence, the lowest rate of heavy drinking, and the lowest level of drinking-related problems.

▶ People have complained about fraternity drinking since 1840.

▶ Most of the economic costs of alcohol and drug problems fall on taxpayers who do not abuse alcohol and drugs.

▶ In 2018, 19%, of 8th graders, 38% of 10th graders, and 53% of 12th graders reported past year use of alcohol.

▶ On weekend nights throughout the United States, 70% of all fatal single-vehicle crashes involve a driver who is legally intoxicated.

▶ Less affluent people drink less than more affluent individuals.

## Learning Objectives

**On completing this chapter, you should be able to:**

❭ Cite some of the latest statistics on the use of alcohol.

❭ Cite the countries with the highest and lowest rates of alcohol consumption.

❭ Discuss the major ways that alcohol is costly to our society.

❭ Discuss the main events of the temperance movement and the Prohibition era.

❭ Define alcoholism and identify the general characteristics of an alcoholic.

❭ Cite some of the cultural differences for defining problem drinkers.

❭ Explain how culture influences views about alcohol.

❭ List four cultural factors that affect our views about alcohol consumption.

❭ List four findings about alcohol consumption and college students.

❭ Provide at least three reasons why the effects of alcohol consumption differ between women and men.

❭ Understand the differences between codependency and enabling behaviors.

❭ List two major factors that alcohol treatment must consider.

# Introduction

First interview:

I am the owner of this liquor store and most customers buy what they need and do not leave me with any negative impressions. However, there are a number of customers, maybe 10% who make impressions on me as well as Cindy [referring to a hired store clerk working at this liquor store]. With this small percentage of customers, you can tell by the look on their faces—often serious-looking faces—that they have a problem with the alcohol they are buying. It's a certain look that tells you they are more than likely to be seriously addicted to alcohol. Such people, both men and women, hand you the bottle they are buying and when they are paying their hand is shaking—like their hands are trembling. You can tell they want to buy the alcohol and go somewhere and gobble it up. These people are short on words, often crabby, expecting a quick purchase, and quickly head out the door. Some are dressed shabbily while others dress normally. Some look poor and with this small percentage many also look like my other working customers. These people [referring to the alleged problem drinkers] . . . usually purchase lower-end beer or hard liquor. Then there are the ones who appear to have worked a steady shift, and they are the ones with that "thirsty look." They are in a hurry to go home or wherever they go and drink it all down. This is what we think about these people. I have to say most of these problem drinkers pick out vodka then when they come up to the counter to get checked out, they pull money out of their pockets and the dollars and change are dropped on the counter for a quick getaway. Others have credit cards, and most of the rejected cards come from these types of drinkers I would label down and out. If the credit card is rejected, they have other ones or quickly leave, go back to their cars, and some passenger in the car hands over money so he or she can make the purchase. Then there are the talkative and lively problem drinkers in this group who often give me the feeling they are covering up a drinking problem. They joke around or mention something just to kill time while I ring up the sale. Funny how these types are quick to get away and drive off to what I think to go back home and drink. I am often left with the impression that all that friendliness is just a cover up, but then my sales associate sometimes disagrees with me after we exchange impressions. Cindy has a female's impression and mine is different at times. We do find it interesting how the majority of times we agree what we think we see in these customers after they have left the store. It's kind of sad at times to know so much and I think sometimes we are supporting their bad habits. *(From Venturelli's research files, male owner of a liquor store a smaller Midwestern town, age 56, November 5, 2015)*

Second interview:

I even knew a professor who would buy pints of whiskey as soon as we would open in the morning. He would drive off and go to your university [referring to the author's university] to teach. He was a heck of a nice fella, always ready with a joke and very pleasant to talk to, but I knew he had a problem with this stuff. *(From Venturelli's research files, female liquor store clerk in a small Midwestern town, age 50, August 9, 1999. Update: The professor with the alleged drinking problem has changed jobs and is no longer at this university.)*

Third interview:

I vividly recall at age 10 seeing at least three or four middle-aged men arrive at my father's tavern as soon as the doors were opened at 8:00 A.M. on most mornings, desperately looking for the morning's first drink of alcohol. I recall my dad would crack a raw egg into an eight-ounce glass. Draft beer and the raw egg filled the glass half full. The reason for the raw egg was to get some breakfast protein and the reason for the half-full glass of beer was because their hands were very shaky and they had to steady the drink to their mouths. Immediately following what my dad referred to as a "full" breakfast were at least several double shots of Jim Beam whiskey. These alcoholic customers had to have the drinks so that they could feel "normal" for the rest of the day. Some would even be dressed in formal attire ready to go off to their office jobs. *(Venturelli's personal observation)*

Fourth interview:

I have this friend who works as a restaurant manager and has a big drinking problem.

On most evenings, he calls as soon as he reaches home from work late at night. Each time, and as he is talking to me on the phone, I can hear the jingling of the ice cubes in his glass. Sometimes he already had a few cocktails before he calls so as soon as he starts talking, I can immediately distinguish by the way he speaks that he is already half-drunk. As he continues drinking and contradicting himself, in mostly a one-way conversation—him talking to me—I have to listen to a lot of nonsensical talk that makes me feel like he is using me as someone to call so he can unload all the problems that went on with his job for the day. After 10 to 15 minutes of listening, I often try to end the conversation by saying, "I have to get up real early tomorrow morning, so I need to get to bed." This usually ends the conversation. I realize he is lonely (living by himself), but why do I have to endure this nearly every night? I guess I feel sorry for him, but it is unfair to be used this way. He often claims he is an alcoholic and says at least he is a functioning alcoholic. I know he puts in many hours at work, and probably because he sees so many of his customers drinking all day long maybe he develops some kind of thirst for alcohol when he is off work. How many times he asks me to take him to the liquor store to buy vodka, and the funny thing is that I hardly drink anymore. Each time I take him to buy liquor on days when he is off work he always comes out with a half-gallon bottle of vodka that is usually consumed within a week. He cannot drive since his driving record is abominable with four DUIs to date. He says in 10 years he will be able to drive again—God help us when he does! At a very young age when he received his first DUI he went off the road completely drunk and hit a barn, actually went through a barn, and killed a steer with his car! I sometimes laugh about this when I picture the accident, but it is really not funny. Just imagine if it was a pedestrian or another car? I know he has a big alcohol problem, but it appears he also knows it without either desiring or seeking help for his alcoholism. I keep imagining what hell it must be if I had to live with him as his roommate. *(From Venturelli's research files, male high school teacher in a small Midwestern town, age 53, July 4, 2010)*

# Alcohol Consumption in the United States

Similar to nearly all societies past and present, alcohol has always been a part of American society. The preceding quotes illustrate how an individual can consume an excessive amount of a psychoactive and addictive substance without necessarily coming to the attention of anyone except perhaps a neighbor or friend, a lone liquor store owner or employee, or even a bar owner and his young son's observation. Furthermore, this same depressant chemical is often not perceived as a drug by many Americans. It is considered more of a social lubricant, something that is "always" consumed at social gatherings and perceived as normal at social gatherings.

Consider these findings from the National Household Survey on Drug and Health, 2018 (Substance Abuse and Mental Health Services Administration [SAMHSA], 2019):

**Figure 8.1A** from the National Household survey on Drug and Health, 2018 (SAMHSA, 2019), indicates the following:

There were 139.8 million **current drinkers** (past month) of alcohol aged 12 or older in 2018, including 67.1 million (48.0% of alcohol users) who were **binge alcohol users** and 16.6 million who were **heavy alcohol users**. (The 2018 estimate of past month alcohol use was similar to the estimates in most years from 2002 to 2017.). Thus, nearly half of current alcohol users were binge drinkers (48.0%), and 1 in 8 current alcohol users were heavy drinkers (11.8%). Among binge

## KEY TERMS

**current drinkers**
at least one drink in the past 30 days; can include binge and heavy use

**binge alcohol users**
a pattern of drinking five or more drinks for men and four or more drinks for women on a single occasion such as at the same time or within two hours of each other on at least one day in the past 30 days; includes heavy use

**heavy alcohol users**
five or more drinks on the same occasion on each of five or more days in the past 30 days or consuming an average of more than one alcoholic beverage per day for women and an average of more than two alcoholic beverages per day for men and any drinking by pregnant women or underage youth

drinkers, about 1 in 4 (24.7%) were heavy drinkers.

**Figure 8.1B** shows the following in regard to *binge alcohol use* in 2017:

- Approximately one in four people age 12 or older (24.5%) were current binge alcohol users.
- Though not shown, this percentage corresponds to about 66.6 million binge drinkers who were age 12 or older. About 1.3 million adolescents ages 12 to 17 were past-month binge drinkers, which corresponds to 5.3% of adolescents.
- Approximately, one in 20 adolescents ages 12 to 17 in 2017 were current binge drinkers.
- The highest percentages of binge alcohol use (36.9%) and heavy alcohol use (9.6%) were among young adults ages 18 to 25, which corresponds to about 12.7 million young adults. (Stated another way, more than a third of young adults in 2017 were current binge drinkers.) About a quarter (24.7%) of adults aged 26 or older were current binge drinkers.

In regard to *heavy alcohol use* in Figure 8.1B, the following findings are noteworthy:

- In 2017, 174,000 adolescents ages 12 to 17 were current heavy drinkers.

- About one out of every 10 young adults ages 18 to 25 (9.6%) were current heavy alcohol drinkers.
- An estimated 6.2% of adults age 26 or older in 2017 were current heavy drinkers.

**Figure 8.1C** shows current, binge, and heavy alcohol use among persons age 12 or older by age in 2018. Note that the 21–25 year olds are the heaviest consumers of alcohol (across the categories of current, binge, and heavy alcohol drinkers).

## Trends in Alcohol Consumption

In a 2013 Gallup poll examining alcohol consumption, it was reported that "Americans who drink alcohol continue to say they most often choose beer (40%) over wine (30%) and liquor (26%). Beer has typically been the preferred alcoholic beverage" (McCarthy, 2017) in prior polls conducted by Gallup.

Other findings are the following:

- Sixty-two percent "of male drinkers say they prefer beer, compared with 19% of female drinkers" (McCarthy, 2017).
- "Women are significantly more likely than men to prefer wine, at 50% for females and 11% for males" (McCarthy, 2017). Wine is also preferred among college-educated adults.

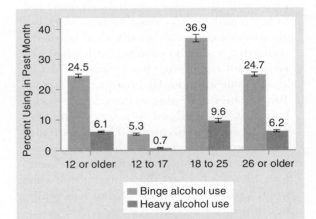

A

139.8 million alcohol users

67.1 million binge alcohol users (48.0% of alcohol users)

16.6 million heavy alcohol users (24.7% of binge alcohol users and 11.8% of alcohol users)

B

Note: Since 2015, the threshold for determining binge alcohol use for males is consuming five or more drinks on an occasion and for females is consuming four or more drinks on an occasion.

**FIGURE 8.1** (A) Current, binge, and heavy alcohol use among people aged 12 or older: 2018. (B) Past month binge and heavy alcohol use among people age 12 or older by age group: percentages, 2017. *(continues)*

(A) Data from Substance Abuse and Mental Health Services Administration (SAMHSA). (2019). *Results from the 2018 National Survey on Drug Use and Health: Detailed tables.* Rockville, MD: Author. Retrieved from https://www.samhsa.gov /data; (B) Data from Substance Abuse and Mental Health Services Administration (SAMHSA). (2019). *Key substance use and mental health indicators in the United States: Results from the 2018 National Survey on Drug Use and Health* (HHS Publication No. PEP19-5068, NSDUH Series H-54). Rockville, MD: Author.

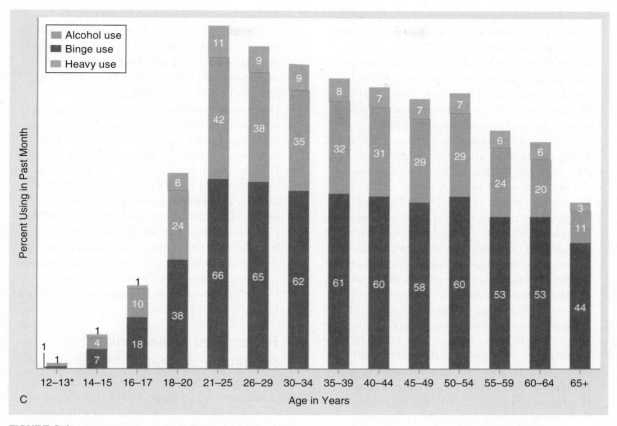

**FIGURE 8.1** (*continued*) (C) Current, binge, and heavy alcohol use among persons age 12 or older by age: 2018.

(C) Data from Substance Abuse and Mental Health Services Administration (SAMHSA). (2019). *Results from the 2018 National Survey on Drug Use and Health: Detailed tables.* Rockville, MD: Author. Retrieved from https://www.samhsa.gov/data

- Thirty-eight percent "of U.S. adults totally abstain from alcohol. That figure has remained below 40% since 1997" (McCarthy, 2017).
- Most Americans believe that moderate drinking does not affect health (Riffkin, 2015).
- Twenty-eight percent "[of Americans polled] . . . say one or two drinks a day is bad for health" (Riffkin, 2015).
- "Americans who drink are more likely to say it is good for health" (Riffkin, 2015).
- "Eight in 10 upper-income American college grads drink alcohol" (Jones, 2015).
- "About half of lower-income Americans drink" (Jones, 2015).
- "Thirty-six percent say alcohol has been a cause of trouble in their family" (Jones, 2014).
- "Americans who attend religious services weekly are less likely than others to drink alcohol, reflecting the centuries-old connection in American history between religion and the perceived immorality of drinking" (Newport, 2019).
- Regarding weekly church attendees. "drinking is no longer the moral and political issue it once was, as other issues—namely, abortion and gay and lesbian relations—have taken their place as major causes activating and animating the Religious Right" (Newport, 2019).
- There are large geographical differences across the world. Alcohol consumption across North Africa and the Middle East is particularly low— in many countries, close to zero. At the upper end of the scale, alcohol intake across Eastern Europe is highest at 14–17 liters (14 liters equals approximately four U.S. liquid gallons and 17 liters equals 4.4 US gallons) per person per year across Belarus, Russia, the Czech Republic, and Lithuania (Ritchie & Roser, 2018).
- In terms of the share of the prevalence (not intensity) of drinking, it is highest across Western Europe and Australia. In 2010, close to 95% of adults in France had drunk alcohol in the preceding year. Again, the prevalence of drinking across North Africa and the Middle East is notably lower than elsewhere. Typically, 5% to 10% of adults across these

regions had consumed alcohol within the preceding year, and this was below 5% in several countries (Ritchie & Roser, 2018).

- When we look at gender differences, we see that men in all countries are more likely to drink than women (Ritchie & Roser, 2018).
- In Madagascar, 65% of drinkers had a heavy session of drinking or binging within the preceding month. Lithuania, Paraguay, Finland, Mongolia, Austria, and Benin all had more than 50% of drinkers having a heavy session within the prior month (Ritchie & Roser, 2018).
- Worldwide, adults (those 21 or older) consume on average five liters[1] of pure alcohol from beer, wine, and spirits per year. The average alcohol consumption is highest in Europe, followed by the Americas and Africa. Alcohol consumption tends to increase with economic development; however, consumption remains low in some regions where the majority of the population is Muslim (GreenFacts, 2009).
- The World Health Organization (WHO) reported that throughout the world, the following ten countries has the highest average alcohol consumption of pure alcohol per capita (per person): Belarus (ranked first with 14.4 liters); Lithuania, (ranked second with 12.9 liters); Grenada (ranked third with11.9 liters); the Czech Republic and France (ranked fourth with 11.8 liters each); Russia (ranked fifth with 11.4 liters); Ireland, Luxembourg, and Slovakia (ranked sixth with 11.4 liters each); Germany and Hungry (ranked seventh with 11.3 liters); Portugal (ranked eighth with 11.0 liters), Poland (ranked ninth with 10.9 liters); Slovenia (ranked 10th with 1.6 liters) and the United States (ranked 25th with (8.7 liters) (Alcohol.org, 2019). Consumption of alcohol was lowest in Egypt and Niger (with 0.3 liter per capita over 15+ years), Bangladesh, Comoros, Saudi Arabia, and Yemen (each with 0.2 liters), Kuwait and Mauritania (with 0.1 liters each) (VinePair, 2019).
- Illicit drug use in 2013 varied by the educational status of adults 18 or older. The rate of current

illicit drug use was lower among college graduates (6.7%) than those with some college education but no degree (10.8%), high school graduates with no further education (9.9%), and those who had not graduated from high school (11.8%) (SAMHSA, 2014).

- Drinking is commonly believed to be associated with poverty, but a Gallup poll found that the people most likely to drink have higher incomes, are younger than 65, do not attend church, live in regions of the United States other than the South, and are more likely to identify themselves as liberals (Newport, 2000).
- Research continues to show that most of the economic burden of alcohol and drug problems falls on the population of taxpayers who do not abuse alcohol and drugs. Government, private insurance, and other members of households bear most of these costs (Miller & Hendrie, 2008).

## ▌ Percentages of the Drinking Population: A Pyramid Model

What percentage of our society drinks alcohol? We can construct a pyramid based on the amount of alcohol consumed, the pattern of drinking, or the "problem" or "illness" dimension (e.g., by attempting to calculate what proportion of Americans are "abusers" or "dependent"). For example, at the beginning of this chapter, several interviews discussed people who bought and consumed liquor and are prime examples of alcohol drinkers who probably imbibe approximately one quart per day. By most definitions, this is a clear diagnostic criterion for a diagnosis of alcoholism. It is interesting that all four of the chapter's opening examples indicate that the alcohol drinkers are apparently functional, or at least they manage to create this impression.

The pyramid in **Figure 8.2** has a base of 35% of people who are **teetotalers**, then a layer of about 13% who occasionally drink, and a top 52% who drink regularly. In 2018, 24.7% (67.1 million) of those age 12 or older reported that they engaged in binge drinking in the past month; 16.6 million people age 12 or older (6.1% of the population) reported that they engaged in heavy alcohol use[2] in the preceding month (SAMHSA, 2019).

---

[1]One liter is equivalent to 0.264172 U.S. liquid gallon or 1.05669 U.S. liquid quart.

[2]Heavy alcohol use is defined as binge drinking on five or more days in the past 30 days.

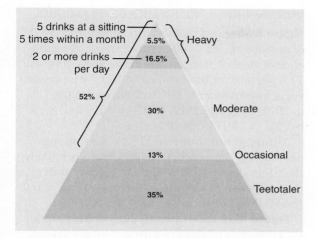

5 drinks at a sitting / 5 times within a month — 5.5% Heavy

2 or more drinks per day — 16.5%

52%

30% Moderate

13% Occasional

35% Teetotaler

**FIGURE 8.2** Broad distribution of drinking behaviors.

Different definitions of what constitutes heavy drinking exist. Thus, if we define heavy drinking differently—for example, as more than two drinks per day—we come up with a much larger slice of the pyramid—three times as large.

## ▪ Prevalence of Drinking in the U.S.

According to the 2015 National Survey on Drug Use and Health (NSDUH), 86% of people age 18 or older reported that they drank alcohol at some point in their lifetime, 70% reported that they drank in the past year, and 56% reported that they drank in the past month (SAMHSA, 2016a).

Regarding binge drinking in 2015, 26.9% of people age 18 or older reported that they engaged in binge drinking in the preceding month; 7.0% reported that they engaged in heavy alcohol use in the past month (SAMHSA, 2016b).

## ▪ Dual Problems: Underage and Adult Drinking

As we saw in Figure 8.1, alcohol consumption does not have age boundaries. Although all states have had a legal drinking age of 21 since 1988, a high percentage of the underage population drinks alcohol. Overall, in looking at a larger and more detailed picture of the percentages and types of groups reporting alcohol use in 2013, the following findings have been reported.

### UNDERAGE ALCOHOL USE

- Alcohol remains the substance most widely used by today's teenagers.
- Alcohol use is more widespread than use of illicit drugs. Nearly three-fifths of 12th grade students (59%) have at least tried alcohol, and nearly one-third (30%) are current drinkers—that is, they reported consuming some alcohol in the 30 days prior to the survey. Even among 8th graders, nearly a quarter (24%) reported some alcohol use in their lifetime, and one in 13 (8.0%) reported being a current (past 30 days) drinker (Miech, et al., 2019).

- Of greater concern than just any use of alcohol is its use to the point of intoxication: In 2018 more than two out of five 12th graders (43%), one-quarter of 10th graders (26%), and about one in 11 of all 8th graders (9.2%) said they had been drunk at least once in their lifetimes (Miech et al., 2019).

- Despite recent declines, by the end of high school six out of every 10 students (59% after a significant three percentage point drop in 2018) have consumed more than just a few sips of alcohol at some time in their lives, and about a quarter (24%) have done so by 8th grade (SAMHSA, 2019).

- An estimated 9.0% of adolescents ages 12 to 17 in 2018 were current alcohol users, which corresponds to 2.2 million adolescents who drank alcohol in the preceding month (SAMHSA, 2019).

- About 1.2 million adolescents age 12 to 17 in 2018 were past-month binge drinkers, which corresponds to 4.7% of adolescents. Thus, about one in 21 adolescents were current binge drinkers (SAMHSA, 2019).

- In 2018, an estimated 2.4 million adolescents age 12 to 17 used alcohol for the first time in the preceding year, which averages to approximately 6,500 adolescents each day who initiated alcohol use (SAMHSA, 2019).

- In 2018, an estimated 131,000 adolescents age 12 to 17 were current heavy drinkers. Stated another way, about one out of 200 adolescents (0.5%) engaged in binge drinking on five or more days in the preceding 30 days (SAMHSA, 2019).

- In 2018, about two out of three adolescents age 12 to 17 perceived great risk of harm from having four or five drinks of alcohol nearly every day (64%) (SAMHSA, 2019).

- An estimated 1.6% (401,000) adolescents age 12 to 17 in 2018 had a past-year alcohol use disorder (SAMHSA, 2019).

- In 2018, about 946,000 adolescents aged 12 to 17 needed substance use treatment in the preceding year. This number corresponds to 3.8% of adolescents, or about 1 in 26 adolescents (SAMHSA, 2019).

- Males and females aged 12 to 20 in 2013 had similar rates of current alcohol use (23% and 22.5%, respectively). However, underage males were more likely than underage females to report binge (15.8% vs. 12.4%) or heavy alcohol use (4.6% vs. 2.7%) (SAMHSA, 2013).

- Students may be more likely to drink and drive on prom and graduation nights, according to a survey of 11th- and 12th-grade students across the country. Nearly all of the students surveyed (90%) said that their peers are more likely to drink and drive on prom night, and 79% reported the same for graduation night. Although another study indicated that "teens aged 16 to 19, published by AAA in 2014, found that 31% to 41% of teens said it was likely that they or their friends would use drugs or alcohol on prom night" (Promises Treatment Centers, 2019). Despite this belief, students do not seem to think that driving on these nights is dangerous. Less than-one third (29%) reported that they believe that driving on prom night comes with a high degree of danger, and 25% said the same for graduation night. These findings suggest that there is a need to provide high school students with prevention messages that paint an accurate picture of the risks and consequences of drinking and driving during prom and graduation season (Center for Substance Abuse Research [CESAR], 2010).

## ALCOHOL USE: AGE 12 OR OLDER BY ETHNICITY AND RACE

- **Figure 8.3A** shows that, among persons age 12 or older in 2018, whites were more likely than other racial or ethnic group to report current use of alcohol (56.7%). The rates were 46.0% for persons reporting two or more races, 41.0% for Hispanics or Latinos, 35.9% for American Indians and Alaska Natives, 43.0% for blacks, and 39.3% for Asians (SAMHSA, 2019).

- In 2019, Asians had the lowest overall rates of binge drinking or heavy use of alcohol rates across all age groups whereas whites had the highest current, binge, and heavy alcohol use.

## DRIVING UNDER THE INFLUENCE OF ALCOHOL

**Figure 8.3B** shows that in 2018, an estimated 8.0% of persons age 12 or older drove under the influence of alcohol at least once in the preceding year. This percentage has been consistent with previous years: approximately 12% in 2008 and 2009; 11% in 2010, 2011, and 2012; 10.9% in 2013; and 8.4% in 2017 (SAMHSA, 2019).

Although not shown in Figure 8.3, among persons age 12 or older, males were more likely than females (10.8% vs. 6.2%) to drive under the influence of alcohol in the preceding year (SAMHSA, 2019).

**Figure 8.3C** shows that in 2013 driving under the influence of alcohol differed by age group. An estimated 3.8% of those age 16 or 17, 10.8% of those age 18 to 20, and 19.7% of those age 21 to 25 reported driving under the influence of alcohol in the preceding year. Note that the 21- to 25-year-old age group had the highest percentage (13.8%) of driving under the influence of alcohol in the preceding year. With increasing age after 26, these rates show a general steady decline in driving under the influence (SAMHSA, 2019).

## EDUCATION AND ALCOHOL USE

- Among adults age 18 or older, the rate of past-month alcohol use increased with increasing levels of education. Among adults in 2013 with less than a high school education, 36.5% were current drinkers. In comparison, 69.2% of college graduates were current drinkers (SAMHSA, 2014).

- Among adults age 18 or older, rates of binge and heavy alcohol use varied by level of education. Among adults in 2013, those who had graduated from college were *less likely* than those with some college education but no degree to be binge drinkers (23.1% vs. 26.4%) or heavy drinkers (6.0% vs. 7.6%) (SAMHSA, 2014).

## AGE DIFFERENCES

Ages 12 to 17:

- *Any alcohol use*—An estimated 9.0% of adolescents 12 to 17 in 2018 were current alcohol users; this corresponds to 2.2 million adolescents who drank alcohol in the preceding month.

- *Binge alcohol use*—About 1.2 million adolescents aged 12 to 17 in 2018 were past-month binge drinkers, which corresponds to 4.7% of adolescents.

- *Heavy alcohol use*—In 2018, an estimated 131,000 adolescents 12 to 17 were current heavy drinkers. Stated another way, about one out of 200 adolescents (0.5%) engaged in binge drinking on five or more days in the preceding 30 days.

Aged 18 to 25:

- *Any alcohol use*— In 2018, an estimated 55.1% of young adults ages 18 to 25 were current alcohol users, which corresponds to about 18.8 million young adults.
- *Binge drinking*—An estimated 34.9% of young adults 18 to 25 in 2018 were binge drinkers in

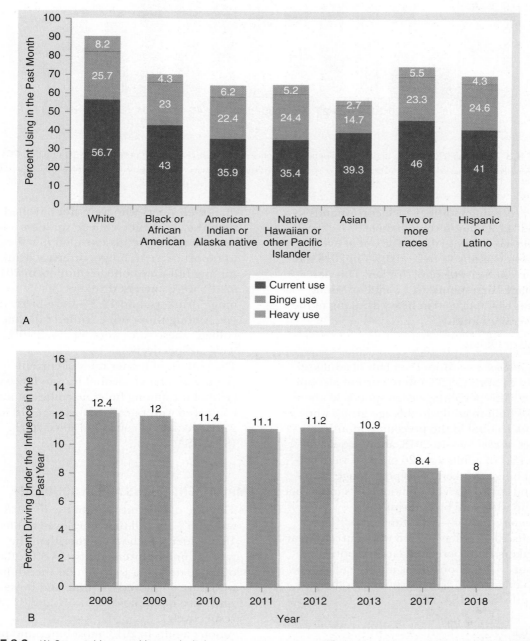

**FIGURE 8.3** (A) Current, binge, and heavy alcohol use among persons age 12 or older by race and ethnicity: 2018. (B) Driving under the influence of alcohol in the past year among persons aged 12 or older in 2008–2013 and 2017–2018. (*continues*)

(A and B) Data from Substance Abuse and Mental Health Services Administration (SAMHSA). (2019). *Key substance use and mental health indicators in the United States: Results from the 2018 National Survey on Drug Use and Health* (HHS Publication No. PEP19-5068, NSDUH Series H-54). Rockville, MD: Author. Retrieved from https://www.samhsa.gov/data/report/2018-nsduh-detailed-tables

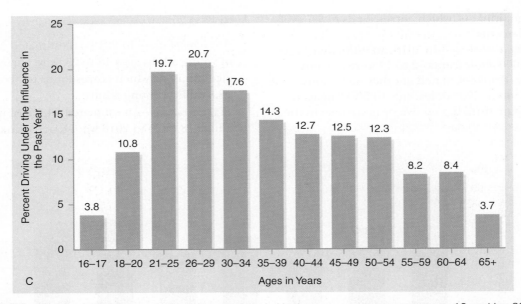

**FIGURE 8.3** *(continued)* (C) Driving under the influence of alcohol in the past year among persons age 16 or older: 2014.

(C) Substance Abuse and Mental Health Services Administration (SAMHSA). (2015). *Results from the 2014 National Survey on Drug Use and Health: Summary of National Findings.* Data from NSDUH Series H-48, HHS Publication No. SMA 14-4863. Rockville, MD: Author.

the preceding month, which corresponds to about 11.9 million young adults.

- *Heavy alcohol use*—About one out of every 11 young adults 18 to 25 (9.0%) in 2018 was a current heavy alcohol drinker. This percentage corresponds to 3.1 million young adults who engaged in heavy drinking in the preceding month

Aged 26 or Older:

- *Any alcohol use*—More than half of adults 26 or older in 2018 (55.3%) were current alcohol users. This percentage corresponds to about 118.8 million adults in this age group who drank alcohol in the preceding month.
- *Binge alcohol use*—In 2018, about a quarter (25.1%) of adults ages 26 or older were current binge drinkers. This percentage corresponds to about 54.0 million adults in this age group who were binge drinkers.
- *Heavy alcohol use*—An estimated 6.2% of adults 26 or older in 2018 were current heavy drinkers. This percentage corresponds to about 13.4 million adults in this age group who engaged in heavy drinking in the past month (SAMHSA, 2019).

## COLLEGE STUDENTS AND ALCOHOL USE

- Young adults ages 18 to 22 who were enrolled full time in college were more likely than their peers who were not enrolled full-time (i.e., part-time college students and persons not currently enrolled in college) to report current, binge, or heavy drinking. Among full-time college students in 2018, 59.9% were current drinkers, 30.0% were binge drinkers, and 12.3% were heavy drinkers. Among those not enrolled full-time in college, these rates were 50.2%, 25.0%, and 9.6%, respectively.
- The pattern of higher rates of current alcohol use, binge alcohol use, and heavy alcohol use among full-time college students compared with rates for others ages 18 to 22 has remained consistent since 2002 (SAMHSA, 2019).

## EMPLOYMENT STATUS AND ALCOHOL USE

- The rate of current alcohol use in 2018 was 64.8% for full-time employed adults 18 or older, which was higher than the rate for unemployed adults (53.8%). Rates of binge drinking were similar for adults who were employed full-time and those who were unemployed (31.5% and 31.3%, respectively).
- Among adults in 2013, most binge and heavy alcohol users were employed. Among the 58.5 million adults who were binge drinkers,

44.5 million (76.1%) were employed either full- or part-time. Among the 16.2 million adults who were heavy drinkers, 12.4 million (76.0%) were employed.

## ALCOHOL AND THE VERY YOUNG

Use of either of the two major licit drugs, alcohol and cigarettes, remains more widespread than the use of any illicit drug. In 2018, 19% of 8th graders, 38% of 10th graders, and 53% of 12th graders reported past year use of alcohol (Miech et al., 2019). Most important was the prevalence of occasions of binge drinking—five or more drinks in a row at least once in the prior two-week period—which was reported by 3.7% of 8th graders, 8.7% of 10th graders, 13.8% of 12th graders, and 38% of college students (Miech et al., 2019). A noteworthy finding is that for 8th, 10th, and 12th graders combined, marijuana usage on a daily basis exceeds alcohol usage.

Of greater concern than just any use of alcohol is its use to the point of inebriation. In 2018, 6.5% of 8th graders, 21% of 10th graders, and 34% of 12th graders said they had been drunk at least once in their lifetime (Miech et al., 2019).

Another measure of heavy drinking asks respondents to report on how many occasions during the last two weeks they had consumed five or more drinks in a row, which is also defined as binge drinking. In 2018, prevalence levels for this behavior were 13.8%, 8.7%, and 3.7% in the 12th, 10th, and 8th grade, respectively (Miech, et al. 2019; see "Point–Counterpoint: Lower the Legal Drinking Age?").

With regard to the three major types of alcohol (beer, wine coolers, and liquor) used by junior high and high school students, alcohol consumption continues to significantly proliferates from the ninth through the 12th grade (Miech, Johnston, O'Malley, Bachman, & Schulenberg, 2015; Miech et al., 2019). In looking at 12th graders' consumption of alcohol, white underage students are much more likely to binge drink (24%) compared with African American students (11%) and Hispanic students (20%). Finally, boys in 12th grade are more likely to drink alcohol on a daily basis compared with girls of the same grade and age; daily use among boys was reported at 1.6%, whereas the rate among girls was reported at 0.5%. Boys are more likely than girls to drink large quantities of alcohol in a single sitting: 16% of 12th-grade males reported drinking five or more drinks in a row two weeks prior to being surveyed, but only 12% of the 12th-grade females reported drinking the same amount (Miech et al., 2019). When reviewing the statistics, keep in mind that females differ from males in terms of their alcohol drinking capacities.

## ▶POINT/COUNTERPOINT

### Lower the Legal Drinking Age?

The United States is one of 20 countries that has set the minimum legal drinking age at 21. **Table 8.1** and the following figure show the exceptions to this minimum age for the consumption of alcohol as of 2019.

A clear majority of 103 countries throughout the world do not have any minimum drinking age to drink alcohol (see Table 8.1). In the next highest number, 66 countries have set the minimum drinking age at 18 years (Hanson, 2019a). Internationally, the average age at which drinking alcohol first occurs is 12 years, and about 80% of young people begin drinking alcoholic beverages regularly at age 15 or younger, according to the World Health Organization (Hanson, 2019a).

Arguments against lowering the legal limit for consuming alcohol are as follows:

- A higher minimum legal drinking age (MLDA) is effective in preventing alcohol-related deaths and injuries among youth. When the MLDA is lowered, injury and death rates increase; when the MLDA is increased, death and injury rates decline (McCartt & Kirley, 2006; Wagenaar, 1993).

- A higher MLDA results in fewer alcohol-related problems among youth, and an MLDA of 21 years saves the lives of more than 1,000 youth each year. Conversely, when the MLDA is lowered, motor vehicle crashes and deaths among youth increase. At least 50 studies have evaluated this correlation (McCartt & Kirley, 2006; Wagenaar, 1993).

*(continues)*

# ►POINT/COUNTERPOINT

## Lower the Legal Drinking Age? (*continued*)

- Research shows that when the MLDA is 21, people younger than 21 drink less overall and continue to do so through their early 20s (O'Malley & Wagenaar, 1991).

- Higher MLDAs reduce traffic fatalities involving drivers 18 to 20 years old by saving approximately 1,000 lives each year (American Medical Association [AMA], 2011).

- Although younger drivers are less likely than adults to drink and drive, their risk of crashing is substantially higher when they do drink and drive (McCartt & Kirley, 2006).

- The evidence is clear that a MLDA can deter underage drinking and driving and reduce alcohol-related crashes among young drivers (McCartt & Kirley, 2006).

Arguments for lowering the legal limit for consuming alcohol are as follows:

- The United States has the strictest youth drinking laws in Western civilization and yet has the most drinking-related problems among its young, and there seems to be a connection between these two facts (Hanson, 2019a).

- A study of a large sample of young people between ages 16 and 19 in Massachusetts and New York after Massachusetts raised its drinking age revealed that average self-reported daily alcohol consumption in Massachusetts did not decline in comparison with New York (Hanson, 2013b).

- Comparison of college students attending schools in states that had maintained for at least 10 years a minimum drinking age of 21 with those in states that had similarly maintained minimum drinking ages below 21 revealed few differences in drinking problems (Hanson, 2013b).

- A study of all 50 states and the District of Columbia found "a positive relationship between the purchase age and single-vehicle fatalities." Thus, single-vehicle fatalities were found to be more frequent in those states with high purchase ages (Hanson, 2013b).

- Comparison of drinking before and after the passage of raised minimum age legislation has generally revealed little impact on behavior. For example, a study that examined college students' drinking behavior before and after an increase in the minimum legal drinking age from 18 to 19 in New York found the law had no impact on underage students' consumption rates, intoxication rates, drinking attitudes, or drinking problems. These studies were

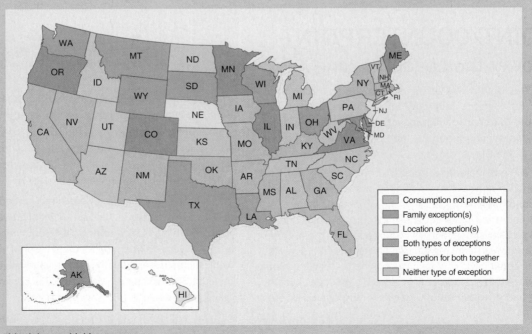

Legend:
- Consumption not prohibited
- Family exception(s)
- Location exception(s)
- Both types of exceptions
- Exception for both together
- Neither type of exception

World minimum drinking ages.

# ►POINT/COUNTERPOINT

## Lower the Legal Drinking Age? (*continued*)

corroborated by other researchers at a different college in the same state (Hanson, 2013b).

- An examination of East Carolina University students' intentions regarding their behavior after the increase of the MLDA to age 21 revealed that only 6% intended to stop drinking, 70% planned to change their drinking location, 21% expected to use a false or borrowed identification to obtain alcohol, and 22% intended to use other drugs. Anecdotal statements by students indicated the belief by some that it "might be easier to hide a little pot in my room than a six pack of beer" (Hanson, 2013b).

- Finally, a summation of drinking by youth below age 21 is also strongly linked with:

  - death from alcohol poisoning;
  - unintentional injuries such as car crashes, falls, burns, and drowning;
  - suicide and violence such as fighting and sexual assault;
  - changes in brain development;
  - school performance problems such as higher absenteeism and poor or failing grades;
  - alcohol dependence later in life; and
  - other risk behaviors such as smoking, abuse of other drugs, and risky sexual behaviors (CDC, 2018a).

Research and the information from sources in this chapter indicate that with regard to under-21 alcohol violations, the United States continues to have serious problems. Thus, we are not any better than most countries regarding the percentage of minors consuming alcohol, despite our unique MLDA of age 21 for alcohol consumption. Instead of prohibiting alcohol consumption to those younger than age 21 (which, to date, continues to be ineffective), perhaps we need to teach moderation at an early age so that the percentage of youth who decide to consume alcohol can learn to do so responsibly. Given that the MLDA of 21 years has not deterred our nation's youth from consuming

alcohol, and in light of younger and younger age groups consuming alcohol, it may be time to reconsider lowering the age limit of alcohol consumption for the following reasons.

1. We can be more in alignment with the majority of countries. Currently, 82 countries allow alcohol consumption at 18 years of age or older.

2. We can eliminate costly, burdensome, and unnecessary underage drinking violations. These infractions with the law include fines, legal costs, imprisonment, court time, legal expenses, and introducing our nation's youth into the criminal justice system (which many believe should remain "lean and mean" so it can effectively prohibit and prosecute serious law violators).

3. We can teach responsible drinking and drinking in moderation, and alcohol consumption can be promoted and taught to be a "normal" part of behavior when eating or socializing with friends (like consuming coffee or fruit juice). Such prevention measures can clearly emphasize that excessive alcohol consumption is a sign of immaturity and lack of self-respect.

How successful do you think a campaign calling for lowering the legal drinking age would be with (1) family members, (2) your school, (3) your community, (4) your city or town, and (5) U.S. society in general? Would it be successful? If yes, why? If no, why not? Have you had any experiences in foreign countries where alcohol consumption was not severely restricted? If so, what did you observe?

In essence, do you think we should try to change the current drinking laws in light of the fact that the current laws continue to be violated by youths under 21? Should the United States become like other progressive nations regarding age limits on the use of alcohol? What are the pros and cons of lowering the drinking rates in the United States? At what specific age should the consumption of alcohol be legal?

Data from American Medical Association (AMA). (2011). Facts about youth and alcohol. Chicago, IL: Author; Hanson, D. J. (2009). Binge drinking. Potsdam, NY: State University of New York, Sociology Department. Retrieved from http://www2.potsdam.edu/hansondj/BingeDrinking.html; Hanson, D. J. (2013a). Minimum legal drinking ages around the world. Alcohol problems and solutions. Retrieved from http://www2.potsdam.edu/hansondj/LegalDrinkingAge .htm; Hanson, D. J. (2013b). Binge drinking. Potsdam, NY: State University of New York, Sociology Department. Retrieved from http://www2.potsdam .edu/hansondj/BingeDrinking.html; McCartt, A. T., & Kirley, B. B. (2006). Minimum purchase age laws: How effective are they in reducing alcohol-impaired driving? Arlington, VA: Insurance Institute for Highway Safety. Retrieved from http://onlinepubs.trb.org/onlinepubs/circulars/ec123.pdf; O'Malley, P. M., & Wagenaar, A. C. (1991). Effects of minimum drinking age laws on alcohol use, related behaviors and traffic crash involvement among American youth: 1976–1987. *Journal of Studies on Alcohol, 52,* 478–491; Wagenaar, A. C. (1993). Minimum drinking age and alcohol availability to youth: Issues and research needs. In M. E. Hilton & B. Bloss (Eds.), *Economics and the prevention of alcohol-related problems* (pp. 175–200); Hanson, D. J. (2019b). Legal drinking ages around the world—You'll be surprised. Potsdam, NY: State University of New York, Sociology Department. Retrieved from https://www.alcohol problemsandsolutions.org/legal-drinking-ages-around-the-world/

**TABLE 8.1** World Minimum Drinking Ages

| None | 16 | 17 | 18 | 19 | 20 | 21 |
|---|---|---|---|---|---|---|
| 1. Angola | 1. Austria (18 in some areas and varies by beverage) | 1. Malta | 1. Albania | 1. Nicaragua | 1. Iceland | 1. American Samoa |
| 2. Anguilla | | | 2. Andorra | 2. South Korea | 2. Japan | 2. Cameroon (18 with a 21 year old) |
| 3. Armenia | | | 3. Angola | | 3. Paraguay | |
| 4. Azerbaijan | 2. Dominica | | 4. Antigua and Barbuda | | | 3. Congo – Brazzaville (18 with a 21 year old) |
| 5. Belgium | 3. British Virgin Islands | | 5. Argentina | | | |
| 6. Bahrain | | | 6. Australia (varies by state) | | | 4. Cote d'Ivoire |
| 7. Barbados | 4. Congo | | | | | 5. Egypt |
| 8. Belarus | 5. Dominica | | 7. Bahamas | | | 6. Guam |
| 9. Belgium | 6. Germany(varies by beverage)* | | 8. Barundi (any age with parent) | | | 7. Indonesia |
| 10. Benin | | | 9. Belize | | | 8. Kazakhstan |
| 11. Bolivia | 7. Guyana (varies by beverage) | | 10. Bermuda | | | 9. Kiribati |
| 12. Bosnia and Herzegovina | 8. Liechtenstein (varies by beverage)* | | 11. Canada (19 in many provinces) | | | 10. Malasia |
| 13. Botswana | | | 12. Chad (any age with parent) | | | 11. Marshal Islands |
| 14. Brazil (19 in some provinces) | 9. Lithuania | | 13. Chile | | | 12. Micronesia |
| 15. Bulgaria | 10. Palestinian Authority | | 14. England (age 5 in private) | | | 13. Mongolia |
| 16. Burkina Faso | 11. Saint Lucia | | 15. Estonia | | | 14. Nauru |
| 17. Cambodia | 12. Saint Vincent and the Grenadines | | 16. Falkland Islands | | | 15. Nepal |
| 18. Cape Verde | | | 17. Finland (varies by beverage) | | | 16. Northern Mariana Islands |
| 19. Czechnia | 13. San Marino | | 18. Fiji (lowered from 21) | | | |
| 20. China | 14. Wales (age 5 in private) | | 19. France (any age in private) | | | 17. Palau |
| 21. Columbia | 15. Zambia (varies by beverage) | | 20. Gabon | | | 18. Samoa (any age with parent) |
| 22. Comoros | | | 21. Grenada (any age in private) | | | 19. Sri Lanka |
| 23. Costa Rica | | | 22. Guatemala | | | 20. U.S. (With six age exceptions. See *World Minimum Drinking Ages* map of the U.S.) |
| 24. Denmark | | | 23. Guyana (varies by beverage) | | | |
| 25. Croatia | | | 24. Honduras | | | |
| 26. Cuba | | | 25. Hungary | | | |
| 27. Cyprus | | | 26. India (varies by state) | | | |
| 28. Denmark | | | 27. Ireland (any age in private residence) | | | |
| 29. Djibouti | | | | | | |
| 30. Dominican Republic | | | 28. Jordan | | | |
| 31. Ecuador | | | 29. Kyrgyzstan | | | |
| 32. El Salvador | | | | | | |
| 33. Equatorial Guinea | | | | | | |
| 34. Eritrea | | | | | | |
| 35. Ethiopia | | | | | | |
| 36. Gambia | | | | | | |
| 37. Greece | | | | | | |

**TABLE 8.1** World Minimum Drinking Ages (*continued*)

| None | 16 | 17 | 18 | 19 | 20 | 21 |
|------|-----|-----|-----|-----|-----|-----|

38. Georgia
39. Gibraltar
40. Greece
41. Guinea-Bissau
42. Haiti
43. Hong Kong
44. Iceland
45. Indonesia
46. Israel
47. Italy
48. Italy
49. Jamaica
50. Kenya
51. Kosovo
52. Latvia
53. Lebanon
54. Liberia
55. Luxembourg
56. Macau
57. Macedonia
58. Madagascar
59. Malawi
60. Moldova
61. Mali
62. Mauritius
63. Moldova
64. Morocco
65. Myanmar
66. Namibia
67. Nepal
68. Netherlands*
69. New Zealand
70. Nicaragua
71. Norway
72. Niger
73. Nigeria
74. Northern Ireland
75. Norway

30. Lebanon (no enforcement generally)
31. Lesoto
32. Lithuania
33. Mexico
34. Mongolia
35. Montenegro
36. Mozambique
37. Nepal
38. North Korea
39. Pakistan (for non-Muslims)
40. Papua New Guinea
41. Philippine
42. Poland
43. Puerto Rico
44. Republic of Congo
45. Samoa (any age with parent)
46. Scotland (any age in private)
47. Seychelles
48. Singapore (any age in private)
49. Slovakia
50. South Africa (any age with parent)
51. South Sudan
52. Swaziland
53. Sweden (none for low proof beverages)
54. Syria
55. Taiwan
56. Tanzania
57. Thailand
58. Tokelau
59. Tonga
60. Turkey

*(continues)*

**TABLE 8.1** World Minimum Drinking Ages (*continued*)

| None | 16 | 17 | 18 | 19 | 20 | 21 |
|------|----|----|----|----|----|----|
| 76. Panama | | | 61. Turkmenistan | | | |
| 77. Peru | | | 62. Ukraine | | | |
| 78. Poland | | | 63. United Arab Emirates (varies by jurisdiction) | | | |
| 79. Portugal | | | | | | |
| 80. Romania | | | 64. U.S. Virgin Islands | | | |
| 81. Russia | | | 65. Vanuatu | | | |
| 82. Rwanda | | | 66. Zambia | | | |
| 83. Sao Tome & Prinipia | | | | | | |
| 84. Senegal | | | | | | |
| 85. Serbia | | | | | | |
| 86. Sierra Leone | | | | | | |
| 87. Slovenia | | | | | | |
| 88. Solomon Islands | | | | | | |
| 89. South Korea | | | | | | |
| 90. Spain | | | | | | |
| 91. Switzerland | | | | | | |
| 92. Turks & Caicos Islands | | | | | | |
| 93. Trinidad and Tobago | | | | | | |
| 94. Timor-Leste | | | | | | |
| 95. Togo | | | | | | |
| 96. Turks & Caicos Islands | | | | | | |
| 97. Uganda | | | | | | |
| 98. Uruguay | | | | | | |
| 99. Uzbekistan | | | | | | |
| 100. Venezuela | | | | | | |
| 101. Vietnam | | | | | | |
| 102. Western Sahara | | | | | | |
| 103. Zimbabwe | | | | | | |

*16 to 18 depending on the percentage of alcohol in the beverage

Data from World Health Organization (WHO). (2004). *Global Status Report: Alcohol policy*. Geneva, Switzerland: World Health Organization.

## ▮ Economic Costs of Alcohol Abuse

Note that "[m]ost of the costs of alcohol abuse result from the adverse effects of alcohol consumption on health" (Buddy T., 2016b). In estimating the costs of alcohol abuse as it relates to illnesses, three major categories that have to be included are: "(1) expenditures on medical treatment (a large proportion of which is for the many medical consequences of alcohol consumption; the remainder is for treatment of alcohol abuse and dependence themselves), (2) the lost productivity that results from workers' abuse of alcohol, and (3) the losses to society from premature deaths that are due to alcohol problems" (Buddy T., 2016b).

In two 2018 National Institute on Alcohol Abuse and Alcoholism (NIAAA) press releases, the gravity of the economic costs was stated as follows:

- An estimated 88,000 people (approximately 62,000 men and 26,000 women) die from alcohol-related causes annually, making alcohol the third leading preventable cause of death in the United States. The first is tobacco, and the second is poor diet and physical inactivity (NIAAA, 2018a).
- In 2014, alcohol-impaired driving fatalities accounted for 31% of overall driving fatalities (9,967 deaths) (NIAAA, 2018a).
- Alcohol is the most widely used drug in the United States, and alcohol problems cost the nation nearly $249 billion each year (NIAAA, 2018a).
- Three-quarters of the total cost of alcohol misuse is related to binge drinking (NIAAA, 2018a).
- More than 10% of U.S. children live with a problematic alcoholic parent, according to a 2012 study (NIAAA, 2018a).
- Women historically consume less alcohol than men, drink alcohol less frequently, and are less likely to develop alcohol-related problems. Yet when women do develop alcohol-related problems, they tend to develop them faster, and their problems are more severe. In fact, women develop higher blood alcohol concentrations than men, even when drinking the same amount of alcohol, which increases their risk of injury and illness from conditions such as alcohol-related liver disease.
- The hidden costs of excessive alcohol consumption in 2010 were as follows (Ingraham, 2015):
  - $82 billion—lost productivity
  - $75 billion—early mortality
  - $28 billion—healthcare costs
  - $25 billion—crime
  - $13 billion—car crashes
  - $28 billion—other costs (Ingraham 2015)
- Seventy-six percent of people with drug or alcohol problems are employed.
- About 19.2 million U.S. workers (15%) reported using or being impaired by alcohol at work at least once in the past year.
- On a per capita basis, the economic impact of excessive alcohol consumption in the United States is approximately $746 per person, most of which is attributable to binge drinking (Centers for Disease Control and Prevention [CDC], 2011).
- According to a study in the journal *Addiction*, in the United States approximately 2.8 million older adults (older than age 50) meet the criteria for alcohol abuse, and this number was expected to reach 5.7 million by 2020 (Yip, 2014).
- Alcohol remained the most common primary substance of abuse among older adults admitted for treatment, but the proportion of admissions reporting alcohol as the primary substance of abuse dropped from 84.6% in 1992 to 59.9% in 2008 (Reardon, 2012).

Problems with reduced productivity of alcohol-abusing employees include the following:

- Employees who use drugs, consume alcohol at work, or drink heavily away from work are more likely than other employees to exhibit job-withdrawal behaviors such as spending work time on nonwork-related activities, taking long lunch breaks, leaving early, or sleeping on the job (Connecticut Business and Industry Association [CBIA], 2016).
- Employees who drink heavily off the job are more likely to experience hangovers that cause them to be absent from work, show up late or leave early, feel sick at work, perform poorly, or argue with coworkers. People with drug or alcohol problems were more likely than others to report having worked for three or more employers in the previous year (CBIA, 2016).

Younger workers who abuse alcohol contribute to the following problems (CBIA, 2016):

- *Increased healthcare costs*: Healthcare costs for employees with alcohol problems are twice those for other employees.
- *Higher risk*: People who abuse drugs or alcohol are three and a half times more likely to be involved in workplace accidents.
- *Reduced productivity*: Lost work productivity (including absenteeism and poor job performance) associated with substance abuse costs the nation an estimated $249 billion a year, accounting for 72% of the total cost of excessive alcohol consumption (Bouchery, Harwood, Sacks, Simon, & Brewer, 2011; CDC, 2011; CDC, 2018a). Categories included in lost productivity are impaired productivity at work, mortality, incarceration of perpetrators, impaired productivity at home, absenteeism,

crime victims, fetal alcohol syndrome, and minimum-wage earners.

- Substance use disorders can exacerbate already costly medical conditions such as heart disease and diabetes, which are more common among older adults.
- Older people who consume alcohol are highly susceptible to the damaging effects of drug–alcohol interactions—not only because they are more likely to be taking multiple medications but also because they metabolize both medications and alcohol more slowly than do younger people.
- Misuse of alcohol by employees contributes to the following (SAMHSA, 2008).
  - *Higher healthcare spending*: Healthcare costs for employees with alcohol problems are twice as those for other employees. Almost half of all trauma and injury visits to hospital emergency rooms are alcohol related, which helps to drive up employers' health-insurance expenditures.
  - *Decreased productivity*: Alcohol problems in the workplace are associated with increased absenteeism, disability, and job turnover. Furthermore, in one survey, 14% of workers said they had to redo work within the last year because of a coworker's drinking.
  - *Increased safety risks*: Up to 40% of industrial fatalities and 47% of industrial injuries can be linked to alcohol consumption and alcoholism. Alcohol-related accidents contribute to more workers' compensation claims, and more claims mean higher insurance premiums.

As mentioned previously, the economic costs of alcohol abuse to society are staggering. A statement by Ting-Kai Li, MD, director of the NIAAA, highlighted the following:

According to the Centers for Disease Control and Prevention, alcohol is the third leading cause of preventable death in the U.S. Even more importantly from a public health perspective, alcohol misuse negatively affects the quality of life for millions of Americans. The World Health Organization ranks alcohol as one of the top ten causes of Disability Adjusted Life Years (DALYs) in the United States. Alcohol also contributes to a number of the other leading causes of DALYs, e.g., motor vehicle accidents, brain and liver disease, and cancer.

According to NIAAA's National Epidemiologic Survey on Alcohol and Related Conditions, over 18 million people ages 18 or older suffer from alcohol abuse or dependence and only 7% of them receive any form of treatment. The consequences of alcohol misuse can affect both drinkers and those around them at all stages of life, from damage due to alcohol exposure of the developing embryo, to injuries, to tissue and organ damage resulting from chronic, heavy alcohol use. Therefore, for NIAAA to achieve its goal of reducing the heavy burden of illness from alcohol misuse, the Institute's research focus must be broader than simply reducing alcohol-related mortality; it must encompass reducing the risk for all of the aforementioned negative alcohol-related outcomes at all stages of life. (Li, 2008, p. 1)

Regarding how the burden of the costs of alcohol abuse is distributed across various segments of society, **Figure 8.4** shows the cost of alcohol abuse with the percentages and categories of $223.5 billion (total cost) from excessive alcohol consumption in the United States in 2006. The following are major factors that contribute to the

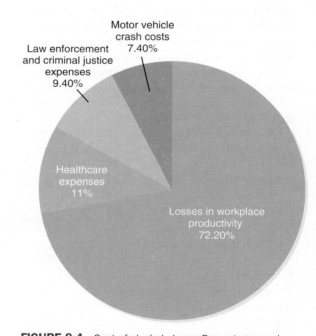

**FIGURE 8.4** Cost of alcohol abuse: Percentages and categories of $223.5 billion (total cost) from excessive alcohol consumption in the United States: 2006.

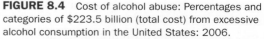

Data from Bouchery, E. E., Harwood, H. J., Sacks, J. J., Simon, C. J., & Brewer, R. D. (2011, November). Economic costs of excessive alcohol consumption in the U.S., 2006. *American Journal of Preventive Medicine, 41*, 516–524. Retrieved from http://www.ajpmonline.org/article/S0749-3797(11)00538-1/fulltext

problem (see Figure 8.4) (Bouchery et al., 2011, unless otherwise noted):

- The cost of excessive alcohol consumption in the United States reached $223.5 billion in 2006. The costs largely resulted from losses in workplace productivity (72.2% of the total cost), healthcare expenses for problems caused by excessive drinking (11.0% of total), law enforcement and other criminal justice expenses related to excessive alcohol consumption (9.4% of total), and motor vehicle crash costs from impaired driving (7.4% of the total) (Bouchery et al., 2011; CDC, 2014); see Figure 8.4.
- Overall, $94.2 billion (42.1%) of the total economic cost of excessive alcohol use was borne by government, including federal, state, and local government agencies, while almost as much $92.9 billion (41.5%) was borne by excessive drinkers and their family members.
- By cost category, excessive drinkers and their households bore 10.3% of the $24.6 billion in total healthcare expenditures related to excessive alcohol consumption. In contrast, government entities bore most (60.9%) of these costs, which is more than the proportion of total healthcare spending that is covered by government (46.1%).
- In contrast, slightly more than half (54.6%) of productivity losses were borne by excessive drinkers and their households, 35.1% by government, and the remainder by others in society.
  - Victims of alcohol-related crimes (including homicide) and nondrinking victims of alcohol-related motor vehicle crashes bear 6% to 9% of the total costs.

Other findings include that the percentage of traffic fatalities that are alcohol related remains at around 40%, according to data from the National Highway Transportation Safety Administration's Fatality Analysis Reporting System (FARS) (CESAR, 2005). In addition, the NIAAA has reported the following:

- Nearly 88,000 people (approximately 62,000 men and 26,000 women) die from alcohol-related causes annually, making it the third leading preventable cause of death in the United States (NIAAA, 2015a).
- In 2013, alcohol-impaired driving fatalities accounted for 10,076 deaths (30.8% of overall driving fatalities) (NIAAA, 2015a).

Current advertisement stressing the need to have a designated driver who does not consume alcohol if others are.

- More than 90% of U.S. adults who drink excessively report binge drinking in the previous 30 days (CDC, 2018b).
- The annual cost of alcohol-related crashes totals more than $44 billion (CDC 2018b).
- Alcohol abuse is estimated to have contributed to 25% to 30% of violent crime (NIAAA, 2000b).
- Alcohol is officially linked to at least half of all highway fatalities, and that figure includes only legal intoxication. In all states, the cutoff for the blood alcohol level is 0.08%. In as many as 70% of all single-vehicle fatal crashes on weekend nights, the driver was legally intoxicated, and this proportion holds during most weekends throughout the United States. Interestingly, this single issue has been the only alcohol problem that has inspired very vocal and effective groups to lobby for stricter enforcement of laws against alcohol-impaired automobile driving. Groups such as Mothers Against Drunk Driving (MADD) and Students Against Drunk Driving (SADD) are the largest prevention organizations in the nation (NIAAA, 2000b).

## History of Alcohol in America

### ■ Drinking Patterns

From a peak in 1830, when the amount of alcohol ingested by the average American was 7.1 gallons per year, use declined continuously until 1871–1880, when the average was 1.72 gallons. Numbers then rose to a high in 1906–1910 of 2.6 gallons and then fell to 1.96 gallons just before Prohibition, 1916–1919. Under Prohibition, less than a gallon of absolute alcohol per person was consumed annually, on average. During the last half of the 20th century, alcohol consumption stayed constant, within the two- to three-gallon range. Wine and beer gained in popularity, whereas the popularity of "spirits" (hard liquor) declined (Hanson, 2009; Lender & Martin, 1987).

## ■ Historical Considerations

Alcoholic beverages have played an important role in the history of the United States as well as in most countries throughout the world. Most likely, fermentation was the first method for making alcohol, dating to around 4200 BC. As early as AD 100, it appears that brandy was the first distilled beverage. In Ireland and Scotland, whiskey was first distilled in the 1400s, and gin began appearing in the 1600s after being initially distilled by a Flemish physician. Other types of liquor also have distinct origins. For example, rum was first invented in Barbados in the 1650s. Bourbon was first made near Georgetown, Kentucky, in the late 1700s. In the United States, the first distillery was established in the 1600s in the area that is now New York City.

In colonial America, alcohol was viewed quite favorably. From an economic standpoint, the manufacturing of rum, "which is the residue left after sugar has been made from sugar cane . . . was introduced to the world, and presumably invented, by the first European settlers in the West Indies (no one knows when it was first produced or by what individual)" (Hanson, 2009). Rum became New England's largest and most profitable industry in the so-called Triangle Trade. It acquired this name because Yankee traders would sail with a cargo of rum to the west coast of Africa, where they bargained the "demon" liquor for slaves. From there, they sailed to the West Indies, where they bartered the slaves for molasses, the raw ingredient for rum. Finally, they took the molasses back to New England, where it was made into rum, thus completing the triangle. For many years, New England distilleries flourished and the slave trade proved highly lucrative (see **Figure 8.5**). "[In] 1657, a rum distillery was operating in Boston. It was highly successful and within a generation the manufacture of rum would become colonial New England's largest and most prosperous industry" (Roueche, 1963, p. 178). This slave trade triangle continued until

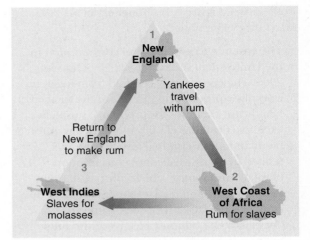

**FIGURE 8.5** Slave trade triangle.

1807, when an act of Congress prohibited the importation of slaves.

From a social standpoint, the consumption of alcohol was seen as a part of life. The colonial tavern "was a key institution, the center of social and political life" (Levine, 1983, p. 66). In the 17th and 18th centuries, alcohol flowed freely at weddings, baptisms, and funerals. Especially in the 18th century, people drank at home, at work, and while traveling. In the 19th century, largely because of the temperance movement, taverns became stigmatized and were viewed as dens where the lower classes, immigrants, and mostly men would congregate. "Any drinking, [Lyman Beecher] argued, was a step toward 'irreclaimable' slavery to liquor" (Lender & Martin, 1987). People in the 19th century began to report that they were addicted to alcohol. This is when the temperance movement had its effect in bringing about a change in attitudes regarding drinking.

### FROM THE TEMPERANCE MOVEMENT (1830–1850) TO THE PROHIBITION ERA (1920–1933)

The time from the temperance movement to the Prohibition era was a highly turbulent period in the history of alcohol in the United States. The period of heaviest drinking in the United States began during President Jefferson's term of office (1801–1809). The nation was going through uneasy times, trying to stay out of the war between Napoleon and the British Empire. The transient population had increased, especially in seaport cities, and migration westward had begun. Heavy drinking had become a major form of recreation and a "social lubricant" at elections and public gatherings. The temperance movement never began with the intention of stopping alcohol consumption but with the goal of encouraging moderation. In fact, in the 1830s, at the peak of this early campaign, temperance leaders (many of whom drank beer and wine) recommended abstinence only from distilled spirits, not from the other forms of alcohol such as beer or wine. This movement developed from several highly vocal spiritual leaders who preached that alcohol harms the nation's health and that alcohol interfered with the spreading of the gospel. Later, as is explained shortly in more detail, the temperance movement turned against all forms of alcohol.

Because the temperance movement was closely tied to the abolitionist movement as well as the African American church, African Americans were preeminent promoters of temperance. Leaders such as Frederick Douglass stated,

> [I]t was as well to be a slave to master, as to whisky and rum. When a slave was drunk, the slaveholder had no fear that he would plan an insurrection; no fear that he would escape to the north. It was the sober, thinking slave who was dangerous, and needed the vigilance of his master to keep him a slave. (Douglass, 1967/1892, p. 133)

Over the next decades, partly in connection with religious revivals, the meaning of temperance was gradually altered from *moderation* to *total abstinence*. All alcoholic beverages were attacked as being unnecessary, harmful to health, and inherently poisonous. Over the course of the 19th century, the demand gradually arose for total prohibition (Austin, 1978).

By the late 19th and early 20th centuries, several countries either passed legislation or created alcohol restrictions. Most of these laws and restrictions eventually failed. In the United States, attempts to control, restrict, or abolish alcohol were made, but they all met with abysmal failure. From 1907 to 1919, 34 states passed prohibition laws. Finally, on a national scale, the 18th Amendment to the Constitution was ratified in 1919 in an attempt to stop the rapid spread of alcohol addiction. In January 1920, alcohol was outlawed. As soon as such a widely used substance became illegal, criminal activity flourished as profiteers sought to satisfy the huge demand for alcohol. Illegal outlets developed for purchasing liquor. Numerous not-so-secret **speakeasies** developed as illegal establishments where people could buy and consume

alcoholic beverages despite the laws of Prohibition. **Bootlegging** was a widely accepted activity. In effect, such involvement in "dens of sin" filled the vacuum for many drinkers during Prohibition.

During the temperance movement and Prohibition period, doctors and druggists prescribed whiskey and other alcohol products known as **patent medicines** (see "Case in Point: The Great American Fraud: Patent Medicines"). By 1928, doctors made an estimated $40 million per year writing prescriptions for whiskey. Patent medicines flourished, with alcohol contents as high as 50%. Whisko, a "nonintoxicating stimulant," was 55 proof (or 27.5% alcohol). Another, Kaufman's Sulfur Bitters, was labeled "contains no alcohol" but was 40 proof (20% alcohol) and did not contain sulfur. There were dozens of others, many of which contained other types of drugs such as opium.

Both Prohibitionists and critics of the law were shocked by the violent gang wars that broke out between rivals seeking to control the lucrative black market in liquor. More important, a general disregard for the law developed. Corruption among law enforcement agents was widespread, and organized crime grew to become an enormous illegitimate business. In reaction to these developments, political support rallied against Prohibition, resulting in its repeal in 1933 by the 21st Amendment. Early in the 20th century, women suffragettes had been prominent temperance organizers; paradoxically, flappers organized against Prohibition and were vital in gathering the signatures for its repeal.

Three main developments occurred because of Prohibition. First, alcohol use continued to diminish for the first two or three years after Prohibition was in effect. This trend had begun several years before the law was passed. More important, after

## KEY TERMS

**speakeasies**
small, often backroom bars where alcoholic beverages were illegally consumed and sold during the Prohibition era from 1920 to 1933 (in some states, Prohibition was longer than this period of time)

**bootlegging**
making, distributing, and selling alcoholic beverages during the Prohibition era

**patent medicines**
the ingredients in these uncontrolled "medicines" were secret, often consisting of large amounts of colored water, alcohol, cocaine, or opiates

# ► CASE IN POINT

## The Great American Fraud: Patent Medicines

In the late 1800s and early 1900s and before the days of U.S. Food and Drug Administration (FDA) legislation, the sale of uncontrolled medicines flourished and became widespread. Many of these products were called *patent medicines*, which meant that the ingredients were secret, not that they were patented. The law of the day seemed to be more concerned with someone's recipe being stolen than with preventing harm to the naive consumer. Some of these patent medicines included toxic ingredients such as acetanilide in Bromo-Seltzer and Orangeine and prussic (hydrocyanic) acid in Shiloh's Consumption Cure.

Most patent medicines appear to have been composed largely of either colored water or alcohol, with an occasional added ingredient such as opium or cocaine. Hostetter's Stomach Bitters with 44% alcohol could easily have been classified as liquor. Sale of Peruna (28% alcohol) was prohibited to Native Americans because of its high alcohol content. Birney's Catarrh Cure contained 4% cocaine. Wistar's Balsam of Wild Cherry, Dr. King's Discovery for Consumption, Mrs. Winslow's Soothing Syrup, and several others contained opiates as well as alcohol.

The medical profession of the middle and late 19th century was ill prepared to do battle with the ever-present manufacturers and distributors of patent medicines. Qualified physicians during this time were rare. Much more common were medical practitioners with poor training and little scientific understanding. In fact, many of these early physicians practiced a brand of medicine that was generally useless and frequently more life threatening than the patent medicines themselves.

In 1905, *Collier's* magazine ran a series of articles called the "Great American Fraud," which warned of the abuse of patent medicines. This brought the problem to the public's attention (Adams, 1906). *Collier's* coined the phrase "dope fiend" from dope, an African word meaning "intoxicating substance." The American Medical Association (AMA) joined in and widely distributed reprints of the *Collier's* story to inform the public about the dangers of these medicines, even though the AMA itself accepted advertisements for patent medicines that physicians knew were addicting. The publicity created mounting pressure on Congress and President Theodore Roosevelt to do something about these fraudulent products. In 1905, Roosevelt proposed that a law be enacted to regulate interstate commerce of misbranded and adulterated foods, drinks, and drugs. This movement received further impetus when Upton Sinclair's book *The Jungle* was published in 1906; this nauseatingly realistic exposé detailed how immigrant laborers worked under appalling conditions of filth, disease, putrefaction, and other extreme exploitations in Chicago's stockyards and slaughterhouses.

Two substances used in patent medicines helped shape attitudes that would form the basis of regulatory policies for years to come: the opium derivatives (narcotic drugs such as heroin and morphine) and cocaine.

This poster advertises one of the patent medicines that contained liberal doses of opium and a high concentration of alcohol. This medicine was widely used to treat tuberculosis (then known as *consumption*) around the turn of the 20th century, when more than 25% of all adult deaths were attributable to this disease. The U.S government finally forced the remedy off the market by 1920.

Data from Adams, S. H. (1905–1906). The great American fraud. *Collier's, 36*(5), 17–18; (10), 16–18; (16), 18–20.

three years of steady decline, the use of distilled liquors rose every year afterward. Further, even minors were becoming addicted to alcohol during this period.

Second, enforcement of laws against alcohol use was thwarted by corrupt law enforcement officials, enforcement was uneven (in some areas of the United States enforcement was lax, whereas in other areas it was strict), and law enforcement experienced more than 50% turnover in its ranks. Corruption of law enforcement officials stands out as a paramount concern. Reportedly, 10% of law enforcement was "on the take" and had to be continually discharged.

Third, among the Western Europeans who immigrated to the United States en masse during this period, the consumption of alcohol was culturally prescribed. Prohibition against alcohol usage to the Italian, German, French, Polish, Irish, and other European-based immigrants was perceived as unnecessary and an infringement of the right to common existence. One 93-year-old Italian American émigré to Chicago exemplified some of these attitudes:

> Well, when we were not allowed to drink because of the government, I thought it was a stupid law. Many of us here in the neighborhood [a fading Italian American community on Chicago's West Side and the original home of Venturelli] made lots of money as "alki cookers."

> We would make the alcohol in our bathtubs and sell to other people or even to those mafia types. Oh, it was horrible cheap and crappy alcohol; if you drank too much the night before, it gave you headaches sometimes for days. On Sunday afternoons, if you walked through this neighborhood in the hot summer days, you could smell the alcohol oozing from people's windows. Nearly everyone my mother's and father's age or older at the time made extra money as alki cookers. It was actually a good law [referring to Prohibition] for making a few bucks to help out the family expenses. No one around here gave a damn about the law, because too many were "on the take" so-to-say . . . and it was not just us [referring to the local Italian Americans]. At least for us when we meet together and eat for fun, alcohol is like the air we breathe. Who the hell is going to change that, especially something so deep? *(From Venturelli's research files, male neighborhood resident, age 93, May 26, 2000)*

Al Capone ("Scarface") (center), the undisputed leader of Chicago's gang scene during Prohibition, made millions of dollars in his bootlegging operations until he was convicted of tax evasion in 1931 and eventually imprisoned in Alcatraz.

## Defining Alcoholics

As discussed at the beginning of this chapter, creating absolute definitions or categories of behavior that represent an alcoholic type is especially difficult because behaviors vary enormously from one person to the next; thus, most behaviors range along a continuum. Adding to this confusion is the fact that some disagreement exists among experts on what the exact criteria should be regarding the definition of an alcoholic. In other words, when can a person be defined as an alcoholic? Is it the daily drinker or the inebriated weekend drinker? What if the excessive drinking involves only one type of liquor such as beer, which is often considered less potent than hard liquor? What if the person is able to maintain a job and provide for his or her family? How does this type of alcoholic compare with an unemployed resident of skid row? In the minds of many Americans, an alcoholic is a derelict who frequents skid rows, train stations, and bus terminals; panders for money; and sleeps on a park bench at night. Yet this stereotypical image of an alcoholic represents only a tiny percentage of the millions of Americans who qualify as alcoholic by any of the accepted medical definitions. The more typical alcoholic, in fact, is similar to the example of the professor or businessman purchasing alcohol at a liquor store described at the opening of this chapter. In effect, most functioning alcoholics are secret or closeted drinkers who look like everyday working people.

## ▌ Cultural Differences

Although more will be presented later in this chapter about the pervasive role that culture plays in drinking behavior, we begin with a quote highlighting cultural differences in interpreting alcohol consumption:

> Even definitions of a "problem drinker" differ from one culture to the next. In Poland, loss of productivity tends to demonstrate a drinking problem, while Californians emphasize drunk driving as an important and sometimes key indicator.... [Among Italian Americans, an inability to provide for one's family because of heavy drinking qualifies a person as an alcoholic.] Some methods of assessing problem drinking look to behavior that leads to a brush with the law. However, drunkenness may or may not lead to disruptive behavior.
>
> In the Netherlands, alcoholic beverage consumption is similar to that in Finland and Poland, but there is much less disruptive or public drinking. In these nations, the actual amount of alcohol consumed is not indicated by the arrest figures, the actual amount consumed (as a separate category), and the number of physical ailments caused by excessive alcohol consumption. Secondly, the social response to drunkenness may not be arrest and conviction. Ireland, for example, has traditionally used psychiatric institutions to control drunkenness. (Osterberg, 1986, p. 83)

Estimates vary, but it is believed that approximately three-fourths of problem drinkers are men and one-fourth are women. The proportion of women has risen in recent years. This increase has occurred for two reasons: (1) Women as problem drinkers are more visible and numerous because they now make up about half of the workforce, and (2) women are more likely to acknowledge the problem and seek treatment, especially if they are in white-collar occupations. Thus, female problem drinkers may now

be more visible and more self-assured as well as more numerous.

Next, in attempting to define alcoholism, we turn to models that speak of the state of addiction. **Alcoholism** is a state of physical and psychological addiction to ethanol, a psychoactive substance. It was once viewed as a vice and dismissed as sinful, but over the years there has been a shift from this perspective to one that views alcoholism as a disease. The sinfulness perspective failed to focus on the fact that alcoholism is an addiction—an illness—and not the result of a lack of personal discipline and morality.

Attempts to expand the basic definition of alcoholism to include symptoms of the condition and psychological and sociological factors have been difficult; no one definition satisfies everyone. In 1980, the World Health Organization defined alcohol dependence syndrome as a syndrome characterized by a state—mental and usually also physical—resulting from drinking alcohol. This state is characterized by behavioral and other responses that include a compulsion to drink alcohol (like an unquenchable thirst) on a continuous or periodic basis to experience its psychic effects and sometimes to avoid the discomfort of its absence; tolerance may or may not be present (National Institute on Alcohol Abuse and Alcoholism [NIAAA], 1980).

Another more classic explanation of alcoholism that remains popular is that "[a]lcoholism is a chronic behavioral disorder manifested by repeated drinking of alcoholic beverages in excess of the dietary and social uses of the community, to an extent that interferes with the drinker's health or his [or her] social or economic functioning" (Keller, 1958, p. 78). Another definition emphasizes that "[a]lcoholism is a chronic, primary, hereditary disease that progresses from an early, physiological susceptibility into an addiction characterized by tolerance changes, physiological dependence, and loss of control over drinking. [In this definition], [p]sychological symptoms are secondary to the physiological disease and not relevant to its onset" (Gold, 1991, p. 99).

A final definition, from Royce and Scratchley (2007), defines "alcoholism as a chronic primary illness or disorder characterized by some loss of control over drinking, with habituation or addiction to the drug alcohol, or causing interference in any major life function, for example: health, job, family, friends, legal or spiritual" (p. 203). In their working definition of alcoholism, Royce and Scratchley list three major factors: "(1) Some

**KEY TERM**

**alcoholism**
a medical condition consisting of a physical and psychological addiction to ethanol (alcohol), a psychoactive substance

loss of control, but it need not be total . . . (2) dependence or need can be psychological or physiological . . . and (3) interference with normal functioning" (p. 203).

In summary, the preceding definitions either list or hint at the following major components of alcoholism (NIAAA, 2007a):

- *Craving*: An overwhelming compulsion to drink even when not feasible, such as at work, while driving a car, while mowing a lawn, and so on.
- *Loss of control and highly impaired*: An inability to limit one's drinking once drinking has begun; for example, one drink only before going to bed is impossible to control.
- *Physical dependence*: The presence of withdrawal symptoms when attempting to abstain from usage. Such symptoms as nausea, sweating, shakiness, and anxiety about the availability of alcohol are common.
- *Tolerance*: A need to continually increase the amount of alcohol consumed to maintain its effects (or to maintain the "buzz").

## ■ Alcohol Abuse and Alcoholism Disorders

When attempting to understand the meaning of chronic drinking, one additional clarification that should be made is to distinguish between **alcohol abuse** and alcoholism. The two explanations of drinking behavior differ as a matter of degree. When speaking of alcohol abuse, the craving, loss of control, and physical dependence just listed as primary manifestations are less prominent and not as pronounced as in alcoholism. There is diminished ability to fulfill obligations and goals; more occasions of drinking at the wrong time, such as while driving; legal problems, such as driving under the influence; and relationship problems. Note that many of these problems that result from alcohol abuse are also experienced by alcoholics, but not all manifestations of alcoholics are experienced by alcohol abusers. For example, an alcoholic may repeatedly argue with family members two or three times per week, whereas an alcohol abuser may have fewer occurrences of the same type of alcohol-inspired arguments with a family member. Thus, even though the alcohol abuser has fewer occasions of uncontrollable drinking than the alcoholic, the drinking remains largely uncontrollable when it occurs. For many years, people with drinking problems were lumped together under the label *alcoholic*, and alcohol abusers were assumed to be suffering

from the same illness. Today, because of greater understanding about addiction and addictive behaviors, the distinction between the two terms leads to a more precise understanding of excessive alcohol abuse (see "Here and Now: Do You Have an Alcohol Use Disorder?").

## ■ Types of Alcoholics

Although written more than five decades ago, Jellinek's (1960) original personality typology (characterizations) differentiating the types of alcoholics remains historically interesting but dated.[3] Jellinek is credited with adding descriptive content in classifying alcohol abuse and its outcomes. Jellinek's categories are as follow.

- *Alpha alcoholism*: Mostly a psychological dependence on alcohol to bolster an inability to cope with life. The alpha type constantly needs alcohol and becomes irritable and anxious when it is not available.
- *Beta alcoholism*: Mostly a social dependence on alcohol. Often, although not exclusively, this type is a heavy beer drinker who continues to meet social and economic obligations. Some nutritional deficiencies can occur, including organic damage such as gastritis and cirrhosis.
- *Gamma alcoholism*: The most severe form of alcoholism. This type of alcoholic suffers from emotional and psychological impairment. Jellinek believed this type of alcoholic suffers from a true disease that progresses from a psychological dependence to physical dependence. Loss of control over when alcohol is consumed and how much is taken

---

[3]Prior to and during the late 1950s and 1960s when Jellinek created his personality typology, the field of psychology was in a disease-centered era regarding alcoholics and alcoholism. Today, with increasing emphasis on using a more person-centered approach, people with alcohol problems in the *Diagnostic and Statistical Manual of Mental Disorders* (DSM-5) (published by the American Psychiatric Association; APA 2013) are referred to as having substance use disorders. We also have to realize that the DSM-5 is used primarily by therapists and psychologists as a diagnostic resource for diagnosing and categorizing mental disorders.

**KEY TERM**

**alcohol abuse**
uncontrollable drinking that leads to alcohol craving, loss of control, and physical dependence but with less prominent characteristics than found in alcoholism

# HERE AND NOW
## Do You Have an Alcohol Use Disorder?

A more recent diagnosis of excessive alcohol use is termed **alcohol use disorder (AUD)** by the National Institute on Alcohol Abuse and Alcoholism (NIAAA): "[p]roblem drinking that becomes severe is given the medical diagnosis of 'alcohol use disorder' or AUD. AUD is a chronic relapsing brain disease characterized by compulsive alcohol use, loss of control over alcohol intake, and a negative emotional state when not using" (NIAAA, 2018b).

The medical diagnosis of AUD must meet certain criteria outlined in the *Diagnostic and Statistical Manual of Mental Disorders* (DSM). In the current edition of the DSM, the DSM-5, anyone meeting any two of the following 11 criteria during the same 12-month period meet the requirements for a diagnosis of AUD. The severity of an AUD diagnosis ranges from mild, moderate, to severe, based on the number of criteria met (NIAAA, n.d.).

To assess whether you or a loved one may have an AUD, here are some critical questions to ask. In the past year have you:

- Had times when you ended up drinking more, or longer, than you intended?

- More than once wanted to cut down or stop drinking—or tried to but could not?

- Spent a lot of time drinking? Or being sick or getting over the aftereffects?

- Experienced craving—a strong need or urge to drink?

- Found that drinking—or being sick from drinking—often interfered with taking care of your home or family? Or caused job troubles? Or school problems?

- Continued to drink even though it was causing trouble with your family or friends?

- Given up or cut back on activities that were important or interesting to you or gave you pleasure in order to drink?

- More than once gotten into situations while or after drinking that increased your chances of getting hurt (such as driving, swimming, using machinery, walking in a dangerous area, or having unsafe sex)?

- Continued to drink even though it was making you feel depressed or anxious or adding to another health problem? Or after having had a memory blackout?

- Had to drink much more than you once did to get the effect you want? Or found that your usual number of drinks had much less effect than before?

- Found that when the effects of alcohol were wearing off, you had withdrawal symptoms, such as trouble sleeping, shakiness, irritability, anxiety, depression, restlessness, nausea, or sweating? Or sensed things that were not there?

If you have any of these symptoms, your drinking may already be a cause for concern. The more symptoms you have, the more urgent the need for change. A health professional can conduct a formal assessment of your symptoms to see if an alcohol use disorder is present.

Ultimately, receiving treatment can improve an individual's chances of success in overcoming an AUD. Talk with your doctor to determine the best course of action for you and see National Institutes of Health (n.d.). and National Institute on Alcohol Abuse and Alcoholism (NIAAA) (n.d.b) for more information.

Data from National Institute on Alcohol Abuse and Alcoholism (NIAAA). (n.d.a). Alcohol use disorder. Rockville, MD: National Institute on Alcohol Abuse and Alcoholism. Retrieved from http://www.niaaa.nih.gov/alcohol-health/overview-alcohol-consumption/alcohol-use-disorders; American Psychiatric Association (APA). (2013). Substance related and addictive disorders. In *Diagnostic and Statistical Manual of Mental Disorders (DSM-5)*, 5th ed., (pp. 481–589). Washington, DC: American Psychiatric Association; Centers for Disease Control and Prevention (CDC). (2018b). Binge drinking. Atlanta, GA: Author. Retrieved from https://www.cdc.gov/alcohol/fact-sheets/binge-drinking.htm

## KEY TERM

**alcohol use disorder (AUD)**
a chronic relapsing brain disease characterized by an impaired ability to stop or control alcohol use despite adverse social, occupational, or health consequences. In the latest *Diagnostic Statistical Manual* (DSM-5), this disorder is further subdivided as mild, moderate, or severe

characterizes the latter phase of this type of alcoholism.

- *Delta alcoholic*: Also called the *maintenance drinker* (Royce, 1989), this type of alcoholic loses control over drinking and cannot abstain for even a day or two. Many wine-drinking countries such as France and Italy contain delta-type alcoholics who sip wine throughout most of their waking hours. Being "tipsy" but never completely inebriated is typical of the delta alcoholic.

- *Epsilon alcoholic*: This type of alcoholic is characterized as a binge drinker. The epsilon-type drinker drinks excessively for a certain period (for days and sometimes weeks) but then abstains completely from alcohol until the next binge period. The dependence on alcohol is both physical and psychological. Loss of control over the amount consumed is another characteristic of this type of alcoholic.
- *Zeta alcoholic*: This category was added to Jellinek's types to describe the moderate drinker who becomes abusive and violent. Although this type also is referred to as a *pathological drinker* or *mad drunk*, zeta types may not be addicted to alcohol.

Another, more recent classification of alcoholism subtypes includes five alcohol-dependent subtypes created by Dr. Moss and colleagues (NIAAA, 2007b). Quoted extensively, the five types follow.

- *Young adult subtype*: 31.5% of U.S. alcoholics. Young adult drinkers, with relatively low rates of co-occurring substance abuse and other mental disorders and a low rate of family alcoholism and who rarely seek any kind of help for their drinking.
- *Young antisocial subtype*: 21% of U.S. alcoholics. These people tend to be in their mid-20s and had early onset of regular drinking and alcohol problems. More than half come from families with alcoholism, and about half have a psychiatric diagnosis of antisocial personality disorder. Many have major depression, bipolar disorder, and anxiety problems. More than 75% smoke cigarettes and marijuana, and many have cocaine and opiate addictions. More than one-third of these alcoholics seek help for their drinking.
- *Functional subtype*: 19.5% of U.S. alcoholics. Typically, they are middle-aged, well-educated, and have stable jobs and families. About one-third have a multigenerational family history of alcoholism, about one-quarter have major depressive illness sometime in their lives, and nearly 50% are smokers.
- *Intermediate familial subtype*: 19% of U.S. alcoholics. Middle-aged, with about 50% from families with multigenerational alcoholism, almost half of these people have had clinical depression, and 20% have had bipolar disorder. Most of these individuals smoke cigarettes,

Many cultural social interactions demand drinking together.

and nearly one in five have had problems with cocaine and marijuana use. Only 25% ever seek treatment for their problem drinking.

- *Chronic severe subtype*: 9% of U.S. alcoholics. Composed mostly of middle-aged individuals who had early onset of drinking and alcohol problems, they have high rates of antisocial personality disorder and criminality. Almost 80% come from families with multigenerational alcoholism. They have the highest rates of other psychiatric disorders, including depression, bipolar disorder, and anxiety disorders, as well as high rates of smoking and marijuana, cocaine, and opiate dependence. Two-thirds of these alcoholics seek help for their drinking problems, making them the most prevalent type of alcoholics in treatment.

Other classifications differentiate alcoholics by their reaction to the drug as quiet, sullen, friendly, or angry types. Another method is to classify alcoholics according to their drinking patterns: occupational, social, escape, and emotional.

## ■ Major Traditional Distinctions Between "Wet" and "Dry" Cultures

Before delving into the next section regarding how culture defines and views the use of alcohol, note that alcohol researchers traditionally distinguished countries as either *wet* or *dry*. In **wet cultures**, alcohol is integrated into daily life and

KEY TERM

**wet cultures**
cultures in which alcohol is integrated into daily life and activities (e.g., is consumed with meals) and is widely available and accessible (e.g., European countries bordering the Mediterranean have traditionally exemplified wet cultures)

activities (e.g., is consumed with meals) and is widely available and accessible. In these cultures, abstinence rates are low, and wine is largely the beverage of preference. European countries bordering the Mediterranean have traditionally exemplified wet cultures.

In **dry cultures**, alcohol consumption is not as common during everyday activities (e.g., it is less frequently a part of meals), and access to alcohol is more restricted. Abstinence is more common, but when drinking occurs, it is more likely to result in intoxication; moreover, wine consumption is less common. Examples of traditionally dry cultures include the Scandinavian countries, the United States, and Canada (Bloomfield, Stockwell, Gmel, & Rehn, 2003). Recent comparative research, however, has found that, especially in Europe, the wet–dry distinction seems to be disappearing and a homogenization of consumption rates and beverage preferences is increasingly evident. Room and Mäkelä (2000) have reconsidered the simple wet–dry dichotomy and have instead proposed a new typology that considers a variety of drinking behaviors, such as the regularity of drinking and the extent of drunkenness. Such a typology may better fit the distinctions in drinking cultures that are emerging today. Nevertheless, the wet–dry dichotomy has represented a scale of extremes on which to measure drinking cultures and around which a fair amount of past research literature has been organized (Bloomfield et al., 2003).

## Cultural Influences

This section explains how views of alcohol are culturally determined—that is, how culture encodes the thoughts, attitudes, values, and beliefs about alcohol and how it influences our behavior regarding the use and abuse of alcohol.

> I started drinking heavily at college after I joined a fraternity. We had many nights of drinking and good times. When I turned 21, I got a part-time job at a pizzeria waiting on tables. It was a fun job in that the owners were

**KEY TERM**

**dry cultures**
cultures in which alcohol consumption is not as common during everyday activities (e.g., it is less frequently a part of meals) and access to alcohol is more restricted; abstinence is more common (e.g., Scandinavian countries, the United States, and Canada)

pretty big drug users and did not care if the student workers drank especially after hours into the early mornings sitting around the bar area after we closed for the night. I kept drinking after graduation and never paid attention to how often and how much I drank. I knew it was a lot of drinking I was doing but I never thought of myself as having an alcohol problem. About 15 years later, I got married and wouldn't you know it, I married a woman who also had a drinking problem. Right now, I am in counseling for alcoholism and though I am trying to slow down on the drinking with the end goal to quit, I get mixed results. On the days I abstain after two days of not drinking, I find my car after work automatically drives to liquor stores. I say automatic because on the days I am not drinking I know each and every liquor store I pass while driving home with a tempting desire to stop in and buy liquor for the night before I get home and have dinner. After a few days I just end up in the parking lot of a liquor store and give up, walk in and buy my hard liquor for another night of drinking. Nearly all of the liquor stores know me by first name and here I am close to 40 years of age and I have a pretty bad alcohol problem. My wife and I make all these promises to quit but we never do it. My wife and I are so bad that we always end up hearing the bartender making the last call for the night. We just never leave until closing time. I am on special types of drugs now that lessen the desire but it's very hard to stop drinking for more than two to three days before we break down and resume our alcohol addiction. We are both talking about going to a rehab center to try and get a grip on stopping the alcohol. Waking up with a hangover is normal at our house, so we are still pretty bad with the drinking. *(From Venturelli's research files, male working as a mortgage loan officer, residing in northwest Indiana, age 37, January 21, 2016)*

Or,
Q:   Do you consider yourself a heavy drinker?
A:   No, I only drink beer.
Q:   But, you are often drunk at night?
A:   Yeah, but it's only beer—it certainly is a lot better than drinking the hard stuff.

These two interviews illustrate a belief shared by many Americans, which is that the milder alcohols such as beer, wine, and wine coolers are outside the domain of potentially addictive types of beverages. Some may even believe that distilled spirits such as vodka, gin, and whiskey are the only types of addictive alcoholic beverages. Finally, the comment that "I don't use and never would use drugs; I only drink" can easily be heard being espoused by a large portion of Americans (probably a majority), who place alcohol in a completely separate category from drugs. However, each 12-ounce bottle of beer is equal to one ounce of liquor. Thus, two beers equal a double shot of bourbon or vodka.

## ■ Culture and Drinking Behavior

Another way of looking at how culture influences us is to stand outside of our culture and see how people behave when intoxicated in our culture and in a variety of other cultures in an effort to understand the real relationship among culture, alcohol, and human beings. A major contribution to our knowledge of intoxicated behavior from an outside perspective comes from the field of cultural anthropology.

As we previously saw in the distinction between wet and dry cultures, how alcohol is used varies culturally. Does culture also affect how or in what way we view alcohol? Why would our culture differ from other cultures in the use and abuse of alcoholic beverages? We focus on these two questions in this section.

Throughout the world, cultures create a climate for the development of attitudes toward most behaviors. Like other behaviors, the use of alcohol is embedded within our culture. Culture does more than contain the attitudes and feelings that people have toward alcohol use—it dictates the variety, the attachment, and the intensity of attitudes that are held toward other people's behavior. For example, in the 1930s, American college students acquired a "reverence for strong drink" (Room, 1984, p. 8). Although for decades many people believed that college students "majored in drinking," students during the 1930s grew to consider heavy use as romantic and adult, resonating with the romantic, heavy-drinking expatriate community of writers in Paris such as Ernest Hemingway.

American culture in general views ethanol-containing beverages as being sexy, mature, and sophisticated, facilitating socializing and enhancing status. Today, many of these beliefs are communicated through the mass media, and advertising is a key medium of communication. Advertising uses positive images to persuade observers to purchase a particular brand of alcohol. For example, what messages are found in newspapers and especially magazines about drinking certain types of wine, bourbon, gin, scotch, and the numerous types of domestic and imported beers? What attitudes are generally conveyed when a sexy, glamorous woman is dressed in formal evening attire standing next to her man in front of a perfectly glowing fireplace, smiling confidently as he stares into her eyes and sips his special-label cognac?

## ■ Culture and Disinhibited Behavior

The concept of **drunken comportment** was first formulated by MacAndrew and Edgerton (1969). *Drunken comportment* refers to the behavior demonstrated while under the influence of alcohol within the norms and expectations of a particular culture. Instead of simply labeling drinking behavior as "drunken behavior," this concept sensitizes us to how drinking behavior is influenced by cultural norms and expectations. For example, in the United States, drinking is comported to mean time out away from duties and obligations. "The symbolism of alcohol in American culture contains this motif of release and remission, as in the emergence of TGIF [Thank God It's Friday]" (Gusfield, 1986, p. 203). Another example is that in some cultures, drinking occurs during celebrations and festivities and as part of religious ceremony. In France and Italy, drinking alcohol occurs while eating with family members.

Alcohol is a **disinhibitor**, which refers to depression of the cerebral cortex functions. When this occurs, it results in a suspension of rational or thoughtful constraints on impulsive behavior. Inhibitions (inner raw feelings and attitudes) are normally controlled through rationality and logical thought processes. The popular image of office Christmas parties at which too much alcohol is consumed and parties that get out of control because of overconsumption of alcohol are examples. People at such events can easily become uncontrollable, loud, impulsive, and just plain irrational. In such situations, outbreaks of arguing

### KEY TERMS

**drunken comportment**
behavior exhibited while under the direct influence of alcohol; determined by the norms and expectations of a particular culture

**disinhibitor**
a psychoactive chemical that depresses thought and judgment functions in the cerebral cortex, which has the effect of allowing relatively unrestrained behavior (as in alcohol inebriation)

and physical and verbal abuse are more likely to occur. Such behavior is disinhibited behavior.

Although all of us know that the alcohol content that is usually measured in terms of alcohol proof has an independent effect on the user, two additional factors contribute to the effects of alcohol: **set and setting** (Goode, 1999; Zinberg, 1984; Zinberg & Robertson, 1972). *Set* is the individual's expectation of what a drug will do to his or her personality. *Setting* is both the physical environment and the social environment in which the drug is consumed. How important are these two distinctions? Some psychologists contend that both set and setting can overshadow the pharmacological effects of most drugs. In fact, set and setting are far more influential in determining a drug user's experience even when less-addictive drugs such as alcohol and marijuana are used, in contrast to more potent addictive drugs such as cocaine and heroin. Good examples of this are when people who drink alcohol say, "I felt that drink right away" or "I drank a lot last night but I had something on my mind and, dude, I was just not in the partying mood."

A review of various ethnographic studies (Marshall, 1983) reveals **pseudointoxicated** behavior (i.e., people acting drunk before or seconds after the bottle is opened or as the drink is consumed) among Tahitians, Rarotongans, Chippewas, Dakotas, Pine Ridge and Teton Sioux, Aleuts, Baffin Island Inuits, and Potawatomi. The frequency of use or the amount consumed has less effect on how drinkers comport themselves; instead, the cultural values, beliefs, mental maps, and norms cause a particular behavioral outcome. Using the terminology of psychology, we would say that it is not the biochemical effects on the brain alone that account for disinhibitory behavior but rather the belief that one has been drinking a substance that has a disinhibitory effect; that is, the mental (cognitive) appraisal of the physiological state allows disinhibited behavior. In using the terminology of sociology and revising a famous sociological axiom, we could say, "What we believe

to be (or personally define as true) is true in its consequences or in the obtained results." Thus, if you believe you are drunk and you act drunk, then you are drunk.

Cultures vary in how they evaluate alcohol consumption. Some religions in the United States view drinking as evil, whereas others view alcohol as a gift from God and use it in religious ceremonies. In some subcultures, excessive use of alcohol is an indication of manhood, strength, and virility; in other subcultures, excessive alcohol use in public is disgusting and embarrassing. Even drug education has different perspectives. Do we emphasize total abstinence or teach people how to drink in moderation? Why such vastly different approaches? Because our culture includes contradictory practices on this front.

Similarly, the views we maintain about alcohol abuse and addiction vary. For example, is alcoholism a disease? Is it prescribed by certain customs within ethnic groups? Does it result from some type of personality flaw? The three concepts discussed in this section—drunken comportment, set and setting, and pseudointoxication—demonstrate that social and cultural contexts exert their influences independently of the effects of alcohol consumption.

## ■ Culture Provides Rules for Drinking Behavior

Many cultures such as traditional Italian and Jewish cultures permit moderate drinking within the family, especially at meals, but disapprove of drunken behaviors. Note that many differences separate these groups. For example, Italians use wine as a food item, whereas it has only ritual value among Orthodox Jews. In one study of Scandinavian nations, by contrast, drinking was considered separated from work. Where drinking at work was permitted, however, it was allowed to go on to the point of intoxication (Makela, 1986). Finnish, Polish, and Russian cultures are associated with binge drinking, whereas French culture is linked with sipping. In the United States, we encounter a vast variety of subgroups; some heavy drinkers may live in a community in which it is not considered excessive to drink with friends out of paper bags on the street in the morning. In other communities, all outdoor drinking is done in either parks, restaurants, bars, or outdoor cafés. Some people may belong to a "workplace culture of drinking" at a particular country club, construction site, or law firm, where "three-martini lunches" are not unheard of. Perhaps this

**set and setting**
*set* refers to the individual's expectation of what a drug will do to his or her personality; *setting* is the physical and social environments where the drug is consumed

**pseudointoxicated**
acting drunk even before alcohol has had a chance to cause its effects

type of drinking is not much different from the habits of teenage peer groups. To be "treated" for this behavior might seem as strange as going into rehab for acting "normal."

## ■ Culture Provides Ceremonial Meaning for Alcohol Use

The first notable work on ceremonial use and ethnic drinking practices was undertaken by Bales (1946), who attempted to explain the different rates of drinking between Jews (low) and Irish (high) in terms of symbolic and ceremonial meanings. For Jews, drinking had familial and sacramental significance, whereas for the Irish it represented male convivial bonding.

A high rate of heavy drinking was observed among the Irish in the 1800s. It was said that these individuals drank because they were Irish. Today, some descendants of the Irish continue to live the stereotype; for them, it represents "Irishness"— they drink because they are Irish. A button displayed on St. Patrick's Day proclaimed, "Today I'm Irish, Tomorrow I'm Hung Over," and a *New York Post* supplement declared this event to be "Three Days of Drinking and Revelry." With regard to Hasidic Jews, the belief is that they can "drink alcohol, [and] it is considered a 'mitzvah' (good deed) when done so on the Sabbath and on holidays" (Answers.com, 2011). Further, as Rabbi Daniel Siegel writes,

> [O]verall, the approach of the Jewish rabbinic tradition is to encourage the moderate use of alcohol, particularly wine, within the frameworks provided by existing commandments which require one to be happy in their fulfillment. Wine is an important part of Sabbath and holiday observances, life cycle celebrations, and the holiday of Purim. In the Hassidic world, a small amount of vodka is a legitimate preparation for listening to the teachings of the rabbi and, in oral traditions, a measured amount of alcohol on a regular basis is considered good for one's health. (Dartmouth Center on Addiction, Recovery, and Education, 2003, p. 3)

## ■ Culture Provides Models of Alcoholism

U.S. citizens define alcoholism as a disease far more often than French Canadians or French people, for example (Babor et al., 1986). Some South Bronx Hispanics have ascribed alcoholism to "spells" and spirits (Garrison & Podell, 1981), the evil eye (*mal ojo*), or witchcraft (*brujeria*). The entire addiction also may be ignored or bypassed;

ulcers, divorce, or car accidents that an alcohol counselor may recognize as alcoholism based may instead be traced directly to supernatural influence. One way or another, if it is attributed to a supernatural cause, a supernatural solution may be called on to cure this problem. Thus, many seek the help of a folk curer (e.g., *espiritista*, *santero*). Some African Americans interpret their problems as a punishment from God and may subscribe to a moral model that conflicts with a disease or other psychiatric or addictive model.

## ■ Cultural Stereotypes of Drinking May Be Misleading

African American drinking patterns run the gamut from middle-class cocktail lounges (as seen in liquor ads in *Ebony*) to blue-collar wakes and birthday parties, to the "bottle gang" of homeless poor. By class, middle-class African American women drinkers are not dramatically different from middle-class white women drinkers; they are typically moderate drinkers, with few nondrinkers and heavy drinkers. Poorer African American female groups have a larger proportion of nondrinkers; among those who do drink, more are heavy drinkers. Breaking it down further, being married, older, and church affiliated has been associated with nonacceptance of heavy drinking (Gary & Gary, 1985; Kinney, 2000). At historically black colleges and universities, blacks have lower levels of alcohol and other types of drug consumption than are observed at colleges and universities with a majority of white students. At all colleges and universities, white students drink significantly more than do African American students (Kinney, 2000).

Gordon, who studied a Connecticut city in 1981, examined three Hispanic groups, all new to the United States and all blue collar. In this group, Dominicans drank less after migration. They emphasized suave or sophisticated drinking, and they saw drunkenness as indecent (without respect). Alcoholics were seen as "sick," perhaps from some tragic experience. Guatemalans drank substantially more after migration: One-third of males were often drunk and binged most weekends. Being drunk was considered glamorous and sentimentalized—like Humphrey Bogart under the hanging lightbulb, alone in a hotel room. These individuals boasted of hangovers, even when they did not have one. The Guatemalan Alcoholics Anonymous (AA) group was alien to Puerto Ricans, who broke down into middle-class, American-style moderate drinkers, depressed and wife-abusing alcoholic welfare recipients, and various sorts of polydrug abusers, including those who entered into the mainland "druggie" youth culture (Gordon, 1981). Among Hispanics in general, men were twice as likely to be involved in heavy drinking as both white and African American males (Kinney, 2000). In fact, African American students have the lowest lifetime, annual, and 30-day prevalence rates for alcohol use; they also tend to have the lowest rates for daily drinking (Miech et al., 2019; National Institute on Drug Abuse [NIDA], 1999). Finally, several conclusive studies that examine the relationship between ethnic identity and the extent of illicit drug use and abuse indicate that illicit drug abuse is more likely to occur in second-generation ethnics (children of parents who immigrated to the United States) with less illicit drug use in successive ethnic generations beyond the second generation (Cheung, 2009; Hjern, 2016; Svensson & Hagquist, 2009). Similar patterns of illicit drug use and abuse are also found in minority groups that are socially and economically disadvantaged in the United States (Gans, 1992; Vaillant, 1966).

Even when looking at physiological responses to alcohol, ethnicity appears to matter. The long-term effects of alcohol dependence are reported to cause more damage to the immune systems of African Americans than other ethnic groups. The greater sensitivity to alcohol and its damaging effects puts this group at an increased risk for infection and, in many cases, at a greater likelihood of death (Research Group News Release, 2016).

## ■ Culture Provides Attitudes Regarding Alcohol Consumption

Although cultures often maintain generalized (normative) attitudes regarding alcohol use and abuse, significant differences in attitudes also exist within cultures (Arkin & Funkhouser, 1992; Inciardi, 1992). The United States is characterized as culturally ambivalent regarding alcohol use (Kinney, 2000); that is, alcohol consumption varies enormously across our culture. Different geographic regions, diverse religious beliefs, and racial and ethnic differences result in confusing attitudes about drinking alcohol. Other factors that contribute to diversity in attitudes include social upbringing, peer-group dynamics, social class, income, education, and occupational differences.

What specific impact do such attitudes have on drinking? As just mentioned, attitudes are responsible for making alcohol consumption acceptable or unacceptable—or even relished as a form of behavior. For example, in one segment of impoverished African American groups, alcohol use and abuse are so common that they have become accepted behavior. The following excerpt describes an accepted pattern of alcohol consumption:

> A party without liquor or a street rap without a bottle is often perceived as unimaginable. These attitudes about drinking are shaped as youth grow up seeing liquor stores in their communities next to schools, churches, and homes. Liquor stores and bootleg dealers frequently permeate the black residential community, where in traditionally white communities they are generally restricted to commercial or business zones. With liquor stores throughout the fabric of black residential life, black youth grow up seeing men drinking in the streets and relatives drinking at home. (Harper, 1986)

Contrast this attitude with orthodox religious and fundamentalist communities in which the use of alcohol and other drugs is strictly prohibited:

> I was raised in a very religious, Seventh-Day Adventist family. My father was a pretty strong figure in our little church of 18 members. My mother stayed home most of the time, living in a way like an Old Testament kind of biblical life, so-to-speak. We were strict vegetarians, and all of us in the family had to be very involved with church life. The first time I ever saw alcohol outside of always hearing how corrupting it was to the mind and the body, was when I was 7. One day the father of a friend of mine—the only non-Adventist family friend I was allowed to play with—was drinking a beer in the kitchen when we walked in. I asked, "What's that?" The father's reply was "This is beer, dear John." I looked strangely at him and pretended to be amused at the father's answer. Actually, inside I remember being very surprised and scared at the same time for I was always told that people who drink alcohol were not doing what God wanted them to do in life. *(From Venturelli's research files, male university student, age 18, May 21, 1993)*

From these contrasting examples, we can see that the values expressed through group and family attitudes regarding drug use are highly significant in determining the extent of alcohol consumption.

### ■ Culture Determines What Is Considered Acceptable Amounts of Drinking

In looking at countries with the heaviest drinking rates, it has been reported that

> [In]early all of the countries with the highest levels of alcohol consumption are located in Eastern Europe. They include Russia and other former Soviet Union nations such as Belarus, Lithuania, Moldova, and Ukraine. The only top-consuming nation not located in Eastern Europe is Andorra, a principality located between France and Spain in the Pyrenees. (Hess, Frohlich, & Callo, 2014)

Specifically, the heaviest-drinking countries in the world, with consumption reported in liters of alcohol per capita (1 gallon equals 3.7854 liters), are, from highest to lowest:

- Belarus—17.5 liters,
- Republic of Moldova—16.8 liters,
- Lithuania—15.4 liters,
- Russian Federation—15.1 liters,
- Romania—14.4 liters,
- Ukraine—13.9 liters,
- Andorra—13.8 liters,
- Hungary—13.3 liters,
- Czech Republic—13.0 liters, and
- Slovakia—13.0 liters (tied for ninth highest with the Czech Republic) (Hess et al., 2014; GraphicMaps, 2018).

Residents in these countries were also often among the most likely to suffer from alcohol use disorders. Five of the heaviest-drinking countries were also among the 10 highest in prevalence for AUDs, which include alcoholism and other forms of health-damaging use of alcohol. Alcohol use disorders often lead to physical problems such as liver cirrhosis and mental illnesses such as depression. The three nations with the highest rates of alcohol use disorders—Hungary, Russia, and Belarus—were also among the 10 heaviest-drinking nations (Hess et al., 2014). Note that life expectancies are shorter in nations with heavy alcohol use. According to Hess et al. (2014), "[A]verage life expectancy at birth in high-income nations was 79.3 years as of 2012, far higher than in almost all of the heaviest drinking nations. In Romania, the average life expectancy was just 68.7 years. In Russia and Ukraine the average life expectancy was below 72 years as well."

In looking at the 10 countries with exceptionally higher amounts of alcohol consumed, we can begin to understand how cultures vary with regard to alcohol consumption and how each country's culture determines what is considered normative (acceptable) alcohol consumption. Pointing out these top 10 alcohol-consuming countries shows how, as a group, these countries vary widely when compared to other countries where alcohol consumption is much lower.

## College and University Students and Alcohol Use

Over the years, alcohol use and consumption rates among college students have remained largely stable, although rates for other drugs show a lot more variance. For example, marijuana use has dramatically risen, fallen, and then risen again. In looking at alcohol consumption and college students, some interesting findings exist. The following annual statistics regarding college drinking by the National Institute on Alcohol Abuse and Alcoholism (NIAAA, 2019b) are especially noteworthy.

- *Death*: 1,825 college students between ages 18 and 24 die from alcohol-related unintentional injuries, including motor vehicle crashes.
- *Injury*: 599,000 students between 18 and 24 are unintentionally injured under the influence of alcohol.
- *Assault*: 696,000 students between 18 and 24 are assaulted by another student who has been drinking.
- *Sexual assault*: 97,000 students between 18 and 24 report experiencing alcohol-related sexual assault or date rape.
- *Unsafe sex*: 400,000 students between ages 18 and 24 have unprotected sex, and more than 100,000 students between ages 18 and 24 report having been too intoxicated to know whether they had consented to having sex.
- *Academic problems*: About one in four college students report academic consequences from drinking, including missing class, falling behind in class, doing poorly on exams or papers, and receiving lower grades overall.
- *Binge drinkers:* In a national survey of college students, binge drinkers who consumed alcohol at least three times per week were roughly six times more likely than those who drank but never binged to perform poorly on a test or project as a result of drinking (40% vs. 7%)

and five times more likely to have missed a class (64% vs. 12%).

- *Alcohol use disorder*: About 20% of college students meet the criteria for an AUD.
- *Health problems and suicide attempts*: More than 150,000 students develop an alcohol-related health problem, and between 1.2% and 1.5% of students indicate that they tried to commit suicide within the past year because of drinking or drug use.
- *Drunk driving*: 3,360,000 students between 18 and 24 drive under the influence of alcohol.
- *Drinking alcohol and driving*: "Over the course of a year, half of the underage students said they drove after drinking and 20% said they drove while drunk. Among 20-year-olds, 43% said they had ridden with a drunk driver" (Health Day, 2019).
- *Vandalism*: About 11% of college student drinkers report that they have damaged property while under the influence of alcohol.
- *Property damage*: More than 25% of administrators from schools with relatively low drinking levels and more than 50% from schools with high drinking levels say their campuses have a "moderate" or "major" problem with alcohol-related property damage.
- *Police involvement*: About 5% of four-year-college students are involved with the police or campus security as a result of their drinking, and 110,000 students between 18 and 24 are arrested for alcohol-related violations such as public drunkenness and driving under the influence.
- *Alcohol abuse and dependence*: 31% of college students met criteria for a diagnosis of alcohol abuse and 6% for a diagnosis of alcohol dependence in the past 12 months, according to questionnaire-based self-reports about their drinking.

Additional findings are as follows:

- College students drink an estimated four billion cans of beer annually.
- The total amount of alcohol consumed by college students each year is 430 million gallons, enough for every college and university in the United States to fill an Olympic-size swimming pool.
- As many as 360,000 of the nation's 12 million undergraduates will die from alcohol-related causes while in school. This is more than the number who will receive master's and doctoral degrees.

- Nearly 40% of all college students are binge drinkers.
- The number of college women who drink to get drunk has more than tripled since the 1980s and increased from 10% to 35%.
- On America's college campuses, alcohol is often responsible for 28% of all students who drop out of college before completing their bachelor's degree.
- Fully 75% of male students and 55% of female students involved in acquaintance rape had been drinking or using drugs at the time.
- For college men, alcohol consumption is inversely related to the size of the institution; that is, male students at smaller institutions consume far more than those at larger institutions. (Lack of social activities could be a precipitating factor.)
- Nearly one-quarter of student's report failing a test or project because of the aftereffects of drinking or doing drugs.
- Although only two in 20 college students are arrested for driving under the influence, "27% of students said they drove while under the influence of alcohol . . . [and this] . . . translates to 2.1 million students" (Boyd, McCabe, & d'Arcy, 2003).
- A related consequence of alcohol abuse is motor vehicle accidents. For young people under age 25, motor vehicle accidents rate as the leading cause of death (Presley, Meilman, & Lyerla, 1996).
- Each year an estimated 1,825 college students between 18 and 24 die from alcohol-related unintentional injuries, including motor vehicle crashes (NIAAA, 2013).
- Although the average cost for book purchases for classes is about $1,000 per year (Weisbaum, 2014), the average student spends about $500 on alcohol each year, and 10% of all college loans are actually used to finance alcohol consumption (Bissonnette, 2010).

On a positive note, a small but significant downward trend has been seen in alcohol use on America's campuses. In 1985, the percentage of college students who had consumed alcohol in the previous 30 days was approximately 80%. By 1990, that number had declined to 74.5%, and it continues to decline each year.

With regard to the prevalence of drinking, more recent findings from the 2017 NSDUH reports 86.3% of people ages 18 or older reported that they drank alcohol at some point in their lifetime; 50.1% reported that they drank in the past year; and 55.9% reported that they drank in the past month (NIAAA, 2019c). However, counterbalancing this positive trend, the use of other illegitimate-type drugs continues to increase. Further, past and more current studies show that although overall alcohol consumption is slowly decreasing, binge drinking remains high on most campuses throughout the United States (English, Shutt, & Oswalt, 2009; NIAAA, 2015a; Wechsler, Dowdall, Davenport, & DeJong, 2000).

Other recent findings (NIAAA, 2016) indicate the following with regard to alcohol use by college students as of 2014.

- *Prevalence of drinking:* 59.8% of full-time college students 18 to 22 drank alcohol in the preceding month compared with 51.5% of other persons of the same age.
- *Prevalence of binge drinking:* 37.9% of college students 18 to 22 engaged in binge drinking (five or more drinks on an occasion) in the past month compared with 33.5% of other persons of the same age.
- *Prevalence of heavy drinking:* 12.2% of college students aged 18 to 22 engaged in heavy drinking (five or more drinks on an occasion on five or more occasions per month) in the past month compared with 9.5% of other persons of the same age.

The Core Institute survey is a validated survey instrument that has been administered to more than one million students—by far the largest sample of college students surveyed. The available figures from this survey (Core Institute, 2014) indicate that, on average, approximately 81.3% of college students consumed alcohol within the year this survey was given, and 68.6% consumed alcohol within the 30 days prior to taking the survey. The average number of drinks that students consumed was 4.4 per week. Approximately 42.8% engaged in binge drinking within 30 days before the Core Institute survey was administered. Of all the drugs reported as being used within a year of when survey was completed (annual prevalence), alcohol was the most heavily abused on college campuses, followed by tobacco (33%) and marijuana (32.5%) (Core Institute, 2014).

## ■ Binge Drinking

A recent Swedish study defines a binge as the consumption of half a bottle of spirit or two bottles of wine on the same occasion. Similarly, a study in Italy found that consuming an average of eight drinks a day was considered normal drinking—clearly not bingeing. In the United Kingdom, bingeing is commonly defined as consuming 11 or more drinks on an occasion. However, in the United States, some researchers have defined bingeing as consuming five or more drinks on an occasion (an *occasion* can refer to an entire day). In the United States, binge drinking is defined as a pattern of drinking that brings blood alcohol concentration levels to 0.08 g/dL. This typically occurs after four drinks for women and five drinks for men—generally within a two-hour period (NIAAA, 2019a).

According to the 2017 National Survey on Drug Use and Health, 53.6% of full-time college students ages 18 to 22 drank alcohol in the past month; 34.8% engaged in binge drinking (five or more drinks on a single occasion for men and four or more drinks on an occasion for women) in the past month; and 9.7% engaged in heavy alcohol use (binge drinking on five or more days in the past month). These rates are higher than those for their noncollege-attending peers (NIAAA, 2019b).

Other major findings from the widely reported study by Wechsler and Wuethrich (2002) brought the issue of binge drinking to the public's attention. Of those surveyed, 84% drank alcohol during the school year, with almost half (44%) categorized as binge drinkers and 19% as frequent binge drinkers. In summary, the finding were:

- One-third (33%) of schools surveyed qualified as high-binge drinking campuses. To be qualified for a high-binge drinking campus, more than half of the students responding to the survey had to indicate they were binge drinkers.
- The strongest predictor for binge drinking was living in a sorority or fraternity house. Eighty percent of sorority women and 86% of fraternity men living in Greek housing qualified as binge drinkers.

Alcohol consumption is routine at many social activities for college students.

Wechsler, Lee, Kuo, & Lee 2000 found that

- the "typical characteristics of binge drinkers include: male, fraternity and sorority members, white, under 24 years of age, involved in athletics, and students who socialize a great deal";
- "students involved in community service, the arts, or studying a great deal were less likely to binge drink"; and
- "less than half of binge drinkers considered religion an important part of their lives."

One may question whether all five-drink episodes qualify as *binge drinking*, a term that calls to mind a weekend of drinking or Jellinek's epsilon alcoholism. However, 11.1% of males and 7.4% of females reported three or more episodes of memory loss during the past year from drug or alcohol use, of which the overwhelming majority were alcohol related, both because alcohol is the major drug consumed by students and because it produces amnesiac episodes. Amnesiac episodes are accepted as symptoms of problem-drinking behavior.

In another national survey of 17,600 students at 140 four-year colleges and universities (and one that is regularly conducted by the Harvard School of Public Health) the findings were as follows (Wechsler et al., 2000, p. 1):

- "Overall, 44% of the students were binge drinkers. Among men, 50% were binge drinkers; among women, the figure was 39%."
- "The main reason given for binge drinking was 'to get drunk.'"
- "White students were over twice as likely to be binge drinkers compared to other racial [and] ethnic groups."
- "Students who said that religious participation is not very important to them were more than twice as likely to be binge drinkers compared to other students."
- "Students who said that athletic participation was very important or important to them were also one-and-a-half times more likely to be binge drinkers."
- "Residents of fraternities or sororities were four times as likely to be binge drinkers compared to other students."

Other alcohol research studies revealed the following:

- Community college students were less likely to engage in binge drinking; 29.9% had binged in the previous two weeks compared with 40.4% of their peers at four-year schools.

It is not unusual for college students to overconsume alcohol when they are partying.

- Approximately one-fourth of all males enrolled at four-year colleges reported three or more binge episodes during the previous two weeks (NIAAA, 2008).
- According to a national survey, almost 60% of college students ages 18 to 22 drank alcohol in the preceding month, and almost two out of three engaged in binge drinking during that same time frame (NIH 2015c).
- Students who lived on campus were more likely to binge drink than those who lived off campus. Furthermore, older, working, off-campus students were less likely to engage in such behavior, lowering their scores in this regard relative to the standard college students (NIAAA, 2008).
- American Indian and Alaska Native students had the highest frequency of drinking episodes, binge drinking, and memory loss, followed (in order) by white, Hispanic, African American, and Asian students.

## ▪ Gender and Collegiate Alcohol Use

Among college students and young adults generally, there are substantial gender differences in alcohol use, with college males drinking the most. In 2014, for example, approximately 50% of all college males reported having five or more drinks in a row over the previous two weeks versus one-third (34%) of college females. Given that the physiological impacts of five drinks are considerably greater for the typical young female versus the typical young male, it is not surprising that we find substantial gender differences in the prevalence of having five or more drinks in a row. Throughout the years, this gender difference has narrowed gradually, with the rate declining somewhat for males and increasing somewhat for females.

The findings from the Core Institute (2014) survey consistently indicate greater frequency of male drinking, frequency of male binge drinking, and consequences of drinking. In a review of the literature addressing gender and student drinking patterns, Berkowitz and Perkins (1987) and Hensel et al. (2014) found a historical pattern of male-dominated college drinking patterns. The transition into college is associated with a doubling of the percentages of those who drink for both genders. Both men and women drink to enhance sociability or social interaction, to escape negative emotions or release otherwise unacceptable ones, and to simply get drunk. "Drinking to get drunk" is generally considered more of a male pursuit. Indeed, males are more frequently associated with binge drinking and negative public consequences than are female drinkers. Severe drunkenness and a customary rowdiness or drunken comportment are normative for male drinkers who binge, with the results including fighting, property damage, and troubles with authorities. The latter were twice as likely to be male problems.

It comes as no surprise that drinking is inversely related to academic achievement. With heavier drinkers, grades suffered for both male and female students. According to the studies cited by Berkowitz and Perkins (1987) for binge drinkers, the impact on impaired academic performance is just as great for women drinkers. More recent information (Core Institute, 2014; De Jong, 1995; Presley et al., 1996; Wechsler, Dowdall, Davenport, & DeJong, 2000; Wechsler, Eun Lee, Kuo, & Lee, 2000) corroborates this finding and shows similar consequences among male and female binge drinkers in terms of health problems, personal injury, and unplanned sexual activity. Over the past few decades, drinking behaviors (amount and percentage of drinking) have been becoming more similar between males and females.

# Alcohol Consumption Patterns of Women

Women are affected by alcohol differently than are men. Women possess greater sensitivity to alcohol, have a greater likelihood of addiction, and develop alcohol-related health problems sooner than men. Why do women respond differently than men to alcohol? Three reasons are (1) women have smaller body sizes (men are generally larger than women); (2) women absorb alcohol sooner than men because on average they possess more body fat, and body fat does not dilute alcohol as well as water (male bodies contain more water); and (3) women possess less of a metabolizing enzyme that functions to get rid of (process out) alcohol.

In Great Britain, the proportion of women drinking has risen steadily since 1984. This increase in drinking still holds true for all age groups with the exception of women older than 65 (Alcohol Concern, 2008). Other notable facts regarding women and drinking can be summarized as follows (Buddy T., 2016a, 2016c; NIAAA, 2000a):

- Although men begin drinking earlier in life, women are more likely than men to start drinking heavily later in life.
- Women are more easily affected by alcohol consumption, both its effects and diseases related to alcoholism—cirrhosis of the liver, stomach cancer, and so on.
- Women become intoxicated faster than men.
- Women's blood-alcohol content increases more quickly than in men.
- Women become dependent or addicted to alcohol more quickly than do men.
- Women develop alcohol liver disease after drinking less than men.
- Women develop alcohol-related brain damage sooner than men.
- Women experience more extensive alcohol-related brain damage than men.
- Women are at higher risk for getting alcohol-related cancers than men.
- Women are more likely to have a fatal alcohol-related auto crash than men.
- Women's alcohol consumption is often similar to that of people they are close to such as a lover or husband.
- Full-time working, professionally oriented women drink at the end of their working day, whereas women who stay at home drink alcohol throughout the day.
- More women in alcohol treatment come from sexually abusive homes (70%), in comparison to men (12%).
- Today, women are more visible and their behavior, especially alcohol consumption, is more observable (e.g., drinking in bars, purchasing alcohol).

**Figure 8.6** shows the prevalence estimate of alcohol use (percentage of any use and binge drinking) among women 18 to 44 in 2016 (CDC 2018). The U.S. average of all the states and territories for any use of alcohol by women is approximately 46%, and average binge drinking is 20% for all

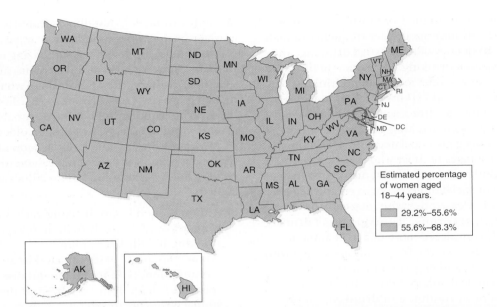

| Location | Any-Alcohol-Use* | Binge drinking |
|---|---|---|
| Alabama | 45.6% | 14.2 |
| Alaska | 57.4% | 21.1 |
| Arizona | 45.2% | 14.7 |
| Arkansas | 45.6% | 16.1 |
| California | 47.9% | 15.7 |
| Colorado | 61.7% | 21.2 |
| Connecticut | 56.5% | 19.6 |
| Delaware | 53.8% | 21 |
| Washington D. C. | 67.9% | 28.9 |
| Florida | 51.5% | 18.1 |
| Georgia | 49.1% | 13.6 |
| Hawaii | 48.5% | 20.9 |
| Idaho | 44.1% | 16.2 |
| Illinois | 56.9% | 22 |
| Indiana | 54.3% | 19.7 |
| Iowa | 60.2% | 24.3 |
| Kansas | 55.6% | 16.3 |
| Kentucky | 43.3% | 16.3 |
| Louisiana | 57% | 18.1 |
| Maine | 60% | 23.5 |
| Maryland | 55.6% | 17.9 |
| Massachusetts | 63.1% | 21.9 |
| Michigan | 57.3% | 21.4 |
| Minnesota | 60.7% | 23.7 |
| Mississippi | 41.6% | 11.9 |
| Missouri | 58.1% | 20.2 |
| Montana | 60.1% | 19.8 |

| Location | Any-Alcohol-Use* | Binge drinking |
|---|---|---|
| Nebraska | 55.7% | 19.9 |
| Nevada | 47.6% | 16.3 |
| New Hampshire | 63.2% | 21.4 |
| New Jersey | 53.4% | 17.6 |
| New Mexico | 47.1% | 15.3 |
| New York | 56.7% | 19.5 |
| North Carolina | 50.6% | 17.3 |
| North Dakota | 65.6% | 25.8 |
| Ohio | 57.2% | 20.8 |
| Oklahoma | 42.6% | 12.3 |
| Oregon | 57.7% | 17.2 |
| Pennsylvania | 61% | 22.4 |
| Rhode Island | 56% | 15.7 |
| South Carolina | 54.6% | 16.6 |
| South Dakota | 59.8% | 23 |
| Tennessee | 53.3% | 16.7 |
| Texas | 47.4% | 17.9 |
| Utah | 29.2% | 11.6 |
| Vermont | 64.6% | 23.5 |
| Virginia | 55.7% | 18.8 |
| Washington | 55% | 17.9 |
| West Virginia | 36.1% | 11.1 |
| Wisconsin | 68.3% | 29.6 |
| Wyoming | 50.4% | 18.7 |
| Guam | 38.7% | 14.7 |
| Puerto Rico | 31.1% | 13.1 |

**FIGURE 8.6** State-specific weighted prevalence estimates of alcohol use (percentage of any alcohol use and binge drinking) among women aged 18–44 years.

Data from Centers for Disease Control and Prevention (CDC). (2018, March 20). Fetal Alcohol Spectrum Disorders (FASDs)—State-level Estimates of Alcohol Use Among Women—2016. Atlanta, GA: Centers for Disease Control and Prevention. Retrieved from https://www.cdc.gov/ncbddd/fasd/data-maps-2016.html

childbearing-age women. When looking at binge drinking rates among women, the state of Wisconsin has the highest percentage (29.6%), and West Virginia has the lowest percentage (11.1%).

Figure 8.6 also shows the following.

- These states and Washington, D.C., have the highest percentages (68.3% to 60%) of childbearing women who drink alcohol (listed from high to low): Wisconsin (68.3%), Washington, D.C. (67.9%), North Dakota (65.6%), Vermont (64.6%), New Hampshire (63.2%), Massachusetts (63.1%), Colorado (61.7%), Pennsylvania (61%), Minnesota (60.7), Iowa 60.2%), Montana (60.1%), and Maine (60%).

- The following states and Washington, D.C., have the highest percentages (20.2% to 29.6%) of childbearing women who binge drink (listed from high to low): Wisconsin (29.6%), Washington, D.C. (28.9%), North Dakota (25.8%), Pennsylvania (22.4%), Illinois (22%), Massachusetts (21.9%), Michigan (21.4%), New Hampshire (21.4%), Colorado (21.2%), Alaska (21.1%), Delaware (21%), Hawaii (20.9%), Ohio (20.8%), and Missouri (20.2%).

As a group, alcohol-abusing women are more likely to drink alone at home. A high incidence of alcohol abuse is found in women who are unemployed and looking for work, whereas less alcohol abuse is likely in women who are employed part-time. Divorced or separated women, women who never marry, and those who are unmarried and living with a partner are more likely to use and abuse alcohol than are married women. Other high-risk groups are women in their 20s and early 30s and women with heavy-drinking husbands or partners. Other researchers (Williams, Stinson, Parker, Harford, & Noble, 1997; Wilsnack, Wilsnack, & Klassen, 1986) found that women who experience depression or encounter problems with fertility or menopausal changes also demonstrate heavier drinking behavior.

Looking at specific age groups, the following conclusions have been drawn:

- The course of alcohol addiction progresses at a faster rate among women than among men. Research shows that "female alcoholics are generally younger than males" (NIDA, 2019).
- For many women, heavy drinking came after a health problem such as depression or reproductive difficulties (Register, Cline, & Shively, 2002).
- Women in the 21- to 34-year-old age group were least likely to report alcohol-related problems if they had stable marriages and were working full-time. In other words, young mothers with full-time occupations reported less reliance on alcohol in comparison to childless women without full-time work (Register et al., 2002).

- Among nonpregnant binge drinkers, binge-drinking prevalence, frequency, and intensity were highest among those aged 18 to 24 years (CDC 2010).
- Women tend to marry men whose drinking habits match their own (NIAAA, 2015b).
- Young women in their 20s and early 30s are more likely to drink than older women. No one factor predicts whether a woman will have problems with alcohol, or at what age she is most at risk. However, there are some life experiences that seem to make it more likely that women will have drinking problems (NIAAA, 2015b).
- Heavy drinking and drinking problems among white women are most common in younger age groups. Among African American women, however, drinking problems are more common in middle age than in youth. A woman's ethnic origins—and the extent to which she adopts the attitudes of mainstream versus her native culture—influence how and when she will drink. Hispanic women who are more "mainstream" are more likely to drink and to drink heavily (i.e., to drink at least once a week and to have five or more drinks at one time) (NIAAA, 2015b).
- Research suggests that women who have trouble with their closest relationships tend to drink more than other women. Heavy drinking is more common among women who have never married, are living unmarried with a partner, or are divorced or separated (note that the effect of divorce on a woman's later drinking may depend on whether she is already drinking heavily in her marriage) (NIAAA, 2015b).
- In the 35- to 49-year-old age group, the heaviest drinkers were divorced or separated women without children in the home.
- In the 50- to 64-year-old age group, the heaviest drinkers were women whose husbands or partners drank heavily.
- Women 65 years or older constitute less than 10% of drinkers with drinking problems.

Alcohol consumption has been found to be higher in women who closely work in traditionally so-called masculine occupations and levels of management such as executives and traditional blue-collar occupations. In April 1995, former First Lady Betty Ford made the following statement:

Today, we know that when a woman abuses alcohol or other drugs, the risk to her health is much greater than it is for a man. Yet there is not enough prevention, intervention, and treatment targeting women. It is still much harder for women to get help. That needs to change. (SAMHSA, 1995, p. 14)

In fact, women risk serious health consequences when they choose to use alcohol and other drugs. Alcohol, in particular, can often be devastating to women's health.

Alcohol not only has a greater immediate effect on women, but also its long-term risks are more dangerous. Some surveys now show that more alcohol consumption occurs among girls 12 to 17 years old than among boys of the same age. This places young women at risk of delaying the onset of puberty, a condition that can wreak havoc in terms of adolescent maturation. "Drinking over the long term is more likely to damage a woman's health than a man's, even if the woman has been drinking less alcohol or for a shorter length of time than a man (NIAAA, 2015b).

Finally, women are more likely than men to combine alcohol with prescription drugs. When the use of other drugs enters into the equation, ovulation may become inhibited and fertility may be adversely affected. Women also risk early menopause when they consume alcohol.

## ■ The Role of Alcohol in Domestic Violence

Domestic violence involves behavior that one person uses against another to control a spouse or partner through fear and intimidation. It can involve physical, sexual, emotional, economic, and psychological abuse; it "includes any behaviors that intimidate, manipulate, humiliate, isolate, frighten, terrorize, coerce, threaten, blame, hurt, injure, or wound someone" (U.S. Department of Justice, 2013).

Abuse can show itself in the following ways.

- *Physical battering.* Attacks can range from bruising to punching to life-threatening choking or use of weapons.
- *Sexual abuse.* A person is forced to have sexual intercourse with the abuser or take part in unwanted sexual activity.
- *Psychological battering.* Psychological violence can include constant verbal abuse, harassment, excessive possessiveness, isolating the victim from friends and family, withholding money, and destruction of personal property (FOE 2005, p. 3).

Much attention was focused on domestic violence in the mid-1990s because of high-profile criminal cases such as those involving the Menendez brothers and O. J. Simpson. The increased emphasis on decreasing domestic violence has inspired much research into its causes and effects, as well as in identifying the common traits of abusers. Studies have found a significant relationship between the incidence of battering and the abuse of alcohol; furthermore, the abuse of alcohol overwhelmingly emerges as a primary predictor of marital violence (Buddy T., 2016d; De Jong, 1995; Drug Strategies, 1999). A study of 2,000 American couples conducted in 1993 showed that rates of domestic violence were as much as 15 times higher in households in which the husband was described as "often" being drunk as opposed to "never" being drunk (Buddy T., 2016d; Collins & Messerschmidt, 1993). Collins & Messerschmidt found that alcohol was present in more than half of all reported incidences of domestic abuse. Further, "[a]nother study . . . [showed] . . . that the percentage of batterers who are under the influence of alcohol when they assault their partners ranges from 48% to 87%, with most research indicating a 60% to 70% rate of alcohol abuse and a 13% to 20% rate of drug abuse" (Buddy T., 2016d).

Domestic violence also creates significant problems for its victims later in life. A study of 472 women by the Research Institute on Addictions found that 87% of female alcoholics had been physically or sexually abused as children (Drug Strategies, 1999; Miller & Downs, 1993; NIAAA, 2015b). Research also shows the following:

On the surface it seems hard to argue with the numbers reported in domestic violence research studies. Ninety-two percent of the domestic abuse assailants reported use of alcohol or other drugs on the day of the assault, according to a recent *JAMA* [*Journal of the American Medical Association*]. (Wechsler, Davenport, Dowdall, Moeykens, & Castillo, 1994)

The insidiousness of domestic violence may exist because of the consistent abuse of alcohol that is associated with both abusers and victims. Given these disturbing statistics, more research and counseling programs focusing on the prevention of alcoholism and subsequent domestic violence are necessary before the very foundations of identity, security, and happiness are forever destroyed. As one reformed alcoholic explains,

> It was really terrible. I would drink by myself in the living room and fight with my wife in other parts of the house. I knew I needed help when I shoved her around on the night of her birthday and threw a wet kitchen washcloth and hit her in the face. Before that night, I never would have done this, but her nagging about my drinking that night got to me more than on other nights and it caused me to lose control. *(From Venturelli's research files, male, age 48, July 2010)*

## ■ Alcohol and Sex

Alcohol use is linked to an overwhelming proportion of unwanted sexual behaviors, including **acquaintance and date rape**, unplanned pregnancies, and sexually transmitted infections, including HIV infections (Abbey, 1990; World Health Organization [WHO], 1996). Factors that immediately come to mind include disinhibition concerning restraints on sexuality, poor judgment, and unconsciousness or helplessness on the part of victims. The links between unwanted sex and substance abuse are subtler than many imagine, however. Although disinhibition, impulsivity, and helplessness are certainly major considerations, other elements come into play as illustrated in the following paragraphs.

A study conducted at an unnamed university in upstate New York and published in the *Journal of Adolescent Health* reports "that 19% of women, nearly one in five, said they had been a victim of attempted or completed rape, either by force or while they were incapacitated due to alcohol or drugs, during their freshman year" (Wallace, 2015). Other dating violence includes physical, psychological, and sexual violence. One in 10 high school students have experienced physical violence from a dating partner in the past year (Adamo & Advocates for Youth, 2014).

The following are additional data that have been reported on sexual and dating violence among young people (Adamo & Advocates for Youth. 2014):

- According to data from the 2011 Youth Risk Behavior Surveillance, nationwide, 8% of students reported that they had been physically forced to have sexual intercourse when they did not want to. Overall, the prevalence of having been forced to have sexual intercourse was higher among female (11.8%) than male (4.5%) students. For 28% of young women who were raped or sexually assaulted, the perpetrator was a former or current intimate partner.
- Young women between ages 16 and 24 experience the highest rate of intimate partner violence. According to one national study, 29% of the young women surveyed who had ever been in a relationship said they had been pressured to have sex or to engage in sexual activity they did not want.
- Most female victims of intimate partner violence were previously victimized by the same offender, including 77% of female victims ages 18 to 24.
- Psychological violence includes uneven power dynamics, control, jealousy, and threats regarding the relationship. In one study, 21% of teens said that they had been in a relationship with someone who wanted to keep them from seeing friends and family. The same study found that 64% of those surveyed had a partner who acted jealous and demanded to know their whereabouts at all times.
- A 2013 study of dating violence among lesbian, gay, bisexual, and transgender (LGBT) youth found that LGBT youth showed significantly higher rates of all types of dating violence victimization and perpetration experiences, compared to heterosexual youth.

Recall the drunken comportment thesis that was introduced in the section on culture and drinking behavior. Some nonreligious ceremonial drinking settings incorporate expectations of disinhibited behaviors, such as at holiday office parties. Drinking is a signal or cue that it is acceptable to be amorous, even sexually aggressive, and that the intoxicated object of one's affections will not object and is disinhibited.

Intoxicated people are not as capable of attending to multiple cues. When cues are ambiguous, drunken men are more likely to miss the ambiguity and to interpret cues as meaning that sex will occur and should be initiated. (Men are generally more likely to interpret friendly cues as sexual

**KEY TERM**

**acquaintance and date rape**
unplanned and unwanted forced sexual attack from a friend or a date partner

signals, but intoxication makes this misunderstanding more likely.) In addition, possible dangers implicit in a private setting, on a date, with a drunken male will not be picked up as often or as easily by the intoxicated and potentially victimized female (Abbey, 1990).

# Alcohol and the Family: Destructive Types of Social Support and Organizations for Victims of Alcoholics

## ▮ Codependency and Enabling

Codependency and enabling generally occur together. **Codependency** (which some call *co-alcoholism*) refers to a relationship pattern, and *enabling* refers to a set of specific behaviors (Doweiko, 2015). Codependency is defined as the behavior displayed by either addicted or non-addicted family members (codependents) who identify with the alcohol addict and cover up the excessive drinking behavior. An example of codependency is when a family member remains silent when empty bottles of vodka, for example, are discovered under a bed or in the garage.

**Enablers** are those close to the alcohol addict who deny or make excuses for enabling the excessive drinking. Often, both codependency and enabling are done by the same person. An example is the husband who calmly conspires and phones his wife's place of employment and reports that his wife has the stomach flu when the reality is that she is too drunk or hung over to realize it is time to go to work.

Such a husband is both codependent and an enabler. He lies to cover up his wife's addiction and enables her not to face her irresponsible drinking behavior. In this example, the husband

is responsible for perpetuating the spouse's addiction. Even quiet toleration of the alcoholic's addiction enables the drinker to continue the drinking behavior.

## ▮ Children of Alcoholics (COAs) and Adult Children of Alcoholics (ACOAs)

Alcoholism is a disease of the family. Not only is there a significant genetic component that is passed from generation to generation, but the drinking problems of a single family member affect all other family members. The family environment and genetics can perpetuate a vicious and destructive cycle. "Alcoholism is also known as a family disease. Alcoholics may have young, teenage, or grown-up children; they have wives or husbands; they have brothers or sisters; they have parents or other relatives. An alcoholic can totally disrupt family life and cause harmful effects that can last a lifetime" (Parsons, 2003). Children living with a nonrecovering alcoholic score lower on measures of family cohesion, intellectual–cultural orientation, active-recreational orientation, and independence. They also usually experience higher levels of conflict within the family.

Research findings indicate the following:

There are 18 million alcoholics in the U.S., according to the National Council on Alcoholism and Drug Dependence. As a result, an estimated 26.8 million children are exposed, at varying degrees, to alcoholism in the family. These children are at higher risk for alcoholism and other drug abuse than are children of non-alcoholics, and are more likely to marry an alcoholic as well. Children of alcoholics or addicts are commonly referred to as "COA." (American Association for Marriage and Family Therapy, 2019)

Approximately 9.7 million children age 17 or younger were living in households with one or more adults who were classified as having a diagnosis of alcohol abuse or dependence within the previous year, according to data from the National Longitudinal Alcohol Epidemiologic Survey. Approximately 70% of these children were biological, foster, adopted, or stepchildren. Therefore, 6.8 million children, or about 15% of children age 17 or younger, meet the formal definition of children of alcoholics (COAs) (Zucker, Donovan, Masten, Mattson, & Moss, 2009).

Children of alcoholics are at high risk of developing the same attachment to alcohol as their

---

**KEY TERMS**

**codependency**
behavior displayed by either addicted or nonaddicted family members (codependents) who identify with the alcohol addict and cover up the excessive drinking behavior, allowing it to continue and letting it affect the codependent's life

**enablers**
those close to the alcohol addict who deny or make excuses for enabling his or her excessive drinking

parents. Alcoholics are more likely than nonalcoholics to have an alcoholic parent, sibling, or other relative.

Within the last decade, both COAs and adult children of alcoholics (ACOAs) have been studied extensively. Here are some major findings concerning these two groups by Zucker et al. (2009, p. 24):

- COAs have an increased risk of alcohol involvement because "[g]enetically transmitted differences in response to alcohol . . . make drinking more pleasurable and/or less aversive" (p. 24).
- "Higher transmission of risky temperamental and behavioral traits . . . lead the COAs into greater contact with earlier and heavier drinking peers" (p. 24).
- COAs are two to four times more likely to develop alcoholism. In addition, both COAs and ACOAs are more likely to marry into families in which alcoholism is prevalent.
- Approximately one-third of alcoholics come from families in which one parent was or is an alcoholic.
- Both physiological and environmental factors appear to place COAs and ACOAs at greater risk of becoming alcoholics.
- COAs and ACOAs exhibit more symptoms of depression and anxiety than do children of nonalcoholic parents.
- Young children of alcoholics exhibit an excessive amount of crying, bed-wetting, and sleep problems such as nightmares.
- Teenagers display excessive perfectionism, hoarding, staying by themselves (loners), and excessive self-consciousness.
- Phobias develop, and difficulty with school performance is not uncommon.

ACOAs have been found to share many characteristics. The following set of ACOA characteristics was developed by Dr. Janel G. Woititz in 1983 (Buddy T., 2015):

- Become isolated.
- Fear people and authority figures.
- Become approval seekers.
- Be frightened of angry people.
- Be terrified of personal criticism.
- Become alcoholics, marry them, or both.
- View life as a victim.
- Have an overwhelming exaggerated sense of responsibility.
- Be concerned more with others than themselves.
- Feel guilty when they stand up for themselves.
- Become addicted to excitement.
- Confuse love and pity.
- "Love" people who need rescuing.
- Stuff their feelings.
- Lose the ability to feel.
- Have low self-esteem.
- Judge themselves harshly.
- Become terrified of abandonment.
- Do anything to hold onto a relationship.
- Become "para-alcoholics" without drinking.
- Become reactors instead of actors.

## Treatment of Alcoholism

Although treatment of alcoholism and treatment of other addictions have somewhat separate historical roots and consequently gave rise to separate therapy systems, governmental authorities, and counselor certifications, they have now merged in most states in the United States. In addition to recognizing that alcohol is a drug addiction, epidemiologically few "pure" alcoholics and drug addicts exist anymore. Most addicts drink in addition to their other drug addictions (making them polydrug users), many alcoholics abuse other drugs, and some move through stages of heroin, methadone, and alcohol use—in that order. Alcoholism and its treatment have a few special features:

- Although addicts remain in denial, the socially acceptable nature of drinking, or even of heavy drinking, makes it easier to maintain denial as a psychological defense. In contrast, it is more difficult to remain in denial of crack addiction.
- Although all addictions could result in **relapsing syndrome**, and most addicts have a tendency to relapse, the social environment that permits or even encourages drinking and the ready availability of alcohol makes it easy to relapse without a radical shift in lifestyle. Again, the alcoholic is buffered within a subcultural (social and cultural) cloud of use. Alcoholics Anonymous remains particularly vigilant in looking for signs of relapse,

KEY TERM

**relapsing syndrome**
returning to the use of alcohol after quitting

advising the alcoholic to "keep the memory regarding the misery of addiction green," to HALT—that is, do not get too *hungry, angry, lonely,* or *thirsty or tired* because these are possible relapse triggers—and not to become isolated from others but to stay in the support system, making phone calls and attending "90 meetings in 90 days."

• Alcohol rehabilitation differs from other addiction treatments mainly in its medical ramifications. Alcoholism is devastating to the liver, muscles, nutritional system, gastrointestinal system, and brain. Alcoholics who have become "dry" only recently may still suffer from pancreatitis, weakness, impaired cognitive capacities, and so forth. The fact that treatment is so structured, simplified, and made into a slogan ("Don't drink and go to meetings," "Keep coming: It works") makes it possible for the bleary and confused, recently dried-out alcoholic to follow. (An AA term for this condition is *mokus.*) Although the cognitive impairment tends to clear up somewhat over a period of six months (unless clear cortical wasting has occurred, a condition known as "wet brain"), the alcoholic is often physically ravaged to an extent that requires years to mend the damage, if it is ever possible.

• The alcoholic is typically more emotionally fragile than other addicts in treatment.

• The other major medical ramification is withdrawal. Withdrawal from alcohol and withdrawal from barbiturates are the two most severe withdrawal syndromes. Before modern medical management techniques, many individuals succumbed to **acute alcohol withdrawal syndrome**.

## ▪ Getting Through Withdrawal

An alcoholic who is well nourished and in good physical condition can go through withdrawal as an outpatient with reasonable safety. However, an acutely ill alcoholic needs medically supervised care. A general hospital ward is best for preliminary treatment. The alcohol withdrawal syndrome is quite similar to that for barbiturates and other sedative hypnotics. Symptoms typically appear within 12 to 72 hours after total cessation of drinking but can appear whenever the blood alcohol level drops below a certain point. The alcoholic experiences severe muscle tremors, nausea, and anxiety. In extremely acute alcohol syndromes, a condition known as **delirium tremens (DTs)** occurs, in which the individual hallucinates, is delirious, and suffers from a high fever and rapid heartbeat. The DTs are an uncommon but life-threatening condition.

Alcohol withdrawal syndrome reaches its peak intensity within 24 to 48 hours. About 5% of the alcoholics in hospitals and perhaps 20% to 25% who suffer the DTs without treatment die. Phenobarbital, chlordiazepoxide (Librium), and diazepam (Valium) are commonly prescribed to prevent withdrawal symptoms. Simultaneously, the alcoholic may need treatment for malnutrition and vitamin deficiencies (especially the B vitamins). Pneumonia is also a frequent complication. After the alcoholic patient is over the acute stages of intoxication and withdrawal, administration of central nervous system depressants may be continued for a few weeks, with care taken not to transfer dependence on alcohol to dependence on the depressants. Long-term treatment with sedatives (such as Librium or Valium) does not prevent a relapse of drinking or assist with behavioral adaptation. A prescription of disulfiram (Antabuse) may be offered to encourage patients to abstain from alcohol; it blocks metabolism of acetaldehyde so that drinking any alcohol will result in a pounding headache, flushing, nausea, and other unpleasant symptoms. The patient must decide about two days in advance to stop taking Antabuse before he or she can drink. Antabuse is an aid to other supportive treatments, not the sole method of therapy.

A current medical approach for treating alcohol dependent patients includes Naltrexone (Naltrexone hydrochloride). Naltrexone a non-addictive compound blocks the euphoric effects and feelings of intoxication. This drug allows alcohol addicted patients to reduce and stop their drinking behaviors and more likely to complete treatments and avoid alcohol relapses (SAMHSA, 2020).

## ▪ Helping the Alcoholic Family Recover

Alcoholism is a pervasive disease that affects the entire family. The family is a system and should be viewed not as disconnected people living together but as people who affect one another and play certain roles, all working to keep the system in balance. In treating alcoholism, family therapy has a strong and bright future. Often family therapists place emphasis on the emotional patterns within alcoholic families, expecting that entire families attend counseling sessions. It is not unusual to have sessions with different generations of alcohol abusers within families. The goal is to break the cycle of alcohol abuse within families:

> Family therapy in substance abuse treatment can help by using the family's strengths and resources to find ways for the person who abuses alcohol or drugs to live without substances of abuse and to ameliorate the impact of chemical dependency on both the patient and the family. Family therapy . . . can help families become aware of their own needs and aid in the goal of keeping substance abuse from moving from one generation to another. (SAMHSA, 2004)

We are all familiar with the stereotype of families in which the oldest child is the "hero," the middle child is "forgotten," and the youngest is the "baby." Whatever the roles of the individuals, when the family includes an alcoholic, it means that a member of the system is ill. The system adapts to dysfunction by rearranging itself around the problem. The family is like a mobile, a sculpture with interdependent parts that revolve around one another. We are not talking about adjusting to a person with a broken leg or diabetes, but someone who is in denial—manipulative, lying, and blaming other family members. By adjusting around the addiction, the family members enable the addict to progress further along the disease path. Roles become exaggerated and distorted. Persons may be blamed, scapegoated, or lost and forgotten. One major adaptation is related to the person who "takes up the slack" by assuming extra responsibilities and taking on the role of a parent or even spouse.

Early family therapy systems research described how the family often acts as a unit. It focused on the disturbed communication patterns within families and the process by which the family throws up a scapegoat, often in the form of a child who is presented as the "identified patient" (Kolevzon & Green, 1985; SAMHSA, 2004). The concept of the "super-responsible one" was first described by Virginia Satir in 1964. In modern

times, popular writing on addiction in the family and codependent roles of children that are carried into adulthood, all of these roles are depicted as especially characteristic of addicted families (SAMHSA, 2004; Satir, 1964; Wegscheider, 1991). Because such roles are so common, many individuals may identify with them and ascribe a variety of ills to their being the offspring of an addict. Many individuals do suffer tremendously from the legacy of family addiction, and some have indeed been cast in one of these roles as a by-product of addiction in the family. However, acting as if only one kind of family or one kind of addicted family exists, which transcends cultural backgrounds, is not much better than saying that all languages or religions are the same. For example, "executive authority" over younger children can be the normal role of the eldest female child in African American families as part of a broader pattern of role flexibility (Brisbane, 1985, 1985–1986). When an older child plays a parental part in the family, it may represent culturally routine behavior or it may indicate a response to addiction in the family.

There is some gain or perceived benefit to the person playing a role and to the system as a whole, in the individual's actions, although this gain may seem indirect and, in fact, be injurious in the long run. Although the super-responsible person may be overburdened and resentful, he or she also feels important, heroic, and capable. Over a period, this role solidifies. Perhaps the hero becomes unable to remember or imagine it any other way. If the alcoholic enters or promises to enter into recovery, it may threaten the benefits to the family member. One of many examples is a wife in a subservient role who relishes, at some level, the power, control, and authority she enjoys with an alcoholic husband or the recognition she

Even after the alcoholic is ready for rehabilitation, the other family members will also need treatment and support.

receives in martyrdom—perhaps her only recognition in life. Another example is the child who is prematurely given executive authority in the family. Without knowing it, the family members may resist change, not only for what they may have to give up, but also because change is always feared. Thus, they may undermine recovery.

The role systems found in alcoholic families can be enmeshed so that everyone is hyper-responsive to and dependent on one another—disorganized, chaotic, or exploded into nothingness. The old-fashioned, middle-class alcoholic family is commonly enmeshed. This situation is more likely to arise if religion represents a barrier to divorce and hence removal of the alcoholic.

A family counselor can help the family members understand the roles they are playing and start a process of change. This recognition allows family members to develop their own identities separate from the roles they have been playing. Two of the techniques used in understanding roles and relationships are **psychodrama** (or **role-playing**) and the **genogram**, a kind of family tree in which behavioral relationships as well as biological relationships are explored (Davis, n.d.).

The family counselor can help the family members figure out their patterns of thinking, which involves certain modes of information processing. In the alcoholic family, these patterns typically involve denial, minimization, rationalization, shame, blame, and projection. Counselors also rely on certain self-statements (see "Here and Now: The 'Top Tens' of Helping Alcoholics and Their Families").

In addition, the family counselor can help family members understand their patterns of communication. Alcoholic family communication is almost certainly a type of abnormal communication characterized by either simple absence of communication (chaotic, destructive, manipulative, and blaming) or a combination of communication methods. What the family does in the public view, visible to the outside world ("front stage"), differs from what goes on when the family is alone ("backstage"). Some individuals may be cut off from communication or embroiled in endless argument and acrimony. Teaching people how to communicate their feelings and opinions in a direct, honest, and nonhurtful way begins the healing process.

The alcoholic family is injured, traumatized, often in debt, and collectively suffering from **posttraumatic stress disorder (PTSD)**. Grief, loss, pain, and rage are present. Healing will not take place overnight and will not occur just because the alcoholic stops drinking. The child, in particular, may have been wounded by violence, neglect, and inconsistent parenting and may have been witness to sex, violence, or depression.

## KEY TERMS

**psychodrama**
family therapy system developed by Jacques Moreno in which significant interpersonal and intrapersonal issues are enacted in a focused setting using dramatic techniques

**role-playing**
therapeutic technique in which group members play assigned parts to elicit emotional reactions

**genogram**
a family therapy technique that records information about behavior and relationships on a type of family tree to elucidate persistent patterns of dysfunctional behavior

**posttraumatic stress disorder (PTSD)**
a psychiatric syndrome in which an individual who has been exposed to a traumatic event or situation experiences persistent psychological stress that may manifest itself in a wide range of symptoms, including reexperiencing the trauma, numbing of general responsiveness, and hyperarousal

# HERE AND NOW

## The "Top Tens" of Helping Alcoholics and Their Families

### 10 "Don'ts"

Don't "persecute" the addict. Confront lovingly.

Don't have the goal of "saving the family."

Don't start sentences with "you never" or "you always."

Don't live in the past or in the future.

Don't make excuses for the alcoholic.

Don't let the alcoholic be the center of your life.

Don't clean up after the alcoholic (literally or figuratively).

Don't protect the alcoholic from the consequences of his or her behavior.

Don't blame, excuse, justify, or rationalize.

Don't join in drinking.

### 10 "Dos"

Set limits, using "I" words (I need to stop).

Set limits empathetically (I know you want me to, but I can't).

Detach, lovingly, from the addict's problems.

Teach parenting skills.

Concentrate on the here and now.

Talk about violence and abuse.

Remember that you didn't cause it, you can't cure it, and you can't control it.

Take life a day at a time.

Give "self" assignments, taking care of yourself.

Accept the right to have your feelings and for others to have their feelings.

### 10 Alcoholic Family Self-Statements

In an actively alcoholic family

"Don't talk" (about how you feel, about what's going on).

"Don't trust."

"Don't feel."

"Alcoholism isn't the cause of our problems."

"Keep the status quo at all costs."

In a family having a hard time becoming used to sobriety:

"We liked you better drunk."

"You're always away at AA meetings."

"Who are these people you're always having coffee with?"

"I felt important feeding my brothers and sisters, Mom."

"I felt important going to the school on Open School Night, Dad."

### 10 Roles for Spouses of Alcoholics

Rescuer

Long-suffering martyr

Blamer, conscience

Fellow drinker

Placater

Overextended, super-responsible one

Composed computer

Sick hypochondriac

Scapegoat ("It's your entire fault")

Avoider

### 10 Roles for Children of Alcoholics

Family hero*

Scapegoat*

Lost child*

Mascot*

Placater

Sick role

Parental child or pseudoparent to younger children

Pseudoparent to alcoholic parent

Pseudospouse to sober parent

Place of refuge (for younger children)

---

*Reproduced from Wegscheider, S. (1991). *Another chance.* Palo Alto, CA: Science and Behavior Books. As seen in Inservice Training Program, Essex County, New Jersey, Professional Advisory Committee on Alcohol and Drug Abuse, November 1993. Prepared by Peter L. Myers, PhD.

# LEARNING PORTFOLIO

## Key Terms

## Discussion Questions

1. Why do you think alcohol has always been part of human existence?

2. Cite three positive and three negative outcomes of alcohol use in our society. Do you think the negatives outweigh the positives? If so, why? If not, why not?

3. Look at the pyramid of drinkers shown in Figure 8.2. How do you think the percentages will change 10 years, 20 years, and 30 years from now? Support your projections.

4. What are three positive and three negative outcomes regarding lowering the legal drinking age to 18?

5. Do you personally believe in the strong independent effects of set and setting and pseudointoxication? Can these psychological processes have more effect on the alcohol user than the alcohol itself? Wherever possible, give personal examples.

6. Why do you think the temperance movement and Prohibition failed? Cite three main reasons that also support the text material.

7. Research reports that LGBTQ and homeless people tend to abuse alcohol more than straight (heterosexual) and non-homeless populations. What are three reasons members of each of these subcultures have a tendency to overconsume alcohol?

8. Why do you think children and younger teens desire to consume alcohol with their peers?

9. After reviewing the different definitions of what is an alcoholic, what definition do you think is the most accurate? Write a clear definition of what you think is a "real" alcoholic.

10. What specific criteria would you include when teaching college students to drink in moderation during freshman orientation?

11. Should alcohol be available on college campuses for those 21 years of age or older? Why or why not?

12. Recall and discuss the question of how you may have unknowingly acted as an enabler for a family member or a friend. Can you cite the reason why you acted like this?

## Summary

1. There were 139.8 million current drinkers (past month) of alcohol age 12 or older in 2018, including 67.1 million (48.0% of alcohol users) who were binge alcohol users and 16.6 million who were heavy alcohol users. (The 2018 estimate of past month alcohol use was similar to the estimates in most years from 2002 to 2017.). Thus, nearly half of current

alcohol users were binge drinkers (48.0%), and one in eight current alcohol users were heavy drinkers (11.8%). Among binge drinkers, about one in four (24.7%) were heavy drinkers.

2. Worldwide, adults age 21 or older consume on average five liters of pure alcohol from beer, wine, and spirits per year. Average alcohol consumption is highest in Europe, followed by the Americas and Africa. It tends to increase with economic development. However, consumption remains low in some regions where the majority of the population is Muslim (GreenFacts, 2009).

3. Among persons 12 or older, whites in 2014 were more likely than other racial and ethnic groups to report current use of alcohol (57.7%). The rates were 49.5% for persons reporting two or more races, 42.3% for American Indians or Alaska Natives, 44.4% for Hispanics, 44.2% for blacks, and 38.7% for Asians (SAMHSA, 2016a).

4. Alcohol is the most widely used drug in the United States, and alcohol problems cost the nation nearly $249 billion each year (NIAAA, 2018a). Three-quarters of the total cost of alcohol misuse is related to binge drinking (NIAAA, 2018a). More than 10% of U.S. children live with an alcoholic problematic parent, according to a 2012 study (NIAAA, 2018a). Seventy-six percent of people with drug or alcohol problems are employed. About 19.2 million U.S. workers (15%) reported using or being impaired by alcohol at work at least once in the past year.

5. Alcohol is officially linked to at least half of all highway fatalities, and that figure includes only legal intoxication. In all states, the cutoff for the blood alcohol level is 0.08%. In as many as 70% of all single-vehicle fatal crashes on weekend nights, the driver was legally intoxicated, and this proportion holds during most weekends throughout the United States. Note that this single issue has been the only alcohol problem that has inspired highly vocal and effective groups to lobby for stricter enforcement of laws against alcohol-impaired automobile driving. Groups such as MADD and SADD are the largest prevention organizations in the nation.

6. In 2000, total costs attributed to alcohol-related motor vehicle crashes were estimated to be $24.7 billion. Expenditures for alcohol-related crime totaled $6.2 billion, and $17.4 billion for crime related to illicit drugs. Alcohol abuse is estimated to have contributed to 25% to 30% of violent crime.

7. The temperance movement was a response to the heaviest drinking period in the United States during President Thomas Jefferson's term in office (1801–1809). The original goal of this movement was to promote moderate use of alcohol. Largely because it was unsuccessful, the temperance movement began advocating total abstinence. Over the course of the 19th century, reformers sought to have complete prohibition enacted into law. Shortly after Prohibition laws were created, making alcohol use illegal, organized crime monopolized the production and sale of alcohol as an illicit drug.

8. There are several accepted definitions of alcoholism. *Alcohol addiction* involves both a physical and psychological dependence on ethanol. Most definitions include chronic behavioral disorders, repeated drinking to the point of loss of control, health disorders, and difficulty functioning socially and economically.

9. The definition of who is a problem drinker varies from one culture to the next. In Poland, a person becomes a problem drinker when there is a loss of productivity. Californians find that drunken-driving violations are a key indication. For Italian Americans, an inability to provide for one's family because of heavy drinking qualifies a person as a problem drinker.

10. Culture influences our view of alcohol and alcohol consumption. Culture dictates the self-definition, attachment, and intensity of our behavior. For example, with regard to drinking, much of how we feel after

ingesting alcohol is determined by social and psychological experiences. In addition to the amount consumed, drunken comportment refers to society's expectations regarding drinking behavior. Set and setting are two important factors affecting alcohol consumption. *Set* refers to the individual's expectation of what a drug will do, and *setting* refers to both the physical environment and the social environment in which the drug is consumed. *Pseudointoxication* refers to the psychological belief regarding how one feels under the effects of alcohol; that is, how inebriated the drinker imagines he or she is from the effects of the consumed alcohol.

11. The broader ways in which culture influences the consumption of alcohol are the following: (a) Culture provides rules for drinking behavior, (b) culture provides ceremonial meaning for alcohol use, (c) culture provides models of alcoholism, (d) cultural stereotypes of drinking may be misleading, (e) culture provides attitudes regarding alcohol consumption, and (f) culture determines what is considered acceptable amounts of drinking.

12. Use of alcohol by college students results in a significant increase in the number of incidents of death, injury, assault, sexual abuse, unsafe sex, academic problems, health problems, suicide attempts, drunk driving, vandalism, property damage, police involvement, and alcohol abuse and dependence. Additional noteworthy findings include the following: (a) college students consume an estimated four billion cans of beer annually, (b) nearly 40% of all college students are binge drinkers, (c) one consequence of alcohol abuse is motor vehicle accidents (which is the leading cause of death in people younger than 25), and (d) 75% of male students and 55% of female students involved in acquaintance rape had been drinking or using drugs at the time.

13. In comparison to men, women possess greater sensitivity to alcohol, are more likely to become addicted, and are more likely to develop health problems earlier in life than men. Three main reasons why women are more sensitive and are more easily affected by alcohol use are (a) their generally smaller bodies, (b) they absorb alcohol sooner than men because they generally have more body fat (fat does not dilute alcohol) and men's bodies contain more water, and (c) women possess less of a metabolizing enzyme that functions to get rid of (process out) alcohol.

14. Codependency and enabling generally occur together. *Codependency* is the behavior that a family member or close friend displays to cover up the excessive drinking. *Enabling* refers to anyone who helps the excessive drinker deny or makes excuses for the excessive drinking.

15. Alcoholism treatment must take into consideration physical withdrawal and denial.

# References

Abbey, A. (1990, Fall). Sex and substance abuse: What are the links? *Eta Sigma Gamman, 22,* 16–18.

Adamo, C., & Advocates for Youth. (2014, March). Young people and dating violence: Teaching healthy relationship skills to protect health and well-being. Washington, DC: Advocates for Youth, March 2014. Retrieved from http://www.advocatesforyouth.org/datingviolence

Adams, S. H. (1905–1906). The great American fraud. *Collier's, 36*(5), 17–18; (10), 16–18; (16), 18–20.

Alcohol Concern. (2008, December). Fact sheet: Women and alcohol—A cause for concern? London, UK.

Alcohol.org. (2019). Global drinking demographics. San Diego, CA: American Addiction Centers Inc. Retrieved from https://www.alcohol.org/guides/global-drinking-demographics/

American Association for Marriage and Family Therapy. (2019). Children of alcoholics. Alexandra, VA: Author. Retrieved from https://www.aamft.org/Consumer_Updates/Children_of_Alcoholics.aspx?WebsiteKey=8e8c9bd6-0b71-4cd1-a5ab-013b5f855b01

American Medical Association (AMA). (2011). Facts about youth and alcohol. Chicago, IL: Author.

American Psychiatric Association (APA). (2013). Substance related and addictive disorders. In *Diagnostic and Statistical*

*Manual of Mental Disorders (DSM-5)*, 5th ed., (pp. 481–589). Washington, DC: American Psychiatric Association.

Answers.com. (2011). Can Hasidic Jews drink alcohol? Retrieved from http://wiki.answers.com/Q/Can_Hasidic_Jews_drink_alcohol

Arkin, E. B., & Funkhouser, J. E. (Eds.). (1992). *Communicating about alcohol and other drugs: Strategies for reaching populations at risk.* OSAP Prevention Monograph No. 5. Rockville, MD: Office of Substance Abuse Prevention, U.S. Department of Health and Human Services.

Austin, G. A. (1978). Perspectives on the history of psychoactive substance use. *National Institute on Drug Abuse Research Issues, 23.* Washington, DC: U.S. Department of Health, Education, and Welfare.

Babor, T. F., Hesselbrock, M., Radouce-Thomas, S., Feguer, L., Ferrant, J. P., & Choquette, K. (1986). Concepts of alcoholism among American, French-Canadian, and French alcoholics. In T. F. Babor (Ed.), *Alcohol and culture: Comparative perspectives from Europe and America* (pp. 98–109). New York, NY: Academy of Sciences.

Bales, R. F. (1946). Cultural differences in rates of alcoholism. *Quarterly Journal of Studies on Alcohol, 6,* 489–499.

Berkowitz, A. D., & Perkins, H. W. (1987, September). Recent research on gender differences in collegiate alcohol use. *Journal of American College Health, 36,* 12–15.

Bissonnette, Z. (2010, September 5). Alcohol and college: How much money are students really drinking? *Daily Finance* (AOL Inc.).

Bloomfield, K., Stockwell, T., Gmel, G., & Rehn, N. (2003). *International comparisons of alcohol consumption.* Bethesda, MD: National Institute on Alcohol Abuse and Alcoholism, National Institutes of Health.

Bouchery, E. E, Harwood, H. J., Sacks, J. J., Simon, C. J., & Brewer, R. D. (2011, November). Economic costs of excessive alcohol consumption in the U.S., 2006. *American Journal of Preventive Medicine, 41,* 516–524. Retrieved from http://www.ajpmonline.org/article/S0749-3797(11)00538-1/fulltext

Boyd, C. J., McCabe, S. E., & d'Arcy, H. (2003, December). A modified version of the cage as an indicator of alcohol abuse and its consequences among undergraduate drinkers. *Substance Abuse, 24,* 221–232.

Brisbane, F. L. (1985, April). Understanding the female child role of family hero in black alcoholic families. *Bulletin of the New York State Chapter of the National Black Alcoholism Council, 4.*

Brisbane, F. L. (1985–1986, Fall–Winter). A self-help model for working with black women of alcoholic parents. *Alcoholism Treatment Quarterly, 2,* 47–53.

Buddy T. (2015, November 1). 13 characteristics of adult children of alcoholics. Retrieved from https://www.verywell.com/common-traits-of-adult-children-of-alcoholics-66557

Buddy T. (2016a). Women and the effects of alcohol: Women at higher risks for serious medical consequences (February 11). Retrieved from https://www.verywell.com/women-and-the-effects-of-alcohol-63794

Buddy T. (2016b). The cost of excessive alcohol use in the U.S. (February 10). Retrieved from https://www.verywell.com/the-cost-of-excessive-alcohol-use-in-the-u-s-67482

Buddy T. (2016c). Alcohol health risks for women (July 13). Retrieved from https://www.verywell.com/alcohol-health-risks-for-women-63799

Buddy T. (2016d). The combination of domestic abuse and alcohol (August 1). Retrieved from https://www.verywell.com/domestic-abuse-and-alcohol-62643

Center for Substance Abuse Research (CESAR). (2005, October 10). Alcohol-related traffic fatalities remain steady at around 40%. Retrieved from http://www.cesar.umd.edu/cesar/cesarfax/vol14/14-41.pdf

Center for Substance Abuse Research (CESAR). (2010, April 26). Nearly all 11th and 12th graders believe their peers are more likely to drink and drive on prom and graduation nights; less than one-third think driving on these nights is dangerous. Retrieved from http://www.cesar.umd.edu

Centers for Disease Control and Prevention (CDC). (2010, May 19). Fetal alcohol spectrum disorders (FASDs)—State-specific weighted prevalence estimates of alcohol use (percentage of any use/binge drinking) among women aged 18–44 years. Retrieved from http://www.cdc.gov/ncbddd/fasd/data.html

Centers for Disease Control and Prevention (CDC). (2011). CDC reports excessive alcohol consumption cost the U.S. $224 billion in 2006. Retrieved from http://www.cdc.gov/media/releases/2011/p1017_alcohol_consumption.html

Centers for Disease Control and Prevention (CDC). (2014). Excessive drinking is draining the U.S. economy. Retrieved from http://www.cdc.gov/features/alcoholconsumption/

Centers for Disease Control and Prevention (CDC). (2018a). Alcohol and public health: Fact sheets–Age 21 minimum legal drinking age (August 3). Atlanta, GA: Author. Retrieved from https://www.cdc.gov/alcohol/fact-sheets/minimum-legal-drinking-age.htm

Centers for Disease Control and Prevention (CDC). (2018b). Binge drinking. Atlanta, GA: Author. Retrieved from https://www.cdc.gov/alcohol/factsheets/binge-drinking.htm

Cheung, Y. W. (2009, July). Approaches to ethnicity: Clearing roadblocks in the study of ethnicity and substance use. *International Journal of Addictions, 28,* 1209–1226.

Collins, J. J., & Messerschmidt, M. A. (1993). Epidemiology of alcohol-related violence. *Alcohol, Health, and Research World, 17,* 93–100.

Connecticut Business and Industry Association (CBIA). (2016, September 23). CBIA healthy connections. Hartford, CT: Author.

Core Institute. (2014, August 25). 2013 annual data: Core alcohol and drug survey long form—Form 194 executive summary. Carbondale, IL: Core Institute, Southern Illinois University. Retrieved from http://core.siu.edu/_common/documents/2013.pdf

Dartmouth Center on Addiction, Recovery, and Education. (2003, August 18). Jewish tradition: Alcohol and Judaism: One view. Retrieved from http://www.dartmouth.edu/~dcare/topics/jewish.html

Davis, L. (n.d.). Acting out your issues through psychodrama. Sierra Tucson. Retrieved from http://sierratucson.crchealth.com/articles/psychodrama/

De Jong, J. (1995, Spring). Scope of the problem: Gender and drinking. *Catalyst* (Higher Education Center for Alcohol and Other Drug Prevention), *1,* 1.

Douglass, F. (1967/1892). *Life and times of Frederick Douglass* (pp. 147–148). New York, NY: Collier Books.

Doweiko, H. E. (2015). *Concepts of chemical dependency,* 9th ed. Belmont, CA: Brooks/Cole, Cengage Learning.

Drug Strategies. (1999). Alcohol and crime. In *Millennium Hangover: Keeping Score on Alcohol.* Retrieved from http://www.drugstrategies.com/pdf/Score99.pdf

English, E. M., Shutt, M. D., & Oswalt, S. B. (2009). Decreasing use of alcohol, tobacco, and other drugs on a college campus: Exploring potential factors related to change. *Journal of Student Affairs Research and Practice, 46.* Retrieved from http://journals.naspa.org/jsarp/vol46/iss2/art3

Gallup. (2013). Alcohol and drinking. Retrieved from http://www.gallup.com/poll/1582/alcohol-drinking.aspx

Gans, H. J. (1992, April). Second-generation decline: Scenarios for the economic and ethnic futures of the post-1965 American immigrants. *Ethnic and Racial Studies, 15,* 173–192.

Garrison, V., & Podell, J. (1981). Community support systems assessment for use in clinical interviews. *Schizophrenia Bulletin, 7,* 1.

Gary, L. E., & Gary, R. B. (1985). Treatment needs of black alcoholic women. *Alcoholism Treatment Quarterly, 2,* 97–113.

Gold, M. S. (1991). *The good news about drugs and alcohol.* New York, NY: Villard Books.

Goode, E. (1999). *Drugs in American society.* Boston, MA: McGraw-Hill, 1999.

Gordon, A. J. (1981). The cultural context of drinking and indigenous therapy for alcohol problems in three migrant Hispanic cultures. *Journal of Studies on Alcohol* (supplement 9), 217–240.

GraphicMaps. (2018, October 10). Which country drinks the most alcohol? Author. Retrieved from https://www.graphicmaps.com/which-country-drinks-the-most-alcohol

GreenFacts. (2009, May 10). Scientific facts on alcohol. Brussels, Belgium: GreenFacts Scientific Board. Retrieved from http://www.greenfacts.org/en/alcohol/index.htm

Gusfield, J. R. (1986). *Symbolic crusade: Status politics and the American temperance movement,* 2nd ed. Chicago, IL: University of Illinois, 1986.

Hanson, D. J. (2009). Binge drinking. Retrieved from http://www2.potsdam.edu/hansondj/BingeDrinking.html

Hanson, D. J. (2013a). Minimum legal drinking ages around the world. Alcohol Problems and Solutions. Retrieved from http://www2.potsdam.edu/hansondj/LegalDrinkingAge.htm.

Hanson, D. J. (2013b). Binge drinking. Potsdam, NY: State University of New York, Sociology Department. Retrieved from http://www2.potsdam.edu/han-sondj/BingeDrinking.html

Hanson, D. J. (2019a). History of alcohol and drinking around the world. Potsdam, NY: State University of New York, Sociology Department. Retrieved from https://www.alcoholproblemsandsolutions.org/history-of-alcohol-and-drinking-around-world/

Hanson, D. J. (2019b). Legal drinking ages around the world—You'll be surprised. Potsdam, NY: State University of New York, Sociology Department. Retrieved from https://www.alcoholproblemsandsolutions.org/legal-drinking-ages-around-the-world/

Harper, F. D. (1986). *The black family and substance abuse.* Detroit, MI: Detroit Urban League.

Health Day. (2019). 1 in 5 college students admitted to drunk driving, study found. Melville, NY: ScoutNews LLC.

Hensel, D., Katherine, T., & Engs, R. (2014, Fall). College student's health, drinking and smoking patterns: What has changed in 20 years? *College Student Journal, 3,* 378–385.

Hess, A. E. M, Frohlich, T. C., & Callo, V. (2014, May 17). The heaviest-drinking countries in the world. *USA Today.* Retrieved from https://www.usatoday.com/story/money/busness/2014/05/17/heaviest-drinking-countries/9146227/

Hingston, R. W., Zha, W., & Weitzman, E. R. (2009, July). Magnitude of and trends in alcohol-related mortality and morbidity among U.S. college students ages 18–24, 1998–2005. *Journal of Studies on Alcohol and Drugs, 16,* 12–20.

Hjern, A. (2016). Illicit drug abuse in second-generation immigrants: A register study in a national cohort of Swedish residents. Stockholm, Sweden: Centre for Epidemiology, National Board of Health and Welfare, 2016. Retrieved from http://sjp.sagepub.com/content/32/1/40.short

Inciardi, J. A. (1992). *The war on drugs II.* Mountain View, CA: Mayfield.

Ingraham, C. (2015, October 16). The hidden cost of your drinking habit. *Washington Post.* Retrieved from https://www.washingtonpost.com/news/wonk/wp/2015/10/16/the-hidden-cost-of-your-drinking-habit/

Jellinek, E. M. (1960). *The disease concept of alcoholism.* New Haven, CT: College and University Press.

Jones, J. M. (2014, July 29). Reports of alcohol-related family trouble remain up in U.S. Washington, DC: Gallup. Retrieved from https://news.gallup.com/poll/174200/reports-alcohol-related-family-trouble-remain.aspx

Jones, J. M. (2015, July 17). Drinking highest among educated, upper-income Americans. Washington, DC: Gallup. Retrieved from https://news.gallup.com/poll/184358/drinking-highest-among-educated-upper-income-americans.aspx

Keller, M. (1958). Alcoholism: Nature and extent of the problem: Understanding alcoholism. *Annals of the American Academy of Political and Social Science, 315,* 1–11.

Kinney, J. (2000), *Loosening the grip,* 6th ed. Boston, MA: McGraw-Hill.

Kolevzon, M. S., & Green, R. G. (1985). *Family therapy models.* New York, NY: Springer.

Lender, M. E., & Martin, J. K. (1987). *Drinking in America,* rev. ed. New York, NY: Free Press.

Levine, H. G. (1983). The good creature of God and the demon rum. *Research Monograph No. 12: Alcohol and Disinhibition: Nature and Meaning of the Link,* pp. 111–161. Rockville, MD: National Institute on Alcohol Abuse and Alcoholism.

Li, T.-K. (2008, March 5). *FY 2009 president's budget request for NIAAA—Director's statement before the House Subcommittee on Labor—HHS Appropriations,* p. 1. Bethesda, MD: National Institute on Alcohol Abuse and Alcoholism.

MacAndrew, C., & Edgerton, R. B. (1969). *Drunken comportment: A social explanation.* Chicago, IL: Aldine.

Makela, K. (1986). Attitudes towards drinking and drunkenness in four Scandinavian countries. In T. F. Babor (Ed.), *Alcohol and culture: Comparative perspectives from Europe and America* (p. 472). New York, NY: New York Academy of Sciences.

Marshall, M. (1983). Four hundred rabbits: An anthropological view of ethanol as a disinhibitor. *Alcohol and Disinhibition: Nature and Meaning of the Link.* NIAAA Research Monograph No. 12. Washington, DC: U.S. Department of Health and Human Services.

McCarthy, J. (2017, July 19). Beer remains the preferred alcoholic beverage in the U.S. Washington, DC: Gallup. Retrieved from https://news.gallup.com/poll/214229/beer-remains-preferred-alcoholic-beverage.aspx

McCartt, A. T., & Kirley, B. B. (2006). Minimum purchase age laws: How effective are they in reducing alcohol-impaired driving? Arlington, VA: Insurance Institute for Highway Safety. Retrieved from http://onlinepubs.trb.org/onlinepubs/circulars/ec123.pdf

Miech, R. A., Johnston, L.D., O'Malley, P. M., Bachman, J. G., & Schulenberg, J. E. (2015). *Monitoring the Future national survey results on drug use, 1975–2014: Volume I, secondary school students.* Ann Arbor, MI: Institute for Social Research, University of Michigan.

Miech, R. A., Johnston, L. D., O'Malley, P. M., Bachman, J. G., Schulenberg, J. E., & Patrick, M. E. (2019). *Monitoring the Future national survey results on drug use, 1975–2018: Volume I, secondary school students.* Ann Arbor, MI: Institute for Social Research, University of Michigan.

Miller, B. A., & Downs, W. R. (1993). The impact of family violence on the use of alcohol by women. *Alcohol, Health, and Research World, 17,* 137–143.

Miller, T., & Hendrie, D. (2008). *Substance abuse prevention dollars and cents: A cost-benefit analysis.* DHHS Pub. No. (SMA) 07-4298. Rockville, MD: Center for Substance Abuse Prevention, Substance Abuse and Mental Health Services Administration.

National Institute on Alcohol Abuse and Alcoholism (NIAAA). (n.d.a). Alcohol use disorder. Rockville, MD: National Institute on Alcohol Abuse and Alcoholism. Retrieved from http://www.niaaa.nih.gov/alcohol-health/overview-alcohol-consumption/alcohol-use-disorders

National Institute on Alcohol Abuse and Alcoholism (NIAAA). (n.d.b). Treatment for alcohol problems: Finding and getting help. Rockville, MD. National Institute on Alcohol Abuse and Alcoholism https://pubs.niaaa.nih.gov/publications/Treatment/treatment.htm

National Institute on Alcohol Abuse and Alcoholism (NIAAA). (1980). *Facts about alcohol and alcoholism.* Washington, DC: U.S. Government Printing Office.

National Institute on Alcohol Abuse and Alcoholism (NIAAA). (1993). Research Monograph No. 25, NIH Pub. No. 93-3513. Bethesda, MD: National Institute on Alcohol Abuse and Alcoholism.

National Institute on Alcohol Abuse and Alcoholism (NIAAA). (2000a). *Are women more vulnerable to alcohol's effects?* Washington, DC: U.S. Department of Health and Human Services.

National Institute on Alcohol Abuse and Alcoholism (NIAAA). (2000b). *10th special report to the U.S. Congress on alcohol and health: Highlights from current research.* Washington, DC: U.S. Government Printing Office.

National Institute on Alcohol Abuse and Alcoholism (NIAAA). (2007a). Frequently asked questions on alcohol abuse and alcoholism.

National Institute on Alcohol Abuse and Alcoholism (NIAAA). (2007b). Researchers identify alcoholism subtypes. Bethesda, MD: Government Printing Office. Retrieved from http://www.nih.gov/news/pr/jun2007/niaaa-28.htm

National Institute on Alcohol Abuse and Alcoholism (NIAAA). (2008, January). *Alcohol research—A lifespan perspective.* Rockville, MD: National Institute on Alcohol Abuse and Alcoholism.

National Institute on Alcohol Abuse and Alcoholism (NIAAA). (2013). College drinking. Rockville, MD: National Institute on Alcohol Abuse and Alcoholism.

National Institute on Alcohol Abuse and Alcoholism (NIAAA). (2015a). *Alcohol facts and statistics.* Rockville, MD: National Institute on Alcohol Abuse and Alcoholism.

National Institute on Alcohol Abuse and Alcoholism (NIAAA). (2015b). *Alcohol: A woman's health issue.* Rockville, MD: National Institute on Alcohol Abuse and Alcoholism.

National Institute on Alcohol Abuse and Alcoholism (NIAAA). (2016, January). Alcohol facts and statistics. Rockville, MD: National Institute on Alcohol Abuse and Alcoholism.

National Institute on Alcohol Abuse and Alcoholism (NIAAA). (2018a). Alcohol facts and statistics. August. Rockville, MD: U.S Department of Health and Human Services and National Institutes of Health,.

National Institute on Alcohol Abuse and Alcoholism (NIAAA). (2018b). Alcohol use disorder. March. Rockville, MD: U.S Department of Health and Human Services and National Institutes of Health. Retrieved from http://www.niaaa.nih.gov/alcohol-health/overview-alcohol-consumption/alcohol-use-disorders

National Institute on Alcohol Abuse and Alcoholism (NIAAA). (2019a). Fall semester—A time for parents to discuss the risks of college drinking. Rockville, MD: U.S Department of Health and Human Services and National Institutes of Health.

National Institute on Alcohol Abuse and Alcoholism (NIAAA). (2019b). College drinking. Rockville, MD:

U.S Department of Health and Human Services and National Institutes of Health.

National Institute on Alcohol Abuse and Alcoholism (NIAAA). (2019c). Alcohol facts and statistics. Rockville, MD: U.S Department of Health and Human Services and National Institutes of Health. Retrieved from https://www.niaaa.nih.gov/publications/brochures-and-fact-sheets/alcohol-facts-and-statistics

National Institute on Drug Abuse (NIDA). (1999). *National survey results on drug use from the Monitoring the Future study, 1975–1998. Volume 1: Secondary school students.* Washington, DC: U.S. Government Printing Office.

National Institute on Drug Abuse (NIDA). (2019, December). Women and alcohol. Washington, DC: National Institutes of Health, U.S. Department of Health and Human Servces. Retrieved from https://www.niaaa.nih.gov/publications/brochures-and-fact-sheets/women-and-alcohol

National Institutes of Health. (n.d.). Rethinking drinking. Bethesda, MD: Author. Retrieved from http://rethinkingdrinking.niaaa.nih.gov

Newport, F. (2019, August 12). Religion and drinking alcohol in the U.S. Washington, DC: Gallup. Retrieved from https://news.gallup.com/opinion/polling-matters/264713/religion-drinking-alcohol.aspx

Newport, F. (2000. November 13–15). Alcohol and drinking. Gallup. Retrieved from http://www.gallup.com/poll/1582/alcohol-drinking.aspx

O'Malley, P. M., & Wagenaar, A. C. (1991). Effects of minimum drinking age laws on alcohol use, related behaviors and traffic crash involvement among American youth: 1976–1987. *Journal of Studies on Alcohol, 52,* 478–491.

Osterberg, E. (1986). Alcohol and culture: Comparative perspectives from Europe and America. *Annals of the New York Academy of Sciences, 472,* 10–21.

Parsons, T. (2003, December 14). Alcoholism and its effect on the family. AllPsych. Retrieved from http://allpsych.com/journal/alcoholism.html

Presley, C., Meilman, P., & Lyerla, R. (1996). *Recent statistics on alcohol and other drug use on American college campuses: 1995–1996.* Carbondale, IL: Southern Illinois University at Carbondale, Core Institute.

Promises Treatment Centers. (2019). Prom night and teen drinking: The facts. Spicewood, TX: Author. Retrieved from https://www.promises.com/contact/

Reardon, C. (2012). The changing face of older adult substance abuse. *Social Work Today, 12,* 8–18.

Register, T. C., Cline, J. M., & Shively, C. A. (2002). Minority women and alcohol use. *Alcohol Research and Health,* 243–244.

Research Group News Release. (2016, July 5). How African-American drinking patterns are more deadly. Retrieved from https://www.verywell.com/african-american-drinking-patterns-more-deadly-63193

Riffkin, R. (2015, July 28). One in five Americans say moderate drinking is healthy. Washington, DC: Gallup. Retrieved from https://news.gallup.com/poll/184382/one-five-americans-say-moderate-drinking-healthy.aspx

Ritchie, H., & Roser, M. (2018). Alcohol consumption. Oxford, UK: Global University of Oxford Change Data Lab and OurWorldInData.org. Retrieved from https://ourworldindata.org/alcohol-consumption

Room, R. (1984). A reverence for strong drink: The Lost Generation and the elevation of alcohol in American Culture. *Journal of Studies on Alcohol, 43,* 540–545.

Room, R., & Mäkelä, K. (2000). Typologies of the cultural position of drinking. *Journal of Studies on Alcohol, 61,* 475–483.

Roueche, B. (1963). Alcohol in human culture. In L. P. Salvatore *(Ed.), Alcohol and civilization* (pp. 167–182). New York, NY: McGraw-Hill.

Royce, J. E. (1989). *Alcohol problems and alcoholism,* rev. ed. New York, NY: Free Press.

Royce, J. E., & Scratchley, D. (2007). *Alcoholism and other drug problems.* New York, NY: Free Press.

Satir, V. (1964). *Conjoint family therapy.* Palo Alto, CA: Science and Behavior Books.

Substance Abuse and Mental Health Services Administration (SAMHSA). (1995, Spring). *Making the link: Alcohol, tobacco, and other drugs and women's health.* Rockville, MD: Author.

Substance Abuse and Mental Health Services Administration (SAMHSA). (2004). SAMHSA unveils guide to introduce substance abuse treatment providers to family therapy. Rockville, MD: Author.

Substance Abuse and Mental Health Services Administration (SAMHSA). (2008). Issue brief 5 for employers: Save money by addressing employee alcohol problems. Rockville, MD: Author.

Substance Abuse and Mental Health Services Administration (SAMHSA). (2013). *National survey on drug use and health* (NSDUH). Table 2.46B—Alcohol use, binge alcohol use, and heavy alcohol use in the past month among persons aged 18 or older, by demographic characteristics: Percentages 2012 and 2013. Rockville, MD: Author. Retrieved from http://www.samhsa.gov/data/sites/default/files/NSDUH-DetTabsPDFWHTML2013/Web/HTML/NSDUH-DetTabsSect2peTabs43to84-2013.htm#tab2.46b

Substance Abuse and Mental Health Services Administration (SAMHSA). (2014). *Results from the 2013 national survey on drug use and health: Summary of national findings.* Rockville, MD: Author.

Substance Abuse and Mental Health Services Administration (SAMHSA). (2016a). *2015 national survey on drug use and health* (NSDUH). Table 2.41B—alcohol use in lifetime, past year, and past month among persons aged 12 or older, by demographic characteristics: Percentages 2014 and 2015. Rockville, MD: Author. Retrieved from https://www.samhsa.gov/data/sites/default/files/NSDUH-DetTabs-2015/NSDUH-DetTabs-2015/NSDUH-DetTabs-2015.htm#tab2-41b

Substance Abuse and Mental Health Services Administration (SAMHSA). (2016b). *2015 national survey on drug use and health* (NSDUH). Table 2.46B—Alcohol use, binge alcohol use, and heavy alcohol use in past month among persons aged 12 or older, by demographic characteristics: Percentages 2014 and 2015. Rockville, MD: Author. Retrieved from https://www.samhsa.gov/data/sites/default/files/NSDUH-DetTabs-2015/NSDUH-DetTabs-2015/NSDUH-DetTabs-2015.htm#tab2-46b.

Substance Abuse and Mental Health Services Administration (SAMHSA). (2019). *Key substance use and mental health indicators in the United States: Results from the 2018 National Survey on Drug Use and Health.* Rockville, MD: Author. Retrieved from https://www.samhsa.gov/data/sites/default/files/cbhsq-reports/NSDUHNationalFindingsReport2018/NSDUHNationalFindingsReport2018.pdf

Substance Abuse and Mental Health Services Administration. (2020, April 30). "Naltrexone." Rockville, MD: Author. Retrieved from https://www.samhsa.gov/medication-assisted-treatment/treatment/naltrexone

Svensson, M., & Hagquist, C. (2009, November). Adolescent alcohol and illicit drug use among first- and second-generation immigrants in Sweden. *Scandinavian Journal of Public Health, 38*: 184–191. Retrieved from https://www.researchgate.net/publication/40026582_Adolescent_alcohol_and_illicit_drug_use_among_first-_and_second-generation_immigrants_in_Sweden

U.S. Department of Justice. (2013, March). Domestic violence. Washington, DC: U.S. Department of Justice, Office on Violence Against Women.

Vaillant, G. E. (1966, June). Parent–child cultural disparity and drug addiction. *Journal of Nervous and Mental Disease, 142,* 534–539. Retrieved from http://journals.lww.com

/jonmd/Citation/1966/06000/PARENT_CHILD
_CULTURAL_DISPARITY_AND_DRUG.4.aspx

VinePair. (2019). Map: What country drinks the most alcohol? New York, NY: Author. Retrieved from https://vinepair .com/articles/map-countries-drink-most-alcohol/

Wagenaar, A. C. (1993). Minimum drinking age and alcohol availability to youth: Issues and research needs. In M. E. Hilton & B. Bloss (Eds.), *Economics and the prevention of alcohol-related problems* (pp. 175–200).

Wallace, K. (2015, May 20). Study has more disturbing findings about campus rape of freshmen women. CNN. Retrieved from http://www.cnn.com/2015/05/20 /living/feat-rape-freshmen-women-new-study/

Wechsler, H., Davenport, A., Dowdall, G., Moeykens, B., & Castillo, S. (1994, December 7). Health and behavioral consequences of binge drinking in college: A national survey of students at 140 campuses. *Journal of the American Medical Association, 272,* 1672–1677.

Wechsler, H., Dowdall, G. W., Davenport, A., & DeJong, W. (2000). *Binge drinking on campus: Results of a national study.* Cambridge, MA: Harvard School of Public Health, Higher Education Center for Alcohol and Other Drug Prevention.

Wechsler, H., Eun Lee, J., Kuo, M., & Lee, H. (2000). *College binge drinking in the 1990s: A continuing problem: Results of the Harvard School of Public Health 1999 college alcohol study.* Cambridge, MA: Harvard School of Public Health.

Wechsler, H., & Wuethrich, B. (2002). *Dying to drink: Confronting binge drinking on college campuses.* Emmaus, PA: Rodale Books.

Wegscheider, S. (1991). *Another chance.* Palo Alto, CA: Science and Behavior Books.

Weisbaum, H. (2014, January 28). College textbook costs more outrageous than ever. CNBC. Retrieved from http://www.cnbc.com/2014/01/28/college-textbook costs-more-outrageous-than-ever.html

Williams, G. D., Stinson, F. S., Parker, D. A., Harford, T. C., & Noble, V. (1997). Demographic trends, alcohol abuse and alcoholism, 1985–1995. Epidemiologic Bulletin No. 15. *Alcohol, Health, and Research World, 11,* 80–83.

Wilsnack, S. C., Wilsnack, R. W., & Klassen, A. D. (1986). Epidemiological research on women's drinking, 1978–1984. *Women and Alcohol: Health-Related Issues.* Research Monograph No. 16. Washington, DC: U.S. Government Printing Office.

World Health Organization (WHO). (1996). Trends in substance use and associated health problems. *Trends in substance use.* Fact Sheet No. 127. Retrieved from http:// www.dronet.org/lineeguida/ligu_pdf/trendsub.pdf

Yip, P. (2014, December 9). More seniors struggling with substance and alcohol abuse. *Dallas Morning News.*

Zinberg, N. E. (1984). *Drug, set, and setting: The basis for controlled intoxicant use.* New Haven, CT: Yale University Press.

Zinberg, N. E., & Robertson, J. A. (1972). *Drugs and the public.* New York, NY: Simon & Schuster.

Zucker, R. A., Donovan, J. E., Masten, A. S., Mattson, M. E., & Moss, H. B. (2009). Developmental processes and mechanisms—Ages 0–10. *Alcohol Research and Health, 32,* 16–29.

# Narcotics (Opioids)

## Did You Know?

▶ The release of natural substances called *endorphins* activate opioid receptors and can mimic the effects of narcotics such as heroin and morphine.

▶ By the end of the 19th century, almost 300,000 Americans were addicted to opiates, primarily because of patent medicines that contained opium products.

▶ Narcotics are among the most potent analgesics available today.

▶ In the past decade, treatment for nonmedical use of prescription pain relievers has increased more than fourfold and currently accounts for two-thirds of prescription abuse in the United States.

▶ Because of concerns about abuse of prescription narcotic analgesics, many clinicians are hesitant to prescribe sufficient quantities of these drugs to adequately manage severe long-term pain.

▶ Addiction to prescription narcotic analgesics rarely happens when these medications are used properly to treat pain.

▶ Evidence suggests that acupuncture reduces pain by activating a natural opioid system.

▶ Many heroin addicts have been exposed to the human immunodeficiency virus (HIV).

▶ Heroin supplies today are more potent, cheaper, and more readily available than a decade ago.

▶ One designer drug, made from the narcotic fentanyl, is 6,000 times more potent than heroin.

▶ Some heroin addicts have to be treated with the narcotics methadone or buprenorphine for the rest of their lives to keep them from abusing heroin.

▶ Dextromethorphan (a common over-the-counter [OTC] cough medicine chemically related to codeine), when taken in high doses, can cause phencyclidine (PCP)-like hallucinations.

## Learning Objectives

**On completing this chapter, you should be able to:**

❭ Describe the principal pharmacological effects of narcotics, their biological targets, and their main therapeutic uses.

❭ Identify the major side effects of narcotics, in particular their abuse potential.

❭ Distinguish between narcotic physical dependence and addiction.

❭ Identify the abuse patterns for heroin.

❭ Outline the stages of heroin dependence.

❭ List the withdrawal symptoms that result from narcotic dependence, list potential treatments, and discuss the significance of tolerance.

❭ Describe and compare the use of methadone and buprenorphine in treating narcotic addiction.

❭ Explain the connection between abuse of prescription opioid narcotic drugs and heroin.

❭ Identify the unique features of fentanyl that make it appealing to illicit drug dealers but dangerous to narcotic addicts.

❭ Describe how "designer" drugs have been associated with narcotics and Parkinson's disease.

❭ Describe why dextromethorphan in cough medicines is abused.

❭ Identify the opioid features of tramadol and its potential for abuse.

# Introduction

In 2018, an estimated 2 million people in the United States had an opioid drug use disorder associated with prescription painkillers, and another 900,000 were abusing heroin (U.S. Department of Health and Human Services, 2019). These facts illustrate that our society is having major problems dealing with nonmedical use of drugs known as *opioid narcotics*. Additional findings that further confirm the extent of the so-called opioid drug epidemic include the following (American Society of Addiction Medicine [ASAM], 2016):

- Approximately 10% of all Americans with a substance use disorder abuse prescription pain relievers.
- It is estimated that almost one-quarter of those who use heroin will become addicted to opioid drugs.
- Of the approximately 47,000 persons in the United States who died from a lethal drug overdose in 2014, 40% were related to prescription opioid pain relievers.
- The treatment admission rate for opioid drug use disorder has increased almost 10-fold in the past decade.
- Of new heroin users exposed to opioid drugs, 80% first misused prescription painkillers.
- In 2014, approximately 500,000 adolescents were nonmedical users of opioid analgesics.
- Most adolescents who have prescription opioid drug use disorder get their drugs for free from a friend or relative.
- Women are more likely to experience chronic pain, use prescribed opioid analgesics, receive higher doses, and use these drugs for longer time periods than men.

The term *narcotic* in general means a central nervous system (CNS) depressant that produces insensibility or stupor. The term has also come to designate those drugs and substances with pharmacological properties related to opium ingredients and their drug derivatives. All opioid narcotics activate opioid receptors and have abuse potential. Narcotics are frequently prescribed for pain relief (**analgesics**), to reduce coughing (**antitussives**), and to reduce diarrhea.

In this chapter, we introduce the opioid narcotics with a brief historical account. The pharmacological properties and therapeutic uses of these drugs are discussed, followed by a description of, and distinction between, their side effects and problems with tolerance, withdrawal, dependence, and addiction. Narcotic abuse, its risks and outcomes, is presented in detail, with special emphasis on heroin. In addition, treatment approaches for narcotic addiction, dependence, and withdrawal are included. This chapter concludes with descriptions of other commonly used opioid narcotics and related drugs.

# What Are Narcotics?

The word *narcotic* has been used to label many substances from opium to marijuana to cocaine. The translation of the Greek word *narkoticos* is "benumbing" or "deadening." The term *narcotic* is sometimes used to refer to a CNS depressant, producing insensibility or stupor, and at other times to refer to an addicting drug. Most people would not consider marijuana among the narcotics today, although for many years it was included in this category. Although pharmacologically cocaine is not a narcotic either, it is still legally classified as such. Perhaps part of this confusion results from the fact that cocaine, as a local anesthetic, can cause a numbing effect.

For purposes of the current discussion, the term *narcotic* is used to refer to those naturally occurring substances derived from the opium poppy and their synthetic substitutes. These drugs are referred to as the **opioid** (or opiate) narcotics because of their association with opium. They have similar pharmacological features, including abuse potential, pain-relieving effects; cough suppression; and reduction of intestinal movement, often causing constipation, but useful in reducing severe diarrhea. Some of the most commonly used opioid narcotics are listed in **Table 9.1**.

**TABLE 9.1** Commonly Used Opioid Narcotic Drugs and Products

| Narcotic Drug | Common or Trade Names | Most Common Uses |
|---|---|---|
| Heroin | Horse, smack, junk (street names) | Abuse |
| Morphine | Several | Analgesia |
| Methadone | Dolophine | Treat narcotic dependence |
| Meperidine | Demerol | Analgesia |
| Oxycodone | Percodan, OxyContin | Analgesia |
| Propoxyphene | Darvon | Analgesia |
| Codeine | Several | Analgesia, antitussive |
| Loperamide | Imodium A-D | Antidiarrheal |
| Diphenoxylate | Lomotil | Antidiarrheal |
| Opium tincture | Paregoric | Antidiarrheal |
| Buprenorphine | Suboxone | Treat narcotic dependence |
| Tramadol | Ultram | Analgesia (considered to have weak, but significant, opioid properties) |

# The History of Narcotics

The opium poppy, *Papaver somniferum*, from which opium and its naturally occurring narcotic derivatives are obtained, has been cultivated for millennia. A 6000-year-old Sumerian tablet has an ideograph for the poppy shown as "joy" plus "plant," suggesting that the addicting properties of this substance have been appreciated for millennia. The Egyptians listed opium along with approximately 700 other medicinal compounds in the famous Ebers Papyrus (circa 1500 BC).

The Greek god of sleep, Hypnos, and the Roman god of sleep, Somnus, were portrayed as carrying containers of opium pods, and the Minoan goddess of sleep wore a crown of opium pods. During the so-called Dark Ages that followed the collapse of the Roman Empire, Arab traders actively engaged in traveling the overland caravan routes to China and to India, where they introduced opium. Eventually, both China and India grew their own poppies.

## ■ Opium in China

The opium poppy had a dramatic impact in China, causing widespread addiction (Frontline, n.d.). Initially, the seeds were used medically, as was opium later. However, by the late 1690s opium was being smoked and used for diversion. The Chinese government, fearful of the weakening of national vitality by the potent opiate narcotic, outlawed the sale of opium in 1729. The penalty for disobedience was death by strangulation or decapitation. Despite these laws and threats, the habit of opium smoking became so widespread that the Chinese government went a step further and forbade its importation from India, where most of the opium poppy was grown. In contrast, the British East India Company (and later the British government in India) encouraged cultivation of opium. British companies were the principal shippers to the Chinese port of Canton, which was the only port open to Western merchants. During the next 120 years, a complex network of opium smuggling routes developed in China with the help of local merchants, who received substantial profits, and local officials, who pocketed bribes to ignore the smugglers.

Everyone involved in the opium trade, but particularly the British, continued to profit until the Chinese government ordered the strict enforcement of the edict against importation. Such actions by the Chinese caused conflict with the British government and helped trigger the Opium War of 1839 to 1842. Great Britain sent in an army, and by 1842, 10,000 British soldiers had won a victory over 350 million Chinese. Because of the war, the island of Hong Kong was ceded

Opium poppies such as these are used as a source for natural opioid narcotic drugs such as heroin, morphine, and codeine.

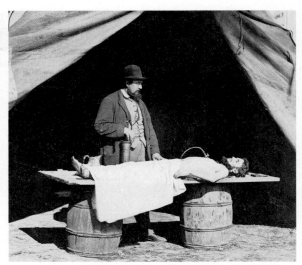

With the development of the hypodermic needle and its use during the Civil War, heroin addiction became more likely and more severe.

to the British, and an indemnity of $6 million was imposed on China to cover the value of the destroyed opium and the cost of the war. In 1856, a second Opium War broke out. Peking was occupied by British and French troops, and China was compelled to make further concessions to Britain. The importation of opium continued to increase until 1908, when Britain and China made an agreement to limit the importation of opium from India (Frontline, n.d.).

## ▌ American Opium Use

Meanwhile, in 1803, a young German named Frederick Serturner extracted and partially purified the active ingredients in opium. The result was 10 times more potent than opium itself and was named *morphine*, after Morpheus, the Greek god of dreams. This discovery increased worldwide interest in opium. By 1832, a second

A famous cartoon showing a British sailor shoving opium down the throat of a Chinese man, which dates back to the Opium War of 1839–1842.

compound had been purified and named *codeine*, after the Greek word for "poppy capsule" (Medical Discoveries, n.d.).

The opium problem was aggravated further in 1853 when Alexander Wood perfected the hypodermic syringe and introduced it first in Europe and then in the United States. Christopher Wren and others had worked with the idea of injecting drugs directly into the body by means of hollow quills and straws, but the approach was never successful or well received. Wood perfected the syringe technique with the intent of preventing morphine addiction by injecting the drug directly into the veins rather than using oral administration (Golding, 1993). Unfortunately, just the opposite happened; injection of morphine increased the potency and the likelihood of dependence (Maurer & Vogel, 1967).

The hypodermic syringe was used extensively during the Civil War to administer morphine to treat pain, dysentery, and fatigue (Kosten & Hollister, 1998). A large percentage of the soldiers who returned home from the war were addicted to morphine (deShazo et al., 2018). Opiate addiction became known as the "soldier's disease" or "army disease."

By 1900, an estimated 300,000 Americans were dependent on opiates (Arablouei & Abdelfatah, 2019). The drug problem then became worse because of (1) Chinese laborers, who brought opium with them to the United States to smoke (it was legal to smoke opium in the United States at that time); (2) the availability of purified

Chinese laborers often smoked heroin at the turn of the 20th century.

morphine and the hypodermic syringe; and (3) the lack of controls on the large number of patent medicines that contained opium derivatives (Karch, 1996). Until 1914, when the Harrison Narcotic Act was passed (regulating opium, coca leaves, and their products), the average opiate addict was a middle-aged Southern white woman who functioned well and was adjusted to her role as a wife and mother. She bought opium or morphine legally by mail order from Sears and Roebuck or at the local store, used it orally, and encountered few problems. Many physicians were addicted as well. One of the best-known morphine addicts was William Holsted, a founder of Johns Hopkins Medical School. Holsted was a highly productive surgeon and innovator, although secretly an addict for most of his career. He became dependent on morphine as a substitute for his cocaine dependence (Brecher, 1972).

Looking for better medicines, chemists found that modifying the morphine molecule resulted

Heroin use by soldiers fighting in Afghanistan is a great concern.

in a more potent compound. In 1898, diacetyl-morphine was placed on the market as a cough suppressant by Bayer. It was to be a "heroic" drug, without the addictive potential of morphine—it thus received the name *heroin*.

Heroin was first used in the United States as a cough suppressant and to combat addiction to other substances (Hubbard, 1998). However, its inherent abuse potential was quickly discovered. When injected, heroin is more addictive than most of the other narcotics because of its ability to enter the brain rapidly and cause a euphoric surge (DiChiara & North, 1992). Heroin was banned from U.S. medical practice in 1924, although it is still prescribed legally as an analgesic or for treatment of narcotic dependence (like methadone) in other countries (Drug War Facts, 2012).

The Vietnam War was an important landmark for heroin use in the United States (Hubbard, 1998). It has been estimated that as many as 40% of the U.S. soldiers serving in Southeast Asia at this time used heroin to combat the frustrations and stress associated with this unpopular military action. Although only 7% of the soldiers continued to use heroin after returning home, those who were addicted to this potent narcotic became a major component of the heroin-abusing population in this country (Golding, 1993).

Smoking heroin became popular in the mid-1980s in response to the acquired immune deficiency syndrome (AIDS) epidemic. This was out of fear that users risked HIV infection from needles during intravenous injections (Hubbard, 1998). The effect resulting from inhalation is as intense as that caused by injection, although a highly pure drug is required for smoking. Smoking continues to be a favorite form of heroin administration today.

As experience has shown, problems with the opiate drugs such as heroin are closely linked with war and its associated miseries and pains. As our country again finds itself in the middle of an extended and increasingly less popular military engagement in the Middle East, particularly Afghanistan, problems with heroin are becoming more and more apparent (RT, 2013). As during previous wars, soldiers turn to drugs like heroin to cope and even to survive emotionally in a war zone. This is reflected in comments such as "Life is unbearable. You don't know whether you're going to be alive in 10 minutes' time or not." "Life has few pleasures; you're uncomfortable . . . the food is pretty awful, the ever-present smell of death and you see some of your closest buddies die before your very eyes." "So life is really unbearable and heroin is cheap" (Edwards, 2010).

# Pharmacological Effects

Even though opioid narcotics have a history of being abused, they continue to be important therapeutic agents.

## ▪ Narcotic Analgesics

The most common clinical use of the opioid narcotics is as analgesics to relieve pain. These drugs are effective against most varieties of pain, including *visceral* (associated with internal organs of the body) and *somatic* (associated with skeletal muscles, bones, skin, and teeth) types. Used in sufficiently high doses, narcotics can even relieve the intense pain associated with some types of cancer (Gutstein & Akil, 2006).

The opioid narcotics relieve pain by activating the same group of receptors that are controlled by the endogenous substances called *endorphins* (Schumacher, Basbaum, & Naidu, 2015). The endorphins are a family of peptides (small proteins) that are released in the brain, in the spinal cord, and from the adrenal glands in response to stress and painful experiences. When released, the endorphins serve as transmitters and stimulate receptors designated as opioid types. Activation of opioid receptors by either the naturally released endorphins or administered narcotic analgesic drugs blocks the transmission of pain through the spinal cord or brain stem and alters the perception of pain in the "pain center" of the brain. Because the narcotics work at multiple levels of pain transmission, they are potent analgesics against almost all types of pain.

Note that the endorphin system appears to be influenced by psychological factors as well. Thus, natural activation of opioid receptors also contributes to the regulation of emotional behaviors such as stress, learning, and memory, as well as the regulation of the brain's reward circuits (Schumacher et al., 2015). Pain relief caused by administration of placebos or nonmedicinal manipulation such as acupuncture may be partly from the natural release of endorphins (Eshkevari & Heath, 2005). This relationship suggests that physiological, psychological, and pharmacological factors are intertwined in pain management through the opioid

system, which makes it impossible to deal with one without considering the others.

Although the narcotics are highly effective analgesics, they do cause some side effects that are particularly alarming; thus, their clinical use usually is limited to the treatment of moderate to severe pain (Schumacher et al., 2015). Other, safer drugs, such as the aspirin-type analgesics, are preferred for pain management when possible. Often, the amount of narcotic required for pain relief can be reduced by combining a narcotic, such as codeine, with aspirin or acetaminophen (the active ingredient in Tylenol). Such combinations reduce the chance of significant narcotic side effects while providing adequate pain relief (Schumacher et al., 2015).

Morphine is a particularly potent pain reliever and often is the analgesic standard to which other narcotics are compared (Gutstein & Akil, 2006). With continual use, tolerance develops to the analgesic effects of morphine and other narcotics, sometimes requiring a dramatic escalation of doses to maintain adequate pain control (Schumacher et al., 2015).

Because pain is expressed in different forms with many different diseases, narcotic treatment can vary considerably. Usually, the convenience of oral narcotic therapy is preferred but often is inadequate for severe pain. For short-term relief from intense pain, narcotics are effective when injected subcutaneously or intramuscularly. Narcotics can also be given intravenously for persistent and potent analgesia or administered by transdermal patches for sustained chronic pain (*Drug Facts and Comparisons*, 2010). Despite the fact that most pain can be relieved if enough narcotic analgesic is properly administered, physicians frequently underprescribe narcotics or are not well trained in proper pain management or how to use the opioid narcotics responsibly (Young & Hobson, 2016). Because of fear of causing narcotic addiction or creating legal problems with federal agencies such as the Drug Enforcement Administration (DEA) (see "Here and Now: A War on Doctors? Are Restrictions on Pain Pills Too Painful?"), many patients in the United States are often inadequately treated for their pain (Alford, 2016). An important rule of narcotic use is that adequate pain relief should not be denied because of concern about the abuse potential of these drugs (Schumacher et al., 2015). Indeed, addiction to narcotics is rare in patients receiving these drugs for therapy unless they have a history of drug

# HERE AND NOW

## A War on Doctors? Are Restrictions on Pain Pills Too Painful?

Many people, especially those patients suffering from pain who are not able to convince their doctors to prescribe sufficient opioid painkillers for adequate relief, believe that the federal government, and the DEA in particular, is scaring health providers from prescribing sufficient pain medications to relieve their suffering. The start of these problems can be traced back to the 1980s when doctors began to embrace the philosophy that relieving pain actually promoted healing. Over the next couple of decades, prescriptions for opioid painkillers escalated dramatically, led by a drug called Oxy-Contin, which reached sales of $1.6 billion in 2003. Related to this escalation of narcotic analgesic prescriptions was the emergence of an illegal market that sold diverted opioid painkillers in the streets, feeding a robust drug trade headed by drug dealers and drug lords. In response to this growing problem, the DEA was perceived as particularly targeting health professionals and discouraged their use of these drugs to treat pain. Some feel that this strategy is somewhat misplaced based on findings that 95% of all illegal prescription drugs sold on the streets are related to thefts from pharmacies, warehouses, and trucks and that only 5% are from illegally diverted prescriptions from health providers. Of course, there are examples of prescribers running "pill mills" in exchange for money, sex, or other drugs, but in reality these are few and far between. It is argued by some that the emphasis on investigating legitimate medical practices is an excessive incursion by law enforcement into medical practice. Thus, there are those who claim that while DEA investigations have done little to curb the access to illegal drug products and have caused many clinicians to either underprescribe for pain management in their patients or have caused them to refuse altogether to prescribe the opioid painkillers for the control of pain.

Courtesy of DEA.

abuse or have an underlying psychiatric disorder (Gutstein & Akil, 2006).

Occasionally, there are outbreaks of abuse of commonly prescribed narcotic products such as OxyContin (Celona, 2007; P&T Community, 2013). This product includes the opiate oxycodone, which has the approximate narcotic potency of morphine and can be obtained with relative ease. Authorities claim that the illegal pills come from doctors' offices, from dealers who fake illness to get legal prescriptions or who are writing phony orders, and from others who steal the supplies from pharmacies. OxyContin has been called *oxys*, *O.C.*, and *killers* on the street and is popular with narcotic abusers because of its rapid and potent effect. However, many, if not most, of those who use prescriptions drugs for nonmedical purposes obtain their painkillers from the medicine cabinets of a family member or a friend (Drug Enforcement Administration [DEA], 2019b). On the street, the drug can cost 10 times its prescription price. Because of its potent ability to suppress respiration, OxyContin appears to have been involved in overdose deaths throughout the country, although there is some evidence that other drugs were also involved in many of these cases.

Critics claim that part of the abuse problem with OxyContin stems from overuse in situations that should be managed by a less potent and less addicting opioid analgesic.

## ■ Other Therapeutic Uses

Opioid narcotics are also used to treat conditions not related to pain. For example, these drugs suppress the coughing center of the brain, so they are effective antitussives. Codeine, a natural opioid narcotic, is commonly included in cough medicine. In addition, opioid narcotics slow the movement of materials through the intestines, a property that can be used to relieve diarrhea but one that can also cause the side effect of constipation (Schumacher et al., 2015). Paregoric contains an opioid narcotic substance and is commonly used to treat severe diarrhea.

When used carefully by the clinician, opioid narcotics are highly effective therapeutic tools. Guidelines for avoiding unnecessary problems with these drugs include the following (Rolfs, 2008; Volkow, 2014a):

- Opioid pain relievers should only be used for pain when severity warrants and after consideration of other nonopioid pain medications such as aspirin, ibuprofen, or acetaminophen (e.g., Tylenol).

- Doses and duration of use should be limited as much as possible while permitting adequate therapeutic care.
- The patient should be counseled to store the medications securely, not share them with others, and to dispose of drugs properly when the pain has subsided and the medication is no longer needed.
- Long-duration opioid drugs should not be used to treat acute pain, except in situations where adequate monitoring can be conducted.
- The use of opioids should be reevaluated if pain persists beyond the anticipated time period for acute pain management.
- A comprehensive evaluation should be conducted before initiating opioid treatment.
- The provider should consider conducting a screen for risk of abuse or addiction before initiating opioid treatment.
- A treatment plan should be established between the doctor and patient that includes measurable goals for reduction of pain and improvement of function.
- The patient and family members, if appropriate, should be informed of the risks and benefits of the opioid treatment. Sometimes a written contract identifying these elements should be prepared and signed.
- Opioid treatment should be discontinued if the terms of the contract are not being met by the patient.
- If significant abuse is suspected, the clinician should discuss the concerns with the patient and help the patient find appropriate treatment.

### ▪ Abuse of Prescription Opioid Painkillers

As already mentioned, the rapid increase in the abuse of prescription opioid painkillers has become a major problem in the United States (Volkow, 2014a, 2014b). An example of what has become all too common is the tragic narcotic overdose death of Leslie Cooper near Portsmouth, Ohio. She was never known to wander the streets or dark alleys to get her opioid narcotics. She received her drugs "legally" from multiple doctors and "pain-management clinics." Her problem with these prescription analgesics started when doctors prescribed potent painkillers to deal with severe discomfort after a difficult surgery. More surgeries

were necessary, which meant continual demand for and access to the opioid pain relievers. Something went terribly wrong, and Leslie paid the price with her life. In her system was found a deadly combination of depressant drugs prescribed for muscle relaxation and depression and two highly potent narcotic analgesics. Leslie fell asleep and did not wake up. This is an example of why the misuse of these painkillers has more than doubled emergency room visits in the past decade (Compton, Jones, & Baldwin, 2016) and also has caused some critics to question whether many doctors who prescribe such drugs are sufficiently trained in proper pain or substance abuse management (Young & Hobson, 2016).

## PRESCRIPTION FOR ABUSE !

*What Makes People Vulnerable?*

For most patients, the responsible use of prescription opioid analgesics is helpful in the management of moderate to severe pain; however, a relatively small population has factors that can increase the danger of becoming addicted to these drugs as much as 25-fold. The risks that lead to this vulnerability include:

- a family history of substance abuse problems, which suggests the likelihood of genetic vulnerability;
- dependence on nicotine, alcohol, or sleeping pills;
- depression;
- the use of psychiatric medications; and
- age younger than 65 years

The value of identifying these risks is that they may help warn clinicians about which patients require special consideration and caution when prescribing narcotics to treat their pain.

Data from American Academy of Pain Medicine. (2007, February 7). Psychiatric factors linked to increased risk for misuse of opioid medications. *23rd Annual Meeting.* Abstract 151; Levran, O., Londono, D., O'Hara, K., Randesi, M., Rotrosen, J., Casasonte, P., ... Kreek, M. J. (2009). Heroin addiction in African Americans: A hypothesis-driven association study. *Genes, Brain and Behavior, 8,* 531–540; Medical News Today. (2010, August 28). Study identifies risk factors for painkiller addiction and links the addiction to genetics. Retrieved from http://www.medicalnewstoday.com/articles/199263.php; Sify News. (2010, August 28). Risk factors for painkiller addiction identified. Retrieved from http://sify.com/news/risk-factors-for-painkiller-addiction -identified-news-scitech-ki3pEjahbic.html; Mayo Clinic. (2019). How opioid addiction occurs. Retrieved from https://www.mayoclinic.org/diseases -conditions/prescription-drug-abuse/in-depth/how-opioid-addiction -occurs/art-20360372

Abuse problems with these narcotic analgesics are partially the result of their popularity and account for more than 207 million prescriptions in the United States each year (Volkow, 2014a, 2014b). This means that these drugs are more readily available, and their use is more widely accepted than ever before. However, it is important to appreciate that when used properly (i.e., as prescribed), the likelihood of becoming addicted to these narcotics for most people is miniscule (likely less than 1%). But there are risk factors that make some patients more likely to have problems with these drugs; for those with these risk factors the rate of addiction jumps to 25% (Sify News, 2010; see "Prescription for Abuse: What Makes People Vulnerable?").

Abuse of prescription opioid narcotics such as OxyContin and illicit narcotics such as heroin might seem to some people quite different because one comes from a doctor and the other from drug dealers in the street. But in reality, because both types of drugs are opiates, they both can cause similar addictions, overdoses, and even death. In fact, a surprising rise in heroin abuse is occurring across the United States, which is likely, in part, because people who become addicted to the prescription opioid painkillers switch to heroin because it is more accessible and easier to obtain.

Heroin also can cost as little as one-fifth the price of prescription medications. All too often heroin overdose deaths appear to have their origins in victims first being exposed to the opioid narcotics during a chronic treatment for pain often associated with sports-related injuries.

## ■ Mechanisms of Action

As previously mentioned, the opioid receptors are the sites of action of naturally occurring endorphin peptide transmitters and are found throughout the nervous system, intestines, and other internal organs. Because narcotic drugs such as morphine and heroin enhance the endorphin system by directly stimulating opioid receptors, these drugs have widespread influences throughout the body.

For example, the opioid receptors are present in high concentration within the limbic structures of the brain. Stimulation of these receptors by narcotics causes release of the transmitter dopamine in the limbic regions of the brain. This effect contributes to the rewarding actions of these drugs and leads to dependence and abuse (Trigo, Martin-Garcia, Berrendero, Robledo, & Maldonado, 2010; Zocchi et al., 2003; see "Signs & Symptoms: Narcotics").

## ■ Side Effects

One of the most common side effects of opioid narcotics is constipation. Other side effects include drowsiness, mental clouding, respiratory depression (suppressed breathing is usually the cause of death from overdose), nausea and vomiting, itching, inability to urinate, a drop in blood pressure, and constricted pupils (Kral & Ghafoor, 2013; Schumacher et al., 2015). This array of seemingly unrelated side effects is the result of widespread distribution of opioid receptors throughout the body and their involvement in many physiological functions (Gourlay, 2004; Trigo et al., 2010). With continual use, tolerance usually develops to some of these undesirable narcotic responses.

Drugs that selectively antagonize the opioid receptors can block the effects of natural opioid systems in the body and reverse the effects of narcotic opiate drugs (Schumacher et al., 2015). When an opioid antagonist such as the drug naloxone is administered alone, it has little noticeable effect. The anti-opioid actions of naloxone become more apparent when the antagonist is injected into someone who has taken a narcotic opioid drug. For example, naloxone will cause (1) a recurrence of pain in the patient using a narcotic for pain relief, (2) the restoration of consciousness and normal breathing in the addict who has overdosed on heroin, and (3) severe withdrawal effects in the opioid abuser who has become dependent on narcotics (Schumacher et al., 2015). Because of the ability of these antagonists to block the effects of opioid drugs, they are also used as treatment for some opioid-dependent patients (Schumacher et al., 2015).

An interesting recent use of opioid antagonists is in the treatment of alcohol dependence. The Food

# SIGNS & SYMPTOMS

## Narcotics

| Possible Signs of Use | Possible Signs of Overdose |
|---|---|
| Euphoria | Low and shallow breathing |
| Drowsiness | Clammy skin |
| Respiratory depression | Convulsions |
| Constricted pupils | Coma |
| Nausea | Death |

and Drug Administration (FDA) has approved the use of naltrexone (a narcotic antagonist) in a regular and extended-release formulation to relieve the craving of alcoholics for excessive alcohol consumption (Schumacher et al., 2015).

## Abuse, Tolerance, Dependence, and Withdrawal

All the opioid narcotic agents that activate opioid receptors have abuse potential and are classified as scheduled drugs (see **Table 9.2**). Their patterns of abuse are determined by the ability of these drugs to cause tolerance, dependence, withdrawal effects, and eventually addiction. However, it is important to recognize that even though a patient treated by these drugs for pain develops physical dependence and experiences significant withdrawal when the drug is abruptly removed, they are not necessarily addicted (Hitti, 2010). In fact, relatively few patients properly receiving the opioid narcotics for pain relief will go on to become truly addicted, even though they may develop physical dependence and are temporarily

uncomfortable when the narcotic treatment is discontinued. This distinction between physical dependence and the compulsive need to use the opioid narcotics despite negative consequences (i.e., addiction) is critically important and needs to be appreciated when providing proper pain management, especially for severe long-term pain conditions (NAABT.org, 2014).

The process of tolerance literally begins with the first dose of a narcotic, but tolerance does not become clinically evident until after two to three weeks of frequent use (either therapeutic or abuse related). Tolerance occurs most rapidly with high doses given in short intervals and is a common result of the extended clinical use of prescription opioid painkillers. It also is caused by abuse of these narcotics in addicted persons. The result of tolerance is that doses of these drugs must be increased (sometimes several-fold) to retain or regain the therapeutic or nonmedicinal narcotic effects. Physical dependence invariably accompanies severe tolerance (Schumacher et al., 2015). Psychological dependence can also develop with continual narcotic use because these drugs can cause euphoria and relieve stress. Such psychological dependence leads to compulsive use (Luscher, 2012). Because all narcotics affect the same opioid systems in the body, developing tolerance to one narcotic drug means the person has cross-tolerance to all drugs in this group.

The development of psychological and physical dependence makes stopping the drug uncomfortable because of the resulting unpleasant withdrawal effects. Someone who has used potent narcotics for a long time, such as a long-term addict, will experience severe withdrawal effects, including exaggerated pain responses, agitation, anxiety, stomach cramps and vomiting, joint and muscle aches, runny nose, and an overall flulike feeling. Although these withdrawal symptoms are not fatal, they are extremely aversive and encourage continuation of the narcotic habit (Schumacher et al., 2015).

Overall, the narcotic opioids have similar actions; there are differences, however, in their potencies, severity of side effects, likelihood of being abused, and clinical usefulness.

**TABLE 9.2** Schedule Classification of Some Common Narcotics

| Narcotic | Schedule |
|---|---|
| Heroin | I |
| Morphine | II, III |
| Methadone | II |
| Fentanyl | II |
| Hydromorphone | II |
| Hydrocodone | II |
| Meperidine | II |
| Codeine | II, III, V |
| Buprenorphine | III |
| Pentazocine | IV |
| Tramadol | Unscheduled |
| Narcotics combined with nonsteroidal anti-inflammatory drugs | III |

Data from Drug Enforcement Administration (DEA). (2013, May). Controlled Substances Schedules. Retrieved from http://www.deadiversion.usdoj.gov/schedules/#list

## ■ Heroin Abuse

"He loved heroin more than it loved him. I was shocked beyond imagining: he was the first of my friends to fall."

—Corey Feldman, "How to Kick Heroin" (2016)

Next to the potent synthetic opioid agonist fentanyl, heroin was a major contributor to nearly opioid-related 50,000 deaths in the United States in 2017 (Durkin, 2018). The likely explanations for this recent rise in popularity include the facts that high-grade heroin has become cheap and readily available (Centers for Disease Control and Prevention [CDC], 2015). In addition, it appears that the rise in heroin use is an indirect consequence of the increase in the abuse of prescription opioid painkillers (Compton et al., 2016). For example, four out of five new heroin users start out by misusing prescription pain relievers (ASAM, 2016). People who abuse prescribed opioid narcotics often increase their consumption of these drugs because they develop tolerance. This makes their habit more expensive and makes it more difficult to obtain enough of the prescription drugs to satisfy their nonmedical (addiction) needs. Consequently, these people frequently switch to street heroin, which is a fraction of the cost while still being reasonably pure and potent. Of course, this switch to heroin increases the risk of getting a bad batch of drug that is much more potent than expected or that contains other drugs that are more dangerous. The unintended outcomes can be, at the least, extremely dangerous and result in a trip to the emergency room or, in the extreme, an accidental overdose fatality. This number for the United States exceeded 100,000 in 2018; however, although an enormous number, it needs to be recognized that it represented an approximately 21% decline from the year before (Newman, 2019).

Heroin is currently classified as a Schedule I drug by the DEA (see Table 9.2). It is not approved for any clinical use in the United States and is one of the most widely abused illegal drugs in the world (United Nations Office on Drugs and Crime [UNODC], 2015). Heroin was illicitly used more than any other drug of abuse in the United States (except for marijuana) until 2000, when it was unseated by cocaine (DiChiara & North, 1992). In 2018, 0.4% of high school seniors reported using heroin, and 0.8% indicated that they had used this drug sometime during their life (Johnston, 2019).

From 1970 through 1976, most of the heroin reaching the United States originated from the Golden Triangle region of Southeast Asia, which includes parts of Burma, Thailand, and Laos. During that period, the United States and other nations purchased much of the legal opium crop from Turkey in an effort to stop opium from being converted into heroin. From 1975 until 1980, the major heroin supply came from opium poppies grown in Mexico. The U.S. government furnished the Mexican government with helicopters, herbicide sprays, and financial assistance to destroy the poppy crop. Changes in political climates shifted the source of supply back to the Golden Triangle and Latin American countries and then to Afghanistan, where 92% of the world's heroin was produced in 2010.

Heroin produced in Afghanistan took a heavy toll on the Afghan people (Christenson, 2010) as well as killing many people around the world (Agence France-Presse, 2010). In addition, it was a substantial problem for U.S. and NATO soldiers fighting in the Afghan War (Edwards, 2010). Even today, heroin-related corruption in the Afghanistan government has made it difficult to effectively control the lucrative heroin trade from this country. Today, the cultivation of the opium poppy remains high in Mexico, making this country the primary supplier of heroin to the United States (DEA, 2018).

## HEROIN COMBINATIONS

As previously mentioned, heroin is typically smuggled into the United States from one of four foreign sources: Mexico, South America, Southeast Asia (e.g., Burma), or Southwest Asia (e.g., Afghanistan). It is carried into the United States hidden in commercial and private vehicles driven from Mexico or Canada or carried by couriers traveling on commercial flights. Pure heroin is a white powder. Other colors, such as brown Mexican heroin, result from incomplete processing of morphine or from adulterants. Heroin is usually "cut" (diluted) with lactose (milk sugar) to give it bulk and thus increase profits. When heroin first enters the United States, it can be up to 95% pure; by the time it is sold to users, its purity can be as low as 3% or (recently) as high as 70% (UNODC, 2015). If users are unaware of the variance in purity and do not adjust doses accordingly, the results can be extremely dangerous and occasionally fatal (Gorner, 2015).

Heroin has a bitter taste, so sometimes it is cut with quinine, a bitter substance, to disguise the fact that the heroin content has been reduced. Quinine can be a deadly adulterant. Part of the "flash," or immediate rush, from direct injection of heroin may be caused by this contaminant. Quinine is an irritant, and it causes vascular damage, acute and potentially lethal

Courtesy of DEA.

Crude heroin is dark, whereas purified heroin is a white powder.

disturbances in heartbeat, depressed respiration, coma, and death from respiratory arrest. Opiate poisoning causes acute pulmonary edema as well as respiratory depression. To counteract the constipation caused by heroin, sometimes mannitol is added for its laxative effect.

Another potentially lethal combination emerges when heroin is laced with the much more potent artificial narcotic fentanyl. This adulterated heroin can be extremely dangerous because of its unexpected potency (DEA, 2018; Gorner, 2015).

Frequently, heroin is deliberately combined with other drugs when self-administered by addicts (DEA, 2018). Heroin is most frequently used with alcohol, but it is often combined with CNS stimulants such as cocaine (Bebinger, 2015). Some crack cocaine smokers turn to heroin to ease the jitters caused by the CNS stimulant. It also has been reported that heroin addicts use cocaine to withdraw or detoxify themselves from heroin by gradually decreasing amounts of heroin while increasing amounts of cocaine. This drug combination is called **speedballing**, and addicts claim the cocaine provides relief from the unpleasant withdrawal effects that accompany heroin abstinence in a dependent user (Bebinger, 2015).

## PROFILE OF HEROIN ADDICTS

An estimated 600,000 to 1 million active heroin addicts live in the United States, a figure that has remained relatively stable despite changes in

the number of infrequent and moderate users. Heroin addicts often search for a better and purer drug—but if they do find an unusually potent batch of heroin, there is a good chance they will get more than they bargained for. Addicts are sometimes found dead with the needle still in a vein after injecting a particularly potent batch of heroin (ASAM, 2016). More than 10,000 deaths occur annually in the United States from heroin overdoses (ASAM, 2016). Death associated with heroin injection is usually because of the concurrent use of alcohol or barbiturates—not the heroin alone—and frequently occur after an addict has gone weeks or months without the drug and injects the same amount of heroin he or she used before, not realizing that tolerance has worn off (Bebinger, 2015).

Hard-core addicts often come together and share a common place where they can stash supplies and equipment for their heroin encounters. These *shooting galleries* serve as gathering places for addicts (Lopez, 2019) and can be set up in homes but are usually located in less established locations such as abandoned cars, cardboard lean-tos, and weed-infested vacant lots. An entrance charge often is required of patrons. Conditions in shooting galleries are notoriously filthy, and these places are frequented by intravenous heroin users with bloodborne infections that can cause AIDS or hepatitis. Because of needle sharing and other unsanitary

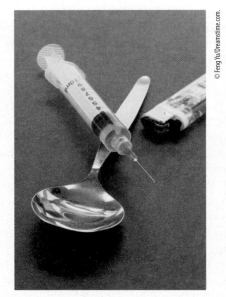

© Feng Yu/Dreamstime.com.

Heroin paraphernalia is usually simple and crude but effective: a spoon on which to dissolve the narcotic and a makeshift syringe to inject it.

practices, shooting galleries have become a place where serious communicative diseases are spread to a wide range of people of different ages, races, genders, and socioeconomic statuses (Nakamura, 2008). In some countries, such as the United Kingdom, and even in U.S. cities such as New York or San Francisco are proposing controversial efforts to develop government-regulated shooting galleries to ensure sanitary conditions and the availability of clean needles for the heroin addicts to prevent their exposure to the dangers of contracting devastating and potentially deadly diseases (Lopez, 2019).

The heroin in shooting galleries is typically prepared by adding several drops of water to the white powder in an improvised container (such as a metal bottle cap) and lightly shaking the container while heating it over a small flame to dissolve the powder. The fluid is then drawn through a tiny wad of cotton to filter out the gross contaminants into an all-too-often used syringe where it is ready for injection.

Some addicts become fixated on the drug's paraphernalia, especially the needle. They can get a psychological high from playing with the needle and syringe. The injection process and syringe plunger action appear to have sexual overtones for them. As one reformed user explained, "I think what I miss more than heroin sometimes is just the ritual of shooting up." A heavy user concurred, explaining, "You get addicted to the needle.... Just the process of sticking something into your vein, having such a direct involvement with your body" ("Mary," 1996, p. 42; Winkler et al., 2011).

## HEROIN AND CRIME

In 1971, the House Select Committee on Crime in the United States released a report on methods used to combat the heroin crisis that arose in the 1950s and 1960s. This report was a turning point in setting up treatment programs for narcotic addicts. The report stated that drug arrests for heroin use had increased 700% since 1961 and that the cost of heroin-related crimes to U.S. society was estimated to exceed $3 billion per year. Other reports since that time have linked heroin addiction with crime (Fisher, 2015).

Currently, many young heroin addicts come from affluent or middle-class white families (Seelye, 2015; see "Here and Now: Heroin's New Terrain"). However, research shows that heavy users (usually addicts who inject their heroin) are frequently poorly educated with minimal

social integration and live in neighborhoods surrounded by poverty (Nandi et al., 2010). Because of these disadvantages, these heroin addicts often have a low level of employment, exist in unstable living conditions, and socialize with other illicit drug users. Clearly, such undesirable living conditions encourage criminal activity. However, the pharmacological effects of heroin itself do not appear to be directly responsible for criminal behavior or associated with violence, but drug seeking in heroin users may result in violence (Deveney, 2019) Thus, there are three other factors that likely contribute to the association between heroin use and crime:

1. The use of heroin encourages antisocial behavior that is crime related. Depressants such as heroin diminish inhibitions and cause people to engage in activities they normally would not. The effects of heroin and its withdrawal make addicts self-centered, demanding, impulsive, and governed by their "need" for the drug.
2. Because heroin addiction is expensive, the user is forced to resort to crime to support the drug habit (McMurran, 2007).
3. A similar personality is driven to engage in both criminal behavior and heroin use. Often, heroin addicts start using heroin about the same time they begin to become actively involved in criminal activity. In most cases, the heroin user has been taking other illicit drugs, especially marijuana or prescription painkillers, years before trying heroin (Reid, Elifson, & Sterk, 2007; Seelye, 2015).

These findings suggest that for many heroin addicts, the antisocial behavior causes the criminal behavior rather than the criminal behavior resulting from the heroin use. Thus, the more a drug such as heroin is perceived as being illegal, desirable, and addictive, the more likely it will be used by deviant criminal populations. However, typical heroin users are not violent, although they may participate in criminal activities to fund their drug habit. Violence is more likely associated with heroin trafficking and distribution because of the criminal groups involved in this activity.

## PATTERNS OF HEROIN ABUSE

It has become apparent that problems with narcotics are no longer confined to the inner cities but have infiltrated suburban areas and small towns

# HERE AND NOW

## Heroin's New Terrain

Courtney Griffin came from a comfortable home in southeastern New Hampshire—hardly the place where one would expect a hard-core heroin "junkie" to live. And yet Courtney's father explained at her funeral that his daughter's death was a consequence of her heroin addiction. He acknowledged her addiction secret and revealed that Courtney had lied, frequently disappeared, and stolen money from her parents to sustain a $400-a-day heroin habit. Her parents tried to "protect" their daughter by never reporting her thefts to the police and by paying her drug-related debts. Despite all of their efforts, Courtney was kicked out of the Marines because of her drug habit and was found dead from a heroin overdose at the home of her boyfriend's grandmother. Courtney was one of many victims of the recent heroin epidemic spreading into suburbs and small towns linked to a recent wave of addictions to prescription painkillers. This heroin epidemic differs demographically from that seen earlier with crack cocaine, which occurred primarily in poor and predominantly black urban areas. Another difference between the two drug epidemics is the public response. For the cocaine scourge, people demanded "zero tolerance" and severe prison terms. However, because the current heroin epidemic is predominantly found in white populations (90%), many of whom are from middle-class homes, families of the heroin "victims" are using their voice and political power to demand a more forgiving approach from government officials and law enforcement agencies: punishment is out and treatment is in.

Information from Seelye, K. (2015, October 30). In heroin crisis, white families seek gentler war on drugs. *The New York Times*. Retrieved from http://www.nytimes.com/2015/10/31/us/heroin-war-on-drugs-parents.html

**TABLE 9.3** Prevalence of Heroin and Other Opioid Abuse Among High School Seniors

| Year | Annual Use (%) | | Lifetime Use (%) | |
|---|---|---|---|---|
| | Heroin | Other Opioids | Heroin | Other Opioids |
| 1995 | 1.1 | 4.7 | 1.6 | 7.2 |
| 1999 | 1.1 | 6.7 | 2.0 | 10.2 |
| 2002 | 1.0 | 9.4* | 1.7 | 13.5* |
| 2007 | 0.9 | 9.2 | 1.5 | 13.1 |
| 2009 | 0.7 | 9.2 | 1.2 | 13.2 |
| 2012 | 0.6 | 7.9 | 1.1 | 12.2 |
| 2015 | 0.4 | 5.4 | 0.8 | 8.4 |
| 2018 | 0.4 | 3.4 | 0.6 | – |

*In 2002, the question text was changed in half of the questionnaire forms. The list of examples of narcotics other than heroin was updated: Talwin, laudanum, and paregoric—all of which had negligible rates of use by 2001—were replaced with Vicodin, OxyContin, and Percocet. The 2002 data presented here are based on the changed forms only; $N$ is one-half of $N$ indicated. In 2003, the remaining forms were changed to the new wording. Data based on all forms beginning in 2003.

Data from Johnston, L. D., Miech, R. A., O'Malley, P. M., Bachman, J. G., Schulenberg, J. E., & Patrick, M. E. (2018). *Monitoring the future*. Retrieved from http://monitoringthefuture.org/pubs/monographs/mtf-overview2018.pdf

and afflict both rich and poor. The following are recent heroin trends (see **Table 9.3**):

- Heroin use among adolescents and young adults, after holding steady through much of the first decade in 2000, is thought to be rising because of decreases in cost and increases in purity and availability (Ramde, 2014).

- Heroin has become purer (60% to 70% purity) and cheaper ($10/bag [around 100 milligrams]) (Ramde, 2014).

- Thanks to the greater purity, new users are able to administer heroin in less efficient ways, such as smoking and snorting, avoiding the dangers of intravenous use (Gray, 2014). Many youths believe that heroin can be used safely if it is not injected.

- Because of its association with popular fashions and entertainment, heroin has been viewed as glamorous and chic, especially by many young people, despite its highly publicized lethal consequences. The look of being "wasted" and unkempt has been referred to as "heroin chic" (Carbone, 2014). However, to some extent this "druggy look" and malnourished appearance has fallen out of fashion within the glamour business because of its highly negative implications and health consequences.
- Approximately 250,000 emergency room visits each year are from heroin overdoses (Polidoro, 2014).

## STAGES OF DEPENDENCE

Initially, the early effects of heroin are often unpleasant, especially after the first injection (Gutstein & Akil, 2006). It is not uncommon to experience nausea and vomiting after administration; gradually, however, euphoria overwhelms the aversive effects (Powell, 2015). The development of a psychological dependence on heroin or other opioid narcotics has two major stages:

1. In the rewarding stage, euphoria and positive effects occur in at least 50% of users. These positive feelings and sensations increase with continued administration and encourage use.
2. Eventually, the heroin or narcotic user must take the drug to avoid withdrawal symptoms that start about six to 12 hours after the last dose. At this stage, it is said that "the monkey is on his back." This stage is psychological dependence. If one grain of heroin (about 65 milligrams) is taken over a two-week period on a daily basis, the user becomes physically dependent on the drug.

## METHODS OF ADMINISTRATION

Many heroin users start by sniffing the powder or injecting it into a muscle (intramuscular) or under the skin ("skin popping"). Because of the increased purity and decreased cost, many of today's heroin users are administering their drug by smoking and snorting (Gray, 2014).

Most established heroin addicts still prefer to **mainline** the drug (intravenous injection) (Kritz, 2015). The injection device can be made from an eyedropper bulb, part of a syringe, and a hypodermic needle. Mainlining drugs causes the thin-walled veins to become scarred; if done frequently, the veins will collapse. Once a vein is collapsed, it can no longer be used to introduce the drug into the blood. Addicts become expert in locating new veins to use: in the feet, the legs, the neck, even the temples. When addicts do not want "needle tracks" (scars) to show, they inject under the tongue or in the groin.

## HEROIN ADDICTS, AIDS, AND HEPATITIS

Intravenous drug use, particularly heroin, substantially increases the likelihood of contracting viral infections associated with HIV, AIDS, and viral hepatitis from contact with infected blood or other body fluids from shared syringes and other injection paraphernalia. Although substituting snorting or smoking for intravenous drug administration reduces the likelihood of contracting these infectious diseases, it is not eliminated because people under the influence of heroin are more likely to be exposed to these diseases through risky sexual behaviors. Injection drug users are among the highest groups for being infected with these body fluid-borne microorganisms and, in turn, are likely to infect many others as they transmit the pathogens to those with whom they associate (NIDA, 2014a).

## HEROIN AND PREGNANCY

Devin acts like any normal 2-year-old. He particularly enjoys the fast-food Chick-fil-A restaurant and playing with the barbecue sauce containers. Looking at Devin gives no clue that his mother had become addicted to prescription painkillers when she discovered her pregnancy. She was urged by her sister to seek professional help immediately. Devin was born on time and was undersized at 5 pounds and 5 ounces. Devin was able to avoid the worst withdrawal symptoms after birth because he was immediately placed on methadone and gradually weaned to allow his small body to adjust to not having the painkillers that his mother had been using throughout her pregnancy. Devin was lucky: other babies under similar circumstances who do not receive proper medical care suffer through serious

**KEY TERM**

**mainline**
to inject a drug of abuse intravenously

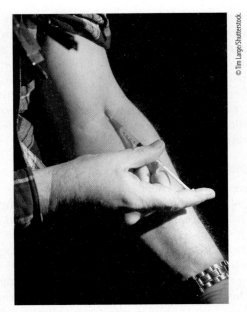

A heroin addict "mainlining" his drug.

feeding problems, vomiting, diarrhea, muscle stiffness, and severe tremors. These babies cry constantly as they experience dangerous narcotic withdrawal, and in extreme cases they may even suffer seizures. (Colon, 2011; NIDA, 2014b)

These withdrawal symptoms in new born infants are often controlled by exposure to opioid drugs specifically developed for treating neonatal abstinence syndrome (NAS) such as buprenorphine (NIDA, 2014b).

Many women use heroin during their pregnancy. In the United States, as many as 7,000 infants are born each year to women who chronically used heroin or other opioid drugs during their pregnancies (Bhuvaneswar, Chang, Epstein, & Stern, 2008). There is no evidence that prenatal exposure to opioid drugs causes overt structural damage, although incidents of lower birthweights or even reduced head size have been reported in infants born to mothers using opioid drugs (Wang, 2010). The most devastating consequence of heroin or opioid use during pregnancy appears to be physical dependence in the newborn, resulting in withdrawal symptoms, usually immediately after birth. As previously mentioned, the NAS are characterized by high-pitched crying, inconsolability, tightened muscle tone, tremors, vomiting, seizures, and even death. Elements of this withdrawal persist for weeks and usually require hospitalization (NIDA, 2014b). Treatment for such withdrawal problems generally includes low doses of a long-lasting opioid narcotic to reduce the intensity of the symptoms and then a gradual tapering of the dose to eventually wean the infant from the drug. For heroin, this typically takes up to two weeks (NIDA, 2014b). In addition, some evidence suggests that use of heroin during pregnancy increases the likelihood of sudden infant death syndrome in offspring (March of Dimes, 2015).

## WITHDRAWAL SYMPTOMS

After the effects of heroin wear off, the addict usually has only a few hours in which to find the next dose before severe withdrawal symptoms begin. A single "shot" of heroin lasts only four to six hours. It is enough to help addicts "get straight," or relieve the severe withdrawal symptoms called *dope sickness,* but is not enough to give a desired high. Withdrawal symptoms start with a runny nose, tears, and minor stomach cramps. The addict may feel as if he or she is coming down with a bad cold (Armstrong, 2016). Between 12 and 48 hours after the last dose, the addict loses all of his or her appetite, vomits, has diarrhea and abdominal cramps, feels alternating chills and fever, and develops goose pimples all over (going "cold turkey"). Between two and four days later, the addict continues to experience some of the symptoms just described, as well as aching bones and muscles and powerful muscle spasms that cause violent kicking motions ("kicking the habit"). After four to five days, symptoms start to subside, and the person may get his or her appetite back. However, attempts to move on in life will be challenging because compulsion to keep using the drug remains strong.

The severity of the withdrawal varies according to the purity and strength of the drug used and the personality of the user. The symptoms of withdrawal from heroin, morphine, and methadone are summarized in **Table 9.4**. Withdrawal symptoms from opioids such as morphine, codeine, meperidine, and others are similar, although the time frame and intensity vary (Schumacher et al., 2015).

## ■ Treatment of Heroin and Other Narcotic Dependence

The ideal result of treatment for dependency on heroin or other narcotics is to help the addict live a normal, productive, and satisfying life without drugs (Volkow, 2014a). Unfortunately, only a minority of heroin addicts receive adequate

**TABLE 9.4** Symptoms of Withdrawal from Heroin, Morphine, and Methadone

| Symptoms | Time in Hours | | |
|---|---|---|---|
| | Heroin | Morphine | Methadone |
| Craving for drugs, anxiety | 4 | 6 | 24–48 |
| Yawning, perspiration, runny nose, tears | 8 | 14 | 34–48 |
| Pupil dilation, goose bumps, muscle twitches, aching bones and muscles, hot and cold flashes, loss of appetite | 12 | 16 | 48–72 |
| Increased intensity of preceding symptoms, insomnia, raised blood pressure, fever, faster pulse, nausea | 18–24 | 24–36 | ≥ 72 |
| Increased intensity of preceding symptoms, curled-up position, vomiting, diarrhea, increased blood sugar, foot kicking ("kicking the habit") | 26–36 | 36–48 | – |

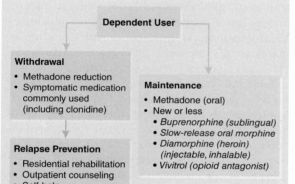

**FIGURE 9.1** Treatment of heroin addiction. The principal aspects of treating heroin addiction include minimizing the highly aversive withdrawal effect (usually with drug adjuncts), preventing relapse (usually with behavioral modification), and, if necessary, providing maintenance support with other opioid-like drugs that have longer action than heroin.

Volkow, N. (2016). America's addiction to opioids: Heroin and prescription drug abuse. National Institute on Drug Abuse Publication. Retrieved from https://www.drugabuse.gov/about-nida/legislative-activities/testimony-to-congress/2016/americas-addiction-to-opioids-heroin-prescription-drug-abuse; Volkow, N. (2016). Prescription opioid and heroin abuse. National Institute on Drug Abuse. Retrieved from www.drugabuse.gov/about-nida/legislative-activities/testimony-to-congress. Accessed February 29, 2020.

treatment for their addiction. Of those who are treated, relatively few become absolutely "clean" from drug use; thus, therapeutic compromise often is necessary (see **Figure 9.1**). In the real world, treatment of heroin dependency is considered successful if the addict does the following:

- stops using heroin;
- no longer associates with dealers or users of heroin;
- avoids dangerous activities often associated with heroin use (such as needle sharing, injecting unknown drugs, and frequenting shooting galleries) (Tur, 2010);
- improves his or her employment status;
- refrains from criminal activity; and
- is able to enjoy normal family and social relationships.

For more than 30 years, many heroin addicts have achieved these goals by substituting a long-lasting synthetic narcotic such as methadone for the short-acting heroin (ASAM, 2015). The maintenance (*substitute*) narcotic is made available to heroin-dependent people through drug treatment centers under the direction of trained medical personnel. The dispensing of the substitute narcotic is tightly regulated by governmental agencies. The rationale for the substitution is that a long-acting drug such as methadone can be conveniently taken once a day to prevent the unpleasant withdrawal symptoms that occur within four hours after each heroin use (ASAM, 2015) (see Table 9.4). Although the substitute narcotic may also have abuse potential and be scheduled by the DEA (see Table 9.2), it is given to the addict in its oral form; thus, its onset of action is too slow to cause a rush like that associated with heroin use, which means that its abuse potential is substantially less. In addition, the cost to society is dramatically reduced. According to one study, an untreated heroin addict costs the community $21,000 for six months, but the cost of methadone maintenance for a person dependent on heroin is only about $3,000 for the same period (Buddy T., 2008; Palm Partners Recovery Center, 2013).

Currently, methadone is approved by the FDA for *opiate maintenance therapy* in the treatment of heroin (or other narcotic) dependency (Volkow, 2014a). It has been used in heroin treatment for more than 30 years. Although it is not the best treatment for every person dependent on an opiate drug, it is an effective tool for managing many heroin addicts. Proper use of methadone has been shown to effectively decrease illicit use of narcotics and other undesirable behavior related to drug dependence. Although methadone does not tend to make users high, it helps heroin addicts by reducing their drug craving (Simon, 2016). Often methadone-assisted therapy will be long term, perhaps for the rest of the addict's life. The methadone is typically well tolerated, although if misused it can be problematic and has been associated with a startling number of overdose deaths across the country (Rudd, Noah, Zibbell, & Mathew, 2016).

A second narcotic, buprenorphine, which is used as an analgesic, also has been approved for treatment of narcotic dependence (Volkow, 2014a). Because buprenorphine is both an opioid agonist and an antagonist, it has minimal potential for dependence and is easy to manage, which makes this drug a desirable substitute for heroin (Schumacher et al., 2015). Efforts are being made to provide education and training to primary care physicians so they will be able to use buprenorphine to treat patients addicted to narcotics in their own offices (Substance Abuse and Mental Health Services Administration [SAMHSA], 2019). This novel strategy opens the door to physicians not yet involved in the treatment of drug addiction to become familiar with substance abuse management, which will hopefully increase opportunities to diagnose and treat these patients. There is considerable discussion as to how buprenorphine products compare to methadone in treatment of dependence on and addiction to opioids in general and heroin in particular. Although these issues clearly require further study, some evidence suggests that buprenorphine is usually the better and safer strategy for detoxification (i.e., treatment of withdrawal) and treatment of infants of opiate-addicted mothers. However, such claims are disputed by some experts in the field (Mental Health Daily, 2015).

A third and decidedly different drug approved in 2010 by the FDA to treat heroin and other opioid addictions is Vivitrol, an extended-release form of naltrexone, an opioid antagonist (MedlinePlus, 2019; Tabachnick, 2015). In 2006, Vivitrol was originally approved as a treatment for alcoholism because of its ability to reduce alcohol craving and its consumption (Tabachnick, 2015). Vivitrol has been found to also reduce craving for narcotic drugs such as heroin. Its administration consists of a monthly deep muscle injection. Some of the potential side effects of using Vivitrol include (1) interference with thinking or reactions, (2) wheezing, (3) enhanced pain, and (4) mood changes (Drugs.com, 2015b).

**Table 9.5** compares the opioids that have been used for maintenance therapy. Other drugs used less frequently for similar maintenance therapy of heroin addicts include slow-release oral morphine and even heroin itself for addicts who do not respond to the other maintenance opioid drugs.

Some people, including some professionals involved in drug abuse therapy, view heroin or narcotic addiction as a "failure of the will" and see methadone treatment as substituting one addiction for another. However, evidence has demonstrated that this approach is highly effective in preventing the spread of infectious diseases such as AIDS and hepatitis and helps the heroin addict return to a normal productive life (McClure, 2009).

**TABLE 9.5** Comparison of Narcotic-Related Drugs Used in Opiate Maintenance Therapy

| Properties | Methadone (agonist) | Buprenorphine (partial agonist) | Vivitrol (antagonist) |
|---|---|---|---|
| Administration | Oral | Oral or sublingual | Injection |
| Frequency of doses | Daily | Daily | Monthly |
| Other uses | Analgesic | Analgesic | Alcohol dependence |
| Physical dependence | Yes | Little | No |
| Causes positive subjective effects | Yes | Yes | No |
| Abuse potential | Yes | Limited | No |

Data from Swan, N. (1993, March/April). Two NIDA-tested heroin treatment medications move toward FDA approval. *NIDA Notes*, 45.

# ► CASE IN POINT

## Heroin Addiction: Not a Joke

**A**rtie Lange, who used to be a "funnyman" on *The Howard Stern Show*, was discovered by his mother bleeding on his Hoboken apartment floor. According to paramedics, Lange had been stabbed nine times with a kitchen knife. Police investigators concluded the wounds were self-inflicted and called it a suicide attempt, although Lange claims he was not trying to commit suicide and that the knife wounds were related to his heroin addiction. It was concluded, that despite treatment, Lange was manifesting self-destructive tendencies that apparently led to this attempt to take his own life. His behavior has been compared to other self-destructive comics such as Chris Farley and John Belushi, who both experienced untimely deaths apparently by accidental causes linked to their drug or heroin use.

Data from Staff. (2012, September 6). Artie Lange says self-inflicted stab wounds were due to heroin addiction. Rehabs.com. Retrieved from http://luxury .rehabs.com/blog/artie-lange-says-self-inflicted-stab-wounds-were-due-to-heroin-addiction/

Unrealistic treatment expectations are sometimes imposed on heroin addicts, leading to high failure rates. For example, some methadone treatment programs distribute inadequate methadone doses to maintain heroin or narcotic abstinence (Recovery Helpdesk, 2010); alternatively, narcotic-dependent patients may be told their methadone will be terminated within six months regardless of their progress in the program. Such ill-advised policies often drive clients back to their heroin habits and demonstrate that many professionals who treat heroin and narcotic dependency do not understand that methadone is not a cure for heroin addiction but a means to achieve a healthier, more normal lifestyle (McClure, 2009).

It also is essential to understand that even proper treatment does not guarantee resolution of heroin or narcotic addiction (see "Case in Point: Heroin Addiction: Not a Joke"). To maximize the possibility of successful treatment, clients often must also participate in regular counseling sessions in combination with medication to help modify the drug-seeking behavior and receive on-site care from professionals, including job training, career development, education, general medical care, and family counseling. This combination of strategies is referred to as *medication-assisted treatment*, and it provides a whole-patient approach for treating these patients, dramatically improving the success rate of narcotic-dependence treatment (SAMHSA, 2015). Although only a small minority of heroin addicts become completely drug abstinent for the rest of their lives, many do have long periods of sustained abstinence after proper treatment (Darke et al., 2015).

# Other Narcotics

A large number of nonheroin narcotics are used for medical purposes. However, many are also distributed in the streets, including morphine, methadone, codeine, hydromorphone (Dilaudid), meperidine (Demerol), and other synthetics (hydrocodone [Vicodin] and oxycodone [OxyContin]). A few of the most commonly abused opioids are discussed briefly in the following sections. Except where noted, they are all Schedule II or III drugs (Schumacher et al., 2015).

## ■ Morphine

As previously noted, morphine is the standard by which other narcotic analgesic agents are measured (Medi-Cal, 2015). It has been used to relieve pain since it was first isolated in 1803. Morphine has about half the analgesic potency of heroin but 12 times the potency of codeine. It is commonly used to relieve moderate to intense pain that cannot be controlled by less potent and less dangerous narcotics. Because of its potential for serious side effects, morphine is generally used in a hospital setting where emergency care can be rendered if necessary. Most pain can be relieved by morphine if high enough doses are used (Schumacher et al., 2015); however, morphine is most effective against continuous dull pain.

The side effects that occur when using therapeutic doses of morphine include drowsiness, changes in mood, and inability to think straight. In addition, therapeutic doses depress respiratory activity; thus, morphine decreases the rate and depth of breathing and produces irregular breathing patterns. Like the other narcotics, it can create an array of seemingly unrelated effects throughout the body, including nausea and vomiting, constipation, blurred vision, constricted pupils, and flushed skin (Bennington-Castro, 2014).

The initial response to morphine is varied. In normal people who are not suffering pain, the first exposure can be unpleasant, with nausea and vomiting being the prominent reactions. However, continual use often leads to a euphoric response and encourages dependence. When injected subcutaneously, the effects of heroin and morphine are almost identical; this situation occurs because heroin is rapidly metabolized in the body into morphine. After intravenous administration, the onset of heroin's effects is more rapid and more intense than that of morphine because heroin is more lipid soluble and enters the brain faster. Because heroin is easier to manufacture and is more potent, it is more popular in illicit trade than morphine. Even so, morphine also has substantial abuse potential and is classified as a Schedule II substance (DEA, 2016).

Tolerance to the effects of morphine can develop rapidly if the drug is used continuously. For example, an addict who is repeatedly administering the morphine to get a "kick" or maintain a high must constantly increase the dose. Such users can build up to incredible doses. Some addicts report using 200 milligrams of morphine daily; the normal analgesic dose of morphine is 50 to 80 milligrams per day. Such high doses are lethal in a person without a tolerance to narcotics.

## ▌ Methadone

Methadone was first synthesized in Germany in 1943, when natural opiate analgesics were not available because opium could not be obtained from Asia during World War II. Methadone was first called *Dolophine*, after Adolf Hitler; one company still uses that trade name. (On the street, methadone pills have been called *dollies*.) As previously described, methadone is often substituted for heroin in the treatment of narcotic-dependent people (*Drug Facts*, 2010). It is an effective analgesic, equal to morphine if injected and more potent if taken orally (*Drug Facts*, 2010).

The physiological effects of methadone are the same as those of morphine and heroin. As a narcotic, methadone produces psychological dependence, tolerance, and then physical dependence and addiction if repeated doses are taken (Schumacher et al., 2015). It is effective for about 24 to 36 hours; therefore, the addict must take methadone daily to avoid narcotic withdrawal. It is often considered as addictive as heroin if injected; consequently, because methadone is soluble in water, it is formulated with insoluble, inert ingredients to prevent it from being injected by narcotic addicts.

Among methadone's most useful properties are cross-tolerance with other narcotic drugs and a less-intense withdrawal response (Preda, 2015). If it reaches a sufficiently high level in the blood, methadone blocks heroin euphoria. In addition, withdrawal symptoms of patients physically dependent on heroin or morphine and the postaddiction craving can be suppressed by oral administration of methadone (Meader, 2010). The effective dose for methadone maintenance is 50 to 100 milligrams per day to treat severe withdrawal symptoms (Preda, 2015).

The value of substituting methadone for heroin lies in its longer action. Because addicts no longer need heroin to prevent withdrawal, they often can be persuaded to leave their undesirable associates, drug sources, and dangerous lifestyles. The potential side effects from methadone are the same as those from morphine and heroin, including constipation and sedation; yet if properly used, methadone is usually a safe drug (*Drug Facts*, 2010).

When injecting methadone, some people feel the same kind of euphoria that can be obtained from heroin. Methadone addicts receiving maintenance treatment sometimes become euphoric if the dose is increased too rapidly. There are cases of people who injected crushed methadone pills and developed serious lung conditions from particles that lodged in the tissue, creating a condition somewhat like emphysema. The number of deaths from methadone overdose in recent years are about one-fifth that of heroin. The reasons for these problems caused by methadone include the following (Zielinski, 2010):

- Large quantities of methadone are being stolen from legitimate businesses such as hospitals and pharmacies for personal use or to sell.
- Excessive amounts of methadone are being accumulated and abused by doctor shopping, prescription fraud, or illegal Internet pharmacy websites.
- It is being misused by patients who received their methadone by legitimate prescriptions for pain.
- Because of increases in pain-management clinics, it has become easier to obtain methadone.

Like heroin, methadone overdoses can be reversed by the antagonist naloxone if the person is treated in time.

# ▪ Fentanyls

The following is a personal account of a young user of one of the most potent opioid narcotics, fentanyl:

> Each patch of fentanyl is designed to provide 72 hours of steady analgesic relief for people suffering from intense, chronic pain—every day. These fentanyl patches can be chewed, have the gel scraped out them and smoked or injected. One young abuser of these fentanyl products claims to have come close to overdosing on many occasions, and frequently passed out, as the drug slowed his breathing and pulse. He explains that these patches have made his pulse drop to 30 beats a minute while giving him the feeling of invincibility. It took the heroin-related deaths of four of his friends and fellow abusers—two of them still in their teens—to convince him to seek help. (Gatehouse & Macdonald, 2015)

The fentanyls belong to a family of highly potent narcotic analgesics (more than 200 times the potency of morphine) that include drugs such as acetylfentanyl, fluranylfentanyl, and carfentanyl and are often administered intravenously for general anesthesia (CDC, 2019). These synthetic opioid narcotics include drugs such as sufentanil and alfentanil (Gutstein & Akil, 2006). Fentanyls are also used in transdermal systems (patches on the skin) and as lollipops in the treatment of chronic pain (Hieatt, 2010). Occasionally, reports surface of individuals abusing a fentanyl patch by licking, swallowing, or even smoking it (Gatehouse & Macdonald, 2015).

An estimated 100 different active forms of fentanyl could be synthesized, but so far only some 10 derivatives have appeared on the street. They are considered to be "designer" drugs. Because of their great potency, ease of production, and low cost, the fentanyls have sometimes been used to replace heroin (DEA, 2019a). Fentanyl-type drugs can appear in the same forms and colors as heroin, so there is nothing to alert users that they have been sold a heroin substitute or a heroin combination (Stewart, 2014). Because of their powerful effects, these drugs are especially dangerous, and incredibly small doses can cause fatal respiratory depression in an unsuspecting heroin user (Stewart, 2014). Hundreds have probably died from overdosing with heroin laced with fentanyl. Because of the enhanced high, addicts are tempted to use these lethal combinations (Stewart, 2014). Because these drugs are sometimes extremely difficult to detect in the blood because of the small quantities used, there is no reliable information regarding the extent of fentanyl abuse. Fentanyl is so potent that abusing the patch has caused overdoses and even death (Gatehouse & Macdonald, 2015).

# ▪ Hydromorphone

Hydromorphone (Dilaudid) is prepared from morphine and used as an analgesic and cough suppressant. It is a stronger analgesic than morphine and is used to treat moderate to severe pain. Nausea, vomiting, constipation, and euphoria may be less marked with hydromorphone than with morphine (Karch, 1996; Way, Fields, & Way, 1998). It is becoming more popular with opiate addicts because of its potency, although combination with other CNS depressants can be fatal. On the street, it is taken in tablet form or injected (Gulur et al., 2015).

# ▪ Oxycodone

Oxycodone (OxyContin) is a moderate narcotic analgesic that in the past decade has been increasingly abused as the proprietary product OxyContin, creating considerable controversy. OxyContin is a long-lasting version of oxycodone and is considered to be an important and effective therapy for the treatment of severe pain from cancer or other lingering diseases. Abuse of OxyContin has been a considerable cause for alarm by officials. Street names for OxyContin include *OC, kicker, OxyCotton,* and *Rushbo* (Rehabs.com, n.d.). This drug can be easily abused by simply crushing the tablet and then ingesting, injecting, inhaling, or placing it rectally. However, recent modifications have made the drug in OxyContin less available by this process, thereby reducing its appeal to those who intend to abuse it (Diep, 2013).

The problems with OxyContin are underscored by a report that 2.3% of high school students in 2015 had abused this drug (Johnston, 2019). Interestingly, the abuse rate by this population for the less-potent Vicodin (hydrocodone plus acetaminophen) was almost double that for OxyContin, likely because of easier access (Johnston, 2019). Deaths and trips to the emergency room caused by OxyContin have been common and are of concern to both medical and law enforcement organizations (Bryan, 2015). As a result, the FDA and DEA control OxyContin at the same level as morphine.

## ▪ Meperidine

Meperidine (Demerol) is a synthetic drug frequently used as an analgesic for treatment of moderate pain; it can be taken in tablet form or injected. This drug is sometimes given too freely by some physicians. Meperidine is about 1/10th as powerful as morphine. Tolerance develops with continued use of the drug, requiring larger doses to maintain its therapeutic action. With continual use, it causes physical dependence. Meperidine addicts may use large daily doses (three to four grams per day) (Addiction Center, n.d.).

## ▪ Hydrocodone

Hydrocodone is a synthetic opioid analgesic typically used to treat moderate to moderately severe pain. It is also used on occasion to help suppress severe coughing often associated with colds and flu. Hydrocodone is available as both immediate- and delayed-release forms and is frequently combined with acetaminophen or ibuprofen for pain relief. It is available in liquid preparations in combination with other drugs such as antihistamines and decongestants, usually to treat colds. Hydrocodone's common side effects are similar to other opioid analgesics and include dizziness, drowsiness, constipation, and nausea and vomiting. Products containing hydrocodone such as Vicodin and Lortab have become extremely popular for both legitimate and illegitimate uses. Consequently, 4.4% of high school seniors reported abusing Vicodin in 2015, but that number decreased to 1.7% in 2018 (Johnston, 2019). The substance abuse rate of hydrocodone led to the changing of the hydrocodone schedule classification from Schedule IV to II in 2014, making it more difficult to prescribe (Pietrangelo, 2015).

## ▪ Buprenorphine

Buprenorphine, a mild to moderate narcotic analgesic, was available as a Schedule V pain reliever for years. As previously discussed, after extensive research this drug was approved in 2002 as an effective medication for the treatment of narcotic abuse and dependence (Schumacher et al., 2015). Buprenorphine has been shown to be effective in relieving the cravings for narcotic pain relievers with minimal tendency to cause addiction itself (Preda, 2015). Although buprenorphine has been reported to have a minimal high when used properly (Preda, 2015), there have been isolated reports of occasional deaths, especially when combined with other CNS depressant drugs (Sansone & Sansone, 2015). Despite buprenorphine's significant safety record and its minimal propensity for abuse, its new FDA-approved indication to treat dependence on other opioid drugs would cause it to be dispensed to patients with drug abuse histories, so the DEA revised its classification, changing buprenorphine to a Schedule III drug.

Of particular importance is the fact that buprenorphine (in the form of Subutex and Suboxone, combinations of buprenorphine and the opioid antagonist, naloxone) has been approved for the treatment of opiate dependence in an office setting. Trained physicians are allowed to treat up to 100 narcotic-dependent patients with buprenorphine in their medical offices. This means that opioid addictions and dependence can now be treated with a prescribed medication by trained primary care physicians in the offices of private doctors. This is an important step in what may become a revolution in addiction treatment, allowing patients to discreetly receive help from a family doctor for their substance abuse problem (Sansone & Sansone, 2015). Although most physicians are not licensed to prescribe Suboxone, many are; consequently, three times more opioid addicts are being treated with Suboxone than methadone, despite the fact that this opioid drug is much more expensive (Svrluga, 2015).

## ▪ MPTP: A "Designer" Tragedy

Attempts to synthesize illicit designer versions of meperidine by street chemists have proved tragic for some unsuspecting drug addicts. In 1976, a young drug addict with elementary laboratory skills attempted to make a meperidine-like drug by using shortcuts in the chemical synthesis. Three days after self-administering his untested drug product, the drug user developed a severe case of tremors and motor problems identical to Parkinson's disease, a neurological disorder generally occurring in the elderly. Even more surprising to attending neurologists was that this young drug addict improved dramatically after treatment with levodopa, a drug that is highly effective in treating the symptoms of traditional Parkinson's disease. After 18 months of treatment, the despondent addict committed suicide. An autopsy revealed he had severe brain damage that was almost identical to that occurring in classical Parkinson's patients. It was concluded that a by-product resulting from the sloppy synthesis of the meperidine-like designer narcotic was responsible for the irreversible brain damage.

This hypothesis was confirmed by a separate and independent event on the West Coast in 1981, when a cluster of relatively young heroin addicts (ages 22 to 42) in the San Francisco area also developed symptoms of Parkinson's disease. All of these patients had consumed a new "synthetic heroin" obtained on the streets, which was produced by attempting to synthesize meperidine-like drugs (Aminoff, 1998; Langston, Ballard, Tetrud, & Irwin, 1983). Common to both incidents was the presence of the compound MPTP, which was a contaminant resulting from the careless synthesis. MPTP is metabolized to a highly reactive molecule in the brain that selectively destroys neurons containing the transmitter dopamine in the motor regions of the basal ganglia. Similar neuronal damage occurs in classical Parkinson's disease over the course of 50 to 70 years, whereas ingestion of MPTP dramatically accelerates the degeneration to a matter of days (Goldstein, 1994). As tragic as the MPTP incident was, it was heralded as an important scientific breakthrough, and MPTP is now used by researchers as a tool to study why Parkinson's disease occurs and how to treat it effectively (Muñoz-Manchado et al., 2015).

## ■ Codeine

Codeine is a naturally occurring constituent of opium and the most frequently prescribed of the narcotic analgesics. It is used principally as a treatment for minor to moderate pain and as a cough suppressant. Maximum pain relief from codeine occurs with 30 to 50 milligrams. Usually, when prescribed for pain, codeine is combined with either a salicylate (such as aspirin) or acetaminophen (Tylenol). Aspirin-like drugs and opioid narcotics interact in a synergistic fashion to give an analgesic equivalence greater than what can be achieved by aspirin or codeine alone.

Although not especially powerful, codeine may still be abused. Codeine-containing cough syrup is currently classified as a Schedule V drug. Because the abuse potential is considered minor, the FDA has ruled that codeine cough products can be sold without a prescription; however, the pharmacist is required to keep them behind the counter and must be asked directly by consumers to provide codeine-containing cough medications. Despite the FDA ruling, many states have more restrictive regulations and require that codeine-containing cough products be available only by prescription.

Although codeine dependence is possible, it is not common; most people who abuse codeine developed narcotic dependence previously with one of the more potent opioids. In general, because of its lower potency, large quantities of codeine are needed to satisfy a narcotic addiction; therefore, it is not commonly marketed on the street (Pietrangelo, 2015).

## ■ Pentazocine

Pentazocine (Talwin) was first developed in the 1960s in an effort to create an effective analgesic with low abuse potential. When taken orally, its analgesic effect is slightly greater than that of codeine. Its effects on respiration and sedation are similar to those of the other opioids, but it does not prevent withdrawal symptoms in a narcotic addict. In fact, pentazocine will precipitate withdrawal symptoms if given to a person on methadone maintenance (Pain Community Centre, n.d.). Pentazocine is not commonly abused because its effects can be unpleasant and result in dysphoria. It is classified as a Schedule IV drug.

## ■ Tramadol

Tramadol (Ultram) was first introduced into the U.S. market in 1995 as a synthetic, moderately effective analgesic sometimes used as a substitute for opioid painkillers (Drugs.com, 2015a). Although tramadol itself causes some activation of opioid receptors in the brain, it appears that its analgesic properties are related to more than just its opioid actions. For example, tramadol alters gamma-aminobutyric acid (GABA), noradrenaline, and serotonin transmitter systems as well in a manner that might contribute to its atypical analgesic properties. For this reason, tramadol may have some antidepressant effects that augment its analgesic abilities (DEA, 2013).

Tramadol is frequently prescribed for patients who either do not respond well or have difficulty with the opioid painkillers. Despite the fact that opioid action likely is not the sole basis of its analgesia, it is significant enough to cause some dependence issues. For example, there is an illegal street market for this substance, where it is known by names such as *chill pills* and *ultra*. There are clinicians who claim that for some patients tramadol can cause a serious opioid-like dependence (DEA, 2013). Such conclusions are based on findings such as the following:

1. From 1998 to 2006 there was a sixfold increase in admissions for treatment of tramadol-related dependence.
2. For teens, tramadol is easier to get than alcohol and easy to sell on the streets.
3. Emergency room visits nationwide that included tramadol as a significant component went from about 5,000 in 2004 to around 20,000 in 2011.
4. There is evidence that regular daily use of tramadol can cause physical dependence and withdrawals when discontinued abruptly (Drugs.com, 2015a).

These increases in tramadol-related problems correspond to an explosion in its popularity, resulting in about 26 million prescriptions being dispensed by retailers in 2008 (Smith, 2010). Tramadol is available as both regular and extended-release tablets (Drugs.com, 2015a).

Even though tramadol is marketed as an opioid drug with low risk of dependence and some health authorities consider it to have a relatively low dependence liability, it is clear that many patients can become addicted to this analgesic (DEA, 2013). Thus, in 2014 the DEA made it a Schedule IV drug (Drugs.com, 2015a). Tramadol has been associated with a wide array of side effects, including diarrhea, constipation, drowsiness, and, in rare instances, even seizures (Medical News Today, 2019).

## Narcotic-Related Drugs

Although not classified as narcotics, the following drugs are either structurally similar to narcotics (dextromethorphan) or are used to treat narcotic withdrawal (clonidine) or overdose (naloxone).

### ■ Kratom

Kratom is a plant that recently received significant media attention because of its recreational as well as medicinal uses, but it is not allowed to be legally marketed in the United States as a drug or dietary supplement. The FDA has published warnings about products that contain kratom, trying to alert consumers about the potential serious side effects associated with its use. Although kratom is still technically "legal" in the United States, the DEA is considering labeling it as a Schedule I drug. The kratom plant is officially known as *Mitragyna speciosa* and grows naturally in Asian countries, including Thailand, Malaysia, Indonesia, and Papua New Guinea. Studies have suggested that some of the pharmacological effects come from kratom's ability to activate the same opioid receptors that are responsible for the abuse, addiction, and analgesic properties of morphine. Recently, the CDC has claimed that some overdose drug deaths in the United States relate to kratom abuse, but usually these deaths also involved the use of other substances such as opioids. There are claims that products that contain kratom can be used to treat pain and opioid withdrawals, but these claims have not been substantiated by the FDA (Webmed, 2019).

### ■ Dextromethorphan

Dextromethorphan is a safe and effective synthetic drug that has been used in cough remedies since the 1960s and can be purchased without prescription. Although its molecular structure resembles that of codeine, this drug does not have analgesic action and does not cause typical narcotic dependence (Consumer Healthcare Products Association [CHPA], n.d.).

Although dextromethorphan is not traditionally considered a major drug abuse problem, approximately 1 million youth and young adults in the United States misuse this medication each year, resulting in many visits to emergency departments (Rosenbaum & Boyer, 2019). Because of these abuse problems, several states prohibit sales of dextromethorphan-containing products to minors (CHPA, n.d.). Overdose of dextromethorphan-containing cough medicines has been reported in the United States and other countries, sometimes resulting in deadly consequences (Logan, Goldfogel, Hamilton, & Kuhlman, 2015; see "Here and Now: Dextromethorphan: Nothing to Cough At"). The principal symptoms of abuse include altered perceptions, sense of floating, hallucinations, visual distortions, and even paranoia and psychotic reactions. Its effects have been described to be similar to those of phencyclidine (PCP) and the general anesthetic ketamine (Rosenbaum & Boyer, 2019).

# HERE AND NOW

## Dextromethorphan: Nothing to Cough At

Two teenage boys who had purchased dextromethorphan through the Internet were found dead in the bedroom of one of the boys after a sleepover. Next to their bodies was a bag labeled "dextromethorphan, not for human consumption." Dextromethorphan appeared to be the only drug in the boys' bodies. Family members revealed that the boys had a history of recreationally using OTC cough medicine, but the habit escalated to using the "pure" stuff. The conclusion from the autopsy was that two healthy young males died from nonspecific findings such as edema in the lungs, air passages, and on the brain associated with extremely high concentrations of dextromethorphan in their bodies consumed for the hallucinogenic effects of the drug.

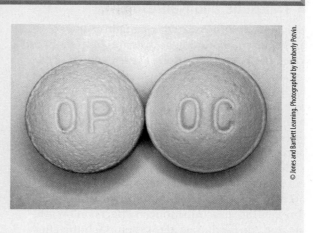

© Jones and Bartlett Learning. Photographed by Kimberly Potvin.

Data from Magnus, E. (2004, March 7). Addicted to cough medicine? *MSNBC News*. Retrieved from http://www.msnbc.msn.com/id/4608341. Accessed March 14, 2011; Traynor, K. (2010). Advisers vote against declaring dextromethorphan a controlled substance. American Society of Health Pharmacists. Retrieved from http://www.ashp.org/import/news/HealthSystemPharmacyNews/newsarticle.aspx?id=3418. Accessed March 14, 2011.

Street names for abused dextromethorphan are *DXM, triple C, Skittles, robo,* and *poor man's PCP* (DEA, 2014). Some suggest that both physical and psychological dependence can occur with dextromethorphan, resulting in withdrawal when its use is discontinued (Mutschler et al., 2010). Dextromethorphan is sometimes mixed with drugs such as alcohol, amphetamines, and cocaine to give unusual psychoactive interactions.

As of 2019, the DEA had taken no steps to restrict the use of dextromethorphan in OTC products; in fact, advisers to the FDA voted against placing this drug in a schedule of controlled substances, which likely will preclude the DEA from making a change in its category (Rosenbaum & Boyer, 2019).

Young people are becoming aware of dextromethorphan's abuse potential from websites on the Internet. A growing number of these sites have promoted dextromethorphan as a powerful OTC mind-altering drug. Included on these sites are personal experiences of users as well as directions on how to use the drug, predictions about what to expect, warning signs of adverse reactions, and instructions on how to extract dextromethorphan from OTC cough medicines (Vaults of Erowid, n.d.).

### ■ Clonidine

Clonidine (Catapres) was created in the late 1970s. It is not a narcotic analgesic and has no direct effect on the opioid receptors; instead, it stimulates receptors for noradrenaline. Its principal use is as an oral antihypertensive (Robertson & Biaggioni, 2015). Clonidine is mentioned here because it is a nonaddictive, noneuphorigenic prescription medication with demonstrated efficacy in relieving some of the physical effects of opiate withdrawal (such as vomiting and diarrhea). However, clonidine does not alter narcotic craving or the generalized aches associated with withdrawal (Addiction Center, 2019). The dosing regimen is typically a seven- to 14-day inpatient treatment for opiate withdrawal. Length of treatment can be reduced to seven days for withdrawal from heroin and short-acting opiates; the 14-day treatment is needed for the longer-acting methadone-type opiates. Because tolerance to clonidine may develop, opiates are discontinued abruptly at the start of treatment. In this way, the peak intensity of withdrawal will occur while clonidine is still maximally effective (DAT, 2013).

One of the most important advantages of clonidine over other treatments for opiate withdrawal detoxification is that it shortens the time for withdrawal to 14 days compared with several weeks or months using standard procedures such as methadone treatment (Addiction Center, 2019). The potential disadvantage of taking clonidine is that it can cause serious side effects of its own, the most serious being significantly lowered blood pressure, which can cause fainting and blackouts (DAT, 2013). Overall, its lack of abuse potential makes clonidine particularly useful in rapid treatment of narcotic dependence; however, the long-term benefit is controversial (Finch, 2015).

## ▮ Naloxone and Naltrexone

Naloxone and the related drug naltrexone are relatively pure narcotic antagonists and have short and long half-lives, respectively. These drugs attach to opiate receptors in the brain and throughout the body. They do not activate the receptors but prevent narcotic drugs such as heroin and morphine from having an effect. By themselves, these antagonists do not cause much change but potently block or reverse the effects of all narcotics.

Because of its antagonistic properties, naloxone is a useful antidote in the treatment of narcotic overdoses; its administration rapidly reverses life-threatening, narcotic-induced effects on breathing and the cardiovascular system (Schumacher et al., 2015). However, if not used carefully, this antagonist will also block the analgesic action of the narcotics and initiate severe withdrawal in narcotic-dependent people (Schumacher et al., 2015). In fact, many individuals dependent on heroin are not interested in using this drug because it can precipitate withdrawal symptoms.

Use of naloxone has been proposed to prevent addicts from experiencing the effects of heroin and other potent opioid narcotics (Schumacher et al., 2015). In fact, as discussed previously in this chapter, an extended form of naloxone (its effects persist for one month) called Vivitrol was approved by the FDA for the treatment of heroin addiction (Rubin, 2010). A recent study found that of those heroin addicts who received six monthly injections, 70% did not go back to heroin use (this was twice the success rate of heroin addicts given placebo), and they claimed that the Vivitrol reduced their cravings for the opiate drug (Tabachnick, 2015). It is critical to appreciate that Vivitrol is not a cure for heroin or opioid dependence in general and that heroin and opioid addicts must also develop good coping skills to stop abusing their narcotic drugs (Tabachnick, 2015)

An interesting use of naloxone has been to combine it with buprenorphine in small quantities (Suboxone). As long as this product is taken as prescribed, the quantity of naloxone is too small to have an antagonistic effect; however, if Suboxone is consumed in high doses—as it would if being abused—there would be sufficient naloxone to block the opioid effect (RxList, 2019). The FDA also has approved Suboxone to reduce the craving for alcohol in the treatment of chronic alcoholism (*Drug Facts*, 2010). Additional reports suggest that

opioid receptors may contribute to other drug addictions such as those caused by nicotine and psychostimulants. At this time, it is not clear if an opioid antagonist like naloxone would be effective in treating these other addictions (American Addiction Centers, 2019).

## Natural Narcotic Substances

Although many herbal preparations can cause drowsiness or have some analgesic properties, few of these actually contain opioid narcotic drugs. The naturally occurring opioid drugs include morphine, codeine, heroin, papaverine, and thebaine and are found only in the opium poppy, *Papaver somniferum*. Although several varieties of opium-yielding poppies exist, they are typically winter crops in the Southern Hemisphere and do best in climates that have warm days and cool nights. All of the plants thrive in sandy soil. Most of the active drugs are found in the seepage from the seed heads located beneath the flower petals of the poppy flowers, although small amounts of these active ingredients are found in other parts of the plant such as the stem and leaves. Although this species of plant can survive in the United States if the environment is rigidly controlled, the vast majority of the supplies of the naturally occurring narcotic drugs are brought into the country either legally and sold as legitimate pharmaceuticals or smuggled across borders and sold as illicit narcotics.

© Hellojan/Shutterstock.

The sap oozing from this opium poppy pod contains the natural narcotic drugs.

# LEARNING PORTFOLIO

## Discussion Questions

1. Why do narcotics have high abuse potential?
2. What are the principal clinical uses of the opioid narcotics?
3. What is the relationship between endorphin systems and the opioid narcotics?
4. Why do the opioid pain relievers account for two-thirds of prescription drug abuse?
5. What effect has the rising abuse of prescription narcotic analgesics had on legitimately prescribing these drugs for pain management?
6. What is the difference between opioid addiction and opioid physical dependence?
7. Why was there a substantial increase in heroin abuse in the United States throughout the 1990s?
8. Why does heroin addiction contribute to criminal activity?
9. What are the principal withdrawal effects when heroin use is stopped in addicts?
10. How does methadone maintenance work for the treatment of narcotic dependence? Discuss a possible drawback to this approach.
11. How does buprenorphine, with and without naloxone, compare to methadone as a treatment for narcotic addictions?
12. How does naloxone alone (e.g., Vivitrol) compare to methadone maintenance treatment for heroin and opioid addiction? Is it of value in treating other drug addictions?
13. What is considered to be successful treatment for heroin addiction?
14. How do morphine and fentanyl compare with heroin?
15. How does tramadol compare to other opioid analgesics?
16. Why is clonidine useful in treating opioid withdrawals?
17. Why is dextromethorphan potentially addicting, and what should the federal government do to stop its abuse?
18. Naloxone is effective in treating alcoholism. What does this suggest about the role of endogenous opioid systems in alcohol dependence?

## Key Terms

## Summary

1. The term *narcotic* refers to naturally occurring substances derived from the opium poppy and their synthetic substitutes. These drugs are referred to as the opioid (or opiate) narcotics because of their association with opium. For the most part, the opioid narcotics possess abuse potential, but they also have important clinical value and are used to relieve all kinds of pain (they are analgesic), suppress coughing (they are antitussive), and stop diarrhea.

2. The principal side effects of the opioid narcotics, besides their abuse potential, include drowsiness and sedation, respiratory depression, nausea and vomiting, constipation, inability to urinate, and sometimes a drop in blood pressure. These side effects can be annoying or even life threatening, so caution is required when using these drugs.

3. Heroin is the most likely of the opioid narcotics to be severely abused; it is easily prepared from opium and has a rapid, intense effect. It is a Schedule I drug.

4. When narcotics such as heroin are first used by people not experiencing pain, the drugs can cause unpleasant, dysphoric sensations. However, euphoria gradually overcomes the aversive effects. The positive feelings increase with narcotic use, leading to psychological dependence. After psychological dependence, physical dependence occurs with frequent daily use, which reinforces the narcotic abuse. If the user stops taking the drug after physical dependence has occurred, severe withdrawal symptoms result.

5. Tolerance to narcotics can occur rapidly with intense use of these drugs. This tolerance can result in the use of incredibly large doses of narcotics that would be fatal to a nontolerant person. This tolerance phenomenon also compromises the therapeutic value of these drugs.

6. Methadone and buprenorphine are frequently used to help narcotic addicts stop using heroin or one of the other highly addicting drugs. Oral methadone relieves the withdrawal symptoms that would result from discontinuing narcotics. Methadone can also cause psychological and physical dependence, but it is less addicting than heroin and easier to control. Buprenorphine is distinct from methadone in that it has been approved for use in primary care settings and may be safer for treating women who use opioid narcotics during pregnancy.

7. Fentanyls are highly potent synthetic opioid narcotics. They can be easily synthesized and converted into drugs that are as much as 3,000 to 6,000 times more potent than heroin itself. Detection and regulation of the illegal fentanyl derivatives by law enforcement agencies are extremely difficult. The fentanyl-type drugs are used as heroin substitutes and have killed narcotic addicts because of their unexpected potency.

8. Attempts to create designer narcotics have led to the synthesis of very potent fentanyl-like drugs that are responsible for many overdose deaths. In addition, attempts to synthesize a meperidine (Demerol) designer drug resulted in the inadvertent creation of MPTP, a highly reactive compound that causes a dramatic onset of Parkinson's disease in its users.

9. Tramadol is an atypical opioid-like analgesic that has some antidepressant actions that might contribute to its effectiveness as a moderately potent pain killer. It likely has fewer addicting properties than most of the other opioid narcotics, but its dramatic rise in popularity has revealed a potential for causing dependence and withdrawal in some patients. Because of these opioid effects, tramadol has been classified by the DEA as a Schedule IV controlled substance.

10. Dextromethorphan is a codeine-related drug used as an antitussive in OTC cough medicines. In extremely high doses, dextromethorphan can cause PCP- or ketamine-like hallucinations and sensory distortions. The abuse of this drug has not been substantial enough to result in its removal or special control by federal agencies.

## References

Addiction Center. (n.d.). Demerol addiction and abuse. Retrieved from https://www.addictioncenter.com/pain killers/demerol/

Addiction Center. (2019). Understanding clonidine. Retrieved from https://www.addictioncenter.com/treatment /medications/clonidine/

Agence France-Presse. (2010, June 8). Afghan heroin took million lives last decade: Russia. Retrieved from http://

www.globalresearch.ca/afghan-heroin-took-million -lives-last-decade-russia/19640

Alford, D. (2016). Opioid prescribing for chronic pain-achieving the right balance through education. *New England Journal of Medicine, 374*, 301–303.

American Academy of Pain Medicine. (2007, February 7). Psychiatric factors linked to increased risk for misuse of opioid medications. *23rd Annual Meeting.* Abstract 151.

American Addiction Centers. (2012, September 6). Artie Lange says self-inflicted stab wounds were due to heroin addiction. Rehabs.com. Retrieved from http://luxury .rehabs.com/blog/artie-lange-says-self-inflicted-stab-wounds-were-due-to-heroin-addiction/

American Addiction Centers. (2019). What drugs are used in addiction rehabilitation treatment? Retrieved from https://americanaddictioncenters.org/addiction -medications

American Society of Addiction Medicine (ASAM). (2015). The national practice guideline for the use of medications in the treatment of addiction involving opioid use. Retrieved from https://www.asam.org/docs/default -source/practice-support/guidelines-and-consensus-docs /asam-national-practice-guideline-supplement.pdf

American Society of Addiction Medicine (ASAM). (2016). Opioid addiction 2016 facts & figures. Retrieved from https://www.asam.org/docs/default-source/advocacy /opioid-addiction-disease-facts-figures.pdf

Aminoff, M. (1998). Pharmacologic management of Parkinsonism and other movement disorders. In B. Katzung *(Ed.), Basic and clinical pharmacology,* 7th ed. (pp. 450–463). Stamford, CT: Appleton and Lange.

Arablouei, R., & Abdelfatah, R. (2019, April 4). A history of opioids in America. NPR. Retrieved from https://www .npr.org/2019/04/04/709767408/a-history-of-opioids -in-america

Armstrong, D. (2016). Dope-sick: A harrowing story of best friends, addiction—and a stealth killer. Stat. Retrieved from https://www.statnews.com/feature/opioid-crisis /dope-sick/

Bebinger, M. (2015, November 13). It's not just heroin: Drug cocktails are fueling the overdose crisis. WBUR's Common Health. Retrieved from http://common-health.wbur.org/2015/11/drug-overdose-cocktails

Bennington-Castro, J. (2014). What is morphine? Everyday Health. Retrieved from http://www.everydayhealth.com /drugs/morphine

Bhuvaneswar, C., Chang, G., Epstein, L., & Stern, T. (2008). Cocaine and opioid use during pregnancy: Prevalence and management. *Primary Care Companion to the Journal of Clinical Psychiatry, 10*, 59–65.

Brecher, E. M. (1972). *Licit and illicit drugs.* Boston, MA: Little, Brown.

Bryan, M. (2015, June 5). Emergency rooms crack down on abusers of pain pills. NPR. Retrieved from http://www.npr .org/sections/health-shots/2015/06/03/411560144 /emergency-rooms-crack-down-on-abusers-of-pain-pills

Buddy T. (2008, December 31). The costs of alcohol and drug treatment. About.com: Alcoholism. Retrieved from http://alcoholism.about.com/od/pro/a/blsam040527 .htm

Capital Blue Cross. (2015, May 1). Treatment of opiate addiction.

Carbone, A. (2014, July 1). Is heroin chic over? *AfterParty Magazine.* Retrieved from https://rehabreviews.com /heroin-chic/

Celona, L. (2007, June 18). "Oxy" Kids Crisis. *New York Post.* Retrieved from http://www.nypost.com/p/news /regional/item_2RyopB29Z8esHu8oe50qkK

Centers for Disease Control and Prevention (CDC). (2015). Today's heroin epidemic. Retrieved from http://www .cdc.gov/vitalsigns/heroin/

Centers for Disease Control and Prevention (CDC). (2019). Synthetic opioid overdose data. Atlanta, GA: Author. Retrieved from https://www.cdc.gov/drugoverdose /data/fentanyl.html

Christenson, S. (2010, May 24). Heroin addiction takes brutal toll on Afghanistan. *San Antonio Express-News.* Retrieved from http://www.mysanantonio.com/news /military/article/Heroin-addiction-takes-brutal-toll-on -Afghanistan-787499.php

Colon, D. (2011, February 16). Number of newborns addicted to painkillers rising. NPR. Retrieved from http://www.npr.org/2011/02/16/133805289/number -of-newborns-addicted-to-painkillers-rising

Compton, W., Jones, C., & Baldwin, G. (2016). Relationship between nonmedical prescription-opioid use and heroin use. *New England Journal of Medicine, 373*, 154–163.

Consumer Healthcare Products Association (CHPA). (n.d.). Dextromethorphan: Preventing teen cough medicine abuse. Retrieved from http://www.chpa.org/dex.aspx

Daily Kos. (2015, April 15). The war on doctors: How the DEA is scaring doctors from prescribing pain medications. Retrieved from http://www.dailykos.com /story/2015/4/15/1375189/-The-War-On-Doctors -How-The-DEA-is-Scaring-Doctors-from-Prescribing -Pain-Medications

Darke, S., Marel, C., Slada, T., Ross, J., Mills, K., & Teesson, M. (2015). Patterns and correlates of sustained heroin abstinence: Findings from the 11-year follow-up of the Australian treatment outcome study. *Journal of Studies on Alcohol and Drugs, 76*, 909–915.

DAT. (2013, February 20). Clonidine treatment for opioid withdrawal. Drug Addiction Treatment. Retrieved from http://www.drugaddictiontreatment.com/types-of-addiction/prescription-drug-addiction/clonidine-treatment-for-opioid-withdrawal/

deShazo, R., Johnson, M., Eriator, I. and Rodenmeyer, K. (2018). Backstories on the US Opioid Epidemic. Good Intentions Gone Bad, an Industry Gone Rogue, and Watch Dogs Gone to Sleep. The American Journal of Medicine, *131*, 595–601.

Deveney, R. (2019). Are heroin addicts violent? The Recovery Village. Retrieved from https://www.therecovery village.com/heroin-addiction/related-topics/are-heroin-addicts-violent/#gref

DiChiara, G., & North, A. (1992, May). Neurobiology of opiate abuse. *Trends in Pharmacological Sciences, 13*, 185–193.

Diep, F. (2013, May 13). How do you make a painkiller addiction-proof? *Popular Science.* Retrieved from http://www.popsci.com/science/article/2013-05/science-un-crushable-oxycontin

Drug Enforcement Administration (DEA). (2013, March). Tramadol. Springfield, VA: Author. Retrieved from http://www.deadiversion.usdoj.gov/drug_chem_info/tramadol.pdf

Drug Enforcement Administration (DEA). (2014, March). Dextromethorphan. Retrieved from https://www.deadiversion.usdoj.gov/drug_chem_info/dextro_m.pdf

Drug Enforcement Administration (DEA). (2016). Controlled substance schedules. Washington, DC: Office of Diversion Control, U.S. Department of Justice. Retrieved from http://www.deadiversion.usdoj.gov/schedules/#list

Drug Enforcement Administration (DEA). (2018). DEA releases 2018 national drug threat assessment. Springfield, VA: Author. Retrieved from https://www.dea.gov/press-releases/2018/11/02/dea-releases-2018-national-drug-threat-assessment-0

Drug Enforcement Administration (DEA). (2019a). The countdown: Fentanyl analogues & the expiring emergency scheduling order. Springfield, VA: Author. Retrieved from https://www.dea.gov/sites/default/files/2019-06/DOJ%20DEA%20Fentanyl%20Expiration%20of%20Temp%20Order_SJC_4June19_final.pdf

Drug Enforcement Administration (DEA). (2019b). National Rx take back 2019. Springfield, VA: Author. Retrieved from https://takebackday.dea.gov/

*Drug Facts and Comparisons.* (2010). Pocket version (pp. 244–247, 520–590). St. Louis, MO: Wolters Kluwer.

Drugs.com. (2015a). Tramadol: Top 8 things you need to know. Retrieved from http://www.drugs.com/article/tramadol-need-to-know.html

Drugs.com. (2015b). Vivitrol. Retrieved from http://www.drugs.com/vivitrol.html

Drug War Facts. (2012). Heroin assisted treatment/heroin management. Retrieved from http://www.drugwarfacts.org/cms/heroin_maintenance#sthash.LJWKNnvQ.dphs

Durkin, E. (2018). US drug overdose deaths rose to record 72,000 last year, data reveals. *The Guardian.* (2018). Retrieved from https://www.theguardian.com/us-news/2018/aug/16/us-drug-overdose-deaths-opioids-fentanyl-cdc

Edwards, M. (2010, June 5). Soldiers at risk of getting hooked on heroin. ABC News [Australia]. Retrieved from http://www.abc.net.au/news/2010-06-03/soldiers-at-risk-of-getting-hooked-on-heroin/853234

Eshkevari, L., & Heath, J. (2005). Use of acupuncture for chronic pain: Optimizing clinical practice. *Holistic Nursing Practice, 19*, 217–221.

Feldman, C. (2015). How to kick heroin. Heroin Quotes. Retrieved from http://www.howtokickheroin.com/heroin-quotes/

Finch, M. (2015, March 4). How to use clonidine for opiate withdrawal. Opiate Addiction Support. Retrieved from http://opiateaddictionsupport.com/how-to-use-clonidine-for-opiate-withdrawal/

Fisher, J. (2015, February 14). Heroin sparks epidemic of thefts. *The News Journal* [delawareonline]. Retrieved from http://www.delawareonline.com/story/news/local/2015/02/14/heroin-fueled-crime-wave/23412993/

Frontline. (n.d.). Opium throughout history. PBS. Retrieved from http://www.pbs.org/wgbh/pages/frontline/shows/heroin/etc/history.html

Gatehouse, J., & Macdonald. N. (2015, June 22). Fentanyl: The king of all opiates, and a killer drug crisis. *Maclean's.* Retrieved from http://www.macleans.ca/society/health/fentanyl-the-king-of-all-opiates-and-a-killer-drug-crisis/

Golding, A. (1993, May). Two hundred years of drug abuse. *Journal of the Royal Society of Medicine, 86*, 282–286.

Goldstein, A. (1994). *Addiction from biology to drug policy* (pp. 137–154). New York, NY: Freeman.

Gorner, J. (2015, October 2). 74 overdoses in 72 hours: Laced heroin may be to blame. *Chicago Tribune.* Retrieved from http://www.chicagotribune.com/news/local/breaking/ct-heroin-overdoses-met-20151002-story.html

Gourlay, G. (2004, December 21). Advances in opioid pharmacology. *Supportive Care for Cancer,* pp. 153–159.

Gray, E. (2014, February 4). Heroin gains popularity as cheap doses flood the U.S. *Time.* Retrieved from http://time.com/4505/heroin-gains-popularity-as-cheap-doses-flood-the-u-s/

Gulur, P., Loury, K., Arnstein, P., Lee, H., McCarthy, P., Coley, C., & Mort, E. (2015, November 1). Morphine versus hydromorphone: Does choice of opioid influence outcomes? *Pain Research and Treatment.* Retrieved from https://www.ncbi.nlm.nih.gov/pmc/articles/PMC4644543/

Gutstein, H., & Akil, H. (2006). Opioid analgesics. In L. Brunton, J. Lazo, and K. Parker *(Eds.), The pharmacological basis of therapeutics,* 11th ed. (pp. 547–590). New York, NY: McGraw-Hill.

Hieatt, K. (2010, May 18). Search for answers in fentanyl death raises more questions. *Virginian-Pilot* [Norfolk, VA]. Retrieved from http://www.pilotonline.com/news/article_be9c67e4-e21d-5ce0-b0d7-5619606a85f2.html

Hitti, M. (2010, August 2). Prescription painkiller addiction: 7 myths. WebMD. Retrieved from http://www.webmd.com/pain-management/features/prescription-painkiller-addiction-7-myths

Hubbard, R. (1998, June). Focus on heroin: Increase in users and changing treatment system present new challenges for services researchers. *Connection* (Association for Health Services Research), pp. 1–2.

Johnston, L. (2019). Monitoring the Future 2018. Retrieved from http://monitoringthefuture.org/pubs/monographs/mtf-overview2018.pdf

Johnston, L. D., Miech, R. A., O'Malley, P. M., Bachman, J. G., Schulenberg, J. E., & Patrick, M. E. (2018). *Monitoring the Future.* Retrieved from http://monitoringthefuture.org/pubs/monographs/mtf-overview2018.pdf

Karch, S. (1996). Narcotics. In *The pathology of drug abuse* (pp. 281–408). New York, NY: CRC.

Kosten, T., & Hollister, L. (1998). Drugs of abuse. In B. Katzun *(Ed.), Basic and clinical pharmacology,* 7th ed. (pp. 516–531). Stamford, CT: Appleton & Lange.

Kral, L., & Ghafoor, V. (2013). Pain and its management. In B. Alldredge et al. (Eds.), *Applied therapeutics: The clinical use of drugs,* 10th ed. (pp. 112–146). Philadelphia, PA: Wolters Kluwer.

Kritz, F. (2015, August 5). What you don't know unless you've been there: Heroin. Addiction.com. Retrieved from https://www.addiction.com/12360/what-you-dont-know-unless-youve-been-there-heroin/

Langston, J., Ballard, P., Tetrud, J., & Irwin, I. (1983). Chronic Parkinsonism in humans due to a product of meperidine—Analogue synthesis. *Science, 219*: 979–980.

Levran, O., Londono, D., O'Hara, K., Randesi, M., Rotrosen, J., Casasonte, P., . . ., & Kreek, M. J. (2009). Heroin addiction in African Americans: A hypothesis-driven association study. *Genes, Brain and Behavior, 8,* 531–540.

Logan, B. K., Goldfogel, G., Hamilton, R., & Kuhlman, J. (2015). Five deaths resulting from abuse of dextromethorphan sold over the Internet. *Journal of Analytical Toxicology, 33,* 99–103. Retrieved from https://academic.oup.com/jat/article/33/2/99/773442

Lopez, G. (2019). Cities are considering safe injection sites. Vox. Retrieved from https://www.vox.com/science-and-health/2018/1/25/16928144/safe-injection-sites-heroin-opioid-epidemic

Luscher, C. (2012). Drugs of abuse. In B. Katzung *(Ed.), Basic and clinical pharmacology* (pp. 565–580). New York, NY: McGraw-Hill.

March of Dimes. (2015). Heroin and pregnancy. Retrieved from http://www.marchofdimes.org/pregnancy/heroin-and-pregnancy.aspx#

"Mary." (1996). *Rolling Stone, 30,* 42–43.

Maurer, D., & Vogel, V. (1967). *Narcotics and narcotic addiction,* 3rd ed. Springfield, IL: Thomas.

Mayo Clinic. (2019). How opioid addiction occurs. Retrieved from https://www.mayoclinic.org/diseases-conditions/prescription-drug-abuse/in-depth/how-opioid-addiction-occurs/art-20360372

McClure, C. (2009). Global drug policy and the HIV/IDU epidemic in Eastern Europe and Central Asia. International AIDS Society. Retrieved from http://www.iasociety.org/Web/WebContent/File/CraigMcClure_SODAK%202009.pdf

McMurran, M. (2007). What works in substance misuse treatments for offenders. *Criminal Behavior and Mental Health, 17,* 225–233.

Meader, N. (2010). A comparison of methadone, buprenorphine and alpha2 adrenergic agonists for opioid detoxification: A mixed comparison meta-analysis. *Drug and Alcohol Dependence, 108,* 110–114.

Medi-Cal. (2015, September 30). Clinical review: Morphine equivalent daily dose to prevent opioid overuse. Retrieved from https://files.medi-cal.ca.gov/pubsdoco/dur/Articles/dured_24035.pdf

Medical Discoveries. (n.d.). Codeine. Retrieved from http://www.discoveriesinmedicine.com/Bar-Cod/Codeine.html

Medical News Today. (2010, August 28). Study identifies risk factors for painkiller addiction and links the addiction to genetics. Retrieved from http://www.medicalnewstoday.com/articles/199263.php

Medical News Today. (2019). What are the side effects of tramadol? Retrieved from https://www.medicalnewstoday.com/articles/325278.php#summary

MedlinePlus. (2019). Naltrexone injection. Retrieved from https://medlineplus.gov/druginfo/meds/a609007.html

Mental Health Daily. (2015, June 10). Methadone vs. subozone: Comparison. Retrieved from https://mentalhealthdaily.com/2015/06/10/methadone-vs-suboxone-comparison/

Muñoz-Manchado, A., Villadiego, J., Romo-Madero, S., Suárez-Luna, N., Bermejo-Navas, A., Rodríguez-Gómez, J. A., . . ., & Toledo-Aral, J. J. (2015). Chronic and progressive Parkinson's disease MPTP model in adult and aged mice. *Journal of Neurochemistry, 136,* 373–387.

Mutschler, J., Koopmann, A., Grosshans, M., Hermann, D., Mann, K., & Kiefer, F. (2010). Dextromethorphan withdrawal and dependence syndrome. *Deutsches Ärzteblatt International, 107,* 537–540.

NAABT.org. (2014, October). Physical dependence and addiction. Retrieved from http://www.naabt.org/addiction_physical-dependence.cfm

National Institute on Drug Abuse (NIDA). (n.d.). Prescription opioids and heroin. Retrieved from https://www.drugabuse.gov/publications/research-reports/relationship-between-prescription-drug-abuse-heroin-use/heroin-use-driven-by-its-low-cost-high-availability

National Institute on Drug Abuse (NIDA). (2014a). Why does heroin use create special risk for contracting HIV/AIDS and hepatitis B and C? Retrieved from https://www.drugabuse.gov/publications/research-reports/heroin/why-are-heroin-users-special-risk-contracting-hivaids-hepatitis-b-c

National Institute on Drug Abuse (NIDA). (2014b). How does heroin use affect pregnant women? Retrieved from https://www.drugabuse.gov/publications/research-reports/heroin/how-does-heroin-abuse-affect-pregnant-women

Nakamura, D. (2008, January 3). City to spend $650,000 on needle exchange programs. *Washington Post.* Retrieved from http://www.washingtonpost.com/wp-dyn/content/article/2008/01/02/AR2008010201905.html

Nandi, A., Glass, T., Cole, S., Chu, H., Galea, S., Celentano, D., . . ., & Mehta, S. H. (2010). Neighborhood poverty and injection cessation in a sample of injection drug users. *American Journal of Epidemiology, 171,* 391–398.

Newman, K. (2019, May 16). Study: Emergency visits for heroin overdoses decline in some states. *U.S. News & World Report.* Retrieved from https://www.usnews.com/news/healthiest-communities/articles/2019-05-16/emergency-visits-for-heroin-overdoses-decline-in-some-states

P&T Community (2013, August 6). FDA approves new formulation for OxyContin. FDA News Release. Retrieved from https://www.ptcommunity.com/news/20100406/fda-approves-new-formulation-oxycontin

Pain Community Centre. (n.d.). Opioids. Retrieved from http://www.paincommunitycentre.org/article/opioids

Palm Partners Recovery Center. (2013, June 11). How do methadone clinics work? Retrieved from http://blog.palmpartners.com/how-do-methadone-clinics-work/

Pietrangelo, A. (2015, March 26). Codeine vs. hydrocodone: Two ways to treat pain. Healthline. Retrieved from http://www.healthline.com/health/pain-relief/codeine-vs-hydrocodone#Overview1

Polidoro, R. (2014, April 8). Infographic: Emergency rooms see increase in heroin patients. NBC News. Retrieved from https://www.nbcnews.com/storyline/americas-heroin-epidemic/infographic-emergency-rooms-see-increase-heroin-patients-n74316

Powell, A. (2015, September 29). Heroin's descent. *Harvard Gazette* [Cambridge, MA]. Retrieved from http://news.harvard.edu/gazette/story/2015/09/heroins-descent/

Preda, A. (2015). Opioid abuse treatment & management. Medscape. http://emedicine.medscape.com/article/287790-treatment

Ramde, D. (2014, July 2). FBI report analyzes Wisconsin's growing heroin problem. *USA Today.* Retrieved from http://www.thenorthwestern.com/story/news/local/2014/07/02/fbi-prices-purity-drugs-fueling-wisconsins-growing-heroin-problem/12030025/

Recovery Helpdesk. (2010). 10 things you should know about methadone: A low methadone dose is not necessarily the best methadone dose. Retrieved from http://www.recoveryhelpdesk.com/2010/05/14/series-10-things-you-should-know-about-methadone-number-10

Rehabs.com. (n.d.). Street names for oxycontin. Retrieved from http://luxury.rehabs.com/oxycontin-addiction/street-names-and-nicknames/

Reid, L., Elifson, K., & Sterk, C. (2007). Ecstasy and gateway drugs: Initiating the use of Ecstasy and other drugs. *Annals of Epidemiology, 17,* 74–80.

Robertson, D., & Biaggioni, I. (2015). Adrenoceptor agonists & sympathomimetic drugs. In B. Katzung & A. Trevor *(Eds.), Basic and clinical pharmacology,* 13th ed. (pp. 133–151). New York, NY: McGraw-Hill.

Rolfs, R. (2008). Utah clinical guidelines on prescribing opioids. Retrieved from http://health.utah.gov/prescription/pdf/Utah_guidelines_pdfs.pdf

Rosenbaum, C., & Boyer, E. (2019). Dextromethorphan abuse and poisoning: Clinical features and diagnosis. UpToDate. Retrieved from https://www.uptodate.com/contents/dextromethorphan-abuse-and-poisoning-clinical-features-and-diagnosis

RT. (2013, April 3). 1mn died from Afghan heroin, drug production "40 times higher" since NATO operation. Retrieved from http://rt.com/news/afghanistan-heroin-production-increased-266

Rubin, R. (2010, October 13). FDA OKs vivitrol to treat heroin, narcotic addictions. *USA Today.* Retrieved from http://www.usatoday.com/yourlife/health/2010-10-14-opioid14_ST_N.htm

Rudd, R., Noah, A., Zibbell, J., & Mathew, G. (2016). Increases in drug and opioid overdose deaths—United States, 2000–2014. *Morbidity and Mortality Weekly Report, 64,* 1378–1382. Retrieved from http://www.cdc.gov/mmwr/preview/mmwrhtml/mm6450a3.htm

RxList. (2019). Suboxone. Retrieved from https://www.rxlist.com/suboxone-drug.htm#description

Sansone, R., & Sansone, L. (2015). Buprenorphine treatment for narcotic addiction: Not without risks. *Innovations in Clinical Neuroscience, 12,* 32–26.

Schumacher, M., Basbaum, A., & Naidu, K. (2015). Opioid analgesics and antagonists. B. Katzung & A. Trevor (Eds.), In *Basic and clinical pharmacology*, 13th ed. (pp. 531–551). New York, NY: McGraw-Hill.

Seelye, K. (2015, October 30). In heroin crisis, white families seek gentler war on drugs. *The New York Times.* Retrieved from http://www.nytimes.com/2015/10/31/us/heroin-war-on-drugs-parents.html

Sify News. (2010, August 28). Risk factors for painkiller addiction identified. Retrieved from http://sify.com/news/risk-factors-for-painkiller-addiction-identified-news-scitech-ki3pEjahbic.html

Simon, D. (2016, March 9). Is methadone an effective treatment for heroin addiction? Yes! Addiction Blog.

Smith, C. (2010, March 28). Experts push for painkiller tramadol to be on controlled list. *Pittsburgh Tribune-Review.* Retrieved from https://archive.triblive.com/news/experts-push-for-painkiller-tramadol-to-be-on-controlled-list/

Stewart, C. (2014, December 20). Overdose deaths tied to potent new drug. *Dayton Daily News* [OH]. Retrieved from https://www.daytondailynews.com/news/crime--law/overdose-deaths-tied-potent-new-drug/mykn7eWgzHJEVRapH1vlKM/

Substance Abuse and Mental Health Services Administration (SAMHSA). (2015, October 27). Substance use disorders. Rockville, MD: Author. Retrieved from http://www.samhsa.gov/disorders/substance-use

Substance Abuse and Mental Health Services Administration (SAMHSA). (2019). Apply for a practitioner waiver. Rockville, MD: Author. Retrieved from https://www.samhsa.gov/medication-assisted-treatment/training-materials-resources/apply-for-practitioner-waiver

Svrluga, S. (2015, January 13). The drug suboxone could combat the heroin epidemic. So why is it so hard to get? *Washington Post.* Retrieved from https://www.washingtonpost.com/local/a-drug-called-suboxone-could-combat-the-heroin-epidemic-so-why-is-it-so-hard-to-get/2015/01/13/4135d08c-812e-11e4-9f38-95a187e4c1f7_story.html

Tabachnick, C. (2005, March 13). Breaking good: Vivitrol, a new drug given as a monthly shot, is helping addicts stay clean. *Washington Post.* Retrieved from https://www.washingtonpost.com/lifestyle/magazine/his-last-shot-will-a-monthly-jab-of-a-new-drug-keep-this-addict-out-of-jail/2015/03/05/7f054354-7a4c-11e4-84d4-7c896b90abdc_story.html

Trigo, J. M., Martin-Garcia, E., Berrendero, F., Robledo, P., & Maldonado, R. (2010). The endogenous opioid system: A common substrate in drug addiction. *Drug and Alcohol Dependence, 108*, 183–194.

Tur, K. (2010, August 19). Saving lives with heroin needles. NBC New York. Retrieved from http://www.nbcnewyork.com/news/local-beat/The-Syringe-Exchange-Saved-My-Life-101112079.html

United Nations Office on Drugs and Crime (UNODC). (2015). World drug report. Vienna, Austria: Author. Retrieved from https://www.unodc.org/documents/wdr2015/World_Drug_Report_2015.pdf

U.S. Department of Health and Human Services. (2019). What is the U.S. opioid epidemic? HHS.Gov/Opioids Retrieved from https://www.hhs.gov/opioids/about-the-epidemic/index.html

Vaults of Erowid. (n.d.). Dextromethorphan. Retrieved from https://www.erowid.org/chemicals/dxm/dxm_basics.shtml

Volkow, N. (2014a). America's addiction to opioids: Heroin and prescription drug abuse. National Institute on Drug Abuse (May 14). Retrieved from https://archives.drugabuse.gov/testimonies/2014/americas-addiction-to-opioids-heroin-prescription-drug-abuse

Volkow, N. (2014b). Prescription opioid and heroin abuse. National Institute on Drug Abuse. (April 29). Retrieved from https://archives.drugabuse.gov/testimonies/2014/prescription-opioid-heroin-abuse

Wang, M. (2010, April 12). Perinatal drug abuse and neonatal drug withdrawal. Medscape. Retrieved from http://emedicine.medscape.com/article/978492-overview

Way, W., Fields, H., & Way, E. L. (1998). Opioid analgesics and antagonists. In B. Katzung (Ed.), *Basic and clinical pharmacology*, 7th ed. (pp. 496–515). Stamford, CT: Appleton & Lange.

WebMD. (2019, June 28). FDA cracks down again on kratom products. Retrieved from https://www.webmd.com/mental-health/addiction/news/20190628/fda-cracks-down-again-on-kratom-products

Winkler, M., Weyers, P., Mucha, R., Stippekohl, B., & Pauli, P. (2011, February). Conditioned cues for smoking elicit preparatory responses in healthy smokers. *Psychopharmacology, 213*, 781–789.

Young, R., & Hobson, J. (2016, February 16). Pain specialist: Many doctors underprescribe for chronic pain. WBUR. Retrieved from http://hereandnow.wbur.org/2016/02/16/underprescribing-opioids-for-pain

Zielinski, N. (2010, August 1). Methadone deaths increase in the US. Examiner.com.

Zocchi, A., Girlanda, E., Varnier, G., Sartori, I., Zanetti, L., Wildish, G., . . . , & Heidbreder, C. A. (2003). Dopamine responsiveness to drugs of abuse: A shell-core investigation in the nucleus accumbens of the mouse. *Synapse, 50*, 293–302.

# Stimulants

## Did You Know?

▶ The first therapeutic use of amphetamines was in inhalers to treat nasal congestion.

▶ Illegal methamphetamine can be easily made from drugs found in common over-the-counter (OTC) decongestants and some herbal products.

▶ Methylphenidate (Ritalin), a drug prescribed to treat children with attention-deficit hyperactivity disorder (ADHD), is sometimes used illegally by college students to suppress fatigue while studying long hours for exams.

▶ Ecstasy has both psychedelic and stimulant properties and is being studied for potential therapeutic action for management of patients with posttraumatic stress disorder (PTSD).

▶ Products such as bath salts, ivory wave, or flakka contain designer amphetamine- and cocaine-like drugs that have not been well studied and are potentially dangerous.

▶ Smoking "freebased" or "crack" cocaine is more dangerous and more addicting than other forms of administration.

▶ Using high doses of amphetamines or cocaine can cause behavior that resembles schizophrenia.

▶ Caffeine is the most frequently used stimulant in the world.

▶ Caffeine is the principal active ingredient in most so-called energy drinks.

▶ Herbal stimulants promoted as "natural highs" contain central nervous system stimulants such as caffeine or guarana.

▶ Ephedrine found in natural herbal products has caused fatal cardiovascular problems in unsuspecting athletes and was removed from the list of approved OTC products by the Food and Drug Administration (FDA). Because ephedrine's chemical structure resembles amphetamine, it can be used to synthesize methamphetamine and also has some mild amphetamine-like actions.

## Learning Objectives

**On completing this chapter, you should be able to:**

〉 Explain how amphetamines work.
〉 Identify the FDA-approved uses for amphetamines.
〉 Recognize the major side effects of amphetamines on brain and cardiovascular functions.
〉 Identify the terms *speed, ice, run, high*, and *tweaking* as they relate to amphetamine use.
〉 Describe the recent changes in the patterns of illicit amphetamine uses in the United States.
〉 Explain what "designer" amphetamines are and how Ecstasy compares to methamphetamine. Also identify the therapeutic potential (good and bad) in the treatment of PTSD.
〉 Discuss the unique dangers of products such as bath salts.
〉 Explain what "club drugs" are.
〉 Describe why stimulants are used as "performance enhancers" and why they should be considered dangerous.
〉 Explain how methylphenidate (e.g., Ritalin) compares to methamphetamine.
〉 Trace the changes in attitude toward cocaine abuse that occurred in the 1980s, and explain why they occurred.
〉 Compare the effects of cocaine with those of amphetamines.
〉 Identify the different stages of cocaine withdrawal.
〉 Discuss the different approaches to treating cocaine dependence.
〉 Identify and compare the major sources of the caffeine-like xanthine drugs.
〉 List the principal physiological effects of caffeine.
〉 Compare caffeine dependence and withdrawal to that associated with the major stimulants.
〉 Describe the beverages known as "energy drinks" and relate their potential risks.
〉 Understand the potential dangers of using herbal stimulants such as ephedra.
〉 Identify the role of the FDA in regulating herbal stimulants.

## Introduction

Stimulants are substances that cause the user to feel energized and experience a sense of increased energy and a state of euphoria or "high." This effect is likely because of the ability of these drugs to release dopamine (Mental Health Daily, 2015a). When used excessively, the user may also feel restless and talkative and have trouble sleeping. High doses administered over the long term can produce personality changes or even induce violent, dangerous, or psychotic behavior. Persons addicted to potent stimulants make notoriously bad decisions that hurt them and their loved ones (Miller, 2016). The following describes the experiences of a stimulant (i.e., methamphetamine) user:

> Rayda Tegen, a 46-year-old mother, was arrested and sentenced to [three] years of prison for smuggling in a pound of methamphetamine into Juneau, Alaska. As she sat in a yellow prison suit, she deeply regretted her very bad decisions causing her to relapse back to using methamphetamine after being clean for 20 years. She isn't exactly sure how it happened. "It wasn't that I woke up one day and said, 'I have a beautiful family, why don't I screw that up. I have a beautiful marriage . . . why don't I throw that down the tubes." Rayda blames herself for her predicament. In fact, she admits that it probably was good thing she was arrested. "Maybe someone would have died from the drugs I was bringing into the state and I would have had to live with that. I couldn't live knowing that I gave someone something that killed them. Or I could have ended up dead."

Many users self-medicate psychological conditions—for example, depression or attention-deficit hyperactivity disorder (ADHD)—with stimulants. Because the initial effects of stimulants are so pleasant, these drugs are repeatedly abused, leading to dependence.

### KEY TERM

**uppers**
CNS stimulants

In this chapter, you will learn about two principal classifications of stimulant drugs. Major stimulants, including amphetamines and cocaine, are addressed first, given their prominent role in current illicit and prescription drug abuse problems in the United States. The chapter concludes with a review of minor stimulants—in particular, caffeine. The stimulant properties of over-the-counter (OTC) sympathomimetics and "herbal highs" also are discussed.

## Major Stimulants

All major stimulants increase alertness, excitation, and euphoria; thus, these drugs are referred to as **uppers**. The major stimulants are classified as either Schedule I ("designer" amphetamines or major ingredients in products such as bath salts) or Schedule II (amphetamine, cocaine, and methylphenidate [Ritalin]) controlled substances because of their abuse potential. Although these drugs have properties in common, they also have unique features that distinguish them from one another (Oregon Health & Science University [OHSU], 2015). The similarities and differences of the major stimulants are discussed in the following sections.

### ▪ Amphetamines

Since the early 2000s, the disturbing images of drug-related violence, methamphetamine lab explosions in residential areas, disastrous effects on teeth and health in general have taken a back seat to the opioid crisis of 2018–2019. It was more than 13 years ago that the federal and state governments aggressively spent millions of dollars and devoted incalculable time and effort to eliminate the meth scourge in this country. These efforts in many ways were successful until recently. However, in the western United States, in places such as Oregon, Montana, Southern California, and along the southern borders of the United States, meth has returned purer, cheaper, and even more lethal than before. Although almost all of the small domestic meth labs of the early 2000s have disappeared, authorities claim there is more meth on the streets today, with more people using it with more deadly consequences than before. Much of the new meth that is showing up on our streets today comes from Mexican drug cartels in large quantities making dealers eager to move their abundant stashes quickly by providing a product that is almost 100% pure and almost impossible for users to resist at $5 a hit. In some states such as Oklahoma, meth-related deaths exceed those caused by opioids (Robles, 2018).

Amphetamines are potent synthetic central nervous system (CNS) stimulants capable of causing dependence because of their euphorigenic properties and ability to eliminate fatigue. Despite their addicting effects, amphetamines can be legally prescribed by physicians for appetite control in weight-loss programs, narcolepsy, and hyperactivity disorders; however, their medical uses are considered to be limited (NIDA, 2015). Consequently, amphetamine abuse occurs in people who acquire their drugs by both legitimate and illicit means.

## THE HISTORY OF AMPHETAMINES

The first amphetamine was synthesized by German pharmacologist L. Edeleano in 1887, but this and several related compounds were not tested in laboratory animals until 1910. Another 17 years passed before Gordon Alles, a researcher looking for a more potent substitute for ephedrine (used as a decongestant at the time), self-administered amphetamine and gave a firsthand account of its effects. Alles found that when inhaled or taken orally, amphetamine dramatically reduced fatigue, increased alertness, and caused a sense of confident euphoria (Grinspoon & Bakalar, 1978).

Because of Alles's impressive findings, the Benzedrine (amphetamine) inhaler became available in 1932 as a nonprescription medication in drugstores across the United States. The Benzedrine inhaler, marketed for nasal congestion, was widely abused for its stimulant action but continued to be available OTC until 1949. Because of a loophole in a law that was passed later, all potent amphetamine-like compounds in nasal inhalers were not withdrawn from the market until 1971 (Grinspoon & Bakalar, 1978; McCaffrey, 1999).

Owing to the lack of restrictions during this early period, amphetamines were sold to treat a variety of ailments, including obesity, alcoholism, bed-wetting, depression, schizophrenia, morphine and codeine addiction, heart block, head injuries, seasickness, persistent hiccups, and caffeine mania. Today, most of these uses are no longer approved as legitimate therapeutics but would be considered forms of drug abuse.

World War II provided a setting in which both the legal and "black market" use of amphetamines flourished (Grinspoon & Bakalar, 1978). Because of their stimulating effects, amphetamines were widely used by the Germans, Japanese, and British in World War II to counteract fatigue. By the end of World War II, large quantities of amphetamines were readily available without prescription in seven types of nasal inhalers (Newman, 2016; "A Social History of America's Most Popular Drugs," n.d.).

In spite of warnings about these drugs' addicting properties and serious side effects, the U.S. armed forces issued amphetamines on a regular basis during the Korean War and, in fact, may still make it available to pilots in the Air Force to relieve fatigue. Amphetamine use became widespread among truck drivers making long hauls, and among the earliest distribution systems for illicit amphetamines were truck stops along major U.S. highways. High achievers under continuous pressure in the fields of entertainment, business, and industry often relied on amphetamines to counteract fatigue ("A Social History," n.d.). Homemakers used them to control weight and to combat boredom from unfulfilled lives. At the height of one U.S. epidemic in 1967, some 31 million prescriptions were written for **anorexiants** (diet pills) alone.

Today, a variety of related drugs and mixtures exist, including amphetamine substances such as dextroamphetamine (Dexedrine), methamphetamine (Desoxyn), and amphetamine itself. Generally, if doses are adjusted, the psychological effects of these various drugs are similar, so they will be discussed as a group. Other drugs with some of the same pharmacological properties are phenmetrazine (Preludin) and methylphenidate (Ritalin). Not only are illicit stimulants a significant drug abuse problem, but also legal stimulants are the second most frequently abused drug on college campuses, with 15% to 20% of college students using these drugs. Common slang terms for amphetamines include *bennies*, *amped*, *black/blue mollies*, *jelly beans*, *speed*, *uppers*, *dexies*, *eyepoppers*, and *lightning* ("Amphetamine Street Names," n.d.).

### KEY TERM

**anorexiants**
drugs that suppress the activity of the brain's appetite center and cause reduced food intake

## HOW AMPHETAMINES WORK

Amphetamines are synthetic chemicals that are similar to natural neurotransmitters such as norepinephrine (noradrenaline), dopamine, and the stress hormone epinephrine (adrenaline). The amphetamines exert their pharmacological effect by increasing the release and blocking the metabolism of these catecholamine substances, as well as serotonin, both in the brain and in nerves associated with the sympathetic nervous system. Because amphetamines cause release of norepinephrine from sympathetic nerves, they are classified as sympathomimetic drugs. The amphetamines generally cause an arousal or activating response (also called the *fight-or-flight response*) that is similar to the normal reaction to emergency situations, stress, or crises. Amphetamines also cause alertness so that the individual becomes aroused and hypersensitive to stimuli and feels "turned on." These effects occur even without external sensory input. This activation may be a highly pleasant experience in itself, but a continual high level of activation may convert to anxiety, severe apprehension, or panic (Luscher, 2015).

Amphetamines have potent effects on dopamine in the reward (pleasure) center of the brain. This action probably causes the "flash" or sudden feeling of intense pleasure that occurs when amphetamine is taken intravenously. Some users describe the sensation as a "whole-body orgasm," and many associate intravenous methamphetamine use with sexual feelings. The actual effect of these drugs on sexual behavior is quite variable and dependent on dose (OHSU, 2015).

## WHAT AMPHETAMINES CAN DO

A curious condition commonly reported with heavy amphetamine use is **behavioral stereotypy**, or "getting hung up." This term refers to a simple activity that is done repeatedly. An individual who is "hung up" will repeat a thought or act for hours. For example, he or she may take objects such as radios or clocks apart and carefully categorize all

the parts, or sit in a tub and bathe all day, persistently singing a note, repeating a phrase of music, or repeatedly cleaning the same object. This phenomenon seems to be peculiar to potent stimulants such as the amphetamines and cocaine. Similar patterns of repetitive behavior also occur in psychotic conditions, which suggests that the intense use of stimulants such as amphetamines or cocaine alters the brain in a manner like that causing psychotic mental disorders (NIDA, 2015) and can lead to violent behavior.

Chronic use of high doses of amphetamines decreases the brain content of the neurotransmitters dopamine and serotonin, a condition that persists for months even after drug use is stopped (Luscher, 2015). These decreases have been shown to reflect damage to the CNS neurons that release these transmitters. Why this neuronal destruction occurs is not clear, although there is evidence that the amphetamines can stimulate production of highly reactive molecules called *free radicals* that, in turn, damage brain cells (NIDA, 2015).

## APPROVED USES

Until 1970, amphetamines were prescribed for a large number of conditions, including depression, fatigue, and long-term weight reduction. In 1970, the Food and Drug Administration (FDA), acting on the recommendation of the National Academy of Sciences, restricted the legal use of amphetamines to three medical conditions: (1) narcolepsy, (2) ADHD, and (3) short-term weight-reduction programs (Newman, 2016).

### NARCOLEPSY

Amphetamine treatment of narcolepsy is not widespread because this condition is a relatively rare disorder. The term **narcolepsy** comes from the Greek words for "numbness" and "seizure." A person who has narcolepsy falls asleep as frequently as 50 times a day if he or she stays in one position for long. Taking low doses of amphetamines helps narcoleptic people stay alert.

### ATTENTION-DEFICIT HYPERACTIVITY DISORDER

ADHD is a common behavioral problem in children and adolescents that involves an abnormally high level of physical activity, an inability to focus attention, and frequent disruptive behavior. Approximately 11% of children ages four to 17 years have been diagnosed with ADHD in the

### KEY TERMS

**behavioral stereotypy**
meaningless repetition of a single activity

**narcolepsy**
condition that causes spontaneous and uncontrolled sleeping episodes

United States (Centers for Disease Control and Prevention, 2016). The drug commonly used to treat children with ADHD is the amphetamine-related methylphenidate, or Ritalin (discussed later in this chapter).

## WEIGHT REDUCTION

The most common use of amphetamines is for the treatment of obesity. Amphetamines and chemically similar compounds are used as anorexiants to help obese or severely overweight people control appetite. Amphetamines are thought to act by affecting the appetite center in the hypothalamus of the brain, which causes the user to decrease food intake. The FDA has approved short-term use of amphetamines for weight-loss programs but has warned of their potential for abuse. Many experts believe that the euphoric effect of amphetamines is the primary motivation for their continued use in weight-reduction programs. Many obese people may have a need for gratification that can be satisfied by the euphoric feeling this drug produces (Ely & Cusack, 2015). If the drug is taken away, these individuals return to food to satisfy their need and sometimes experience "rebound," causing them to gain back more weight than they lost. Some persons who become addicted to amphetamine-like substances begin illicit use of these drugs by trying to either prevent weight gain or lose weight on their own without the guidance of a physician (American Psychiatric Association [APA], 2013).

## SIDE EFFECTS OF THERAPEUTIC DOSES

The two principal side effects of therapeutic doses of amphetamines are abuse, which has already been discussed, and cardiovascular toxicities. Many of these effects derive from the amphetamine-induced release of epinephrine from the adrenal glands and norepinephrine from the nerves associated with the sympathetic nervous system. The effects include increased heart rate, elevated blood pressure, and damage to vessels, especially small veins and arteries (Newman, 2016). In users with a history of heart attack, coronary arrhythmia, or hypertension, amphetamine toxicity can be severe or even fatal.

## CURRENT MISUSE

Amphetamine drugs can be readily and inexpensively synthesized in makeshift laboratories for illicit sale, can be administered by several routes,

and cause a more sustained effect than cocaine, so they have become more popular than cocaine in many parts of the United States (Johnston, 2019). Surveys suggest that there was a decline in the abuse of amphetamines in the late 1980s and early 1990s in parallel with a similar trend in cocaine abuse (Johnston, 2019). By 2002, these declines were replaced by a rise in the number of persons abusing amphetamines to 11.1%. However, abuse again declined, as indicated by the finding that 7.7% of high school seniors used amphetamines in 2015 (Johnston, 2019). Of those who abuse amphetamines and become addicted, many end up in the criminal justice system (Federal Bureau of Investigation, 2015). However, as previously mentioned, recently there appears to be a resurgent pattern of meth use and its associated criminal activity, and the full impact of this associated shift in meth trafficking is yet to be determined (Newman, 2019) (see "Here and Now: Revisiting the Returning Meth Criminal Problem").

Because of the potential for serious side effects, U.S. medical associations have asked all physicians to be more careful about prescribing amphetamines. Use is currently recommended only for narcolepsy and some cases of hyperactivity in children (Newman, 2016). In spite of FDA approval, most medical associations do not recommend the use of amphetamines for weight loss.

Amphetamine abusers commonly administer a dose of 10 to 30 milligrams. Besides the positive effects of this dose—the high—it can cause hyperactive, nervous, or jittery feelings that encourage the use of a depressant such as a benzodiazepine, barbiturate, or alcohol to relieve the discomfort of being "wired" (Mental Health Daily, 2015c).

A potent and commonly abused form of amphetamine is **speed**, an illegal methamphetamine available as a white, odorless, bitter-tasting crystalline powder for injection. Methamphetamine is a highly addictive stimulant that is much cheaper and longer lasting than cocaine. In 2019, a single hit of meth cost around $5 for almost 100% drug purity, whereas cocaine costs were two to three times greater for drugs with much

**KEY TERM**

**speed**
injectable methamphetamine used by drug addicts

# HERE AND NOW

## Revisiting the Returning Meth Criminal Problem

The return of the meth problem in the shadow of the opioid threats has law enforcement agencies across the country highly concerned about how to stretch limited budgets and employee power to effectively address the criminal consequences of coincidental use of these two distinct types of drugs of abuse. The criminal effects of the resurging meth patterns are particularly problematic because of the involvement of Mexican drug cartels, the large quantities of pure drug being moved into the United States across the borders, and the dramatic reduction in drug cost for the abuser. The consequence of these patterns is that meth is highly available and widely used, making it the biggest contributor to local violent and property crimes in communities especially, but not exclusively, in the western United States. Authorities complain that the dramatic proliferation of meth quantity and availability has hampered local law enforcement efforts because of the national reduction of recruitment and retention of law enforcement officers in this country.

These elevated meth quantities have caused a shift in methods of drug distribution from individual dealers working on the streets to area businesses such as restaurants, auto body shops, clothing stores, and even nurseries as side businesses whose owners are "solid citizens" with families and solid reputations in their communities. Such stores and commercial outlets have become part of drug-trafficking organizations and are able to quietly transport large quantities of drug-related cash back to Mexico and the cartels without detection. Around 2000, the fight against meth was all about following up anonymous tips concerning potent smells and even occasional fires and explosions in neighborhoods that involved rundown homes that served as residences for unknown groups and often turned out to be makeshift laboratories for "cooking" large quantities of meth on the streets to support the drug habits of the "cookers." Current investigations are long term and based more on investigation teams using covert strategies in order to close down large international gang-directed activities for meth selling and trafficking.

Newman, K. (2019, March). Meth from Mexico a growing problem for law enforcement. *U.S. News & World Report*. Retrieved from https://www.usnews.com/news/healthiest-communities/articles/2019-03-12/meth-from-mexico-a-growing-problem-for-law-enforcement

less purity and shorter action (Bezrutczyk, 2019). The profit for the speed manufacturer is substantial enough to make illicit production financially attractive at $10 to $20 a dose; it is sometimes known as the "poor man's cocaine" (KCI.org, n.d.). Despite this image of being a particular problem of the working class, there are many examples of rich and famous people who also have abused this potent stimulant (see "Here and Now: Meth—A Powerful Drug Abused by Powerful People").

Methamphetamine is relatively easy and inexpensive to make. Historically, many illicit manufacturers have been individuals without expertise in chemistry. Such people, referred to as *cookers*, could produce methamphetamine batches by using cookbook-style recipes (often obtained in

## KEY TERM

**precursor chemicals**
chemicals used to produce a drug

jail or over the Internet). The most popular recipes used common OTC ingredients—ephedrine, pseudoephedrine, and phenylpropanolamine—as **precursor chemicals** for the methamphetamine. To discourage the illicit manufacture of this potent stimulant, the Comprehensive Methamphetamine Control Act was passed in the United States in October 1996. This law increased penalties for trafficking in methamphetamine and in the precursor chemicals used to create this drug and gave the government authority to regulate and seize these substances (Drug Enforcement Administration [DEA], n.d.). When discovered, the local so-called meth or speed labs were raided by law enforcement agencies. In 2003, the DEA funded the cleanup of approximately 12,000 illegal local methamphetamine labs, most of which were in the western United States. This number decreased to 3,866 in 2008 (Doyle, 2010). It is not surprising that these operations posed a serious threat to neighbors and residents, especially children, in the structures that contain the labs. Law enforcement personnel and firefighters are

# HERE AND NOW

## Meth—A Powerful Drug Abused by Powerful People

Meth is a strong stimulant that can have debilitating and tragic consequences to anyone who becomes addicted to its potent rewarding effects. Included in those groups who seem to be particularly susceptible to the devastating impact of meth use disorder are celebrities from all walks of life and all skills, including actors and actresses, musicians and vocalists, authors, athletes, political and military leaders, and even religious cult leaders. The following are some of the most famous people who have found themselves trapped in the addictive seduction of this psychostimulant:

- Lindsay Lohan was known as one of the greatest child and teen stars of the 1990s and early 2000s. Because of her highly erratic behavior, she was accused by her father in 2011 of smoking either crack of meth.

- Robert Downey, Jr., the iconic star who portrayed the role of *Iron Man* in some of the *Avenger* series was arrested for possession of cocaine and meth in November 2000. He claims he has been sober from his abuse of these substances for the past few years and that the strongest drug he currently uses is espresso.

- Marilyn Monroe, exclaimed by some as the best movie actress in film history, regularly received meth injections by "Dr. Feelgood" Jacobson, who also treated famous author Truman Capote and President John F. Kennedy with a similar meth-containing concoction.

- Truman Capote, author of best-selling books such as *In Cold Blood* and *Breakfast at Tiffany's*, described meth injections as "instant euphoria" and the crash during withdrawal as "falling down a well." Abuse of meth and other drugs is thought to have contributed to his death from liver failure.

- Britney Spears, described by some as one of the most outstanding female vocalists since 2000, was accused by her former lawyer of shaving her head to avoid detection of meth during a defamation trial.

- Andre Agassi, an international tennis star, failed a drug test in 1997 and claimed his assistant had spiked his water bottle with meth. However, nearly 10 years later he acknowledged in his autobiography that in fact "meth made him feel so alive, so hopeful, with such energy." But his meth use helped to destroy his tennis career and his family life.

- Adolf Hitler, German fuhrer (leader) during World War II, is known to have become dependent on meth found in products such as Pervitin," as well as daily injections of meth itself. Hitler had this "power drug" distributed to German troops during the war to create super soldier machines by reducing their fatigue and empathy and increasing their aggression. His heavy abuse of meth may have contributed to his increased psychotic behavior in the later parts of World War II and his eventual expression of Parkinson's disease.

- John F. Kennedy, one of the most popular presidents in U.S. history, received daily injections of meth combined with vitamins and hormones from a German physician named Max Jacobson, also known as "Dr. Feelgood," to help deal with crippling diseases such as chronic back pain, colitis, and Addison's disease. He thought that use of this meth concoction gave him the stamina necessary to reinforce his youthful and energetic image.

© Ron Frehm/AP Images.

Data from Friedman, A., & Rocher, F. (2013, September 22). A history of celebrities getting caught with meth. Complex. Retrieved from https://www.complex.com/pop-culture/2013/09/celebrities-caught-with-meth/; "Famous people with meth problems." (n.d.). Ranker. Retrieved from https://www.ranker.com/list/famous-crystal-users/celebrity-lists

also at risk when dealing with methamphetamine labs because of ignitable, corrosive, reactive, and toxic chemicals that might explode, start a fire, emit toxic fumes, or cause serious injury at the site. The toxic chemicals involved in meth synthesis create fumes that contaminate neighboring buildings, water supplies, and soil. These labs were especially dangerous when set up in poorly ventilated rooms.

Although enforcement of the Comprehensive Methamphetamine Control Act was successful in dramatically decreasing the number of small neighborhood meth labs in the United States, over the long run it apparently had minimal effect on actual supplies of this drug for illegal sales. Thus, methamphetamine is currently being smuggled across the U.S. border from Mexico in enormous quantities and is being manufactured by criminal organizations from chemicals diverted by the ton from Asian pharmaceutical companies (Longmire, 2016; Morris, 2018; Thornton, 2015). Currently, the vast majority of meth is imported by drug cartels, keeping supplies abundant, purity high, and costs low (Morris, 2018).

### PATTERNS OF HIGH-DOSE USE

Amphetamines can be taken orally, intravenously, or by smoking. The intensity and duration of effects vary according to the mode of

administration. The methamphetamine addict frequently uses chronic, high doses of amphetamines intravenously and can be infected with human immunodeficiency virus (HIV) (Massanella et al., 2015). Another approach to administering amphetamines is smoking **ice**, which can cause effects as potent, but perhaps more prolonged and erratic, than intravenous doses. The initial effect (after five to 30 minutes) of these potent stimulants is called the **rush** and includes a racing heartbeat and elevated blood pressure, metabolism, and pulse. During this phase, the user has powerful impressions of pleasure and enthusiasm. The next stage is the **high** (four to 16 hours after drug use) when the person feels aggressively smarter, energetic, talkative, and powerful and may initiate and complete highly ambitious tasks. The amphetamine addict tries to maintain the high for as long as possible, with continual drug use leading to extended mental and physical hyperactivity; this is referred to as a **run** or **binge**, and it can last from three to 15 days. Persistent use of these drugs, such as methamphetamine, to maintain the high for long periods of time is called **tweaking**. The tweaker often has neither slept nor eaten much for three to 15 days and can be extremely irritable and paranoid and have an elevated body temperature, a condition known as **hyperpyrexia**. This is a potentially dangerous stage for medical personnel or law enforcement officers because if the tweaker becomes agitated, he or she can respond violently to the efforts of others to help. To relieve some of the side effects of the extensive use of methamphetamine, tweakers often use a depressant such as alcohol, barbiturates, benzodiazepines, or opioid narcotics (Center for Substance Abuse Research, 2013). The consequences of such a drug combination are to intensify negative feelings and worsen the dangers of the drug. Tweakers are frequently involved in domestic violence and often injure their children and partners. Withdrawal follows for 30 to 90 days and includes feelings of depression and lethargy. During this phase, cravings can be intense and the abuser may even become suicidal. Because a dose of methamphetamine often relieves these symptoms, many addicts in treatment return to abusing this stimulant (Narconon, 2016a).

After the first day or so of a run, unpleasant symptoms become prominent as the dosage is increased. Symptoms commonly reported at this stage are teeth grinding, disorganized patterns

### KEY TERMS

**ice**
smokable form of methamphetamine

**rush**
initial pleasure after amphetamine use that includes racing heartbeat and elevated blood pressure

**high**
condition lasting four to 16 hours after drug use; includes feelings of energy and power

**run**
intense use of a stimulant, consisting of multiple administrations over a period of days

**binge**
similar to a run but usually of shorter duration

**tweaking**
repeated administration of methamphetamine to maintain a high

**hyperpyrexia**
elevated body temperature

of thought and behavior, stereotypy, irritability, self-consciousness, suspiciousness, and fear. Hallucinations and delusions that are similar to a paranoid psychosis and indistinguishable from schizophrenia can occur (Narconon, 2016a). The person is likely to show aggressive and antisocial behavior for no apparent reason, although recent brain-imaging studies have revealed that addictions to the amphetamines can cause long-term damage to the brain's inhibitory control centers (NIDA, 2014). Severe chest pains, abdominal discomfort that mimics appendicitis, and fainting from overdosage are sometimes reported. "Cocaine bugs" represent one bizarre effect of high doses of potent stimulants such as amphetamines: the user experiences strange feelings like insects crawling under the skin. The range of physical and mental symptoms experienced from low to high doses is summarized in "Signs and Symptoms: Summary of the Effects of Amphetamines on the Body and Mind."

Toward the end of the run, adverse symptoms dominate. When the drug is discontinued because the supply is exhausted or the symptoms become too unpleasant, an extreme crash can occur that is followed by prolonged sleep, sometimes for several days. On awakening, the person is lethargic, hungry, and often severely depressed. The amphetamine user may overcome these unpleasant effects by smoking ice or injecting speed, thereby initiating a new cycle (APA, 2013).

Continued use of massive doses of amphetamine often leads to considerable weight loss, sores on the skin, poor oral hygiene and deterioration of the teeth, nonhealing ulcers, liver disease, hypertensive disorders, cerebral hemorrhage (stroke), heart attack, kidney damage, and seizures (NIDA, 2015). For some of these effects, it is impossible to tell if they are caused by the drug, poor eating habits, or other factors associated with the lifestyle of people who inject methamphetamine.

Speed freaks are generally unpopular with the rest of the drug-taking community, especially "acid-heads" (addicts who use lysergic acid diethylamide [LSD]), because of the aggressive, unpredictable behavior associated with use of potent stimulants (Roberts, 2015). In general, drug abusers who take high doses of these agents, such as amphetamines or cocaine, are more likely to be involved in violent crimes than those who abuse other drugs (Substance Abuse and Mental Health Services Administration [SAMHSA], 2010). Heavy users are generally unable to hold steady jobs because of their drug habits and often have

# SIGNS & SYMPTOMS

## Summary of the Effects of Amphetamines on the Body and Mind

| | Body | Mind |
|---|---|---|
| Low dose | Increased heartbeat | Decreased fatigue |
| | Increased blood pressure | Increased confidence |
| | Decreased appetite | Increased feeling of alertness |
| | Increased breathing rate | Restlessness, talkativeness |
| | Inability to sleep | Increased irritability |
| | Sweating | Fearfulness, apprehension |
| | Dry mouth | Distrust of people |
| | Muscle twitching | Behavioral stereotypy |
| | Convulsions | Hallucinations |
| | Fever | Psychosis |
| High dose | Death from overdose | |

a parasitic relationship with the rest of the illicit drug-using community.

Although claims have been made that amphetamines do not cause physical dependence, it is almost certain that depression (sometimes suicidal), lethargy, muscle pains, abnormal sleep patterns, and, in severe cases, suicide attempts occur after high chronic doses as part of withdrawal (Addiction Center, 2016c). During withdrawal from amphetamine use, the dependent user often turns to other drugs for relief (Cantwell & McBride, 1998). Rebound from the amphetamines is opposite to that experienced with withdrawal from CNS depressants.

Although the effects of amphetamines on the unborn fetus are difficult to evaluate and are not fully understood (Davies, 2015), some human studies suggest that there is a possibility of serious problems in the offspring. This research shows that babies born to methamphetamine-using mothers are much more likely to be preterm and less likely to survive. In addition, almost 40% of the meth-exposed babies are at least temporarily removed from their mothers to be adopted or placed in child protective services or foster care (Mothers Against Methamphetamine, n.d.). Studies on the long-term effects on the offspring of methamphetamine moms have been more difficult to conduct but suggest that brain structures are altered, particularly if these women are also consuming alcohol. These congenital problems could lead to long-term cognitive or behavioral problems (Mothers Against Methamphetamines, n.d.). The methamphetamine-abusing expectant mothers are also vulnerable to serious pregnancy problems of their own such as uncontrolled high blood pressure and delivery complications (Harding, 2010).

Evidence suggests that repeated high-dose use of amphetamines such as methamphetamine by adolescents or adults causes long-term and perhaps permanent damage to both the dopamine and serotonin neurotransmitter systems of the brain (Northrop & Yamamoto, 2015). This brain damage may result in persistent episodes of psychosis as well as long-lasting memory, motor impairment, and cognitive deficits (Recovery.org, 2015). Abuse of amphetamines often seriously damages personal relationships with friends, associates, and even family members. Particularly disturbing is the use of methamphetamine by young mothers. Moms on meth have claimed that use of this stimulant makes them feel invincible and as if they can run around the world—and

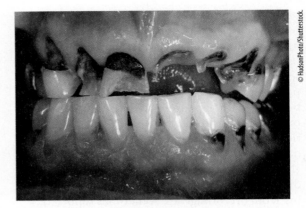

Devastation of oral structures, known as *meth mouth*, is sometimes associated with methamphetamine addiction.

then do it again. They claim to lose weight, but they also can lose their instinct to mother their children as they become obsessed with the drug (Holt, 2005). Consequently, children are being exposed to dangerous levels of this drug in many forms (see "Here and Now: Small Town, Big Problems: The Female Methamphetamine Epidemic") at a tremendous emotional cost (see "Signs and Symptoms: A Daughter's Plea to a Meth Mother").

## TREATMENT

Admissions for treatment of methamphetamine addiction more than doubled from 2000 to 2005, but admissions have decreased by approximately 50% since 2013 (SAMHSA, 2015). This is at least partially the result of restricting access to the decongestant drugs used to synthesize methamphetamine (SAMHSA, 2015). However, more recent findings suggest that Mexican methamphetamine labs are finding ways to get around the laws and avoid detection, resulting in a significant resurgence in methamphetamine supplies and purity in the United States. Currently, 8% of all admissions to treat substance use disorder are linked to the amphetamines and for the most part include persons 20 to 44 years of age (SAMHSA, 2015).

The dependence disorder caused by the amphetamines is hard but not impossible to treat successfully. Many methamphetamine addicts have significant impairment of their decision-making ability and do not self-refer but are forced into treatment by drug courts and other components of the criminal justice system (National Association of Drug Court Professionals, 2015). Currently, the most effective

# HERE AND NOW

## Small Town, Big Problems: The Female Methamphetamine Epidemic

Methamphetamine has caused a drug-related epidemic never before experienced in this country. Its abuse and devastating social effects have taxed public social services in unanticipated ways. One of the most striking aspects of this drug's abuse is its appeal to young adult women, many of whom have children or were using methamphetamine when they were pregnant and will have to deal with the potential damage to their offspring. Typically, the number of women seeking treatment for drug addiction is considerably lower than the number of men in the same situation; however, in many regions roughly equal numbers of men and women seek help for methamphetamine as their primary addiction. Clearly, the destructive influence of methamphetamine abuse is taking an enormous toll on homes and families. Consequently, criminal justice systems for women offenders have been overwhelmed.

Women who are addicted to methamphetamine often do not do well in conventional drug treatment programs. Because of the potent addicting properties of this drug, they typically struggle with the requirements of probation or parole and often end up back in prison, and their children end up in family services and foster care. Although it is not clear why this stimulant is so

seductive to young women, women who use methamphetamine typically have:

- a history of chronic unemployment,
- a live-in partner who also uses drugs,
- a history of physical and sexual abuse,
- a history of suicide attempts,
- motivation to use methamphetamine for weight control, and
- psychiatric drug-related problems.

For female methamphetamine addicts, "this drug is a massive black hole. It's swallowing these people alive and takes a miracle to put these families back together again."

Data from "Escalation in methamphetamine use also leads to escalation in social service." (2005, February 14). *Health & Medicine Week*; Khazan, O. (2015a). Into the body of another. *The Atlantic* (May 8). Retrieved from http://www.theatlantic.com/health/archive/2015/05/into-the-body-of-another/392522/; Rowan-Szal, G., Joe, G., Simpson, W., Greener, J., & Vance, J. (2009). During-treatment outcomes among female methamphetamine-using offenders in prison-based treatments. *Journal of Offender Rehabilitation, 48*, 388–401.

# SIGNS & SYMPTOMS

## A Daughter's Plea to a Meth Mother

One can only imagine the frustration, anger, and pain that are suffered by the children of mothers who are addicted to methamphetamine. The children's lives are filled with uncertainty, such as the lies of parents who swear that they are clean or will stop their drug habit because they "love their children so much and they don't want to hurt them anymore," but their addiction always seems to crowd out the "love for the child."

Often the children try to tough it out and smile on the outside even though on the inside they being torn apart. How long should a child have to tolerate this emotional and even physical abuse? When does it become too much and how can a child escape? Recently a poem was posted on the Internet that beautifully expressed these terrible struggles of a child with a mother who is a drug addict.

"My mother vs. meth." (n.d.). Addiction Poem about Family. Retrieved from www.familyfriendpoems.com/poem/my-mother-vs-meth

treatments for amphetamine addiction are behavioral interventions to help modify thinking patterns, improve cognitive skills, change expectations, and increase coping with life's stressors.

Amphetamine support groups also appear to be successful as adjuncts to behavioral therapies. To date, no well-established pharmacological treatments for amphetamine dependency have been developed (Elkashef et al., 2008; Kishi, Matsuda, Iwata, & Correll, 2013). Approaches used for cocaine have been tried with some success. Antidepressant medication may help relieve the depression that occurs during early stages of withdrawal (Woolston, 2016).

The persistence of the effects of methamphetamine makes this addiction especially difficult to address effectively. The word on the street has been that many of the effects of this stimulant are permanent, and its cognitive damage might be irreversible. Although there is ample evidence that hard-core use of methamphetamine for extended periods has devastating effects on decision-making, impulsivity, memory, and other functions, evidence is accumulating that suggests that recovery from these effects is possible. However, effective treatment is not simple or cheap and typically requires more than a year of intense

intervention consisting of drug abstinence; cognitive, emotional, and motivational rehabilitation; and often career and skills development (Woolston, 2016).

## AMPHETAMINE COMBINATIONS

As previously mentioned, amphetamines are frequently used in conjunction with a variety of other drugs such as barbiturates, benzodiazepines, alcohol, and heroin ("Methamphetamine Mixing," n.d.). Amphetamines intensify, prolong, or otherwise alter the effects of LSD, and the two types of drugs are sometimes combined. The majority of speed users have also had experience with a variety of psychedelics or other drugs. In addition, people dependent on opiate narcotics frequently use amphetamines or cocaine (see "Signs and Symptoms: Morning Meth and a Heroin Night" (Dembosky, 2019). These combinations

# SIGNS & SYMPTOMS
## Morning Meth and a Heroin Night

"Kim" has been routinely snorting METN (methamphetamine) for more than two decades. She describes the meth experiences as helping her to feel normal or, as she calls it, her "Oh! There I am" moments. These normal moments became "not so normal" distortions and eventually made her dysfunctional and unable to cope with the stress and pain that seemed to define her life. Kim sought professional help, and as she was weaning herself off meth, she became aware of heroin and felt that it could replace her meth habit by calming her down and helping her walk away from the agitation and paranoia that had become so routine with her frequent tweaking episodes. The heroin did change her life, but not how Kim expected: instead of being able to walk away from the potent stimulation of meth, Kim became addicted to both drugs for which she required complicated and expensive integrated treatment. Kim was a child of the '90s meth wave and now she has become a member of the new meth epidemic currently creating problems across the country, but especially in the West. Scientists and clinician who track illicit drug use patterns express concern that this new meth crisis was

precipitated by the opioid epidemic. This trend is confirmed by reports that opioid users who claim also to be using meth has dramatically increased from 19% in 2011 to 34% in 2017. Possible reasons for this trend include: (1) synergistic interactions between these two seeming opposite categories of CNS pharmacology; (2) substitution for the opioids when unavailable or too expensive; and (3) attempting to balance out the opioid sedation with a meth stimulation. These explanations sound similar to the common custom in our society to wake up in the morning with the stimulation of coffee (i.e., caffeine) and drink a glass of wine to calm down at night. The meth and heroin combination is colloquially known as a "goofball." Kim explains this pattern of stimulant and depressant mixing as follows: "You're balancing, trying to figure out your own prescription to how to make you feel good." Unfortunately, users of the "goofball" approach to feel normal or to try to sustain "balance" in their lives rarely recognize the severe and sometimes deadly consequences of such naïve experimenting with two extremely powerful and deadly substances.

Dembosky, A. (2019, June 17). Meth in the morning, heroin at night: Inside the seesaw struggle of dual addiction. NPR. Retrieved from https://www.npr.org/sections/health-shots/2019/06/17/730803759/meth-in-the-morning-heroin-at-night-inside-the-seesaw-struggle-of-dual-addiction are sometimes called **speedballs** or **goofballs** (Hawaii Island Recovery, 2019).

## "DESIGNER" AMPHETAMINES

Underground chemists can readily synthesize drugs that mimic the psychoactive effects of amphetamines. Although the production of such drugs declined in the early 1990s, their use by American teens surged in the late 1990s and early 2000s, as reflected in the fact that more than 9% of high school seniors used the designer amphetamine known as MDMA (methylenedioxymethamphetamine) or Ecstasy in 2001. This rate decreased dramatically to 3% in 2005, reflecting a concern about its potential harmful effects. However, the rate of annual use rose to 5.3% in 2011 but dropped back again to 2.2% in 2018, suggesting that the concerns about the risk of recreational use of the designer amphetamines have been vacillating (Johnston, 2019).

Designer amphetamines sometimes differ from the parent compound by only a single element. These *synthetic spinoffs* pose a significant abuse problem because often several different designer amphetamines can be made from the parent compound and still retain the abuse potential and physical risks of the original substance (Baumann & Volkow, 2016).

For many years, the production and distribution of designer amphetamines were not illegal, even though they were synthesized from controlled substances. In the mid-1980s, however, the DEA actively pursued policies to curb their production and sale. Consequently, many designer amphetamines were outlawed under the Substance Analogue Enforcement Act of 1986, which makes illegal any substance that is similar in structure or psychological effect to any substance already scheduled if it is manufactured, possessed, or sold with the intention that it be consumed by human beings (Beck, 1990).

The principal types of designer amphetamines are the following:

- derivatives from amphetamine and methamphetamine that retain the CNS stimulatory effects, such as methcathinone ("cat") or mephedrone (methyl-methcathinone); and
- derivatives from amphetamine and methamphetamine that have prominent psychedelic effects in addition to their CNS stimulatory action such as MDMA (Ecstasy).

Because the basic amphetamine molecule can be easily synthesized and readily modified, hundreds of new amphetamine-like drugs known as *new psychoactive substances* (NPSs) have appeared on the streets around the world (United Nations Office on Drugs and Crime [UNODC], 2015). Although these designer amphetamines are thought of as new drugs when they first appear, in fact most were originally synthesized from the 1940s to the 1960s by pharmaceutical companies trying to find new decongestant and anorexiant drugs to compete with the other amphetamines. Some of these compounds were found to be too toxic to be marketed but have been rediscovered by "street chemists" and sold to unsuspecting victims trying to experience a new sensation. **Table 10.1** lists some of these designer amphetamines.

Some designer drugs of abuse that are chemically related to amphetamine include DOM (STP), methcathinone (called *cat* or *bathtub speed*), mephedrone (methylmethcathinone, called *meow meow* or *drone*, and found in products such as ivory wave or bath salts), MDA, and MDMA (or methylenedioxymethamphetamine, called *Ecstasy, X, E, XTC*, or *Adam*). As of 2018, most, if not all, of these drugs had been classified as Schedule I agents.

## MDMA (ECSTASY)

Among the designer amphetamines, MDMA, or Molly, continues to be the most popular (Juergen, 2020). It gained widespread popularity in the United States throughout the 1980s; its use peaked in 1987 despite its classification as a Schedule I drug in 1985 by the DEA. At the height of its use, 39% of the undergraduates at Stanford University reported having used MDMA at least once (Randall, 1992a). In the late 1980s and early 1990s, use of MDMA declined in this country, but about this time it was "reformulated." This reformulation was not in a pharmacological sense but in a cultural context.

## KEY TERMS

**speedballs**
combinations of amphetamine or cocaine with an opioid narcotic, often heroin

**goofballs**
stimulant plus potent opioid drug like heroin

**TABLE 10.1** Designer Amphetamines

| Amphetamine Derivative | Properties |
| --- | --- |
| Methcathinone ("cat") | Properties like those of methamphetamine and cocaine |
| Methylenedioxymethamphetamine (MDMA or "Ecstasy") | Stimulant and hallucinogen |
| Methylenedioxyamphetamine (MDA) | More powerful stimulant and less powerful hallucinogen than MDMA |
| 4-methylaminorex | CNS stimulant like amphetamine |
| *N,N*-dimethylamphetamine | One-fifth the potency of amphetamine |
| 4-thiomethyl-2,5-dimethoxyamphetamine | Hallucinogen |
| Para-methoxymethamphetamine | Weak stimulant |
| Mephedrone | Potent stimulant and hallucinogen (found in products such as bath salts) |
| α-Pyrrolidinopentiophenone ("flakka," "5-dollar insanity") | Potent stimulant and hallucinogen |

The *rave* scene in England provided a new showcase for MDMA (Randall, 1992a). Partygoers attired in Dr. Seuss–style "Cat in the Hat" hats and psychedelic jumpsuits paid $20 to dance all night to heavy, electronically generated sound mixed with computer-generated video and laser light shows. An Ecstasy tablet could be purchased for the sensory enhancement caused by the drug (Randall, 1992b). At one time, it was estimated that as many as 31% of English youth 16 to 25 years old had used Ecstasy (Grob, Poland, Chang, & Ernst, 1996). The British rave counterculture and its generous use of Ecstasy were exported to the United States in the early 1990s. High-tech music and video trappings were encouraged by low-tech laboratories that illegally manufactured the drug and shipped it into this country. Because of these sensory-enriched environments, Ecstasy became the drug of choice for many young people in the United States (Cloud, 2000) and globally (UNODC, 2009) who wee looking for a novel "chemical" experience. To this day, the rave phenomenon continues to be a major attraction to youthful participants and an excuse for heavy MDMA use and its associated overdose emergencies (Lin, 2015).

International seizures of MDMA in 2007 were almost double those reported for 1998 (Power, 2015; UNODC, 2009). However, compared to methamphetamine, global seizures of Ecstasy have been low and were less than five tons annually from 2009 to 2013 (UNODC, 2015). Currently, more than 90% of these illegal drugs originate in European countries such as the Netherlands and Belgium, which are the principal sources for Ecstasy smuggled into the United States (UNODC, 2009). However, the number of U.S. homegrown labs that produce MDMA and methamphetamine recently increased, despite the fact that the process of making MDMA is hazardous and the chemicals used for synthesis are difficult to obtain (Friends of Narconon, 2010).

Because of its frequent association with raves, clubs, and bars, MDMA is known as a club drug. At its peak in 2001, Ecstasy was used by 9.2% of all U.S. high school seniors; since this time, its abuse has been reduced by more than half (Johnston, 2019).

Some observers have compared the rave culture and its use of MDMA to the acid-test parties of the 1960s and the partygoers' use of LSD and amphetamines ("Ecstasy Overdoses at a New Year's Eve Rave," 2010). Some say this drug is not likely to cause significant dependence for most casual users, but intense use appears to possibly lead to addiction. Part of the explanation for the dramatic reduction in MDMA use by young populations is likely a reaction to some highly publicized overdoses of Ecstasy and a perceived increase in the risk of this drug (Johnston, 2019).

MDMA was inadvertently discovered in 1912 by chemists at E. Merck in Darmstadt, Germany (Grob et al., 1996). No pharmaceutical company has ever manufactured MDMA for public marketing, and the FDA has never approved it for therapy. MDMA was first found by the DEA on the streets in 1972 in a drug sample bought in Chicago (Beck, 1990). The DEA earnestly began gathering data on MDMA abuse a decade later, which led to its classification as a Schedule I substance in 1985, despite the highly vocal opposition of psychiatrists who had been giving

MDMA to patients since the late 1970s to facilitate communication, acceptance, and fear reduction (Beck, 1990). A growing number of health professionals believe that MDMA should be made available to clinicians for the treatment of some psychiatric disorders such as fear and anxiety (Skomorowsky, 2015; Stone, 2019; Waugh, 2015). In fact, with FDA approval, small trial studies have been conducted to test the safety of this drug and its potential value in treating conditions such as PTSD in combination with psychotherapy is currently being evaluated in Phase 3 studies. Although the outcome of these clinical trials has yet to be determined by the FDA, the researchers have publicly stated that they are hopeful that MDMA treatment will be an effective option to relieving the suffering of highly stressed patients (Stone, 2019). It is likely that the increased public support for such MDMA studies is partly the result of increased success of states to pass laws that allow the legal use of marijuana and some of its active hallucinogenic ingredients to treat similar stress-related problems (Doblin, 2019).

MDMA and related designer amphetamines are somewhat unique from other amphetamines in that, besides causing excitation, they have prominent psychedelic effects (Drugs.com, 2014). These drugs have been characterized as combining the properties of amphetamine and LSD (Drugs.com, 2014; Luscher, 2015). The psychedelic effects of MDMA are likely caused by the release of the neurotransmitter serotonin (Drugs.com, 2014). After using hallucinogenic amphetamines, the mind is often flooded with irrelevant and incoherent thoughts and exaggerated sensory experiences and is more receptive to suggestion.

MDMA often is viewed as a "smooth amphetamine" and does not appear to cause the severe

Dancers at a rave often consume Ecstasy for sensory enhancement.

depression, "crash," or violent behavior often associated with frequent high doses of the more traditional amphetamines (Drug Policy Alliance, 2015b). As previously mentioned, MDMA was originally thought to be nonaddictive; however, some reports suggest that addiction does occur when high doses of this drug are used (Addiction Center, 2016a). Many users tend to be predominantly positive when describing their initial MDMA experiences. They claim the drug causes them to dramatically drop their defense mechanisms or fear responses while feeling increased empathy for others (Nutt, 2015). Combined with its stimulant effects, this action often increases intimate communication and association with others. However, heavy users often experience adverse effects such as loss of appetite, teeth grinding, muscle aches and stiffness, sweating, rapid heartbeat, hostility, anxiety, and altered sleep patterns (Davis, 2015). In addition, fatigue can be experienced for hours or even days after use. In high doses, MDMA can cause panic attacks and severe anxiety (Davis, 2015). Evidence suggests that high doses can significantly damage serotonin neurons or other systems in the brain and cause long-term memory deficits and psychological disturbances in some people (Davis, 2015). The duration of these high-dose CNS effects has not been determined and may vary based on the intensity of the bingeing (Hahn, 2015).

Recreational use of Ecstasy has been linked to physical emergencies and even occasional fatalities that are similar to those caused by amphetamines and cocaine (Hahn, 2015). The leading causes of deaths associated with MDMA use appear to be complications from hyperthermia (related to heatstroke), metabolic problems, and underlying heart problems (Juergen, 2019).

Because of its frequent association with raves, clubs, and bars, MDMA is known as a *club drug*.

Because of its popularity, occasional spin-off Ecstasy drugs show up in dance clubs frequented by young people such as *n*-benzylpiperazine, or BZP. This drug is sold in the shape of cartoon characters and has a chemistry that resembles that of MDMA. BZP is not available in pharmacies but can be purchased over the Internet and has been used in the club scene since the 1990s. However, the pharmacology of this drug looks more like that of the amphetamines than MDMA because its stimulant effects cause feelings of euphoria, alertness, and increased energy. With high doses, BZP induces a state of paranoia and anxiety accompanied by increased heart rate, blood pressure, and body temperature. However, when combined with another MDMA spin-off drug called TFMPP (trifluoromethylphneylpiperazine), it has MDMA-like effects (Keoni, 2015).

## METHYLPHENIDATE: A SPECIAL AMPHETAMINE

Methylphenidate (Ritalin) is related to the amphetamines but is a relatively mild CNS stimulant, especially when used orally. Although used as a treatment to alleviate depression, research now casts doubt on its effectiveness. It is effective in treating narcolepsy (a sleep disorder). As explained previously, Ritalin has also been found to help calm children and adults suffering from ADHD, which is characterized by an inability to focus attention and increased impulsivity, making it difficult to stay on task. ADHD can also result in impaired learning abilities and lead to social and personal frustrations (Storebo et al., 2015; WebMD, n.d.). Like Adderall (amphetamine) and Provigil (modafinil), Ritalin is routinely used to treat ADHD in both children and adults. Use of these drugs can improve scholastic performance in 70% of those with ADHD. Ritalin is frequently the drug of choice for this indication (Zheng et al., 2015). The stimulant potency of Ritalin lies between that of caffeine and amphetamine. Although it is not used much on the street by hard-core drug addicts, there are increasingly more frequent reports of use by high school and college students because of claims that it helps them to "study better," "party harder," and enhance their "performance" in general (Addiction Center,

2016b). It is important that methylphenidate be taken only as prescribed to avoid problems of dependence or addiction (Mayo Clinic, 2016). Recent statistics from the *Monitoring the Future* survey suggest that 2.0% of high school seniors used this drug for nonmedical purposes in 2015 (Johnston, 2016). Because of its potential for abuse, some critics claim its medical use in the treatment of childhood ADHD may increase the likelihood that patients will later abuse drugs; however, recent studies have not been able to confirm or disprove these claims, and clearly more research is needed to address this concern (Humphreys, Eng, & Lee, 2013).

High doses of Ritalin can cause tremors, seizures, and strokes. Ritalin has been classified as a Schedule II drug like the other prescribed amphetamines. Its principal mechanism of action is to block the reuptake of dopamine and noradrenaline into their respective neurons; thus, its pharmacological action is more like cocaine than methamphetamine.

## PERFORMANCE ENHANCERS

**Performance enhancers** is a term frequently used to describe stimulants such as amphetamines or methylphenidate, and other drugs that are taken to increase physical or mental endurance to embellish personal performance and achieve a more positive outcome (Khazan, 2015b). As illustrated in the following real-life example, some college students have come to rely on these drugs to get through the stressful challenges of school:

Janell (real name withheld), a college sophomore, is only one of all too many students who pray for a miracle every finals week to help them cram in the studying time to survive this very demanding ritual. The miracle that Janell, and others like her, are hoping for comes from the stimulant effects of drugs such as Ritalin and Adderall. Recognizing the use of these substances comes with significant risk, Janell says, "I am afraid that if I keep taking Adderall during stressful times, I will become addicted." Although these "performance enhancing" drugs can be legally prescribed, the way Janell is using them is not medically sanctioned and can do her great harm. But, despite the potential for very serious consequences for this form of drug abuse, Janell responds, "If you expect me to pass five major tests in one week, you better believe

**KEY TERM**

**performance enhancers**
drugs taken to increase physical or mental endurance to embellish one's performance

that I am going to take Adderall. I need to get in the zone. Nothing else seems to work for me." (Keenan, 2010)

Unfortunately, many students and adults do not appreciate the full adverse potential of this practice, or they choose to ignore the possibility that they might become addicted, experience psychosis, or have a severe cardiovascular reaction if they routinely use the prescription stimulants for illegal nonmedical purposes (Oremus, 2013). If these drugs are not being obtained legally by prescription, then how do those who use them as performance enhancers obtain them? Often the supply comes from other students who have ADHD and a legitimate prescription and are willing to sell or give away their extra pills (see "Prescription for Abuse: Colleges Are Laboratories for Drug Neuroenhancing").

There is no argument that the popularity of these performance-enhancing substances has been increasing with many college and even high school students (Ricker & Nicolino, 2010);

however, the value and safety of this practice are being debated (Khazan, 2015b).

## BATH SALTS: A POTPOURRI OF POTENT STIMULANTS

The term *bath salts* is often used to describe a group of stimulant-containing products that frequently include synthetic drugs related to synthetic cathinones (e.g., khat) such as mephedrone, methylenedioxypyrovalerone (MDPV), flakka (α-pyrrolidinopentiophenone [α-PVP]), and other not-yet-identified analogs (NIDA, 2016a; Nordrum, 2015). Because these designer drugs of the amphetamine class typically have not been well studied in either humans or laboratory animals, their pharmacological effects are not precisely known. However, recent reports suggest that abuse of bath salts–related products can have both the stimulant and addicting properties of methamphetamine, with the hallucinogenic actions of MDMA or LSD (Hadlock et al., 2011). The following account in

---

## PRESCRIPTION FOR ABUSE

### Colleges Are Laboratories for Drug Neuroenhancing

Everyone agrees that unsupervised use of stimulants to help with studying or to improve one's performance in other intellectual or physical ways is potentially dangerous, but does it actually help improve the likelihood of success in the classroom, on the playing field, or in the workplace? The answer to this question is being debated, but there is good evidence that those who have some degree of ADHD do benefit from stimulant medications such as Adderall, Modafinil, or Ritalin and will perform better in academic endeavors (Khazan, 2015b). But what about everyone else? It is said that college campuses have become laboratories for researching pharmacological neuroenhancement. Although evidence is equivocal, a commentary in 2008 in a prestigious journal called the use of cognitive enhancement drugs inevitable and stated, "Society must respond to the growing demand . . . by rejecting the idea that 'enhancement' is a dirty word." The authors of this article went on to clarify that their statement was intended to encourage a rational and realistic approach to what they perceived as an

inevitability; that is, that in the future our society will realize that these cognitive enhancing drugs are "increasingly useful for improved quality of life and extended work productivity" (Sederer, 2009). Others counter with the argument that "advocates fail to recognize the severe personal and societal consequences that such availability would generate, looking instead to a pharmaceutical solution that would, in the end, cause more problems than it would solve" (Hessert, Medvecz, Miller, & Richard, 2009).

© Photos.com.

Hessert, A., Medvecz, A., Miller, J., & Richard, J. (2009, June 4). The new performance enhancing drugs. Neuroanthropology. Retrieved from http://neuroanthropology .net/2009/06/04/the-new-performance-enhancing-drugs; Khazan, O. (2015b). The rise of work-doping. *The Atlantic* (August 27). Retrieved from http://www .theatlantic.com/health/archive/2015/08/the-rise-of-work-doping/402373/; Sederer, L. (2010, June 1). Paying the piper: Brain "neuroenhancers." Huffington Post. Retrieved from http://www.huffingtonpost.com/lloyd-i-sederer-md/paying-the-piper-brain-ne_b_209702.html

the general press illustrates this point. In 2015, a teenager in Florida who had recently taken the amphetamine-like drug flakka ran while naked and covered in blood at police officers screaming that she was both the Devil and God. Another flakka user in Florida tried to climb over a 10-foot fence to get into the Fort Lauderdale police station and slipped and fell, impaling himself through the buttocks on a sharp fence post. It required several hours to remove him from the post (Nordrum, 2015).

Bath salts often are packaged in colorful small plastic or foil containers, frequently marketed as "Not for Human Consumption," and labeled as "Plant Food" or "Jewelry Cleaner." Buyers typically self-administer the contents of these products orally, by inhalation, or even by injection, even though some of the stimulant ingredients in these products have been classified as Schedule I substances by the federal government, and other ingredients have not even been identified yet. Common product names are Bloom, CloudNine, and Vanilla Sky, just to mention a few (NIDA, 2016a). The use of these products has resulted in thousands of alarming visits to emergency rooms across the United States by persons with a syndrome known as *excited delirium* and symptoms, including paranoia, hallucinations, psychotic behavior, dehydration, muscle damage, kidney failure, and even death (NIDA, 2016a). Government and law enforcement agencies are working hard to develop strategies to address the persistent problems associated with bath salts (NIDA, 2016a).

## ▪ Cocaine

In the past, cocaine eradication was considered a top priority. This cocaine policy reflected the fact that from 1978 to 1987 the United States experienced the largest cocaine epidemic in history. Antisocial and criminal activities related to the effects of this potent stimulant were highly visible and widely publicized.

In the 1980s, cocaine use was not believed to cause dependency because it does not cause gross withdrawal effects as do alcohol and narcotics (Goldstein, 1994). In fact, a 1982 article in *Scientific American* stated that cocaine was "no more habit forming than potato chips" (Van Dyck & Byck, 1982). This perception has clearly been proven false; cocaine is so highly addictive that it is readily self-administered not only by human beings but also by laboratory animals (Mandt, Copenhagen, Zahniser, & Allen, 2015). Surveys suggested that

2.7 million chronic and 3.0 million casual cocaine users lived in the United States as of 2007. There is no better substance than cocaine to illustrate the "love–hate" relationship that people can have with drugs. Many lessons can be learned by understanding the impact of cocaine and the ensuing social struggles as people and societies try to determine their proper relationship with this substance.

### THE HISTORY OF COCAINE USE

Cocaine has been used as a stimulant for thousands of years. Its history can be classified into three eras based on geographic, social, and therapeutic considerations. Learning about these eras can help us understand current attitudes about cocaine (Dryden-Edwards, 2019).

### THE FIRST COCAINE ERA

The first cocaine era was characterized by an almost harmonious use of this stimulant by South American Indians living in the regions of the Andes Mountains and dates back to around 2500 BC in Peru. It is believed that the stimulant properties of cocaine played a major role in the advancement of this isolated civilization, providing its people with the energy and motivation to realize dramatic social and architectural achievements while enduring tremendous hardships in barren, inhospitable environments. The *Erythroxylum coca* shrub (cocaine is found in its leaves) was held in religious reverence by these people until the time of the Spanish conquistadors (Foundation for a Drug-Free World, n.d.).

The first written description of coca chewing in the New World was by explorer Amerigo Vespucci in 1499:

> They were very brutish in appearance and behavior, and their cheeks bulged with the

An Andean Indian chews coca leaves.

leaves of a certain green herb, which they chewed like cattle, so that they could hardly speak. Each had around his neck two dried gourds, one full of that herb in their mouth, the other filled with a white flour-like powdered chalk. . . . [This was lime, which was mixed with the coca to enhance its effects.] When I asked . . . why they carried these leaves in their mouth, which they did not eat, . . . they replied it prevents them from feeling hungry, and gives them great vigor and strength. (Aldrich & Barker, 1976, p. 3)

Ironically, there are no indications that these early South American civilizations had significant social problems with cocaine, unlike the difficulties it has caused contemporary civilizations. There are three possible explanations for their lack of significant negative experiences with coca:

1. The Andean Indians maintained control of the use of cocaine. For these people, coca could only be used by the conquering aristocracy, chiefs, royalty, and other designated honorables (Aldrich & Barker, 1976).
2. These Indians used the unpurified, and less potent, form of cocaine in the coca plant.
3. Chewing the coca leaf was a slow, sustained form of oral drug administration; therefore, the effect was much less potent and less likely to cause serious dependence than the snorting, intravenous injection, or smoking techniques most often used today.

Ad created in 1894 by Jules Chéret.

The "refreshing" element in Vin Mariani was coca extract.

© Everett Collection/Shutterstock.

Sigmund Freud was an early advocate of cocaine, which he referred to as "cure-all."

### THE SECOND COCAINE ERA

A second major cocaine era began in the 19th century. During this period, scientific techniques were used to determine the pharmacology of cocaine and identify its dangerous effects. It was also during this era that the threat of cocaine to society—both its members and institutions—was first recognized (DiChiara, 1993; Musto, 1998). At about this time, scientists in North America and Europe began experimenting with a purified, white, powdered extract made from the coca plant.

In the last half of the 19th century, Corsican chemist Angelo Mariani removed the active ingredients from the coca leaf and identified cocaine. This purified cocaine was added into cough drops and into a special Bordeaux wine called Vin Mariani (Musto, 1998). The pope gave Mariani a medal in appreciation for the fine work he had done developing this concoction. The cocaine extract was publicized as a magical drug that would free the body from fatigue, lift the spirits, and cause a sense of well-being, and the cocaine-laced wine became widely endorsed throughout the civilized world (Fischman & Johanson, 1996). Included in a long list of luminaries who advocated this product for an array of ailments were the Czar and Czarina of Russia; the Prince and Princess of Wales; the kings of Sweden, Norway, and Cambodia; commanders of the French and English armies; President McKinley of the United States; H. G. Wells; August Bartholdi (sculptor of the Statue of Liberty); and some 8,000 physicians.

The astounding success of this wine attracted imitators, all making outlandish claims. One of these cocaine tonics was a nonalcoholic beverage named Coca-Cola, which was made from African kola nuts and advertised as the "intellectual beverage and temperance drink"; it contained four to 12 milligrams per bottle of the stimulant (DiChiara, 1993). By 1906, Coca-Cola no longer contained detectable amounts of cocaine, but caffeine had been substituted in its place. In 1884, the esteemed Sigmund Freud published his findings on cocaine in a report called *Uber Coca*. Freud enjoyed the way cocaine made him feel and recommended this "magical drug" for an assortment of medical problems, including depression, hysteria, nervous exhaustion, digestive disorders, hypochondria, "all diseases which involve degeneration of tissue," and drug addiction (PBS Newshour, 2011).

In response to a request by Freud, a young Viennese physician, Karl Köller, studied the ability of cocaine to cause numbing effects. He discovered that it was an effective local anesthetic that could be applied to the surface of the eye and permitted minor surgery to be conducted without pain. This discovery of the first local anesthetic had tremendous worldwide impact. Orders for the new local anesthetic, cocaine, overwhelmed pharmaceutical companies.

Soon after the initial jubilation over the virtues of cocaine came the sober realization that with its benefits came severe disadvantages. As more people used cocaine, particularly in tonics and patent medicines, the CNS side effects and abuse liability became painfully evident. By the turn of the 20th century, cocaine was being processed from the coca plant and purified routinely by drug companies. People began to snort or inject the purified form of this popular powder, which increased both its effects and its dangers. The controversy over cocaine exploded before the American public in newspapers and magazines.

As medical and police reports of cocaine abuse and toxicities escalated, public opinion demanded that cocaine be banned. In 1914, the Harrison Act misleadingly classified both cocaine and coca as narcotic substances (cocaine is a stimulant) and outlawed their uncontrolled use.

Although prohibited in patent and nonprescription medicines, prescribed medicinal use of cocaine continued into the 1920s. Medicinal texts included descriptions of therapeutic uses for cocaine to treat fatigue, vomiting, seasickness, melancholia, and gastritis. However, they also included lengthy warnings about excessive cocaine use, "the most insidious of all drug habits" (Aldrich & Barker, 1976).

Little of medical or social significance occurred for the next few decades (Fischman & Johanson, 1996). The medicinal use of cocaine was replaced mostly by the amphetamines during World War II because cocaine could not be supplied from South America. Cocaine is not easily synthesized, so even today most cocaine, both legal and illegal, continues to come from Columbia, Peru, and Bolivia ("Drug Supplies: Track Marks," 2016). During this period, cocaine continued to be employed for its local anesthetic action, was available on the black market, and was used recreationally by musicians, entertainers, and the wealthy. Because of the limited supply, the cost of cocaine was prohibitive for most would-be consumers. Cocaine abuse problems continued as a minor concern until the 1980s.

### THE THIRD COCAINE ERA

With the 1980s, came the third major era of cocaine use. This era started much like the second in that the public and even the medical community were naive and misinformed about the drug. Cocaine was viewed as a glamorous substance and portrayed by the media as the drug of celebrities. Its use by prominent actors, athletes, musicians, and other members of a fast-paced, elite society was common knowledge. By 1982, more than 20 million Americans had tried cocaine in one form or another, compared with only 5 million in 1974 (Green, 1985).

The following is an example of a report from a Los Angeles television station in the early 1980s, which was typical of the misleading information being released to the public:

> Cocaine may actually be no more harmful to your health than smoking cigarettes or drinking alcohol; at least that's according to a [six]-year study of cocaine use [described in *Scientific American*]. It concludes that the drug is relatively safe and, if not taken in large amounts, it is not addictive. (Byck, 1987)

With such visibility, an association with prestige and glamour, and what amounted to indirect endorsements by medical experts, the stage was set for another epidemic of cocaine use. Initially, the high cost of this imported substance limited its use. With increased demand, however, came increased supply, and prices tumbled from an unaffordable $100 per "fix" to an affordable $10. The epidemic began.

By the mid-1980s, cocaine permeated all elements of society. No group of people or part of the country was immune from its effects. Many tragic stories were told of athletes, entertainers, corporate executives, politicians, fathers and mothers, high school students, and even children using and abusing cocaine. It was no longer the drug of the laborer or even the rich and famous. It was everybody's drug and everybody's problem (Golding, 1993). As one user recounted,

> It started out with me selling. I loved money; figured I could sell a little cocaine. I didn't use. I had a child to consider. I looked respectable. . . . Then I fell for a customer. A heavy user. I started using with him. Big mistake. . . . Later, when I got honest, I could see he was in love with my cocaine, not me. . . . Soon I didn't take care of my child. . . . I was always in that triple cycle: about to get high, was high, or was crashing. . . . Then my supplier didn't get paid. Dangerous. I wasn't together enough to deal and I owed money everywhere. . . . I wanted to stop, so why couldn't I? What was up with that? Denial, addiction's long shadow, is vital to the addict's psyche. Without it, we quit or commit suicide. . . . I began to look bad, smell bad and talk bad. I couldn't see over the piles of shame to life without coke. . . . I was no longer able to fake normal. I was too scary, a low-bottom addict who didn't have a key to my name (no car, no house, no office). . . . Somehow I go to detox. Somehow, I began the slow climb back to civilization. It was [six] months before the fog lifted. Six months before I could think in a straight line. I don't refer to myself as normal. Most of the people I sold to are now dead or destroyed. (Barnes, 2013)

Cocaine availability decreased sharply in the United States in 2009, resulting in an increase in price for a pure gram of cocaine from about $95 in 2006 to $175 toward the end of 2009. The purity of cocaine also diminished during this time, from 68% to 46%. The reasons for the shortages of cocaine at this time were thought to relate to several factors, including decreased production in Colombia and increased seizures of cocaine destined for Mexico and trafficking into the United States (Beckhusen, 2013). However, it

is important to appreciate that these trends can reverse themselves quickly and that the United States by far is the largest consumer of cocaine in the world (Baynes, 2019).

## COCAINE PRODUCTION

Because cocaine is derived from the coca plant, which is imported from the Andean countries, the problems with this drug in the United States have had profound effects on several South American countries. With the dramatic rise in U.S. cocaine demand in the early 1980s, coca production in South America increased to meet that demand. The coca crop is by far the most profitable agricultural venture in some of these countries. In addition, it is easily cultivated and maintained (the coca plant is a perennial and remains productive for decades) and can be harvested several times a year (two to four on average). The coca harvest has brought many jobs and some prosperity to these struggling economies; however, it has come at a significant environmental cost from the slash-and-burn techniques used to clear spots for coca bush cultivation and resulting in deforestation and damaging soil (UNODC, 2015).

U.S. coca-eradication program allegedly has seriously influenced the fragile economies of poor Latin American countries, such as Bolivia and Peru, causing anti-American sentiment, especially in poor rural communities that depend on money from their coca crops (Briceno, 2015). This is illustrated by the following account of a poor coca farmer in Peru:

> Duran uses a machete to harvest coca leaves from a plot of small plot of land damaged by a U.S.-backed eradication campaign that affected almost 500,000 Peruvians. "This is what we live off," Duran complains, "Nobody buys anything but coca." Duran and her family tried planting and selling bananas after their coca harvested was destroyed by the eradication effort but could not make enough money to survive so they returned to planting and selling coca which was much more lucrative and easier to manage. A local counter-narcotics police who is charged with enforcing the coca elimination policies sympathizes with the frustrations of these poor farmers and claims, "They are very poor people. They drop to their knees and beg us to leave them a little (coca), because that's what they live off." (Briceno, 2015)

In addition, the spraying of herbicides from U.S.-piloted aircraft to destroy coca harvests is suspected of posing health hazards to the native populations. Because of these problems, there is evidence that the attempts by the U.S. government to control cocaine abuse by eliminating coca crops have been frustrating. Despite this, coca bush cultivation has declined to its lowest level since the mid-1980s. It appears that some of this decline in cocaine cultivation is the result of successful law enforcement efforts (UNODC, 2015).

Trafficking of illegal cocaine is highly profitable and often extremely dangerous (see "Here and Now: Bloody 'Drug War' Fought in Streets of Mexico"). Because of the highly addictive nature of cocaine and the profits associated with the illegal purchasing and selling of this drug, criminal groups frequently engage in violent struggles for control of the cocaine market. For example, Central America has become the location for some of the most deadly cities in the world, causing Honduras to be designated as the country with the highest homicide rate in the world at 82 murders per 100,0000 people (Drug Policy Alliance, 2015a). In some ways, it is like playing whack-a-mole. As efforts to shut down drug cartels in Mexico intensify, the cartels tend to pop up elsewhere. As a result, drug-related crime has been increasing in Caribbean countries. For example, with increased cocaine seizures in Columbia and Mexico, the Dominican Republic has developed into a main transit point for shipping this drug into both the United States and Europe (Baynes, 2019; "Dominican Republic Emerges," 2013). Solutions are elusive, and it is clear that without a significant reduction in demand the profit from producing, trafficking, and selling cocaine will remain high and attractive to illegal and dangerous groups.

## COCAINE PROCESSING

As previously noted, cocaine is one of several active ingredients from the leaves of the *Erythroxylum coca* plant. The leaves are harvested two to four times per year and used to produce coca paste, which contains as much as 80% cocaine. The paste is processed in clandestine laboratories to form a pure, white hydrochloride salt powder. Purified cocaine is often **adulterated** (or *cut*) with substances such as powdered sugar, talc, arsenic, lidocaine, strychnine, and methamphetamine before it is sold on the streets. Adverse responses

### KEY TERM

**adulterated**
when contaminated substances are mixed in drugs to dilute them

# HERE AND NOW
## Bloody "Drug War" Fought in Streets of Mexico

Drug cartels ship hundreds of tons of cocaine to the United States. Because of the billions of dollars that can be made from this illegal market, gangs fight each other for control of cocaine production and merchandising. This competition frequently turns violent. In Mexico, approximately 164,000 people were killed between 2007 and 2014, with more than half likely associated with the drug wars. Such blatant violence has become almost a way of life in some parts of Mexico, but perhaps the most shocking aspect of these acts of wanton homicide is that most of the victims had nothing whatsoever to do with the drug cartels or the government forces fighting each other over drug-related issues. These people just happened to be in the wrong place at the wrong time and were innocently killed.

Such violence has everyone wondering how this can be stopped. Is victory even possible in the war against the drug cartels?

© Bernardino Hernandez/AP/Shutterstock.

Data from Breslow, J. (2015). The staggering death toll of Mexico's drug war. *Frontline*. Retrieved from http://www.pbs.org/wgbh/frontline/article/the-staggering-death-toll-of-mexicos-drug-war/; Grillo, I. (2016, January 15). Why cartels are killing Mexico's mayors. *The New York Times*. Retrieved from http://www.nytimes.com/2016/01/17/opinion/sunday/why-cartels-are-killing-mexicos-mayors.html?_r=0

Courtesy of Orange County Police Department, Florida.

Cocaine is often sold in a form that appears like small rocks.

to street cocaine are sometimes caused by the additives, not the cocaine itself. The resultant purity of the cut material ranges from 10% to 85% (Stewart, 2013).

Cocaine is often sold in the form of little pellets called *rocks* or as flakes or powder. If it is in pellet form, it must be crushed before use. Street names used for these cocaine products have included *big flake, crack, gold dust, lime, Snow White, snow cones, white powder,* and *white mosquito* (Buddy T., 2019).

## CURRENT ATTITUDES AND PATTERNS OF ABUSE

Given contemporary medical advances, we now have a greater understanding of the effects of cocaine and its toxicities and the dependence it produces. The reasons why people abuse cocaine are better understood as well. For example, it has been suggested that some chronic cocaine users are self-medicating their psychiatric disorders, such as depression, attention-deficit disorders, and

anxiety (Gorelick, 2015). Such knowledge helps in identifying and administering effective treatment. The hope is that society will never again be fooled into thinking that cocaine abuse is glamorous or an acceptable form of entertainment. Attempts are being made to use this understanding (either recently acquired or merely relearned) to educate people about the true nature of cocaine. Surveys have revealed that, in general, cocaine use has become less acceptable (see **Figure 10.1**). From 1992 to 1999, cocaine use rose among high school seniors but leveled off to about 4% to 5% during much of the first decade of the 2000s, dropping to 1.5% by 2018 (Johnston, 2019). A recent corresponding reduction in other markers of cocaine use includes decreases in chronic and frequent users, treatment admissions, and accidental overdoses. Possible explanations for this reduction include (1) reduced Colombian coca available for cocaine production, (2) the crackdown on cocaine traffickers in Mexico because of drug-related violence, (3) increased non-U.S. demand for cocaine, and (4) reduced U.S. demand for this potent stimulant.

## COCAINE ADMINISTRATION

Cocaine can be administered orally, inhaled into the nasal passages, injected intravenously, or smoked. The form of administration is important in determining the intensity of cocaine's effects, its abuse liability, and the likelihood of toxicity (DEA, 2015).

Oral administration of cocaine produces the least potent effects; most of the drug is destroyed in the gut or liver before it reaches the brain. The result is a slower onset of action with a milder,

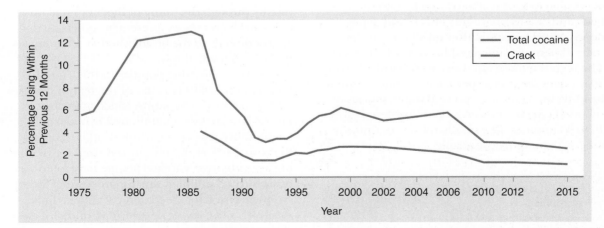

**FIGURE 10.1** Trends in cocaine and crack use by high school seniors, 1990–2018. These data represent the percentages of high school seniors surveyed who reported using cocaine during the year.

Data from Johnston, L. (2019). *Monitoring the Future 2018*. Retrieved from http://monitoringthefuture.org/pubs/monographs/mtf-overview2018.pdf

more sustained stimulation. This form is least likely to cause health problems and dependence. South American Indians still take cocaine orally to increase their strength and for relief from fatigue. Administration usually involves prolonged chewing of the coca leaf, resulting in the consumption of about 20 to 400 milligrams of the drug (Narconon, 2016b). Oral use of cocaine is not common in the United States.

*Snorting* involves inhaling cocaine hydrochloride powder into the nostrils, where deposits form on the lining of the nasal chambers (Narconon, 2016b). Substantial CNS stimulation occurs in several minutes, persists for 30 to 40 minutes, and then subsides. The effects occur more rapidly and are shorter lasting and more intense than those achieved with oral administration because more of the drug enters the brain more quickly. Because concentrations of cocaine in the body are higher after snorting than after oral ingestion, the side effects are more severe. One of the most common consequences of snorting cocaine is rebound depression—a *crash*—that is of little consequence after oral consumption. As a general rule, the intensity of the depression correlates with the intensity of the euphoria.

According to studies performed by the National Institute on Drug Abuse (NIDA), 10% to 15% of those who try intranasal (snorting) cocaine go on to heavier forms of dosing, such as intravenous administration. Intravenous administration of cocaine is a relatively recent phenomenon because the hypodermic needle was not widely available until the late 1800s. This form of administration contributed to many of the cocaine problems that appeared at the turn of the 20th century. Intravenous administration allows large amounts of cocaine to be introduced rapidly into the body and causes severe side effects and dependence. Within seconds after injection, cocaine users experience an incredible state of euphoria. The high is intense but short lived; within 15 to 20 minutes the user experiences dysphoria and is heading for a crash. To prevent these unpleasant rebound effects, cocaine is readministered every 10 to 30 minutes. Readministration continues as long as there is drug available (NIDA, 2013).

## KEY TERM

**freebasing**
conversion of cocaine into its alkaline form for smoking

This binge activity resembles that seen in the methamphetamine *run*, except it is usually shorter in duration. When the cocaine supply is exhausted, the binge is over. Several days of abstinence may separate these episodes. The average cocaine addict binges once to several times a week, with each binge lasting four to 24 hours. Cocaine addicts claim that all thoughts turn toward cocaine during binges; everything else loses significance. This pattern of intense use is how some people blow all of their money on cocaine.

**Freebasing** is a method of reducing impurities in cocaine and preparing the drug for smoking. It produces a type of cocaine that is more powerful than normal cocaine hydrochloride. One way to freebase is to treat the cocaine hydrochloride with a liquid base such as sodium carbonate or ammonium hydroxide. The cocaine dissolves, along with many of the impurities commonly found in it (such as amphetamines, lidocaine, sugars, and others). A solvent such as petroleum or ethyl ether is added to the liquid to extract the cocaine. The solvent containing the cocaine floats to the top and is drawn off with an eyedropper; it is placed in an evaporation dish to dry, and crystalized cocaine residue is then crushed into a fine powder, which can be smoked in a special glass pipe (RehabPathway, n.d.).

The effects of smoked cocaine are as intense or even more intense than those achieved through intravenous administration. The onset is nearly instantaneous, the euphoria is dramatic, the depression is severe, the side effects are dangerous, and the chances of dependence are high. The reason for these intense reactions to inhaling cocaine into the lungs is that the drug passes rapidly through the lining of the lungs and into the many blood vessels present; it is then carried almost directly to the brain, where it accumulates quickly (RehabPathway, n.d.).

Freebasing became popular in the United States in the 1980s because of the fear of diseases such as AIDS and hepatitis, which are transmitted by sharing contaminated hypodermic needles. But freebasing involves other dangers. Because the volatile solvents required for freebasing are explosive, careless people have been seriously burned or killed during processing. Street synonyms used for freebased cocaine include *snow coke*, *rocks*, *candy*, *nuggets*, *sleet*, and *tornado* (Sclar, 2019).

Freebasing paraphernalia. A water pipe is often used to smoke freebased cocaine, or *crack*. Cocaine administered by smoking is extremely potent and fast-acting; the effect lasts for 10 to 15 minutes, after which depression occurs. This is the most addicting form of cocaine.

## CRACK COCAINE

Beginning in 1985 and 1986, a special type of freebased cocaine known as **crack** appeared on the streets (RehabPathway, n.d.). By 1999, approximately 2.7% of high school seniors had tried crack. As of 2018, this number was down to 0.6% (Johnston, 2019). Crack can be smoked without the dangerous explosive solvents mentioned earlier in the discussion of freebasing. It is made by taking powdered cocaine hydrochloride and adding sodium bicarbonate (baking soda) and water. The paste that forms removes impurities as well as the hydrochloride from the cocaine. The substance is then dried into hard pieces called *rocks* that may contain as much as 90% pure cocaine. Like freebased cocaine, crack is usually smoked in a glass water pipe. When the fumes are absorbed into the lungs, they act rapidly, reaching the brain within eight to 10 seconds. An intense rush or high results, and later a powerful state of depression or crash occurs. The high may last only three to five minutes, and the depression may persist from 10 to 40 minutes or longer in some cases. As soon as crack is smoked, the nervous system is greatly stimulated by the release of dopamine, which seems to be involved in the rush. Cocaine prevents resupply of this neurotransmitter, which may trigger the crash.

Because of the abrupt and intense release of dopamine, smoked crack is viewed as a drug with tremendous potential for addiction and antisocial behavior (RehabPathway, n.d.). Some users consider it to be more enjoyable than cocaine administered intravenously. Crack and cocaine marketing and use are often associated with criminal activity such as robberies and homicides (RehabPathway, n.d.).

In general, crack use has been more common among African American and Hispanic populations than among white Americans. Of special concern is the use of crack among women during pregnancy. Children born under these circumstances have been referred to as *crack babies*. Even though the effects of crack on fetal development are not fully understood, many clinicians and researchers have predicted that these crack babies will impose an enormous social burden as they grow up. However, other experts have expressed concern that the impact of cocaine on the fetus is grossly overstated and have suggested that behavioral problems seen in these children are more a consequence of social environment than direct pharmacological effects. This issue is discussed in greater detail later in this section.

It is not coincidental that the popularity of crack use paralleled the AIDS epidemic in the mid-1980s. Because crack administration does not require injection, theoretically the risk of contracting HIV from contaminated needles is avoided. Even so, HIV infection still occurs in crack users because many crack smokers also use cocaine intravenously, thereby increasing their chances of becoming infected with HIV. Another reason for HIV infection (as well as other sexually transmitted diseases such as syphilis and gonorrhea) among crack users is the dangerous sexual behaviors in which these people engage (Science Daily, 2010). Not only is crack commonly used as payment for sex, but also its users are much

## KEY TERM

**crack**
already processed and inexpensive "freebased" cocaine ready for smoking

less inclined to be cautious about their sexual activities while under the influence of this drug (Ladd & Petry, 2003).

## MAJOR PHARMACOLOGICAL EFFECTS OF COCAINE

Cocaine can profoundly affect several vital systems in the body (RehabPathway, n.d.). With the assistance of modern technology, the mechanisms whereby cocaine alters body functions have become better understood. Such knowledge may eventually lead to better treatment of cocaine dependence.

Most of the pharmacological effects of cocaine use stem from enhanced activity of catecholamine (dopamine, noradrenaline, adrenaline) and serotonin transmitters. It is believed that the principal action of the drug is to block the reuptake and inactivation of these substances following their release from neurons. Such action prolongs the activity of these transmitter substances at their receptors and substantially increases their effects. The summation of cocaine's effects on these four transmitters causes CNS stimulation (RehabPathway, n.d.). The increase of noradrenaline activity following cocaine administration increases the effects of the sympathetic nervous system and alters cardiovascular activity.

## CNS EFFECTS

Because cocaine has stimulant properties, it has antidepressant effects as well. Some users self-administer cocaine to relieve severe depression or the negative symptoms of schizophrenia, but in general its short-term action and abuse liability make cocaine unsatisfactory for the treatment of depression disorders. The effects of stimulation appear to increase both physical and mental performance while masking fatigue. High doses of cocaine cause euphoria (based on the form of administration) and enhance the sense of strength, energy, and performance. Because of these positive effects, cocaine has intense reinforcing properties that encourage continual use and dependence (RehabPathway, n.d.).

Cocaine addicts can often distinguish between the two phenomena of the rush and the high associated with cocaine administration. Both the rush and the high peak about three minutes after use. The rush seems to be associated with elevated heart rate, sweating, and feelings of "speeding" or "being out of control"; the high includes feelings of euphoria, self-confidence, well-being, and sociability. Drug craving also occurs rapidly and is evident as soon as 12 minutes after administration. Interestingly, brain scans of cocaine users have demonstrated that specific brain regions are associated with these drug effects; thus, the rush and craving are linked with different regions of the limbic system in the brain (Stocker, 1999).

The feeling of exhilaration and confidence caused by cocaine can easily become transformed into irritable restlessness and confused hyperactivity (APA, 2013). In addition, high chronic doses alter personality, frequently causing psychotic behavior that resembles paranoid schizophrenia (RehabPathway, n.d.). For example, in her interview with Peter Venturelli, a 17-year-old female explained that a cocaine-abusing friend "was so coked up that he carved the word 'pain' in his arm and poured coke on it. He thought it symbolized something." In addition, cocaine use heightens the risk of suicide, major trauma, and violent crimes (RehabPathway, n.d.). In many ways, the CNS effects of cocaine resemble those of amphetamines, although perhaps with a more rapid onset, a more intense high (partially because of the manner in which the drugs are administered), and a shorter duration of action (APA, 2013). Besides dependence, other notable CNS toxicities that can be caused by cocaine use include headaches, temporary loss of consciousness, seizures, and death.

## CARDIOVASCULAR SYSTEM EFFECTS

Cocaine can initiate pronounced changes in the cardiovascular system by enhancing the sympathetic nervous system, increasing the levels of adrenaline, and causing vasoconstriction (Luscher, 2015). The initial effects of cocaine are to increase heart rate and elevate blood pressure. While the heart is being stimulated and working harder, the vasoconstriction effects deprive the cardiac muscle of needed blood (Fischman & Johanson, 1996). Such a combination can cause severe heart arrhythmia (an irregular contraction pattern) or heart attack. Other degenerative processes have also been described in the hearts and blood vessels of chronic cocaine users (Kloner & Rezkalla, 2003). In addition, the vasoconstrictive action of this sympathomimetic can damage other tissues, leading to stroke, lung damage in those who smoke cocaine, destruction of nasal cartilage in those who snort the drug, and injury to the gastrointestinal tract (Goodger, Wang, & Pogrel, 2005).

## LOCAL ANESTHETIC EFFECTS

Cocaine was the first local anesthetic used routinely in modern-day medicine (Drasner, 2012). Some people speculate that in ancient times the Indians of the South American Andes Mountains used cocaine-filled saliva from chewing coca leaves as a local anesthetic for surgical procedures (Aldrich & Barker, 1976), although this assumption has been contested by others (Byck, 1987). Even so, cocaine is still used as a local anesthetic for minor pharyngeal (back part of the mouth and upper throat area) surgery because of its good vasoconstriction (reduces bleeding) and topical, local numbing effects. Although relatively safe when applied topically, significant amounts of cocaine can enter the bloodstream and, in sensitive people, cause CNS stimulation, toxic psychosis, or, on rare occasions, death (Mayo Clinic, 2010).

## COCAINE WITHDRAWAL

Considerable debate has arisen as to whether cocaine withdrawal actually happens and, if so, what it involves. With the most recent cocaine epidemic and the high incidence of intense, chronic use, it has become apparent that nervous systems do become tolerant to cocaine and that, during abstinence, withdrawal symptoms occur (Narconon, 2013). In fact, because of CNS dependence, the use of cocaine is less likely to be stopped voluntarily than is the use of many other illicit drugs (Sofuoglu, Dudish-Poulsen, Brown, & Hatsukami, 2003). Certainly, if the withdrawal experience is adverse enough, a user will be encouraged to resume the cocaine habit.

The extent of cocaine withdrawal is proportional to the duration and intensity of use. The physical withdrawal symptoms are relatively minor compared with those caused by long-term use of CNS depressants and by themselves are not considered to be life threatening (MedlinePlus, 2007).

Short-term withdrawal symptoms include depression (chronic cocaine users are 60 times more likely to commit suicide than nonusers), sleep abnormalities, craving for the drug, agitation, and anhedonia (inability to experience pleasure). Long-term withdrawal effects include a return to normal pleasures, accompanied by mood swings and occasional craving triggered by cues in the surroundings (APA, 2013; Mendelson & Mello, 1996; Narconon, 2013).

Of particular importance to the treatment of chronic cocaine users is that abstinence after bingeing appears to follow three unique stages, each of which must be dealt with in a different manner to prevent relapse. These phases are classified as phase 1 or *crash* (occurs 24 hours to two days after drug use is stopped), phase 2 or *withdrawal* (one to 10 weeks), and phase 3 or *extinction* (indefinite). The basic features of these phases are outlined in **Table 10.2** (APA, 2013).

## TREATMENT OF COCAINE DEPENDENCE

Cocaine dependence is classified as a psychiatric disorder by the American Psychiatric Association (APA, 2013) and results in many persons seeking treatment for drug addiction (Platt, Rowlett, & Spealman, 2002). Treatment of this condition has improved as experience working with these patients has increased. Even so, success rates vary for different programs. The problem with program assessments is that they often do not take into account patients who drop out. Also, no clear-cut criteria for qualifying success have been established. For example, is success considered to be abstaining from cocaine for one year, two years, five years, or forever?

No one treatment technique has been found to be significantly superior to others or universally effective (MedlinePlus, 2010; NIDA, 2010), nor is there a particularly effective medication

**TABLE 10.2** Cocaine Abstinence Phases

| Phase 1: "Crash" | Phase 2: Withdrawal | Phase 3: Extinction |
|---|---|---|
| 24–48 hours since last binge | 1–10 weeks since last binge | Indefinite since last binge |
| *Initial*: Agitation, depression, anorexia, suicidal thoughts | *Initial*: Mood swings, sleep returns, some craving, little anxiety | Normal pleasure, mood swings, occasional craving, cues trigger craving |
| *Middle*: Fatigue, no craving, insomnia | *Middle and late*: Anhedonia, anxiety, intense craving, obsessed with drug seeking | |
| *Late*: Extreme fatigue, no craving, exhaustion | | |

Data from Garwin, F. (1991). Cocaine addiction: Psychology and neurophysiology. *Science, 251*, 1580–1586.

to treat cocaine addiction (Platt et al., 2002). Consequently, substantial disagreement exists as to the best strategy for treating cocaine dependency. Efforts are ongoing by federal agencies and scientists to find effective therapy for cocaine addiction. Most treatments are directed at relieving craving. Major differences in treatment approaches include (1) whether outpatient or inpatient status is deemed appropriate, (2) which drugs and what dosages are used to treat patients during the various stages of abstinence, and (3) what length of time the patient is isolated from cocaine-accessible environments.

It is important to treat each individual patient according to his or her unique needs. Questions that need to be considered when formulating a therapeutic approach include the following:

- Why did the patient begin using cocaine, and why has dependency occurred?
- What is the severity of abuse?
- How has the cocaine been administered?
- What is the psychiatric status of the patient? Are there underlying or coexisting mental disorders, such as depression or attention-deficit disorder?
- What other drugs are being abused along with the cocaine?
- What is the patient's motivation for eliminating cocaine dependence?
- What sort of support system (family, friends, coworkers, and so on) will sustain the patient in the abstinence effort?

## OUTPATIENT VERSUS INPATIENT APPROACHES

The decision as to whether to treat a patient who is dependent on cocaine as an outpatient or an inpatient is based on several factors. For example, inpatient techniques allow greater control than outpatient treatment; thus, the environment can be better regulated, the training of the patient can be more closely supervised, and the patient's responses to treatment can be more closely monitored. In contrast, the advantages of the outpatient approach are that supportive family and friends are better able to encourage the patient, the surroundings are more comfortable and natural, and potential problems that might occur when the patient returns to a normal lifestyle are more likely to be identified. In addition, outpatient treatment is less expensive.

Cocaine-dependent patients should be matched to the most appropriate strategy based on their personality, psychiatric status, and the conditions

of their addiction. For instance, a cocaine addict who lives in the inner city, comes from a home with other drug-dependent family members, and has little support probably would do better in the tightly controlled inpatient environment. However, a highly motivated cocaine addict who comes from a supportive home and a neighborhood that is relatively free of drug problems would probably do better on an outpatient basis.

## THERAPEUTIC DRUG TREATMENT

Several drugs have been used to treat cocaine abstinence, some of which are themselves active on dopamine systems, but none has been found to be universally effective (NIDA, 2016b). Besides relieving acute problems of anxiety, agitation, and psychosis, drugs can diminish cocaine craving; this effect is achieved by giving drugs such as bromocriptine or levodopa, which stimulate the dopamine transmitter system, or the narcotic buprenorphine. As mentioned, the pleasant aspects of cocaine likely relate to its ability to increase the activity of dopamine in the limbic system. When cocaine is no longer available, the dopamine system becomes less active, causing depression and anhedonia, which result in a tremendous craving for cocaine. The intent of these cocaine substitutes is to stimulate dopamine activity and relieve the cravings. Although this approach sometimes works initially, it is temporary. In the third phase of cocaine abstinence, antidepressants such as desipramine are effective for many cocaine-dependent patients in relieving underlying mood problems and occasional cravings.

The beneficial effects of these drugs are variable and not well studied (NIDA, 2016b), and there is some debate over their use. At best, drugs are only adjuncts in the treatment of cocaine dependence. Successful treatment of cocaine abuse requires intensive counseling; strong support from family, friends, and coworkers; and a highly motivated patient (NIDA, 2016b). It is important to realize that a complete "cure" from cocaine dependence is not likely; ex-addicts cannot return to cocaine and control its use.

## RECOVERY FROM COCAINE DEPENDENCE

Although numerous therapeutic approaches exist for treating cocaine addiction, successful recovery is not likely unless the individual will substantially benefit by giving up the drug. Research has shown that treatment is most likely to succeed in patients who are middle class, employed, and married; for example, 85% of addicted medical professionals recover from cocaine addiction. These people can usually be convinced that they have too much to lose in their personal and professional lives by continuing their cocaine habit. In contrast, a severely dependent crack addict who has no job, family, home, or hope for the future is not likely to be persuaded that abstinence from cocaine would be advantageous, so therapy is rarely successful. As previously mentioned, there currently is no uniformly effective pharmacological treatment available to deal with long-term cocaine addiction, although intensive research to identify such therapeutic agents is under way (NIDA, 2016b).

## POLYDRUG USE BY COCAINE ABUSERS

Treatment of most cocaine abusers is complicated by the fact that they are *polydrug* (multiple drug) users. It is unusual to find a person who abuses only cocaine. For example, many cocaine abusers also use alcohol (Pennings, Leccese, & Wolff, 2002). In general, the more severe the alcoholism, the greater the severity of the cocaine dependence. Alcohol is used to relieve some of the unpleasant cocaine effects such as anxiety, insomnia, and mood disturbances (Pennings et al., 2002). This drug combination can be dangerous for several reasons:

- The presence of both cocaine and alcohol (ethanol) in the liver results in the formation of a unique chemical product called *cocaethylene*, which is created in the reaction of ethanol with a cocaine metabolite. Cocaethylene often is found in high levels in the blood of victims of fatal drug overdoses and appears to enhance the euphoria as well as the cardiovascular toxicity of cocaine (Bazuaye-Ekwuyasi, Ogunbilege, Kaphalia, Eltorky, & Okorodudu, 2015).
- Both cocaine and alcohol can damage the liver, so their toxic effects on the liver are likely to add together when the drugs are used in combination (Pennings et al., 2002).
- The likelihood of damaging a fetus is enhanced when both drugs are used together during pregnancy (Pennings et al., 2002).
- Cardiovascular stress is increased in the presence of both drugs (Pennings et al., 2002).

Like users of amphetamines, cocaine abusers frequently coadminister narcotics such as heroin; this combination is called a *speedball* and has

been associated with a high risk for HIV infection (NIDA, 2013). Cocaine users sometimes combine their drug with other depressants such as benzodiazepines or marijuana to help reduce the severity of the crash after their cocaine binges. Codependence on cocaine and a CNS depressant can complicate treatment but must be considered. Some of the street names for cocaine mixtures include *banana* or *bazooka* (laced marijuana or cigarettes), *bipping* (snorting heroin and cocaine together), *bump* (mixing with ketamine), *candy flipping on a string* (mixing with methcathinone or inhalants), and *spaceball* (mixing with PCP) (SoberRecovery, 2015).

## COCAINE AND PREGNANCY

One consequence of widespread cocaine abuse is that since the mid-1980s many babies in the United States have been born to mothers who used cocaine during pregnancy (Fitzgerald, 2013). Cocaine use during pregnancy is highest in poor, inner-city regions. Many of these **cocaine babies** have been abandoned by their mothers and left to the welfare system for care. It is still not clear exactly what types of direct effects cocaine has on the developing fetus (Winkel, 2010). Some early studies have been criticized because (1) the pregnant populations examined were not well defined and properly matched, (2) use of other drugs (such as alcohol) with cocaine during pregnancy was often ignored, and (3) the effects of poor nutrition, poor living conditions, and traumatic lifestyles were not considered when analyzing the

### KEY TERM

**cocaine babies**
infants born to women who used cocaine during their pregnancies

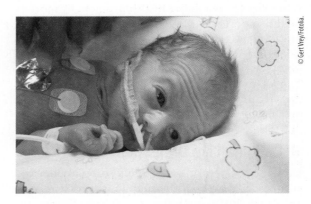

Infants born to crack-using mothers are often premature.

results. Because of these problems, much of the earlier work examining prenatal effects of cocaine is flawed, and the conclusions are questionable (Fitzgerald, 2013).

Cocaine use during pregnancy is known to cause vasoconstriction of placental vessels, thereby interfering with oxygen and nutrient exchange between mother and child, or contraction of the uterine muscles, resulting in trauma or premature birth. Even so, recent studies have suggested that prenatal cocaine exposure does not cause any long-term specific disorder or condition and its long-term effect is no greater than that of "poverty." However, some observers suggest that prenatal cocaine exposure may have minor effects on sustained attention and behavioral self-regulation (Fitzgerald, 2013; Nonacs, 2015). It is likely that this controversy is not yet resolved and will require additional study.

## Minor Stimulants

Minor stimulants enjoy widespread use in the United States because of the mild lift in mood provided by their consumption. The most popular of these routinely consumed agents are methyl-xanthines (commonly called *xanthines*) such as caffeine, which are consumed in beverages made from plants and herbs. On average, in the United States the range of daily caffeine consumption is from 20 milligrams for two- to five-year-olds and up to 220 milligrams for 50- to 64-year-olds (Lutz, 2015). Other minor stimulants are contained in OTC medications such as cold and hay fever products. Because of their frequent use, some dependence on these drugs can occur; however, serious dysfunction because of dependence is infrequent. Consequently, abuse of xanthines such as caffeine is not viewed as a major health problem by most health experts ("Is Caffeine Bad for You?" 2015). However, recently concerns have been raised that many people, especially adolescents and young adults, do not appreciate that caffeine is a drug and consume it more like food, resulting in side effects and even trips to the emergency room (Hitti, 2006).

### ■ Caffeine-Like Drugs (Xanthines)

Caffeine is a naturally occurring stimulant derived from more than 60 different plants (Caffeine Informer, 2016) and is the world's most frequently

**TABLE 10.3** Caffeine Content of Beverages and Chocolate

| Beverage | Caffeine Content (milligrams/cup) | Amount (oz.) |
|---|---|---|
| Brewed coffee | 90–135 | 5 |
| Instant coffee | 35–164 | 5 |
| Decaffeinated coffee | 1–6 | 5 |
| Tea | 25–70 | 5 |
| Cocoa | 5–25 | 5 |
| Coca-Cola | 45 | 12 |
| Pepsi-Cola | 38 | 12 |
| Mountain Dew | 70 | 12 |
| Energy drinks | 80–160 | 8–16 |
| Excedrin (OTC medication) | 65 | |
| NoDoz (OTC medication) | 34 | |
| Vivarin (OTC medication) | 200 | |
| Chocolate bar | 1–35 | 1 |

Reproduced from MedicineNet. (2010). Caffeine. Retrieved from http://www.medicinenet.com/caffeine/article.htm

used stimulant and perhaps its most popular drug ("Is Caffeine Bad for You?" 2015). Beverages and foods containing caffeine are consumed by almost all adults and children living in the United States today (see **Table 10.3**). Almost 80% of the world's population consumes caffeine daily (MedicineNet, 2010). The most common sources of caffeine include coffee beans, tea plants, kola nuts, maté leaves, guarana paste, yoco bark, and an array of herbal and so-called natural products.

Although the consumption of caffeine-containing drinks can be found throughout history, the active stimulant caffeine was identified by German and French scientists in the early 1820s. Caffeine was described as a substance with alkaloid (basic) properties that was extracted from green coffee beans and referred to as *kaffebase* by Ferdinand Runge in 1820 (Gilbert, 1984). In the course of the next 40 to 60 years, caffeine was identified in several other genera of plants that were used as sources for common beverages. These included tea leaves (originally the caffeine-like drug was called *thein*), guarana paste (originally the drug was called *guaranin*), Paraguay tea or maté, and kola nuts. Certainly, the popularity of these beverages over the centuries attests to the fact that most consumers find the stimulant effects of this drug desirable.

## THE CHEMICAL NATURE OF CAFFEINE

Caffeine belongs to a group of drugs that have similar chemical structures and are known as the **xanthines**. Besides caffeine, other xanthines include theobromine (which means "divine leaf"), discovered in cacao beans (used to make chocolate) in 1842, and theophylline (which means "divine food"), isolated from tea leaves in 1888. These three agents have unique pharmacological properties (which are discussed later), with caffeine being the most potent CNS stimulant.

## BEVERAGES CONTAINING CAFFEINE

To understand the unique role that caffeine plays in U.S. society, it is useful to gain perspective on its most common sources: unfermented beverages.

## COFFEE

Coffee is derived from the beans of several species of *Coffea*. The most widely grown species, *Coffea arabica*, grows as a shrub or small tree and reaches four to six meters in height when growing wild. Coffee beans are primarily cultivated in South America and East Africa and constitute the major cash crop for exportation in several developing countries.

The name *coffee* was likely derived from the Arabian word *kahwa* or named after Ethiopian prince Kaffa. From Ethiopia, the coffee tree was carried to Arabia and cultivated (Kihlman, 1977); it became an important element in Arabian civilization and is mentioned in writings dating back to AD 900.

Coffee probably reached Europe through Turkey and was likely used initially as a medicine. By the middle of the 17th century, coffeehouses had sprung up in England and France—places to relax, talk, and learn the news. These coffeehouses turned into the famous "penny universities" of the early 18th century where, for a penny a cup, you could listen to some of the great literary and political figures of the day.

Coffee was originally consumed in the Americas by English colonists, although tea was initially preferred. Tea was replaced by coffee following the Revolutionary War. Because tea had become a symbol of English repression, the switch to coffee was more a political statement than a change in taste. The popularity of coffee grew as U.S. boundaries moved west. In fact,

daily coffee intake continued to increase until it peaked in 1986, when annual coffee consumption averaged 10 pounds per person. Although there are concerns about the side effects associated with caffeine, this beverage still plays a major role in the lifestyles of most Americans (Caffeine Informer, 2016; MedicineNet, 2010), with approximately 56% of adults in the United States being coffee drinkers in 2006 (HealthResearchFunding.org, 2014).

## TEA

Tea is made from the *Camellia sinensis* plant, which is native to China and parts of India, Burma, Thailand, Laos, and Vietnam. Tea contains two xanthines: caffeine and theophylline. As with coffee, the earliest use of tea is not known.

Although apocryphal versions of the origin of tea credit Chinese Emperor Shen Nung for its discovery in 2737 BC, the first reliable account of the use of tea as a medicinal plant appears in an early Chinese manuscript written around AD 350. The Dutch brought the first tea to Europe in 1610, where it was accepted rather slowly; with time, it was adopted by the British as a favorite beverage and became an integral part of daily life. In fact, the tea trade constituted one of the major elements of the English economy. Tea revenues made it possible for England to colonize India and helped to bring on the Opium Wars in the 1800s, which benefited British colonialism.

The British were constantly at odds with the Dutch as they attempted to monopolize the tea trade. Even so, the Dutch introduced the first tea into America at New Amsterdam (modern-day New York City) around 1650. Later, the British gained exclusive rights to sell tea to the American colonies. Because of the high taxes levied by the British government on tea being shipped to America, tea became a symbol of British rule.

## SOFT DRINKS

The second most common source of caffeine is soft drinks. In general, the caffeine content per 12-ounce serving ranges from 30 to 60 milligrams (see Table 10.3). Soft drinks account for most of the caffeine consumed by U.S. children and teenagers; for many people, a can of cola has replaced

**KEY TERM**

**xanthines**
family of drugs that includes caffeine

the usual cup of coffee. Recently, because of its general acceptance, caffeine has been added to juices, water, and even combined with alcoholic drinks (Caffeine Informer, 2016).

Supercaffeinated energy drinks—with names like 357 Super Magnum, Wired X344, 5-Hour Energy, Adrenalin Shot, All City NRG, and Amp Lightening Charge—have dramatically increased in popularity (ShapeFit, n.d.). Approximately 30% to 60% of students 12 to 20 years of age regularly consume these energy drinks (Nowak & Jasionowski, 2015). Although manufacturers of these high-dose caffeine drinks claim they do not specifically target teenagers in their marketing strategies, most of the advertisements for these products are commonly shown on television stations with a high percentage of adolescents in their viewing base (Edmond, 2015).

The reality is that adolescents are heavy consumers of these so-called energy drinks and do not appreciate how high the caffeine doses are in these caffeine-rich products. This is evident from the reports by poison control systems and emergency rooms of dramatic increases in calls and visits by young people complaining of caffeine-related overdose symptoms such as shakiness, tremors, dizziness, nausea, vomiting, agitation, increased heart rate, and elevated blood pressure (Goodman, 2011).

Another concern relates to observations that consumption of these drinks is associated with what has become known as *toxic jock* behavior: a combination of behaviors that reflect an inclination to engage in dangerous risk taking such as unprotected sex, substance abuse, and violence— behaviors perceived as expressions of masculinity. These observations do not mean that the caffeine causes this poor decision making, but it does appear that kids who are heavily involved in consuming these beverages are more likely to ignore basic rules of common sense related to their health and safety (Levant, Parent, McCurdy, & Bradstreet, 2015).

As mentioned previously, caffeine also has been added to alcoholic beverages with names such as Four Loco and Joose. Despite claims by the manufacturers that a combination of caffeine and alcohol is "generally recognized as safe," evidence has been accumulating that, especially in underage consumers, these products pose a significant health risk. After a year-long review of evidence, complaints, and claims, the FDA concluded that this drug combination may mask

feelings of drunkenness, prompting consumers to engage in dangerous activities such as driving while under the influence of alcohol. As a result of the FDA's conclusion, caffeine–alcohol combination products have been removed from the market (Caffeine Informer, 2014).

## SOCIAL CONSEQUENCES OF CONSUMING CAFFEINE-BASED BEVERAGES

It is impossible to accurately assess the social impact of consuming beverages containing caffeine, but certainly the subtle (and sometimes not so subtle) stimulant effects of the caffeine present in these drinks have some social influence. These beverages have become integrated into social customs and ceremonies and are recognized as traditional drinks.

Today, drinks containing caffeine are consumed by many people with ritualistic devotion first thing in the morning, following every meal, and at frequent interludes throughout the day known as "coffee breaks" or "tea times." The immense popularity of these products is certainly a consequence of the stimulant actions of caffeine. Both the dependence on the "jump-start" effect of caffeine and the avoidance of unpleasant withdrawal consequences in the frequent user ensure the continual popularity of these products.

## OTHER NATURAL CAFFEINE SOURCES

Although coffee and tea are two of the most common sources of natural caffeine in the United States, other caffeine-containing beverages and food are popular in different parts of the world. Some of the most common include guarana from Brazil; maté from Argentina, southern Brazil, and Paraguay; and kola nuts from West Africa, the West Indies, and South America (Nierenberg, 2015).

## CHOCOLATE

Although chocolate contains small amounts of caffeine (see Table 10.3), the principal stimulant in chocolate is the alkaloid theobromine, named after the cocoa tree, *Theobroma cacao.* (*Theobroma* is an Aztec word meaning "fruit of the gods.") The Aztecs thought highly of the fruit and seed pods from the cacao tree, and they used the beans as a medium of exchange in bartering. The Mayans adopted the food and made a warm drink from the beans that they called *chocolatl* (meaning "warm drink"). The original chocolate drink was a thick concoction that had to be eaten with a spoon. It was unsweetened because the Mayans apparently did not know about sugarcane.

Hernán Cortés, the conqueror of Mexico, took some chocolate cakes back to Spain with him in 1528, but the method of preparing them remained a secret for nearly 100 years. Not until 1828 did the Dutch work out a process to remove much of the fat from the kernels to make a chocolate powder that was the forerunner of the cocoa we know today. The cocoa fat, or cocoa butter as it is called, was later mixed with sugar and pressed into bars. In 1847, the first chocolate bars appeared on the market. By 1876, the Swiss had developed milk chocolate, which is highly popular in today's confectioneries.

## OTHER SOURCES OF CAFFEINE

Although the consumption of beverages is by far the most common source of xanthines, many popular OTC products contain significant quantities of caffeine. For example, many OTC analgesic products (e.g., Anacin and Excedrin) contain approximately 30 to 60 milligrams of caffeine per tablet. Higher doses of 100 to 200 milligrams per tablet are included in stay-awake (NoDoz) and "picker-upper" (Vivarin) products (Kirkwood & Melton, 2012; Wilkinson, 2012). The use of caffeine in these OTC drugs is highly controversial and has been criticized by clinicians who are unconvinced of caffeine's benefits. Some critics believe that the presence of caffeine in these OTC drugs is nothing more than a psychological gimmick to entice customers through mild euphoric effects provided by this stimulant. Caffeine is also sometimes added to nonbeverage products such as vaporizers, patches, soups, gummy candies, and hot sauces (Ramsey, 2015).

Despite this criticism, it is likely that caffeine has some analgesic (pain-relieving) properties of its own (Dunwiddie & Masino, 2001). Studies suggest that 130 milligrams, but not 65 milligrams, of caffeine is superior to a placebo in relieving non-migraine headaches. In addition, the presence of caffeine has been shown to enhance aspirin-medicated relief from surgical pain (such as tooth extraction). Based on such findings, some clinicians recommend the use of caffeine in the management of some types of headaches and minor to moderate pains (Derry, Derry, & Moore, 2015).

## PHYSIOLOGICAL EFFECTS OF THE XANTHINES

The xanthines significantly influence several important body functions. Although the effects of these drugs are generally viewed as minor

and short term (Food Insight, 2015), these drugs can be dangerous when used in high doses or by people who have severe medical problems (Nierenberg, 2015). The following sections summarize the responses of the major systems to xanthines.

## CNS EFFECTS

Among the common xanthines, caffeine has the most potent effect on the CNS, followed by theophylline; for most people, theobromine has relatively little influence. Although the CNS responses of users can vary considerably, in general 100 to 200 milligrams of caffeine enhances alertness, causes arousal, and diminishes fatigue (Galanter & Boushey, 2015). Caffeine is often used to block drowsiness and facilitate mental activity, such as when cramming for examinations into the early hours of the morning. In addition, caffeine stimulates the formation of thoughts but does not improve learning ability in the wide-awake student. The effects of caffeine are most pronounced in unstimulated, drowsy consumers (Food Insight, 2015). The CNS effects of caffeine also diminish the sense of boredom (MedicineNet, 2010). Thus, people engaged in dull, repetitive tasks such as assembly-line work or nonstimulating and laborious exercises such as listening to a boring professor often consume caffeinated beverages to help compensate for the tedium. Most certainly, xanthine drinks are popular because they cause these effects on brain activity.

Adverse CNS effects usually occur with doses greater than 300 milligrams per day. Some of these include insomnia, increased tension, anxiety, and initiation of muscle twitches. Doses above 500 milligrams can be dysphoric (unpleasant) and can cause panic sensations, chills, nausea, and clumsiness. Extremely high doses of caffeine, from five to 10 grams, frequently result in seizures, respiratory failure, and death (APA, 2013).

## CARDIOVASCULAR AND RESPIRATORY EFFECTS

Drugs that stimulate the brain usually stimulate the cardiovascular system as well. The response of the heart and blood vessels to xanthines is dependent on dose and previous experience with these mild stimulants. Tolerance to the cardiovascular effects occurs with frequent use (MedicineNet, 2010). With low doses (100 to 200 milligrams), heart activity can increase, decrease, or do nothing; at higher doses (more than 500 milligrams), the rate of contraction of the heart increases. Xanthines usually cause minor vasodilation in

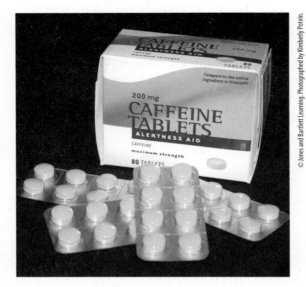

© Jones and Bartlett Learning. Photographed by Kimberly Potvin.

OTC caffeine products frequently contain the equivalent of two to three cups of coffee and are used to stay awake.

most of the body. In contrast, the cerebral blood vessels are vasoconstricted by the action of caffeine. In fact, cerebral vasoconstriction likely accounts for this drug's effectiveness in relieving some minor vascular headaches caused by vasodilation of the cerebral vessels. For most consumers the effects of caffeine on the cardiovascular system are minor, but for some people with underlying heart disease, caffeine can be dangerous ("Teen Girl Dies of 'Caffeine Toxicity,'" 2012).

Among the xanthines, theophylline has the greatest effect on the respiratory system, causing air passages to open and facilitate breathing. Because of this effect, tea has often been recommended to relieve breathing difficulties, and theophylline is frequently used to treat asthma-related respiratory problems.

### OTHER EFFECTS

The xanthines also have noteworthy—albeit mild—effects on other systems in the body. They cause a minor increase in the secretion of digestive juices in the stomach, which can be significant to individuals suffering from stomach ailments such as ulcers. These drugs also increase urine formation (as any heavy tea drinker undoubtedly knows).

### KEY TERM

**caffeinism**
symptoms caused by taking high chronic doses of caffeine

### CAFFEINE INTOXICATION

Consuming occasional low doses of the xanthines (the equivalent of four to five cups of coffee—around 400 milligrams—per day) is relatively safe for most users (Nierenberg, 2015). However, frequent use of high doses causes psychological as well as physical problems called **caffeinism**. This condition is found in about 10% of the adults who consume coffee (APA, 2013).

The CNS components of caffeine intoxication are recognized as "caffeine use disorder" in the criteria established by the American Psychiatric Association (2013) in the fifth edition of its *Diagnosis and Statistical Manual of Mental Disorders* (DSM-5). The essential features of this disorder are restlessness, nervousness, excitement, insomnia, flushed face, diuresis, muscle twitching, rambling thoughts and speech, and stomach complaints. These symptoms can occur in some sensitive people following a dose as low as 250 milligrams per day. Caffeine doses in excess of one gram per day may cause muscle twitching, rambling thoughts and speech, heart arrhythmias, and motor agitation. With higher doses, hearing ringing in the ears and seeing flashes of light can occur. Some researchers suggest that consuming large quantities of caffeine is associated with cancers of the bladder, ovaries, colon, and kidneys. These claims have not been reliably substantiated, and some evidence suggests that in moderation caffeine may protect against some cancers (Mozes, 2015).

One problem with many such studies is that they assess the effect of coffee consumption on cancers rather than the effect of caffeine itself. Because coffee contains so many different chemicals, it is impossible to determine specifically the effect of caffeine in such research. Other reports claim that caffeine promotes cyst formation in women's breasts. Although these conclusions have been challenged, some clinicians advise patients with breast cysts to avoid caffeine (American Cancer Society, 2015). Finally, some reports, but not all, indicate that extremely high doses of caffeine given to pregnant laboratory animals can cause stillbirths. However, studies found that moderate consumption of caffeine (less than 300 milligrams per day) did not significantly affect human fetal development. Generally, expectant mothers are advised to avoid or at least reduce caffeine use during pregnancy just to be safe.

Based on the information available, no strong evidence exists to suggest that moderate use of caffeine leads to disease. In fact, some research has suggested that moderate caffeine consumption may even reduce the risk of degenerative diseases of the brain such as Parkinson's disease and Alzheimer's disease (Van Dam, 2015). There are, however, implications that people with existing severe medical problems—psychiatric disorders (such as severe anxiety, panic attacks, and schizophrenia), cardiovascular disease, and possibly breast cysts—may be at greater risk when consuming caffeine. Realistically, other elements such as alcohol and fat consumption and smoking are much more likely to cause serious health problems (Van Dam, 2015).

## CAFFEINE DEPENDENCE

Caffeine causes limited dependence, which, for most people, is relatively minor compared with that of the potent stimulants; thus, the abuse potential of caffeine is much lower and dependence is less likely to interfere with normal daily routines (Food Insight, 2015). Despite this, caffeine use is thought to be possibly habit forming in some people (Haupt, 2012). Consequently, 50% of those consuming one to three cups of coffee each day develop headaches when withdrawing, and 10% become significantly depressed, anxious, or fatigued without their coffee. Some people experience elements of withdrawal every morning before their first cup and claim caffeine gives them an edge at work or in school (Hartney, 2013). However, caffeine is so readily available

**TABLE 10.4** Caffeine-Withdrawal Syndrome

| Symptom | Duration |
|---------|----------|
| Headache | Several days to 1 week |
| Decreased alertness | 2 days |
| Decreased vigor | 2 days |
| Fatigue and lethargy | 2 days |
| Nervousness | 2 days |

Bethea, A. (2015, February). The duration of caffeine withdrawal symptoms. LiveStrong.com. Retrieved from http://www.livestrong.com/article/399329-the-duration-of-caffeine-withdrawal-symptoms/

and socially accepted (almost expected) that the high quantity of consumption has produced many modestly dependent users and occasionally a trip to the emergency room (see "Here and Now: Caffeine Emergencies").

The degree of physical dependence on caffeine is highly variable but is related to dose. With typical caffeine withdrawal, adverse effects can persist for several days (see **Table 10.4**). Although these symptoms are unpleasant, they usually are not severe enough to prevent most people from giving up their coffee or cola drinks if motivated. It is noteworthy, however, that many of those patients who are treated for caffeinism relapse into their caffeine-consuming habits (Wheeler, 2010).

# HERE AND NOW
## Caffeine Emergencies

Caffeine can easily be purchased online in a pure concentrated powder form. One teaspoon of such a preparation contains a quantity of caffeine comparable to that found in 25 cups of coffee and about four times that considered to be a safe daily dose. Because of this highly concentrated caffeine source, Dr. Glenn Greeting, an emergency physician from Penn State Hershey Medical Center, has been quoted as saying that caffeine powder is even more concerning than powdered alcohol. Proof of this concern includes recent reports that the use of powdered caffeine has caused numerous caffeine overdoses nationwide resulting in hospitalization and two deaths. Signs of the caffeine overdose include symptoms such as rapid, erratic heartbeats; extreme agitation; vomiting; and even seizures. It has been difficult for the FDA to manage these products because powdered caffeine is classified as a dietary supplement and thus not directly regulated by the FDA. However, the FDA has put out an advisory that pure powdered caffeine should be avoided and that its adverse effects are much more severe than consuming too much coffee, tea, or other caffeinated beverage. The FDA has also advised parents that teenagers and young adults are particularly attracted to these products.

Data from Dallas, E. (2015, February 27). E.R. physician raises concerns about powdered caffeine. HealthDay. Retrieved from http://consumer.healthday.com/kids-health-information-23/adolescents-and-teen-health-news-719/er-physician-raises-concerns-about-powdered-caffeine-696703.html; Food and Drug Administration (FDA). (2019). Pure and highly concentrated caffeine. Silver Spring, MD: Author. Retrieved from https://www.fda.gov/food/dietary-supplement-products-ingredients/pure-and-highly-concentrated-caffeine

## VARIABILITY IN RESPONSES

Caffeine is eventually absorbed entirely from the gastrointestinal tract after oral consumption. In most users, 90% of the drug reaches the bloodstream within 20 minutes and is quickly distributed into the brain and throughout the body. The rate of absorption of caffeine from the stomach and intestines differs from person to person by as much as sixfold. Because of the wide variations in the rate at which caffeine enters the blood from the stomach, this likely accounts for much of the variability in response to this drug (Mental Health Daily, 2015b).

## ■ OTC Sympathomimetics

Although often overlooked, the sympathomimetic decongestant drugs included in OTC products such as cold, allergy, and diet aid medications have stimulant properties like those of caffeine. For most people, the CNS impact of these drugs is minor, but for those people who are sensitive to these drugs, they can cause jitters and interfere with sleep. For such individuals, OTC products containing the sympathomimetics should be avoided before bedtime.

The common OTC sympathomimetics are shown in **Table 10.5** and include ephedrine, pseudoephedrine, and phenylephrine. In the past, these drugs have been referred to as "look-alikes," suggesting they have effects similar to the more potent stimulants such as amphetamine. Although much less potent than amphetamines (even though they can be used as precursor chemicals to make methamphetamine), these

**TABLE 10.5** Common OTC Sympathomimetics

| Drug | OTC Product (Form) |
|------|--------------------|
| Ephedrine | Before being removed from market, drug was used as a decongestant (oral, nasal spray, or nasal drops) and for weight loss |
| Naphazoline | Decongestant (nasal spray or nasal drops) |
| Oxymetazoline | Decongestant (nasal spray or nasal drops) |
| Phenylephrine | Decongestant (oral, nasal spray, nasal drops, or eye drops) |
| Pseudoephedrine | Decongestant (oral) |
| Tetrahydrozoline | Decongestant (eye drops) |

Data from Scolaro, K. (2012). Disorders related to colds and allergy. In *Handbook of Nonprescription Drugs*, 17th ed. (pp. 179–204). Washington, DC: American Pharmaceutical Association.

minor stimulants can be abused and have caused deaths. Attempts to keep these drugs from being promoted as potent stimulants resulted in passage of the federal and state Imitation Controlled Substances Acts. These statutes prohibit the packaging of OTC sympathomimetics to look like amphetamines.

Despite these laws, occasionally other products containing the OTC sympathomimetics are promoted on the street as "harmless speed" and "OTC uppers." It is likely that use of such products can lead to the abuse of more potent stimulants.

As previously mentioned in the chapter, some of the sympathomimetics that are included in cold medicines can be readily converted into methamphetamine. For this reason, since 2006 federal statutes have required these products be secured in a locked case behind the counter and sold in limited quantities ("Reduction in Meth Lab Seizures," 2015).

## ■ Herbal Stimulants

Some OTC sympathomimetics occur naturally and are also found in herbal stimulants or dietary supplements sold by mail and in novelty stores, beauty salons, health-food stores, online, and sometimes by health professionals, including physicians (Myers, 2014). (To appreciate this point, perform an Internet search for "herbal stimulant.") These pills have been sold under many names, including *rave herbal stimulant*, *legal herbal weed*, and *herbal ecstasy* and often contain stimulants such as ephedrine, ephedra, or ma huang. These products are promoted as natural highs to be used as diet aids, energy boosters, or performance enhancers for athletics. Excessive use of these products can cause seizures, heart attacks, and strokes (Food and Drug Administration [FDA], 2018). In fact, several deaths and many cases of severe reactions have been reported in the United States from excessive use of these products (FDA, 2013). The death of a Major League Baseball player (see "Here and Now: Diet Pills Are Russian Roulette for Athletes") resulted in particularly strong pressure to ban OTC products, including dietary supplements, containing either the herb ephedra or the active ingredient ephedrine (Grace, 2006). In response to these pressures, the FDA banned the use of ephedrine or ephedra in OTC products; however, it is difficult to actually remove herbal stimulants from the marketplace because of a 1994 federal law that prohibits such action until

# HERE AND NOW
## Diet Pills Are Russian Roulette for Athletes

Steve Bechler, a 23-year-old pitcher for the Baltimore Orioles of the American League, died in 2003 after collapsing on the field during running drills due to "multiple organ failure resulting from heat stroke," according to his autopsy report. Ephedrine was found in Bechler's body and likely contributed to his death. He was reported to be using an ephedrine supplement called Xenadrine RFA-1. Although advised not to use it by his trainer, Bechler was taking this ephedrine-containing product to get his weight down after being criticized by coaches for being too heavy and not performing well in preseason drills. A teammate explained that heavy athletes like Bechler are under a lot of pressure to control their weight to make big-league teams. Although at the time of Bechler's death use of ephedrine was not prohibited by Major League Baseball, it was prohibited by the National Football League (NFL) in 2002. The NFL's ban came after Korey Stringer, a lineman for the Minnesota Vikings who was taking an ephedrine product, died after collapsing during a training camp workout in 2001. In 2004, ephedrine in OTC

© Fernando Medina/Stringer/Getty Images Sport/Getty Images.

dietary supplements was made illegal by the FDA after reports of 22 deaths and 800 incidents of serious toxicity caused by OTC ephedrine.

the FDA conclusively proves the dangers of these substances (Miller & Longtin, 2010). Numerous lawsuits have been filed against herbal companies that manufactured products containing ma huang and the drug ephedrine. These legal actions claim that such products have caused serious illness and even death. Several of these lawsuits have been settled out of court, reportedly for millions of dollars. Even before the FDA ban, because ephedrine can be converted into methamphetamine, the Comprehensive Methamphetamine Control Act passed in 1996 regulated the amount of ephedrine that could be purchased or sold at one time (Sprague, Harrod, & Teconchuk, 1998). Because the ephedrine molecule resembles that of the amphetamines, it is not surprising that this drug has some mild amphetamine-like properties.

# Global Stimulant Abuse

Like the United States, other countries have been seriously impacted by the abuse of stimulant drugs, causing governments and law enforcement agencies around the world and international organizations such as the United Nations Office on Drugs and Crime to search for solutions (UNODC, 2015). For the most part, these drugs are referred to as *amphetamine-type stimulants* (ATSs) or cocaine and their various forms. The ATS drugs include amphetamines such as methamphetamine, methcathinone, and MDMA and related substances.

## ■ Stimulant Production

Because most ATS drugs are synthetics, they can be produced anywhere and are relatively inexpensive. As previously mentioned, for this reason these drugs are often perceived as a "poor-man's cocaine." The global market for ATS drugs continues to be dominated by methamphetamine, and the market for this drug is expanding in East Asia and Southeast Asia. The total quantity of ATS drug seizures is approaching 150 tons per year (UNODC, 2015). In contrast, the global market for Ecstasy is smaller, especially in the Americas, and is currently most active in Eastern Asia (UNODC, 2015).

In contrast, because cocaine is a natural substance derived from a plant, its production

Organizations of the United Nations such as its Office on Drugs and Crime work with countries around the world to identify critical drug problems and to develop global solutions that cross international borders.

is limited to those regions that have climate and geographic conditions conducive to coca cultivation. The countries that produce the vast majority of the world's cocaine supply are Bolivia, Peru, and Colombia. The global cocaine supply decreased to 845 metric tons in 2008. These recent declines were largely due to a 28% reduction in cocaine production in Colombia as a result of pressure from the United States (UNODC, 2009).

## ▪ Global Stimulant Consumption

It is roughly estimated that globally 27 million persons suffer from substance use disorders, with only one-sixth of those having access to treatment (UNODC, 2015). These intense users are likely heavily dependent on their drug of choice, cause a serious drain on public health and law enforcement resources, and would benefit from proper treatment.

Different drugs tend to cause problems for different global regions. Marijuana is particularly troubling for Africa and Australia; heroin is especially problematic for Asia and Europe; the ATS drugs are a major problem for Asia, North America, and Australia; and cocaine causes the greatest problem in North and South America, with the United States being the largest consumer in absolute numbers. By comparison, the ATS drugs are consumed by almost twice as many people around the world (about 35 million annually) as cocaine (about 17 million). The proliferation of new psychoactive substances (NPSs) pose a special challenge in that little is known regarding their health and social risks. The short- and long-term effects of these drugs often have not been well studied, making it difficult to treat and warn about their use (UNODC, 2015).

## ▪ Global Drug Policy

Like the United States, most countries around the world are looking for solutions to the personal and social consequences of drug abuse in general and the stimulant problems in particular. Lively discussions about demand, production, and trafficking occur between countries to try to stem the tide of drug abuse and addiction and their devastating consequences. The causes are many and the solutions are complex and evasive. There are heated discussions between nations on topics such as (1) who is principally at fault for the problems (i.e., the nations that produce or consume), (2) whether these drugs should be legalized or at least be decriminalized, and (3) whether taxing of such drug products be used to raise needed public revenues. The international discussions resemble those occurring throughout the United States. What has become evident to everyone is that although specific solutions are difficult, all nations are in this together. Drug problems and drug policies to address these problems cross national borders, impacting global efforts to find solutions; thus, to be successful in our attempts to mitigate these drug problems, we must have global cooperation and work together.

# LEARNING PORTFOLIO

## Discussion Questions

1. How are methamphetamine and Ecstasy similar, and how do they differ?

2. Should children be taken from mothers who are addicted to methamphetamine or cocaine?

3. How is the resurfacing of methamphetamine use connected to the epidemic with opioid drugs?

4. Why is methamphetamine abuse increasing despite the fact that small local methamphetamine labs have all but disappeared?

5. What have past experiences taught us about cocaine? Do you think we have finally learned our lesson concerning this drug?

6. If clinical trials demonstrate that MDMA is effective in the treatment of stress and anxiety, should the FDA approve its use by prescription? What would be the effect on recreational MDMA use by young people if the FDA approved MDMA for treating PTSD?

7. Why does the method of cocaine administration make a difference in how a user is affected by this drug? Use examples to substantiate your conclusions.

8. Why do people smoke cocaine, and what are the major toxicities caused by the use of high doses of this stimulant?

9. How is cocaine dependence treated? What are the rationales for the treatment?

10. How does caffeine compare with cocaine and amphetamine as a CNS stimulant?

11. Because of caffeine's potential for abuse, do you think the FDA should control it more tightly? Defend your answer.

12. Do you feel that herbal stimulants such as ephedra should have been removed from OTC products?

13. How do global efforts to address stimulant abuse problems affect the people and policies in the United States?

14. Why is it disturbing to have so many NPSs becoming globally available?

## Key Terms

| | |
|---|---|
| adulterated | 350 |
| anorexiants | 331 |
| behavioral stereotypy | 332 |
| binge | 336 |
| caffeinism | 362 |
| cocaine babies | 357 |
| crack | 353 |
| freebasing | 352 |
| goofballs | 341 |
| high | 336 |
| hyperpyrexia | 336 |
| ice | 336 |
| narcolepsy | 332 |
| performance enhancers | 344 |
| precursor chemicals | 334 |
| run | 336 |
| rush | 336 |
| speed | 333 |
| speedballs | 341 |
| tweaking | 336 |
| uppers | 330 |
| xanthines | 359 |

## Summary

1. Amphetamines, originally developed as decongestants, are potent stimulants. Some amphetamines have been approved by the FDA as (a) diet aids to treat obesity, (b) treatment for narcolepsy, and (c) treatment for attention-deficit hyperactivity disorder in children.

2. In therapeutic doses, amphetamines can cause agitation, anxiety, and panic because of their effects on the brain; in addition, they can cause an irregular heartbeat, increased blood

pressure, heart attack, or stroke. Intense, high-dose abuse of these drugs can cause severe psychotic behavior, stereotypy, and seizures, as well as the severe cardiovascular side effects just mentioned.

3. *Speed* refers to the use of intravenous methamphetamine. *Ice* is smoked methamphetamine. A *run* is a pattern of intense, multiple dosing over a period of days that can cause serious neurological, psychiatric, and cardiovascular consequences.

4. Tweakers are individuals who repeatedly self-administer methamphetamine to maintain the high. They often have not slept or eaten for days, are highly irritable, and sometimes are paranoid or even violent.

5. "Designer" amphetamines are chemical modifications of original amphetamines and are included in the category of new psychoactive substance. Some designer amphetamines such as Ecstasy have some abuse potential and are marketed on the street under exotic and alluring names.

6. Ecstasy and related NPSs have both psychedelic and stimulant properties because of their ability to release serotonin and dopamine in the brain. This combination of pharmacological effects makes these drugs particularly attractive to younger populations engaging in sensory-rich activities such as dances called *raves*.

7. There appears to be a renewed effort to get FDA approval of MDMA for therapeutic use, especially to treat stress conditions such as PTSD. This probably is loosely associated with the fact that this country has become more accepting of efforts to legalize other hallucinogenic drugs such as marijuana for medical and recreational purposes.

8. In the early 1980s, cocaine was commonly viewed by the U.S. public as a relatively safe drug with glamorous connotations. By the mid-1980s, it became apparent that cocaine was a highly addictive drug with dangerous side effects.

9. The CNS and cardiovascular effects of both amphetamines and cocaine are similar. However, the effects of cocaine tend to occur more rapidly, be more intense, and wear off more quickly than those of amphetamines.

10. The intensity of the cocaine effect and the likelihood of dependence occurring are directly related to the means of administration. Going from least to most intense effect, the modes of cocaine administration include chewing, snorting, injecting, and smoking (or freebasing).

11. *Crack* is cocaine that has been converted into its "freebase" form intended for smoking.

12. Cocaine withdrawal goes through three main stages: (a) the *crash*, or the initial abstinence phase consisting of depression, agitation, suicidal thoughts, and fatigue; (b) *withdrawal*, including mood swings, craving, anhedonia, and obsession with drug seeking; and (c) *extinction*, when normal pleasure returns and cues trigger craving and mood swings.

13. Treatment of cocaine dependence is highly individualistic and has variable success. The principal strategies include both inpatient and outpatient programs. Drug therapy often is used to relieve short-term cocaine craving and to alleviate mood problems and long-term craving. Psychological counseling and support therapy are essential components of treatment.

14. Caffeine is the most frequently consumed stimulant in the world. It is classified as a xanthine (methylxanthine) and is added to many different types of beverages, including water, and has even been added to alcoholic drinks. It is also included in some OTC medicines such as analgesics and so-called stay-awake products. Caffeine causes minor stimulation of cardiovascular activity, kidney function (it is a diuretic), and gastric secretion.

15. Dependence on caffeine can occur in people who regularly consume large doses. Withdrawal can cause headaches, agitation, and tremors. Although unpleasant, withdrawal from caffeine dependence is much less severe than withdrawal from amphetamine and cocaine dependence.

16. OTC sympathomimetics such as ephedrine have been consumed in high doses. Although not as potent as the major stimulants, recreational use of these drugs can be dangerous. Because of those potential dangers, the FDA has prohibited the use of ephedrine in OTC products.

17. Stimulant abuse and addiction are problems that are global in nature. Because these drugs are manufactured around the world and trafficked across international borders, it is impossible to find lasting solutions to these problems without working with other countries to help stem the production and smuggling of these illegal substances.

# References

Addiction Center. (2016a). Ecstasy addiction and abuse. Retrieved from https://www.addictioncenter.com/drugs/ecstasy/

Addiction Center. (2016b). Ritalin addiction, abuse and treatment. Retrieved from https://www.addictioncenter.com/stimulants/ritalin/

Addiction Center. (2016c). Treatment for meth addiction. Retrieved from https://www.addictioncenter.com/drugs/meth/withdrawal-detox/

Aldrich, M., & Barker, R. (1976). In S. J. Mule (Ed.), *Cocaine: Chemical, biological, social and treatment aspects* (pp. 3–10). Cleveland, OH: CRC.

American Cancer Society. (2015). Fibrosis and simple cysts. Retrieved from https://www.cancer.org/cancer/breast-cancer/non-cancerous-breast-conditions/fibrosis-and-simple-cysts-in-the-breast.html

American Psychiatric Association. (2013). *Diagnostic and statistical manual of mental disorders*, 5th ed. Washington, DC: American Psychiatric Association.

"Amphetamine street names." (n.d.). Amphetamines.com. Retrieved from http://amphetamines.com/street-names/

Barnes, L. (2013, January 1). An addict's story: Cocaine and the crash. *The Citizen* [Auburn, NY]. Retrieved from http://auburnpub.com/lifestyles/an-addict-s-story-cocaine-and-the-crash/article_aadd6bc1-5678-542a-9cb3-f256a3631981.html

Baumann, M., & Volkow, N. (2016). Abuse of new psychoactive substances: Threats and solutions. *Neuropsychopharm, 41*, 663–665.

Baynes, C. (2019). US vows to help world's largest cocaine producer curb "deeply concerning" rise in cultivation. *The Independent* [London, UK]. Retrieved from https://www.independent.co.uk/news/world/americas/colombia-us-cocaine-production-coca-leaf-mike-pompeo-ivan-duque-drugs-a8710131.html

Bazuaye-Ekwuyasi, E. A., Ogunbilege, J. O., Kaphalia, B. S., Eltorky, M. A., & Okorodudu, A. O. (2015). Comparative effects of cocaine and cocaethylene on alveolar epithelial type II cells. *Toxicology Mechanisms and Methods, 25*, 604–613.

Beck, J. (1990). The public health implications of MDMA use. In S. Peroutka (Ed.), *Ecstasy* (pp. 77–103). Norwell, MA: Kluwer.

Beckhusen, R. (2013, April). As Colombian drug gangs collapse, Mexican cartels get tons of cheap coke. *WIRED.* Retrieved from http://www.wired.com/dangerroom/2013/04/colombian-bacrim-gangs/

Bethea, A. (2015, February). The duration of caffeine withdrawal symptoms. LiveStrong.com. Retrieved from http://www.livestrong.com/article/399329-the-duration-of-caffeine-withdrawal-symptoms/

Bezrutczyk, D. (2019). How much do drugs cost: The steep price of addiction. Addiction Center. Retrieved from https://www.addictioncenter.com/drugs/how-much-do-drugs-cost/

Breslow, J. (2015). The staggering death toll of Mexico's drug war. *Frontline.* Retrieved from http://www.pbs.org/wgbh/frontline/article/the-staggering-death-toll-of-mexicos-drug-war/

Briceno, F. (2015, August 17). Eradication spells misery for Peru's coca farmers. AP News. Retrieved from https://apnews.com/89563c1baf5344b996c914da07a43eb3

Buddy, T. (2019). Common street names for cocaine. VeryWellMind. Retrieved from https://www.verywellmind.com/common-street-names-for-cocaine-66696

Byck, R. (1987). Cocaine use and research: Three histories. In S. Fisher (Ed.), *Cocaine: Chemical and behavioral aspects* (pp. 3–17). London, UK: Oxford University Press.

Caffeine Informer. (2014). Alcohol and energy drinks: The dangers of mixing. Retrieved from http://www.caffeineinformer.com/alcoholic-energy-drinks-the-list

Caffeine Informer. (2016). Caffeine content of drinks. Retrieved from http://www.caffeineinformer.com/the-caffeine-database

Cantwell, B., & McBride, A. (1998). Self-detoxification by amphetamine-dependent patients: A pilot study. *Drug and Alcohol Dependence, 49*, 157–163.

Center for Substance Abuse Research. (2013, October 29). Methamphetamine.

Centers for Disease Control and Prevention. (2016). Data and statistics about ADHD. Retrieved from http://www.cdc.gov/ncbddd/adhd/data.html

Cloud, J. (2000, June 5). The lure of Ecstasy. *Time, 155*, 60.

Dallas, E. (2015, February 27). E.R. physician raises concerns about powdered caffeine. HealthDay. Retrieved from http://consumer.healthday.com/kids -health-information-23/adolescents-and-teen-health -news-719/er-physician-raises-concerns-about-powdered -caffeine-696703.html

Davies, J. (2015, September 3). Prenatal methamphetamine exposure. RainbowKids. Retrieved from http://www .rainbowkids.com/adoption-stories/prenatal-metham phetamine-exposure-1239

Davis, K. (2015, July 22). MDMA (Ecstasy): Facts, effects and hazards. Medical News Today. Retrieved from http:// www.medicalnewstoday.com/articles/297064.php

Dembosky, A. (2019, June 17). Meth in the morning, heroin at night: Inside the seesaw struggle of dual addiction. NPR. Retrieved from https://www.npr.org/sections /health-shots/2019/06/17/730803759/meth-in-the -morning-heroin-at-night-inside-the-seesaw-struggle -of-dual-addiction

Derry, C. J., Derry, S., & Moore, R. A. (2015). Caffeine as an analgesic adjuvant for acute pain in adults. Cochrane Database of Systematic Reviews. Retrieved from https:// pubmed.ncbi.nlm.nih.gov/22419343/

DiChiara, G. (1993). Cocaine: Scientific and social dimensions. *Trends in Neurological Sciences, 16,* 39.

Doblin, R. (2019). Mental health is getting the psychedelic treatment. Aspen Ideas Festival. Retrieved from https:// www.aspenideas.org/articles/mental-health-is-getting -the-psychedelic-treatment

"Dominican Republic emerges as drug trafficking center of the Caribbean." (2013, January 23). Huffington Post. Retrieved from http://www.huffingtonpost.com/2013 /01/23/dominican-republic-emerge_n_2533210.html/

Doyle, M. (2010, July 6). Report: 2006 anti-meth law reduced number of U.S. labs. McClatchy. Retrieved from https:// www.mcclatchydc.com/news/crime/article24587128 .html

Drasner, K. (2012). Local anesthetics. In B. Katzung, S. Masters, & A. Trevor (Eds.), *Basic and clinical pharmacology,* 12th ed. (pp. 449–464). New York, NY: McGraw-Hill Medical.

Drug Enforcement Administration (DEA). (n.d.). Methamphetamine lab incidents, 2004–2014. Springfield, VA: Author.

Drug Enforcement Administration. (2015). Drugs of abuse: Cocaine. Retrieved from https://www.dea.gov /pr/multimedia-library/publications/drug_of_abuse .pdf#page=47

Drug Policy Alliance. (2015a). The international drug war. Retrieved from http://www.drugpolicy.org/drug-traffic king-latin-america

Drug Policy Alliance. (2015b). 10 facts about MDMA. Retrieved from http://www.drugpolicy.org/sites/default /files/DPA_Fact_Sheet_10_Facts_about_MDMA.pdf

Drugs.com. (2014). MDMA: What is MDMA? Retrieved from http://www.drugs.com/illicit/mdma.html

"Drug supplies: Track marks." (2016, April 2). *The Economist.* Retrieved from http://www.economist.com/news /science-and-technology/21695861-chemists-find -previously-unknown-sources-cocaine-track-marks

Dryden-Edwards, R. (2019). Cocaine abuse. eMedicineHealth. Retrieved from http://www.emedicinehealth .com/cocaine_abuse/article_em.htm

Dunwiddie, T., & Masino, S. (2001). The role and regulation of adenosine in the central nervous system. *Annual Review of Neuroscience, 24,* 31–55.

"Ecstasy overdoses at a New Year's Eve rave, Los Angeles, California, 2010." (2010). *Journal of the American Medical Association, 304,* 629–632.

Edmond, J. (2015, March 6). Teenage TV audiences and energy drink advertisements. Medical Xpress. Retrieved from http://medicalxpress.com/news/2015-03-teenage -tv-audiences-energy-advertisements.html

Elkashef, A., Vocci, F., Hanson, G., White, J., Wickes, W., & Tiihonen, J. (2008). Pharmacotherapy of methamphetamine addiction: An update. *Substance Abuse, 29,* 31–49.

Ely, A., & Cusack, A. (2015). The binge and the brain. New York, NY: Dana Foundation. Retrieved from http://www .dana.org/Cerebrum/2015/The_Binge_and_the_Brain/

"Escalation in methamphetamine use also leads to escalation in social service." (2005, February 14). *Health & Medicine Week.*

"Famous people with meth problems." (n.d.). Ranker. Retrieved from https://www.ranker.com/list/famous -crystal-users/celebrity-lists

Federal Bureau of Investigation. (2015, December 31). Aryan Brotherhood methamphetamine operation dismantled. Retrieved from https://www.fbi.gov/news/stories/aryan -brotherhood-methamphetamine-operation-dismantled

Fischman, M., & Johanson, C. (1996). Cocaine. In C. Schuster & M. Kuhar (Eds.), *Pharmacological aspects of drug dependence: Towards an integrated neurobehavior approach handbook of experimental pharmacology* (pp. 159–195). New York, NY: Springer-Verlag.

Fitzgerald, S. (2013, July 22). "Crack baby" study ends with unexpected but clear results. *The Inquirer* [Philadelphia]. Retrieved from http://articles.philly.com/2013-07-22 /news/40709969_1_hallam-hurt-so-called-crack-babies -funded-study

Food and Drug Administration (FDA). (2013). Stimulant potentially dangerous to health, FDA warns. Retrieved from http://www.fda.gov/ForConsumers/Consumer Updates/ucm347270.htm

Food and Drug Administration. (2018, September 21). Herbal stimulants give kicks around world. Retrieved from https://www.fda.gov/food/dietary-supplement -products-ingredients/pure-and-highly-concentrated -caffeine

Food and Drug Administration (FDA). (2019). Pure and highly concentrated caffeine. Silver Spring, MD: Author. Retrieved from https://www.fda.gov/food/dietary -supplement-products-ingredients/pure-and-highly -concentrated-caffeine

Food Insight. (2015, August 27). Everything you need to know about caffeine. Washington, DC: International Food Information Council Foundation. Retrieved from http://www.foodinsight.org/everything-about-caffeine -science-amount-safety

Foundation for a Drug-Free World. (n.d.). The truth about cocaine. Los Angeles, Ca: Author. Retrieved from http://www.drugfreeworld.org/drugfacts/cocaine/a -short-history.html

Friedman, A., & Rocher, F. (2013, September 22). A history of celebrities getting caught with meth. Complex. Retrieved from https://www.complex.com/pop-culture /2013/09/celebrities-caught-with-meth/

Friends of Narconon. (2010). Ecstasy/MDMA manufacturing and statistics. Retrieved from http://www.friends ofnarconon.org/drug_education/news/latest_news /ecstasy%10mdma_manufacturing_and_statistics

Galanter, J., & Boushey, H. (2015). Drugs used in asthma. In B. Katzung and A. Trevor (Eds.), *Basic and clinical pharmacology*, 13th ed. (pp. 336–351). New York, NY: McGraw-Hill.

Garwin, F. (1991). Cocaine addiction: Psychology and neurophysiology. *Science, 251,* 1580–1586.

Gilbert, R. (1984). Caffeine consumption. In G. Spiller (Ed.), *The methylxanthine beverages and foods: Chemistry, consumption, and health effects* (pp. 185–213). New York, NY: Liss.

Golding, A. (1993, May). Two hundred years of drug abuse. *Journal of the Royal Society of Medicine, 86,* 282–286.

Goldstein, A. (1994). *Addiction from biology to drug abuse.* New York, NY: Freeman.

Goodger, N., Wang, J., & Pogrel, M. (2005). Palatal and nasal necrosis resulting from cocaine misuse. *British Dental Journal, 198,* 333–334.

Goodman, B. (2011, November 22). Energy drinks send thousands to the ER each year. WebMD. Retrieved from http://www.Webmd.com/mental-health/alcohol -abuse/news/20111121/energy-drinks-send-thousands -to-the-er-each-year

Gorelick, D. (2015, August 7). Cocaine use disorder in adults: Epidemiology, pharmacology, clinical manifestations, medical consequences, and diagnosis. UpToDate. Retrieved from http://www.uptodate.com/contents /cocaine-use-disorder-in-adults-epidemiology -pharmacology-clinical-manifestations-medical -consequences-and-diagnosis

Grace, F. (2006, May 9). FDA wants ephedra ban restored. CBS News. Retrieved from http://www.cbsnews.com /news/fda-wants-ephedra-ban-restored/

Green, E. (1985, November). Cocaine, glamorous status symbol of the "jet set," is fast becoming many students' drug of choice. *Chronicle of Higher Education, 31*(11), 1, 34–35.

Grillo, I. (2016, January 15). Why cartels are killing Mexico's mayors. *The New York Times.* Retrieved from http://www.nytimes.com/2016/01/17/opinion/sunday /why-cartels-are-killing-mexicos-mayors.html?_r=0

Grinspoon, L., & Bakalar, J. (1978). The amphetamines: Medical use and health hazards. In D. Smith (Ed.), *Amphetamines: Use, misuse and abuse* (pp. 18–33). Boston, MA: Hall.

Grob, C., Poland, R., Chang, L., & Ernst, T. (1996). Psychobiological effects of 3,4-methylenedioxymethamphetamine in humans: Methodological considerations and preliminary observations. *Behavioral Brain Research, 73,* 103–107.

Hadlock, G., Webb, K., McFadden, L., Chu, P., Ellis, J., Allen, S., . . . , et al. (2011). 4-methylmethcathinone (mephedrone): Neuropharmacological effects of a designer stimulant of abuse. *Journal of Pharmacology and Experimental Therapeutics, 339,* 530–536.

Hahn, I. (2015, March 25). MDMA toxicity. Medscape. Retrieved from https://emedicine.medscape.com /article/821572-overview#a5

Harding, A. (2010, July 29). Meth use in pregnancy endangers mom and baby. Reuters Health News. Retrieved from http://www.reuters.com/article/2010/07/29/us -meth-pregnancy-idUSTRE66S5M720100729

Hartney, E. (2013, January 20). What to expect from caffeine withdrawal. VeryWellMind. Retrieved from http:// addictions.about.com/od/Caffeine/a/What-To-Expect -From-Caffeine-Withdrawal.htm

Haupt, A. (2012, April 17). Signs of caffeine addiction. *U.S. News & World Report.* Retrieved from http://health .usnews.com/health-news/articles/2012/04/17/signs -of-caffeine-addiction

Hawaii Island Recovery. (2019, October 22). Speedballs claim the life of baseball great Ken Caminiti. Retrieved from http://www.hawaiianrecovery.com/speedballs -claim-the-life-of-baseball-great-ken-caminiti.html

HealthResearchFunding.org. (2014). 24 remarkable caffeine consumption statistics. Retrieved from http://healthresearchfunding.org/remarkable-caffeine-consumption-statistics/

Hessert, A., Medvecz, A., Miller, J., & Richard, J. (2009, June 4). The new performance enhancing drugs. Neuroanthropology. Retrieved from http://neuroanthropology.net/2009/06/04/the-new-performance-enhancing-drugs

Hitti, M. (2006, October 16). Caffeine abuse: Buzz gone wrong. WebMD. Retrieved from http://www.webmd.com/content/article/128/117124

Holt, L. (2005, October 8). Former meth addicts Jenny Madonecky and Faye Benner speak about crystal meth addiction. *Saturday Today Show* (NBC).

Humphreys, K., Eng, T., & Lee, S. (2013, May 29). Stimulant medication and substance use outcomes. *JAMA Psychiatry*. Retrieved from https://leelab.psych.ucla.edu/wp-content/uploads/sites/44/2015/10/Humphreys_2013_Stimulant.pdf

"Is caffeine bad for you?" Medical News Today. Retrieved from http://www.medicalnewstoday.com/articles/271707.php

Johnston, L. (2019). *Monitoring the Future 2018*. Retrieved from http://monitoringthefuture.org/pubs/monographs/mtf-overview2018.pdf

Juergen, J. (2020, April 29). Ecstasy addiction and drug abuse. Addiction Center. Retrieved from https://www.addictioncenter.com/drugs/ecstasy/

KCI.org. (n.d.). Methamphetamine FAQ. Retrieved from http://www.kci.org/meth_info/faq_meth.htm

Keenan, B. (2010, April 22). Adderall is "secret miracle" for illegal use. *The Breeze* [Harrisonburg, WV]. Retrieved from http://www.breezejmu.org/article_8d88baa4-757c-554f-9d36-9e48c47fb35a.html

Keoni, J. (2015). New synthetic drug: Trifluoromethylphenylpiperazine (RFMPP). New Roads. Retrieved from http://newroadstreatment.com/trifluoromethylphenylpiperazine-tfmpp/

Khazan, O. (2015a). Into the body of another. *The Atlantic* (May 8). Retrieved from http://www.theatlantic.com/health/archive/2015/05/into-the-body-of-another/392522/

Khazan, O. (2015b). The rise of work-doping. *The Atlantic* (August 27). Retrieved from http://www.theatlantic.com/health/archive/2015/08/the-rise-of-work-doping/402373/

Kihlman, B. (1977). *Caffeine and chromosomes*. Amsterdam, The Netherlands: Elsevier.

Kirkwood, C., & Melton, S. (2012). Insomnia, drowsiness and fatigue. In D. Krinsky (Ed.), *Handbook of nonprescription drugs* (pp. 867–883). Washington, DC: American Pharmacists Association.

Kishi, T., Matsuda, Y., Iwata, N., & Correll, C. (2013). Antipsychotics for cocaine or psychostimulant dependence: Systematic review and meta-analysis of randomized, placebo-controlled trials. *Journal of Clinical Psychiatry, 74,* 1169–1180.

Kloner, R., & Rezkalla, S. (2003). Cocaine and the heart. *New England Journal of Medicine, 348,* 487–488.

Ladd, G., & Petry, N. (2003). Antisocial personality in treatment-seeking cocaine abusers: Psychosocial functioning and HIV risk. *Journal of Substance Abuse Treatment, 24,* 323–330.

Levant, R., Parent, M., McCurdy, E., & Bradstreet, T. (2015). Moderated mediation of the relationships between masculinity ideology, outcome expectations, and energy drink use. *Health Psychology, 34,* 1100–1106.

Lin, R. (2015, August 10). Q&A ER doctors: Drug-fueled raves too dangerous and should be banned. *Los Angeles Times.* Retrieved from http://www.latimes.com/local/lanow/la-me-ln-why-some-er-doctors-want-to-end-raves-in-los-angeles-county-20150810-story.html

Longmire, S. (2016, February 15). Historic METH bust At Arizona border crossing could signal cartel conflict. Breitbart. Retrieved from http://www.breitbart.com/big-government/2016/02/15/historic-meth-bust-at-arizona-border-crossing-could-be-major-cartel-signal/

Luscher, C. (2015). Drugs of abuse. In B. Katzung & A. Trevor (Eds.), *Basic and clinical pharmacology,* 13th ed. (pp. 552–566). New York, NY: McGraw Hill Medical.

Lutz, A. (2015, April 6). Here's how much caffeine people consume at every age. *Business Insider.* Retrieved from http://www.businessinsider.com/caffeine-consumption-by-age-2015-4

Mandt, B., Copenhagen, L., Zahniser, N., & Allen, R. (2015). Escalation of cocaine consumption in short and long access self-administration procedures. *Drug and Alcohol Dependence, 149,* 166–172.

Massanella, M., Gianella, S., Schrier, R., Dan, J. M., Pérez-Santiago, J., Oliveira, M. F., . . . , Morris, S. R. (2015). Methamphetamine use in HIV-infected individuals affects T-cell function and viral outcome during suppressive antiretroviral therapy. *Scientific Reports, 5,* 13179. Retrieved from http://www.nature.com/articles/srep13179

Mayo Clinic. (2010, December 15). Cocaine (topical route). Retrieved from http://www.mayoclinic.com/health/drug-information/DR600467

Mayo Clinic. (2016). Methylphenidate (oral route). Retrieved from http://www.mayoclinic.org/drugs-supplements/methylphenidate-oral-route/proper-use/drg-20068297

McCaffrey, B. (1999, May). Methamphetamine. Washington, DC: Office of National Drug Control Policy. NCJ-1756677, 1–3.

MedicineNet. (2010). Caffeine. Retrieved from http://www.medicinenet.com/caffeine/article.htm

MedlinePlus. (2007). Cocaine withdrawal. Bethesday, MD: U.S. National Library of Medicine. Retrieved from https://medlineplus.gov/ency/article/000947.htm

MedlinePlus. (2010, November 15). Cocaine withdrawal. Retrieved from http://www.nlm.nih.gov/medlineplus/ency/article/000947.htm

Mendelson, J., & Mello, N. (1996). Management of cocaine abuse and dependence. *New England Journal of Medicine, 334*, 965–972.

Mental Health Daily. (2015a). How to increase dopamine levels. (April 17). Retrieved from http://mentalhealthdaily.com/2015/04/17/how-to-increase-dopamine-levels/

Mental Health Daily. (2015b). How long does caffeine stay in your system? (October 21). Retrieved from http://mentalhealthdaily.com/2015/10/21/how-long-does-caffeine-stay-in-your-system/

Mental Health Daily. (2015c). Stimulant psychosis: Causes, symptoms, and treatment. (April 20). Retrieved from http://mentalhealthdaily.com/2015/04/20/stimulant-psychosis-causes-symptoms-treatment/

"Methamphetamine mixing." (n.d.). TheGoodDrugsGuide.com. Retrieved from http://www.thegooddrugsguide.com/methamphetamine/mixing.htm

Miller, E. (2016). Addict-turned-convict: "We are the unwanted." *Juneau Empire* [Alaska]. Retrieved from https://www.juneauempire.com/news/addict-turned-convict-we-are-the-unwanted/

Miller, H., & Longtin, D. (2010, March 23). Death by dietary supplement. Forbes.com. Retrieved from http://www.forbes.com/2010/03/23/dietary-supplemetns-herbal-fda-opinions-contributors-henry-i-miller-david-longtin.html

Morris, F. (2018, October 25). Methamphetamine roils rural towns again across the U.S. NPR. Retrieved from https://www.npr.org/sections/health-shots/2018/10/25/656192849/methamphetamine-roils-rural-towns-again-across-the-u-s

Mothers Against Methamphetamine. (n.d.). Crystal meth: They call it "Ice." Retrieved from http://www.mamasite.net/index.php?main_page=page&id=53&chapter=0

Mozes, A. (2015, August 17). New findings on coffee and cancer risk. CBS News. Retrieved from http://www.cbsnews.com/news/new-findings-on-coffee-and-cancer-risk/

Musto, D. (1998). International traffic in coca through the early 20th century. *Drug and Alcohol Dependence, 49*, 145–156.

Myers, G. (2014). Top 10 over-the-counter drugs that will get you higher than marijuana. TopTenz. Retrieved from http://www.toptenz.net/top-10-over-the-counter-drugs-that-will-get-you-higher-than-marijuana.php

"My mother vs. meth." (n.d.). Addiction Poem about Family. Retrieved from www.familyfriendpoems.com/poem/my-mother-vs-meth

Narconon. (2013). Does cocaine have withdrawal symptoms? Retrieved from http://www.narconon.org/drug-rehab/does-cocaine-have-withdrawal-symptoms.html

Narconon. (2016a). Methamphetamine/meth addiction info. Retrieved from http://www.narconon.org/drug-information/methamphetamine-addiction.html

Narconon. (2016b). Cocaine information. Retrieved from http://www.narconon.org/drug-information/cocaine-coke.html

National Association of Drug Court Professionals. (2015). Drug courts work. Retrieved from https://www.nadcp.org/treatment-courts-work/

National Institute on Drug Abuse (NIDA). (2013, April). What is cocaine? Retrieved from https://www.drugabuse.gov/publications/drugfacts/cocaine

National Institute on Drug Abuse (NIDA). (2014, March 20). Methamphetamine alters brain structures, impairs mental flexibility. *NIDA Notes.* Retrieved from https://www.drugabuse.gov/news-events/nida-notes/2014/03/methamphetamine-alters-brain-structures-impairs-mental-flexibility

National Institute on Drug Abuse (NIDA). (2015). Methamphetamine. Retrieved from https://www.drugabuse.gov/drugs-abuse/methamphetamine

National Institute on Drug Abuse (NIDA). (2016a). Bath salts. Retrieved from http://teens.drugabuse.gov/drug-facts/bath-salts

National Institute on Drug Abuse (NIDA). (2016b). What is cocaine? Retrieved from http://www.drugabuse.gov/publications/research-reports/cocaine-abuse-addiction

Newman, K. (2019, March). Meth from Mexico a growing problem for law enforcement. *U.S. News & World Report.* Retrieved from https://www.usnews.com/news/healthiest-communities/articles/2019-03-12/meth-from-mexico-a-growing-problem-for-law-enforcement

Newman, T. (2016, March 18). Amphetamine: Uses, side effects and contraindications. Medical News Today. Retrieved from http://www.medicalnewstoday.com/articles/221211.php

Nierenberg, C. (2015, October 5). 10 interesting facts about caffeine. Live Science. Retrieved from http://www.livescience.com/52383-interesting-facts-about-caffeine.html

Nonacs, R. (2015, May 12). Prenatal cocaine exposure and its effect on the developing brain. Boston, MA: Massachusetts General Hospital/Harvard Medical School, Center for Women's Mental Health. Retrieved from https://womensmentalhealth.org/posts/prenatal-cocaine-exposure-and-its-effect-on-the-developing-brain/

Nordrum, A. (2015, November 17). Flakka drug addiction 2015: Scientists say dangerous recreational drug is as addictive as bath salts. *International Business Times*. Retrieved from http://www.ibtimes.com/flakka-drug-addiction-2015-scientists-say-dangerous-recreational-drug-addictive-bath-1927327

Northrop, N., & Yamamoto, B. (2015, March 4). Methamphetamine effects on blood-brain barrier structure and function. *Frontiers of Neuroscience*. Retrieved from http://journal.frontiersin.org/article/10.3389/fnins.2015.00069/full

Nowak, D., & Jasionowski, A. (2015). Analysis of the consumption of caffeinated energy drinks among Polish adolescents. *International Journal of Environmental Research and Public Health, 12*, 7910–7921.

Nutt, D. (2015). Making a medicine out of MDMA. *British Journal of Psychiatry, 204*, 4–6.

Oregon Health & Science University (OHSU). (2015). OHSU researchers discover how cocaine, amphetamines disrupt the brain's normal functioning. Portland, OR: Author.

Oremus, W. (2013, March 27). The new stimulus package. Slate. Retrieved from http://www.slate.com/articles/technology/superman/2013/03/adderall_ritalin_vyvanse_do_smart_pills_work_if_you_don_t_have_adhd.html

PBS Newshour. (2011, October 17). Cocaine: How "miracle drug" nearly destroyed Sigmund Freund, William Halsted. Retrieved from https://www.pbs.org/newshour/show/cocaine-how-miracle-drug-nearly-destroyed-sigmund-freud-william-halsted

Pennings, E., Leccese, A., & Wolff, F. (2002). Effects of concurrent use of alcohol and cocaine. *Addiction, 97*, 773–783.

Platt, D., Rowlett, J., & Spealman, R. (2002). Behavioral effects of cocaine and dopaminergic strategies for preclinical medication development. *Psychopharmacology, 163*, 265–282.

Power, M. (2015). Ecstasy in 2015. Mixbag. Retrieved from http://www.mixmag.net/feature/ecstasy-in-2015

Ramsey, L. (2015, September 21). 9 crazy ways to get a caffeine fix without taking a single sip of coffee. *Business Insider*. Retrieved from http://www.businessinsider.com/ways-to-get-caffeine-without-coffee-2015-9

Randall, T. (1992a). Ecstasy-fueled "rave" parties become dances of death for English youths. *Journal of the American Medical Association, 268*, 1505–1506.

Randall, T. (1992b). "Rave" scene, ecstasy use, leap Atlantic. *Journal of the American Medical Association, 268*, 1506.

Recovery.org. (2015, January). Long term effects of crystal meth abuse. Retrieved from http://www.recovery.org/forums/discussion/285/long-term-effects-of-crystal-meth-abuse

Reduction in meth lab seizures following adoption of meth-resistant NEXAFED. (2015). *Pharmacy Times*. 2015. Retrieved from https://www.pharmacytimes.com/publications/issue/2015/January2015/R681_January2015

RehabPathway. (n.d.). Crack addiction and treatment. Retrieved from https://www.rehabpathway.com/crack/

Ricker, R., & Nicolino, V. (2010, June 21). Adderall: The most abused prescription drug in America. Huffington Post. Retrieved from http://www.huffingtonpost.com/dr-ronald-ricker-and-dr-venus-nicolino/adderall-the-most-abused_b_619549.html

Roberts, T. (2015). Built for speed? The Vaults of Erowid. Retrieved from https://www.erowid.org/chemicals/meth/meth_writings1.shtml

Robles, F. (2018, February 13). Meth, the forgotten killer, is back. And it's everywhere. *The New York Times*. Retrieved from https://www.nytimes.com/2018/02/13/us/meth-crystal-drug.html

Rowan-Szal, G., Joe, G., Simpson, W., Greener, J., & Vance, J. (2009). During-treatment outcomes among female methamphetamine-using offenders in prison-based treatments. *Journal of Offender Rehabilitation, 48*, 388–401.

Science Daily. (2010, April 1). Crack and cocaine use a significant HIV risk factor for teens. Retrieved from http://www.sciencedaily.com/releases/2010/03/100331141006.htm

Sclar, K. (2019). Street names and nicknames for cocaine. Rehabs.com. Retrieved from https://luxury.rehabs.com/cocaine-addiction/street-names-and-nicknames/#crack

Scolaro, K. (2012). Disorders related to colds and allergy. In *Handbook of Nonprescription Drugs*, 17th ed. (pp. 179–204). Washington, DC: American Pharmaceutical Association.

Sederer, L. (2010, June 1). Paying the piper: Brain "neuroenhancers." Huffington Post. Retrieved from http://www.huffingtonpost.com/lloyd-i-sederer-md/paying-the-piper-brain-ne_b_209702.html

ShapeFit. (n.d.). Caffeine in energy drinks—How much caffeine is in your drink? Retrieved from http://www.shapefit.com/diet/caffeine-energy-drinks.html

Skomorowsky, A. (2015, March 10). How Molly works in the brain. *Scientific American*. Retrieved from http://www.scientificamerican.com/article/how-molly-works-in-the-brain/

SoberRecovery. (2015, March 12). Cocaine street names. Retrieved from http://www.soberrecovery.com/addiction/cocaine-street-names/

"A social history of America's most popular drugs." (n.d.). Frontline. Retrieved from http://www.pbs.org/wgbh/pages/frontline/shows/drugs/buyers/socialhistory.html

Sofuoglu, M., Dudish-Poulsen, S., Brown, S., & Hatsukami, D. (2003). Association of cocaine withdrawal symptoms with more severe dependence and enhanced subjective response to cocaine. *Drug and Alcohol Dependence, 69,* 273–282.

Sprague, J., Harrod, A., & Teconchuk, A. (1998, May). The pharmacology and abuse potential of ephedrine. *Pharmacy Times,* pp. 72–80.

Stewart, S. (2013, January 3). Mexico's cartels and the economics of cocaine. Stratfor. Retrieved from https://www.stratfor.com/weekly/mexicos-cartels-and-economics-cocaine

Stocker, S. (1999). Cocaine activates different brain regions for rush versus craving. *NIDA Notes, 13,* 7–10.

Stone, W. (2019, August 21). MDMA, or Ecstasy, shows promise as a PTSD treatment. *Scientific American.* Retrieved from https://www.scientificamerican.com/article/mdma-or-ecstasy-shows-promise-as-a-ptsd-treatment/#

Storebo, O. J., Krogh, H. B., Ramstad, E., Moreira-Maia, C. R., Holmskov, M., Skoog, M., . . . , & Gluud, C. (2015). Methylphenidate for attention-deficit/hyperactivity disorder in children and adolescents. *BMJ, 351,* 351. Retrieved from http://www.bmj.com/content/351/bmj.h5203

Substance Abuse and Mental Health Services Administration (SAMHSA). (2010). Chapter 5—Medical aspects of stimulant use disorders. Rockville, MD: Author. Retrieved from http://www.ncbi.nlm.nih.gov/books/NBK64323/

Substance Abuse and Mental Health Services Administration (SAMHSA). (2015). *Treatment episode data set (TEDS): 2003–2013.* Rockville, MD: Author. Retrieved from http://www.samhsa.gov/data/sites/default/files/2003_2013_TEDS_National/2003_2013_Treatment_Episode_Data_Set_National.pdf

"Teen girl dies of 'caffeine toxicity' after downing 2 energy drinks." (2012, March 21). Today Health. Retrieved from http://www.today.com/health/teen-girl-dies-caffeine-toxicity-after-downing-2-energy-drinks-506441

Thornton, K. (2015, November 30). Report finds meth epidemic in full force in San Diego County. Los Angeles, CA: Southern District of California. Retrieved from https://www.justice.gov/usao-sdca/pr/report-finds-meth-epidemic-full-force-san-diego-county

United Nations Office on Drugs and Crime (UNODC). (2009). *World drug report 2009.* Vienna, Austria: Author.

United Nations Office on Drugs and Crime (UNODC). (2015). *World drug report 2015.* Vienna, Austria: Author. Retrieved from https://www.unodc.org/documents/wdr2015/World_Drug_Report_2015.pdf

Van Dam, R. (2015). Ask the expert: Coffee and health. Harvard T. H. Chan School of Public Health. Retrieved from http://www.hsph.harvard.edu/nutritionsource/2015/02/23/ask-the-expert-coffee-and-health-2/

Van Dyck, C., & Byck, R. (1982, March). Cocaine. *Scientific American, 246*(3), 128–141. Retrieved from https://pubmed.ncbi.nlm.nih.gov/7043731/

Waugh, R. (2015, September 9). MDMA "could be used to treat mental illness," scientists say. *Metro* [London, UK]. Retrieved from http://metro.co.uk/2015/09/09/mdma-could-be-used-to-treat-mental-illness-scientists-say-5383241/

WebMD. (n.d.). Ritalin. Retrieved from http://www.webmd.com/drugs/2/drug-9475/ritalin-oral/details

Wheeler, R. (2010). Hooked on caffeine? Everyday Health. Retrieved from http://www.everydayhealth.com/addiction/hooked-on-caffeine.aspx

Wilkinson, J. (2012). Headache. In D. Krinsky (Ed.), *Handbook of nonprescription drugs* (pp. 67–86). Washington, DC: American Pharmacists Association.

Winkel, B. (2010, October 25). Real crack babies. Treatment Solutions Network, Connections for Recovery. Retrieved from http://www.treatmentsolutions.com/real-crack-babies/

Woolston, M. (2016). Treatment for methamphetamine addiction. HealthDay. Retrieved from http://consumer.healthday.com/encyclopedia/substance-abuse-38/drug-abuse-news-210/treatment-for-methamphetamine-addiction-648262.html

Zheng, Y., Liang, J.-M., Gao, H.-Y., Yang, Z.-W., Jia, F.-J., et al. (2015). An open-label, self-control, prospective study on cognitive function, academic performance, and tolerability of osmotic-release oral system methylphenidate in children with attention-deficit hyperactivity disorder. *Chinese Medical Journal* [English]. *128,* 2988–2997.

CHAPTER **11**

# Tobacco

## Did You Know?

▶ Approximately 21.5% of the U.S. population age 12 or older reports current (past-month) use of a tobacco product.

▶ Tobacco use is the leading preventable cause of death in the United States.

▶ Tobacco kills approximately 480,000 U.S. citizens each year. This represents nearly one in five deaths.

▶ More than 10 times as many U.S. citizens have died prematurely from cigarette smoking than have died in all the wars fought by the United States during its history.

▶ Nicotine is just one of thousands of chemicals found in cigarette smoke.

▶ Approximately 2,000 young people in the United States will begin smoking today.

▶ Several smoking-cessation aids are available, including nicotine gum, patches, nasal sprays, and inhalers. In addition, newer prescription drugs are now used to help with smoking cessation.

## Learning Objectives

**On completing this chapter, you should be able to:**

❯ Describe the social and economic costs of smoking in the United States.

❯ Describe the history of tobacco use.

❯ Explain how the quality of leaf tobacco has changed since the mid-1950s.

❯ Describe the pharmacological effects of nicotine.

❯ List several disease states caused by cigarette smoking.

❯ Explain the consequences of environmental tobacco smoke on nonsmokers.

❯ List several reasons why individuals smoke.

❯ List several strategies that aid in smoking cessation.

❯ Describe current issues concerning vaping and its potential health consequences.

# Introduction to Tobacco Use: Scope of the Problem

Tobacco use is the leading preventable cause of death in the United States, accounting for an estimated 480,000 deaths per year (Centers for Disease Control and Prevention [CDC], 2019b). The impact of nicotine addiction in terms of morbidity, mortality, and economic costs to society is staggering. Smoking-related illness in the United States costs more than $300 billion each year, including nearly $170 billion for direct medical care for adults. Additional costs total more than $156 billion in lost productivity, including $5.6 billion in lost productivity from secondhand smoke exposure (CDC, 2019a). These high costs will likely continue and increase in the future because it is estimated that each day approximately 2,000 people younger than age 18 start smoking, and an estimated 300 become daily smokers (CDC, 2019b, 2019e).

Tobacco is the leading cause of preventable death (CDC, 2019b). Approximately 5.6 million children alive today in the United States will ultimately die early from smoking if more is not done to reduce current smoking rates (CDC, 2019b). Smoking cigarettes kills more individuals in the United States than alcohol, car accidents, guns, human immunodeficiency virus (HIV), and illegal drugs combined (American Cancer Society, 2018). More than 10 times as many U.S. citizens have died prematurely from cigarette smoking than have died in all the wars fought by the United States (CDC, 2018a).

Although much of this chapter deals with tobacco use in the United States, it is noteworthy that tobacco is used throughout the world. The World Health Organization (WHO) estimates that tobacco use kills 8 million people each year, of whom 7 million are the result of direct tobacco exposure, and more than 1.2 million are nonusers exposed to secondhand smoke (WHO, 2019).

## ▪ Current Tobacco Use in the United States

In 2018, an estimated 58.8 million Americans, or 21.5% of the population age 12 or older, reported current (i.e., past month) use of a

The WHO estimates that tobacco kills 8 million people per year worldwide. Early exposure increases the chance that young people will become regular adult smokers.

tobacco product. Among these individuals, 2.1 million smoked tobacco in pipes, 8.0 million used smokeless tobacco, 12.2 million smoked cigars, and 47 million smoked cigarettes (Substance Abuse and Mental Health Services Administration [SAMHSA], 2019). In 2017, approximately 28.6% of males and 16.6% of females age 12 or older were current users of any tobacco product (SAMHSA, 2018).

In 2017, current cigarette use among individuals age 12 or older by U.S. region were as follows: approximately 19.9% of the population in the Midwest, 19.1% in the South, 15.0% in the West, and 16.8% in the Northeast. Level of educational attainment is also correlated with cigarette smoking: 33.0% of adults age 26 or older who did not complete high school smoke cigarettes, whereas only 13.2% of college graduates smoke (SAMHSA, 2018).

Approximately 249 billion cigarettes were purchased in the United States in 2017, with four companies responsible for 92% of sales: Philip Morris USA, Reynolds American, Inc., ITG Brands, and Liggett Group. This represents a 3.5% decrease from the 258 billion sold in 2016 (CDC, 2019a).

Several investigators have suggested that tobacco can serve as a gateway drug—that is, its use may lead to the use of other drugs. Although this possibility remains controversial, it is noteworthy that research indicates that cigarette smokers are more likely to use illicit drugs than are nonsmokers. For example, in 2017, among persons age 12 or older, 28.1% of past-month cigarette smokers reported concurrent use of an illicit drug compared with 7.5% of persons who were not current cigarette smokers (SAMHSA, 2018).

## ■ Cigarette Smoking: A Costly Addiction

The past 25 years have been marked by a steady decline in cigarette consumption. Still, an estimated 34.3 million Americans age 18 or older were current cigarette smokers in 2017 (SAMHSA, 2018), even though this single behavior will result in death or disability for many of its users.

As previously noted, tobacco use is responsible for approximately 480,000 deaths each year in the United States. Between 2005 and 2009, cigarette smoking caused an annual estimate of 133,300 deaths from ischemic heart disease, 137,989 deaths from lung cancer, 36,000 deaths from other forms of cancer, 100,600 deaths from chronic pulmonary obstructive disease, and 15,300 deaths from stroke. (CDC, 2018b) (see **Figure 11.1**). In fact, as just noted, cigarette smoking kills more individuals in the United States than alcohol, car accidents, guns, AIDS, and illegal drugs combined (American Cancer Society, 2018).

Overall mortality rates decline the longer ex-smokers abstain from smoking. Individuals who quit smoking, regardless of their age, increase their life expectancy compared to those who

continue to smoke. Those who quit between 25 and 34 years of age live approximately 10 years longer. Individuals who quit between ages 35 and 44 live approximately nine years longer. Individuals who quit between ages 45 and 54 live approximately six years longer, and those who quit between ages 55 and 64 live approximately four years longer (National Cancer Institute [NCI], 2017, and references therein).

# The History of Tobacco Use

Like alcohol, tobacco has a long history of use in the Americas and is indigenous to the United States. In fact, tobacco was one of the New World's contributions to the rest of humanity. The word *tobacco* may have come from *tabacco*, which was a two-pronged tube used by the natives of Central America to take snuff. Columbus reported receiving tobacco leaves from the natives of San Salvador in 1492. However, the native peoples had been smoking the leaves for many centuries before Columbus arrived. Practically all native people—from Paraguay to Quebec—used tobacco. The Mayans regarded tobacco smoke as divine incense that would bring rain in the dry season. The oldest known representation of a smoker is a stone carving from a Mayan temple, which shows a priest puffing on a ceremonial pipe. The Aztecs also used tobacco in folk medicine and religious ritual.

Indeed, Native Americans used tobacco in every manner known: smoked as cigars and cigarettes (wrapped in corn husks) and in pipes, as a syrup to be swallowed or applied to the gums, chewed and snuffed, and administered rectally as a ceremonial enema (O'Brien, Cohen, Evans, & Fine, 1992; Schultes, 1978).

In the 1600s, Turkey, Russia, and China all imposed death penalties for smoking. In Turkey, smoking was introduced in the 1600s, spread in popularity, and instantly created two camps. On the one hand, poets praised tobacco as one of four elements of the world of pleasure that also included opium, coffee, and wine. On the other hand, religious leaders were violently opposed to this substance. They created the legend that tobacco grew from Mohammed's spittle after he was bitten by a viper, sucked out the venom, and spat.

Murad (Amurath) IV, known as Murad the Cruel, who reigned during 1623–1640, executed many of his subjects caught smoking.

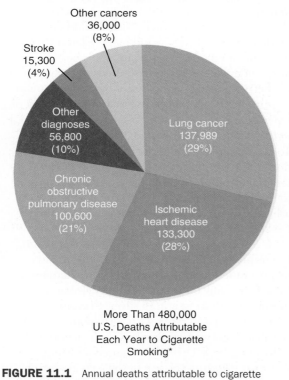

**FIGURE 11.1** Annual deaths attributable to cigarette smoking, 2005–2009.

*Average annual number of deaths 2005–2009.

Reproduced from Centers for Disease Control and Prevention (CDC). (2018b). Health effects infographics. Retrieved from www.cdc.gov/tobacco/infographics/health-effects/index.htm

Other cancers
36,000
(8%)

Stroke
15,300
(4%)

Other diagnoses
56,800
(10%)

Chronic obstructive pulmonary disease
100,600
(21%)

Lung cancer
137,989
(29%)

Ischemic heart disease
133,300
(28%)

More Than 480,000
U.S. Deaths Attributable
Each Year to Cigarette
Smoking*

Whenever the Sultan went on his travels or on a military expedition, his halting-places were always distinguished by a terrible increase in the number of executions. Even on the battlefield, he was fond of surprising men in the act of smoking . . . he would punish them by beheading, hanging, quartering, or crushing their hands and feet and leaving them helpless between the lines.... Nevertheless, in spite of all the horrors of this lust [smoking] that seemed to increase with age, the passion for smoking still persisted.... Even the fear of death was of no avail with the passionate devotees of the habit. (Corti, 1931)

The Romanov tsars publicly tortured smokers and exiled them to Siberia. The Chinese decapitated anyone caught dealing in tobacco with the "outer barbarians." Yet smoking continued to grow to epidemic proportions. Despite their opposition to anything foreign, the Chinese became the heaviest smokers in Asia, thus facilitating the later spread of opium smoking. Thus, no nation whose population has learned to use tobacco products has been successful in outlawing their use or getting people to stop.

Snuffing first became fashionable in France during the reign of Louis XIII and spread throughout the European aristocracy. Snuffing was regarded as daintier and more elegant than constantly exhaling smoke. Louis XIV, however, detested all forms of tobacco, and would not permit its use in his presence. (He would have banned it, but he needed the tax revenue that tobacco brought in.) His sister-in-law, Charlotte of Orleans, was one of the few at court who agreed with him. As she wrote to her sister, "It is better to take no snuff at all than a little; for it is certain that he who takes a little will soon take much, and that is why they call it 'the enchanted herb,' for those who take it are so taken by it that they cannot go without it." Napoleon is said to have used seven pounds of snuff per month (Corti, 1931).

## ▌ Popularity in the Western World

When tobacco reached Europe, it was at first merely a curiosity, but its use spread rapidly. Europeans had no name for the process of inhaling smoke, so they called this "drinking" smoke. Perhaps the first European to inhale tobacco smoke was Rodrigo de Jerez, a member of Columbus's crew. He had seen people smoking in Cuba and brought the habit to Portugal. When he smoked in Portugal, his friends, seeing smoke coming from his mouth, believed he was possessed by the devil. As a result, he was placed in jail for several years (Heimann, 1960; O'Brien et al., 1992).

In 1559, the French ambassador to Portugal, Jean Nicot, grew interested in this novel plant and sent one as a gift to Catherine de Medici, queen of France. The plant was named *Nicotiana tabacum* after him.

The next several hundred years saw a remarkable increase in the use of tobacco. Portuguese sailors smoked it and left tobacco seeds scattered around the world. Over the next 150 years, the Portuguese introduced tobacco to trade with India, Brazil, Japan, China, Arabia, and Africa. Many large tobacco plantations around the world were started by the Portuguese at this time.

An early Christian religious leader, Bishop Bartolome de las Casas (1474–1566), reported that Spanish settlers in Hispaniola (modern Haiti and the Dominican Republic) smoked rolled tobacco leaves in cigar form like the natives. When the bishop asked about this disgusting habit, the settlers replied that they found it impossible to give up.

As the use of tobacco spread, so did the controversy about whether it was bad or good. Tobacco use inspired the first major drug controversy of global dimensions. As a medicine, tobacco was at first almost universally accepted. Nicholas Monardes, in his description of New World plants (dated 1574), recommended tobacco as an infallible cure for 36 different maladies. It was described as a holy, healing herb—a special remedy sent by God to humans.

Opponents of tobacco use disputed its medicinal value. They pointed out that tobacco was used in the magic and religion of Native Americans. Tobacco was attacked as an evil plant, an invention of the devil. King James I of England was fanatically opposed to smoking. In an attempt to limit tobacco use, he raised the import tax on tobacco and also sold the right to collect the tax (Austin, 1978; O'Brien et al., 1992).

Nevertheless, tobacco use increased. By 1614, the number of tobacco shops in London had mushroomed to more than 7000, and demand for tobacco usually outstripped supply. Tobacco was literally worth its weight in silver; to conserve it, users smoked it in pipes with very small bowls. Use of tobacco grew in other areas of the world as well.

In 1642, Pope Urban VIII issued a formal decree forbidding the use of tobacco in church under penalty of immediate excommunication. This decree was in response to the fact that priests and worshippers had been staining church floors with tobacco juice. One priest in Naples sneezed so hard after taking snuff that he vomited on the altar in full sight of the congregation. In response, Pope Innocent X issued another edict against tobacco use in 1650, but the clergy and the laity continued to take snuff and smoke. Finally, in 1725, Pope Benedict XIII, himself a smoker and "snuff-taker," annulled all previous edicts against tobacco (Austin, 1978).

## ■ History of Tobacco Use in America

Tobacco played a significant role in the successful colonization of the United States (Langton, 1991). In 1610, John Rolfe was sent to Virginia to set up a tobacco industry. At first, the tobacco planted in Virginia was a native species, *Nicotiana rustica*, that was harsh and did not sell well. But in 1612, Rolfe managed to obtain some seeds of the Spanish tobacco species *Nicotiana tabacum*, and by 1613 the success of the tobacco industry and the Virginia colony was ensured.

The history of tobacco smoking in the United States is rich in terms of the tremendous number of laws, rules, regulations, and customs that have arisen around the habit of smoking. Many states have had laws prohibiting the use of tobacco by young people as well as women of any age. In the 1860s, for instance, it was illegal in Florida for anyone younger than 21 to smoke cigarettes. A 20-year-old caught smoking could be taken to court and compelled to reveal his source (the cigarette "pusher"). In Pennsylvania, as in South Carolina, any child not informing on his or her cigarette supplier was a criminal.

Cigars became popular in the United States in the early 1800s. Cigar manufacturers fought the introduction of cigarettes for many years. They spread rumors that cigarettes contained opium, were made with tobacco from discarded cigar butts, were made with paper made by Chinese lepers, and so on. By about 1920, however, cigarette consumption started to exceed that of cigars.

The introduction of the cigarette-rolling machine in 1883 spurred cigarette consumption because cigarettes became less expensive. In 2017, nearly 249 billion cigarettes were sold in the United States, a decrease from 258 billion sold in 2016 (CDC, 2019a).

## ■ Tobacco Production

Although there are more than 60 species of tobacco, *Nicotiana tabacum* is the primary tobacco species cultivated in the United States. Its mature leaves are 1 to 2.5 feet long. The nicotine content ranges from 0.3% to 7.0%, depending on the variety, leaf position on the stalk (the higher the position, the more nicotine), and growing conditions.

After harvesting and drying, tobacco leaves are shredded, blown clean of foreign matter and stems, remoisturized with glycerin or other chemical agents, and packed in huge tobacco silos. The tobacco is stored to age for one to two years, during which time the tobacco becomes darker and loses moisture, nicotine, and other volatile substances. When aging has been completed, moisture is again added and the tobacco is blended with other varieties.

There are many types of tobacco, with varying characteristics of harshness, mildness, and flavor. *Bright*, also called *flue-cured* or *Virginia*, has traditionally been among the most common types used in cigarettes. (Flue-cured tobacco is cured with heat transmitted through a flue without exposure to smoke or fumes.) Developed just before the Civil War, this technique made tobacco smoke more readily inhalable.

The amount of leaf tobacco in a cigarette has declined since 1956. There are at least two reasons for this drop. The first reason is the use of reconstituted sheets of tobacco. Parts of the tobacco leaves and stems that were discarded in earlier years are now ground up; combined with many other ingredients to control factors such as moisture, flavor, and color; and then rolled out as a flat, homogenized sheet of reconstituted tobacco. This sheet is then shredded and mixed with regular leaf tobacco, thus reducing production costs. Nearly one-fourth of the tobacco in a cigarette comes from tobacco scraps made into reconstituted sheets. (See "Here and Now: What Is in Tobacco Smoke?")

A second technological advance has further reduced the amount of tobacco needed. This process, called *puffing*, is based on freeze-drying the tobacco and then blowing in air or an inert gas such as carbon dioxide. The gas expands or puffs up the plant cells so they take up more space, are lighter, and can absorb additives better. Additives may include extracts of tobacco, as well as nontobacco flavors such as licorice, cocoa, fruit, spices, and floral compositions. (Licorice was first used in tobacco as a preservative around 1830 and became appreciated only later as a sweetener.) Synthetic flavoring compounds also may be used.

In the 1870s, a "cigarette girl" could roll about four cigarettes per minute by hand. When James Duke leased and improved the first cigarette-rolling machine in 1883, he

## HERE AND NOW
### What Is in Tobacco Smoke?

Tobacco smoke contains chemicals that are harmful to smokers and nonsmokers alike. Of the more than 7,000 chemicals in tobacco smoke, at least 250 are known to be harmful, including hydrogen cyanide, carbon monoxide, and ammonia. Among these 250 harmful chemicals, more than 69 have been found to be carcinogens, including arsenic, benzene, ethylene oxide, and vinyl chloride. Other suspected carcinogens in tobacco include formaldehyde, benzo[↑]pyrene, and toluene.

Data from National Cancer Institute (NCI). (2017). Harms of cigarette smoking and health benefits of quitting. Retrieved from https://www.cancer.gov/about-cancer/causes-prevention/risk/tobacco/cessation-fact-sheet#r6

could make about 200 cigarettes per minute. This advance was the last link in the chain of development leading to the modern American blended cigarette. By 2006, cigarette-rolling machines could roll 20,000 cigarettes per minute (Edwards, 2015).

Tar and nicotine levels in cigarettes have dropped considerably over the years (Bartecchi, MacKenzie, & Shrier, 1995; Palfai & Jankiewicz, 1991). Most cigarettes today are low-tar and low-nicotine types. The filter tip, in which the filter is made of cellulose or in some cases charcoal, has also become common; the vast majority of all cigarettes sold currently in the United States have filter tips. The filter does help remove some of the harmful substances in smoke, but most pass through into the mouth and lungs, including carbon monoxide. The health consequences of many of the substances found in cigarettes have not been adequately analyzed.

© Kevin Largent/Fotolia.com.

Use of spittoons (placed on the floor at the ends of a table) was considered an advancement in public conduct.

### ■ Government Regulation

In the early 1960s, attitudes toward tobacco use began to change in the United States. Before this time, tobacco was perceived as being devoid of any negative consequences. After years of study and hundreds of research reports about the effects of smoking, however, the Advisory Committee to the U.S. Surgeon General reported in 1964 that cigarette smoking is a cause of lung cancer and laryngeal cancer in men, a probable cause of lung cancer in women, and the most important cause of chronic bronchitis. The committee stated, "[C]igarette smoking is a health hazard of sufficient importance in the United States to warrant appropriate remedial action." In 1965, Congress passed legislation setting up the National Clearinghouse for Smoking and Health. This organization had the responsibility of monitoring, compiling, and reviewing the world's medical literature on the health consequences of smoking.

This clearinghouse published reports in 1967, 1968, and 1969. The statistical evidence presented in 1969 made it difficult for Congress to avoid warning the public that smoking was dangerous to their health. Since November 1, 1970, all cigarette packages and cartons have had to carry this label: "Warning: The Surgeon General Has Determined That Cigarette Smoking Is Dangerous to Your Health." In 1984, Congress enacted legislation requiring cigarette advertisements and packages to post four distinct warnings that were to be rotated every three months.

Further pressure on Congress prompting laws that prohibited advertising for tobacco on radio and television after January 2, 1971. The intent was to limit the media's ability to make smoking seem glamorous and sophisticated. The loss in revenue to radio and television was enormous.

The 1979 publication of *Smoking and Health: A Report of the Surgeon General* gave what was then up-to-date information on research about the effects of tobacco on cardiovascular disease, bronchopulmonary disease, cancer, peptic ulcer, and pregnancy. It also emphasized the increase in smoking by women and girls over the preceding 15 years. The 1981 U.S. Surgeon General's report, *The Changing Cigarette*, gave further information, and the 1985 report, *The Health Consequences of Smoking*, gave research findings showing the relationship among smoking in the workplace, cancer, and chronic lung disease.

Over the years, private insurance companies, as well as state and federal agencies, have paid billions of dollars to cover healthcare costs presumably resulting from diseases caused by tobacco use. A series of lawsuits has forced large tobacco companies to compensate for some of these losses. In a landmark settlement in 1998, 47 states reached an agreement with five major tobacco companies to pay a settlement estimated at exceeding $200 billion. Important features of this "Master Settlement Agreement" include the following (U.S. Department of Agriculture [USDA], 2001):

- limitations on advertising,
- ban on cartoon characters in advertising,
- ban on "branded" merchandise,
- limitations on sponsorship of sporting events,
- disbanding of tobacco trade organizations, and
- funds designated to support antismoking measures and research to reduce youth smoking.

All 50 states have enacted laws that restrict the purchase, possession, and use of tobacco products by minors. Although no state has completely banned the sale of tobacco products through vending machines, none allow such sales to minors. In fact, many states have created additional restrictions intended to reduce youth access to vending machines. Some have banned the placement of vending machines in areas accessible to young people and allow their placement only in bars, liquor stores, adult clubs, and other adult-oriented establishments.

Since 1985, numerous other reports on smoking and health by the U.S. Surgeon General have been issued; they invariably repeat the assertions about the devastating effects of cigarette smoking.

In June 2009, President Barack Obama signed legislation that granted the Food and Drug Administration (FDA) the authority to regulate tobacco products. This law, the Family Smoking Prevention and Tobacco Control Act, gave the FDA broad authority to restrict tobacco sales and marketing to youth. Further, it required disclosure of ingredients in tobacco products and smokeless tobacco product warning labels. It also ensured that "modified risk" claims are supported by scientific evidence. Its provisions ban sales to minors, vending-machine sales (except in some facilities that are available to adults only), and the sale of packages of fewer than 20 cigarettes. Further, the act banned tobacco-brand sponsorships of sports and entertainment events or other social or cultural events, as well as free giveaways of sample cigarettes and brand-name nontobacco promotional items (FDA, 2019a).

In August 2016, the FDA finalized a rule that extended its regulatory authority to all tobacco products, including electronic cigarettes (e-cigarettes), cigars, and hookah and pipe tobacco. The rule bans free tobacco samples. It requires health warnings on roll-your-own tobacco and cigarette tobacco (FDA, 2019b). Despite restrictions, tobacco marketing and production remain a major industry in the United States (see "Here and Now: Economic Trends and Tobacco").

# HERE AND NOW
## Economic Trends and Tobacco

According to the CDC, "in 2017, tobacco companies spent $9.06 billion marketing cigarettes and smokeless tobacco in the United States. This amount translates to more than $25 million each day, or more than $1 million every hour."

Further, "although U.S. tobacco production has decreased significantly since the 1980s (from nearly 180,000 tobacco-growing farms to about 10,000 in 2012), the United States continues to be a leading producer of tobacco leaves."

Centers for Disease Control and Prevention (CDC). (2019a). Economic trends in tobacco. Retrieved from http://www.cdc.gov/tobacco/data_statistics/fact_sheets/economics/econ_facts/index.htm

# Pharmacology of Nicotine

In 1828, **nicotine** was discovered to be one component of tobacco. This alkaloid is one of more than 7,000 chemicals found in the smoke from tobacco products such as cigarettes (NCI, 2017). When smoked, nicotine enters the lungs and is then absorbed into the bloodstream. In both (**tobacco chewing**) and dipping (**snuff dipping**), nicotine is absorbed through the mucous lining of the mouth.

The amount of nicotine absorbed into the body varies according to several factors:

- the exact composition of the tobacco used,
- how densely the tobacco is packed in the cigarette and the length of the cigarette smoked,
- whether a filter is used and the characteristics of the filter,
- the volume of smoke inhaled, and
- the number of cigarettes smoked throughout the day.

Depending on how tobacco is taken, the rate at which it enters the bloodstream varies widely. Cigarette smoking results in rapid distribution of nicotine throughout the body; it reaches the brain within 10 seconds of inhalation. A typical smoker will take 10 puffs on a cigarette during the 5 minutes that the cigarette is lit. Thus, a person who smokes one pack (20 cigarettes) each day gets 200 "hits" of nicotine to the brain each day (National Institute on Drug Abuse [NIDA], 2019). In contrast, cigar and pipe smokers typically do not inhale the smoke; nicotine is absorbed more slowly through the lining of the mouth.

## ▌ Effects of Nicotine on the Central Nervous System

Nicotine produces an intense effect on the central nervous system. Research has demonstrated that nicotine activates the brain circuitry in regions responsible for regulating feelings of pleasure. In particular, nicotine increases the release of the neurotransmitter dopamine in the so-called reward or pleasure pathways of the brain. This effect likely contributes to the abuse potential of the stimulant.

The pharmacokinetic properties of nicotine also enhance its abuse potential. Cigarette smoking allows nicotine to enter the brain rapidly, with drug levels peaking within 10 seconds of inhalation. The acute effects of this rapid increase in brain concentration dissipate within a few minutes, causing the smoker to continue to dose frequently throughout the day in an effort to maintain the pleasurable effects of the drug.

## ▌ Other Effects of Nicotine

In addition to its direct effects in the brain, nicotine increases the respiration rate at low dose levels because it stimulates the receptors in the carotid artery (in the neck) that monitor the brain's need for oxygen. It also stimulates the cardiovascular system by releasing epinephrine, which increases coronary blood flow, heart rate, and blood pressure. The effect is to raise the oxygen requirements of the heart muscle. Initially, nicotine stimulates salivary and bronchial secretions; it then inhibits them.

Nicotine has been used as an insecticide, and at higher concentrations it can be extremely toxic. Symptoms of nicotine poisoning include vomiting, abdominal cramps, mental confusion, and breathing difficulty. Respiratory failure from the paralysis of muscles usually brings on death. The average smoker takes in one to two milligrams of nicotine from every cigarette (NIDA, 2019).

# Cigarette Smoking

Smoking leads to disease and damages nearly every organ in the body. Cigarette smokers not only tend to die at an earlier age than nonsmokers but also have a higher probability of developing certain diseases, including cardiovascular disease, cancer, bronchopulmonary disease, and other illnesses, which are described in the following sections. Cigarette smoking shortens the lives of male smokers by approximately 12 years and female smokers by approximately 11 years (American Cancer Society, 2018).

## KEY TERMS

**nicotine**
alkaloid derived from the tobacco plant

**tobacco chewing**
absorption of nicotine through the mucous lining of the mouth

**snuff dipping**
placing a pinch of tobacco between the gums and the cheek

## ■ Cardiovascular Disease

Overwhelming evidence shows that cigarette smoking increases the risk of cardiovascular disease. Smoking causes coronary heart disease, a leading cause of death in the United States. In fact, compared with nonsmokers, smoking increases the risk of coronary heart disease two to four times. Smoking damages blood vessels and can make them thicken and grow narrower, thus promoting hypertension. Smoking can promote blood-clot formation. A stroke occurs when a clot blocks the blood flow to part of the brain or when a blood vessel in or around the brain bursts. Smoking increases the likelihood of a stroke by two to four times (CDC, 2018a).

## ■ Cancer

Smoking tobacco causes an estimated 90% of all lung cancer deaths. Cigarette smoking is a major cause of cancers of the bladder, pancreas, cervix, esophagus, stomach, mouth, and kidney. The risk of lung cancer in men who smoke is 25 times greater than the risk for nonsmokers; the risk for women smokers is approximately 25.7 times greater than for nonsmokers (CDC, 2018a).

## ■ Bronchopulmonary Disease

Cigarette smoking is the leading cause of bronchopulmonary disease, which includes a host of lung ailments. Lung diseases caused by smoking include chronic obstructive pulmonary disease (COPD), which includes emphysema and chronic bronchitis. Tobacco smoke can trigger asthma attacks. Smokers are 12 to 13 times more likely to die from COPD than nonsmokers (CDC, 2018a).

## ■ Effects on Pregnancy

Women who smoke during pregnancy are at an increased risk of miscarriage. Smoking during pregnancy can cause a baby to be born prematurely or have low birth weight. It is a risk factor of sudden infant death syndrome (SIDS). Babies born to women who smoke are more likely to have certain birth defects, including defects of the mouth or lip (CDC, 2019d).

## ■ "Light" Cigarettes

Light cigarettes include those with cellulose acetate filters to trap tar, small holes in the filter tip to dilute smoke with air, and pores to allow toxic chemicals to escape. These are no less hazardous

Cigarette smoking is a leading cause of bronchopulmonary disease.

than regular cigarettes (NCI, 2010b). Smoking machines indicate that they reduce tar levels and should be of some limited benefit. However, many smokers lose this benefit because they often smoke more cigarettes per day, increase the puff number and volume, or block the filter holes with their fingers or lips (see "Here and Now: The Truth About Light Cigarettes").

## ■ Electronic Cigarettes

E-cigarettes are devices designed to deliver nicotine or other substances to a user as a vapor. These products often resemble cigarettes, cigars, or pipes. For individuals who desire to use e-cigarettes without others noticing, some devices are designed to look like pens or USB memory sticks. E-cigarettes are generally composed of a rechargeable battery-operated heating element, a replaceable cartridge that may contain nicotine (or other chemicals), and an atomizer that, when heated, converts the contents of the cartridge into a vapor. The user can then inhale the vapor, a process that can be referred to as **vaping** (see "Here and Now: Vaping Rising Among Adolescents and Teenagers").

### KEY TERM

**vaping**
inhaling or exhaling the vapor produced by an electronic cigarette or similar device

# HERE AND NOW

## The Truth About Light Cigarettes

Many smokers choose low-tar, mild, or light cigarettes because they believe that these cigarettes may be less harmful to their health than regular or full-flavor cigarettes. Unfortunately, light cigarettes do not reduce the health risks of smoking. The only way to reduce risk to oneself and others is to stop smoking completely. Common questions concerning light cigarettes include the following:

**Q.** Are light cigarettes less hazardous than regular cigarettes?

**A.** No. Light cigarettes are no safer than regular cigarettes. According to the National Cancer Institute, tar exposure from a light cigarette can be just as high as that from a regular cigarette if the smoker takes deeper, longer, or more frequent puffs.

**Q.** Why would someone smoking a light cigarette take bigger puffs than with a regular cigarette?

**A.** Features of cigarettes that reduce the yield of machine-measured tar also reduce the yield of nicotine. Thus, smokers may take larger and more frequent puffs, inhale more deeply, or smoke extra cigarettes each day to get enough nicotine to satisfy their craving.

**Q.** Are machine-measured tar yields misleading?

**A.** Yes. The ratings cannot be used to predict how much tar a smoker will actually take in because the way the machine smokes a cigarette is not necessarily the same as how an individual smokes. Taking deeper, longer, and more frequent puffs will lead to greater tar exposure.

**Q.** Do light cigarettes cause cancer?

**A.** Yes. People who smoke any kind of cigarette are at much greater risk of lung cancer than people who do not smoke.

Data from National Cancer Institute (NCI). (2010b). Light cigarettes and cancer risk. Retrieved from http://www.cancer.gov/about-cancer/causes-prevention/risk/tobacco/light-cigarettes-fact-sheet

# HERE AND NOW

## Vaping Rising Among Adolescents and Teenagers

According to the 2018 *Monitoring the Future* (MTF) study that is sponsored by the National Institute on Drug Abuse, there was a dramatic increase in the number of teenagers who tried vaping during 2017.

In vaping, including e-cigarettes, a battery-powered device heats a liquid into an inhalable aerosol. The vapor frequently contains nicotine but may also contain marijuana or tetrahydrocannabinol, hash oil, or other substances. The vapor may also contain flavored propylene glycol or flavored glycerin. Many flavors that are attractive to teenagers are available, including milk chocolate cream, cinnamon, vanilla, buttered popcorn, strawberry and banana, and mint.

According to MTF, approximately 37% of 12th graders reported vaping in 2018, up from 28% in 2017. The percentage of 12th graders indicating that they vaped "just flavoring" in the past year also increased to 25.7% in 2018 from 20.6% in 2017. However, according to NIDA, "it is unclear if teens know what is in the vaping devices they are using, since the most popular devices do not have nicotine-free options, and some labeling has been shown to be inaccurate."

This increase in vaping was not limited to nicotine. For example, marijuana and tetrahydrocannibinol vaping increased significantly as this new method of using marijuana has become more mainstream. In 2018, prevalence of marijuana and tetrahydrocannibinol vaping in the last 12 months increased 1.3, 4.2, and 3.6 percentage points in 8th, 10th, and 12th grades to levels of 4.4%, 12.4%, and 13.1%, respectively.

Noteworthy, the perceived availability of vaping devices and liquids among 8th and 10th graders was high, with 45.7% and 66.6%, respectively, indicating that the devices are "fairly easy" or "very easy" to get.

According to MTF, adolescents associate little risk of harm with vaping. Levels of perceived risk among adolescents for regular use of e-cigarettes or regular vaping of nicotine rank near the lowest of all substances, with little change in recent years.

On September 6, 2019, the Centers for Disease Control and Prevention announced an investigation into "multistate outbreak of severe pulmonary disease associated with e-cigarette product (devices, liquids, refill pods, and/or cartridges) use." As of that date, more than 450 possible cases of lung illness associated with the use of e-cigarette products had been reported to CDC from 33 states and one U.S. territory. While this investigation is ongoing, the CDC suggested that individuals consider not using e-cigarette products.

Centers for Disease Control and Prevention (CDC). (2019). Outbreak of lung illness associated with using e-cigarette projects. Retrieved from https://www.cdc.gov/tobacco/basic_information/e-cigarettes/severe-lung-disease.html

Miech, R. A., Johnston, L. D., O'Malley, P. M., Bachman, J. G., Schulenberg, J. E., & Patrick, M. E. (2019). *Monitoring the Future national survey results on drug use, 1975–2017. Vol. I, Secondary school students*. Ann Arbor, MI: University of Michigan, Institute for Social Research. Retrieved from http://monitoringthefuture.org/pubs.html#monographs

National Institute on Drug Abuse (NIDA). (2018). Teens using vaping in record numbers. Retrieved from https://www.drugabuse.gov/news-events/news-releases/2018/12/teens-using-vaping-devices-in-record-numbers

National Institutes of Health (NIH). (2019, February). Vaping rises among teens. NIH News in Health. Retrieved from https://newsinhealth.nih.gov/2019/02/vaping-rises-among-teens

# Tobacco Use and Exposure Without Smoking

## ■ Smokeless Tobacco

Although it is customary to associate the effects of tobacco use with smoking, millions of nonsmokers experience tobacco effects through their use of smokeless tobacco products.

There are two main forms of smokeless tobacco in the United States. The first, **chewing tobacco**, comes in the form of loose leaf, a plug, or a twist. The second, **snuff**, is finely ground tobacco that can be moist or dry (NCI, 2010c). Most smokeless tobacco users place the product in their cheek or between their cheek and gum. Users suck or chew the tobacco and then spit out the juices. Thus, smokeless tobacco is often called *spitting tobacco*.

Smokeless tobacco contains powerful chemicals that can injure tissues in the mouth and throat. The following findings have been made regarding smokeless tobacco (NCI, 2010c):

- Smokeless tobacco use can lead to nicotine addiction and dependence.
- Smokeless tobacco contains at least 28 cancer-causing agents (carcinogens).
- Smokeless tobacco is strongly associated with leukoplakia, a precancerous lesion of the soft tissues in the mouth that consists of a white patch or plaque.
- Smokeless tobacco increases the risk of developing cancer of the oral cavity, esophagus, and pancreas.

Several smokeless tobacco products have entered the U.S. market, including snus (a form of moist snuff) and "dissolvable" products that can take the form of breath mints or strips. These products are available in a range of flavors, which research suggests may make the products more attractive to young adults (Choi, Fabian, Mottey, Corbett, & Forster, 2012). These products can be more appealing than traditional smokeless tobacco products because they do not require spitting and can be used discreetly.

## ■ Secondhand Smoke

The health of individuals who neither smoke nor chew is also adversely affected by tobacco, specifically, through exposure to **secondhand smoke**, also known as **environmental tobacco smoke**. Secondhand smoke includes a mixture of smoke that comes directly from the lighted tip of a

**KEY TERMS**

**chewing tobacco**
tobacco leaves shredded and twisted into strands for chewing purposes

**snuff**
finely ground smokeless tobacco that can be moist or dry

**secondhand smoke**
smoke released into the air from a lighted cigarette, cigar, or pipe tip and exhaled mainstream smoke

**environmental tobacco smoke**
term referring to secondhand smoke

cigarette, cigar, or pipe and smoke that has been exhaled (CDC, 2018c). Studies of smoking and its effects have directed increased attention to secondhand smoke because smokers and nonsmokers alike breathe in the burning tobacco smoke that pollutes the air. This type of smoke contains thousands of chemicals, including approximately 70 carcinogens (CDC, 2018c).

Exposure to secondhand smoke has serious health consequences. Since 1964, approximately 2.5 million nonsmokers have died from health problems caused by exposure to secondhand smoke. Breathing secondhand smoke has immediate harmful effects on the cardiovascular system of nonsmokers. It is estimated that secondhand smoke caused nearly 34,000 heart disease deaths each year during 2005–2009 among adult nonsmokers in the United States (CDC, 2018c).

Of note, children are particularly vulnerable to secondhand smoke. In children, it contributes to ear infections, more frequent and severe asthma attacks, and an increased risk for SIDS (CDC, 2018c).

# Reasons for Smoking and the Motivation to Quit

## ▮ Reasons for Smoking

Nicotine dependency through cigarette smoking is not only one of the most common forms of drug addiction but also one responsible for numerous deaths. As noted previously, in the United States more deaths each year are caused by tobacco use than by AIDS, illegal drug use, murders, alcohol use, suicides, and motor vehicle injuries combined. Tobacco use continues despite the fact that, since the 1960s, medical research and government assessments have clearly proved that smoking leads to premature death.

When tobacco users are asked why they smoke, their answers are often quite similar:

- It is relaxing.
- It decreases the unpleasant effects of tension, anxiety, and anger.
- It satisfies the craving.
- It is a habit.
- It provides stimulation, increased energy, and arousal.

- It allows the manipulation of objects that have become satisfying habits (the cigarette, pipe, and so on).

In addition,

- Parents or siblings smoke.
- A close friend or boyfriend or girlfriend smokes.

Tobacco use fosters dependence for several reasons:

- The habit can be rapidly and frequently reinforced by inhaling tobacco smoke.
- The rapid metabolism and clearance of nicotine allow for frequent and repeated use, which is encouraged by the rapid onset of withdrawal symptoms.
- Smoking has complex pharmacological effects—both central and peripheral—that may satisfy a variety of the needs of the smoker.
- Some groups offer psychological and social rewards for use, especially the peer groups of young people.
- Smoking patterns can be generalized; that is, the smoker becomes conditioned to smoke with specific activities. For example, some smokers feel the need to smoke after a meal, when driving, and so on.
- Smoking is reinforced by both pharmacological effects and ritual.
- No marked impairment in performance occurs. In fact, smoking enhances performance in some cases. (Nicotine produces a state of alertness, prevents deterioration of reaction time, and improves learning.)

These reasons not only may explain why people continue to smoke but also reveal why it is often difficult for them to stop.

Smokers appear to regulate their intake of nicotine. For example, the smoker of a low-nicotine cigarette often smokes more and inhales more deeply. The average one-pack-a-day smoker is estimated to self-administer thousands of pulses (one pulse per inhalation) of nicotine to nicotinic receptors in the brain per year. This rate greatly surpasses the stimulation rate of any other known form of substance abuse. A habit that is reinforced as frequently and as easily as smoking is hard to break.

Other factors responsible for creating the addiction to nicotine follow:

- Cigarettes are readily available.
- No equipment other than a lighter or match is needed.
- Cigarettes are portable and easy to store.
- Cigarettes are legal for individuals 18 years of age or older.
- Other rewarding behaviors can occur while smoking (e.g., drinking, socializing, and eating).

## ■ Benefits of Cessation

Individuals who stop smoking greatly reduce their risk for disease and premature death. Although the health benefits are greater for people who stop at earlier ages, cessation is beneficial at all ages. As previously noted, individuals who quit between 25 and 34 years of age live approximately 10 years longer. Individuals who quit between ages 35 and 44 live approximately nine years longer. Individuals who quit between ages 45 and 54 live approximately six years longer, and those who quit between ages 55 and 64 live approximately four years longer (National Cancer Institute [NCI], 2017, and references therein).

According to the National Cancer Institute (2017), immediate health benefits of quitting smoking are significant and include the following:

- a return to normalcy of heart rate and blood pressure (which are abnormally high while smoking);
- a decline of carbon monoxide in the blood within hours;
- improved circulation, production of less phlegm, and decreased rate of coughing and wheezing within weeks; and
- substantial improvements in lung function within several months.

In addition, according to the CDC (2019c), cessation of smoking is associated with reductions in the following:

- the risk for lung and other types of cancer;
- the risk for heart disease, stroke, and peripheral vascular disease;
- respiratory symptoms such as coughing, wheezing, and shortness of breath;
- the risk of developing chronic obstructive pulmonary disease;
- the risk for infertility in women; and
- the risk of having a low-birth-weight baby

## ■ The Motivation to Quit

Quitting smoking is easy. I've done it a thousand times.
—*Mark Twain*

When habitual smokers stop smoking, particularly without the use of smoking-cessation aids, they may experience a variety of unpleasant withdrawal effects, including craving for tobacco, irritability, restlessness, sleep disturbances, gastrointestinal disturbances, anxiety and impaired concentration, judgment, and psychomotor performance. The onset of nicotine withdrawal symptoms may occur within hours or days after quitting and may persist from a few days to several months. Frustration over these symptoms leads many people to start smoking again. The intensity of withdrawal effects may be mild, moderate, or severe; it is not always correlated with the amount smoked.

The National Cancer Institute (2010a) has several recommendations of alternative activities that ex-smokers might try as aids to handle the cravings associated with quitting and get through the withdrawal period. These include the following:

- reminding oneself that cravings will pass;
- avoiding situations and activities that one normally associates with smoking;
- chewing on carrots, pickles, sunflower seeds, apples, celery, or sugarless gum or hard candy as a substitute for smoking so as to keep one's mouth occupied and thus perhaps diminish the psychological craving to smoke; and
- repeatedly taking a deep breath through one's nose and exhaling slowly through one's mouth.

In addition to behavioral modifications, several pharmacological interventions are available to someone wanting to quit smoking. These include nicotine replacement therapy (e.g., nicotine gums, patches, lozenges, inhalers, or sprays) and agents such as bupropion (Zyban) and varenicline (Chantix).

### NICOTINE GUM

Nicotine gum can be purchased over the counter without a prescription. Chewing the gum allows for the rapid absorption of nicotine through the mucous membranes of the mouth. Users chew the gum until noting a peppery taste, and then hold it against the cheek to permit faster absorption. The user will chew on and off for about 20 to 30 minutes.

Significant advantages afforded by nicotine gum are that it is easy to use and allows the user to control the dose of nicotine by controlling the number of pieces chewed each day. Individuals gradually decrease the number of pieces chewed each day, with a goal of complete abstinence from the drug. Side effects of the gum can include a bad taste, throat irritation, nausea (if the gum is swallowed), jaw discomfort (if chewed too rapidly), and racing heartbeat.

### NICOTINE PATCHES

Nicotine patches, also known as *transdermal nicotine systems*, are available without a prescription. The patch, which is directly applied and worn on the skin, releases a continuous flow of small doses of nicotine to quell the desire for cigarette-provided nicotine. The method of delivering nicotine to the skin reduces the withdrawal symptoms as the smoker attempts to quit. As the nicotine doses are lowered over a course of weeks, the smoker is weaned away from nicotine. The most common side effects are mild skin irritations such as redness and itching.

### NICOTINE NASAL SPRAYS, INHALERS, AND LOZENGES

Nicotine nasal sprays rapidly deliver nicotine to the bloodstream as it is absorbed through the membranous lining of the nasal passages. These are easy to use and give immediate relief of withdrawal symptoms. The most common side effects of using the spray include coughing, sinus irritation, runny nose, watery eyes, sneezing, and throat irritation. It is generally not recommended for individuals with asthma, allergies, or other pulmonary problems.

A nicotine inhaler consists of a small plastic tube that contains a nicotine plug. When the user puffs on the inhaler, the plug provides nicotine vapor into the mouth. One advantage to the inhaler is that the action of puffing mimics some of the behaviors associated with smoking. Side effects associated with its use include coughing and throat irritation.

Nicotine lozenges are alternatives to sprays and inhalers. Potential side effects can include sore throat and heartburn. Lozenges are available without a prescription. In the United States, nicotine inhalers and nasal sprays are available by prescription only (Smokefree.gov, n.d.).

### VARENICLINE AND BUPROPION

Varenicline acts at receptors in the brain affected by nicotine. Common side effects include nausea, constipation, vomiting, difficulty sleeping, and strange dreams. Other serious side effects can include changes in behavior, depressed mood, hostility, and suicidal thoughts.

Bupropion also helps patients abstain from smoking by acting at brain nicotine receptors. Noteworthy, this agent is also used as an antidepressant. Its side effects can include dry mouth, headaches, and dizziness. Other serious potential side effects can include changes in behavior, depressed mood, hostility, suicidal thoughts, seizures, and irregular heartbeat.

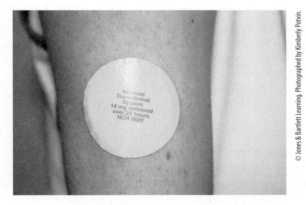

A transdermal patch, an example of a popular therapy for quitting smoking.

© Jones & Bartlett Learning. Photographed by Kimberly Potvin.

# Smoking Prohibition Versus Smokers' Rights

In response to the banning of smoking from certain public facilities throughout the United States, people who want to continue smoking have formed action groups to press their right to smoke. Although these groups have made some modest gains, the trend toward restricting and banning cigarette smoking remains strong. Antismoking groups have been highly successful in their own efforts, and restrictions on the sale of cigarettes and tobacco products remain tight. Many states have banned smoking in worksites, restaurants, and bars.

# HERE AND NOW

## Taxing Cigarettes Decreases Tobacco Consumption

The Centers for Disease Control and Prevention asserts that "increasing the price of tobacco products is the single most effective way to reduce consumption." According to the World Health Organization, "A tax increase that increases tobacco prices by 10% decreases tobacco consumption by about 4% in high-income countries and about 5% in low- and middle-income countries. Similarly, the CDC estimates that a 10% increase in price reduces overall cigarette consumption by 3% to 5%. Further, the CDC reported research suggesting that youth and young adults are two to three times more likely to respond to increases in price than adults.

Centers for Disease Control and Prevention (CDC). (2019a). Economic trends in tobacco. Retrieved from http://www.cdc.gov/tobacco/data_statistics/fact_sheets/economics/econ_facts/index.htm

World Health Organization (WHO). (2019). Tobacco. Retrieved from https://www.who.int/news-room/fact-sheets/detail/tobacco

# LEARNING PORTFOLIO

## Key Terms

## Discussion Questions

1. If smoking is the most preventable cause of disease and premature death in the United States, why do people continue to smoke?
2. How effective are the health warning labels on cigarette packages?
3. List and define the diseases that cigarette smokers are most likely to contract.
4. What effects does maternal smoking have on the fetus?
5. Why is smokeless tobacco perceived as safer than other forms of tobacco?
6. Who is most likely to smoke and why?
7. Why do people who smoke become dependent on tobacco?
8. Assess the major methods for quitting smoking. Which methods are most likely to succeed?
9. Do you think smokers should have the right to smoke in public places? Explain.
10. Discuss if or how the use of e-cigarettes and vaping should be regulated.

## Summary

1. Nicotine is a highly addictive substance.
2. Approximately 21.5% of the U.S. population age 12 or older reports current use of a tobacco product.
3. Nicotine is the substance in tobacco that causes dependence. This drug initially stimulates and then depresses the central nervous system.
4. The amount of tobacco absorbed varies according to five factors: (a) the exact composition of the tobacco being used, (b) how densely the tobacco is packed in the cigarette and the length of the cigarette smoked, (c) whether a filter is used and the characteristics of the filter, (d) the volume of the smoke inhaled, and (e) the number of cigarettes smoked throughout the day.
5. Cigarette smoking is an addiction that is costly in several ways. For instance, each year approximately 480,000 deaths in the United States are attributed to cigarette smoking.
6. Chewing tobacco and snuff are types of smokeless tobacco products that are commonly referred to as "spitting tobacco." Chewing tobacco consists of tobacco leaves that are shredded and twisted into strands and then either chewed or placed in the cheek between the lower lip and gum. Snuff is finely ground smokeless tobacco that can be moist or dry.

**7.** Cigarette smokers tend to die at an earlier age than nonsmokers. They also have a greater probability of contracting various illnesses, including various types of cancers, chronic bronchitis and emphysema, diseases of the cardiovascular system, and peptic ulcers. In addition, smoking has adverse effects on pregnancy and may harm the fetus.

# References

American Cancer Society. (2018). Health risks of smoking tobacco. Retrieved from https://www.cancer.org/cancer/cancer-causes/tobacco-and-cancer/health-risks-of-smoking-tobacco.html

Austin, G. A. (1978). *Perspectives on the history of psychoactive substance use.* Washington, DC: National Institute on Drug Abuse.

Bartecchi, C. E., MacKenzie, T. D., & Shrier, R. W. (1995, May). The global tobacco epidemic. *Scientific American,* p. 49.

Centers for Disease Control and Prevention (CDC). (2018a). Health effects of cigarette smoking. Retrieved from https://www.cdc.gov/tobacco/data_statistics/fact_sheets/health_effects/effects_cig_smoking/index.htm

Centers for Disease Control and Prevention (CDC). (2018b). Health effects infographics. Retrieved from www.cdc.gov/tobacco/infographics/health-effects/index.htm

Centers for Disease Control and Prevention (CDC). (2018c). Secondhand smoke facts. Retrieved from http://www.cdc.gov/tobacco/data_statistics/fact_sheets/secondhand_smoke/general_facts/

Centers for Disease Control and Prevention (CDC). (2019a). Economic trends in tobacco. Retrieved from http://www.cdc.gov/tobacco/data_statistics/fact_sheets/economics/econ_facts/index.htm

Centers for Disease Control and Prevention (CDC). (2019b). Fast facts. Retrieved from http://www.cdc.gov/tobacco/data_statistics/fact_sheets/fast_facts/index.htm

Centers for Disease Control and Prevention (CDC). (2019c). Quitting smoking. Retrieved from http://www.cdc.gov/tobacco/data_statistics/fact_sheets/cessation/quitting/

Centers for Disease Control and Prevention (CDC). (2019d). Substance use during pregnancy. Retrieved from http://www.cdc.gov/reproductivehealth/maternalinfanthealth/tobaccousepregnancy/index.htm

Centers for Disease Control and Prevention (CDC). (2019e). Youth and tobacco use. Retrieved from http://www.cdc.gov/tobacco/data_statistics/fact_sheets/youth_data/tobacco_use/index.htm

Choi, K., Fabian, L., Mottey, N., Corbett, A., & Forster, J. (2012). Young adults' favorable perceptions of snus, dissolvable tobacco products, and electronic cigarettes: Findings from a focus group study. *American Journal of Public Health, 102*(11), 2088–2093.

Corti, E. C. (1931). *A history of smoking.* London, UK: Harrap and Company.

Edwards, P. (2015). What everyone gets wrong about the history of cigarettes. Vox Technology. Retrieved from http://www.vox.com/2015/3/18/8243707/cigarette-rolling-machines

Food and Drug Administration (FDA). (2019a). Family Smoking and Prevention Tobacco Control Act—An overview. Retrieved from https://www.fda.gov/tobacco-products/rules-regulations-and-guidance/family-smoking-prevention-and-tobacco-control-act-overview

Food and Drug Administration (FDA). (2019b). The facts on the FDA's new tobacco rule. Retrieved from https://www.fda.gov/consumers/consumer-updates/facts-fdas-new-tobacco-rule

Heimann, R. K. (1960). *Tobacco and Americans.* New York, NY: McGraw-Hill.

Langton, P. A. (1991). *Drug use and the alcohol dilemma.* Boston, MA: Allyn & Bacon.

Miech, R. A., Johnston, L. D., O'Malley, P. M., Bachman, J. G., Schulenberg, J. E., & Patrick, M. E. (2019). *Monitoring the Future national survey results on drug use, 1975–2017. Vol. I, Secondary school students.* Ann Arbor, MI: University of Michigan, Institute for Social Research. Retrieved from http://monitoringthefuture.org/pubs.html#monographs

National Cancer Institute (NCI). (2010a). How to handle withdrawal symptoms and triggers when you decide to quit smoking. Retrieved from http://www.cancer.gov/cancertopics/factsheet/Tobacco/symptoms-triggers-quitting

National Cancer Institute (NCI). (2010b). Light cigarettes and cancer risk. Retrieved from http://www.cancer.gov/about-cancer/causes-prevention/risk/tobacco/light-cigarettes-fact-sheet

National Cancer Institute (NCI). (2010c). Smokeless tobacco and cancer. Retrieved from http://www.cancer.gov/cancertopics/factsheet/Tobacco/smokeless

National Cancer Institute (NCI). (2017). Harms of cigarette smoking and health benefits of quitting. Retrieved from https://www.cancer.gov/about-cancer/causes-prevention/risk/tobacco/cessation-fact-sheet#r6

National Institute on Drug Abuse (NIDA). (2018). Teens using vaping in record numbers. Retrieved from https://www

.drugabuse.gov/news-events/news-releases/2018/12/teens-using-vaping-devices-in-record-numbers

National Institute on Drug Abuse (NIDA). (2019). Tobacco, nicotine and e-cigarettes. Retrieved from https://www.drugabuse.gov/publications/research-reports/tobacco-nicotine-e-cigarettes

National Institutes of Health (NIH). (2019, February). Vaping rises among teens. NIH News in Health. Retrieved from https://newsinhealth.nih.gov/2019/02/vaping-rises-among-teens

O'Brien, R., Cohen, S., Evans, G., & Fine, J. (1992). *The encyclopedia of drug abuse*, 2nd ed. New York, NY: Facts on File and Greenspring.

Palfai, T., & Jankiewicz, H. (1991). *Drugs and human behavior.* Dubuque, IA: William C. Brown.

Schultes, R. E. (1978). Ethnopharmacological significance of psychotropic drugs of vegetal origin. In W. G. Clark & J. del Guidice, *Principles of psychopharmacology*, 2nd ed. (pp. 41–70). New York, NY: Academic Press.

Smokefree.gov. (n.d.). Using nicotine replacement therapy. Bethesda, MD: National Institutes of Health, National Cancer Institute. Retrieved from https://smokefree.gov/tools-tips/medications-can-help-you-quit/using-nicotine-replacement-therapy

Substance Abuse and Mental Health Services Administration (SAMHSA). (2018). 2017 National Survey on Drug Use and Health: Detailed tables. Substance Abuse and Mental Health Services Administration, Rockville, MD: Author.

Substance Abuse and Mental Health Services Administration (SAMHSA). (2019). Key substance use and mental health indicators in the United States: Results from the 2018 National Survey on Drug Use and Health. Rockville, MD: Author. Retrieved from https://www.samhsa.gov/data/sites/default/files/cbhsq-reports/NSDUHNationalFindingsReport2018/NSDUHNationalFindingsReport2018.pdf

U.S. Department of Agriculture (USDA). (2001). *Trends in the cigarette industry after the master settlement agreement.* Washington, DC: Economic Research Service.

World Health Organization (WHO). (2019). Tobacco. Retrieved from https://www.who.int/news-room/fact-sheets/detail/tobacco

CHAPTER **12**

# Hallucinogens (Psychedelics)

## Did You Know?

▶ Hallucinogens were abused by relatively few people in the United States until the social upheaval of the 1960s.

▶ Some hallucinogens such as lysergic acid diethylamide (LSD) and the herb *Salvia divinorum* have been used and recommended by psychiatrists to assist in psychotherapy with certain patients.

▶ Ecstasy has been tested in clinical trials for its ability to treat posttraumatic stress disorder (PTSD).

▶ Hallucinogens such as LSD do not tend to be physically addicting.

▶ Evidence has strongly suggested that ketamine is a unique antidepressant that has relatively fast therapeutic actions in depressed patients who are not effectively managed by other treatment strategies.

▶ The senses are grossly exaggerated and distorted under the influence of hallucinogens.

▶ Abuse of Ecstasy increased dramatically from 1996 to 2000 because of its popularity as a "club drug" and its use at "rave" parties, but its use has since declined over concerns about its potential side effects.

▶ For some users, hallucinogens can cause frightening, nightmarish experiences referred to as "bad trips."

▶ Phencyclidine (PCP) and ketamine were originally developed as general anesthetics, but because of their ability to cause psychosis their use in humans is either prohibited or tightly limited.

▶ Abuse of high doses of over-the-counter (OTC) cough medicines that contain dextromethorphan is a problem with young populations and can cause a PCP-like hallucinogenic or psychotic effect.

## Learning Objectives

**On completing this chapter, you should be able to:**

❯ Explain why hallucinogens became so popular during the 1960s.

❯ Describe how hallucinogens alter the senses.

❯ Outline how psychedelic, stimulant, and anticholinergic effects are expressed in the three principal types of hallucinogens.

❯ Describe why some psychotherapists believe that MDMA and other hallucinogens may be beneficial for their patients and how public approval of marijuana likely will affect this movement.

❯ Explain the reasons for Ecstasy's recent fluctuations in patterns of use.

❯ Explain how hallucinogens differ from other commonly abused drugs in terms of their addicting properties and their ability to cause dependence.

❯ Describe the effects that environment and personality have on the individual's response to hallucinogens.

❯ Explain what is meant by the term *club drugs* and describe particular problems associated with their use.

❯ Characterize how PCP differs from other hallucinogens and why it is so dangerous.

❯ Explain the similarities between PCP and ketamine.

❯ Describe the recreational and legal status of *Salvia divinorum*.

## Introduction

The following is a summary of issues to consider when caring for someone under the influence of a high dose of a hallucinogen:

> Because persons under the influence of hallucinogens may exhibit very diverse and rapidly changing behaviors ranging from euphoria to agitation and aggression, it is important to be calm and reassuring while trying to "talk them down." Patients presenting with an acute panic reaction should be placed in a quiet nonthreatening environment with minimal stimuli. In extreme situations because of potentially fatal consequences associated with the cardiovascular system, it may even be necessary to either chemically or physically restrain the person to keep [him or her] from self-injury or from hurting someone nearby. Hospitalization may be necessary in difficult situations to control circumstances and allow for required stabilizing therapy. (D'Orazio, 2018)

This description from an experienced treatment provider illustrates the sensory and emotional distortions that can be caused by using **hallucinogens** or **psychedelics**. The word *psychedelic* comes from the Greek root meaning "mind revealing." In this chapter, we begin with a brief historical review of the use of hallucinogens, tracing the trend in the United States from the 1960s to today. Next, the nature of hallucinogens and the effects they produce are examined. The rest of the chapter addresses the various types of psychedelic agents—lysergic acid diethylamide (LSD), phenylethylamines (including Ecstasy), anticholinergics, natural products, and other miscellaneous substances.

### KEY TERMS

**hallucinogens**
substances that alter sensory processing in the brain, causing perceptual disturbances, changes in thought processing, and depersonalization

**psychedelics**
substances that expand or heighten perception and consciousness

## The History of Hallucinogen Use

People have known and written about drug-related hallucinations for centuries. Throughout the ages, individuals who saw visions or experienced hallucinations were perceived as being holy or sacred, as receiving divine messages, or possibly as bewitched and controlled by the devil. There are many indications that medicine men, shamans, witches, oracles, and perhaps mystics and priests of various groups were familiar with drugs and herbs that caused such experiences, which today are known as *hallucinogens* (Parish, 2015).

Before the 1960s, several psychedelic substances, such as mescaline from the peyote cactus, could be obtained from chemical supply houses with no restriction in the United States. Abuse of hallucinogens did not become a major social problem in this country until this decade of racial struggles, the Vietnam War, and violent demonstrations. Many individuals frustrated with the hypocrisy of "the establishment" tried to "turn on and tune in" by using hallucinogens as pharmacological crutches.

Psychedelic drugs became especially popular when some medical professionals, such as then-Harvard psychology professor Timothy Leary, reported that these drugs allowed users to get in touch with themselves and achieve a peaceful inner serenity. At the same time, it became well publicized that the natural psychedelics (such as mescaline and peyote) for many years had been used routinely by some Native Americans religious groups for enhancing spiritual experiences. This factor contributed to the mystical, supernatural aura associated with hallucinogenic agents and added to their enticement for the so-called dropout generation.

Protests against the Vietnam War in the 1960s and 1970s often included the use of hallucinogens.

Because of their widespread use, this and similar drugs were seen as inducing a form of psychosis-like schizophrenia (American Psychiatric Association [APA] 2013). The term **psychotomimetic** was coined to describe these compounds; this term means "psychosis mimicking" and is still used in medicine today. The basis for the designation is the effects of these drugs, which induce mental states that impair an individual's ability to recognize and respond appropriately to reality.

By the mid-1960s, federal regulatory agencies had become concerned with the misuse of hallucinogens and the potential emotional damage caused by these drugs. Access to hallucinogenic agents was restricted, and laws against their distribution were passed. Despite the problems associated with these psychedelics, some groups demanded that responsible use with therapeutic benefits was possible and that trained clinicians be allowed legal access to these substances (Begola & Schillerstrom, 2019). For example, some hallucinogens have been proposed for treatment of patients suffering terminal diseases such as cancer to help them deal with the fear of death (Begola & Schillerstrom, 2019).

## ■ The Native American Church

The hallucinogen peyote plays a central role in the ceremonies of Native Americans who follow a religion that is a combination of Christian doctrine and Native American religious rituals. Members of this church are found as far north as Canada. They believe that God made a special gift of this sacramental plant to them so that they might commune more directly with Him. The first organized peyote church was the First-Born Church of Christ, incorporated in 1914 in Oklahoma. The Native American Church of the United States was chartered in 1918 and is currently the largest such group with approximately 100,000 to 200,000 members (Hilleary, 2019).

Because of the religious beliefs of the members of the Native American Church concerning the powers of peyote, when Congress legislated against its use in 1965, it allowed room for religious use of this psychedelic plant. The American Indian Religious Freedom Act of 1978 was an attempt by Congress to allow the members of the Native American Church access to peyote based on constitutional guarantees of religious freedom. Because of controversy inspired by the original piece of legislation, an amendment to the 1978 act

Peyote is used as a sacramental plant by members of the Native American Church as part of their religious ceremonies.

was signed in 1994, which specifically protected the use of peyote in Native American Church ceremonies. This amendment prohibits the use of peyote for nonreligious purposes (Native American Church, 2008). However, despite these efforts by Congress to resolve this issue, controversies continue to arise (see "Case in Point: Peyote and the Rights of Native Americans").

## ■ Timothy Leary and the League of Spiritual Discovery

In 1966, three years after being fired by Harvard University because of his controversial involvement with hallucinogens (Associated Press, 1999), Timothy Leary undertook a strategy based on the right to freedom of religion established in the

**KEY TERM**

**psychotomimetics**
substances that cause psychosis-like symptoms

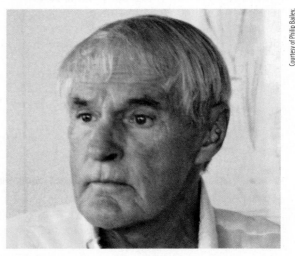

Timothy Leary advocated the legalization of LSD in the 1960s.

# ► CASE IN POINT

## Peyote and the Rights of Native Americans

**T**wo Native Americans living in Oregon worked for a drug-rehabilitation facility. They consumed portions of a small cactus referred to as *peyote* regularly as part of their religious beliefs. The organization they worked for found out about the counselors' practice and terminated their employment. The Native Americans filed for unemployment benefits but were denied by the state's unemployment office, which claimed they were dismissed because of misconduct. The employees sued the state

and lost. The case was appealed to the U.S. Supreme Court, which ruled against the Native Americans, concluding that an individual's religious affiliation does not exclude him or her from complying with valid laws. Several years later, individual states started to pass their own laws that created religious exemptions to this law. This led to the passage of the Religious Freedom Restoration Act, which requires the federal government to "not substantially burden religious exercise without compelling justification."

Sterbenz, C. (2015, April 3). Indiana's religious freedom law was inspired by Native Americans' right to smoke peyote. Business Insider. Retrieved from http://www.businessinsider.com/where-did-indianas-religious-freedom-law-come-from-2015-4

---

U.S. Constitution to maintain legitimate access to LSD. He began a religion called the League of Spiritual Discovery; LSD was the sacrament. This unorthodox religious orientation to the LSD experience was presented in a manual called *The Psychedelic Experience* (Leary, Metzner, & Alpert, 1964), which was based on the *Tibetan Book of the Dead*. It became the "bible" of the psychedelic drug movement.

The movement grew, but most members used street LSD and did not follow Leary's directions. Leary believed that the hallucinogenic experience was only beneficial under proper control and guidance. But most members of this so-called religion merely used the organization as a front to gain access to an illegal drug. Federal authorities did not agree with Leary's freedom of religion interpretation and in 1969 convicted him of possession of marijuana and LSD and sentenced him to 20 years in prison (Biography, n.d.). Before being incarcerated, Leary escaped to Algeria and wandered for a couple of years before being extradited to the United States. He served several years in jail and was released in 1976.

Even in his later years, Leary continued to believe that U.S. citizens should be able to use hallucinogens without government regulation. He died in 1996 at age 75, revered by some but despised by others (Associated Press, 1999; "Many Were Lost," 1996).

## Hallucinogen Use Today

Today, the use of hallucinogens (excluding marijuana) is mostly a young-adult phenomenon. Although the use rate has not returned to that

of the late 1960s and early 1970s (approximately 16%), in high school seniors use in 2018 was 4.3% (Johnston, 2019) (see **Table 12.1**).

## The Nature of Hallucinogens

Agreement has not been reached on what constitutes a hallucinogenic agent (Cormier 2016), for several reasons. First, a variety of seemingly unrelated drug groups can produce hallucinations, delusions, or sensory disturbances under certain conditions. For example, besides the traditional hallucinogens (such as LSD), high doses of anticholinergics, cocaine, amphetamines, and steroids can also cause hallucinations (Goldsmith, 2015).

In addition, responses to even the traditional hallucinogens can vary tremendously from person to person and from experience to experience

Hooton, 2015.

**TABLE 12.1** Trends in the Use of LSD and All Hallucinogens by 8th, 10th, and 12th Graders: 1994–2018

| | Substance | Used During Year (%) | | | | | | |
|---|---|---|---|---|---|---|---|---|
| | | **1994** | **1996** | **2006** | **2010** | **2012** | **2015** | **2018** |
| **8th Graders** | LSD | 2.4 | 3.5 | 0.9 | 1.2 | 0.8 | 0.9 | 0.9 |
| | All hallucinogens | 2.7 | 4.1 | 2.1 | 2.2 | 1.6 | 1.3 | 1.4 |
| **10th Graders** | LSD | 5.2 | 6.9 | 1.7 | 1.9 | 1.7 | 2.0 | 2.0 |
| | All hallucinogens | 5.8 | 7.8 | 4.1 | 4.2 | 3.5 | 3.1 | 2.7 |
| **12th Graders** | LSD | 6.9 | 8.8 | 1.7 | 2.6 | 2.4 | 2.9 | 3.2 |
| | All hallucinogens | 7.6 | 10.1 | 4.9 | 5.5 | 4.8 | 4.2 | 4.3 |

Data from Johnston, L. D. (2019). *Monitoring the future*. Ann Arbor, MI: University of Michigan, Institute for Social Research. Retrieved from http://monitoringthefuture.org/pubs/monographs/mtf-overview2018.pdf

(see "Signs & Symptoms: Hallucinogens"). Multiple mechanisms are involved in the actions of these drugs, which contribute to the array of responses that they can cause. These drugs most certainly influence the complex inner workings of the human mind and have been described as psychedelic, **psychotogenic**, or psychotomimetic (Cormier, 2016). The feature of hallucinogens that distinguishes them from other drug groups is their ability to alter perception, thought, and feeling in such a manner that does not normally occur except in dreams or during experiences of extreme religious exaltation (Cormier, 2016). We examine these characteristics throughout this chapter.

## ■ Sensory and Psychological Effects

In general, LSD is considered the prototype agent against which other hallucinogens are measured (Cormier, 2016). Typical users experience several stages of sensory experiences; they can go through all stages during a single "trip" or, more likely, will pass through only some. These stages are as follows:

- heightened, exaggerated senses;
- loss of control;
- self-reflection; and
- loss of identity and a sense of cosmic merging.

LSD users describe the transitions they experience while under this potent hallucinogen as going from normal, to highly colorful, to extremely emotional and uncontrolled, to demonic, and then to becoming merged with what is outside one's head. This is reflected in a series of facial self-portraits drawn by a young lady on LSD (see Hooton, 2015, for an example).

### ALTERED SENSES

An associated sensation caused by LSD-like hallucinogens is **synesthesia**, a crossover phenomenon between senses. For example, sound develops visual dimensions, and vice versa, enabling the user to see sounds and hear colors. These altered sensory experiences are described

## SIGNS & SYMPTOMS
### Hallucinogens

| Possible Signs of Use | Extreme Reactions |
|---|---|
| Heightened senses | Increased body temperature (MDMA) |
| Loss of control | Electrolyte imbalance |
| Loss of identity | Cardiac arrest |
| Illusions and hallucinations | A nightmare-like trip (LSD) |
| Altered perception of time and distance | Unable to direct movement, feel pain, or remember |

## KEY TERMS

**psychotogenics**
substances that initiate psychotic behavior

**synesthesia**
a subjective sensation or image of a sense other than the one being stimulated, such as an auditory sensation caused by a visual stimulus

as a heightened sensory awareness and relate to the first component of the psychedelic state (Sapolsky, 2015).

## LOSS OF CONTROL

The second feature of LSD also relates to altered sensory experiences and a loss of control (Buddy T., 2012). The user cannot determine whether the psychedelic trip will be a pleasant, relaxing experience or a "bad trip," with recollections of hidden fears and suppressed anxieties that can precipitate neurotic or psychotic responses. The frightening reactions may persist for a few minutes or several hours and be mildly agitating or extremely disturbing. Some bad trips can include feelings of panic, confusion, suspicion, helplessness, and a total lack of control. The following example illustrates how terrifying a bad trip can be:

> I was having problems breathing [and] my throat was all screwed up. The things that entered my mind were that I was dead and people were saying good-bye, because they really meant it. I was witnessing my own funeral. I was thinking that I was going to wake either in the back seat of a cop car or in the hospital. (*From Venturelli's files, male, age 19*)

Replays of these frightening experiences can occur at a later time, even though the drug has not been taken again; such recurrences are referred to as **flashbacks**, or *hallucinogen-persisting perception disorder*. However, the frequency and severity of these experiences are controversial (Ferro, 2013).

It is not clear what determines the nature of the sensory response. Perhaps it relates to the state of anxiety and personality of the user or the nature of his or her surroundings. It is interesting that Timothy Leary tried to teach his "drug disciples" that "turning on correctly means to understand the many levels that are brought into focus; it takes years of discipline, training and discipleship" ("Celebration #1," 1966). He apparently felt that, with experience and training, you could control the sensory effects of the hallucinogens. This is

### KEY TERM

**flashbacks**
recurrences of earlier drug-induced sensory experiences in the absence of the drug

an interesting possibility but has never been well demonstrated.

## SELF-REFLECTION

During the period when sensory effects predominate, self-reflection also occurs. While in this state, the user becomes aware of thoughts and feelings long hidden beneath the surface, forgotten, or repressed. Some claim that this new perspective can lead to valid insights that are useful psychotherapeutic exercises (Johnstad, 2015).

Some psychotherapists have used or advocated the use of psychedelics for this purpose since the 1950s, as described many years before by Sigmund Freud, to "make conscious the unconscious" (Snyder, 1974, p. 44). Although a case can be made for the psychotherapeutic use of this group of drugs, the Food and Drug Administration (FDA) has not yet approved any of these agents for psychiatric use; it has, however, approved clinical trials to study the psychedelic and stimulant drug Ecstasy (MDMA) to evaluate if it would be useful in the treatment of posttraumatic stress disorder (PTSD). These studies are supported by an organization known as the Multidisciplinary Association for Psychedelic Studies and are speculated to require 10 years at a cost of $15 million to complete. If approved, the intent is to use MDMA as an adjunct to psychotherapy because of its ability to increase feelings of empathy (Wing, 2015).

Although considerable caution is still needed because of the somewhat unpredictable nature of these drugs, other small studies are examining the effects of psychedelic drugs, including psilocybin and LSD, to treat emotional problems such as depression in cancer patients, obsessive–compulsive disorder, and end-of-life anxiety. Some of the reported results have been encouraging, but they are only preliminary and still small-scale. Some are concerned that some of the reported benefits have been exaggerated by scientists turned evangelists who are anxious to make these drugs routine therapeutics. Only time will tell how or if the medical and scientific community will react to the "new science" that is promoted as evidence that psychedelics have an important therapeutic role to play in modern-day medicine. Clearly, this is a controversy that is far from being resolved.

## LOSS OF IDENTITY AND COSMIC MERGING

The final features that set the psychedelics apart as unique drugs are the mystical and spiritual aspect of the drug experience. Because consumption of hallucinogen-containing plants has often been part of religious ceremonies, it is likely that this sense of cosmic merging and union with all humankind correlates to the exhilaratingly spiritual experiences described by many religious mystics.

The loss of identity and personal boundaries caused by hallucinogens is not viewed as being spiritually enticing by everyone. In particular, for individuals who have rigid, highly ordered personalities, the dissolution of a well-organized and well-structured world is terrifying because the drug destroys the individual's emotional support. Such an individual finds that the loss of a separate identity can cause extreme panic and anxiety. During these drug-induced panic states, which in some ways are similar to schizophrenia, people have committed suicide and homicide. These tragic reactions are part of the risk of using hallucinogens and explain some of the FDA's hesitancy to legalize or authorize them for psychotherapeutic use (Horgan, 2015).

### ■ Mechanisms of Action

As with most drugs, hallucinogens represent the proverbial "double-edged sword." These drugs may cause potentially useful psychiatric effects for many people. However, the variability in positive versus negative responses, coupled with a lack of understanding about what factors are responsible for the variables, suggests that these drugs may be dangerous for some patients and difficult to manage (Horgan, 2019).

Some researchers have suggested that all hallucinogens act at a common central nervous system (CNS) site to exert their psychedelic effects. Although this hypothesis has not been totally disproven, there is little evidence to support it. The fact that so many different types of drugs can cause hallucinogenic effects suggests that multiple mechanisms are likely responsible for their actions.

The most predictable and typical psychedelic experiences are caused by LSD or similar agents. Consequently, these agents have been the primary focus of studies intended to elucidate the nature of hallucinogenic mechanisms. Although LSD has effects at several CNS sites, ranging from the spinal cord to the cortex of the brain, its effects on the neurotransmitter serotonin most likely account for its psychedelic properties. That LSD and similar drugs alter serotonin activity has been proven; how they affect this transmitter is not so readily apparent.

Although many experts believe that changes in serotonin activity are the basis for the psychedelic properties of most hallucinogens, a case can be made for the involvement of norepinephrine, dopamine, acetylcholine, and perhaps other transmitter systems as well. Only additional research will be able to sort out this complex but important issue (Kyzar, Stewart, & Kalueff, 2016).

## Types of Hallucinogenic Agents

Because of recent technological developments, understanding of hallucinogens has advanced. However, the classification of these drugs remains somewhat arbitrary. Many agents produce some of the pharmacological effects of the traditional psychedelics such as LSD and mescaline.

A second type of hallucinogen includes those agents that have amphetamine-like molecular structures (referred to as *phenylethylamines*) and that possess some stimulant action. Hallucinogens in this group include drugs such as dimethoxymethylamphetamine (DOM), methylenedioxyamphetamine (MDA), methylenedioxymethamphetamine (MDMA or Ecstasy), and likely mephedrone (methylmethcathinone). These agents vary in their hallucinogenic or stimulant properties. MDA is more like an amphetamine (stimulant), MDMA is more like LSD (hallucinogen), and the drug mephedrone has potent properties of both (Hadlock et al., 2011). In large doses, however, each phenylethylamine causes substantial CNS stimulation. Some of the drugs that belong to this group of hallucinogens are undergoing FDA-approved clinical trials for psychotherapy in the management of conditions such as PTSD (Sessa, Higbed, & Nutt, 2019).

The third major group of hallucinogens comprises the anticholinergic (antimuscarinic) drugs, which block some of the receptors for the neurotransmitter acetylcholine. Almost all drugs that antagonize these receptors cause hallucinations in high doses. Many of these potent anticholinergic hallucinogens are naturally occurring and have been known, used, and abused for millennia (D'Orazio, 2015).

### ■ Traditional Hallucinogens: LSD Types

The LSD-like drugs are considered to be the prototypical hallucinogens and are used as the basis of comparison for other types of agents with

Courtesy of Philip Bailey.

Albert Hofmann first synthesized LSD and later proposed its use in psychotherapy.

psychedelic properties. Included in this group are LSD itself and some hallucinogens derived from plants, such as mescaline from the peyote cactus, psilocybin from mushrooms, dimethyltryptamine (DMT) from seeds, and myristicin from nutmeg. Because LSD is the principal hallucinogen, its origin, history, and properties are discussed in detail, providing a basis for understanding the other psychedelic drugs.

## LYSERGIC ACID DIETHYLAMIDE

Lysergic acid diethylamide is a relatively new drug, but similar compounds have existed for a long time. For example, accounts from the Middle Ages tell about a strange affliction that caused pregnant women to abort and others to develop strange burning sensations in their extremities. Today, we call this condition **ergotism** and know it is caused by eating grains contaminated by the ergot fungus. This fungus produces compounds related to LSD called the *ergot alkaloids* (National Institute on Drug Abuse [NIDA], 2007a). Besides the sensory effects, the ergot substances can cause hallucinations, delirium, and psychosis.

In 1938, Albert Hofmann, a scientist for Sandoz Pharmaceutical Laboratories of Basel, Switzerland, worked on a series of ergot compounds in a search for active chemicals that might be of medical value. Lysergic acid was similar in structure to a

compound called *nikethamide*, a stimulant, and Hofmann tried to create slight chemical modifications that might merit further testing. The result of this effort was the production of lysergic acid diethylamide. Hofmann's experience with this new compound gave insight into the effects of this drug (Liester, 2014).

Soon after LSD was discovered, the similarity of experiences with this agent to the symptoms of schizophrenia were noted, which prompted researchers to investigate correlations between the two (Weber, 2006). The hope was to use LSD as a tool for producing an artificial psychosis to aid in understanding the biochemistry of psychosis (NIDA, 2001). Interest in this use of LSD has declined because it is generally accepted that LSD effects differ from natural psychoses.

The use of LSD in psychotherapy has also been tried in treating alcoholism, autism, paranoia, schizophrenia, depression, and various other mental and emotional disorders (Devlin, 2015; Weber, 2006). Even though there continues to be advocates for the therapeutic use of LSD (as discussed previously in this chapter), the administration of LSD for clinical objectives has not been approved for general use because of its limited proven successes, legal restrictions, difficulty in obtaining the pure drug, adverse reactions to the drug (bad trips can occur under controlled as well as uncontrolled conditions), and rapid tolerance buildup in some patients. However, there has been a recent resurgence in research on combining low doses of LSD with psychotherapy to treat depression, compulsive disorders, and chronic pain (Alcohol and Drug Foundation [ADF], 2018). Researchers conducting small studies claim that for some patients the drug can be a catalyst to help change perception of problems and make the patient more responsive to the behavioral therapies (ADF, 2018). No one believes that this approach will be a panacea or universally effective, and even the strongest of advocates emphasize that it is important to use only low doses for relatively short periods of time.

Nonmedical interest in LSD and related drugs began to grow during the 1950s and peaked in the 1960s, when LSD was used by millions of young Americans for chemical escape. On rare occasions, a bad trip would cause a user to feel terror and panic; these experiences resulted in well-publicized tragedies (ADF, 2018).

As with other hallucinogens, the use of LSD by teenagers declined somewhat over the 1970s and

## KEY TERM

**ergotism**
poisoning by toxic substances from the ergot fungus *Claviceps purpurea*

1980s but began to rise again in the early 1990s. The reason for this rise was thought to relate to a decline in the perceived dangers of using LSD and an increase in peer approval. However, the reasons for recent dramatic drops in LSD use remain unclear (Johnston, 2019; see Table 12.1). Of high school seniors sampled in 1975, 11.3% had used LSD sometime during their life; that number declined to 6.9% in 1994, rebounded to 8.8% in 1996, and tumbled to 3.2% in 2018. LSD users are typically college or high school students, white, and middle class and consider themselves to be risk-takers.

### SYNTHESIS AND ADMINISTRATION

LSD is a complex molecule that requires about one week to be synthesized. Because of the sophisticated chemistry necessary for its production, LSD is not manufactured by local illicit laboratories but requires the skills of a trained chemist. Because of LSD's potency, it has been difficult to locate illicit LSD labs; small quantities of LSD are sufficient to satisfy the demand and can be easily transported without detection. The last publicized major LSD lab seizure in the United States was in 2000 when a Drug Enforcement Agency (DEA) raid in Kansas resulted in a temporary 95% decrease in LSD supplies (Anders, 2015).

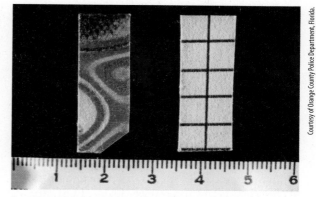

Courtesy of Orange County Police Department, Florida.

Small quantities of LSD are applied to squares of absorbent blotter paper to be chewed or swallowed.

The physical properties of LSD are not distinctive. In its purified form, LSD is colorless, odorless, and tasteless. It can be purchased in several forms, including tiny tablets (about 1/10th the size of aspirins and called *microdots*), capsules, thin squares of gelatin called window panes, or more commonly dissolved and applied to paper as "blotter acid" and cut up into 0.25-inch squares for individual dosing (Partnership for Drug-Free Kids, n.d.). Each square is swallowed or chewed and represents a single dose. One gram of LSD can provide approximately 10,000 individual

# HERE AND NOW

## Microdosing, the New Hallucinogenic Fad?

Recently, a new approach to using hallucinogens such as LSD called *microdosing* entails consuming small quantities of substances like LSD and psilocybin that are 10% to 20% the doses used for typical psychedelic experiences such as the classic "trip." Users claim that it is best to take the drugs every four days in order to experience "subtle internal yet profound shifts." Microdosers have reported improvements in mood, productivity, and creativity; enhanced focusing; and decreased reactivity. Some have explained these results as a "rebalancing." Researchers evaluating self-reported testimonies report that the general response of users is that they "feel better and experience an actual movement towards increased health or wellness." However, as of yet there has been no reported peer-reviewed studies that investigate if and how microdosing works.

As of now, all that is known comes from anecdotal stories and personal testimonies.

© CSP_Bialasiewicz/age fotostock.

Data from Gregoire, C. (2017, January 24). Everything you wanted to know about microdosing (but were afraid to ask). *Science*. Retrieved from http://www.huffingtonpost.com/entry/psychedelic-microdosing-research_us_569525afe4b09dbb4bac9db8

doses and be sold on the streets for $10,000 to $100,000. Although LSD usually is taken by mouth, it is sometimes injected. It costs $1 to $10 per dose (Freeman, n.d.).

### PHYSIOLOGICAL EFFECTS

Like many hallucinogens, LSD is remarkably potent. A common dose today is 10 to 30 micrograms, referred to as *microdosing*, compared with a typical dose of 150 to 300 micrograms in the 1960s (see "Here and Now: Microdosing, the New Hallucinogenic Fad?"). This difference in dose likely explains why today fewer users of LSD are experiencing severe side effects (Smith, 2015). In monkeys, the lethal dose has been determined to be about five milligrams per kilogram of body weight.

When taken orally, LSD is readily absorbed and diffused into all tissues. It passes through the placenta into the fetus and through the blood–brain barrier. The brain receives about 1% of the total dose. Within the brain, LSD is particularly concentrated in the hypothalamus, the limbic system, and the auditory and visual reflex areas. Electrodes placed in the limbic system show an "electrical storm," or a massive increase in neural activity, that might correlate with the overwhelming flood of sensations and the phenomenon of synesthesia reported by the user (Sample, 2016). LSD also activates the sympathetic nervous system; shortly after the drug is taken body temperature, heart rate, and blood pressure rise; the person sweats; and the pupils of the eyes dilate. Its effects on the parasympathetic nervous system increase salivation and nausea (Liester, 2014). These systemic effects do not appear to be related to the hallucinogenic properties of the drug.

The effect of LSD begins within 30 to 90 minutes after ingestion and can last up to 12 hours. Tolerance to the effects of LSD develops more rapidly and lasts longer than tolerance to other hallucinogens (Liester, 2014). Tolerance develops quickly to repeated doses, probably because of a change in sensitivity of the target cells in the brain rather than a change in its metabolism. Tolerance wears off within a few days after the drug is discontinued. Because there are no withdrawal symptoms, a person does not become physically dependent, but some psychological dependency on LSD can occur (Liester, 2014).

### BEHAVIORAL EFFECTS

Because LSD alters several systems in the brain, its behavioral effects are many and variable among individuals (Liester, 2014). The following sections address common CNS responses to this drug.

### Creativity and Insight

Researchers experimenting with LSD are often interested in learning whether LSD helps expand the mind, increasing insight and creativity (Liester, 2014). This question is extremely difficult to answer because no one has ever determined the origin of insight and creativity. Moreover, each of us views these qualities differently.

Subjects under the influence of LSD often express the feeling of being more creative, but creative acts such as drawing and painting are hindered by the motor impairment caused by LSD. The products of artists under the influence of the drug usually prove to be inferior to those produced before the drug experience. Paintings done in LSD creativity studies have been described as reminiscent of "schizophrenic art."

In an often-cited study, creativity, attitude, and anxiety tests on 24 college students found that LSD had no objective effect on creativity, although many of the subjects said they felt they were more creative (McGlothin, Cohen, & McGlothin, 1967). This paradox is noted in several studies of LSD use. The subjects believe they have more insight and provide better answers to life's problems, but they do not or cannot demonstrate this increase objectively. Overt behavior is not modified, and these new insights are short-lived unless they are reinforced by modified behavior.

In spite of these results, some researchers still contend that LSD can enhance the creative process. For example, Oscar Janigar, a psychiatrist at the University of California at Los Angeles, claimed to have determined that LSD does not produce a tangible alteration in the way a painter paints; thus, it does not turn a poor painter into a good one. However, Janigar claimed that LSD does alter the way the painter appraises the world and allows the artist to "plunge into areas where access was restricted by confines of perceptions" and consequently becomes more creative (Tucker, 1987, p. 16).

### Adverse Psychedelic Effects

Remember: There is no typical pattern of response to LSD. The experience varies for each user as a function of the person's set, or expectations, and setting, or environment, during the experience (Liester, 2014). Two of the major negative responses are described as follows (Liester, 2014):

1. The psychotic adverse reaction is an intense, nightmarish experience. The subject may have complete loss of emotional control and experience paranoid delusions, hallucinations, panic attacks, psychosis, and catatonic seizures. In rare instances, some of these reactions are prolonged, lasting days.
2. The nonpsychotic adverse reaction may involve varying degrees of tension, anxiety, fear, depression, and despair but not as intense a response as the "freak-out."

A person with deep psychological problems or a strong need to be in conscious control or one who takes the drug in an unfavorable setting is more likely to have an adverse reaction than a person with a well-integrated personality. Severe LSD behavioral toxicity can be treated with tranquilizers or a sedative such as a benzodiazepine.

### Perceptual Effects

Because the brain's sensory processing is altered by a hallucinogenic dose of LSD, many kinds of unusual illusions can occur. Some users report seeing shifting geometrical patterns mixed with intense color perception; others observe the movement of stationary objects, such that a speck on the wall appears as a large blinking eye or an unfolding flower. Interpretation of sounds can also be scrambled; a dropped ashtray may become a gun fired at the user, for instance. In some cases, LSD alters perceptions to the extent that people feel they can walk on water or fly through the air. The sensation that the body is distorted and even coming apart is another common effect, especially for novice users. Thoughts of suicide and sometimes actual attempts can be caused by use of LSD as well , although recent studies have challenged these conclusions and suggest that under some conditions LSD may even reduce psychological stress (Hendricks, 2015).

Many LSD users find their sense of time distorted, such that hours may be perceived as years or an eternity. As previously discussed, users may also have a distorted perception of their own knowledge or creativity; for instance, they may feel their ideas or work are especially unique, brilliant, or artistic. When analyzed by a person not on LSD or explained after the trip is over, however, these ideas or creations are almost always quite ordinary.

In sum, LSD alters perception such that any sensation can be perceived in the extreme. An experience can be incredibly beautiful and

Courtesy of Dr. Glen Hanson.

This head was sculpted by a university student while under the influence of LSD.

uplifting. However, sometimes the experience can be extremely unpleasant.

### Flashbacks

The flashback, or *hallucinogen-persisting perception disorder*, is an interesting but poorly understood phenomenon of LSD use. Although usually thought of as being adverse, sometimes flashbacks are pleasant and even referred to as "free trips." During a flashback, sensations caused by previous LSD use return, although the subject is not using the drug at the time (Rega, 2015).

There are three broad categories of negative LSD-related flashbacks:

1. *body trip*—recurrence of an unpleasant physical sensation;
2. *bad mind trip*—recurrence of a distressing thought or emotion; and
3. *altered visual perception*—the most frequent type of recurrence, consisting of seeing dots, flashes, trails of light, halos, false motion in the peripheral field, and other sensations.

Flashbacks are most disturbing because they come on unexpectedly. Some have been reported years after use of LSD; for most people, however, flashbacks usually subside within weeks or months after taking LSD. The duration of a flashback is variable, lasting from a few minutes to several hours (NIDA, 2010).

Although the precise mechanism of flashbacks is unknown, physical or psychological stresses and some drugs such as marijuana may trigger these experiences (Clark, 2015). It has been proposed that flashbacks are an especially vivid form of memory that becomes seared into the subconscious mind because of LSD's effects on the brain's transmitters.

Treatment consists of reassurance that the condition will go away and use of a sedative such as diazepam (Valium), if necessary, to treat the anxiety or panic that can accompany the flashback experience.

### GENETIC DAMAGE AND BIRTH DEFECTS

Experiments conducted in the mid-1960s suggested that LSD could cause birth defects, based on the observation that when LSD was added to a suspension of human white blood cells in a test tube the chromosomes of these cells were damaged. From this finding, it was proposed that when LSD was consumed by humans it could damage the chromosomes of the male sperm or female egg or the cells of the developing infant. Such damage theoretically could result in congenital defects in offspring (Dishotsky, Loughman, Mogar, & Lipscomb, 1971).

Carefully controlled studies conducted after news of LSD's chromosomal effects were made public did not support this hypothesis. Experiments revealed that, in contrast to the test tube findings, there is no chromosomal damage to white blood cells or any other cells when LSD is given to a human being (Dishotsky et al., 1971).

Studies have also shown that there are no carcinogenic or mutagenic effects from using LSD in experimental animals or human beings, with the exception of the fruit fly. (LSD is a mutagen in fruit flies if given in doses that are equivalent to 100,000 times the hallucinogenic dose for people.) Teratogenic effects occur in mice if LSD is given early in pregnancy. LSD may be teratogenic in rhesus monkeys if it is injected in doses (based on body weight) exceeding at least 100 times the usual hallucinogenic dose for humans. In other studies, women who took street LSD, but not those given pure LSD, had a higher rate of spontaneous abortions and births of malformed infants; this finding suggests that contaminants in adulterated LSD were responsible for the fetal effects and not the hallucinogen itself (Dishotsky et al., 1971).

### EARLY HUMAN RESEARCH

In the 1950s, the U.S. government—specifically, the Central Intelligence Agency and the U.S. Army—became interested in reports of the effects of mind-altering drugs, including LSD. Unknown to the public at the time, these agencies conducted tests on human beings to learn more about such compounds and determine their usefulness in conducting military and clandestine missions. These activities became public when a biochemist, Frank Olson, killed himself in 1953 after being given a drink laced with LSD. Olson had a severe psychotic reaction and was being treated for the condition when he jumped out of a 10th-story window. His family was told only that he had committed suicide. The connection to LSD was not uncovered until 1975. The court awarded Olson's family $750,000 in damages in 1976.

In 1976, the extent of these studies was revealed; nearly 585 soldiers and 900 civilians had been given LSD in poorly organized experiments in which participants were coerced into taking this drug or not told that they were receiving it. Powerful hallucinogens such as LSD can cause serious psychological damage in some subjects, especially when they are unaware of what is happening (OneLuckySoul, 2015; Remsberg, 2010; Willing, 2007).

The legal consequences of these LSD studies continued for years. In 1987, a New York judge awarded $700,000 to the family of a mental patient who killed himself after having been given LSD without an explanation of the drug's nature. The judge said that there was a "conspiracy of silence" among the Army, the Department of Justice, and the New York state attorney general to conceal events surrounding the death of the subject, Harold Blauer (Doyle 1987).

### MESCALINE (PEYOTE)

Mescaline is one of approximately 30 psychoactive chemicals that have been isolated from the peyote cactus and used for centuries in the Americas (see "Here and Now: Peyote: An Ancient Indian Way"). One of the first reports on the peyote plant was made by Francisco Hernandez to the court of King Philip II of Spain. King Philip was interested in reports from the earlier Hernán Cortés expedition about strange medicines the natives used and sent Cortés to collect information about herbs and medicines. Cortés worked on this project from 1570 to 1575 and reported on the use of more than 1,200 plant remedies, as well as the existence of many hallucinogenic plants. He was

# HERE AND NOW

## Peyote: An Ancient Indian Way

Members of the Native American Church use the buttons of the hallucinogenic peyote cactus to brew a sacramental tea as sacred to them as the bread and wine of the Christian Eucharist is to Catholics. As described by one member, "Peyote is a gift given to the Indians, but its ways cannot be obtained overnight. It has to be done with sincerity. It becomes part of your way of life. One has to walk that walk." Those who accept this form of worship believe that respectful use of peyote can be a gateway to the realm of the spirit, visions, and guidance. The use of peyote as part of the latest New Age craze is very disturbing to members of this church and is viewed almost as a form of sacrilege.

Data from Mims, B. (1999, July 1). "Peyote: When the ancient Indian way collides with a New Age craze." *Salt Lake Tribune, 258*, A-10; Native American Church. (2008). Millennium purification and emergence. Strawberry Plains, TN: Author. Retrieved from http://www.nativeamericanchurch.com; Ojibwa. (2019, November 24). Suppressing peyote in 1918. Native American Netroots. Retrieved from http://nativeamericannetroots.net/diary/tag/peyote

one of the first to record the eating of parts of the peyote cactus and the resulting visions and mental changes.

In the 17th century, Spanish Catholic priests asked their Indian converts to confess to the use of peyote, which they believed was used to conjure up demons. However, nothing stopped its use. By 1760, use of peyote had spread into what is now the United States. Peyote has been confused with another plant, the mescal shrub, which produces dark red beans that contain an extremely toxic alkaloid called *cytisine*. This alkaloid may cause hallucinations, convulsions, and even death. In addition, a mescal liquor is made from the agave cactus. Partly because of misidentification with the toxic mescal beans, the U.S. government outlawed the use of both peyote and mescaline for everyone except members of the Native American Church (Ojibwa, 2015). Mescaline has been used for decades by this group as part of their religious sacrament. Research has suggested that long-term religious use of peyote does not have significant psychological effects or cause problems with cognitive performance in Native Americans (Halpern, Sherwood, Hudson, Yurgelun-Todd, & Pope, 2005).

Mescaline is the most active drug in peyote and belongs to the family of phenylethylamine compounds such as MDMA. It induces intensified perception of colors and euphoria in the user. However, as Aldous Huxley said in *The Doors of Perception* (1954), his book about his experimentation with mescaline, "Along with the happily transfigured majority of mescaline takers there is a minority that finds in the drug only hell and purgatory." After Huxley related his experiences with mescaline, it was used by an increasing number of people.

## PHYSIOLOGICAL EFFECTS

The average dose of mescaline that will cause hallucinations and other physiological effects is from 300 to 600 milligrams. It may take up to 20 peyote (mescal) buttons (ingested orally) to get 600 milligrams of mescaline.

Based on animal studies, scientists estimate that a lethal dosage is 10 to 30 times greater than that which causes behavioral effects in human beings. (About 200 milligrams is the lowest mind-altering dose.) Death in animals results from convulsions and respiratory arrest. Mescaline is perhaps 1,000 to 3,000 times less potent than LSD and 30 times less potent than another common hallucinogen, psilocybin (Mathias, 1993). Psilocybin is discussed later in this chapter.

© Martyn Vickery/Alamy Images.

The peyote cactus contains a number of drugs. The best known is mescaline.

Mescaline's effects include dilation of the pupils (**mydriasis**), increase in body temperature, anxiety, visual hallucinations, and alteration of body image. The last effect is a type of hallucination in which parts of the body may seem to disappear or to become grossly distorted. Mescaline induces vomiting in many people and some muscular relaxation (sedation). Apparently, there are few aftereffects or drug hangover feelings at low doses. Higher doses of mescaline slow the heart and respiratory rhythm, contract the intestines and the uterus, and cause headache, difficulty in coordination, dry skin with itching, and hypertension (high blood pressure) (DEA, 2015).

Mescaline users report that they lose all awareness of time. As with LSD, the setting for the trip influences the user's reactions. Most mescaline users prefer natural settings, most likely because of the historical association of this drug with Native Americans and their nature-related spiritual experiences (often under the influence of this drug). The visual hallucinations achieved depend on the individual. Colors are at first intensified and may be followed by hallucinations of shades, movements, forms, and events. The senses of smell and taste are enhanced. Some people claim (as with LSD) that they can "hear" colors and "see" sounds such as the wind. Synesthesia occurs naturally in a small percentage of cases. At low to medium doses, a state of euphoria is reported, often followed by a feeling of anxiety and less frequently by depression. Occasionally, users observe themselves as two people and experience the sensation that the mind and the body are separate entities. Some people have had cosmic experiences that are profound—almost religious—and in which they discover a sense of unity with all creation. People who have this sensation often believe they have discovered the meaning of existence.

### MECHANISM OF ACTION

Within 30 to 120 minutes after ingestion, mescaline reaches a maximum concentration in the brain. The effects may persist for as long as 9 or 10 hours. Hallucinations may last up to two hours and are usually affected by the dose level. About half the dose is excreted unchanged after six hours and can be recovered in the urine for

### KEY TERM

**mydriasis**
pupil dilation

reuse (if peyote is in short supply). A slow tolerance builds up after repeated use, and there is cross-tolerance to LSD. As with LSD, mescaline intoxication can be alleviated or stopped by taking a dose of chlorpromazine (Thorazine), a tranquilizer, and to a lesser extent by taking diazepam (Valium). Like LSD, mescaline probably exerts much of its hallucinogenic effects by altering serotonin systems (Delgado, 2013).

Common street names for mescaline include *Big Chief, Blue Caps, Buttons, Cactus, Moon,* and *San Pedro* (Bezrutczyk, 2019). Analysis of street samples of mescaline obtained recently in many U.S. cities shows that the chemical sold rarely is authentic. Regardless of color or appearance, these street drugs are usually other hallucinogens, such as LSD, DOM, or PCP. If a person decides to take hallucinogenic street drugs, "let the buyer beware." Not only is the actual content often different and potentially much more toxic than bargained for (street drugs are frequently contaminated), but also the dosage is usually unknown even if the drug is genuine.

### PSILOCYBIN

The drug psilocybin has a long and colorful history. Its principal source is the *Psilocybe mexicana* mushroom of the "magic" variety (DEA, 2015). It was first used by some of the early natives of Central America more than 2,000 years ago. In Guatemala, statues of mushrooms that date back to 100 BC have been found. The Aztecs later used the mushrooms for ceremonial rites. When the Spaniards came into Mexico in the 1500s, the natives were calling the *Psilocybe mexicana* mushroom "God's flesh." Because of this seeming sacrilege, the natives were harshly treated by the Spanish priests.

Gordon Wasson identified the *Psilocybe mexicana* mushroom in 1955. The active ingredient was extracted in 1958 by Albert Hofmann, who also synthesized LSD. During research, Hofmann wanted to make certain he would feel the effects of the mushroom, so he ate 32 of them, weighing 2.4 grams (a medium dose by Native American standards), and then recorded his hallucinogenic reactions (Burger, 1968).

Timothy Leary also tried psilocybin mushrooms in Mexico in 1960; apparently, the experience influenced him greatly. On his return to Harvard, he carried out a series of experiments using psilocybin with student groups. Leary was careless in experimental procedures and did some work in uncontrolled situations. His actions caused a major administrative upheaval, ending in his departure from Harvard.

One of Leary's questionable studies was the Good Friday experiment in which 20 theological students were given either a placebo or psilocybin in a double-blind study (i.e., neither the researcher nor the subjects know who gets the placebo or the drug), after which all attended the same 2.5-hour Good Friday service. The experimental group reported mystical experiences, whereas the control group did not (Pahnke & Richards, 1966). Leary believed that the experience was of value and that, under proper control and guidance, the hallucinatory experience could be beneficial.

Psilocybin is not common on the street. Generally, it is administered orally and is eaten either fresh or dried. Accidental poisonings are common for those who mistakenly consume poisonous mushrooms rather than the hallucinogenic variety.

The dried form of these mushrooms contains from 0.2% to 0.5% psilocybin. The hallucinogenic effects produced are quite similar to those of LSD, and there is a cross-tolerance among psilocybin, LSD, and mescaline, suggesting they have similar mechanisms of action. The effects caused by psilocybin vary with the dosage taken. Up to four milligrams cause a pleasant experience, relaxation, and some body sensation. In some subjects, higher doses cause considerable perceptual and body image changes, accompanied by hallucinations.

Although psilocybin has been reported to be helpful in the treatment of depression for some people (Jacoby, 2015), in extreme cases psilocybin can cause mental problems (NIDA, 2015). Psilocybin stimulates the autonomic nervous system, dilates the pupils, and increases body temperature. Some evidence suggests that psilocybin is metabolized into psilocin, which is more potent and may be the principal active ingredient. Psilocin is found in mushrooms, albeit in small amounts. Like the other hallucinogens, psilocybin apparently causes no physical dependence (Delgado, 2013; NIDA, 2001).

## TRYPTAMINES

Some compounds related to the tryptamine class of drugs (molecules that resemble the neurotransmitter serotonin) have hallucinogenic properties and can exist naturally in herbs, fungi, and animals or can be synthesized in the

The *Psilocybe* mushroom is the source of the hallucinogens psilocybin and psilocin.

laboratory. Some of the newer tryptamines are available for purchase over the Internet, but their effects are not well understood. Many, but not all, of these compounds are Schedule I drugs and illegal (Araujo, Carvalho, Bastos Mde, Guedes de Pinho, & Carvalho, 2015). Two examples are discussed in this section.

### DIMETHYLTRYPTAMINE

DMT is a short-acting hallucinogen found in the seeds of certain leguminous trees native to the West Indies and parts of South America (Schultes, 1978) and is reported to occur naturally in the human body in low quantities (Horgan, n.d.). It is also prepared synthetically in illicit laboratories and is reported to have both beneficial and terrifying adverse effects (Horgan, n.d.). For centuries, the powdered seeds have been used as a snuff called *cohoba* in pipes and snuffing tubes. Haitian natives claim that, under the influence of the drug, they can communicate with their gods. Its effects occur rapidly and may last less than one hour, which has earned it the nickname the "businessman's lunch break" (Carollo, 2010).

DMT has no effect when taken orally; it is inhaled either as smoke from the burning plant or in vaporized form. DMT is sometimes added to parsley leaves or flakes, tobacco, or marijuana to induce its hallucinogenic effect. The usual dose is 60 to 150 milligrams. In structure and action, it is similar to psilocybin, although it is not as powerful. Like the other hallucinogens discussed, DMT does not cause physical dependence.

### FOXY

The synthetic substance 5-methoxy-N, N-diisopropyltryptamine, but more commonly referred to as *Foxy*, is a relatively new hallucinogen.

This drug has been used at raves and clubs in Arizona, California, New York, and Florida. It was added to the DEA Schedule I category in 2004. At lower doses, Foxy can cause euphoria; at higher doses, its effects are similar to LSD, causing hallucinations and psychedelic experiences (DEA, 2002). Foxy is typically consumed orally in doses of six to 20 milligrams, but it may also be smoked (National Drug Intelligence Center [NDIC], n.d.).

### NUTMEG

High doses of nutmeg can be intoxicating, causing symptoms such as drowsiness, stupor, delirium, and sleep. Prison inmates have known about this drug for years, so in most prisons use of spices such as nutmeg is restricted. It is typically young people who experiment with nutmeg to get a cheap high, but because of the frequent unpleasant side effects, abusers often end up either in an emergency room or calling a poison control center and usually are not interested in trying nutmeg again. Needless to say, nutmeg is not perceived as a major drug abuse problem by authorities (Szalavitz, 2010).

Nutmeg contains 5% to 15% myristica oil, which is responsible for the physical effects. Myristicin (about 4%), which is structurally similar to mescaline, and elemicin are probably the most potent psychoactive ingredients in nutmeg. Myristicin blocks release of serotonin from brain neurons. The exterior covering of the nutmeg seed also contains the hallucinogenic compound myristicin.

Two tablespoons of nutmeg (about 14 grams) taken orally cause a rather unpleasant trip with a dreamlike stage. Rapid heartbeat, dry mouth, and thirst are experienced as well. Agitation, apprehension, and a sense of impending doom may last about 12 hours, with a sense of unreality persisting for several days (Rahman, Fazilah, & Effarazah, 2015).

## ▮ Phenylethylamine Hallucinogens

The phenylethylamine drugs are chemically related to amphetamines. Phenylethylamines have varying degrees of hallucinogenic and CNS stimulant effects, which are likely related to their ability to release serotonin and dopamine, respectively. Consequently, the phenylethylamines that predominantly release serotonin are dominated by their hallucinogenic action and are more LSD like, whereas those more inclined to release dopamine are dominated by their stimulant effects and are amphetamine like.

### DIMETHOXYMETHYLAMPHETAMINE

The basic structure of DOM—or STP, an acronym for "serenity, tranquility and peace"—is amphetamine. Nonetheless, it is a fairly powerful hallucinogen that seems to work through mechanisms similar to those found with mescaline and LSD. In fact, the effects of DOM are similar to those caused by a combination of amphetamine and LSD, with the hallucinogenic effects of the drug overpowering the amphetamine-like physiological effects. Like other hallucinogens, DOM is not considered to be particularly addicting, and users experience tolerance with multiple drug exposures (Leonard, 2015). The following is an excerpt from a user who experienced a bad trip with DOM:

> I like to think of myself as an experienced psychonaut (someone who uses a lot of psychoactive substances).... Yesterday, I took 5 milligrams of DOM.... I was excited to spend the whole day ... exploring new neural connections.... The first 4 hours were enjoyable.... Then all at once, something big shifted ... I found the visual image of myself literally ripped in half.... I felt like I was being dragged down to the very depths of hell. Death was everywhere.... I felt like I was being drenched in blood, almost drowning in it.... My consciousness continued to explode.... I was sobbing hysterically.... I felt my body become a vessel for all pain.... Several times over the next several hours, I was sure that I myself was dying.... Every 15 minutes or so, my body would go into convulsions.... I was convinced that I would never be the same.... I had become self-injurious and suicidal.... Finally around 21 hours, and still going strong, I (took) a Seroquel which axed the trip ... I certainly will never be taking this chemical again, and am questioning whether or not my journeys with these types of drugs are at an end. I am grateful to be alive and ... have my sanity back. (Psychonaut, 2015)

### "DESIGNER" AMPHETAMINES

The hybrid actions of so-called designer amphetamines as psychedelic stimulants not only make them a particularly fascinating topic for research but also provide a unique experience described by drug abusers as a "smooth amphetamine," or an

**entactogen** (implying that the pleasurable sensation of touch is enhanced). This characterization likely accounts for their popularity (Weaver, Hopper, & Gunderson, 2015).

## 3,4-METHYLENEDIOXYAMPHETAMINE

MDA was first synthesized in 1910 and is structurally related to both mescaline and amphetamine. Early research found that MDA is an anorexiant (causing loss of appetite), as well as a mood elevator in some people. Further research has shown that the mode of action of MDA is similar to that of amphetamines and a metabolite of MDMA (Zhou, 2016). It causes additional release of the neurotransmitters serotonin, dopamine, and norepinephrine (Baggott et al., 2010).

In the past, MDA was used as an adjunct to psychotherapy. In one study, eight volunteers who had previously experienced the effects of LSD under clinical conditions were given 150 milligrams of MDA. Effects of the drug were noted between 40 and 60 minutes following ingestion by all eight subjects. The subjective effects following administration peaked at the end of 90 minutes and persisted for approximately 8 hours. None of the subjects experienced hallucinations, perceptual distortion, or closed-eye imagery, but they reported that the feelings the drug induced had some relationship to those previously experienced with LSD. The subjects found that both drugs induced an intensification of feelings, increased perceptions of self-insight, and heightened empathy with others during the experience. Most of the subjects also felt an increased sense of aesthetic enjoyment at some point during the intoxication. Seven of the eight subjects said they perceived music as "three-dimensional" (Naranjo, Shulgin, & Sargent, 1967).

On the street, MDA has been called the *love drug* because of its effects on the sense of touch and the attitudes of the users. Users often report experiencing a sense of well-being (likely a stimulant effect) and heightened tactile sensations (likely a hallucinogenic effect) and thus increased pleasure through sex and expressions of affection. Those under the influence of MDA frequently focus on interpersonal relationships and demonstrate an overwhelming desire or need to be with or talk to people. Some users say they have a pleasant "body high"—more sensual than cerebral and more empathetic than introverted. For these reasons, MDA is sometimes used by persons attending raves, much like MDMA or Ecstasy (Baggott et al., 2010).

The unpleasant side effects most often reported are nausea, periodic tensing of muscles in the neck, tightening of the jaw and grinding of the teeth, and dilation of the pupils. Street doses of MDA range from 100 to 150 milligrams. Serious convulsions and death have resulted from larger doses, but in these cases the quantity of MDA was not accurately measured. Ingestion of 500 milligrams of pure MDA has been shown to cause death. The only reported adverse reaction to moderate doses is a marked physical exhaustion lasting as long as two days (Marquardt, DiStefano, & Ling, 1978).

An unpleasant MDA experience should be treated the same as a bad trip with any hallucinogen. The person should be "talked down" (reassured) in a friendly and supportive manner. The use of other drugs is rarely needed, although medical attention may be necessary.

Under the Comprehensive Drug Abuse Prevention and Control Act of 1970, MDA is classified as a Schedule I substance; illegal possession is a serious offense.

## METHYLENEDIOXYMETHAMPHETAMINE

MDMA is a modification of MDA but is thought to have more psychedelic and less stimulant activity (e.g., euphoria) than its predecessor. MDMA is also structurally similar to mescaline. The popular names for MDMA are *Ecstasy* or *Molly*, which is slang for "molecular" (NIDA, 2016b).

MDMA was synthesized in 1912 to suppress appetite, but its bizarre side effects caused its withdrawal from development until it became widely used in the 1980s (Adam, 2006). This designer amphetamine can be produced easily, although the process can be hazardous and the chemicals used for the synthesis are difficult to obtain (Plummer, Breadon, Pearson, & Jones, 2016). Although the synthesis can be done by local illicit laboratories (Plummer et al., 2016), most of the MDMA supplies in this country are smuggled in from outlaw drug laboratories in European countries such as the Netherlands (Meadow, 2015). The unusual psychological effects it produces are part of the reason for its popularity. The drug causes euphoria, increased energy, increased sensitivity

**KEY TERM**

**entactogen**
a drug that enhances the sensation and pleasure of touching

to touch, and lowered inhibitions. Many users claim it intensifies emotional feelings without sensory distortion and that it increases empathy and awareness of the user's body and the aesthetics of the surroundings. Some consider MDMA to be an aphrodisiac. Because MDMA lowers defense mechanisms and reduces inhibitions, it has even been used during psychoanalysis. In fact, recently there have been reports that an initial FDA-approved clinical trial has demonstrated that MDMA was effective in the treatment of 10 or 12 patients suffering from PTSD. Obviously this represents a small study, and the results must be confirmed by other much larger clinical trials (NIDA, 2016b).

MDMA—popularized in the 1980s by articles in *Newsweek* (Adler, 1985), *Time* (Toufexis, 1985), and other magazines—seems to vacillate in popularity as reflected by its episodic coverage in the national news media as a drug with euphoric effects, potential therapeutic value, and lack of serious side effects. MDMA is commonly used by college-aged students and young adults (Johnston, 2019). Because of its effect of enhancing sensations, MDMA has been used as part of a countercultural rave scene, including high-tech music and laser light shows. Observers report that MDMA-linked rave parties are reminiscent of the acid parties of the 1960s and 1970s. The latest cycle of MDMA popularity peaked in 2003, when it was being used annually by 3.6% of high school seniors. However, because of reports of MDMA neurotoxicity and persistent negative side effects, use of this drug has decreased dramatically, and in 2018 had been used by only 0.5% of high school seniors (Johnston, 2019).

Because of the widespread abuse of MDMA, the DEA prohibited its use by formally placing it on the Schedule I list in 1988. At the time of the ban, it was estimated that as many as 200 physicians were using the drug in psychotherapy (Greer & Tolbert, 1990). It is interesting that many mental health professionals are still advocating for the use of this drug to treat conditions such as PTSD; in fact, it is currently the subject of FDA-approved clinical trials for this very purpose (Stone, 2019). MDMA is often referred to as a *club drug* because of its frequent use at rave dances, clubs, and bars. It costs 25 to 50 cents to produce a tablet of Ecstasy in Europe, but on the street that same tablet costs $20 to $30 (Scinto, 2013).

MDMA is usually taken orally, but it is sometimes snorted or even occasionally smoked. After the high starts, it may persist for minutes or even an hour, depending on the person, the purity of the drug, and the environment in which it is taken. When coming down from an MDMA-induced high, people often take small oral doses known as *boosters* to get high again. If they take too many boosters, they become extremely fatigued the next day. The average dose is about 75 to 150 milligrams; toxic effects have been reported at higher doses. Some statistics suggest that almost 50% of the tablets sold as MDMA actually contain other drugs such as aspirin, caffeine, cocaine, methamphetamine, or pseudoephedrine (NIDA, 2016b).

Many possible harmful side effects of MDMA have been reported. Use of high doses can cause psychosis and paranoia (NIDA, 2010). Some negative physiological responses caused by recreational doses include dilated pupils, dry mouth and throat, clenching and grinding of teeth (resulting in the use of baby pacifiers), muscle aches and stiffness, fatigue, insomnia, agitation, and anxiety. Some of these reactions can be intense and unpredictable. Under some conditions, death can be caused by hyperthermia (elevated body temperature), instability of the autonomic nervous system, underlying cardiovascular problems, or kidney failure (NIDA, 2016b).

Several studies have demonstrated long-term damage to serotonin neurons in the brain following a single high dose of either MDMA or MDA, which may result in impaired memory, diminished ability to process information, and heightened impulsivity. Although the behavioral significance of this damage in people is not clear, caution using this drug is warranted at this time (Drug-Dangers, 2016).

Experts continue to debate the addictive properties of MDMA. Some claim this drug is like LSD,

Ecstasy is frequently used at "raves" to increase sensory stimulation and the pleasure of touching.

© Maxim Blinkov/Dreamstime.com.

with little likelihood of causing physical dependence, whereas others claim its properties are likely to be more amphetamine like, and suggest that of those who use MDMA routinely some have developed dependence (Juergens, 2019; NIDA, 2010). Part of the difficulty in sorting out this controversy is that most moderate MDMA users also use other drugs, making it difficult to determine which effects are specifically attributable to the MDMA. The potential of MDMA to cause addiction and dependence is likely somewhere between that of amphetamine and LSD. Because of its ability to cause euphoria and release dopamine in the brain, it is highly probable that heavy use or administration by smoking or injection can cause significant dependence (NIDA, 2016b).

## ■ Anticholinergic Hallucinogens

The anticholinergic hallucinogens include naturally occurring alkaloid (bitter organic base) substances that are present in plants and herbs found around the world. These drugs are often mentioned in folklore and in early literature as being added to potions. They are thought to have played a role in the death of the Roman emperor Claudius, and Shakespeare refers to them in the poisoning of Hamlet's father. Historically, they have been the favorite drugs used to eliminate inconvenient people. Hallucinogens affecting the cholinergic neurons also have been used by South American Indians for religious ceremonies (Schultes & Hofmann, 1980) and were probably used in witchcraft to give the illusion of flying, to prepare sacrificial victims, and provide a powerful kick to give some types of marijuana ("superpot") (Black Witch Coven, n.d.).

The family of plants that includes potatoes, the Solanaceae, contains most of these mind-altering drugs. The following three potent anticholinergic compounds are commonly found in these plants: (1) scopolamine, or hyoscine; (2) hyoscyamine; and (3) atropine. Scopolamine may produce excitement, hallucinations, and delirium even at therapeutic doses. With atropine, doses bordering on toxic levels are usually required to obtain these effects (Garden Spot, 2013). All of these active alkaloid drugs block some acetylcholine receptors.

These alkaloid drugs can be used as ingredients in cold symptom remedies because they have a drying effect and block production of mucus in the nose and throat. They also prevent salivation; therefore, the mouth becomes uncommonly dry and perspiration may stop. Atropine may increase the heart rate by 100% and dilate the pupils markedly, causing inability to focus on nearby objects. Other annoying side effects of these anticholinergic drugs include constipation and difficulty urinating. These inconveniences tend to discourage excessive abuse of these drugs for their hallucinogenic properties. Usually, people who abuse these anticholinergic compounds are receiving the drugs by prescription (Anderson, 2016).

Anticholinergics can cause drowsiness by affecting the sleep centers of the brain. At large doses, a condition occurs that is similar to a psychosis, characterized by delirium, loss of attention, mental confusion, and sleepiness (Anderson, 2016). Hallucinations may also occur at higher doses. At extremely high doses, paralysis of the respiratory system may cause death.

Although hundreds of plant species naturally contain anticholinergic substances and consequently can cause psychedelic experiences, only a few of the principal plants are mentioned here.

### ATROPA BELLADONNA: *THE DEADLY NIGHTSHADE PLANT*

Knowledge of *Atropa belladonna* is ancient, and its use as a drug is reported in early folklore. The name of the genus, *Atropa*, is the origin for the drug name *atropine* and indicates the reverence the Greeks had for the plant. Atropos was one of the three Fates in Greek mythology, whose duty it was to cut the thread of life when the time came. This plant has been used for thousands of years by assassins and murderers. In *Tales of the Arabian Nights*, unsuspecting potentates were poisoned with atropine from the deadly nightshade or one of its relatives. Fourteen berries of the deadly nightshade contain enough drug to cause death.

The species name, *belladonna*, means "beautiful woman." In early Rome and Egypt, girls with large pupils were considered attractive and friendly. To create this condition, they would put a few drops of an extract of this plant into their eyes, causing the pupils to dilate (Garden Spot, 2013). Belladonna has also enjoyed a reputation as a love potion.

### MANDRAGORA OFFICINARUM: *THE MANDRAKE*

*Mandragora officinarum*, commonly known as *mandrake*, contains several active psychedelic alkaloids: hyoscyamine, scopolamine, atropine, and mandragorine. Mandrake has been used as a love potion for centuries but has also been known for its toxic properties. In ancient folk medicine, mandrake was used to treat many ailments in spite of its side effects. It was recommended as a sedative, to relieve nervous conditions, and to relieve pain (University of Toronto, 2014), as portrayed in the 2006 movie *Pan's Labyrinth*.

The root of the mandrake is forked and, when viewed with a little imagination, may resemble the human body (as portrayed in the *Harry Potter and the Chamber of Secrets* movie in 2002). Because of this resemblance, it has been credited with human attributes, which gave rise to many superstitions in the Middle Ages about its magical powers. Shakespeare referred to this plant in *Romeo and Juliet*. In her farewell speech, Juliet says, "And shrieks like mandrakes torn out of the earth, that living mortals hearing them run mad."

### HYOSCYAMUS NIGER: *HENBANE*

*Hyoscyamus niger*, or henbane, contains both hyoscyamine and scopolamine. In AD 60, Pliny the Elder spoke of henbane: "For this is certainly known, that if one takes it in drink more than four leaves, it will put him beside himself" (Jones, 1956). Henbane was also used in the orgies, or *bacchanalias*, of the ancient world.

Although rarely used today, henbane has been given medicinally since early times. It was frequently used to cause sleep, although hallucinations often occurred if given in excess. It was likely included in witches' brews and deadly concoctions during the Dark Ages (WebMD, n.d.).

### DATURA STRAMONIUM: JIMSONWEED

The *Datura* genus of the Solanaceae family includes a large number of related plants found worldwide. The principal active drug in this group is scopolamine; there are also several less active alkaloids.

Throughout history, these plants have been used as hallucinogens by many societies. They are mentioned in early Sanskrit and Chinese writings and were revered by the Buddhists. There is also some indication that the priestess (oracle) at the ancient Greek Temple of Apollo at Delphi was under the influence of this type of plant when she made prophecies (Schultes, 1970). Before the supposed divine possession, she appeared to have chewed leaves of the sacred laurel. A mystic vapor

© Richard Thornton/ShutterStock, Inc.

*Datura stramonium*, or jimsonweed, is a common plant that contains the hallucinogenic drug scopolamine.

was also reported to have risen from a fissure in the ground. The sacred laurel may have been one of the *Datura* species, and the vapors may have come from burning these plants.

**Jimsonweed** gets its name from an incident that took place in 17th-century Jamestown and is a contraction of "Jamestown weed." British soldiers ate this weed while trying to capture Nathaniel Bacon, who had made seditious remarks about the king. Jimsonweed is still occasionally consumed by young people who are searching for an inexpensive hallucinogenic experience. Because this wild weed grows in most parts of the United States, it is relatively easy to find and is free. This plant has been referred to by names such as *angel's trumpet*, *locoweed*, and *stinkweed*. The hallucinogenic effects from this plant mainly result from two powerful anticholinergic drugs, atropine and scopolamine, found in the roots. Often the person who consumes the jimsonweed in a stew or other brew ends up in the emergency room complaining of hallucinations, confusion, dilated pupils, and rapid heartbeat. Because of the unpleasant side effects, abuse of jimsonweed is not considered a major drug abuse problem, but most emergency rooms will occasionally see an unsuspecting

### KEY TERM

**jimsonweed**
a potent hallucinogenic plant

young person who foolishly experiments with jimsonweed for a cheap and natural high and gets much more than expected (Woolcott, 2015).

## ■ Other Hallucinogens

Technically, any drug that alters perceptions, thoughts, and feelings in a manner that is not normally experienced except in dreams can be classified as a hallucinogen. Because the brain's sensory input is complex and involves several neurotransmitter systems, drugs with many diverse effects can cause hallucinations (Parish, 2015).

Four agents that do not conveniently fit into the principal categories of hallucinogens are discussed in the following sections.

### PHENCYCLIDINE

PCP users can be so psychotic when they're brought in that they can't provide any history.... Some PCP users are transferred to the psych unit from the trauma unit, where they had pins put in their legs because they jumped out a window. Some complain of chest pains days after arriving, and when we do an x-ray we find broken ribs. PCP is also an anesthetic, so other injuries often aren't discovered until after it wears off. (Inpatient Director, Einstein Hospital psychiatric unit)

The use of PCP added to marijuana (referred to as wet marijuana) can be particularly destructive causing extreme hyperactivity, physical violence, strokes, cardiac arrests, heart attacks and seizures. (Citizens' Commission, 2015)

PCP is considered by many experts as the most dangerous of the hallucinogens. Developed in the late 1950s as an intravenous anesthetic, it was found to be effective but had serious side effects such as precipitating schizophrenia-like symptoms, which caused it to be discontinued for human use. Sometimes when people were recovering from PCP anesthesia, they experienced delirium and manic states of excitation lasting 18 hours. PCP is currently a Schedule II drug and is legitimately available only as an anesthetic for animals. It has even been banned from veterinary practice since 1985, however, because of its high theft rate. Most if not all PCP used in the United States today is produced illegally (Davis, 2016a).

Street PCP is mainly synthesized from readily available chemical precursors in clandestine

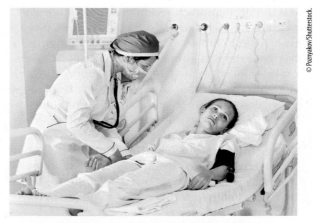

Persons on PCP often have psychotic episodes leading to their admission into psychiatric wards.

laboratories. PCP first appeared on the street drug scene in 1967 as the *PeaCe Pill*. In 1968, it reappeared in New York as a substance called *hog*. By 1969, PCP was found under a variety of guises. It was sold as angel dust and sprinkled on parsley for smoking. Today, it is sold on the streets under many different slang names, including *angel dust, Butt Naked, Purple Rain, Yellow Fever,* and *Zombie* to mention a few (Bezrutczyk, 2019).

In the late 1960s, PCP began to find its way into a variety of street drugs sold as psychedelics. By 1970, authorities observed that phencyclidine was used widely as a main ingredient in psychedelic preparations. It has frequently been used to lace or substitute for LSD, mescaline, marijuana, tobacco, or cocaine (Citizens' Commission, 2015; MacLaren, n.d.). These drug combinations can cause particularly alarming and sometimes dangerous behaviors (Citizens' Commission, 2015).

One difficulty in estimating the effects or use patterns of PCP is caused by variance in drug purity. Also, there are about 30 **analogs** of PCP, some of which have appeared on the street. PCP has so many other street names that people may not know they are using it, or they may have been deceived when buying what they thought was LSD or marijuana (Schmetzer, 2015). Users may not question the identity of the substances unless they have a bad reaction.

PCP is available as a pure, white crystalline powder or as tablets or capsules. However, because

### KEY TERM

**analogs**
drugs with similar structures

it is usually manufactured in makeshift laboratories, it is frequently discolored by contaminants from a tan to brown with a consistency ranging from powder to a gummy mass. PCP can be taken orally, smoked, sniffed, or injected, but currently the preferred form of administration is smoking, often as an additive to marijuana referred to as *wet weed* (Schmetzer, 2015). By smoking PCP, the experienced user is better able to limit his or her dosage to a desired level. After smoking, the subjective effects appear within one to five minutes and peak within the next five to 30 minutes. The high lasts about four to six hours followed by a six- to 24-hour "comedown" (Anderson, 2018).

Since 1990, the use of PCP has remained relatively stable, with the reported annual use by high school seniors at 1.4% in 1991 and 1.1% in 2018 (Johnston, 2019).

## PHYSIOLOGICAL EFFECTS

Although PCP may have hallucinogenic effects, it can cause a host of other physiological actions, including stimulation, depression, anesthesia, and analgesia. The effects of PCP on the CNS vary greatly. At low doses, the most prominent effect is similar to that of alcohol intoxication, with generalized numbness. As the dose of PCP increases, the person becomes even more insensitive and may become fully anesthetized. Large doses can cause coma, convulsions, and death (Anderson, 2018).

The majority of peripheral effects are apparently related to activation of the sympathetic nervous system. Flushing, excess sweating, and a blank stare are common, although the size of the pupils is unaffected. The cardiovascular system reacts by increasing blood pressure and heart rate. Other effects include side-to-side eye movements (called *nystagmus*), muscular incoordination, double vision, dizziness, nausea, and vomiting (Anderson, 2018). These symptoms occur in many people who take medium to high doses.

## PSYCHOLOGICAL EFFECTS

PCP has unpleasant effects most of the time it is used—so why do people use it repeatedly as their drug of choice?

PCP has the ability to markedly alter the person's subjective feelings; this effect may be reinforcing, even though the alteration is not always positive. Some say use of PCP makes them feel godlike and powerful (Maier, 2003). There is an element of risk, not knowing how the trip will turn out. PCP may give the user feelings of strength, power, and invulnerability (NIDA, 2007b). Other positive effects include heightened sensitivity to outside stimuli, a sense of stimulation and mood elevation, and dissociation from surroundings. Also, PCP is a social drug; virtually all users report taking it in groups rather than during a solitary experience. PCP also causes serious perceptual distortions. Users cannot accurately interpret the environment or their own emotions and as a result may take absurd actions such as throwing themselves at moving police cars, mutilating themselves, or assaulting others without provocation.

Chronic users may take PCP in "runs" extending over two to three days, during which time they do not sleep or eat. In later stages of chronic administration, users may develop outright paranoia, unpredictable violent behavior, and auditory hallucinations (Anderson, 2018). Law enforcement officers claim to be more fearful of suspects on PCP than of suspects on other drugs of abuse. Often such people seem to have superhuman strength and are totally irrational and extremely difficult—even dangerous—to manage (NIDA, 2015).

It is claimed by some that PCP has no equal in its ability to produce brief psychoses similar to schizophrenia. The psychoses—induced with moderate doses given to normal, healthy volunteers—last about two hours and are characterized by changes in body image, thought disorders, estrangement, autism, and occasionally rigid inability to move (**catatonia**, or catalepsy). Subjects report feeling numb, have great difficulty differentiating between themselves and their surroundings, and complain afterward of feeling extremely isolated and apathetic. They are often violently paranoid during the psychosis (Anderson, 2018).

When PCP was given experimentally to hospitalized chronic schizophrenics, it made them much worse not for a few hours but for six weeks. PCP is not just another hallucinogen—many authorities view it as much more dangerous than other drugs of abuse (Maier, 2003).

## MEDICAL MANAGEMENT

The diagnosis of a PCP overdose is frequently missed because the symptoms often closely resemble those of an acute schizophrenic episode. Simple, uncomplicated PCP intoxication can be managed with the same techniques used in other

## KEY TERM

**catatonia**
a condition of physical rigidity, excitement, and stupor

psychedelic drug cases. It is important to have a quiet environment, limited but focused contact with an empathic person capable of determining any deterioration in the patient's physical state, protection from self-harm, and the availability of hospital facilities. Talking down is not helpful; the patient is better off isolated from external stimuli as much as possible.

Valium is often used for its sedating effect to prevent injury to self and to staff and also to reduce the chance for severe convulsions. An antipsychotic agent (e.g., haloperidol [Haldol]) is frequently administered to make the patient manageable (Schmetzer, 2015).

The medical management of a comatose or convulsing patient is more difficult. The patient may need external respiratory assistance and external cooling to reduce fever. Blood pressure may have to be reduced to safe levels and convulsions controlled. Restraints and four to five strong hospital aides are often needed to prevent the patient from injuring him- or herself or the medical staff. After the coma lightens, the patient typically becomes delirious, paranoid, and violently assaultive.

### EFFECTS OF CHRONIC USE

Chronic PCP users may develop a tolerance to the drug; thus, a decrease in behavioral effects and toxicity can occur with frequent administration. Different forms of dependence may occur when tolerance develops. Users may complain of vague cravings after cessation of the drug. In addition, long-term difficulties in memory, speech, and thinking persist for six to 12 months in the chronic user (MacLaren, n.d.). These functional changes are accompanied by personality deficits such as social isolation and states of anxiety, nervousness, and extreme agitation (APA, 2013; Buddy 2019).

### KETAMINE

Ketamine is considered a club drug (NIDA, 2016a). Its annual use in 2012 by high school seniors was 1.5% and 0.7% in 2018 (Johnston, 2019). Almost all persons who abuse ketamine are polydrug users (Bracchi et al., 2015), and those who abuse it chronically lose cognitive function and experience a deteriorating sense of well-being (Morgan, Muetzelfeldt, & Curran, 2010). Ketamine, like PCP, was originally developed for its general anesthetic properties. Its effects resemble those of PCP except they are more rapid and less potent (Frohlich & Van Horn, 2016). Depending on the dose, ketamine can have many effects,

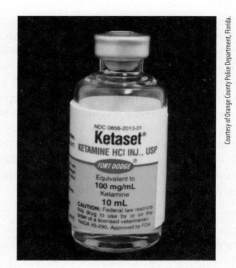

Ketamine is frequently used as a general anesthetic for veterinary procedures.

ranging from feelings of weightlessness to out-of-body or near-death experiences. Ketamine, often referred to as *Special K*, has been abused as a date-rape drug like other CNS depressants such as Rohypnol or gamma-hydroxybutyrate (GHB) (Cunha, n.d.). Abuse of ketamine has been reported in many cities throughout the United States, and the drug is sometimes snorted as a substitute for cocaine. Several deaths have been linked to ketamine overdoses (Smith, 2016).

Despite its potential as a drug of abuse, recent studies have suggested that it is gaining ground as a promising antidepressant for some cases of major depression, which is the leading cause of disability worldwide. When given to someone severely depressed, it can rapidly reduce major impulses of committing suicide (suicidality), especially if anxiety is also involved (Meisner, 2019). In contrast, other more conventional strategies of managing major depression with antidepressant medications or behavioral talk therapies can require months of treatment before gaining relief. It is not understood how ketamine's antidepressant efforts work in such a dramatic fashion, suggesting it may be through a new, yet undiscovered mechanism (Meisner, 2019).This novel use of ketamine may have a success rate for treating severe depression as high as 75% and often highly profound. For example, consider the following report by a depressed patient known as Ted:

> I had situations [of depression] where I just wasn't getting out of bed, I was completely dysfunctional and it was shredding my relationship with my wife.... I'd get hypercritical

of myself and my surroundings.... I was prescribed Wellbutrin, a pretty common antidepressant ... (and other antidepressants as well).... Some antidepressants would lift the veil (of depression) a little bit. It would be gray instead of pitch black, ... I was skeptical about ketamine and thought it would also fail ... but I was willing to try almost anything at that point ... (after ketamine infusion the veil) completely goes away.... After my first infusion, when I realized it had worked, I felt so relieved. (Landsbaum, 2016)

However, the improvement caused by ketamine is temporary, and subsequent ketamine treatments are required every few days or weeks (Landsbaum, 2016).

### DEXTROMETHORPHAN

Dextromethorphan is the active ingredient used in many OTC cough medicines because of its ability to suppress the cough reflex (Durbin, 2019).

Although harmless in low recommended doses, if consumed in high quantities (approximately 10 times the recommended dose), it can cause some hallucinogenic effects much as do PCP and ketamine, as well as other symptoms, such as confusion, nervousness, irritability, numbness, disorientation, and stomach pain (Durbin, 2019). The effects of dextromethorphan can vary and have been described as ranging from a mild stimulant effect to a complete dissociation from one's body, and they can last for several hours. Abuse of dextromethorphan is typically done by teenagers and is sometimes referred to as *roboing* (Durbin, 2019). Recreational use of cough medicines containing this drug was 3.2% in high school seniors in 2018 (Johnston, 2019). This practice of consuming high doses of cough medicine can be extremely dangerous and on occasions even fatal (see "Prescription for Abuse: Cough Medicine Abuse—Nothing to Be Sneezed At"). Most young people who abuse cough medicines are abusing other substances

## PRESCRIPTION FOR ABUSE

### Cough Medicine Abuse—Nothing to Be Sneezed At

Although abuse of cough medicine has not been considered serious enough by the FDA or other federal agencies to do anything more than issue warnings, many parents are concerned because cough syrup abuse seems to be on the rise among teens because it is cheap and readily available. It is generally known by young people that high doses of cough medicines that contain the drug dextromethorphan can cause euphoria, some stimulation, and even hallucinations. However, what is not appreciated by many potential young consumers is that high-dose abuse of these products can have serious negative consequences. For example, some of the cough syrups also contain other ingredients such as the analgesic drug acetaminophen (the active ingredient in Tylenol). When consumed in high doses (as would be the case if someone were to ingest 10 times the recommended dose of an acetaminophen-containing cough medicine to achieve a high), the high doses of acetaminophen can cause permanent and even fatal damage to the liver. In addition, high doses of dextromethorphan itself cause a dissociative effect (e.g., confusion), loss of motor

© Dana Rothstein/Dreamstime.com.

control, nausea, dizziness, fever, hypertension, and difficulty breathing. For long-term abusers, dependence on the dextromethorphan can occur, causing significant withdrawal symptoms such as insomnia, dysphoria, and depression. Finally, cough medicine overdoses often are accompanied by alcohol use, resulting in potentially life-threatening interactions such as severe depressed breathing.

Data from Narconon. (n.d.). Signs and symptoms of dextromethorphan abuse. Retrieved from http://www.narconon.org/drug-abuse/dextromethorphan-signs-symptoms.html

such as marijuana, LSD, or Ecstasy. This surprisingly high rate of abuse for cough medicines has caused some to suggest that these products be removed from shelves and placed behind pharmacy counters or sold only to consumers over age 18. Laws prohibiting sales of these cough medicines to minors have been passed in states such as California, New Jersey, New York, and several others. However, although the FDA has considered these strategies on the national level, as of yet its advisory panel of medical experts has advised against their implementation (Consumer Healthcare Products Association [CHPA], 2016).

### MARIJUANA

Marijuana is known to be the most popular illicit drug of abuse in the United States, with more than 20 million regular users. Whether marijuana should be classified as a hallucinogen is somewhat controversial. Part of this controversy results from the variable effects caused by smoking marijuana between users. Based on the user and the doses consumed, marijuana can have stimulant, depressant, or hallucinogenic effects (sometimes more than one at the same time). This mixture of actions is probably related to the fact that cannabinoid receptors (targets for tetrahydrocannabinol-like ingredients in marijuana) are found in the parts of the brain related to functions such as pleasure, memory, cognitive function, concentration, coordination, and sensory, space, and time perceptions. High doses of tetrahydrocannabinol (THC) or its analogs (the approximately 66 THC-like chemicals found in the marijuana plant) can cause the user to lose contact with reality and result in bizarre and unusual behaviors. In general, marijuana manifests hallucinogenic effects significantly less than those caused by LSD, PCP, or mescaline, but it can distort emotions and sensory perceptions in pleasant or abnormal dysphoric ways, especially in users who already have underlying mental health problems (Hallucinogens.com, n.d.). Another controversial issue relates to the claims that marijuana has potential therapeutic benefits in the treatment in conditions such as chronic pain, weight loss, and nausea in people with cancer, acquired immunodeficiency syndrome (AIDS), neurological disorders, PTSD, and anxiety disorders. Such claims are the main reasons why many states have approved marijuana and its cannabinoid ingredients for "medical" and even "recreational" use. A comprehensive summary of the status of "legal use" of marijuana and its products throughout the states of America as of June 2019 is found in the State Medical Marijuana Laws (National Conference of State Legislatures, 2019). Although many anecdotal reports support these and other therapeutic uses for marijuana, few of these claims have actually been substantiated by well-conducted, controlled, and peer-reviewed scientific studies. A highly regarded comprehensive scientific summary of such claims and their confirmed validity is provided in the National Academy of Science publication entitled *The Health Effects of Cannabis and Cannabinoids: The Current State of Evidence and Recommendations for Research* (Academies of Science, 2017). See Chapter 13 in this text for more details concerning the status of our understanding and use of marijuana and related substances.

# Natural Substances

## ■ Naturally Occurring Hallucinogens

Many plants contain naturally occurring hallucinogens. As already discussed, examples of such substances include mescaline from the peyote cactus, psilocybin from *Psilocybe* mushrooms, and anticholinergic drugs such as atropine from the deadly nightshade plant, mandrake, or jimsonweed. Although some of these plants have been used for medicinal purposes for centuries, typically the therapeutic benefit has not been a consequence of the hallucinogenic effects of the substance. For example, anticholinergic drugs usually cause CNS depression and induce sleep; therefore, herbs that contain these drugs have been used as sleep potions. The hallucinogenic properties of some natural products such as peyote are viewed as positive by some cultures. As noted early in this chapter, peyote is employed in a religious context as a sacrament for the Native American Church. In the United States today, the hallucinogen-containing natural substances are generally not viewed as therapeutic and are more likely to be used for their mind-altering properties as recreational drugs by adolescents. Each year thousands of incidents of accidental consumption of these hallucinogenic plants are reported in the United States (see "Case in Point: Jimsonweed Toxicity in Maryland"), most frequently by children and kids trying to get high (Diaz, 2016). Some users claim that because these are natural rather than synthetic sources of a hallucinogenic episode, it somehow makes the

## ► CASE IN POINT

### Jimsonweed Toxicity in Maryland

Jimsonweed is a natural herb with medicinal purposes that include treatment for asthma, muscle spasms, and whooping cough. It also causes a cluster of annoying and even dangerous side effects. Because of these toxic effects, intentional and unintentional use of jimsonweed can often result in an unexpected visit to an emergency room. For example, six adults of the same family were admitted to a Maryland hospital emergency room suffering from extreme hallucinations, incoherence, dilated pupils (causing blurred vision), extremely rapid heartbeats,

and, in one case, unconsciousness. The symptoms lasted several hours, and the patients remained in the hospital two to four days. Follow-up investigations discovered that all of the patients had consumed a meal of homemade stew that included jimsonweed. The preparer of the stew inadvertently included cuttings from a jimsonweed plant outside the kitchen door without knowledge of the plant's toxic consequences. Such emergency experiences are all too frequent results of ignorance about this natural but potent hallucinogen.

Data from Russell, J. (2010). Jimsonweed poisoning associated with a homemade stew. *Morbidity and Mortality Weekly Report, 59*, 102–104. Atlanta, GA: Centers for Disease Control and Prevention. Retrieved from http://www.cdc.gov/mmwr/preview/mmwrhtml/mm5904a3.htm

experience more rewarding and desirable. There is no evidence that the natural-versus-synthetic features of a hallucinogen are responsible for the quality of a drug-induced hallucination. Frequently, consumption of these seeds and weeds causes severe hallucinations, dry mouth, hyperthermia, seizures, and occasionally death (Leinwand, 2006; Russell, 2010; Wagner, 2015).

### ■ Salvia divinorum

Occasionally, obscure hallucinogenic herbs make their way into the culture of hallucinogenic substance users. This migration has become easier because of the Internet and specialized websites that provide information (some accurate and much anecdotal) and the means to acquire these typically natural substances. For example, a relatively recent hallucinogenic fad has been the use of the Mexican herb *Salvia divinorum*, a drug that did not reach the United States until the late 1980s. In 2009, this plant was abused by 5.7% of high school seniors in the United States, but by 2018 the abuse rate of this plant decreased to 0.9% (Johnston, 2019). This bright, leafy green plant is usually smoked but can also be chewed, crushed, or mixed in a drink (Fernandez, 2008). This relatively unknown plant is referred to as *diviner's mint*. Although it has become illegal in many states because of its intense hallucinations, out-of-body experiences, and short-term memory loss, the federal government has not yet outlawed this hallucinogenic plant (Poncelet, 2019), although some states have restricted its use. Promotions for these products include advertising claims such as "The Mazatec people have preserved Salvia divinorum

and the knowledge surrounding its use for hundreds of years. We are privileged to have them share their sacred herb with us" (Jones, 2001, p. A14). The dried herb sells for $10 to $60 a hit, depending on the quality and purity of the product (Detrick, 2010). The substance typically makes the user introverted while "altering the consciousness in unusual ways" (Vince, 2006). The herb can have dramatic effects on perception that are similar to those seen with LSD (Poncelet, 2019), causes hallucinations when chewed or smoked (Poncelet, 2019), and, also like LSD, has been proposed for use in treating some mental health conditions (Medical News Today, 2019). It typically is not used in social settings and frequently is used only once because for some people the effects can be quite unpleasant, often triggering a lack of coordination and frightening perceptions (Poncelet, 2019). Because of its frequent negative consequences, this herb is not viewed as particularly addicting for most people (Detrick, 2010; Pienciak, 2003). However, some users describe a pleasant experience that is "almost innocent and quaint," with one teenage user describing the effects of salvia as causing "Ferris wheels, flying pigs, and fairies wearing a green dress" (Fernandez, 2008). More recent reports from some scientists researching the active ingredient salvinorum A suggest that this drug may be useful in treating conditions such as depression, stress management, and even drug addiction itself. Much more research needs to be conducted to determine which, if any, of these claims are clinically significant (Davis, 2016b; Johnson, MacLean, Caspers, Prisinzano, & Griffiths, 2016).

# LEARNING PORTFOLIO

## Discussion Questions

1. Why were substances with hallucinogenic properties used by ancient religions and cults?
2. Would you expect natural hallucinogens such as peyote to have fewer adverse effects than other hallucinogens? Why or why not?
3. Why would a drug with both stimulant and hallucinogenic effects have peculiar abuse potential, especially to young people?
4. Why do some users find psychedelic experiences terrifying, whereas others find them desirable?
5. Do you think the federal government is justified in covering up information about the benefits of hallucinogens to convince people to stop using these drugs? Defend your answer.
6. How do the side effects of LSD compare with those of the CNS stimulants, especially with regards to addiction?
7. Why has MDMA been so popular, especially among young people?
8. Do you think scientists should research psychedelic drugs such as LSD and MDMA to determine if they have medicinal value? What are the advantages and disadvantages of doing this, and what role should the FDA play?
9. Why is PCP more dangerous than LSD?
10. How do PCP and ketamine compare?
11. Should severe depression be treated with ketamine?
12. What is the best way to convince people that hallucinogenic drugs of abuse can be harmful?
13. What is a flashback, and how is it caused?
14. Should *Salvia divinorum* be more tightly controlled by the federal government?

## Key Terms

## Summary

1. Many drugs can exert hallucinogenic effects. The principal hallucinogens include LSD types, phenylethylamines, and anticholinergic agents. The four major effects that occur from administering LSD are (a) heightened senses, (b) loss of sensory control, (c) self-reflection or introspection, and (d) loss of identity or sense of cosmic merging.
2. Hallucinogens exaggerate sensory input and cause vivid and unusual visual and auditory effects.
3. The classic hallucinogens, such as LSD, cause predominantly psychedelic effects. Phenylethylamines are related to amphetamines, such as Ecstasy, and cause varying combinations of psychedelic and stimulant effects. Anticholinergic

drugs such as scopolamine, antihistamines, or herbs such as *Salvia divinorum* can also produce psychedelic effects when taken in high doses, but because of their annoying side effects, they are not usually abused recreationally.

4. One prominent effect of hallucinogens is self-reflection. The user becomes aware of thoughts and feelings that had been forgotten or repressed. It is claimed that some experiences help to clarify motives and relationships and cause periods of greater openness. These effects have been promoted by some psychiatrists as providing valid insights useful in psychotherapy, especially for managing conditions such as PTSD, anxiety disorders, and depression.

5. The classic hallucinogens do not cause physical dependence. Although some tolerance can build up to the hallucinogenic effects of drugs such as LSD, withdrawal effects are usually minor.

6. The environment plays a major role in determining the sensory response to hallucinogens. Environments that are warm, comfortable, and hospitable tend to create a pleasant sensory response to the psychedelic effects of these drugs. Threatening, hostile environments are likely to lead to intimidating, frightening "bad trips."

7. In some users, high doses of LSD can cause a terrifying destruction of identity, resulting in panic and severe anxiety that resembles schizophrenia. Another psychological feature commonly associated with LSD is the flashback phenomenon. LSD use can cause recurring, unexpected visual and time distortions that last a few minutes to several hours. Although unusual, flashbacks can occur months to years after use of the drug.

8. Designer amphetamines such as MDMA (Ecstasy) have been included in the so-called club drug phenomenon. MDMA has been used frequently by young people to enhance the sensory experience of raves and the nightclub scene. Although viewed by some as harmless and even therapeutic, evidence of potentially serious negative physiological and neurological consequences suggests that these drugs can be extremely dangerous in high doses and under some conditions.

9. Hallucinogens purchased on the street are often poorly prepared and contaminated with adulterant substances. This practice of cutting the pure drugs with other stimulant or hallucinogenic substances also makes use of street hallucinogens extremely dangerous and unpredictable.

10. PCP differs from the other traditional hallucinogens in several ways: (a) it is a general anesthetic in high doses; (b) it causes schizophrenia-like psychosis and can produce incredible strength and extreme violent behavior, making users difficult and dangerous to manage; (c) management of the severe psychological reactions to PCP requires drug therapy, whereas treatment of other hallucinogens often requires only reassurance, talking down, and supportive therapy; and (d) reactions to overdoses include fever, convulsions, and coma. Ketamine is related to but less potent than PCP and shares many of its pharmacological effects.

11. Other substances also abused for their hallucinogenic properties include dextromethorphan, a common OTC anticough medication, and some natural herbs, such as *Salvia divinorum*, that are promoted over the Internet.

# References

Academies of Science. (2017, January 12). *The health effects of cannabis and cannabinoids: The current state of evidence and recommendations for research*. Washington, DC: National Academies of Science, Health and Medicine Division. Retrieved from http://nationalacademies.org/hmd/reports/2017/health-effects-of-cannabis-and-cannabinoids.aspx

Adam, D. (2006, August 18). Truth about Ecstasy's unlikely trip from lab to dance floor. *The Guardian* [London, UK]. Retrieved from http://guardian.co.uk/uk/2006/aug/18/topstories3.drugsandalcohol

Alcohol and Drug Foundation (ADF). (2018, July 19). LSD as a therapeutic treatment. North Melbourne, Victoria, Australia: Author. Retrieved from https://adf.org.au/insights/lsd-therapeutic-treatment/

Adler, J. (1985, April 15). Getting high on Ecstasy. *Newsweek*, p. 15.

American Psychiatric Association (APA). (2013). *Diagnostic and statistical manual of mental disorders*, 5th ed. Washington, DC: Author.

Anders, C. (2015, January 2). There really is an LSD Shortage, and here's why. Gizmodo. Retrieved from http://io9.gizmodo.com/there-really-is-an-lsd-shortage-and-heres-why-1677123866

Anderson, L. (2016, February 10). Anticholinergic drugs to avoid in the elderly. Drugs.com. Retrieved from http://www.drugs.com/article/anticholinergic-drugs-elderly.html

Anderson, L. (2018, April 26). Phencyclidine (PCP). Drugs.com. Retrieved from https://www.drugs.com/phencyclidine.html

Araujo, A., Carvalho, F., Bastos Mde, L., Guedes de Pinho, P., & Carvalho, M. (2015). The hallucinogenic world of tryptamines: An updated review. *Archives of Toxicology, 89*, 1151–1173.

Associated Press. (1999, July 1). 60s icon Timothy Leary cooperated with the FBI. *Salt Lake Tribune, 258*, A-10.

Baggott, M., Siegrist, J., Galloway, G., Robertson, L., Coyle, J., & Mendelson, J. (2010, December 2). Investigating the mechanisms of hallucinogen-induced visions using 3,4-methyleneamphetamine (MDA): A randomized controlled trial in humans. *PLoS One, 5*(12): e14074. doi: 10.1371/journal.pone.001407. Retrieved from http://www.plosone.org/article/info%3Adoi%2F10.1371%2Fjournal.pone.0014074

Begola, M., & Schillerstrom, J. (2019, September). Hallucinogens and their therapeutic use. *Psychiatric Practice, 25*, 334–343.

Bezrutczyk, D. (2019, November). Drug street names. Addiction Center. Retrieved from https://www.addictioncenter.com/drugs/drug-street-names/

Biography. (n.d.). Timothy Leary, psychologist (1920-1996). Biography.com. Retrieved from http://www.biography.com/people/timothy-leary-37330#film-tv-tech

Black Witch Coven. (n.d.). Belladonna. Herbs & Oils. Retrieved from http://blackwitchcoven.com/the-most-deadly-magick-herbs-1/

Bracchi, M., Stuart, D., Castles, R., Khoo, S., Back, D., & Boffito, M. (2015). Increasing use of "party drugs" in people living with HIV on antiretrovirals: A concern for patient safety. *AIDS, 29*, 1585–1592.

Buddy T. (2012, January 12). What are the effects of LSD? VeryWellMind. Retrieved from http://alcoholism.about.com/cs/lsd/f/lsd_faq04.htm

Buddy T. (2019, September 3). What to know about PCP use. VeryWellMind. Retrieved from https://www.verywellmind.com/basic-facts-about-pcp-67498

Burger, A. (Ed.). (1968). Quotes from Albert Hofmann. *Drugs affecting the central nervous system: Psychotomimetic agents*, vol. 2. New York, NY: Dekker.

Carollo, K. (2010, October 25). Georgetown students arrested for manufacturing illegal drug in dorm room. ABC News. Retrieved from http://abcnews.go.com/Health/MindMoodNews/georgetown-university-students-busted-illegal-drug-manufacturing/story?id=11963382

"Celebration #1." (1966). *The New Yorker, 42*, 43.

Center for Substance Abuse Research (CESAR). "Dextromethorphan (DXM)." 2005. Retrieved from http://www.cesar.umd.edu/cesar/drugs/dxm.asp

Citizens' Commission. (2015, March 24). PCP laced marijuana: Creating psychosis and psychiatric commitment. Citizens Commission on Human Rights, Florida. Retrieved from http://www.cchrflorida.org/pcp-laced-marijuana-creating-psychosis-and-psychiatric-commitment/

Clark, C. (2015, May 10). LSD could take you on a trip to Alice in Wonderland syndrome. BrainBlogger. Retrieved from http://brainblogger.com/2015/05/10/lsd-could-take-you-on-a-trip-to-alice-in-wonderland-syndrome/

Consumer Healthcare Products Association (CHPA). (2016, February). OTC cough medicine abuse prevention." February 2016. Retrieved from http://www.google.com/url?sa=t&rct=j&q=&esrc=s&source=web&cd=1&ved=0ahUKEwjG6aeq5oTNAhVT2GMKHb2tDIgQFggcMAA&url=http%3A%2F%2Fwww.chpa.org%2FPP_CoughMedAbusePrevention.aspx&usg=AFQjCNHa9n3wY0ktG8HHqiJt3SlFO8jjZQ&bvm=bv.123325700,d.cGc

Cormier, Z. (2016). Brain scans reveal how LSD affects consciousness. *Nature*. Retrieved from https://www.nature.com/news/brain-scans-reveal-how-lsd-affects-consciousness-1.19727

Cunha, J. (n.d.). Date rape drugs facts. MedicineNet.com. Retrieved from http://www.medicinenet.com/date_rape_drugs/article.htm

Davis, K. (2016a). PCP (phencyclidine): Facts, effects and health risks. Medical News Today, January 22. Retrieved from http://www.medicalnewstoday.com/articles/305328.php

Davis, K. (2016b). Salvia: What are the effects? Medical News Today, May 2. Retrieved from http://www.medicalnewstoday.com/articles/309735.php

Delgado, J. (2013). Intoxication from LSD and other common hallucinogens. UpToDate. Retrieved from http://www.uptodate.com/contents/intoxication-from-lsd-and-other-common-hallucinogens

Detrick, B. (2010, December 23). Salvia takes a starring role. *The New York Times.* Retrieved from http://www.nytimes.com/2010/12/26/fashion/26noticed.html?_r=1

Devlin, H. (2015, March 5). Psychedelic drugs like LSD could be used to treat depression, study suggests. *The Guardian* [London, UK]. Retrieved from https://www.theguardian.com/science/2015/mar/05/psychedelic-drugs-like-lsd-could-be-used-to-treat-depression-study-suggests

Diaz, J. (2016). Poisoning by herbs and plants: Rapid taxonomic classification and diagnosis. *Wilderness & Environmental Medicine, 27,* 136–152.

Dishotsky, N. I., Loughman, W. D., Mogar, R. E., & Lipscomb, W. R. (1971). LSD and genetic damage. *Science, 172,* 431–440.

Doyle, J. U.S. Held Responsible for Death in Secret Army Drug Testing. AP NEWS (1987). Retrieved from https://apnews.com/2e5220ecb195844edacfbffdb0a37a5a

D'Orazio, J. (2015). Hallucinogen toxicity treatment and management. Medscape. Retrieved from http://emedicine|.medscape.com/article/814848-treatment#d10

D'Orazio, J. (2018). Hallucinogen toxicity. Medscape. Retrieved from http://emedicine.medscape.com/article/814848-overview

DrugDangers. (2016). MDMA (Molly) parental warning. Retrieved from http://www.drugdangers.com/MDMA-molly-parental-warning.htm

Drug Enforcement Administration (DEA). (2002, October). Trippin' on tryptamine. Intelligence Brief. Document No. DEA-02052.

Drug Enforcement Administration (DEA). (2015). Drugs of abuse. Retrieved from https://www.dea.gov/pr/multimedia-library/publications/drug_of_abuse.pdf

Durbin, K. (2019, March 4). Dextromethorphan. Drugs.com. Retrieved from https://www.drugs.com/dextromethorphan.html

Fernandez, D. (2008, June 26). Salvia becoming "drug du jour" for some teens; Hallucinogenic herb Salvia divinorum causes concern as young adults use it to get a cheap high. Salvia. Retrieved from http://www.salvia.net/articles.php?id=29

Ferro, S. (2013, August). Are acid flashbacks a myth? *Popular Science.* Retrieved from http://www.popsci.com/science/article/2013-08/fyi-can-acid-trip-really-give-you-flashbacks

Freeman, S. (n.d.). How LSD works. Howstuffworks. Retrieved from http://www.howstuffworks.com/lsd.htm

Frohlich, J., & Van Horn, J. (2016). Ketamine and dissociatives: Comparisons with schizophrenia. In V. Preedy (Ed.), *Neuropathology of drug addictions and substance misuse,* vol. 2 (pp. 649–657). Cambridge, MA: Elsevier.

Garden Spot. (2013, July 17). Auntie Dogma's garden spot. Retrieved from https://auntiedogmasgardenspot.wordpress.com/2013/07/17/atropa-belladonna-belladonna-nightshade-plant-guide/

Goldsmith, N. (2015, January 23). Neurotransmitters and the integral approach to reality. Psychedelic Press UK. Retrieved from http://psypressuk.com/2015/01/23/neurotransmitters-and-the-integral-approach-to-reality/

Greer, G., & Tolbert, R. (1990). The therapeutic use of MDMA. In S. J. Peroutka (Ed.), *Ecstasy: The clinical, pharmacological and neurotoxicological effects of the drug MDMA* (p. 28). Boston, MA: Kluwer.

Gregoire, C. (2017, January 24). Everything you wanted to know about microdosing (but were afraid to ask). *Science.* Retrieved from http://www.huffingtonpost.com/entry/psychedelic-microdosing-research_us_569525afe4b09dbb4bac9db8

Hadlock, G., Webb, K., McFadden, L., Chu, P., Ellis, J., Allen, S. C., . . . , & Fleckenstein, A. E. (2011). 4-methylmethcathinone (mephedrone): Neuropharmacological effects of a designer stimulant of abuse. *Journal of Pharmacology and Experimental Therapeutics, 339,* 530–536.

Halpern, J., Sherwood, A., Hudson, J., Yurgelun-Todd, D., & Pope, H. (2005). Psychological and cognitive effects of long-term peyote use among Native Americans. *Biological Psychiatry, 58,* 624–631.

Hallucinogens.com. (2016). Is marijuana a hallucinogen? Retrieved from http://hallucinogens.com/what-are-hallucinogens/is-marijuana-a-hallucinogen/

Hendricks, P. (2015, March 9). Psychedelic drug use could reduce psychological distress, suicidal thinking. Johns Hopkins Medicine. Retrieved from http://www.hopkinsmedicine.org/news/media/releases/psychedelic_drug_use_could_reduce_psychological_distress_suicidal_thinking

Hilleary, C. (2019). Native American church works to conserve, sustain peyote. VOA. Retrieved from https://www.voanews.com/usa/native-american-church-works-conserve-sustain-peyote

Hooton, C. (2015, August 27). Different stages of the 9-hour trip to show its effects. *Independent* [London, UK]. Retrieved from http://www.independent.co.uk/arts-entertainment/art/news/girl-takes-lsd-draws-herself-over-different-stages-of-the-9-hour-trip-to-show-its-effects-10474372.html

Horgan, J. (n.d.). The psychedelic sorcerer. Retrieved from http://www.johnhorgan.org/the_psychedelic_sorcerer_15289.htm

Horgan, J. (2019, February 9). As psychedelics revival rolls on, don't downplay bad trips. *Scientific American.* Retrieved from http://blogs.scientificamerican.com/cross-check/as-psychedelics-revival-rolls-on-don-t-downplay-bad-trips/

Huxley, A. (1954). *The doors of perception.* New York, NY: Harper.

Jacoby, S. (2015). How these 4 illegal drugs are treating mental illness. Refinery 29. Retrieved from http://www.refinery29.com/2015/03/83909/psychedelics-mental-illness-treatment

Johnson, M., MacLean, K., Caspers, M., Prisinzano, T., & Griffiths, R. (2016). Time course of pharmacokinetic and hormonal effects of inhaled high-dose Salvinorin A in humans. *Psychopharmacology, 30,* 323–329.

Johnstad, P. (2015). User perceptions of mental health consequences of hallucinogen use in self-identified spiritual contexts. NAD Research Report. Retrieved from http://bora.uib.no/bitstream/handle/1956/11901/nsad-2015-0053-1.pdf?sequence=3

Johnston, L. D. (2019). *Monitoring the future.* Ann Arbor, MI: University of Michigan, Institute for Social Research. Retrieved from http://monitoringthefuture.org/pubs/monographs/mtf-overview2018.pdf

Jones, R. (2001, July 9). New cautions about an herb that's hip, hallucinogenic and legal. *The New York Times,* p. A-14.

Jones, W. H. S. (1956). *Natural history.* Cambridge, MA: Harvard University Press.

Juergens, J. (2019). Ecstasy addiction and abuse. Addiction Center. Retrieved from https://www.addictioncenter.com/drugs/ecstasy/

Kyzar, E. Stewart, A., & Kalueff, A. (2016). Effects of LSD on grooming behavior in serotonin transporter heterozygous (sert +/−) mice. *Behavioral Brain Research, 296,* 47–52.

Landsbaum, C. (2016). What it's like to have your severe depression treated with a hallucinogenic drug. *New York.* Retrieved from http://nymag.com/scienceofus/2016/03/what-its-like-to-treat-severe-depression-with-a-hallucinogenic-drug.html

Leary, T., Metzner, R., & Alpert, R. (1964). *The psychedelic experience.* New Hyde Park, NY: University Books.

Leinwand, D. (2006, November 1). Jimson weed users chase high all the way to the hospital. *USA Today.* Retrieved from https://addictionandrecoverynews.wordpress.com/2006/11/07/jimson-weed-users-chase-high-all-the-way-to-hospital/

Leonard, M. (2015). DOM, DOB, STP, 2C-b, 2C-e, 2C-I, MDA. Streetdrugs.org. Retrieved from http://www.streetdrugs.org/dom-dob-stp-2c-b-2c-e-mda/

Liester, M. (2014). A review of lysergic acid diethylamide (LSD) in the treatment of addictions: Historical perspectives and future prospects. *Current Drug Abuse Reviews, 7,* 146–156.

MacLaren, E. (n.d.). The effects of PCP use. DrugAbuse.com. Retrieved from http://drugabuse.com/library/the-effects-of-pcp-use/

Maier, T. (2003, February 17). PCP is rearing its ugly head again. *Insight on the News,* pp. 4–6.

Many were lost because of Leary. (1996, June 3). Letters (to the editor). *USA Today,* p. 12-A.

Marquardt, G. M., DiStefano, V., & Ling. L. L. (1978). Pharmacological Effects of (S)-, and (R)-MDA. In R. C. Stillman & R. E. Willette (Eds.), *The psychopharmacology of hallucinogens.* New York, NY: Pergamon.

Mathias, R. (1993, March–April). NIDA research takes a new look at LSD and other hallucinogens. *NIDA Notes, 8,* 6.

McGlothin, W., Cohen, S., & McGlothin, M. S. (1967). Long-lasting effects of LSD on normals. *Archives of General Psychiatry, 17,* 521–532.

Meadow, M. (2015, October 15). European MDMA vs. American Molly: The winner is clear. YOUREDM. Retrieved from https://www.youredm.com/2015/10/15/european-mdma-vs-american-molly-the-winner-is-clear/

Medical News Today. (2019, December 31). Salvia: What are the effects? Retrieved from https://www.medicalnewstoday.com/articles/309735.php

Meisner, R. (2019, May 22). Ketamine for major depression: New tool, new questions. Cambridge, MA: Harvard Health Publishing, Harvard Medical School. Retrieved from https://www.health.harvard.edu/blog/ketamine-for-major-depression-new-tool-new-questions-2019052216673

Mims, B. (1999, July 1). "Peyote: When the ancient Indian way collides with a New Age craze." *Salt Lake Tribune, 258,* A-10.

Morgan, C., Muetzelfeldt, L., & Curran, H. (2010). Consequences of chronic ketamine self-administration upon neurocognitive function and psychological wellbeing: A 1-year longitudinal study. *Addiction, 105,* 121–133.

Naranjo, C., Shulgin, A. T., & Sargent, T. (1967). Evaluation of 3,4 methylenedioxyamphetamine (MDA) as an adjunct to psychotherapy. *Medicina et Pharmacologia Experimentalis, 17,* 359–364.

Narconon. (n.d.). Signs and symptoms of dextromethorphan abuse. Retrieved from http://www.narconon.org/drug-abuse/dextromethorphan-signs-symptoms.html

National Conference of State Legislatures. (2019, October 16). State medical marijuana laws. NCSL. Retrieved from https://www.ncsl.org/research/health/state-medical-marijuana-laws.aspx

National Drug Intelligence Center (NDIC). (n.d.). Foxy fast facts. Retrieved from https://www.justice.gov/archive/ndic/pubs6/6440/6440p.pdf

National Institute on Drug Abuse (NIDA). (2001, March). Hallucinogens and dissociative drugs. NIDA Research Report Series. NIH Publication No. 01-4209. Rockville, MD: Author.

National Institute on Drug Abuse (NIDA). (2007a). Info-Facts. LSD. Rockville, MD: Author. Retrieved from http://nida.nih.gov/Infofax/lsd.html

National Institute on Drug Abuse (NIDA). (2007b). PCP/phencyclidine. Rockville, MD: Author. Retrieved from http://nida.nih.gov/Infofax/pcp.html

National Institute on Drug Abuse (NIDA). (2010, December). "NIDA InfoFacts: LSD." Rockville, MD: Author.

National Institute on Drug Abuse (NIDA). (2015, February). Hallucinogens and dissociative drugs. Rockville, MD: Author. Retrieved from https://www.drugabuse.gov/publications/research-reports/hallucinogens-dissociative-drugs/where-can-i-get-more-scientific-information-hallucinogens-diss

National Institute on Drug Abuse (NIDA). (2016a). Club drugs. Rockville, MD: Author. Retrieved from https://www.drugabuse.gov/drugs-abuse/club-drugs

National Institute on Drug Abuse (NIDA). (2016b). Drug-Facts: MDMA (Ecstasy/Molly) [February]. Rockville, MD: Author. Retrieved from https://www.drugabuse.gov/publications/drugfacts/mdma-ecstasymolly

Native American Church. (2008). Millennium purification and emergence. Strawberry Plains, TN: Author. Retrieved from http://www.nativeamericanchurch.com

Ojibwa. (2015, January 1). Suppressing Indian religions in 1915. Native American Netroots. Retrieved from http://nativeamericannetroots.net/diary/tag/peyote

Ojibwa. (2019, November 24). Suppressing peyote in 1918. Native American Netroots. Retrieved from http://nativeamericannetroots.net/diary/tag/peyote

OneLuckySoul. (2015). The LSD experiments of the 1950s and 60s [videos & documentaries]. Retrieved from http://oneluckysoul.blogspot.com/2015/02/the-lsd-experiments-of-1950s-and-60s.html

Pahnke, W. N., & Richards, W. A. (1966). Implications of LSD and experimental mysticism. *Journal of Religion and Health, 5,* 175–208.

Parish, B. (2015, November 23). Hallucinogen use. Medscape. Retrieved from http://emedicine.medscape.com/article/293752-overview

Partnership for Drug-Free Kids. (n.d.). Drug guide: LSD. Drugfree.org. Retrieved from http://www.drugfree.org/drug-guide/lsd

Pienciak, R. (2003, July 25). DEA issues warning for legal herb stronger than LSD. *Daily News* [New York].

Plummer, C., Breadon, T., Pearson, J., & Jones, O. (2016). The synthesis and characterization of MDMA from a catalytic oxidation of material isolated from black pepper reveals potential route specific impurities. *Science and Justice, 56,* 223–230.

Poncelet, B. (2019). What to know about Salvia divinorum use. VeryWellMind. Retrieved from htts://www.verywellmind.com/salvia-divinorum-a-legal-trip-3200920

Psychonaut. (2015). 20 hours in waking hell, or, my experience with DOM. Retrieved from https://www.reddit.com/r/Psychonaut/comments/2u4i8t/20_hours_in_waking_hell_or_my_experience_with_dom/

Rahman, N., Fazilah, A., & Effarizah, M. (2015). Toxicity of nutmeg (myristicin): A review. *International Journal on Advanced Science Engineering Information Technology, 5,* 61–64. Retrieved from http://insightsociety.org/ojaseit/index.php/ijaseit/article/viewFile/518/pdf_20

Rega, P. (2015). LSD toxicity. Medscape. Retrieved from http://emedicine.medscape.com/article/1011615-overview

Remsberg, R. (2010, December 1). Found in the archives: Military LSD testing. NPR. Retrieved from http://www.npr.org/blogs/pictureshow/2010/12/01/131724898/lsd-testing

Russell, J. (2010). Jimsonweed poisoning associated with a homemade stew. *Morbidity and Mortality Weekly Report, 59,* 102–104. Atlanta, GA: Centers for Disease Control and Prevention. Retrieved from http://www.cdc.gov/mmwr/preview/mmwrhtml/mm5904a3.htm

Sample, I. (2016, April 11). LSD's impact on the brain revealed in groundbreaking images. *The Guardian* [London, UK]. Retrieved from https://www.theguardian.com/science/2016/apr/11/lsd-impact-brain-revealed-groundbreaking-images

Sapolsky, R. (2015, March 25). Synesthesia: Tasting sounds and smelling sights. *Wall Street Journal.* Retrieved from http://www.wsj.com/articles/synesthesia-tasting-sounds-and-smelling-sights-1427298999

Schmetzer, A. (2015, December 29). Phencyclidine (PCP)-related psychiatric disorders. Medscape. Retrieved from http://emedicine.medscape.com/article/290476-overview

Schultes, R. E. (1970). The plant kingdom and hallucinogens (part III). *Bulletin on Narcotics, 22,* 25–53.

Schultes, R. E. (1978). Ethnopharmacological significance of psychotropic drugs of vegetal origin. In W. G. Clark &

J. del Giudice (Eds.), *Principles of psychopharmacology*, 2nd ed. New York, NY: Academic Press.

Schultes, R. E., & Hofmann, A. (1980). *The botany and chemistry of hallucinogens*, 2nd ed. Springfield, IL: Thomas.

Scinto, M. (2013, January 28). Inside the lucrative world of ecstasy smuggling. *New York Post*. Retrieved from http://www.nypost.com/p/news/opinion/opedcolumnists/riding_the_train_wxKKIdsE4zYejiWxK5AoUO

Sessa, B., Higbed, L., & Nutt, D. (2019). A review of 3,4-methylenedioxymethamphetamine (MDMA)-assisted psychotherapy. *Frontiers in Psychiatry, 10,* 138.

Smith, K. (2016). Ketamine symptoms and warning signs. AddictionCenter. Retrieved from https://www.addictioncenter.com/drugs/hallucinogens/ketamine/

Smith, P. (2015, June 12). Microdosing: A new, low-key way to use psychedelics. Alternet. Retrieved from http://www.alternet.org/drugs/microdosing-new-low-key-way-use-psychedelics

Snyder, S. H. (1974). *Madness and the brain.* New York, NY: McGraw-Hill.

Sterbenz, C. (2015, April 3). Indiana's religious freedom law was inspired by Native Americans' right to smoke peyote. Business Insider. Retrieved from http://www.businessinsider.com/where-did-indianas-religious-freedom-law-come-from-2015-4

Stone, W. (2019, August 21). MDMA, or Ecstasy, shows promise as a PTSD treatment. *Scientific American.* Retrieved from https://www.scientificamerican.com/article/mdma-or-ecstasy-shows-promise-as-a-ptsd-treatment/#

Szalavitz, M. (2010, December 24). Can you get high on gingerbread? The truth about nutmeg. *Time.* Retrieved from http://healthland.time.com/2010/12/24/high-on-ginger bread-truth-about-nutmeg/

Toufexis, A. (1985, June 10). A crackdown on Ecstasy. *Time,* p. 64.

Tucker, R. (1987, November). Acid test. *Omni,* p. 16.

University of Toronto. (2014). Contain powerful alkaloids ex 6 scopolamine from…History Drug Discovery. Retrieved from https://www.coursehero.com/search/results/607088436/c353efa24e95a72f7e/

Vince, G. (2006, September 30). Legally high. *New Scientist,* pp. 40–45.

Wagner, R. (2015). Tropane alkaloid poisoning. Medscape. Retrieved from http://emedicine.medscape.com/article/816657-overview#a4

Weaver, M., Hopper, J., & Gunderson, E. (2015). Designer drugs 2015: Assessment and management. *Addiction Science and Clinical Practice, 10,* 1–9.

Weber, B. (2006, October 6). Prairie LSD studies coined "psychedelic." *Toronto Star,* p. A8.

WebMD. (n.d.). Vitamins and supplements. Retrieved from https://www.webmd.com/vitamins/index

Willing, R. (2007, April 6). Researchers tested pot, LSD on Army volunteers. *USA Today.* Retrieved from http://www.usatoday.com/news/washington/2007-04-05-army-experiments_N.htm

Wing, N. (2015). DEA approves study of psychedelic drug MDMA in treatment of seriously ill patients. Huffington Post. Retrieved from http://www.huffingtonpost.com/2015/03/18/dea-mdma-study_n_6888972.html

Woolcott, I. (2015). Jimson weed Datura stramonium poisonous herbal medicine. Shamanism. Retrieved from http://www.shamanicjourney.com/jimson-weed-datura-stramonium-poisonous-herbal-medicine

Zhou, S. (2016). *Cytochrome P450 2D6, structure, function, regulation and polymorphism.* Boca Raton, FL: CRC Press.

# CHAPTER 13
# Marijuana

## Did You Know?

▶ George Washington grew marijuana plants at Mount Vernon for medicine and rope making.

▶ An estimated 43.5 million Americans aged 12 or older in 2018 used marijuana in the past year. This number of past-year marijuana users corresponds to 15.9% of the population.

▶ In some states, marijuana is one of the largest cash-producing crops. For example, California produces nearly 33% of the marijuana in the United States; it is worth an estimated $5.1 billion in 2019, making it the state's largest cash crop.

▶ Marijuana grows wild in many U.S. states today.

▶ Research shows that many users have difficulty learning and remembering what they have learned when they are "high."

▶ An April 2018 Pew Research Center poll found that around six in 10 Americans (62%) say the use of marijuana should be legalized.

▶ In 2018, 80% said marijuana was easy or extremely easy to get, 44% said there was great risk of harm in regular use, and approximately 26% reported using once or more in the past 30 days.

▶ The "high" experienced by using marijuana varies not only according to the quality of the drug, the user's expectations, and the physical surroundings where the drug is taken but also according to how the drug is taken, whether it is smoked, inhaled through a vaporizer, or ingested (eaten).

## Learning Objectives

**On completing this chapter, you should be able to:**

❯ Explain what marijuana is and why it remains so attractive and controversial.

❯ Differentiate between the effects of low and high doses of marijuana.

❯ List the potential effects marijuana use has on the body.

❯ Explain how marijuana use can become psychologically addictive.

❯ Describe how tolerance and dependence affect the response to marijuana and its use.

❯ Describe the medical uses of marijuana.

❯ Identify which age groups are most likely to use marijuana.

❯ Identify the major characteristics of first-time marijuana users.

❯ Explain how the perceived danger of marijuana use has changed with regard to high school seniors and younger age groups.

❯ Differentiate between prior and current beliefs regarding the effects of chronic marijuana use.

## Introduction

When compared to more addictive types of drugs, marijuana is often perceived as a benign drug. In 2018, marijuana was the third most used drug with 27.7 million monthly users (SAMHSA, 2019). In 2018, marijuana ranked second after alcohol for past-year use with 3.1 million new users (8,400 first-time users each day) (SAMHSA, 2019). Further. the most common illicit drug use disorder (SUD) was marijuana with 4.4 million people. How benign is this drug?

The following interviews reveal different degrees of use and commitment in using this drug.

### ▪ First Interview

I was first tried marijuana when I was in college. I would do it with two of my college friends several evenings each week. Back then it was fun to be buzzed! Then when I went to law school, I would continue to smoke weed with other undergrads living off campus usually late at night in law school. I also did this about three times weekly. It was great to get away from classes and homework, smoke and drink a little before going to bed, it was nice to just to change venues from the pressures of law school. I continued to occasionally smoke while practicing law with my law partner late at night when we closed the law office. I did not do it as often because of the time it took to service my clients with their many legal problems. Eight years later my dad suddenly died, and my mom was getting up there in age, so I had her move in with me. She had a lot of arthritis, some rheumatism, as well heart problems. My brothers and their wives did not know it, but I found that a few puffs of weed seemed to help her cope with aging. About two years later, I had a former friend of mine who knew drug dealers and I purchased electronic versions of marijuana and with my mom we both started vaping several times a week. Vaping marijuana is less expensive than purchasing dried marijuana. It seems to be stronger than regular marijuana, but my mom likes vaping to ease aging. No one knows she does this because in Milwaukee and the state of Wisconsin it remains an illegal drug. I have a valid reason for letting her vape marijuana given her age and deteriorating health. My brothers would really be upset if they knew that my mom and I use marijuana. All of my older brothers are against using any type of recreational drugs as you call it. For a long time now, I continue to enjoy the buzz, plus my mom is therapeutically helped from the effects of this drug. I certainly do not have any internal problems using this drug for my own relaxation and recreational pursuits. (*From Venturelli's research files, male attorney, age 41, July 5, 2019*)

### ▪ Second Interview

My kids know that I still smoke dope, and I know they are used to me doing this since from the day they were born. I never hid this habit of mine. I am now 59, and I never even thought of quitting. You see I started back in the late 60s when I was 17 years old. My wife does not do it as much as I do. Usually a couple of times a week, late at night I go outside on the deck and take a few hits. I don't think it is much different than having a drink. Why I have always done it, so what is the big deal? I have a few friends about my age who do the same thing and we don't bother anyone, we work 5 and often 6 days a week at our full-time jobs, and only do this away from work, and as I said only a few times a week. I ask again, what's the big deal? Now society may look down on me, but at this age, I don't give a rat's ass what society thinks. I don't tell anyone about this long-time habit that brings me relief and relaxation and outside of a few friends, my wife, and kids, no one else knows that I do this. As you asked, I really don't care what the law says; I will always do it until I die. It is so natural for me to do this that I don't even think about breaking drug laws. This is a private matter between my family and me. My kids don't smoke dope, and I never thought I would have kids who would not. Especially when I grew up in the 60s, everyone I knew smoked dope and I never thought it would change, but today the world is different, so I keep to myself with my habits. To me, honestly professor, if marijuana is outlawed and if I wanted to say smoke oregano then they should outlaw oregano. Outlawing a naturally growing plant is just plain stupid. What threat to the world is my smoking weed? I just think this law-making marijuana illegal is ridiculous, especially when smoking it is viewed as a violation of law. What a stupid law it is and how effective this law is in that I have smoked dope all my life. (*From Venturelli's research files, male, living in a Midwestern rural area, August 10, 2010*)

## ■ Third Interview

We used to have one great big bong and fill it with dope [referring to marijuana], and all of us in someone's fraternity room would each take hits from the bong. Today, it's a different life altogether. I am working three different jobs, one teaching at a junior high school, [one] working at a film production studio, and my third claim to fame is my job as a part-time waiter. . . . I feel that I wasted many nights by just "smokin'," "dopin'," and "drinkin'" back during those college days. I sometimes think that I could have accomplished a lot more if I would not have inhaled so much dope. If I had to do it over again I would not have wasted so much time. *(From Venturelli's research files, male, age 28, August 9, 1996)*

The preceding interviews illustrate contrasting views regarding marijuana usage as a subcultural phenomenon. The first and second interviews present "die-hard" users who refuse to relinquish their use of this drug. These individuals have been using marijuana for many years and consider it an essential recreational drug. Conversely, the third interviewee expresses some regret over the time "wasted" while becoming intoxicated with marijuana when he could have been pursuing other, more career-oriented activities.

## Marijuana: History and Trends

Although marijuana is potentially less addictive, it is one of the few drugs that remains controversial. (As an example of the controversy that surrounds this drug, see "Here and Now: Legalizing Recreational and Medicinal Marijuana Use.") It is difficult to wade through the emotion, politics, and rigidity found in the writings on marijuana to tease out the objective, clinical reality. In the United States, extreme views go back to the 1930s, when the film *Reefer Madness* portrayed an after-school marijuana "club" for high school

## HERE AND NOW

### Legalizing Recreational and Medicinal Marijuana Use

Recent developments in legalizing recreational and medical marijuana use include the following:

- An April 2018 Pew Research Center poll found that "[a]bout six in 10 Americans (62%) say the use of marijuana should be legalized, reflecting a steady increase over the past decade, according to a new Pew Research Center survey. The share of U.S. adults who support marijuana legalization is little changed from about a year ago—when 61% favored it—but it is double what it was in 2000 (31%)" (Hartig & Geiger, 2018).

- Regarding the legalization of marijuana significantly varies across the generations, "[m]ajorities of Millennials (74%), Gen Xers (63%) and Baby Boomers (54%) say the use of marijuana should be legal. Members of the Silent Generation continue to be the least supportive of legalization (39%), but they have become more supportive in the past year" (Hartig & Geiger, 2018).

- "The District of Columbia [DC] and 11 states— Alaska, California, Colorado, Illinois, Maine, Massachusetts, Michigan, Nevada, Oregon, Vermont, and Washington—have adopted the most expansive laws legalizing marijuana for recreational use" (Governing, 2019).

- Political party members also vary in their view of marijuana legalization. Republicans have split attitudes regarding this drug in that "45% . . . [are] . . . in favor of legalizing marijuana and 51% . . . [are] . . . opposed. The percentage "of Republicans saying marijuana should be legal has increased from 39% in 2015. Independents who lean toward the Republican Party are far more likely than Republicans to favor marijuana legalization (59% vs. 45%)" (Hartig & Geiger, 2018).

- "By wide margins, the public views marijuana as less harmful than alcohol, both to personal health and to society more generally" (Pew Research Center, 2014).

- Even though support for the legalization of marijuana continues to grow, "[m]ore than half (54%) say that legalizing marijuana would lead to more underage people trying it" (Pew Research Center, 2014).

- "On a personal level, most Americans say that, if marijuana were legal, they would be bothered by people using the drug in public (63%), though fewer (41%) would be bothered if a store or business selling marijuana opened in their neighborhood. Just 15% would be bothered if people used marijuana in their own homes" (Pew Research Center, 2014).

*(continues)*

## HERE AND NOW

### Legalizing Recreational and Medicinal Marijuana Use (*continued*)

- "[Y]oung people are less likely than older Americans to say that drug abuse is a crisis nationally" (Pew Research Center, 2014).

- Finally, current findings also indicates that 63% of Americans say that state governments moving away from mandatory prison terms for nonviolent

drug crimes is a good thing, while just 32% say these policy changes are a bad thing. This is a substantial shift from 2001 when the public was evenly divided (47% good thing vs. 45% bad thing) (Pew Research Center, 2014).

Data from Pew Research Center. Governing. (2019). State marijuana laws in 2019 map. Washington, DC: eRepublic. Retrieved from https://www.governing.com /gov-data/safety-justice/state-marijuana-laws-map-medical-recreational.html; Hartig, H., & Geiger, A. W. (2018, October 8). About six-in-ten Americans support marijuana legalization. Washington, DC: Pew Research Center; Pew Research Center. (2014, April 2). Section 1: Perceptions of drug abuse, views of drug policies. Washington, DC: Author. Retrieved from https://www.people-press.org/2014/04/02/section-1-perceptions-of-drug-abuse-views-of-drug-policies/

students in suits and ties who became hallucinatory, homicidal, violent, and suicidal; such symptoms were highly exaggerated. As a complete contradiction, in the same decade, the Rastafarian religion spread among Jamaican agricultural workers, who named marijuana a holy plant:

[In] *Ganja in Jamaica* (Rubin & Comitas, 1975) [the book] focused its findings to refute the claim that marijuana users damaged their productive capability. The study found that most rural Jamaicans who smoked ganja (marijuana) were extraordinarily diligent peasants who invested impressive amounts of time and energy in multiple income-bearing schemes every day of the year. Starting before sunrise, they tended livestock and poultry; farmed gardens; hired out their labor for wages; exchanged goods and services in an indigenous marketing system; maintained churches, self-help associations, political parties, guilds, schools, and households; and sometimes, at night, clandestinely cleared acres of forest to cultivate marijuana. They listened to the radio,

watched television, and read newspapers to perform better as citizens in a modern democracy. These active, clear-sighted economic strategists and community builders depended on a heavy daily intake of ganja for nourishment as "brain food," and relied on it specifically to improve production. Adult Jamaican marijuana smokers consumed some six or more large "spliffs" (hand-rolled cigars) of ganja a day, or a few ounces. They also consumed it in teas, tisanes, and tonics. As employers, they preferred to pay their employees ganja rather than money and encouraged its use in the workplace. (Rubin & Comitas, 1975, cited in Hamid, 1998, p. 61)

Marijuana consists of the dried and crushed leaves, flowers, stems, and seeds of the *Cannabis* plant. The three main strains are **Cannabis sativa**, **Cannabis indica**, and **Cannabis ruderalis**. They differ "in their chemical composition, physiological aesthetic, and medical application" (ProCon.org, 2012a). *C. sativa* originates from Colombia, Mexico, Jamaica, South Africa, Thailand, and Southeast Asia and generally causes

Close-ups of growing marijuana plants of the *Cannabis indica* strain. This type of marijuana often is used for legal and illegal human consumption as a mind-altering drug.

uplifting and energetic feelings, stimulates the appetite, and provides pain relief from certain ailments (Kaplan, 2017; Bridgeman & Abazia, 2017). Some users believe that it enhances creativity:

> *Sativa* dominant marijuana strains tend to have a more grassy type odor to the buds providing an uplifting, energetic and "cerebral" high that is best suited for daytime smoking. A *sativa* high is one filled with creativity and energy as being high on *sativa* can spark new ideas and creations. Many artists take advantage of the creative powers of *Cannabis sativa* to create paintings. (Smoker, 2014)

This strain is grown in countries that have hotter climates. It has a brighter green color than the *C. indica* strain and has narrower leaves and reaches an average height of more than six feet.

*C. indica* originates from hash-producing countries (e.g., Afghanistan, Pakistan, India, Turkey, Morocco, and Tibet) (ProCon.org, 2012a), and its effects include relaxation of the body, stress relief, and calmness and serenity (Budfacts.com, 2009). Some believe that *C. indica* is effective as a pain reliever and as a treatment for insomnia (Smoker, 2014). Medical marijuana patients often smoke *C. indica* buds in the late evening or right before bed (Smoker, 2014). Unlike *C. sativa*, *C. indica* grows well in warm, not hot, climates, and the plants are shorter (less than six feet tall) and darker green in color with wider leaves (Weedist, 2012). The tetrahydrocannabinol (THC) content in the two strains differs, with the *C. indica* strain generally having a lower THC content (Weedist, 2012).

Though *C. ruderalis* as a distinct species of marijuana has been somewhat controversial in that some botanists believe that it descends from *C. indica* species that adapted "to the harsh climates and the shorter growing seasons of the northern regions where it originates" (Hyde, 2015). "According to Jorge Cervantes, grow guru and author of *The Cannabis Encyclopedia*, 'Botanists disagree as to whether *C. ruderalis* qualifies as a separate species or subspecies'" (Hyde, 2015).

*Cannabis ruderalis* is native to areas in Asia, Central/Eastern Europe, and specifically Russia, where botanists used the term "ruderalis" to classify the breeds of hemp plant that had escaped from human and cultivation, adapting to the extreme environments found in these climates. Originally, *cannabis ruderalis* was considered a wild breed of cannabis. However, in recent years it has been brought indoors to influence new hybrid varieties. (Hyde, 2015)

Finally, of the three species, C. *ruderalis* is generally not grown for recreational use because it has the lowest amount of THC concentrations—between 7% and 8% cannabadiol (CBD). The most important strengths breeders find with C. *ruderalis* include the following:

- It is tolerant of colder climates and its autoflowering traits are within the shortest growing periods of the three main species.
- *C. ruderalis* can be crossbred with either *indica* or *sativa* strains to improve crop yields.

## KEY TERMS

**Cannabis sativa**
biological name of one of three major species of marijuana; originates from Colombia, Mexico, Thailand, and Southeast Asia; generally causes uplifting and largely psychological or mental energetic feelings, as well as providing pain relief for certain ailments

**Cannabis indica**
biological name of one of three major species of marijuana that originates from hash-producing countries (e.g., Afghanistan, Morocco, and Tibet); its effects include relaxation of the body, stress relief, and calmness and serenity; is known to cause a strong body high

**Cannabis ruderalis**
biological name of one of three major species of marijuana that is native to Asia and Central and Eastern Europe. This species has adapted to shorter growing seasons and the environments found in these three climates

Photo illustration of the three major species of marijuana (left to right, cannabis sativa, Indica, and ruderalis)

Sativa          Indica          Ruderalis

The 3 marijuana strains

- "The *ruderalis* subspecies can contain higher levels of CBD and be useful for medicinal markets, as long as sophisticated extraction equipment is used."
- "[*R*]*uderalis* strains . . . [are] . . . more suitable for use in clothing, or textiles" (Cannabismarketcap, 2019).

Finally, cannabis strains are available across the whole spectrum—from pure sativas to pure indicas, and in every combination in between—from 30% sativa–70% indica to 80% sativa–20% indica and many other combinations (BudFacts.com, 2009).

These three main *cannabis* species have been cultivated for thousands of years. Smoking the dried and crushed leaves, stems, and seeds produces sedative and mind-altering effects that vary according to the potency of the variety of cannabis used.

Usage in the United States began in the 1920s, rose during the 1960s and 1970s, and fell in every year from 1978 until 1991. From 1991 on, however, usage began to climb. In this chapter, we review the history, past and current usage trends, attitudes, and controversies surrounding marijuana (including the amotivational syndrome and the current debate regarding the legalization of marijuana for medical purposes) and its physiological and behavioral effects on the user.

## ▮ Marijuana: Polemic Growth and Expansion

As the rich history in this section will reveal, the trends and economic impact of marijuana are noteworthy. Historically, many societies discovered marijuana as a valued crop when they realized that the plant's woody stems, known as *hemp*, yielded a fiber that could be used to make cloth or rope. The extensive use and economic impact of marijuana continues to the present day as exemplified by many states now allowing marijuana as a cash crop. In fact, according to the former head of the legalization group National Organization for the Reform of Marijuana Laws (NORML), the annual marijuana crop "is now the nation's most valuable, worth more than cultivation of corn and wheat combined" (Join Together Staff, 2006). Further, *Reuters* reported "that public-policy analyst Jon Gettman estimated the value of the U.S. marijuana crop at $35 billion annually, with California, Tennessee, Kentucky, Hawaii, and Washington each producing more than $1 billion worth of the illegal drug each year." The market for legal cannabis is growing rapidly, increasing by 74% in 2014 (Ferner, 2015). *Markets Insider* reports,

> The marijuana industry is booming in the United States, stating that there was ". . . $52 billion in sales . . . [and] . . . the industry posted the 76% increase in cannabis jobs this year." Recreational marijuana use is legal in 10 U.S. states, while medicinal marijuana is legal in 30. (Evans, 2019)

In looking at just one state, estimates put the annual California marijuana crop at $13.8 billion per year, exceeding the combined value of corn ($23.3 billion) and wheat ($7.5 billion) (Drug Science, 2019; Venkataraman, 2006). California produces nearly 33% of the marijuana in the United States that is worth an estimated $5.1 billion in 2019, making it the state's largest cash crop ("California Cannabis Market," 2018).

## ▮ Historical Roots of Marijuana

The name *cannabis* comes from the Greek word for hemp. Initially, the Spaniards brought cannabis to the Western Hemisphere as a source of fiber and seeds. For thousands of years, the seeds have been pressed to extract a reddish oil used for medicinal and euphorigenic purposes (Abood & Martin, 1992; Iversen, 1993). The plants (both male and female) also produce a resin with active ingredients that affect the central nervous system (CNS). Marijuana contains hundreds of chemical compounds, but only a few found in the resin are responsible for producing the euphoric high.

Even the original uses of marijuana remain controversial. Botanists have never been able to trace cannabis to its origins, although some think it originated in Asia. Ancient Chinese documents contain the earliest recorded name of hemp—*ma*, meaning "fiber-producing plant," as well as "valuable" or "endearing." The term *ma* was still used as late as 1930. In the late 1970s, during an archeological dig in Gansu, the seat of Chinese civilization, workers uncovered cannabis seeds stored in an earthen jar.

Ayurvedic documents from 600 BC describe an intoxicating resin from the plant. Fifth-century BC Greek historian Herodotus recorded that the Scythians burned the tops of the plant, producing a narcotic smoke. An AD first-century Greek physician wrote that hemp was made into intoxicating cakes, perhaps the forerunners of the marijuana brownies of 1960s fame (Pollan, 1998).

Other sources report that the first known record of marijuana use is in the *Book of Drugs*, written about 2737 BC by Chinese emperor Shen Nung; he prescribed marijuana for treating gout, malaria, gas pains, and absentmindedness. The Chinese apparently had much respect for the plant. They obtained fiber for clothes and medicine from it for thousands of years.

Around 500 BC, another Chinese book of treatments referred to the medical use of marijuana. Nonetheless, the plant got a bad name from the moralists of the day, who claimed that youngsters became wild and disrespectful from the recreational use of ma. They called it the "liberator of sin" because, under its influence, the youngsters refused to listen to their elders and did other scandalous things. Although the Chinese recognized ma's medical usefulness, they eventually banned it because of its unpredictable intoxicating effects. Later, because of rampant use, it was legalized again.

India also has a long and varied history of marijuana use. It was an essential part of Indian religious ceremonies for thousands of years. The well-known *Rigveda* (a collection of Sanskrit hymns) and other chants describe the use of *soma*, which some believe was marijuana. Early writings describe a ritual in which resin was collected from the plants. After fasting and purification, certain men ran naked through the cannabis fields. The clinging resin was scraped off their bodies, and cakes were made from it and used in feasts. For centuries, missionaries in

India tried to ban the use of marijuana, but they were never successful because its use was heavily ingrained in the culture. From India, the use of marijuana spread throughout Asia, Africa, Europe, and the Americas, with English settlers bringing it to the American colonies.

Assyrian records dating back to 650 BC refer to a drug called *azulla* that was used for making rope and cloth and was consumed to experience euphoria. The ancient Greeks also knew about marijuana. Galen described the general use of hemp in cakes, which, when eaten in excess, produced narcotic effects. Herodotus described the Scythian custom of burning marijuana seeds and leaves to produce a narcotic smoke in steam baths. It was believed that breathing the smoke from the burning plants would cause frenzied activity. Groups of people stood in the smoke, laughed, and danced as it took effect.

One legend about cannabis is based on the travels of Marco Polo in the 12th century. Marco Polo told of the legendary Hasan Ibn-Sabbah, who terrorized a part of Arabia in the early 1100s. His men were some of the earliest political murderers, and he ordered them to kill under the influence of hashish, a strong, unadulterated cannabis derivative. The cult was called the *hashishiyya*, from which came the word *hashish*. (The word *assassin* may be derived from the name of Sheik Hasan, who was a political leader in the 10th century.) It is unlikely, however, that using hashish can turn people into killers. Experience suggests that people tend to become sleepy and indolent rather than violent after eating or smoking hashish or another of the strong cannabis preparations available in Arabia (Abel, 1989).

Despite Napoleon's strict orders to the contrary, his troops brought hashish to France after their campaign in Egypt at the beginning of the 19th century. By the 1840s, the use of hashish, as well as opium, was widespread in France, and efforts to curb its spread were unsuccessful.

In North America, hemp was planted near Jamestown in 1611 for use in making rope. By 1630, half of the winter clothing at the settlement was made from hemp fibers. There is no evidence that hemp was used medicinally at this time. Hemp was also valuable as a source of fiber for clothing and rope for the Pilgrims at Plymouth. To meet the demand for fiber, a law was passed in Massachusetts in 1639 requiring every household to plant hemp seed. However, it took much manual labor to work the hemp fiber into usable form, resulting in a chronic shortage of fiber for fishnets and the like (Abel, 1989).

George Washington cultivated a field of hemp at Mount Vernon, and there is some indication that it was used for medicine as well as for making rope. In his writings, Washington once mentioned that he forgot to separate the male and female plants, a process usually done because the female plant produces more resin if it remains unpollinated.

In the early 1800s, U.S. physicians used marijuana extracts to produce a tonic intended for both medicinal and recreational purposes. This practice changed in 1937 with passage of the Marijuana Tax Act. The Marijuana Tax Act was modeled after the Harrison Act of 1914 and considered marijuana a narcotic and subject to the same legal controls as cocaine and the opiates. Like these opiates, marijuana distributors had to register and pay a tax to legally import, buy, or sell this drug (Musto, 1999). As a result, the Marijuana Tax Act prohibited the use of this drug as an intoxicant and regulated its use as a medicine.

Most of the abuse of marijuana in the United States during the early part of the 20th century took place near the Mexican border and in the ghetto areas of major cities. Cannabis was mistakenly considered a narcotic, like opium, and legal authorities treated it as such (Abood & Martin, 1992). In 1931, Harry Anslinger, who was the first appointed head of the Bureau of Narcotics and later would become responsible for the enforcement of marijuana laws, believed that the problem was slight (Musto, 1999; Venturelli, 2016). By 1936, however, he claimed that the increase in the use of marijuana was of great national concern (Anslinger & Cooper, 1937) (see **Figure 13.1**). Anslinger set up an informational program that ultimately led to the federal law that banned marijuana. The following sensationalized statement was part of Anslinger's campaign to outlaw the drug:

> What about the alleged connection between drugs and sexual pleasure? . . . What is the real relationship between drugs and sex? There isn't any question about marijuana being a sexual stimulant. It has been used throughout the ages for that: in Egypt, for instance. From what we have seen, it is an aphrodisiac, and I believe that the use in colleges today has sexual connotations. (Anslinger & Cooper, 1937, p. 19)

In addition, during this time, some otherwise usually accurate magazines reported that marijuana was partly responsible for crimes of violence. In 1936, *Scientific American* reported that "marijuana produces a wide variety of symptoms in the user, including hilarity, swooning, and

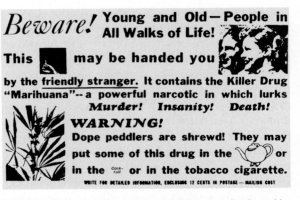

**FIGURE 13.1** This antimarijuana poster was distributed by the Federal Bureau of Narcotics in the late 1930s.

Courtesy of Wisconsin Historical Society, WHS-56411.

sexual excitement. Combined with intoxicants, it often makes the smoker vicious, with a desire to fight and kill" ("Marijuana menaces youth," 1936; Venturelli, 2016). A famous poster of the day titled "The Assassination of Youth" was effective in molding attitudes against drug use.

Largely because of the media's influence on public opinion, Congress passed the Marijuana Tax Act in 1937. However, because of the discussions and debates before the passage of the 1970 Comprehensive Drug Abuse Prevention and Control Act, which replaced or updated all other laws concerning narcotics and dangerous drugs, the Marijuana Tax Act of 1937 was declared unconstitutional in 1969 because it classified marijuana as a narcotic. Marijuana has not been classified as a narcotic since 1971 (Venturelli, 2016).

In the early 1900s, marijuana was brought across the U.S. border by Mexican laborers who entered the United States seeking jobs. From the border areas of the United States, recreational use of marijuana spread mainly through the American Southwest. Such use reached major cities in Texas and surrounding states as well as many African American communities in these cities. Heavy users of marijuana included a subpopulation of jazz musicians as well as other "bohemian types" who led less-structured existences in unconventional jobs and occupations (e.g., artists, entertainers, poets, criminals). Thus, before the 1960s, marijuana use was largely confined to small segments of African American urban youth, jazz musicians, and artists and writers who belonged to the 1950s Beat Generation. Use rose tremendously in the 1960s, when it was closely associated with the hippie counterculture, which categorized marijuana as a psychedelic (consciousness-expanding) sacrament. It spread into other youth categories during the 1970s, until approximately 1978. In each year from 1978 until 1991, marijuana use fell. After 1991, researchers and prevention specialists were astounded to see a rise in usage among youth (Venturelli, 2016).

Marijuana still grows wild in many U.S. states today. Curiously, one reason for the survival of this supply is that, during World War II, the fiber used to make rope (sisal) was hard to import, so the government paid subsidies to farmers who grew hemp. Much of today's crop comes from these same plants. Another reason for the spread of the plants is that, until recently, the seeds were used in birdseed. Leftover seed was discarded in the garbage and thus spread to landfill dumps, where it sprouted. Birdseed containing marijuana seeds is still available, but the seeds are sterilized so that they cannot germinate.

The Indian Hemp Drug Commission Report in the 1890s and the 1930 Panama Canal Zone Report on marijuana stressed that available evidence did not prove marijuana as dangerous as it was popularly thought; these reports were given little publicity, however, and for the most part were disregarded. In 1944, a report was issued by the LaGuardia Committee on Marijuana, which consisted of 31 qualified physicians, psychiatrists, psychologists, pharmacologists, chemists, and sociologists appointed by the New York Academy of Medicine. They stated in one key summary that marijuana was not the killer many thought it to be:

> It was found that marijuana in an effective dose impairs intellectual functioning in general. . . . Marijuana does not change the basic personality structure of the individual. It lessens inhibition and this brings out what is latent in his thoughts and emotions but it does not evoke responses that would otherwise be totally alien to him. . . . Those who have been smoking marijuana for years showed no mental or physical deterioration that may be attributed to the drug. (Solomon 1966, p. 37)

Much of the early research conducted did not consider the potency of marijuana. As a result, findings from various studies are often conflicting and difficult to compare. Because the quality of marijuana varies so greatly, it is impossible to know the amount of drug taken without analyzing the original material and the leftover stub or "roach." Conditions such as type of seed, soil moisture and fertility, amount of sunlight, and temperature all affect the amounts of active ingredients found in the resulting marijuana plant.

## Current Use of Marijuana

As reported previously, current users of marijuana are estimated to be 43.5 million Americans aged 12 or older in 2018. This number of past-year marijuana users corresponds to 15.9% of the population (Substance Abuse and Mental Health Services Administration [SAMHSA], 2019). **Table 13.1** from the National Survey on Drug Use and Health (NSDUH) reported that among persons aged 12 or older, the overall rate of past-year marijuana use was 13.5% in 2015, 13.9% in 2016, 15.0% in 2017, and 15.9% in 2018 (SAMHSA, 2019). Throughout these four years, the number of people using marijuana continually increased in past-year usage among persons aged 12 or older.

Other age group differences in marijuana use are the following (SAMHSA, 2019):

- Aged 12 to 17: In 2018, about one in eight adolescents aged 12 to 17 (12.5%) were

**TABLE 13.1** Percentage of Past Year Marijuana Users among People Aged 12 or Older: 2002–2018

| Age | 02 | 03 | 04 | 05 | 06 | 07 | 08 | 09 | 10 | 11 | 12 | 13 | 14 | 15 | 16 | 17 | 18 |
|---|---|---|---|---|---|---|---|---|---|---|---|---|---|---|---|---|---|
| ≥12 | 11.0[+] | 10.6[+] | 10.6[+] | 10.4[+] | 10.3[+] | 10.1[+] | 10.4[+] | 11.4[+] | 11.6[+] | 11.5[+] | 12.1[+] | 12.6[+] | 13.2[+] | 13.5[+] | 13.9[+] | 15.0[+] | 15.9 |
| 12–17 | 15.8[+] | 15.0[+] | 14.5[+] | 13.3 | 13.2 | 12.5 | 13.1 | 13.7[+] | 14.0[+] | 14.2[+] | 13.5[+] | 13.4[+] | 13.1 | 12.6 | 12.0 | 12.4 | 12.5 |
| 18–25 | 29.8[+] | 28.5[+] | 27.8[+] | 28.0[+] | 28.1[+] | 27.5[+] | 27.8[+] | 30.8[+] | 30.0[+] | 30.8[+] | 31.5[+] | 31.6[+] | 31.9[+] | 32.2[+] | 33.0[+] | 34.9 | 34.8 |
| ≥26 | 7.0[+] | 6.9[+] | 7.0[+] | 6.9[+] | 6.9[+] | 6.8[+] | 7.0[+] | 7.7[+] | 8.0[+] | 7.9[+] | 8.6[+] | 9.2[+] | 10.1[+] | 10.4[+] | 11.0[+] | 12.2[+] | 13.3 |

+Difference between this estimate and the 2018 estimate is statistically significant at the .05 level.

Data from Substance Abuse and Mental Health Services (SAMHSA). (2019). Key substance use and mental health indicators in the United States: Results from the *2018 National Survey on Drug Use and Health*. Rockville, MD: Author. Retrieved from https://www.samhsa.gov/data/sites/default/files/cbhsq-reports/NSDUHNationalFindingsReport2018/NSDUHNationalFindingsReport2018.pdf

past-year users of marijuana. This represents approximately 3.1 million adolescents who used marijuana in the preceding year.

- Aged 18 to 25: In 2018, more than a third of young adults 18 to 25 (34.8%) were past-year users of marijuana, or about 11.8 million young adults.
- Aged 26 or older: In 2018, an estimated 13.3% of adults 26 or older were past-year users of marijuana, which represents about 28.5 million adults in this age group.

**Figure 13.2A** shows the past-year marijuana initiates among persons ages 12 or older and mean age at first use of marijuana among past-year initiates. In 2018, there were 3.1 million past first-time uses of marijuana. From 2012 through 2018 the number of past-year initiates generally increased each year beginning in 2012. Thus, there were more past-year initiates each year.

**Figure 13.2B** shows the mean age at first use of marijuana among past-year initiates ages 12 to 49 from 2011 to 2017. The mean age of first use in 2017 was 19.7 years of age. Beginning in 2011 the mean age was 17.5 and each year beyond, the age of first use steadily increased through 2017. Additional notable findings regarding the initiation of marijuana use are the following (SAMHSA, 2019):

- In 2018, about 3.1 million people aged 12 or older used marijuana for the first time in the past 12 months. This number averages to about 8,400 new marijuana users each day.
- In 2018, an estimated 1.3 million adolescents aged 12 to 17 used marijuana for the first

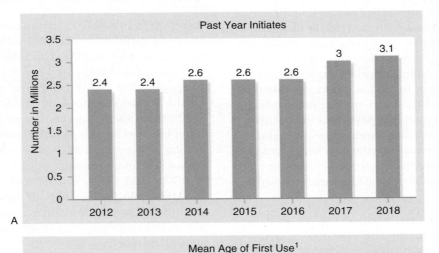

A

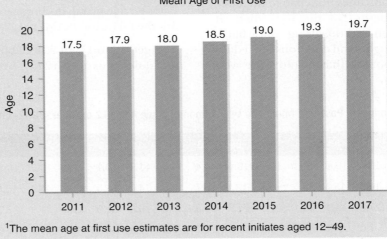

B

[1]The mean age at first use estimates are for recent initiates aged 12–49.

**FIGURE 13.2   (A)** Past-year marijuana initiates among persons age 12 or older and mean age at first use of marijuana among past-year initiates and **(B)** ages 12–49: 2011–2017.

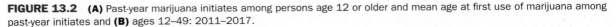

Data from Substance Abuse and Mental Health Services Administration (SAMHSA). (2018) *2017 National Survey on Drug Use and Health: Detailed Tables*. Rockville, MD: Author; Substance Abuse and Mental Health Services (SAMHSA). (2019). Key substance use and mental health indicators in the United States: Results from the *2018 National Survey on Drug Use and Health*. Rockville, MD: Author. Retrieved from https://www.samhsa.gov/data/sites/default/files/cbhsq-reports /NSDUHNationalFindingsReport2018/NSDUHNationalFindingsReport2018.pdf

time in the past year, which translates to approximately 3,700 adolescents each day who initiated marijuana use.

- In 2018, 1.2 million young adults aged 18 to 25 initiated marijuana use in the past year, or an average of about 3,300 recent initiates per day in this age group.
- An estimated 525,000 adults aged 26 or older in 2018 initiated marijuana use in the past year, which rounds to the estimate of 0.5 million initiates in this age group. This number averages to about 1,400 recent initiates per day in this age group.
- Finally, consistent with the pattern for cigarette and alcohol use, the majority of people in 2018 who initiated marijuana use in the past year were aged 12 to 25.

As **Table 13.2** shows, the frequency of marijuana use is strongly correlated with age. The age group reporting the highest lifetime (51.5%), past-year (34.8%), and past-month (22.1%) use is by those 18 to 25 years old. For the 26-and-older age group, marijuana use drops sharply for the past-year (8.8%) and past-month (5.4%) categories.

**TABLE 13.2** Marijuana Use Reported by Americans During Their Lifetime, the Past Year, and the Past Month, According to Age: 2018

| Age (Years) | Lifetime (%) | Past Year (%) | Past Month (%) |
|---|---|---|---|
| 12–17 | 15.4 | 12.5 | 6.7 |
| 18–25 | 51.5 | 34.8 | 22.1 |
| 26 or older | 47.8 | 13.3 | 8.6 |

Data from Substance Abuse and Mental Health Services (SAMHSA). (2019). Key substance use and mental health indicators in the United States: Results from the *2018 National Survey on Drug Use and Health*. Rockville, MD: Author. Retrieved from https://www.samhsa.gov/data/sites/default/files/cbhsq-reports/NSDUHNationalFindings Report2018/NSDUHNationalFindingsReport2018.pdf

## ■ Recent Trends in Use of Marijuana: 8th, 10th, and 12th Graders

In regard to marijuana, in 2018, the percentage of 8th-, 10th-, and 12th-grade students (see **Figure 13.3A**) shows the percentage who used in the last 12 months from 1995 through 2018. **Figure 13.3B** shows the percentage of grade

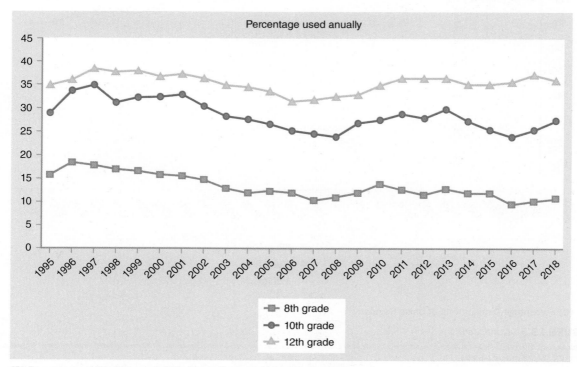

**(A)** Percentage of 8th-10th, and 12th Grage Students Using Marijuana Annually

**FIGURE 13.3** Marijuana trends: Percentages of marijuana use, risk, disapproval for 8th-, 10th-, and 12th-grade students. (*continues*)

Data from Johnston, L. D., Miech, R. A., O'Malley, P. M., Bachman, J. G., Schulenberg, J. E., & Patrick, M. E. (2019). *Monitoring the Future: National survey results on drug use 1975–2018: Overview, key findings on adolescent drug use*. Ann Arbor, MI: University of Michigan, Institute for Social Research.

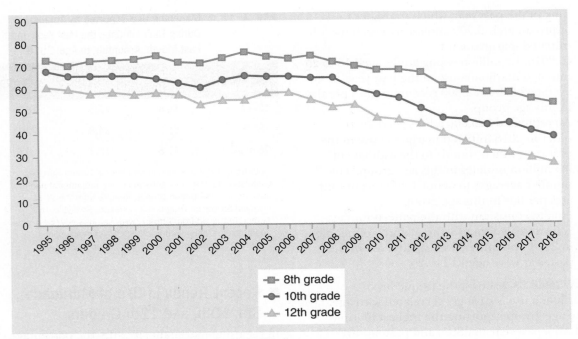

**(B)** Percentage Seeing "Great Risk" of Regular Use of Marijuana

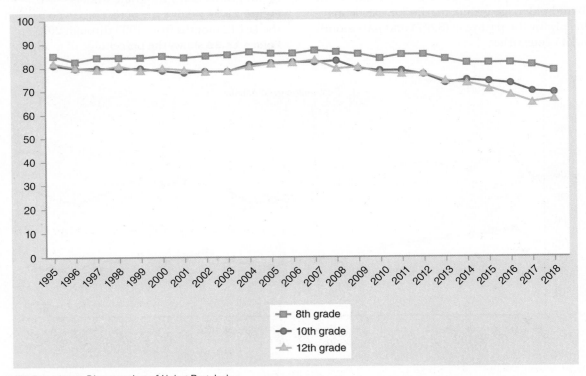

**(C)** Percentage Disapproving of Using Regularly

**FIGURE 13.3**   (*continued*).

Data from Johnston, L. D., Miech, R. A., O'Malley, P. M., Bachman, J. G., Schulenberg, J. E., & Patrick, M. E. (2019). *Monitoring the Future: National survey results on drug use 1975 -2018: Overview, key findings on adolescent drug use.* Ann Arbor, MI: University of Michigan, Institute for Social Research.

school students seeing great risk in using marijuana regularly from 1995 through 2018. **Figure 13.3C** shows the percentage disapproving of the use of marijuana on a regular basis from 1995 through 2018. **Figure 13.3D** shows the trends in perceived availability, perceived risk, regular use of marijuana, and prevalence of use in past 30 day in grade 12.

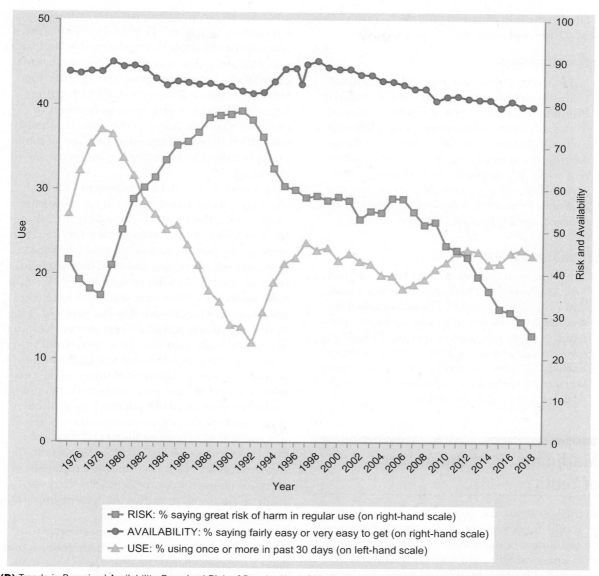

**(D)** Trends in Perceived Availability, Preceived Risk of Regular Use of Marijuana and Prevalence of Use in Past 30 Days in Grade 12

**FIGURE 13.3** *(continued)*.

Data from Miech, R. A., Johnston, L. D., O'Malley, P. M., Bachman, J. G., Schulenberg, J. E., & Patrick, M. E. (2019). *Monitoring the Future National Survey Results on Drug Use, 1975–2018: Volume I, Secondary school students.* Ann Arbor, MI: University of Michigan, Institute for Social Research. Retrieved from http://monitoringthefuture.org/pubs/monographs/mtf-vol1_2018.pdf

In looking at the percentage who used in the last 12 months, major findings are the following.[1]

- *Marijuana use*—In 2018 for 8th-, 10th-, and 12th-grade students using marijuana annually: 12th graders are the highest users, averaging approximately 35% usage. Tenth graders rank second, with the highest users averaging approximately 28%. Eighth graders are the lowest users of annual marijuana use and average approximately 12%.

- *"Great risk" in using marijuana regularly*—In 2018, approximate positive responses to this statement were 53% for 8th graders, 39% for 10th graders, and 23% for 12th graders.
- *Percentage disapproving of using marijuana regularly*—79% for 8th graders, 70% for 10th graders, and 68% for 12th graders.
- *Trends in perceived availability, perceived risk of regular use of marijuana and prevalence of use in past 20 days for 12th graders*—In 2018, 80% said marijuana was easy to get, 44% said there was great risk of harm in regular use, and approximately 26% reported using once or more in the past 30 days.

---

[1] Not all bulleted findings are displayed in Figure 13.3a, b, c, & d.

Finally, the following two interviews convey what figures and percentages cannot capture

### FIRST INTERVIEW

What, weed? It's so easy to get. In fact, many times [referring to junior high school] I didn't even have to buy, it would be offered in the morning, at lunchtime, and whenever we get together, even after school it is there. Among the users (and we know each other real well), it's as common as sharing candy. *(From Venturelli's research files, male first-year high school student in a medium-sized town in the Midwest, age 15, June 19, 2000)*

### SECOND INTERVIEW

No, I don't smoke it often, but I know over half my friends smoke it two or three times a week and on weekend nights. It's not unusual for several of my friends to smoke up before partying. I usually take a hit or two, but I wouldn't even do that if it weren't for my friends always having it. *(From Venturelli's research files, male senior in high school in a medium-sized town in the Midwest, age 17, July 16, 2010)*

## Marijuana: Is It the Assassin of Youth?

In the late 1930s, the poster "Marijuana: Assassin of Youth" made a clever play on words, bringing up reminders of the Middle Eastern *hashashin* cult, whose terrible exploits were attributed to their use of hashish (marijuana resin). At the time, marijuana was incorrectly classified as a narcotic like opium and morphine. Amotivational syndrome, lassitude, poor driving skills the day after smoking, educational failure, and dependence may not quite add up to "assassination," as wildly exaggerated in *Reefer Madness*. The poster was right, however, in associating use of this drug with young people, among whom marijuana is popular in both local peer groups and broad youth cultures.

### ▌ Major Factors Affecting Marijuana Use

The mass media, parental role models, perceived risk, availability, and peers have the most direct influence on the development of youth's attitudes regarding drug use. An estimated 8.3 million children—11.9%—live with at least one parent (biological, step, adoptive, or foster) who had abused or was dependent on alcohol or an illicit drug in the past year (Center for Substance Abuse Research [CESAR], 2010a). These findings become worrisome when we consider that marijuana is the most frequently used illicit drug and that parental use of marijuana is a significant influence on teens' use of this drug.

In a study by Kandel and colleagues (2001), when parents had used marijuana at some time in their lives, their teen children were 40% more likely to have used the drug in their lifetime than teens whose parents had never used marijuana. Moreover, when parents had used marijuana in the past year, their children were twice as likely to have used in the same time period, as were teens whose parents had not used in the past year. This same study also found that when parents had used marijuana in the past year, their teen children were more likely to have used marijuana in the past year compared with the children of parents who had used at some time in their life but not in the last year. Similarly, parental use of other drugs, such as alcohol, nicotine, and cocaine, was also found to have an impact on their teen children's use of marijuana. More important, the perceived risk is the most important influence on teen marijuana use. In the Kandel et al. (2001) study, it was found to be five times more important than parental use.

As shown in Figure 13.3A, when comparisons are made among 8th, 10th, and 12th graders, marijuana use rises sharply by 12th grade. One main reason for this is because children in lower grades are less likely to have friends and access to friends who use marijuana (as well as access to other major drugs of abuse). Marijuana has been almost universally available to U.S. high school seniors (from 83% to 90%) since at least 1990 (Johnston, O'Malley, Bachman, & Schulenberg, 2009), and nearly half of youth aged 12 to 17 reported easy access to marijuana (Johnston, O'Malley, Bachman, & Schulenberg, 2013). With easy access to marijuana, it is not surprising that "[n]early 80% of high school seniors don't consider occasional marijuana use harmful—the highest rate since 1983—and [one] in 15 smoke nearly every day" (Leger, 2012).

Beginning several years before age 13 (early adolescence), peers and peer groups begin to exert the most influence (Bauman & Ennett, 1996; Greenblatt, 1999; Heitzeg, 1996; Scholastic, 2016; Steinberg, 2011; Tudor, Petersen, & Elifson, 1987; Venturelli, 2000). In fact, even in acquiring the drug, one finding stated that "[m]arijuana distribution relies primarily on informal dealing through social networks" (CESAR, 2007). More than one-half (58%) of household residents who had used marijuana in the past year reported that they most recently obtained their marijuana for free, compared to 39% who reported purchasing it. Nearly all marijuana users (89%) reported getting their most recent acquisition from a friend or relative. Unlike users of more expensive drugs such as cocaine and heroin, the majority of people who used marijuana in the past year (58%) gave away or shared some of their most recent acquisition (CESAR, 2007).

Research shows that it is unlikely that an individual will use drugs when his or her peers do not use them. Marijuana use, in particular, is a group-motivated behavior that is strongly affected by peer pressure and influence. In effect, habitual drug users are likely to belong to drug-using groups. In contrast, people who do not use belong to groups in which drug use is perceived as an unacceptable and devious form of social recreation. Learning theory explains how peers can influence one another; drug-using peer members serve as role models, legitimizing use. Peers in such groups are saying, in essence, "It's perfectly normal to use drugs." This, in turn justifies usage.

In addition to these major factors (mass media, parental role models, perceived risk, availability, and peer influences), six other factors must be taken into account as influencing drug use:

1. *structural factors* such as age, gender, family background, and religious beliefs;
2. *social and interactional factors* such as the type of interpersonal relationships, friendship cliques, and drug use within the peer group setting;
3. *setting* such as the type of community and neighborhood (physical location where drugs are used);
4. *attitudinal factors* such as personal beliefs and attitudes regarding drug use, and *personality factors* such as self-esteem, level of security versus insecurity, and maturation level;
5. *participation in after-school activities* is associated with higher levels of academic achievement and self-esteem, as well as lower levels of substance use (SAMHSA, 2007b, 2017).

Regardless of family income, youths aged 12 to 17 who did not participate in any activities had higher rates of past-month cigarette and illicit drug use than those who participated in four, six, seven, or more activities (SAMHSA, 2007b, 2016, 2017).

6. Finally, even the *amount of religious involvement* affects illicit drug use (which includes marijuana use). With regard to religious involvement and substance use, adults who reported that religious beliefs are a critically important part of their lives were less likely to use illicit drugs in the past month than those who reported that religious beliefs are not an important part of their lives (6.1% vs. 14.3%) (SAMHSA, 2007a, 2016). Other researchers have also identified religiosity as an important protective factor against substance use (Brigham Young University, 2008; Center on Addiction and Substance Abuse, 2001; Kendler, Gardner, & Prescott, 1997; SAMHSA, 2016; Wallace, Myers, & Osai 2004).

Keep in mind these factors can easily overlap; they are not separate and distinct. Sociologists have long studied "youth cultures" (Coleman, 1961). In the 1970s, sociologists began to examine different subcultures of youth in terms of the behaviors that symbolically represent the group, in which participation in drug use is a ritual that marks entrance into the group and out of childhood—a rite of passage. Typically, U.S. high school culture includes a leading clique, often associated with team sports, whose members might be called *jocks*, and a marginal, deviant, or rebellious group (Eckert, 1989). In some cases, the latter group is associated with marijuana use. In the mid-1960s, hippies were perceived as a group whose members were part of a counterculture committed to unconventional values, pacifism, and communalism, in addition to psychedelic drugs. By 1970, this name denoted broader segments of youth who adhered merely to hippie styles of clothing and drug use (Buff, 1970). By the 1980s, marijuana use was identified with subgroups of youth often called *burnouts*. In many communities studied by sociologists, burnouts came from all social levels but were often overrepresented in upper-middle classes, and they were marginal or rebellious within the educational system, if not dropouts (Eckert, 1989; Gaines, 1992).

A common example of polydrug use (alcohol and marijuana).

Membership in such marijuana-using subcultures often bonds the youth to ongoing and persistent drug use.

## Is Marijuana a Gateway Drug?

Gateway drugs are drugs that serve as the gate or path that usually precedes the use of other illicit drugs such as tobacco, marijuana, heroin, and LSD. This concept is often referred to as the *gateway theory*, *gateway hypothesis*, or *gateway effect*. Gateway drugs, or drugs of entry, serve to initiate a novice user into the drug-using world. Although the linkage is not biochemical, common gateway drugs include tobacco, inhalants, alcohol, anabolic steroids, Ritalin, and prescription painkillers (i.e., prescription opioid medications) (Benson, 2010; National Institutes of Health [NIH], 2011).

The claim that marijuana use often leads to the use of other more serious drugs such as heroin remains controversial (Gardner, 1992; Hanson, 2019). A Rand press release reported that the gateway theory does not explain the progression to other more addictive drugs; instead, "[t]he people who are predisposed to use drugs and have the opportunity to use drugs *are more likely* than others to use both marijuana and harder drugs. . . . Marijuana typically comes first because it is more available" (Rand Drug Policy Research Center, 2002). Thus, instead of assuming that marijuana, alcohol, and other more commonly used drugs are simply gateway drugs responsible for leading to more serious drugs, it is more likely that factors such as (1) the age when teens have opportunities to use marijuana and other drugs, (2) associated opportunities,

and (3) the willingness, mindset, or predisposition to use drugs may be better predictors of the progression from less addictive to more addictive and powerful types of drugs.

For example, the gateway theory cannot explain the fact that although it is true that many heroin addicts began drug use with marijuana, it is also true that many, if not most, also used coffee and cigarettes. Millions of marijuana users never go beyond the gateway drugs used: "There are only a few thousand opiate addicts in Great Britain, yet there are millions who have tried cannabis" (Gossop, 1987, p. 9).

Nevertheless, the gateway theory may offer a plausible explanation as to why a small percentage of marijuana users progress to hard drugs such as cocaine or heroin. In many cases, it may be unlikely that the use of marijuana as well as other drugs considered to be gateway drugs would be the *principal cause* for progressing to harder and more addictive types of drugs.

Youth who turn to drugs are usually seriously alienated individuals. Thus, progression from marijuana to other drugs is more likely to depend on peer-group composition, family relationships, social class, and the age at which drug use begins (Indiana Prevention Resource Center, 1996).

Note, however, that many, if not most, young drug users do eventually leave drug-using groups and abandon their drug-using behavior, a process sometimes called *maturing out*. An example that often typifies maturing out is found in the following interviews.

### ▪ First Interview

Up until I started my full-time job after graduation from college I was smoking weed and at parties using other even worse types of drugs without any hesitation. Even during my senior year in high school I was smoking weed nearly every day and graduated with a B average. But then, once I joined this company I am still working at today, they were drug testing, so I quit everything. I just did not want to risk a good paying job that I liked for drugs. Plus the embarrassment of not passing a drug test, when my dad is a CEO in the company I am working at. Now, I am even a Boy Scout leader and known as the Scout who is totally against any unnecessary drug use. What a change from those younger days! *(From Venturelli's research files, male working for a major corporation in Chicago, age 29, May 12, 2010)*

## ■ Second Interview

I first started with marijuana when I was 13. Friends of mine were also smoking cigarettes whenever we got together to smoke weed. It was easy to try cigarettes after smoking weed so at around age 14 or 15 I added cigarettes to my weed smoking. From there and in enjoying the highs alcohol was my next drug of choice. Pills and snorting my best friend's Ritalin crushed into power was added to my favorite drugs. I guess you could say that one led to another, but I never went to snorting coke because it was so expensive and I figured I progressed enough in my drug usage and didn't need to add yet another drug to my drugs of choice. I was 24 when I decided to quit playing around with all these drugs and only drink alcohol occasionally now. *(From Venturelli's research files, male working at a health club in Valparaiso, Indiana, age 29, April 6, 2013)*

# Misperceptions of Marijuana Use

In a world in which marijuana can be considered either an assassin or a sacrament, and in which it is associated with membership in prized or despised peer groups, it is not surprising that estimates of its use vary widely and are often inaccurate. Parents, for example, tend to underestimate their children's use of drugs. Findings from one study indicated that "only 14% of the parents interviewed thought their children had experimented with marijuana while 38% of the teenagers said they had tried it" (Wren, 1996, p. 1). In the same survey, 52% of teenagers reported having been offered drugs, whereas 34% of the parents thought their children might have been offered drugs. Another more recent study indicated that "[o]nly 10% of parents think their own teens drank alcohol within the last year, and 5% believe their teens smoked marijuana in the last year, according to the latest poll by the University of Michigan's C.S. Mott Children's Hospital" (Melina, 2011). Reports from the 2010 *Monitoring the Future* survey reported that 29% of 10th graders had used marijuana within the past year (Johnston, O'Malley, Bachman, & Schulenberg, 2012).

Other recent research indicates that parents who more carefully and consistently monitor their children and maintain more open communication are more likely to underestimate their children's risky behavior. "[Further,] parents of adolescents who perceived themselves as better than average in school performance and who participated in religious services were more likely to underestimate adolescents' substance use" (Hongmei et al., 2006, p. 1).

Interestingly, another report by the former president of the National Center on Addiction and Substance Abuse at Columbia University stated the following with regard to baby-boomer parents (parents born between 1946 through 1964):

Almost half know someone who uses illegal drugs; a third have friends who use marijuana. Almost half expect their children to try illegal drugs, and 65 percent of those who smoked pot regularly when young believe their kids will try drugs. . . . [A]lmost half of the parents don't think they can have much influence on whether their kids will use drugs. (Califano, 1996, p. 19)

Even with regard to users' perceptions of other users, beliefs about marijuana remain distorted. College students tend to have exaggerated misperceptions of use, believing that their peers use marijuana much more than is true (Berkowitz, 1991; Johnston et al., 2009; Sorden, 2011). For example, at one campus in northern New Jersey, two-thirds of students reported never using marijuana, yet most students polled believed that the average student uses marijuana once per week. Other research also shows a widespread misperception in usage of marijuana. In 2005, in a randomly selected sample of 3639 college students, a large proportion (51%) of undergraduate students overestimated the use of marijuana among their peers on campus (McCabe, 2008).

These findings of misperception in the use of marijuana are important because actual marijuana usage remains high for the time being. Recent findings show that marijuana continues to be the most commonly used illicit drug with an estimated 43.5 million Americans aged 12 or older in 2018 used marijuana in the past year. This number of past year marijuana users corresponds to 15.9% of the population. The percentage of the population in 2018 who used marijuana was higher than the percentages from 2002 to 2017. This increase in marijuana use among people aged 12 or older reflects increases in marijuana use among both young adults aged 18 to 25 and adults 26 or older (SAMHSA, 2019).

## Characteristics of Cannabis

In 1753, Carolus Linnaeus, a Swedish botanist, classified marijuana as *Cannabis sativa* (see **Figure 13.4**). Some botanists believe that *C. sativa* is a single species and the other species are merely variants (Schultes, 1978). Other botanists think that there are three distinct species, namely, *C. sativa*, *C. indica*, and *C. ruderalis*.

*Cannabis sativa* grows well in many parts of the world. It is the tallest of the three *cannabis* species and can reach 20 to 25 feet high when grown outdoors. Because of its height, it has long been cultivated for its lengthy fibers, which can be used to make rope or cloth. It is not as bushy as *C. indica*, and thus plants can be cultivated more closely together (Rosenthal, 2010).

*C. indica* is the bushiest of the three *cannabis* species and in the middle with regard to height, rarely exceeding 10 feet. *C. indica* has a higher ratio of THC to CBD ratio than *C. sativa*. This means that it produces a much heavier "stone" and more of a body high compared to *C. sativa*. The resin of *C. indica* is thought to be the most potent, but potency is influenced by climate, soil, and breeding. *C. indica* produces a higher yield than *C. sativa* and reaches maturity more quickly (Rosenthal, 2010).

The Russian botanist D. E. Janichevsky discovered *C. ruderalis* in Eastern Europe. It is the shortest of the three species, reaching 24 inches at most, and is able to grow in cold climates. Unlike the other two varieties, it is able to switch from vegetative growth to flowering once it has grown five to seven sets of leaves. This is important because it means that flowering in this species is not affected by day length. Breeders have crossed *C. ruderalis* with the other two varieties to create a heavy budding plant that will grow in cooler conditions. The hybrid plants are shorter and mature more quickly that *C. sativa* and *C.*

### KEY TERM

**sinsemilla**
meaning "without seeds," this marijuana is made from the buds and flowering tops of female plants and is one of the most potent types

**FIGURE 13.4** Marijuana plants.
© skydie/Shutterstock.

*indica* but have a lower THC content (Rosenthal, 2010).

Cannabis is *dioecious*, meaning there are male and female plants. After the male plant releases its pollen, it usually dies. In any case, even before the male plant dies, cultivators of marijuana often eliminate or remove the male plants before the female plant has been pollinated.

Cannabis plants produce more than 421 different chemicals, many of which have not yet been identified. Tetrahydrocannabinol, or THC, is the primary mind-altering (psychoactive) agent in marijuana (Abood & Martin, 1996; National Institute on Drug Abuse [NIDA], 2009; Swan, 1996) and appears to be important for the reinforcing properties of this substance (Kelly, Foltin, Enurian, & Fischman, 1994). THC is most highly concentrated in the flowering tops and upper leaves of the female plant. When crushed, the flowering tops, or *buds*, produce a resin that contains the THC. THC concentrations are usually highest in the buds of the female cannabis plant, followed by the leaves. The seeds and stalks have much lower THC levels and are of limited commercial value (Cannabis Information and Support, 2013).

In cultivated marijuana crops, as previously mentioned, male plants are eradicated from the growing fields so that they cannot pollinate the female plants. The lack of pollination makes the potency of female plants increase dramatically.

There are approximately four derivatives (or "spin-offs") from marijuana plants. The first derivative, **sinsemilla** (meaning "without seeds" in Spanish), is one of the most potent types of marijuana in the United States, with an average THC content of 9.6% but reaching as high as 24%.

Sinsemilla is produced from the buds of the flowering tops of female plants (NIDA, 1998). Varieties of sinsemilla that have a high THC content include "hydro" (which means grown in water), "blueberry," and "kind bud." Through selective breeding, breeders have developed new strains of marijuana, such as 8 Miles High, Albert Walker, Black Pineapple Kush, Cantatonic Incognito, Diesel Mange Haze, Girl Scout Cookies, Elephant Stomper, Snowcap, Satori, Purple Urkle, Big Budda Cheese, Trainwreck, Trinity, and GDP Grand Daddy Purple. Many of these new varieties have much higher THC contents (Rosenthal, 2010).

One interviewee provided noteworthy insight regarding comparing these more potent varieties with more generic types of marijuana by stating the following:

> Smoking those *primo* buds [referring to the more potent types of marijuana] ... is like the difference between eating strip steak versus filet mignon. The THC content of these more specialized types of marijuana is more like a quantum leap in the quality of marijuana. These strains are very mellow in taste and they are potent as hell.... [The interviewee also humorously added] and the cost difference is every bit like paying for filet mignon, but this upgrade in quality is totally worth the extra cost. *(From Venturelli's research files, male, commodities stock broker, age 36, residing in Chicago, February 28, 2016)*

In a report by the University of Mississippi Potency Monitoring Project, dated December 2008 through March 2009, the average potency of all marijuana in the United States was 8.52% (5.62% domestic and 9.57% nondomestic). Nondomestic varieties include Jamaican, Colombian, Mexican, and Canadian, which averaged 9.57% THC. "Out of 788 domestic and nondomestic samples seized between 2008 and 2009 the average was 8.52% THC" (ElSohly, 2009, p. 6). "For comparison, the national average of marijuana's THC content in 1978 was 1.37%, in 1988 it was 3.59%, in 1998 4.43%, and in 2008 8.49%" (ProCon, 2012b).

Other more recent research presented at a meeting of the American Chemical Society in Denver reported that the potency (THC content) is continually increasing. The main finding of the new analysis was that potency has risen by a factor of three in the last few decades. "As far as potency goes, it's been surprising how strong a lot of the marijuana is," says researcher and study lead Andy LaFrate. "We've seen potency values close to 30 percent THC, which is huge." Potency used to be around 10% or less, but it's been bred upward over the years, presumably because the market has demanded it (Walton, 2015).

This dramatic increase in the potency of marijuana results from "[m]ore efficient agriculture—new methods of harvesting and processing marijuana plants—has made pot about 20 times more potent than the marijuana on the street in the 1960s and 1970s, drug treatment experts and law officials say" (Henneberger, 1994, p. F-18). Further, the quantities of other, more potent types of marijuana such as sinsemilla and hydro are increasingly readily available in illegal drug markets. In addition, recently developed **drug-trafficking organizations (DTOs)**—which are complex illegal organizations with highly defined command-and-control structures—produce, transport, and/or distribute large quantities of one or more illicit drugs.

Another finding is the following:

> Marijuana produced in Mexico remains the most widely available in the United States. High potency marijuana has also entered the U.S. drug market from Canada. Another source for marijuana in the United States is domestically grown marijuana, which includes both indoor and outdoor operations. Groups [such as identified DTOs] operating from Mexico employ a variety of transportation and concealment methods to smuggle marijuana into the United States. Most of the marijuana smuggled into the United States is concealed in vehicles—often in false compartments—or hidden in shipments of legitimate agricultural or industrial products. Marijuana is also smuggled across the border by rail, horse, raft, and backpack. Canada is becoming a source country for indoor-grown, high potency (15% to 25% THC) marijuana destined for the United States. Such indoor-grow operations have become an enormous and lucrative illicit industry, producing a potent

## KEY TERM

**drug-trafficking organizations (DTOs)**
complex organizations with highly defined command-and-control structures that produce, transport, or distribute large quantities of one or more illicit drugs

form of marijuana that has come to be known as "BC Bud." (Office of National Drug Control Policy, 2003)

Finally, not only are there many more types of marijuana available today in comparison to 20 years ago from illegal drug markets, but also the types and quality of marijuana seeds for growing marijuana plants have multiplied. One website among many devoted to selling high-quality marijuana seeds on the internet is BC Bud Depot in Ontario, Canada, which greets shoppers with the following:

Welcome to the BC Bud Depot. View our entire seed bank listing here. Along with breeding the world's best marijuana seeds for fast and discreet delivery worldwide, the BC Bud Depot also collaborates with other world renowned breeders to bring you the very best and most comprehensive marijuana seed bank in the world today. Find everything you need here, from CC Bud Depot and Reeferman seeds, to European breeders like T.H. Seeds, Soma, DNA Genetics and Delta-9 Labs. Take a look at our awards cabinet and sign up for our newsletter for amazing monthly specials and limited time offers. (BC Bud Depot, n.d.)

**Hashish** (or hasheesh) is the second cannabis derivative; it contains a pure form of resin. This type of marijuana consists of the sticky resin from the flowers of the female plant. Domestic samples of resin had an average of 12.14% THC, nondomestic had 7.03% THC, and the average of all samples seized, which includes samples with much higher amounts of THC, was 20.76% THC (ElSohly, 2009). Historically, hashish users have represented a somewhat small percentage of the cannabis user population in the United States

compared to Europe, where its use is much more prevalent. Hashish often is produced in Lebanon, Afghanistan, and Pakistan.

The third cannabis derivative is **marijuana wax** or **cannabis wax**, which is also known as *wax, ear wax, butter, honey oil, shatter, BHO* (which stands for "butane honey oil" or "butane hash oil"), and *dabs*. To date, this is one of the most powerful and most potent (90% pure THC) (Way of Leaf, 2019) types of marijuana on both the illegal and legal drug markets (in states where marijuana has either been decriminalized or medically sanctioned). Smoking or vaporizing this type of marijuana "leads to a quicker, stronger high," and "wax is said to be the strongest form of marijuana on the market" (Kimble, 2013). However, making marijuana wax is no easy task:

Amateur chemists be warned: making marijuana wax is not a kitchen-friendly (or, for that matter, user-friendly) activity. The marijuana is placed into a long tube or pipe, which is then hit with a rush of highly flammable butane—yes, like lighter fluid. The butane is used to extract THC, marijuana's active ingredient, in a hardened, extremely potent form that resembles wax, hence the name. For anyone familiar with how hash is made, it's a similar, yet more dangerous, process. (Kimble, 2013)

A more recent description:

[C]annabis wax is one of the most sought-after concentrates because the highest quality versions contain a THC content that's equivalent to 15–20 joints! While there are plants available with a THC content of 30%, many wax concentrates have over 90% THC. (Way of Leaf, 2019)

Reports from users indicate that marijuana wax is highly hallucinogenic in comparison to smoking common marijuana plant leaves and flowering buds. Some say that the effects also include intense visions and intense physical effects (Ghaly, 2015), passing out, and high levels of impairment. Wax sells for approximately $45 per gram on the street and $50 to $55 in a dispensary, "compared to $20 to $60 for an eighth of an ounce, roughly 3.5 grams, of plant marijuana depending the quality" (Pinto, 2016).

A fourth cannabis derivative is *ganja*, which is produced in India. This preparation consists of the dried tops of female plants. *Ganja* is also used as a slang term for marijuana (as are *pot, herb,*

## KEY TERMS

**hashish**
cannabis product made from the pure resin from the flowers of female plants with high amount of THC (the average THC content of all samples seized was 12.14% and often ranges from 7.03% [nondomestic] to 20.76%)

**marijuana wax or cannabis wax**
extremely potent cannabis spin-off made by using butane to extract the THC content, producing a "waxy" residue that is smoked or vaporized; has THC levels of approximately 90% and is highly hallucinogenic, often resulting in high levels of physical and mental impairment

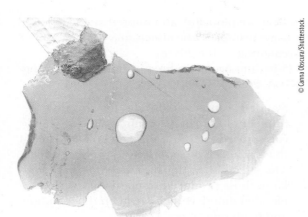

© Canna Obscura/Shutterstock.

Marijuana wax

*weed, grass, boom, Mary Jane, gangster,* or *chronic*). In fact, there are more than 200 slang terms for marijuana.

# Electronic Cigarettes or E-Cigarettes or Vaping

Key Facts about Use of E-Cigarette or Vaping Products (CDC, 2019):

- **Electronic cigarettes** or **e-cigarettes**—are also called *vapes, e-hookahs, vape pens, tank systems, mods,* and *electronic nicotine delivery systems.*
- Using an e-cigarette product is commonly called **vaping**.
- E-cigarettes work by heating a liquid to produce an aerosol that users inhale into their lungs.
- The liquid can contain nicotine, THC, and CBD oils, and other substances and additives. THC is the psychoactive mind-altering compound of marijuana that produces the "high" (CDC, 2019).

It should not be a major surprise that adolescent vaping from 2017 to 2018 were the largest ever recorded in the past 40 years for any adolescent substance use outcome in the United States (Schulenberg et al., 2019). Between 2017 and 2018, vaping marijuana increased from 1.6% to 2.6% among 8th graders, from 4.3% to 7.0% among 10th graders, from 4.9% to 7.5% among 12th graders, from 5.2% to 10.9% among college students, and from 6.6% to 9.3% among young adults. Each one-year increase was significant; as with vaping nicotine, the rise of vaping marijuana

among college students is especially notable. In fact, the doubling from 5.2% in 2017 to 10.9% in 2018 of 30-day prevalence of vaping marijuana among college students is among the largest one-year proportion increases for any substance since *Monitoring the Future* (MTF) began in 1975 (Schulenberg et al., 2019).

Vaping is making substantial inroads among adolescents, no matter the substance vaped, said Miech. In 2018 we saw substantial increases in vaping across all substances, including nicotine, marijuana, and adolescents who reported vaping "just flavoring." Factors that make vaping so attractive to youth include its novelty and the easy concealability of the latest vaping devices, which better allows youth to vape without adults knowing about it. If we want to prevent youth from using drugs, including nicotine, vaping will warrant special attention in terms of policy, education campaigns, and prevention programs in the coming years. (Miech et al., 2019)

Across 8th-, 10th-, and 12th-graders, the overall rates of vaping other substances, including marijuana, are second only to alcohol among substances surveyed. Their daily marijuana use continues to outpace daily cigarette use across grades, reflecting a steep decline in daily cigarette use and fairly stable daily marijuana use. Part of the reason for the popularity of vaporizers among teens is their low perceived risk: for the specific vaporizer device of an e-cigarette, less than 23% of students in all grades see a "great risk" in regular vaporizer use, one of the lowest levels of perceived risk measured in the survey (Schulenberg et al., 2019).

## ■ Dangers of Vaping

Lung injuries and deaths have recently occurred linked to the use of e-cigarettes and vaping products. "As of November 2019, the CDC has

**KEY TERMS**

**electronic cigarettes** or **e-cigarettes**
electronic nicotine-delivery systems; also called *vapes, e-hookahs, vape pens, tank systems, mods,* and *electronic nicotine delivery systems*

**vaping**
using an e-cigarette product to consume tobacco and some forms of marijuana

confirmed 2,290 vaping related lung injury cases, with 47 deaths" (Radcliffe, 2019). In "earlier data on 514 patients, about 77% reported using THC-containing products in the 30 days prior to the start of their symptoms. However, 16% reported using only nicotine-containing products" (Radcliff, 2019). Thus, the majority of patients with lung injuries are from vaping marijuana. Some of the lung injuries had signs of *bronchiolitis obliterans*, often referred to as *popcorn lung disease*, which consists of tiny airways (bronchioles) that are severely inflamed (Radcliff, 2019). Specifically, the CDC has identified vitamin E acetate as a chemical of concern among people with lung injuries associated with e-cigarette, or vaping, product use (CDC, 2019). Finally, the CDC recommends that people should not use THC-containing e-cigarette or vaping products particularly from informal sources like friends, or family, or in-person, or online dealer. Acetate should not be added to e-cigarette or vaping products; when vaporized and inhaled, it is extremely harmful to the lungs (CDC, 2019).

# Synthetic Marijuana

In recent years, psychoactive drugs such as Spice and K2 have become available. Such drugs are referred as **synthetic marijuana** because they are composed of herbal materials that have been sprayed with one or more of the designer chemicals that fall into the cannabinoid family (i.e., they are related to chemicals found in the marijuana plant). The synthetic cannabinoids are often marketed as "fake weed" and as a safe, legal alternative to marijuana. Users smoke the dried plant material that has been sprayed with synthetic cannabinoids or mix the sprayed plant material with marijuana or brew it as tea. Other users buy synthetic cannabinoid products as liquids that can be vaporized in e-cigarettes. Some experts think that synthetic cannabinoids have

**KEY TERM**

**synthetic marijuana**
human-made mind-altering chemicals that are either sprayed on dried, shredded plant material so they can be smoked (herbal incense) or sold as liquids to be vaporized and inhaled in e-cigarettes and other devices (liquid incense); also known as *fake weed*

much more powerful, and unpredictable, effects. In some instances, the effects may even be life threatening (NIH, 2015a).

Other important findings include the following (NIDA, 2018; NIH, 2015a):

- Synthetic cannabinoids refer to a growing number of human-made mind-altering chemicals sprayed on dried, shredded plant material that is smoked or vaporized to produce a high.
- The effects of synthetic cannabinoids are similar to those produced by marijuana, such as elevated mood, relaxation, altered perception, and symptoms of psychosis.
- Use of synthetic cannabinoids can cause serious mental and physical health problems, such as rapid heart rate, vomiting, violent behavior, and suicidal thoughts.
- The effects of synthetic cannabinoids can be unpredictable and severe or even life threatening.
- The psychotic effects from synthetic cannabinoids include extreme anxiety, confusion, paranoia, and hallucinations.
- Synthetic cannabinoids can be addictive, and behavioral therapies and medications have not been tested for treatment of addiction to these products.

Until March 2011, these drugs were not scheduled by the Drug Enforcement Administration (DEA), so they were readily and legally available on the Internet and in head shops, gas stations, and so on. However, the DEA scheduled some of the most widely used chemicals beginning March 1, 2011, making their possession and sale illegal. Subsequent laws have expanded the list of banned chemicals (Johnston et al., 2018).

## ▮ Trends in Use: High School and Youth

The MTF study first addressed the use of synthetic marijuana in its 2011 survey by asking 12th graders about their use of such products in the prior 12 months (which would have covered a considerable period of time prior to the drugs being scheduled) (Johnston et al., 2018).

Annual prevalence was found to be 11.4%, making synthetic marijuana the second most widely used class of illicit drug after marijuana itself among 12th graders at that time. In 2012, for the first time, 8th and 10th graders were asked about their use of synthetic marijuana; their annual prevalence rates also were high at 4.4% and 8.8%, respectively. Use in all three grades dropped in 2013, with a sharp and significant decline among 12th graders and significant declines for both 10th and 12th graders in 2014. These sharp declines continued through 2017 among both 8th and 10th graders, but halted among 12th graders. Annual prevalence in 2017 was down to 2.0%, 2.7%, and 3.7% for the three grades, reflecting a dramatic drop in use since 2012 (Johnston et al., 2018)

### ■ Perceived Risk

All three grades were asked whether they associated great risk with trying synthetic marijuana once or twice. As can be viewed in Figure 13.3D, the level of perceived risk for experimental use was quite low in 2012 (between 24% and 25%) but rose some, particularly among 12th graders, to 36% in 2016. (The percent would have been higher if those answering "Can't say, Drug unfamiliar" were excluded.) In 2017 there was a slight decline in perceived risk in all three grades, including a significant one in 8th grade. The availability of these drugs over the counter probably had the effect of communicating to teens that they must be safe when they are not (Johnston et al., 2019).

# The Behavioral Effects of Marijuana Use

This section will discuss the "high" experienced from marijuana, the subjective euphoric effects of this drug, how the use of marijuana affects driving performance and critical-thinking skills, and the amotivational syndrome that appears to be a characteristic effect of marijuana use.

### ■ The High

The widely held belief of the 1930s that marijuana was a destructive assassin of youth is no longer considered valid for casual or occasional users of this drug. In most individuals, low to moderate doses of cannabis produce euphoria and a pleasant state of relaxation (Goldstein, 1994). What are the common effects experienced from marijuana use? After a few delayed moments of forcibly holding the smoke in the lungs, most users suddenly experience the high. In this state of euphoria, the user experiences a dry mouth, elevated heartbeat, and some loss of coordination and balance, coupled with slower reaction times and a feeling

of euphoria (mild to elevated intoxication). Blood vessels in the eyes expand, which accounts for reddening of the eyes. Some people experience slightly elevated blood pressure, which can double the normal heart rate. These effects can become intensified when other drugs, such as LSD or psychedelic ("magic") mushrooms, are combined with the marijuana.

The state of euphoria that results from the high is usually mild and short lived; a typical high from one joint may last from two to three hours. Subjectively, the user experiences altered perception of space and time, impaired memory of recent events, and impaired physical coordination (Abood & Martin, 1992). (More of these subjective effects are discussed at length in the next section.) An occasional high is not usually hazardous unless the person attempts to drive a car, operate heavy machinery, fly a plane, or function in similar ways requiring coordination, good reflexes, or quick judgment (Nahas & Latour, 1992). Even low doses of marijuana alter perception—for example, being able to judge the speed of an approaching vehicle or how much to slow down on an exit ramp. As one user put it:

> In trying to describe the high, it's not like an alcohol high. In an alcohol high, you are a lot more uncoordinated if drinking a lot. With weed, it's like reality changes—you add a lot more bass so-to-speak to what you see, hear, think, and feel. The reality is tempered with some distortion that to me and many others is pleasurable. You know how you feel after three or four very strong drinks [referring to alcoholic beverages]. Well take two more of those drinks and then look around the room you are in. Now, the difference between alcohol and weed is that you can walk to the bathroom quite well while under the influence of weed, while with alcohol you walk carefully so that no one notices that you are just about drunk. Weed is a mind high while alcohol is more of a body high. *(Venturelli's research files, female professionally employed and residing in San Francisco, age 23, May 19, 2000)*

Three additional interviews attempted to compare the high from marijuana with the effects of alcohol.

First interview:

> The marijuana high is also not nearly as harsh on the body. Being high doesn't give you that

painful hangover as alcohol does. The actual high is very functional; I tend to do some of my best work (after burning a "dubbie") in that state [of mind]. It is part of the lifestyle of marijuana. [In contrast], alcohol makes me (and most people I know) very unproductive when the "buzz" is reached. *(From Venturelli's research files, male undergraduate student at a Midwestern university, age 21, August 10, 2000)*

Second interview with the same person a day later:

There seems to be a small misconception about the effects of marijuana and alcohol. For me, anyway, in looking at the physical "buzz" you get from alcohol, it is very physically disabling. You get drunk and stumble around, your lips loosen up, and you say things that you would not normally say. I find that marijuana has more of a calming effect. It makes you relaxed, a little more perceptive to some stimuli, and obviously less perceptive to other stimuli. It is a light feeling, but not overwhelming to the equilibrium. *(From Venturelli's research files, same student as above, August 11, 2000)*

Third interview:

I can't drink much, because I feel the effects of alcohol more than the average person. I also don't like the effects of being high on alcohol. I feel very loopy and uncoordinated. Then, the next morning after drinking the night before is very unpleasant for me with headaches and sometimes even nausea. This is why I like to smoke weed. With weed you don't have all the impairment, the sick feelings, and you don't wake all messed up. I also have great conversations with people who are high on marijuana and find myself in a good mood while high. Also with regard to impairment, I would never drive under the influence of alcohol, but with marijuana, I have no problem driving. I even had a police officer stop me one night when my tail light was out on one side while on weed, and he never detected my marijuana high. He just wrote me a warning notice. Now, if it were alcohol, he probably would have become suspicious. Everyone is different, and this is my take on comparing these two drugs. *(From Venturelli's research files, female student at a Midwestern university, age 22, September 9, 2010)*

In describing how the effects of THC in marijuana can enhance feelings, one source provided the following:

*Cannabis* use can increase focus and concentration, making a person's moods, sensations, and experience seem more intense. Your heart may feel like it's pounding, the music is fantastic, this is the best dessert you've ever eaten and, wow, get a load of how beautiful nature is. The problem is that if you're concentrating on something that's negative, you can intensify that feeling, as well. Fortunately, something else will come along and distract you with another thought to pursue, if you so choose. And if your fleeting idea feels like the answer to the world's problems, please write it down. It's profundity might escape you later, but it will feel good if it turns out you're right. (Norris & Conrad, n.d)

An acute dose of cannabis can produce adverse reactions, ranging from mild anxiety to panic and paranoia in some users. These reactions occur most frequently in individuals who are under stress or who are anxious, depressed, or borderline schizophrenic (Nahas & Latour, 1992). Documented research indicates the following:

Acute cannabis toxicity results in difficulty with coordination, decreased muscle strength, decreased hand steadiness, postural hypotension, lethargy, decreased concentration, slowed reaction time, slurred speech, and conjunctival injection. Large doses of THC may produce confusion, amnesia, delusions, hallucinations, anxiety, and agitation, but most episodes remit rapidly. Chronic users may experience paranoia, panic disorder, fear, or dysphoria. (Aydin & Fulton, 2015)

Such effects also may also be experienced by users who accidentally take much more than they feel they can handle.

Although the more potent varieties can cause acute cannabis toxicity, extreme reactions can also occur because of ingesting marijuana treated (or "laced") with such things as opium, PCP, or other additives. Based on limited evidence from survey studies, mild or often adverse reactions can be experienced by regular users that are mainly self-treated and usually go unreported (see "Signs and Symptoms: Specific Indicators of Marijuana Use").

## ■ Subjective Euphoric Effects

**Subjective euphoric effects** associated with marijuana use refer to the ongoing social and psychological experiences incurred while intoxicated by marijuana. These effects of intoxication include both the user's altered state of consciousness and his or her perceptions. Subjective effects in experienced users include a general sense of relaxation and tranquility, coupled with heightened sensitivity to sound, taste, and emotionality. For inexperienced users, the subjective effects can vary from those similar to experienced users to some anxiety from anticipation of the effects. Often, the high depends on the **set and setting** (Goode, 1999; Zinberg, 1984; Zinberg & Robertson, 1972). *Set* is the individual's expectation of what a drug will do to his or her personality (state of mind and mood). *Setting* is both the physical and the social environment in which the drug is consumed (surroundings where the drug is taken, including the people in the immediate environment when the drug is consumed). Some users report occasional similarities to the typical hallucinogenic high, emphasizing much less intensity. How closely the marijuana high resembles a hallucinogenic high depends on the amount of THC absorbed from marijuana. For example, higher amounts of THC found in more

### KEY TERMS

**subjective euphoric effects**
ongoing social and psychological experiences incurred while intoxicated with marijuana

**set and setting**
*set* refers to the individual's expectation of what a drug will do to his or her personality; *setting* is the physical and social environments where the drug is consumed

# SIGNS & SYMPTOMS

## Specific Indicators of Marijuana Use

- A sweet odor similar to burnt rope in room, on clothes, and so on.
- Roach: The small butt end of a marijuana cigarette.
- Joint: Looks like a hand-rolled cigarette; usually the ends are twisted or crimped.
- Roach clips: Holders for the roach could be any number of common items such as paper clips, bobby pins, or hemostats. They also could be of a store-bought variety in a number of shapes and disguises.
- Herb or marijuana grinder: Usually a round device in which solid marijuana is placed that can grind the bud into fine bits so that marijuana joints or blunts can be made.

- Seeds or leaves in pockets or possession.
- Plastic baggies, either with some amount of marijuana inside the baggie or an empty baggie often found in pant or shirt pockets.
- Rolling papers or pipes, usually hidden somewhere.
- Eye drops: For disguising red eyes.
- Excessive use of incense, room deodorizers, or breath fresheners.
- Bong: A device for smoking cannabis, tobacco, or other herbal substance. A bong is filled with water as a filter to cool the smoke.
- Devices for storing the substance such as film canisters, boxes or cans, a dugout (containing a one hitter device), or pill bottles (fully formed buds of marijuana or high-end strains may be distributed in pill bottles to protect their shape and size).
- Eating binges: An after effect for some marijuana users.
- Appearance of intoxication, yet no smell of alcohol.
- Excessive laughter.
- Initial use (first hour): Animated behavior (loud or excessive talking).
- Hours later: Fatigue or drowsiness.

© iStock/Thinkstock.

potent types of marijuana, like sinsemilla, hydro, and kind bud, more clearly mimic a hallucinogenic high. These effects are especially evident when considering the extent to which the senses of hearing, vision, sound, and taste are distorted by use of highly potent forms of marijuana.

As mentioned previously, recent, potent varieties of marijuana with higher than usual THC content include GSC, Kosher Kush, Ghost OG, Bruce Banner, Ghost Train Haze, Chemdog, Original Glue, The White, Death Star, White Fire OG, Headband, Cherry Pie, and LA Confidential (Rahn, 2015). Other marijuana strains rated as the most potent include Grandfather OG, Chewdawg, Irish Crème, White Tahoe Cookies, and Strawberry Banana (Doctor, 2019).

Some marijuana users become highly attached to these euphoric effects by desiring and looking forward to repeating these effects. Such users often pride themselves on their extensive knowledge of this drug and maintain interest in discussing past experiences of "when I was really high" or "let me tell you about that night we smoked hydro. . . ." Devotees stay current with developments in the marijuana field by avidly reading monthly issues of magazines devoted to marijuana (the art of marijuana use) and frequently scan the Internet for information and conversations in chat rooms about the best varieties of marijuana, the best growing techniques, announcements of hemp festivals, advice, and information regarding current laws, fines, and other information. A vivid example of such an enthusiast is recalled in the following observation:

> This author recalls visiting a neighbor one evening and noticing that one of the visitors sat very quietly with a pleasant smile while several intense conversations were occurring. I recall noticing this student because he sat very quietly appearing somewhat distant and occasionally displaying several facial gestures in either approval or disapproval of comments and suggestions during the ongoing conversations. About [one] hour into my visit, while others continued having multiple conversations, I directed my attention to this "quiet" individual with some introductory comments. He made minimal responses in the conversation. As others were discussing multiple topics, several of the guests began talking about drug use. Immediately, this quiet and reserved individual became very lively and began talking about the best types of marijuana on campus. Within several minutes, I literally saw a

transformation in his involvement with the ongoing conversation. He was incessantly talking about marijuana and dominated the conversation with his many insights about the drug. I realized, prior to the topic of drug use and marijuana, he probably did not have much interest in the other topics. However, when we "hit" what appeared to be an interesting topic, which was a passion for marijuana use, an intensive amount of enthusiasm emerged. Clearly, this former "quiet young man" had transformed and clearly appeared to be quite a connoisseur about the varieties and the subjective euphoric effects of marijuana. By his overall conversational enthusiasm, he appeared quite content in letting us know how much he knew about this topic—and it was an extensive amount of knowledge. *(Observation from Venturelli visiting a neighbor's home in a small Midwestern town, June 9, 2010)*

Why is marijuana so attractive to many individuals? One quote from an interview illustrates the extensive psychological and social reinforcement experienced by marijuana users:

> It's the high that I particularly like. Everything becomes mellower. Everyday tensions are released or submerged by more inner-like experiences. I can review the day and how happy or miserable I feel. Actually, when I am thinking and I am high on grass, I always feel that my thoughts are profound. You think from another perspective, one that numbs the more reality-based everyday strains. On the other hand, there are moments when this drug affects your mood and channels it [in] different ways. You have moments when you either feel sad, happy, angry (in a more contemplative way), or worried. These moods are both good and bad. If for the moment you feel good, then your mood is positive. If you feel down, your mood is negative in a particular way. If I am with friends and we are all sharing the bong or joint or pipe, we laugh a lot together. It's a type of drug that makes you more jovial, more introspective, and friendly, gregarious *(From Venturelli's research files, male personnel manager, age 40, August 20, 1996)*

As documented, marijuana enthusiasts have a strong attachment to their passionate feelings surrounding the use of marijuana. Psychologists believe the drug user becomes attached and habituated to the drug largely through the reinforcement of pleasurable feelings. If these subjective euphoric experiences were to become largely negative, attachment to and repeated use of this drug would cease. Thus, the theory of **differential association** applies. This theory, developed by Edwin H. Sutherland in his classic publication in 1939 (revised in 1947), attempts to explain the causes of delinquent behavior. Sociologists define the term *differential association* as the process by which individuals become socialized into the perceptions and values of a group. Differential association can apply to drug use. In using this drug, the camaraderie, the conversations and banter that often occur among friends, is often perceived as a fun activity. It can include the perception that marijuana relieves boredom or stress or is the perfect drug for just hanging out, chilling, partying, and getting high together. Specifically, the definition of differential association can include the behavioral satisfaction derived from friends who use marijuana. In this situation, getting high with others is the positive reward that solidifies the user to his or her friends and the drug.

## ■ Driving Performance

Some evidence[2] shows that the ability to perform complex tasks, such as driving, can be impaired while under the influence of marijuana (Couper & Logan, 2004; "Do Marijuana and Driving Mix?" 2010; Goldstein, 1994; Mathias, 1996; NIH, 2015b). Research indicates that "cannabis consumption impairs motor coordination, reaction time, sensory perceptions and glare recovery" (Teen Challenge, 2000, p. 1). This effect has been demonstrated in laboratory assessments of driving-related skills such as eye–hand coordination and reaction time, in driver simulator studies, in test-course performance, and in actual street driving situations (Chait & Pierri, 1992; Couper & Logan, 2004; Mathias, 1996; NIH, 2015b; Teen Challenge, 2000). Other research summarizes the key impairments with driving under the influence of marijuana as deficiencies in "attentiveness, vigilance, perception of time and speed, and use of acquired knowledge" (Sewell, Poling, & Sofuoglu, 2009).

One study tested the effects of known amounts of marijuana, alcohol, or both on driving. The subjects drove a course rigged with various traffic problems. Driving skills deteriorated among those who had used either drug, but the greatest deterioration was observed in subjects who had taken both. In another test, 59 subjects smoked marijuana until they were intoxicated and then were given sobriety tests on the roadside by highway patrol officers. Overall, 94% of the subjects did not pass the test 90 minutes after smoking, and 60% failed at 150 minutes, even though the blood THC was much lower at this time (Hollister, 1986). Another, more recent study indicated that "[m]arijuana significantly impairs judgment, motor coordination, and reaction time, and studies have found a direct relationship between blood THC concentration and impaired driving ability" (NIDA, 2016).

Another study detailing results from driving performance found that the short-term effects of marijuana use include problems with memory and learning, distorted perception, difficultly in thinking and problem-solving, and loss of coordination (National Highway Traffic Safety Administration, 2004). Heavy users may have increased difficulty sustaining attention, shifting attention to meet the demands of changes in the environment, and registering, processing, and using information. In general, laboratory performance studies indicate that sensory functions are not highly impaired, but perceptual functions are significantly affected. The ability to concentrate and maintain attention is decreased during marijuana use, and impairment of hand–eye coordination is dose related over a wide range of dosages. Impairment in retention time and tracking, subjective sleepiness, distortion of time and distance, vigilance, and loss of coordination in divided attention tasks have been reported. Note, however, that subjects can often "pull themselves together" to concentrate on simple tasks for brief periods of time, but that significant performance impairments are usually observed for at least one to two hours following marijuana use, and residual effects have been reported for up to 24 hours (Couper and Logan, 2004; see also NIDA, 2010b).

Another, slightly less critical study of city driving

showed that drivers who drank alcohol overestimated their performance quality [often by speeding and overconfidence] whereas those who smoked marijuana underestimated it

---

[2] Other, more recent published research contradicts impaired driving under the influence of marijuana; see InsuranceInformation Institute (2019) and NORML (2019).

[slower speed and more cautious driving]. . . . Drivers under the influence of marijuana retain insight in their performance and will compensate where they can, for example, by slowing down or increasing effort. As a consequence, THC's adverse effects on driving performance appear relatively small. Still we can easily imagine situations where the influence of marijuana smoking might have an exceedingly dangerous effect; i.e., emergency situations which put high demands on the driver's information processing capacity, prolonged monotonous driving, and after THC has been taken with other drugs, especially alcohol. (U.S. Department of Transportation, 1993)

Research reported by the Drug Enforcement Administration (DEA, 2013) indicates the following:

- More than "3,000 fatally injured drivers in Australia showed that when marijuana was present in the blood of the driver they were much more likely to be at fault for the accident. And the higher the THC concentration, the more likely they were to be culpable" (p. 43).
- "A study in the *British Medical Journal* on the consequences of cannabis impaired driving found that drivers who consume cannabis within [three] hours of driving are nearly twice as likely to cause a vehicle collision as those who are not under the influence of drugs or alcohol" (p. 41).
- "A study in the *Epidemiologic Reviews* by researchers from Columbia University found that drivers who get behind the wheel after smoking pot run more than twice the risk of getting into an accident" (p. 42).
- "In 2009, marijuana was the most prevalent drug found in this population—approximately 28% of fatally injured drivers who tested positive tested positive for marijuana" (p. 42).

Other, more recent findings by the Canadian Centre on Substance Abuse include the following (Beirness & Porath-Waller, 2015):

- Among young drivers, driving after using cannabis is more prevalent than driving after drinking.

**KEY TERM**

**drugged driving**
operating a motor vehicle with a measurable quantity or quantities of a legal or an illegal drug in the driver's body, which most often results in impaired driving

- Cannabis impairs the cognitive and motor abilities necessary to operate a motor vehicle and doubles the risk of crash involvement.
- After alcohol, cannabis is the most commonly detected substance among drivers who die in traffic crashes.
- Cannabis use is not uncommon among drivers involved in collisions.
- The police have the tools and authority required to detect and arrest drivers who are impaired by cannabis.

Other research regarding drug-impaired driving indicated that U.S. Census data found that "there are 13 million driving-aged teenagers and, with 23% of teens admitting to driving under the influence of alcohol, marijuana or other drugs" (Liberty Mutual Insurance, 2013). This same study revealed that 75% of teens claimed marijuana use has no impact on their driving ability. Another interesting report pointing to the severity of teens driving under the influence stated that in 2007 the Maryland Adolescent Survey indicated that 11.1% of the state's licensed adolescent drivers reported driving under the influence of marijuana on three or more occasions, and 10% reported driving while using a drug other than marijuana (not including alcohol) (NIDA, 2010b).

**Drugged driving** is defined as operating a motor vehicle with a measurable quantity (or quantities) of a legal or illegal drug in the driver's body, which most often results in impaired driving. "After alcohol, marijuana is the drug most often found in the blood of drivers involved in crashes" (NIDA, 2019). Medical data indicate a connection between drugged driving and accidents.

Use of illicit drugs or misuse of prescription drugs can make driving a car unsafe—just like driving after drinking alcohol. In 2017, 21.4 million people age 16 or older drove under the influence of alcohol in the preceding year, and 12.8 million drove under the influence of illicit drugs. It's hard to measure how many crashes are caused by drugged driving, but estimates show that almost 44% of drivers in fatal car crashes tested positive for drugs (NIDA, 2019).

A study of patients in a shock trauma unit who had been in collisions revealed that 15% of those who had been driving a car or motorcycle had been smoking marijuana, and another 17% had both THC and alcohol in their blood. In 2009, an estimated 12% of persons aged 12 or older (30.2 million persons) drove under the influence of alcohol at least once in the past year (NIDA, 2010b), and another major study found that 33% of fatally injured drivers with known test results tested positive for at least one drug (Dupont, 2011).

Research conducted by the University of Auckland, New Zealand, proves the link between marijuana use and car accidents. The research found that habitual cannabis users were 9.5 times more likely to be involved in crashes, with 5.6% of people who had crashed having taken the drug, compared to 0.5% of the control group (Blows et al., 2005).

A study published by researchers at the University of Maryland Medical Center Shock Trauma Center indicated that during the 90-day study about half of the drivers admitted to the shock trauma center tested positive for drugs other than alcohol. In addition, one in four drivers admitted to the shock trauma unit tested positive for marijuana. According to the researchers,

> This population-based case-control study indicates that habitual use of marijuana is strongly associated with car crash injury. The nature of the relationship between marijuana use and risk-taking is unclear and needs further research. The prevalence of marijuana use in this driving population was low, and acute use was associated with habitual marijuana use, suggesting that intervention strategies may be more effective if they are targeted towards high use groups (Blows et al., 2005, p. 605)

One notable interview presents us with a negative experience regarding use of marijuana and driving experiences:

> One time I smoked some real strong dope at my friend's house, then had to drive back home, which was [two] miles in one direction. I remember wigging out [panicking] in trying to get home. There were moments when I did not know where I was until I would see the next marker of my neighborhood. I remember having seconds of panic because I did not know where I was; then suddenly, I would notice a neighborhood restaurant or some other marker that said I was right around my neighborhood. I took smaller streets on the way home and even took a longer way home because I was freaking out about the cops—what if one would spot me? This was bogus thinking because how the hell would anyone suddenly spot me while driving home? Well, that's an example of wigging out

on weed. But, I still don't think that even that time I would be getting into an accident. I was so freaked out that I was extra careful not to speed, pass stop signs, or violate any law for fear of being seen. If anything, I drive slower when I am really high, not more dangerously. *(From Venturelli's research files, male college student in a Midwestern town, age 20, July 19, 2000)*

In contrast to this student's beliefs, scientific research indicates that some perceptual or other performance deficits resulting from marijuana use may persist for some time after the high, and users who attempt to drive, fly, operate heavy machinery, perform surgery, and so on may not recognize their impairment because they do not feel intoxicated. States such as California have established testing procedures to detect the presence of THC in urine or blood samples from apparently intoxicated drivers.

If the use of marijuana becomes more socially acceptable (or perhaps even legal everywhere) and penalties for simple possession become more lenient, it is likely that individuals will feel less inclined to hide their drug use. Unfortunately, it follows that these individuals may also be more inclined to drive while high, endangering themselves and others.

## ■ Critical-Thinking Skills

Marijuana has been found to have a negative impact on critical-thinking skills. Research by NIDA shows that heavy marijuana use impairs critical skills related to attention, memory, and learning. Another study showed that even alertness, coordination, and reaction time were impaired by marijuana usage (Couper & Logan, 2004; National Clearinghouse on Alcohol and Drug Information [NCADI], 1998; NIDA, 2010a). Impairment from marijuana continues even after discontinuing use of the drug for at least 24 hours (Brown & Massaro, 1996).

In the same study (Brown & Massaro, 1996), researchers compared 65 heavy users (using approximately every other day) with light users (using once or twice per week). Heavy users made more mistakes and had greater difficulty sustaining attention, shifting attention to meet the demands of challenges in the environment, and registering, processing, and using information compared with light users (Brown & Massaro, 1996; Fuller, 2008; Norton, 2009). In addition, heavy users had greater difficulty completing the tests, which specifically measured aspects of attention, memory, and learning such as intellectual functioning, abstraction ability, attention span, verbal fluency, and learning and recalling abilities (Brown & Massaro, 1996; Teen Challenge, 2000). One researcher stated, "If you could get heavy users to learn an item, then they could remember it; the problem was getting them to learn it in the first place" (Brown & Massaro, 1996, p. 3). The researchers surmised that marijuana alters brain activity because residues of the drug persist in the brain or because a withdrawal syndrome follows the euphoric effects of the marijuana.

In another study, researchers tested the cognitive functioning of 65 marijuana-using college students. Residual impairments were seen in the 24 hours after use in terms of sustaining attention and shifting attention and hence in registering, organizing, and using information (NIDA, 2010a; Pope & Yurgulen-Todd, 1996). This study, which was undertaken during the 1990s, is significant because it was carefully controlled. The unresolved question is whether these memory impairments are short term or long term. These noteworthy findings complement many other similar findings that identified protracted cognitive impairment among heavy users of marijuana (Fuller, 2008; NCADI, 1998; Norton, 2009).

## ▮ Amotivational Syndrome

The so-called **amotivational syndrome** (sometimes referred to as *antimotivational syndrome*) is a flashpoint of controversy about marijuana although not as newsworthy as that regarding medical legalization. Amotivational syndrome refers to a belief that heavy use of marijuana causes a lack of motivation or "impaired desire" and reduced productivity. Specifically, users show apathy, poor short-term memory, difficulty in concentration, and a lingering disinterest in pursuing goals (Abood & Martin, 1992; Right Diagnosis, 2010).

In the past (emphasis on *past*), this syndrome received considerable negative attention. People who are high, or stoned, lack the desire to perform hard work and are not interested in doing difficult tasks. There is some evidence of this behavior in regular marijuana users (Nahas &

KEY TERM

**amotivational syndrome**
controversial syndrome whose proponents claim that heavy marijuana use causes a lack of motivation and reduced productivity

Latour, 1992). Overall, although not solely the result of cannabis use, chronic users have lower grades in school, are more likely to be absent from classes, and are likely not to complete assignments and to drop out of school (Hardcastle, 2007; Henneberger, 1994; Liska, 1997). In terms of age, the earlier someone begins smoking marijuana, coupled with heavier use, the more likely the amotivational characteristics will prevail and the more difficult it will be to cease using this drug.

Although the effects of marijuana per se are somewhat responsible for creating this syndrome, other factors contribute as well. For instance, is the lack of motivation caused by the drug itself, or is it that poorly motivated people begin using marijuana, which then further exacerbates their lack of motivation? Surveys show that a sizable number of marijuana users and their peer groups tend to be alienated from society and are likely to be classified as nonconformists or as rebellious youth. They may, in fact, choose pleasure and nonconformity rather than goal-directed behavior. Another challenge to the concept of amotivational syndrome argues that the lack of motivation may simply be the result of the effects of marijuana while under its influence and not any type of longer-term or unique syndrome (Iverson, 2005; Johns, 2001).

Advocates of marijuana legalization stress data that tend to debunk research on amotivational syndrome. One institute that supports legalization, the Lindesmith Center, published a study asserting that college students who are users have higher grades than nonusers (Zimmer & Morgan, 1997). How can we account for the discrepancies between this study and others, not to mention the clinical experiences of students, who often report academic repercussions of heavy use? One factor in the explanation is sociocultural:

In the New York–New Jersey metro region, there are "druggy" schools and "drinking" schools. The "druggy" schools are more upper-middle class, liberal arts schools, artsy types, latter-day hippies, etc. The boozer campuses are filled with blue-collar and lower-middle-class kids—sometimes big fraternity schools. Frontloading at basketball games, comas after pledge parties. . . . Not as good educational backgrounds as the artsy potheads, who went to better schools, private schools, read a lot, or heard a lot at dinner before college, so they get by with their profs. However, the potheads ratchet down into easier majors, and they get crummier grades as they get into regular use. *(Interview with Pearl Mott for a prevention newsletter, prevention specialist, Drug Prevention Programs in Higher Education, Washington, D.C., October 1994)*

A second methodological factor complicating drug research among such students is simply that academic failures stay in "F" categories for only one or two semesters. Many then disappear from statistics entirely via academic attrition.

A more serious challenge to the notion of amotivational syndrome comes from the same ethnographic research that was mentioned at the beginning of this chapter. The most well-known of these investigations was carried out by Vera Rubin and Labros Comitas and reported in their book *Ganja in Jamaica* (1975). Follow-up studies were done in Jamaica (Dreher, 1982; Hamid, 1998) and Costa Rica (Carter, 1980; Pollan, 1998). None of these works found that chronic use impaired occupational or other functioning; in fact, the main point of the Jamaican studies was that users defined this drug as helpful and motivating for work—a "motivational syndrome." This work is often cited to counter amotivational syndrome claims. By this logic, dropping out of the rat race is a cultural posture, with marijuana being secondary to or, at most, reinforcing the drift away from a mainstream lifestyle.

The Jamaican and Costa Rican subjects, however, were not observed engaging in an academic, cognitively complex, or rapid reflex activity, nor were they found in occupations that were competitive and striving for mobility.

Typical effects of amotivational syndrome.

© Sanjmur/Dreamstime.com.

Rather, these subjects were involved in repetitive, physical labor involving sugarcane cutting. In such a context, marijuana drug use functions to provide a pleasant stimulation that counters the monotony and physical discomfort of such labor.

When studies in other cultures contradict the American notion of amotivational syndrome, we are left to be cautious in making a direct assumption that marijuana use per se leads to such a syndrome, especially given that one strain of marijuana, *C. indica*, causes sedation, whereas another strain, *C. sativa*, causes stimulation. More than likely, if we agree that the amotivational syndrome does manifest itself in marijuana users, it may be a direct result of a particular strain of marijuana. As discussed previously, keep in mind that *C. indica* differs

---

## ▶ CASE IN POINT

### A Letter to an Editor: No Valid Reason to Ban Marijuana

**A**n Associated Press release printed in the *Kentucky Enquirer* had the head of the White House Office of Drug Control Policy, Gil Kerlikowske, President Obama's so-called drug czar, extolling the necessity of continuing the prohibition of marijuana. The reasons he cites for continuing the 70-year war on marijuana smokers are a clear indication that history is correct in judging marijuana prohibition as one of the greatest policy failures in the history of the federal government. The letter is as follows.

Below is a veteran soldier responding to Gil Kerlikowske.

Those who support prohibition started in 1933 at the end of alcohol prohibition to shift all the

bad outcomes of alcohol use to marijuana. The films and newspaper stories of the day claimed that using marijuana leads to violence, murder, and insanity. Think of the movie, "Reefer Madness." Cut to the present and the Drug Czar is reduced to claiming that marijuana causes lung cancer, and that marijuana use is the cause of a significant amount of traffic accidents. The lung cancer, marijuana connection is a myth that grows out of the fact that tobacco smoking causes lung cancer therefore marijuana smoking should too. With this in mind, the Government originally supported the work of Dr. Donald Tashkin. His study on marijuana smoking and head, neck, and lung cancer was expected to be a slam-dunk for the

*(continues)*

# ► CASE IN POINT

## A Letter to an Editor: No Valid Reason to Ban Marijuana (*continued*)

Government. The problem is that the results of Dr. Tashkin's and other studies is that the opposite is true. Dr. Tashkin's study showed that people who regularly use marijuana get head, neck, and lung cancer at the same rate as people who do not smoke at all. He reported that marijuana seemed to have an anti-cancer effect and acted as a cancer preventer. One would think medical researchers would be all over this like "stink on poopy" looking for a cancer cure, but the forces of prohibition continue to block research, even though compassion for one's fellow men and the saving of lives would indicate the opposite.

Mr. Kerlikowske's claim about marijuana being the cause of a significant amount of traffic accidents is a "fact" that he must have pulled out of a lower opening. There is no data to support this. Again, what studies have been done on this angle do not support his claim. Studies have found that marijuana smokers get into accidents as often as those who do not use marijuana. Think about it! I returned to Northern Kentucky in 1996. I watch local news at least once a day and read the paper every day.

In the 14 years since 1996, I have seen only one report of a marijuana caused traffic accident. If I remember right, a young man had blown through an intersection and someone was killed in the resulting accident. The local media reported that the driver had been smoking marijuana and that was the cause of the accident. A follow up report later claimed the driver was texting when he blew the intersection. You have to ask yourself that if there are so many marijuana's caused accidents, where are all the marijuana accident stories, arrests, trials, and incarcerations.

Marijuana prohibition is an idea that has lived long past the point of being something that is "good" for America. Marijuana use is not as Reagan said that it's the greatest threat faced by America. The end of the federal ban on marijuana is long overdue. It has no basis in science or logic, costs billions of tax dollars, and causes more harm than good. At a time when Americans need jobs and economic growth, we are shooting ourselves in the foot by continuing to suppress the marijuana/hemp industry, an industry that could go a long way in creating jobs and economic activity worth billions of dollars.

M.Sgt. Thomas Vance, USAF Ret., Alexandria

### Questions to Consider

1. What is your initial reaction to this letter?

2. Like the firmly established link between lung cancer and smoking tobacco, can a similar argument can be made between smoking marijuana and lung cancer? Explain.

3. Do you think the "forces of prohibition" are masking potential benefits of using marijuana, as the writer claims? Explain.

4. What is your opinion about using marijuana and driving? Do you think drivers under the influence are adversely affected by the effects of this drug? Explain.

5. How do you generally feel about people who use marijuana?

6. How much of a threat to society is marijuana use? Should marijuana be decriminalized? If yes, why? Should it remain illegal? If so, what penalties should apply and why?

from *C. sativa*. Also, there is great likelihood that in Jamaica, the stimulation caused by *C. sativa* (which is the most common variety of marijuana in Jamaica) may explain why these sugarcane field workers under the effects of this particular strain of marijuana are able to work long hours. (For additional information on how marijuana affects personality, see "Case in Point: A Letter to an Editor: No Valid Reason to Ban Marijuana.")

# Therapeutic Uses and the Controversy Over Medical Marijuana Use

Although the use of marijuana for medical purposes is far more accepted than it was at the turn of this century, controversy remains about the medical uses of marijuana. Basically,

# HOLDING THE LINE

## States Are Allowing Cannabis Buyers' Clubs

Despite federal drug laws prohibiting the cultivation, possession, use, and sale of marijuana, 33 states plus the District of Columbia have recently enacted the legalization of recreational and medical marijuana. The 33 states are Alaska, Arizona, Arkansas, California, Colorado, Connecticut, Delaware, Florida, Hawaii, Illinois, Louisiana, Maine, Maryland, Massachusetts, Michigan, Minnesota, Missouri, Montana, Nevada, New Hampshire, New Jersey, New Mexico, New York, North Dakota, Ohio, Oklahoma, Oregon, Pennsylvania, Rhode Island, Utah, Vermont, Washington, and West Virginia (ProCon.org, 2019). Out of 325,719,178 of U.S. population as of March 17, 2018 (ProCon.org, 2019), the estimated number of medical marijuana users would be 2,132,777 (ProCon.org, 2019).

Why should medically ill patients, those afflicted with AIDS and associated wasting, lack of appetite, nausea, arthritis, hepatitis C, migraines, multiple sclerosis, muscle spasms, chronic pain, glaucoma, and other illnesses (such as posttraumatic stress disorder, depression, or bipolar disorder) or those suffering the deleterious effects of chemotherapy or radiation not be able to legally purchase marijuana if they find relief from the effects of their illnesses? The first cannabis buyers' club began in 1996 when the voting citizens of Marin County, California, passed "Proposition 215, which authorized the use of medical marijuana . . . for those who have a doctor's recommendation" (Nolde, 2002). The main problem facing this club in Marin County, and all the other cannabis buyers' clubs throughout the United States, is that although these 23 states and DC have legalized such enterprises, they continue to violate federal drug laws, causing a conflict between federal and state law. At times, the clubs can be ordered closed by a superior court judge, resulting in federal agents raiding the clubs, confiscating the marijuana, and arresting the owners and operators of these establishments.

To date, this cyclical pattern of raids and arrests by federal officials continues to sporadically occur because of this rift between state and federal laws. The clubs are either for-profit or nonprofit organizations whose sole intent is to distribute marijuana for medicinal purposes when prescribed by a licensed physician. Many of the buyers (known as *patients*) report relief and satisfaction from their use of marijuana. For example, a man named Clay Shinn, 46, was diagnosed with AIDS in 1992. At the time of his interview, he had been going to the Marin Alliance's Cannabis Buyers' Club for five years. "It's made a major difference in my life," he said. After taking his [AIDS] medication morning, afternoon, and evening, he said, "I was always getting nauseated. . . . I could set my watch by it. I hate it. God, it's awful. Now I don't barf anymore" (Nolde, 2002). Another interviewee, who is an arthritic, HIV-positive cabaret performer, said, "After I leave here . . . I won't feel my pain" (Goldberg, 1996). Another man, the club's director, reiterated that, "'You have to be sick or dying' . . . If you are, with a doctor's note to prove that you have AIDS or cancer or another condition with symptoms that marijuana is known to alleviate, Mr. Peron [the club's director] is willing to sell some relief" (Goldberg, 1996). Finally, Dennis Peron, the founder of the San Francisco Buyers' Club, stated, "We have over 400 senior citizens that come here for arthritis, glaucoma, pain, etc. We have an old woman trapped in her wheelchair, day in and day out. Marijuana makes her feel a little bit better. I don't require a letter of diagnosis for people 65 or older—things wear out—or for people who are blind or deaf, as they say it helps their other senses" (Fuhrman, 1995).

What are your views regarding the prescribed use of marijuana, especially when these clubs or cooperatives provide seriously ill patients with a safe and reliable source of medical cannabis information and patient support? What about buying clubs for recreational use of marijuana—are your views similar to buying clubs selling marijuana only for medicinal purposes? Would you support a cannabis buyers' club or cooperative in your community that sells medical marijuana and recreational marijuana? What are your views regarding federal laws that prohibit such establishments while states pass laws allowing these establishments to legally operate? How do you think this current problem of the illegality on the federal level should be resolved? Finally, how do you think this dilemma will be resolved in your lifetime?

Data from Nolde, H. (2002, July 1). Medical pot war rages on. *Marin Independent Journal*. Retrieved from http://cannabisnews.com/news/13/thread13278.shtml; Fuhrman, R. A. (1995). Cannabis buyers' club flourishes in 'Frisco." San Francisco, CA: Cannabis Buyers' Club; Goldberg, C. (1996, February 26). Marijuana club helps those in pain. *The New York Times*. Retrieved from http://query.nytimes.com/gst/fullpage.html?res=9C06E6DF1139F936A15751C0A960958260&sec=&spon=&pagewanted=all; ProCon.org. (2013). How many people in the United State use medical marijuana? Santa Monica, CA: Author. Retrieved from http://medicalmarijuana.procon.org/view.answers.php?questionID=001199; ProCon.org. (2018, May 17). Number of legal medical marijuana patients. Santa Monica, CA: Author; ProCon.org. (2019, July 24). Legal medical marijuana states and DC. Santa Monica, CA: Author.

**medical marijuana** provides cannabis, primarily the THC from the cannabis plant, as a drug to calm or relieve symptoms of an illness. At the heart of this controversy is the use of an illicit drug for medical purposes. However, the desire to use cannabis in this fashion is nothing new. Between 1840 and 1900, European and American medical journals published more than 100 articles on the therapeutic use of the drug known then as *Cannabis indica* (or Indian hemp) and now as *marijuana*. It was recommended as an appetite stimulant, muscle relaxant, analgesic, hypnotic, and anticonvulsant. As late as 1913, Sir William Osler recommended it as the most satisfactory remedy for migraines (Grinspoon & Bakalar, 1995).

Marijuana was used to treat a variety of human ills in folk and formal medicine for thousands of years in South Africa, Turkey, South America, and Egypt, as well as such Asian countries as India, Malaysia, Myanmar, and Siam. Thus, marijuana, known as *cannabis* back then, has a 5,000-year-old medical history that came to an abrupt end in the United States by passage of the Marijuana Tax Act of 1937. When the Marijuana Tax Act became law, marijuana was legally classified as a narcotic, and medical use of this substance effectively ceased at that time. Only since 1990 has there been organized renewed interest in possible medical uses for cannabis. Because of potential clinical uses for marijuana, enforcement of laws prohibiting the use of this substance has been controversial (see "Holding the Line: Despite Federal Drug Laws Prohibiting the Cultivation, Possession, Use, and the Sale of Marijuana, States Sanction Cannabis Buyers' Clubs").

Marijuana has been shown to be effective in the treatment of certain types of medical conditions. However, because medications exist that are at least as effective and without abuse potential such as legally approved **Marinol** (dronabinol), to date, none of these applications have been approved by the Food and Drug Administration (FDA). The potential medical uses that have been described by researchers (Abood & Martin, 1992; Consroe & Sandyk, 1992; Iversen, 1993) and proponents (ProCon. org, 2012a) for the medical uses of marijuana are described in the following sections.

### ■ Reduction in Intraocular (Eye) Pressure

**Glaucoma**, the second-leading cause of blindness, is caused by uncontrollable eye pressure (Julian, 1994; National Eye Institute, 2010). Marijuana lowers glaucoma-associated intraocular pressure, even though it does not cure the condition or reverse blindness (Goldstein, 1995; Green, 2006; Loria, 2018; NIDA, 2010c).

### ■ Cancer

Recent animal studies have shown that marijuana extracts may help kill certain cancer cells and reduce the size of others. Evidence from one cell culture study suggests that purified extracts from whole-plant marijuana can slow the growth of cancer cells from one of the most serious types of brain tumors. Research in mice showed that treatment with purified extracts of THC and CBD, when used with radiation, increased the cancer-killing effects of the radiation (Loria, 2018; NIH, 2015c; Scott, Dalgleish, & Liu, 2014).

In November 2010, Arizona began to issue cards that allow the users to purchase marijuana for medicinal purposes.

---

**KEY TERMS**

**medical marijuana**
use of the THC in cannabis as a drug to calm or relieve symptoms of an illness

**Marinol**
FDA-approved synthesized THC in capsule form (dronabinol); primarily used to treat nausea and vomiting; often prescribed to people diagnosed with AIDS

**glaucoma**
potentially blinding eye disease causing continual and increasing intraocular pressure

## ■ Antiasthmatic Effect

Some research indicates that short-term marijuana smoking improves breathing for asthma patients. Marijuana smoke dilates the lungs' air passages (bronchodilation). Other findings also show, however, that the lung-irritating properties of marijuana smoke seem to offset its benefits. The adverse effects of marijuana smoke remain controversial (NIDA, 2006, 2010c). Regardless, marijuana may still prove useful when other drugs are not effective because of the different mode of action in causing bronchodilation.

Another study made a distinction between short-term and long-term marijuana smoking, emphasizing a distinction: "Short-term exposure to marijuana is associated with bronchodilation. However, physiologic data were inconclusive regarding an association between long-term marijuana smoking and airflow obstruction measures. Long-term marijuana smoking is associated with increased respiratory symptoms suggestive of obstructive lung disease" (Barclay & Vega, 2007).

## ■ Pain Control

Marijuana can ease pain.

Marijuana is quite effective for the chronic pain that plagues millions of Americans, especially as they age. Part of its allure is that it is clearly safer than opiates (it is impossible to overdose on and far less addictive) and it can take the place of NSAIDs such as Advil or Aleve, if people can't take them due to problems with their kidneys or ulcers or GERD. (Grinspoon, 2018)

In particular, it can ease the pain of multiple sclerosis, and nerve pain in general. (Loria, 2018)

## ■ Muscle-Relaxant Effect

Some studies indicate that muscle spasms are relieved when patients with muscle disorders such as multiple sclerosis use marijuana. Researchers have found that the key medicinal ingredients of cannabis, THC and CBD, have beneficial effects in treating muscle spasms and spasticity. "Many patients report that medical cannabis is effective in relieving their muscle spasms. Medical cannabis may also be effective in alleviating uncontrollable and debilitating muscle tremors. Some patients with severe spasticity report that medical cannabis

is the only treatment that allows them to function" (Loria, 2018; Grinspoon, 2018).

## ■ Antiseizure Effect

Marijuana has both convulsing and anticonvulsant properties and has been considered for use in preventing seizures associated with epilepsy. In studies with animal models, the cannabinoids reduced or increased seizure activities, depending on how the experiments were conducted. One or more of the components of marijuana may be useful in combination with other standard antiseizure medication. "New evidence suggests that a chemical derived from marijuana may be an effective treatment for patients with drug-resistant forms of epilepsy" (Kwon, 2016). The Epilepsy Foundation, comprising parent advocates, proposes that cannabis should be a legalized treatment option for physicians and patients dealing with epilepsy (Loria, 2018; Rabinski, 2015).

## ■ Antidepressant Effect

Some research studies have suggested that cannabis is a promising remedy for treating physical and mental conditions. "Neuroscientists from the University of Buffalo's Research Institute on Addictions found that endocannabinoids—chemical compounds in the brain that activate the same receptors as THC, an active compound in marijuana—may be helpful in treating depression that results from chronic stress" (Gregoire, 2015). The use of cannabis—marijuana—stabilized moods and reduced symptoms of depression (Gregoire, 2015; Loria, 2018; Wilde, 2015).

## ■ Analgesic Effect

Published testimonials have reported that marijuana can relieve the intense pain associated with migraine and chronic headaches or inflammation (Green, 2006; Grinspoon & Bakalar, 1995). Among chronic pain populations, survey data indicate that use of cannabis is common, and clinical trials have indicated that inhaled marijuana can alleviate neuropathic pain (Cone, Kaplan, Black, Robert, & Moser, 2008; Gardner, 2010; Green, 2006; NORML, 2013). In South Africa, native women smoke cannabis to dull the pain of childbirth (Hamid, 1998; Solomon, 1966). The pain-relieving potency of marijuana has not been carefully studied and compared with other analgesics such as narcotics or aspirin-type drugs.

### ▮ Antinauseant

Marijuana can relieve the nausea that accompanies chemotherapy known as *chemotherapy-induced nausea and vomiting* (CINV) for cancer treatment (Havelka, 2017 NIDA, 2010c; Robson, 2001).

> Overpowering. That's how cancer patients describe the onslaught that occurs within the first 24 hours after starting chemotherapy. . . . The most dreaded side effect is the extreme bouts of nausea and vomiting (called emesis). This isn't just regular [CINV]. It is severe and usually occurs right away, with a peak window of 6–24+ hours after treatment. (Havelka, 2017)

In summary, the use of cannabinoids derived from cannabis "activates a neurotransmitter that decreases the sensation of nausea" (Havelka, 2017).

### ▮ Appetite Stimulant

Marijuana is also a powerful appetite stimulant (NIDA, 2010c; NORML, n.d.). The stimulant effects on appetite are seen as useful for patients with human immunodeficiency virus, AIDS wasting syndrome, or dementia, as well as those with eating disorders (NORML, n.d.; Sewester, 1993).

### ▮ Alzheimer's Disease and Dementia

"The 2006 study, published in the journal *Molecular Pharmaceutics,* found that THC (the active chemical in marijuana) slows the formation of amyloid plaques by blocking the enzyme in the brain that makes them. These plaques kill brain cells and are associated with Alzheimer's" (Loria, 2018).

## Short-Term Consequences of Smoking Marijuana

Discomforts associated with smoking marijuana include dry mouth, dry eyes, increased heart rate, and visible signs of intoxication such as bloodshot eyes and puffy eyelids (Brown University Health Education, 2007). Marijuana overactivates the parts of the brain that contain receptors (a protein molecule that receives chemical signals from outside a cell). In cell biology, a receptor is a structure on the surface of a cell (or inside a cell) that selectively receives and binds a specific substance. The high (altered state of consciousness) occurs when receptors in the brain are affected

by the THC in marijuana (NIH, 2015d). Other short-term effects of marijuana use include the following (NIH, 2015d):

- altered senses (e.g., seeing brighter colors),
- altered sense of time,
- changes in mood,
- impaired body movement,
- difficulty with thinking and problem-solving, and
- impaired memory.

## Long-Term Consequences of Smoking Marijuana

Marijuana affects brain development. When teenagers begin using marijuana, the drug may reduce thinking, memory, and learning functions and affect how the brain builds connections between the areas necessary for these functions. Marijuana's effects on these abilities may last a long time or may even be permanent (NIH, 2015d).

Long-term consequences, lasting longer than intoxication, and cumulative effects of chronic abuse of smoking marijuana include the following.

- *Respiratory problems*: Many of these problems are the same as for cigarette smokers. Persistent coughing, symptoms of bronchitis, and more frequent chest colds are possible symptoms from the 400-plus chemicals (some carcinogenic) in marijuana smoke. "Researchers report that marijuana cigarettes release five times as much carbon monoxide into the bloodstream and three times as much tar into the lungs of smokers as tobacco cigarettes" (American Lung Association, 2019; Marijuana Detox, 2008; NIDA. 2010c).
- *Memory and learning*: Regular marijuana use compromises the ability to learn and to remember information by impairing the ability to focus, sustain, and shift attention. One study also found that long-term use reduces the ability to organize and integrate complex information. Marijuana impairs short-term memory and decreases motivation to accomplish tasks, even after the high is over.
- *Fertility*: Long-term marijuana use suppresses the production of hormones that help regulate the reproductive system. For men, this can cause decreased sperm counts, and the heaviest users can experience erectile

dysfunction. Women may experience irregular periods from heavy marijuana use.

- *Mental effects*: Long-term marijuana use has been linked to mental illness in some users, such as temporary hallucinations, temporary paranoia, and worsening symptoms in patients with schizophrenia (NIH, 2015d).
- *Addictive properties*: For a small percentage of people who use it, long-term marijuana use can lead to addiction (NIDA, 2010c). Researchers estimate that about 9% of marijuana users become addicted and that this number is higher among those who start their marijuana use at a young age (about 17%) and among daily users (25% to 50%) (NIDA, 2012; NIH, 2015e). Both animal and human studies show physical and psychological withdrawal symptoms from marijuana, including irritability, restlessness, insomnia, nausea, and intense dreams. The withdrawal syndrome has been described as being similar to that of nicotine withdrawal, with people trying to quit reporting irritability, sleeping difficulties, cravings, and anxiety (NIDA, 2010c; NIH, 2015e). Tolerance to marijuana also builds up rapidly. Heavy users need eight times higher doses to get the same effects as infrequent users. It is estimated that 10% to 14% of users will become *heavily* dependent during the addiction process. More than 120,000 people in the United States seek treatment for marijuana addiction every year (Brown University Health Education, 2007).

All of these effects have either been disputed or shown to be exaggerated by proponents who are in favor of medical marijuana. Proponents for medical marijuana argue that "its illegality [marijuana] . . . imposes much anxiety and expense on suffering people, forces them to bargain with illicit drug dealers, and exposes them to the threat of criminal prosecution" (Grinspoon & Bakalar, 1995, p. 1876). For a list of states currently allowing the use of marijuana for medical purposes, see the "Holding the Line" feature earlier in this chapter.

## The Physiological Effects of Marijuana Use

Although the literature on marijuana use repeatedly states that "in 5,000 years of medical and nonmedical use, marijuana has not caused a single overdose death" (Grinspoon & Bakalar, 1995,

p. 1875), the effects of marijuana use should not be overlooked. We begin by examining the effects of marijuana on the lungs.

When marijuana smoke is inhaled into the lungs, THC, the psychoactive ingredient, leaves the blood rapidly through metabolism and efficient uptake into the tissues. THC and its metabolites tend to bind to proteins in the blood and remain stored for long periods in body fat. Five days after a single dosage of THC, 20% remains stored, whereas 20% of its metabolites remain in the blood (Indiana Prevention Resource Center, 1996). Complete elimination of a single dose can take up to 30 days. Measurable levels of THC in blood from chronic users often can be detected for several days or even weeks after their last marijuana cigarette (joint).

When marijuana is smoked, THC is rapidly absorbed into the lungs and transported to the brain, with THC reaching the brain within as little as 14 seconds after inhalation. Marijuana is metabolized more efficiently through smoking than via intravenous injection or oral ingestion.

A summary of major findings regarding the inhalation of marijuana smoke compiled by the CDC concludes that "[s]moke from marijuana contains many of the same toxins, irritants, and carcinogens as tobacco smoke. Smoking marijuana can also lead to a greater risk of bronchitis, cough, and phlegm production. These symptoms generally improve when marijuana smokers quit" (CDC, 2018).

Smoking is also three to five times more potent than these two methods (Jones, 1980; Kaplan & Whitmire, 1995). Other findings that compare the amounts of marijuana with tobacco conclude that "three to four joints a day is about as harmful to your lungs as smoking a pack of cigarettes a day" (Reaney, 2000, p. 1).

Some of the effects of cannabis described in the following sections are unquestionably toxic in that they can either directly or indirectly produce adverse health effects. Other effects may be beneficial in treating some medical conditions. The use of marijuana, THC, and synthetic cannabinoids, either alone or in combination with other drugs, continues to be discussed and investigated for treating pain, inflammation, glaucoma, nausea, and muscle spasms (Iversen, 1993; NIDA, 2010c).

### ■ Effects on the Brain

As THC enters the brain, it causes the user to feel euphoric—or high—by acting on the brain's reward system, which is made up of regions that govern the response to pleasurable things like sex and chocolate, as well as to most drugs of abuse. THC activates the reward system in the same way that nearly all drugs of abuse do: by stimulating brain cells to release the chemical dopamine (NIDA, 2010c). THC affects the nerve cells in the part of the brain where memories are formed. This makes it hard for the user to recall recent events (such as what happened a few minutes ago). It is hard to learn while high—a working short-term memory is required for learning and performing tasks that call for more than one or two steps (NIDA, 2007, 2010c).

An interesting finding by researchers reported that, among a group of long-time heavy marijuana users in Costa Rica, people had great trouble when asked to recall a short list of words (a standard test of memory). People in that study group also found it difficult to focus their attention on the tests given to them.

As people age, they normally lose nerve cells in a region of the brain that is important for remembering events. Chronic exposure to THC may hasten the age-related loss of these nerve cells. In one study, researchers found that rats exposed to THC every day for eight months (about one-third of their lifespan) showed a loss of brain cells comparable to rats that were twice their age. It is not known whether a similar effect occurs in humans. Researchers are still learning about the many ways that marijuana could affect the brain (NIDA, 2007).

When someone smokes marijuana, THC artificially stimulates the cannabinoid receptors (CBRs), disrupting the function of natural or endogenous cannabinoids. An overstimulation of these receptors in key brain areas produces the marijuana high, as well as producing other effects on mental processes. Over time, this overstimulation can alter the function of CBRs, which, along with other changes in the brain, can lead to addiction and to withdrawal symptoms when drug use stops (NIDA, 2010c).

## KEY TERMS

**altered perceptions**
changes in the interpretation of stimuli resulting from marijuana use

**munchies**
hunger experienced while under the effects of marijuana

## ■ Effects on the Central Nervous System

The primary effects of marijuana—specifically, THC—are on CNS functions. The precise CNS effects of consuming marijuana or administering THC can vary according to the expectations of the user, the social setting, the route of administration, and previous experiences (Abood & Martin, 1992; Jaffe, 1990). Smoking a marijuana cigarette can alter mood, coordination, memory, and self-perception. Usually, such exposure causes some euphoria, a sense of well-being, and relaxation. Marijuana smokers often claim heightened sensory awareness and **altered perceptions** (particularly a slowing of time), symptoms associated with hunger (the **munchies**), and a dry mouth (Hubbard, Franco, & Onaivi, 1999; Swan, 1994). High doses of THC or greater exposure to marijuana can cause hallucinations, delusions, and paranoia (American Psychiatric Association [APA], 1994; Goldstein, 1995; Hubbard et al., 1999; NIDA, 2007). Some users describe anxiety after high-dose exposure. Because of the availability and widespread use of marijuana, psychiatric emergencies from marijuana overdose are becoming somewhat common. Long-term, chronic users often show decreased interest in personal appearance or goals (part of the amotivational syndrome discussed previously in this chapter) as well as an inability to concentrate, make appropriate decisions, and recall information from short-term memory (Abood & Martin, 1992; Block, 1996).

The precise classification of THC is uncertain because the responses to marijuana are highly variable and appear to have elements of all three major groups of drugs of abuse. Consequently, marijuana use can cause euphoria and paranoia (like stimulants), drowsiness and sedation (like depressants), and hallucinations (like psychedelics). It is possible that THC alters several receptor or transmitter systems in the brain; this action would account for its diverse and somewhat unpredictable effects.

The dramatic discovery of a specific receptor site in the brain for THC, the cannabinoid receptor (previously mentioned), suggests that a selective endogenous marijuana system exists in the brain and is activated by THC when marijuana is consumed (Hudson, 1990; NIDA, 2007). Some researchers speculate that an endogenous fatty-acid–like substance called *anandamide* naturally works at these marijuana sites; efforts are being made to characterize this neurotransmitter (Iversen, 1993; NIDA, 2010c). From this discovery, a group of new therapeutic agents could be developed that can selectively interact with the marijuana receptors, resulting in medical benefits without the side effects that generally accompany marijuana use (Iversen, 1993; Swan, 1994).

## ■ Effects on the Respiratory System: Smoking Marijuana

Marijuana is often smoked like tobacco and also can cause damage to the lungs (Adams & Martin, 1996; Consroe & Sandyk, 1992; NIDA, 2010c). When smoking tobacco, nearly 70% of the total suspended particles in the smoke are retained in the lungs. Because marijuana smoke is inhaled more deeply than tobacco smoke, even more tar residues may be retained with its use.

Smoke is a mixture of tiny particles suspended in gas, mostly carbon monoxide. These solid particles combine to form a residue called *tar*. Cannabis produces more tar (as much as 50% more) than an equivalent weight of tobacco and is smoked in a way that increases the accumulation of tar (Jones, 1980).

More than 140 chemicals have been identified in marijuana smoke and tar. A few are proven carcinogens; many others have not yet been tested for carcinogenicity. The carcinogen benzopyrene, for example, is 70% more abundant in marijuana smoke than in tobacco smoke. When cannabis tar is applied to the skin of experimental animals, it causes precancerous lesions similar to those caused by tobacco tar. Similarly, whenever isolated lung tissue is exposed to these same tars, precancerous changes result (Hollister, 1986; Jones, 1980; Turner, 1980).

Special white blood cells in living lung tissue—alveolar macrophages—play a role in removing debris from the lungs. When exposed to smoke from cannabis, these cells are less able to remove bacteria and other foreign debris.

Smoking only a few marijuana cigarettes a day for six to eight weeks can significantly impair pulmonary function. Laboratory and clinical evidence often indicate that heavy use of marijuana causes cellular changes, and those heavy users have a higher incidence of such respiratory problems as laryngitis, pharyngitis, bronchitis, asthmalike conditions, cough, hoarseness, and dry throat (Goldstein, 1995; Hollister, 1986). Some reports emphasize the potential damage to pulmonary function that can occur from chronic marijuana use (NIDA, 1991). Evidence suggests that many 20-year-old smokers of both hashish and tobacco

have lung damage comparable to that found in heavy tobacco smokers older than 40. It is believed that the tar from tobacco and marijuana has damaging effects, but it is not known whether smokers who use both products suffer synergistic or additive effects (Hollister, 1986; Jones, 1980).

## ■ Effects on the Respiratory System: Vaporizing Marijuana

As just presented, the evidence shows that smoking marijuana clearly appears to be hazardous to the respiratory system, having the most negative impact on the lungs. A newer method of use—vaporizing marijuana—is slowly increasing among users, even though one major study of 6,883 people surveyed showed that "only 152 participants (2.2%) reported vaporizing as their primary method for cannabis use" (Earleywine & Smucker Barnwell, 2007, p. 3). However, another survey found that 18% of e-cigarette users in Connecticut high schools had "vaped" marijuana or used an e-cigarette to get high and that more than one-quarter of those students who described themselves as dual users of e-cigarettes and marijuana had used the devices to get high (Thompson, 2015).

Cannabis smoke contains gaseous and particulate matter with the potential to create symptoms of respiratory problems. Although cannabis smoke creates fewer problems than cigarette smoke, increasing its safety has the potential to improve quality of life. One step toward increasing the safety of cannabis involves the use of vaporizers. Vaporizers heat cannabis to temperatures that cause the release of cannabinoids in a fine mist without creating the toxins associated with combustion. Although vaporizers are not common knowledge in popular culture, a recent photograph of one appeared in the *New England Journal of Medicine*, and information about the machine is becoming more available. A vaporizer has the potential to increase the safety of cannabis use, but data from human users appear only rarely (Earleywine & Smucker Barnwell, 2007). Research suggests that "the respiratory effects of cannabis can decrease with the use of a vaporizer. The data reveal that respiratory symptoms like cough, phlegm, and tightness in the chest increase with cigarette use and cannabis use, but are less severe among users of a vaporizer" (Earleywine & Smucker Barnwell, 2007, p. 3).

The cost of a vaporizer unit can usually run several hundred dollars and more. Using a vaporizer for marijuana use may decrease respiratory problems, but other hazards continue to exist. Users who replace smoking marijuana with vaporizing marijuana continue to run the risk of marijuana dependence (addiction), impaired driving skills, and cognitive, mainly short-term memory, impairment. Also, users often mix smoking with vaporizing, resulting in increased usage. Thus, although pulmonary damage is likely to be minimized when using a vaporizer, other deleterious consequences from marijuana use are continued and even increased.

## ▪ Effects on the Cardiovascular System

In human beings, cannabis causes both *vasodilation* (enlarged blood vessels) and an increase in heart rate related to the amount of THC consumed (Abood & Martin, 1992; NIDA, 2000, 2010c). The vasodilation is responsible for the reddening of the eyes often seen in marijuana smokers. In physically healthy users, these effects, as well as slight changes in heart rhythm, are transitory and do not appear to be significant. In patients with heart disease, however, the increased oxygen requirement from an accelerated heart rate may have serious consequences. The effect of cannabis on people with heart rhythm irregularities is not known. Because of vasodilation caused by marijuana use, abnormally low blood pressure can occur when standing. In addition, if a user stands up quickly after smoking, a feeling of lightheadedness or fainting may result. Chronic administration of large doses of THC to healthy volunteers shows that tolerance develops to the increase in heart rate and vasodilation.

People with cardiovascular problems seem to be at an increased risk when smoking marijuana (Hollister, 1986; NIDA, 2010c). Marijuana products also bind hemoglobin, limiting the amount of oxygen that can be carried to the heart tissue. In a few cases, this deficiency could trigger heart attacks in susceptible people (Palfai & Jankiewicz, 1991). The National Academy of Sciences' Institute of Medicine recommends that people with cardiovascular disease avoid marijuana use because there are still many unanswered questions about its effects on the cardiovascular system (Mack & Joy, 2001).

A demonstration of a marijuana vaporizer.

## ▪ Effects on Sexual Performance and Reproduction

Drugs may interfere with sexual performance and reproduction in several ways (Hanson, 2011). They may alter sexual behavior, affect fertility, damage the chromosomes of germ cells in the male or female, or adversely affect fetal growth and development.

The Indian Hemp Commission (Taylor, 1963, 1966), which wrote the first scientific report on cannabis, commented that it had a sexually stimulating effect like alcohol. However, the report also said that cannabis was used by Asian Indian ascetics to destroy the sexual appetite. This apparent discrepancy may be a dose-related effect. Used occasionally over the short term, marijuana may act as an **aphrodisiac** by decreasing CNS inhibitions. In addition, the altered perception of time under the influence of the drug could make the pleasurable sensations appear to last longer than they actually do.

Marijuana affects the sympathetic nervous system, increasing vasodilation in the genitals

**KEY TERM**

**aphrodisiac**
compound that is believed to cause sexual arousal

and delaying ejaculation. Some biologists and public health researchers believe that frequent high doses of marijuana adversely impacts **spermatogenesis**.

> Studies of marijuana abuse in humans and animal models of exposure to marijuana suggest that marijuana smoking adversely impacts spermatogenesis. Data is less clear for moderate consumption levels and multiple studies have found higher serum testosterone concentrations among marijuana consumers. (Nassan et al., 2019)

While other researchers found that in the comparison between men who have smoked marijuana during any period of their lifetime versus men who never inhaled this drug had

> significantly higher concentrations of sperm, . . . according to new research led by Harvard T.H. Chan School of Public Health. The study, conducted in the Fertility Clinic at Massachusetts General Hospital, also found that there was no significant difference in sperm concentrations between current and former marijuana smokers. (Arvizu, Mínguez-Alarcón, Williams, & Hauser, 2019)

Despite these effects, there are no documented reports of children with birth defects in which the abnormality was linked to the father's marijuana use. It is possible that damaged sperm cells are incapable of fertilization (so that only normal sperm cells reach the egg) or that the abnormal sperm appearance is meaningless in terms of predicting birth defects. When marijuana use stops, the quality of sperm gradually returns to normal over several months.

Less-reliable data are available on the effects of cannabis on female libido, sexual response (ability to respond to sexual stimulation with vaginal lubrication and orgasm), and fertile reproductive (menstrual) cycles (Consroe & Sandyk, 1992; Grinspoon, 1987). However, some researchers have found that heavy marijuana use in women may inhibit ovulation and that use during pregnancy can harm the development of the fetus, resulting in neurobehavioral and physical abnormalities, and increase the chance of a premature birth (Silverberg, 2007). Data from the Reproductive Biology Research Foundation show that chronic smoking of cannabis (at least three times per week for the preceding six months) adversely affects the female reproductive cycle. Results with women were correlated with work in rhesus monkeys; it

was found that THC blocks ovulation (because of effects on female sex hormones).

Data on the effects of marijuana use during pregnancy and lactation are inconclusive. Some evidence suggests that the use of this drug by pregnant women can result in intrauterine growth retardation, which is characterized by increased fetal mortality, prolonged labor, low-birth-weight babies (Foley, 2007), and behavioral abnormalities in newborns (Fernandez-Ruiz, Rodriguez de Fonseca, Navarro, & Ramos, 1992; Nahas & Latour, 1992; Roffman & George, 1988). THC and other cannabinoids pass through the blood–placenta barrier and concentrate in the fetus's fatty tissue, including its brain. Ethical considerations prevent duplication of the experiment in humans.

Women who smoke marijuana during pregnancy also often use other drugs such as alcohol, tobacco, and cocaine, which are all known to have adverse effects on the developing fetus. Because multiple drugs are used, it is difficult to isolate the specific effects of marijuana during pregnancy. Like many other substances, THC is taken up by the mammary glands in lactating women and is excreted in the breast milk. Effects of marijuana in the breast milk on human infants have not been determined (Christina, 1994; Murphy & Bartke, 1992).

In studies on mice and rats (but not humans), the addition of THC to pregnant animals decreased litter size, increased fetal reabsorption, and increased the number of reproductive abnormalities in the surviving offspring (Dewey, 1986). The offspring of the drug-treated animal mothers had reduced fertility and more testicular abnormalities. The dose of cannabinoids used in these studies was higher than that used by humans. Clearly, pregnant women should be advised against using marijuana, even though there are few direct data on its prenatal effects in humans (Dewey, 1986; Foley, 2007; Murphy & Bartke, 1992).

## ■ Tolerance and Dependence

It has been known for many years that tolerance to some effects of cannabis builds rapidly in animals—namely, the drug effect becomes less

**KEY TERM**

**spermatogenesis**
biological development involving the production of mature sperm cells that occurs in the male gonad of a sexually reproducing organism (Biology Online, 2020)

intense with repeated administration. Frequent use of high doses of marijuana or THC in humans produces similar tolerance. For example, increasingly higher doses must be given to obtain the same intensity of subjective effects and increased heart rate that occur initially with small doses (Abood & Martin, 1992; NIDA, 2010c).

Frequent high doses of THC also can produce mild physical dependence. Healthy subjects who smoke several joints a day or who are given comparable amounts of THC orally experience irritability, sleep disturbances, weight loss, loss of appetite, sweating, and gastrointestinal upsets when drug use is stopped abruptly. However, not all subjects experience this mild form of withdrawal.

It is much easier to show psychological dependence in heavy users of marijuana (Abood & Martin, 1992; Hollister, 1986; NIDA, 2010c). Psychological dependence involves an attachment to the euphoric effects of the THC content in marijuana and may include craving for the drug. The subjective psychological effects of marijuana intoxication include a heightened sensitivity to and distortion of sight, smell, taste, and sound; mood alteration; and diminished reaction time.

### DIAGNOSIS: CANNABIS DEPENDENCE

In general, outright cannabis addiction, with obsessive drug seeking and compulsive drug-taking behavior, is relatively rare with low-THC cannabis. Contributing to this is the fact that the less potent forms of marijuana are the most readily available in the United States, resulting in most chronic users in this country having little problem controlling or eliminating their cannabis habit if they so desire.

*The Diagnostic and Statistical Manual of Mental Disorders*, fifth edition (*DSM-5*), recognizes a diagnosis of cannabis dependence. It is characterized by compulsive use and hours per day spent acquiring and using the substance. Compulsive users persist in their use despite knowledge of physical problems (e.g., chronic cough related to smoking) or psychological problems (e.g., excessive sedation resulting from repeated use of high doses) (APA, 2013).

## ∎ Chronic Use

Research on chronic use of marijuana (repeated daily use of this drug) in the 1970s indicated the possibility of three types of damage: (1) chromosomal damage (Stenchever, Kunysz, & Allen, 1974), (2) cerebral atrophy (shrinking of the brain) (Campbell et al., 1971), and (3) lowered

capacity of white blood cells to fight disease (Suciu-Foca, Armand, & Morishima, 1974). These findings have all been contradicted or refuted by subsequent research. The only finding that appears credible is that heavy use of this drug impairs lung capacity (Bloodworth, 1987; Henneberger, 1994; Kaplan & Whitmire, 1995; NIDA, 2010c; Oliwenstein, 1988; Swan, 1994). Other evidence indicates that chronic, heavy use of cannabis can lead to unforeseen calamities in some users (see "Case in Point: Chronic Marijuana Use").

We have pointed out that marijuana produces a variety of psychoactive effects. One of those effects is sedation of unwanted emotional states such as anxiety, which are inevitable given the conflicts and turmoil of living in our fast-paced society today. As with the chronic use of any psychoactive drug that produces sedating effects, normal emotional and psychosocial development can be arrested by heavy marijuana consumption. For example, a youth who is usually high at a party avoids the anxieties and embarrassments of introspective and critical interpersonal interactions but instead will be interested in thrill-seeking behavior such as romantic and sexual involvements, experimentation with and heavy use of other drugs, and other types of more daring experiences.

From years of research with this drug, we find that heavy and chronic use of marijuana can easily compromise cognitive functions such as short-term memory, concentration, moderately taxing problem-solving, and even spiritual growth and development. Often, the more serious costs in using this drug are that the individual acquires a poor record for development and advancement of learning, as is often expected in educational settings (schools, colleges, trade schools, and universities). Another cost that is more serious is the retardation in emotional development. Such types of development are often obscured by being high all the time. Further, in such chronic use cases, much time is wasted seeking the pleasures and sometimes the longed-for thrills derived from the habitual use of marijuana.

The amotivational syndrome, in fact, can be deconstructed into the sedation, depression, and cognitive impairment discussed throughout this chapter. The user who is experiencing a subjective euphoric effect, enjoying the presence and social reinforcement of peers, feeling no pain, and remaining cognitively unfocused finds it difficult to intellectually grasp the learned experiences

## ► CASE IN POINT

### Chronic Marijuana Use

The following comments show how marijuana use can become a disturbing habit:

I guess you could say it was peer pressure. Back in 1969, I was a sophomore in college, and everyone was smoking "dope." The Vietnam War was in progress, and most students on college campuses were heavily involved in the drug scene. I first started smoking marijuana when my closest friends did. I was taught by other students who already knew how to enjoy the effects of "pot."

I recall that one of my fellow students used to supply me with "nickel bags," and many users nicknamed him "God." How did he get such a name? Because he sold some very potent marijuana that at times caused us to hallucinate.

I used pot nearly every day for about a year and a half, and hardly an evening would pass without smoking dope and listening to music. Smoking marijuana became as common as drinking alcohol. I used it in the same manner a person has a cocktail after a long day. At first, I liked the effects of being "high," but later I became so accustomed to the stuff that life appeared boring without it.

After graduating, my college friends went their separate ways, and I stopped using marijuana for a few years. A year later, in graduate school, a neighborhood friend reintroduced me to the pleasure of smoking pot. I began to use it again but not as often. Whenever I experienced some pressure, I would use a little to relax.

After finishing my degree, I found myself employed at an institution that at times was boring. Again, I started using pot at night to relax, and somehow it got out of control. I used to smoke a little before work and sometimes during lunch. I thought all was well until one day I got fired because someone accused me of being high on the job.

Soon afterward, I came to the realization that the use of marijuana can be very insidious. It has a way of becoming psychologically addictive, and you don't even realize it. When I was high, I thought that no one knew, and that I was even more effective with others. Little did I know, I was dead wrong and fooling no one. *(From Venturelli's research files, male, age 39, May 1990)*

In May 2013, this same interviewee, now 62 years of age, was asked if he had any additional remarks about the interview he gave in May 1990. He said the following:

How time flies! Now it's been 23 years since I was interviewed. I can say that as a very recent retired man I still occasionally dabble in pot smoking and still enjoy it. I did quit for many years, but about 9 years ago, a lifelong friend of mine was visiting and I asked him to get me some so we could "fire one up after a long time." We did that and it was nothing but memory lane while we were smoking it. We had a good time talking and laughing about things we did during those as you say [referring to the interviewer] days of chronic marijuana use.

What I really like about the pot these days is that you have real quality and really powerful stuff. Several puffs and you can get really stoned. My friend picked up some blueberry marijuana and it was really powerful. I only had a few puffs during the first few hours I tried it with him and I was really high. Very potent stuff for sure. Thank God we did not have this stuff when I was doing it a lot in my younger days. I think I really would have been totally addicted. Back when I was young, we had stuff that was effective in achieving a buzz but not feeling it so strongly as the stuff my friend brought me. Get this: he got it from his grandchild when he told him to get him some because he was visiting me.

I want to emphasize, I only smoke marijuana about once or twice a month now and I am very careful to not like it too much because as I said in my first interview back in 1990, I really had a problem years ago. It's real good today and think that there must be a lot more addiction to this drug today in comparison to when I was young when we did not have such potent stuff. *(Second interview with same interviewee on May 12, 2013, from Venturelli's research files, male, age 62)*

from such developmental delays. Although many do mature out of use, this step may occur only after years of development have slipped away, never to be regained. Sometimes treatment interventions are necessary to get the subject into a drug-free state and reunited with non–drug-using peer groups.

In concluding this chapter, we note that the history of this drug indicates that usage and availability will remain widespread despite all the efforts to eradicate its existence. Even with every prevention effort to date, marijuana remains the most popular illicit drug, topped only by alcohol and tobacco, which are licit drugs.

# LEARNING PORTFOLIO

## Key Terms

## Discussion Questions

1. What are the sociologial and psychological reasons why the very young continue to use marijuana at alarming rates despite the illegality of usage?

2. Do you believe that prosecution for marijuana where marijuana is prohibited should be more or less rigid than it currently is? Explain.

3. Debate whether marijuana use adversely affects driving capabilities.

4. Either directly interview or imagine interviews with several users and nonusers of marijuana. How do you think they would answer the question of whether their critical-thinking skills are adversely affected by this drug?

5. Among marijuana users, do you believe that the amotivational syndrome exists as a syndrome? Interview several users and try to either add to the characteristics of this syndrome from your interviews or modify the syndrome as discussed in this chapter.

6. In light of the information in "Holding the Line," do you believe the sale of marijuana for medical or recreational purposes will ever be completely legalized at the state and federal levels in all 50 states? Why or why not for medical purposes, and why or why not for recreational purposes?

7. What is your reaction to legalizing marijuana as a controlled substance? Give reasons either for or against legalization.

8. Do you believe consistent use of marijuana changes the user's personality? If so, what do you think are the changes?

9. Summarize how marijuana affects the brain, CNS, respiratory system, cardiovascular system, and sexual performance and reproduction.

10. Debate how much family upbringing and attachment to a religion affect later drug use.

11. From reading this chapter, try to explain why most heroin users have used marijuana, whereas the vast majority of marijuana users never advance to such highly addictive drugs.

12. Explain how a user of cannabis might develop psychological dependence.

13. Do you believe that use of marijuana is more or less harmful than use of tobacco products? Should they be regulated differently?

14. Why do you think that in 2018 youth marijuana attitudes were more accepting of marijuana use and that perceived risk of regular marijuana use declined in all three grades (8th, 10th, and 12th) (Johnston et al., 2019)?

# Summary

1. Marijuana consists of the dried and crushed leaves, flowers, stems, and seeds of the *cannabis* plant. Tetrahydrocannabinol is the primary mind-altering (psychoactive) ingredient in marijuana. There are three main strains: *Cannabis sativa, Cannabis indica,* and *Cannabis ruderalis.* They differ "in their chemical composition, physiological aesthetic, and medical application" (ProCon.org, 2012a). *C. sativa* originates from Colombia, Mexico, Jamaica, South Africa, Thailand, and Southeast Asia and generally causes uplifting and energetic feelings, stimulates the appetite, and provides pain relief from certain ailments (Budfacts.com, 2009). It is cultivated in hot climates. It is a brighter green than the *C. indica* strain and has narrower leaves. It reaches an average height of more than six feet when grown outdoors. *C. indica* originates from hash-producing countries (e.g., Afghanistan, Pakistan, India, Turkey, Morocco, and Tibet) (ProCon.org, 2012a), and its effects include body relaxation, stress relief, and calmness and serenity (Budfacts.com, 2009). *C. indica* is grown in warm, not hot, climates; the plants are shorter (less than six feet tall) and darker green in color and with wider leaves (Weedist, 2012). The THC content in the two strains differs, with *C. indica* generally having a lower THC content (Weedist, 2012). *C. ruderalis* has the lowest amount of THC of the three main strains, although it tolerates a wide variety of climates. This species is native to Asia and Central and Eastern Europe and has adapted to short growing seasons in these extreme three climates (Hyde, 2015).

2. There are approximately four cannabis derivatives (or spin-offs). The first derivative, *sinsemilla,* includes the more potent strains that are available today. Hashish is the second derivative; it contains a pure form of resin produced from the flowers of female cannabis plants. A third, more recent derivative from cannabis is *marijuana wax.* To date, this is one of the most powerful and most potent (80% pure THC) types of marijuana on the illegal and legal drug markets. Smoking or vaporizing this type of marijuana "leads to a quicker, stronger high" (Kimble, 2013). It is thought to be the strongest form of marijuana on the market. A fourth derivative is *ganja,* which is produced in India. This preparation consists of the dried tops of female plants. *Ganja* is also used as a slang term for marijuana. There are more than 200 slang terms for marijuana.

3. Marijuana remains controversial for the following reasons: (a) a high percentage of the U.S. population uses this drug; (b) it continues to be illegal in most states; (c) 33 states and the District of Columbia have legalized the sale of marijuana for medical purposes, although the use and sale of marijuana in these states remains *illegal at the federal level*; (d) marijuana accounts for a large number of arrests for simple possession; (e) it is one of the least addictive types of drugs; and (f) most marijuana users do not graduate to other, more addictive illicit drugs.

4. The effects of marijuana can vary according to the user's expectations and where the drug is consumed (surroundings). At low doses, such as when smoked, ingested (eaten), or vaporized, the *C. indica* strain often has a sedative effect. At higher doses, it can produce hallucinations and delusions.

5. As with tobacco, heavy use of marijuana can impair pulmonary function, cause chronic respiratory diseases (such as bronchitis and asthma), and promote lung cancer. Marijuana causes vasodilation and a compensatory increase in heart rate. The effects of marijuana on sexual performance and reproduction are controversial. Some studies have indicated this substance enhances sexual arousal.

6. Tolerance to the CNS and cardiovascular effects of marijuana develops rapidly with

repeated use. Although physical dependence and associated withdrawal are minor, psychological dependence can be significant in chronic, heavy users.

7. Tetrahydrocannabinol (THC), the active ingredient in marijuana, has been used to treat a variety of seemingly unrelated medical conditions. This drug is indicated for treatment of nausea and vomiting in cancer patients receiving chemotherapy and for treatment of anorexia (lack of appetite) in AIDS patients. Other potential therapeutic uses for THC include relief of intraocular pressure associated with glaucoma, as an antiasthmatic drug, as a muscle relaxant, as an antiseizure drug, as an antidepressant, as a tumor-reducing agent, and as an analgesic to relieve migraines and other types of pain.

8. The age groups most likely to use marijuana are the following: (a) highest lifetime use, adults between 18 and 25 years of age (51.9%), and (b) highest past-year (31.6%) and past-month (19.1%) use in the 18- to 25-year age category. There is a sharp drop in past-year and past-month use in the 26-and-older age group.

9. The NSDUH reported that among persons aged 12 or older the overall rate of past-year marijuana use was 13.5% in 2015, 13.9% in 2016, 15.0% in 2017, and 15.9% in 2018 (SAMHSA, 2019).

10. Drugged driving is defined as operating a motor vehicle with a measurable quantity (or quantities) of a legal or an illegal drug in the driver's body, which most often results in impaired driving. Recent findings reported by the Canadian Centre on Substance Abuse note that (a) among young drivers, driving after using cannabis is more prevalent than driving after drinking; (b) cannabis impairs the cognitive and motor abilities necessary to operate a motor vehicle and doubles the risk of crash involvement; (c) after alcohol, cannabis is the most commonly detected substance among drivers who die in traffic crashes; (d) cannabis use is not uncommon among drivers involved in collisions; and (e) the police have the tools and authority required to detect and arrest drivers who are impaired by cannabis (Beirness & Porath-Waller, 2015).

11. Currently, 33 states are medical marijuana states (along with DC) that have enacted laws to legalize medical marijuana: Alaska, Arizona, Arkansas, California, Colorado, Connecticut, Delaware, Florida, Hawaii, Illinois, Louisiana, Maine, Maryland, Massachusetts, Michigan, Minnesota, Missouri, Montana, Nevada, New Hampshire, New Jersey, New Mexico, New York, North Dakota, Ohio, Oklahoma, Oregon, Pennsylvania, Rhode Island, Utah, Vermont, Washington, and West Virginia (ProCon.org, 2019). Out of 325,719,178 of the U.S. population as of March 17, 2018 (ProCon.org, 2019), the *estimated* number of medical marijuana users would be 2,132,777 (ProCon.org, 2019).

12. Marijuana affects brain development. When marijuana users begin using as teenagers, the drug may reduce thinking, memory, and learning functions and affect how the brain builds connections between the areas necessary for these functions. Marijuana's effects on these abilities may last a long time or even be permanent (NIH, 2015d).

13. Long-term consequences of regularly using marijuana include respiratory problems, memory and learning impairments, problems with fertility, mental effects (hallucinations, paranoia, and disorganized thinking). Marijuana can become an addictive drug.

14. Legalization of the medical use of marijuana entails permitting physicians to prescribe marijuana for medical problems with the idea that terminally ill as well as other types of sick patients could be given the option of smoking marijuana as opposed to taking the already-approved Marinol (dronabinol), an FDA-approved version of THC in capsule form.

# References

Abel, E. L. (1989). *Marijuana: The first twelve thousand years.* New York, NY: Plenum.

Abood, M., & Martin, B. (1992, May). Neurobiology of marijuana abuse. *Trends in Pharmacological Sciences, 13,* 201–206.

Abood, M. E., & Martin, B. R. (1996, May). Molecular neurobiology of the cannabinoid receptor. *International Review of Neurobiology, 39,* 197–219.

Adams, I. B., & Martin, R. R. (1996). Cannabis: Pharmacology and toxicology in animals and humans. *Addiction, 91,* 1585–1614.

American Lung Association. (2019, August 7). Marijuana and lung health. Chicago, IL: Author. Retrieved from https://www.lung.org/stop-smoking/smoking-facts/marijuana-and-lung-health.html

American Psychiatric Association (APA). (1994). *Diagnostic and statistical manual of mental disorders,* 4th ed. Washington, DC: Author.

American Psychiatric Association (APA). (2013). *Diagnostic and statistical manual of mental disorders,* 5th ed. Washington, DC: Author.

Anslinger, H. J., & Cooper, C. R. (1937, July). Marijuana: Assassin of youth. *American Magazine, 124,* 19–20, 150–153.

Arvizu, M., Mínguez-Alarcón, L., Williams, P., & Hauser, R. (2019, February 5). Marijuana smoking linked with higher sperm concentrations. Cambridge, MA: Harvard T. H. Chan School of Public Health. Retrieved from https://www.hsph.harvard.edu/news/press-releases/marijuana-smoking-sperm-counts/

Aydin A., & Fulton, J. A. (2015, August 12). Cannabinoid poisoning. Medscape. Retrieved from http://emedicine.medscape.com/article/833828-overview

Barclay, L., & Vega, C. (2007, February 19). Marijuana use linked to bronchodilation and respiratory symptoms. Medscape. Retrieved from http://www.medscape.org/viewarticle/552405

Bauman, K. E., & Ennett, S. T. (1996, February). On the importance of peer influence for adolescent drug use: Commonly neglected considerations. *Addiction, 91,* 185–198.

BC Bud Depot. (n.d.). Welcome to the BC Bud Depot. Retrieved from https://www.bcbuddepot.com

Beirness, D. J., & Porath-Waller, A. J. (2015). Clearing the smoke on cannabis: Respiratory effects of cannabis smoking. Ottawa, Ontario, Canada: Canadian Centre on Substance Abuse. Retrieved from https://www.ccsa.ca/clearing-smoke-cannabis-respiratory-effects-cannabis-smoking

Benson, J. (2010, August 30). Prescription painkillers now gateway drugs to hard drug use. NaturalNews.com. Retrieved from http://www.naturalnews.com/029606_prescription_opioids_gateway_drugs.html

Berkowitz, A. (1991). Following imaginary peers: How norm misperceptions influence student substance abuse. In G. Lindsay and G. Rulf (Eds.), *Project direction* (Module No. 2, pp. 12–15). Muncie, IN: Ball State University.

Biology Online. (2020). "Spermatogenesis." Retrieved from https://www.biologyonline.com/dictionary/spermatogenesis

Block, R. I. (1996). Does heavy marijuana use impair human cognition and brain function? *Journal of the American Medical Association, 275,* 560–561.

Bloodworth, R. C. (1987). Major problems associated with marijuana use. *Psychiatric Medicine, 3,* 173–184.

Blows, S., Ivers, R. Q., Connor, J., Ameratunga, S., Woodward, M., & Norton, R. (2005). Marijuana use and car crash injury. *Society for the Study of Addiction, 100,* 605–611.

Bridgeman, M. B., & Abazia, D. T. (2017, March). Medicinal cannabis: History, pharmacology, and implications for the acute care. Setting. *Pharmacy and Therapeutics, 42,* 180–188. Retrieved from https://www.ncbi.nlm.nih.gov/pmc/articles/PMC5312634/

Brigham Young University. (2008, October 1). News release: National study finds religiosity curbs teen marijuana use by half. Provo, UT: Author.

Brown, M. W., & Massaro, S. (1996, February 20). *Attention and memory impaired in heavy users of marijuana.* Rockville, MD: National Institute on Drug Abuse.

Brown University Health Education. (2007). Marijuana. Retrieved from https://www.brown.edu/campus-life/health/services/promotion/alcohol-other-drugs-other-drugs/marijuana

Buff, J. (1970). Greasers, dopers, and hippies: Three responses to the adult world. In L. Howe (Ed.), *The white majority* (pp. 60–70). New York, NY: Random House.

Califano, J. A. (1996, September 23). Dangerous indifference to drugs. *Washington Post,* p. A-19.

"California cannabis market expected to reach $5.1 billion market value." (2018, June 19). MarketNewsUpdates. Retrieved from https://www.prnewswire.com/news-releases/california-cannabis-market-expected-to-reach-51-billion-market-value-685917412.html

Campbell, A. G., Evans, M., Thomson, J. L., & Williams, M. J. (1971). Cerebral atrophy in young cannabis smokers. *Lancet, 19,* 1219–1225.

Cannibismarketcap. (2019, April 23). Understanding cannabis: Sativa vs. indica vs. ruderalis. [Blog post]. Retrieved from https://www.cannabismarketcap.io/blog/understanding-canna bis-sativa-vs-indica-vs-ruderalis

Cannabis Information and Support. (2013, April 1). Cannabis potency. Retrieved from http://ncpic.org.au/ncpic/publications/factsheets/article/cannabis-potency

Carter, E. (1980). *Cannabis in Costa Rica.* Philadelphia, PA: Institute for the Study of Human Issues.

Center for Substance Abuse Research (CESAR). (2007, March 19). Marijuana distribution relies primarily on generosity of friends and family. CESAR FAX 16. Retrieved from http://www.cesar.umd.edu/cesar/cesarfax/vol16/16-11.pdf

Center for Substance Abuse Research (CESAR). (2010a). More than one in ten children in the U.S. live with substance-abusing or substance-dependent parent. CESAR FAX 18, May 11. Retrieved from http://www.cesar.umd.edu/cesar/cesarfax/vol18/18-18.pdf

Center on Addiction. (2001). Casa report: Spirituality and religion reduce risk of substance abuse. Retrieved from http://www.casacolumbia.org/absolutenm/templates/PressReleases.aspx?articleid=115&zoneid=48

Centers for Disease Control and Prevention (CDC). (2018, February 27). Marijuana: How can it affect your health? Atlanta, GA: Author. Retrieved from https://www.cdc.gov/marijuana/health-effects.html

Centers for Disease Control and Prevention (CDC). (2019, November 26). Outbreak of lung injury associated with the use of e-cigarette, or vaping, products. Atlanta, GA: Author. Retrieved from https://www.cdc.gov/tobacco/basic_information/e-cigarettes/severe-lung-disease.html

Chait, L., & Pierri, J. (1992). Effect of smoked marijuana on human performance: A critical review. In L. Murphy & A. Bartke (Eds.), *Marijuana/cannabinoids, neurobiology and neurophysiology* (pp. 387–424). Boca Raton, FL: CRC Press.

Christina, D. (1994). *Marijuana: Personality and behavior.* Tempe, AZ: Do It Now.

Coleman, J. S. (1961). *The adolescent society.* New York, NY: Free Press of Glencoe.

Cone, E. J., Kaplan, Y. H., Black, D. L., Robert, T., & Moser, F. (2008). Urine drug testing of chronic pain patients: Licit and illicit drug patterns. *Journal of Analytic Toxicology, 32,* 532–543.

Consroe, P., & Sandyk, R. (1992). Potential role of cannabinoids for therapy of neurological disorders. In L. Murphy & A. Bartke (Eds.), *Marijuana/cannabinoids, neurobiology and neurophysiology* (pp. 459–524). Boca Raton, FL: CRC Press.

Couper, F. J., & Logan, B. K. (2004, March). *Cannabis/Marijuana (Δ⁹-tetrahydro-cannabinol, THC).* Drugs and Human Performance Fact Sheets. Washington, DC: National Highway Traffic Safety Administration.

Dewey, W. L. (1986). Cannabinoid pharmacology. *Pharmacological Reviews, 38,* 48–50.

"Do marijuana and driving mix?" (2010, June 7). TheWeek. Retrieved from http://theweek.com/article/index/203778/do-marijuana-and-driving-mix

Doctor, V. (2019, March 13). 2019 strongest marijuana strain, according to experts. International Business Times. Retrieved from https://www.ibtimes.com/2019-strongest-marijuana-strains-according-experts-2774932

Dreher, M. C. (1982). *Working men and ganja: Marijuana use in rural Jamaica.* Philadelphia, PA: Institute for the Study of Human Issues.

Drug Enforcement Administration (DEA). (2013, April). The DEA position on marijuana. Washington, DC: Author. Retrieved from http://www.justice.gov/dea/docs/marijuana_position_2011.pdf

Drug Science. (2019). Marijuana production in the United States (2006)—Comparison with other cash crops. London, UK: Author.

Dupont, R. L. (2011, March 31). Drugged driving research: A white paper. Rockville, MD: Institute for Behavior and Health. Retrieved from http://www.whitehouse.gov/sites/default/files/ondcp/issues-content/drugged-driving/nida_dd_paper.pdf

Earleywine, M., & Smucker Barnwell, S. (2007, April 16). Decreased respiratory symptoms in cannabis users who vaporize. *Harm Reduction Journal, 4,* 1–6.

Eckert, P. (1989). *Jocks and burnouts: Social categories and identity in the high school.* New York, NY: Teachers College, Columbia University.

ElSohly, M. (2009). *Quarterly report: Potency monitoring projected.* Report 104, December 16, 2008 thru March 15, 2009. Oxford, MS: School of Pharmacy, University of Mississippi.

Evans, P. (2019, May 7). 8 incredible facts about the booming US marijuana industry. Markets Insider. Retrieved from https://markets.businessinsider.com/news/stocks/weed-us-marijuana-industry-facts-2019-5-1028177375

Fernandez-Ruiz, J., Rodriguez de Fonseca, F., Navarro, M., & Ramos, J. (1992). Maternal cannabinoid exposure and brain development: Changes in the ontogeny of dopaminergic neurons. In L. Murphy & A. Bartke (Eds.), *Marijuana/cannabinoids, neurobiology and neurophysiology* (pp. 118–164). Boca Raton, FL: CRC Press.

Ferner, M. (2015, January 28). Legal marijuana is the fastest-growing industry in the U.S.: Report. Huffington Post. Retrieved from http://www.huffingtonpost.com/2015/01/26/marijuana-industry-fastest-growing_n_6540166.html

Foley, M. R. (2007). Drug use during pregnancy. *Merck Manuals Online Edition.* Whitehouse Station, NJ: Merck & Co.

Retrieved from http://www.merck.com/mmhe/sec22/ch259/ch259a.html

Fuhrman, R. A. (1995). Cannabis buyers' club flourishes in 'Frisco." San Francisco, CA: Cannabis Buyers' Club.

Fuller, D. (2008, October). Adolescent brain function adversely affected by marijuana use. Medical News Today. Retrieved from http://www.medicalnewstoday.com/articles/125443.php

Gaines, G. (1992). *Teenage wasteland: Suburbia's dead-end kids.* New York, NY: Harper Perennial.

Gardner, A. (2010, August 30). Study: Smoking pot may ease chronic pain. CNN.com. Retrieved from http://www.cnn.com/2010/HEALTH/08/30/health.pot.reduce.pain/index.html

Gardner, E. (1992). Cannabinoid interaction with brain reward systems: The neurobiological basis of cannabinoid abuse. In L. Murphy & A. Bartke (Eds.), *Marijuana/cannabinoids, neurobiology and neurophysiology* (pp. 275–335). Boca Raton, FL: CRC Press.

Ghaly, S. J. (2015, October 31). What is marijuana wax? Herb. Retrieved from http://www.thestonerscookbook.com/2015/10/31/what-is-marijuana-wax/

Goldberg, C. (1996, February 26). Marijuana club helps those in pain. *The New York Times.*

Goldstein, A. (1994). *Addiction from biology to drug policy.* New York, NY: Freeman.

Goldstein, F. (1995). Pharmacological aspects of substance abuse. *Remington's pharmaceutical sciences,* 19th ed. Easton, PA: Mack.

Goode, E. (1999). *Drugs in American society.* Boston, MA: McGraw-Hill.

Gossop, M. (1987). *Living with drugs,* 2nd ed. Aldershot, UK: Wildwood House.

Governing. (2019). State marijuana laws in 2019 map. Washington, DC: eRepublic. Retrieved from https://www.governing.com/gov-data/safety-justice/state-marijuana-laws-map-medical-recreational.html

Green, C. A. (2006). Gender and use of substance abuse treatment services. *Alcohol Research and Health, 29,* 55–62.

Greenblatt, J. C. (1999, July). *Adolescent self-reported behaviors and their association with marijuana use.* Rockville, MD: National Clearinghouse for Alcohol and Drug Information.

Gregoire, C. (2015, February 6). New study finds marijuana to be effective against depression. Huffington Post. Retrieved from http://www.huffingtonpost.com/2015/02/06/marijauna-depression_n_6622126.html

Grinspoon, L. (1987, November). Marijuana. *Harvard Medical School Mental Health Letter, 4,* 1–4.

Grinspoon, P. (2018, January 15). Medical marijuana. Cambridge, MA: Harvard Health Publishing. Retrieved from https://www.health.harvard.edu/blog/medical-marijuana-2018011513085

Grinspoon, P. (2020, April 10). Medical marijuana. Cambridge, MA: Harvard Health Publishing. Retrieved from https://www.health.harvard.edu/blog/medical-marijuana-2018011513085

Grinspoon, L., & Bakalar, J. B. (1995). Commentary, marijuana as medicine: A plea for reconsideration. *Journal of the American Medical Association, 273,* 1875–1876.

Hamid, A. (1998). *Drugs in America: Sociology, economics, and politics.* Gaithersburg, MD: Aspen.

Hanson, D. J. (2011, July 28). Pharmaceuticals and sexual performance. Addiction Inbox. Retrieved from http://addiction-dirkh.blogspot.com/2010/09/sex-drugs-and-sex.html

Hanson, D. J. (2019). Stepping stone theory of alcohol and drugs (Discover here what it is. Potsdam, NY: State University of New York, 2019. Retrieved from https://www.alcoholproblemsandsolutions.org/stepping-stone-theory/

Hardcastle, M. (2007, March 15). Marijuana use can threaten teen's academic success. About.com. Retrieved from http://teenadvice.about.com/od/marijuanause/a/marijana1.htm

Hartig, H., & Geiger, A. W. (2018, October 8). About six-in-ten Americans support marijuana legalization. Washington, DC: Pew Research Center.

Havelka, J. (2017, July 26). How cannabis is used for nausea and vomiting relief. Leafly. Retrieved from https://www.leafly.com/news/health/marijuana-for-nausea-and-vomiting-relief

Heitzeg, N. (1996). *Deviance: Rulemakers and rulebreakers.* St. Paul, MN: West Publishing.

Henneberger, M. (1994, February 6). Pot surges back: It's like a whole new world. *The New York Times,* pp. C19, F-18.

Hollister, L. E. (1986). Health aspects of *Cannabis. Pharmacological Reviews, 38,* 39–42.

Hongmei, Y., Stanton, B., Cottrel, L., Kaljee, L., Galbraith, J., . . . , & Wu, Y. (2006, September). Parental awareness of adolescent risk involvement: Implications of overestimates and underestimates. *Journal of Adolescent Health, 39,* 353–361.

Hubbard, J. R., Franco, S. E., & Onaivi, E. S. (1999). Marijuana: Medical implications. *American Family Physician, 283,* 231–240.

Hudson, R. (1990, August 9). Researchers identify gene that triggers marijuana's "high." *Wall Street Journal,* p. B2.

Hyde, W. (2015, June 4). What is *Cannabis ruderalis?* Leafly. Retrieved from https://www.leafly.com/news/cannabis-101/what-is-cannabis-ruderalis

Indiana Prevention Resource Center. (1996). *Factline on: Marijuana*. Bloomington, IN: Author.

Iversen, L. (1993). Medicinal use of marijuana. *Nature, 365*, 12–13.

Iverson, L. (2005). Long-term effects of exposure to *Cannabis. Current Opinion in Pharmacology, 5*, 69–72.

Jaffe, J. H. (1990). Drug addiction and drug abuse. In A. Gilman, T. Rall, A. Nies, & P. Taylor (Eds.), *The pharmacological basis of therapeutics*, 8th ed. (pp. 522–575). New York, NY: Pergamon.

Johns, A. (2001). Psychiatric effects of *Cannabis. British Journal of Psychiatry, 178*, 116–122.

Johnston, L. D., Miech, R. A., O'Malley, P. M., Bachman, J. G., Schulenberg, J. E., & Patrick, M. E. (2018). *Monitoring the Future: National survey results on drug use: 1975–2017: Overview key findings on adolescent drug use*. Ann Arbor, MI: University of Michigan, Institute for Social Research.

Johnston, L. D., Miech, R. A., O'Malley, P. M., Bachman, J. G., Schulenberg, J. E., & Patrick, M. E. (2019). *Monitoring the Future: National survey results on drug use 1975–2018: Overview, key findings on adolescent drug use*. Ann Arbor, MI: University of Michigan, Institute for Social Research.

Johnston, L. D., O'Malley, P. M., Bachman, J. G., & Schulenberg, J. E. (2009). *Monitoring the Future: National survey results on drug use*. Bethesda, MD: National Institute on Drug Abuse.

Johnston, L. D., O'Malley, P. M., Bachman, J. G., & Schulenberg, J. E. (2012). *Monitoring the Future: National survey results on drug use, 1975–2011: Volume I, Secondary school students*. Ann Arbor, MI: University of Michigan, Institute for Social Research.

Johnston, L. D., O'Malley, P. M., Bachman, J. G., & Schulenberg, J. E. (2013), *Monitoring the Future: National survey results on drug use, 1975–2012: Volume I, Secondary school students*. Ann Arbor, MI: University of Michigan, Institute for Social Research.

Join Together Staff. (2006, December 19). Biggest U.S. cash crop: Marijuana. Partnership for Drug-Free Kids. Retrieved from http://www.drugfree.org/join-together /drugs/biggest-us-cash-crop

Jones, R. T. (1980). Human effects: An overview. In *Marijuana research findings: 1980*. NIDA Research Monograph No. 31. Washington, DC: National Institute on Drug Abuse.

Julian, B. S. (1994). alt.hemp *Cannabis*/marijuana FAQ. Amherst, MA: University of Massachusetts at Amherst. Retrieved from http://www.faqs.org/faqs/drugs/hemp -marijuana

Kandel, D. B., Griesler, P. C., Lee, G., Davies, M., & Shaffsan, C. (2001). *Parental influences on adolescent marijuana use and the baby boom generation: Findings from the 1995–1996 national household surveys on drug abuse*. Rockville, MD: Substance Abuse and Mental

Kaplan, L. F., & Whitmire, R. (1995, May 21). Pot—It's potent, prevalent and preventable. *Salt Lake Tribune, 250*, 9.

Kaplan, R. (2017, November 22). The different type of medical marijuana. Denver, CO: Buddy Boy Brands. Retrieved from https://www.buddyboybrands.com/blog /different-types-of-medical-marijuana

Kelly, T., Foltin, R., Enurian, C., & Fischman, M. (1994). Effects of THC on marijuana smoking, drug choice and verbal report of drug liking. *Journal of Experimental Analysis of Behavior, 61*, 203–211.

Kendler, K. S., Gardner, C. O., & Prescott, C. A. (1997). Religion, psychopathology, and substance use and abuse: A multimeasure, genetic-epidemiologic study. *American Journal of Psychiatry, 154*, 322–329.

Kimble, J. (2013, October 22). Everything you need to know about marijuana wax. Complex. 22 October 2013. Retrieved from http://www.complex.com/pop -culture/2013/10/marijuana-wax-facts-info/marijuana -wax-nicknames

Kwon, D. (2016, January 22). Can cannabis treat epileptic seizures? *Scientific American*. Retrieved from https:// www.scientificamerican.com/article/can-cannabis-treat -epileptic-seizures/

Leger, D. L. (2012, December 20). Survey: 1 in 15 high school students smoking pot. *USA Today*. Retrieved from http:// www.usatoday.com/story/news/nation/2012/12/19 /national-drug-survey-youth-marijuana/1779563/

Liberty Mutual Insurance. (2013, April 24). One in four teens admits to driving under the influence and many believe it does not impact their safety. Boston, MA: Author. Retrieved from https://www.libertymutualgroup .com/about-lm/news/news-release-archive/articles /one-in-four-teens-admits-to-driving-under-the-influence -and-many-believe-it-does-not-impact-their-safety

Liska, K. (1997). *Drugs and the human body*, 5th ed. Upper Saddle River, NJ: Prentice Hall.

Loria, K. (2018, March 7). 23 health benefits of marijuana. Business Insider. Retrieved from https://www .businessinsider.com/health-benefits-of-medical -marijuana-2014-4

Mack, A., & Joy, J. (2001). *Marijuana as medicine? The science beyond the controversy*. Washington, DC: National Academy Press.

Marijuana Detox. (2008). Marijuana facts. Retrieved from http://www.marijuana-detox.com/m-facts.htm

"Marijuana menaces youth." (1936). *Scientific American, 154*, 151.

Mathias, R. (1996, January–February). Marijuana impairs driving-related skills and workplace performance. *NIDA Notes, 11*, 6.

McCabe, S. E. (2008, May). Misperceptions of nonmedical prescription drug use: A web survey of college students. *Addictive Behavior, 33*, 713–724.

Melina, R. (2011, September 13). Not my kid: Parents severely underestimate teens' drug and alcohol use. Live Science. Retrieved from http://www.livescience.com/16037-parents-underestimate-kids-substance.html

Miech, R. A., Johnston, L. D., O'Malley, P. M., Bachman, J. G., Schulenberg, J. E., & Patrick, M. E. (2019). *Monitoring the Future National Survey Results on Drug Use, 1975–2018: Volume I, Secondary school students.* Ann Arbor, MI: University of Michigan, Institute for Social Research.

Murphy, L., & Bartke, A. (1992). Effects of THC on pregnancy, puberty, and the neuroendocrine system. In L. Murphy & A. Bartke (Eds.), *Marijuana/cannabinoids, neurobiology and neurophysiology* (p. 539). Boca Raton, FL: CRC Press.

Musto, D. F. (1999). *The American disease: Origins of narcotic control*, 3rd ed. New York, NY: Oxford University Press.

Nahas, G., & Latour, C. (1992). The human toxicity of marijuana. *Medical Journal of Australia, 156*, 495–497.

Nassan, F. L., Arvizu, M, Minguez-Alarcón, L., Williams, P. L., Attaman, J., Petrozza, . . . , & Chavarro, J., for the EARTH Study Team. (2019). Marijuana smoking and markers of testicular function among men from a fertility centre. *Human Reproduction* Retrieved from https://insights.ovid.com/human-reproduction/hurep/2019/04/000/marijuana-smoking-markers-testicular-function/13/00004683

National Clearinghouse on Alcohol and Drug Information (NCADI). (1998, November). *Marijuana: Facts parents need to know.* Rockville, MD: Author.

National Eye Institute. (2010). *Facts about glaucoma.* Bethesda, MD: U.S. Department of Health and Human Services and National Institutes of Health.

National Highway Traffic Safety Administration. (2004). Cannabis/marijuana. In F. J. Couper and B. K. Logan (Eds.), *Drugs and human performance fact sheets.* Washington, DC: Author.

National Institute on Drug Abuse (NIDA). (1991). Drug abuse and drug abuse research. Washington, DC: Author.

National Institute on Drug Abuse (NIDA). (1998). Marijuana: Facts parents need to know. Rockville, MD: Author.

National Institute on Drug Abuse (NIDA). (2000, March 29). What is marijuana? Bethesda, MD: Author. Retrieved from http://www.nida.nih.gov/infofax/marijuana.html

National Institute on Drug Abuse (NIDA). (2006, October 21). Marijuana smoking is associated with a spectrum of respiratory disorders. Bethesda, MD: Author.

National Institute on Drug Abuse (NIDA). (2007, August). Marijuana: Facts parents need to know. Bethesda, MD: Author.

National Institute on Drug Abuse (NIDA). (2009). InfoFacts: Marijuana. Bethesda, MD: Author.

National Institute on Drug Abuse (NIDA). (2010a). Does marijuana use affect driving? (December). Bethesda, MD: Author. Retrieved from http://www.drugabuse.gov/publications/marijuana-abuse/does-marijuana-use-affect-driving

National Institute on Drug Abuse (NIDA). (2010b). DrugFacts: Drugged driving (December). Bethesda, MD: Author. Retrieved from http://www.drugabuse.gov/publications/drugfacts/drugged-driving

National Institute on Drug Abuse (NIDA). (2010c). Marijuana: Letter from the director. (September). Bethesda, MD: Author. Retrieved from http://www.drugabuse.gov/PDF/RRMarijuana.pdf

National Institute on Drug Abuse (NIDA). (2012, December). Drug facts: Marijuana. Bethesda, MD: Author.

National Institute on Drug Abuse (NIDA). (2015, December). *Monitoring the Future Study*: Overview of findings 2015. Bethesda, MD: Author. Retrieved from https://www.drugabuse.gov/related-topics/trends-statistics/monitoring-future/monitoring-future-survey-overview-findings-2015

National Institute on Drug Abuse (NIDA). (2016, August). Does marijuana use affect driving? Bethesda, MD: Author.

National Institute on Drug Abuse (NIDA). (2018, February). Synthetic cannabinoids (K2/Spice). Bethesda, MD: Author. Retrieved from https://www.drugabuse.gov/publications/drugfacts/synthetic-cannabinoids-k2spice

National Institute on Drug Abuse (NIDA). (2019, March). Drugged driving. Bethesda, MD: Author. Retrieved from https://www.drugabuse.gov/publications/drugfacts/drugged-driving

National Institutes of Health (NIH). (2011, November 2). NIH study examines nicotine as a gateway drug. Bethesda, MD: Author. Retrieved from http://www.nih.gov/news/health/nov2011/nida-02.htm

National Institutes of Health (NIH). (2015a). Drug facts: Synthetic cannabinoids. Bethesda, MD: Author.

National Institutes of Health (NIH). (2015b). Effects of marijuana—With and without alcohol—on driving performance. Bethesda, MD: Author. Retrieved from https://www.drugabuse.gov/news-events/news-releases/2015/06/effects-marijuana-without-alcohol-driving-performance

National Institutes of Health (NIH). (2015c). Drug facts: Marijuana as medicine. Bethesda, MD: Author. Retrieved from https://www.drugabuse.gov/publications/drugfacts/marijuana-medicine

National Institutes of Health (NIH). (2015d). Drug facts: What is marijuana? Bethesda, MD: Author. Retrieved from https://www.drugabuse.gov/publications/drugfacts/marijuana

National Institutes of Health (NIH). (2015e). Is marijuana addictive? Bethesda, MD: Author. Retrieved from https://www.drugabuse.gov/publications/research-reports/marijuana/marijuana-addictive

National Organization for the Reform of Marijuana Laws (NORML). (n.d.). Medical use. Retrieved from http://norml.org/marijuana/medical

National Organization for the Reform of Marijuana Laws (NORML). (2013, January 30). Chronic pain. Retrieved from http://norml.org/library/item/chronic-pain

"No valid reason to ban marijuana." (2010, August 9). *The Enquirer* [Cincinnati, OH].

Nolde, H. (2002, July 1). Medical pot war rages on. *Marin Independent Journal*. Retrieved from http://cannabisnews.com/news/13/thread13278.shtml

Norris, M., & Conrad, C. (n.d.). The experience of getting high. Amsterdam, The Netherlands: Cannabis Consumers Campaign. Retrieved from http://cannabisconsumers.org/reports/gettinghigh.php

Norton, A. (2009, July–August). Address client myths about marijuana: Professionals can counteract mixed messages in society that impede healing. *Addiction Professional, 4,* 32–34.

Office of National Drug Control Policy. (2003). Drug facts: Marijuana. Washington, DC: Office of National Drug Control.

Oliwenstein, L. (1988). The perils of pot. *Discover, 9,* 18.

Palfai, T., & Jankiewicz, H. (1991). *Drugs and human behavior.* Dubuque, IA: William C. Brown.

Pew Research Center. (2013, April 4). Majority now supports legalizing marijuana. Retrieved from http://www.people-press.org/2013/04/04/majority-now-supports-legalizing-marijuana/

Pew Research Center. (2014, April 2). Section 1: Perceptions of drug abuse, views of drug policies. Washington, DC: Author.

Pinto, F. G. (2016, February 4). What is marijuana wax? 7 things you may not know about dabs, shatter, and honey oil." NJ.com. Retrieved from http://www.nj.com/news/index.ssf/2016/02/pro-marijuana_advocates_debate_officials_warnings.html

Pollan, M. (1998, March–April). Medical marijuana: Can it help you? Should it be legal? A report from California. *Herbs for Health,* pp. 38–50.

Pope, H. G. Jr., & Yurgulen-Todd, D. (1996). The residual cognitive effects of heavy marijuana use in college students. *Journal of the American Medical Association, 275,* 521–527.

ProCon.org. (2012a, June 11). Medical marijuana: What are the differences between *Cannabis indica* and *Cannabis sativa,* and how do they vary in their potential medical utility? Retrieved from http://medicalmarijuana.procon.org/view.answers.php?questionID=000638#answer-id-011092

ProCon.org. (2012b). Is marijuana significantly more potent now than in the past? (February 7).

ProCon.org. (2013). 20 legal medical marijuana states and DC. Retrieved from http://medicalmarijuana.procon.org/view.resource.php?resourceID=000881

ProCon.org. (2018, May 17). Number of legal medical marijuana patients. Santa Monica, CA: Author.

ProCon.org. (2019, July 24). Legal medical marijuana states and DC. Santa Monica, CA: Author.

Rabinski, G. (2015, September 14). How does cannabis treat epilepsy? *Whaxy.*

Radcliffe, S. (2019, November 21). Vaping lung disease: Over 2,200 cases reported, teen gets "popcorn lung." New York, NY: Healthline. Retrieved from https://www.healthline.com/about?ref=footer#contact-us

Rahn, B. (2015, October 22). What are the strongest cannabis strains? Leafly. Retrieved from https://www.leafly.com/news/strains-products/what-are-the-strongest-cannabis-strains

Rand Drug Policy Research Center. (2002, December 26). Rand releases study on marijuana "gateway effect."

Reaney, P. (2000, March 20). Getting high may not be so harmless after all. Reuters Limited.

Right Diagnosis. (2010, August). Amotivational syndrome. Health Grades. Retrieved from http://www.wrongdiagnosis.com/a/amotivational_syndrome/intro.htm#whatis

Robson, P. (2001). Therapeutic aspects of cannabis and cannabinoids. *British Journal of Psychiatry, 178,* 107–115.

Roffman, R. A., & George, W. H. (1988). Cannabis abuse." In D. M. Donovan & G. A. Marlatt (Eds.), *Assessment of addictive behaviors* (pp. 78–86). New York, NY: Guilford.

Rosenthal, C. T. (2010). *Marijuana grower's handbook.* Oakland, CA: Quick American Publishing.

Rubin, V., & Comitas, L. (1975). *Ganja in Jamaica: A medical anthropological study of chronic marijuana use.* Paris, France: Mouton.

Scholastic. (2016). Peer pressure: Its influence on teens and decision making. Retrieved from http://headsup.scholastic.com/students/peer-pressure-its-influence-on-teens-and-decision-making

Schulenberg, J. E., Johnston, L. D., O'Malley, P. M., Bachman, J. G., Miech, R. A., & Patrick, M. E. (2019). *Monitoring the Future national survey results on drug use, 1975–2018: Volume II, College students and adults ages 19–60.* Ann Arbor, MI: University of Michigan, Institute for Social Research.

Schultes, R. E. (1978). Ethnopharmacological significance of psychotropic drugs of vegetal origin. In W. G. Clark & J. del Giudice (Eds.), *Principles of psychopharmacology,* 2nd ed. New York, NY: Academic Press, 1978.

Scott, K. A, Dalgleish, A. G., & Liu, W. M. (2014). The combination of cannabidiol and Δ9-tetrahydrocannabinol enhances the anticancer effects of radiation in an orthotopic murine glioma model. *Molecular Cancer Therapy, 13,* 2955–2967.

Sewell, R. A., Poling, J., & Sofuoglu, M. (2009). The effect of cannabis compared with alcohol on driving. *American Journal of Addictions, 18,* 185–193. Retrieved from http://www.ncbi.nlm.nih.gov/pmc/articles/PMC2722956/

Sewester, S. (1993). *Drug facts and comparisons.* St. Louis, MO: Kluwer.

Silverberg, C. (2007, July 5). Sex and marijuana. About.com.

Smoker, J. (2014, April 20). What is the difference between indica and sativa marijuana plants? The Weedblog. Retrieved from http://www.theweedblog.com/the-difference-between-indica-and-sativa-marijuana-plants/

Solomon, D. (Ed.). (1966). *The marihuana papers.* New York, NY: New American Library.

Sorden, S. (2011, October 7). The promise of social norming. John's Addiction.

Steinberg, L. (2011, February 3). How peers affect the teenage brain. *Psychology Today.* Retrieved from https://www.psychologytoday.com/us/blog/you-and-your-adolescent/201102/how-peers-affect-the-teenage-brain

Stenchever, M. A., Kunysz, T. J., & Allen, M. A. (1974, January). Chromosome breakage in users of marijuana. *American Journal of Obstetrics and Gynecology, 118,* 106–113.

Substance Abuse and Mental Health Services Administration (SAMHSA). (2007a). The NHSDA report: Religious involvement and substance use among adults. Rockville, MD: Author.

Substance Abuse and Mental Health Services Administration (SAMHSA) (2007b). The NHSDA report: Youth activities, substance use, and family income (April 19). Rockville, MD: Author.

Substance Abuse and Mental Health Services (SAMHSA). (2016, January). *Building on strengths: Tools for improving positive outcomes among boys and young men of color.* Rockville, MD: Author.

Substance Abuse and Mental Health Services (SAMHSA). (2017, March). Focus on prevention. Rockville, MD: Author. Retrieved from https://store.samhsa.gov/product/Focus-on-Prevention/sma10-4120

Substance Abuse and Mental Health Services Administration (SAMHSA). (2018). *2017 National Survey on Drug Use and Health: Detailed tables.* Rockville, MD: Author.

Substance Abuse and Mental Health Services (SAMHSA). (2019). Key substance use and mental health indicators in the United States: Results from the *2018 National Survey on Drug Use and Health.* Rockville, MD: Author. Retrieved from https://www.samhsa.gov/data/sites/default/files/cbhsq-reports/NSDUHNationalFindingsReport2018/NSDUHNationalFindingsReport2018.pdf

Suciu-Foca, N., Armand, J. P., & Morishima, A. (1974). Inhibition of cellular immunity in marijuana smokers. *Science, 183,* 419–420.

Sutherland, E. H. (1939). *Principles of criminology,* 3rd ed. (4th ed., 1947). Philadelphia, PA: Lippincott.

Swan, N. (1994, February–March). A look at marijuana's harmful effects. *NIDA Notes, 9,* 3–4.

Swan, N. (1996, March–April). Facts about marijuana and marijuana abuse. *NIDA Notes, 11,* 15.

Taylor, N. (1963). *Narcotics: Nature's dangerous gifts.* New York, NY: Dell.

Taylor, N. (1966). The pleasant assassin: The story of marijuana. In D. Solomon (Ed.), *The marihuana papers.* New York, NY: Signet Books.

Teen Challenge. (2000). *Drugs: Frequently asked questions.* South Australia: Pragin Press.

Thompson, D. (2015, September 7). Teens using e-cigarettes to "vape" pot, survey finds. HealthDay. Retrieved from http://consumer.healthday.com/public-health-information-30/marijuana-news-759/teens-using-e-cigarettes-to-smoke-pot-survey-finds-703025.html

Tudor, C. G., Petersen, D. M., & Elifson. K. W. (1987). An examination of the relationships between peer and parental influences and adolescent drug use. In C. D. Chambers, J. A. Inciardi, D. M. Petersen, H. A. Siegal, & O. Z. White *(Eds.), Chemical dependencies: Patterns, costs, and consequences.* Columbus, OH: Ohio University Press.

Turner, C. E. (1980). Chemistry and metabolism. In *Marijuana Research Findings: 1980.* NIDA Research Monograph No. 31. Washington, DC: National Institute on Drug Abuse.

U.S. Department of Transportation. (1993, November). *Marijuana and actual driving performance: Effects of THC on driving performance.* Washington, DC: National Highway Traffic Safety Administration.

Venkataraman, N. (2006, December 18). Marijuana called top U.S. cash crop. ABC News. Retrieved from http://abcnews.go.com/Business/story?id=2735017

Venturelli, P. J. (2000). Drugs in schools: Myths and Reality. In W. Hinkle & S. Henry *(Eds.), The Annals of the American Academy of Political and Social Science* (pp. 72–87). Thousand Oaks, CA: Sage Publications.

Venturelli, P. J. (2016). Drug use as a socially constructed problem. In H. H. Brownstein (Ed.), *The handbook of drugs and society* (pp. 177–196). West Sussex, UK: John Wiley & Sons.

Wallace, J. M., Myers, V. L., & Osai, E. R. (2004). *Faith matters: Race/ethnicity, religion and substance use.* Baltimore, MD: Annie E. Casey Foundation.

Walton, A. G. (2015, March 25). New study shows how marijuana's potency has changed over time. *Forbes.* Retrieved from http://www.forbes.com/sites/alicegwalton/2015/03/23/pot-evolution-how-the-makeup-of-marijuana-has-changed-over-time/#3b8c32745579

Way of Leaf. (2019, November 20). Cannabis wax; Everything you need to know in one resource. Piscataway, NJ: Yoad Development and Technology. Retrieved from https://www.marijuanabreak.com/cannabis-wax

Weedist. (2012, August 12). Cannabis 101: Differences between sativa and indica marijuana. Retrieved from http://www.weedist.com/2012/08/differences-between-sativa-and-indica-marijuana/

Wilde, C. (2015, February 4). *RIA neuroscience study points to possible use of medical marijuana for depression.* Buffalo, NY: University of Buffalo. Retrieved from http://www.buffalo.edu/news/releases/2015/02/004.html

Wren, C. S. (1996, February 20). Youth marijuana use rises. *The New York Times,* p. 1.

Zimmer, L., & Morgan, J. P. (1997). *Marijuana myths, marijuana facts: A review of the scientific evidence.* New York, NY: Lindesmith Center.

Zinberg, N. E. (1984). Drug, set, and setting: The basis for controlled intoxicant use. New Haven, CT: Yale University Press.

Zinberg, N. E., & Robertson, J. A. (1972). *Drugs and the public.* New York, NY: Simon & Schuster.

CHAPTER **14**

# Inhalants

## Did You Know?

▶ More than 1,000 different commercial and household products are commonly abused in the United States.

▶ Ordinary household products are misused as inhalants: glues and adhesives, nail polish remover, gasoline, paint thinner, spray paint, butane lighter fluid, propane gas, typewriter correction fluid, household cleaners, cooking sprays, deodorants, whipping cream aerosols, marking pens, and air conditioning coolants.

▶ Inhalant abuse is typically a problem of adolescents and teenagers.

▶ Each year, young people in this country die of inhalant abuse or suffer severe consequences, including permanent brain damage and damage to the heart, kidneys, and liver.

▶ Inhalant abusers can die suddenly and without warning; even first-time abusers have died from sniffing inhalants.

## Learning Objectives

**On completing this chapter, you should be able to:**

⟩ Understand that inhalant use is not harmless and that even one-time use could lead to sudden sniffing death syndrome.

⟩ List the household and commercial products that are most often abused as inhalants.

⟩ Describe the principal means of using household and commercial products as inhalants.

⟩ Identify signs of abuse.

⟩ Examine the current patterns of abuse among various groups.

⟩ List the dangers of inhalant abuse.

## Introduction

Inhalants are **volatile** substances that elicit psychological or physiological changes when introduced into the body via the lungs. They are rarely administered by any other route. Most cause intoxicating or **euphorigenic** effects or both. Many of these substances were never intended to be used by humans as drugs; consequently, they are not often thought of as having abuse potential. However, abuse of inhalants is a serious public health problem; according to data obtained for the *Monitoring the Future* (MTF) study sponsored by the National Institute on Drug Abuse (NIDA), 8.7% of 8th graders have misused an inhalant at least once in their lifetime. Among 10th and 12th graders, lifetime reported use was 6.5% and 4.4%, respectively (Miech et al., 2019). This lifetime frequency of inhalant abuse among 8th graders surpasses the frequency of abuse of such highly publicized drugs as cocaine (1.4%) and amphetamines (5.9%). For comparison, lifetime marijuana or hashish use was 13.9% in this age group (Miech et al., 2019).

According to the Substance Abuse and Mental Health Services Administration (SAMHSA), in 2018, an estimated 576,000 people aged 12 or older had used inhalants for the first time in the past 12 months, which averages to approximately 1,600 people per day. This same survey reported that in 2018 an estimated 308,000 adolescents aged 12 to 17 used inhalants for the first time in the past year. This number averages to approximately 840 adolescents each day who initiated inhalant use. These numbers were similar to the estimates for 2015–2017 (SAMHSA, 2019).

The vast majority of adolescents do not use inhalants. For example, in 2015, 97.3% did not report past year use of inhalants. Among adolescents who did use inhalants, more than half of

adolescents aged 12 to 17 who used inhalants in the past year, 59.0 % had indicated that they used these agents on one to 11 days, and 19.3 % indicated that they had used these agents 12 to 49 days. Further, approximately 14% of past-year inhalant users had used on 50 to 99 days in the past year. Approximately 8% of adolescents who used inhalants in the past year had used inhalants on 100 or more days in the past year (Lipari, 2017).

A widespread misconception is that inhalant abuse is a harmless phase that occurs commonly during normal childhood and teenage development and as such is not worthy of significant concern because young people will grow out of it without experiencing harm. On the contrary, numerous adolescents and teenagers in the United States die or are seriously injured each year as a result of inhalant abuse. Even first-time users may die from sudden sniffing death syndrome (SSDS), a condition characterized by serious cardiac **arrhythmia** occurring during or immediately after inhaling. Accurate statistics regarding the number of inhalant-associated deaths and injuries each year are unavailable, in part because medical examiners often attribute deaths from inhalant use to suicide, suffocation, or accidents. Nevertheless, every year young people in the United States die from inhalant abuse, and many more suffer severe consequences, such as damage to the brain, heart, kidneys, and liver (U.S. Consumer Product Safety Commission, n.d.).

Most inhalants are household or commercial products composed of several different chemicals. These compounds can act alone or synergistically to exert toxic effects. The potential of these agents to cause harm is compounded by the high concentrations of these substances absorbed in the body by inhalation and the tendency for these often lipid-rich (oily or fatty) substances to be retained in lipid-containing vital organs. Another important consideration is that the users are often developmentally immature and so can be more susceptible to the toxic effects of inhalants. The summation of these factors makes inhalants dangerous substances of abuse.

## KEY TERMS

**volatile**
readily evaporated at low temperatures

**euphorigenic**
having the ability to cause feelings of pleasure and well-being

**arrhythmia**
an irregular heartbeat

## History of Inhalants

The modern era of inhalant abuse can be traced to 1776, when British chemist Joseph Priestley synthesized nitrous oxide (Kennedy & Longnecker, 1990), a colorless gas with a slightly sweet odor and no noticeable taste. Roughly 20 years later, he and Humphry Davy suggested correctly that the gas might be useful as an anesthetic, and experiments were conducted to test this possibility.

Dentists contributed greatly to the introduction of nitrous oxide as an anesthetic. At a stage show in the 1840s, dentist Horace Wells noticed that one of the persons involved in the show injured himself while under the influence of nitrous oxide yet felt no pain. Wells was so impressed by this anesthetic effect that he subsequently allowed his own tooth to be extracted while under the influence of the gas. His experiment was a success; Wells did not experience pain. He went on to attempt to demonstrate his discovery at Massachusetts General Hospital in Boston; unfortunately, the patient cried out during the procedure and the experiment was deemed unsuccessful (Kennedy & Longnecker, 1990). Nevertheless, word of this demonstration and others like it spread, ultimately leading to the use of nitrous oxide and other volatile anesthetics as legitimate medical therapy.

Over the years, it was discovered that many chemicals, in addition to nitrous oxide, could be inhaled so as to alter psychological function. Such abuse of inhalants came to public attention in the 1950s when the news media reported that young people were getting high from sniffing glue. The term *glue sniffing* is still used today, but it is often used to describe inhalation of many products besides glue. In fact, more than 1,000 different products are misused as inhalants (U.S. Consumer Product Safety Commission, n.d.). These chemicals are not regulated like other drugs of abuse; hence, they are readily available to young people. This category of drugs can be classified into three major groups: volatile substances, anesthetics, and nitrites.

# Types of Inhalants

## ■ Volatile Substances

Over the past 50 years, the number of products containing volatile substances has increased substantially. This category of agents includes aerosols (e.g., spray paints, hair sprays, deodorants, vegetable oil sprays), art or office supplies (e.g., correction fluids, felt-tip marker fluids), adhesives (e.g., airplane and other glues), fuels (e.g., propane, gasoline), and industrial or household solvents (e.g., nail polish remover, paint thinners, dry-cleaning fluids). Some volatile substances exist as gases (e.g., nitrous oxide, the propellant in whipping cream cans), whereas others are liquids that vaporize at room temperature (e.g., gasoline). In some cases, the abuser inhales vapors directly from their original containers (called *sniffing* or *snorting*). Still others inhale volatile solvents from plastic bags (called *bagging*) or from old rags or bandannas soaked in the solvent fluid and held over the mouth (called *huffing*).

Acute effects of the volatile chemicals that are commonly abused include initial nausea with some irritation of airways causing coughing and sneezing. Low doses often bring a brief feeling of lightheadedness, mild stimulation followed by a loss of control, lack of coordination, and disorientation accompanied by dizziness and possible hallucinations. In some instances, higher doses can produce relaxation, sleep, or even coma. If inhalation is continued, dangerous **hypoxia** may occur and cause brain damage or death. In other cases, SSDS can occur. Other potential toxic consequences of inhaling such substances include hypertension and damage to the cardiac muscle, peripheral nerves, brain, and kidneys. In addition, chronic users of inhalants frequently lose their appetite, are continually tired, and experience nosebleeds. If use of inhalants persists, some of the damage may become irreversible (see "Here and Now: Chronic Solvent Abuse, Brain Abnormalities, and Cognitive Deficits").

### AEROSOLS

Chemicals associated with aerosol sprays are popular among young inhalant abusers. They include spray paints, deodorant and hair sprays, vegetable oil sprays for cooking, and fabric protector sprays (NIDA, 2012). Aerosol sprays are often abused not because of the effects produced by their principal ingredients, but because of the effects of their propellant gases. Inhalation of aerosol preparations can be dangerous because these devices are capable of generating high concentrations of the inhaled chemicals, much greater than those released more slowly from liquid products.

KEY TERM

**hypoxia**
state of oxygen deficiency

# HERE AND NOW
## Chronic Solvent Abuse, Brain Abnormalities, and Cognitive Deficits

Chronic inhalant abuse has long been associated with neurological damage and cognitive abnormalities that can range from mild impairment to severe dementia. In fact, the severity of these problems can be greater than for drugs often considered by the general population as being more harmful. For example, a 2002 report published by Neil Rosenberg of the University of Colorado Health Sciences Center found that chronic solvent abusers performed worse than chronic users of other drugs (especially cocaine and alcohol) on tests of working memory and executive function. In this study, abusers inhaled primarily vapors from spray paint containing toluene and averaged more than 10 years of abuse. More than half of the group reported near daily inhalant intoxication.

According to Rosenberg,

[T]he extensive neurological damage and cognitive impairments we found among chronic solvent abusers in our study could limit their ability to control their behavior and perceive problems associated with their substance abuse. . . . Some of the brain damage and cognitive deficits seen in both primary inhalant and cocaine abusers in the study could stem from the heavy use of alcohol that was common among both groups. . . . However, the diffuse white matter changes and abnormalities found in the thalamus have not been seen in alcohol abusers and are clearly from solvent abuse.

Data from Mathias, R. (2002, November). Chronic solvent abusers have more brain abnormalities and cognitive impairments than cocaine abusers. *NIDA Notes, 17*(4). Retrieved from http://archives.drugabuse.gov/NIDA_notes/NNVol17N4/Chronic.html. Accessed February 17, 2011; Rosenberg, N. L., Grigsby, J., Dreisbach, J., Busenbark, D., & Grisby, P. (2002). Neuropsychologic impairment and MRI abnormalities with chronic solvent abuse. *Journal of Clinical Toxicology, 40*, 21–34.

## TOLUENE

Toluene is a chemical found in some glues, paints, thinners, nail polishes, and typewriter correction fluid. It is a principal ingredient in *Texas Shoeshine* (a shoe spray) (NIDA, 2012). Toluene is detectable in the arterial blood within 10 seconds of inhalation exposure (National Highway Traffic Safety Administration [NHTSA], n.d.). Because this molecule is highly lipid soluble, it is rapidly absorbed by the brain, heart, and liver. Accordingly, toluene abuse can cause brain damage. Other damage can include impaired cognition and gait disturbances. Loss of coordination, equilibrium, hearing, and vision can also occur. Liver and kidney damage have also been reported (NIDA, 2012). Of note, at least one study indicates that toluene activates dopaminergic activity in the brain (NIDA, 2012). The dopamine system is important for the rewarding effects of nearly all drugs of abuse.

## BUTANE AND PROPANE

Butane and propane are found commonly in hair and paint sprays and lighter fluid. Serious burn injuries (because of flammability) and SSDS have resulted from their abuse (NIDA, 2012).

## GASOLINE

Because of gasoline's widespread availability, young people, often in rural settings, sometimes abuse it. Gasoline is a mixture of volatile chemicals, and can include toluene and benzene. Because it is a mixture of chemicals, the intentional inhalation of gasoline can be especially dangerous. Benzene is an organic compound that causes impaired immunologic function, bone marrow injury, increased risk of leukemia, and reproductive system toxicity (NIDA, 2012). Furthermore, gasoline is highly flammable; as with butane and propane, fires and serious burn injuries have resulted when gasoline inhalation has been combined with smoking of marijuana, tobacco, or other drugs.

### FREON

Freon and other related agents are used in many products, including refrigerators, air conditioners, and airbrushes. Their inhalation can cause not only serious liver damage but also SSDS (NIDA, 2012). Inhaling these agents also poses other dangers; freeze injuries can occur when individuals inhaling Freon lose consciousness, leaving unprotected skin in close proximity to cold. In one serious but rare case, a 16-year-old male attempted to get high by inhaling airbrush propellant. The patient lost consciousness. When he awoke, he discovered that his tongue and lips were frozen and that he had suffered serious burns on his larynx, vocal cords, trachea, bronchi, and esophagus (Kuspis & Krenzelok, 1999).

## ■ Anesthetics

When used properly, other forms of inhalants with abuse potential are important therapeutic agents. Included in this category are anesthetics

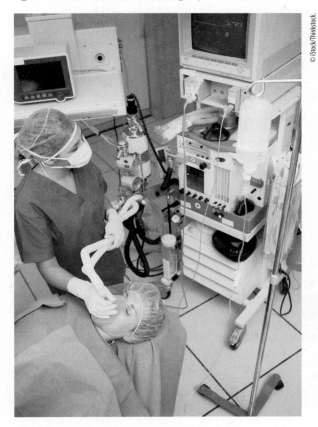

© iStock/Thinkstock.

Anesthetics are an example of an inhalant.

such as ether, chloroform, halothane, and nitrous oxide. Only nitrous oxide is available widely enough to be a significant abuse concern. This colorless gas is used for minor outpatient procedures in offices of both physicians and dentists. It is often referred to as *laughing gas* because it can cause giggling and laughter in the patient receiving it. It is also found in products used in cars to boost octane levels in racing cars (NIDA, 2012). Because it is readily accessible, health professionals themselves or their staff are most likely to abuse nitrous oxide.

In addition to being found in a clinical setting, nitrous oxide can also be sold in large balloons from which the gas is released and inhaled for its mind-altering effects. It is also found in small cylindrical cartridges used as charges for whipped cream dispensers. These cylinders and other plastic containers filled with nitrous oxide are referred to as *whippets*. Although significant abuse problems of nitrous oxide are infrequent, there are occasional reports of severe hypoxia (i.e., a lack of oxygen) or death from acute overdoses. Nitrous oxide can also cause loss of sensation, limb spasms, altered perception and motor coordination, blackouts resulting from blood pressure changes, and reduced cardiac function (NIDA, 2012).

## ■ Nitrites

Nitrites are chemicals that cause vasodilation. Owing to this property, the prototype of this group, amyl nitrite, has been used in the past to treat angina. Nitrites have been abused most commonly as sexual enhancers. Nitrites were first abused in the 1960s when ampules of the compound were available over the counter. The ampules were popped between the fingers (hence, the name *poppers*) and held to the nostrils for inhalation.

Although the use of nitrites is now prohibited by the Consumer Product Safety Commission, they can still be obtained in small bottles labeled as "video head cleaner," "room odorizer," "leather cleaner," or "liquid aroma" (NIDA, 2012). The use of amyl and the related butyl nitrite has decreased dramatically from an annual use among 12th graders of 6.5% in 1979 to only 0.9% in 2009. Since then, the MTF study (an ongoing series of national surveys of American adolescents and adults that has provided important data concerning drug usage for more than 30 years; see Miech et al., 2019) has ceased to monitor usage because of this low prevalence.

## ❚ Legislation

Inhalants of abuse are generally not regulated as controlled substances. However, at least 37 states have enacted laws regulating inhalant and aerosol sales or abuse (National Inhalant Prevention Coalition [NIPC], 2012).

# Current Patterns and Signs of Abuse

Inhalants, particularly gases and aerosols, are often among the first drugs that young children misuse. The inhalants are popular for several reasons:

- They are legally obtained.
- They are readily available in most households and workplaces.
- They are inexpensive.
- They are easy to conceal.
- Most users are uninformed about the potential dangers.

In addition, inhalation is popular because it generally causes feelings of intoxication and euphoria much more rapidly than do agents such as alcohol.

## ❚ Adolescent and Teenage Usage

Adolescents most commonly use inhalants, with usage decreasing as students grow older. For example, according to the 2015 MTF study (Miech et al., 2019), 1.8% of 8th graders reported using inhalants within the past month, whereas only 1.0% of 10th graders and 0.7% of high school seniors reported a similar pattern of use (see **Table 14.1**). By comparison, in 2015, past-month use among college students was 0.2%. One reason for this age difference is that older

individuals often view use of inhalants with disdain and consider it unsophisticated and a "kid's habit."

Lifetime inhalant use among 12th graders in 2018 was 4.4%, compared with 6.5% among 10th graders. Of considerable concern are reports that inhalant abuse can begin in small children (Spiller & Krenzelok, 1997). Imitation of older siblings or neighbors often accounts for this initial exposure. Hence, education efforts should be directed at young children as well as adolescents and their parents.

## ❚ Gender, Race, Socioeconomics, and Abuse

According to the 2017 National Survey on Drug Use and Health, a greater percentage of men (0.8%) than women (0.5%) aged 12 or older have used an inhalant during the past year. However, that gender difference is diminishing as evidenced by recent findings that rates of past-year inhalant use were greater among females (2.4%) than males (2.2%) ages 12 to 17. Approximately 5.1% of American Indian or Alaskan Natives ages 12 to 17 have abused an inhalant at least once. Non-Hispanic whites, Hispanics or Latinos, blacks or African Americans, and Asian individuals ages 12 to 17 abused inhalants at least once in their lifetime at rates of 9.0%, 8.0%, 8.5%, and 7.7%, respectively (SAMHSA, 2018).

## ❚ Signs of Inhalant Abuse

Individuals under the influence of inhalants are often uncoordinated and disoriented and appear drunken, as if they had consumed alcohol. Red and watery eyes, slurred speech, nausea, headaches, and nosebleeds are also common. Rashes around the nose and mouth or unexplained paint on the hands and mouth can be signs of

**TABLE 14.1** Inhalant Use Among 8th, 10th, and 12th Graders

|  | 8th Graders (%) | | | 10th Graders (%) | | | 12th Graders (%) | | |
|---|---|---|---|---|---|---|---|---|---|
|  | 2016 | 2017 | 2018 | 2016 | 2017 | 2018 | 2016 | 2017 | 2018 |
| Lifetime | 7.7 | 8.9 | 8.7 | 6.6 | 6.1 | 6.5 | 5.0 | 4.9 | 4.4 |
| Annual | 3.8 | 4.7 | 4.6 | 2.4 | 2.3 | 2.4 | 1.7 | 1.5 | 1.6 |
| 30 day | 1.8 | 2.1 | 1.8 | 1.0 | 1.1 | 1.0 | 0.8 | 0.8 | 0.7 |

Data from Miech, R. A., Johnston, L. D., O'Mailey, P. M., Bachman, J. G., Schulenberg, J. E., & Patrick, M. E. (2019). *Monitoring the Future: National survey results on drug use, 1975–2018. Volume I, secondary school students*. Ann Arbor, MI: University of Michigan, Institute for Social Research. Retrieved from http://monitoringthefuture.org/pubs/monographs/mtf-vol1_2018.pdf

inhalant abuse. Other signs include smelling a chemical odor in the room or in unusual containers (e.g., soda cans, plastic bags), finding cans of aerosol whipped cream that will not foam, or discovering air conditioners that do not work. In addition, children who are frequent users of inhalants:

- often collect an unusual assortment of chemicals (such as glues, paints, thinners and solvents, nail polish, liquid eraser, and cleaning fluids) in bedrooms or with belongings;
- have breath that occasionally smells of solvents;
- often have the sniffles similar to a cold but without other symptoms of the ailment;
- appear drunk for short periods of time (15 to 60 minutes) but recover quickly; and
- do not do well in school and are often unkempt.

Other signs of inhalant abuse can include the following:

- sitting with a pen or marker near nose;
- constantly smelling clothing sleeves;
- hiding rags, clothes, or empty containers of the potentially abused products in closets, boxes, and other places;
- possessing chemical-soaked rags, bags, or socks; and
- abusable household items missing.

# Dangers of Inhalant Abuse

The dangers of inhalant abuse stretch beyond simply the direct physical damage to the heart, lungs, liver, and brain. Other dangers can include death by choking on one's own vomit or by fatal injury from accidents, including car crashes (NIDA, 2012).

Use of inhalants by pregnant women also may put newborns at risk of developmental deficits. Although it is not yet possible to link prenatal exposure to specific inhalants with a specific birth defect, case reports have documented developmental abnormalities in offspring of mothers who chronically abuse inhalants (NIDA, 2012).

According to NIDA (2012), many individuals who have abused inhalants for prolonged periods over many days report a strong need to continue inhalant use. A mild withdrawal syndrome and compulsive use can occur with long-term inhalant abuse.

A survey of 43,000 U.S. adults indicates that inhalant users, on average, initiate use of alcohol, cigarettes, and almost all other drugs at younger ages than those who do not abuse inhalants. Further, these individuals display a higher lifetime prevalence of substance use disorders, including prescription drug abuse, when compared with substance abusers without a history of inhalant use (NIDA, 2012).

## LEARNING PORTFOLIO

### Key Terms

| | |
|---|---|
| arrhythmia | 484 |
| euphorigenic | 484 |
| hypoxia | 485 |
| volatile | 484 |

## Discussion Questions

1. Name the three types of inhalants and list examples of each type. List the dangerous side effects associated with the misuse of each type of inhalant.
2. Why are inhalants widely abused?
3. What is sudden sniffing death syndrome?
4. What chemical properties of inhalants make these agents particularly dangerous?
5. Who is most likely to abuse inhalants?
6. List several signs of inhalant abuse.
7. List several dangers of inhalant abuse other than the direct physical damage done by the chemical itself.

## Summary

1. Inhalants are volatile substances that cause intoxicating or euphorigenic effects, and sometimes both. Most were never intended to be used as drugs and are not often thought of as having abuse potential. However, inhalant abuse is a serious public health problem. Hundreds of adolescents and teenagers in the United States die or are seriously injured each year as a result of inhalant abuse. Even first-time users can die from a condition referred to as sudden sniffing death syndrome (SSDS).
2. Most inhalants are household or commercial products composed of several different fat-soluble chemicals that can act alone or synergistically to exert toxic effects. These agents can be classified into three groups: volatile substances, anesthetics, and nitrites.
3. Volatile substances include aerosols, adhesives, fuels, and household solvents. Abusers inhale vapors directly from their original containers (called *sniffing* or *snorting*), from plastic bags (called *bagging*), or from old rags or bandannas soaked in the solvent fluid and held over the mouth (called *huffing*). Abuse of these agents can cause damage to the liver, brain, kidneys, and immune system, as well as SSDS.
4. Anesthetics include ether, chloroform, halothane, and nitrous oxide. When used properly, these forms of inhalants are important therapeutic agents; however, their misuse can cause severe hypoxia and death.
5. Inhalants are popular because they are legally obtained, readily available, inexpensive, and easy to conceal.
6. Inhalant abuse is typically a problem of adolescents and teenagers.

**7.** Signs of inhalant abuse include a drunken appearance, watery eyes, nausea, headaches, and nosebleeds. Rashes around the nose and mouth or unexplained paint on the hands and mouth can be signs of inhalant abuse. Other signs can include smelling a chemical odor in the room or in unusual containers (e.g., soda cans, plastic bags), finding cans of aerosol whipped cream that will not foam, or discovering air conditioners that do not work.

## References

Kennedy, S. K., & Longnecker, D. E. (1990). History and principles of anesthesiology. In A. G. Gilman, T. W. Rall, A. S. Nies, & P. Taylor (Eds.), *The pharmacological basis of therapeutics* (p. 269). New York, NY: Pergamon Press.

Kuspis, D. A., & Krenzelok, E. P. (1999). Oral frostbite injury from intentional abuse of a fluorinated hydrocarbon. *Journal of Toxicology and Clinical Toxicology, 37*, 873–875.

Lipari, R. N. (2017, June). The CBHSQ report: Understanding adolescent inhalant use. Retrieved from https://www.samhsa.gov/data/sites/default/files/report_3095/ShortReport-3095.html

Mathias, R. (2002, November). Chronic solvent abusers have more brain abnormalities and cognitive impairments than cocaine abusers. *NIDA Notes, 17*(4). Retrieved from http://archives.drugabuse.gov/NIDA_notes/NNVol17N4/Chronic.html

Miech, R. A., Johnston, L. D., O'Mailey, P. M., Bachman, J. G., Schulenberg, J. E., & Patrick, M. E. (2019). *Monitoring the Future: National survey results on drug use, 1975–2018. Volume I, secondary school students.* Ann Arbor, MI: University of Michigan, Institute for Social Research. Retrieved from http://monitoringthefuture.org/pubs/monographs/mtf-vol1_2018.pdf

National Highway Traffic Safety Administration (NHTSA). (n.d.). Drugs and human performance fact sheets: Toluene. Retrieved from https://www.wsp.wa.gov/breathtest/docs/webdms/DRE_Forms/Publications/drug/Human_Performance_Drug_Fact_Sheets-NHTSA.pdf

National Inhalant Prevention Coalition (NIPC). (n.d.). Inhalant laws by state—Which states give jail time and fines for inhalant abuse. Retrieved from http://www.inhalants.org/laws.htm

National Institute on Drug Abuse (NIDA). (2012, July). *Inhalants.* Retrieved from http://www.drugabuse.gov/publications/research-reports/inhalant-abuse

Rosenberg, N. L., Grigsby, J., Dreisbach, J., Busenbark, D., & Grisby, P. (2002). Neuropsychologic impairment and MRI abnormalities with chronic solvent abuse. *Journal of Clinical Toxicology, 40*, 21–34.

Spiller, H. A., & Krenzelok, E. P. (1997). Epidemiology of inhalant abuse reported to two regional poison centers. *Clinical Toxicology, 35*, 167–173.

Substance Abuse and Mental Health Services Administration (SAMHSA). (2018). *Results from the 2017 National Survey on Drug Use and Health: Detailed tables.* Rockville, MD: Author.

Substance Abuse and Mental Health Services Administration (SAMHSA). (2019). Key substance use and mental health indicators in the United States: Results from the 2018 National Survey on Drug Use and Health. Rockville, MD: Author.

U.S. Consumer Product Safety Commission. (n.d.). A parent's guide to preventing inhalant abuse. Retrieved from https://www.cpsc.gov/safety-education/safety-guides/containers-and-packaging/parents-guide-preventing-inhalant-abuse

## CHAPTER 15

# Over-the-Counter, Prescription, and Herbal Drugs

© FOTOGRIN/Shutterstock.

## Did You Know?

▶ More than 100 ingredients and 700 drug products that are now available over the counter (OTC) were available only by prescription 30 years ago.

▶ Pharmacists can provide useful counseling in selecting appropriate OTC products.

▶ Careless, excessive use of some OTC medications can cause addiction, physical dependence, tolerance, and withdrawal symptoms.

▶ When used together, prescription drugs or drugs of abuse can interact with OTC or herbal drugs in dangerous and sometimes even lethal ways.

▶ Most herbal (natural) remedies are popular products that, despite containing drugs, are available without a prescription and by law are excluded from routine OTC regulation by the Food and Drug Administration (FDA).

▶ More people die in the United States from adverse reactions to legal medications than from all illegal drug use.

▶ Every day more than 130 deaths occur in the United States from prescription drugs, the majority of which are linked to opioid painkillers.

▶ Many college students take stimulant prescription drugs to either get high or enhance their academic performance.

▶ Most generic drugs are as effective as but substantially less expensive than their proprietary counterparts.

## Learning Objectives

**On completing this chapter, you should be able to:**

❯ Outline the general differences between prescription and nonprescription drugs.

❯ Explain why the Food and Drug Administration (FDA) occasionally switches prescription drugs to over-the-counter (OTC) status.

❯ Describe potential abuse problems with OTC, prescription, and herbal drugs.

❯ Identify some of the most popular drugs that have been switched to OTC.

❯ Discuss the potential problems of making more effective OTC drugs available to the public for self-care.

❯ Describe the type of information that is included on the labels of nonprescription medicines.

❯ Discuss the rules for safe use of nonprescription drugs.

❯ Determine the difference between herbal products and OTC medications.

❯ Explain why the FDA has removed ephedrine and ephedra from its list of approved OTC products.

❯ Compare problems of abuse and addiction of illicit and prescription drugs, and explain why prescription abuse has become so widespread.

❯ Discuss the type of information that should be communicated between doctor and patient to avoid unnecessary drug side effects.

❯ Explain how prescription drugs should be disposed of properly.

❯ Explain the advantages and disadvantages of generic and proprietary drugs.

❯ Explain which prescription drugs are most likely to be abused and why.

❯ Discuss the connection between abuse of opioid prescription drugs and management of chronic pain.

# Introduction

Most Americans would agree that the cost of prescription drugs is out of control. Some medication consumers even travel to foreign countries like Canada or Mexico to get cheaper, more affordable drug prices. To illustrate the problem, the average cost of brand-name (proprietary) drugs has more than tripled in the past 10 years. The question is, Why is this happening? Drug manufacturers claim it is because of the high costs of research development for new drugs; however, this does not explain why the cost for a century-old medication like the life-saving drug insulin (essential for type 1 diabetics survival) has increased approximately 600% since 2002 (Consumer Action News, 2020). Because of this crisis, programs to help families afford critical medication have been created by both government and philanthropic organizations. In addition, consumer and legislative efforts have targeted drug companies as well as policy makers to apply pressure for the development of more rational and affordable drug products to improve management of major critical diseases (Consumer Action News, 2020).

Currently, American healthcare providers are able to prescribe in excess of 10,000 different prescription medications, with more than 30% of U.S. adults consuming at least five medications. Although properly prescribed drugs have dramatically improved the management of many minor and serious diseases, their frequent use also comes with significant risks referred to as *adverse drug events* (ADEs). Each year these ADEs result in approximately 700,000 visits to emergency departments and 100,000 hospitalizations (PSNet, 2015), underscoring the need for careful management of these medications and consideration of their benefit-to-risk ratio.

Over-the-counter (OTC) and prescription drugs have been viewed differently by the public since these classifications were formally established by the Durham–Humphrey Amendment of 1951. In general, we view OTC medications as less effective, relatively free from side effects, and rarely abused; in contrast, we often consider prescription drugs as much more potent, typically used for more serious medical conditions, and frequently dangerous. For more information on the classification and management of drug categories see Chapter 3, "Drug Use, Regulation, and the Law."

However, distinctions between prescription and nonprescription drugs, which at one time appeared to be obvious, have become blurred by changes in public demand and federal policies. Because of escalating health costs and a growing interest in self-care, people today want access to effective medications, and government agencies such as the FDA are responding to their demands. Consequently, as mentioned in Chapter 3, the FDA has been involved in switching some 106 effective and relatively safe prescription medications to OTC status at a savings of $146 billion annually ("From Prescription Pad to Store Shelf," 2019). In fact, more than 700 drug products sold OTC today were available only by prescription 30 years ago ("From Prescription Pad," 2019). Overall, OTC drugs are used by more than 75% of households, which each spend approximately $338 annually (Consumer Healthcare Products Association [CHPA], 2019).

It is likely that in the future other drugs (albeit much less frequently) will be removed from behind the pharmacist's counter and made available for public access as nonprescription medications. Some possibilities for switching from prescription to OTC that have been suggested by health experts include drugs to treat migraine headaches, high cholesterol, benign enlarged prostate glands, and allergic rhinitis (Center for Drug Evaluation and Research, 2019; Page, 2015). These shifts of drugs between prescription and nonprescription status emphasize the somewhat arbitrary nature of classifying drugs as prescription and OTC and remind us that similar care should be taken with all medications to achieve maximal benefit and minimal risk.

In this chapter, we begin by discussing OTC (nonprescription) drugs. The first topic encompasses policies regarding OTC drug regulation and is followed by a discussion of safe self-care with nonprescription drug products. Explanations of some of the most common medications in this category, including herbal (natural) remedies, conclude the section on OTC drugs. The second part of this chapter provides a general overview of prescription drugs. The consequences of misusing prescription drugs, as well as ways to avoid such problems, are discussed. A brief presentation of some of the most commonly prescribed drugs ends the chapter.

# OTC Drugs

Today, more than 100,000 different OTC products, including more than 1,500 active ingredients, are available to treat everything from age spots to halitosis; they account for 60% of the annual drug purchases in this country (CHPA, 2016b). An estimated 60% of the population routinely self-medicates with these drug products. The top five OTC categories by sales account for approximately 60% of the total OTC purchases: respiratory drugs ($8.8 billion), oral care ($4.3 billion) analgesics products ($4.3 billion), drugs for gastrointestinal ailments such as heart burn ($3.2 billion), and antiperspirants ($3.0 billion), (Stone, 2019).

Some of the 80 major drug classes currently approved for OTC status are shown in **Table 15.1**. OTC remedies are nonprescription drugs that may be obtained and used without the supervision of a physician or other health professional. Nevertheless, for some people, certain OTC products can be dangerous when used alone or in combination with other drugs. Although some OTC drugs are highly beneficial in the self-treatment of minor to moderate uncomplicated health problems, others are of questionable therapeutic value, and their usefulness is often misrepresented by manufacturers.

**TABLE 15.1** Some Major Drug Classes Approved by the FDA for OTC Status

| Drug Class | Effects |
| --- | --- |
| Analgesics and anti-inflammatories | Relieve pain, fever, and inflammation |
| Cold remedies | Relieve cold symptoms |
| Antihistamines and allergy products | Relieve allergy symptoms |
| Stimulants | Diminish fatigue and drowsiness |
| Sedatives and sleep aids | Promote sleep |
| Antacids | Relieve indigestion from rebound activity |
| Laxatives | Relieve self-limiting constipation |
| Antidiarrheals | Relieve minor, self-limiting diarrhea |
| Gastric secretion blockers | Relieve heartburn |
| Topical antimicrobials | Treat skin infections |
| Bronchodilators and antiasthmatics | Assist breathing |
| Dentifrices and dental products | Promote oral hygiene |
| Acne medications | Treat and prevent acne |
| Sunburn treatments and sunscreens | Treat and prevent skin damage from ultraviolet rays |
| Dandruff and athlete's foot medications | Treat and prevent specific skin conditions |
| Contraceptives and vaginal products | Prevent pregnancy and treat vaginal infections |
| Ophthalmics | Promote eye hygiene and treat eye infections |
| Vitamins and minerals | Provide diet supplements |
| Antiperspirants | Promote body hygiene |
| Hair growth stimulators | Promote hair growth |

Data from OTC Monograph Reform. (2020). OTC review/Drug monographs. Washington, DC: Consumer Healthcare Products Association. Retrieved from https://www.chpa.org/OTCReview.aspx

## ▪ Abuse of OTC Drugs

Although the consequences of abusing OTC drugs can be substantial, relatively speaking, the occurrence rate of such abuse is low. However, there are notable exceptions, such as cough medicines and decongestants (National Institute on Drug Abuse [NIDA], 2019a).

Because these drugs are usually available on demand, perceived as being exceptionally safe, and poorly understood by the general public, their abuse patterns differ somewhat from those seen with the so-called hard-core drugs of abuse; nevertheless, they can be equally harmful. Even though the OTC products generally have a greater margin of safety than their prescription counterparts, issues of abuse need to be considered (Juergens, 2019). For example, many OTC drugs when misused can cause physical and psychological dependence. Nonprescription products that can be severely habit forming include nasal and ophthalmic (eye) decongestants, laxatives, antihistamines, sleep aids, and antacids. Of particular abuse concern are OTC stimulants such as ephedrine that can be severely toxic by themselves or can be used as precursors to the synthesis of extremely addicting and dangerous amphetamines. In fact, because of these concerns, the FDA ruled in 2012 that ephedrine could no longer be included in OTC or in most herbal products (Quinn, 2019), and most states require that cold products containing amphetamine precursors be safeguarded behind the counter (Cunningham et al., 2012). It is not unusual to find that persons who regularly abuse OTC products are more likely to go on to abuse prescription or even illegal drugs as well (Juergens, 2019).

Because use of OTC products is unrestricted, the patterns of abuse are impossible to determine accurately. However, these products are more likely to be abused by members of the unsuspecting general public who inadvertently become dependent due to excessive self-medication than by hard-core drug addicts who obtain the most potent drugs of abuse by illicit means.

## ▪ Federal Regulation of OTC Drugs

In the United States, the Food and Drug Administration is responsible for regulating OTC drugs through the Center for Drug Evaluation and Research. Under the direction of the FDA, the active ingredients in OTC drugs have been and continue to be evaluated and classified according to their effectiveness and safety.

The FDA has attempted to make even more drugs available to the general public by switching some frequently used and safe prescription medications to OTC status. This policy is in response to public demand to have access to effective drugs for self-medication and has resulted in approximately 106 successful switches, leading to 700 new OTC products (Food and Drug Administration [FDA], n.d., 2016c). This policy helps cut medical costs by eliminating the need for costly visits to healthcare providers for treatment of minor, self-limiting ailments (CHPA, 2016a). A few of the more notable drugs that have been switched from prescription to nonprescription status since 1985 are naproxen (analgesic, anti-inflammatory—Aleve), hydrocortisone (anti-inflammatory steroid—Cortaid), loperamide (antidiarrheal—Imodium), miconazole (antifungal—Monistat 7), cimetidine (heartburn medication—Tagamet), increased-strength minoxidil (hair growth stimulant—Rogaine), nicotine patch (smoking cessation aid—Nicotrol), orlistat (weight loss—Alli), lansoprazole (gastric acid reducer—Prevacid), diphenhydramine (sleep aid—Sominex), levonorgestrel (contraception—Plan B), cetirizine (allergy—Zyrtec), triamcionolone (24-hour corticosteroid nasal spray for allergies—Nasocort Allergy 24 HR), oxybutynin (overactive bladder for women—Oxytrol), and esomeprozole (24-hour relief of esophageal reflux—Nexium 24 HR) (FDA, n.d., 2016c).

A major concern of health professionals is that reclassification of safe prescription drugs to OTC status will result in overuse or misuse of these agents. The reclassified drugs may tempt individuals to self-medicate rather than seek medical care for potentially serious health problems or encourage the use of multiple drugs at the same time, increasing the likelihood of dangerous interactions (CHPA, 2016a; FDA, 2016c).

However, because there has been no evidence of significant problems, effective and safe prescription drugs will probably continue to be made available OTC, although the rate of switching prescription drugs to OTC status does appear to be slowing.

## ▪ OTC Drugs and Self-Care

Of the approximately 3.5 billion health problems treated in the United States annually, almost 2 billion can be treated with an OTC drug (CHPA, 2016a). This fact demonstrates that the public frequently engages in medical self-care with OTC products. Self-care with nonprescription medications occurs because we decide that we have a health problem that can be adequately self-medicated without involving a health professional. Proper self-care assumes that the individual has made a correct diagnosis of the health problem and is informed enough to select the appropriate OTC product. If done correctly, self-care with OTC medications can provide significant relief from minor, self-limiting health problems at minimal cost and can save billions of dollars that would otherwise be spent on expensive health care and prescription drugs (CHPA, 2016a). However, a lack of understanding about the nature of the OTC products—what they can and cannot do—and their potential side effects can result in harmful misuse. For this reason, it is important that those who consume OTC medications be fully aware of their proper use. This goal usually can be achieved by reading product labels carefully and asking questions of health professionals such as pharmacists and physicians. Potential problems associated with the use of OTC medicines include (1) delay in seeking proper medical care for serious illnesses, (2) risk of drug or herbal interactions, (3) unassessed potential for adverse effects in individual users, and (4) potential for abuse, dependence, and misuse (American College of Preventive Medicine, 2016).

## OTC LABELS

Information about proper use of OTC medications is required to be cited on the drug label and is regulated by the FDA. Required label information, referred to as the *statement of identity* includes (1) intended action, (2) statement of general pharmacological action or intended

action, (3) indications for use including proper directions, and (4) cautions or warnings to those at greatest risk when taking the medication. FDA regulations require that this information be readily intelligible to the lay public and easily read (FDA, 2019) (see **Figure 15.1**). Many consumers experience adverse side effects because they either choose to ignore the warnings on OTC labels or simply do not bother to read them. For example, as previously mentioned, excessive or inappropriate use of some nonprescription drugs can cause drug dependence; consequently, people who are always dropping medication in the eyes "to get the red out" or popping antacids like dessert after every meal are likely dependent. They continue to use OTC products to avoid unpleasant eye redness or stomach acidity, which are likely withdrawal consequences of excessive use of these medications ("Cold and Flu Overview," 2016).

## RULES FOR PROPER OTC DRUG USE

The OTC marketplace for drugs operates differently than does its prescription counterpart. The use of OTC drugs is not restricted, and consumers are responsible for making correct decisions about these products. Thus, to a large degree, the consumer sets policy and determines use patterns.

Because there are no formal controls over the use of OTC drugs, abuse often occurs. In extreme situations, the abuse of OTC medication can be extremely troublesome, even causing structural damage to the body and, on rare occasions, death. Proper education about the pharmacological features of these agents is necessary if consumers are to make intelligent and informed decisions about OTC drug use. To reduce the

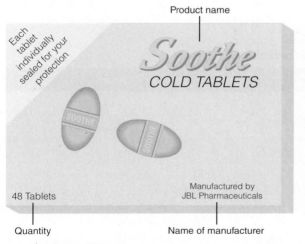

**FIGURE 15.1** OTC label. Certain information must appear on the labels of OTC medicinal products.

incidence of problems, the following rules should be observed when using nonprescription products (Hussar, 2016):

- Make sure your self-diagnosis is accurate.
- Chose products with the fewest appropriate ingredients.
- Always know what you are taking. Identify the active ingredients in the product.
- Know the effects. Be sure you know both the desired and potential undesired effects of each active ingredient.
- Read and heed the warnings and cautions.
- The warnings are not intended to scare but to protect.
- Do not use OTC drug products for more than one to two weeks. If the problem being treated persists beyond this time, consult a health professional.
- Be particularly cautious if you are also taking prescription or herbal drugs. Serious interactions between OTC drugs and these medications frequently occur. If you have a question, be sure to find out the answer.
- If you have questions, ask a pharmacist. Pharmacists are excellent sources of information about OTC drugs. They possess up-to-date knowledge of OTC products and can assist consumers in selecting correct medications for their health needs. Ask them to help you.
- Most important—If you don't need it, don't use it!

## ▌ Types of OTC Drugs

It is impossible to provide a detailed description of the hundreds of active ingredients approved by the FDA for OTC distribution; however, the following includes a brief discussion of the most common OTC drugs available in the United States.

### INTERNAL ANALGESICS

Each year Americans spend more than $4.3 billion on internal (taken by mouth) analgesics (CHPA, 2020). Most of this is spent on salicylates (aspirin products—e.g., Anacin, Bayer), acetaminophen (Tylenol, Datril, Pamprin, Panadol), ibuprofen (Advil, Nuprin), and ibuprofen-like drugs such as naproxen (Aleve). The compositions of common OTC internal analgesics are provided in **Table 15.2**.

### THERAPEUTIC CONSIDERATIONS

The internal analgesic products are effective in treating several common ailments (Borazan & Furst, 2015).

- *Analgesic action*: The OTC analgesics effectively relieve mild to moderate somatic pain associated with musculoskeletal structures such as bones, skin, teeth, joints, and ligaments. Pains that are relieved by the use of these drugs include headaches, toothaches, earaches, and muscle strains. In contrast, these drugs are not effective in the treatment of severe pain or pain associated with internal organs such as the heart, stomach, and intestines.
- *Anti-inflammatory effects*: Use of high doses (two to three times the analgesic dose) of the salicylates and ibuprofen relieves the symptoms of inflammation such as those associated with arthritis. In contrast, even high doses of acetaminophen have little anti-inflammatory action. Because of this anti-inflammatory effect, these drugs are frequently compared with a group of natural, highly potent anti-inflammatory compounds, the steroids. To distinguish drugs such as the salicylates and ibuprofen from steroids, these drugs are

**TABLE 15.2** Compositions of OTC Internal Analgesics (Dose per Unit)

| Product | Aspirin (mg) | Acetaminophen (mg) | Ibuprofen (mg) | Other |
|---|---|---|---|---|
| Bayer Aspirin | 325 | – | – | – |
| Ecotrin | 325 | – | – | Coated tablet |
| Tylenol, Children's | – | 80 | – | – |
| Advil | – | – | 200 | – |
| Motrin IB | – | – | 200 | – |
| Motrin, Children's | – | – | 200 | – |
| Aleve | – | – | – | Naproxen (220 mg) |

Wilkinson, J. (2012). Headache. In D. Krinsky et al. (Eds.), *Handbook of Nonprescription Drugs*, 17th ed. (pp. 67–86). Washington, DC: American Pharmacists Association.

often called *nonsteroidal anti-inflammatory drugs* (NSAIDs).

- *Antipyretic effects*: The OTC analgesics such as aspirin and acetaminophen reduce fever but do not alter normal body temperature. Such drugs are called *antipyretics*. The frequent use of these drugs to eliminate fevers is controversial. Some clinicians believe that low-grade fever may be a defense mechanism that helps destroy infecting microorganisms such as bacteria and viruses, so interfering with fevers may hamper the body's ability to rid itself of infection-causing microorganisms. Because no serious problems are associated with fevers of 102°F or lower, they are probably better left unmedicated.
- *Side effects*: When selecting an OTC analgesic drug for relief of pain, inflammation, or fever, possible side effects should be considered. Although salicylates such as aspirin are frequently used, they can cause problems for both children and adults (see "Signs & Symptoms: Common Side Effects of OTC NSAIDs"). Because of their side effects, salicylates are not recommended for (1) children because of the potential for Reye syndrome, (2) people suffering from gastrointestinal problems such as ulcers, and (3) people who have bleeding problems, are taking anticlot medication, are scheduled for surgery, or are near term in pregnancy because salicylates interfere with blood clotting and prolong bleeding.

For minor aches and pains, acetaminophen substitutes adequately for salicylates, has no effect on blood clotting, and does not cause stomach irritation. In addition, acetaminophen does not influence the occurrence of Reye syndrome, a potentially deadly complication of colds, flu, and chickenpox in children up to age 18 who are using salicylates (Wilkinson, 2012). However, even acetaminophen, if used in high doses, can have serious health consequences. Concern that excessive use of acetaminophen can cause permanent and even fatal liver damage has caused the FDA to put out warnings to consumers of acetaminophen-containing products to avoid the use of high doses of this drug (Brennan, 2015).

### CAFFEINE AND OTHER ADDITIVES

Many OTC analgesic products contain caffeine. Caffeine may relieve the negative element of pain because of its stimulant effect, which may be perceived as pleasant and energizing. The combination of caffeine with OTC analgesics may enhance pain relief (Baratloo et al., 2016) and be especially useful in treating vascular headaches because of the vasoconstrictive properties on cerebral blood vessels caused by this stimulant. In most OTC analgesic products—for example, Anacin and Excedrin—the amount of caffeine is less than that found in one-fourth to one-half cup of coffee (about 30 milligrams/tablet). Other ingredients—such as antacids, antihistamines, and decongestants—sometimes included in OTC pain-relieving products have little or no analgesic

# SIGNS & SYMPTOMS

## Common Side Effects of OTC NSAIDs

| Drugs | System Affected | Side Effects |
|---|---|---|
| Salicylates | Gastrointestinal | Can cause irritation, bleeding; aggravate ulcers |
| | Blood | Interfere with clotting; prolong bleeding |
| | Ears | Chronic high doses cause ringing (tinnitus) and hearing loss |
| | Pediatric | Can cause Reye's syndrome |
| Acetaminophen | Liver | High acute doses or chronic exposure can cause severe damage |
| Ibuprofen (includes other, newer NSAIDs) | Gastrointestinal | Similar to salicylates but less severe |
| | Blood | Similar to salicylates but less severe |
| | Kidneys | Damage in elderly or those with existing kidney disease |

Data from Borazan, N., & Furst, D. (2015). Nonsteroidal anti-inflammatory drugs, disease-modifying antirheumatic drugs, nonopioid analgesics, and drugs used in gout. In B. Katzung and A. Trevor (Eds.), *Basic and clinical pharmacology*, 13th ed. (pp. 618–641). New York, NY: McGraw-Hill.

action and usually add little to the therapeutic value of the medication. A recent development for OTC analgesic products was FDA permission to advertise pain-relieving products effective in the relief of migraine headaches. Although these products have been found to provide relief from minor migraine headaches, they do not contain any new breakthrough drugs; these products contain previously available ingredients, such as aspirin, ibuprofen, and caffeine, just in higher doses (e.g., Migraine Extra Strength Excedrin).

## UPPER RESPIRATORY MEDICINES (I.E., COLD, COUGH, ALLERGY AND ASTHMA)

More than $8.8 billion are spent annually for OTC drugs to treat upper-respiratory problems such as cold, coughs, flu, allergies, and asthma (CHPA, 2020). The incidence of the common cold varies with age. Children between one and five years of age are most susceptible; each child averages six to 12 respiratory illnesses per year, most of which are common colds. Individuals 25 to 30 years old average six respiratory illnesses a year, and older adults average two or three. The declining incidence of colds with age is a result of the immunity that occurs after each infection with a cold virus; thus, if reinfected with the same virus, the microorganism is rapidly destroyed by the body's defense system and the full-blown symptoms of a cold do not occur ("Common Cold Risk Factors," 2016).

Most colds have similar general symptoms. In the first stage, the throat and nose are dry and scratchy; in the second stage, secretions accumulate in the air passages, nose, throat, and bronchial tubes. The second stage is marked by continuous sneezing, nasal obstruction, sore throat, coughing, and nasal discharge. There may be watering and redness of the eyes and pain in the face (particularly near the sinuses) and ears. One of the most bothersome symptoms of the common cold is the congestion of the mucous membranes of the nasal passages, largely because of capillary dilation, which causes these blood

vessels to enlarge and become more permeable. Such vascular changes allow fluids to escape, resulting in drainage and also inflammation from fluid-swollen tissues ("Cold and Flu Overview," 2016).

There has been a problem of young people abusing these OTC products. Recent surveys suggest that up to 3.4% of high school seniors used cough medicine with dextromethorphan to get high in 2018, although this represents a decline from the 6.9% reported in 2006 (Johnston, 2019). This practice is sometimes referred to as *robotripping* or *skittling*. Common side effects include confusion, dizziness, excessive sweating, stomach pain, numbness, and blurred vision.

## DECONGESTANTS

The cold and allergy products we use are principally formulated with such drugs as decongestants (sympathomimetics), antihistamines (chlorpheniramine and pheniramine), and analgesics (aspirin, acetaminophen, and naproxen). **Table 15.3** lists the ingredients found in many common OTC cold and allergy products.

Antihistamines reduce congestion caused by allergies, but their effectiveness in the treatment of virus-induced colds is controversial. In high doses, the anticholinergic action of antihistamines also decreases the secretion of mucus, relieving the runny nose; however, this action is probably insignificant at the lower recommended doses of OTC preparations (Stoppler, 2016). An anticholinergic drying action may actually be harmful because it can lead to a serious coughing response. Because of their anticholinergic effects, antihistamines also may cause dizziness, drowsiness, impaired judgment, constipation, and dry mouth; they sometimes are abused because of psychedelic effects resulting from high-dose consumption. Because of the limited usefulness and the side effects of antihistamines for treating colds, decongestant products without such agents are usually preferred for these viral infections. In contrast, antihistamines

**TABLE 15.3** Compositions of Common OTC Cold and Allergy Products (Dose per Tablet)

| Product | Sympathomimetic | Analgesic |
| --- | --- | --- |
| Afrin | Oxymetazoline (0.05%) | — |
| Alka-Seltzer Plus | Phenylephrine (7.8 mg) | Aspirin (325 mg) |
| Tylenol Cold | Pseudoephedrine (5 mg) | Acetaminophen (325 mg) |
| Aleve-D Sinus | Pseudoephedrine (120 mg) | Naproxen (220 mg) |

Data from Scolaro, K. (2012). Disorders related to colds and allergies. In D. Krinsky et al. (Eds.), *Handbook of nonprescription drugs*, 17th ed. (pp. 180–204). Washington, DC: American Pharmacists Association.

are especially useful in relieving allergy-related congestion and symptoms.

The sympathomimetic drugs used as decongestants cause nasal membranes to shrink because of their vasoconstrictive effect, which reduces the congestion caused by both colds and allergies. Such drugs can be used in the form of sprays or drops (topical decongestants) or systemically (oral decongestants) (see **Table 15.4**). FDA-approved sympathomimetics include pseudoephedrine, phenylephrine (probably the most effective topical), and oxymetazoline (Scolaro, 2012). A substantial problem associated with the sympathomimetic decongestant ingredients in cold medicines is that they can easily be chemically converted into methamphetamine. For this reason, the federal government passed the Combat Methamphetamine Epidemic Acts of 2005 and

**TABLE 15.4** Compositions of OTC Topical Decongestants (Drug Concentrations)

| Product | Sympathomimetic |
| --- | --- |
| Afrin | Oxymetazoline (0.05%) |
| Neo-Synephrine | Phenylephrine (0.5%) |
| Vicks Sinex | Oxymetazoline (0.05%) |

Data from Scolaro, K. (2012). Disorders related to colds and allergies. In D. Krinsky et al. (Eds.), *Handbook of nonprescription drugs*, 17th ed. (pp. 180–204). Washington, DC: American Pharmacists Association.

2010, which requires keeping these decongestant products behind the counter and keeping records of those who purchase these medications (see "Here and Now: Fighting the 'Common Cold' Pills"). In addition to the

# HERE AND NOW

## Fighting the "Common Cold" Pills

It is becoming harder and harder to get those pills we all buy to fight the common cold. This problem is not because drugs like Sudafed are themselves particularly addicting; rather, the concern arises because of what they can become, and this is leading to the imposition of tighter controls on these popular decongestants. Because ingredients in OTC cold medicines such as pseudoephedrine can easily be converted into methamphetamine, these products have been bought in large quantities to be used in makeshift meth labs across the country. As a result, law enforcement agencies and even Congress itself have pointed out these drugs' potential dangers. Besides requiring that these OTC products be kept behind the counter in pharmacies, there have been attempts to pass local and national legislation to limit purchases of these drugs to about 9 grams (roughly 300 pills) in a 30-day period. This quantity of pseudoephedrine can be turned into approximately 25 doses of methamphetamine. Such restrictions have made it difficult for small neighborhood meth labs to obtain sufficient quantities of precursor ingredients to cook their dangerous brew, resulting in their disappearance for the most part. Mexican drug cartels have filled the gap with large quantities of methamphetamine manufactured in Mexico and smuggled across the border in combination with potent opioid drugs such as heroin and fentanyl. The cartels are using dummy corporations and false labeling to bring ordinary cold, flu, and allergy medicines into Mexico from China, India, and Belgium and converting the ingredients from these common decongestants into large quantities of methamphetamine for illicit sale. Despite efforts by both the Mexican and U.S. governments, these trafficking groups are highly resilient, keep ahead of the law, and have become the primary source for illegal U.S. methamphetamine.

© Jorge Saenz/AP/Shutterstock.

Data from Booth, W., & O'Connor, A. (2010, November 28). Mexican cartels emerge as top source for U.S. meth. *Washington Post*. Retrieved from http://www.washingtonpost.com/wp-dyn/content/article/2010/11/23/AR2010112303703.html?sid=ST2010112303730; Cooper, C. (2016, March 31). Methamphetamine abuse and illegal trafficking remain a persistent threat across the state. *Cronkite News/Arizona PBS*. Retrieved from https://cronkitenews.azpbs.org/2016/03/31/methamphetamine-abuse-and-illegal-trafficking-remain-a-persistent-threat-across-the-state/; Elena, M. (2016, March 10). Mexican drug cartel's crystal meth ingredient may be from Belgian pharma execs. *Latin Post*. Retrieved from http://www.latinpost.com/articles/118030/20160310/mexican-drug-cartels-crystal-meth-ingredient-belgian-pharma-execs.htm; Bebinger, M. (2019, July 29). Seizures of methamphetamine are surging in the U.S. *NPR*. Retrieved from https://www.npr.org/sections/health-shots/2019/07/29/745061185/seizures-of-methamphetamine-are-surging-in-the-u-s.

federal laws, many states have also passed their own statutes to regulate the sale of precursors used to make methamphetamine. The control varies from state to state, and many of these local laws are more rigid than the federal regulations (FDA, 2016b; NIDA, 2016b).

Someone using decongestant nasal sprays frequently can experience **congestion rebound** because of tissue dependence. After using a nasal spray regularly for longer than the recommended period of time, the nasal membranes adjust to the effect of the vasoconstrictor and become congested when the drug is not present. One can become hooked and use the spray more and more with less and less relief until one's tissues no longer respond and the sinus passages become almost completely obstructed (FamilyDoctor.org, n.d.). Allergists frequently see new patients who are addicted to nasal decongestant sprays and are desperate for relief from congestion. This problem can be prevented by using nasal sprays sparingly and for no longer than the recommended time.

Orally ingested sympathomimetic drugs give less relief from congestion than the topical medications but are less likely to cause rebound effects. In contrast, systemic administration of these drugs is more likely to cause cardiovascular problems (i.e., stimulate the heart, cause arrhythmia, increase blood pressure, and cause stroke).

### ANTITUSSIVES

Other drugs used to relieve the common cold are intended to treat coughing. The cough reflex helps clear the lower respiratory tract of foreign matter, particularly in the later stages of a cold. There are two types of cough: productive and nonproductive. A *productive cough* removes mucous secretions and foreign matter so that breathing becomes easier and the infection clears up. A *nonproductive* or *dry cough* causes throat irritation;

© Leah-Anne Thompson/ShutterStock, Inc.

The common cold accounts for 20% of all acute illnesses in the United States.

this type of cough is of little cleansing value. Some types of cough suppressant (antitussive) medication are useful for treating a nonproductive cough but should not be used to suppress a productive cough (Pain Assist, 2016).

Two kinds of OTC preparations are available to treat coughing:

1. **Antitussives** such as codeine, dextromethorphan, and diphenhydramine (an antihistamine) that act on the central nervous system (CNS) to raise the threshold of the cough-coordinating center, thereby reducing the frequency and intensity of a cough
2. **Expectorants** such as guaifenesin and terpin hydrate theoretically (but not effectively) increase and thin the fluids of the respiratory tract in an attempt to soothe the irritated respiratory tract membranes and decrease the thickness of the accumulated secretions so that coughing becomes more productive

**Table 15.5** lists commonly used OTC antitussives and their compositions. Often, the tickling sensation in the throat that triggers a cough can be eased by sucking on a cough drop or hard candy, which stimulates saliva flow to soothe the irritated membranes. Unless the cough is severe, sour hard candy often works just as well as more expensive cough lozenges.

Like other medications, cough remedies have a psychological value. Many patients with

### KEY TERMS

**congestion rebound**
withdrawal from excessive use of a decongestant that results in congestion

**antitussives**
drugs that block the coughing reflex

**expectorants**
substances that stimulate the secretion of mucus and diminish its viscosity

**TABLE 15.5** Compositions of Common OTC Antitussives

| Product | Antitussive | Expectorant |
|---|---|---|
| Delsym | Dextromethorphan | — |
| Humibid | — | Guaifen |
| Vicks Cough Drops | — | Guaifen |
| Robitussin DM Cough | Dextromethorphan | Guaifen |

Data from Scolaro, K. (2012). Disorders related to colds and allergies. In D. Krinsky et al. (Eds.), *Handbook of nonprescription drugs*, 17th ed. (pp. 180–204). Washington, DC: American Pharmacists Association.

respiratory tract infections claim that they cough less after using cough remedies, even when it is objectively demonstrated that the remedies reduce neither the frequency nor the intensity of the cough. Cough remedies work partly by reducing patients' anxiety about the cough and causing them to believe that their cough is lessening. Someone who believes in the remedy, often can get as much relief from a simple, inexpensive product as from the most sophisticated and costly one. If a cough does not ease in a few days, a doctor should be consulted (Pain Assist, 2016).

As previously mentioned, abuse of antitussive products by teenagers is a significant problem in some regions of this country. This abuse likely relates to the fact that in high doses the antitussive ingredient dextromethorphan can have an effect that resembles that of phencyclidine (PCP) (see "Here and Now: The Dextromethorphan Trip"). Up to 10% of young people use high doses of antitussives that contain dextromethorphan to get high (Johnston, 2019). Even though possession of cough medicines is not controlled, the National Institute on Drug Abuse advises parents to control access to cough and cold medications at home to prevent this potential problem (NIDA, 2016a).

### WHAT REALLY WORKS?

With all of the advances in medicine today, there is still no cure for the common cold. In most cases, the best treatment is plenty of rest, increased fluid intake to prevent dehydration and facilitate productive coughing, humidification of the air if it is dry, gargling with diluted saltwater (two teaspoons per quart), an analgesic to relieve the accompanying headache or muscle ache, and perhaps an occasional decongestant if nasal stuffiness is unbearable. In contrast, allergy symptoms are best relieved by antihistamines.

# HERE AND NOW

## The Dextromethorphan Trip

Dextromethorphan is the antitussive ingredient frequently found in nonprescription cough medicine. Because of pharmacological properties that resemble those of PCP, OTC cough medicines are sometimes abused by teenagers and young adults. The following was a posting on Bluelight with "advice" from a so-called experienced dextromethorphan user to the "beginner" illustrating the unpredictability and potential dangers of abusing this drug:

> Don't start getting anxious before your first "trip." Use the search engine and look up dextromethorphan. . . . There are a few things you need to know. . . . It can be enlightening, scary, dull, crazy. . . . It is not a classical psychedelic. Mixing different things will give you different results. Tripping with some friends, listening to a Dead album might be perfect. Spazzing out to EMTs and police, because

you don't understand what's going on is quite different. . . . I don't recommend mixing other drugs [the] first time. . . . Don't drink ALCOHOL. . . . Everyone is different. My "good time" could suck for you.

© Cheryl Casey/Shutterstock.

Data from Allen, J. (2010, September 14). Over-the-counter cough medicines escape FDA restrictions. *ABC Good Morning America*. Retrieved from http://abcnews.go.com/Health/Wellness/dextromethorphan-ingredient-robitussin-cough-medicines-escapes-fda-restrictions/story?id=11638160. Accessed March 16, 2011.

## SLEEP AIDS

The inability to sleep—insomnia—is a major problem in the United States, as illustrated by the following facts ("Insomnia Statistics," 2016):

- People today sleep 20% less than they did in the early 20th century.
- Approximately one-third of the population will suffer from some form of insomnia during their lifetime.
- The majority of Americans lose sleep because of stress and anxiety.
- Women are twice as likely to have problems sleeping as men.
- Some forms of insomnia have a genetic basis.
- Approximately 90% of the people who suffer from depression also have sleep problems.
- Approximately 10 million Americans use sleep aids.
- People suffering from sleep deprivation are more likely to become overweight or obese.
- The U.S. Surgeon General's office reports that sleep disorders cost our economy more than $15 billion per year in additional health costs.
- Each employee with sleep problems cost his or her employer approximately $3,200 more in healthcare costs than those employees who have normal sleep patterns, resulting in a total expense of about $150 billion.

These drugs should not be used as a sleep aid for young children because they can be unpredictable or even dangerous in this population. For example, the parents of a young child were traveling cross-country. They knew the trip would be long and the child would likely grow tired and cranky. To keep the child quiet and manageable, the parents used Benadryl, an allergy medication that contains an antihistamine to cause sedation. Instead of going to sleep, the medicated child became excited and uncontrollable, resulting in a difficult journey for the rest of the family (personal communication to Hanson, 2016). The drugs commonly used in OTC sleep aids are antihistamines, particularly diphenhydramine (Soong, 2016). Although antihistamines have been classified as OTC category I sleep aid ingredients, their usefulness in treating significant sleep disorders is limited. At best, some people who suffer mild, temporary sleep disturbances caused by problems such as physical discomfort, short-term disruption in daily routines (such as jet lag), and extreme emotional upset might experience temporary relief. However, even for those few who initially benefit from these agents, tolerance develops within four days. For long-term sleep problems, OTC sleep aids are of no therapeutic value and are rarely recommended by health professionals (Soong, 2016). Actually, their placebo benefit is likely more significant than their actual pharmacological benefit. Usually counseling and psychotherapy are more effective approaches for resolving chronic insomnia than OTC or even prescription sleep aid drugs (Bushak, 2016).

Because antihistamines are CNS depressants, in low doses they can cause sedation and antianxiety action. Although in the past some OTC products containing antihistamines were promoted for their relaxing effects (e.g., Quietworld, Compoz), currently no sedatives are approved for OTC marketing. The FDA decided that the earlier products relieved anxiety by causing drowsiness, and thus were not legitimate sedatives. Because of this ruling, medications that are promoted as antianxiety products are no longer available without a prescription. However, antihistamines have been added to an array of other OTC drug products marketed for the purpose of causing relaxation or promoting sleep; such products include analgesics (e.g., Excedrin PM), cold medicines (e.g., Tylenol Cold Multisymptom Nighttime), Midol Complete, and many others (Kirkwood & Melton, 2012; Scolaro, 2012; Shimp, 2012). The rationale for such combinations is questionable and their therapeutic value unsubstantiated.

## MELATONIN

The hormone melatonin is currently being used by millions to induce sleep or help the body's natural clock readjust after the effects of jet lag. Melatonin was referred to as the "all-natural nightcap of the 1990s." Although most users of this hormone want assistance in falling asleep, some people claim that melatonin also slows the aging process, stimulates the immune system, and enhances the sex drive. Melatonin is a naturally occurring hormone and is also found in some foods. Under the 1994 Dietary Supplement and Education Act, melatonin is considered a dietary supplement and is not regulated by the FDA. Despite the popularity of melatonin products, the efficacy of supplemental melatonin as a sleep aid or to help with jet lag is minimal at best (Bonnet & Arand, 2016). Products containing melatonin should be used cautiously, if at all (National Center for Complementary and Integrative Health, 2019).

## STIMULANTS

Some OTC drugs are promoted as stay-awake (e.g., NoDoz) or energy-promoting (e.g., Vivarin) products (Kirkwood & Melton 2012). In general, these medications contain high doses of caffeine (100 to 200 milligrams per tablet). Although it is true that CNS stimulation by ingesting significant doses of caffeine can increase the state of alertness during periods of drowsiness, the repeated use of such an approach is highly suspected.

For example, college students sometimes rely on such products to repeatedly enhance mental endurance during cramming sessions for examinations. In fact, at one western U.S. university, the back page of a quarterly class schedule, printed and distributed by the university, included a full-page advertisement for the OTC stimulant Vivarin with the caption, "Exam Survival Kit." The implications of such promotions are obvious and disturbing. Because of faculty objections, the advertisement was not run again at the university. Although moderate doses (around 200 milligrams) may help on test scores, excessive caffeine (more than 400 milligrams) causes anxiety and actually can significantly impair memory (Miller, 2016).

Routine use of stay-awake or energy-promoting products to enhance performance at work or in school can lead to dependence, resulting in withdrawal when the person stops using the drug. Most health professionals agree that there are more effective and safer ways to deal with fatigue and drowsiness—for example, managing time efficiently and getting plenty of rest (Kirkwood & Melton 2012).

## SYMPATHOMIMETICS

Mild OTC sympathomimetics have been marketed as safe stimulants and as legal alternatives to cocaine and other illicit stimulants. The principal ingredients found in the mild stimulants are drugs such as phenylephrine and caffeine. The same drugs are also found in OTC decongestants and diet aids (Miller & Bartels, 2012; Scolaro, 2012). Ephedrine, a naturally occurring stimulant (i.e., from the ephedra plant), and phenylpropanolamine were withdrawn from OTC use because of their potential toxicity on the cardiovascular system (Cleveland Clinic, 2016).

Although much less potent than amphetamines, high doses of OTC stimulants can cause anxiety, restlessness, throbbing headaches, breathing problems, and tachycardia (rapid heartbeat). There have been reports of death from heart arrhythmias, cerebral hemorrhaging, and strokes, as previously discussed, from excessive ephedrine use.

## GASTROINTESTINAL MEDICATIONS

The gastrointestinal (GI) system consists principally of the esophagus, stomach, and intestines and is responsible for the absorption of nutrients and water into the body, as well as the elimination of body wastes. The function of the GI system can be altered by changes in eating habits, stress, infection, and diseases such as ulcers and cancers. Such problems may affect appetite, cause discomfort or pain, result in nausea and vomiting, and alter the formation and passage of stools from the intestines.

A variety of OTC medications are available to treat GI disorders such as indigestion (antacids), heartburn (gastric-secretion blockers), constipation (laxatives), and diarrhea (antidiarrheals) ("Stomach and GI," 2016). However, before individuals self-medicate with nonprescription drugs, they should be certain that the cause of their GI problem is minor, self-limiting, and does not require professional care. Because antacids are the most frequently used of the GI nonprescription drugs, they are discussed next.

## ANTACIDS AND ANTIHEARTBURN MEDICATION

More than $3 billion is spent each year on antacids and heartburn medications that claim to give relief from heartburn and indigestion caused by excessive eating or drinking and to provide long-term treatment of chronic peptic ulcer disease (CHPA, 2020). It is estimated that as much as 50% of the population has had one or more attacks of **gastritis**, often referred to as *acid indigestion, heartburn, upset stomach*, and *sour* or *acid stomach*. These attacks often result from acid rebound and occur one to two hours after eating; by this time, the stomach contents have passed into the small intestine, leaving the gastric acids to irritate or damage the lining of the empty stomach. Heartburn, or gastroesophageal reflux, occurs after exposure of the lower esophagus to these irritating gastric chemicals.

## KEY TERM

**gastritis**
inflammation or irritation of the gut

Some cases of severe, chronic acid indigestion may progress to peptic ulcer disease. Peptic ulcers (open sores) most frequently affect the duodenum (first part of the intestine) and the stomach. Although this condition is serious, it can be treated effectively with antacids, which are often combined with drugs available OTC or by prescription such as cimetidine (Tagamet), ranitidine (Zantac), and famotidine (Pepcid). A person with acute, severe stomach pain; chronic gastritis; blood in the stools (common ulcer symptoms); diarrhea; or vomiting should see a physician promptly and should not attempt to self-medicate with OTC antacids (Sandi, 2016).

Most bouts of acid rebound, however, are associated with overeating or consuming irritating foods or drinks; these self-limiting cases can usually be managed safely with OTC antacids (such as sodium bicarbonate, calcium carbonate, aluminum salts, and magnesium salts). Because of their alkaline (opposite of acidic) nature, the nonprescription products neutralize gastric acids and give relief.

Generally speaking, OTC antacid preparations are safe for occasional use at low recommended doses, but excessive use can cause serious problems.

In addition, all antacids can interact with other drugs; they may alter the GI absorption or renal elimination of other medications. For example, some antacids inhibit the absorption of some vitamins and the minerals calcium and iron; thus, these products should not be taken at the same time. Consequently, patients using prescription drugs should consult with their physicians before taking OTC antacids (Sandi, 2016).

Heartburn can be treated effectively with low doses of Tagamet, Zantac, or Pepcid. These drugs were switched to OTC status in the mid-1990s and help reduce gastric secretions (Zweber & Berardi, 2012).

## DIET AIDS

In U.S. society, being slim and trim are prerequisites to being attractive. Despite the social desirability of being thin, it is estimated that in the United States 40% of adults and 19% of children and adolescents are obese (more than 20% above the ideal body weight) (Faberman, 2019). Being obese has been linked to many medical problems such as cardiovascular disease, some cancers, diabetes, chronic fatigue, and an array of aches and pains, not to mention psychological disorders such as depression (DerSarkissian, 2016). Popular remedies for losing weight often include fad diets advertised in supermarket journals, expensive weight-loss programs, or prescription or OTC diet aids.

Using drugs as diet aids is highly controversial (Anderson, 2016). Many experts view them as useless or even dangerous. Drugs marketed as diet aids are supposed to depress the appetite, which helps users maintain low-calorie diets. The most effective of these agents are called **anorexiants**. Potent anorexiants such as amphetamine-like

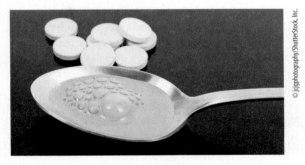

More than $3 billion is spent each year on heartburn medications in the United States and antacids such as this.

© jcjgphotography/ShutterStock, Inc.

**anorexiants**
drugs that suppress the activity of the brain's appetite center, causing reduced food intake

In 2019 approximately 20% to 30% of the people in the United States were obese and 50% were overweight.

© Wendy Nero/ShutterStock, Inc.

drugs (including the once-popular diet aid fen-phen), can cause dangerous side effects and are available only by prescription. The appetite-suppression effects of prescription anorexiants are usually temporary, after which tolerance often builds. Thus, even prescription diet aid drugs are usually effective for only a short period. There are no wonder drugs to help the obese lose weight permanently.

The most potent and most frequently used OTC diet aid ingredients were the sympathomimetic drugs phenylpropanolamine and ephedrine, but several years ago the FDA removed both drugs from all OTC products ("Urban Legends," 2010). The current OTC diet aids are minimally effective and of no value in the treatment of significant obesity; they typically contain high doses of caffeine and sometimes natural ingredients such as *bitter orange*, which contains the mild sympathomimetic synephrine. Despite their minimal value, frequent use of high doses of the OTC diet aid products is a common practice by weight-conscious female high school and college students. As one college sophomore who routinely carried a package of Dexatrim in her purse said, "Popping two or three of these before an important date helps me to eat like a bird and appear more petite" (personal communication to Hanson). Interestingly, this same woman also occasionally induced vomiting after eating because of her fear that she was gaining weight. Such weight-management practices are extremely worrisome and may be part of strategies of young people suffering from eating disorders such as anorexia and bulimia (Mayo Clinic, 2016).

### SKIN PRODUCTS

Because the skin is so accessible and readily visible, most people are sensitive about its appearance. These cosmetic concerns are motivated by attempts to look good and preserve a youthful appearance. Almost 25% of the world's population has some form of skin disease with conditions such as eczema, rashes, and acne accounting for the majority of these issues (Science Daily, 2019). Only a few of the most commonly used products are mentioned here: acne medications, sun products, and basic first-aid products.

### ACNE MEDICATIONS

Acne is the most common skin disorder that affects adolescents. It typically occurs during puberty in response to the secretion of the male hormone androgen, which is produced by both males and females. Acne is typically a chronic inflammation caused by bacteria trapped in plugged sebaceous (oil) glands and hair follicles. This condition consists of whiteheads, pimples, nodules, and, in more severe cases, pustules, cysts, and abscesses. Moderate to severe acne can cause unsightly scarring on the face, back, chest, and arms and should be treated aggressively by a dermatologist with drugs such as antibiotics (tetracycline) and potent **keratolytics**, such as Retin-A (retinoic acid), vitamin A, or Accutane (isotretinoin). Usually, minor to moderate acne does not cause scarring or permanent skin damage and often can be safely self-medicated with OTC acne medications (Lynn, Umari, Dunnick, & Dellavalle, 2016).

Several nonprescription approaches to treating mild acne are available, including the following.

- *Sebum removal*: Oil and fatty chemicals (sebum) can accumulate on the skin and plug the sebaceous glands and hair follicles. Use of OTC products such as alcohol wipes (e.g., Stri-Dex) can help remove such accumulations.
- *Peeling agents*: The FDA found several keratolytic agents safe and effective for treatment of minor acne: benzoyl peroxide (Oxy 10 Daily Wash), salicylic acid (Neutrogena Rapid Defense), resorcinol, and sulfur (DDF Sulfur), alone or in combination. These drugs help to prevent acne eruptions by causing the **keratin layer** of the skin to peel or by killing the bacteria that cause inflammation associated with acne. If multiple concentrations of a keratolytic are available, then it is better to start with a lower concentration and move up to the higher one, allowing the skin to become accustomed to the caustic action of these products. The initial exposure may worsen the appearance of acne temporarily, but the acne usually improves with continual use of these products.

### SUN PRODUCTS

The damaging effects of sun exposure on the skin have been well publicized in recent years. It is now clear that the ultraviolet (UV) rays associated with

### KEY TERMS

**keratolytics**
caustic agents that cause the keratin skin layer to peel

**keratin layer**
outermost protective layer of the skin

sunlight have several adverse effects on the skin. Skin cancer is the most common cancer in the United States. Most cases are a direct consequence of exposure to UV rays, which cause cumulative skin damage over time (American Academy of Dermatology, 2016).

The majority of cases will be cancers of skin cells called *basal cell* or *squamous cell carcinomas* (Crosby & O'Neal, 2012). These cancers usually are easily removed by minor surgery, and patients have a good prognosis for recovery. However, about 0.5% of the population will suffer a much more deadly form of skin cancer called *melanoma*. Melanomas are cancers of the pigment-forming cells of the skin, called *melanocytes*, and spread rapidly from the skin throughout the body, ultimately causing 75% of skin cancer–related deaths. Almost 10,000 deaths occur from melanomas each year (American Academy of Dermatology, 2016).

Another long-term concern related to UV exposure is premature aging. Skin frequently exposed to UV rays such as during routine tanning experiences deterioration associated with the aging process. Elastin and collagen fibers are damaged, causing a loss of pliability and elasticity in the skin and resulting in a leathery, wrinkled appearance (MedlinePlus, 2019).

Because of these damaging effects of sun exposure, an array of protective sunscreen products is available OTC. Most sunscreens are formulated to screen out the shorter UVB rays. Because they deeply penetrate the skin, the longer UVA rays likely contribute to melanoma as well as chronic skin damage, causing skin to wrinkle, sag, and lose tone; consequently, many of the newer sunscreens block the UVA rays as well (American Academy of Dermatology Association, 2019).

The protection afforded by sunscreens is designated by a **sun protection factor (SPF) number**. This designation tells users the relative length of time they can stay in the sun before burning, and includes ratings of two to 11 (minimum), 12 to 30 (moderate), and greater than 30 (high) (Crosby & O'Neal, 2012). For example, proper application of a product with an SPF of 10 allows users to remain in the sun without burning 10 times longer than if it was not applied. Remember that

the SPF designation does not indicate protection against UVA rays. Although there currently is no convenient rating system to assess UVA screening, products with SPF ratings of 15 or greater usually offer some protection against the longer UV radiation. In addition, a compound called *avobenzone* appears to offer the fullest protection against UVA rays. Because the natural pigment in the skin affords some UV protection, people with fair complexions (less skin pigmentation) require products with higher SPF numbers than do darker-skinned people.

People who want complete protection from UVB exposure can use OTC sunblockers, which prevent any tanning. Sunscreen ingredients in high concentrations essentially become sunblockers. In addition, an opaque zinc oxide ointment is a highly effective and inexpensive sun-blocking product and is available OTC.

### SKIN FIRST-AID PRODUCTS

A variety of unrelated OTC drugs are available as first-aid products for the self-treatment of minor skin problems such as burns, sunburns, and wounds (Drugs.com, 2016). Included in this category of agents are the following products:

- local anesthetics such as benzocaine (e.g., Dermoplast) to relieve the discomfort and pain of burns or trauma;
- antibiotics and antiseptics such as bacitracin (Polysporin), neomycin (Neosporin), betadine, and tincture of iodine to treat or prevent skin infections; and
- antihistamines (Benadryl) or corticosteroids (hydrocortisone [Cortaid]) to relieve itching or inflammation associated with skin rashes, allergies, or insect bites

These first-aid skin products can be effective when used properly. In general, side effects to such topical products are few and minor when they do occur.

## ▌ OTC Herbal (Natural) Products

The World Health Organization reports that 80% of people worldwide use herbal products as part of their primary health care. Herbal products are a unique category of OTC remedies that account for almost $8 billion a year in U.S. sales (Saper, 2019). They are unique because, despite the presence of active ingredients, there is little or no federal regulation (Drugs.com, 2015) because of a 1994 law supported by the dietary supplement industry called the Dietary Supplement Health and Education

Act (National Library of Medicine, 2010). This law requires the government to demonstrate that substances in the herbal products are harmful before such products can be removed from the market; thus, the burden of proof lies with the FDA, not the manufacturer (Rickert, 2012).

This act also (1) makes the manufacturer responsible for its product's safety, (2) explains how product literature is used for product promotion, and (3) describes what can be included on labels. Because of these regulations, manufacturers cannot use terms such as *diagnose*, *treat*, *prevent*, or *cure* to describe their herbal products. Companies can, however, make claims about affecting body function. For example, manufacturers of glucosamine cannot claim their product helps cure arthritis, but they can say products with glucosamine help the joints function better (National Library of Medicine, 2010). Because of the lack of regulation, these products often are not scientifically tested, and they vary considerably in both the quantity and quality of active ingredients (National Library of Medicine, 2010). Herbal products have been viewed with considerable skepticism by many experts who argue that "assertions, speculation and testimonials do not substitute for evidence" when it comes to establishing the value of a drug (McQueen & Orr, 2012).

In the past few years, some changes in attitude toward herbal products have occurred. More people, including a few traditional health professionals, believe that some herbs may be useful in treating minor health problems (McQueen & Orr, 2012; Saper, 2019). However, physicians are typically not taught about herbal medicines in medical school and are generally perceived as being ignorant about herbal products and knowing little about their therapeutic value or their ability to

Herbal products have become popular and widely accepted.

interact with prescribed drugs (Brunner, 2010). Despite greater acceptance, the fact that most people who use herbs to treat medical conditions still consider prescription drugs to be considerably more effective suggests there exists persistent skepticism regarding these products, even among consumers (Lampert, 2013).

Frequent uses of herbal products include treatment of anxiety, chronic fatigue, arthritis, and digestive problems. Another common use of these natural products is to elevate mood. The most popular herbs for these purposes are St. John's wort, S-adenosylmethionine (SAM-e), and kava kava (Hume & Strong, 2006; Williams, Girard, Jui, Sabina, & Katz, 2005) (see "Here and Now: Herbal Options"). It is generally thought that although these products do have some effect in the treatment of minor to moderate depression and anxiety, there is no evidence they elevate a normal, undisturbed mood or that they are particularly effective against severe mood disturbances (National Center for Complementary and Alternative Medicine [NCCAM], 2013). A major risk of self-administering these remedies for mood disorders is that some of the people self-treating their depression are severely emotionally unstable. Overall, depression leads to approximately 20,000 suicides in this country each year. Another considerable problem of self-medicating with herbal products for mood disorders is the lack of standardization for these substances. A recent survey revealed that the actual amount of active SAM-e per pill in products claiming to contain 200 milligrams of active ingredient ranged from 80 to 250 milligrams. For these reasons, it is almost universally recommended that patients with serious emotional disturbances, especially depression, be diagnosed by a mental health professional even though

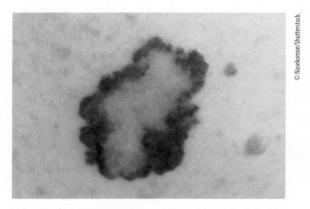

This skin cancer is melanoma and is caused by excessive exposure to ultraviolet light.

# HERE AND NOW
## Herbal Options

With the increasing popularity of herbal products, an array of choices has become available for dealing with many common, usually self-limiting health problems. The following is a list of some of the most popular of these medicinal herbs (Saper, 2019).

### Echinacea

*Common claim:* Stimulates immune system and helps fight infections.

*Common use:* Reduce cold symptoms and help accelerate recovery.

*Effectiveness:* May shorten the duration of a cold but does not prevent it; however, even this is controversial.

*Concerns:* Relatively well tolerated, but fatigue and sleepiness occasionally occur.

### Garlic

*Common claim:* Inhibits production of cholesterol and reduces blood sugar.

*Common use:* Treat diabetes and prevent cardiovascular disease.

*Effectiveness:* Most studies do not find garlic effective against serious diseases.

*Concerns:* Mild stomach discomfort and possible interaction with blood-thinning (anticlotting) prescription drugs occur.

### Ginkgo Biloba

*Common claim:* Improves memory.

*Common use:* Often promoted to enhance memory for patients with Alzheimer's disease.

*Effectiveness:* At best helps to prevent some mental decline in Alzheimer's patients but does not appear to reverse memory loss or help normal or age-related memory losses.

*Concerns:* Can interact with blood-thinning medications such as aspirin.

### Glucosamine and Chondroitin

*Common claim:* Contribute to joint strength.

*Common use:* Relieve the discomfort of arthritis.

*Effectiveness:* Provide moderate relief from the pain of arthritis and may help to slow progress of the disease.

*Concerns:* May interact with blood thinners and adversely affect adult-onset diabetes.

### Saw Palmetto

*Common claim:* Relieves discomforts associated with prostate gland.

*Common use:* Shrink enlarged prostate and facilitate urination.

*Effectiveness:* Provides relief for most men within a month of use.

*Concerns:* Well tolerated by most men.

### SAM-e

*Common claim:* Helps regulate brain transmitters such as dopamine.

*Common use:* Relieve symptoms of depression.

*Effectiveness:* Some evidence that it relieves moderate depression.

*Concerns:* Side effects are typically mild such as stomach upset, insomnia, and nervousness. Can be expensive, ranging from $55 to $260 per month.

### St. John's Wort

*Common claim:* Elevates mood.

*Common use:* Treats mild to moderate depression.

*Effectiveness:* Appears to relieve some cases of mild depression for the short term.

*Concerns:* Recent alert from the FDA warns about interactions with numerous medications, such as other antidepressants and birth-control pills.

### Ginseng

*Common claim:* Increases energy.

*Common use:* Treats fatigue and enhances performance.

*Effectiveness:* There may be some mild stimulation, but there is no evidence of enhanced performance.

*Concerns:* Well tolerated for the most part, although there are some reports of minor addiction.

Data from McQueen, C., & Orr, R. (2012). Natural products. In D. Krinsky et al. (Eds.), *Handbook of nonprescription drugs*, 17th ed. (pp. 967–1006). Washington, DC: American Pharmacists Association; National Center for Complementary and Alternative Medicine (NCCAM). (2013, June 10). Herbs at a glance. Retrieved from http://nccam.nih.gov/health/herbsataglance.htm

some of these professionals may find use of the natural products to be acceptable for treatment of mild emotional problems.

Other concerns with herbal products include the possibility of interaction with other OTC and prescription medications, especially in the elderly population (Landro, 2016; NCCAM, 2013). This is becoming more problematic as the routine use of herbs becomes common, especially because unscrupulous manufacturers may deceive customers into thinking that these products are perfectly safe and do not really contain any drugs but "only natural ingredients." Products containing herbs such as garlic, ginkgo biloba, and ginseng have been shown to interact with some drugs. A notable example of drug interactions has been reported with St. John's wort, kava, and Echinacea, which alter the metabolism of drugs used to treat heart failure, asthma, infections, blood clots, and cancer (Landro, 2016). Despite such potentially dangerous interactions with prescriptions, 70% of patients claim they do not advise physicians that they regularly use herbal products (Landro, 2016).

Finally, lack of regulation has encouraged such a lackadaisical attitude concerning herbs that their use has been trivialized to the extent that they and their associated active drugs are now being included in foods and marketed in both health-food stores and supermarkets. Recent snacks, cereals, and beverages spiked with medicinal herbs include ginseng ginger ale, kava kava corn chips, Echinacea fruit drinks, and ginkgo biloba chocolate bars. These products, sometimes referred to as *functional foods*, are typically packaged in colorful containers with cartoon figures that are likely to appeal to kids and accompanied by subtle suggestive promotions implying that they can "support emotional and mental balance." The exact quantities of herbal substances added to such food and snack products and their actual effects (if any) are difficult to monitor. Although concerned, regulatory agencies are uncertain as to how to deal with the potential problems associated with this marketing strategy (Brophy & Schardt, 2010).

### HERBALS AND ABUSE

Despite the lack of governmental control, drugs found naturally in plants or herbs can have serious side effects or can be abused. In fact, some of the most powerful substances of abuse are extracted from plants, including drugs such as cocaine (*Erythroxylum coca*), marijuana (*Cannabis sativa*), peyote (*Lophophora williamsii*), and tobacco (*Nicotiana tabacum*). These substances are mentioned to emphasize the point that being associated with herbs and natural products does not exclude a drug from being abused. Of concern in this section are unregulated herbal products and their potential for abuse and addiction. As a general

rule, if a substance (including a natural product) elevates mood, causes a feeling of energy, or brings on a feeling of relaxation and relief from stress, it likely has potential for abuse. Based on these principles, the herbal products most likely to be abused include those containing ma huang, ginseng, kava kava, and ephedrine (NCCAM, 2013). Of course, with addiction typically comes high-quantity use and a greater chance of serious side effects. Even though serious abuse of herbal products is possible, it does not occur frequently; when it does occur, it is generally relatively easy to treat.

## Prescription Drugs

The Durham–Humphrey Amendment of 1951 established the criteria that are still used today to determine whether a drug should be used only under the direction of a licensed health professional such as a physician. According to this piece of legislation, drugs are controlled with prescriptions if they are (1) habit forming, (2) not safe for self-medication, (3) intended to treat ailments that require the supervision of a health professional, or (4) new and without an established safe track record (Katzung, 2015b). Currently, more than 10,000 prescription products are sold in the United States, representing approximately 1,500 different drugs, with 20 to 50 new medications approved each year by the FDA. In 2019, nearly 70% of US adults ages 40 to 79 used at least one prescription drug in the previous 30 days, and 20% were concurrently using at least five or more prescription medications (Hales, 2019). In 2010, 3.9 billion drug prescriptions were written at a cost of about $300 billion and since then this cost has risen almost 50% (Bartholow, 2010; Hales, 2019; Kaiser Family Foundation, 2010). With statistics like these, it is not surprising that the United States leads the world in prescription drug consumption on a per capita basis (Hanson, 2010). It also is not surprising that many drug consumers have difficulty affording required prescriptions. For example, a 48-year-old mother of five children tells the story of how she recently was forced to rush to an emergency room in Maine while driving her car with children because of an episode of hyperglycemia (elevated blood sugar because of insufficient insulin in the blood) resulting from a cutback in her diabetic medication. The reduction in her use of these essential drugs was not voluntary but imposed because of her inability to afford the dramatic monthly rise in cost of insulin to $300 (Gill, 2019). Similar stories are being told throughout the United States because of what appears to be uncontrolled factors making many prescription drugs unaffordable for patients who depend on access to these medications to address serious medical problems. The following are suggestions of possible strategies to help mitigate this drug crisis in the United States (Kamal, Cox, & McDermott, 2019):

- Make it easier for cheaper generic drugs to get to market.
- Require drug companies to better inform consumers by including drug prices in ads.
- Allow the government to negotiate with drug companies for lower competitive prices.
- Allow Americans to get cheaper drugs from other countries such as Canada and Mexico.
- Increasing taxes on drug companies whose prices are unreasonably high.
- End tax breaks given to drug companies for their advertising expenses.

Because of their specialized training, physicians, dentists, and, under certain conditions, podiatrists, physician assistants, nurse practitioners, pharmacists, and optometrists, are granted drug-prescribing privileges. The health professionals who write prescriptions are expected to accurately diagnose medical conditions requiring therapy, consider the benefits and risks of drug treatment for the patient, and identify the best drug and safest manner of administering it. The responsibility of the health professional does not conclude with the writing of a prescription; in many ways, it only just begins. Professional monitoring to ensure proper drug use and evaluate the patient's response is crucial for successful therapy.

## ▌ Prescription Drug Abuse

A 23-year-old man had been a football star in his high school and was excited about receiving a full football scholarship to Ohio State University. Although majoring in engineering, his dream was to play in the National Football League. Unlike many of his football friends in high school, this young man had stayed clean from opioid drugs such as heroin and prescription analgesics until a car accident a month before graduation. Because of the emotional trauma and severe pain from the major car crash, his life plans were shattered. He dealt with all of his mental and physical problems by consuming large quantities of the hydrocodone opioid narcotic drug his orthopedic surgeon continued to prescribe long after medical treatment

ended. One day his father could not rouse him and called an ambulance. Fortunately, emergency treatment at the local hospital saved his life and also made both him and his parents aware of his drug crisis. He weaned himself off of the pills, and they all entered family therapy. Happily, after a year of treatment, this young man was ready to get on with his life and successfully entered college with the support of his family (Satel, 2019). This real life story is a typical example of abuse problems that have resulted in more than 130 opioid overdose deaths in the United States every day (NIDA, 2019b; Schiller, Goyal, Cao, & Mechanic, 2019). In many places, abuse of prescription drugs, particularly of the opioid category, is a greater problem than use of illicit drugs. This is supported by the fact that the overall cost of prescription painkiller abuse over 15 years has been $72 billion (Leslie, Ba, Agbese, Xing, & Liu, 2019).

The three classes of prescription drugs most likely to be abused, in order of their abuse frequency, are narcotic analgesics, CNS depressants, and stimulants (used to treat obesity and attention-deficit hyperactivity disorder [ADHD]). Particularly troubling is what appears to be an exploding epidemic of abusing prescription narcotic painkilling drugs such as OxyContin and Vicodin (Johnston, 2016; U.S. Department of Health and Human Services, 2016). Headlines announcing a celebrity seeking treatment for dependence on or even death because of these drugs are becoming disturbingly routine (see "Here and Now: Another Celebrity Death from Prescription Drug Abuse"). In fact, as previously mentioned, abuse of prescription narcotics appears to be the leading problem with prescription drugs. Often young people abuse a combination of these prescribed drugs, and their sources include the medicine cabinets in their parents' or friends' homes or the Internet from "web pharmacies" that do not require legitimate prescriptions (Journey Pure, 2015). This is a problem with youth and adults from all backgrounds.

To deal with this escalating problem, it is important to determine why nonmedical prescription drug abuse occurs. Although there are many general and personal explanations for why a person takes medications not prescribed for them, the most frequent are as follow (Health Day, 2012; McCabe, Boyd, & Teter, 2009):

- 13% abuse the prescription drugs for recreation, usually to get high or to try to feel better;
- 39% try to self-medicate a preexisting medical or emotional problem with someone else's

# HERE AND NOW

## Another Celebrity Death from Prescription Drug Abuse

The music megastar known as Prince (Prince Rogers Nelson) died from a prescription overdose on April 21, 2016. Authorities confirmed that the 57-year-old rock star was addicted to pain medications. However, at his death little was known about his past use of these drugs or how he was able to obtain them. An autopsy revealed no trauma and no evidence of foul play. His death was also ruled not an act of suicide but accidental. It is believed his abuse of these opioid analgesics began after a hip surgery several years before because of his energetic stage performances. Friends have revealed that at the time of death attempts were being made to persuade Prince to enroll in a treatment program to deal with his opioid drug addiction. Reports from the medical examiner's office claim that the cause of Prince's death was self-administration of the powerful opioid narcotic fentanyl. This opioid analgesic is the most potent of all the opioid drugs prescribed for pain relief: approximately 100 times more potent than morphine and 20 to 40 times more potent than heroin. Although it is often used to manage cancer-related pain, because of its potency and rapid action it has become a favorite drug for narcotic abusers. Because of fentanyl's potency and low cost (it is cheaper than heroin), drug dealers often add it to their street drugs to enhance their effects. In high doses or in combination with other CNS-depressing drugs, fentanyl can kill in seconds. This certainly is not the first time that fentanyl has contributed to the narcotic overdose death of an unsuspecting user, and it certainly will not be the last.

© Anthony Correia/Shutterstock.

Data from Hayes, A. (2016). Prince died from fentanyl overdose. WebMD. Retrieved from http://www.webmd.com/mental-health/addiction/news/20160602 /prince-fentanyl-overdose; Sickles, J. (2016). Prince cause of death: Opioid overdose, tests reportedly show. Yahoo News. Retrieved from https://www.yahoo .com/news/prince-cause-death-000000903.html. Accessed January 9, 2020.

prescription medication (e.g., use a benzodiazepine to relieve anxiety);

- 48% have elements of both of the first two explanations; and
- prescription abuse can be part of a bigger picture of substance abuse that includes the abuse of other drugs (both licit and illicit). One drug may be used to either embellish or relieve withdrawal from another drug of abuse (e.g., benzodiazepines taken to relieve the withdrawal from alcohol) (NIDA, 2016c).

Dealing with suspected abuse of prescription medication can pose a difficult management problem for physicians and pharmacists. It has become such a major issue that some third-party payers (i.e., health insurance companies) have implemented tight monitoring procedures. Those who try to fraudulently obtain controlled substances with valid and invalid prescriptions include persons from all walks of life.

In the United States, young people frequently abuse prescription drugs. One trend is the so-called pharm party, where high school students get together and try to get high on a mixture of prescription drugs followed by a chaser of alcohol (Fuller, 2020) (see "Here and Now: Pharm Parties and Russian Roulette"). However, young people rarely obtain the drugs by theft, fraud, or doctor shopping, although occasionally unscrupulous doctors will write prescriptions without questions for money (Fuller, 2020). Instead, they usually obtain their prescription drugs from peers, friends, or family members or sometimes purchase them from rogue Internet pharmacies. In some areas, the problem is so severe that high schools have implemented programs to prevent such sharing.

Abusers of prescription drugs often have multiple addictions, including dependence on caffeine, alcohol, or nicotine. In addition, once a pharmacy is recognized as an easy target, word spreads and other abusers often begin to frequent the same store. Signs of patients with drug-seeking behavior include the following:

- use of altered or forged prescriptions;
- claims that a prescription has been lost and a physician is unavailable for confirmation;

# HERE AND NOW
## Pharm Parties and Russian Roulette

One expression of prescription drug abuse is seen with high school students who bring samples of prescription drugs from home and dump them into a common bowl. The teens then grab a handful and pop them into their mouths like trail mix and swallow. The objective is to try to produce bizarre feelings and unusual highs. The mixtures often include medications such as antidepressants, stimulants, sleeping pills, antianxiety drugs, and narcotic pain relievers. One doctor described the activity as "Russian roulette," only with pills instead of bullets. The source of the drugs is often parents' or grandparents' medicine cabinets that frequently are filled with years of drug accumulation. For example, one 15-year-old said he wanted to be "cool" and told his friends that he could get some Percocets out of his stepdad's bottle. He explained that his stepdad had undergone many surgeries, so he had a lot of pills. The young man explained that the pills went down quickly and the smooth buzz was free and everyone thought it was safe. Soon other friends joined the group and each would bring medicines from their own homes—a little

Vicodin here, some OxyContin there, usually with some whiskey and vodka to wash it down. As word got around, other friends joined the "cool" group and more prescription drugs were pooled and the activity had escalated into a pharm party. Although at first everything seemed innocent and fun, the group soon learned that using large quantities and mixed assortments of drugs that belong to someone else can be disastrous and even deadly.

Fuller, K. (2020, January). Pharming: Pill parties for teens. *Psychology Today*. Retrieved from https://www.psychologytoday.com/us/blog/happiness-is-state-mind/201809/pharming-pill-parties-teens

- frequent visits to emergency rooms or clinics for poorly defined health problems;
- visits made to a pharmacy late in the day, on weekends, or just before closing;
- alteration of doses on a legitimate prescription;
- loud, abusive, and insulting behavior;
- use of several names; and
- being particularly knowledgeable about drugs.

## ▪ Prescription Abuse and Pregnancy

Babies born to mothers addicted to prescription drugs have become the youngest victims of the prescription abuse epidemic. In excess of 22,000 babies are born annually who are physically dependent on the prescription analgesics to which their mothers are addicted and experience withdrawal after birth (NIDA, 2015). This disturbing outcome includes a newborn who within days after birth, for no apparent reason, experienced vomiting with diarrhea, extreme

irritability and shaking, inability to sleep, trouble eating, and frequent shrieking from pain. Infants such as this are manifesting withdrawal symptoms caused by their in utero exposure to the drugs (usually prescription narcotics) the mother consumed in large quantities during pregnancy. Although these infants are sometimes described as addicted to their mothers' drugs, this is inaccurate. Their bodies have become physically dependent on the substances the newborns were exposed to during development; after birth their bodies are abruptly removed from drug exposure and thrown into a withdrawal reaction. These drug-dependent babies should remain in the hospital for weeks or months while they are gradually weaned from the drug on which they are physically dependent. These babies put a tremendous financial strain on our healthcare systems, costing an average of about $50,000 per child. As stated by a maternal–fetal medicine specialist, "They are the innocent victims. They had no control over it and yet they suffer tremendously for it" (Olian, 2012).

# ■ Necessary Drug Information for Healthcare Providers

Many unnecessary side effects and delays in proper care are caused by poor communication between the health professional and the patient or by a doctor's lack of knowledge concerning the patient's medical history when a drug is prescribed. The smaller a drug's margin of safety (i.e., the difference between therapeutic and toxic doses), the more critical it becomes that the doctor has all relevant information regarding the patient's medical needs and vulnerabilities. The following is a brief overview of principles to help ensure that the health professional has the necessary information to properly prescribe and manage drug use for the patient.

Doctor–patient communication must be reciprocal. We tend to think that patients listen while doctors talk when it comes to deciding on the best medication for treatment. To ensure a proper diagnosis, precise and complete information from the patient is also essential. In fact, if a doctor is to select the best and safest drug for a patient, he or she needs to know everything possible about the medical problems to be treated. In addition, the patient should provide the doctor with a complete medical and drug history, particularly if there has been a problem with the patient's cardiovascular system, kidneys, liver, or mental functions. Other information that should be shared with the doctor includes previous drug reactions as well as a complete list of drugs routinely being used, including prescription, nonprescription, and herbal products. In this regard, more and more states are establishing database systems that include up-to-date information concerning prescription drug histories that allow monitoring of what has been prescribed and dispensed to individual patients. Currently, most states have passed legislation authorizing, and in some cases mandating, such programs, but making these databases real time can be extremely expensive and must adequately address issues such as patient confidentiality (Small, 2013; Vestal, 2016). However, it is hoped that eventually there will be a nationwide program that allows pharmacies, doctors, and other medical personnel to contribute to and access information from the prescription drug history of their patients so they can avoid dangerous and unnecessary prescribing practices and be aware of potential prescription abuse problems.

The patient needs to be educated about proper drug use. If the doctor does not volunteer this information, then the patient should insist on answers to the following questions:

- *What is being treated?* This question does not require a long, unintelligible scientific answer. It should include an easy-to-understand explanation of the medical problem.
- *What is the desired outcome?* The patient should know why the drug is being prescribed and what the drug treatment is intended to accomplish. It is difficult for the patient to become involved in therapy if he or she is not aware of its objectives.
- *What are the possible side effects of the drug?* This answer does not necessitate an exhaustive list of every adverse reaction ever recorded in the medical literature; however, it is important to realize that adverse drug reactions to prescription drugs are common. In the United States, more people die from adverse reactions to legal medications than succumb to all illegal drug use. It is estimated that approximately 20,000 people die while another 2.1 million are seriously injured in this country each year from reactions to legal medications (Alton, 2016). In general, if adverse reactions occur in more than 1% of users, this should be mentioned to the patient. In addition, the patient should be made aware of ways to minimize the occurrence of side effects (e.g., to minimize nausea, an irritating drug should not be taken on an empty stomach), as well as what to do if a side effect occurs (e.g., if a rash occurs, call the doctor immediately).

© LiquidLibrary.

To maximize benefit and minimize risk, there must be proper doctor–patient communication.

- *How should the drug be taken to minimize problems and maximize benefits?* This answer should include details on how much, how often, and how long the drug should be taken.

- *How should the drug be disposed of?* This should include a discussion of the facts concerning proper and safe elimination of prescription drugs (see "Here and Now: Do Not Flush! Do Not Pour!").

# HERE AND NOW
## Do Not Flush! Do Not Pour!

Most of us have prescription drugs we no longer need sitting in our medicine cabinets or in other unsecured places. Often these medications have long passed their recommended expiration dates or intended use, but because of ignorance or neglect they become forgotten and a potential risk to an inquisitive child, to someone who is tempted to use them for medical purposes other than those for which they were prescribed, or to someone who is desperately looking to steal drugs to satisfy a substance abuse problem. To avoid these undesirable outcomes and to prevent water pollution, it is important for patients to be educated about the proper use and disposal of their prescription drugs. For safe management of prescription drugs, the following guidelines should be observed:

- *Don't flush unused prescription drugs down the toilet or pour them down the drain.* Some drugs that are disposed of in our sewers end up in our water systems, causing pollution and damaging the environment. This is not a desirable way to dispose of prescription substances.

- *Don't throw unused prescription drugs into the garbage.* Because abuse of some of the prescription drugs such as opioid painkillers is common, often persons with substance abuse problems check the garbage cans of acquaintances and strangers alike for unused drugs that satisfy their intense cravings.

- *Prescription drugs still being used should be safely secured.* Keeping in mind the potential danger and abuse of many prescription drugs, it is important that these substances be stored in a secure place that can be locked and is inaccessible to children and unintended users.

- *Disposal of unused prescription drugs at approved permanent collection sites is preferred.* Steel-mounted metal drug disposal bins are usually available at approved pharmacies, hospitals, or law enforcement stations and offices. The prescription drugs can be anonymously deposited in the bins for frequent removal by authorized personnel and then transferred to special facilities for incineration (Drug Enforcement Administration [DEA], 2018).

- *Prescription medicines can be safely disposed of at home.* If there is no access to a permanent collection site, then safe disposal at home can be achieved by mixing all unused drugs with an undesirable substance such as coffee grounds, moist unused cat litter, or spoiled food and putting it into a sealable plastic bag. The bag should be wrapped with duct tape or placed in a solid container. If the medications are solid, water should be added to dissolve them before mixing. The container should then be thrown away on the day of garbage collection. When disposing of the drug container, be sure all identifying personal information has been removed or destroyed.

In 2014, the Drug Enforcement Administration (DEA) posted a final ruling for the public entitled the Disposal Act, which gives the DEA authority to create and enforce regulations that allow prescription drug users to deliver unused pharmaceutical controlled substances to appropriate facilities (such as pharmacies) for safe and effective disposal (DEA, 2014). The objective is to encourage public and private users of these drugs to eliminate unnecessary controlled medications in an efficient, secure, and convenient manner, thereby minimizing the likelihood of illegal diversion and abuse of these products (DEA, 2018).

© D. Pimborough/Shutterstock.

This is a secure drug disposal box now available in some pharmacies throughout the country for secure disposal of unused controlled prescription substances.

# HERE AND NOW

## OBRA '90: The Evolving Role of Pharmacists in Drug Management

In 1990, the U.S. Congress passed section 4401 of the Omnibus Budget Reconciliation Act (commonly referred to as OBRA '90), which substantially altered the role of pharmacists in drug management. This act designated the pharmacist as the key player in improving the quality of drug care for patients in this country. Because OBRA '90 is federal legislation, it can require drug-related services for Medicare patients only; however, most states have recognized that similar services should be made available to all patients and have enacted legislation to that end. OBRA '90 requires pharmacists to conduct a drug use review (DUR) for each prescription to improve the outcome of drug therapy and reduce adverse side effects. The DUR program describes four basic professional services that a pharmacist must render whenever a drug prescription is filled:

- Prescriptions and patients' records must be screened to avoid problems caused by drug duplications, adverse drug–drug interactions, medical complications, incorrect drug doses, and incorrect duration of drug treatment.

Patients should be counseled regarding the following:

- How to safely and effectively administer the drug.
- Common adverse effects and interactions with other drugs, food, and so forth.
- How to avoid problems with the drug.
- How to monitor the progress of drug therapy.
- How to store the drug properly.
- Whether a refill is intended.
- What to do if a dose is missed.

Patient profiles, including information on disease, a list of medications, and the pharmacist's comments relevant to drug therapy, must be maintained. This information should be stored in computer files for future reference.

Documentation must record if the patient refuses consultation from the pharmacist or if a potential drug therapy problem is identified and the patient is warned.

*Note:* In 2019, the OBRA '90 act was still being enforced (see Vivian & Fink, 2019).

Data from Abood, R. (1992). OBRA '90: Implementation and enforcement. *NABP U.S. Pharmacists, State Boards—A Continuing Education Series*. Park Ridge, IL: National Association of Pharmacy.

---

Although it is a health professional's legal and professional obligation to communicate this information, patients frequently leave the doctor's office with a prescription that gives them legal permission to use a drug but without the knowledge of how to use it properly. Because of this all-too-common problem, pharmacists have been mandated by legislation referred to as the Omnibus Budget Reconciliation Act of 1990 to provide the necessary information to patients on proper drug use (Centers for Medicare and Medicaid Services, 2016) (see "Here and Now: OBRA '90: The Evolving Role of Pharmacists in Drug Management"). Patients should be encouraged to ask questions of those who write and fill prescriptions.

### ■ Drug Selection: Generic Versus Proprietary

Although it is the primary responsibility of the doctor or healthcare provider to decide which drug is most suitable for a treatment, often an inexpensive choice can be as effective and as safe as a more costly option. This statement frequently is true when choosing between generic and proprietary drugs. The term **generic** refers to the common name of a drug that is not subject to trademark rights; in contrast, **proprietary** denotes medications marketed under specific brand names (FDA, 2016a). For example, diazepam is the generic designation for the proprietary name Valium. Often, the most common proprietary name associated with a drug is the name given when it is initially released for marketing. Because such drugs are almost always

## KEY TERMS

**generic**
official, nonpatented, nonproprietary name of a drug

**proprietary**
brand or trademark name that is registered with the U.S. Patent Office

covered by patent restrictions for several years when first sold to the public, they become identified with their first proprietary names. After the patent lapses, the same drug often is also marketed by its lesser known generic designation (Stoppler, 2010).

Because the pharmaceutical companies that market the generic products usually have not invested in the discovery or development of the drug, they often charge much less for their version of the medication. This situation contrasts with that of the original drug manufacturer, which may have invested as much as $2.6 billion for research and development. Even though the generic product frequently is less expensive, because of FDA regulations the quality is not inferior to the related proprietary drug; thus, substitution of generic for proprietary products usually does not compromise therapy (Desai, 2019).

Because of reduced cost, generic products have become popular. Currently, generic drugs account for approximately 80% of prescriptions dispensed (Stone, 2013), up from 57% in 2004, and they cost approximately 80% less than corresponding proprietary drugs (FDA, 2016a). Because of the high demand, all states have laws that govern the use and substitution of generic drugs; unfortunately, the laws are not all the same. Some states have positive laws that require pharmacists to substitute a generic product unless the physician gives specific instructions

not to do so. Other states have negative laws that forbid substitution without the physician's permission. Some physicians use convenient prescription forms with "May" or "May Not" substitution boxes that can be checked when the prescription is filled out.

## ▮ Common Categories of Prescription Drugs

Of the approximately 10,000 different prescription drugs available in the United States, the top 50 drugs in sales account for almost 30% of all new and refilled prescriptions. As an example, a list of the 10 top-selling prescription drugs for 2019 is shown in **Table 15.6**. The following includes a brief discussion of some of the more popular prescription drug groups used in the United States. This list is not intended to be all-inclusive but gives only a sampling of common prescription products.

### ANALGESICS

The prescription analgesics consist mainly of narcotic and NSAID types. The narcotic analgesics most often dispensed to patients by prescription are (1) codeine and hydrocodone (e.g., Lortab, Vicodin), (2) the moderate-potency agents pentazocine (e.g., Talwin) and oxycodone (e.g., Percodan), and (3) the high-potency drug morphine. All narcotic analgesics are scheduled drugs because of their abuse potential and are effective

**TABLE 15.6** The Top 10 Prescription Drugs by U.S. Sales: 2019

| Rank | Proprietary Name | Generic Name | Principal Clinical Use | Fair Price ($) |
|---|---|---|---|---|
| 1 | Lipitor | Atorvastatin | Statin to treat high cholesterol | 13 |
| 2 | Levothyroxine | Synthroid | Thyroid hormone for replacement | 20 |
| 3 | Lisinopril | Zestril | ACE inhibitor for hypertension | 7 |
| 4 | Gabapentin | Neurontin | Treats seizures or nerve pain | 13 |
| 5 | Amlodipine | Norvasc | Calcium channel blockers for hypertension | 8 |
| 6 | Albuterol | Proventil | Prevents bronchospasms | 10 |
| 7 | Hydrocodone + acetaminophen | Vicoden | Moderate opioid analgesic | 4.7 |
| 8 | Omeprazole | Prilosec | Proton pump inhibitor | 10 |
| 9 | Amoxicillin | Amoxil | Broad-spectrum penicillin | 9 |
| 10 | Losartan | Cozaar | Treats hypertension | 10 |

Data from GoodRx. (2019, July). The GoodRx top 10. Retrieved from https://www.goodrx.com/drug-guide

against most types of pain. The narcotic analgesic products are often combined with aspirin or acetaminophen (e.g., Lortab and Vicodin are combinations of hydrocodone and acetaminophen) to enhance their pain-relieving actions. These are the most likely prescription drugs to be abused and can cause severe substance dependence and devastate lives when not managed properly (see "Here and Now: A Blackbox for Painkillers"). Unfortunately, because of concern about abuse of the prescription painkillers, many patients with legitimate pain symptoms are inadequately treated to relieve their extreme discomfort out of prescribers' fears that they may be contributing to the development of a narcotic addict (American Academy of Family Physicians, 2019; Dowell, Haegerich, & Chou, 2016).

The NSAIDs constitute the other major group of analgesics available by prescription. The pharmacology of these drugs is similar to that of the OTC compound ibuprofen, previously discussed in this chapter. These medications are used to relieve inflammatory conditions such as arthritis and are effective in relieving minor to moderate musculoskeletal pain (pain associated with body structures such as muscles, ligaments, bones, teeth, and skin). These drugs have no abuse potential and are not scheduled; several are also available OTC (see the discussion of OTC analgesics). Their principal adverse side effects include stomach irritation, kidney damage, tinnitus (ringing in the ears), dizziness, and swelling from fluid retention. Most prescription NSAIDs have similar pharmacological side effects. Included in the group of prescription NSAIDs are ibuprofen (e.g., Motrin), naproxen (e.g., Anaprox), indomethacin (e.g., Indocin), sulindac (e.g., Clinoril), mefenamic acid

# HERE AND NOW

## A Black Box for Opioid Painkillers

Experts and government officials claim that opioid abuse, severe dependence, and overdose consequences have reached epidemic levels in the United States and elsewhere. Consequently, the FDA has been called on to do its part to reverse these disturbing trends. In response to these expectations, the FDA has announced label changes on prescription opioid medications that are designed to educate prescribers and patients about the potential dangers related to use of both extended-release and long-acting opioids intended for use once or twice a day and immediate-release opioids intended for use every four to six hours. The FDA has mandated two types of label changes. First, the FDA now requires the placement of a "black box" advisory on all single-drug opioid analgesics that includes precautions about the potentially serious consequences of misuse, abuse, addiction, and overdose deaths, as well as warnings about the risks of chronic use of opioids during pregnancy and the association with neonatal withdrawal syndrome. Second, the FDA has mandated changes in the labeling of opioid analgesics so that labels now include information related to a drug's (1) indications, (2) limitations of use, (3) serious risks, and (4) safety information concerning potentially harmful drug interactions that can affect the CNS, adrenal glands, and sex hormone levels. Although not yet included, it is anticipated that after review of causes for life-threatening opioid overdose consequences, the FDA also will require the addition of label information on the potentially serious outcomes related to opioid interactions with antianxiety drugs (e.g., benzodiazepines). In addition to these required label changes for opioid painkiller products, the FDA is also considering its role in promoting the use of the opioid antagonist drug naloxone as a rescue medication to prevent opioid overdose death and expanding access to the use of medication-assisted treatment with drugs such as methadone and buprenorphine.

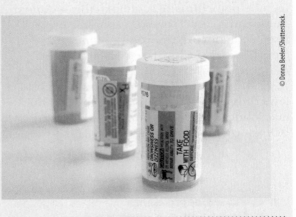

© Donna Beeler/Shutterstock.

Data from Food and Drug Administration (FDA). (2016d, March 22). FDA announces enhanced warnings for immediate-release opioid pain medications related to risks of misuse, abuse, addiction, overdose and death. Retrieved from http://www.fda.gov/NewsEvents/Newsroom/Press Announcements/ucm491739.htm

(e.g., Ponstel), tolmetin (e.g., Tolectin), piroxicam (e.g., Feldene), and ketoprofen (e.g., Orudis) (Borazan & Furst, 2015).

## ANTIBIOTICS

Drugs referred to by the layperson as "antibiotics" are more accurately described by the term *antibacterials*, although the more common term will be used here. For the most part, antibiotics are effective in treating infections caused by microorganisms classified as bacteria. Bacterial infections can occur anywhere in the body, resulting in tissue damage, loss of function, and ultimately death if untreated. Even though bacterial infections continue to be the most common serious diseases in the United States and throughout the world today, the vast majority of these can be cured with antibiotic treatment.

Close to 100 different antibiotic drugs are available. They differ from one another in (1) whether they kill bacteria (*bactericidal*) or stop their growth (*bacteriostatic*) and (2) the species of bacteria that are sensitive to their antibacterial action. Antibiotics that are effective against many species of bacteria are classified as *broad-spectrum types*, whereas those antibiotics that are relatively selective and effective against only a few species of bacteria are considered *narrow-spectrum types*.

Although most antibiotics are well tolerated by patients, they can cause very serious side effects, especially if not used properly. For example, the penicillins have a wide margin of safety for most patients, but 5% to 10% of the population is allergic to these drugs, and life-threatening reactions can occur in sensitized patients if penicillins are used.

The most common groups of antibiotics include penicillins (e.g., amoxicillin—Amoxil, Augmentin, and Trimox), cephalosporins (e.g., cephalexin), fluoroquinolones (e.g., ciprofloxacin—Cipro), tetracyclines (e.g., minocycline—Minocin), aminoglycosides (e.g., streptomycin), sulfonamides (e.g., sulfamethoxazole—Bactrim and Septra), and macrolides (e.g., erythromycin—E-Mycin) (Chemotherapeutic Drugs, 2015).

### KEY TERM

**tricyclic antidepressants**
most commonly used group of drugs to treat severe depression

## ANTIDEPRESSANTS

Severe depression is characterized by diminished interest or pleasure in normal activities accompanied by feelings of fatigue, pessimism, and guilt, as well as sleep and appetite disturbances and suicidal desires (American Psychiatric Association, 2013). Major depression afflicts approximately: (1) 6% to 7% of the population at any one time, (2) 3.2 million adolescents (~13%), (3) 20% of females, and (4) 6.8% males, and it is estimated that about 23% of the population will become severely depressed during their lives (Centers for Disease Control and Prevention [CDC], 2016a; National Institute of Mental Health [NIMH], 2019). This high prevalence makes depression the most common psychiatric disorder. According to the American Psychiatric Association's (2013) classification in the *Diagnostic and Statistical Manual of Mental Disorders*, fifth edition, several types of depression exist, based on their origin.

- *Endogenous major depression*: A genetic disorder that can occur spontaneously and results from transmitter imbalances in the brain.
- *Depression associated with bipolar mood disorder*—that is, manic–depressive disorder.
- *Drug-induced depression*: The depressive symptoms are associated with the ingestion, injection, or inhalation of a substance (e.g., drug abuse, toxin, psychotropic medication, or other medication), and the symptoms persist beyond the expected length of physiological effects, intoxication, or withdrawal period. The relevant depressive disorder should have developed during or within one month after use of the depression-inducing substance.
- *Reactive depression*: The most common form of depression, which is a response to situations of grief, personal loss, illness, and other highly stressful situations.

Antidepressant medication is typically used to treat endogenous major depression, although on occasion these drugs are used to treat other forms of depression if they are resistant to conventional therapy (DeBatista, 2015).

Several groups of prescription antidepressant medications are approved for use in the United States (DeBatista, 2015). The most commonly used category is the **tricyclic antidepressants**. Included in this group are drugs such as amitriptyline (Elavil), imipramine (Tofranil), and nortriptyline (Pamelor). Although usually well tolerated, the tricyclic antidepressants can cause annoying side effects because of their anticholinergic activity. These adverse reactions include drowsiness, dry mouth, blurred vision, and constipation. Tolerance to these side effects usually develops with continued use.

The second group of drugs used to treat depression is referred to as the **monoamine oxidase inhibitors (MAOIs)**. Historically, these agents have been backup drugs for the tricyclic antidepressants. Because of their annoying and sometimes dangerous side effects, as well as problems interacting with other drugs or even food, the MAOIs have become less popular with clinicians. These drugs can have deadly interactions with many of the stimulants of abuse such as methamphetamine, cocaine, and Ecstasy. Drugs belonging to this group include phenelzine (Nardil) and tranylcypromine (Parnate).

Agents from a third, somewhat disparate group of antidepressants that are safer and have fewer side effects than the tricyclic or MAOI antidepressants are especially popular. They include fluoxetine (Prozac), sertraline (Zoloft), paroxetine (Paxil), uvoxamine (Luvox), bupropion (Wellbutrin), trazodone (Desyrel), and duloxetine (Cymbalta). Although the side effects and margin of safety of these groups of antidepressants may differ, in general they all appear to have similar therapeutic benefits. Of this third group of antidepressants, Prozac is the best known and used to be the most frequently prescribed antidepressant; in 2003 it was the 11th most frequently prescribed drug in the United States. However, by 2009 it had been replaced by other antidepressants such as Lexapro (escitalopram). Although most commonly used to treat depression, Prozac has also been prescribed by physicians to treat more than 30 other conditions ranging from drug addiction (although not found to be generally effective) to kleptomania. The vast majority of these uses are neither proven to be effective nor approved by the FDA.

## ANTIDIABETIC DRUGS

**Diabetes mellitus** is likely the leading metabolic endocrine disease in this country; it afflicts approximately 29 million people in the United States (21 million diagnosed and 8 million undiagnosed), with 86 million Americans considered "prediabetic" (i.e., in early stages but likely to progress to full expression) (American Diabetes Association, 2016). It is the result of insufficient or ineffective activity of insulin, a hormone secreted from the pancreas (Kennedy & Mashirani, 2015). Because of the lack of insulin, untreated diabetics have severe problems with cellular and systemic metabolism and elevated blood sugar (called **hyperglycemia**). The two major types of diabetes are type 1 and type 2. **Type 1 diabetes** is caused by total destruction of the insulin-producing cells in the pancreas and usually begins in juveniles, although it occasionally begins during adulthood. In contrast, **type 2 diabetes**, which used to be called *adult-onset diabetes*, typically occurs after age 40 and is frequently associated with obesity. Recently, however, because severe obesity is occurring more often in younger persons (about 17% of Americans), an epidemic of type 2 diabetes has erupted in adolescents (Woolston, 2016), making

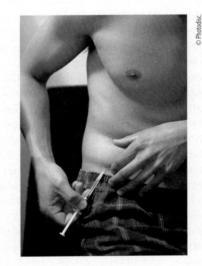

© Photodisc.

Insulin is self-administered by diabetic patients in subcutaneous injections.

## KEY TERMS

**monoamine oxidase inhibitors (MAOIs)**
drugs used to treat severe depression

**diabetes mellitus**
disease caused by elevated blood sugar from insufficient insulin

**hyperglycemia**
elevated blood sugar

**type 1 diabetes**
disease associated with complete loss of insulin-producing cells in the pancreas

**type 2 diabetes**
disease usually associated with obesity; does not involve a loss of insulin-producing cells

Obesity in young children has reached epidemic status and is causing type 2 diabetes to occur at a younger age.

the term *adult-onset diabetes* less meaningful. In type 2 diabetes, the pancreas is able to produce insulin, but insulin receptors no longer respond normally to this hormone (Woolston, 2016). In both types of diabetes mellitus, drugs are administered to restore proper insulin function.

Because people with type 1 diabetes are unable to produce or release insulin, these patients are universally treated with subcutaneous injections of insulin one to three times per day, depending on their needs. Usually the levels of sugar (glucose) in the blood are evaluated to determine the effectiveness of treatment. Insulin products are characterized by their onset of action (either rapid or delayed onset) and duration (short to long) (Kennedy & Masharani, 2015).

The strategy for treating type 2 diabetics is somewhat different. For many of these patients, the symptoms of diabetes and problems of insufficient insulin function subside with proper diet, weight management, and exercise. If an appropriate change in lifestyle does not correct the diabetes-associated problems, drugs called **oral hypoglycemic** (meaning they are taken by mouth and lower blood sugar) are often prescribed. These drugs, which stimulate the release of additional insulin from the pancreas, include popular drugs such as rosiglitazone (Avandia). A major

concern is that although these drugs are effective in controlling glucose levels, some of them might increase the incidence of cardiovascular disease (Kennedy, 2012). If the diabetic symptoms are not adequately controlled with the oral hypoglycemic drugs, then type 2 diabetics are treated with insulin injections, as are type 1 patients. The treatment of diabetes has improved substantially in recent years because of new, more selective, and more effective drugs that control glucose blood levels (Kennedy & Masharani, 2015).

## ANTIULCER DRUGS

**Peptic ulcers** are sores that recur in the lining of the lower stomach (gastric ulcer) or most often in the upper portion of the small intestine (duodenal ulcer). Secretions of gastric acids and digestive enzymes are necessary for ulcer development. Because gastric secretions are involved in developing peptic ulcers, several drug types are useful in ulcer treatment.

Antacids help relieve acute discomfort from ulcers by neutralizing gastric acidity. These drugs are discussed in greater detail in the OTC section of this chapter. Prescription drugs that block gastric secretion have been the mainstay of ulcer treatment. Because the endogenous chemical histamine is important in regulating gastric secretions, drugs that selectively block the activity of gastric histamine (called H2 blockers) substantially reduce secretion of gastric acids and digestive enzymes. The popular drugs cimetidine (Tagamet), ranitidine (Zantac), and famotidine (Pepcid) function in this manner. Because Tagamet, Zantac, and Pepcid are used so frequently, that they have been switched to OTC status by the FDA—not to treat ulcers but to relieve heartburn (esophageal reflux) (McQuaid, 2015).

Although the exact causes of peptic ulcers are not completely understood, it is widely accepted that the bacteria *Helicobacter pylori* play a role. Because of the involvement of these microorganisms, most clinicians treat patients with recurring ulcers with multiple antibiotics to eliminate these bacteria (McQuaid, 2015).

## BRONCHODILATORS

Drugs that widen air passages (bronchi) facilitate breathing in patients with air-passage constriction or obstruction. Such drugs are called **bronchodilators** and are particularly useful in relieving respiratory difficulty associated with asthma. Asthmatic patients frequently experience bouts of intense coughing, shortness of breath, tightness in the chest, and wheezing resulting in breathing difficulties. Many of the symptoms of asthma result from an increased sensitivity of the airways to irritating substances and can result in serious asthma attacks that are life threatening if not treated promptly (Galanter & Boushey, 2015). Two major categories of bronchodilators are the sympathomimetics known as **beta-adrenergic stimulants**—for example, isoproterenol (Isuprel) and albuterol (Proventil, Ventolin)—and xanthines (caffeine-like drugs) such as theophylline and its derivatives. These drugs relax the muscles of the air passages, cause bronchodilation, and facilitate breathing. In the early 1990s, some bronchodilators were switched to OTC status, such as Bronkaid Mist and Primatene Mist. These contain relatively low amounts of epinephrine and are safe and effective when used for mild, intermittent disease. Typically these OTC medications should not be used by patients with cardiovascular disease (Schiffman, 2013) and may dangerously interact with sympathomimetic stimulants of abuse such as cocaine and the amphetamines.

## CARDIOVASCULAR DRUGS

Cardiovascular disease has been the leading cause of death in the United States for the past several decades. Consequently, of the 20 top-selling drugs in this country, four are medications for diseases related to the cardiovascular system (see Table 15.6). The following are brief discussions of the major categories of cardiovascular drugs (National Heart, Lung, and Blood Institute, 2016).

### ANTIHYPERTENSIVE AGENTS

An estimated 29% of U.S. adults have **hypertension** (persistent elevated high blood pressure) (Benowitz, 2015). Because hypertension can result in serious damage to the heart, kidneys, and brain, this condition needs to be treated aggressively. Treatment should consist of changes in lifestyle, including exercise and diet, but usually also requires drug therapy. Two of the principal classes of antihypertensive agents are diuretics and direct vasodilators (Benowitz, 2015):

- *Diuretics* lower blood pressure by eliminating sodium and excess water from the body. Included in this category is hydrochlorothiazide.
- *Direct vasodilators* reduce blood pressure by relaxing the muscles in the walls of blood

vessels that cause vasoconstriction, thereby dilating the blood vessels and decreasing their resistance to the flow of blood. Drugs included in this category are calcium-channel blockers such as diltiazem (Cardizem), verapamil (Calan), nifedipine (Procardia); inhibitors of the enzyme that synthesizes the vasoconstricting hormone, angiotensin II (enalapril or Vasotec); and drugs that block the vasoconstricting action of the sympathetic nervous system such as clonidine (Catapres) and prazosin (Minipress).

### ANTIANGINAL AGENTS

When the heart is deprived of sufficient blood (a condition called **ischemia**), the oxygen requirements of the cardiac muscle are not met and the breakdown of chemicals caused by the continual activity of the heart results in pain; this viselike chest pain is called **angina pectoris**. The most frequent cause of angina is obstruction of the coronary vessels (Katzung, 2015a). Angina pectoris frequently occurs in patients with hypertension; left untreated, the underlying blockage of coronary vessels can result in heart attacks. All the drugs used to relieve or prevent angina decrease the oxygen deficit of the heart either by decreasing the amount of work required of the heart during normal functioning or by increasing the blood supply to the heart (Katzung, 2015a). The three types of drugs prescribed for treating angina pectoris are (1) calcium-channel blockers such as verapamil (Calan), diltiazem (Cardizem); (2) nitrates and nitrites such as amylnitrite (Vaporate), nitroglycerin (Transderm-Nitro), and (3) blockers of the sympathetic nervous system, specifically classified as beta-adrenergic blockers such as atenolol (Tenormin) and propranolol (Inderal) (Katzung, 2015).

## KEY TERMS

**beta-adrenergic stimulants**
Drugs that stimulate a subtype of adrenaline and noradrenaline receptors

**hypertension**
elevated blood pressure

**ischemia**
when tissue is deprived of sufficient blood and oxygen

**angina pectoris**
severe chest pain usually caused by a deficiency of blood to the heart muscle

## DRUGS TO TREAT CONGESTIVE HEART FAILURE

When the cardiac muscle is unable to pump sufficient blood to satisfy the oxygen needs of the body, **congestive heart failure** occurs. This condition causes an enlarged heart, decreased ability to exercise, shortness of breath, and accumulation of fluid (**edema**) in the lungs and limbs (Katzung, 2015c). The principal treatment for congestive heart failure consists of drugs that improve the heart's efficiency, such as digoxin (Lanoxin) (Katzung, 2015c).

Drugs that cause vasodilation are also sometimes used successfully to reduce the work required of the heart as it pumps blood through the body. Among the drugs causing vasodilation are those already discussed in conjunction with other heart conditions such as hypertension and angina pectoris such as enalapril (Vasotec).

## CHOLESTEROL- AND LIPID-LOWERING DRUGS

Cholesterol and some types of fatty (lipid) molecules can accumulate in the walls of arteries and narrow the openings of these blood vessels. Such arterial changes cause hypertension, heart attacks, strokes, and heart failure and are the leading cause of death in the United States, costing about $380 billion annually (Pharmaletter, 2016). These health problems can often be avoided by adopting a lifestyle that includes a low-fat and low-cholesterol diet combined with regular, appropriate exercise (Malloy & Kane, 2012). However, sometimes lifestyle changes are insufficient; in such cases, cholesterol-lowering drugs can be used to prevent the damaging changes in blood vessel walls. The drugs most often used include lovastatin (Mevacor), cholestyramine (Questran), and niacin (vitamin B3) (Malloy & Kane, 2015).

## HORMONE-RELATED DRUGS

Hormones are released from endocrine (ductless) glands and are important in regulating metabolism, growth, tissue repair, reproduction, and other vital functions. When there is a deficiency or excess of specific hormones, body functions can be impaired, causing abnormal growth, imbalance in

metabolism, disease, and often death. Hormones, or hormone-like substances, are sometimes administered as drugs to compensate for an endocrine deficiency and to restore normal function. This is the case for (1) insulin used to treat diabetes (see the previous discussion for more details), (2) levothyroxine (Synthroid, an artificial thyroid hormone—see top 10 favorite drugs in Table 15.6) to treat **hypothyroidism** (insufficient activity of the thyroid gland), and (3) conjugated estrogens (Premarin) to relieve the symptoms caused by estrogen deficiency during menopause.

Hormones also can be administered as drugs to alter normal body processes. Thus, drugs containing the female hormones estrogen and progesterone (norethindrone, ethinyl estradiol [Ortho Novum]), can be used as contraceptives to alter the female reproductive cycles and prevent pregnancy. Another example involves drugs related to corticosteroids (hormones from the cortex of the adrenal glands), which are often prescribed because of their immune-suppressing effects. In high doses, the corticosteroid drugs (e.g., triamcinolone [Kenalog]) reduce symptoms of inflammation and are used to treat severe forms of inflammatory diseases, such as arthritis (Ogbru, 2016). Finally, hormone-linked drugs such as etanercept (Enbrel), which depress the important immune mediator, tissue necrosis factor, have also become popular for suppressing serious inflammatory diseases such as arthritis (see Table 15.6).

## SEDATIVE-HYPNOTIC AGENTS

About 12.5% of U.S. adults use sedative-hypnotics annually, and 2% use them daily (Sola, 2010). Some popular sleeping medications include Ambien (zolpidem), Lunesta (eszopiclone), Rozerem (ramelteon), Sona (carisoprodol), and Silenor (doxepin). If one is not careful, these drugs can be used excessively for reducing stress and aiding sleep, leading to addictions and adverse consequences. Benzodiazepines commonly prescribed for these purposes are clonazepam (Klonopin) and lorazepam (Ativan) (Trevor, 2015).

## STIMULANTS

One of the most common uses for prescription stimulants is the treatment of ADHD. This neurobehavioral disorder is the most common mental health problem in children, affecting approximately 10% of all school-aged children in the United States (CDC, 2016b), the majority of whom are male (Quinlan, 2016). Of those children diagnosed with ADHD, many will continue to manifest associated impairment into adolescence and even

## KEY TERMS

**congestive heart failure**
when the heart is unable to pump sufficient blood for the body's needs

**edema**
swollen tissue because of an accumulation of fluid

**hypothyroidism**
when the thyroid gland does not produce sufficient hormone

adulthood, although the expression of the symptoms of hyperactivity may be replaced with inattention (NIMH, 2016). The most frequent treatments for ADHD include (1) stimulants such as methylphenidate (Ritalin) and amphetamine (Adderall), which have been proven to improve attention while controlling impulsivity and disruptive behaviors; (2) nonstimulants (such as Atomoxetine-Strattera), which are typically used as a backup for the stimulants because of fewer side effects; and, less often, (3) antidepressants that affect the neurotransmitters norepinephrine and dopamine. Of some concern is the dramatic increase in stimulant prescriptions for ADHD treatment and whether they are the best drug choice for treating ADHD patients (Keshavan, 2016). This rise in ADHD-related medication use has corresponded with a disturbing increase in the use of these stimulants without prescriptions. It has been estimated that approximately 21 million people aged 12 or older in the United States are prescribed these stimulants annually, and in 2018 these drugs were abused by approximately 5% of high school seniors, many of whom were not the legal recipients of the prescriptions (Johnston, 2019).

Perhaps the most troubling issue is the trend for college students to abuse these short-acting stimulants to enhance performance while studying to prepare for examinations or stay awake to party well into the night (Awad, 2013). Another common reason for this group to abuse these drugs is to lose weight because of their appetite-suppressing actions. The increase of stimulant abuse by college students probably reflects an assumption that these agents must be safe or they would not be prescribed by physicians. Because of this growing problem, scientists and drug companies are working to develop nonaddicting medications to treat ADHD.

### DRUGS TO TREAT HIV

Of relevance to our discussion on prescription drugs are recent advances in pharmacological management of this disease. Although no cure for HIV or immunization against this virus is available yet, some drug therapies can delay the onset or dramatically slow the progression of this infection. The first drugs to be used effectively in AIDS therapy were the transcriptase inhibitors such as zidovudine (AZT) and stavudine (Zerit), which block a unique enzyme essential for HIV replication (Flexner, 2006). Another group of anti-AIDS drugs called the *protease inhibitors* prevent HIV maturation; they include aquinavir. The protease inhibitors are particularly effective when used in combination with the transcriptase inhibitor drugs (Flexner, 2006). Most current strategies for AIDS therapy include drug combinations based on issues such as viral susceptibility, drug toxicity, drug metabolism, drug-interaction potential, and medical conditions of the patient. More than 20 anti-HIV drugs from six different mechanistic classes can be used in combination-drug treatments. These include drug categories such as the transcriptase inhibitors, protease inhibitors, fusion inhibitors, and CCR5 antagonists. Strategies for more effective drug treatments are continually being developed. Research suggests that, if done properly, antiviral treatment is more than 80% effective in suppressing the symptoms of AIDS and preventing death (Panel on Antiretroviral Guidelines for Adults and Adolescents, 2016).

## Common Principles of Drug Use

Probably the most effective way to teach people not to use drugs improperly is to help them understand how to use drugs correctly. This goal can be achieved by educating the drug-using public about prescription, OTC, and herbal drug products. If people can appreciate the difference between the benefits of therapeutic drug use and the negative consequences of drug misuse or abuse, they will be more likely to use medications in a cautious and thoughtful manner. To reach this level of understanding, patients must be able to communicate freely with health professionals. Before prescription or OTC drugs are purchased and used, patients should have all questions answered about the therapeutic objective, the most effective mode of administration, and side effects. Education about proper drug use greatly diminishes drug-related problems and unnecessary healthcare costs.

To minimize problems, before using any drug product, the patient should be able to answer the following questions:

- Why am I using this drug?
- How should I be taking this drug?
- What are the active ingredients in this drug product?
- What are the most likely side effects of this drug?
- How long should this drug be used?
- How should this drug be disposed of?

A major factor in the escalation of prescription drug misuse is that excess unused medications are not dealt with appropriately and are readily available to those who would abuse them

## PRESCRIPTION FOR ABUSE

### Invitation for Prescription Abuse

Michael was polite, clean-cut, and a typical white-collar professional. To consider him a drug addict would be unthinkable, and yet Michael would be the first to admit his drug addiction on prescription medication is as strong and debilitating as an addiction to illegal drugs such as cocaine and heroin. Michael became extremely skilled in his ability to feign back pain in a doctor's office or emergency room so he could walk away with a prescription for potent narcotic painkillers. When asked if he drove himself to the office, Michael would always say no, so he could also get an injection of the potent narcotic Demerol. If he had difficulty getting a medication from legitimate or forged prescriptions, Michael would steal pills from easy targets in the suburbs. For example, at garage sales he would ask to use the bathroom, and unsuspecting homeowners would nicely open their houses to him and leave him unsupervised. People trying to sell their house would usually invite him in as a prospective buyer, and, as he looked around unattended, he would sneak into a bathroom or bedroom and rifle through medicine cabinets and dresser drawers for drugs to satisfy his cravings. Michael tells of one experience when he went to an open house pretending to be an interested buyer.

When the owner wasn't looking, Michael slipped into a bedroom and snatched a large bottle of Vicodin and an unfilled prescription next to a wheelchair and crutches. At the peak of his addiction, Michael was consuming up to 120 narcotic painkillers a day. Michael explains that using large quantities of these prescriptions was not all that difficult. He claims that "doctors and psychiatrists would hand out drugs like candy," and people were so unsuspecting that it was easy to take unsecured prescription drugs from bathrooms and bedrooms.

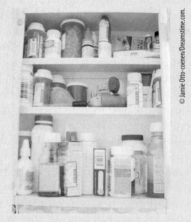

© Jamie Otto-coenen/Dreamstime.com.

Data from Sotonoff, J. (2010, July 26). Addiction began with prescription drugs he got from your homes. *Chicago Daily Herald*. Retrieved from http://prev.dailyherald.com/story/?id=396310. Accessed January 10, 2020.

---

or use them in a dangerous fashion. This problem can be prevented by complying with the following guidelines from the Office of National Drug Control Policy that explain how to manage and dispose of these extra drugs (Siler et al., n.d.):

- Do not flush medications. The Environmental Protection Agency has declared that flushing drugs down the toilet results in high levels of many medications in community water supplies, causing health problems for people, animals, and the environment.
- Realize that many of these prescription medications are in high demand on the Internet and the street, are often sold for a considerable amount of money, and can be tempting to young people. Consequently, teens frequently raid home medicine cabinets to use these drugs for pharm parties, where the pills are mixed together and shared or sold to friends and acquaintances. For these reasons, all prescription drugs should be stored in a

secure (even locked) place ("Only Federal Prevention Message," 2010).

- Do not dispose of your medications or their containers with labels in the trash. The bright labels of these bottles are highly visible in garbage cans and landfills and contain important personal information that can be used to steal your identity.
- The FDA recommends placing unused prescription medications into a plastic bag with moist coffee grounds or cat litter before disposing of the pills or tablets in the garbage. The moisture from the coffee grounds or cat litter will help dissolve the capsules, pills, or tablets, making them unusable.
- Many communities have secured drop-off boxes that are attended by certified law enforcement personnel. Medications left in these boxes are collected by authorized personnel and properly disposed of. Locations of these drop-off containers can usually be determined by checking with local police.

# LEARNING PORTFOLIO

## Discussion Questions

1. Why are some prescription drugs appropriate for switching to OTC status?
2. What should the FDA use as a standard of safety when evaluating OTC and prescription drugs?
3. What role should the pharmacist play in providing information about OTC and prescription drugs to patients?
4. What type of formal training should be required before a health professional is allowed to prescribe drugs?
5. What kinds of questions should be asked by a health professional to ensure that a patient sufficiently understands how to use a drug properly and safely?
6. What are the basic rules for using OTC drugs properly?
7. Why is abuse of prescription drugs such a common problem?
8. Why are the opioid painkillers the most frequently abused of the prescription drugs?
9. How should users of prescription drugs handle their medications to prevent their abuse by others?
10. Why are some people more likely to abuse prescription drugs than illegal substances?
11. Even though some antibiotics have a wide margin of safety, currently there is no systemic antibiotic available OTC. Why is the FDA not willing to make some of these drugs available on a nonprescription basis?
12. Should herbal remedies be required to be safe and effective by the FDA like other OTC drug products?
13. What role, if any, should the FDA have in regulating herbal products?

## Summary

1. Prescription drugs are available only by recommendation of an authorized health professional such as a physician. Nonprescription (OTC) drugs are available on request and do not require approval by a health professional. In general, OTC medications are safer than their prescription counterparts, but they often are less effective.
2. The FDA's switching policy is an attempt to make available more effective medications to the general public on a nonprescription basis. This policy has been implemented in response to the interest in self-treatment by the public and in an attempt to reduce healthcare costs.
3. Drugs switched by the FDA to OTC status include ulcer medications such as cimetidine (Tagamet) and ranitidine (Zantac), medications for asthma and allergies, the contraceptive levonorgestrel (Plan B), and the weight-loss drug orlistat (Ally).

## Key Terms

4. Potential problems caused by making more effective drugs available OTC include over-use and inappropriate use, leading to dependence and other undesirable side effects. For example, these more effective drugs could encourage self-treatment of medical problems that usually require professional care.

5. Information on OTC product labels is crucial for proper use of these drugs and thus is regulated by the FDA. Product labels must list the active ingredients and their quantities in the product. Labels must also provide instructions for safe and effective treatment with the drug, as well as cautions and warnings.

6. Many herbal products contain active drugs and have become highly popular. The lack of regulation makes these remedies difficult to assess for either efficacy or safety.

7. Although OTC drug products can be useful for treatment of many minor to moderate self-limiting medical problems, when used without proper precautions they can cause problems.

8. The principal drug groups available OTC are used in the treatment of common but minor medical problems and include analgesics, cold remedies, allergy products, mild stimulants, sleep aids, antacids, laxatives, antidiarrheals, antiasthmatics, acne medications, sunscreens, contraceptives, and nutrients.

9. For drugs to be prescribed properly, patients need to provide complete and accurate information about their medical condition and medical history to their physicians. In turn, providers need to communicate to patients what is being treated, why the drug is being used, how it should be used for maximum benefit, and what potential side effects can occur.

10. Proprietary drug names can be used legally only by the drug company that has trademark rights. Often, the original proprietary name becomes the popular name associated with the drug. Because the pharmaceutical company that develops a drug is trying to recover its investment, a newly marketed proprietary drug is expensive. Once the patent rights expire, other drug companies can also market the drug but under a different name; often, the common, generic name is used because it cannot be trademarked. The generic drugs are less expensive because the manufacturers do not need to recover any significant investment. The FDA requires the less expensive generic drug to be as effective and safe as the proprietary counterpart.

11. Of the approximately 1,500 different prescription drugs currently available in the United States, the most commonly prescribed groups are analgesics, antibiotics, antidepressants, drugs used for diabetes, antiulcer drugs, bronchodilators, drugs used to treat cardiovascular diseases, hormone-related drugs, and sedative-hypnotics.

12. Abuse of prescription drugs is a serious problem in the United States. Some patients try to persuade clinicians or pharmacists to make prescription medications available by using deceit or intimidation. Legal drugs obtained in this manner are often used to relieve drug dependence or to reduce withdrawal symptoms from illicit substances. Those who abuse prescription drugs often abuse other substances as well such as alcohol, tobacco, and even illicit drugs.

13. To help reduce prescription abuse, those who use these drugs legitimately should make sure their medications are securely stored and that unused prescriptions are disposed of properly.

# References

Abood, R. (1992). OBRA '90: Implementation and enforcement. *NABP U.S. Pharmacists, State Boards—A Continuing Education Series*. Park Ridge, IL: National Association of Pharmacy.

Alton, L. (2016, February 9). FDA warns: Drugs cause over 2 million "adverse" reactions per year. *Natural Health, 365*. Retrieved from http://www.naturalhealth365.com/fda-big-pharma-drug-interaction-1736.html

American Academy of Dermatology. (2016). Skin cancer, incidence rates.

American Academy of Dermatology Association. (2019). Sunscreen FAQS. Schaumburg, IL: Author. Retrieved from https://www.aad.org/sun-protection/sunscreen-faqs

American Academy of Family Physicians. (2019). Pain management and opioid abuse resources. Leawood, KS: Author. Retrieved from https://www.aafp.org/patient-care/public-health/pain-opioids/resources.html

American College of Preventive Medicine. (2016). Over-the-counter medications time tool.

American Diabetes Association. (2016). Statistics about diabetes. Retrieved from http://www.diabetes.org/diabetes-basics/statistics/

American Psychiatric Association. (2013). *Diagnostic and statistical manual of mental disorders*, 5th ed. Washington, DC: Author.

Anderson, W. (2016). Can a drug or surgery solve your weight problem? Huffpost. Retrieved from http://www.huffingtonpost.com/william-anderson-ma-lmhc/can-a-drug-or-surgery-sol_b_7486428.html

Awad, S. (2013, April 17). ADHD medication stimulates controversy. Technician. Retrieved from http://www.technicianonline.com/article_c5a144c6-a004-11e2-9ff0-0019bb30f31a.html

Baratloo, A., Rouhipour, A., Forouzanfar, M., Safari, S., Amiri, M., & Negida, A. (2016). The role of caffeine in pain management: A brief literature review. *Anesthesiology and Pain Medicine, 6*, e33139.

Bartholow, M. (2010, May 11). Top 200 prescription drugs of 2009. *Pharmacy Times*. Retrieved from https://www.pharmacytimes.com/publications/issue/2010/may2010/rxfocustopdrugs-0510

Bebinger, M. (2019, July 29). Seizures of methamphetamine are surging in the U.S. NPR. Retrieved from https://www.npr.org/sections/health-shots/2019/07/29/745061185/seizures-of-methamphetamine-are-surging-in-the-u-s

Benowitz, N. (2015). Antihypertensive agents. In B. Katzung & A Trevor (Eds.), *Basic and clinical pharmacology*, 13th ed. (pp. 169–190). New York, NY: McGraw-Hill.

Bluelight. (2016). Basic drug discussion. Retrieved from http://www.bluelight.org/vb/threads/785632-Dxm-trip

Bonnet, M., & Arand, D. (2016). Behavioral and pharmacologic therapies for chronic insomnia in adults. UpToDate. Retrieved from http://www.uptodate.com/contents/treatment-of-insomnia

Booth, W., & O'Connor, A. (2010, November 28). Mexican cartels emerge as top source for U.S. meth. *Washington Post*. Retrieved from http://www.washingtonpost.com/wp-dyn/content/article/2010/11/23/AR2010112303703.html?sid=ST2010112303730

Borazan, N., & Furst, D. (2015). Nonsteroidal anti-inflammatory drugs, disease-modifying antirheumatic drugs, nonopioid analgesics, and drugs used in gout. In B. Katzung and A. Trevor (Eds.), *Basic and clinical pharmacology*, 13th ed. (pp. 618–641). New York, NY: McGraw-Hill.

Brennan, Z. (2015). FDA amends liver warning labeling guidance for some OTC drugs containing acetaminophen. Regulatory Affairs Professionals Society (RAPS). 2015. Retrieved from http://www.raps.org/Regulatory-Focus/News/2015/11/16/23608/FDA-Amends-Liver-Warning-Labeling-Guidance-for-Some-OTC-Drugs-Containing-Acetaminophen/

Brophy, B., and & D. Schardt, D. (2011). Functional foods. HighBeam Research.

Brunner, S. (2010). Are doctors knowledgeable about herbal medicines? Medical News Today. Retrieved from http://www.medicalnewstoday.com/articles/184716.php

Bushak, L. (2016, May 3). Psychotherapy is better than sleeping pills for insomnia treatment: Report. Medical Daily. Retrieved from http://www.medicaldaily.com/insomnia-treatment-psychotherapy-sleeping-pills-384574

Center for Drug Evaluation and Research. (2019). Prescription to over-the-counter (OTC) switch list. Silver Spring, MD: Food and Drug Administration. Retrieved from https://www.fda.gov/about-fda/center-drug-evaluation-and-research-cder/prescription-over-counter-otc-switch-list

Centers for Disease Control and Prevention (CDC). (2016a). Depression in the U.S. household population 2009–2012. Atlanta, GA: Centers for Disease Control and Prevention. Retrieved from https://www.cdc.gov/nchs/fastats/depression.htm

Centers for Disease Control and Prevention (CDC). (2016b). Attentiondeficit/hyperactivity disorder (ADHD). Retrieved from http://www.cdc.gov/ncbddd/adhd/data.html

Centers for Medicare and Medicaid Services. (2016). We're putting patients first. Retrieved from https://www.cms.gov/

Chemotherapeutic Drugs. (2015). In B. Katzung & A. Trevor (Eds.), *Basic and clinical pharmacology,* 13th ed. (pp. 767–970). New York, NY: McGraw-Hill.

Cleveland Clinic. (2016). Over-the-counter and herbal remedies for weight loss. Retrieved from http://my.clevelandclinic.org/health/healthy_living/getting_fit/hic_Maintaining_a_Healthy_Weight/hic_Over-the-Counter_and_Herbal_Remedies_for_Weight_Loss

"Cold and flu overview." (2016). WebMD. Retrieved from http://www.webmd.com/cold-and-flu/

"Common Cold Risk Factors." Health Guide. *The New York Times*. (June 14, 2016). Retrieved from. http://www.nytimes.com/health/guides/disease/common-cold/risk-factors.html

Consumer Action News (2020, January 2). Prescription drug cost crisis (Fall 2019). Retrieved from https://www.consumer-action.org/news/articles/prescription-drug-cost-crisis-fall-2019

Consumer Healthcare Products Association (CHPA). (2016a). Statistics on OTC use. Retrieved from http://www.chpa.org/marketstats.aspx

Consumer Healthcare Products Association (CHPA). (2016b). OTC review/Drug monographs. 2016b. Retrieved from http://www.chpa.org/OTCReview.aspx

Consumer Healthcare Products Association (CHPA). (2019). Statistics on OTC use. Retrieved from https://www.chpa.org/MarketStats.aspx

Consumer Healthcare Products Association (CHPA). (2020). OTC sales by category 2015–2018. Retrieved from https://www.accessdata.fda.gov/scripts/cdrh/cfdocs/cfCFR/CFRSearch.cfm?CFRPart=201&showFR=1&subpartNode=21:4.0.1.1.2.3

Cooper, C. (2016, March 31). Methamphetamine abuse and illegal trafficking remain a persistent threat across the state. Cronkite News/Arizona PBS. Retrieved from https://cronkitenews.azpbs.org/2016/03/31/methamphetamine-abuse-and-illegal-trafficking-remain-a-persistent-threat-across-the-state/

Crosby, K., & O'Neal, K. (2012). Prevention of sun-induced skin disorders. In D. Krinsky et al. (Eds.), *Handbook of nonprescription drugs*, 17th ed. (pp. 707–722). Washington, DC: American Pharmacists Association.

Cunningham, J. K., Callaghan, R. C., Tong, D., Liu, L. M., Li, H. Y., & Lattyak, W. J. (2012). Changing over-the-counter ephedrine and pseudoephedrine products to prescription only: Impacts on methamphetamine clandestine laboratory seizures. *Drug and Alcohol Dependency*, 126, 55–64.

DeBatista, C. (2015). Antidepressant agents. In B. Katzung & A. Trevor (Eds.), *Basic and clinical pharmacology*, 13th ed. (pp. 510–527). New York, NY: McGraw-Hill.

DerSarkissian, C. (2016). Health risks linked to obesity. WebMD. Retrieved from http://www.webmd.com/diet/obesity/obesity-health-risks

Desai, R. (2019). Comparative effectiveness of generic and brand-name medication use: A database study of US health insurance claims. PLoS Medicine. Retrieved from https://www.ncbi.nlm.nih.gov/pmc/articles/PMC6415809/

Dowell, D., Haegerich, T., & Chou, R. (2016). CDC guideline for prescribing opioids for chronic pain—United States, 2016. *Morbidity and Mortality Weekly Report*, 65, 1–49. Retrieved from http://www.cdc.gov/mmwr/volumes/65/rr/rr6501e1.htm

Drug Enforcement Administration (DEA). (2014). Disposal of Controlled Substances; Final Rule. 21 CFR Parts 1300, 1301, 1304 et al. *Federal Register, 79*. Retrieved from http://www.deadiversion.usdoj.gov/fed_regs/rules/2014/2014-20926.pdf

Drug Enforcement Administration (DEA). (2018). DEA national prescription takeback. Springfield, VA: Author. Available https://takebackday.dea.gov/

Drugs.com. (2015). 18 herbal supplements with risky drug interactions. Retrieved from http://www.drugs.com/slideshow/herb-drug-interactions-1069

Drugs.com. (2016). Over-the-counter medications. Retrieved from https://www.drugs.com/otc/

Elena, M. (2016, March 10). Mexican drug cartel's crystal meth ingredient may be from Belgian pharma execs. Latin Post. Retrieved from http://www.latinpost.com/articles/118030/20160310/mexican-drug-cartels-crystal-meth-ingredient-belgian-pharma-execs.htm

Faberman, R. (2019). U.S. obesity rates reach historic highs, ethnic, gender and geographic disparities. Trust for America's Health. Retrieved from https://www.tfah.org/report-details/stateofobesity2019/

FamilyDoctor.org. (n.d.). Decongestants: OTC relief for congestion. Retrieved from http://familydoctor.org/familydoctor/en/drugs-procedures-devices/over-the-counter/decongestants-otc-relief-for-congestion.html

Flexner, C. (2006). Antiretroviral agents and treatment of HIV infection. In L. Brunton, J. Lazo, & K. Parker (Eds.), *The pharmacological basis of therapeutics*, 11th ed. (pp. 1273–1314). New York, NY: McGraw-Hill.

Food and Drug Administration (FDA). (n.d.). Prescription to over-the-counter (OTC) switch list. Retrieved from https://wayback.archive-it.org/7993/20170722193547/https://www.fda.gov/AboutFDA/CentersOffices/OfficeofMedicalProductsandTobacco/CDER/ucm106378.htm

Food and Drug Administration (FDA). (2016a). Generic drug facts. Retrieved from http://www.fda.gov/drugs/resourcesforyou/consumers/buyingusingmedicinesafely/understandinggenericdrugs/ucm167991.htm

Food and Drug Administration (FDA). (2016b). Legal requirements for the sale and purchase of drug products containing pseudoephedrine, ephedrine, and phenylpropanolamine. Retrieved from https://www.fda.gov/drugs/information-drug-class/legal-requirements-sale-and-purchase-drug-products-containing-pseudoephedrine-ephedrine-and

Food and Drug Administration (FDA). (2016c). Now available without a prescription. Retrieved from http://www.fda.gov/Drugs/ResourcesForYou/Consumers/ucm143547.htm

Food and Drug Administration (FDA). (2016d, March 22). FDA announces enhanced warnings for immediate-release opioid pain medications related to risks of misuse, abuse, addiction, overdose and death. Retrieved from http://www.fda.gov/NewsEvents/Newsroom/PressAnnouncements/ucm491739.htm

Food and Drug Administration (FDA). (2019). Labeling requirements for over-the-counter drugs." CFR Title 21—Food and Drugs Chapter I—Subchapter C—Drugs: General, Part 201 Labeling. Retrieved from https://www.accessdata.fda.gov/scripts/cdrh/cfdocs/cfCFR/CFRSearch.cfm?CFRPart=201&showFR=1&subpartNode=21:4.0.1.1.2.3

"From Prescription Pad to Store Shelf." (2019). Optum Retrieved from https://www.optum.com/health-insights/prescription-vs-otc.html

Fuller, K. (2020, January). Pharming: Pill parties for teens. *Psychology Today*. Retrieved from https://www.psychologytoday.com/us/blog/happiness-is-state-mind/201809/pharming-pill-parties-teens

Galanter, J., & Boushey, H. (2015). Drugs used in asthma. In B. Katzung & A. Trevor (Eds.), *Basic and clinical pharmacology*, 13th ed. (pp. 336–353). New York, NY: McGraw-Hill.

Gill, L. (2019). The shocking rise of prescription drug prices. *Consumer Reports*. Retrieved from https://www.consumerreports.org/drug-prices/the-shocking-rise-of-prescription-drug-prices/

GoodRx. (2019, July). The GoodRx top 10. Retrieved from https://www.goodrx.com/drug-guide

Hales, C. (2019). Prescription drug use among adults aged 40–79 in the United States and Canada. Hyattsville, MD: National Center for Health Statistics. Retrieved from https://www.cdc.gov/nchs/products/databriefs/db347.htm

Hanson, D. (2010, July 28). U.S. leads world in prescription drug use. Addiction Inbox. Retrieved from http://addiction-dirkh.blogspot.com/2010/07/us-leads-world-in-prescription-drug-use.html

Hayes, A. (2016). Prince died from fentanyl overdose. WebMD. Retrieved from http://www.webmd.com/mental-health/addiction/news/20160602/prince-fentanyl-overdose

Health Day. (2012, June 19). More mental health woes in college kids who abuse prescription drugs. *U.S. News & World Report*. Retrieved from https://consumer.healthday.com/mental-health-information-25/depression-news-176/more-mental-health-woes-in-college-kids-who-abuse-prescription-drugs-665719.html

Hume, A., & Strong, K. (2006). Botanical medicines. In I. Bernardi (Ed.), *Handbook of nonprescription drugs*, 15th ed. (pp. 1103–1136). Washington, DC: American Pharmacists Association.

Hussar, D. (2016). Overview of over-the-counter drugs. Merck manual: Consumer version. Retrieved from http://www.merckmanuals.com/home/drugs/over-the-counter-drugs/overview-of-over-the-counter-drugs

"Insomnia statistics." (2016). The Better Sleep Guide. Retrieved from http://www.better-sleep-better-life.com/insomnia-statistics.html

Johnston, L. (2019). *Monitoring the Future*. Retrieved from http://monitoringthefuture.org/pubs/monographs/mtf-overview2018.pdf

Journey Pure. (2015). The dangers of pharm parties. 12 Keys Rehab. 2015. Retrieved from http://www.12keysrehab.com/blog/dangers-of-pharm-parties

Juergens, J. (2019). Over the counter (OTC) drug addiction, abuse and treatment. Addiction Center. Retrieved from https://www.addictioncenter.com/drugs/over-the-counter-drugs/

Kaiser Family Foundation. (2010, May). Prescription drug trends fact sheet. Retrieved from http://www.kff.org/rxdrugs/upload/3057-08.pdf

Kamal, R., Cox, C., & McDermott, D. (2019). What are the recent and forecasted trends in prescription drug spending? Health System Tracker, 2019. Retrieved from https://www.healthsystemtracker.org/chart-collection/recent-forecasted-trends-prescription-drug-spending/

Katzung, B. (2015a). Vasodilators and the treatment of angina pectoris." In B. Katzung & A. Trevor (Eds.), *Basic and clinical pharmacology*, 13th ed. (pp. 191–207). New York, NY: McGraw-Hill.

Katzung, B. (2015b). Development and regulation of drugs. In B. Katzung & A. Trevor (Eds.), *Basic and clinical pharmacology*, 13th ed. (pp. 69–77). New York, NY: McGraw-Hill.

Katzung. B. (2015c). Drugs used in heart failure. In B. Katzung & A. Trevor (Eds.), *Basic and clinical pharmacology*, 13th ed. (pp. 209–223). New York, NY: McGraw-Hill.

Kennedy, M. (2012). Pancreatic hormones and antidiabetes drugs. In B. Katzung (Ed.), *Basic and clinical pharmacology*, 12th ed. (pp. 743–768). New York, NY: McGraw-Hill Medical.

Kennedy, M. S., & Masharani, U. (2015). Pancreatic hormones and antidiabetic drugs. In B. Katzung & A. Trevor (Eds.), *Basic and clinical pharmacology*, 13th ed. (pp. 723–746). New York, NY: McGraw-Hill.

Keshavan, M. (2016, May 23). Tasty and easy to take, a new ADHD alarms some psychiatrists. Retrieved from https://www.statnews.com/2016/05/23/adhd-drug-concerns/

Kirkwood, C., & Melton, S. (2012). Insomnia, drowsiness, and fatigue." In D. Krinsky et al. (Eds.), *Handbook of nonprescription drugs*, 17th ed. (pp. 867–883). Washington, DC: American Pharmacists Association.

Lampert, P. (2013, May 14). Consumer skepticism growing regarding "all natural" food claims. CISION PR Newswire. Retrieved from http://www.prnewswire.com/news-releases/consumer-skepticism-growing-regarding-all-natural-food-claims-207362511.html

Landro, L. (2016, February 29). How your supplements interact with prescription drugs. *Wall Street Journal*. Retrieved from http://www.wsj.com/articles/what-you

-should-know-about-how-your-supplements-interact
-with-prescription-drugs-1456777548

Leslie, D. L, Ba, D. M., Agbese, E., Xing, X., & Liu, G. (2019). The economic burden of the opioid epidemic on states: The case of Medicaid. AJMC 2019. Retrieved from https://www.ajmc.com/journals/supplement/2019/deaths-dollars-diverted-resources-opioid-epidemic/the-economic-burden-opioid-epidemic-on-states-case-of-medicaid

Lynn, D., Umari, T., Dunnick, C., & Dellavalle, R. (2016). The epidemiology of acne vulgaris in late adolescence. *Adolescent Health, Medicine, and Therapeutics*, 7, 13–25.

Malloy, M., & Kane, J. (2015). Agents used in dyslipidemia." In B. Katzung & A. Trevor (Eds.), *Basic and clinical pharmacology*, 13th ed. (pp. 602–615). New York, NY: McGraw-Hill, 2015.

Mayo Clinic. (2016). Eating disorders. Retrieved from http://www.mayoclinic.org/diseases-conditions/eating-disorders/symptoms-causes/dxc-20182875

McCabe, S., Boyd, C., & Teter, C. (2009). Subtypes of nonmedical prescription drug misuse. *Drug and Alcohol Dependence, 102*, 63–70.

McQuaid, K. (2015). Drugs used in the treatment of gastrointestinal diseases. In B. Katzung and A. Trevor (Eds.), *Basic and clinical pharmacology*, 13th ed. (pp. 1052–1083). New York, NY: McGraw-Hill.

McQueen, C., & Orr, R. (2012). Natural products. In D. Krinsky et al. (Eds.), *Handbook of nonprescription drugs*, 17th ed. (pp. 967–1006). Washington, DC: American Pharmacists Association.

MedlinePlus. (2019). Skin aging. Bethesda, MD: U.S. National Library of Medicine. Retrieved from https://medlineplus.gov/skinaging.html

Miller, M. (2016). Is caffeine before an exam a good or bad idea? Viter Energy. Retrieved from https://www.goviter.com/search?q=Miller+Is+Caffeine+before+an+Exam+a+Good

Miller, S., & Bartels, C. (2012). Overweight and obesity. In D. Krinsky et al. (Eds.), *Handbook of nonprescription drugs*, 17th ed. (pp. 488–505). Washington, DC: American Pharmacists Association.

National Center for Complementary and Alternative Medicine (NCCAM). (2013, June 10). Herbs at a glance.

National Center for Complementary and Integrative Health. (2019, October). Melatonin: What you need to know. Bethesda, MD: Author. Retrieved from https://nccih.nih.gov/health/melatonin

National Heart, Lung, and Blood Institute. (2016). Other names for coronary heart disease. Bethesda, MD: Author. Retrieved from http://www.nhlbi.nih.gov/health/health-topics/topics/cad/names

National Institute of Mental Health (NIMH). (2016). Attention deficit hyperactivity disorder. Retrieved from http://www.nimh.nih.gov/health/topics/attention-deficit-hyperactivity-disorder-adhd/index.shtml

National Institute of Mental Health (NIMH). (2019). Major depression. Bethesda, MD: Author. Retrieved from https://www.nimh.nih.gov/health/statistics/major-depression.shtml

National Institute on Drug Abuse (NIDA). (2015). Dramatic increases in maternal opioid use and neonatal abstinence syndrome. Rockville, MD: Author. Retrieved from https://www.drugabuse.gov/related-topics/trends-statistics/infographics/dramatic-increases-in-maternal-opioid-use-neonatal-abstinence-syndrome

National Institute on Drug Abuse (NIDA). (2016a). Overdose death rates. Rockville, MD: Author. Retrieved from https://www.drugabuse.gov/related-topics/trends-statistics/overdose-death-rates

National Institute on Drug Abuse (NIDA). (2016b). DrugFacts: Cough and cold medicine abuse. Rockville, MD: Author. Retrieved from https://www.drugabuse.gov/publications/drugfacts/cough-cold-medicine-abuse

National Institute on Drug Abuse (NIDA). (2016c). Extended-release naltrexone lowers relapse rates in ex-offenders. Rockville, MD: Author. Retrieved from https://www.drugabuse.gov/news-events/news-releases/2016/03/extended-release-naltrexone-lowers-relapse-rates-in-ex-offenders

National Institute on Drug Abuse (NIDA). (2019a). Over-the-counter medicines. Rockville, MD: Author. Retrieved from https://www.drugabuse.gov/drugs-abuse/over-counter-medicines

National Institute on Drug Abuse (NIDA). (2019b). NIDAMED clinical resources. Rockville, MD: Author. Retrieved from https://www.drugabuse.gov/nidamed-medical-health-professionals

Ogbru, O. (2016). Corticosteroid drugs: Systemic, oral, injections, and types. MedicineNet.com. Retrieved from http://www.medicinenet.com/corticosteroids-oral/article.htm

Olian, K. (2012, July 5). Prescription drug addiction among women becoming "monstrous tidal wave." NBC News. Retrieved from http://rockcenter.nbcnews.com/_news/2012/07/05/12570381-prescription-drug-addiction-among-pregnant-women-becoming-monstrous-tidal-wave?lite

"Only federal prevention message about prescription drugs: Lock up or throw out." (2010, March 15). *Alcoholism & Drug Abuse Weekly*. Retrieved from https://onlinelibrary.wiley.com/doi/10.1002/adaw.20225

OTC Monograph Reform. (2020). OTC review/Drug monographs. Washington, DC: Consumer Healthcare

Products Association. Retrieved from https://www.chpa.org/OTCReview.aspx

Page, M. (2015, February). "Rx-to-OTC switches: Trends to watch." Pharmacy Times.

Pain Assist. (2016). Differentiating dry cough and wet cough based on causes, symptoms, treatment. Retrieved from http://www.epainassist.com/chest-pain/lungs/differentiating-dry-cough-and-wet-cough

Panel on Antiretroviral Guidelines for Adults and Adolescents. (2016). Guidelines for the use of antiretroviral agents in HIV-1-infected adults and adolescents. Washington, DC: Department of Health and Human Services. Retrieved from at http://www.aidsinfo.nih.gov/ContentFiles/Adultand AdolescentGL.pdf

Pharmaletter. (2016). Costs and consequences of not treating high cholesterol in the USA. Retrieved from http://www.thepharmaletter.com/article/costs-and-consequences-of-not-treating-high-cholesterol-in-the-usa

PSNet. (2015). Medication errors. Rockville, MD: Agency for Healthcare Research and Quality. Retrieved from https://psnet.ahrq.gov/primers/primer/23/medication-errors

Quinlan, C. (2016). "Our understanding of ADHD is changing." ThinkProgress.org.

Quinn, E. (2019). Are all ephedrine supplements banned? VeryWellFit. Retrieved from https://www.verywellfit.com/sports-supplements-ephedrine-and-athletic-performance-3119368

Rickert, E. (2012). Legal and regulatory issues in self-care pharmacy practice. In D. Krinsky (Ed.), *Handbook of nonprescription drugs*, 17th ed. (pp. 53–64). Washington, DC: American Pharmacists Association.

Sandi, B. (2016). OTC reflux medications: Concerns for patients and proactive roles for compounding pharmacists. Glendale, CA: Pharmaceutica North America.

Saper, R. (2019). Overview of herbal medicine and dietary supplements. UptoDate. Retrieved from https://www.uptodate.com/contents/overview-of-herbal-medicine-and-dietary-supplements

Satel, S. (2019). The truth about painkiller addiction. *The Atlantic*. Retrieved from https://www.theatlantic.com/ideas/archive/2019/08/what-america-got-wrong-about-opioid-crisis/595090/

Schiffman, G. (2013). Asthma: Over-the-counter treatment. MedicineNet. Retrieved from http://www.medicinenet.com/asthma_over_the_counter_treatment/article.htm

Schiller, E. Y., Goyal, A., Cao, F., & Mechanic, O. (2019). Opioid overdose. StatPearls. Retrieved from https://www.ncbi.nlm.nih.gov/books/NBK470415/

Science Daily. (2019, March 20). Skin diseases are more common than we think. Science Daily. Retrieved from https://www.sciencedaily.com/releases/2019/03/190320102041.htm

Scolaro, K. (2012). Disorders related to colds and allergies. In D. Krinsky et al. (Eds.), *Handbook of nonprescription drugs*, 17th ed. (pp. 180–204). Washington, DC: American Pharmacists Association.

Shimp, L. (2012). Disorders related to menstruation. In D. Krinsky et al. (Eds.), *Handbook of nonprescription drugs*, 17th ed. (pp. 139–158). Washington, DC: American Pharmacists Association.

Sickles, J. (2016). Prince cause of death: Opioid overdose, tests reportedly show. Yahoo News. Retrieved from https://www.yahoo.com/news/prince-cause-death-000000903.html

Siler, S., Duda, S., Brown, R., Gbemudu, J., Weier, S., & Glaudemans, J. (n.d.). Safe disposal of unused controlled substances. Washington, DC: Avalere Health. Retrieved from http://www.ncdoi.com/osfm/safekids/Documents/OMD/SafeDisposalOfUnusedControlledSubstances Report.pdf

Small, J. (2013, April 15). Funds to run out for database that monitors prescription drug usage. Pasadena, CA: KPCC. Retrieved from http://www.scpr.org/news/2013/04/15/36829/funds-to-run-out-for-database-that-monitors-prescr/

Sola, C. (2010). Sedative, hypnotic, anxiolytic use disorders. Medscape. Retrieved from http://emedicine.medscape.com/article/290585-overview

Soong, J. (2016). Sleeping pills: Prescription or OTC? WebMD. Retrieved from http://www.webmd.com/sleep-disorders/living-with-insomnia-11/sleeping-pills

Sotonoff, J. (2010, July 26). Addiction began with prescription drugs he got from your homes. *Chicago Daily Herald*. Retrieved from http://prev.dailyherald.com/story/?id=396310

"Stomach and GI." (2016). *U.S. News & World Report*. Retrieved from http://health.usnews.com/health-products/stomach-and-gi-10

Stone, K. (2013). Top generic drug companies. The Balance. Retrieved from http://pharma.about.com/od/Generics/a/Top-Generic-Drug-Companies.htm

Stone, K. (2019). List of best-selling over-the-counter (OTC) drugs. VeryWellHealth. Retrieved from https://www.verywellhealth.com/top-selling-otc-drugs-by-category-2663170

Stoppler, M. (2010, December 29). Generic drugs, are they as good as brand names? MedicineNet.com. Retrieved from http://www.medicinenet.com/script/main/art.asp?articlekey=46204

Stoppler, M. (2016). Cold, flu, allergy treatments. Medicine Net.com. Retrieved from http://www.medicinenet.com/cold_flu_allergy/article.htm

Trevor, A. (2015). Sedative-hypnotic drugs. In B. Katzung & A. Trevor (Eds.), *Basic and clinical pharmacology*, 13th ed. (pp. 369–381). New York, NY: McGraw-Hill.

"Urban legends: Phenylpropanolamine recall." (2010). About.com.

U.S. Department of Health and Human Services. (2016). What is the U.S. opioid epidemic? Retrieved from https://www.hhs.gov/opioids/about-the-epidemic/index.html

Vestal, C. (2016). States require opioid prescribers to check for "doctor shopping." PEW Stateline. Retrieved from http://www.pewtrusts.org/en/research-and-analysis/blogs/stateline/2016/05/09/states-require-opioid-prescribers-to-check-for-doctor-shopping

Vivian, J., & Fink, J. (2019, December). OBRA'90 at sweet sixteen: A retrospective review. U.S. Pharmacist. Retrieved from https://www.uspharmacist.com/article/obra-90-at-sweet-sixteen-a-retrospective-review

Wilkinson, J. (2012). Headache. In D. Krinsky et al. (Eds.), *Handbook of Nonprescription Drugs*, 17th ed. (pp. 67–86). Washington, DC: American Pharmacists Association.

Williams, A., Girard, C., Jui, D., Sabina, A., & Katz, D. (2005). SAMe as treatment for depression: A systemic review. *Clinical Investigation of Medicine, 28*, 132–139.

Woolston, M. (2016). Type 2 diabetes and kids: The growing epidemic. HealthDay. Retrieved from https://consumer.healthday.com/encyclopedia/diabetes-13/misc-diabetes-news-181/type-2-diabetes-and-kids-the-growing-epidemic-644152.html

Zweber, A., & Berardi, R. (2012). Heartburn and dyspepsia. In D. Krinsky (Eds.), *Handbook of nonprescription drugs*, 17th ed. (pp. 221–235). Washington, DC: American Pharmacists Association.

## CHAPTER 16

# Drug Use in Subcultures of Special Populations

© FOTOGRIN/Shutterstock.

## Did You Know?

▶ As a subcultural group, athletes are much more likely to abuse performance-enhancing (ergogenic drugs) to enhance athletic performance.

▶ Studies have shown that athletes are less likely than nonathletes to use other drugs of abuse such as marijuana, alcohol, barbiturates, cocaine, and hallucinogens In general, men tend to use drugs more than women, yet women are more likely to become addicted to drugs.

▶ In comparison to men, women are more reluctant to seek substance abuse treatment.

▶ Approximately 70% of women in drug abuse treatment report histories of physical and sexual abuse, with victimization beginning before age 11 and occurring repeatedly.

▶ Adolescents who abuse drugs often have other co-occurring mental health problems.

▶ The major reasons adolescents use drugs are to cope with boredom, unpleasant feelings, emotions, and stress or to relieve depression and reduce tension and alienation.

▶ After marijuana and alcohol, prescription and over-the-counter (OTC) drugs are the most commonly abused substances by Americans 14 and older.

▶ Suicide is more likely to be attempted by those adolescents who turn to alcohol and other drugs to help them cope with serious emotional and personality conflicts and frustrations.

▶ Street gangs, outlaw motorcycle gangs, and prison gangs are the primary distributors of illegal drugs in the United States.

▶ Alcohol use is implicated in one-third to two-thirds of sexual assaults and acquaintance or date rapes among teens and college students.

▶ According to a national survey, almost 60% of college students ages 18 to 22 years drank alcohol in the past month, and more than 60% of those who drank engaged in binge drinking during that same time frame.

▶ More than 1.2 million people in the United States are living with human immunodeficiency virus (HIV) infection, and almost 12.8% are unaware of their infection.

▶ Gay, bisexual, and other men who have sex with men (MSM) of all races and ethnicities remain the population most profoundly affected by HIV.

▶ An HIV-infected individual may not manifest symptoms of acquired immune deficiency syndrome (AIDS) for as many as 10 to 12 years after the initial infection, and during this dormant period the person is highly contagious.

▶ Licit and illicit drugs can easily be purchased via Internet websites.

## Learning Objectives

**On completing this chapter, you should be able to:**

❭ Know which drugs are most likely to be abused by athletes and why.

❭ Describe the use of drug testing in athletic competitions.

❭ Identify where users obtain anabolic steroids.

❭ Describe the purpose and goals of the Adolescents Training and Learning to Avoid Steroids (ATLAS) prevention program.

❭ Explain two major ways the history of drug abuse among women differs from that of men.

❭ Explain the major reasons why adolescents use substances of abuse.

❭ Explain which types of parents are more likely to raise drug-abusing adolescents.

❭ List the types of drugs adolescents are most likely to abuse.

❭ List two major findings from research regarding drug use by college students.

❭ Know what "club drugs" are and how they are used.

❭ Explain how drug abuse contributes to the spread of HIV and AIDS.

❭ Know the key statistics regarding HIV and AIDS.

❭ List the major strategies to prevent HIV infection.

❭ Know how the use of alcohol and other drugs is presented in popular movies and songs.

❭ Understand how users can access the Internet to purchase licit and illicit types of drugs.

# Introduction

Although similarities appear in the patterns of addiction among drug users, the development of drug use, initial and extent of drug use, dependence, and often eventual abuse of drugs varies from individual to individual. When attempting to understand common patterns and possible causes of drug use, examining the subcultures of special populations provides a more organized understanding of commonalities within such subgroups. A **subculture** is defined as a special population or subgroup whose members share similar values, attitudes, and patterns of related behaviors that differ from those of other subcultures in the larger population. For example, from a subcultural perspective, a group of drug-using adolescents from a particular locality in a city or town is not much different from a group of divorced women meeting to discuss coping with separation and suddenly being single. Both of these are distinct subcultures in that their members are involved with similar experiences, concerns, and goals. As a result, these subcultural groups comprising special populations share a significant amount of similar values and attitudes.

Even though many subcultures are so broad and diverse that not all members may be consciously aware of one another as a distinct subculture, from an **outsider's perspective** these groupings are perceived as distinct subcultures with similar behavior patterns.

An **insider's perspective** refers to participants who use drugs within their group and are the participants inside the drug-using group. The members of a drug-using subculture are continually experiencing ongoing activity within their group. Group members maintain an insiders' perspective and are often surrounded by other group members who share the same inside perspective. Outsiders such as conventional members of society and law enforcement officials are composed of groups who challenge and largely oppose drug use and perceive drug use as deviant behavior. In summary, *insiders are looking at their drug use behavior from inside the group norms, and outsiders are looking at this same group from outside the boundaries of the group*. This distinction between insiders and outsiders is important for understanding drug use because the often-clashing perspectives between insiders and outsiders result in vastly different perspectives and, by extension, vastly different beliefs about drug-using behavior.

Sociologists often refer to a subculture as a "world within a world." Subcultures create and provide their members with lifestyle patterns that are observable, fairly consistent, and interwoven. Viewing a drug-using group as a subculture offers a way to look for more generalized and distinctive patterns of drug use. In looking at the subcultures of drug users, we can begin to logically and methodically examine the reasons why individuals within various subcultures might initially use and persist in using drugs. Further, insider internal and external types of forces continually shape and affect members of a drug-using subculture.

*Internal subcultural forces* affecting drug users include the following:

- shared in-group attitudes about people who do and do not use drugs (drug users versus nonusers);
- compatibility with other members of the peer group (often peer members share complementary personality traits);
- shared attitudes favorable to drug use despite conventional society's view that such behavior is deviant and violates law;
- addiction to drugs or, at minimum, habitual drug usage; and
- a common secrecy about drug use (who you can and cannot trust in knowing about your drug usage).

*External subcultural forces* affecting drug users include the following:

- preoccupation with law enforcement while procuring the drugs and while under the effects of illicit drugs;
- a desire to identify other users and dealers of illicit drugs, such as verifying the dependability

## KEY TERMS

**subculture**
subgroup within the population whose members share similar values and patterns of related behaviors that differ from other subcultures and the larger population

**outsider's perspective**
viewing a group or subculture from outside the group and viewing the group and its members as an observer; looking "in" at the members

**insider's perspective**
viewing a group or subculture from inside the group; seeing members as they perceive themselves

of the drug dealer (who best to deal drugs with and who has the best quality drugs);

- constant preoccupation regarding drug supply and when to keep in touch with drug dealer(s) and concern about acquiring a new supply of their drug of choice; and
- some preoccupation with being viewed or observed using or acting "high" in public, at work, at school, or at a social function where drug use would be perceived as deviant social behavior.

To further understand how similar patterns of drug use or abuse occur, in this chapter we look at drug use and users from both outsiders' and insiders' perspectives from the vantage point of the members belonging to a distinct subculture and how their behavior is perceived by society. This chapter focuses on and examines drug use, drug dependence, and drug abuse in the following seven drug-using subcultures:

1. athletes and those involved in sports;
2. women;
3. adolescents;
4. college students;
5. those affected by the human immunodeficiency virus (HIV) and acquired immune deficiency syndrome (AIDS);
6. a certain percentage of professional actors, actresses, and music celebrities; and
7. Internet users who are seeking and purchasing illicit drugs.

## Athletes, Doping, and Drug Abuse

Drug abuse among athletes has been reported as far back as the Greek Olympics in 776 BC, when it was noted that competitors were ingesting certain substances to gain ground against their fellow competitors (Shavin, 2016).

Major drug substances that are most often monitored by agencies are divided into . . . three classes. . . . *Central nervous system stimulants* such as bupropion, nicotine, phenylephrine, phenylpropanolamine, sinephrine, and pipradrol; *narcotics* [such as] hydrocodone, tramadol, talpentadol; and *glucocorticoids*, banned in competition through all ways of administration. Also, telmisartan, a angiotensin II antagonist class on AT1 receptors and meldonium substance used in angina pectoris, can be included in the same category. Central

nervous system stimulants as well as narcotics will not be used in competitions, while glucocorticoids, meldonium and telmisartan are banned both outside and in competitions. (Vlad, Hancu, Popescu, & Lungu, 2018)

To enhance athletic performance, the primary substances used are "[n]arcotics and analgesics, anabolic steroids, hormones, selective androgen receptor modulators are among the most frequently utilized substances" (Vlad et al., 2018).

Using performance-enhancing drugs for increased athletic ability is known as **doping** (National Institute on Drug Abuse [NIDA], 2009). In sport, doping

is the deliberate or inadvertent use by an athlete of a substance or method banned by the International Olympic Committee (IOC). [The International Federation of Sports Medicine] supports the prohibition of doping to protect athletes from the:

- unfair advantage, which may be gained by those athletes who use banned substances or methods to enhance performance;
- possible harmful side effects, which some substances or methods can produce;
- quicker recovery from an injury; and
- increasing muscle mass and better endurance. (Vlad et al., 2018)

In the past, reports revealed that "'[d]oping' among world-class competitors is rampant . . . and the governing bodies of individual sports, as well as the International Olympic Committee, turn a blind eye" (Begley et al., 1999, p. 49). The reasons boil down to winning in sports, especially when millisecond differences exist between gold and silver medals. The differences between the two medals "can amount to millions in endorsement contract and appearance fees" (Begley et al., p. 49), and apparently the world of professional sports and "drugs [performance-enhancing drugs] go together like socks and sweat" (p. 49). Charles Yesalis, an epidemiologist at Pennsylvania State University at University Park, stated,

More recent findings continue to support the continual prevalence of doping in professional

**KEY TERM**

**doping**
use of performance-enhancing drugs to increase athletic ability

sports. The doping phenomenon in sports is increasing and diversifying, as are the drugs used for doping. There is a permanent race among those who invent new doping methods and sports ethics organizations that are searching for more performant methods to detect them. Unfortunately, most of the times, those in the first category are always one step ahead. (Vlad et al., 2018)

In addition,

Elite athletes stay away from traditional anabolic steroids. They use testosterone creams or gels, which dramatically reduce the chance of being caught, in conjunction with insulin or insulin-like growth factor.... The supplement industry has exploded since the passage of the Dietary Supplement Health and Education Act in 1994. . . . Anyone can buy substances like testosterone, human-growth hormone (HGH), and insulin-like growth factor over the Internet. One site requires a doctor's prescription but will sell one to any customer for $100 or someone can just walk down to the local GNC, like Mr. Jackson's teammates at Florida State. There, one can buy muscle-building steroid "precursors" like androstenedione and creatine monohydrate. (Suggs, 2003, p. 36)

More recently, however, findings indicate that since 2007 antidoping agencies introduced the concept of a *biological passport*, a record of the substances found normally in an athlete's blood and urine that is created by repeated sampling over time. By comparing the results of a blood test administered right before a competition to the passport, officials can determine if an athlete has been using erythropoietin (EPO) or other performance-enhancing drugs (Harris, 2013).

As a result, the use of muscle-building steroid *precursors* such as androstenedione and creatine monohydrate are now detectable in drug testing.

Athletes may come into contact with performance-enhancing substances inadvertently or intentionally. For example, some athletes may inadvertently (or allegedly inadvertently) consume a pharmaceutical that is banned from competition, either because the ingredients or manufacturing method are kept secret or because it is protected by trademark or copyright (also known as a **proprietary medicine**). Other athletes may deliberately consume such substances for misuse as a recreational drug or deliberately consume them to enhance their performance (Docherty, 2008).

To further our understanding of why athletes are willing to risk using these drugs, it is necessary to further explore their mindsets.

To excel in athletic competition is admirable. Most high school, college, amateur, and professional athletes participate in sports for the opportunity to pit their abilities against those of their peers and to experience the satisfaction that comes from playing to their potential. Others do so to satisfy a desire for recognition and fame. Unfortunately, that creates some athletes who are determined to win at any cost. And they may use that determination to justify the use of anabolic steroids despite evidence that these drugs can inflict irreversible physical harm and have significant side effects (New York State Department of Health, 2010).

Young athletes receive exaggerated attention and prestige in almost every university, college, high school, and junior high school in the United States. Pressure to excel or be the best is placed on athletes by parents, peers, teachers, coaches, school administrators, news media, and the surrounding community. The importance of sports is frequently distorted and even used by some to evaluate the quality of educational institutions (Lawn, 1984; New York State Department of Health, 2010) or the quality of living conditions in a city. Athletic success can determine the level of financial support these institutions receive from local and state governments, alumni, and other private donors; thus, winning in athletics often translates into fiscal stability and institutional prosperity.

For the athlete, success in sports means psychological rewards such as the admiration of peers, school officials, family, and the community. In addition, athletic success can mean financial rewards such as scholarships, paid living expenses in college, advertising endorsement opportunities, and, for a few, incredible salaries as professional athletes. With the rewards of winning, athletes have to deal with the added pressures of not winning: "What will people think of me if I lose?" "When I lose, I let everybody down."

**KEY TERM**

**proprietary medicine**
pharmaceutical medicine that is protected from commercial competition because the ingredients or manufacturing method is kept secret or because it is protected by trademark or copyright

"Losing shows that I am not as good as everyone thinks." These pressures on young, immature athletes can result in poor coping responses. Being better than competitors, no matter the cost, becomes the driving motivation, and doing one's best is no longer sufficient. Such attitudes may lead to serious risk-taking behavior in an attempt to develop an advantage over the competition; this situation can include using drugs to improve performance.

Canadian sprinter Ben Johnson, once known as the fastest human in history, was banned for life from competitive running in March 1993 (Begley et al., 1999; Hoberman & Yesalis, 1995). Five years earlier, at the 1988 Seoul Olympics, Johnson was stripped of a world record for the 100-meter dash and forfeited the gold medal when his urine tested positive for steroids (D'Souza, 2018). Because of the first incident, Johnson was suspended from competition for two years. However, in 1992, the 31-year-old sprinter was attempting a comeback, with speeds that approached his world record times. In January 1993, a routine urine test determined Johnson was again using steroids to enhance his athletic performance (Ferrente, 1993). More recently, "Johnson, 51, has admitted to years of steroid use, but still feels he was unfairly picked out for vilification at a time of widespread drug use in athletics. 'I was nailed on a cross, and 25 years later I'm still being punished,' he [Johnson] . . . said" ("Ben Johnson," 2013).

Another incident involving the use of steroids that ended in shocking tragedy was the case of wrestler Chris Benoit's double murder-suicide.

Evidence proved that the professional wrestler asphyxiated his son and wife before he hanged himself in a basement weight room using a cord from one of the weight machines (ESPN.com, 2007; Wright, 2009). When going through Benoit's house, investigators found several prescription steroid medications (Donaldson-Evans, 2007). One side effect of anabolic steroids is extreme anger (Donaldson-Evans, 2007).

After Major League Baseball (MLB) implemented a new steroid policy, 83 players were suspended. "Guys did steroids because it was easy to get away with" (Anonymous, as told by Penn, 2005, p. 292). According to a player who chose to remain anonymous, "So many people were doing it that it didn't feel like cheating. If anything, it felt like leveling the field. . . . I juiced because I love playing more than anything else in the world, and I would have pretty much done anything to keep my career going" (Anonymous, 2005, p. 297).

Widely publicized incidents such as these concerning illicit use of so-called **ergogenic** (performance-enhancing) drugs by professional and amateur athletes have created intense interest in the problem of drug abuse in sport (Begley et al., 1999; Merchant, 1992; see "Point/Counterpoint: How the 'Juice' Was and Is Flowing in Baseball").

### KEY TERM

**ergogenic**
drugs that enhance athletic performance

---

## ▶ POINT/COUNTERPOINT

### How the "Juice" Was and Is Flowing in Baseball

**W**e embrace instant gratification in the United States. We are a society that embraces "bigger, faster, stronger" and winning at all costs (Dvorchak, 2005). This concept now applies to professional sports. A sampling from news sources reveals the following:

- "Jose Canseco, a Major League Baseball player for the Oakland Athletics and Texas Rangers (among other teams), wrote a tell-all book titled *Juiced*, in which he exposed not only the rampant use of performance-enhancing substances in baseball. . . . A steroid devotee since the age of 20,

Canseco goes beyond admitting his own usage . . . [to claiming that] he often injected [Mark] McGwire while they were teammates. . . . According to Canseco, steroids and human growth hormone gave McGwire and Sammy Sosa (whose own usage was 'so obvious, it was a joke') the strength, stamina, regenerative ability, and confidence they needed for [the] record setting home run duels often credited with restoring baseball's popularity after the 1994 strike" (Canseco, 2005).

- "[S]everal star athletes, including New York Yankees slugger Jason Giambi, have reportedly told a federal grand jury investigating the [Bay Area Laboratory Cooperative] that they used illegal steroids,

*(continues)*

# ▶POINT/COUNTERPOINT

## How the "Juice" Was and Is Flowing in Baseball (*continued*)

prompting Congress to hold hearings on the testing policies of all the major sports leagues" (Coile, 2005).

- "Seattle Mariners minor-league outfielder Jamal Strong was suspended for 10 days . . . making him the fourth player to test positive under Major League Baseball's new policy on performance-enhancing drugs" (ESPN.com, 2005).

- "McGwire's shameful refusal to answer questions about his alleged steroid use before a congressional committee and Bonds' unbelievable claim that he did not know that substances rubbed into his body were steroids clearly suggest deceit and dishonesty" (Eilek, 2005).

- "Performance-enhancing drugs (PEDs) have once again taken a toll on the professional sports world with yesterday's suspensions of 13 Major League Baseball players, including Alex Rodriguez—the highest paid player in professional baseball" (Woemer, 2013).

- "Rodriguez was suspended in August for an unprecedented 211 games for his connection to the now defunct Biogenesis anti-aging clinic linked to providing 14 players with performance-enhancing drugs. His suspension came since he violated the joint drug agreement and the collective bargaining agreement. A-Rod had the harshest punishment of all the players as Ryan Braun received a 65-game ban while the other 12 players each accepted and served 50-game suspensions" (Smollins, 2013).

- "According to baseball reporter Ken Rosenthal, Major League Baseball has suspended 12 players in relation to the Biogenesis case.... [That 2013 case involved a recently defunct clinic, Biogenesis of America, which provided PEDs to MLB players] . . . Nelson Cruz, Jhonny Peralta,

Antonio Bastardo, Jordany Valdespin, Everth Cabrera, Francisco Cervelli, Jesus Montero, Sergio Escalona, Fautino De Los Santos, Cesar Puello, Fernando Martinez, and Jordan Norberto will all be suspended. All 12 players have accepted their 50-game suspensions" (Lengel & Busfield, 2013).

### Questions to Consider

1. Are professional sports players entitled to claim records set if they were on drugs during their successful career? If they are entitled to their accomplishments regardless of their drug usage, how would it affect non–drug-using players? Is it fair to the sport and to the fans supporting the players? If they are not entitled to their accomplishments under drugged conditions, what should the penalty be?

2. Do you think that all players in professional sports should be continuously tested for drugs? Should this policy be extended to high school and college sports players as well? If so, what should the penalties for drug violations be?

3. What if we find clear evidence that some currently admired major sports figures who scored big-time records in the past were using steroids or other performance-enhancing drugs while setting new and impressive records? Should anything be done about such evidence? If so, what penalties should the athletes receive? If not, why should we let them remain unblemished?

4. Are the real victims of this tragedy America's youth? Have athletes such as McGwire and Rodriguez betrayed the young people who admire and emulate them? Do you think America's youth are affected by their drug use in professional sports?

5. Does this scandal about professional sports and drug use suggest anything about the findings by the Centers for Disease Control and Prevention that steroid use among high school students more than doubled from 1991 to 2003?

Data from Amazon.com. (2005). Editorial reviews. Retrieved from http://www.amazon.com/exec/obidos/asin/0060746408/ref=bxgy; ESPN.com. (2005, April 26). Strong suspended for performance-enhancing drugs. ESPN Sports. Retrieved from http://sports.espn.go.com/mlb/news/story?id=2046762; Coile, Z. (2005, April 27). House bill seeks to toughen steroid rules: Athletes in all leagues would be held to the strict standards used in Olympics. *San Francisco Chronicle*, pp. 1–2; Dvorchak, R. (2005, April 27). Former Steeler Courson outlines solutions for steroid use. Black and Gold. Retrieved from http://blackandgoldworld.blogspot.com/2005/04/robert-dvorchak-courson-outlines.html; Eilek, R. (2005, April 17). Pro sports keep heads in sand on steroids. *San Diego Union Tribune*; Smollins, M. (2013, November 1). Alex Rodriguez Biogenesis case: MLB CEO Rob Manfred calls A-Rod career "sad and tarnished," claims Rodriguez PED use "longer than any other player." *Sports World News*. Retrieved from http://www.sportsworldnews.com/articles /6205/20131101/alex-rodriguez-biogenesis-case-mlb-ceo-rob-manfred-calls-a-rod-career-sad-tarnished-claims-rodriguez-ped-use-longer-than-any-other -player.htm; TheScore.com. (2013, August 5). MLB suspends 12 players in Biogenesis case; Woemer, A. (2013, August 6). MLB players' use of performance enhancing drugs comes with serious health risks. *FoxNews.com*. Retrieved from http://www.foxnews.com/health/2013/08/06/mlb-players-use -performance-enhancing-drugs-comes-with-serious-health-risks/; D'Souza, M. (2018). 10 famous athletes who were caught doping. *Edgar*. Retrieved from https://edgardaily.com/articles/10-famous-athletes-caught-doping/

A case of steroid use in professional sports involves Alexander Emmanuel "Alex" Rodriguez. Born in 1975, Rodriquez was an MLB player for the Seattle Mariners, Texas Rangers, and New York Yankees. He was considered one of the best players in baseball history. In 2007, he signed a 10-year, $252 million contract (Britannica.com, 2010) with the Yankees. However, Rodriguez was dogged by accusations of steroid use:

> The Slugger [Rodriguez] who might someday become baseball's all-time home run king remembered more details about performance-enhancing drugs Tuesday, saying his cousin repeatedly injected him from 2001–03 with a mysterious substance from the Dominican Republic. "I didn't think they were steroids" the New York Yankees star said. Later, he admitted, "I knew we weren't taking Tic Tacs." (Blum, 2009, p. A11)

It was at this press conference that Rodriguez made "his second public attempt to explain a 2003 positive drug test while with Texas … while his cousin persuaded him to use 'boli'—a substance he said the cousin obtained without a prescription and without consulting doctors or trainers" (Blum, 2009, p. A11).

> Rodriguez was suspended from the MLB for steroid use, but recently in an effort to reverse the suspension, the three-time American League Most Valuable Player sued MLB, its players' union, and a Yankees team physician. The Yankees and Rodriguez issued a joint statement on Tuesday [referring to February 10, 2015]. . . . "Alex initiated the meeting and apologized to the organization for his actions over the past several years," the statement said. "There was an honest and frank discussion on all of the issues. As far as the Yankees are concerned, the next step is to play baseball in spring training." Rodriguez, who turns 40 in July, is set to make $61 million over the next three years, thanks to a 10-year $275 million contract he signed in 2007. (McSpadden, 2015)

Finally, one of the most shocking cases was that of bicyclist Lance Armstrong, who was stripped of his record-holding *seven* Tour de France titles that he received from 1999 to 2005—because of doping. Armstrong stated that doping was required to become a record holder (Leicester, 2013). Armstrong also stated that "his life has been ruined by the U.S. Anti-Doping Agency investigation that exposed as lies his years of denials that

he and his teammates doped" (Gleeson, 2019; Leicester 2013).

## ■ Laws Intended to Stop the Use of Performance-Enhancing Drugs in Professional Sports

Originally established in 1999, The **World Anti-Doping Agency (WADA)** is "an international independent agency composed and funded equally by the sport movement and governments of the world" (WADA, 2020). In brief, the WADA was created "[a]fter the events that shook the world of cycling in the summer of 1998, the International Olympic Committee (IOC) decided to convene a World Conference on Doping, bringing together all parties involved in the fight against doping" (WADA, 2020).

The **World Anti-Doping Code** is the core document that harmonizes antidoping policies, rules, and regulations within sport organizations and among public authorities around the world. It works in conjunction with five International standards that aim to foster consistency among antidoping organizations in various areas: testing, laboratories, therapeutic use exemptions (TUEs), the List of Prohibited Substances and Methods, and the protection of privacy and personal information.

This code has proven to be a powerful and effective tool in harmonizing antidoping efforts worldwide since it came into force on January 1, 2004 (WADA, 2009).

One revision of the code provides provisions for increased sanctions, greater flexibility (the accused athlete has the option to provide evidence that the substance used was not intended to enhance performance), clear listing and definition of specified substances violating the rules, incentives to come forward and report personal usage or use by other athletes of performance-enhancing drugs, financial sanctions (including clearly specified periods of ineligibility), and WADA's right to appeal to a Court of Sport Arbitration (WADA, 2009). Another more recent revision strengthened the code to be a more vigorous

**KEY TERMS**

**World Anti-Doping Agency (WADA)**
organization with a mission to lead a collaborative worldwide movement for doping-free sport

**World Anti-Doping Code**
core document providing a framework for harmonized antidoping policies, rules, and regulations within sport organizations and among public authorities

tool protecting the rights of the clean athlete worldwide (WADA, 2015).

In 2020 the World Anti-Doping Agency (WADA) stipulated a revised Code of Compliance listing the following (WADA, 2020, unless otherwise noted):

- "To date, more than 600 sport organizations have accepted the World Anti-Doping Code. These organizations include the International Olympic Committee (IOC), the International Paralympic Committee, all Olympic sport international federations (IFs) and all IOC-recognized IFs, national Olympic and Paralympic Committees, national antidoping organizations."
- Code of Compliance monitoring: "Overseeing acceptance, implementation, and compliance of the Code, the core document that glues together antidoping policies, rules, and regulations worldwide."
- Education: "Preventative methods such as values-based education programs targeted at young athletes, coaches, doctors, trainers, and parents on the dangers and consequences of doping, as well as the legal and social ramifications, are increasingly prevalent in antidoping programs."
- Antidoping coordination: Coordinating antidoping activities globally through its central clearinghouse, the antidoping administration and management system.
- Global antidoping development: "Through its regional antidoping organization . . . program, WADA is developing a clean sport culture in parts of the world previously untouched by antidoping programs."
- Athlete outreach: "Engaging with athletes, their entourage, and all those involved in sport on the world stage, WADA's Athlete Outreach program aims to raise awareness while ensuring athletes are involved and part of the solution."
- Cooperation with law enforcement: "Working closely with government, law enforcement, and antidoping organizations . . . to facilitate evidence gathering and information sharing."
- Other initiatives: "Conducting a wide range of other activities including independent observer missions at major sports events."
- WADA monitors implementation of and compliance with the code (WADA, 2015).

## ■ Drugs Used by Athletes

A very memorable interview:

> Yes, the steroids I used certainly made me get bigger. I was going out for football and I had just made the team, so I kept using them and the results were phenomenal. Now, [two] years later, I won't be graduating. Several months ago, they removed a tumor on my liver, but they didn't get all the cancer. I am going home at the end of this semester. My parents want me to stay with them for the time I have left. When I go, I only have one wish—I want to die big and always be known as Big Jim. *(From Venturelli's research files, male, age 20, December 13, 1996)*

Studies have shown that athletes are less likely than nonathletes to use other drugs of abuse such as marijuana, alcohol, barbiturates, cocaine, and hallucinogens (Hoberman & Yesalis, 1995; Substance Abuse and Mental Health Services Administration [SAMHSA], 2007). However, with regard to the types of drugs athletes are prone to use and abuse, there is some disagreement. A study by Yusko et al. (2008, p. 281) found that "[m]ale student athletes were at high risk for heavy drinking and performance-enhancing drug use. Considerable in-season versus out-of-season substance use fluctuations were identified in male and female student athletes."

Regardless of whether alcohol use and abuse is more or less likely in college athletes, athletes *are* much more likely than other populations to take drugs that enhance (physically or psychologically) or are thought to enhance competitive performance. These drugs include stimulants such as amphetamines and cocaine and an array of drugs with presumed ergogenic effects such as anabolic steroids (Bell, 1987; NIDA, 2006b). Some of the major drugs abused by athletes are listed in **Table 16.1** along with their desired effects. The sections that follow discuss the drugs that are most frequently self-administered by athletes in an effort to improve their competitive performance.

### ANABOLIC STEROIDS

Anabolic steroids are a group of synthetic (human-made) drugs that are chemically similar to cholesterol and related to the testosterone, the male hormone (NIDA, 2018a), and its artificial derivatives. A more recent definition states that "[a]nabolic steroids are synthetic variations of the

**TABLE 16.1** Partial List of Ergogenic Substances* and Expected Effects

| Drugs | Expected Results |
|---|---|
| Amino acids | Stimulate natural production of growth hormone and increase strength |
| Amphetamines and cocaine | Increase strength, alertness, and endurance |
| Anabolic steroids | Increase muscle mass and strength |
| Androl-50 (Oxymetholone) | Increase the amount of the hormone (erythropoietin) involved in production of red blood cells |
| Asthma medication | Improve breathing |
| B-complex vitamins | Enhance body metabolism and increase energy |
| Beta-blockers | Reduce hand tremor and stimulate growth hormone |
| Caffeine | Reduce fatigue |
| Chromium | Enhance carbohydrate metabolism |
| Creatine | Increase strength, gain weight, increase muscle mass |
| Dianabol (methandrostenolone) | Increase muscle mass and fat reduction |
| Ephedrine | Improve breathing and increase energy |
| Equipoise (boldenone undecylenate) | Increase endurance, muscle mass, and the production of red blood cells in the body |
| Furosemide | Mask steroid use and enable rapid weight loss |
| Methylphenidate | Enhance alertness and endurance |
| Deca-Durabolin (nandrolone decanoate) | Increase muscle mass |
| Over-the-counter decongestants | Increase endurance and energy |
| Oxandrin (oxandrolone) | Promote growth of muscle tissue |
| Protein powders | Gain more muscle, gain weight, maintain weight, recover from workouts |
| Testosterone (testosterone cypionate) | Replace testosterone that the body is missing |
| Tetrahydrogestrinone (THG) | A difficult-to-detect designer steroid used to increase muscle bulk and muscle strength and speed muscle recovery |
| Thyroid hormone | Enhance metabolism |

* Ergogenic drugs are substances that are used to enhance athletic performance.

Data from Brandenburg, J. R. (2004, January 1). The use of ergogenic aids among high school athletes in eastern Kentucky [Thesis]. Huntington, WV: Marshall University. Retrieved from http://mds.marshall.edu/cgi/viewcontent.cgi?article=1509&context=etd; Harlan, R., & Garcia, M. (1992). Neurobiology of androgen abuse. In R. Watson (Ed.), *Drugs of abuse and neurobiology* (p. 186). Boca Raton, FL: CRC Press; National Institute on Drug Abuse (NIDA). (2018a). DrugFacts: What are anabolic steroids? (August). Retrieved from https://www.drugabuse.gov/publications/drugfacts/anabolic-steroids; Krans, M., & Nall, R. (2016, August 9). Performance enhancers: The safe and the deadly. *Healthline*. Retrieved from https://www.healthline.com/health/performance-enhancers-safe-deadly

male sex hormone testosterone. The proper term for these compounds is *anabolic-androgenic steroids*. 'Anabolic' refers to muscle building, and 'androgenic' refers to increased male sex characteristics" (NIDA, 2016a). Common names for anabolic steroids include *gear, juice, roids*, and *stackers* (NIDA, 2016a, 2018b).

Steroids are used medically for treatment of certain diseases such as certain types of anemia, hormonal issues such as delayed puberty, diseases that cause muscle loss such as cancer and AIDS, some breast cancers, and testosterone deficiency (NIDA, 2016a). Although illegal when taken for nonmedical purposes, steroids have been used illegally by both athletes and nonathletes since the late 1950s to improve athletic ability and physical appearance because steroids have performance-enhancing and bodybuilding properties. Steroids are taken orally or injected into the muscles. Although males and females both use steroids, males have higher rates of use (NIDA, 2009, 2016a; SAMHSA, 1999b).

Naturally occurring male hormones, or *androgens*, are produced by the testes in males. These hormones are essential for normal growth and development of male sex organs as well as secondary sex characteristics such as muscular development, male hair patterns, voice changes, and fat distribution. The androgens are also necessary for appropriate growth spurts during adolescence (Olin, 1994). The principal accepted therapeutic use for androgens is for hormone replacement in males with abnormally functioning testes. In such cases, the androgens are administered before puberty and for prolonged periods during puberty to stimulate proper male development (Olin, 1994).

## MAJOR REASONS FOR THE ABUSE OF ANABOLIC STEROIDS

In light of a finding on the sources of banned substances in sports, it was reported that "[a]thletes may obtain banned medicines from physicians, pharmacists, retail outlets, health and lifestyle magazines, gymnasiums, coaches, family members, fellow athletes, the Internet, and the black market" ("Doping in Sports," 2011). The major reason for the use and abuse of anabolic steroids is that many athletes use them to improve athletic performance (Burke & Davis, 1992; NIDA, 2006b, 2016a). Under some conditions, androgen-like drugs can increase muscle mass and strength. Athletes may also use steroids to increase their muscle size or reduce their body fat (NIDA, 2006b).

Studies have found that some athletes who abuse steroids to boost their muscle size have experienced physical or sexual abuse. In one series of interviews with male weightlifters, 25%

who abused steroids reported memories of childhood physical or sexual abuse. Similarly, female weightlifters who had been raped were found to be twice as likely to report use of anabolic steroids or another purported muscle-building drug, compared with those women who had not been raped. Moreover, almost all of those who had been raped reported that they markedly increased their bodybuilding activities after the attack (NIDA, 2006b).

Adolescent steroid abuse has been found to be part of a pattern of high-risk behaviors. Steroid-abusing adolescents have also been found to take risks such as drinking and driving, carrying a gun, driving a motorcycle without a helmet, and abusing other illicit drugs.

In conclusion, conditions such as **muscle dysmorphia** (a behavioral syndrome that causes individuals to have a distorted image of their bodies, perceiving themselves as looking small and weak even when they may be large and muscular), a history of physical or sexual abuse, or a history of engaging in high-risk behaviors have all been associated with an increased risk of initiating or continuing steroid abuse (see **Figure 16.1**).

A more recent study determined that 1,084,000 Americans or 0.5% of adult population said they had used anabolic steroids (NIDA, 2018a). The most commonly abused steroids are in two categories: oral and injectable. Oral steroids include the following (USDOJ, 2004):

- Anadrol (oxymetholone),
- Oxandrin (oxandrolone),

### KEY TERM

**muscle dysmorphia**

behavioral syndrome that causes men to have distorted images of their bodies, perceiving themselves as looking small and weak, even when they may be large and muscular; women with this condition think they look fat and flabby, even though they may actually be lean and muscular

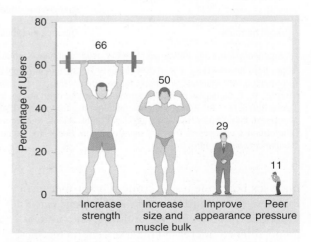

**FIGURE 16.1** Reasons for nonmedical steroid use by college students.

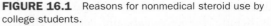

© Leonard Zhukovsky/Shutterstock.

Besides risking their health, athletes who choose to dope should remember that they are role models. Seventy-three percent of youth want to be like a famous athlete; 53% of youth say it is common for famous athletes to use banned substances to get ahead.

- Dianabol (methandrostenolone), and
- Winstrol (stanozolol).

Injectable steroids include the following:

- Deca-Durabolin (nandrolone decanoate),
- Durabolin (nandrolone phenylpropionate),
- Depo-Testosterone (testosterone cypionate),
- Equipoise (boldenone undecylenate), and
- Tetrahydrogestrinone (THG).

Competition for scholarships and entry into professional sports are major factors that influence young athletes to use steroids (Scott, Wagner, & Barlow, 1996). However, a 2019 *Monitoring the Future* (MTF) study by the Institute for Social Research at the University of Michigan reported that only 1.5% of 8th graders and 1.60% of 10th and 12th graders used steroids (Miech et al., 2019). Encouraging results indicate that steroid use among adolescents in 8th, 10th, and 12th grade is holding steady when comparing to previous years (Miech et al., 2019).

Although a vast majority of anabolic steroid users are male, women involved in bodybuilding and strength and endurance sports also abuse these drugs. In another study, among high school seniors, 3.2% of the males reported steroid use in the past year compared with 1.1% of the females. These statistics are much lower among 19- to 32-year-olds (0.4%), with males accounting for all steroid use.

A 2014 college survey by the National Collegiate Athletic Association (NCAA) found that usage of stimulants, including ephedrine and amphetamines, and anabolic steroids had risen slightly during survey years 2009 and 2013. However, in 2018, the overall percentage of anabolic steroids used by females within the last 12 months was 0.1% and males was 1.1% (Miech et al., 2019). The following are more recent findings regarding NCAA students:

- Substance use is typically highest among Division III student athletes and for most substances appears to be on the rise relative to trends in Division I and Division II.
- With the exception of alcohol use, substance use is higher among male student athletes.
- Excessive drinking (10 or more drinks in one sitting) is six times higher in male student athletes than in female student athletes.
- Contrary to popular belief, excessive drinking overall is going down among student athletes. Chewing tobacco use has remained relatively consistent and is currently being used at a higher level than cigarettes. Cigarette use is declining.
- Marijuana is used most among Division III student athletes at a rate approximately 10% higher than Division I and Division II student athletes.
- Compared with general college student cohorts, student athletes are using cigarettes, marijuana, amphetamines, cocaine, and synthetic marijuana at lower rates (NCAA, 2014).

### PATTERNS OF ABUSE

Geographical factors appear to have little to do with the use of anabolic steroids among athletes. In both inner-city and suburban schools, all athletes are equally attracted to these drugs. However, some athletes are more inclined to abuse anabolic steroids than others. For example, football players have the highest rate of abuse, and track athletes have one of the lowest (NCAA, 2014).[1] In a survey conducted by the NCAA of 11 member colleges and universities, 9% of football players self-reported abuse of steroids compared to only 4% of track and field athletes

[1]Even the usage rates of other major drugs such as alcohol, marijuana, and cocaine within the three divisions at educational institutions are noteworthy and problematic. The National Collegiate Athletic Association (NCAA) reports the following usage rates among college athletes: Division I—78% alcohol, 16% marijuana, and 1.5% cocaine usage; Division II—79% alcohol, 20% marijuana, and 1.3% cocaine usage; Division III—83% alcohol, 29% marijuana, and 2.6% cocaine usage (NCAA, 2014).

(National Institutes of Health [NIH] & NIDA, 1998). A study by WADA that examined blood samples taken between 2003 and 2008 across all professional sports found the following (Burn-Murdoch, 2012):

- Of the 26 sports included in the 2012 Olympic Games, the worst offender in terms of the rate of findings per sample (averaged across all 8 years) is cycling at 3.71%.
- The second highest rate—3.05%—was found among boxers. Badminton had the lowest rate of usage-indication findings per sample, at 0.87%.
- Footballers were the most tested athletes in terms of the total number of samples (30,398), followed by athletics (competitive running, jumping, throwing, and walking) (25,013), cycling (21,427), and aquatics (13,138).

Another study using a more indirect method of interviewing known as *self-reporting* found rates three times higher than the percentages just reported (Burn-Murdoch, 2012). In addition, the likelihood of abusing these drugs increases as the level of competition increases. Colleges and universities are in one of three divisions—I, II, or III. Educational institutions in Division I "have to sponsor at least seven sports for men and seven for women (or six for men and eight for women) with two team sports for each gender. Each playing season has to be represented by each gender as well" (NCAA, 2015).

Educational institutions in Division II "have to sponsor at least five sports for men and five for women (or four for men and six for women), with two team sports for each gender, and

each playing season represented by each gender" (NCAA, 2015).

Division III institutions have to sponsor at least five sports for men and five for women, with two team sports for each gender, and each playing season represented by each gender. There are minimum contest and participant minimums for each sport. Division III athletics features student athletes who receive no financial aid related to their athletic ability and athletic departments are staffed and funded like any other department in the university. Division III athletics departments place special importance on the impact of athletics on the participants rather than on the spectators. (NCAA, 2015)

In general, usage patterns for anabolic steroids vary considerably according to athletes' motivation, the level of competition, the type of sport, and the pressure for winning.

The pattern of use usually consists of self-administering doses that are one to 100 times greater than dosages used for legitimate medical conditions (U.S. Department of Justice [USDOJ], 2004). Users take nonmedical anabolic-androgenic steroids in cycles, which are periods of use lasting six to 12 weeks or longer. **Stacking** these drugs means combining two or more different steroids and mixing oral and injectable types. **Cycling** refers to taking multiple doses for a period of time, stopping for a time, and then restarting to take steroids. **Plateauing** refers to alternating, overlapping, or substituting with another steroid to avoid developing a tolerance. **Pyramiding** refers to slowly increasing the dose or frequency of steroid misuse, reaching a peak amount, and then gradually tapering off to zero (NIDA, 2018a). There is no scientific evidence that any of these practices reduce the harmful medical consequences of these drugs.

To combat such unwanted side effects of steroids as severe skin rashes and development of irreversible masculine traits in women, as well as sudden anger and explosive physical aggressiveness (known as *roid rage* in men), other drugs such as diuretics, antiestrogens, human chorionic gonadotropin, and antiacne medication are often taken concurrently. This pattern of use is referred to by users as an **array**. In general, power athletes prefer stacking, whereas bodybuilders prefer cycling. (See **Table 16.2**, which lists classes of drugs banned by the NCAA, drugs and

## KEY TERMS

**stacking**
combining two or more different types of steroids

**cycling**
taking doses of steroid for a period of time, stopping for a time, and then restarting

**plateauing**
developing tolerance to the effects of anabolic steroids

**pyramiding**
slowly increasing the dose or frequency of steroid abuse, reaching a peak amount, and then gradually tapering off

**array**
use of other drugs while taking anabolic steroids to avoid possible side effects

**TABLE 16.2** 2019–20 NCAA Banned Substances

### The NCAA bans the following classes of drugs:

a. Stimulants

b. Anabolic Agents

c. Alcohol and Beta Blockers (banned for rifle only)

d. Diuretics and Other Masking Agents

e. Narcotics

f. Cannabinoids

g. Peptide hormones, growth factors, related substances and mimetics

h. Hormone and metabolic modulators (anti-estrogens)

i. Beta-2 Agonists

*Note:* Any substance chemically/pharmacologically related to all classes listed above and with no current approval by any governmental regulatory health authority for human therapeutic use (e.g., drugs under preclinical or clinical development or discontinued, designer drugs, substances approved only for veterinary use) is also banned. The institution and the student athlete shall be held accountable for all drugs within the banned drug class regardless of whether they have been specifically identified. Examples of substances under each class can be found at www.ncaa.org/drugtesting. There is no complete list of banned substances.

### Substances and Methods Subject to Restrictions

· Blood and gene doping

· Local anesthetics (permitted under some conditions)

· Manipulation of urine samples

· Beta-2 agonists (permitted only by inhalation with prescription)

· Tampering of urine samples

### NCAA Nutritional/Dietary Supplements

*Warning:* Before consuming any nutritional/dietary supplement product, review the product and its label with your athletics department staff!

· Nutritional/Dietary supplements, including vitamins and minerals, are not well regulated and may cause a positive drug test.

· Student athletes have tested positive and lost their eligibility using nutritional/dietary supplements.

· Many nutritional/dietary supplements are contaminated with banned substances not listed on the label.

· Any product containing a nutritional/dietary supplement ingredient is taken at your own risk.

Athletics department staff should provide guidance to student-athletes about supplement use, including a directive to have any product checked by qualified staff members before consuming. The NCAA subscribes only to Drug Free Sport AXISTM for authoritative review of label ingredients in medications and nutritional/dietary supplements. Contact the Drug Free Sport AXIS at 877-202-0769 or www.dfsaxis.com (password ncaa1, ncaa2 or ncaa3).

### Some Examples of Substances in Each NCAA Banned Drug Class

THERE IS NO COMPLETE LIST OF BANNED SUBSTANCES.

DO NOT RELY ON THIS LIST TO RULE OUT ANY LABEL INGREDIENT.

### Stimulants

Amphetamine (Adderall); caffeine (guarana); cocaine; ephedrine; methamphetamine; methylphenidate (Ritalin); synephrine (bitter orange); dimethylamylamine (DMAA, methylhexanamine); "bath salts"(mephedrone); Octopamine; hordenine; dimethylbutylamine (DMBA, AMP, 4-amino methylpentane citrate); phenethylamines (PEAs); dimethylhexylamine (DMHA, Octodrine); heptaminol etc. Exceptions: Phenylephrine and pseudoephedrine are not banned.

### Anabolic Agents

(sometimes listed as a chemical formula, such as 3,6,17-androstenetrione): Androstenedione; boldenone; clenbuterol; DHEA (7-Keto); epitrenbolone; testosterone; etiocholanolone; methasterone; methandienone; nandrolone; norandrostenedione; stanozolol; stenbolone; trenbolone; SARMS (ostarine, ligandrol, LGD-4033, S-23, RAD140)); DHCMT (oral turinabol); etc.

### Alcohol and Beta Blockers

(banned for rifle only)

Alcohol; atenolol; metoprolol; nadolol; pindolol; propranolol; timolol; etc.

*(continues)*

**TABLE 16.2** 2019–20 NCAA Banned Substances (*continued*)

**Diuretics and Masking Agents**

Bumetanide; chlorothiazide; furosemide; hydrochlorothiazide; probenecid; spironolactone (canrenone); triameterene; trichlormethiazide; etc. *Exceptions:* Finasteride is not banned

**Narcotics**

Buprenorphine; dextromoramide; diamorphine (heroin); fentanyl, and its derivatives; hydrocodone; hydromorphone; methadone; morphine; nicomorphine; oxycodone; oxymorphone; pentazocine; pethidine

**Cannabinoids**

Marijuana; tetrahydrocannabinol (THC); synthetic cannabinoids (e.g., spice, K2, JWH-018, JWH-073)

**Peptide Hormones, Growth Factors, Related Substances, and Mimetics**

Growth hormone (hGH); human chorionic gonadotropin (hCG); erythropoietin (EPO); IGF-1 (colostrum, deer antler velvet); ibutamoren; etc. *Exceptions:* Insulin, Synthroid are not banned.

**Hormone and Metabolic Modulators (Anti-Estrogens)**

Anastrozole; tamoxifen; formestane; ATD; SERMS (clomiphene, nolvadex); Arimidex; clomid; evista; fulvestrant; aromatase inhibitors (Androst-3,5-dien-7,17-dione), letrozole; GW1516; cardarine; etc.

**Beta-2 Agonists**

Bambuterol; formoterol; salbutamol; salmeterol; higenamine; norcoclaurine; etc.

Any substance that is chemically related to one of the above classes, *even if it is not listed as an example, is also banned!*

Information about ingredients in medications and nutritional/dietary supplements can be obtained by contacting Drug Free Sport AXIS, 877-202-0769 or www.dfsaxis.com password ncaa1, ncaa2, or ncaa3.

*It is the student-athlete's responsibility to check with the appropriate or designated athletics staff before using any substance.*

Reproduced with permission from National Collegiate Athletic Association (NCAA). (2020). 2019–20 NCAA banned drugs. Retrieved from http://www.ncaa.org/sport-science-institute/topics/2019-20-ncaa-banned-substances. Accessed February 23, 2020.

procedures subject to restrictions, and examples of NCAA banned substances in each drug class.)

Because steroid use has been prohibited by all legitimate sporting organizations, urine testing just before an athletic event has become commonplace (Lukas, 1993). Steroid-using athletes attempt to avoid detection by trying to fool the tests. These highly questionable strategies include the following (Lukas, 1993; Merchant, 1992):

- New designer drugs constantly become available that can escape detection and put athletes willing to cheat one step ahead of authorities' testing efforts. To detect early use of designer steroids and provide more accurate baseline standards for each athlete, testing laboratories store data from each drug-testing sample. These samples are then used as reference points for future testing, thereby eliminating the possibility that a person tests positive simply because he or she has naturally elevated levels of testosterone when compared to the general population. Long-term use of designer steroids suppresses levels endogenous steroids in urine samples, which could be the first indication that an athlete is taking a designer steroid (NIDA, 2018b).

- By using a substance only during training for the athletic events and discontinuing its use several weeks before a competition, an athlete may be able to allow the drug to disappear from the body. Because oral steroids are cleared from the body faster than the injectable types, they are usually discontinued two to four weeks before competition, and the injection steroids are stopped three to six weeks before competition.

- Drugs such as probenecid can block the excretion of steroids in the urine. Probenecid often is used in an attempt to mask (cover up) anabolic steroids when drug tests are taken. Probenecid "[d]ecreases entry of steroids into the urine" (USDOJ, 2004). Current drug testing can detect the use of these drugs.

- Adulterant chemicals can be added to the urine such as Drano, Clorox, ammonia, or eye drops to invalidate the tests.

Some of the most recent types of drugs that athletes use, even though they are all banned by WADA, are listed in **Table 16.3**. This table summarizes the 2013 list of prohibited performance-enhancing substances banned by the World Anti-Doping Code—International Standard.

**TABLE 16.3** World Anti-Doping Code 2016 List of Prohibited Substances and Methods*

Substances and methods prohibited at all times (in and out of competition)

**Prohibited Substances**

*S0 Non-Approved Substances*

Any pharmacological substance which is not addressed by any of the subsequent sections of the List and with no current approval by any governmental regulatory health authority for human therapeutic use (e.g. drugs under pre-clinical or clinical development or discontinued, designer drugs, substances approved only for veterinary use) is prohibited at all times.

*S1 Anabolic Agents*

Anabolic agents are prohibited.

1. Anabolic androgenic steroids (AAS)
   a. Exogenous[1] AAS, including: (e.g. 1-Androstenediol (5α-androst-1-ene-3β,17β-diol); 1-Androstenedione (5α-androst-1-ene-3,17-dione); 1-Testosterone (17β-hydroxy-5α-androst-1-en-3-one); 4-Hydroxytestosterone (4,17β-dihydroxyandrost-4-en-3-one); 19-Norandrostenedione (estr-4-ene-3,17-dione); Bolandiol (estr-4-ene-3β,17β-diol); Bolasterone, etc., etc.
   b. Endogenous[2] AAS when administered exogenously: Androstenediol (androst-5-ene-3β,17β-diol); Androstenedione (androst-4-ene-3,17-dione); Dihydrotestosterone (17β-hydroxy-5α-androstan-3-one); Prasterone (dehydroepiandrosterone, DHEA, 3β-hydroxyandrost-5-en-17-one); etc., etc.
2. Other Anabolic Agents including but not limited to Clenbuterol, selective androgen receptor modulators (SARMs, e.g., andarine and ostarine), tibolone, zeranol, and zilpaterol, etc.

*S2 Peptide Hormones, Growth Factors, Related Substances, and Mimetics*

The following substances and other substances with similar chemical structure or similar biological effect(s) are prohibited:

1. Erythropoietin-receptor agonists: 1.1 Erythropoiesis-stimulating agents (ESAs) including Darbepoietin (dEPO); Erythropoietins (EPO); EPO-Fc; EPO-mimetic peptides (EMP), e.g. CNTO 530 and peginesatide; methoxy polyethylene glycol-epoetin beta (CERA), etc.

*S3 Beta-2 Agonists*

All beta-2 agonists, including all optical isomers (e.g., d- and l- where relevant) are prohibited.

Except:

· Inhaled salbutamol (maximum 1600 micrograms over 24 hours);
· Inhaled formoterol (maximum delivered dose 54 micrograms over 24 hours); and
· Inhaled salmeterol in accordance with the manufacturers' recommended therapeutic regimen.

The presence in urine of salbutamol in excess of 1000 ng/mL or formoterol in excess of 40 ng/mL is presumed not to be an intended therapeutic use of the substance and will be considered as an Adverse Analytical Finding (AAF) unless the Athlete proves, through a controlled pharmacokinetic study, that the abnormal result was the consequence of the use of the therapeutic inhaled dose up to the maximum indicated above.

*S4 Hormone and Metabolic Modulators*

The following hormone and metabolic modulators are prohibited:

1. Aromatase inhibitors including, but not limited to: 4-Androstene-3,6,17 trione (6-oxo); Aminoglutethimide; Anastrozole; Androsta-1,4,6-triene-3,17-dione (androstatrienedione); Exemestane; Formestane; Letrozole; Testolactone.
2. Selective estrogen receptor modulators (SERMs) including, but not limited to: Raloxifene; Tamoxifen; Toremifene.
3. Other anti-estrogenic substances including, but not limited to: Clomiphene; Cyclofenil; Fulvestrant, etc., etc.

*S5 Diuretics and Masking Agents*

The following diuretics and masking agents are prohibited, as are other substances with a similar chemical structure or similar biological effect(s).

Including, but not limited to:

· Desmopressin; probenecid; plasma expanders, e.g. glycerol and intravenous administration of albumin, dextran, hydroxyethyl starch and mannitol.
· Acetazolamide; amiloride; bumetanide; canrenone; chlortalidone; etacrynic acid; furosemide; indapamide; metolazone; spironolactone; thiazides, e.g. bendroflumethiazide, chlorothiazide and hydrochlorothiazide; triamterene and vaptans, e.g. tolvaptan.

*(continues)*

**TABLE 16.3** World Anti-Doping Code 2016 List of Prohibited Substances and Methods* (*continued*)

**Except**

· Drospirenone; pamabrom; and ophthalmic use of carbonic anhydrase inhibitors (e.g. dorzolamide, brinzolamide).

· Local administration of felypressin in dental anaesthesia.

The detection in an Athlete's Sample at all times or In-Competition, as applicable, of any quantity of the following substances subject to threshold limits: formoterol, salbutamol, cathine, ephedrine, methylephedrine and pseudoephedrine, in conjunction with a diuretic or masking agent, will be considered as an Adverse Analytical Finding unless the Athlete has an approved TUE for that substance in addition to the one granted for the diuretic or masking agent.

**Prohibited Methods**

*M1 Manipulation of Blood and Blood Components*

The following are prohibited:

1. The Administration or reintroduction of any quantity of autologous, allogenic (homologous) or heterologous blood, or red blood cell products of any origin into the circulatory system.

2. Artificially enhancing the uptake, transport or delivery of oxygen. Including, but not limited to: Perfluorochemicals; efaproxiral (RSR13) and modified haemoglobin products, e.g. haemoglobin-based blood substitutes and microencapsulated haemoglobin products, excluding supplemental oxygen.

3. Any form of intravascular manipulation of the blood or blood components by physical or chemical means.

*M2 Chemical and Physical Manipulation*

The following are prohibited:

1. Tampering, or Attempting to Tamper, to alter the integrity and validity of Samples collected during Doping Control. Including, but not limited to: Urine substitution and/or adulteration, e.g. proteases.

2. Intravenous infusions and/or injections of more than 50 mL per 6 hour period except for those legitimately received in the course of hospital admissions, surgical procedures or clinical investigations.

*M3 Gene Doping*

The following, with the potential to enhance sport performance, are prohibited:

1. The transfer of polymers of nucleic acids or nucleic acid analogues;

2. The use of normal or genetically modified cells.

[1] "Exogenous" refers to a substance which is not ordinarily produced by the body naturally.

[2] "Endogenous" refers to a substance which is ordinarily produced by the body naturally.

* This table has been abbreviated from WADA's 2016 Prohibited List The List of Prohibited Substances and Methods is the World Anti-Doping Agency's (WADA) International Standard identifying substances and methods prohibited in-competition, out-of-competition, and in particular sports. The complete and current List can be found on WADA's website at http://www.usada.org/wp-content /uploads/wada-2016-prohibited-list-en.pdf. Please be advised that the official text of the List shall be maintained by WADA and, in the event of any discrepancy between this extract and the List, the official WADA List shall prevail.

Reproduced and abbreviated from World Anti-Doping Code. (2016, January 1). *International standard: Prohibited list.* Montreal, Canada: World Anti-Doping Agency (WADA). Retrieved from http://www.usada.org/wp-content/uploads/wada-2016-prohibited-list-en.pdf

## EFFECTS OF ANABOLIC STEROIDS

Low to moderate doses of anabolic steroids have little effect on the strength or athletic skills of the average adult. However, when high doses are used by athletes during intense training programs, these drugs cause significant gains in lean body mass (i.e., muscle) and strength while decreasing fat (Lukas, 1993; NIDA, 2018a). Because most of these effects are transient and will disappear when steroid use is stopped, athletes feel compelled to continue using them and become psychologically dependent, and it can easily lead to a substance use disorder. A substance use disorder occurs

when a person continues to misuse steroids, even though there are serious consequences for doing so (NIDA, 2018a). The drugs are most likely to benefit athletes in contact and strength sports in which increased muscle mass provides an advantage, such as weightlifting and football; anabolic steroids are less likely to benefit athletes involved in sports requiring dexterity and agility such as baseball and tennis.

The risks associated with anabolic steroids have long-term effects. Most certainly, the higher the doses and the longer the use, the greater the potential damage these drugs can do to the body. Adverse effects largely depend on "[a]ge, sex, the anabolic steroid used, amount used, and duration of use" (Drug Enforcement Administration [DEA], 2015, p. 77). The following adverse effects are associated with heavy steroid use (10 to 30 times the therapeutic dose):

- Anabolic steroid use can stunt the ultimate height an individual achieves.
- In boys, steroid use can cause early sexual development, acne, and stunted growth (if adolescents use steroids before their growth spurt).
- In adolescent girls and women, anabolic steroid use can induce permanent physical changes such as voice deepening, increased facial and body hair growth, menstrual irregularities, male pattern baldness, and lengthening of the clitoris.
- In men, anabolic steroid use can shrink testicles, reduce sperm count, enlarge the male breast tissue, cause sterility, and increase the risk of prostate cancer.
- In both men and women, anabolic steroid use can cause high cholesterol levels, which may increase the risk of coronary artery disease, strokes, and heart attacks.
- Anabolic steroid use can also cause acne and fluid retention.
- Oral preparations of anabolic steroids, in particular, can damage the liver.
- Abusers who inject steroids run the risk of contracting various infections because of nonsterile injection techniques, sharing of contaminated needles, and the use of steroid preparations manufactured in nonsterile environments. All these factors put users at risk for contracting viral infections such as human immunodeficiency syndrome (HIV) and AIDS or hepatitis B or C and bacterial infections at the sight of injection.
- Abusers may also develop endocarditis, a bacterial infection that causes a potentially fatal inflammation of the heart lining (DEA, 2015, p. 77).

Additional adverse side effects include the following:

- psychological side effects, including irritability, outbursts of anger, mania, psychosis, and major depression;
- persistent unpleasant breath odor (NIDA, 2018a); and

- swelling of the feet or lower limbs (National Clearinghouse for Alcohol and Drug Information, 1999).

People who abuse steroids may experience withdrawal symptoms when they stop their use, including mood swings, fatigue, restlessness, loss of appetite, sleep problems, decreased sex drive, and steroid cravings (NIDA, 2016, 2018a).

Finally, several substances produce effects similar to those of anabolic steroids. These include human growth hormone, clenbuterol, gonadotropins, and erythropoietin (DEA, 2015).

## LAWS AND PENALTIES FOR ANABOLIC STEROID ABUSE

The first reported use of anabolic steroids to improve athletic performance was in 1954 by the Russian weightlifting team. These drugs' performance-enhancing advantages were quickly recognized by other athletes, and it has been estimated that as many as 90% of weightlifting competitors in the 1960 Olympic Games used some form of steroid (Toronto, 1992). Because of the widespread misuse and associated problems with the use of these drugs, anabolic steroids were classified as Schedule III controlled drugs in 1991 in the United States (Merchant, 1992).

The Anabolic Steroids Control Act of 1990 placed anabolic steroids into Schedule III of the Controlled Substances Act (CSA) as of February 27, 1991. Under this legislation, anabolic steroids are defined as any drug or hormonal substance chemically and pharmacologically related to testosterone (other than estrogens, progestins, and corticosteroids) that promotes muscle growth.

The possession or sale of anabolic steroids without a valid prescription is illegal. Federal law states that simple possession of illicitly obtained anabolic steroids carries a maximum penalty of one year in prison and a minimum $1,000 fine if it is an individual's first drug offense. Second-time offenders face fines of $2,500 and a maximum of two years in prison. For individuals with more than two prior convictions, the fine is doubled to a minimum of $5,000 and a possible three-year prison term. Note that simple possession is any amount. The maximum penalty for trafficking anabolic steroids is five years in prison and a fine of $250,000 if it is the individual's first felony drug offense. If it is the person's second felony drug offense, then the maximum period of imprisonment and the maximum fine both double (Anabolics.com, 2016; USDOJ, 2004).

The penalties just described are for federal offenses; individual states also impose fines and penalties for illegal use of anabolic steroids. State executive offices have also recognized the seriousness of steroid abuse and other drugs of abuse in schools. For example, the state of Virginia enacted a new law that will allow student drug testing as a legitimate school drug-prevention program. Other states and individual school districts are considering implementing similar measures (Anabolics.com, 2016; USDOJ, 2004).

### SOURCES OF STEROIDS

Where do the anabolic steroids come from? About 50% of the anabolic steroids used in the United States are prescribed by doctors; the other 50% are obtained from the black market. Black market sources of steroids include drugs diverted from legitimate channels, smuggled from foreign countries—including Brazil, Italy, Mexico, Great Britain, Portugal, France, and Peru (NIDA, 1996)—that are designated for veterinarian use; and inactive counterfeits (USDOJ, 1991–1992). A primary source for steroids in the United States is the state of Baja California in Mexico (Yesalis & Cowart, 1998). The steroids are manufactured in Mexico City and shipped to pharmacies in Baja. Some health food stores and mail-order firms also offer products with names similar to the prescription anabolic steroids such as Dynabdin, Metrobolin, and Diostero. These sham steroids contain only vitamins, amino acids, or micronutrients (Merchant, 1992; NIDA, 2006b). More recent findings regarding the origins of steroids indicate that

> [m]ost illicit steroids are smuggled into the [United States] from abroad. Steroids are also illegally diverted from legitimate sources (theft or inappropriate prescribing). The Internet is the most widely used means of buying and selling anabolic steroids. Steroids are also bought and sold at gyms, bodybuilding competitions, and schools from teammates, coaches, and trainers. (DEA, 2015)

Most steroids used for nonmedical purposes are obtained illegally. A major federal report indicates that sources of illicit steroids fall into three rough categories: (1) smuggled steroids manufactured licitly or illicitly abroad, (2) drugs legally manufactured in this country and diverted to illicit sales at various places in the distribution chain, and (3) drugs clandestinely produced domestically. Small minorities of users obtain their drugs by prescription. Actual doses are often difficult to estimate because the product may have been produced in an uncontrolled laboratory with unknown quality control, may have been intended for veterinary use with its human equivalent doses not known, or may be counterfeit (NIH & NIDA, 1998). Another source noted that the majority of young people report that steroids are easily available through their friends and coaches (McCaffrey, 1999).

### STIMULANT USE AMONG ATHLETES

Reports often appear in news media of football, basketball, and baseball players who have tested positive in drug-screening evaluations or who have been suspended from competition because of drug abuse. In 1986, reports of cocaine-related deaths of sports figures included basketball star Len Bias and professional football player Don Rogers. Perhaps such sports tragedies helped convince some U.S. youth of the dangers of stimulant abuse and contributed to the decline in drug abuse in the late 1980s (Johnston, O'Malley, & Bachman, 1993). Clearly, no one—not even an athlete—is immune from the risks of these drugs (see "Case in Point: When Drugs Enter the Boxing Ring").

Amphetamines and cocaine are abused to improve athletic skills (McDonald, 1995). However, it is not clear if stimulants actually enhance athletic performance or merely the athlete's perception of performance. Many athletes believe these drugs promote quickness, enhance endurance, delay fatigue, increase self-confidence and aggression, and mask pain (Hoberman & Yesalis, 1995). In fact, some studies have shown that stimulants can improve some aspects of athletic performance, especially in the presence of fatigue (NIDA, 1996).

Although some athletes would never consider using hard stimulants such as cocaine and amphetamines, milder stimulants that are legal and available over the counter (OTC) may be thought to be acceptable. Such stimulants include caffeine and OTC decongestants (e.g., phenylpropanolamine and phenylephrine). These drugs can be a double-edged sword for the athlete. Their use can reduce fatigue, give a sense of energy, and even mask pain. Nevertheless, in high doses, especially when combined, they can cause nervousness, tremors, and restlessness; impair concentration; accelerate dehydration; and interfere with sleep ("OTC Drugs and Athletes," 1992). Some athletic competitions limit permissible blood levels of caffeine and do not allow the use of OTC stimulants such as decongestant drugs.

► **CASE IN POINT**

## When Drugs Enter the Boxing Ring

Retired former heavyweight boxing champion Mike Tyson admitted to being under the influence of illicit drugs during major fights and even admitted to using "a fake penis to avoid detection" to pass drug tests (Swaine, 2013; Tyson, 2014). In his tell-all memoir, Tyson writes, "I was a full-blown cokehead" and that he "was high before taking to the ring for a match against Lou Savarese in Glasgow in June 2000" (Swaine, 2013; Tyson, 2014). Further, "Tyson explained he had taken cocaine before a notorious televised press conference with Lennox Lewis in New York in January 2002, which descended into an onstage brawl between the rival camps" (Swaine, 2013). Tyson writes that he lost his mind during this event and that he was so drugged up that he lost control and attacked another heavyweight (Lewis) that resulted in him biting into "one of Lewis's legs" (Swaine, 2013).

Tyson, the youngest boxer ever to win the [World Boxing Council, World Boxing Association, and International Boxing Federation] heavyweight titles, said he regrets that his drug use led to "Herculean" mood swings. After several years of rehabilitation treatment—between staging a one-man show, appearing in the film *The Hangover*, and socializing with A-list celebrities such as Victoria Beckham—Tyson said in August this year that he was close to death due to his chronic alcoholism. (Swaine, 2013)

Swaine, J. (2013, November 12). Mike Tyson admits to being high on drugs during major fights, and using a fake penis to avoid detection. *The Telegraph* [London, UK]. Retrieved from http://www.telegraph.co.uk/sport/othersports/boxing/10444998/Mike-Tyson-admits-to-being-high-on-drugs-during-major-fights-and-using-a-fake-penis-to-avoid-detection.html; Tyson, M. (2014, January 3). Fighting to kick the habit. *The New York Times*. Retrieved from https://www.nytimes.com/2014/01/04/opinion/mike-tyson-fighting-to-kick-the-habit.html?auth=login-email&login=email

## MISCELLANEOUS ERGOGENIC DRUGS

Most athletic organizations have banned the use of anabolic steroids and stimulants and are using more effective screening procedures to detect offenders. A result of this clampdown has been the search for alternative performance-enhancing drugs by athletes who feel a need for such pharmacological assistance. The following are brief discussions of a few of these substitute ergogenic substances.

### CLENBUTEROL

At the 1992 Olympic Games in Barcelona, Spain, at least four athletes, including German world sprint champion Katrina Krabbe, were disqualified from competition for using the drug clenbuterol to enhance their athletic performance (Merchant, 1992). Not legally available in the United States, this drug is known as *Doper's Delight* and is supposed to improve breathing and increase strength. Currently, most athletic urine examinations test for it.

### ERYTHROPOIETIN

Clinically, erythropoietin (EPO) is a drug used to treat patients with anemia (Kennedy, 2000). Because it stimulates the production of red blood cells (the oxygen-carrying cells in the blood), it is thought that this drug enhances oxygen use and produces additional energy. EPO was used as a substitute for blood doping before it became detectable. *Blood doping* is when athletes attempt to increase their number of red blood cells by reinfusing some of their own blood (which has been stored) before an athletic event. EPO can now be detected through testing. In the past, it was reportedly used by athletes engaged in endurance activities such as long-distance cycling.

The drug is not without dangers. EPO use thickens the blood by increasing the number of red blood cells. The increased blood thickness elevates the risk of blood clots, heart attacks, and strokes. It can also cause problems when the heart rate slows down such as during sleep (Quinn, 2016).

### HUMAN GROWTH FACTOR AND HUMAN GROWTH HORMONE

Athletes sometimes abuse hormones such as **human growth factor (HGF)** or its synthetic version, **human growth hormone (HGH)**. HGH also is

## KEY TERMS

**human growth factor (HGF)**
natural hormone that stimulates normal growth

**human growth hormone (HGH)**
designer drug synthetic version of HGF; also referred to as simply *GH* (growth hormone)

referred to simply as *GH* (growth hormone). HGF, also known as *somatotropin*, is a hormone naturally secreted by the pituitary gland at the base of the brain that helps to achieve normal growth potential of muscles, bones, and internal organs. Some athletes claim that release of natural HGF can be simulated by using drugs such as levodopa (used to treat Parkinson's disease), clonidine (used to treat hypertension), and amino acids. Athletes use commercially prepared HGH because it cannot be distinguished from naturally occurring HGF (Kennedy, 2000).

Use of this hormone by athletes is limited, however, by its high cost. The benefits of HGF to athletic performance are controversial, although the potential side effects are substantial, including abnormal growth patterns (called *acromegaly*), diabetes, thyroid gland problems, heart disease, and loss of sex drive (Merchant, 1992).

The synthetic HGH is available in the form of a structured steroid-type analog sold in vials; this product is used to build muscle tissue, with corresponding decreases in body fat, without exercise (McDonald, 1995). HGH is probably the most potent anabolic agent ever discovered, but it is also one of the most expensive. In fact, HGH is so expensive that until the mid-1990s "its use in the United States was confined to pediatric endocrinologists who used it to treat undersized children" (McDonald, 1995, p. C1). To date, tests are capable of detecting HGH in the blood ("What Is a Growth Hormone Stimulation Test?" 2008). In addition, the side effects of this drug remain largely unknown. As a result, this drug is highly vulnerable to abuse.

### BETA (β)-ADRENERGIC BLOCKERS

The β-adrenergic blockers are drugs that affect the cardiovascular system and are frequently used to treat hypertension. They have been used in sports because they reduce heart rate and signs of nervousness, which, in turn, quiets hand tremors. Consequently, these drugs are most likely to be used by individuals participating in sports that require steady hands such as competitive shooting. The use of these drugs

**KEY TERM**

**Adolescents Training and Learning to Avoid Steroids (ATLAS) program**
an anabolic abuse prevention educational program that empowers student athletes to make the right choices about steroid use

is prohibited by most athletic organizations (Kennedy, 2000; Merchant, 1992).

### GAMMA-HYDROXYBUTYRATE

The substance gamma-hydroxybutyrate (GHB) is found naturally in the brain and has been used in England to treat insomnia. Athletes and bodybuilders have used GHB to increase muscle mass and strength (Kennedy, 2000). Although the actual effects of the compound are not known, it has been reported to cause euphoria and increase the release of growth hormone. Acute poisoning with GHB has occurred, causing hospitalization; other adverse effects can include headaches, nausea, vomiting, muscle jerking, and even short-term coma, though full recovery has been universal ("Bodybuilding Drug Yields 'High,'" 1992; "Multistate Outbreak," 1994). Prolonged use may cause withdrawal (insomnia, anxiety, and tremor). GHB is especially dangerous when combined with central nervous system (CNS) stimulants such as amphetamines and cocaine (USDOJ, 2004).

## ■ Prevention of Abuse

If the problem of drug abuse among athletes is to be dealt with effectively, sport programs must be designed to discourage inappropriate drug use and assist athletes who have developed drug abuse problems. Coaches and administrators should make it clear to sport participants that substance abuse will never give athletes a competitive advantage in their programs and will not be tolerated. The **Adolescents Training and Learning to Avoid Steroids (ATLAS) program**, which was developed by Dr. Linn Goldberg of Oregon Health & Science University in Portland, is one of the most successful prevention programs for steroid abuse:

> The Adolescent[s] Training and Learning to Avoid Steroids Program (ATLAS) was designed to lower the use of anabolic steroids among high school athletes. The program combined classroom and weight-training sessions, to teach students about strength training, nutrition, and risk factors for steroid use. Overall, the ATLAS program was found to reduce the use of steroids. (Child Trends, 2009)

More specifically,

> Athletes Training and Learning to Avoid Steroids (ATLAS) is a drug prevention and health promotion program for adolescent high school athletes that emphasizes the negative impact of anabolic steroids, alcohol,

and other drugs on immediate sports performance. The program is integrated into team practice sessions and consists of a seven-session classroom curriculum and seven weight room skill training sessions. Coaching staff or surrogates administer the classroom curriculum which includes subjects such as risk factors of steroid use, strength training and sports nutrition, as well as skills to refuse steroids and other substances. In addition, nutritional recommendations and false claims of over the counter supplements are discussed. Parents attend a single evening meeting centered on program goals. (Blueprints for Healthy Youth Development, 2020)

Athletes, coaches, and team leaders are trained to educate team members about the effects of anabolic steroid abuse. Because adolescents already know that anabolic steroids build muscles and can increase athletic abilities, both desirable and adverse effects of steroid use are taught. Research has shown that information about anabolic steroids that fails to acknowledge potential benefits creates a credibility gap that can make youth distrustful of the prevention program. The program consists of three components—classroom, weight training, and parent information—to "give the student athletes the knowledge and skills to resist steroid use and achieve their athletic goals in more effective, healthier ways" (Goldberg et al., 1996, p. 1555):

1. The classroom component consists of football coaches and student leaders conducting highly interactive sessions that explore the effects of steroids, the elements of sports nutrition, and strength-training alternatives to steroid use. In this setting, while the coaches introduce topics and act as leaders, the students are exploring and learning from one another (Goldberg, et al. 1996).
2. In the weight-training component, research staff members conduct seven hands-on sessions that teach the students proper weight-training techniques (Goldberg et al., 1996).
3. The parent-information component consists of discussions and information sessions with parents. The staff provides nutrition guidelines and seeks compliance while stressing the best nutrition for the athletes and their families. Parents become more vigilant against steroid use and learn to enjoy well-balanced and nutritious meals (Goldberg et al., 1996).

Briefly summarized, results indicate that the students who participated in this program—in comparison with a control group (a group of students not participating in the program)—(1) knew more about proper exercise, (2) had a clear understanding of the dangers of using steroids and had become much more sensitized to the harmful effects of such drugs, (3) held more unfavorable views of others' use of anabolic steroids, and (4) were more likely to avoid unhealthy eating (such as frequenting fast-food restaurants) (Child Trends, 2009; Goldberg et al., 1996).

Major outcomes to date include the following.

Drug Use Intentions and Behaviors

- Decreased likelihood of lifetime steroid use at posttest and one-year follow-up, but the differences are not significant.
- Decreased likelihood of alcohol and other drug use at the one-year follow-up.
- Decreased likelihood of new occurrences of drinking and driving at the one-year follow-up.

Health Promotion Behaviors Found at Posttest and One-Year Follow-Up

- Heightened perception of coach intolerance to drug use.
- Improved nutrition knowledge and behaviors.
- Enhanced strength training self-efficacy.
- Less likely to believe advertisements for sports supplements and positive steroid use images.
- Reduction in sport supplement use at one-year follow-up.

Significant Program Effects on Risk and Protective Factors

- Greater self-reported ability to refuse drug offers from peers.
- Greater knowledge of the effects of steroids and alcohol.
- Stronger beliefs about the harmful effects of anabolic steroid use and perceived greater susceptibility to their effects (Blueprints for Healthy Youth Development, 2016).

# Drug Use Among Women

In the recent past, little was known about the patterns of female drug abuse. In general, most clinical drug abuse research, including treatment and rehabilitation outcomes, was either conducted in male populations with the results extrapolated to women or the research was done in general populations with little regard to gender influences (Chilet-Rosell, 2014; Dicker & Leighton, 1994; Klee & Jackson, 2002; Lin, 1994; NIDA, 2006a; U.S. Department of Health and Human Services [USDHHS] & NIDA, 1999). Most researchers considered drug abuse to be a male problem. Today, the research focusing on women and drug use is better, but a greater amount of study is still needed. Even today, scientists performing even basic research with animals generally prefer male animal models to avoid the hormonal complexities of female animals. However, a growing concern for the importance of the unique emotional, social, biochemical, and hormonal features in females has caused researchers to acknowledge the importance of gender differences. Further, women and men may face unique issues when it comes to substance use as a result of both sex and gender. *Sex differences* result from biology, or being genetically female or male, whereas *gender differences* are based on culturally defined roles for men and women, as well as those who feel uncomfortable identifying with either category. Gender roles influence how people perceive themselves and how they interact with others. Sex and gender can also interact with each other to create even more complex differences between men and women (NIDA, 2015a).

Scientists who study substance use have discovered special sex-related issues related to hormones, menstrual cycle, fertility, pregnancy, breastfeeding, and menopause that can impact women's struggles with drug use. In addition, women themselves experience unique gender issues and reasons for using drugs that may include, for example, controlling weight, fighting exhaustion, coping with menstrual and pregnancy pain, and self-treating mental health problems (NIDA, 2015a).

## ■ Women Are More Concerned About Drug Use Than Men

Women express greater initial concerns about drug use than men, although "most recent studies suggest that gender either has no effect on treatment initiation, or, if it has an effect, women are more likely than men to initiate treatment" (Green, 2006, p. 6). When asked whether drug abuse is a greater problem now than five years earlier, 51% of women and 42% of men answered

"yes" (Drug Strategies, 1998). When asked whether drug use is a big concern among youth, 58% of women and 48% of men answered "yes" (Drug, Strategies 1998). Further, 58% of women and 50% of men thought it was wrong to reduce prevention funds while increasing prison funds (Drug Strategies, 1998). One reason for this discrepancy may be that women traditionally have been primary caregivers; therefore, they feel more responsible about issues that can plague their communities and their families and often feel the need to be more vocal and in positions that maintain harmony within the family setting (Green, 2006). Women also generally express more concerns about safety issues than men because they are more likely to be victims of violent crimes such as muggings or sexual assaults.

## ■ Patterns of Drug Use: Comparing Females with Males

Recent surveys comparing male and female drug use patterns confirm that differences exist among the licit and illicit drug-using populations. **Table 16.4** compares annual female and male drug use among respondents ages 19 to 30 in 2018. The research findings in this table indicate the following gender-related differences in drug use (Johnston, O'Malley, Bachman, Schulenberg, & Miech, 2015):

- Overall, use of illicit drugs is consistently lower in females (40.8%) than in males (43.9%).
- The most common types of abused drugs (in descending order) for females were alcohol (83.2%), flavored alcoholic beverages (57.2%), any illicit drug use (40.8%), marijuana (36.9%), binge drinking (five or more drinks in a row in the preceding two weeks) (27.4%), cigarettes (20.2%), and any illicit drug other than marijuana (17.4%).
- Males have higher annual prevalence rates for nearly all illicit drugs. They are at least twice as likely to use synthetic marijuana (not shown in table), hallucinogens, LSD, hallucinogens other than LSD, salvia (not shown in table), heroin, heroin with a needle, GHB (not shown in table), ketamine (not shown in table), bath salts (not shown in table), and steroids.
- All three measures of cocaine use showed higher rates of use by male than 19- to 30-year-old females. Annual cocaine use was reported

**TABLE 16.4** Annual Percentage Use of Various Types of Drugs by Gender Among Respondents Ages 19 to 30 Years, 2018

|  | Males | Females | Totals* |
|---|---|---|---|
| Any illicit drug (nonmedical use)[†] | 43.9 | 40.8 | 42.0 |
| Alcohol | 81.5 | 83.2 | 82.5 |
| Flavored alcoholic beverages | 48.9 | 57.2 | 53.9 |
| Marijuana | 40.0 | 36.9 | 38.1 |
| Binge drinking (five or more drinks in a row in last two weeks) | 36.6 | 27.4 | 31.2 |
| Cigarettes | 25.9 | 20.2 | 22.5 |
| Any illicit drug other than marijuana | 22.0 | 17.4 | 19.2 |
| Amphetamines, adjusted[‡] | 9.1 | 6.4 | 7.5 |
| Cocaine | 7.4 | 5.0 | 5.9 |
| Other cocaine | 7.3 | 5.1 | 5.9 |
| Hallucinogens | 6.9 | 4.1 | 5.3 |
| Tranquilizers[‡] | 4.3 | 4.1 | 4.2 |
| MDMA (Ecstasy, Molly) | 4.6 | 3.6 | 4.0 |
| Narcotics other than heroin[‡] | 4.3 | 3.1 | 3.6 |
| LSD | 4.9 | 2.8 | 3.6 |
| Hallucinogens other than LSD | 4.5 | 2.4 | 3.3 |
| Sedatives (barbiturates)[‡] | 2.9 | 2.3 | 2.5 |
| Methamphetamines | 1.3 | 0.9 | 1.0 |
| Inhalants | 1.0 | 0.6 | 0.8 |
| PCP | [§] | 0.9 | 0.6 |
| Steroids | 1.1 | 0.1 | 0.5 |
| Crystal methamphetamine (ice) | 0.5 | 0.3 | 0.4 |
| Heroin | 0.5 | 0.1 | 0.3 |
| Crack | 0.4 | 0.1 | 0.2 |
| Heroin (with a needle) | [§] | 0.1 | [§] |
| Heroin (without a needle) | [§] | 0.2 | 0.1 |

*Notes:*
* Drugs listed in totals column are rank ordered from highest to lowest percent of usage.
[†] Use of any illicit drug includes any use of marijuana, hallucinogens, cocaine, heroin or other narcotics, amphetamines, sedatives (barbiturates), or tranquilizers not under a doctor's orders.
[‡] Nonprescription use
[§] Rate of less than 0.05%

Data from Schulenberg, J. E., Johnston, L. D., O'Malley, P. M., Bachman, J. G., Miech, R. A., & Patrick, M. E. (2019). *Monitoring the Future National Survey Results on Drug Use, 1975–2018: Volume II, College students and adults ages 19–60*. Ann Arbor, MI: University of Michigan, Institute for Social Research.

by 7.4% of males and 5.0% of females, and crack use by 0.4% of males and 0.1% of females.

- Other large gender differences among those 19 to 30 were found in daily marijuana use (9.0% for males vs. 5.2% for females), daily alcohol use (7.4% vs. 4.1%), and occasions of drinking five or more drinks in a row in the preceding two weeks (43% vs. 26%).
- A particularly large gender difference exists in measures of *extreme* binge drinking 10 or more drinks on at least one occasion in the preceding two weeks was 17.2% for males versus 7.7% for females. The rate for having 15 or more drinks was 7.0% for males and 1.4% for females.
- Ecstasy (MDMA [Ecstasy, Molly]) use was slightly higher among males than among females, with annual prevalences of 4.6% and 3.6%, respectively.
- Annual prevalence of narcotics use other than heroin outside of medical supervision was also slightly higher among males than females (4.3% vs. 3.1%). The gender difference for OxyContin was 3.0% for males versus 2.3% for females.
- The use of amphetamines was slightly higher among males than among females, with annual prevalence's of 9.1% and 6.4%, respectively.
- Steroid use among young adults was much more prevalent among males than females, as was true for 12th graders. Among 12th graders in 2018, 2.6% of males reported steroid use in the past year versus 0.9% of females. For 19- to 30-year-olds, use by males remained higher than females (1.1% for males vs. 0.1% for females).

Recent findings regarding gender differences among 8th, 10th, and 12th graders in 2018 are as follows (Miech et al., 2019):

- Males have considerably higher prevalence than females on most illicit drugs—at least by 12th grade. The annual prevalence for 12th grade males, compared to 12th grade females, is more than twice as high for hallucinogens, LSD, hallucinogens other than LSD, salvia, crack, Ritalin, methamphetamine, crystal methamphetamine (ice), ketamine, and steroids.
- Annual prevalence for amphetamine use is higher among females than among males in

grade 8, but it becomes higher for males by 12th grade.
- Among 12th graders, males are somewhat more likely to report using some illicit drug other than marijuana during the preceding year (13.9% for males versus 9.7% for females). In 8th and 10th grades, the prevalence levels do not differ much by gender.
- Frequent alcohol use tends to be somewhat higher among males in 12th grade. Among 12th graders, daily alcohol use is reported by 1.6% of males versus 0.5% of females. Similarly, binge drinking is reported by 16% of males versus 12% of females, and being drunk in the past 30 days is reported by 19% of males versus 16% of females.
- Vaping nicotine in the past year follows the common pattern of higher prevalence among males as compared to females in 12th grade at 33% vs. 27%. Prevalence differences by gender were negligible at the younger grades.
- The use of anabolic steroids is concentrated among males in 12th grade, with prevalence levels of 1.5% for males compared to 0.4% for females. In both 10th and 8th grade, gender differences are negligible.

### College Bound Versus Noncollege Bound Adolescents (8th, 10th, and 12th Graders)

- Significant ratio differences are found between college-bound and noncollege-bound students for annual prevalence of use on virtually all illicit drugs other than marijuana; ratios tend to be highest in the earlier grades, with the noncollege-bound having higher annual prevalences.
- Among 12th graders in 2018, use of any illicit drug other than marijuana in the prior year was almost 50% higher for the noncollege-bound compared to college-bound youth at 16% and 11%, respectively.
- Levels of frequent alcohol use are also considerably higher among the noncollege-bound. For example, daily drinking is reported by 2.4% of the noncollege-bound 12th graders versus 0.7% of the college-bound.
- At all three grade levels, noncollege-bound students are more likely to use steroids compared to college-bound students.
- By far, the largest and most dramatic difference in substance use between the college- and noncollege-bound involves cigarette smoking—0.8% of college-bound 12th graders

report smoking a half-pack or more daily compared to 3.1% of the noncollege-bound.

- Vaping of all substances is higher for the noncollege-bound youth.

The following findings are pertinent to adults and gender differences in substance use and abuse:

To date, there is extensive evidence of the differences between women and men regarding substance use. Epidemiological studies show that even though women are less likely to initiate drug use than men, they start earlier and are more susceptible to develop an addiction. Women are also more vulnerable to drug-related pathologies, such as liver and cardiovascular diseases, and are more exposed to sexual and physical abuse and violence and to sexually transmitted diseases. At the same time studies of gender differences in drug treatment show that reasons why women and men seek help are often dissimilar, and that psychological, biological and social gender differences are important factors for the success of diverse types of treatment and for retention into treatment. (United Nations Interregional Crime and Justice Research Institute, 2013, p. 1)

Although some similarities appear between genders in drug usage rates for specific types of drugs, the general differences in the prevalence rates for females and males compel researchers to look for explanations so that we can better understand and deal with gender-related drug abuse problems.

## ■ Female Roles, Seeking Treatment, and Drug Addiction

Women are expected to take on more responsibilities than in my mother's day. Not only are we expected to work like men, but we also take care of the house, worry about the children, and get dinner on the table. If the house needs cleaning, everyone looks at the woman of the house. Men still have these expectations. I know things are changing with more equality between the sexes, but real equality of responsibilities has yet to occur. After everyone gets to bed on weekdays, I have a few drinks in order to calm me down before I go to bed. *(From Venturelli's research files, female employed full-time, age 43, June 30, 1996)*

Another interview revealed the following:

When we first married my husband used to help me with housework. However, several years later he gradually slacked off with helping me with house cleaning. I really cannot fully blame him because this happened when his job become increasingly demanding and on weekends he had to catch up with his loss of sleep during his demanding workweek. I complained at the time that it was a lot of work doing it all alone. Shortly after I continually complained we decide to hire a cleaning service. However, I have to admit, whenever we have company over, the pressure to make the house look good is always on me and even most guests look at me when they complement how nice and clean our house is. So, it's not just who does the housework and how we divide the work to maintain it, it's how people traditionally look at women as being responsible for cleanliness and order inside the home *(From Venturelli's research files, female nurse practitioner, age 41, residing in Chesterton, Indiana, March 2016).*

## ■ Gender Differences in Drug Use

Data from Schulenberg et al. (2019) indicate the following:

- Men's use of most drugs remain consistently and modestly higher for most drugs than women.
- Over the long term, male and female differences narrowed for some drugs among young adults in each of these three age bands: 19–22, 23–26, and 27–30.
- Daily marijuana use in 2018 was at or near historic highs for both men and women across the three age groups: 10.2% and 6.1%, respectively for 19- to 22-year-old males and females; 9.9% and 6.3% respectively for 23- to 26-year-old males and females; and 10.8% and 6.6% respectively for 27-30-year olds.
- In all three age bands, use of synthetic marijuana by men tended to be higher than use by women. Annual prevalence in 2018 for the 19–22 age group was 2.5% for men and 1.5% for women.
- For LSD usage in 2018, use decreased significantly for men (3.4%) and leveled for women (2.4%).
- MDMA (Ecstasy and Molly) exhibited little or no gender difference in any of the three age

bands before use began to grow in the late 1990s. In 2017 and 2018, use declined among men and reduced the gender difference (4.9% for men, 3.0% for women in 2018).

- In 2018, men had higher rates of cocaine use (6.7%) than women 4.5%. Crack followed a different pattern, with men having slightly higher rates than women.
- In the same year, there was little differences between heroin use by men (0.1%) and women (0.5%).
- Similarly, OxyContin usage rates varied little between men (2.0%) and women (2.1%).
- With regard to daily drinking of alcohol, men have always had higher percentages than women, but gender differences decreased gradually in the two younger age groups. In 2018, it was 8.1% for men versus 4.6% for women.

Women's drinking patterns are different from men's. They face greater risks than men because of the following:

- Women typically start to have alcohol-related problems at lower drinking levels than men;
- Women typically weigh less than men; and
- Pound for pound, women have less water in their bodies than men do, and alcohol resides predominantly in body water.

Recent research indicates that most people who have a substance use problem do not receive treatment. In comparing men with women, women are at a greater disadvantage for receiving substance abuse treatment:

Although males abuse drugs at an earlier age and more frequently than females, females tend to become addicted more quickly once they are introduced to drugs—a phenomenon known as "telescoping." Women tend to relapse at higher rates than men after going through rehab, and they tend to suffer from more serious consequences to their health, occupational status, relationships, and finances. ("A Study of Drug Addiction Between Genders," 2016)

In 2011, about 609,000 of the 1.84 million admissions to substance abuse treatment programs were female (33.1%) and 1.23 million were male (66.9%). In general, the proportions of female and male admissions were similar for each of the seven age categories examined. Other major findings regarding female substance abuse treatment include the following:

- No meaningful gender differences were found by race or ethnicity. Specifically, the majority of female and male admissions (66.4 and 58.2%, respectively) were non-Hispanic white. The percentages of female and male admissions that were non-Hispanic black and Hispanic were similar (SAMHSA, 2014a).
- Alcohol was the most commonly reported primary substance of abuse by females (33.3%) and males (42.3%) being admitted to programs. Among females, alcohol was followed by heroin (15.3%), marijuana (14.6%), and prescription pain relievers (13.8%); among males, the next most frequently reported substances were marijuana (19.9%), heroin (15.0%), and prescription pain relievers (7.8%) (SAMHSA, 2014b).
- Marijuana was reported as the primary substance of abuse less frequently by females than by males among admissions ages 12 to 17 (60.8 vs. 80.7%) and 18 to 24 (22.1 vs. 33.4%). There was no variation by gender in primary marijuana abuse among admissions ages 25 or older (SAMHSA, 2014a).
- The proportions of female and male admissions reporting methamphetamines or amphetamines as their primary substance of abuse were similar across all age groups, with the exception of those ages 18 to 24. Specifically, among admissions ages 18 to 24, 8.9% of female admissions reported primary methamphetamine or amphetamine abuse compared with 3.7% of male admissions (SAMHSA, 2014a).
- The highest proportions of primary abuse of prescription pain relievers (e.g., oxycodone) were found among admissions age 18 to 24 and 25 to 34. In the 25 to 34 age group, 19.0% of female admissions and 12.2% of male admissions reported prescription pain relievers as their primary substance of abuse. In terms of the effect size, however, the differences between male and female admissions in these age groups were negligible. The only meaningful difference by effect size between males and females was observed among admissions ages 65 or older. Within the 65 or older age group, the proportion of female admissions reporting primary abuse of prescription pain relievers was nearly three times

that of their male counterparts (7.2 vs. 2.8%) (SAMHSA, 2014b).

Another study indicated that the major reasons reported why women ages 18 to 49 who needed did not receive treatment were as follows (National Survey on Drug Use and Health [NSDUH], 2007; SAMHSA, 2010):

- not ready to stop using (36%);
- cost or insurance barriers (34%);
- social stigma (29%);
- did not feel a need for treatment or believed they could handle the problem without treatment (15.5%);
- did not know where to go for treatment (13.2%);
- did not have the time for treatment (4.7%);
- believed treatment would not help (2.7%); and
- other access barriers (15.7%).

To appreciate the impact of drug abuse on women and the reasons why they are more reluctant to seek substance abuse treatment, we must understand the uniqueness of female roles in our society. Relative to drug abuse problems, women today often experience a double standard. Women suffering from drug addictions are often perceived as less tolerant than comparably addicted men (Erickson & Murray, 1989). Because of these social biases, women are afraid of being condemned and are less likely to seek professional help for their own personal drug abuse problems; they also are more likely to report feeling shame or embarrassment because they are in substance abuse treatment (Green, 2006). In addition, family, friends, and associates are less inclined to provide drug-dependent women with important emotional support (Klee & Jackson, 2002; NSDUH, 2007; USDHHS & NIDA, 1999).

The image of the alcoholic woman has always been that of one who is boisterous, flirtatious, effusive, and sometimes loudmouthed. This may be who she becomes on occasion, but more often she is secluded in the privacy of her apartment or staying home after getting the kids off to school or having just come home from the office, classroom, or business. She is shy, reclusive to a point, alienated, retrospective, and lacking in self-esteem. Later in her drinking, she may become self-pitying, resentful, and even childishly cruel because of alcohol usage (Kirkpatrick, 1999).

Because of their unique socioeconomic and family roles, women are especially vulnerable to emotional disruptions resulting from divorce, loneliness, and professional failures. Studies suggest that such stresses aggravate tendencies for women to abuse alcohol and other substances (Brady & Ashley, 2005; Kirkpatrick, 1999; Korolenko & Donskih, 1990). More specifically, "women drink from a feeling of inadequacy and from a need for love, the kind of love not found within a sexual relationship but, rather, a love that is deeper and more primal" (Kirkpatrick, 1999, p. 1; see also Verhaak, Lintsen, Evers, & Braat, 2010).

In addition, drug addiction can occur in some women as a result of domestic adversities. Consequently, there is a high prevalence of drug dependence in women who are victims of sexual or physical abuse (Ladwig & Anderson, 1989). "Approximately 70% of women in drug abuse treatment report histories of physical and sexual abuse, with victimization beginning before 11 years of age and occurring repeatedly" (SAMHSA, 1999a, p. 1). These physical and emotional traumas result in or are precursors to factors leading to drug abuse such as low self-esteem, self-condemnation, anxiety and personal conflicts, dysfunctional dependencies, and overwhelming feelings of guilt (Kirkpatrick, 1999; Verhaak et al., 2010). In addition, because of the crucial nurturing roles women hold, drug abuse problems can be particularly damaging to family stability.

Another unique role for women in drug abuse situations is that of a spouse, significant other, or mother of a drug addict. Often, in both traditional and nontraditional family relationships, women are expected to be nurturing, understanding, and willing to sacrifice to preserve the integrity of the family. If a family member becomes afflicted by drug dependence, the wife or mother is viewed as a failure. In other words, if the woman had maintained a good home and conducted her domestic chores properly, the family member would not have been driven to drugs (Green, 2006; Klee & Jackson, 2002; USDHHS & NIDA, 1999).

Despite the disruption and considerable stress caused by drug addiction in the home, women continue to bear the burden of raising children, performing domestic chores, and keeping the family together. In addition, women in such circumstances are frequently put at great physical risk. The risk is from an addicted spouse who becomes abusive to his partner or from exposure to sexually transmitted infections such as HIV or hepatitis transmitted by a careless infected partner. The anxiety and frustrations resulting from these stressful circumstances can encourage women themselves to become dependent as they seek emotional relief by using drugs.

## ▪ Women's Responses to Drugs

Research continues to lag regarding how women respond to substances of abuse. "Women have traditionally been underrepresented in clinical trials. In order to translate recent advances in our understanding of the molecular and physiological bases of sex differences into new therapeutics and health practices, sound sex-specific clinical data are imperative" (Schiebinger, 2003). Although the situation is slowly changing, the trend in drug abuse studies is still to avoid female populations; the effects of the drugs in men are still extrapolated to women. Even when drug abuse research is conducted on women, frequently the woman's response is not the primary concern; rather, the objective is to determine the effects of a drug on a fetus during pregnancy or an infant during nursing (Klee & Jackson, 2002; NSDUH, 2007; USDHHS & NIDA, 1999).

Although it generally can be assumed that the physiological and drug responses of men and women are similar, some distinctions should be recognized. For example, one study compared the risk for lung cancer in men and women after a lifetime of cigarette smoking. It was found that female smokers were twice as likely to get lung cancer as males who had smoked an identical number of cigarettes in their lifetimes ("Women Smokers," 1994). Another study indicated that women are *three* times more likely to contract lung cancer than men when smoking the same number of cigarettes (Kirkpatrick, 1999). These differences clearly indicate that cigarette smoking is far more dangerous for women than for men. Finally, women's unique responses to drugs includes a finding discovered by researchers at the University of California at San Francisco that women respond to a class of painkillers called *kappa opioids*, which are ineffective in men (University of California, San Francisco, 2000).

### DRUG ABUSE AND REPRODUCTIVE HEALTH

An important physiological distinction that sets women apart from men in terms of taking drugs is their ability to bear children. Because of this unique function, men and women have different endocrine (hormone) systems and reproductive organs and structures, and women have varied drug responses based on their reproductive state. The unique features of women have a substantial impact on the response to drug abuse in the presence and absence of pregnancy:

> Long term drug abuse may make it difficult to have children in the future and cause short-term hormone problems. Worse yet, long-term drug abuse can cause difficulty having children later in life. The effects of drug abuse on your reproductive system are numerous. Drug use during pregnancy or conception may cause a baby to be born with an addiction or cause physical and mental disabilities. (Drug and Alcohol Rehab Florida, 2012)

Drug abuse patterns can influence the outcome of pregnancy even if they occur before a woman becomes pregnant. For example, women who are addicted to heroin are more likely to have poor health, including chronic infections, poor nutrition, and sexually transmitted infections such as human immunodeficiency virus HIV, which can damage the offspring if pregnancy occurs. If substances are abused during pregnancy, they may directly affect the fetus and adversely alter its growth and development. The incidence of substance abuse during pregnancy is not known precisely, but undoubtedly hundreds of thousands of children have been exposed to drugs in utero. The effects of individual drugs of abuse taken during pregnancy are not discussed in depth in this chapter, but several specific observations merit reiteration here (Centers for Disease Control and Prevention [CDC], 2015, unless otherwise noted).

- Cocaine is a substantial threat for both the pregnant woman and her fetus. Although many specific claims for the fetal effects of cocaine are controversial, several observations appear legitimate: Cocaine use increases the likelihood of miscarriage when used during pregnancy (Drug and Alcohol Rehab Florida, 2012), cocaine use in the late stages of pregnancy can cause cardiovascular or CNS complications in the baby at birth and immediately thereafter. In addition, because of its vasoconstrictor effects, cocaine may deprive the fetal brain of oxygen, resulting in strokes and permanent physical and mental damage to the child.

- The impact of alcohol consumption during pregnancy has been well documented and publicized (Mathias, 1995). When alcohol is consumed by the mother, it crosses the placenta, but the effect of this drug on the fetus is highly variable and depends on the quantity of alcohol consumed, the timing of the exposure, maternal drug metabolism, maternal state of health, and the presence of other drugs. A particularly alarming consequence of high alcohol intake during pregnancy is an aggregate of physical and mental defects called *fetal alcohol syndrome*. Characteristics of this syndrome include low birth weight, abnormal facial features, mental retardation, and retarded sensorimotor development. In addition to its direct effects on the fetus, alcohol has played a major role in many unwanted pregnancies or has resulted in women's exposure to sexually transmitted infections. As a CNS depressant, alcohol impairs judgment and reason and thus encourages sexual risk-taking that normally would not occur. The results are all too frequently tragic for women (SAMHSA, 1999a).
- Tobacco use, primarily smoking, during pregnancy is an avoidable health hazard in the United States.
- Some experts suggest cigarette smoking during pregnancy may pose a greater risk to the fetus than cocaine. Tobacco use by pregnant women may interfere with blood flow to the fetus, deprive it of oxygen and nutrition, and disrupt development of its organs—particularly the brain. Smoking harms many aspects and every phase of reproduction. Despite having greater increased knowledge of the adverse health effects of smoking during pregnancy, many pregnant women and girls continue to smoke.
- Of women who smoked three months before pregnancy, 55% quit during pregnancy. Among women who quit smoking during pregnancy, 40% relapsed within six months after delivery.
- Approximately 10% of women reported smoking during the last three months of pregnancy.
- Smoking during pregnancy can cause a baby to be born too early or to have low birth weight, making it more likely the baby will be sick and have to stay in the hospital longer. A few babies may even die.
- Smoking during and after pregnancy is a risk factor of sudden infant death syndrome (SIDS). SIDS is an infant death for which a cause of the death cannot be determined.
- Babies born to women who smoke are more likely to have certain birth defects such as cleft lip or cleft palate.
- Also of significant concern is the possibility that exposure of nonsmoking pregnant women to secondhand tobacco smoke may damage fetuses.
- Drugs of abuse that have been associated with abnormal fetal development when used during pregnancy include alcohol, barbiturates, benzodiazepines, amphetamines, marijuana, methamphetamine, and cocaine—and even caffeine when consumed in high doses.

Clearly, women should be strongly urged to avoid all substances of abuse, especially during pregnancy.

## ■ Sex and Gender Differences in Substance Use

### WOMEN AND ALCOHOL

In general, men have higher rates of alcohol use, including binge drinking. However, young adults are an exception: girls 12 to 20 have slightly higher rates of alcohol misuse and binge drinking than their male counterparts.

Drinking over the long term is more likely to damage a woman's health than a man's, even if the woman has been drinking less alcohol or for a shorter length of time. Comparing people with alcohol use disorders, women have death rates 50 to 100 percent higher than do men, including deaths from suicides, alcohol-related accidents, heart disease, stroke, and liver disease.

In addition, there are some health risks that are unique to female drinkers. For example, heavy drinking is associated with increased risk of having unprotected sex, resulting in pregnancy or disease, and an increased risk of becoming a victim of violence and sexual assault. In addition, drinking as little as one drink per day is associated with a higher risk of breast cancer in some women, especially those who are postmenopausal or have a family history of breast cancer.

Men and women metabolize alcohol differently due to differences in gastric tissue activity. In fact, after drinking comparable amounts of alcohol, women have higher blood ethanol concentrations. As a result, women become intoxicated from smaller quantities of alcohol than men. (NIDA, 2020)

Prior research indicated that, as a rule, women are less likely than men to develop severe alcohol dependence; thus, only 25% of the alcoholics in the United States are female. Women are also likely to initiate their drinking patterns later in life than men (Green, 2006; SAMHSA, 2014b). "Women are older than men are when they begin drinking to intoxication, but once they develop a pattern of regular intoxication, they encounter drinking-related problems more quickly than men and lose control over their drinking more quickly than men" (Green, 2006). Interesting ethnic patterns of alcohol consumption have been reported in females, with black and white women manifesting similar drinking patterns. Although the proportions are similar, black women are more likely to completely abstain from alcohol than white women are.

Women who are dependent on alcohol are often more harshly judged than men with similar difficulties. Alcoholic males are more likely to be excused because their drinking problems are often perceived as being caused by frustrating work conditions, family demands, economic pressures, or so-called nagging wives and children. In contrast, women with drinking problems are often perceived as spoiled or pampered, weak, deviant, or immoral. Such stigmas cause women to experience more guilt and anxiety about their alcohol dependence and discourage them from admitting their drug problems and seeking professional help (Kirkpatrick, 1999).

The principal reasons for excessive alcohol consumption in women range from loneliness, boredom, and domestic stress in the housewife drinker to financial problems, sexual harassment, lack of challenge, discrimination, and powerlessness in the career woman. Depression is often associated with alcohol problems in women, although it is not clear whether this condition is a cause or an effect of excessive alcohol use.

### WOMEN'S PHYSIOLOGICAL RESPONSES TO ALCOHOL

Health consequences for excessive alcohol consumption appear to be more severe for women than for men. For example, alcoholic women are more likely to suffer premature death than alcoholic men. In addition, liver disease is more common and occurs at a younger age in female drinkers than in male alcoholics. In general, higher morbidity rates are experienced by alcoholic women than by their male counterparts.

Several explanations have been suggested for the higher rate of adverse effects seen in female alcoholics. Their higher blood alcohol concentrations may be the result of a smaller blood volume and more rapid absorption into the bloodstream after drinking. Alternatively, slower alcohol metabolism in the stomach and liver might cause more alcohol to reach the brain and other organs as well as prolong exposure to the drug following consumption (Goldstein, 1995). Studies have shown that for a woman of average size, one alcoholic drink has effects equivalent to two drinks in an average-size man.

### DEALING WITH WOMEN'S ALCOHOL PROBLEMS

Alcohol consumption varies considerably in women, ranging from total abstinence or an occasional drink to daily intake of large amounts of alcohol. Clearly, much is yet to be learned about the cause of some women's excessive drinking and dependence on alcohol. The role of genetic factors in predisposing women to alcohol-related problems is still unclear. The environment is certainly a major factor contributing to excessive alcohol consumption in women. It is well established that depression, stress, and trauma encourage alcohol consumption because of the antianxiety and amnesic properties of this drug. Because of unreasonable societal expectations and numerous socioeconomic disadvantages, women are especially vulnerable to the emotional upheavals that encourage excessive alcohol consumption.

As with all drug-dependence problems, prevention is the preferred solution to alcohol abuse by women. Alcohol usually becomes problematic when it is no longer used occasionally to enhance social events but used daily to deal with personal problems. Such alcohol dependence can best be avoided by using constructive techniques to manage stress and frustrations. Because of unique female roles and society's expectations, women especially need to learn to be assertive with family members, associates in the workplace (including bosses), and other contacts in their daily routines. By expecting and demanding equitable treatment and consideration in personal and professional activities, stress and anxiety can often be reduced. Education, career training, and development of communication abilities can be particularly important in establishing a sense of self-worth. With these skills and confidence, women are better able to manage problems associated with their lives and less likely to resort to drugs for an escape.

### WOMEN AND PRESCRIPTION DRUGS

A recent report states,

Misuse of, abuse of and dependence on prescription drugs are major health problems for women. Two-thirds of all tranquilizers, such as diazepam (Valium), chlordiazepoxide (Librium) and alprazolam (Xanax), are prescribed to women. Other examples of prescription drugs used frequently by women include sedatives such as triazolam (Halcion) and estazolam (ProSom); analgesics like meperidine (Demerol) or other types of painkillers such as oxycodone mixed with aspirin (Percodan) or guaifenesin mixed with codeine (Brontex); and stimulants such as methylphenidate (Ritalin), sibutramine (Meridia) and dextroamphetamine (Dexedrine). ("Substance Abuse," 2016)

Women are more likely than men to suffer depression, anxiety, and panic attacks (Anxiety and Depression Association of America, 2016); be unable to express anger; be victims of physical and sexual abuse; and be subject to overwhelming guilt feelings (Kirkpatrick, 1999). Consequently, they are also more likely to take and become addicted to the prescription drugs used in treating these disorders. Because these drugs are used as part of psychiatric therapy and under the supervision of a physician, drug dependence frequently is not recognized and may be ignored for months or even years. This type of legitimate drug abuse occurs most often in elderly women and includes the use of sedatives, antidepressants, and antianxiety medications. A recent study found that one in four women older than age 60 takes at least one of these drugs daily and that some of them develop serious drug problems (Drug Strategies, 1998). Excessive use of these drugs by older women results in side effects such as insomnia, mood fluctuations, and disruption of cognitive and motor functions that can substantially compromise the quality of life.

## ■ Treatment of Drug Dependence in Women

As previously discussed, women are less likely than men to seek treatment for and rehabilitation from drug dependence (Kirkpatrick, 1999; SAMHSA,

2010). Possible reasons for their reluctance are as follows:

* In more traditional families, women have unique roles with high expectations. They are expected to assume demanding and ongoing responsibilities such as motherhood, child-rearing, and family maintenance that cannot be postponed and often cannot be delegated to others, even temporarily. Consequently, many women feel that they are too essential for the well-being of other family members to leave the home and seek time-consuming treatment for drug abuse problems.
* Drug treatment centers often are not well designed to handle the unique health requirements of females—thus, women face more obstacles. These obstacles involve barriers to treatment entry, treatment engagement, and long-term recovery (Holdcroft, 2007; NIDA, 1999). Women have been shown to have greater health needs than men because of more frequent respiratory, genitourinary (associated with the sex and urinary organs), and circulatory problems. If drug-treatment centers are not capable of providing the necessary physical care, women are less likely to participate in associated drug abuse programs.
* Women are also more likely to relapse when their romantic partners are substance users (Rubin, Stout, & Longabaugh, 1996).
* Drug-dependent women are more inclined to be unemployed than their male counterparts and more likely to be receiving public support. The implications of this difference are twofold. First, because concerns about one's job often motivate drug-dependent workers to seek treatment, this issue is less likely to be a factor in unemployed women. Second, without the financial security of a job, unemployed women may feel that good treatment for their drug problems is unaffordable.

The unique female requirements must be recognized and considered if women are to receive adequate treatment for drug dependence. Some considerations on how to achieve this objective include the following (Futures, 2016, unless otherwise noted):

* availability of female-sensitive services;
* nonpunitive and noncoercive treatment that incorporates supportive behavioral change approaches;

- treatment for a wide range of medical problems, mental disorders, and psychosocial problems (NIDA, 1999);
- provision of childcare during treatment because many women drug abusers are likely to be the primary caregivers for their children;
- offering supportive network-based therapy rather than confrontational therapy; and
- inclusion of alternative therapies that focus on creativity such as art or music therapy.

The role of motherhood needs to be used in a positive manner in drug-treatment strategies. For most women, motherhood is viewed with high regard and linked to self-esteem. Approximately 90% of female drug abusers are in their childbearing years, and many have family responsibilities. Consequently, treatment approaches need to be tailored to allow women to fulfill their domestic responsibilities and satisfy their female and maternal motivations and obligations.

Women dependent on drugs often lack important coping skills. Even today, a significant percentage of women lead restricted, almost isolated, lives that focus entirely on domestic responsibilities and thus face limited alternatives for dealing with stressful situations. Under these restrictive circumstances, the use of drugs to cope with anxieties and frustrations is highly appealing. To enhance their ability to cope, drug-dependent women need to develop communication and assertiveness skills. Further, many need to be encouraged to control situations rather than allow themselves to be controlled by the situation. Specific techniques that have proven useful in coping management are exercise (particularly relaxation types), relaxing visual imagery, personal hobbies, and outside interests that require active participation. Many drug-dependent women require experiences that divert their attention from the source of their frustrations while affording them an opportunity to succeed and develop a sense of self-worth.

Finally, one research study found that the most effective treatment for women included a mutually supportive therapeutic environment that addressed the following issues: psychopathology (such as depression), a woman's role as mother, interpersonal relationships, and the need for parenting education (Werner, Young, Dennis, & Amatetti, 2007). Another study found that cocaine-using women whose children were living with them during residential treatment remained in the treatment programs significantly longer than women whose children were not living with them at the facility. Thus, having children in the treatment facility provides opportunities to assess and meet women's needs, which in turn affects the women's prognosis (Holdcroft, 2007; NIDA, 1999).

## ■ Prevention of Drug Dependence in Women

The best treatment for drug addiction is prevention. To help prevent drug problems in women as opposed to men, socioeconomic disadvantages need to be recognized as factors that make women more vulnerable to drug dependence, especially on prescription medication. Women need to learn that nondrug approaches are often more desirable for dealing with situational problems than prescribed medications. For example, for older women suffering loneliness, isolation, or depression, it is better to encourage participation in outside interests such as hobbies and service activities. In addition, social support and concern should be encouraged from family, friends, and neighbors. Such nonmedicinal approaches are preferred over prescribing sedatives and hypnotics to cope with emotional distresses. Similarly, medical conditions such as obesity, constipation, and insomnia should be treated by changing lifestyle, eating, and exercise habits rather than using drug "bandage therapy."

When women are prescribed drugs, they should ask about the associated risks, especially as they relate to drug abuse potential. Frequently, drug dependency develops insidiously and is not recognized by either the patient or the attending physician until it is already firmly established. If a woman taking medication is aware of the potential for becoming dependent and is instructed on how to avoid its occurrence, then the problems of dependence and abuse can frequently be averted.

## Drug Use Among Adolescents

I love waking up in the morning and smoking a nice fat joint. I live above the garage now, and my mom lives across the yard from the garage. This is a great living arrangement! I go to my room a few hours before crashing on many school nights, get high, drink some vodka that my older brother buys for me, then finally crash. In the morning, I always wake myself up so my mom stays away from my room, and my hideaway stash box is always locked. I roll me a joint and get a little high before I greet mom in the morning for a quick breakfast. I think she gets high too, but if I ask her and she says "no," what if she then asks me and gets all suspicious and shit? Besides, my Uncle Prentice always gets high with me, so I still think my mom really does not care about smoking weed. In fact, I know she is more worried about me drinking and driving than my friend "Mary Jane" [nickname for marijuana]. That's just my private life and no one needs to know. *(From Venturelli's research files, male residing in Chicago, age 18, July 10, 2000)*

From ages 13 through 18, adolescents are more likely to experience heightened psychological, social, and biological changes (National Institute of Mental Health, 2012; Office of the Surgeon General, 2007). Often, such internal and external changes are manifested by emotional outbursts. Why do such changes and urges arise? The adolescent's body is stretching, growing, and sometimes appearing out of control from the hormonal changes of puberty. These changes have an impact on drug use and abuse by adolescents:

Adolescent drug abusers have unique needs stemming from their immature neurocognitive and psychosocial stage of development. Research has demonstrated that the brain undergoes a prolonged process of development and refinement from birth through early adulthood. Over the course of this developmental period, a young person's actions go from being more impulsive to being more reasoned and reflective. In fact, the brain areas most closely associated with aspects of behavior such as decision-making, judgment, planning, and self-control undergo a period of rapid development during adolescence and young adulthood. (NIDA, 2012)

Adolescents who abuse drugs often have other co-occurring mental health problems. These disorders can include any one or combination of the following: attention-deficit hyperactivity disorder (ADHD), oppositional defiant disorder, conduct problems, and depressive and anxiety disorders (NIDA, 2012).

One perspective regarding early adolescent identity formation characterizes it as a developmental stage teeming with storm and stress in which adolescents are uncertain and confused about who or what they are becoming. They often are confused as to their worth to family, peers, society, and even to themselves (Kantrowitz & Wingert, 1999). Adding to the frustration of growing up, the cultural status of adolescents is poorly defined. They find themselves trapped in a "no man's land" between the acceptance, simplicity, and security of childhood and the stress, complexities, expectations, independence, and responsibilities of adulthood. Not only do adolescents have difficulty deciding who and what they are, but also adults are equally unsure as to how to deal with these transitional human beings. Although the grown-up world tries to push adolescents out of the secure nest of childhood, it is not willing to bestow the full membership and rights of adulthood on them (Johnson, Hoffmann, & Gerstein, 1996; Kantrowitz & Wingert, 1999).

Because of their uniquely rapid development, several developmental issues are particularly important to evolving adolescents (Elmen & Offer, 1993; Johnson et al., 1996; Kantrowitz & Wingert, 1999; Office of the Surgeon General, 2007; Von Der Haar, 2005):

- discovering and understanding their distinctive identities;
- "feeling awkward or strange about one's self and one's body" (American Academy of Child and Adolescent Psychiatry, 2006);
- forming more intimate and caring relationships with others;
- conflicts with parents over the need for independence;
- increased interest in sexuality and concern with heterosexual versus homosexual identities;
- "experimentation with sex and drugs (cigarettes, alcohol, and marijuana)" (American Academy of Child and Adolescent Psychiatry, 2006);
- establishing a sense of autonomy;
- coming to terms with the hormone-related feelings of puberty and expressing their sexuality;
- learning to become productive contributors to society; and
- feeling alone and alienated.

Because of all of this developmental confusion, "normal" behavior for the adolescent is difficult to define precisely. Experts generally agree that persistent low self-esteem, depression, feelings of alienation, and other emotional distur-bances can be troublesome for teenagers (Von Der Haar, 2005). However, most adolescents are relatively well adjusted and are able to cope with **sociobiological changes**.

Emotionally stable adolescents relate well to family and peers and function productively within their schools, neighborhoods, and com-munities. The majority of adolescents experi-ence transient problems, which they are able to resolve, but some become deeply disturbed and are unable to grow out of their problems without counseling and therapy. Those adolescents who are unable or unwilling to ask for assistance often turn to destructive devices such as drugs, juvenile delinquency, or violence (Kantrowitz & Wingert, 1999) for relief from their emotional dilemmas.

Another perspective regarding adolescent identity development outlines specific stages and statuses regarding identity development (Butler, 2010). Butler (2010) identifies the following major developmental stages for drug-using adolescents:

- "*Identity diffusion* is the status of adolescents who have not made a commitment to a par-ticular identity." Often these adolescents drift in and out of drug use because of their attach-ment to drug-using peers.
- "*Identity foreclosure* involves committing to an identity prematurely without exploration or choice." For example, this might occur when adolescents join drug-using or drug-dealing gangs and foreclose on drug usage largely because drugs are viewed positively. For exam-ple, such adolescents foreclose by identifying when higher-status gang members who are insistent on drug use or drug dealing.
- "*Identity moratorium* is a stage of active explo-ration coupled with low commitment to a particular identity." This can be an interesting, exciting, and potentially dangerous time for an adolescent who identifies with drug users or dealers, resulting in conflict with parents and authority figures. Adolescents in this stage of identity development have freedom to explore and develop their identities with drug users and dealers.

**KEY TERM**

**sociobiological changes**
belief that biological forces (largely genes) have a direct influence on the root causes of social psychological behavior

- "*Identity achievement* is said to occur when the adolescent, having had the opportunity to closely explore an identity, chooses that identity with a high degree of commitment." An example would be gang members who are accepted as members of a gang or social group involved in drug use or drug dealing.

Adolescents living in neighborhoods infested with drugs, who have fellow gang members involved in drug use, or associate with drug-using friends in neighborhoods where drug use is not common can experience each of these stages in their drug use and abuse.

## ■ Consequences of Underage Drug Use

According to the Office of the Surgeon General (2007), some of the well-known consequences of underage drug use by adolescents are:

- Alcohol poses a greater risk than any other drug, including marijuana, to the largest number of teens, largely because of alcohol's availability.
- Underage alcohol use is the major cause of death from injuries among young people. Each year, approximately 5,000 people under age 21 die as a result of underage drinking; this includes about 1,900 deaths from motor vehicle crashes, 1,600 as a result of homicides, and 300 from suicide, as well as hundreds from other injuries such as falls, burns, and drowning.
- Alcohol use increases the risk of carrying out or being a victim of a physical or sexual assault.
- Underage alcohol use can affect the body in many ways. The effects of alcohol and other drug use ranges from hangovers to death from alcohol or from other drug abuse.
- Alcohol and other drugs can lead to other problems such as bad grades in school and run-ins with the law.
- Alcohol and other drugs affect how well a young person judges risk and makes sound decisions such as driving while under the influence and riding with a driver under the influence.
- Alcohol and other drugs play a role in risky sexual activity, which can increase the chance of teen pregnancy and sexually transmitted infections (STIs), including HIV.
- Alcohol can harm the growing brain. (Current research clearly shows that the brain continu-ously develops from birth through the teen years into the mid-20s.)

# ■ Why Adolescents Use Drugs

Although there is no such thing as a typical substance-abusing adolescent, certain physiological, psychological, and sociological factors are often associated with drug problems in this subcultures (Johnson et al., 1996; Johnston, O'Malley, Bachman, & Schulenberg, 2009). In looking at an array of explanations regarding why adolescents use drugs, one study by Columbia University's National Center on Addiction and Substance Abuse found that children ages 12 to 17 who are frequently bored are 50% more likely to smoke, drink, get drunk, and use illegal drugs. In addition, kids with $25 or more a week in spending money are nearly twice as likely to smoke, drink, or use drugs as children with less money. Anxiety is another risk factor. The study found that youngsters who said that they were highly stressed were twice as likely as low-stress kids to smoke, drink, or use drugs ("Boredom, Stress, Money Linked to Drug Abuse," 2003).

Remember that not all drug use by adolescents means therapy is necessary or even desirable. More traditional proven and accepted explanations stress that most excessive drug use that often leads to abuse by adolescents results from the desire to experience new behaviors and sensations, a passing fancy of maturation, an attempt to relieve peer pressure, feelings of alienation, or an inclination to enhance a social setting with chemistry (Jayson, 2007; Kantrowitz & Wingert, 1999). Most of these adolescent users will not go on to develop problematic dependence on drugs and, for the most part, should be watched but not aggressively confronted or treated. The adolescents who usually have significant difficulty with drug use are those who turn to drugs for extended support as coping devices and become drug reliant because they are unable to find alternative, less destructive solutions to their problems. Several major factors can contribute to serious drug dependence in adolescents (Archambault, 1992; Johnson et al., 1996; Walsh & Shenkman, 1992).

Research indicates that the most important factor influencing drug use among adolescents is peer drug use (Bahr, Marcos, & Maughan, 1995; Jayson, 2007; Kandel, 1980; NIDA, 1999; Swadi, 1992; Winters, 1997; Yoder, 2015). Other primary factors that can either increase or decrease drug use include how teens perceive the risk of drug use, social approval, and the availability of drugs (CRC Health Group, 2007).

Consequently, eventual transition to heavier substance use also directly correlates with peer use (Steinberg, Fletcher, & Darling, 1994). Conversely, individuals whose peer groups do not use or abuse drugs are less likely to use drugs themselves (Venturelli, 2000). Research has identified a correlation between strong family bonds and nondrug-using peer groups (NIDA, 1999). "Adolescents with higher [stronger] family bonds are less likely than adolescents with lower [weaker] bonds to have close friends who use drugs" (Bahr et al., 1995, p. 466). In addition, family bonding is highly correlated with educational commitment. In essence, family bonding influences choice of friends and educational goals and aspirations (Bahr et al., 1995). However, three noteworthy differences exist between male and female adolescents (Teen Challenge, 2000):

1. Males demonstrate a stronger association between educational achievement and family bonds.
2. Among females, peer drug use is negatively associated with family bonds, so peer drug use and family bonds are not likely to influence the use of licit and illicit drugs by females.
3. The impact of age on peer drug use (the younger the age, the more vulnerable to peer pressure) and on the amount of alcohol consumed can be predicted with slightly greater accuracy for males than females.

A significant proportion of adolescents are more likely to use recreational types of drugs because they experience such psychological disorders as stress, tension, role confusion, anxiety, and alienation (Teen Challenge, 2000). Psychological differences among adolescents who are frequent drug users, experimenters, and abstainers often can be traced to early childhood, the quality of parenting in their homes, and their home environment. It has been suggested that certain types of parents are more likely to raise children at high risk for substance abuse (Archambault, 1992). Children from families where a parent or caregiver is suffering from alcohol abuse often suffer from guilt, anxiety, embarrassment, an inability to have close relationships, confusion, anger, and depression (American Academy of Child and Adolescent Psychiatry, 2011).

For example, an alcoholic adolescent usually has at least one parent of the following types.

- *Alcoholic*: This parent serves as a negative role model for the adolescent. The child sees the parent dealing with problems by consuming drugs. Even though drinking alcohol is not illegal for adults, it sends the message that drugs can solve problems. The guilt-ridden alcoholic parent is unable to provide the child with a loving, supportive relationship. In addition, the presence of the alcoholic parent is often disruptive or abusive to the family and creates fear or embarrassment in the child.

- *Nonconsuming and condemning*: This type of parent not only chooses to abstain from drinking but also is judgmental about drinkers and condemns them for their behavior. Such persons, who are often referred to as *teetotalers*, have a rigid, moralistic approach to life. Their black-and-white attitudes frequently prove inadequate and unforgiving in an imperfect, gray world. Children in these families can feel inferior and guilty when they are unable to live up to parental expectations, and they may resort to drugs to cope with their frustrations.
- *Hypercritical*: Parents are continually incessantly critical about their children. These parents are unrealistic with their child's abilities, continually pushing their children to accomplish goals that are beyond their children's ability and often beyond what the parents have ever accomplished. This includes athletic, academic, and career choices of their children. In addition, sibling rivalries are caused by such overly critical parents.
- *Overly protective*: Often resembling so-called helicopter parents who are hyperprotective of their children, they hover over their children to the point where their children are unable to learn from their mistakes. Overly protective parents do not allow their children to learn from mistakes; children often end up lacking self-confidence about their own talents and abilities.

The principal influence for learned behavior is usually the home; therefore, several other family-related variables can significantly affect an adolescent's decision to start, maintain, or end a drug habit (Kinney, 2000; Lawson & Lawson, 1992). For example, adolescents usually learn their attitudes about drug use from family models. In other words, what are the drug-consuming patterns of parents and siblings? Adolescents are more likely to develop drug problems if other members of the family (1) are excessive in their drug consumption whether legal or illegal, (2) approve of the use of illicit drugs, or (3) use drugs as a problem-solving strategy.

Sociological factors that damage self-image can also encourage adolescent drug use. Feelings of rejection may cause poor relationships with family members, peers, school personnel, and coworkers.

Ethnic differences sometimes contribute to a poor self-image because people of minority races or cultures are frequently socially excluded and are sometimes viewed as being inferior and undesirable by the majority population. This type of negative message is difficult for adolescents to deal with. Sometimes, to ensure acceptance, adolescents adopt the attitudes and behaviors of their affiliated groups. If a peer group or a gang, views drug use as cool, desirable, or even necessary, then members (or those desiring membership) feel compelled to conform and become involved in drugs.

## ■ Patterns of Drug Use in Adolescent Families

Growing minorities of younger teenagers are being exposed to drug use within their own families. One study reported that "20% of . . . 600 teens in drug treatment in New York, Texas, Florida, and California said they have shared drugs other than alcohol with their parents, and that about 5% of the teens actually were introduced to drugs—usually marijuana—by their moms and dads" (Leinwand, 2000, p. 1). In 1999, Partnership for a Drug-Free America reported similar alarming findings (Leinwand, 2000).

Years ago, alcohol may have been shared between parents and their children in a low percentage of cases; however, today there are parents who either have been or are currently using illicit drugs and appear to be influencing their children in the use of these drugs. Currently, this occurs in a small minority of families. Nevertheless, it remains shocking.

Jason, 17, a recovering addict from an upper-middle-class family in Simi Valley, California, says he wishes his father had been more of a parent and less of a buddy when it came to marijuana:

[Jason] made his drug purchase: a $5 bag of pot. Jason says his father walked by his room's open door as he was stashing it in a dresser drawer. [His father then] "told about his marijuana use," Jason says. "We went into his [dad's] office, and he had a (water pipe) and we got high together." [Jason reports that at the time, he] "thought it was sooo cool." (Leinwand, 2000, p. 2)

In another example, 15-year-old La'kiesha of Southern California is the third generation of a family in which members have become addicted to drugs. La'kiesha said her grandmother smoked pot regularly and gave her a few puffs when she was five years old to settle her down before bedtime (Leinwand, 2000).

In a more recent survey of participants in 70 Phoenix House drug-treatment programs in the United States, researchers found that "[o]ne in five drug abusers in some treatment programs in the United States received their first taste of these illegal substances from their parents, usually before the age of 18" (Livni, 2013). Drug-treatment candidates completing the survey were "19 times more likely to have been introduced to illicit drugs by a family member than a professional drug dealer," with 20% obtaining the drugs from their parents, and, of these, 6% using heroin with them (Livni, 2013).

## ■ Noteworthy Findings Regarding Teen Drug Use

At the onset, regarding drug use white students have the highest lifetime and annual prevalence levels among the three major racial and ethnic groups (whites, Hispanics, and African Americans) for many substances, including marijuana, LSD, hallucinogens other than LSD, MDMA (Ecstasy, Molly), and nonmedical use of narcotics other than heroin, amphetamines, and tranquilizers (Miech et al., 2019).

Recent surveys regarding drug use patterns found that, in 2018, by the 12th grade approximately 47.8% had used any illicit drug(s), 58.5% of the teens had used alcohol, approximately 23.8% had used cigarettes, approximately 43.6% had used marijuana, 8.6% had used amphetamines, and 4.4% had used inhalants. See **Table 16.5**, which details 8th, 10th, and 12th graders' use of drugs from 2015 through 2018.

In addition, a 2018 MTF study indicated that, 15.5% of 12th graders had abused prescription drugs consisting of opioid-, depressant-, and stimulant-types of drugs and that both "prescription and over-the-counter drugs are the most

**TABLE 16.5** Drug Use Among 8th, 10th and 12th Graders

Data show the percentages of 8th, 10th, and 12th graders who used both licit and illicit types of drugs in 2015, 2016, 2017, and 2018.

| | 8TH GRADERS | | | | 10TH GRADERS | | | | 12TH GRADERS | | | |
|---|---|---|---|---|---|---|---|---|---|---|---|---|
| | 2015 | 2016 | 2017 | 2018 | 2015 | 2016 | 2017 | 2018 | 2015 | 2016 | 2017 | 2018 |
| *Any Illicit Drug* | | | | | | | | | | | | |
| Lifetime | 20.5 | 17.2 | 18.2 | 18.7 | 34.7 | 33.7 | 34.3 | 36.3 | 48.9 | 48.3 | 48.9 | 47.8 |
| Annual | 14.8 | 12.0 | 12.9 | 13.4 | 27.9 | 26.8 | 27.8 | 29.9 | 38.6 | 38.3 | 39.9 | 38.8 |
| 30-day | 8.1 | 6.9 | 7.0 | 7.3 | 16.5 | 15.9 | 17.2 | 18.3 | 23.6 | 24.4 | 24.9 | 24.0 |
| *Alcohol (Any Use)* | | | | | | | | | | | | |
| Lifetime | 26.1 | 22.8 | 23.1 | 23.5 | 47.1 | 43.4 | 42.2 | 43.0 | 64.0 | 61.2 | 61.5 | 58.5 |
| Annual | 21.0 | 17.6 | 18.2 | 18.7 | 41.9 | 38.3 | 37.7 | 37.8 | 58.2 | 55.6 | 55.7 | 53.3 |
| 30-day | 9.7 | 7.3 | 8.0 | 8.2 | 21.5 | 19.9 | 19.7 | 18.6 | 35.3 | 33.2 | 33.2 | 30.2 |
| *Cigarettes (Any Use)* | | | | | | | | | | | | |
| Lifetime | 13.3 | 9.8 | 9.4 | 9.1 | 19.9 | 17.5 | 15.9 | 16.0 | 31.1 | 28.3 | 26.6 | 23.8 |
| Annual* | — | — | — | — | — | — | — | — | — | — | — | — |
| 30-day | 3.6 | 2.6 | 1.9 | 2.2 | 6.3 | 4.9 | 5.0 | 4.2 | 11.4 | 10.5 | 9.7 | 7.6 |

*(continues)*

**TABLE 16.5** Drug Use Among 8th, 10th and 12th Graders (*continued*)

Data show the percentages of 8th, 10th, and 12th graders who used both licit and illicit types of drugs in 2015, 2016, 2017, and 2018.

| | 8TH GRADERS | | | | 10TH GRADERS | | | | 12TH GRADERS | | | |
|---|---|---|---|---|---|---|---|---|---|---|---|---|
| | 2015 | 2016 | 2017 | 2018 | 2015 | 2016 | 2017 | 2018 | 2015 | 2016 | 2017 | 2018 |
| *Marijuana and Hashish* | | | | | | | | | | | | |
| Lifetime | 15.5 | 12.8 | 13.5 | 13.9 | 31.1 | 29.7 | 30.7 | 32.6 | 44.7 | 44.5 | 45.0 | 43.6 |
| Annual | 11.8 | 9.4 | 10.1 | 10.5 | 25.4 | 23.9 | 25.5 | 27.5 | 34.9 | 35.6 | 37.1 | 35.9 |
| 30-day | 6.5 | 5.4 | 5.5 | 5.6 | 14.8 | 14.0 | 15.7 | 16.7 | 21.3 | 22.5 | 22.9 | 22.2 |
| *Inhalants* | | | | | | | | | | | | |
| Lifetime | 9.4 | 7.7 | 8.9 | 8.7 | 7.2 | 6.6 | 6.1 | 6.5 | 5.7 | 5.0 | 4.9 | 4.4 |
| Annual | 4.6 | 3.8 | 4.7 | 4.6 | 2.9 | 2.4 | 2.3 | 2.4 | 1.9 | 1.7 | 1.5 | 1.6 |
| 30-day | 2.0 | 1.8 | 2.1 | 1.8 | 1.2 | 1.0 | 1.1 | 1.0 | 0.7 | 0.8 | 0.8 | 0.7 |
| *Amphetamines* | | | | | | | | | | | | |
| Lifetime | 6.8 | 5.7 | 5.7 | 5.9 | 9.7 | 8.8 | 8.2 | 8.6 | 10.8 | 10.0 | 9.2 | 8.6 |
| Annual | 4.1 | 3.5 | 3.5 | 3.7 | 6.8 | 6.1 | 5.6 | 5.7 | 7.7 | 6.7 | 5.9 | 5.5 |
| 30-day | 1.9 | 1.7 | 1.7 | 1.8 | 3.1 | 2.7 | 2.5 | 2.4 | 3.2 | 3.0 | 2.6 | 2.4 |
| *Hallucinogens* | | | | | | | | | | | | |
| Lifetime | 2.0 | 1.9 | 1.9 | 2.2 | 4.6 | 4.4 | 4.2 | 3.9 | 6.4 | 6.7 | 6.7 | 6.6 |
| Annual | 1.3 | 1.2 | 1.1 | 1.4 | 3.1 | 2.9 | 2.8 | 2.7 | 4.2 | 4.3 | 4.4 | 4.3 |
| 30-day | 0.6 | 0.6 | 0.5 | 0.6 | 0.9 | 0.9 | 1.1 | 0.8 | 1.6 | 1.4 | 1.6 | 1.4 |
| *Cocaine* | | | | | | | | | | | | |
| Lifetime | 1.6 | 1.4 | 1.3 | 1.4 | 2.7 | 2.1 | 2.1 | 2.6 | 4.0 | 3.7 | 4.2 | 3.9 |
| Annual | 0.9 | 0.8 | 0.8 | 0.8 | 1.8 | 1.3 | 1.4 | 1.5 | 2.5 | 2.3 | 2.7 | 2.3 |
| 30-day | 0.5 | 0.3 | 0.4 | 0.3 | 0.8 | 0.4 | 0.5 | 0.6 | 1.1 | 0.9 | 1.2 | 1.1 |
| *Crack* | | | | | | | | | | | | |
| Lifetime | 1.0 | 0.9 | 0.8 | 0.9 | 1.1 | 0.8 | 0.8 | 1.0 | 1.7 | 1.4 | 1.7 | 1.5 |
| Annual | 0.5 | 0.5 | 0.5 | 0.4 | 0.7 | 0.4 | 0.6 | 0.6 | 1.1 | 0.8 | 1.0 | 0.9 |
| 30-day | 0.3 | 0.2 | 0.3 | 0.2 | 0.3 | 0.2 | 0.3 | 0.3 | 0.6 | 0.5 | 0.6 | 0.5 |
| *Steroids* | | | | | | | | | | | | |
| Lifetime | 1.0 | 0.9 | 1.1 | 1.1 | 1.2 | 1.3 | 1.1 | 1.2 | 2.3 | 1.6 | 1.6 | 1.6 |
| Annual | 0.5 | 0.5 | 0.6 | 0.6 | 0.7 | 0.7 | 0.7 | 0.6 | 1.7 | 1.0 | 1.1 | 1.1 |
| 30-day | 0.3 | 0.3 | 0.3 | 0.3 | 0.4 | 0.3 | 0.3 | 0.4 | 1.0 | 0.7 | 0.8 | 0.8 |
| *Heroin* | | | | | | | | | | | | |
| Lifetime | 0.5 | 0.5 | 0.7 | 0.6 | 0.7 | 0.6 | 0.4 | 0.4 | 0.8 | 0.7 | 0.7 | 0.8 |
| Annual | 0.3 | 0.3 | 0.3 | 0.3 | 0.5 | 0.3 | 0.2 | 0.2 | 0.5 | 0.3 | 0.4 | 0.4 |
| 30-day | 0.1 | 0.2 | 0.2 | 0.1 | 0.2 | 0.2 | 0.1 | 0.1 | 0.3 | 0.2 | 0.3 | 0.2 |

*No data at time of printing.

Data from Johnston, L. D., Miech, R. A., O'Malley, P. M., Bachman, J. G., Schulenberg, J. E., & Patrick, M. E. (2019). *Monitoring the Future National Survey Results on Drug Use: 1975–2018: Overview, key findings on adolescent drug use*. Ann Arbor, MI: University of Michigan, Institute for Social Research.

commonly abused substances by Americans age 14 and older, after marijuana and alcohol" (NIDA, 2019).

Teens are turning away from street drugs and the stigma that goes along with using them, and abusing prescription drugs to get the same type of high. Many young people are under the false notion that prescription and OTC drugs are medically safer, when in fact, they can be just as dangerous and addictive as street drugs. (Miech et al., 2019; National Education Association and Health Information Network, 2013)

For young adolescents, major sources of obtaining prescription drugs without medical supervision are:

"Given for free by a friend" and "bought from a friend" are the two most common methods for obtaining amphetamines and tranquilizers. For all. . . [of the]. . . three drugs. . . [amphetamine-, tranquilizer- and narcotic-types of drugs]. . . "given or bought from friends" is considerably more frequently mentioned than "given for free by a relative" or "bought from a relative." *Clearly the informal peer network is a major source of these drugs for adolescents, a far more common source than any family network.*

"From a prescription I had" is a relatively common source for narcotic drugs at 32%, fairly similar to "bought from a friend" at 26%. "From a drug dealer/stranger" is not a common source for amphetamine users (14%), tranquilizer users (25%), or narcotic users (17%).

Finally, the least likely sources are "bought from a relative" and "bought on the Internet." The Internet is mentioned as a source by only 8.2% of the users of amphetamines, 5.3% of the users of tranquilizers, and 3.6% of the users of narcotics other than heroin. This may be in part because young people this age are usually living at home and do not want to risk their parents intercepting a shipped package containing illicit drugs. The Internet may well be an important source for older people, especially those who sell these drugs. (Miech et al. 2019)

The four most common sources for obtaining prescription drugs (namely, amphetamines, tranquilizers, and narcotics other than heroin) from 2017 through 2018 for 12th graders were as follows:

- "Given for free by a friend or relative" (43.7%)
- "Bought from a friend or relative" (37.8%)

- "Bought from drug dealer/stranger" (18.8%)
- "Took from friend/relative without asking" (10.1%)

Surprisingly, only 5.7% of adolescents "bought prescription drugs on the Internet" (Miech et al., 2019). Clearly, the informal network of family and friends continues to be the major sources for the supply of these drugs for adolescents.

Finally, "ADHD medications such as Adderall (which contains the stimulant amphetamine) are increasingly popular among young people who take them believing it will improve their school performance" (NIDA, 2020). This also is a dangerous trend. "Teens are also abusing stimulants like Adderall and anti-anxiety drugs like Xanax because they are readily available and perceived as safer than street drugs," said one White House drug czar ("Teen Prescription Drug Abuse," 2007). The extent of naiveté is best illustrated by the interview of one female in Indiana, as reported in the *Daily News* [Muncie, IN], on November 6, 2006: "It's not like I'm taking cocaine or crack—it's OK, these are pharmaceutical drugs made by professionals who know what they are doing" (National Youth Anti-Drug Media Campaign, 2007). Another study found that

[t]he classes of prescription drugs most commonly abused are: opioid pain relievers, such as Vicodin or Oxycontin; stimulants for treating Attention Deficit Hyperactivity Disorder (ADHD), such as Adderall, Concerta, or Ritalin; and central nervous system (CNS) depressants for relieving anxiety, such as Valium or Xanax. The most commonly abused OTC drugs are cough and cold remedies containing dextromethorphan. (NIDA, 2013)

The use of drugs for recreational purposes by young people is of special concern. In looking at adolescent drug use, the following findings are noteworthy (SAMHSA, 2019, unless otherwise noted):

- An estimated 9.0% of adolescents 12 to 17 in 2018 were current alcohol users, which corresponds to 2.2 million adolescents who drank alcohol in the preceding month. The percentage of adolescents who were current alcohol users in 2018 was lower than the percentages in most years from 2002 through 2017.
- In 2018, an estimated 131,000 adolescents 12 to 17 were current heavy drinkers. Stated another way, about one out of 200 adolescents (0.5%) engaged in binge drinking on five or more days in the past 30 days.

- In 2018, an estimated 672,000 adolescents aged 12 to 17 smoked cigarettes in the past month. This number of adolescents who were current cigarette smokers corresponds to 2.7% of adolescents. The percentage of adolescents who were past-month cigarette smokers declined from 13% in 2002 (or about one in eight adolescents) to 2.7% in 2018 (or about one in 37).
- Approximately 4.2 million adolescents 12 to 17 in 2018 were past-year illicit drug users, which corresponds to about one in six adolescents (16.7%).
- In 2018, about one in eight adolescents 12 to 17 (12.5%) were past-year users of marijuana. This represents approximately 3.1 million adolescents who used marijuana in the past year.
- In 2018, 112,000 adolescents 12 to 17 were past-year users of cocaine, including about 4,000 users of crack. These numbers correspond to 0.4% of adolescents who used cocaine in the past year and less than 0.1% who used crack.
- In 2018, about 369,000 adolescents 12 to 17 were past-year misusers of prescription stimulants, corresponding to about 1.5% of adolescents.
- In 2018, about 460,000 adolescents 12 to 17 misused prescription tranquilizers or sedatives in the past year, which corresponds to about 1.8% of adolescents. The percentage of adolescents in 2018 who misused tranquilizers or sedatives in the past year was similar to the percentages in 2015 to 2017.
- Among adolescents 12 to 17 in 2018, 2.8% misused prescription pain relievers corresponding to 695,000 adolescents. The percentage of adolescents in 2018 who misused prescription pain relievers in the past year was lower than the percentages in 2015 and 2016 but similar to the percentage in 2017.
- Among adolescents aged 12 to 17 in 2018, 2.8% misused opioids, which corresponds to 699,000 adolescents. The percentage of adolescents in 2018 who misused opioids in the past year was lower than the percentages in 2015 and 2016 but similar to the percentage in 2017.

As we can see from these statistics, alcohol and marijuana use is more widespread than the use of other drugs. Of greater concern than just any use of alcohol is its use to the point of inebriation: 18% of 8th graders, 37% of 10th graders, and 54.2% of 12th graders said they had been drunk at least once in their lifetime.

## TEEN DRUG USE OF OTC AND PRESCRIPTION DRUGS

Each year, "more teens die from prescription drugs than heroin [and] cocaine combined" ("Teen Drug and Alcohol Abuse Facts and Statistics," 2015). Some OTC and prescription cough and cold medicines contain active ingredients that are psychoactive (mind-altering) at higher-than-recommended dosages and are frequently abused for this purpose. These products may also contain other drugs, such as expectorants and antihistamines, which are dangerous at high doses and compound the dangers of abuse. When teens were asked about past-year cough medicine drug use by the 2015 *Monitoring the Future* survey, researchers found that 1.60% of 8th graders, 3.30% of 10th graders, and 4.60% of 12th graders used cough and cold medicine (most often Dextromethorphan, or DXM) and codeine syrup (most often promethazine-codeine cough syrup) to get high (NIDA, 2016b). Products with DXM include Alka Selter Plus, Coricidin, Dimtapp, Mucinex DM, Robitussin NyQuil, Coricidin, and Robitussin.

Cough and cold medicines are usually consumed orally in tablet, capsule, or syrup form. They may be mixed with soda for flavor and are often abused in combination with other drugs such as alcohol or marijuana. Because they are easily purchased in drugstores without a prescription, cough syrups, pills, and gel capsules containing DXM—particularly "extra-strength" forms—are frequently abused by young people (who refer to the practice as *robotripping* or *skittling*) (NIDA, 2014).

This type of drug abuse is of particular concern, given the easy access teens have to these products. Teens who abuse prescription or OTC drugs may also be abusing other substances. Sometimes they abuse prescription and OTC drugs together with alcohol or other drugs, which can lead to dangerous consequences, including death. Teens are abusing prescription drugs because they are widely available, free, or inexpensive, and the teens believe the drugs are not as risky as street drugs. The majority of teens who abuse these products say they get them for free, usually from friends and relatives, and often without their knowledge. Because these drugs are so readily available, teens who otherwise would not touch street drugs might abuse prescription drugs.

## ■ Adolescent Versus Adult Drug Abuse

Adolescent patterns of drug abuse are different from drug use patterns in adults (Moss, Kirisci, Gordon, & Tarter, 1994). The uniqueness of adolescent drug abuse means that drug-dependent teenagers usually are not successfully treated with adult-directed therapy. For example, compared with adults who abuse drugs, drug-using adolescents are more likely to (1) be involved in criminal activity and at earlier ages, (2) have other members of the family who abuse drugs, (3) be associated with a dysfunctional family that engages in emotional or physical abuse of its members, and (4) begin drug use because of curiosity or peer pressure (Bahr et al., 1995; Daily, 1992b; Hoshino, 1992; Steinberg et al., 1994; Teen Challenge, 2000). Such differences need to be considered when developing adolescent-targeted treatment programs.

## ■ Adolescents: Consequences and Coincidental Problems

Researchers have concluded that the problem of adolescent drug use is a symptom and not a cause of personal social maladjustment. Even so, because of the pharmacological actions of drugs, routine use can contribute to school and social failures, unintended injuries (usually automobile-related), criminal and violent behavior, sexual risk-taking, depression, and suicide (Curry & Spergel, 1997).

Serious drug abuse is usually the result of emotional instability, so the consequences of the underlying disorders may be expressed with chemical dependence, making diagnosis and treatment more difficult. The undesirable coincidental problems may include self-destruction, risk-taking, abuse, or negative group behaviors. Some of these adolescent problems and their relationship to drug abuse are discussed in the following sections.

### ADOLESCENT SUICIDE

Current research shows that although no cause-and-effect relationship exists between use of alcohol or other drugs and suicide, such drugs are often contributing factors (Destinations to Recovery, 2014; see also American Academy of Child and Adolescent Psychiatry, 2013; Minnesota Institute of Public Health, 1995). Adolescents are particularly vulnerable to suicide actions; in fact, white males between 14 and 20 years of age are the most likely to commit suicide in the United States (Daily, 1992b). Further, the teenage suicide rate has doubled since 1980 (Siegel & Senna, 1997; Siegel & Welsh, 2009). "Suicides among young people continue to be a serious problem. Each year in the [United States], thousands of teenagers commit suicide. Suicide is the third leading cause of death for 15- to-24-year-olds, and the sixth leading cause of death for 5- to-14-year-olds" (American Academy of Child and Adolescent Psychiatry, 2004). From 20% to 36% of suicide victims have a history of alcohol abuse or were drinking shortly before their suicide. Some experts have described severe chemical dependence as a form of slow, drug-related suicide. For clinicians, every case of serious drug addiction conceals a suicidal individual because all drug abuse inevitably constitutes a game of life and death similar to "Russian roulette," which comes back into fashion at certain times and under certain circumstances (Bergeret, 1981).

Clearly, many teenagers who abuse alcohol and other drugs possess a self-destructive attitude (Destinations to Recovery, 2014), as this quote from an online chat with Dr. David Shaefer, a teen suicide expert, demonstrates: "[T]wo-thirds of all suicides amongst boys occur in boys who are abusing alcohol or other drugs; so the link between suicide and alcohol and certain drugs, like cocaine and Ecstasy and other stimulant drugs, is a very close one" (Schaefer, Hilton, Ekstrand, & Keogh, 1993, p. 39). According to Shaeffer, adolescents who attempt suicide are more likely to (1) have disciplinary problems and then abuse alcohol and feel even more depressed, (2) be anxious and not display any bad behavior problems, or (3) have a perfectionist attitude and never be satisfied with their outcomes. Nearly all suffer from depression before their suicide attempts. Females generally differ from males in that they are prone to even greater amounts of depression with fewer cases of alcohol or other drug abuse. Finally, another study based on extensive survey data suggests that "between 12 and 25 percent of school age youth consider suicide or make plans to commit suicide . . . [and that] the rate of youth suicide is on an upward path, tripling between 1950 and 1990" (Bussing-Burks, 2013). This research also states that alcohol and drug use increases the likelihood of suicidal thoughts and attempts (Bussing-Burks, 2013).

Besides posing a direct health threat because of their physiological effects, drugs of abuse can precipitate suicide attempts from their pharmacological impacts. Several studies have found a high correlation between acute suicidal behavior and drug use (Buckstein et al,. 1993; Destinations to Recovery, 2014). One report noted that adolescent alcoholics have a suicide rate 58 times greater than the national average (Buckstein et al., 1993). In another study, 30% of adolescent alcoholics had made suicide attempts, although 92% admitted to a history of having suicidal thoughts (Daily, 1992b). The incidence of suicide in drug-consuming adolescents may be high because both types of behavior are the consequence of an inability to develop fundamental adult attributes of confidence, self-esteem, and independence. When drug use does not make up for their need for these characteristics, the resulting frustrations are intensified and ultimately played out in the suicide act.

Most adolescents experiment with drugs for reasons not related to antisocial or deviant behavior but because of curiosity, a desire for recreation, boredom, peer pressure, a desire to gain new insights and experiences, or an urge to heighten social interactions. These adolescents are not likely to engage in self-destructive behavior. In addition, adolescents from "healthy" family environments are not likely to attempt suicide. Specifically, Daily (1992b) stated that the families least likely to have suicidal members are those that do the following:

- express love and show mutual concern,
- are tolerant of differences and overlook failings,
- encourage the development of self-confidence and self-expression,
- have parents who assume strong leadership roles but are not autocratic,
- have interaction characterized by humor and good-natured teasing, and
- are able to serve as a source of joy and happiness to their members.

Suicide is more likely to be attempted by those adolescents who turn to alcohol and other drugs to help them cope with serious emotional and personality conflicts and frustrations. These susceptible teenagers represent approximately 5% of the adolescent population (American Academy of Child and Adolescent Psychiatry, 2013; Beschner & Friedman, 1985; Siegel & Senna, 1997; Siegel & Welsh, 2009). Wright (1985) found that four features significantly contribute to the likelihood of suicidal thought in high school students:

1. Parents with interpersonal conflicts who often use an adolescent child with drug problems as the scapegoat for family problems;
2. Fathers who have poor and often confrontational relationships with their children;
3. Parents who are viewed by their adolescent children as being emotionally unstable, usually suffering from perpetual anger and depression; and
4. A sense of frustration, desperation, and inability to resolve personal and emotional difficulties through traditional means.

Clearly, it is important to identify those adolescents who are at risk for suicide and to provide immediate care and appropriate emotional support.

## SEXUAL VIOLENCE AND DRUGS

Alcohol use has been closely associated with almost every type of sexual abuse in which the adolescent is victimized. "For the perpetrator, being under the influence may remove both physical and psychological inhibitors which keep people from acting out violently. They may also use alcohol or drugs as an excuse for criminal behavior" (Wisconsin Coalition Against Sexual Assault, 1997, p. 13). For example, alcohol is by far the most significant factor in date, acquaintance, and gang rapes involving teenagers (Office of the Surgeon General, 2007; Parrot, 1988; Prendergast, 1994). The evidence for alcohol involvement in incest is particularly overwhelming. Approximately 4 million children in the United States live in incestuous homes with alcoholic parents. In addition, 42% of drug-abusing female adolescents have been victims of sexual abuse (Daily, 1992a). It is estimated that almost half of the offenders consume alcohol before molesting a child and at least one-third of the perpetrators are chronic alcoholics (Baltieri & de Andrad, 2008). Finally, 85% of child molesters were sexually abused themselves as children, usually at the same age as their victims, and the vast majority of these molesters abused drugs as adolescents (Daily, 1992a).

These disturbing associations illustrate the relationship between drugs and violent sexual behavior both in terms of initiating the act and because of the act. The effects of such sexual violence are devastating and far-reaching. Thus, incest victims are more likely than the general population to abuse drugs as adolescents and to engage in anti-social delinquency, prostitution, depression, and suicide (Daily, 1992a).

## GANGS AND DRUGS

The disturbing involvement of adolescents in gangs and gang-related activities and violence is a social phenomenon that first became widely recognized in the 1950s and 1960s. Hollywood, for example, introduced America to the problems of adolescent gangs in the classic movies *Blackboard Jungle* and *West Side Story*. Although the basis for gang involvement has not changed over the years, the levels of violence and public concern have increased dramatically. Many communities consider gang-related problems to be their primary social issue (Henslin, 2014). Access to sophisticated weaponry and greater mobility have drawn unsuspecting neighborhoods and innocent bystanders into the often-violent clashes of **intragang** and **intergang** warfare. Individuals and communities have been reacting angrily to this growing menace. To deal effectively with the threats of gang-initiated violence and crime, however, it is important to understand why gangs form, what their objectives are, how they are structured, and how to discourage adolescent involvement.

Children often join gangs because they are neglected by their parents, lack positive role models, and fail to receive adequate adult supervision. Other motivations for joining a gang include peer pressure, low self-esteem, and the perceived easy acquisition of money from gang-related drug dealing and other criminal activities.

In comparison to traditional, formal youth organizations, juvenile gangs may appear disorganized. Research shows, however, that verbal rules, policies, customs, and hierarchies of command are rigidly observed within the gang. Thus, common values and attitudes exist:

- Gang membership is usually defined in socio-economic, racial, and ethnic terms, and adolescents involved have similar backgrounds.
- Gang members are distinguished by a distinctive and well-defined dress code. Violation of this code by members, or mimicking of the dress code by nongang members, can result in ostracism, ridicule, physical abuse, and violence.
- Leadership and seniority within the gang are defined by vested time in belonging to the gang, age, loyalty, and demonstrated delinquent cleverness (often related to drug dealing and other crimes).
- Gang members use gang slang to ensure camaraderie and group loyalty.

Although a stable home life does not ensure that an adolescent will not become involved with gang-related activity, a strong family environment and guidance from respected parents and guardians are clearly deterrents (Lale, 1992). Many gang members are children from dysfunctional, broken, or single-parent homes. Many parents are aware of their children's gang involvement but lack the skill, confidence, and authority to deter their teens' gang or drug involvement. To make matters worse, ineffective parents often discourage or even interfere with involvement by outside authorities because of misdirected loyalty to their children or to avoid embarrassment to their family and community.

Because troubled adolescents are often estranged from their families, they are particularly influenced by their peer groups. These teenagers are most likely to associate with groups whose members have similar backgrounds and problems and who make them feel accepted. Because of this vulnerability, adolescents may become involved with local gangs. In summary, gangs offer the following:

- fellowship and camaraderie,
- identity and recognition,
- membership and belonging,
- family substitution and role models,
- security and protection,
- diversion and excitement,
- friendships and structure,
- money and financial gain for relatively little effort, and
- ability to live the crazy life (*vida loca*) (Sanders, 1994; Shelden, Tracy, & Brown, 2001) or *locura* (craziness) (Shelden, Tracy, & Brown, 2004).

In the United States, estimates of the total number of existing gangs vary widely. There are at least 30,000 gangs and more than 800,000 active

## KEY TERMS

**intragang**
between members of the same gang
**intergang**
between members of different gangs

gang members in the United States. Gangs conduct criminal activity in all 50 states and all U.S. territories. Although most gang activity is concentrated in major urban areas, gangs also are proliferating in rural and suburban areas of the country as gang members flee increasing law enforcement pressure in urban areas or seek more lucrative drug markets. This proliferation in nonurban areas increasingly is accompanied by violence and threatens society in general (National Drug Intelligence Center [NDIC], 2009).

Sadly, despite recent declines, gangs have a strong presence in schools:

In 2009, about 20 percent of students ages 12–18 reported that gangs were present at their school during the school year. This was a decrease from the 23 percent of students who reported a gang presence in 2007. A higher percentage of students from urban schools (31 percent) reported a gang presence at their school in 2009 than students from suburban and rural schools (17 percent and 16 percent, respectively). (National Center for Education Statistics, 2011)

In Chicago alone, estimates have ranged from 12,000 to 120,000 gang members. In 2012, it was reported that "Chicago is the gang capital of the United States. According to the Chicago Crime Commission, a 2012 Chicago Police Department gang audit found there are more than 600 gang factions in the city, with a minimum combined membership of 70,000" (CBS News, 2013). Spergel (1990) provided the following percentages of those who are reportedly in gangs within a particular school population in the Chicago area: "5% of the elementary school youths, 10% of all high school youths, 20% of those in special school programs, and, more alarmingly perhaps, 35% of those between 16 and 19 years of age who have dropped out of school" (Shelden et al., 2004, p. 29). Keep in mind that these data are for just one city.

Street gangs, outlaw motorcycle gangs (OMGs), and prison gangs in prisons are the primary distributors of illegal drugs in the United States. Gangs also smuggle drugs into the United States and produce and transport drugs within the country, supplying most major drug dealers.

Street gang members convert powdered cocaine into crack cocaine and produce most of the phencyclidine (PCP) available in the United States. Gangs, primarily OMGs, also produce marijuana

and methamphetamine. In addition, gangs smuggle in large quantities of cocaine and marijuana and lesser quantities of heroin, methamphetamine, and MDMA (Ecstasy) into the United States from foreign sources of supply. Gangs primarily transport and distribute powdered cocaine, crack cocaine, heroin, marijuana, methamphetamine, MDMA, and PCP in the United States.

Located throughout the country, street gangs vary in size, composition, and structure. Large, nationally affiliated street gangs pose the greatest threat because they smuggle, produce, transport, and distribute large quantities of illicit drugs throughout the country and are extremely violent. As previously mentioned, local street gangs in rural, suburban, and urban areas pose a growing threat (NDIC, 2009).

One recent survey claims that 27% of public-school students ages 12 to 17 attend schools that are both gang and drug infested. That means 5.7 million students attend schools that are both gang and drug dominated. Nearly 50% of all public-school students report drug use or sales on school grounds (Funk, 2010). Research shows that teenage gangs are becoming major players in the drug trade (Siegel & Senna, 1997; Siegel & Welsh, 2009). Two of the largest gangs in Southern California, the Bloods and the Crips, are examples of this trend. Estimated membership in these two gangs exceeds 20,000. In the past, organized crime families maintained a monopoly on the Asian heroin market. Today, youth gangs have entered this trade, for two reasons: (1) Recent efforts and successes in prosecuting top mob bosses by criminal justice officials have created opportunities for new players, and (2) demand has grown for cocaine and synthetic drugs that are produced locally in many U.S. cities. In Los Angeles and most major large cities, drug-dealing gangs maintain "rock houses" or "stash houses" (where crack cocaine is used and sold) that serve as selling and distribution centers for hard drugs. The crack cocaine found in these rock houses is often supplied or run by gang members (Siegel & Senna, 1997; Siegel & Welsh, 2009).

To a lesser extent, other less-violent gangs with smaller memberships are also involved in drug dealing. However, research shows that news media may exaggerate the percentage of gangs involved in drug dealing. In the past, citywide drug dealing by tightly organized "supergangs" appeared to be on the decline and was being superseded by the activities of loosely organized, neighborhood-based groups (Siegel & Senna, 1997). In the past, the main reason for this shift was that federal and state law enforcement of drug laws have forced drug dealers to become "flexible, informal organizations [rather] than rigid vertically organized gangs with . . . [leaders] who are far removed from day-to-day action [on the street]" (Siegel & Senna, 1997, p. 409).

Other past findings were that

[l]arge trafficking organizations dominate the illicit drug market. These groups include the "families" of America's La Cosa Nostra, as well as an array of more recently identified crime groups such as the Sicilian "Mafia," outlaw motorcycle gangs, and groups based in the Nigerian and Colombian communities. . . . Organized crime groups involved in drug trafficking, however, share a central feature with other organized crime groups in that they consist of a core criminal group and a specialized criminal support designed to facilitate illicit activity. (Gonzales, McEnery, Sheehan, & Mellody, 1986, p. 71)

Levitt and Venkatesh's (2000) research involving criminal gangs in Chicago revealed that the gang's turf they studied

for most of the time period examined is a [12]-square block area bordered by major thoroughfares on all sides. Most of the drug dealing is conducted along the edges of the territory on or near one of the major streets. The gang sells perhaps 30 percent of the drugs to those living within the [12]-block area— most of the remaining purchasers come from a relatively limited geographic range. In this particular area, few buyers come from the suburbs. (p. 763)

Drug use and gang-related activities are often linked, but the relationship is highly variable (Curry & Spergel, 1997; Fagan, 1990). Clearly, problems with drugs exist without gangs, and gang-related activities can occur despite the absence of drugs; however, because they have common etiologies, their occurrences are often intertwined. Most adolescents who are associated with gangs are knowledgeable about drugs. Many gang members have experimented with drugs, much like other adolescents their age. However, the hard-core gang members are more likely to be engaged not only in drug use but also in drug dealing as a source of revenue to support the gang-related activities (Lale, 1992; Siegel & Senna, 1997). The types of drugs used and their significance and functions vary from gang to gang (Fagan, 1990; Siegel & Senna, 1997). For example, many Latino gangs do not profit from drug trafficking but are primarily interested in using hard-core drugs such as heroin and PCP. In contrast, African American gangs tend to be more interested in the illicit commercial value of drugs and often engage in dealing crack and other forms of cocaine.

### PREVENTING ADOLESCENT GANG INVOLVEMENT

The most effective way to prevent adolescent gang involvement is to identify at an early age at-risk children and provide them with lifestyle alternatives. Important components of such strategies follow:

- Encourage parental awareness of gangs and teach parents how to address problems in their own families that may encourage gang involvement.
- Provide teenagers with alternative participation in organizations or groups that satisfy their needs for camaraderie, participation, and emotional security in a constructive way. These groups can be organized around athletics, school activities, career development, or service rendering.
- Help children develop coping skills that will enable them to deal with the frustration and stress in their personal lives.
- Educate children about gang-related problems and help them understand that, like becoming involved with drugs, young people who join gangs create more problems for themselves, and gang membership is not a solution to their personal or family problems.

## ■ Prevention, Intervention, and Treatment of Adolescent Drug Problems

As with most health problems, the sooner drug abuse is identified in the adolescent, the greater the likelihood the problem can be resolved. It can be difficult to recognize signs of drug abuse in teenagers because their behavior can be erratic and unpredictable even under the best of circumstances. In fact, many of the behavioral patterns that occur coincidentally with drug problems are also present when drugs are not a problem. However, frequent occurrence or clustering of these behaviors may indicate the presence of substance abuse. The behaviors that can be warning signs include the following (Archambault, 1992; Hazelden Betty Ford Foundation, 2020):

- abruptly changing their circle of friends,
- experiencing major mood swings,
- continually challenging rules and regulations,
- overreacting to frustrations,
- being particularly submissive to peer pressures,
- sleeping excessively,
- keeping late hours,
- withdrawing from family involvement,
- letting personal hygiene deteriorate,
- becoming isolated,
- engaging in unusual selling of possessions,
- manipulating family members,
- becoming abusive toward other members of the family, and
- frequently coming home at night high.

## PREVENTION OF ADOLESCENT DRUG ABUSE

Logically, the best treatment for drug abuse is to prevent the problem from starting. This approach, referred to as **primary prevention**, typically has been viewed as total abstinence from drug use. Informational scare tactics are frequently used as a component of primary prevention strategies. These messages often focus on a dangerous (although in some cases rare) potential side effect and present the warning against drug use in a graphic and frightening fashion. Although this approach may scare naive adolescents away from drugs, many adolescents today, especially if they are experienced, question the validity of the scare tactics and ignore the message.

Another form of primary prevention is to encourage adolescents to become involved in formal groups such as structured clubs or organizations in an effort to reduce the likelihood of substance abuse (Howard, 1992). Group memberships can help adolescents develop a sense of belonging and contributing to a productive, desirable objective. This involvement can also provide the adolescent with the strength to resist undesirable peer pressures. In contrast, belonging

## KEY TERMS

**primary prevention**
preventing the use of any drug (total abstinence)

**secondary prevention**
preventing casual or recreational drug use from advancing to drug dependence

to informal groups such as gangs—groups with loose structures and ill-defined, often antisocial objectives—can lead to participation in poorly chaperoned parties, excessive sexual involvement, and nonproductive activities. Adolescent members of such poorly defined organizations tend to drink alcohol at an earlier age and are more likely to use other substances of abuse.

Some experts claim that primary prevention against drug use is unrealistic for many adolescents. They believe that no strategy is likely to stop adolescents from experimenting with alcohol or other drugs of abuse, especially if these substances are part of their home environment (e.g., if alcohol or tobacco is routinely used) and are viewed as normal, acceptable, and even expected behaviors (Howard, 1992). For these adolescents, it is important to recognize when drug use moves from experimentation or a social exercise to early stages of a problem and to prevent serious dependence from developing. This approach, referred to as **secondary prevention**, consists of teaching adolescents (1) about the early signs of abuse, (2) how to assist peers and family members with drug problems, and (3) how and where help is available for people with drug problems (Archambault, 1992). Regardless of the prevention approach used, adolescents need to understand that drugs are never the solution for emotional difficulties, nor are they useful for long-term coping.

## TREATMENT OF ADOLESCENT DRUG ABUSE

To provide appropriate treatment for adolescent drug abuse, the severity of the problem must be ascertained. The criteria for such assessments include the following:

- differentiating between abuse and normal adolescent experimentation with drugs,
- distinguishing between minor abuse and severe dependency on drugs, and
- distinguishing among behavioral problems resulting from (1) general behavioral disorders such as juvenile delinquency, (2) intellectual disability, and (3) drugs of abuse.

There is no single best approach for treating adolescent substance abuse. Occasionally, the troubled adolescent is admitted to a clinic and treated on an inpatient basis. The inpatient approach is expensive and creates a temporary artificial environment that may be of limited value in preparing adolescents for the problems to be faced in their real homes and neighborhoods. However, the advantage of an inpatient approach is that adolescents can be managed better and their behavior can be more tightly monitored and controlled (Hoshino, 1992). A more practical and routine treatment approach is to allow adolescents to remain in their natural environment and to provide the necessary life skills to be successful at home, in school, and in the community. For example, adolescents being treated for drug dependence should be helped with:

- schoolwork so that appropriate progress toward high school graduation occurs,
- career skills so adolescents can become self-reliant and learn to care for themselves and others, and
- family problems and learning to communicate and resolve conflicts.

If therapy is to be successful, improving the environment of the drug-abusing adolescent becomes important. This aspect of treatment includes disassociating the adolescent from groups (such as gangs) or surroundings that encourage drug use and promoting association with healthy and supportive groups (such as a nurturing family) and experiences (such as athletics and school activities). Although desirable, such separation is not always possible, especially if the family and home environment are factors that encourage abuse; the likelihood of therapeutic success is substantially diminished under these circumstances.

Therapeutic objectives often are facilitated by positive reinforcement that encourages life changes that eliminate access to and use of drugs. This goal frequently can be achieved by association with peers who have similar drug and social problems but are motivated to make positive changes in their life. Group sessions with such peers are held under the supervision of a trained therapist and consist of members sharing problems and solutions (Hoshino, 1992). Other options include holistic therapies such as acupuncture, homeotherapy, massage therapy, aromatherapy, yoga, nutrition therapy, and many more alternatives that were once marginalized by the medical profession (Apostolides, 1996).

Another useful approach is to discourage use of drugs by reducing their reinforcing effects. This result can sometimes be achieved by substituting a stronger positive or negative reinforcer. For example, if adolescents use drugs because they believe these substances cause good feelings and help them cope with emotional problems, it may be necessary to replace the drug-taking behavior with other activities that make the adolescent feel good without the drug (such as participation in sports or recreational activities). Negative reinforcers, such as parental discovery and punishment or police apprehension, may discourage drug use by teenagers who are willing to conform and respect authorities; however, negative approaches are ineffective deterrents for nonconforming, rebellious adolescents. Negative reinforcers also do not tend to discourage adolescent use of substances that are more socially acceptable such as alcohol, tobacco, and even marijuana (Howard, 1992).

Regardless of the treatment approach, adolescents must meet several basic objectives if therapy for their drug dependence is to be successful (Daily, 1992b):

- They must come to realize that drugs do not solve problems; they only make the problems worse.
- They must understand why they turned to drugs in the first place.
- They must be convinced that abandoning drugs grants them greater independence and control over their own lives.
- They must understand that drug abuse is a symptom of underlying problems that need to be resolved.

## ■ Summary of Adolescent Drug Abuse

Drug abuse by adolescents is particularly problematic in the United States. The teenage years are filled with experimentation, searching, confusion, rebellion, poor self-image, and insecurity. If not managed properly, these attributes can cause inappropriate coping and lead to problems such as drug dependence, gang involvement, violence, criminal behavior, and suicide. Clearly, early detection of severe underlying emotional problems and application of effective early preventive therapy are important for proper management. Approaches to treating drug abuse problems must be individualized because each adolescent is a unique product of physiological, psychological, and environmental factors.

Almost as important as early intervention for adolescent drug abuse problems is recognizing when treatment is unnecessary. We should not be too quick to label all young drug users as antisocial and emotionally unstable. In most cases, teenagers who have used drugs are merely experimenting with new emotions or exercising their newfound freedom. In such situations, nonintervention is usually better than therapeutic meddling. For the most part, if adolescents are given the opportunity, they will work through their own feelings, conflicts, and attitudes about substance abuse, and they will develop a responsible philosophy concerning the use of these drugs.

# Drug Use Among College Students

This section focuses on college undergraduate use of alcohol, with additional emphasis on the use and abuse of illicit drugs by college students currently attending institutions of higher education.

**Table 16.6** compares trends in the annual use of various types of licit and illicit drugs by full-time college students with annual usage by others who

**TABLE 16.6** Annual Prevalence of Drug Use for Full-Time College Students Versus Others Among Respondents One to Four Years beyond High School: 2018*

|  | Percentage of Full-Time College Students | Percentage of Others, 1 to 4 Years Beyond High School |
|---|---|---|
| Any illicit drug** | 44.9 | 44.1 |
| Any illicit drug** other than marijuana | 18.2 | 17.8 |
| Alcohol | 59.8 | 50.1 |
| Marijuana | 42.3 | 41.4 |
| Synthetic marijuana | 1.6 | 2.3 |
| Cigarettes | 15.3 | 27.0 |
| Vaping | 32.2 | 31.6 |
| Amphetamines+ | 8.5 | 4.8 |
| Ritalin | 1.3 | 2.6 |
| Adderall | 11.1 | 8.1 |
| Methamphetamine | 0.4 | 1.2 |
| Other narcotics other than heroin | 2.7 | 3.1 |
| OxyContin | 1.6 | 1.3 |
| Vicodin | 1.4 | 1.6 |
| Tranquilizers | 3.5 | 3.7 |
| Hallucinogens | 5.2 | 6.8 |
| LSD | 4.2 | 6.0 |
| MDMA (Ecstasy, Molly) | 4.4 | 2.8 |
| Cocaine | 5.3 | 4.2 |
| Crack | 0.4 | 0.3 |
| Sedatives+ (barbiturates) | 1.5 | 3.1 |
| Inhalants | 1.3 | 1.1 |
| Ketamine | 0.9 | 0.8 |
| Heroin | Less than 0.05% | 0.5 |

* All full-time college entries, except for the first two percentage entries, are college from highest to lowest.

** Use of any illicit drug includes use of marijuana, hallucinogens, cocaine, or heroin or any use of other narcotics, amphetamines, sedatives (barbiturates), or tranquilizers not under a doctor's orders.

+ Only drug use that was not under a doctor's orders is included here.

Data from Schulenberg, J. E., Johnston, L. D., O'Malley, P. M., Bachman, J. G., Miech, R. A., & Patrick, M. E. (2019). *Monitoring the Future National Survey Results on Drug Use, 1975–2018: Volume II, College students and adults ages 19–60.* Ann Arbor, MI: University of Michigan, Institute for Social Research. Retrieved from http://www.monitoringthefuture.org//pubs/monographs/mtf-overview2019.pdf

are the same age (one to four years beyond high school) but are not attending college. Overall, Table 16.6 shows the following noteworthy prevalence trends (Schulenberg et al., 2019):

- Noncollege youth (designated as others in Table 16.6) had significantly higher rates of nonprescription drug use for the following drugs: cigarettes, methamphetamine, hallucinogens and LSD, and sedatives (barbiturates).
- Full-time college students of the same age had significantly higher rates of drug use for the following drugs: alcohol, amphetamines, Adderall, hallucinogens, MDMA (Ecstasy and Molly), and cocaine.
- College students also had a higher prevalence (29%) of *binge drinking* (five or more drinks in a row at least once in the past two weeks) than their noncollege peers (25%) in 2018. Similarly, more college students (38%) reported having *been drunk* in the prior 30 days, compared to noncollege respondents (24%). Both groups had relatively low *daily*

*drinking* prevalence, with it being similar in 2018 among college students (2.4%) and non-college youth (2.6%). Back in high school, college-bound students, especially in earlier grades, were far less likely to drink alcohol at any level compared to their noncollege-bound peers, thus both relative and absolute increases in most indexes of alcohol use among college students in the first few years following high school are quite striking and point to full-time college attendance as a risk factor for binge drinking.

- From 2012 to 2018, about one in 10 college students (9.5%) reported having *10 or more drinks in a row* at least once in the prior two weeks, and 3.1% reported *15 or more drinks in a row* at least once in the prior two weeks. The noncollege respondents had similar respective rates (10.2% and 5.2%). Clearly, this type of extreme binge drinking is worrisome among both college students and noncollege youth.

- In 2018, 58% of both college students and noncollege youth reported using *flavored alcoholic beverages* in the prior year.

- Prevalence rates for annual vaping of nicotine prevalence was considerably higher among college men (34%) than women (21%); among noncollege youth, it was slightly higher among men than women (22% versus 19%). Thirty-day prevalence was much higher for college men than women (22% versus 12%); among noncollege youth it was similar for men and women (12% versus 13%). Thus, based on 2018 data, college men were at particularly high risk for this rapidly increasing risky health behavior.

- The prevalence of vaping marijuana in 2018 was *higher* among college students than among noncollege youth. For the two groups respectively, annual prevalence was 20% and 11%; 30-day prevalence was 10.8% and 7.9%, respectively (Schulenberg et al., 2019).

- Annual marijuana use was similar among college men (43%) and women (42%) in 2018, and the same was true for 30-day marijuana use (24% and 25%, respectively). Among noncollege youth, annual use was higher for women (44%) than men (39%); and the same was true for 30-day use (30% and 23%, respectively)). In contrast, daily marijuana use was about twice as high among college men (8.4%) compared to college women (4.3%) and also higher for noncollege men (12.4%) than women (9.7%), although the prevalence of daily use for both genders was much higher for the noncollege than college group.

- Overall use of marijuana use by college students in MTF (Schulenberg et al., 2019) survey data on drug use in college-age adults ages 19 to 22 shows an increase in marijuana use in the preceding five years, including vaping with marijuana, as well as a significant increase in nicotine vaping.

- The use of hallucinogens was somewhat higher among noncollege youth in 2018. Among noncollege youth and college students, respectively, annual use of hallucinogens was 6.8% and 5.2%, annual use of LSD was 6.0% and 5.2%, and annual use of hallucinogens other than LSD was 4.3% and 2.5%. However, as previously mentioned, annual use of MDMA (Ecstasy, Molly) was higher among college students (4.4%) than noncollege youth (2.8%).

- Among college students in 2018, annual prevalence of use of any illicit drug was similar for men and women (45% for each), and the same was true for 30-day use (26% and 27%, respectively). For noncollege youth, annual prevalence was higher for women than for men (46% and 41%, respectively); and the same was true for 30-day use (31% and 24%, respectively).

- Among college students, annual prevalence of any hallucinogens in 2018 was more than twice as high for men than for women (8.2% vs. 3.4%), and the same was true for LSD specifically (6.8% vs. 2.6%). Among noncollege respondents, the gender gap was narrower; annual prevalence was similar or slightly higher for men than for women for use of any hallucinogens (7.2% vs. 6.5%), for use of LSD specifically (6.3% vs. 5.8%),

- Annual cocaine use in 2018 was higher among college men (7.0%) than women (4.3%); it was similar among noncollege men (4.5%) and women (4.0%).

In summary, the prevalence of illicit drug use tended to be similar among 19- to 22-year-old college students *and* noncollege youth in 2018. This was true for annual prevalence of marijuana (42% and 41%, respectively) and for any illicit drug other than marijuana (18% for both).

In looking at gender differences, many licit and illicit drugs were used by a higher proportion of college men than college women in 2018, with the largest proportional differences occurring for daily marijuana use, extreme binge drinking, 30-day vaping of nicotine, and annual hallucinogen use. However, for prevalence of annual and 30-day marijuana use in 2018, college men and women were similar. Gender differences for the noncollege segment were more mixed, with noncollege women having higher annual and 30-day prevalence of using marijuana and any illicit drug other than marijuana, as well as higher annual prevalence of amphetamine and MDMA (Ecstasy, Molly) use, but noncollege men had higher prevalence of daily marijuana use, extreme binge drinking, annual marijuana vaping, and annual hallucinogen use. Compared with noncollege men, college men were more frequent users of alcohol and amphetamines (particularly Adderall outside of medical supervision) and more likely to vape marijuana and nicotine but considerably less likely to use marijuana daily; this same pattern generally held for noncollege versus college women. Finally, the most striking difference between the college and noncollege segments

remains for cigarette smoking, with noncollege men and women showing much higher use than college men and women.

**Table 16.7** shows yearly trends in drug use among U.S. college students from 2015 through 2018 (Schulenberg et al., 2019). This table details the percentages of college students who used drugs in the 12 months before the surveys were administered. The main finding is that the category of any illicit drug remained fairly constant from 2015 to 2018—approximately 43.9%, when averaging the four years of surveying. The following list shows that drug usage in each of the categorical designations is generally moderately either holding steady, decreasing, or increasing in usage.

Drugs Declining in Use from 2015 to 2018

- alcohol
- heroin
- amphetamines
- Ritalin
- tranquilizers
- sedatives (barbiturates)
- inhalants

**TABLE 16.7** Trends in Annual Use of Drugs Among College Students 1 to 4 Years Beyond High School (Percentage Who Used in the Past 12 Months Except as Noted): 2015–2018

|  | 2015 | 2016 | 2017 | 2018 |
|---|---|---|---|---|
| Approximate weighted *N* | 1020 | 870 | 880 | 900 |
| Any illicit drug* | 41.4 | 42.8 | 42.4 | 45.2 |
| Any illicit drug other than marijuana* | 18.5 | 19.7 | 18.1 | 18.0 |
| Alcohol | 79.0 | 78.9 | 75.8 | 74.6 |
| Cigarettes | 20.1 | 18.7 | 16.7 | 15.5 |
| Marijuana | 37.9 | 39.3 | 38.3 | 42.6 |
| **Hallucinogens** | 4.3 | 4.5 | 4.1 | 5.1 |
| LSD | 3.0 | 3.1 | 2.8 | 4.1 |
| MDMA (Ecstasy, molly), revised | 4.2 | 4.7 | 2.5 | 4.3 |
| **Amphetamines⁺** | 9.7 | 9.8 | 8.6 | 8.3 |
| Ritalin | 2.0 | 2.4 | 1.4 | 1.3 |
| Adderall | 10.7 | 9.9 | 9.4 | 11.0 |
| Provigil | – | – | – | – |
| Methamphetamine | 0.5 | 0.0 | 0.4 | 0.4 |
| Crystal Methamphetamine (ice) | – | – | 0.4 | – |

| | | | | |
|---|---|---|---|---|
| **Cocaine** | 4.3 | 4.0 | 4.8 | 5.2 |
| Crack | 0.2 | 0.0 | 0.2 | 0.4 |
| **Narcotics (other than Heroin)** | 3.3 | 3.8 | 3.1 | 2.7 |
| OxyContin | 1.5 | 1.9 | 1.7 | 1.6 |
| Vicodin | 1.6 | 1.3 | 1.1 | 1.5 |
| Tranquilizers | 4.3 | 4.9 | 3.6 | 3.5 |
| Sedatives (barbiturates)[+] | 2.3 | 2.1 | 1.9 | 1.5 |
| Inhalants | 0.6 | 0.2 | 1.7 | 1.3 |
| Heroin | 0.1 | 0.2 | 0.0 | - |
| GHB | - | - | - | - |
| Ketamine | 0.6 | 0.5 | 0.3 | 0.9 |

* Use of any illicit drug includes any use of marijuana, hallucinogens, cocaine, or heroin, or any use of other narcotics, amphetamines, sedatives (barbiturates), or tranquilizers not under a doctor's orders.

[+] Only drug use that was not under a doctor's orders is included here.

[-] no data available

Schulenberg, J. E., Johnston, L. D., O'Malley, P. M., Bachman, J. G., Miech, R. A., & Patrick, M. E. (2019). *Monitoring the Future National Survey Results on Drug Use, 1975–2018: Volume II, College students and adults ages 19–60.* Ann Arbor, MI: University of Michigan, Institute for Social Research.

### Drugs Holding Relatively Steady from 2015 to 2018

- any illicit drug
- any illicit drug other than marijuana
- MDMA (Ecstasy)
- methamphetamine
- narcotics (other than heroin)
- ketamine

### Drugs Increasing in Use from 2015 to 2018

- marijuana
- hallucinogens
- LSD
- Adderall
- cocaine

## ▌ Reasons for College Students' Drug Use

**Figure 16.2A** shows the primary reasons why a sample survey of 53,622 male and female college students used alcohol and other drugs (38.8% male, 63.2% female). The major reasons cited in this sample survey were (1) breaks the ice (75.1%), (2) enhances social activity (74.6%), (3) gives people something to do (73.0%), (4) gives people something to talk about (67.3%), (5) allows people to have more fun (62.5%), (6) peer bonding (62.4%), (7) male bonding (60.6%), (8) facilitates sex (51.2%), (9) female bonding (52.9%), and (10) makes it easier to deal with stress (43.6%) (Southern Illinois University Carbondale [SIUC]/Core Institute, 2014, p. 5) (see **Figure 16.2B**). Although not shown in this figure, this same survey revealed the following regarding alcohol (SIUC/Core Institute, 2014, p. 1):

- 81.3% of the students consumed alcohol in the past year ("annual prevalence");
- 68.4% of the students consumed alcohol in the past 30 days ("30-day prevalence");
- 61.3% of underage students (younger than 21) consumed alcohol in the previous 30 days; and
- 43.9% of students reported binge drinking in the previous two weeks. (A binge is defined as consuming five or more drinks in one sitting.)

Key findings on the use of illegal drugs included the following (SIUC/Core Institute, 2014, p. 1):

- 32.8% of the students have used marijuana in the past year ("annual prevalence");
- 19.5% of the students are current marijuana users ("30-day prevalence");

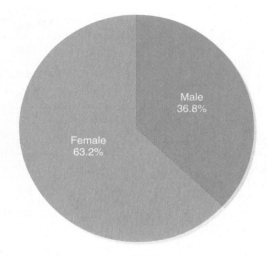

n = 53.622

A. Gender (Students Completing Survey)

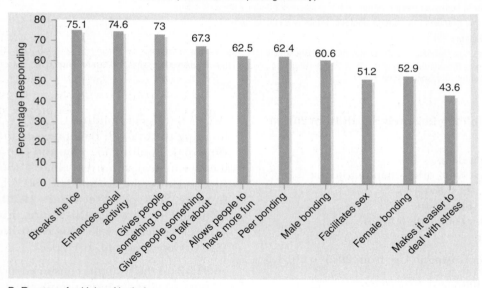

B. Reasons for Using Alcohol

**FIGURE 16.2** Sample of major reasons for using alcohol and other drugs.

Data from Southern Illinois University Carbondale [SIUC]/Core Institute. (2014, April 23). *2012 annual reference group, core alcohol and drug survey long form—Form 194, Executive Summary*. Carbondale, IL: Author.

- 11.8% of the students have used an illegal drug other than marijuana in the past year ("annual prevalence"); and
- 6.2% of the students are current users of illegal drugs other than marijuana ("30-day prevalence").

The most frequently reported illegal drugs used in the past 30 days were the following (SIUC/Core Institute, 2014, p. 1):

- 19.5% marijuana (pot, hash, hash oil),
- 2.9% amphetamines (diet pills, speed), and
- 1.7% designer drugs (Ecstasy, MDMA).

Demographically, approximately 83.3% of the students taking this survey were between ages 18 and 22, and 93.3% were full-time students. Approximately 28.4% were freshmen, 21.8% were sophomores, 22.9% were juniors, 22.4% were seniors, 3.6% were graduates, and 0.9% were other.

In addition, 49.5% lived off campus, and 54.5% worked part time or full time. It is likely that these results regarding college students' use of alcohol and other drugs would be similar to those found on other larger state university campuses in the United States.

# ■ Additional Noteworthy Findings Regarding Drug Use by College Students

The following sections describe the most recent significant studies and findings regarding the use of drugs by college students.

## PATTERNS OF ALCOHOL AND DRUG USE

Research reviews of undergraduates' substance use and abuse and the prevalence patterns of alcohol and other drug use found that alcohol is the most popular substance used by undergraduates (American Addiction Centers, 2020; Johnston et al., 2016; Leinwand, 2007b; SIUC/Core Institute, 2014). According to McMurtrie (2014), "[T]he binge-drinking rate among college students has hovered above 40 percent for two decades, and signs are that partying is getting even harder. More students now drink to get drunk, choose hard liquor over beer and drink in advance of social events. For many the goal is to black out." Another reported, "According to a national survey, almost 60 percent of college students ages 18–22 drank alcohol in the past month, and almost [two out of three] (over 60%) of them engaged in binge drinking during that same time frame" (NIDA, 2015b).

Common heavy drinking settings include the following (Stewart, 2013):

- fraternity parties
- drinking in conjunction with athletic events
- drinking in residence halls
- drinking in off-campus housing areas with a high proportion of students
- drinking in bars adjacent to campus

Alcohol use has been associated with serious and acute problems such as alcoholism, poor academic performance, drinking and driving, and criminalistic behavior (e.g., driving while intoxicated, vandalism, violence) (NIDA, 2015b).

College students vary greatly in their use of alcohol and their beliefs about its positive and negative effects. Studies show that two major drinking patterns appear dominant among college students: (1) drinking related to impulsivity, disinhibition, and sensation-seeking; and (2) drinking to manage negative emotional states such as depression (National Institute on Alcohol Abuse and Alcoholism [NIAAA], 2005a).

Summarized in the following list are other significant findings regarding alcohol and other drug use.

- Approximately 32% college students indicated they had engaged in high-risk binge drinking in the preceding two weeks. In addition, approximately 41% of college students reported being intoxicated in the preceding month (Schulenberg et al., 2019).
- Of all students, 43% reported drinking in a high-risk manner at some point in their college careers, and 20% students reported drinking in a high-risk manner often (Gloucester County College, 2013).

Academic Problems

- About one in four college students report academic consequences from drinking, including missing class, falling behind in class, doing poorly on exams or papers, and receiving lower grades overall. In a national survey of college students, binge drinkers who consumed alcohol at least three times per week were roughly six times more likely than those who drank but never binged to perform poorly on a test or project as a result of drinking (40% vs. 7%) and five times more likely to have missed a class (64% vs. 12%) (NIAAA, 2017).

Other Occurrences

- *Death*: Each year, 1,825 college students between ages 18 and 24 die from alcohol-related unintentional injuries, including motor vehicle crashes (Hingson, Zha, & Weitzman, 2009; NIAAA, 2005a; NIDA, 2015b).
- *Injury*: Each year, 599,000 students between ages 18 and 24 are unintentionally injured while under the influence of alcohol (Hingson et al., 2009; NIAAA, 2005a).
- *Assault*: Each year, 696,000 students between 18 and 24 are assaulted by another student who has been drinking (Hingson et al., 2009; NIAAA, 2005b, 2017; NIDA, 2015b).
- *Sexual assault*: Each year, 97,000 students between 18 and 24 are victims of alcohol-related sexual assault or date rape (NIAAA, 2005b, 2017; NIDA, 2015b). Researchers estimate that alcohol use is implicated in one-third to two-thirds of sexual assaults and acquaintance or date rape cases among teens and college students.

- *Unsafe sex*: Each year, 400,000 students between ages 18 and 24 have unprotected sex, and more than 100,000 students between 18 and 24 report having been too intoxicated to know

- *Health problems and suicide attempts*: More than 150,000 students develop an alcohol-related health problem each year (Hingson et al., 2009), and between 1.2% and 1.5% of students indicate that they tried to commit suicide within the past year because of drinking or drug use (NIAAA, 2005a).

- *Drunk driving*: Each year, 3,360,000 students between 18 and 24 drive under the influence of alcohol (Hingson et al., 2009; NIAAA, 2005a).

- *Vandalism*: About 11% of college student drinkers report that they have damaged property while under the influence of alcohol (SAMHSA, 2011).

- *Property damage*: More than 25% of administrators from schools with relatively low drinking levels and more than 50% from schools with high drinking levels say their campuses have a "moderate" or "major" problem with alcohol-related property damage (SAMHSA, 2011).

- *Police involvement*: About 5% of four-year college students are involved with the police or campus security as a result of their drinking (Wechsler et al., 2002), and 110,000 students between ages 18 and 24 are arrested each year for an alcohol-related violation such as public drunkenness or driving under the influence (SAMHSA, 2011).

- *Alcohol abuse and dependence*: In the preceding 12 months, 31% of college students met criteria for a diagnosis of alcohol abuse and 6% for a diagnosis of alcohol dependence, according to questionnaire-based self-reports about their drinking (NIAAA, 2005a).

- *Alcohol use disorder (AUD)*: About 20% of college students meet the criteria for an AUD (NIDA, 2015b).

- *Binge drinking*: Young adults 18 to 25 are most likely to binge or drink heavily; 54% of the drinkers in this age group binge, and about one in four are heavy drinkers (SAMHSA, 2011).

- *Victimization*: About four in 10 violent crimes against college students were committed by offenders who were perceived by victims to be using drugs or alcohol (National Crime Victims' Rights Week Resource Guide, 2007).

- *Death*: About 1,825 college students between 18 and 24 die from alcohol-related unintentional injuries, including motor vehicle crashes (NIAAA, 2017).

- *Housing*: The amount and proportion of alcohol consumed by college students varies depending on where they live. Drinking rates are highest in fraternities and sororities, followed by on-campus housing (e.g., dormitories, residence halls). Students who live independently off site (e.g., in apartments) drink less, and commuting students who live with their families drink the least (NIAAA, 2005b).

## PREDICTING DRUG USE FOR FIRST-YEAR COLLEGE STUDENTS

One of the best predictors of drug use for first-year college students was drug use during a typical month in the senior year of high school. Overall, college students responding to a questionnaire were found to use marijuana less frequently than they did in high school. Further, alcohol use increased early in the college years. Although the frequency of alcohol use increased, the number of times that college students got drunk did not rise. Most of these students found new friends in college with whom they got drunk. Alcohol and drug use depended on the choice of new college friends (Leibsohn, 1994; Wadley, 2014).

A more recent study examined personality disposition to risky behavior as a predictor of first-year college drinking. A survey of 418 first-year college students at the University of Kentucky revealed that students with a preponderance of sensation-seeking predispositions (risk-taking) were more likely to drink more frequently, consume greater quantities of alcohol, and experience negative outcomes from drinking than those students scoring significantly lower on the UPPS-P Impulsive Behavior Scale, the positive urgency measure, and the Drinking Styles Questionnaire. Sensation-seeking students experienced more lack of control (i.e., dyscontrol) stemming from extreme positive mood swings, and it was during these periods that alcohol consumption rapidly increased (Cyders, Flory, Rainer, & Smith, 2009).

## DORMITORIES FOR NON-DRUG-USING STUDENTS

In 1988, Rutgers University was one of the first universities to create a dormitory for students who were recovering addicts and who wanted to stay away from the alcohol-charged atmosphere of conventional dormitories. The dormitory at Rutgers maintains strict rules and careful management (Witham, 1995). Other universities offer similar variations for on-campus living. In 1989, the University of Michigan opened a substance-free housing facility and set aside 500 dormitory spaces; 1,200 students applied for these spaces (Belsie, 1995). More recent findings indicate that "now that substance-free housing is commonplace, a handful of campuses, including Rutgers, have gone [even] further, offering 'recovery' housing for students who have been in treatment for addiction" (Altschuler, 2017; Lewin, 2005). Today, substance-free housing has become a nationwide choice. This type of housing is found "at dozens of campuses nationwide, from huge state universities like the University of Michigan to Ivy League schools like Dartmouth and small liberal arts colleges like Vassar" (Lewin, 2005). For example,

> a junior at Earlham College who asked that his name not be used . . . [said,] "When I got to college, I didn't want to have to worry about having all that stuff in my face [in reference to having to live with drunk and drugged students in the dorm]. I've been in wellness housing my whole time here. I could handle normal housing now, but I like the people I live with, and there's a very good atmosphere. (Lewin, 2005)

Further, on some campuses, large numbers of entering freshmen prefer substance-free living accommodations, mainly dormitories as well as other types of housing. "At Dartmouth, for example, about 400 of the 1,075 incoming freshmen requested it, compared with only about 200 of the 2,200 sophomores, juniors and seniors who live on campus" (Lewin, 2005). A recent online search in 2016 by the author for substance-free dormitories on college campuses listed approximately 40 U.S. colleges and universities offering such housing, including Bucknell University, California State University–Monterey Bay, Colby-Sawyer College, Indiana University of Pennsylvania, James Madison, Julliard School, Rutgers, the State University of New Jersey–New Brunswick, and the University of New Hampshire (CollegeXpress.com, 2016).

## POPULARITY OF CERTAIN TYPES OF DRUGS: COLLEGE, NONCOLLEGE, AND 12TH GRADERS

Marijuana and psilocybin mushrooms are two types of illicit recreational drugs whose popularity appeared to grow in the 1990s and that remain popular on most college campuses. Referred to as *soft drugs*, these substances are commonly used on most college campuses (Ravid, 1995).

> I know my older brothers told me that when they were at this same college I am now attending "shrooms" [referring to psilocybin mushrooms] were not that easy to get and the better types of weed were very infrequent back [seven] years ago. Well, today it's really different! Even at this smaller university it's all a matter of finding the right dude to hook you up. I have a hook-up that always has blueberry, which is a small percentage *Sativa* and nearly all *Indica*. He is in partnership with a friend in Michigan who grows only this kind. It is expensive but oh is it worth it. You certainly don't need much like the other stuff that is weaker. It is awesome stuff. The "shrooms" are not as frequent and several times I had to go to another friend's campus to get them. *(From Venturelli's research files, male attending a smaller comprehensive university in the Midwest, age 22, June 12, 2013)*

Other significant findings in 2018 in *Monitoring the Future: College Students and Adults Survey Results* include the following (Schulenberg et al., 2019).

- Alcohol use: 60%
- Daily drinking: 3.7% in 1994 and 2.4% in 2018
- Been drunk in the past 30 days: 38%
- Binge drinking in past two weeks: 29%
- Extreme binge drinking or high-intensity drinking (10 or more drinks in a row within two weeks): 9.5%
- Cigarettes (past month): 1.9% of college students and 10.1% of noncollege peers
- Marijuana (past month): 25% of college students and 27% on noncollege students
- Near daily marijuana use (past month): 5.9% of college students and 10.9% on noncollege students
- Vaping nicotine: (past month): 26% of college students and 21% of noncollege peers
- Vaping marijuana and vaping nicotine: college students had higher percentages than noncollege students

**Rohypnol** (flunitrazepam), also known as the *date-rape drug*, is one of six drugs referred to as *club drugs*. The other club drugs are MDMA (Ecstasy or Molly), gamma-hydroxybutyrate (GHB), ketamine, methamphetamine, and LSD. Club drugs are used by individuals at all-night dance parties such as raves or trances, dance clubs, and bars. All of these drugs are colorless, tasteless, and odorless. They can be added discreetly to beverages by individuals who may want to intoxicate or sedate others (NIDA, 2000, 2015c). In cases of sexual assault or rape, the small white Rohypnol pills are slipped into a person's drink, causing the person to black out and have no memories of events that occurred while he or she was under the influence of the drug. A minority of undergraduates also use the drug to intensify the effects of marijuana and alcohol. One problem with identifying whether this drug has been given to an unwilling recipient is that Rohypnol can be detected only for 60 hours after ingestion (Lively, 1996).

Rohypnol belongs to a class of drugs known as *benzodiazepines* (such as Valium and Xanax). Although this drug is not approved for prescription use in the United States, it is approved and used in more than 60 countries as a treatment for insomnia, as a sedative, and as a presurgery anesthetic (NIDA, 2000).

### ■ Recommendations for Reducing Drug Use and Abuse on College Campuses

There is an elevated risk of increased drug use and abuse when students move to a college campus. Approaches to minimize increased drug use include the following (Ross & Dejong, 2008, p. 3):

● *Alcohol-free options*: "offer and promote social, recreational, extracurricular, and public service options that do not include alcohol and other drugs."

### KEY TERMS

**Rohypnol**

"date-rape drug" that is used on some college campuses to commit sexual assault; the three most common date rape drugs are Rohypnol (flunitrazepam), GHB (gamma-hydroxybutyrate), and ketamine

**antiretroviral therapy (ART)**

maintaining a regimen of taking a combination of several antiretroviral medicines to slow the rate at which HIV infects the body

● *Normative environment*: "create a social, academic, and residential environment that supports health-promoting norms."
● *Alcohol availability*: "limit alcohol availability both on and off campus."
● *Alcohol marketing and promotion*: "restrict marketing and promotion of alcohol beverages both on and off campus."
● *Policy development and enforcement*: "develop and enforce campus policies and enforce local, state, and federal laws, and make sure everyone knows what the policies are."

## HIV and AIDS

Acquired immune deficiency syndrome came to the attention of medical authorities in the United States on June 4, 1981, in a newsletter from the Centers for Disease Control and Prevention (CDC) in Atlanta, Georgia (Zuger, 2000). The human immunodeficiency virus, the virus that causes AIDS, was not discovered until 1983. The following is the current state of the HIV and AIDS epidemic from a global perspective (World Health Organization [WHO], 2019).

### ■ Global HIV: Data and Trends

● There were approximately 37.9 million people living with HIV at the end of 2018.
● Because of gaps in HIV services, 770,000 people died from HIV-related causes in 2018, and 1.7 million people were newly infected.
● HIV continues to be a major global public health issue, having claimed more than 32 million lives so far. However, with increasing access to effective HIV prevention, diagnosis, treatment and care, including for opportunistic infections, HIV infection has become a manageable chronic health condition, enabling people living with HIV to lead long and healthy lives.
● As a result of concerted international efforts to respond to HIV, coverage of services has been steadily increasing. In 2018, 62% of adults and 54% of children living with HIV in low- and middle-income countries were receiving lifelong **antiretroviral therapy (ART)**.
● A great majority (82%) of pregnant and breastfeeding women living with HIV also received ART, which not only protects their health but also ensures prevention of HIV transmission to their newborns.

- For the first time, individuals from key population groups and their sexual partners accounted for more than half of all new HIV infections globally (an estimated 54%) in 2018. For the Eastern European, Central Asian, Middle Eastern, and North African regions, these groups accounted for around 95% of new HIV infections.
- Key populations infected include men who have sex with men (MSM), people who inject drugs, people in prisons and other closed settings, sex workers and their clients, and transgender people.
- In addition, given their life circumstances, a range of other populations may be particularly vulnerable and at increased risk of HIV infection, including adolescent girls and young women in Southern and Eastern Africa and indigenous peoples in some communities.
- More than two thirds of all people living with HIV live in the World Health Organization's (WHO's) designated African Region (25.7 million). Although HIV is prevalent among the general population in this region, an increasing number of new infections occur among key population groups.
- There is no cure for HIV infection. However, effective antiretroviral (ARV) drugs can control the virus and help prevent onward transmission to other people.
- At the end of 2018, an estimated 79% of people living with HIV knew their status, 62% were receiving ART, and 53% had achieved suppression of the HIV virus with no risk of infecting others.
- In June 2019, 24.5 million people were accessing ARV therapy.
- Between 2000 and 2018, new HIV infections fell by 37% and HIV-related deaths fell by 45%, with 13.6 million lives saved by ART. This achievement was the result of great efforts by national HIV programs supported by civil society and international development partners (WHO, 2019).
- According to the Joint United Nations Programme on HIV and AIDS (UNAIDS) (2020), key populations and their sexual partners account for:
  - 54% of new HIV infections globally,
  - more than 95% of new HIV infections in Eastern Europe and Central Asia,
  - 3% to 95% of new HIV infections in the Middle East and North Africa,
  - 88% of new HIV infections in Western and Central Europe and North America,
  - 78% of new HIV infections in Asia and the Pacific,
  - 65% of new HIV infections in Latin America,
  - 64% of new HIV infections in Western and Central Africa,
  - 47% of new HIV infections in the Caribbean, and
  - 25% of new HIV infections in Eastern and southern Africa (UNAIDS, 2020).
- Every week, around 6,000 young women 15- to 24-years-old become infected with HIV.
- In sub-Saharan Africa, four in five new infections among adolescents 15–19 years of age are in girls. Young women aged 15–24 years are twice as likely to be living with HIV than men.
- More than one-third (35%) of women around the world have experienced physical or sexual violence at some time in their lives.
- In some regions, women who have experienced physical or sexual intimate partner violence are 1.5 times more likely to acquire HIV than women who have not experienced such violence.

Although cases have been reported in all regions of the world, almost all those living with HIV (97%) reside in low- and middle-income countries, which are disproportionately found in sub-Saharan Africa. The HIV epidemic not only affects the health of individuals but also impacts households, communities, and the development and economic growth of nations. Many of the countries hardest hit by HIV also suffer from other infectious diseases, food insecurity, and other serious problems. According to the World Health Organization, most people living with HIV or at risk for HIV do not have access to prevention, care, or treatment, and there is still no cure (UNAIDS, 2015).

Despite these challenges, there have been successes and promising signs. New global efforts have been mounted to address the epidemic, particularly since 2010. Prevention has helped reduce HIV prevalence rates in a small but growing number of countries, and new HIV infections are declining. In addition, the reported number of people with HIV receiving antiretroviral therapy treatment in resource-poor countries is as follows: "In 2018, 62% [47% to 74%] of all people living with HIV were accessing treatment. Sixty-two percent [47% to 75%] of adults aged 15 years and older living with HIV had access to treatment, as did 54% [37% to 73%] of children aged 0–14 years" (UNAIDS, 2020).

## ▪ U.S. HIV and AIDS: Data and Trends

In the United States, HIV.gov ("U.S. Statistics," 2020) provides the following estimates with regard to populations with HIV/AIDS:

- Approximately 1.1 million people in the United States are living with HIV today. About 14% of them (one in seven) do not know they have HIV and need testing.
- HIV continues to have a disproportionate impact on certain populations, particularly racial and ethnic minorities and gay and bisexual men.
- In 2018, 37,832 people received an HIV diagnosis in the United States and six dependent areas. The annual number of new diagnoses decreased 11% from 2010 to 2017 among adults and adolescents in the 50 states and the District of Columbia. However, trends varied for different groups of people. Gay and bisexual men are the population most affected by HIV. In 2018:
  - Gay and bisexual men accounted for 69% of all HIV diagnoses in the United States and 86% of diagnoses among males.
  - Black or African American gay and bisexual men accounted for the largest number of HIV diagnoses (9,499) followed by Hispanics or Latinos (7,543) and whites (6,423).
  - Among all gay and bisexual men, HIV diagnoses remained stable from 2010 to 2017, but trends varied by race or ethnicity.
  - HIV diagnoses among black or African American gay and bisexual men remained stable.
  - HIV diagnoses among white gay and bisexual men decreased 19%.
  - HIV diagnoses among Hispanics or Latino gay and bisexual men increased 17%.
- Heterosexuals and people who inject drugs also continue to be affected by HIV. In 2018:
  - Heterosexuals accounted for 24% of HIV diagnoses.
  - Heterosexual men accounted for 7% of HIV diagnoses, and heterosexual women accounted for 16% of HIV diagnoses.
  - People who inject drugs accounted for 7% of HIV diagnoses. Men who inject drugs accounted for 4% of HIV diagnoses, and women who inject drugs accounted for 3% of new diagnoses ("U.S. Statistics," 2020).
  - By risk group, *gay, bisexual, and other men who have sex with men* (MSM) of all races and ethnicities remain the population most profoundly affected by HIV.

## ▪ Race and Ethnicity: Data and Trends

- Blacks or African Americans and Hispanics or Latinos are disproportionately affected by HIV. In 2018:
  - Blacks or African Americans accounted for 42% (16,067) of HIV diagnoses and 13% of the population.
  - Hispanics or Latinos accounted for 27% (9,673) of HIV diagnoses and 18% of the population.

## ▪ The Nature of HIV Infection and Related Symptoms

AIDS, which is caused by HIV, is a disease in which the body's immune system breaks down and is unable to fight off certain infections known as *opportunistic infections* and other illnesses that take advantage of a weakened immune system.

The symptoms of HIV vary by stage of infection. Though people living with HIV tend to be most infectious in the first few months after being infected, many are unaware of their status until the later stages (WHO, 2019). In the early stage of HIV infection, often referred to as the *HIV syndrome*, the symptoms can include the following (WHO 2019):

- fever,
- headache,
- fatigue,
- swollen lymph glands,
- sore throat, and
- skin rash.

Without treatment, those infected could also develop severe illnesses such as tuberculosis, cryptococcal meningitis, severe bacterial infections, and cancers such as lymphomas and Kaposi's sarcoma (WHO, 2019).

Many of these symptoms can also be symptoms of mononucleosis (mono), other STIs, or viral hepatitis. Only an HIV test can determine if a person displaying any combination of these symptoms has contracted HIV. Symptoms for HIV as it advances and worsens include the following (AIDS.gov, 2012; WHO, 2019):

- swollen lymph glands,
- diarrhea that is frequent or ongoing,
- frequent high fevers (over 100°F),
- shaking chills,
- shortness of breath,
- blurred and distorted vision,

- unplanned or rapid weight loss,
- ongoing fatigue,
- ulcerated skin in the mouth,
- soaking night sweats,
- cough,
- headaches, and
- skin rashes or bumps.

When a person is infected with HIV, the virus enters the body and lives and multiplies primarily in the white blood cells (see **Figure 16.3**). These immune cells normally protect us from disease. The hallmark of HIV infection is the progressive loss of a specific type of immune cells called *T-helper* or *CD4+ cells*.

As the virus multiplies, it damages or kills CD4+ and other cells, weakening the immune system and leaving the individual vulnerable to numerous opportunistic infections and other illnesses ranging from pneumonia to cancer. The CDC defines someone as having a clinical diagnosis of AIDS if he or she has tested positive for HIV and has one or both of the following conditions (Schernoff & Smith, 2001):

- The person has experienced at least one AIDS-related infection or illness.
- The number of CD4+ cells has reached or fallen below 200 per cubic millimeter of blood (a measurement known as a *T-cell count*).

As mentioned previously, the HIV-positive individual's immune system becomes severely compromised as the CD4+ helper T lymphocytes

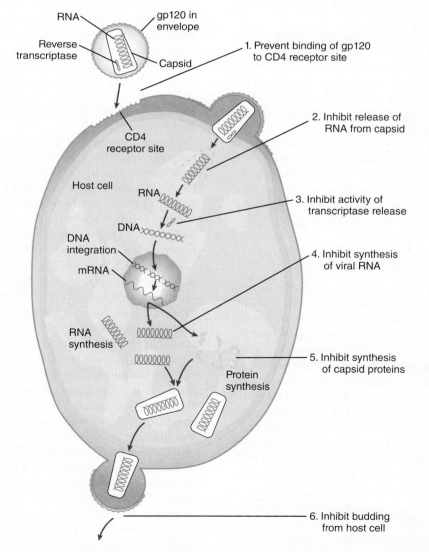

**FIGURE 16.3**  Disrupting the cell's normal functioning line, HIV survives by invading white blood cells and turning them into virus factories. Approaches for developing anti-HIV therapies focus on interfering with the replication of HIV.

and macrophages are destroyed. Because these immune cells are crucial in identifying and eliminating infection-causing microorganisms such as bacteria, fungi, and viruses, their deficiency substantially increases the likelihood and severity of infectious diseases. Progression of the disease brings weight loss, infections in the throat (thrush) and skin (shingles), and other opportunistic infections or cancer (e.g., Kaposi's sarcoma). Infections become increasingly difficult to control with medication, and consequently severe opportunistic infections such as pneumonia, meningitis, hepatitis, and tuberculosis occur and eventually lead to death. The likelihood of introducing these opportunistic infections into the body increases in patients who are injection drug users because they often share injection equipment such as needles and syringes that are contaminated with disease-causing microorganisms.

An HIV-infected individual may not manifest symptoms of AIDS for as many as eight to ten years after initial infection. Further, after an AIDS diagnosis, people who do not have treatment typically survive for three years. Although the HIV-infected individual may experience no symptoms, he or she is highly contagious.

After an individual has become infected, he or she may have a brief flulike illness, usually within six to 12 weeks. It is not known what determines the length of the latency period, or when symptoms are not present. The asymptomatic period eventually ends, however, and signs of immune disorder appear.

## ▪ Diagnosis and Treatment

It is crucial that HIV-infected people be aware of their condition to avoid activities that might transmit the infection to others. Testing for the presence of infection has been available since 1985 and is done by determining whether the body is producing antibodies against HIV. Further, since 1996, newspapers, magazines, radio, and television have been advertising a take-at-home HIV antibody test. (These advertisements are not as widely publicized today, but the test can readily be found on the Internet.) The presence of these specific antibodies indicates HIV

infection. If an individual is infected, it takes six to 12 weeks after the HIV exposure before the body produces enough antibodies to be detected in currently available tests. If the antibody is not present within six months after HIV exposure, then it is likely that infection did not occur (Pietroski, 1993).

Although the tests for HIV infection are reliable, false negatives (i.e., an indication that no HIV is present even though the individual is infected) and false positives (i.e., an indication that the individual is infected even though no HIV is present) occur in one out of 30,000 tests. Because testing positive for HIV is currently perceived as eventually life threatening and is a highly emotional diagnosis, great effort is made to ensure confidentiality of the test results. The blood specimens to be tested are coded, and the personnel conducting the tests are not allowed to divulge the results to anyone but the individual who was tested. The issue of confidentiality is controversial, however. It often is difficult to decide who has the right to know when HIV has been detected (see "Point–Counterpoint: Who Should Know the Results of Your HIV Test If You Test Positive?").

After a positive HIV diagnosis, the best way to lengthen one's life is to immediately begin drug treatments. The first prescription drug treatment for AIDS, azidothymidine (AZT), was introduced in 1987. In 1996, **protease inhibitors** came in the market. When combined with AZT and other drugs, protease inhibitors resulted in miraculous remissions of desperately ill AIDS patients (Zuger, 2000). Further, it appears that with such drug combinations levels of HIV in the blood in newly infected patients remain exceedingly low (Zuger, 2000). Although the drug combinations do not rid the body of infected cells, results indicate that HIV infections could become as manageable as diabetes (Crowley, 1996).

More advanced class of drugs such as those used in ART now consist of six main types of drugs that can be used. A most recent class of drugs termed *nucleoside–nucleotide reverse transcriptase inhibitors* (NRTIs) represents the latest class of drugs to treat HIV and AIDS diagnoses.

Today, people in the United States and other developed countries can use several drugs to treat HIV infection and AIDS. Some of these are designed to treat the opportunistic infections and illnesses that affect people with HIV or AIDS. In addition, several types of drugs seek to prevent HIV from reproducing and destroying the body's

KEY TERM

**protease inhibitors**
major breakthrough class of drugs used to treat HIV-infected individuals

# ▶POINT/COUNTERPOINT

## Who Should Know the Results of Your HIV Test If You Test Positive?

**M**ost people would probably want to keep such results private, but would your opinion about HIV-positive people keeping their results confidential change in the following circumstances?

- You require first aid after a serious auto accident, and the emergency medical technician assisting is HIV positive.
- Your doctor is HIV positive.
- Your dentist is HIV positive.
- Your manicurist is HIV positive.
- Your massage therapist is HIV positive.
- Your severely handicapped daughter's elementary school teacher is HIV positive.
- Your lover is HIV positive.
- Your tattoo artist is HIV positive.
- Your jeweler who is about to pierce your daughter's ears is HIV positive.
- Your boxing partner is HIV positive.
- Your jail cellmate is HIV positive.

Arguments for not disclosing HIV-positive results to anyone other than the person undergoing HIV screening are that reporting such results to others would (1) cause many people not to take the test for fear of disclosure to others; (2) possibly cause loss of employment (if the results require mandatory reporting to supervisors or managers); (3) unnecessarily stigmatize the HIV-positive person, exposing an infected person to social ostracism and gossip and potentially creating fear and panic in others; and (4) potentially destroy a partner or marriage relationship if the significant other or spouse is notified.

Arguments for mandatory disclosure to others potentially affected by the results of this disease include (1) to protect domestic or marital partners, (2) to protect others from HIV-positive workers who could infect them (such as surgeons who are involved in invasive bodily care or procedures), and (3) to honor the public's right to know of the threat of contracting this terminal disease.

Currently, employers cannot legally terminate a worker for being HIV positive. In cases of direct potential threat to the public, an HIV-positive worker can be reassigned to a different position. Also, in most cases, employers cannot legally inquire about HIV test results. An exception to this is the military and prison, where mandatory testing is required. What is your opinion about this issue?

The sooner an HIV-positive person begins drug treatment, the more effective the treatment may be. Knowing this, should HIV-positive individuals be required to inform past sexual partners and people with whom they have shared needles so that these people can be tested (known as *partner notification* or *contact tracing*)?

If an HIV-positive surgeon is going to operate on you, your mother, your father, or your child, do you have the right to know? What are the rights of the HIV-positive individual versus the rights of the public?

immune system. Reverse transcriptase inhibitors attach to an HIV enzyme called *reverse transcriptase*. The two major categories of reverse transcriptase inhibitors are the NRTIs and non-nucleoside reverse transcriptase inhibitors (NNRTIs) (EBSCO, 2013).

Medications used to treat HIV infection (antiretroviral drugs) help many people with HIV lower the levels of virus in their blood—their *viral loads*—to undetectable levels. ART treatment with combinations of these medications slows the rate at which HIV multiplies in the body and may decrease the chance that an infected person will transmit HIV to others through sex. However, the risk of spreading infection is still not zero, which means that persons with HIV who are taking

ART, or persons who are in a relationship with someone who has HIV and is taking ART, should still use proven prevention methods such as condoms (CDC, 2010c).Many HIV patients are taking several of these drugs in combination, a form of ART known as **highly active antiretroviral therapy (HAART)**. When successful, combinations or "cocktail" therapy can reduce the level of HIV in the bloodstream to extremely low—even undetectable—levels and sometimes enable the

**KEY TERM**

**highly active antiretroviral therapy (HAART)**
maintaining a regimen of more recent types of medications to slow the rate at which HIV infects the body

body's CD4+ immune cells to rebound to normal levels (American Foundation for AIDS Research [amfAR], 2001). Approximately a decade ago the drug regimen was quite difficult:

> I take the famous drug "cocktail" and have to wake myself up in the middle of the night around [four] in the morning, then go back to sleep. I am used to it. I know it is a pain in the neck, but I think that despite this, the side effects can even be worse at times. I really don't want to go into it; it's depressing. The bright side: I am still alive after [nine] years since diagnosed with AIDS; I am not dead yet. *(From Venturelli's research files, male bartender in Chicago, age 52, May 18, 2000)*

An update regarding the treatment of HIV and AIDS reveals that

> [i]t wasn't until 1995, with the development of a second class of anti-HIV drugs, that we began to make real progress in controlling the pandemic. These drugs target the HIV protease, an enzyme involved in processing HIV proteins into their functional forms. Today, 20 out of the 21 USDA-approved antiretroviral drugs target either the reverse transcriptase or the viral protease. With the introduction of multiple antiretroviral therapies, clinicians began a treatment regime known as HAART . . . that involves combinations of [three to four] drugs at once. Despite the fact that there might be viruses resistant to one drug, they can still be suppressed by one of the other drugs being used. Just as the probability of getting struck by lightning twice in a row is much lower than getting struck once, the probability of finding a virus resistant to multiple drugs is much lower than being resistant to one. By reducing the probability of resistance, HAART was finally able to increase patient lifespan by suppressing viral replication and curbing immune cell loss. Although HAART has been very successful in preventing those infected with HIV from progressing to AIDS, it is not a cure, thus making prevention of new HIV cases a critical component of the strategy against HIV/AIDS. (Clark, 2010)

As a therapy regimen, HAART results in a dramatic reduction in the incidence of AIDS and death in individuals infected with HIV (MyDNA.com, 2005). Beginning a decade ago, patients took approximately 37 pills per day; a few years later it was a 14-pill-a-day regimen. A few years ago, in the majority of cases, only three pills had to be taken each day ("AIDS Fear," 2003). One source estimated the annual cost of care with HAART at about $10,000 to $12,000 per year (Bartlett, 2006). Today, similar drugs requiring one pill per day are available. One recent example is a drug called *bictegravir–emtricitabine–tenofovir alafenamide* (Biktarvy). "Biktarvy is indicated as a complete regimen for the treatment of HIV-a infection in adult and pediatric patients" (Gilead, 2019). However, this expensive drug is out of reach for most patients because the cost for Biktarvy oral tablets (mg-200 mg-25mg) is around $3,390 for a supply of 30 tablets. Prices are for cash-paying customers only and are not valid with insurance plans. Biktarvy is available as a brand name drug only; a generic version is not yet available (Drugs.com, 2020).

In a recent review, the average yearly cost was approximately $14,000 to $20,000. With the life expectancy for HIV patients increasing, the lifetime cost of treatment in today's terms is estimated at more than a half-million dollars (Aguirre, 2012).

A recent new class of medicines known as *integrase inhibitors* was discovered that is highly efficient in controlling HIV (Chong, 2006). "Integrase inhibitors are a type of antiretroviral therapy, which has advanced a long way in a short time. Because of these advances, HIV is now a manageable disease for most people (Morris, 2020). "Integrase inhibitors prevent HIV, or human immunodeficiency virus, from replicating by blocking its ability to patch its DNA onto cells" (Chong, 2006, p. A9). When combined with two other drugs, tenoflovir and lamivudine, it appears promising. Used as part of a drug cocktail, "the amount of HIV in 90% of patients . . . [was reduced to] undetectable levels in 24 weeks" (Chong, 2006, p. A9).

The different classes of antiretroviral drugs include:

- non-nucleoside reverse transcriptase inhibitors,
- nucleoside reverse transcriptase inhibitors,
- protease inhibitors,
- entry inhibitors, and
- integrase inhibitors.

Newer AIDS drugs have produced the following findings:

- "Entry inhibitors that work by preventing HIV from entering healthy CD4+ cells (T-cells) in the body" (POZ, 2011).
- Entry inhibitors (including fusion inhibitors) "work differently than many of the approved anti-HIV drugs—the protease inhibitors . . . , the . . . NRTIs . . . , and the . . . NNRTIs—which are active against HIV after it has infected a CD4 cell" (POZ, 2011).
- "Entry [and] fusion inhibitors . . . stops the virus from entering cells. Two drugs in this class have been approved by the Food and Drug Administration . . . : maraviroc, an entry inhibitor, and enfuvirtide, a fusion inhibitor" (amfAR, 2010).
- Integrase inhibitors affect the way HIV works in the body.
- As an ART, integrase inhibitors are a type of antiretroviral therapy that has advanced a long way in a short time. Because of these advances, HIV is now a manageable disease for most people.
- "Integrase inhibitors prevent an HIV enzyme called *integrase* from inserting HIV's genetic information into the virus's target cell."
- Newer drugs halt the progression of HIV to AIDS.
- In 1996, the total life expectancy for a 20-year-old person with HIV was 39 years. In 2011, the total life expectancy bumped up to about 70 years (Scaccia & Madell, 2020).

Unfortunately, many health-insurance companies continue to actively issue restrictive amendments on their policies that cap reimbursement for such expensive drug therapies. As a result, infected individuals with extensive debt obligations and patients without health insurance are often unable to afford the latest drug therapy.

A successful prognosis for HIV infection and AIDS relies on three factors: (1) initiation of a drug regimen as soon as possible after an HIV-positive diagnosis, (2) strict adherence to medical advice and treatment, and (3) maintenance of a healthy diet without drug use or abuse in order to avoid taxing the immune system.

## ▪ Who Is at Risk for AIDS?

Although anyone can become infected with HIV, its routes of transmission are limited to blood, semen, vaginal fluid, and possibly some other body fluids (Grinspoon, 1994). Before the advent of AZT, mothers were more likely to pass the virus to their children prenatally or through breast milk. HIV is a virus that is not likely to survive outside of the body. Consequently, it is not spread by casual contact such as by shaking hands, touching, hugging, or kissing (although "deep" kissing with an infected person is not recommended. In addition, it does not spread through food or water, by sharing cups or glasses, by coughing and sneezing, or by using common toilets. It is not spread by mosquitoes or other insects.

The following populations are at greatest risk for contracting HIV:

- Men with a history of having had multiple homosexual or bisexual partners. Men who have sex with men account for more than half of all new HIV infections in the United States each year (53%) as well as nearly half of people living with HIV (48%) (CDC, 2010a). Although new HIV infections have declined among both heterosexuals and injection drug users, infections among MSM have been steadily increasing since the early 1990s (CDC, 2010a).
- Injecting drug users and their sexual partners.
- Heterosexuals with multiple partners.
- Infants born to HIV-infected women (approximately 10% of all HIV-positive mothers have HIV-positive babies).
- People who receive contaminated blood products such as transfusions or treatment of blood disorders. (Blood banks have improved the screening of their blood supplies since 2010.)

See **Figures 16.4** and **16.5** for a detailed breakdown of categories of estimated new HIV infections by transmission category and by type of exposure for men and adult and adolescent females in 2018. Figure 16.4 shows that approximately 70% of men with AIDS reported sex with men, and approximately 8% of people reported injection drug use. An estimated 3% of cases were attributed to male-to-male sexual contact and injection drug use, 24% were attributed to heterosexual contact, and other risk exposures accounted for the remaining 1% of cases. Figure 16.5 shows that in 2018 the majority of diagnoses of HIV infection (84.7%) among females aged 13 or older were attributed to heterosexual contact, regardless of age group; 14.7% attributed to their exposure to injection drug use; and less than 1% reported another type of exposure. Heterosexual contact is with a person known

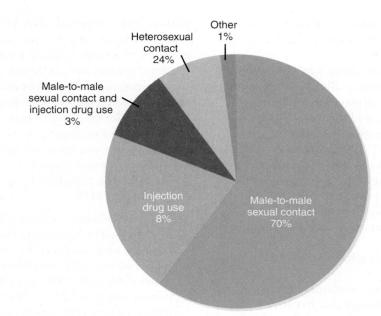

**FIGURE 16.4**   Estimated new HIV infections by transmission category: 2018 (*n* = 46,173).

Data from Centers for Disease Control and Prevention (CDC). (2019b, November 30). *HIV Surveillance Report, 2018* (Preliminary). Retrieved from https://www.cdc.gov/hiv/pdf/library/reports/surveillance/cdc-hiv-surveillance-report-2018-vol-30.pdf

to have or be at high risk for, HIV infection. Other transmission categories include blood transfusion, perinatal exposure, and risk factor not reported or not identified (CDC, 2019a).

Although not shown in Figure 16.5, the percentages attributed to heterosexual contact were higher among females 20 to 24 years of age (83.6%) than among other age groups.

### ▮ Women and Men Acquiring HIV from Drug Use

Contracting HIV is closely associated with drug abuse problems. As previously mentioned, individuals addicted to illicit drugs are currently the second largest risk group for contracting HIV. As Figure 16.5 shows, at the end of 2018 an

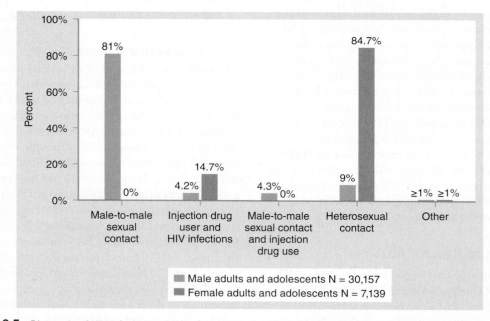

**FIGURE 16.5**   Diagnosis of HIV infections of male and female adults and adolescents by transmission categories, 2018 (*n* = 7139).

Data from Centers for Disease Control and Prevention (CDC). (2019b, November 30). *HIV Surveillance Report, 2018* (Preliminary). Retrieved from https://www.cdc.gov/hiv/pdf/library/reports/surveillance/cdc-hiv-surveillance-report-2018-vol-30.pdf

estimated 84.7% of adult and adolescent females 13 or older living with a diagnosis of HIV in the United States were women who were infected with HIV through heterosexual contact, and 14.7% of adults and adolescent females contracted HIV from injection drug use. Regarding men and women combined together, Figure 16.4 shows that 70% contracted HIV as a result of male-to-male sexual contact, 24% acquired HIV through heterosexual contact, and 8% acquired HIV from injection drug use.

HIV infections among women are attributable to injection drug and other substance use, either directly through sharing drug injection equipment contaminated with HIV or indirectly through engaging in high-risk behaviors such as unprotected sex or while under the influence of drugs or alcohol (CDC, 2013, 2020a). Several reasons account for the high incidence of this deadly infection in the drug-abusing population.

## INTRAVENOUS DRUGS

Injected drugs are those introduced into the bloodstream using a needle and syringe. Sharing drug preparation or injecting equipment increases the risk of exposure to HIV-infected blood. If an injected-drug user shares injecting equipment with a person who is HIV positive, that person's blood and the HIV virus can contaminate the needle or spread to the drug solution. The HIV virus can then be injected directly into the user's body if the infected needle and syringe are reused (AIDS.gov, 2014).

HIV-infected blood can also get into drug solutions through the following means (AIDS.gov, 2014; "Substance Use and HIV Risk," 2018):

- sharing needles;
- using blood-contaminated syringes to prepare drugs;
- reusing water;
- reusing bottle caps, spoons, or other containers ("cookers") to dissolve drugs into water and to heat drugs solutions; and
- reusing small pieces of cotton or cigarette filters ("cottons") to filter out particles that could block the needle.

Intravenous drug use has become an important factor in the spread of AIDS in the United States. Men who inject drugs accounted for 4% of HIV diagnoses, and women who inject drugs accounted for 3% of new diagnoses ("Substance Use," 2018). "Drugs can be taken in a variety of ways including drinking, smoking, snorting,

and rubbing, but it is the injection of drugs that creates the biggest risk of HIV transmission" (AVERT.org, 2013). Among severely addicted populations, intravenous drug use is often undertaken with little regard to hygiene, and injection paraphernalia such as needles, syringes, and cotton are frequently shared with other drug addicts (Millstein, 1993). Sharing HIV-contaminated injection equipment can easily result in the transmission of this virus. Sharing syringes is the second-riskiest behavior for getting HIV. Receptive anal sex is the riskiest (CDC, 2019a).

The likelihood of an intravenous drug user contracting AIDS is directly correlated with (1) the frequency of drug injections, (2) the number of partners with whom injection equipment is shared, (3) the frequency of needle sharing, and (4) the frequency of injections in locations where there are high AIDS infection rates such as in shooting galleries or crack houses (AIDS.gov, 2014; Booth, Watters, & Chitwood, 1993). Finally, "Sharing needles, syringes, or other injection equipment also puts people at risk for getting viral hepatitis. People who inject drugs (PWID). . . should talk to a doctor about getting a blood test for hepatitis B and C and getting vaccinated for hepatitis A and B" (CDC, 2019a).

## CRACK COCAINE

Cocaine is a powerfully addictive stimulant drug. The powdered form of cocaine is either inhaled through the nose (snorted) or dissolved in water and injected into the bloodstream. Crack is a form of cocaine that has been processed to make a rock crystal that users smoke. Use of crack increases the risk of contracting HIV because it can cause users to engage in risky sexual behaviors. When their financial resources are exhausted because of their drug purchases, users may turn to other ways to get the drug, such as trading sex for drugs or money, which increases their HIV-infection risk (AIDS.gov, 2014).

Compared to nonusers, crack cocaine users report the following:

- a greater number of recent and lifetime sexual partners,
- infrequent condom use,
- using more than one substance, and
- being less responsive to HIV-prevention programs.

Use of crack (Ciba Foundation, 1992), as well as other substances, such as alcohol, methamphetamine, Ecstasy, ketamine, GHB, and poppers, can alter the user's judgment and impair decisions about sex or other drug use, resulting in poor judgment and increased engagement in high-risk activities such as injection drug use and sexual risk-taking (AIDS.gov, 2014; Beard & Kunsman, 1993; Inciardi, Lockwood, & Pottieger, 1993). In particular, the use of crack and methamphetamine continue to be associated with high rates of HIV infection (AIDS.gov, 2014; Campsmith, Nakashima, & Jones, 2000). One study found that "[i]n poor, inner-city communities young smokers of crack cocaine, particularly women who have sex in exchange for money or drugs, are at a high risk for HIV infection. Crack use promotes the heterosexual transmission of HIV" (Edlin et al., 1994). As previously mentioned, crack addicts often exchange sex for drugs or money to purchase drugs (Inciardi et al., 1993; Mathias, 1993). These dangerous activities frequently occur in populations with an already high rate of HIV infection. Once infected, almost half of crack users continue to use sex to obtain their drugs and thus become sources of HIV infection for others (Diaz & Chu, 1993).

## ▮ Youth: HIV and AIDS

The CDC reports that young people in the United States are at persistent risk for HIV infection. The following are the numbers regarding HIV and AIDS diagnoses in young people (CDC, 2020b):

- In 2018, youths 13 to 24 made up 21% of the 37,832 new HIV diagnoses in the United States and dependent areas.
- Most new HIV diagnoses among youth were among young gay and bisexual men.
- From 2010 to 2017, HIV diagnoses decreased 10% among youth overall in the 50 states and the District of Columbia. Although trends varied for different groups of youth, HIV diagnoses declined for groups most affected by HIV, including young black or African American gay and bisexual men.
- Youths were the least likely to be aware of their infection compared to any other age group.
- In 2017, there were 149 deaths among youth with diagnosed HIV in the United States and dependent areas. These deaths may be the result of any cause.

- Nationwide, 19% of all students who are currently sexually active (had sexual intercourse during the previous three months) and 20% of male students who had sexual contact with other males drank alcohol or used drugs before their most recent sexual intercourse. Young people may have sex without protection (such as using a condom or taking medicine to prevent HIV) when under the influence of drugs or alcohol.
- Nationwide, 46% of all sexually active high school students and 48% of male students who had sexual contact with other males did not use a condom the last time they had sexual intercourse.
- Nearly one-quarter (24%) of male students who had sexual contact with other males reported sexual intercourse with four or more persons during their lives, compared to 10% of all students. The more sexual partners one has, the more likely sex will be with someone who has HIV and does not know it.
- Blacks or African Americans and Hispanics or Latinos are disproportionately affected by HIV compared to other racial and ethnic groups. Also, transgender women who have sex with men are among the groups at highest risk for HIV infection, and injection drug users remain at significant risk for getting HIV.

The risk of HIV and AIDS is especially notable for minority and ethnic groups. Continual HIV prevention outreach and education efforts, including programs on abstinence and delaying the initiation of sex, are required as new generations replace the generations that benefited from earlier prevention strategies.

Other important findings include the following:

- Adolescents who are most vulnerable to HIV infection include those who are homeless or runaways, juvenile offenders, and school dropouts (CDC, 2010b, 2020b).
- Worldwide, sexual intercourse is by far the most common mode of HIV transmission. In the United States, however, as many as half of all new HIV infections are associated either directly or indirectly with injection drug use (i.e., using HIV-contaminated needles to inject drugs or having sexual contact with an HIV-infected drug user) (amFAR, 2010).

Three of the principal ways adolescents become infected with HIV are as (1) high-risk sexual activity (unprotected sexual intercourse is reported by more than half of adolescents by age 17), (2) injection of substances of abuse, and (3) sex with multiple partners (CDC 2004a, 2004b, 2010b, 2016; Schaefer et al., 1993). Clearly, young people must be better educated about HIV, its transmission, and potential consequences before this epidemic becomes even more disastrous in adolescents.

## ■ What to Do About HIV and AIDS

Yep, I live with it [being HIV positive] and my partner is HIV negative. We are pretty careful with sex. The drugs they have today are really effective. Luckily I did not contract HIV until two years ago before I met my current partner. I had older friends who did not make it twelve years ago while others I knew had this disease and were able to survive until the medication became a lot more effective. I do give presentations about having HIV/AIDS to organizations that have a majority of their members who are either gay or bisexual. I figure, why not do some good for the world and help others understand that safe sex is the only way to have sex. I have written pamphlets on safe sex from an insider's perspective and give out these pamphlets and other written material each time I make a presentation. *(From Venturelli's research files, male pharmacist, age 29, June 10, 2013)*

To date, the combination of various types of protease inhibitors and antiretroviral therapy medications is the most promising treatment for remaining relatively healthy with HIV. Although protease inhibitors do not completely rid the body of HIV antibodies, this category of drugs is usually successful in holding the virus at low levels in the bloodstream. The current lack of a permanent cure makes prevention the most important element in dealing with the AIDS problem. There are two main strategies for preventing HIV:

1. *People should be encouraged to adopt safer sexual behavior.* Some of the steps to help achieve this include (a) avoiding multiple sex partners, especially if they are strangers or only casual acquaintances; (b) avoiding risk-taking sexual behavior that may allow HIV transmission such as unprotected vaginal, oral, and anal intercourse; and (c) encouraging individuals who choose to continue high-risk sexual behaviors to use condoms or insist that their sexual partner use a condom.

2. *Drug abusers should be educated about their risk of contracting AIDS.* They should be encouraged to reduce their risk by (a) abstaining from injecting drugs, (b) not sharing injection paraphernalia or always using clean needles (if available through needle-exchange programs), (c) not sharing drugs with groups with high rates of HIV infection such as those in shooting galleries or crack houses, and (d) disinfecting the equipment (cleaning and boiling equipment for at least 15 minutes) between uses if they continue to share injection equipment.

It has also been proposed that AIDS prevention efforts particularly be focused on younger gay men and injection drug users who have multiple sex partners in the high-density AIDS neighborhoods found in many large metropolitan cities throughout the United States. Even with this focused approach, no one should be fooled into thinking that the HIV and AIDS problem will be eliminated. Everyone should approach potential sexual partners with some degree of caution, especially because an HIV carrier may be unaware of infection or be reluctant to admit being a carrier for fear of abandonment. One thing is evident: If any doubt exists, we strongly recommend both partners being tested several times in a row before engaging in potentially life-threatening sexual contact.

# The Entertainment Industry and Drug Use

Musicians sing about guzzling liquor and movie stars puff cigarettes and take drugs on the big screen. However, federal officials ask, Where is the unglamorous side of substance use—the hangovers, slurred speech, or trouble with the law ("Alcohol, Tobacco, or Drugs," 1999)? Drug use has a tendency to be displayed or fueled (depending on your perspective) by popular culture. In this section, we discuss two important genres of popular culture—movies and music—as one electronic subculture that depicts and promotes drug use.

At the Lollapalooza music festival in July 1997 in an amphitheater in Massachusetts, the mostly white, suburban teen crowd cheered wildly when rap group Cypress Hill pushed a six-foot-tall bong, or water pipe, onstage. The group sold five million copies of its first two albums, one of which included songs titled "Legalize It," "Hits from the Bong," and "I Wanna Get High" (Winters, 1997).

In a research study for Columbia's Center on Addiction and Substance Abuse, 76% of 12- to 17-year-olds indicated that the entertainment industry encouraged illegal drug use. One 16-year-old daily marijuana user said, "All I know is that almost every song you listen to says something about [drug use]. It puts it into your mind constantly.... When you see the celebrities doing it, it makes it seem okay" (Winters, 1997, p. 41).

Beginning in the early 1990s, the jazz, rock, and rap music industries experienced a heroin epidemic. Although many other rock stars before Kurt Cobain used and abused drugs, Cobain's struggle with heroin and his 1994 suicide appear to have glamorized the use of this drug.

> The number of top alternative bands that have been linked to heroin through a member's overdose, arrest, admitted use, or recovery is staggering: Nirvana, Hole, Smashing Pumpkins, Everclear, Blind Melon, Skinny Puppy, 7 Year Bitch, Red Hot Chili Peppers, Stone Temple Pilots, Breeders, Alice in Chains, Sublime, Sex Pistols, Porno for Pyros, and Depeche Mode. (Schoemer, 1996, p. 50)

Together these bands have sold more than 60 million albums—"that's a heck of a lot of white, middle-class kids in the heartland" (Schoemer, 1996, p. 50).

A more recent example of normalizing recreational drug use:

> Miley Cyrus, for example, would post photos of herself on Instagram using hashtags such as "#drugaddict" and "#alcoholic." Rappers Wiz Khalifa and Snoop Dogg constantly post and discuss their affinity toward marijuana, almost making it a characteristic of who they are as a person: over 7% of Snoop Dogg's Instagram content involves the use or mentioning of drugs and alcohol. Over 76% of teenagers across America are on Instagram,

and often follow their favorite singers and celebrities. Constant exposure to this type of content is what causes its normalization: the drug use itself is glamorized, but which of these celebrities is acknowledging its consequences? Very, very few. (Scottsdale Recovery Center, 2018)

There was past where excessive drug use and glamorization of drugs occurred, characterized in the following manner.

> Since the 1970s, addiction has become something which the music industry has, in the main, been happy to see swept under the carpet. Perhaps partly because the drug of choice during the "great rave explosion" of the late 1980s and 1990s was Ecstasy, which is not considered physically addictive, the last few decades have been short on songs about addiction. There is a sizeable tranche celebrating drug indulgence, from bands like Happy Mondays, Black Grape, and Primal Scream, but the only one I can recall confronting the possibility of addiction is Oasis's "Morning Glory," which deals with the need for artificial energy in ambivalent fashion. ("Music and Drugs," 2013)

And with regard to rap music in particular, the following has been noted:

> Rap music has been shown to be a particular problem when it comes to the promotion of drugs. A study conducted by researchers at the University of California, Berkeley, found that there has been a sixfold increase in the number of references to drugs in the lyrics of rap songs over the past 20 years. Denise Herd, associate dean of students at the School of Public Health and the author of the study, says it is an alarming trend considering that rap artists are role models for so many young people. In addition, the discussion of drug use in these song lyrics is often in code, which means kids understand them and parents do not. (Ridings, 2014)

Other music genres also promote the use of drugs:

> In a surprise appearance at the Deadmau5 music festival in 2012, Madonna asked the crowd if anyone had seen Molly, which is another name for MDMA or ecstasy. Music videos are also a culprit in promoting drug

use, including videos such as Black Mountain's "Old Fangs," The Dandy Warhols' "Not If You Were the Last Junkie on Earth," Jarvis Cocker's "Synchronize," and Wavves' "No Hope Kids." (Ridings, 2014)

In the latest twist of how recreational drug use was glamorized in the past, current undercurrents of change are increasingly becoming more of a reality in the music world of rap music. An example of what currently appears to be the change within the rap music subculture is that "Many rappers who grew up around drugs have positively portrayed substance use in their music. However, in recent years, some young rap artists have detailed the consequences of addiction and mental illness to spread awareness and eliminate stigma related to substance use disorders" (Gonzales, 2020). Other of the many examples of this change include the following (Gonzales, 2020):

In February 2016, rapper Macklemore released "The Unruly Mess I've Made," a record in which addiction is a recurring topic. A few months later, he met with President Barack Obama at the White House to discuss the realities of this disease.

For years, rap music has glorified substance use, portraying getting high as an activity with little consequence. Although this trend continues, more rappers today are using their platforms to spread awareness for addiction and mental illness.

"Rap artists began releasing music that talked about the risks of crack and powdered cocaine. Kool Moe Dee and Public Enemy rapped about the perils of crack use, and Melle Mel said powdered cocaine users had "nothing to gain except killing your brain" in his song "White Lines (Don't Don't Do It)."

When looking at the "world" of rap music, we find varying eras of change in how drug use is perceived by rappers. In summary, the children of earlier rappers lived under the conditions of drug use and drug addiction of their parents, which resulted in a modification of the glamour of drug use and abuse. This newer generation of rappers interpreted their dismal surroundings and lives differently than their parents, which affected their views of drugs use and abuse and was expressed in their rap lyrics.

Other reports regarding drug use in the music industry show some change. The past president of CBS Records International and CBS Records reiterates that "[i]n the '80s, drug use was more prevalent, . . . [t]oday, it's more spotty" (Paoletta, 2004). Reasons cited for this change in drug use include growing awareness of the numbers of tragic drug overdoses and deaths of past musicians coupled with increasing pressures, demands, and cutthroat competition to remain musically successful. "Today, there is a lot more demand for an artist's time," says Flom, who has been sober since 1987. "Artists must perform at the top of their game at all times." Further, according to Warner Bros. senior vice president Liz Rosenberg, "artists on drugs can definitely slow down the promotional process. In the publicity world, this has a very strong impact" (Paoletta, 2004).

Finally, more so today, "in the ever-changing addiction scene, alcohol is a continuing problem. But doctors and counselors say such prescription painkillers as Vicodin and OxyContin have eclipsed street drugs (cocaine, heroin) during the past five years" (Paoletta, 2004).

How pervasive is drug use in today's popular movies and music? A research study found that the top types of celebrities who died from drug abuse between 1970 and 2015 were musicians (38.6%), actors (23.2%), and athletes (15.5%) (Johannes, Blackwenn, Schnakenberg, Skatulla, & Weckbecker, 2016). Other research shows there is much substance abuse in popular movies and music. Studies revealed that 98% of movies reviewed depicted illicit drugs, alcohol, tobacco, or OTC and prescription medicines. Alcohol and tobacco appeared in more than 90% of movies, and illicit drugs appeared in 22%. About one-fourth (26%) of the movies that depicted illicit drugs contained explicit, graphic portrayals of their preparation or ingestion. Substance use was almost never a central theme, and few movies ever specified motivations for use. Less than one-half (49%) of the movies portrayed short-term consequences of substance use, and about 12% depicted long-term consequences. Of the 669 adult major characters featured in the 200 movies studied, 5% used illicit drugs, 25% smoked tobacco, and 65% consumed alcohol. At least two major characters used illicit drugs in 12% of the movies, tobacco in 44%, and alcohol in 85% (Office of National Drug Control Policy, 1999).

© s_bukley/ShutterStock, Inc.

Snoop Dogg consuming a drug. Do such pictures have any effect on viewers?

One list of the 10 top drinking movies included *The Room* (2003), *Where the Dead Go to Die* (2012), *The Party* (1968), *Dazed and Confused* (1993), *Hot Shots! Part Deux* (1993), *Death Bed: The Bed that Eats* (1977), *The Last Horror Film* (1982), *The Big Lebowski* (1998), *The Langoliers,* 1995), *Seven Days to Live* (2000), *Killer Klowns from Outer Space* (1988), and *The Hangover* (2009) (Krishnan, 2019).

In all of these movies, which spanned the 20th and 21st centuries, displayed "[l]ots of people [were] drinking lots of alcohol" (Goodykoontz, 2011). A good number of these movies remain popular with movie buffs. Another news article discussing cocaine use on film sets noted that author Bob Woodward, who with Carl Bernstein first chronicled the Watergate scandal that brought down President Nixon, wrote a "detailed biography of [John] Belushi (*Wired: The Short Life and Fast Times of John Belushi*): "'lots of cocaine' was used on set both by some of the actors and members of the production team. Then, when the film came to be released, the mostly negative reviews couldn't help making indirect references to drugs" (Brown, 2013).

The following summarizes recent research findings along with other reported findings on how alcohol and other types of recreational drugs coincide with genres of music and film:

- A . . . study of music popular among adolescents from 1996–1997 revealed that nearly half (47%) of all rap/hip hop . . . songs mentioned alcohol (Roberts, Henriksen, Chritenson, Kelly & Wilson, 1999).
- Further, both alcohol and illicit drug use is also associated with other genres of music, such as heavy metal, rock, and techno (Chen, Miller, Grube, & Walters, 2006).
- "Certain drugs and the drug-dealing lifestyle are featured prominently in different types of music, . . . ." (SAMHSA, 2014).
- According to studies, adolescent listeners are most likely to abuse drugs after hearing song lyrics relating to chemical dependence. For example, teenagers who listen to music about marijuana are at a greater risk of marijuana use (Murray, 2018).
- A recent survey showed that "Many individuals at music festivals note drinking alcohol, smoking Marijuana, and using MDMA to increase the experience" (Murray, 2018).
- For example, "Cannabis users reported that they experienced greater pleasure from music when they used cannabis containing cannabidiols than when these compounds were absent" (University of Liverpool, 2018).
- Certain styles of music match the effects of certain drugs. Amphetamine, for example, is often matched with fast, repetitive music, as it provides stimulation, enabling people to dance quickly. MDMA's (ecstasy) tendency to produce repetitive movement and feelings of pleasure through movement and dance is also well known (University of Liverpool, 2018).

These findings clearly indicate that both movies and songs continue to reflect widespread use of alcohol and other drugs in our culture. Furthermore, their influence on public audiences continues to affect values and attitudes about the use and abuse of drugs. One executive director of a Washington, D.C., area youth group, said, "It's becoming increasingly difficult to administer our preventive drug programs because the youth culture has changed in a manner that a lot more of popular music idolizes the use of marijuana and hallucinogens and that has a profound effect on young people" (Haywood, 1996, p. 14).

Another top administrator at the Center for Substance Abuse Prevention of the Substance Abuse and Mental Health Services Administration agreed: "Our pop culture is sending a lot of pro-drug messages" (Haywood, 1996). A more recent study supporting alcohol use in popular music found that

> [t]oday's popular music often celebrates excessive drinking as a fun, beneficial pastime, even highlighting select booze brands in many lyrics, a new study finds. Hip-hop, rap, R&B and country songs included references to Patron tequila, Hennessy cognac, Grey Goose vodka, and Jack Daniel's whiskey, which is featured in half of the songs that mentioned alcohol. . . . Music can have a particularly powerful influence, the researchers said, because American teens spend about two and a half hours each day listening to music. (HealthDay, 2013)

In addition to these observations and findings, the major findings noted earlier with regard to substance use in movies and songs support the amount of alcohol and other drugs used in these two major types of electronic and audio media.

# The Internet Motivating Drug Use

As of 2018 in the United States, 98% of young adults aged 18 to 29 and 97% of those 30 to 49 years old use the Internet (Clement, 2020a). In 2019, most popular mobile social networking apps in the United States were mainly Facebook (90.9%), mainly Instagram (64.9%), Facebook Messenger (56.9%), Twitter (43.6%), Pinterest (35.8%), mainly Twitter (43.6%), Pinterest (35.8%), and Reddit (25.6%) (Clement, 2020b).

For recreational drug users, the top drug-related information sources were the Internet (74%), friends (75.3%), dealers (38.2%), radio and TV (17.1%), and magazines (15.7%) (Stetina, Reinhold, Cornelia, Tamara, & Kryspin-Exner, 2008). Note how recreational drug users primarily relied on the Internet and secondarily relied on friends and acquaintances for drug information and usage.

The Internet maintains a unique subculture of drug enthusiasts. Drug use information found online includes how to roll superjoints, bake marijuana-laced brownies, grow "magic" psilocybin mushrooms, and create formulas for making amphetamine-like drugs; where to purchase the latest equipment for indoor growing of marijuana; and where to obtain catalogs that offer drug paraphernalia for sale. Similarly, magazines such as *High Times* and *Hemp Times* claim growing numbers of subscribers. These magazines devote most of their articles, features, advice columns, hemp festival information, and advertisements to the pleasures of drug consumption. Further, chat rooms devoted to finding, growing, purchasing, and making drug substances are growing in popularity. Those who do not use illicit drugs are often oblivious to the chat rooms and exchange of information found on the Internet:

> "The Internet is great at proliferating this sort of [drug] information almost faster than law enforcement can really keep track of it," says Robert J. Bell, a coordinator inside the [Drug Enforcement Administration's] synthetic drug department. Once the recipe makes its way online, anyone with the financial means can order chemicals in bulk, usually from China and Southeast Asia. (Vargas-Cooper, 2012, p. 64)

A more recent and alarming occurrence is the boom in illicit drug sales online. Prescription drugs are being sold without a prescription over the Internet. Often solicitations are in the form of spam (unsolicited emails), with some people receiving multiple offers each day. The International Narcotics Control Board reported recently that "90% of online drug sales take place without a medical prescription" and that "[t]he illicit trade over the Internet has been identified as one of the major sources for prescription medicines abused by children and adolescents in certain countries such as the United States" (Join Together Online & BBC News, 2005). In addition,

> [b]illions of [doses of] controlled substances—some of them highly potent drugs such as oxycodone, equivalent to morphine, and fentanyl, which is many times stronger than morphine [as well as Viagra, Xanax, and OxyContin to name a few]—are being sold by unlicensed Internet pharmacies. (Join Together Online & BBC News, 2005)

Other reports indicated the following:

Despite new efforts to regulate Internet pharmacies, 85% of sites selling controlled drugs do not require a prescription. Most orders filled by the 365 Internet pharmacies examined were for controlled substances, especially benzodiazepines like Xanax and Valium, according to the report by the National Center on Addiction and Substance Abuse at Columbia University in New York. (Seetharaman, 2008)

According to the *Global Drugs Survey* 2015, which examines data from 100,000 responses across 50 countries, one-quarter of the 11,750 people who said they had bought drugs online had done so in 2014, more than any other year. . . . The report states: "As we suspected, access to lots of drugs for some . . . leads to experimentation with new drugs and extended drug repertoires, which may not be a good thing for some people. (Palmer, 2015)

MDMA, LSD, and forms of cannabis such as *hydro* or *herbal* are the most popular drugs purchased online. According to the Global Drugs Survey previously noted, when given access to drugs to buy online, the ones people appear to choose are the "traditional illicit" drugs that are "tried, tested, desirable, familiar and probably safer" (Palmer, 2015). Overall, the Global Drugs Survey states that "reduced rates of exposure to violence, less adulterated drugs, more confidence in product quality and removal from street dealing were clear benefits" of using the dark Web to purchase drugs (Palmer, 2015).

In addition, *USA Today* reported that "more than 10 million online messages written by teens in the past year shows they regularly chat about drinking alcohol, smoking pot, partying and hooking up" (Leinwand, 2007a). "Many of the teens who posted messages about drugs or alcohol often traded information about using illicit substances without getting hurt or caught. Some teens debated drug legalization and the drinking age. Other teens recounted their partying experiences, including sexual liaisons while drunk or high" (Leinwand, 2007a).

More recently, a yearly study by the National Center on Addiction and Substance Abuse at Columbia University, which studies situations, circumstances, and factors associated with teen substance abuse, found that

75 percent of teens said that seeing pictures on social networks of peers partying with alcohol or marijuana encourages other teens to want to party like that as well. Nearly half of teens surveyed said they have seen pictures

on Facebook or other social networking sites of kids getting drunk, passing out, or using drugs. Among teens who have seen the pictures, 47 percent said that it seems like those pictured are having a good time. (Duncan, 2012)

## ■ Social Networking Motivating Drug Use

A new form of peer pressure has emerged. *Peer pressure* has been defined as collective human behavior where the norms of a group persuade and motivate naive group members to seek and act out certain forms of behavior to achieve peer acceptance and approval. There now appears to be an additional form of peer pressure to use recreational drugs. The National Center on Addiction and Substance Abuse at Columbia University conducted a survey of 12- to 17-year-olds asking whether they spent any time on social media sites. They found that the vast majority (70%) of the teens surveyed used the sites and that 40% of all teens had "seen pictures on those sites of kids drinking or using drugs and that half of those teens were not yet teens—they were 13 years old or younger" (Reuters & Fox News Network, 2011).

According to a National Center on Addiction and Substance Abuse study,

90% of teens are initially exposed to pictures of their peers drinking, using drugs or passing out on social media before they reach the age of 15 years old. Teens who are exposed to these types of images are three times likelier to consume alcohol, and it's four times as likely that they'll use marijuana. Just as disturbingly, these teens are able to access mind-altering substances, including prescription drugs, more readily than teens who don't use social media. These teenagers are also more likely to have friends who abuse prescription and illegal drugs. ("How Does Social Media Influence Teen Drug Abuse?" 2016)

It appears that the popularity and use of drugs largely through peer pressure can be linked to teen social media websites. Research shows that as result of smartphones "24% of teen go online 'almost constantly'" (Lenhart, 2015). The top social media platforms for American teens are Facebook (71%), Instagram (52%), Snapchat (41%), and Twitter (33%).

# The Dark Web and Anonymous Drug Purchasing

## ■ The Dark Web: The Place to Anonymously Purchase Illicit Drugs?

The Internet has different layers, but most Internet users are only aware of websites that they can navigate to mainly via Google, Bing, Yahoo!, and DuckDuckGo or online databases and academic journals. In reality, most search engines just scrape the surface of the World Wide Web. There is actually much more to the web:

> When you surf the web, you really are just floating at the surface. Dive below and there are tens of trillions of pages—an unfathomable number—that most people have never seen. They include everything from boring statistics to human body parts for sale (illegally). (CNN Money, 2014)

> The deep web is estimated to be 500× the size of the Surface Web. ("The Deep Web," 2020)

How can you access and dip below the surface of the World Wide Web? A vast network is revealed once a user installs a **Tor browser** or The Onion Router (Tor) on a computer. With the Tor browser, users can browse the web anonymously, including the most hidden section of the web that can only be accessed with software that that makes the user's location anonymous (CNN Money, 2014). The Tor browser enables users to access the **Tor network** or **The Onion Router (Tor)**: "The Tor network disguises your identity by moving your traffic across different Tor servers and encrypting that traffic so it isn't traced back to you. Anyone who tries would see traffic coming from random nodes on the Tor network, rather than your computer" (Klosowski, 2014).

According to one description,

> Tor . . . [is] the darkest corner of the Internet. It's a collection of secret websites (ending in .onion) that require special software to access them. People use Tor so that their web activity can't be traced—it runs on a relay system that bounces signals among different Tor-enabled computers around the world. (Pagliery, 2014)

The Tor network largely consists of illegal porn, political dissidence, stolen credit cards, and drugs

(Pagliery, 2014). Others list the primary contents of the dark web via **Tor network or Onion Router** as consisting of black markets, selling or brokering transactions involving drugs, weapons, counterfeit currency, stolen credit card details, cyberarms, forged documents, unlicensed pharmaceuticals, steroids, and other illicit goods as well as the sale of legal products.

One alarming and controversial underground website that could only be accessed using a **Tor network** was Silk Road, which was a website that came into existence in February 2011:

> Silk Road, a digital black market that sits just below most Internet users' purview, does resemble something from a cyberpunk novel. Through a combination of anonymity technology and a sophisticated user-feedback system, Silk Road makes buying and selling illegal drugs as easy as buying used electronics—and seemingly as safe. It's Amazon—if Amazon sold mind-altering chemicals. . . .

> Here was just a small selection of the 340 items available for purchase on Silk Road by anyone, right now: a gram of Afghani hash; one-eighth of an ounce of "sour 13" weed; 14 grams of Ecstasy; 0.1 grams tar heroin. A listing for "Avatar" LSD includes a picture of blotter paper with big blue faces from the James Cameron movie on it. The sellers are located all over the world, a large portion from the U.S. and Canada. . . .

> Sellers feel comfortable openly trading hardcore drugs because the real identities of those involved in Silk Road transactions are utterly obscured. If the authorities wanted to [identify] Silk Road's users with computer forensics, they'd have nowhere to look. TOR (a specialized Internet browser) masks a user's tracks on the site. The site urges sellers to "creatively disguise" their shipments and vacuum seal any drugs that could be detected through smell. As for transactions, Silk Road doesn't accept credit cards, PayPal, or any other form of payment that can be traced

**KEY TERM**

**Tor network or The Onion Router (Tor)**
browser used to access an online network that disguises the user's identity by moving the user's traffic across different Tor servers and encrypting the traffic so that it cannot be traced back to the user's location

or blocked. The only money good here is Bitcoin. (Chen, 2011)

On October 2, 2013, after almost three years in operation as an Amazon-like marketplace for the purchase of illicit drugs over the Internet, Silk Road's alleged administrator, Ross Ulbricht, was arrested in California. The Federal Bureau of Investigation (FBI) shut down the online drug marketplace and seized billions of dollars in Bitcoin (the currency used for purchasing drugs on Silk Road) (Franceschi-Bicchierai, 2013). Although this particular website was eliminated by law enforcement officials, other types of illicit online drug marketplaces may emerge throughout the world in the years ahead given the extensive amount of money and profits confiscated by the FBI's successful sting operation. The following confirms this prediction:

> Maybe it should be no big surprise, but hours after Silk Road was shut down, web users were flocking to online forums with one question: "Where can I buy my drugs now?" The answer? Take your pick. Sites with names like Sheep Marketplace, Black Market Reloaded and Deep Bay were just some of the ones being mentioned as possibilities. (Goss, 2013)

Another report after the Silk Road website was shut down claimed the following:

> One Silk Road moderator, Libertas, posted a long, heartfelt letter to the community urging them to go on. "We have the power to fight these agents of oppression, to fight the governments that task them with that oppression, and with the fires that Silk Road has stoked in our hearts and minds we must do just that," he wrote. "No doubt we will all regroup elsewhere, and I look forward to seeing all of you again, still free and still engaging in free trade

without government interference into your personal affairs." (Jeffries, 2013)

Currently, it appears that Silk Road did become a symbolic blueprint that has fueled other Internet drug mass marketplaces.

The dark web has only grown in the years since the FBI seized the Silk Road's servers and arrested its creator in late 2013. At that time, the site had roughly 12,000 listings for items ranging from marijuana to ecstasy to heroin to counterfeit documents. The largest dark web market today, Alphabay, has far more than 300,000 listings, including more than 240,000 for drugs alone. It also offers other wares—like weapons and stolen data—that the Silk Road did not (Greenberg, 2017).

Clearly, the Internet is a more recent source for marketing illicit drugs for anyone having access to computers, and this audience includes younger teens and adults. Legal suppliers appear to be fueling the trade by providing their products to unlicensed Internet pharmacies that sell these legally restricted types of drugs (Join Together Online & BBC News, 2005). The potential impact of acquiring illicit drugs from Internet sites was emphasized by a journalist warning that we should "[f]orget the drug dealer on the corner, teens are increasingly turning to the Internet to get high" (Fiore, 2008).

Although the Internet serves as an immensely valuable medium for learning, conducting business, communicating, and making information available, it is also used by a growing number of drug users as a forum for exchanging and learning about the latest information and techniques of drug consumption and recently for purchasing illicit drugs. Individuals who use the Internet for this type of information should be particularly wary because it is difficult, if not impossible, for harmful myths and fallacies posted on the web to be regulated.

# LEARNING PORTFOLIO

## Discussion Questions

1. What are two strengths and two weaknesses of studying subcultures from (a) an insider's perspective and (b) an outsider's perspective?
2. What are the primary drugs abused by athletes?
3. What are the principal effects and side effects of steroids?
4. What factors encourage drug use by athletes?
5. From the world of steroid abusers, define and give an example of each of the following terms: *stacking, cycling, plateauing, pyramiding,* and *array.*
6. Argue both for and against drug testing in sports.
7. What types of penalties do you think should be used against athletes who abuse drugs?
8. Review the ATLAS steroid prevention program. Do you have any suggestions for how it can improve its methods for lessening steroid use among adolescents? How effective do you think this program would be at your college or university?
9. List the reasons why women are more concerned than men about drug use and abuse. Can you add several reasons not mentioned in this chapter?
10. Do you believe that drug-prevention programs should be created uniquely for males and females? Support your answer.
11. What aspects of the female role encourage the use of substances of abuse?
12. Should pregnant women who abuse drugs be punished? Why or why not?
13. Why are women who have been or are being sexually abused more likely to become addicted to drugs?
14. Why are adolescents especially vulnerable to drug abuse problems?
15. List three reasons why you think adolescents from upper-middle-class socioeconomic backgrounds become drug abusers.
16. What types of parents are most likely to have children who develop drug abuse problems?
17. How do adolescent drug abuse patterns differ from those in adults?
18. In what way are drugs of abuse associated with juvenile gang activity?
19. Should all adolescents who use drugs of abuse be treated for drug dependence? Why or why not?
20. Do you think that it is realistic to expect drug abusers to change their habits to prevent the spread of AIDS? Why or why not?
21. John was caught by city police growing psilocybin (hallucinogenic) mushrooms in his off-campus college apartment. Should John be punished by his college or university, in

## Key Terms

addition to the punishment that will be meted out by the criminal justice system? Why or why not?

22. What if you discover that your roommate is HIV positive? How would you handle this situation?

23. Do you think that the excessive use of alcohol and other drugs in movies influences viewers? Why or why not? Similarly, are people who enjoy rap or rock music affected by lyrics that refer to drug use and abuse? Why or why not?

24. Do you believe that drug information found on the Internet, such as in chat rooms devoted to the use of certain drugs (e.g., where to purchase equipment for growing marijuana, OTC stimulant pills, or psilocybin mushrooms), promote drug use? Why or why not?

25. What do you think is the future in using the dark web to purchase illicit drugs?

## Summary

1. The most common drugs abused by athletes are ergogenic (performance-enhancing) substances such as anabolic steroids, androstenedione, and Dianabol (methandrostenolone). They include the anabolic steroids for building muscle mass and strength and CNS stimulants to achieve energy, quickness, and endurance.

2. Drug testing is conducted for most professional athletic competitions and usually includes screens for steroids and stimulants. Unlike years ago, nearly all performance-enhancing drugs are now detectable. Even though athletes often go to great lengths to avoid detection, it is virtually impossible to mask drug usage tests.

3. About 50% of the anabolic steroids used in the United States are prescribed by doctors; the other 50% are obtained from the black market, which includes an unknown percentage that are purchased on Internet websites. Currently, the Internet is the most widely used means of buying and selling anabolic steroids. Steroids are also bought and sold at gyms, bodybuilding competitions, and schools through teammates, coaches, and trainers. Black market steroids include drugs diverted from legitimate channels smuggled from foreign countries (e.g., Brazil, Italy, Mexico, Great Britain, Portugal, France, and Peru) that are designated for veterinarian use or inactive counterfeits.

4. The Athletes Training and Learning to Avoid Steroids (ATLAS) program was developed to promote drug prevention and health promotion among adolescent high school athletes. It emphasizes the negative impact of anabolic steroids, alcohol, and other drugs on immediate sports performance. Athletes, coaches, and team leaders are trained to educate team members about the effects of anabolic steroid abuse. They emphasize both desirable and adverse effects of steroid use so that adolescents well know how anabolic steroids build muscles and can increase athletic abilities.

5. Women who use drugs are uniquely affected by their sexual and gender differences when compared to men. The most common types of abused drugs (in descending order) for females were alcohol (83.2%), flavored alcoholic beverages (57.2%), any illicit drug use (40.8%), marijuana (36.9%), binge drinking (five or more drinks in a row in the last two weeks) (27.4%), cigarettes (20.2%), and any illicit drug other than marijuana (17.4%).

6. In general, women are more likely than men to (a) be concerned about drugs and drug use, (b) believe in drug prevention programs such as needle exchange and testing reckless drivers for drug use, and (c) speak with their children about drug use.

7. There is a high prevalence of drug dependence in women who are victims of sexual or physical abuse. Approximately 70% of women in drug abuse treatment report histories of physical abuse, with victimization beginning at 11 years of age and occurring repeatedly. Further, women and men have

different endocrine (hormone) systems and reproductive organs and structures, and women's responses to drugs vary according to their reproductive state.

8. For women to receive adequate treatment for drug dependence, certain considerations must be met: (a) availability of female-sensitive services, (b) nonpunitive and noncoercive treatment that incorporates supportive behavioral change approaches, and (c) treatment for a wide range of medical problems, mental disorders, and psychosocial problems.

9. Most adolescents who use substances of abuse are going through normal psychosocial development and will not develop problematic dependence on these drugs. The adolescent users who have difficulty with drugs often lack coping skills to deal with their problems, have dysfunctional families, possess poor self-images, or feel socially and emotionally insecure.

10. Parents who are most likely to raise drug-abusing adolescents are (a) either drug abusers themselves or are vehemently against recreational drug use, (b) overly demanding and authoritarian, (c) overly protective, and (d) unable to communicate effectively with their children.

11. Recent surveys regarding drug use patterns found that by 12th grade approximately 66.0% of teens had used alcohol, approximately 34.4% had used cigarettes, approximately 44.4% had used marijuana, and 6.5% had used inhalants in 2014. A *Monitoring the Future* survey indicated that, in 2015, 18.30% of 12th graders had abused prescription drugs and that, after marijuana and alcohol, prescription and over-the-counter drugs were the most commonly abused substances by Americans age 14 and older.

12. Research continues to show that the most important factor influencing drug use among adolescents is peer drug use.

13. People who become gang members were often neglected by their parents, lacked positive role models, and failed to receive adequate adult supervision. Other motivations for joining a gang include peer pressure, low self-esteem, and perceived easy acquisition of money from gang-related drug dealing and other criminal activities.

14. The major reasons cited by college students for their use of drugs were: (a) breaks the ice, (b) enhances social activity, (c) gives people something to do, (d) gives people something to talk about, (e) allows people to have more fun, (f) peer bonding, (g) male bonding, (h) facilitates sex, (i) female bonding, and (j) makes it easier to deal with stress.

15. Two interesting findings from research regarding drug use by college student subcultures are that (a) the best predictor of drug use for first-year college students is drug use during a typical month in the senior year of high school and (b) recreational drug use usually does not begin in college but has already been established in high school. A more recent finding includes personality dispositions to risky behavior as a predictor of first-year college drinking (mainly impulsivity and sensation-seeking types of students).

16. Club drugs include MDMA (Ecstasy or Molly), GHB, Rohypnol, ketamine, methamphetamine, and LSD. The term *club drug* is derived from the use of these drugs at all-night dance parties such as raves or trances, dance clubs, and bars. All these drugs are colorless, tasteless, and odorless. Individuals who want to intoxicate, sedate, and later sexually take advantage of others can furtively add them to beverages.

17. Estimated new HIV infections in 2018 by transmission category are male-to-male sexual contact (70%), heterosexual contact (24%), injection drug use (8%), male-to-male sexual contact and injection drug use (3%), and other causes (not specified) (1%).

18. Approximately 1.1 million people in the United States are living with HIV today. About 14% of them (one in seven) do not know it and need testing.

19. Black or African American gay and bisexual men accounted for the largest number of HIV diagnoses (9,499), followed by Hispanic or Latinos (7,543) and whites (6,423).

20. Among all gay and bisexual men, HIV diagnoses remained stable from 2010 to 2017, but trends varied by race and ethnicity.

21. Major ways to prevent contracting HIV include (a) engaging in safe (protected) sexual behavior, (b) avoiding use of contaminated drug paraphernalia and especially use of intravenous drugs, (c) avoiding use of drugs in groups with high rates of HIV infection, and (d) frankly discussing past sexual histories with potential sexual partners and, if in any doubt, having potential partners be tested for HIV several times in a row.

22. The extent of alcohol and drug use in movies and songs is startling. One study found that 98% of reviewed movies depicted illicit drugs, alcohol, tobacco, or OTC or prescription medicines. In this same detailed study, alcohol appeared in 93% of the movies and in 17% of the songs; tobacco appeared in 89% of movies but only 3% of songs. The lyrics of 63% of rap songs versus about 10% of the lyrics in other categories had substance references.

23. More recent reports regarding drug use in the music industry show change. Reasons cited for this change in drug use include growing awareness of the numbers of tragic drug overdoses and deaths of past musicians coupled with increasing pressures, demands, and cutthroat competition to remain musically successful.

24. New media influences contribute to drug use. An underground website called Silk Road came into existence in February 2011. It was like an eBay or Amazon in the world of drug purchasing over the Internet. It was shut down by the FBI in 2013. Although the Internet serves as an immensely valuable medium for learning, conducting business, communicating, and making information available, it is also used by a growing number of drug users as a forum for exchanging and learning about the latest information and techniques of drug consumption and recently for purchasing illicit drugs.

25. The Internet is considered to be the latest burgeoning source of information about using illicit drugs. The Internet has a layer beyond what we know as the World Wide Web. Using software known as The Onion Router (Tor), people can access the Tor network, much of which consists of illegal porn, political dissidence, stolen credit cards, and drugs.

# References

Aguirre, J. C. (2012, July 27). Cost of treatment still a challenge for HIV patients in U.S. NPR. Retrieved from http://www.npr.org/blogs/health/2012/07/27/157499134/cost-of-treatment-still-a-challenge-for-hiv-patients-in-u-s

"AIDS fear: Complacency—Infection rate is on rise for first time since 1994." (2003, August 21): *Post-Tribune* [Crown Point, IN], p. A-10.

AIDS.gov. (2012, June 6). HIV/AIDS 101: Signs and symptoms. Washington, DC: U.S. Department of Health and Human Services. Retrieved from http://aids.gov/hiv-aids-basics/hiv-aids-101/signs-and-symptoms/

AIDS.gov. (2014, January 14). How can using drugs put me at risk for getting or transmitting HIV? Washington, DC: U.S. Department of Health and Human Services. Retrieved from at https://www.aids.gov/hiv-aids-basics/prevention/reduce-your-risk/substance-abuse-use/

"Alcohol, tobacco, or drugs used in 98% of popular movies." (1999, April 29) *News Tribune*, pp. 7–8, 14.

Altschuler, C. (2017, October 13). College using sober dorms to combat alcohol, drug addiction. *Chicago Tribune*. Retrieved from https://www.chicagotribune.com/lifestyles/sc-fam-sober-dorms-1017-story.html

American Academy of Child and Adolescent Psychiatry. (2004). *Facts for families: Teen suicide.* Washington, DC: Author. Retrieved from http://www.aacap.org/cs/root/facts_for_families/teen_suicide

American Academy of Child and Adolescent Psychiatry. (2006). *Facts for families: Normal adolescent development.* Number 57. Washington, DC: Author.

American Academy of Child and Adolescent Psychiatry. (2011). *Teens: Alcohol and other drugs.* Number 3. Washington, DC: Author.

American Academy of Child and Adolescent Psychiatry. (2013). *Facts for families guide: Teen suicide.* Number 10. Washington, DC: Author.

American Addiction Centers. (2020). College drug abuse. Brentwood, TN: Author.

American Foundation for AIDS Research (amfAR). (2001). *Facts about HIV/AIDS, 2001.* New York, NY: Body Health Resources Corporation.

American Foundation for AIDS Research (amfAR). (2010). *Facts for life: What you and the people you care about need to know about HIV/AIDS.* New York, NY: Author.

Anabolics.com. (2016). Steroid laws. Humble, TX: Dynamic Sports Nutrition. Retrieved from http://www.anabolics.com/pages/Steroid-Laws#.VxsgGaMrKS4

Anonymous, as told by Penn, N. (2005, September). Confession: Why I juiced. *Gentleman's Quarterly,* pp. 292–297.

Anxiety and Depression Association of America. (2016, August). Facts and statistics. Silver Spring, MD: Author. Retrieved from https://www.adaa.org/about-adaa/press-room/facts-statistics

Apostolides, M. (1996, September–October). How to quit the holistic way. *Psychology Today, 29,* 30–43, 75–76.

Archambault, D. (1992). Adolescence, a physiological, cultural and psychological no man's land. In G. Lawson & A. Lawson (Eds.), *Adolescent substance abuse, etiology, treatment and prevention* (pp. 11–28). Gaithersburg, MD: Aspen.

AVERT.org. (2013). Injecting drug users and HIV/AIDS. Retrieved from http://www.avert.org/hiv-injecting-drug-users.htm

Bahr, S. J., Marcos, A. C., & Maughan, S. L. (1995). Family, educational and peer influences on alcohol use of female and male adolescents. *Journal of Studies on Alcohol, 56,* 457–469.

Baltieri, D. A., & de Andrad, A. G. (2008). Alcohol and drug consumption and sexual impulsivity among sexual offenders. In J. V. Fenner (Ed.), *Sexual offenders: Management, treatment and bibliography* (pp. 73–96). New York, NY: Nova Science.

Bartlett. J. G. (2006). Ten years of HAART: Foundation for the future. Medscape. Retrieved from https://www.medscape.org/viewarticle/523119

Beard, B., & Kunsman, V. (1993, September–October). A cause for concern: Alcohol-induced risky sex on college campuses. *Prevention Pipeline, 6,* 24.

Begley, S., Brant, M., Dickey, C., Helmstaedt, K., Nordland, R., & Hayden, T. (1999, February 15). The real scandal. *Newsweek, 133,* 48–54.

Bell, J. (1987, March). Athletes' use and abuse of drugs. *The Physician and Sports Medicine, 15,* 99–108.

Belsie, L. (1995, August 30). Temperance movement hits college dorms. *Christian Science Monitor, 87,* 1–2.

"Ben Johnson: I was nailed on a cross for taking steroids at Seoul Olympics—25 years later I'm still being punished." (2013, September 24). *The Daily Telegraph* [London, UK]. Retrieved from http://www.telegraph.co.uk/sport/othersports/athletics/10329995/Ben-Johnson-I-was-nailed-on-a-cross-for-taking-steroids-at-Seoul-Olympics-25-years-later-Im-still-being-punished.html

Bergeret, J. (1981). *Young people, drugs . . . and others.* Rockville, MD: United Nations Office for Drug Control and Crime Prevention.

Beschner, G., & Friedman, A. (1985). Treatment of adolescent drug abusers. *International Journal of the Addictions, 20,* 977–993.

Blueprints for Healthy Youth Development. (2020). *Athletes Training and Learning to Avoid Steroids (ATLAS).* Boulder CO: Blueprints for Healthy Youth Development, Institute of Behavioral Science, University of Colorado Boulder. Retrieved from https://www.blueprintsprograms.org/programs/64999999/athletes-training-and-learning-to-avoid-steroids-atlas/

Blum, R. (2009, February 18). Rodriguez: "Amateur hour." *Post-Tribune* [Crown Point, IN], p. A11.

"Bodybuilding drug yields 'high.'" (1992, June). *Pharmacy Times,* p. 14.

Booth, R., Watters, J., & Chitwood, D. (1993). HIV risk-related sex behaviors among injection drug users, crack smokers, and injection drug users who smoke crack. *American Journal of Public Health, 83,* 1144–1148.

"Boredom, stress, money linked to drug abuse." (2003, August 20). *Chesterton/Valparaiso Post Tribune* [IN], pp. A1, A8.

Brady, T. M., & Ashley, O. S. (Eds.). (2005). *Women in substance abuse treatment: Results from the Alcohol and Drug Services Study (ADSS).* DHHS Pub. No. SMA 04–3968, Analytic Series A–26. Rockville, MD: Substance Abuse and Mental Health Services Administration, Office of Applied Studies.

Brandenburg, J. R. (2004, January 1). The use of ergogenic aids among high school athletes in eastern Kentucky [Thesis]. Huntington, WV: Marshall University. Retrieved from http://mds.marshall.edu/cgi/viewcontent.cgi?article=1509&context=etd

Britannica.com. (2010, October 31). Alex Rodriguez. Encyclopedia Britannica Online. Retrieved from http://www.britannica.com/EBchecked/topic/914723/Alex-Rodriguez

Brown, A. M. (2013, July 22). Drug use on film sets—You'd be amazed by how much of it goes on. *The*

*Telegraph* [London, UK]. Retrieved from http://blogs .telegraph.co.uk/news/andrewmcfbrown/100021797 /drug-use-on-film-sets-%E2%80%93-youd-be-amazed -by-how-much-of-it-goes-it-on/

Buckstein, D., Brent, D., Perper, J., Moritz, G., Baugher, M., Schweers, J., et al. (1993). Risk factors for completed suicide among adolescents with a lifetime history of substance abuse: A case-control study. *Acta Psychiatrica Scandinavia, 88*, 403–408.

Burke, C., & Davis, S. (1992, June). Anabolic steroid abuse. *Pharmacy Times*, pp. 35–40.

Buurman, W. (2010, August). "When drugs and music overlap." *Matters of Substance*, 20. NZ (New Zealand) Drug Foundation. Retrieved from https://www.drug foundation.org.nz/matters-of-substance/august-2010 /when-drugs-and-music-overlap/

Burn-Murdoch, J. (2012, July 4). Doping in Olympic events: How does each sport compare? *The Guardian* [London, UK]. Retrieved from http://www.guardian. co.uk/sport/datablog/2012/jul/04/olympics-2012 -athletics

Bussing-Burks, M. (2013, July 9). Alcohol and drug use increases suicidal behaviors. National Bureau of Economic Research. Retrieved from http://www.nber.org /digest/aug02/w8810.html

Butler, A. (2010, May). Adolescent identity development: Who we are. Ithaca, NY: Cornell University Family Life Development Center and ACT Youth Center of Excellence. Retrieved from http://www.actforyouth.net /resources/n/n_adol_identity/

Campsmith, M. L., Nakashima, A. K., & Jones, J. L. (2000, October 1). Association between crack cocaine use and high-risk sexual behaviors after HIV diagnosis. *Journal of Acquired Immune Deficiency Syndrome, 25*, 192–198.

Canseco, J. (2005). *Juiced: Wild times, rampant 'roids, smash hits, and how baseball got big*. New York, NY: HarperCollins.

CBS News. (2013, May 21). By the numbers: Chicago-Area gangs. CBS Interactive.

Centers for Disease Control and Prevention (CDC). (2004a). *Estimated AIDS cases among male adolescents and young adults by exposure category, diagnosed through 2002, United States*. Atlanta, GA: Author.

Centers for Disease Control and Prevention (CDC). (2004b). *HIV/AIDS surveillance report, 2003*. Vol. 15. Atlanta, GA: Author.

Centers for Disease Control and Prevention (CDC). (2010a). *HIV and AIDS in America: A snapshot*. Atlanta, GA: Author.

Centers for Disease Control and Prevention (CDC). (2010b). *HIV in the United States*. Atlanta, GA: Author.

Centers for Disease Control and Prevention (CDC). (2010c). *Questions and answers on the use of HIV medications to help prevent the transmission of HIV*. Atlanta, GA: Author.

Centers for Disease Control and Prevention (CDC). (2013). HIV among women: Fact sheet. Atlanta, GA: Author.

Centers for Disease Control and Prevention (CDC). (2015). Substance use during pregnancy. (September 9). Atlanta, GA: Author. Retrieved from http://www.cdc .gov/reproductivehealth/maternalinfanthealth /tobaccousepregnancy/

Centers for Disease Control and Prevention (CDC). (2016, April 27). HIV among youth. Atlanta, GA: Author.

Centers for Disease Control and Prevention (CDC). (2019a). Injection drug use and HIV risk. (August). Atlanta, GA: Author. Retrieved from https://www.cdc .gov/hiv/pdf/risk/cdc-hiv-idu-fact-sheet.pdf

Centers for Disease Control and Prevention (CDC). (2019b, November 30). *HIV Surveillance Report, 2018* (Preliminary). Retrieved from https://www.cdc.gov/hiv/pdf /library/reports/surveillance/cdc-hiv-surveillance -report-2018-vol-30.pdf

Centers for Disease Control and Prevention (CDC). (2019c, November). *HIV surveillance Report, 2018* (Preliminary); vol. 30. Retrieved from http://www.cdc.gov/hiv/library /reports/hiv-surveillance.html

Centers for Disease Control and Prevention (CDC). (2020a). HIV and women. (April 2). Atlanta, GA: Author. Retrieved from https://www.cdc.gov/hiv/group /gender/women/index.html

Centers for Disease Control and Prevention (CDC). (2020b). HIV and youth. (April 6). Atlanta, GA: Author.

Chen, A. (2011, June 1). The underground website where you can buy any drug imaginable. Kotaku. Retrieved from https://www.wired.com/2011/06/silkroad-2

Chen, M-J, Miller, B. A., Grube, J. W., & Walters, E. D., (2006, May). "Music substance use, and aggression." *Journal of Studies Alcohol and Drugs, 67*, 373–381.

Chilet-Rosell, E. (2014). Gender bias in clinical research, pharmaceutical marketing, and the prescription of drugs. Bethesda, MD: Global Health Action. Retrieved from https://www.ncbi.nlm.nih.gov/pmc/articles/PMC 4262757/

Child Trends. (2009). Adolescents Training and Learning to Avoid Steroids program (ATLAS). Bethesda, MD: Author.

Chong, J.-R. (2006, August 13). Study casts positive light on AIDS drug. *Los Angeles Times* (reported in *Post-Tribune* [Crown Point, IN]), p. A9.

Ciba Foundation. (1992). AIDS and HIV infection in cocaine users. In G. Block & J. Whelan (Eds.), *Cocaine: Scientific and social dimensions* (pp. 181–194). New York, NY: Wiley.

Clark, E. (2010). *HIV progress and prevention.* Boston, MA: Science in the News (SITN), Harvard Graduate School of Arts and Sciences.

Clement, J. (2020a). U.S. adult Internet usage reach 2000–2018, by age group. Statista. Retrieved from https://www.statista.com/statistics/184389/adult-internet-users-in-the-us-by-age-since-2000/

Clement, J. (2020b). Most popular social media apps in the U.S. 2029, by reach. Statista. Retrieved from https://www.statista.com/statistics/579334/most-popular-us-social-networking-apps-ranked-by-reach/

CNN Money. (2014). What is the deep web? Retrieved from http://money.cnn.com/infographic/technology/what-is-the-deep-web/?iid=EL

Coile, Z. (2005, April 27). House bill seeks to toughen steroid rules: Athletes in all leagues would be held to the strict standards used in Olympics. *San Francisco Chronicle,* pp. 1–2

CollegeExpress.com. (2016). Schools offering substance-free housing. Retrieved from http://www.collegexpress.com/lists/list/schools-offering-substance-free-housing/1663/

CRC Health Group. (2007). Drug use among youth: Facts and statistics. Retrieved from http://www.adolescent-substance-abuse.com

Crowley, G. (1996, December 2). Targeting a deadly scrap of genetic code. *Newsweek,* pp. 68–69.

Curry, D. G., & Spergel, I. A. (1997). Gang homicide, delinquency, and community. In G. L. Mays (Ed.), *Gangs and gang behavior* (pp. 314–336). Chicago, IL: Nelson-Hall.

Cyders, M. A., Flory, K., Rainer, S., & Smith, G. T. (2009). The role of personality dispositions to risky behavior in predicting first-year college drinking. *Addiction, 104,* 193–202.

Daily, S. (1992a). Alcohol, incest, and adolescence. In G. Lawson & A. Lawson (Eds.), *Adolescent substance abuse, etiology, treatment and prevention* (pp. 251–266). Gaithersburg, MD: Aspen.

Daily, S. (1992b). Suicide solution: The relationship of alcohol and drug abuse to adolescent suicide. G. Lawson & A. Lawson (Eds.), In *Adolescent substance abuse, etiology, treatment and prevention* (pp. 233–250). Gaithersburg, MD: Aspen.

Destinations to Recovery. (2014, September 25). Teen alcohol and drug use—How it impacts suicide rates. Woodland Hills, CA: Author.

Diaz, T., & Chu, S. (1993). Crack cocaine use and sexual behavior among people with AIDS. *Journal of the American Medical Association, 269,* 2845–2846.

Dicker, M., & Leighton, E. A. (1994). Trends in the U.S. prevalence of drug-using parturient women and drug-affected newborns, 1979 through 1990. *American Journal of Public Health, 84,* 1433.

Docherty, J. R. (2008). Pharmacology of stimulants prohibited by the World Anti-Doping Agency (WADA). *British Journal of Pharmacology, 154,* 606–622.

Donaldson-Evans, C. (2007, June 27). Wrestler Chris Benoit double murder-suicide: Was it "roid rage"? FoxNews.com. Retrieved from http://www.foxnews.com/printer_friendly_story/0,3566,286834,00.html

"Doping in sports—a deadly game." (2011). TheAthlete.org. Retrieved from http://www.theathlete.org/doping-in-sport.htm

Drug and Alcohol Rehab Florida. (2012, October 8). The effects of drug abuse on your reproductive system. Retrieved from http://www.drugrehabfl.net/the-effects-of-drug-abuse-on-your-reproductive-system/

Drug Enforcement Administration (DEA). (2015). *Drugs of abuse.* Washington, DC: Author. Retrieved from http://www.dea.gov/pr/multimedia-library/publications/drug_of_abuse.pdf#page=76

Drug Strategies. (1998). Drug use and attitudes. In *Keeping score* (pp. 4–10). Washington, DC: Author. Retrieved from http://www.drugstrategies.com/wp-content/uploads/2014/05/ks_1998.pdf

Drugs.com. (2020). Biktarvy prices, coupons and patient assistance programs. Retrieved from https://www.drugs.com/price-guide/biktarvy

D'Souza, M. (2018). 10 famous athletes who were caught doping. *Edgar.* Retrieved from https://edgardaily.com/articles/10-famous-athletes-caught-doping/

Duncan, K. (2012). Online-only: Survey finds some kids use drugs, drink during school day. *The Nation's Health, 42.* Retrieved from http://thenationshealth.aphapublications.org/content/42/9/E46.full

Dvorchak, R. (2005, April 27). Former Steeler Courson outlines solutions for steroid use. Black and Gold. Retrieved from http://blackandgoldworld.blogspot.com/2005/04/robert-dvorchak-courson-outlines.html

EBSCO. (2013). Reverse transcriptase inhibitors. Retrieved from https://healthlibrary.epnet.com/GetContent.aspx?token=e0498803-7f62-4563-8d47-5fe33da65dd4&chunkiid=111797

Edlin, B. R., Irwin, K. L., Faruque, S., McCoy, C. B., Word, C., Serrano, Y., . . . , & Holmberg, S. D. (1994, November 24). Intersecting epidemics—Crack cocaine use and HIV infection among inner-city young adults. *New England Journal of Medicine, 331,* 1422–1427.

Eilek, R. (2005, April 17). Pro sports keep heads in sand on steroids. *San Diego Union Tribune.*

Elmen, J., & Offer, D. (1993). Normality, turmoil and adolescence. In P. Tolan & B. Cohler (Eds.), *Handbook of clinical research and practice with adolescents* (pp. 5–19). New York, NY: Wiley.

Erickson, P. G., & Murray, G. F. (1989). Sex differences in cocaine use and experiences: A double standard revived? *American Journal of Drug and Alcohol Abuse, 15,* 135–152.

ESPN.com. (2005, April 26). Strong suspended for performance-enhancing drugs. Retrieved from http://sports.espn.go.com/mlb/news/story?id=2046762

ESPN.com. (2007, July 27). Steroids discovered in probe slayings, suicide. Retrieved from http://sports.espn.go.com/espn/news/story?id=2917133

Fagan, J. (1990). Social processes of delinquency and drug use among urban gangs. In C. R. Huff (Ed.) *Gangs in America* (pp. 183–213). Newbury Park, CA: Sage.

Ferrente, R. (1993, March 8). Ben Johnson retires from running after positive test. NPR.

Fiore, M. (2008, September 9). Using the Internet to get high. FoxNews.com. Retrieved from http://www.foxnews.com/story/0,2933,419582,00.html

Franceschi-Bicchierai, L. (2013, October 4). The Silk Road online drug marketplace by the numbers. Mashable. Retrieved from http://mashable.com/2013/10/04/silk-road-by-the-numbers/

Funk, L. (2010, August 19). Shocking school drug and gang survey. Democraticunderground.com. Retrieved from http://www.democraticunderground.com/discuss/duboard.php?az=view_all&address=389x8980990

Futures. (2016). Why drug addiction differs in men and women. Futures of Palm Beach. Retrieved from https://www.futuresofpalmbeach.com/addictions/why-drug-addiction-differs-in-men-and-women/

Gilead. (2019). BIKTARVY prescribing information. Foster City, CA: Author. Retrieved from https://www.biktarvyhcp.com/efficacy-resistance/treatment-naive

Gleeson, S. (2019, May 24). Lance Armstrong "wouldn't change a thing" on doping before "most colossal meltdown." *USA Today.* Retrieved from https://www.usatoday.com/story/sports/cycling/2019/05/24/lance-armstrong-wouldnt-change-thing-doping-scandal/1219465001/

Gloucester County College. (2013). Crime prevention and safety: Alcohol and drug abuse on campus. Sewell, NJ: Author. Retrieved from http://www.gccnj.edu/security/crime_prevention_safety/alcohol_and_drug_abuse.cfm

Goldberg, L., Elliot, D., Clarke, G. N., MacKinnon, D. P., Moe, E., Zoref, L., . . . , & Lapin, A. (1996). Effects of a multidimensional anabolic steroid prevention intervention: The Adolescents Training and Learning to Avoid Steroids (ATLAS) program. *Journal of the American Medical Association, 276,* 1555–1562.

Goldstein, F. (1995). Pharmacological aspects of substance abuse. In A. R. Genaro and M. Easton (Eds.), *Remington's pharmaceutical sciences,* 19th ed. (pp. 780–794). Easton, PA: Mack.

Gonzales, M., McEnery, K., Sheehan, T., & Mellody, S. (1986). *America's habit: Drug abuse, drug trafficking, and organized crime.* Washington, DC: President's Commission on Organized Crime.

Gonzales, M. (2020, November 27). Rap music and substance use: Addiction and mental health. DrugRehab.com. Retrieved from https://www.drugrehab.com/featured/substance-use-and-rap-music/

Goodykoontz, B. (2011, October 27). "Big Lebowski," "Animal House" make list of 10 top drinking movies. *Chicago Sun-Times.* Retrieved from http://www.suntimes.com/entertainment/movies/8442007-421/big-lebowski-arthur-animal-house-among-top-drinking-movies-ever-made.html

Goss, D. (2013, October 4). Web's black market peddles drugs, guns and more. CNN Tech. Retrieved from at http://www.cnn.com/2013/10/04/tech/web/internet-black-market/index.html

Green, C. A. (2006). *Gender and use of substance abuse treatment services* (pp. 1–12). Bethesda, MD: National Institute on Alcohol Abuse and Alcoholism.

Greenberg, A. (2017, May 23). The Silk Road creator's life sentence actually boosted dark web drug sales. *Wired.* Retrieved from https://www.wired.com/2017/05/silk-road-creators-life-sentence-actually-boosted-dark-web-drug-sales/

Grinspoon, L. (1994, January). AIDS and mental health—Part 1. *Harvard Mental Health Letter, 10,* 1–4.

Harlan, R., & Garcia, M. (1992). Neurobiology of androgen abuse. In R. Watson (Ed.), *Drugs of abuse and neurobiology* (p. 186). Boca Raton, FL: CRC Press.

Harris, W. (2013). 10 performance-enhancing drugs that aren't steroids. HowStuffWorks. Retrieved from http://science.howstuffworks.com/10-performance-enhancing-drugs.htm

Haywood, R. L. (1996, September 9). Why more young people are using drugs. *Jet* (p. 90).

Hazelden Betty Ford Foundation. (2020). Early warning signs of teen substance use. Center City, MN: Author. Retrieved from https://www.hazeldenbettyford.org/articles/warning-signs-teen-substance-use

HealthDay. (2013, August 23). Alcohol dominates in pop music lyrics: Study. Baltimore, MD: Johns Hopkins Bloomberg School of Public Health. Retrieved from https://consumer.healthday.com/general-health-information-16/alcohol-abuse-news-12/alcohol-dominates-in-pop-music-lyrics-study-679680.html

Henslin, J. M. (2014). *Social problems: A down-to-earth approach*, 11th ed. Upper Saddle River, NJ: Pearson Higher Education.

Hingson, R. W., Zha, W., & Weitzman, E. R. (2009). Magnitude of and trends in alcohol-related mortality and morbidity among U.S. college students ages 18–24, 1998–2005. *Journal of Studies on Alcohol and Drugs*, Suppl. No. 16, pp. 12–20.

Hoberman, J. M., & Yesalis, C. E. (1995, February). The history of synthetic testosterone. *Scientific American*, 272(2), 76–81.

Holdcroft, A. (2007). Gender bias in research: How does it affect evidence based medicine? *Journal of the Royal Society of Medicine, 100*, 2–3.

Hoshino, J. (1992). Assessment of adolescent substance abuse. In G. Lawson & A. Lawson (Eds.), *Adolescent substance abuse, etiology, treatment and prevention* (pp. 87–104). Gaithersburg, MD: Aspen, 1992.

Howard, M. (1992). Adolescent substance abuse: A social learning theory perspective. In G. Lawson & A. Lawson (Eds.), *Adolescent substance abuse, etiology, treatment and prevention* (pp. 29–40). Gaithersburg, MD: Aspen.

"How does social media influence teen drug abuse?" (2016, April 17). Keys Rehab. Retrieved from http:// www.12keysrehab.com/blog/how-does-social-media -influence-teen-drug-abuse/

Inciardi, J. A., Lockwood, D., & Pottieger, A. E. (1993). *Women and crack-cocaine*. New York, NY: Macmillan.

Jayson, S. (2007, April 5). Expert: Risky teen behavior is all in the brain. *USA Today*. Retrieved from http://www .usatoday.com/news/health/2007-04-04-teen-brain_N .htm

Jeffries, A. (2013, October 4). After Silk Road's demise, online drug dealing moves to new sites. The Verge. Retrieved from http://www.theverge.com/2013/10/4 /4799770/drug-dealers-set-up-mini-silk-roads-after -federal-bust

Johnson, R. A., Hoffmann, J. P., & Gerstein, D. R. (1996, July). *The relationship between family structure and adolescent substance use*. Rockville, MD: Substance Abuse and Mental Health Services Administration, Office of Applied Studies.

Johnston, L. D., Miech, R. A., O'Malley, P. M., Bachman, J. G., Schulenberg, J. E., & Patrick, M. E. (2019). *Monitoring the Future National Survey Results on Drug Use: 1975–2018: Overview, key findings on adolescent drug use*. Ann Arbor, MI: University of Michigan, Institute for Social Research.

Johnston, L. D., O'Malley, P. M., & Bachman, J. G. (1993). *National Survey Results from the Monitoring the Future Study, 1975–1992*. Rockville, MD: National Institute on Drug Abuse.

Johnston, L. D., O'Malley, P. M., Bachman, J. G., & Schulenberg, J. E. (2009). *Monitoring the Future: National results on adolescent drug use 1975–2008. Volume I: Secondary school students 2008*. Bethesda, MD: National Institute on Drug Abuse.

Johnston, L. D., O'Malley, P. M., Bachman, J. G., Schulenberg, J. E., & Miech, R. A. (2015). *Monitoring the Future: National survey results on drug use, 1975–2014: Volume 2, College students and adults ages 19–55*. Ann Arbor, MI: University of Michigan, Institute for Social Research.

Johnston, L. D., O'Malley, P. M., Miech, P. M., Bachman, R. A., & Schulenberg, J. E. (2016). *Monitoring the Future national survey results on drug use, 1975–2015: Overview, key findings on adolescent drug use*. Ann Arbor, MI: University of Michigan, Institute for Social Research.

Johannes, J. M., Blackwenn, M., Schnakenberg, R., Skatulla, P., & Weckbecker, K. (2016, December 9). Drug-related celebrity deaths: A cross-sectional study. *Substance Abuse Treatment Prevention Policy, 22* [online]. Retrieved from https://www.ncbi.nlm.nih.gov/pmc /articles/PMC5148833/

Join Together Online & BBC News. (2005). *Illicit drug sales booming online*. Boston, MA: Boston University School of Public Health.

Kandel, D. B. (1980). Drug and drinking behavior among youth. *Annual Review of Sociology, 6*, 235–285.

Kantrowitz, B., & Wingert, P. (1999, May 10). Beyond Littleton: How well do you know your kid? *Newsweek*.

Kennedy, M. C. (2000). Newer drugs used to enhance sporting performance. *Medical Journal of Australia, 273*, 314–317.

Kinney, J. (2000). *Loosening the grip*, 6th ed. Boston, MA: McGraw-Hill.

Kirkpatrick, J. (1999). *The woman alcoholic*. Quakertown, PA: Women for Sobriety.

Klee, H., & Jackson, M. (2002). *Drug misuse and motherhood*. New York, NY: Routledge.

Klosowski, T. (2014, February 21). What is Tor and should I use it? Lifehacker. Retrieved from http://lifehacker .com/what-is-tor-and-should-i-use-it-1527891029

Korolenko, C. P., & Donskih, T. A. (1990). Addictive behavior in women: A theoretical perspective. *Drugs and Society, 4*, 39–65.

Krans, M., & Nall, R. (2016, August 9). Performance enhancers: The safe and the deadly. *Healthline*. Retrieved from https://www.healthline.com/health/performance -enhancers-safe-deadly

Krishnan, A. (2019, February 5). 12 best drinking movies of all time. *The Cinemaholic*, p. 5. Retrieved from https:// www.thecinemaholic.com/best-movies-watch-drunk/

Ladwig, G. B., & Anderson, M. D. (1989). Substance abuse in women: Relationship between chemical dependency of women and past reports of physical and/or sexual abuse. *International Journal of the Addictions, 24,* 739–754.

Lale, T. (1992). Gangs and drugs. In G. Lawson & A. Lawson (Eds.), *Adolescent substance abuse, etiology, treatment and prevention* (pp. 267–281). Gaithersburg, MD: Aspen.

Lawn, J. (1984). *Team up for drug prevention with America's young athletes.* Washington, DC: U.S. Department of Justice, Drug Enforcement Administration.

Lawson, G., & Lawson, A. (1992). Etiology. In G. Lawson & A. Lawson (Eds.), *Adolescent substance abuse, etiology, treatment and prevention* (pp. 1–10). Gaithersburg, MD: Aspen.

Leibsohn, J. (1994). The relationship between drug and alcohol use and peer group associations of college freshmen as they transition from high school. *Journal of Drug Education, 24,* 177–192.

Leicester, J. (2013, June 28). Lance Armstrong considers himself Tour de France record-holder still, believes doping needed to win. Huff Post. Retrieved from http://www.huffingtonpost.com/2013/06/28/lance -armstrong-tour-de-france_n_3515081.html

Leinwand, D. (2000, August 27). 20% say they used drugs with their mom or dad. *USA Today.*

Leinwand, D. (2007a). Study: Drug chat pervasive online— Teens use Internet to share stories, get how-to advice. *USA Today.* (June 19). Retrieved from http://www .usatoday.com/printedition/news/20070619/a_online19 .art.htm

Leinwand, D. (2007b). College drug use, binge drinking rise. *USA Today.* (March 15). Retrieved from http:// usatoday30.usatoday.com/news/nation/2007-03-15 -college-drug-use-N.htm

Lengel, D., & Busfield, S. (2013, August 5). Alex Rodriguez and 12 other payers suspended in Biogenesis PEDs scandal. *Guardian* [London, UK].

Lenhart, A. (2015, April 9). Teens, social media & technology overview 2015. Pew Research Center. Retrieved from http://www.pewinternet.org/2015/04/09/teens -social-media-technology-2015/

Levitt, D., & Venkatesh, S. A. (2000). An economic analysis of a drug-selling gang's finances. *Quarterly Journal of Economics, 115,* 755–789.

Lewin, T. (2005, November 6). Does it work? Substance-free dorms; Clean living on campus. *The New York Times.* Retrieved from http://www.nytimes.com/2005/11/06 /education/edlife/work.html

Lin, A. Y. F. (1994, November). Should women be included in clinical trials? *Pharmacy Times, 10,* 27.

Lively, K. (1996, June 28). The "date-rape drug": Colleges worry about reports of growing use of Rohypnol, a sedative. *Chronicle of Higher Education, 42,* A29.

Livni, E. (2013, August 24). Some parents introduce kids to drugs. ABC News. Retrieved from http://abcnews .go.com/Health/story?id=118024

Lukas, S. (1993). Urine testing for anabolic-androgenic steroids. *Trends in Pharmacological Sciences, 14,* 61–68.

Mathias, R. (1993, May–June). Sex-for-crack phenomenon poses risk for spread of AIDS in heterosexuals. *NIDA Notes, 8,* 8–11.

Mathias, R. (1995, January–February). NIDA survey provides first national data on drug use during pregnancy. *NIDA Notes, 10,* 6–7.

McCaffrey, B. R. (1999, October 21). McCaffrey announces strategy to fight drug use in sports. *Daily Washington File.*

McDonald, M. (1995, June 22). Fast, strong, dead? *Salt Lake Tribune, 250,* C1, C8.

McMurtrie, B. (2014, December 14). Why colleges haven't stopped binge drinking. *The New York Times.* Retrieved from http://www.nytimes.com/2014/12/15/us/why -colleges-havent-stopped-binge-drinking.html?_r=0

McSpadden, K. (2015, February 10). Yankees slugger A-Rod apologizes for misconduct. *Time.* Retrieved from http://time.com/3704481/alex-rodriguez-yankees-mlb -apology-baseball/

Merchant, W. (1992, October). Medications and athletes. *American Druggist,* pp. 6–14.

Miech, R. A., Johnston, L. D., O'Malley, P. M., Bachman, J. G., Schulenberg, J. E., & Patrick, M. E. (2019). *Monitoring the Future national survey results on drug use, 1975– 2018: Volume 1, secondary school. students.* Ann Arbor, MI: University of Michigan, Institute for Social Research. Retrieved from http://monitoringthefuture.org/pubs /mono graphs/mtf-vol1_2018.pdf

Millstein, R. (1993, March 25). *Community alert bulletin.* Rockville, MD: National Institute on Drug Abuse.

Minnesota Institute of Public Health. (1995, Spring). *Alcohol and other drugs and suicide.* Mounds View, MN: Minnesota Department of Human Services, Chemical Health Division.

Morris, S. Y. (2020). Integrase inhibitors for HIV. New York, NY: Healthline Media. Retrieved from https://www .healthline.com/health/hiv-aids/integrase-inhibitors

Moss, H., Kirisci, L., Gordon, H., & Tarter, R. (1994). A neuro-psychological profile of adolescent alcoholics. *Alcoholism: Clinical and Experimental Research, 18,* 159–163.

"Multistate outbreak of poisonings associated with illicit use of GHB." (1994, May–June). *Prevention Pipeline, 7,* 95–96.

Murray, K. (2018, May 31). "Drugs and music: Are your favorite songs fueling your addiction?" AddictionCenter

.com. Retrieved from https://www.addictioncenter.com /community/drugs-and-music/

"Music and drugs—It's a hard habit to break." (2013, November 10). *The Independent* [London, UK]. Retrieved from http://www.independent.co.uk/arts-entertainment /music/features/music-and-drugs--its-a-hard-habit-to -break-2327654.html

MyDNA.com. (2005). *News center: HAART therapy slows progression to AIDS*. Washington, DC: American Medical Association.

National Center for Education Statistics. (2011). Indicators of school crime and safety: 2011: Indicator 8: Students' reports of gangs at school. Washington, DC: U.S. Department of Education, Institute of Education Sciences, and National Center for Education Statistics. Retrieved from http://nces.ed.gov/programs/crimeindicators /crimeindicators2011/ind_08.asp

National Clearinghouse for Alcohol and Drug Information. (1999). *Drugs of abuse*. Rockville, MD: Substance Abuse and Mental Health Services Administration.

National Collegiate Athletic Association (NCAA). (2014, August). NCAA student-athlete substance use study: Executive summary August 2014. Indianapolis, IN: Author. Retrieved from http://www.ncaa.org/about /resources/research/ncaa-student-athlete-substance -use-study-executive-summary-august-2014

National Collegiate Athletic Association (NCAA). (2015). Divisional differences and the history of multidivision classification. Indianapolis, IN: Author. Retrieved from http://www.ncaa.org/about/who-we-are/membership /divisional-differences-and-history-multidivision -classification

National Collegiate Athletic Association (NCAA). (2020). 2019–20 NCAA banned drugs. Retrieved from http:// www.ncaa.org/sport-science-institute/topics/2019-20 -ncaa-banned-substances

National Crime Victims' Rights Week Resource Guide. (2007). Campus crime. Arlington, VA: National Center for Victims of Crime. Retrieved from https://www.ncjrs .gov/ovc_archives/ncvrw/2007/pdf/overview.pdf

National Drug Intelligence Center (NDIC). (2009). *Drugs and gangs: Fast facts, questions and answers*. Washington, DC: Author.

National Education Association and Health Information Network. (2013). *RX for understanding: Preventing prescription drug abuse*. Retrieved from http://www .gadoe.org/Curriculum-Instruction-and-Assessment /Curriculum-and-Instruction/Documents/Prescription %20Drug%20Abuse%20Prevention%20Program _Grades%209-12%20Lesson%20Plans.pdf

National Institute of Mental Health. (2012). The teen brain: Still under construction. Bethesda, MD: Author.

National Institute on Alcohol Abuse and Alcoholism (NIAAA). (2005a). High-risk drinking in college: What we know and what we need to learn. Bethesda, MD: Author. Retrieved from http://www.collegedrinking prevention.gov/niaaacollegematerials/panel01/execsum _01.aspx

National Institute on Alcohol Abuse and Alcoholism (NIAAA). (2005b). Living arrangements. Retrieved from http://www.collegedrinkingprevention.gov/NIAAA CollegeMaterials/TaskForce/Factors_01.asp

National Institute on Alcohol Abuse and Alcoholism (NIAAA). (2017). College drinking. Bethesda, MD: Author. Retrieved from https://pubs.niaaa.nih.gov /publications/CollegeFactSheet/CollegeFactSheet.pdf

National Institute on Drug Abuse (NIDA). (1996). *Anabolic steroid abuse*. Rockville, MD: Author.

National Institute on Drug Abuse (NIDA). (1999). *Drug abuse and addiction research: The sixth triennial report to Congress*. Rockville, MD: Author.

National Institute on Drug Abuse (NIDA). (2000, March 30). Club drugs: Community alert bulletin. *NIDA Notes*, p. 14.

National Institute on Drug Abuse (NIDA). (2006a). *News-Scan for October 13, 2006—Women and substance abuse issue*. Bethesda, MD: Author.

National Institute on Drug Abuse (NIDA). (2006b). *Research report series—Anabolic steroid abuse*. Bethesda, MD: Author.

National Institute on Drug Abuse (NIDA). (2009). *NIDA InfoFacts: Steroids (anabolic-androgenic)*. Bethesda, MD: Author.

National Institute on Drug Abuse (NIDA). (2012, December). *Principles of drug addiction treatment: A research-based guide*, 3rd ed. Bethesda, MD: Author.

National Institute on Drug Abuse (NIDA). (2013, May). DrugFacts: Prescription and over-the-counter medications. Retrieved from https://www.drugabuse.gov /publications/drugfacts/prescription-over-counter -medications

National Institute on Drug Abuse (NIDA). (2014). Drug-Facts: Cough and cold medicine abuse. (May). Retrieved from https://www.drugabuse.gov/publications/drug facts/cough-cold-medicine-abuse

National Institute on Drug Abuse (NIDA). (2015a). Drug-Facts: Sex and gender differences in substance use. (September). Retrieved from https://www.drugabuse .gov/publications/drugfacts/substance-use-in-women

National Institute on Drug Abuse (NIDA). (2015b). College drinking. (December). Bethesda, MD: Author.

National Institute on Drug Abuse (NIDA). (2015c). Drug and alcohol use in college-age adults in 2014. (December). Retrieved from https://www.drugabuse .gov/related-topics/trends-statistics/infographics/drug -alcohol-use-in-college-age-adults-in-2014

National Institute on Drug Abuse (NIDA). (2016a). Drug-Facts: What are anabolic steroids? (March). Retrieved from https://www.drugabuse.gov/publications/drug facts/anabolic-steroids

National Institute on Drug Abuse (NIDA). (2016b). Cough and cold medicine (DXM and codeine syrup). (April 28). Bethesda, MD: Author.

National Institute on Drug Abuse (NIDA). (2018a). Drug-Facts: What are anabolic steroids? (August). Retrieved from https://www.drugabuse.gov/publications/drugfacts /anabolic-steroids

National Institute on Drug Abuse (NIDA). (2018b). Steroids and other appearance and performance enhancing drugs (APEDs). (February). Bethesda, MD: National Institutes of Health. Retrieved from https://www .drugabuse.gov/publications/research-reports/steroids -other-appearance-performance-enhancing-drugs-apeds /how-are-anabolic-steroids-tested-in-athletes

National Institute on Drug Abuse (NIDA). (2019, May). Prescription drugs. Retrieved from https://teens.drug abuse.gov/drug-facts/prescription-drugs

National Institute on Drug Abuse (NIDA). (2020, January). Sex and gender differences in substance use. Bethesda, MD: Author. Retrieved from https://www.drugabuse .gov/publications/research-reports/substance-use-in -women/sex-gender-differences-in-substance-use

National Institutes of Health (NIH) & National Institute on Drug Abuse (NIDA). (1998). *Drug abuse and drug abuse research: Executive summary.* Rockville, MD: Substance Abuse and Mental Health Services Administration.

National Survey on Drug Use and Health (NSDUH). (2007, October 4). *The NSDUH report: Substance use treatment among women of childbearing age.* Research Triangle Park, NC: Office of Applied Studies, Substance Abuse and Mental Health Services Administration and RTI International.

National Youth Anti-Drug Media Campaign. (2007). The 411 on Rx drugs. Retrieved from http://www .theantidrug.com/drug_info/prescription_411.asp

New York State Department of Health. (2010). Anabolic steroids and sports: Winning at any cost. Retrieved from http://www.health.state.ny.us/publications/1210

Office of National Drug Control Policy. (1999). *Substance use in popular movies and music.* Rockville, MD: Author.

Office of the Surgeon General. (2007). Surgeon General's call to action to prevent and reduce underage drinking. Washington, DC: U.S. Department of Health and Human Services. Retrieved from http://www .surgeongeneral.gov/topics/underagedrinking /familyguide.pdf

Olin, B. R. (1994). *Drug facts and comparisons* (pp. 109–109c). St. Louis, MO: Kluwer.

"OTC drugs and athletes." (1992, June). *Pharmacy Times*, p. 16.

Pagliery, J. (2014, March 10). The deep web you don't know about. CNN Money. Retrieved from http://money.cnn .com/2014/03/10/technology/deep-web/index.html

Palmer, E. (2015, June 8). Silk Road: More people buying drugs online following close of illegal dark web market. *International Business Times.* Retrieved from http://www .ibtimes.co.uk/silk-road-more-people-buying-drugs-online -following-close-illegal-dark-web-market-1504985

Paoletta, M. (2004, May 21). Music industry coming to grips with addiction. *Today.* Retrieved from http://www .today.com/id/5033438#.Un8j5JSEayW

Parrot, A. (1988). *Date rape and acquaintance rape.* New York, NY: Rosen.

Pietroski, N. (1993, August). Counseling HIV/AIDS patients. *American Druggist*, pp. 50–56.

POZ. (2011, September 16). Entry inhibitors (including fusion inhibitors). Retrieved from http://www.aidsmeds .com/archive/EIs_1627.shtml

Prendergast, M. L. (1994). Substance use and abuse among college students: A review of recent literature. *Journal of American College Health, 43,* 99–113.

Primack, B. A., Dalton, M. A., Carroll, M. V., Agarwal, A. A., & Fine, M. J. (2008). Content analysis of tobacco, alcohol, and other drugs in popular music. *Archives of Pediatrics and Adolescent Medicine, 162,* 169–205.

Quinn, E. (2016, September 6). EPO and blood doping in sports. Very Well. Retrieved from https://www.verywell .com/epo-and-blood-doping-in-sports-3120522

Ravid, J. (1995, October 19). The hard-core curriculum. *Rolling Stone, 719,* 99.

Reuters & Fox News Network. (2011, August 24). Facebook linked to teenage drinking, drug use. Retrieved from http://www.foxnews.com/tech/2011/08/24/report -links-social-networking-sites-to-teenage-drinking-drug -use/

Ridings, A. (2014, February 25). How music glamorizes drug use. New Beginnings Adolescent Recovery Center. Retrieved from http://newbeginningsteenhelp.com /blog/music-glamorizes-drug-use

Roberts, D. F., Henriksen, L., Christenson, P. G., Kelly, M., Carbone, S., & Wilson, A. B. (1999). Substance use in popular movies and music. Office of National Drug Control Policy; Washington, DC: *Google Scholar.*

Ross, V., & Dejong, W. (2008, March). *Alcohol and other drug abuse among first-year college students* (pp. 1–8). Newton,

MA: Higher Education Center for Alcohol and Other Drug Abuse and Violence Prevention.

Rubin, A., R. Stout, L., & Longabaugh, R. (1996). Gender differences in relapse situations. *Addiction, 91*(Suppl.), S111–S120.

Sanders, W. B. (1994). *Gangbangs and drive-bys.* New York, NY: Aldine De Gruyter.

Scaccia, A., & Madell, R. (2020). Facts about HIV: Life expectancy and long-term outlook. Healthline. Retrieved from https://www.healthline.com/health/hiv-aids/life -expectancy#takeaway

Schaefer, M. A., Hilton, J. F., Ekstrand, M., & Keogh, J. (1993, November–December). Relationship between drug use and sexual behaviors and the occurrence of sexually transmitted diseases among high-risk male youth. *Sexually Transmitted Diseases, 20,* 39–47.

Schernoff, M., & Smith, R. A. (2001, July). HIV treatments: A history of scientific advance. *Body Positive, 14,* 1–7.

Schiebinger, L. (2003). Women's health and clinical trials. *Journal of Clinical Investigation, 112,* 973–977. Retrieved from https://www.jci.org/articles/view/19993

Schoemer, K. (1996, August 26). Rockers, models and the new allure of heroin. *Newsweek,* pp. 24–36.

Schulenberg, J. E., Johnston, L. D., O'Malley, P. M., Bachman, J. G., Miech, R. A., & Patrick, M. E. (2019). *Monitoring the Future National Survey Results on Drug Use, 1975–2018: Volume II, College students and adults ages 19–60.* Ann Arbor, MI: University of Michigan, Institute for Social Research.

Scott, D. M., Wagner, J. C., & Barlow, T. W. (1996). Anabolic steroids use among adolescents in Nebraska schools. *American Journal of Health-System Pharmacy, 53,* 2068–2072.

Scottsdale Recovery Center. (2018). The glamorization of drug use in the entertainment industry. Scottsdale, AZ: Author. Retrieved from https://scottsdalerecovery .com/the-glamorization-of-drug-use-in-the-entertainment -industry/

Seetharaman, D. (2008, July 9). Study: Addictive drugs easily ordered online. *USA Today.* Retrieved from http:// www.usatoday.com/news/health/2008-07-09-online -pharmacies_N.htm

Shavin, N. (2016, August 3). The ancient history of cheating in the Olympics. *Smithsonian Magazine.*

Shelden, R. G., Tracy, S., & Brown, W. (2001). *Youth gangs in American society.* Belmont, CA: Wadsworth/Thomson Learning.

Shelden, R. G., Tracy, S. K., & Brown, W. B. (2004). *Youth gangs in American society,* 3rd ed. Belmont, CA: Wadsworth/Thomson Learning.

Siegel, L., & Senna, J. (1997). *Juvenile delinquency,* 6th ed. St. Paul, MN: West.

Siegel, L. J., & Welsh, B. C. (2009). *Juvenile delinquency: Theory, practice, and law,* 10th ed. Belmont, CA: Wadsworth/ Cengage Learning.

Smollins, M. (2013, November 1). Alex Rodriguez Biogenesis case: MLB CEO Rob Manfred calls A-Rod career "sad and tarnished," claims Rodriguez PED use "longer than any other player." *Sports World News.* Retrieved from http://www.sportsworldnews.com /articles/6205/20131101/alex-rodriguez-biogenesis -case-mlb-ceo-rob-manfred-calls-a-rod-career-sad -tarnished-claims-rodriguez-ped-use-longer-than-any -other-player.htm

Southern Illinois University Carbondale [SIUC]/Core Institute. (2014, April 23). *2012 annual reference group, core alcohol and drug survey long form—Form 194, Executive Summary.* Carbondale, IL: Author.

Spergel, I. A. (1990). *Youth gangs: Problem and response.* Chicago, IL: University of Chicago, School of Social Service Administration.

Steinberg, L., Fletcher, A., & Darling, N. (1994). Parental monitoring and peer influences on adolescent substance use. *Pediatrics, 93,* 1060–1064.

Stetina, B. U., Reinhold, R., Cornelia, S., Tamara, L. M., & Kryspin-Exner, I. (2008). Exploring hidden populations: Recreational drug users. *Cyberpsychology: Journal of Psychosocial Research on Cyberspace, 2*(1). Retrieved from https://cyberpsychology.eu/article/view/4208/3249

Stewart, K. (2013, May). Facts and myths about college drinking: A serious problem with serious solutions. Prevention Research Center. Retrieved from http://resources .prev.org/documents/FactsMythsCollegeDrinking.pdf

"A study of drug addiction between genders." (2016). The Recovery Village. Retrieved from https://www.the recoveryvillage.com/drug-addiction/study-between -genders/

"Substance abuse." (2016). New York, NY: National Women's Health Resource Center. Retrieved from http:// www.healthywomen.org/condition/substance-abuse

Substance Abuse and Mental Health Services Administration (SAMHSA). (1999a). *Making the connection between substance abuse and HIV/AIDS prevention for women of color and youth.* Rockville, MD: Author.

Substance Abuse and Mental Health Services Administration (SAMHSA). (1999b). *Tips for teens: About steroids.* Rockville, MD: Author.

Substance Abuse and Mental Health Services Administration (SAMHSA). (2007). National Survey on Drug Use and Health (NSDUH-2007. Office of Applied Studies. Rockville, MD: Substance Abuse and Mental Health Services Administration.

Substance Abuse and Mental Health Services Administration (SAMHSA). (2010, January 7). *The TEDS (Treatment*

*Episode Data Set) report: Trends in Adult female substance abuse treatment admissions reporting primary alcohol abuse: 1992 to 2007.* Rockville, MD, Author.

Substance Abuse and Mental Health Services Administration (SAMHSA). (2011). *Results from the 2010 National Survey on Drug Use and Health: Summary of national findings.* NSDUH Series H-41, HHS Pub. No. (SMA) 11-4658. Rockville, MD: Author.

Substance Abuse and Mental Health Services Administration (SAMHSA). (2014a). *Results from the 2013 National Survey on Drug Use and Health: Summary of national findings* NSDUH Series Ho-48, HHS Pub. No. (SMA) 14-4863. Rockville, MD: Author.

Substance Abuse and Mental Health Services Administration (SAMHSA). (2014b). The TEDS report: Gender differences in primary substance of abuse across age groups. Rockville, MD: Author.

Substance Abuse and Mental Health Services Administration. (2015). *Improving cultural competence.* Treatment Improvement Protocol (TIP) Series, No. 59. Bethesda, MD: Author.

Substance Abuse and Mental Health Services Administration (SAMHSA). (2019). *Key substance use and mental health indicators in the United States: Results from the 2018 National Survey on Drug Use and Health.* HHS Publication No. PEP19-5068, NSDUH Series H-54. Rockville, MD: Author.

"Substance use and HIV risk." (2018, August 27). Washington, DC: U. S. Department of Health and Human Services and Minority HIV/AIDS Fund. Retrieved from https://www.hiv.gov/hiv-basics/hiv-prevention/reducing-risk-from-alcohol-and-drug-use/substance-use-and-hiv-risk

Suggs, W. (2003, March 14). Deadly fuel: As supplements and steroids tempt and endanger more athletes, what are colleges doing? *Chronicle of Higher Education, 49,* A36–A38.

Swadi, H. (1992). Relative risk factors in detecting adolescent drug abuse. *Drug and Alcohol Dependence, 29,* 253–254.

Swaine, J. (2013, November 12). Mike Tyson admits to being high on drugs during major fights, and using a fake penis to avoid detection. *The Telegraph* [London, UK]. Retrieved from http://www.telegraph.co.uk/sport/othersports/boxing/10444998/Mike-Tyson-admits-to-being-high-on-drugs-during-major-fights-and-using-a-fake-penis-to-avoid-detection.html

Teen Challenge. (2000). *Drugs: Frequently asked questions.* South Australia: Pragin Press.

"Teen drug and alcohol abuse facts and statistics." (2015). Teendrugsrehabs.com. Retrieved from http://www.teendrugrehabs.com/facts-and-stats/

"Teen prescription drug abuse reportedly holding steady." (2007, February 14). *USA Today.*

"The deep Web, the dark web & Tor: How to surf the secret Internet. Who is Hosting This? (2020, March 2). Retrieved from https://www.whoishostingthis.com/blog/2017/03/07/tor-deep-web/

Toronto, R. (1992, July 6). Young athletes who use "enhancing" steroids risk severe physical consequences. *Salt Lake Tribune, 244,* C-5.

Tyson, M. (2014, January 3). Fighting to kick the habit. *The New York Times.* Retrieved from https://www.nytimes.com/2014/01/04/opinion/mike-tyson-fighting-to-kick-the-habit.html?auth=login-email&login=email

UNAIDS. (2015). Fact sheet 2015. Geneva, Switzerland: Author. Retrieved from https://www.unaids.org/sites/default/files/media_asset/20150901_FactSheet_2015_en.pdf

UNAIDS. (2020). Fact sheet—World Aids Day 2019. Geneva, Switzerland: Author. Retrieved from https://www.unaids.org/sites/default/files/media_asset/UNAIDS_FactSheet_en.pdf

United Nations Interregional Crime and Justice Research Institute. (2013). Dawn: Promoting gender-based drug prevention and recovery. Geneva: Switzerland: Author.

University of California, San Francisco. (2000, March 15). Pain drug reveals what most already know—Men's and women's brains are simply different. ScienceDaily. Retrieved from www.sciencedaily.com/releases/2000/03/000315075845.htm

University of Liverpool. (2018, January 20). The link between drugs and music explained by science. Liverpool L69 3BX, United Kingdom: Author. Retrieved from https://news.liverpool.ac.uk/2018/01/30/link-drugs-music-explained-science/

U.S. Department of Health and Human Services (USDHHS) & National Institute on Drug Abuse (NIDA). (1999). *Drug abuse and addiction research: The sixth triennial report to Congress. NIDA research priorities and highlights, role of research: Women's health and gender differences.* Washington, DC: U.S. Government Printing Office.

U.S. Department of Justice (USDOJ). (1991–1992). *Anabolic steroids and you.* Washington, DC: Demand Reduction Section, Drug Enforcement Administration.

U.S. Department of Justice (USDOJ). (2004). *Steroid abuse in today's society*. Springfield, VA: Office of Diversion Control, DEA. 2004. Retrieved from http://www.deadiversion.usdoj.gov/pubs/brochures/steroids/professionals/

"U.S. statistics." (2020, January 16). HIV.gov. Washington, DC: U.S. Department of Health and Human Services and Centers for Disease Control and Prevention. Retrieved from https://www.hiv.gov/hiv-basics/overview/data-and-trends/statistics

Vargas-Cooper, N. (2012, July–August). Bath salts. *Spin*, pp. 58–64, 94.

Venturelli, P. J. (2000). Drugs in schools: Myths and reality. In W. H. Hinkle & S. Henry (Eds.), *The Annals of the American Academy of Political and Social Science, 567*, 72–87. Thousand Oaks, CA: Sage.

Verhaak, C. M., Lintsen, A. M. E., Evers, A. W. M., & Braat, D. D. M. (2010). Who is at risk of emotional problems and how do you know? Screening of women going for IVF treatment. *Human Reproduction, 25*, 1234–1240.

Vlad, R. A., Hancu, G., Popescu, G. C., & Lungu, L. A. (2018). Doping in sports, a never-ending story? *Advanced Pharmacology Bulletin, 8*, 529–534.

Von Der Haar, C. M. (2005). *Social psychology: A sociological perspective*. Upper Saddle River, NJ: Pearson Education.

Wadley, J. (2014, September 8). College student' use of marijuana on the rise, some drugs declining. *Michigan News*. Retrieved from https://news.umich.edu/college-students-use-of-marijuana-on-the-rise-some-drugs-declining/

Walsh, F., & Shenkman. M. (1992). Family context of adolescence. In G. Lawson & A. Lawson (Eds.), *Adolescent substance abuse, etiology, treatment and prevention* (pp. 149–171). Gaithersburg, MD: Aspen.

Wechsler, H., Lee, J. E., Kuo, M., Seibring, M., Nelson, T. F., & Lee, H. P. (2002). Trends in college binge drinking during a period of increased prevention efforts: Findings from four Harvard School of Public Health study surveys, 1993–2001. *Journal of American College Health, 50*, 203–217.

Werner, D., Young, N. K., Dennis, K., & Amatetti, S. (2007). *Family-centered treatment for women with substance use disorders—History, key elements and challenges*. Rockville, MD: Substance Abuse and Mental Health Services Administration (SAMHSA).

"What is a growth hormone stimulation test?" (2008, August 14). WebMD.com. Retrieved from http://www.webmd.com/a-to-z-guides/growth-hormone

Winters, P. A. (1997). *Teen addiction*. San Diego, CA: Greenhaven Press.

Wisconsin Coalition Against Sexual Assault. (1997). *Sexual violence and sexual abuse*. Madison, WI: Wisconsin Coalition Against Sexual Assault.

Witham, D. (1995, November 10). Recovery in the dorm: Rutgers University's special housing for addicted students. *Chronicle of Higher Education, 42*, A-33.

Woemer, A. (2013, August 6). MLB players' use of performance enhancing drugs comes with serious health risks. *FoxNews.com*. Retrieved from http://www.foxnews.com/health/2013/08/06/mlb-players-use-performance-enhancing-drugs-comes-with-serious-health-risks/

"Women smokers run high risk for lung cancer." (1994, May–June). *Prevention Pipeline, 7*, 7.

World Anti-Doping Agency (WADA). (2009). The code. Retrieved from https://www.wada-ama.org/en/what-we-do/the-code

World Anti-Doping Agency (WADA). (2015). The code. Retrieved from https://www.wada-ama.org/en/what-we-do/the-code

World Anti-Doping Agency (WADA). (2020). Who we are. Retrieved from https://www.wada-ama.org/en/who-we-are

World Health Organization (WHO). (2019, November 15). HIV/AIDS: Key facts. Geneva, Switzerland: Author.

Wright, H. (2009, June 29). Steroids in sports: The rise and fall of great athletes. BR. Retrieved from https://bleacherreport.com/articles/209217-steroids-in-sports-the-rise-and-fall-of-great-athletes

Wright, L. (1985). Suicidal thoughts and their relationship to family stress and personal problems among high school seniors and college undergraduates. *Adolescence, 20*, 575–580.

Yesalis, C. E., & Cowart, J. S. (1998). *The steroids game*. Champaign, IL: Human Kinetics.

Yoder, R. (2015, April 28). Causes of teen drug use: It's not just peer pressure. Palm Beach, FL: Palm Beach Institute.

Yusko, D. A., Buckman, J. F., White, H. R., & Pandina, R. J. (2008, November–December). Alcohol, tobacco, illicit drugs, and performance enhancers: A comparison of use by college student athletes and nonathletes. *Journal of American College Health, 57*, 281–290.

Zuger, A. (2000, August 8). Epidemic: An overview. *The New York Times*. Retrieved from http://www.nytimes.com/library/national/science/aids/aids-overview.html

## CHAPTER 17

# Drug Abuse Prevention

© FOTOGRIN/Shutterstock.

## Did You Know?

▶ Drug prevention is aimed at reducing risk factors such as early aggressive behavior, lack of parental supervision, the lure of gang membership, drug availability, and poverty.

▶ Comprehensive prevention programs simultaneously involving the community, school, and family are more effective than single-unit programs.

▶ The harm-reduction drug-prevention model that is practiced in the Netherlands is a preventive model that meets drug users on their own turf in dealing with drug use and abuse.

▶ Among people 12 or older in 2014 who had substance use disorders (SUDs), 17.0 million (nearly four out of five) had an alcohol use disorder, and 7.1 million (about one in every three) had an illicit drug use disorder.

▶ Drug-prevention programs must distinguish among early experimenters, nonproblem drug users, undetected committed or secret users, problem users, and former users.

▶ Students in drug-prevention programs who have difficulty saying "no" to the nonmedical use of drugs need refusal skills training and peer-resistance training.

▶ Drug education actually began in the 1830s with the temperance movement.

▶ Drug courts are a newer form of drug prevention in which drug defendants are more likely to undergo treatment (rehabilitation) than incarceration (punishment).

▶ Other strategies for dealing with drug use include the alternatives approach and meditation.

## Learning Objectives

**On completing this chapter, you should be able to:**

❯ List the 10 most prominent factors influencing individuals with regard to alcohol and other drug use.

❯ Identify and briefly explain the three major types of drug-prevention programs.

❯ Describe the five types of drug users that have to be considered before implementing a drug-prevention program.

❯ List the five levels of comprehensive prevention programs for drug use and abuse.

❯ Identify the three family factors that can prevent initiation to drugs or extensive drug use.

❯ List the four prevention-program models found in higher education.

❯ Describe the main goals of the following large-scale drug-prevention programs: the BACCHUS Network, D.A.R.E., and drug courts.

❯ Describe two alternative prevention strategies or agendas for replacing drug use.

# Introduction

When someone tells another person "Just don't do drugs" and, if that person is addicted to, say, cocaine like I was, that comes across as an ignorant answer. You cannot just quit when you are addicted because even the idea of addiction continually blocks the possibility of casually deciding to stop using the drug. A lot has to go into the day you actually stop using the drug. First of all, the craving for the drug continually reminds you to do it maybe just a few more times. Then, your life appears to be less engaging because your body is missing the chemical properties of the drug that it became accustomed to and this affects your level of depression. So you have to sort of go through that slow abstinence period—you are without the drug and sometimes you can only deal with abstaining 1 hour at a time for the first week or so. Then slowly, ever so slowly, for me at least, the addict has to rebuild her or his daily living without the drug. It's just not easy. If it were, most people addicted to drugs would probably quit on their own. Especially when you realize that you are not controlling the drug, the drug is controlling you. Just remember, most addicts continually deceive (lie to) themselves and others that they are not "really" addicted. Do you know how hard it is to become aware that these lies are part of the addiction? Before the extended therapy I had, no one could convince me that the daily cocaine I was snorting and smoking was bad. *(From Venturelli's research files, female academic administrator in higher education who has been drug free for three years, age 37, June 21, 2000)*

A second interview revealed the following:

I started doing cocaine at age 52. One night, I was having a few beers with a friend of mine and another friend of his over at his apartment. I know I was older than both of them were since they were in their early thirties. After the first few beers, this friend of mine went into his bedroom and came out into the living room with a bag of coke. Soon as he entered the room, he threw the bag into my lap and said, "Do you want to try some of this?" I told them I never did this drug and said, "Okay I will try it once." All I remember that night is that I kept doing lines and often said, "Boy, this stuff is so easy to do—nothing to it." When the night was over, I got back into my car and went home. After that night, I started buying the coke each week and for over 2 years had spent thousands of dollars. It became a nightly thing to do. One day, I decided to stop buying coke since I was very worried about all the money I had been charging to my credit card as cash advances. For the first few nights it was difficult to not go out and pick up coke from a dealer I had gotten to know quite well. This dealer kept calling asking who I was buying from since he hadn't seen me in over a week. I repeatedly tried telling him that I was quitting and had no other dealer but he would not believe me. This added to the difficulty in giving up the drug but I did it. It was "cold turkey" and I had succeeded since now it has been 5 years and I never bought my supply again since that one night when I decided to quit. It is so easy to do this drug and become attached to it. I don't think I was really addicted when I was doing it, but I sure did it often. My problem was more of a mental attachment to the drug. I think I was certainly close to a serious addiction but the cost of the drug, using money I did not have, forced me to quit. In my case, the best prevention is to never start doing this drug or any other drug that is easy to do and makes you feel so good when you are doing it. I have several friends who continue to use this drug mostly on weekends. I am glad I am not in their shoes anymore. *(From Venturelli's research files, male mechanical engineer, age 59, November 5, 2010)*

A third interview:

I met this guy in an introductory sociology class since we both sat near each other during class. About a month later we had our first test coming up so we decided to study together over several nights. We were both first-semester seniors majoring in engineering and felt uneasy about this course since both of us had very little exposure to social science courses and we felt such courses are really different from the more scientific and quantitative courses we were familiar with in our major. The first night we reviewed what we thought were things we had to know for the test and spent time reviewing both the text and class notes we had written. The second night we met in his dorm room instead of the library. We talked about many things in between our studying and got to know each during the 4 days of studying together. On the third night we decided to take a break and meet at a Johnny's [a pseudonym] over a few drinks and just chill out together. As we were drinking beers and shots Tim [a pseudonym], asked me if I ever did drugs. I indicated that I drink alcohol and smoked a lot of weed, tried acid several times, and did Ecstasy during my first year at college. Tim revealed his past drug use, which not only included the drugs I had experienced plus several other drugs I never tried before. He indicated that at the moment he had some cocaine in his dorm room and asked if I wanted to try it with him. I did have one too many beers that night so I agreed to try cocaine back at his dorm room since his roommate went home over the weekend and he assured me that it was a safe drug and not addictive in trying it once. We ended up leaving the bar and went to his room right after that conversation. In his room he said it was better to cook it up and smoke it and at the time little did I know that my first use of this drug was not snorting cocaine but really smoking crack. We smoked it for hours and I loved it. The effects were so pleasurable. I could go on about how many times we did this in the weeks and months afterward but the most important thing is that I really got hooked on cooking up cocaine nearly every night, even after this friend of mine dropped out of school. We also had a thing going on with each other in that I learned to like getting high with Tim that I think made the use of this drug even more appealing and repetitive. A year later I sought help and went to NA [Narcotics Anonymous] and successfully weaned myself off this drug after relapsing the first time and in my second attempt I finally stopped this horribly addictive drug. Addiction is something that consumes you with whatever is your drug of choice. My grades suffered and luckily my uncle hooked me up with NA that he was familiar with as a drug counselor and kept it secret from my parents, who would have died in knowing that in a few short months I was crack addict. What helped me was when Tim left campus and I was all alone doing this drug on my own. I think if Tim would not have left campus I probably would have continued using this drug. As you commented [referring to the interviewer] I had lost my support person when Tim was no longer on campus and moved back to St. Louis, which helped me face my addiction. This was a very slow process to accept the realization that I had to quit this drug. I had to confront this demon on my own, and though I missed Tim after he left campus, it was very helpful in getting me to stop, plus, of course NA was also very influential in quitting. Addiction comes on slowly and when it gets a hold of you I think most addicts continually deny their addiction. It is truly a disorder that can destroy your life. *(From Venturelli's research files, male electrical engineer, age 26, currently residing in Chicago, January 13, 2016)*

This chapter explores and provides information on doing *something* about drug use and abuse. With so many potential causes for the unnecessary and nonmedical use of psychoactive substances, it becomes increasingly important to discuss methods, programs, and strategies that prevent, cease the use, or, at the very least, significantly moderate the habitual or addictive nonmedical use of drugs.

**Figure 17.1** shows many of the potential environmental factors involved in what influences **alcohol and other drug (AOD)** use. The core in this figure starts with the individual, and each concentric zone represents clusters of factors that influence an individual's views, attitudes, and behaviors toward drug use. With so many factors, each having an independent potential effect on the individual, you can see why comprehensive prevention programs involving the community, school, and family are more effective than single-unit programs such as having a mandatory drug-education program in elementary grades without other complementary and overlapping drug programs in the community and the family. Prevention research clearly shows that "we must attend to all factors; prevention that focuses on only one or two factors and ignores or discounts the rest is likely to fail to have a long-term, permanent impact" (Tinzmann & Hixson, 2006, p. 3).

Through comprehensive prevention programs that are multifaceted and complementary, we are able to more effectively tease out which factors are most influential. The televised commercial in the early 1990s that showed two eggs frying in a pan: "This is your brain . . . this is your brain on drugs," sponsored by the Partnership for a Drug-Free America, was an early attempt at prevention through a disturbing analogy. Although its effect

**KEY TERM**

**AOD**
alcohol and other drugs

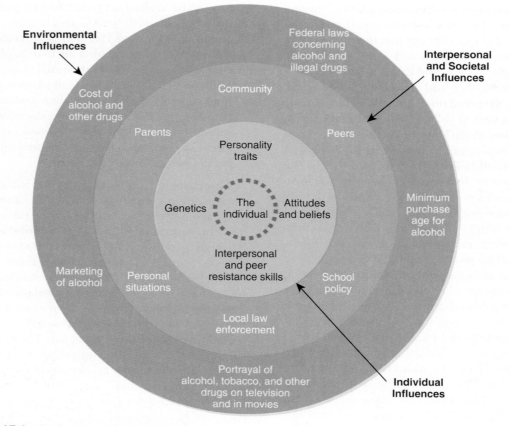

**FIGURE 17.1** Potential Factors that Influence Alcohol and Other Drug Use.

Reproduced from U.S. Department of Health and Human Services, Office of Substance Abuse Prevention. (1989). Factors that influence alcohol and other drug use. In *Prevention Plus II: Tools for creating and sustaining drug-free communities.* DHHS Publication No. 89-1649. Rockville, MD: Author. Distributed by the National Clearinghouse for Alcohol and Drug Information.

was poor on drug users, who had never felt their brains frying, it was an initial step toward innovative prevention efforts.[1] Was it worth the airtime? Can the success of these programs be adequately measured?

In 1997, 15 states thought prevention of alcohol and other drug abuse was important enough to maintain certified prevention-specialist credentialing. Today, a bewildering variety of

programs exists from coast to coast in school districts, churches, and other communities, all with the goal of preventing initial drug use or halting use before it becomes a problem.

## How Serious Are the Problems of Substance Use Disorders?

**Substance use disorders (SUDs)** occur when the recurrent use of alcohol or other drugs (or both) causes clinically significant impairment, including health problems, disability, and failure to meet major responsibilities at work, school, or home. In looking at drug dependence, the severity of this problem can be highlighted by the following findings (Substance Abuse and Mental Health Services Administration [SAMHSA], 2019):

New Past Year Drug Initiates, 2018

- The illicit drugs with the largest number of recent past year initiates from high to low aged 12 or older are:

---

[1]In 2010 this organization changed its name to *the Partnership for Drug-Free Kids.* "The new name reflects the nonprofit's commitment to swerving and supporting parents and families" (Feliz, 2010).

**KEY TERM**

**substance use disorders (SUDs)**
when the recurrent use of alcohol or other drugs (or both) causes clinically significant impairment, including health problems, disability, and failure to meet major responsibilities at work, school, or home

- alcohol—4.9 million new users (13,400 first time users each day);
- marijuana—3.1 million new users (8,400 first time users each day);
- prescription pain relievers—1.9 million new misusers (5,200 first time users each day);
- tried a cigarette for first time approximately—1.8 million (5,000 first time users each day);
- prescription tranquilizers—1.2 million new misusers (3,300 first time users each day);
- hallucinogens—1.1 million new users (3,100 first time users each day);
- prescription stimulants—1.0 million new misusers (2,700 first time users each day day); and
- cocaine—874,000 new users (2,400 first time users each day).

### Substance Use Among People with Mental Health Issues, 2018

- Substance use was more common among both adolescents and adults who had a mental health issue than among those who did not. About one in 16 adolescents aged 12 to 17 in 2018 (6.1%) with a past-year major depressive episode (MDE )smoked cigarettes in the past month compared with 2.1% of those without a past-year MDE. In addition, adolescents with an MDE were more likely than those without an MDE to binge drink in the preceding month (8.5 vs. 4.1%) and to use an illicit drug in the past year (32.7 vs. 14.0%).
- Among adults aged 18 or older in 2018, an estimated 28.1% of adults with any mental illness (AMI) and 37.2% of adults with severe mental illness (SMI) were cigarette smokers in the past month compared with 16.3% of those without any mental illness. In addition, 31.3% of adults with AMI and 32.3% of adults with SMI were binge drinkers in the past month compared with 25.3% of adults with no mental illness.

### Co-Occurring Mental Health Issues and Substance Use Disorders, 2018

- Approximately 358,000 adolescents (1.5% of all adolescents) had a substance use disorder (SUD) and an MDE in the preceding year, including 288,000 adolescents (1.2% of all adolescents) who had an SUD and an MDE with severe impairment.
- In 2018, an estimated 9.2 million adults 18 or older (3.7% of all adults) had both AMI and at least one SUD in the past year

### Substance Use Disorders (SUDs), 2018

- Approximately 20.3 million people 12 or older had an SUD related to their use of

Example of an advertisement aimed at alerting parents about the dangers of early drug use.

alcohol or illicit drugs in the past year, including 14.8 million people who had an alcohol use disorder and 8.1 million people who had an illicit drug use disorder.
- The 21.5 million people who had SUDs in 2014 represent 8.1% of those 12 or older.
- The most common illicit drug use disorder was marijuana use disorder (4.4 million people).
- An estimated 2.0 million people had an opioid use disorder, which includes 1.7 million people with a prescription pain reliever use disorder and 0.5 million people with a heroin use disorder.

### Substance Use Treatment, 2018

- An estimated 21.2 million people aged 12 or older needed substance use treatment. This number translates to about one in 13 people who needed treatment (7.8%). About one in 26 adolescents aged 12 to 17 (3.8%), about one in seven young adults aged 18 to 25 (15.3%), and one in 14 adults aged 26 or older (7.0%) needed treatment.

### Percentage Perceiving "Great Risk" from Substance Use, Age 12 or Older, 2018

- Heroin use—using once or twice a week, 94.3%;
- Cocaine—use once or twice a week, 86.5%;
- Cigarettes—smoking one or more packs of cigarettes per day, 71.8%;
- Alcohol—having four or five drinks of alcohol nearly every day, 68.5%; and
- Marijuana—smoking once or twice a week, 30.6%.

After reviewing the actual numbers and percentages of new drug use initiates, mental health issues among substance users, mental health issues and substance use disorder, substance use treatment, and the percentage of "great risk" from substance use, we can now better understand the need to discuss drug prevention in this chapter.

## The Critical Importance of Early Childhood Substance Abuse Prevention

### ■ Drug Prevention

"In the broadest sense, prevention is organized activity designed to avoid or decrease health problems" (Wilson & Kolander, 2011, p. 7). In addition to this definition of prevention, we add that, in this chapter, **drug prevention** is aimed at preventing or decreasing not only health problems but also social and personal problems. When both licit and illicit types of drugs are used or abused for nonmedical purposes, they compromise psychological, social, and biological behavior. In the remaining sections of this chapter, we will review what drug prevention entails.

### ■ Why Drug Abuse Prevention in Early Childhood?

The first overarching principle drawn from the research reviewed for this resource is that intervening early in childhood can alter the life course trajectory of children in a positive direction (NIDA, 2016).

The major influences include one—*genetic factors*—inherited by his or her biological parents, that influences a person's development

### KEY TERMS

**drug prevention**
preventing or decreasing health problems, including social and personal problems, caused by drug dependency

**protective factors**
factors associated with preventing the potential for drug abuse such as self-control, parental support and parental supervision, academic competence, antidrug-use policies, and strong neighborhood attachment

**risk factors**
factors associated with increased risk of drug use such as early aggressive behavior, lack of parental supervision, the lure of gang membership, drug availability, and poverty

through the course of life, a person's abilities, personality, physical health, and vulnerability to risk factors for behavioral problems such as substance abuse (NIDA, 2016). Second is the *environment* or *the context* that directly influences the young child's early development and socialization. This also includes the following: siblings, relatives, and friends of parents who continually interact with the child; wider physical, social, economic, and historical realities such as the family's socioeconomic status and the affluence and safety of the community in which the family lives. Finally, early and substantial effect factors also include when a child grows older and enters school as an example of a wider environment having important influences on the child and his or her predisposition and attitudes directly and indirectly affecting the child (NIDA, 2016).

## Risk Factors and Protective Factors

From a broad perspective, when considering any drug-prevention program both **protective factors** and **risk factors** have to be considered. "Protective factors are those associated with reduced potential for drug use, and risk factors are those that make drug use more likely" (National Institute on Drug Abuse [NIDA], 2002). Examples of protective factor can include parental support and parental supervision (NIDA, 2014).

The following are the main principles that have to be considered when planning effective drug-prevention programs (quoted extensively from NIDA, 2003, p. 7; NIDA, 2014; and Robertson, Robertson, David, Rao, & NIDA, 2003, unless otherwise noted).

Drug-prevention programs should enhance protective factors and reverse or reduce risk factors.

*Protective factors* include the following:

- strong and positive family bonds,
- parental monitoring of children's activities and peers,
- clear rules of conduct consistently enforced within the family,
- involvement of parents in the lives of their children,
- success in school performance,
- strong bonds in institutions such as schools and religious organizations, and
- adoption of conventional norms about drug use.

*Risk factors* include the following:

- *maternal smoking and drinking* (NIDA, 2016);
- chaotic home environment, particularly in homes where parents abuse substances or suffer from mental illnesses;
- ineffective parenting, especially with children with difficult temperaments or conduct disorders;
- lack of parent–child attachments and nurturing;
- inappropriately shy or aggressive behavior in the classroom;
- failure in school performance;
- poor social coping skills;
- affiliations with peers displaying deviant behaviors;
- perceptions of approval of drug-using behaviors in family, work, school, peer, and community environments (NIDA, 2002); and
- poor self-control and aggressive behavior.

The risk of becoming a drug abuser involves the relationship among the number and type of risk factors (e.g., deviant attitudes and behaviors) and protective factors (e.g., parental support).

- The potential impact of specific risk and protective factors changes with age. For example, risk factors within the family have greater impact on a younger child, whereas association with drug-abusing peers may be a more significant risk factor for an adolescent.
- Early intervention with risk factors (e.g., aggressive behavior and poor self-control) often has a greater impact than later intervention by changing a child's life path (trajectory) away from problems and toward positive behaviors.
- Although risk and protective factors can affect people of all groups, these factors can have a different effect depending on a person's age, gender, ethnicity, culture, and neighborhood environment.
- Prevention programs should address all forms of drug abuse, alone or in combination, including the underage use of legal drugs (e.g., tobacco, alcohol), the use of illegal drugs (e.g., marijuana, heroin), and the inappropriate use of legally obtained substances (e.g., inhalants), prescription medications, or over-the-counter (OTC) drugs.
- Prevention programs should address the type of drug abuse problem in the local community, target modifiable risk factors, and strengthen identified protective factors.
- Prevention programs should be tailored to address risks specific to population or audience characteristics such as age, gender, and ethnicity to improve program effectiveness.

There are three levels of drug-prevention programs, each suited to different types of drug users. **Primary drug-prevention programs** are aimed at either nonusers who need to be "inoculated" against potential drug use or at helping at-risk individuals avoid the development of addictive behaviors. For example, primary prevention often targets at-risk youth who may live in areas where licit and illicit types of drugs are rampant, youth who may come from problem families, or youth who are surrounded by drug-abusing peers.

The other two major types of drug-prevention programs are **secondary drug-prevention programs**, which consist of uncovering potentially harmful substance use before the onset of overt symptoms or problems or targeting newer drug users with a limited or early history of drug use, and **tertiary drug-prevention programs**, which focus directly on intervention and target chemically dependent individuals who need treatment. Tertiary prevention involves treating the medical consequences of drug abuse and facilitating entry into treatment so further disability is minimized.

Primary, secondary, and tertiary programs are usually used in combination because, in most settings, all three types of drug users constitute the targeted population. **Table 17.1** further illustrates these levels of drug prevention and corresponding suggested activities. What can be accomplished is listed under each type of prevention—primary, secondary, and tertiary.

## KEY TERMS

**primary drug-prevention programs**
drug-prevention programs with a broad range of activities aimed at reducing the risk of drug use among nonusers and ensuring continued nonuse and helping at-risk individuals avoid the development of addictive behaviors

**secondary drug-prevention programs**
programs that consist of uncovering potentially harmful substance use before the onset of overt symptoms or problems or targeting newer drug users with a limited history of use; the main goal is to target at-risk groups, experimenters, and early-abuse populations

**tertiary drug-prevention programs**
drug-prevention programs focusing on intervention and targeting chemically dependent individuals who need treatment; tertiary prevention involves treating the medical consequences of drug abuse and facilitating entry into treatment so further disability is minimized (basically the same as drug abuse treatment)

**TABLE 17.1** Levels of Drug Prevention and Suggested Activities

| Primary Prevention (Risk Reduction Before Abuse) | |
|---|---|
| Intrapersonal factors | Affective education (emotional literacy) |
| | Resilience training |
| | Values clarification |
| | Personal and social skills development |
| | Assertiveness skills training |
| | Refusal skills |
| | Drug information and education |
| Small group factors | Peer mentoring, counseling, outreach, modeling |
| | Conflict resolution |
| | Curriculum infusion |
| | Activities demonstrating misperception of peer norms |
| | Alternatives to use: recreational, cultural, athletic |
| | Strengthening families |
| Systems level | Strengthening school–family links |
| | Strengthening school–community group links |
| | Strengthening community-support systems |
| | Media advocacy efforts, reducing alcohol marketing |
| **Secondary Prevention (Intervening in Early Abuse)** | |
| | Assessment strategies: identification of abuse subgroups and individual diagnoses |
| | Early intervention coupled with sanctions |
| | Teacher–counselor–parent team approach |
| | Developing healthy alternative youth culture |
| | Recovering role models |
| **Tertiary Prevention (Intervening in Advanced Abuse)** | |
| | Assessment and diagnosis |
| | Referral into treatment |
| | Case management |
| | Reentry |

# Considering the Audience and Approach

It is important to be aware that drug users vary in their exposure and past histories of substance use or abuse. The audience for drug prevention comprises both users and nonusers. In analyzing the population of users, the following categories can be used:

- nonusers;
- early experimenters;
- nonproblem drug users (i.e., those who abuse drugs on occasion, mostly for recreational purposes);
- undetected, committed, or secret users (i.e., those who abuse drugs and have no interest in stopping their drug use);
- problem users who are often drug dependent or addicted to drugs; and
- former users.

Role models, counselors, teachers, and anyone else involved in drug-prevention programs must consider the different types of substance users and abusers. Therefore, drug-prevention programs must cater to the specific needs of these groups. For nonproblem users, drug-education programs should examine the abuse of drugs and reinforce the message that uncontrolled use leads to abuse. For committed users, drug education should aim to prevent or delay drug abuse. Former users should be given information that will reinforce their decision to stop abusing drugs.

Several questions should be considered by a professional planning a prevention program. To what type of audience should the drug information be targeted? Youth or adults? Peers or parents? Should information focus on knowledge, attitudes, or behavior? Should the program emphasize and recommend abstinence or responsible use? In most cases, it is appropriate for drug prevention to focus on knowledge, attitudes, and behavior; the three are clearly related. For instance, if the goal is to increase knowledge, should we assume that attitudes and behavior would change accordingly, or should knowledge about the harmful effects of drugs be kept separate from attitudes and behavior? For example, if you learn that smoking marijuana is a health hazard that is equal to or more destructive than smoking cigarettes, does this knowledge limit the satisfaction you derive from smoking marijuana with friends? Some would say yes. Unfortunately, many would say no. In fact, knowledge about the harmful effects of certain types of drugs has little effect on the personal attitudes and habits of most people. Most cigarette smokers are aware of the health hazards before they start smoking, but this does not always stop them from starting or becoming addicted.

Drug-education programs have to direct their attention to a small range of behavioral objectives. They will not be effective if they address too many issues. Drug-prevention programs also must decide whether they will stress total abstinence or responsible use. Abstinence is radically different from responsible use. A program cannot advocate both. Information and scare tactics alone have no effect on drug use. Educational prevention models have been modified lately to achieve the following goals:

- Convey the message that society is inconsistent concerning drug use. For example, certain drugs that cause serious harm to a large percentage of the population are legal, whereas other drugs that have less impact are illegal.
- Convey that the reasons for drug use are complex and that drug users vary.
- Demonstrate to youth that young and old alike are affected by role models because attitudes regarding drug use are often patterned from family members who are role models.
- Acknowledge that other influential role models in music, sports, art, drama, business, and education who use and abuse drugs can affect attitudes toward drug use.

# Prevention Research: Key Findings

## ■ Costs of Substance Abuse

According to the National Institute on Drug Abuse, "Abuse of tobacco, alcohol, and illicit drugs is costly to our Nation, exacting more than $740 billion annually in costs related to crime, lost work productivity and health care" (NIDA, 2020).

The National Institute on Drug Abuse (2007, 2020) reported the following key findings regarding drug abuse prevention:

- *Addiction is a complex disease.* No single factor can predict who will become addicted to drugs. Addiction is influenced by a tangle of factors involving genes, environment, and age of first use. Recent advances in genetic research have enabled researchers to begin to uncover which genes make people more vulnerable, which protect a person against addiction, and how genes and environment interact. A more recent report said, "Addiction is a chronic disease characterized by drug seeking and use that is compulsive, or difficult to control, despite harmful consequences" (NIDA, 2018).
- *Addiction is a developmental disease.* It usually begins in adolescence or even childhood when the brain continues to undergo changes. The prefrontal cortex—located just behind the forehead—governs judgment and decision-making functions and is the last part of the brain to develop. This may help explain why teens are prone to risk-taking, why they are particularly vulnerable to drug abuse, and why exposure to drugs at this critical time may affect the possibility of future addiction.
- *Prevention and early intervention work best.* The developmental years might also present opportunities for resiliency and for receptivity to intervention that can alter the course of addiction. We already know many of the risk factors that lead to drug abuse and addiction—mental illness, physical or sexual abuse, aggressive behavior, academic problems, poor social skills, and poor parent–child relations. This knowledge, combined with better understanding of the motivational processes at work in the young brain, can be applied to prevent drug abuse from starting or to intervene early to stop it when warning signs emerge.

## ■ An Example of Drug Prevention at Central High in Elmtown

This section describes how a school-based prevention program is implemented and demonstrates that programs must be comprehensive and multifaceted to be successful.

Let us stand in the shoes of a parent and teacher committee trying to design a primary prevention program for students at Central High in Elmtown. The group has some prevention research materials that it received from the National Clearinghouse for Alcohol and Drug Information (NCDI). After some thought, most members of the committee decide not to address individual, personal risk factors that may generate anxieties, conflicts, or painful or threatening feelings. They have spoken with some students and ascertained that most of the 9th and 10th graders—even those who tend toward rebelliousness and avant-garde styles—are against taking drugs. Although many students feel this way, there are trends in the school that worry the committee members. Some popular 11th- and 12th-grade peer group leaders are drug users, and drug sales have been occurring on school grounds. The presence and availability of drugs and the beginning of a drug-using atmosphere make it more likely that some of the younger students will initiate use.

In brainstorming sessions, different committee members suggest ways to help these students avert initiation of drug use. Depending on their thinking, theoretical perspective, and exposure to prevention models, members come up with the following ideas:

- Students need to be grounded in good, solid knowledge about the negative effects and dangers of drugs as provided in a drug-education course or, more subtly, in a curriculum concerning drug effects and drug-using behaviors (also covered later in this chapter in the section on higher education).
- Students with low self-esteem will feel uncomfortable asserting individual choices or points of view that deviate from those held by peers or peer leaders. Bolstering a positive self-image would allow such students to refuse drugs.
- Students who have low expectations regarding their ability to refuse drugs will be least likely to actually refuse. The school might try to increase their *self-efficacy*; that is, their belief that their behaviors are powerful and will have results.
- Students just do not know how to say "no" and need refusal skills training or peer-resistance training.
- Although a clique leadership may set a tone that is receptive to drug use, the quiet antidrug students probably represent a silent majority. These students often misperceive and exaggerate the amount of recreational drug use that occurs in their school. If the antidrug students are shown that their own attitudes and beliefs are actually in the majority, they will see that the "emperor has no clothes."
- A more confrontational approach involves removing drugs from the school environment

by infiltrating the student body or using informants to gather information about who is distributing drugs. Dealers and users can then be identified or counseled and their parents notified. The school could make the decision to go as far as having the student arrested or expelled.

With so many options put forth, some committee members become frustrated and fear that a sufficient program will never be created. Some have experienced alcoholism in their families and fear that many of these approaches are ineffective for helping students who are already experimenting.

Seeing a disaster brewing, the committee chair makes a call to the Division of Substance Abuse Services in the state's health department to inquire about drug-prevention programs. The operator refers the call to the prevention specialists at the agency, who are linked to the National Prevention Network, which is part of the National Association of State Alcohol and Drug Abuse Directors. A specialist schedules a meeting with the committee, in which she makes the following points:

- A prevention needs assessment is helpful and necessitates using validated survey instruments to determine the patterns of behavior and attitudes regarding drug use among the student body.
- A combination of primary and secondary prevention would be good for the majority of the student body, and group treatment for substance abuse should be made available at an adolescent outpatient clinic. The outpatient clinic will assess some students who are well on their way to addiction and refer them into inpatient treatment. Because this intervention occurs when the student is at an advanced abuse state, this is considered tertiary prevention.

Notice how all three types of approaches—primary, secondary, and tertiary—are necessary to implement a comprehensive prevention strategy.

The specialist brought along a staff member of the Local Council on Alcoholism and Drug Dependence, an affiliate of the National Council on Alcoholism and Drug Dependence (NCADD) branch serving a three-county region of the state. Thousands of branches of NCADD exist in the United States, and their goal is to help local groups design and implement prevention programs. Many branches have developed specialized programs for teens, children, women, and the elderly. The staff member conducts preliminary sessions with the prevention committee and arranges to sign an affiliation agreement with the school administration whereby NCADD will act as a consultant to the school, aiding it in designing a prevention program to fit its particular needs. It will design a project, which will be based on a needs assessment that incorporates a survey of chemical attitudes and use and interviews with parents, teachers, and students. The project design will include the program objectives, a method and management plan, a timeline, and an evaluation component.

To help those members bewildered by the many possible factors identified by the committee in its brainstorming session (such as self-esteem, self-efficacy, and refusal skills), the staff member invites the committee to sample several available, attractive packages of user-friendly activities, such as the following:

- Broad-brush packages that cover a variety of personal choice and primary prevention areas (Holstein, Cohen, & Steinbroner, 1995; Legal Action Center, 2016) and
- More targeted strategies that might include a training package to be implemented by a consultant hired by the school district to address issues such as assertiveness training.

Assertiveness-training skills, which include a variety of personal and social skills, enable people to communicate their needs and feelings in an open, direct, and appropriate manner while still recognizing the needs and feelings of others. They make people feel more powerful and better about themselves (that is, less like doormats), and they offer strategies for saying "no" without hurting, provoking, or manipulating others (Alberti & Emmons, 1988). Assertive behavior contrasts with hostile or belligerent behavior, passive and helpless behavior, and passive–aggressive or indirect manipulation. The exercises included in assertiveness training are nonthreatening, concrete, direct, and enjoyable.

Many intrapersonal prevention concepts, or personal and social skills development concepts, have come and gone, with a trendy buzzword accompanying each one in the year it was introduced. Many of these concepts overlap, such as *life skills training, self-esteem, self-efficacy, resilience training,* and *assertiveness training* (McIntyre, White, & Yoast, 1990; Norman, 1994). The danger lies in employing them as gimmicks or slogans that accomplish little. Nevertheless, as Botvin and

others have shown, personal and skills training that is carefully based on known cognitive and behavioral change factors, if carefully put into place, can indeed make a difference (Botvin & Griffin, 2005; Botvin & Wills, 1985; Shiffman & Wills, 1987). It also is true that almost any positive lifestyle activity is likely to act as an alternative to participating in a drug-using subculture.

In essence, "[p]revention programs should address all forms of drug abuse, alone or in combination, including the underage use of legal drugs (e.g., tobacco or alcohol); the use of illegal drugs (e.g., marijuana or heroin); and the inappropriate use of legally obtained substances (e.g., inhalants), prescription medications, or over-the-counter drugs" (NIDA, 2014).

# Comprehensive Prevention Programs for Drug Use and Abuse

Comprehensive drug-prevention programs range from broad approaches at the societal level to narrower programs at the community, school, family, and individual levels. Comprehensive prevention programs can include ideological and institutional approaches, methods, and perspectives regarding drug prevention. In essence, comprehensive drug-prevention programs are broad based, affecting both single and multiple groups in a society, and can also include entire societies in how they approach and deal with the problem of drug use and abuse. Next we explore major types of comprehensive drug-prevention programs and varying levels.

## ■ Harm Reduction Model

The **harm-reduction model** is a broad and comprehensive model that involves society-wide prevention. As an approach to drug use and addiction, this model is practiced in some cities in the Netherlands and the United Kingdom. It is described by Westermeyer (n.d.) as an addiction model that connects "with the addicted community, by having an 'open door policy' that

KEY TERM

**harm-reduction model**
society-wide approach to drug use and abuse that focuses on reducing the harm experienced by the drug user or abuser as well as the harm to society

welcomes addicts to take part in services, regardless of level of motivation for change, goals or personal ideology." In a sense, it is a model that meets addicts on their own level.

Westermeyer (n.d.) identifies three central beliefs of the harm reduction model:

1. Excessive behaviors occur along a continuum of risk ranging from minimal to extreme. Addictive behaviors are not all-or-nothing phenomena. Although a drug or alcohol abstainer has a lower risk of harm than a drug or alcohol user, a moderate drinker is causing less harm than a binge drinker; a crystal methamphetamine smoker or sniffer is causing less harm than a crystal injector.
2. Changing addictive behavior is a stepwise process, with complete abstinence being the final step. Those who embrace the harm-reduction model believe that any movement in the direction of reduced harm—no matter how small—is positive in and of itself.
3. Sobriety simply is not for everybody. This statement requires the acceptance that many people live in horrible circumstances. Some are able to cope without the use of drugs; others use drugs as a primary means of coping. Until we are in a position to offer an alternative means of survival to these individuals, we are in no position to cast moral judgment. The health and well-being of the individual are of primary concern; if individuals are unwilling or unable to change addictive behavior at this time, they should not be denied services. *Attempts should be made to reduce the harm of their habits as much as possible.*

According to Westermeyer, the Dutch (who created this approach to prevention of drug use and abuse) have "an 80% connection rate with the addicted population," whereas in the United States we are 80% disconnected from our addicted populations. In fact, through our punitive model in dealing with drug users, the strongest connection we have with the addicted population in the United States comes when they are arrested and jailed.

According to the Harm Reduction Coalition,

"was founded in 1993 and incorporated in 1994 by a working group of needle exchange providers, advocates, and drug users. Today, we are strengthened by an extensive and diverse network of allies who challenge the persistent stigma faced by people who use drugs and advocate for policy and public health reform. (Harm Reduction Coalition, n.d.)

Harm reduction incorporates a spectrum of strategies from safer use to managed use to abstinence to meet drug users "where they're at," addressing conditions of use along with the use itself. Because harm reduction demands that interventions and policies designed to serve drug users reflect specific individual and community needs, there is no universal definition of or formula for implementing harm reduction.

The Harm Reduction Coalition has set forth the following principles as being critical to the success of harm-reduction programs:

- accepts, for better and for worse, that licit and illicit drug use is part of our world and chooses to work to minimize its harmful effects rather than simply ignore or condemn them;
- understands drug use as a complex, multi-faceted phenomenon that encompasses a continuum of behaviors from severe abuse to total abstinence, and acknowledges that some ways of using drugs are clearly safer than others;
- establishes quality of individual and community life and well-being—not necessarily cessation of all drug use—as the criteria for successful interventions and policies;
- calls for the nonjudgmental, noncoercive provision of services and resources to people who use drugs and the communities in which they live in order to assist them in reducing attendant harm;
- ensures that drug users and those with a history of drug use routinely have a real voice in the creation of programs and policies designed to serve them;
- affirms drugs users themselves as the primary agents of reducing the harms of their drug use and seeks to empower users to share information and support each other in strategies that meet their actual conditions of use;
- recognizes that the realities of poverty, class, racism, social isolation, past trauma, sex-based discrimination, and other social inequalities affect both people's vulnerability to and capacity for effectively dealing with drug-related harm; and
- does not attempt to minimize or ignore the real and tragic harm and danger associated with licit and illicit drug use.

Harm reduction seeks to reduce the harms of drug policies dependent on an overemphasis on interdiction, such as arrest, incarceration, establishment of a felony record, lack of treatment, lack of adequate information about drugs, the expansion of military source control intervention efforts in other countries, and intrusion on personal freedoms. Harm reduction also seeks to reduce the harms caused by an over-emphasis on prohibition, such as increased purity, black market adulterants, black market sale to minors, and black market crime. A harm reduction strategy seeks to protect youth from the dangers of drugs by offering factual, science-based drug education and eliminating youth's black market exposure to drugs. A harm reduction approach advocates lessening the harms of drugs through education, prevention, and treatment. Finally, harm reduction seeks to restore basic human dignity to dealing with the disease of addiction. (AlcoholAnswers.org, 2013)

## Community-Based Drug Prevention

We begin by defining community-based prevention.

### ■ What Is Community-Based Prevention?

Many different types of people do prevention activities within a community. Some are prevention professionals, or people who have been formally trained and certified in substance abuse prevention. They can be paid by an organization to do this work.

Community-based programs are broad and take into account the community's youth, parents, businesses, media, schools, law enforcement, religious or fraternal groups, civic or volunteer groups, health-care professionals, and government agencies with expertise in the field of substance abuse. The primary goal of community-based prevention is to provide coordinated programs among the numerous agencies and organizations involved in prevention.

Prevention requires communities to conduct a structured review of current prevention programs to determine (1) whether the programs in place were examined and tested according to rigorous scientific standards during their development and (2) whether these programs incorporate the basic principles of prevention that have been identified in research. Usually, prevention programs at the community level ask the following questions

(Robertson, David, Rao, & NIDA, 2003; Sloboda & David, 1999):

- Does the program have components for the individual, the family, the school, the media, community organizations, and healthcare providers? Are the program components well integrated in theme and content so that they reinforce rather than duplicate one another?
- Does the prevention program use media and community-education strategies to increase public awareness, attracting community support, reinforcing the school-based curriculum for students and parents, and keeping the public informed of the program's progress?
- Are interventions carefully designed to reach different at-risk populations, and are they of sufficient duration to make an impact?
- Does the program follow a structured organizational plan that progresses from needs assessment through planning, implementation, and review to refinement, with feedback to and from the community at all stages?
- Are the objectives and activities specific, time limited, feasible (in terms of available resources), and integrated so that they work together across program components and can be used to evaluate program progress and outcomes?

Often these programs set up prevention policy boards to oversee planning and implementation. Boards should include representatives from law enforcement, juvenile justice, education, recreation, social services, private industry, health and mental health agencies, churches, civic organizations, and other community agencies that serve youth and families. They should also include one or several youth members. "The community can be a target group, especially when there is extensive community denial or lack of awareness, lack of clear policies, poor law enforcement, and so on. Public awareness campaigns, political action, and similar efforts are appropriate at this level of prevention" (Tinzmann & Hixson, 2006, pp. 2, 3).

Community prevention programs can also direct their attention to changing the legal and social environment regarding **alcohol, tobacco, and other drug (ATOD)** supplies and toward youth (Center for Prevention Research and

Development, 2000). This effort also includes individual and environmental strategies. For example, an environmental approach to reducing underage drinking might involve training clerks to insist on proper age identification when selling alcoholic beverages. An individual approach might involve education efforts such as a media campaign aimed at discouraging young people from drinking (Silver Gate Group & Robert Wood Johnson Foundation, 2001).

Other community-based strategies include the following:

- strengthening the enforcement of existing legal regulations of ATOD sales and use;
- educating merchants and servers about alcohol and tobacco sales laws;
- regulating legislation regarding the sale of alcohol and tobacco to minors;
- implementing use-and-lose laws that allow for the suspension of the driver's license of a person younger than 21 following a conviction for any alcohol or drug violation (e.g., use, possession, or attempt to purchase with or without false identification); and
- imposing regulations on location and density of retail outlet—that is, monitoring the number of unsupervised vending machines dispensing cigarettes to minors in a given community and monitoring the number of retail establishments selling alcohol and tobacco near schools.

Community-based prevention programs recently have been endorsed, having been found to be not only viable but also cost-effective:

Drug use prevention programmes are effective when they respond to the needs of a community, involve all the relevant sectors, and are based on evidence; effective programmes should also incorporate strong monitoring and evaluation components. Such programmes are also cost effective.... If other costs to society were to be counted, such as the costs resulting from crime, unemployment, and ill health, the cost effectiveness of good drug use prevention programmes is likely to be even greater. (United Nations Office on Drugs and Crime [UNODC], 2011)

A community-based organization that must be mentioned is the Community Anti-Drug Coalitions of America (CADCA), which was organized in 1992. Since then, CADCA has demonstrated that when all sectors of a community come together, social change happens. According to CADCA,

CADCA represents over 5,000 community coalitions that involve individuals from key sectors including schools, law enforcement, youth, parents, healthcare, media and others. We have members in every U.S. state and territory and more than 30 countries around the world. The CADCA coalition model emphasizes the power of community coalitions to prevent substance misuse through collaborative community efforts. We believe that prevention of substance use and misuse before it starts is the most effective and cost-efficient way to reduce substance use and its associated costs (CADCA, 2020).

CADCA provides the following core services:

- training and technical assistance,
- dissemination and coalition relations,
- research and evaluation,
- public policy and advocacy,
- membership and communicating,
- special events and conferences, and
- international programs.

In conclusion, community prevention emphasizes comprehensive drug abuse prevention programs that include multiple components such as the use of media, drug education in schools, parent education, community organizations, and formulation of drug-related health policy. In essence, community drug prevention seeks to reduce drug abuse by informing, coordinating, and decreasing the level of drug use at the community level.

## ▪ School-Based Drug Prevention

Education has been used extensively in the past to control the use and abuse of drugs, especially alcohol and tobacco. Drug education actually began in the late 1800s, when most states required that the harmful effects of certain drugs be taught. An example of an early educational attempt to curb or stop drug abuse is the temperance movement of the late 19th century. The Women's Christian Temperance Union and the Anti-Saloon League taught that alcohol consumption was harmful and contrary to Christian morality.

Years ago, when drug prevention was first attempted, most substance abuse experts thought that schools should be responsible for educating the public about the dangerous use and eventual abuse of drugs because education is the main objective of schooling. Schools began teaching about drug use, but in the beginning drug prevention focused on individual factors such as the dangers of particular types of drugs, the dangers of trusting individuals who sell drugs, and other scare tactics. One problem with this approach was that students varied enormously with regard to their drug experiences. Often the students had already tried the dangerous drugs and had experienced only pleasurable effects with few negative consequences. Their experiences occurred before their exposure to drug-prevention programs that relied on negative information, which is generally known as the **scare tactic or fear-based approach**. Many self-reported use surveys revealed that these programs were not successful. With such audiences of drug users, the warnings are short-lived, not believed, or perceived as exaggerations. Today the use of evidence-based drug education is "based on life skills that offer personal, social, resistance and communication skills, as well as information about the short-term effects of drugs through a series of sessions offered by trained teachers" (UNODC, 2011). Another more recent study reported that "[e]valuation has shown fear-based approaches not to be effective. Programmes depending only on information provision or only on boosting self-esteem also appear to be ineffective. Interactive teaching also seems to be necessary for success, with more didactic approaches generally unsuccessful" (Claire, 2013, p. 23).

School-based programs that are the most successful

> [p]rovide information about drugs and alcohol, in particular correcting misperceptions about how common and acceptable substance misuse is among the young people's peer group (normative education). They also teach interpersonal skills to help handle realistic situations where alcohol or drug are available. Examples with strong evidence base include the Life Skills training programme, developed in the United States, and Unplugged, tested in a large scale evaluation across several European countries. (Claire, 2013, p. 23)

It is equally important that school prevention programs include teacher training on good classroom-management practices such as rewarding appropriate student behavior. Such techniques help foster students' positive behavior, achievement, academic motivation, and school bonding (NIDA, 2014).

**Table 17.2** summarizes the most popular, common, school-based drug-prevention programs, including the premise, strategies, and effectiveness of the following approaches: (1) cognitive, (2) affective, (3) combined cognitive and affective, (4) social learning and cognitive-behavioral, and (5) normative education. Table 17.2 also details the strengths (if any) and weaknesses of each approach.

Finally, two more recent successful school drug-prevention programs that "speak" to their audiences are the Athletes Training and Learning to Avoid Steroids (ATLAS) for males and Athletes Targeting Healthy Exercise and Nutrition Alternatives (ATHENA) for females. These two programs target teenage athletes and specifically focus on addressing steroid abuse and other unhealthy behaviors (e.g., drinking and driving). These two programs leverage the influence of coaches and peer groups to highlight proper sports nutrition, strength training, and other positive alternatives to using drugs to improve performance and build confidence. ATLAS and ATHENA have now been adopted by schools in 29 states and Puerto Rico and have been endorsed by Congress as exemplary prevention programs (NIDA, 2007).

## SCHOOL-BASED PREVENTION POLICIES FOCUSED ON ENFORCEMENT

Grounded in **prohibitionist philosophy** and the law enforcement approach, and largely devoid of public health perspectives and strategies, the following measures have been used to prevent and reduce substance use among students:

- antismoking policies,
- zero-tolerance policies,
- drug searches, and
- drug testing.

These law enforcement approaches aimed at middle school and high school students across the United States began in 1987 when Congress

## KEY TERMS

**scare tactic or fear-based approach**
dug-prevention information based on emphasizing the extreme negative effects of drug use—scaring the audience of potential and current drug users and abusers into not using drugs

**prohibitionist philosophy (regarding drug use)**
reducing or stopping unwanted drug use by legally banning and punishing drug use

**TABLE 17.2** Summary of Common School-Based Drug-Prevention Approaches

| Approach | Premise | Strategies | Effectiveness |
|---|---|---|---|
| Cognitive | If youth understand the dangers of AOD, they will not use them. | Teach pharmacology of alcohol and other drugs, how they are used, long-range consequences of use—usually through scare tactics. | Seldom effective; sometimes detrimental—arouses curiosity and encourages experimentation. Dire facts are not credible; knowledge alone does not counteract peer pressure. Knowledge is necessary but not sufficient; focus on more immediate physical or social consequences may work. |
| Affective | High self-esteem, values consistent with nonuse, and good problem-solving and decision-making skills help youth avoid AOD. | Raise self-esteem. Teach values and life skills. Typically, do not include AOD information. | Do not decrease rate of use. Some community members and parents protest teaching values and decision-making. Need to include AOD* information. |
| Combined cognitive and affective | Students need both information and life skills to avoid AOD use. | Teach problem-solving, decision-making, and peer pressure–resistance skills and provide explicit information about AOD to connect life skills and AOD use and consequences. | Little consistent effect on reducing AOD use, although some successes have been reported. |
| Social learning, cognitive-behavioral | AOD use usually begins in a social setting between grades 5 and 9, usually with peers, but sometimes adults. Youth need skills for resisting these pressures (based on Bandura's social learning theory). | Teach how to identify pressures from peers, media, advertising, and families. Teach resistance skills and model counterarguments. Students role-play pressure situations and actively practice resisting. | Sometimes effective, especially if peers are involved in instruction and when students already have other fairly well-developed social skills. Little evidence that effects last. |
| Normative education | Youth overestimate the extent of AOD use among peers and thus may use AOD to feel part of the group. | Correct misconceptions, demonstrate actual norms through discussion, and develop nonuse norms. | Success with some drugs; not especially effective with alcohol. Some youngsters may believe that fewer peers use AOD than actually do and may come to feel AOD use is more acceptable than they did before entering the program. |

*AOD: Alcohol and other drugs

Data from Tinzmann, M. B., & Hixson, J. (2006). *What does research say about prevention?* Oak Brook, IL: North Central Regional Educational Laboratory.

enacted the Drug-Free Schools and Communities Act (DFSCA). Several law enforcement approaches today are in force in many schools, representing more activist and some say hard-line prohibitionist approaches for reducing and preventing drug use. In many communities across the United States, as well as in many countries throughout the world, there is a wide variety of opinions regarding their success for curbing recreational drug use, which includes student use of tobacco, alcohol, and other drugs.

## CURRICULUM-BASED DRUG-EDUCATION OBJECTIVES

To educate students about the dangers of drug use, school-based drug-education programs and objectives have been implemented in most U.S. school curricula. Specific educational topics have been established for use at the elementary, middle school, high school, and college levels.

The elementary level includes the following topics:

- drugs versus poisons;
- effects of alcohol, tobacco, and marijuana on the body;
- differences between candy and drugs;
- drug overdoses;
- dangers of experimentation;
- how to say "no" to peers offering drugs; and
- reasons for taking drugs—curing illness, pleasure, escape, parental use, and ceremony.

At the middle school level, the topics expand to include the following:

- how peer pressure works;
- how to say "no" to peer pressure;
- how drugs affect the body, physiologically and psychologically;
- where to seek help when needed;
- attitudes toward drug use;
- how to have fun without drugs;
- harmful effects of tobacco, alcohol, and marijuana on the body;
- stress management and building positive self-esteem;
- how advertisers push drugs;
- consequences of breaking drug laws;
- differences among wine, beer, and distilled spirits;
- family drug use;
- family drinking problems and family members who may have drug addiction problems;
- images of violence and drug use in rock and rap music; and
- teenage drug abuse and associated problems.

Topics at the high school and college level include the following:

- responsible use of medications;
- how drugs affect the body and the mind;
- legal versus illegal drugs;
- drinking and driving;
- drug effects on the fetus;
- recreational drug use;
- ways of coping with problems—anger and stress management;
- how to detect problem drug users;
- drug education, prevention, and treatment;
- positive and negative role models;
- how to build positive self-esteem;
- criminal sanctions for various types of drug use;
- binge drinking;
- drugs and driving;
- date rape; and
- addiction to drugs and alcoholism.

## PRINCIPAL QUESTIONS FOR SCHOOL-BASED PROGRAMS

The following questions should be asked to improve the outcomes of drug-education programs:

- Do the school-based programs reach children from kindergarten through high school? If not, do they at least reach children during the critical middle school or junior high years?
- Do the programs contain multiple years of intervention (all through the middle school or junior high years)?
- Do the programs use a well-tested, standardized intervention with detailed lesson plans and student materials?
- Do the programs use age-appropriate interactive teaching methods (modeling, role-playing, discussion, group feedback, reinforcement, extended practice)?
- Do the programs foster social bonding to the school and community?
- Do the programs teach social competence (communication, self-efficacy, assertiveness) and drug-resistance skills that are culturally and developmentally appropriate?
- Do the programs promote positive peer influence?
- Do the programs promote antidrug social norms?
- Do the programs emphasize skills-training teaching methods?
- Do the programs include an adequate "dosage" (10 to 15 sessions in year 1 and another 10 to 15 booster sessions)?
- Is there periodic evaluation to determine whether the programs are effective?

## ■ Family-Based Prevention Programs

Primary family risk factors that predispose youth to find drugs attractive include the following:

- chaotic home environments, particularly in which parents abuse substances or suffer from mental illnesses;
- ineffective parenting, especially with children with difficult temperaments and conduct disorders; and
- lack of mutual attachments and nurturing.

In addition, "[r]esults from longitudinal studies of children, particularly those children most at risk for problems, indicate that families can protect children and youth against drug use and abuse through effective family management practices that impart skills young people can use in resisting social pressures to use drugs" (National Institutes of Health [NIH] & NIDA, 1998, p. 49).

Although the just-listed risk factors are the primary risk factors, *protective factors*—the factors that can insulate against drug use—include the following:

* strong parent–child bonds,
* parental monitoring with clear rules of conduct within the family unit and involvement of parents in the lives of their children,
* open communication of values within the family,
* high levels of supervision and monitoring,
* no inconsistent disciplining from lackadaisical to extreme enforcement of rules and no saying one thing and then doing another, and
* consistent high levels of parental warmth, affection, and emotional support.

Research shows that protective family factors can moderate the effects of risk factors (Cleveland, Collins, Lanza, Greenberg, & Feinberg, 2010; NIDA, 2003). The risk of associating with peers who use drugs can be offset by protective family factors such as parent conventionality, maternal adjustment, and strong parent–child attachment.

Prevention at the family level needs to stress parent–child interaction strategies, communication skills, child management practices, and family management skills. Research has also shown that parents need to take a more active role in their children's lives. This includes talking to their children about drugs, monitoring their activities, getting to know their friends, and understanding their problems and personal concerns (NIH & NIDA, 1998). Such interactive techniques are deemed most effective when, for example, peer discussion groups and parent role-playing are used, which allows for active involvement in learning about drug abuse and reinforcing skills (NIDA, 2014).

### PREVENTION PRINCIPLES FOR FAMILY-BASED PROGRAMS

In conclusion, family-based prevention programs need to do the following:

KEY TERM

**harm-reduction psychotherapy**
an alternative therapy based on harm-reduction philosophy and aimed at reducing negative consequences associated with drug use that accepts abstinence of drug use or less use of a drug by gaining control over drug abusive behavior

* reach families of children at each stage of development;
* train parents in behavioral skills to:
  * reduce conduct problems in children;
  * improve parent–child relations, including positive reinforcement, listening and communication skills, and problem-solving;
  * provide consistent discipline and rule-making;
  * monitor children's activities during adolescence;
* include an educational component for parents with drug information for them and their children;
* focus on families whose children are in kindergarten through 12th grade to enhance protective factors; and
* provide access to counseling services for families at risk.

### ▪ Individual-Based Drug Prevention and Treatment: Harm-Reduction Psychotherapy

Another approach is **harm-reduction psychotherapy**, which is an alternative therapy based on harm-reduction philosophy aimed at reducing negative consequences associated with drug use that accepts abstinence of drug use or less use of a drug by gaining control over drug abusive behavior. Harm-reduction psychotherapy uses several treatment models that can be used in outpatient settings, residential treatment, homeless programs, traditional drug treatment programs, medical services, community outreach programs among other service delivery settings. According to Tatarsky (2002, p. 10):

> Harm reduction is a. . . [therapeutic]. . . framework for helping drug and alcohol users who cannot or will not stop completely—the majority of users—reduce the. harmful consequences of use. Harm reduction accepts that abstinence may be the best outcome for many but relaxes the emphasis on abstinence as the only acceptable goal and criterion of success. Instead, smaller incremental change in the direction of reduced harmfulness of drug use are accepted.

This type of therapy treatment emphasizes collaboration, respect, and self-determination, which differs from traditional addiction treatment. Traditional drug treatment programs generally follow a 12-step program (much like Alcoholics

# ▶ CASE IN POINT

## Lessons from Prevention Research

Prevention programs are generally designed for use in a particular setting such as at home, at school, or within the community but can be adapted for use in several settings. In addition, programs are also designed with the intended audience in mind: for everyone in the population, for those at greater risk, and for those already involved with drugs or other problem behaviors. Some programs can be geared for more than one audience (NIDA, 2014).

Principle 1: Prevention programs should enhance protective factors and reverse or reduce risk factors.

- This includes the risk of becoming a drug abuser.
- The potential impact of specific risk and protective facts changes with age.
- Early intervention should be done with certain risk factors such as aggressive behavior and poor self-control.
- Risk and protective factors change and vary with a person's age, gender, ethnicity, culture, and environment.

Principle 2: Prevention programs should address all forms of drug abuse, alone or in combination, including the underage use of legal drugs (e.g., tobacco or alcohol), the use of illegal drugs (e.g., marijuana or heroin), and the inappropriate use of legally obtained substances (e.g., inhalants), prescription medications, or OTC drugs.

Principle 3: Prevention programs should address the type of drug abuse problem in the local community, target modifiable risk factors, and strengthen identified protective factors.

Principle 4: Prevention programs should be tailored to address risks specific to population or audience characteristics such as age, gender, and ethnicity to improve program effectiveness.

Principle 5: Family-based prevention programs should enhance family bonding and relationships and include parenting skills; practice in developing, discussing, and enforcing family policies on substance abuse; and training in drug education and information

Principle 6: Prevention programs can be designed to intervene as early as infancy to address risk factors

for drug abuse such as aggressive behavior, poor social skills, and academic difficulties.

Principle 7: Prevention programs for elementary school children should target improving academic and social-emotional learning to address risk factors for drug abuse such as early aggression, academic failure, and school dropout. Education should focus on the following skills:

- self-control,
- emotional awareness,
- communication,
- social problem-solving, and
- academic support, especially in reading.

Principle 8: Prevention programs for middle or junior high and high school students should increase academic and social competence with the following skills):

- study habits and academic support,
- communication,
- peer relationships,
- self-efficacy and assertiveness,
- drug-resistance skills,
- reinforcement of antidrug attitudes, and
- strengthening of personal commitments against drug abuse.

Principle 9: Prevention programs aimed at general populations at key transition points such as the transition to middle school can produce beneficial effects even among high-risk families and children. Such interventions do not single out at-risk populations and therefore reduce labeling and promote bonding to school and community.

Principle 10: Community prevention programs that combine two or more effective programs such as family-based and school-based programs can be more effective than a single program alone.

Principle 11: Community prevention programs reaching populations in multiple settings—for example, schools, clubs, faith-based organizations, and the media—are most effective when they present consistent, community-wide messages in each setting.

Principle 12: When communities adapt programs to match their needs, community norms, or differing cultural

*(continues)*

▶ **CASE IN POINT**

## Lessons from Prevention Research (*continued*)

requirements, they should retain core elements of the original research-based intervention, which include:

- structure (how the program is organized and constructed),
- content (the information, skills, and strategies of the program), and
- delivery (how the program is adapted, implemented, and evaluated).

Principle 13: Prevention programs should be long term with repeated interventions (i.e., booster programs) to reinforce the original prevention goals. Research shows that the benefits from middle school prevention programs diminish without follow-up programs in high school.

Principle 14: Prevention programs should include teacher training on good classroom-management practices such as rewarding appropriate student behavior. Such techniques help foster students' positive behavior, achievement, academic motivation, and school bonding.

Principle 15: Prevention programs are most effective when they employ interactive techniques such as peer discussion groups and parent role-playing that allow for active involvement in learning about drug abuse and reinforcing skills.

Principle 16: Research-based prevention programs can be cost-effective. Similar to earlier research, recent research shows that for each dollar invested in prevention, a savings of up to $10 in treatment for alcohol or other substance abuse can be seen (NIDA, 2014).

Anonymous and Narcotics Anonymous) and often use varying amounts of confrontation and coercion in their treatment programs. (For another example of a semi- or quasi-type of harm-reduction drug prevention and treatment method, see "Case in Point: A New Alternative to Conventional Drug Prevention and Treatment: A Nontreatment Program for Alcohol and Drug Abuse.")

## Drug Prevention Programs in Higher Education

The seriousness of alcohol and other drug use on college campuses is underscored by the following findings (California Polytechnic State University, 2016):

- According to the Core Institute, an organization that surveys college drinking practices, 300,000 of today's college students will eventually die of alcohol-related causes such as drunken-driving accidents, cirrhosis of the liver, various cancers, and heart disease.
- Of today's first-year college students, 159,000 will drop out of school next year because of alcohol or other drug-related reasons.
- Almost one-third of college students admit to having missed at least one class because of their alcohol or drug use.

- One night of heavy drinking can impair a person's ability to think abstractly for up to 30 days, limiting the ability to relate textbook reading to classroom discussions or to think through processes such as football plays.

As these statistics indicate, the use of alcohol and other drugs is a serious problem within the college or university environment. Major problems on college campuses resulting from such drug abuse include property damage, poor academic performance, damaged relationships, unprotected sexual activity, physical injuries, date rape, and suicide (Ansari, Stock, & Mills, 2013; Perkins, 1997).

It is obvious that with all of these negative findings regarding alcohol and other drug use on college campuses, prevention programs are vital. Next we review the major prevention programs that currently exist in higher education.

### ■ Overview and Critique of Existing Prevention Programs

This next section will review and critique four drug-prevention program models in higher education. The four program models are:

1. the information-only or awareness model,
2. the attitude change model or affective education model,
3. the social influences model, and
4. the ecological or person-in-environment model.

The first model, the **information-only or awareness model**, is based solely on teaching about drug information, primarily the effects of using different types of drugs. This model heavily relies on making students knowledgeable about various drugs. The second model, the **attitude change or affective education model**, works on attitude change and the role of self-esteem regarding drug use and abuse. The third model, the **social influences model**, focuses on how to use resistance skills when drugs are readily available in a student's environment, taking into account such social psychological factors as prior socialization and peer pressure. The fourth model, the **ecological or person-in-environment (PIE) model**, looks at how changes in a student's social environment can affect attitudes about drugs and drug use.

## INFORMATION-ONLY OR AWARENESS MODEL

One of the earliest preventive interventions, this model is based on the belief that if people are given extensive information about the harmful effects of drugs it will change their attitudes about use and abuse. This model assumes that people are rational enough to seriously curtail or stop drug use based on information. Obviously, today we know that, at most, the majority of drug users exposed to the information-only or awareness model become more knowledgeable about the effects of drugs, but this approach has little influence on the use of habitual or addictive-type drugs.

## ATTITUDE CHANGE OR AFFECTIVE EDUCATION MODEL

The attitude change or affective education model assumes that people use drugs because they have low self-esteem (alcoholrehab.com, 2016; Gonzalez & Clement, 1994). As a result, prevention focuses on strengthening self-image, building positive self-esteem, and boosting self-confidence. A problem with this model is that attitudes often are resistant to change and fluctuate depending on such environmental influences as peer and party settings. Attitudes that were formed in an educational setting (drug and alcohol classes) are abandoned in substance use settings.

## SOCIAL INFLUENCES MODEL

The social influences model assumes that substance abuse results from multiple influences. Although outside influences are perceived as major influences, inner influences—such as prior socialization, a vulnerability to pleasing others,

and a need to be accepted by friends and peers—are likewise taken into account. This prevention strategy emphasizes peer-resistance and inoculation techniques. Techniques primarily include the following (European Monitoring Centre for Drugs and Drug Addiction, 2010; Gonzalez & Clement, 1994; National Crime Prevention Centre, 2019):

- offering factual information about the consequences of drug use;
- guiding development of skills to recognize outer and inner pressures to use drugs and methods and techniques to resist usage;
- communicating correct information about the extent of drug use by students of similar ages;
- modeling, rehearsing, and reinforcing skills for resisting drugs when friends or peers expect compliance; and
- persuading students to try these resistance approaches and techniques in classroom or group settings and in peer group settings away from the classroom.

By far, this method has been more successful than the information-only and attitude change models. Although it works best when it begins at the junior high school level, refresher courses should be administered at least every two years. Some research findings indicate that although this method is least effective with alcohol consumption, it is effective with marijuana and cigarette smoking (Gonzalez & Clement, 1994).

## ECOLOGICAL OR PERSON-IN-ENVIRONMENT MODEL (PIE)

This model is one of the newest types of prevention programs. "Interventions based on this model have multiple components and are designed to

**KEY TERMS**

**information-only or awareness model**
assumes that teaching about the harmful effects of drugs will change attitudes about use and abuse

**attitude change or affective education model**
assumes that people use drugs because of lack of self-esteem

**social influences model**
assumes that drug users lack resistance skills

**ecological or person-in-environment (PIE) model**
stresses that changes in the environment change people's attitudes about drugs

address individuals and the policies, practices, and social norms that affect students on campuses or in the community" (Gonzalez & Clement, 1994, p. 3). In other words,

> This perspective is based on the notion that an individual and his or her behavior cannot be understood adequately without consideration of the various aspects of that individual's environment (social, political, familial, temporal, spiritual, economic, and physical). A person-in-environment perspective is said to provide a more adequate framework for assessing an individual and his or her presenting problem and strengths than an approach that focuses solely on changing an individual's behavior or psyche, or one that focuses solely on environmental conditions. (Kondrat, 2015)

Developed from human ecology, the ecological or person-in-environment (PIE) model stresses that changes in the environment change people. Although the ecological or PIE model does not ignore substance use from individual causes such as personal beliefs and perception of risk, it does primarily focus on the causes from the social environment (Hansen, 1997; Kondrat, 2015). According to Hansen (1997), "The central tenet [belief] of social ecology is that individual behavior is mainly the result of socialization; to change the behavior, we must change the social institutions that shape it" (p. 6). Hansen also stated "the strongest predictors of alcohol and drug abuse among young people are social" (p. 6).

This perspective emphasizes that it is important to take into account all of the environments that may have an impact on drug use. Friends, acquaintances, roommates, and classmates in dorms, sororities, and fraternities and at parties, cafes, and nightspots can influence students (U.S. Department of Education, 1994).

As a result, this model advocates the following drug-prevention strategies (Gonzalez & Clement, 1994):

- dissemination of drug information;
- cognitive and behavioral skills training for youth, parents, and professionals;

## KEY TERM

**social-ecological model**
variant of the ecological or person-in-environment model that takes into account multiple factors regarding drug use and abuse and focuses on the complex interplay among individuals, relationships, communities, and societal factors

- mass media programming;
- development of grassroots citizen interest groups;
- leadership training for key organization and community officials; and
- policy analysis and reformulation.

In applying this model to the college campus, we find that college campuses have long served as an environment for initiating and perpetuating drug use and abuse. Fraternity drunkenness, for example, was decried as early as 1840 (Horowitz, 1987). In 1988, an 18-year-old student attending Rutgers University died of alcohol poisoning at a fraternity party. In a television interview following the incident, then-Chancellor Edward Bloustein described fraternities as "organized conspiracies dedicated to the consumption of alcohol" (Hansen 1997, p. 5).

Using the ecological or person-in-environment model as a preventative measure can alleviate drug use and abuse on college campuses, lessening the vast majority of vandalism, fights, accidents, sexually transmitted infections, unplanned pregnancies, racial bias incidents, date rape, and at least one-third of academic attrition often caused by drug use and abuse (Koss, Gidycz, & Wisniewski, 1987). Although campus prevention programs and research date back several decades, such efforts remained isolated and sporadic until the late 1970s. All campuses now have medium to extensive alcohol and other drug-prevention programs in effect. Tailoring this type of prevention to college environments is certainly worthy of consideration.

Finally, a variant of this model, which was originally formulated to focus on violence (Centers for Disease Control and Prevention, 2009), takes into account other, larger factors regarding drug use and abuse. The **social-ecological model** considers the complex interplay among individuals, relationships, communities, and societal factors. This model (refocused by this author to more directly apply to drug use) emphasizes multiple interacting factors that put individuals at risk for experiencing and later becoming addicted to drug use. The main focus takes into consideration not just individual influencing factors but also the particular drug user's social relationships (e.g., presence of many friends who use drugs), the community, and societal factors (e.g., chaotic drug-infested societies where drug dealing and drug use are common). The social-ecological model includes multiple influencing factors in a person's environment.

# Examples of Large-Scale Drug Prevention Programs

## ■ The BACCHUS Peer Education Network and NASPA

In 1975, an organization known as Boosting Alcohol Consciousness Concerning the Health of University Students (BACCHUS) was developed as a national student organization. Soon BACCHUS realized that many of its affiliates were members of sororities and fraternities, so it renamed the organization then known as BACCHUS and GAMMA (Greeks Advocating Mature Management of Alcohol) to the **BACCHUS Network** effective July 1, 2005. A more recent description includes the following:

> BACCHUS is a network of more than 8,000 student leaders and advisors who work with over four million peers on more than 330 campuses nationwide. Our Members are found on four-year public colleges and universities, private and two-year institutions, historically Black colleges and universities, predominantly Hispanic population campuses, and tribal colleges. (BACCHUS Network, 2013)

In January 2014, the BACCHUS Network officially merged with the National Association of Student Personnel Administrators (NASPA)—Student Affairs Administrators in Higher Education to "provide outstanding resources, professional development, and technical assistance to an even broader community of college and university professionals and students" (NASPA, 2016a).

The **BACCHUS Initiatives of NASPA–Student Affairs Administrators in Higher Education** program was focused on supporting student leadership and peer education on health and safety issues—no matter the peer education group name, specialized health interest, or social affiliation (NASPA, 2016a).

As an organization, NASPA is "the leading association for the advancement, health, and sustainability of the student affairs profession. Our work provides high-quality professional development, advocacy, and research for 15,000 members in all 50 states, 25 countries, and [eight] U.S. territories" (NASPA, 2016b).

The original goal of BACCHUS was to prevent alcohol abuse. Today, the program has broadened its goals to include other student health and safety issues and actively promotes student- and young adult–based, campus and community-wide leadership on healthy and safe lifestyle decisions concerning alcohol abuse, tobacco use, illegal drug use, unhealthy sexual practices, and other high-risk behaviors.

This nonprofit organization devotes a substantial portion of its resources and activities to the following goals on university-affiliated campuses (BACCHUS Network, 2011):

- Create and foster a thriving network of institutions and young adult–led peer education groups supporting health and safety initiatives;
- Empower students and administrators to voice their opinions and needs to create healthier and safer campus communities;
- Develop and promote cutting-edge resources and health promotion campaigns that support peer education, campus leadership, and activism on health and safety issues;
- Provide exceptional conferencing and training opportunities for students, young adults, and professionals to support health and safety strategies;
- Encourage national forums on young adult health and safety concerns;
- Promote and disseminate research and effective strategies that better help campuses and communities address health and safety issues; and
- Advocate for effective and sensible policies and practices for campus and community health and safety issues.

The BACCHUS philosophy is that students can play a uniquely effective role—unmatched by professional educators—in encouraging their

---

**KEY TERMS**

**BACCHUS Network**

a former (prior to 2014) national and international association of college and university peer-education programs focused on alcohol abuse prevention and other related student health and safety issues

**BACCHUS Initiatives of NASPA–Student Affairs Administrators in Higher Education**

reformulated BACCHUS Network that is currently managed by NASPA that continues to support higher education student leadership and peer education on health and safety issues

peers to consider, talk honestly about, and develop responsible habits and attitudes toward high-risk health and safety issues. The organization now hosts four websites to assist students in their prevention efforts.

> The BACCHUS Network is a university and community-based network focusing on comprehensive health and safety initiatives. It is the mission of this 501(C)(3) non-profit organization to actively promote student and young adult based, campus and community-wide leadership on healthy and safe lifestyle decisions concerning alcohol abuse, tobacco use, illegal drug use, unhealthy sexual practices and other high-risk behaviors. (Southwestern Illinois College, n.d.)

The organization focuses prevention and fosters and aids students information about the organization's activities, services, conferences, campaigns, and resource materials.

In 2013, the BACCHUS Network claimed 120 educational resources and training materials offered by its organization. In addition, each affiliate group received health-issue campaigns that, when used in combination, lay the foundation for a year-round prevention program:

- National Collegiate Alcohol Awareness Week (alcohol and high risk drinking)
- Tobacco Prevention and Cessation (control, policy, programs, advocacy)
- Impaired Driving Prevention (designated driver, safe ride, laws, awareness)
- Sexual Responsibility Awareness (sexual health, HIV/AIDS-STIs and relationship issues)
- Safe Spring Break (alcohol, impaired driving, predatory drugs, sun safety, personal safety)

Campaigns consist of health-topic message promotion and resource manuals that contain the latest research and data, program-delivery ideas, model programs, and marketing strategies (BACCHUS Network, 2013).

Most recently, the Bacchus Network has fine-tuned itself as a university and community-based network focusing on comprehensive health and safety initiatives. Its mission is to actively promote student and young adult–based, campus and community-wide leadership on healthy and safe lifestyle decisions concerning alcohol abuse, tobacco use, illegal drug use, unhealthy sexual practices and other high-risk behaviors.

## ▮ Fund for the Improvement of Postsecondary Education Drug-Prevention Programs

In 1987, a huge explosion of campus drug-prevention programs began. It was sparked by a $14 billion annual budget for college drug prevention placed in the Drug-Free Schools and Communities Act of 1986 (now titled the Safe and Free Schools and Communities Act). The funding was parceled out by the U.S. Department of Education's Fund for the Improvement of Postsecondary Education (FIPSE). FIPSE awarded about 100 grants per year from 1987 until 1996 via a grant competition that called for colleges to mount institution-wide drug-prevention programs. The guiding philosophy included the following points:

- A small, isolated program was seen as making little difference, but a comprehensive program reaching into several areas of the institution could send many consistent anti-use messages that would eventually reach critical mass and change the campus environment.
- There should be well-known, top-down administrative support for prevention programming.
- There should be well-written and carefully implemented policies about chemical use on campus.

The hundreds of new programs, whose administrators met and interacted in annual grantee conferences, generated the sense that there was a national prevention movement in higher education. The Network of Colleges and Universities Dedicated to Prevention of Alcohol and Other Drug Abuse was founded, incorporating 900 institutions. The network is supported by the Higher Education Center for Alcohol and Other Drug Prevention funded by the U.S. Department of Education, which provides a range of materials and newsletters (Ryan, Colthurst, & Segars, 1995). Unfortunately, such large-scale efforts when evaluated years later (at the turn of the century) indicated that federally funded drug prevention on most college campuses had mixed results, often indicating weak success; as a result, most of the funding programs were discontinued.

In addition, "many college and universities have implemented prevention programs, or, within counseling centers, intervention efforts to meet the needs of the institution and it students" (Larimer, Kilmer, & Lee, 2005, p. 446). This finding by researchers also indicates that although implementing such individually based, specific college and university prevention programs is commendable, implementing new drug-prevention programs without evaluating the impact of these programs is totally lacking on most college campuses. In other words, colleges or universities also need to rigorously assess and evaluate the effectiveness of their drug-prevention programs, coupling their drug-prevention programs with assessment.

From more than a decade of experience, several exemplary approaches emerged. These strategies might be the predominant focus of a program or one of a number of complementary components of a comprehensive effort. These strategies are addressed next.

### PEER-BASED EFFORTS

Student peers can be involved in a number of ways: as educators, mentors, counselors, or facilitators of prevention and outreach work. Such an approach multiplies manpower tremendously, reaches those students who are apt to become lost in the flow, is not perceived as an outside or authoritarian intrusion, speaks the language of students, and works to change the predominant cultural tone on campus. Peers can conduct classroom presentations, work informational tables or drop-in centers, create prevention newsletters, and establish links to community groups. It is important to carefully train and supervise peer facilitators. Many peer programs are based in residence halls, taking advantage of the training of residence hall assistants and peer facilitators (BACCHUS & GAMMA, 1994).

### CURRICULUM INFUSION

Infusion of a skill or topic across the curriculum has been used in conjunction with classes on writing skills, gender issues, and other areas. Curriculum infusion can be undertaken at individual institutions or as a consortium project. The advantage of curriculum infusion is that it involves faculty members, achieves open discussion of drug issues in the classroom as part of the normal educational process, and stimulates critical thinking about drug issues.

### IMPROVISATIONAL THEATER GROUPS

Improvisational theater groups that tackle health and wellness issues can be lively, stimulating, and provocative, often breaking through peer and institutional denial and bringing issues home to students with a dramatic emotional impact. Improvisational topics can include date rape, sexually transmitted disease, children of alcoholics on campus, and denial of chemical dependency.

### STRATEGIES TO CHANGE MISPERCEPTIONS OF USE

Social psychologists Alan Berkowitz and Wesley Perkins, both of Hobart and William Smith Colleges, have conducted influential research illustrating that students often have incorrect estimates (exaggerated misperceptions) of drug use by their peers (Perkins 1991, 1997; Perkins & Berkowitz, 1986). Thus, they misperceive the peer norms governing drug use, which may lead them to follow imaginary peers. This idea is a modification of the traditional understanding that peers influence peers. It follows logically that activities demonstrating the accurate use pattern to students and correcting misperceptions will indirectly affect overall use patterns. These efforts have included simply publicizing the results of alcohol and drug use surveys and awarding prizes for coming up with correct estimates.

### ALTERNATIVE EVENTS

Alternative events such as alcohol-free cocktail parties ("mocktail" parties), alcohol-free gatherings, and indoor rock climbing—especially as alternatives to presporting events and holiday parties—help avoid some events that are traditionally associated with chemical abuse.

### PROGRAMS THAT CHANGE MARKETING OF ALCOHOL ON AND NEAR CAMPUSES

Until recently, institutions of higher education were a major focus of alcohol marketing. Alcoholic beverage producers sponsor many campus events, and these companies buy considerable newspaper advertising. One report indicates,

> Alcohol advertising is pervasive in college sporting events. According to a recent report in *USA Today*, "NCAA tournament games led all other sports events in alcohol-related TV advertising in 2002, with 939 ads costing $28 million. That compares with a combined 925 ads aired during the Super Bowl, World Series, college bowl games and the NFL's Monday Night Football." (StateUniversity.com, 2011)

Beginning in 1991,

> The OIG [Office of Inspector General of the U.S.] . . . reviewed the voluntary codes then in effect under the auspices of the Beer Institute, the Wine Institute, the Distilled Spirits Council of the United States (DISCUS) . . ., and an alcohol industry umbrella group, the Century Council. In particular, the review looked

at the elements of the voluntary codes that were related to "youth appeal." . . . The OIG concluded: "While the industry advertising standards purport to guide alcohol advertisers towards responsible behavior, they fail to prevent advertising considered to have youth appeal." (Office of Inspector General, 1991, p. 14, in Jernigan & O'Hara, 2004)

Further, "Like The Beer Institute, the DISCUS code calls for advertising not to be placed where most of audience is reasonably expected to be below the legal purchase age." In addition, distilled spirits companies are told not to advertise on "college or university campuses," including their newspapers; however, marketing activities are allowed if they are "in licensed retail establishments located on such campuses" (Jernigan & O'Hara, 2004).

From these findings and the fact that most students on college campuses are underage with regard to purchasing and using alcohol, there is pressure on the alcohol industry to restrict influencing students about alcohol on college campuses with the likelihood that today it is "bad business to promote alcohol on college campuses."

In implementing programs and policies that make a difference, the following are examples of the strategies many colleges and universities are implementing that can have a positive influence on the campus culture regarding alcohol and other drug abuse (U.S. Department of Education, 2008):

- forming partnerships with local communities to ensure that alcohol is not served to minors or to intoxicated students;
- strengthening academic requirements;
- scheduling classes on Fridays (this strategy emphasizes the importance of academics and discourages the alcohol fueled partying that may occur on Thursday nights if students do not need to attend classes on Fridays);
- keeping the library and recreational facilities open longer;
- eliminating alcohol-industry support for athletics programs (accepting such funds can be seen as sending a mixed message to students);
- restricting alcohol promotions and advertising on campus and in campus publications,

especially promotions or ads that feature low-cost drinks;
- monitoring fraternities to ensure compliance with alcohol policies and laws;
- providing a wide range of alcohol-free social and recreational activities;
- disciplining repeat offenders and those who engage in unacceptable behavior associated with substance use;
- notifying parents when students engage in serious or repeated violations of alcohol or other drug policies or laws; and
- launching a media campaign to inform students about the actual amount of drinking that occurs on campus because most students overestimate the number of their classmates who drink and the amount that they drink.

Finally, it is better to embed prevention messages within an overall wellness perspective. Students are concerned about health and wellness issues, not programs that come off as dogmatic or preachy, moralizing, exaggerating, and nagging—perhaps reminding them of life at home.

## ▌ Drug Abuse Resistance Education (D.A.R.E.)

One major drug-prevention program that had high hopes for success was the school-based drug-education programs incorporated into our nation's school districts—**Drug Abuse Resistance Education (D.A.R.E.)**.

Established in 1983, D.A.R.E. operates in about 75% of all school districts across the United States and in numerous foreign countries. In addition to the D.A.R.E. elementary school curriculum, the D.A.R.E. program includes middle school and high school curricula that reinforce lessons taught at the elementary school level. "In fiscal year 2000, the Department of Justice's Bureau of Justice Assistance, which supports various substance abuse prevention programs for youth, provided about $2 million for D.A.R.E. regional training centers to support the training of new police officers that help deliver the D.A.R.E. program lessons" (quoted from U.S. Government Accountability Office [GAO] in Common Sense for Drug Policy, 2009).

D.A.R.E. program shows mixed evaluations:

D.A.R.E. (Drug Abuse Resistance Education) administers a school-based substance abuse, gang, and violence prevention program in 75% of US school districts and in 48 countries (as of 2013). Since 1983, police officers

KEY TERM

**Drug Abuse Resistance Education (D.A.R.E.)**
drug-education program presented in elementary and junior high and middle schools nationwide by police officers

have taught the D.A.R.E. program to over 200 million K–12 students worldwide—approximately 114 million in the United States alone. Proponents say that D.A.R.E. has helped prevent drug use in elementary, middle, and high school students. They contend that D.A.R.E. improves social interaction between police officers, students, and schools, is the most prevalent substance abuse prevention program in the United States, and is popular with kids and parents. Opponents say that dozens of peer-reviewed studies conclude the D.A.R.E. program is ineffective at preventing kids from using drugs. They contend that D.A.R.E. causes kids to ignore legitimate information about the relative harms of drugs, and that D.A.R.E. is even associated with increased drug use. (ProCon.org, 2013)

The D.A.R.E. website stated the following about this program: "Launched in 1983, D.A.R.E. is a comprehensive K–12 education program taught in thousands of schools in America and 52 other countries. D.A.R.E. curricula address drugs, violence, bullying, Internet safety, and other high risk circumstances that today are too often a part of students' lives" (D.A.R.E., 2016).

Evaluations of this program show that, on a short-term basis, D.A.R.E. improved students' views of themselves and increased their sense of personal responsibility. However, the program has *not* yielded a measurable, significant change in drug use (Rosenbaum & Hanson, 1998; Vogt, 2003). Moreover, this drug-education program has shown a strong inconsistency between students' self-reported attitudes about drug use and their actual use (Clayton, Cattarello, Cay, & Walden, 1991; Ennett, Tobler, Ringwalt, & Flewelling, 1994; Vogt, 2003).

The most recent report on D.A.R.E. is that it has shrunken to operating "in 441 Utah public schools and was presented to more than 232,000 Utah children last year, but its ineffectiveness has been repeatedly demonstrated" (Anderson, 2019). The same author adds a final blow to the D.A.R.E program "DARE does not prevent, and may actually lead to, increased drug abuse" (Anderson, 2019). In addition, WSAW-TV in Wausau, Wisconsin, reported the following about D.A.R.E.

It used to be called Drug Abuse Resistance Education but now the D.A.R.E. program in north central Wisconsin is evolving into helping students make better decisions.

D.A.R.E. now stands for Define, Assess, Respond, Evaluate how to respond to different situations and problems. It's a way to tackle all areas of a student's life and even something they can take with them to adulthood. (Will, 2018)

See "Holding the Line: D.A.R.E.: Frustrating and Poor Results from a National Drug Prevention Program" for more information on the D.A.R.E. program.

One major problem was that "over the past decade, a flurry of studies—by the U.S. surgeon general and the General Accounting Office, among others—found no significant difference in drug use between D.A.R.E. graduates and students never exposed to the curriculum" (Vogt, 2003, p. 1; see also Plant, Robertson, Plant, & Miller, 2011). Further, regarding graduates of the D.A.R.E. program, one official said, "I can't tell you how many kids told me D.A.R.E. introduced them to drugs. The problem with D.A.R.E., other than that it's a multimillion-dollar conglomerate in the business of selling T-shirts, is that it takes the burden off parents to raise their kids [drug free]" (Vogt, 2003, p. 3).

Another major problem that was identified is that the D.A.R.E. drug-education program is presented in the classroom by fully uniformed police officers. Although the officers are well intentioned and their efforts are commendable, they are hardly a mechanism for transmitting new norms that would find converts among students, except perhaps those already successfully socialized (Gopelrud, 1991). More important, uniformed police officers used as teachers "sends the wrong message that drugs are a law enforcement issue, rather than a public health issue" (Zeese & Lewin, 1998, p. 1).

## ■ Drug Courts: Partly Legal and Partly Rehabilitative?

Although **drug courts** vary in organization, in scope, and at what point intervention occurs, the underlying premise is that drug possession and use is not only a law enforcement and criminal

KEY TERM

**drug courts**
promising and popular nationwide approach to prevention in which the primary purpose is to include treatment programs and options instead of only punishment for drug offenses

# HOLDING THE LINE

## D.A.R.E.: Frustrating and Poor Results from a National Drug Prevention Program

In 1995, a disturbing study published by a group of researchers at the University of Michigan and backed by the U.S. Department of Health and Human Services and the National Institute on Drug Abuse (NIDA) showed that the use of illicit drugs by young people had been rising steadily since 1992. The results of this study were even more perplexing because overall drug use had been declining over the same period. The increase was happening despite several seemingly successful efforts to combat drug abuse with high-powered prevention programs.

Since the 1980s, most funds allocated for drug prevention have been spent in three areas: criminal justice, major advertising campaigns, and D.A.R.E. Law enforcement professionals who work with hardcore addicts, especially in poor urban neighborhoods, have favored compulsory preventive programs. According to William N. Brownsberger, former assistant state attorney general in the Massachusetts Narcotics and Special Investigations Division, addicts who are forced against their will to enter and remain in therapy can overcome their addiction. Roughly 90% of all addicts are arrested at least once every year, giving the criminal justice system plenty of opportunities to help them kick their habits.

One highly visible persuasive effort to end drug abuse has been the advertising campaign created by the Partnership for a Drug-Free America. The nation's advertising industry developed the partnership and funded it by collaborating with advertisers and a variety of health and educational agencies. The goal was to promote images designed to make drug use look "uncool," especially to younger people. In addition to the creative services donated by advertising agencies, media organizations donated more than $2 billion of public service and advertising space to the partnership between the late 1980s and 1990s.

In the early 1990s, the partnership commissioned surveys to measure the effect of its media campaign on students in the Los Angeles and New York City school systems. On both coasts, increased exposure to the partnership's messages appeared to dramatically change students' attitudes toward drugs. At the same time, however, the number of students who admitted using drugs actually increased.

Another high-visibility persuasive effort has been the nationwide D.A.R.E. program, which was launched in Los Angeles in 1983. "D.A.R.E.'s curriculum reflects mainstream theories about the best way to reduce drinking, smoking, and drug use by children. . . . The program began as collaboration between the Los Angeles Police Department and the city's school district" (Miller 2001, p. A14). Using role-playing techniques and resistance training, uniformed police officers become social workers, talking with students in their classrooms, educating them about the dangers of drugs, and giving them the tools to resist temptation or peer pressure. They generally teach 17 classroom sessions.

Today most school-based prevention programs, including D.A.R.E., assume that adolescents need grown-ups' help in resisting social pressures to use [drugs]. Therefore, they try to correct children's exaggerated beliefs about the prevalence of drug use among their peers. They offer them information about the physical and social effects of using and they try to impart "resistance skills" for making and acting on thoughtful decisions (Miller 2001, p. A14).

Although D.A.R.E. was the most popular drug-education program ever developed for children, increasing numbers of critics claim that its benefits, if any, are short lasting. Most D.A.R.E. training begins in the fifth grade. At this age, students accept most of what they hear. By middle school, however, the effectiveness of D.A.R.E. begins to erode. By high school, many students resist participation in the program. According to a researcher from the Research Triangle Institute in Durham, North Carolina, which conducted a $300,000 study on the impact of D.A.R.E., "Unless there's some sort of booster session that reinforces the original curriculum, the effects of most drug use prevention programs decay rather than increase over time." The findings of numerous research studies conducted on D.A.R.E.'s effectiveness suggest that D.A.R.E. students were no less likely to use drugs than students who had not gone through the program (Ennett et al., 1994; Vogt, 2003). Some have even claimed that the D.A.R.E. program teaches kids to become curious about illicit drug use or actually motivates them to do drugs (Vogt, 2003). Further, "Among the notable quotations from researchers: 'is well established that D.A.R.E doesn't work' Gilbert Botvin, Cornell Medical Center. 'Research shows that, no, D.A.R.E. hasn't been effective in reducing drug use' William Modzeleski, top drug-education official at the Department of Education" (Plant et al., 2011, p. 147).

*(continues)*

# HOLDING THE LINE

## D.A.R.E.: Frustrating and Poor Results from a National Drug Prevention Program (*continued*)

Another major negative finding came from the U.S. Government Accountability Office (GAO), which released a review of current research findings regarding alcohol and other drug abuse prevention programs, particularly D.A.R.E., in 2003:

> The six long-term evaluations of the D.A.R.E. elementary school curriculum that we reviewed found no significant differences in illicit drug use between students who received D.A.R.E. in the fifth or sixth grade (the intervention group) and students who did not (the control group). Three of the evaluations reported that the control groups of students were provided other drug use prevention education. All of the evaluations suggested that D.A.R.E. had no statistically significant long-term effect on preventing youth illicit drug use. Of the six evaluations we reviewed, five also reported on students' attitudes toward illicit drug use and resistance to peer pressure and found no significant differences between the intervention and control groups over the long term. Two of these evaluations found that the D.A.R.E. students showed stronger negative attitudes about illicit drug use and improved social skills about illicit drug use about 1 year after receiving the program. These positive effects diminished over time. (U.S. Government Accountability Office [GAO], 2003, p. 2)

In this same report, seven school districts using the D.A.R.E. program were intensely analyzed. The findings indicated that "No statistically significant differences were observed between the intervention and control schools on students' past year marijuana use [two] years after the intervention" (GAO, 2003, p. 5).

Further, "[a]s D.A.R.E. America celebrated its 20th anniversary, the nation's most widely used school-based drug-prevention program was struggling with a credibility crisis that has devastated the organization financially

and threatens its survival" (Vogt, 2003). Reports indicate that many school districts throughout the country have abandoned the program, finding D.A.R.E. to be ineffective in curbing both licit and illicit drug use.

Because of the diminishing returns from various drug-prevention programs, in late 1996, during President Clinton's administration, a compulsory drug test for teenagers who are applying for their driver's licenses was proposed. Like everything else, the proposal had both supporters and critics. Although this tactic may be part of the answer, prevention programs that have measurable, long-lasting effects remain difficult to find.

As mentioned previously, the most recent information from WSAW-TV in Wausau, Wisconsin, reported that

> [it] used to be called Drug Abuse Resistance Education but now the D.A.R.E. program in north central Wisconsin is evolving into helping students make better decisions.
>
> D.A.R.E. now stands for Define, Assess, Respond, Evaluate how to respond to different situations and problems. It's a way to tackle all areas of a student's life and even something they can take with them to adulthood (Will, 2018).

*Proponents* say that in the past D.A.R.E. helped prevent drug use in elementary, middle, and high school students. They contend that D.A.R.E. did improve social interaction between police officers, students, and schools, was the most prevalent substance abuse prevention program in the United States, and is popular with kids and parents.

*Opponents* say that dozens of peer-reviewed studies conclude the D.A.R.E. program is ineffective at preventing kids from using drugs. They contend that D.A.R.E. causes kids to ignore legitimate information about the relative harms of drugs, and that D.A.R.E. is even associated with increased drug use. (ProCon.org, 2014)

Data from Brownsberger, W. N. (1996, October 20). Just say "criminal justice." *Boston Globe*; Ennett, S. T., Tobler, N. S., Ringwalt, C. L., & Flewelling, R. L. (1994). How effective is drug abuse resistance education? A meta-analysis of Project D.A.R.E. outcome evaluations. *American Journal of Public Health, 84*, 1394–1401; Gordon, P. (1996a, July). The truth about D.A.R.E. *Buzz Magazine*; Gordon, P. (1996b). Can Madison Avenue really save America by making illegal drugs totally uncool? *Buzz Magazine.* (August); Miller, D. W. (2001, October 19). D.A.R.E. reinvents itself—With help from its social-scientist critics. *Chronicle of Higher Education, 48*, A12–A14; Plant, M., Robertson, R., Plant, M., & Miller, P. (2011). *Drug nation: Patterns, problems, panics, and politics.* Oxford, UK: Oxford University Press; ProCon.org. (2014, February 4). Is the D.A.R.E. program good for America's kids (K–12)? Retrieved from http://dare.procon.org/; U.S. Government Accountability Office (GAO). (2003, January 15). *Youth illicit drug use prevention: D.A.R.E. long-term evaluation and federal efforts to identify effective programs.* GAO-03-172R. Washington, DC: Author; Vogt, A. (2003, January 26). Now Many "Just Say No" to D.A.R.E. *Chicago Tribune*, pp. 1, 3; Will, B. (2018, August 29). D.A.R.E. program is evolving. Grand Rapids, WI: WSAW-TV. Retrieved from https://www.wsaw.com/content/news/DARE-program-is-evolving--491995011.html

justice problem but also a public health problem (Sherin & Mahoney, 1996).

> As the name implies, drug courts are specifically for persons with substance use disorders. These court programs offer individuals the opportunity to enter long-term drug treatment and agree to court supervision rather than receiving a jail sentence. The intensive program requires participants to maintain recovery, take on responsibilities, and work towards lifestyle changes. Under the supervision and authority of the court, their progress is monitored. Ultimately, drug courts reduce crime and affect real, positive change in people's lives. (NDCRC, 2020)

Even though adult drug courts vary in target population, program model, and resources, they are generally based on a comprehensive model involving the following (National Institute of Justice (NIJ), 2016):

- offender screening and assessment of risks, needs, and responsivity;
- judicial interaction;
- reduce recidivism among participants (Franco, 2010);
- reduce substance abuse among participants (Franco, 2010);
- rehabilitate participants to improve their chances of successful reintegration into society by providing social services such as employment, job training, education, and housing assistance (Franco, 2010);
- monitoring (e.g., drug testing) and supervision;
- graduated sanctions and incentives; and
- treatment and rehabilitation services.

In *drug court programs*, criminal justice agencies collaborate closely with the substance abuse treatment community and other societal institutions to design and operate the program. Drug courts are often managed by multidisciplinary teams composed of judges, prosecutors, defense attorneys, community corrections, social workers, and treatment service professionals. Stakeholders such as law enforcement, the family, and the community are encouraged to participate in hearings, programming, and graduation events (NIJ, 2016).

The key goal is to divert substance abusers into supervised community treatment centers in an attempt to eliminate the destructive behavior. A committee usually composed of a judge, the

district attorney, a public defender, the probation department, and treatment center officials determines whether treatment is needed and the type and length of treatment.

**Table 17.3** presents the results of a research evaluation of a multisite adult drug court program. The 20 sampled drug courts were evaluated based on the staffing characteristics and frequency of staffing, who attended the staffing, participation in the staffing, who ran the staffing, who made the final decisions on participant response, length of time in minutes of staffing meetings, and the average discussion time in minutes per case (Zweig, 2011). Table 17.3 shows that 75% of the sampled drug courts held weekly staff meetings; that the judges, project or resource coordinators, defense attorneys, and prosecutors primarily attended the staff meetings and that the judges ran the staffing meetings in 55% of the 20 courts sampled. (See Table 17.3 for more detailed findings.)

At the first National Drug Court Conference, one researcher reported, "These courts rely on strong collaboration among judges, prosecutors, defense lawyers, and related supporting agencies (such as case management, corrections, pretrial services, probation), on the one hand, and a partnership with treatment agencies (or providers) and other community organizations and representatives on the other" (Goldkamp, 1993, p. 33). The treatment phase generally consists of (1) detoxification (removal of physical dependence on drugs from the body), (2) stabilization (treating the psychological craving for the drug), and (3) aftercare (helping the defendant obtain education or job training, find a job, and remain drug free) (Office of Justice Programs, 2000).

As of 2020, more than 3,000 drug courts were were operating in the United States and U.S. territories, resulting in a drug court within the boundaries of every state. "Since their inception in 1989, drug courts programs have expanded from serving just adults, to include juvenile drug treatment courts, DUI/DWI courts, family drug courts, and others" (NDCRC, 2020); (see **Figure 17.2** for total drug courts operating in the United States). Approximately half of drug courts (51%) targeted adult offenders, and 14% served juveniles. The other drug courts were categorized as family treatment (9%), tribal healing to wellness (4%), designated DWI (8%), campus (0.2%), reentry drug (1%), federal

**TABLE 17.3** Observed Drug Court Team Staffing Meetings at 20 Drug Court Sites

| Staffing Characteristics | Results (%) | Staffing Characteristics | Results (%) |
|---|---|---|---|
| *Frequency of Staffing* | | Project/resource coordinator(s) | 3.7 |
| Every other week | 10 | Defense attorney(s) | 2.7 |
| Weekly | 75 | Prosecutor(s) | 2.7 |
| More than once a week | 15 | Treatment liaison(s) | 3.8 |
| *Who Attends the Staffing*[1] | | Case manager(s) | 3.3 |
| Judge(s) | 100 | Probation officer(s) | 2.9 |
| Project or resource coordinator(s) | 85 | *Who Runs the Staffing* | |
| Defense attorney(s) | 85 | Judge | 55 |
| Prosecutor(s) | 80 | Project/resource coordinator | 35 |
| Treatment liaison(s) | 70 | Both | 10 |
| Case manager(s) | 50 | *Who Made the Final Decisions on Participant Response* | |
| Probation officer(s) | 50 | | |
| *Others* | | Judge(s) | 75 |
| Clerk(s) | 20 | Team consensus | 25 |
| Law enforcement (police/corrections) | 15 | *Length of Staffing Meeting (in Minutes)*[2] | |
| Drug court administration | 15 | Mean across courts | 64.85 |
| Mental health | 10 | Range across courts | 13.00–170.00 |
| Health department | 5 | *Average Discussion per Case (in Minutes)* | |
| *Participation in the Staffing (Scale of 1 to 5)* | | Mean across courts | 2.64 |
| Judge(s) | 4.9 | Range across courts | 0.60–6.00 |

[1]Multisite Adult Drug Court Evaluation (MADCE) team observers rated the level of participation of each drug court team member on a scale of 1 to 5, with 1 being "did not participate" and 5 being "participated thoroughly."

[2]This reflects the length of the staffing meeting observed; the MADCE team made every effort to observe the whole meeting.

Data from Zweig, J. M. (2011). Description of the drug court sites in the multi-site adult drug court evaluation. In S. B. Rossman, J. M. Zweig, D. Kralstein, K. Henry, P. M. Downey, & C. Lindquist (Eds.), *The multi-site adult drug court evaluation: The drug court experience* (pp. 8–23). Washington, DC: Urban Institute Justice Policy Center.

drug (9%), federal veterans treatment (0.2%), veterans treatment (0.7%), and co-occurring disorder (1%) (National Drug Court Resource Center [NDCRC], 2014).

The following types of drug courts are currently in existence (see also **Table 17.4** for the types and numbers of drug courts in the United States and its territories in 2014):

- adult,
- juvenile,
- family treatment,
- tribal healing to wellness,
- designated DWI,
- campus,
- reentry drug,
- federal drug,
- federal veterans treatment,
- veterans treatment, and
- co-occurring disorder.

Eligible drug offenders can be sent to drug court instead of moving through the traditional justice system. Drug courts put individuals in treatment and closely supervise them throughout the process.

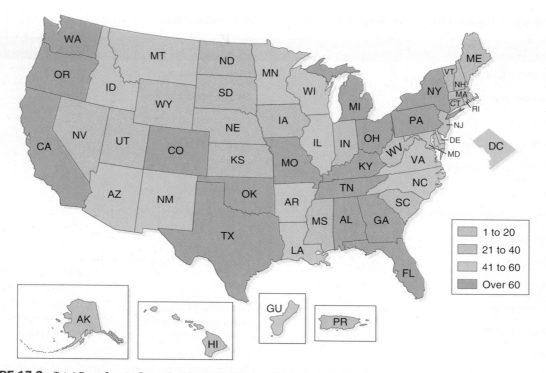

**FIGURE 17.2**   Total Drug Courts Operating the United States (Adult, Juvenile, Family, Tribal, and Veterans Programs).

Data from American University. (2014). Drug court technical assistance. Washington, DC: Bureau of Justice Assistance Project. Retrieved from https://www.american.edu/spa/jpo/initiatives/drug-court/

**TABLE 17.4**  Types and Numbers of U.S. Drug Courts Operating in the United States and Its Territories (as of June 30, 2014)

| Court Type | Number |
|---|---|
| Adult[i] | 1,538 |
| Juvenile[ii] | 433 |
| Family treatment | 303 |
| Tribal healing to wellness | 119 |
| Designated DWI | 242 |
| Campus | 6 |
| Reentry drug | 36 |
| Federal drug | 29 |
| Federal veterans treatment | 6 |
| Veterans treatment | 220 |
| Co-occurring disorder | 36 |
| Total drug courts | 2,968 |

[i]436 are hybrid DWI/drug courts.

[ii]Juvenile drug courts try to address the unique circumstances surrounding adolescent delinquency.

National Institute of Justice (NIJ). (2012). Drug court locations in the United States as of December 31, 2011. Washington, DC: U.S. Department of Justice (USDOJ), Office of Justice Programs. Retrieved from http://www.nij.gov/topics/courts/drug-courts/

For a minimum term of one year, participants are:

- provided with intensive treatment and other services they require to get and stay clean and sober;
- held accountable by the drug court judge for meeting their obligations to the court, society, themselves and their families;
- regularly and randomly tested for drug use;
- required to appear in court frequently so that the judge may review their progress; and
- rewarded for doing well or sanctioned when they do not live up to their obligations. (National Association of Drug Court Professionals [NADCP], 2011b)

What is the target population of drug court participants? Drug courts are expected to have the greatest effects for high-risk offenders who have more severe antisocial backgrounds or poorer prognoses for success in standard treatments:

Such high-risk individuals ordinarily require a combined regimen of intensive supervision, behavioral accountability, and evidence-based treatment services, which drug courts are specifically structured to provide. Consistent with the predictions of the Risk Principle, drug courts have been shown to have the greatest effects for high-risk participants who were relatively younger, had more prior felony convictions, were diagnosed with antisocial personality disorder, or had previously failed in less intensive dispositions. (Marlowe, 2010, p. 3)

One report stated,

A recent survey of more than 120 evaluations of drug court programs showed that they outperformed virtually all other strategies that have been attempted for drug offenders within the [one to two] years that courts typically monitor offenders. Offenders who graduated from drug courts had significant reductions in rearrest rates and in charges for serious crimes. Data show that within the first year of release, 43.5% of drug offenders are rearrested, whereas only 16.4% of drug court graduates are rearrested. (Office of National Drug Control Policy, 2007, p. 25)

Drug court programs have spread rapidly since the first drug court was established in 1989 (Franco, 2010). Today, we are at the point where each state has multiple drug courts.

Overall, defendants participating in drug court sentencing have had lower rearrest rates, and there are statistically significant differences in disposition between those assigned to drug court and comparison groups. Seventy-five percent of drug court graduates are arrest free 2 years after leaving the court, and drug courts reduce crime 35% more than other court options (NADCP, 2011a). "Rigorous studies examining long-term outcomes of individual Drug Courts have found that reductions in crime last at least [three] years and can endure for over 14 years" (NADCP, 2011a).

Those assigned to drug courts are less likely to face further prosecution or to serve probation or short jail terms. Finally, using a drug court and its system of administering treatment within a legal atmosphere is more cost-effective than criminal courts. In 2007, for every federal dollar invested in drug court programs, $9 was leveraged in state funding (NADCP, 2011a).

Another report on the cost-effectiveness of such programs stated that

[e]valuations of the net costs and benefits of drug courts nationwide generally find that drug courts save taxpayer dollars compared to simple probation and/or incarceration, primarily due to reductions in arrests, case processing, jail occupancy and victimization costs. While not all persons diverted to drug court would have

otherwise been sentenced to prison, for those individuals who are incarcerated, the average annual cost is estimated to be $23,000 per inmate, while the average annual cost of drug court participation is estimated to be $4,300 per person. (King & Pasquarella, 2009, p. 7)

Early research suggested that the successes of drug courts should be viewed with caution because much of the effectiveness of these courts occurred early: The courts were in operation fewer than 10 months, and these courts were highly selective regarding the defendants allowed to participate. The criticism was that the courts tended to select violators who would have a better chance for rehabilitation. Today, however, evidence exists that such criticisms are no longer valid: "By 2006, the scientific community had concluded beyond a reasonable doubt from advanced statistical procedures called meta-analyses that Drug Courts reduce criminal recidivism, typically measured by fewer re-arrests for new offenses and technical violations" (Marlowe, 2010, p. 1).

Further, at a 2009 Annual Conference of the American Society of Criminology, research showed that

[i]n addition to significantly less involvement in criminal activity, the Drug Court participants also reported significantly less use of illegal drugs and heavy use of alcohol. These self-report findings were confirmed by saliva drug tests, which revealed significantly fewer positive results for the Drug Court participants at the 18-month assessment (29% vs. 46%, $p < .01$). The Drug Court participants also reported significantly better improvements in their family relationships, and non-significant trends favoring higher employment rates and higher annual incomes. These findings confirm that Drug Courts elicit substantial improvements in other outcomes apart from criminal recidivism. (Marlowe, 2010, p. 2).

Another significant finding regarding the cost-effectiveness of adult drug courts is that "[t]he result has been net economic benefits to local communities ranging from approximately $3,000 to $13,000 per Drug Court participant" (Marlowe, 2010, p. 3).

A noteworthy and promising finding regarding drug courts is the emphasis on treating drug addiction and criminal behavior instead of simply punishing without treating drug-related juvenile delinquency and criminalistic behavior, as had been standard before drug courts were established.

# Problems with Assessing the Success of Drug-Prevention Programs

Both the National Institute on Drug Abuse (NIDA) and individual researchers have evaluated the multitude of drug abuse prevention programs in the United States. The general conclusions of these studies are as follows:

- Few programs have demonstrated clear success or have adequately evaluated themselves.
- The relationships among information about drugs, attitudes toward use, and actual use are unclear in these programs.

Some key factors that are crucial to developing successful programs include the following:

- Prevention must be coordinated at different levels. Successful programs involve families, schools, and communities. In some cases, these efforts are not coordinated.
- The program must be integrated into the ongoing activities of schools, families, and community organizations. Superficial introduction of drug-prevention strategies has limited effects. For instance, distributing literature door to door, making in-class presentations regarding the harmful effects of drugs, and posting banners and slogans warning of the consequences of drug abuse in communities are not successful methods. Instead, programs that are comprehensive and community-wide, integrated into neighborhood clubs, organizations, and church activities, are more likely to have a long-term impact on preventing drug use. A clear example is the yearly Great American Smoke-out launched against tobacco use.
- Personal autobiographical and social experience accounts of former drug abusers should be included in drug information that is distributed. Recipients of drug-prevention information should be given real-life accounts of use, abuse, despair, and successful drug rehabilitation. Just receiving drug information alone has little impact, either initially or over the long term.

In looking at the future of substance abuse prevention, it is important to include a summary from drug-prevention experts, who advocate the following:

Prevention experts across the spectrum of strategies agree that the future of prevention must focus on education and collaboration. Education includes additional research to advance policy and intervention efforts. It also involves educating communities and policymakers regarding the importance and effectiveness of prevention. Collaboration means not only developing a comprehensive approach across the spectrum of prevention strategies, but also recognizing that substance abuse prevention is intrinsically tied to other outcomes, including mental health, academic success, and violence prevention. Collaboration within and among the health care, education, and judicial systems is needed for success. (Berk, 2013)

# Other Viable Alternatives to Drug Use

It has been suggested that people have an innate need to alter their conscious state. This belief is based on the observation that, as part of their normal play, preschoolers deliberately whirl themselves dizzy and even momentarily choke each other to lose consciousness (Wilson & Wilson, 1975). Some young children progress to discovering and using chemicals (such as sniffing shoe polish or gasoline) to alter consciousness and learn to be secretive about this behavior. They learn to be circumspect or come to feel guilty and repress the desire to alter consciousness when adults catch them in these activities.

If this desire to alter the state of consciousness is inherent in human beings, then the use of psychoactive drugs, legal or illegal, in adulthood is natural. Drug abuse is, therefore, a logical continuation of a developmental sequence that goes back to early childhood (Carroll, 1977; Siegel, 2005; Weil, 2004).

One question in response to this is why, even if there is an innate desire to alter consciousness, do only some people progress to abusing chemical substances? It appears that people who do not abuse psychoactive drugs have found positive alternatives to altering consciousness; they feel no need to take chemical substances for this purpose. Involvement in activities such as Boy Scouts and Girl Scouts, youth sports teams, music groups, the YMCA and YWCA, drug-free video game centers, drug-free dances, environmental and historical preservation projects, and social and service projects are viable alternatives to drug use. The rationale for these programs is that youth will find these activities engaging enough to forgo alcohol and drug use (Forman & Linney, 1988).

This strategy is known as the **alternatives approach**. Workers in the drug abuse field tend to agree on its effectiveness. They note that young ex-abusers of common illicit drugs are more likely to stop when they gain satisfaction from exploring positive alternatives rather than from a fear of consequent harm. The alternatives approach assumes the following (Cohen, 1971):

- People abuse drugs voluntarily to fill a need or basic drive.
- Most people abuse drugs for negative reasons. They may be dealing with negative feelings or situations such as relieving boredom, anxiety, depression, tension, or other unpleasant emotional and psychological states. They may be rebelling against authority, trying to escape feelings of loneliness or inadequacy, or trying to be accepted by peers. Peer pressure is extremely important as an inducing force.
- Some people who abuse drugs believe the experience is positive. They may feel that their sensual experiences or music enjoyment is enhanced or that they have achieved altered states of consciousness, or they may simply experience a sense of adventure. Some people may want to explore their own consciousness and reasons for the attraction to drug use.

Whether the reasons for drug use are positive or negative, the effects sought can be achieved through alternative, nondrug means. Such means are preferable to drug use and more constructive because the person is not relying on a psychoactive substance for satisfaction; rather, he or she is finding satisfaction based on personal achievements. Ideally, this approach should lead to a lifetime of self-satisfaction.

**Table 17.5** lists various types of experiences, the motives for such experiences, the probable drugs of abuse with which they are associated, and alternatives to these drugs. As shown in the table, any constructive activity can be considered an alternative to drug abuse. For example, a young person who needs an outlet for increased physical energy might respond better to dance and movement training or a project in preventive medicine than working on ecological projects. In a large

alternatives program established in Idaho, the following activities were planned during a month: arts and crafts, karate, reforestation, backpacking, Humane Society dog show, horseback riding, creating artwork for posters for various programs, astronomy, camping, and volunteering in a local hospital.

## ■ Meditation

Some of the most intriguing research about the brain is being done on the state of the mind during **meditation**. In certain countries such as India, people have long histories of being able to achieve certain goals through meditation. The word *yoga* is derived from the Sanskrit word for "union" or "yoking," meaning the process of discipline by which a person attains union with the absolute. In a sense, it refers to the use of the mind to control itself and the body.

Meditation involves brain wave activity centered on ponderous, contemplative, and reflective thought. An individual who meditates is able to decrease oxygen consumption within a matter of minutes by as much as 20%, a level usually reached only after four to five hours of sleep. However, meditation is physiologically different from sleep, based on the electroencephalograph (EEG) pattern and rate of decline of oxygen consumption. Along with the decreased metabolic rate and EEG changes, there also is a marked decrease in blood lactate. Lactate is produced by metabolism of skeletal muscle, and the decrease is probably the result of reduced activity of the sympathetic nervous system during meditation. Heart rate and respiration also are slowed.

## ■ The Natural Mind Approach

Some people who take drugs eventually look for other methods of maintaining the valuable parts of the drug experience. These people may learn to value the meditation high and abandon drugs.

KEY TERMS

**alternatives approach**
an approach emphasizing the exploration of positive alternatives to drug abuse based on replacing the pleasurable feelings gained from drug abuse with involvement in social and educational activities

**meditation**
state of consciousness in which there is a constant level of awareness focusing on one object—for example, yoga or Zen Buddhism

**TABLE 17.5** Experiences, Motives, and Possible Alternatives for a Drug Abuser

| Experience | Corresponding Motives | Drugs Abused | Possible Alternatives |
|---|---|---|---|
| Physical | Desire for physical well-being: physical relaxation, relief from sickness, desire for more energy | Alcohol, sedative-hypnotics, stimulants, marijuana | Athletics, dance, exercise, hiking, diet, carpentry, outdoor work, swimming, hatha yoga |
| Sensory | Desire to magnify sensorium: sound, touch, taste, need for sensual or sexual stimulation | Hallucinogens, marijuana, alcohol | Sensory awareness training, sky diving, experiencing sensory beauty of nature, scuba diving |
| Emotional | Relief from psychological pain: attempt to resolve personal problems, relief from bad mood, escape from anxiety, desire for emotional insight, liberation of feeling and emotional relaxation | Narcotics, alcohol, barbiturates, sedative-hypnotics | Competent individual counseling, well-run group therapy, instruction in psychology of personal development |
| Interpersonal | Desire to gain peer acceptance, break through interpersonal barriers, "communicate"; defiance of authority figures | Any, especially alcohol, marijuana | Expertly managed sensitivity and encounter groups, well-run group therapy, instruction in social customs, confidence training, emphasis on assisting others (e.g., YMCA or YWCA volunteers) |
| Social | Desire to promote social change, find identifiable subculture, tune out intolerable environmental conditions (e.g., poverty) | Marijuana, psychedelics | Social service community action in positive social change; helping the poor, aged, infirm, or young; tutoring handicapped individuals; ecology action; YMCA or YWCA Big Brother and Big Sister programs |
| Political | Desire to promote political change (out of desperation with the social-political order) and to identify with antiestablishment subgroup | Marijuana, psychedelics | Political service, lobbying for nonpartisan projects (e.g., Common Cause); fieldwork with politicians and public officials |
| Intellectual | Desire to escape boredom, out of intellectual curiosity, to solve cognitive problems, gain new understanding in the world of ideas, research one's own awareness | Stimulants, sometimes psychedelics | Intellectual excitement through reading, debate, and discussion; creative games and puzzles; self-hypnosis; training in concentration |
| Creative-aesthetic | Desire to improve creative performance, enhance enjoyment of art already produced (e.g., music); enjoy imaginative mental productions | Marijuana, stimulants, psychedelics | Nongraded instruction in producing or appreciating art, music, drama, and creative hobbies |
| Philosophical | Desire to discover meaningful values, find meaning in life, help establish personal identity, organize a belief structure | Psychedelics, marijuana, stimulants | Discussions, seminars, courses on ethics, the nature of reality, relevant philosophical literature; explorations of value systems |
| Spiritual-mystical | Desire to transcend orthodox religion, develop spiritual insights, reach higher levels of consciousness, augment yogic practices, take a spiritual shortcut | Psychedelics, marijuana | Exposure to nonchemical methods of spiritual development; study of world religions, mysticism, meditation, yogic techniques |

Data from U.S. Department of Health and Human Services, Office of Substance Abuse Prevention. (1989). Factors that influence alcohol and other drug use. In *Prevention Plus II: Tools for creating and sustaining drug-free communities*. DHHS Publication No. 89-1649. Rockville, MD: Author. Distributed by the National Clearinghouse for Alcohol and Drug Information.

In looking at Table 17.5, we can see how the use of different types of drugs can be replaced with possible alternatives by a drug abuser. Long-term drug users sometimes credit their drug experiences with having given them a taste of their potential, even though continued use has diminished the novelty of drug use. After these individuals become established in careers, they claim to have grown out of chemically induced altered states of consciousness. As Andrew Weil (2004) put it, "One does not see any long-time meditators give up meditation to become acid heads" (p. 72).

Although chemical highs are effective means of altering the state of consciousness, they interfere with the most worthwhile states of altered consciousness because they reinforce the illusion that highs come from external, material agents rather than from within your own nervous system.

Some people have difficulty using meditation as an alternative to drugs because, to be effective, meditation takes practice and concentration; in contrast, the effects of drugs are immediate. Nevertheless, it is within everyone's potential to meditate.

# LEARNING PORTFOLIO

## Key Terms

## Discussion Questions

1. Figure 17.1 lists many factors that can influence drug use. Design and detail a drug-prevention program by selecting any one of the concentric circles; include all factors within that circle and how you would deal with these factors.

2. Look at the findings in the section of this chapter titled "How Serious Are the Problems of Substance Use Disorders?" Which findings regarding dependence did you think were better in explaining the problem of drug dependence? Why?

3. Comment on the harm-reduction model as presented here and in other literature you may have read. What are the major strengths and weaknesses of this model in comparison to the way drug users or abusers are viewed in the United States? Why do you think the U.S. government largely remains opposed to this approach? How do you think the problem of drug use and abuse in the United States would change if it were to adopt the harm-reduction model?

4. What would you emphasize in a primary prevention program for middle school students? High school students? College students?

5. How would you design a drug-prevention program for undetected committed or secret users? What would you emphasize? Similarly, how would you design a drug-prevention program for addicted drug users? What would you emphasize?

6. Which do you think is more likely to work today in drug-prevention programs for America's youth: teaching moderate use or total abstinence? Explain why.

7. Your work supervisor says, "We received a much smaller amount of money than expected from the federal government to create a drug-prevention program. You should focus on either a community-based approach, a school-based approach, a family-based approach, or an individual-based approach or harm-reduction psychotherapy prevention program." Which type of approach would you select? Explain your choice.

8. After learning the history of past large-scale prevention organizations such as BACCHUS Initiatives of NASPA–Student Affairs Administrators in Higher Education, can you think of some type of program that would be beneficial for monitoring and curbing drug abuse on college campuses that would work today? Sketch out and discuss what some of the goals of such a drug-prevention program that could possibly work on today's college campuses.

9. List and explain three major strengths of drug courts in comparison with traditional criminal courts in the United States. Do you perceive any potential problems with preferring drug courts to criminal courts?

10. From everything you read in this chapter about the D.A.R.E. drug-prevention program, what do you think are the major problems with this comprehensive drug-prevention program? How would you improve it program in our current society today?

11. What is your assessment of using the alternatives approach and meditation for preventing drug use? Do you think it would be effective for alleviating drug use? Why or why not?

## Summary

1. The 10 most prominent factors affecting an individual's use of drugs are (a) genetics, (b) personality traits, (c) attitudes and beliefs, (d) interpersonal and peer resistance skills, (e) community, (f) peers, (g) school policy, (h) local law enforcement, (i) personal situations, and (j) parents.

2. The seriousness of the problem with regard to drug dependence is highlighted by the fact that in 2014 approximately 21.5 million people or older had an SUD in the preceding year, including 17.0 million people with an alcohol use disorder and 7.1 million people with an illicit drug use disorder. An estimated 4.2 million people had a past-year disorder related to marijuana use, and 1.9 million people had disorders related to nonmedical past-year use of prescription pain relievers. Approximately 2.6 million people 12 or older had both an alcohol use disorder and an illicit drug use disorder in the past year; thus, among people aged 12 or older in 2014 who an SUD in the past year, nearly four out of five had an alcohol use disorder and about one out of three had an illicit drug use disorder. About one in eight people 12 or older who had SUDs in the preceding year had both an alcohol use disorder and an illicit drug use disorder. An estimated 1.3 million adolescents aged 12 to 17 had an SUD in 2014 (5.0% of adolescents). In 2014, 5.7 million young adults 18 to 25 had an SUD (16.3% of young adults). An estimated 14.5 million adults aged 26 or older in 2014 had an SUD (7.1% of adults aged 26 or older). The approximately 4.2 million people 12 or older in 2014 who had a marijuana use disorder in the preceding year represented 1.6% of those aged 12 or older. The estimated 1.9 million people 12 or older in 2014 who had a pain reliever use disorder represent 0.7% of the people aged 12 or older. About 913,000 people aged 12 or older in 2014 had a cocaine use disorder, which represents 0.3% of the people 12 or older. About 586,000 people aged 12 or older in 2014 had a heroin use disorder, which represents 0.2% of the people aged 12 or older.

3. The three major types of prevention programs are primary, secondary, and tertiary.

4. Five major types of drug users that drug-prevention programs have to recognize before assembling a program are (a) early experimenters, (b) nonproblem drug users and recreational users, (c) undetected committed or secret users, (d) problem users, and (e) former users.

5. The five levels of comprehensive prevention programs for drug use and abuse are (a) the harm-reduction model, (b) community-based prevention, (c) school-based prevention, (d) family-based prevention, and (e) individual-based drug prevention and treatment and harm-reduction psychotherapy.

6. Proactive family factors can moderate the effects of drug risk factors. The risk of associating with peers who use drugs can be offset by protective family factors, such as parent conventionality, maternal adjustment, and strong parent–child attachment.

7. Five primary prevention programs that exist in higher education are the (a) information-only or awareness model, (b) attitude change model or affective education model, (c) social influences model, (d) ecological or person-in-environment model, and (e) social-ecological model.

8. Three of today's large-scale prevention programs are (a) the BACCHUS Initiatives of NASPA–Student Affairs Administrators in

Higher Education, a national and international association of college and university peer-education programs focused on alcohol abuse prevention and other related student health and safety issues; (b) D.A.R.E., a nationwide drug-prevention program presented in middle and junior high schools by police officers that has shown severe shortcomings; and (c) drug courts, a promising and popular nationwide approach to prevention in which the primary purpose is to include treatment programs and options instead of only punishment for drug offenses.

9. Two additional possibilities for lessening or eliminating drug use are the alternatives approach and meditation. Alternatives to drug abuse are based on replacing the euphoria and pleasure gained by being high with involvement in social, recreational, and educational activities. Meditation is producing a state of consciousness in which there is a constant level of satisfying awareness that is rewarding in itself without artificial inducements (drugs). Yoga and Zen Buddhism are examples.

# References

Alberti, R. E., & Emmons. M. L. (1988). *Your perfect right.* San Luis Obispo, CA: Impact.

AlcoholAnswers.org. (2013). *Harm reduction philosophy.* Farmington, CT: National Alliance of Advocates for Buprenorphine Treatment.

Alcoholrehab.com. (2016). Addiction and low self-esteem. Alcohol Rehab. Retrieved from http://alcoholrehab.com /addiction-articles/addiction-and-low-self-esteem/

American University. (2014). Drug court technical assistance. Washington, DC: Bureau of Justice Assistance Project. Retrieved from https://www.american.edu/spa /jpo/initiatives/drug-court/

Anderson, R. (2019). Replace DARE with programs that really work. Salt Lake City, UT: Author. Retrieved from http://rockyanderson.org/writings-main/writings-2 /published/replace-dare-with-programs-that-really-work/

Ansari, W. E., Stock, C., & Mills, C. (2013, October). Is alcohol consumption associated with poor academic achievement in university students? *International Journal of Preventive Medicine, 4,* 1175–1188.

BACCHUS & GAMMA. (1994). *Community college guide to peer education.* Denver, CO: The BACCHUS and GAMMA Peer Education Network.

BACCHUS Network. (2011). Mission statement. Retrieved from https://oregontechsfcdn.azureedge.net/oregontech /integrated-student-health-center-documents/what-is -bacchus.pdf?sfvrsn=3d5fb960_2

BACCHUS Network. (2013). About the BACCHUS Network. Retrieved from http://www.bacchusnetwork.org/about -the-network.html

Berk, B. (2013, March). *Effective substance abuse prevention: Why it matters, what works, and what the experts see for the future.* Santa Rosa, CA: Center for Applied Research Solutions. Retrieved from http://www.ca-cpi.org/docs/Publications /Other/EffectiveSubstanceAbusePrevention_March2013 .pdf

Botvin, G. J., & Griffin, K. W. (2005). School-based programs. In J. H. Lowinson, P. Ruiz, R. B. Millman, & J. G. Langrod (Eds.), *Substance abuse: A comprehensive textbook,* 4th ed. (pp. 1211–1228). Philadelphia, PA: Lippincott Williams & Wilkins.

Botvin, G. J., & Wills, T. A. (1985). Personal and social skills training: Cognitive-behavioral approaches to substance abuse prevention. In *Prevention research: Deterring drug abuse among children and adolescents.* NIDA Research Monograph No. 64. Rockville, MD: National Institute on Drug Abuse.

Brownsberger, W. N. (1996, October 20). Just say "criminal justice." *Boston Globe.*

California Polytechnic State University. (2016). Sobering statistics. Health and Counseling Services. Retrieved from http://www.hcs.calpoly.edu/pulse/students/alc _awareness/statistics

Carroll, E. (1977). Notes on the epidemiology of inhalants. In C. W. Sharp & M. L. Brehm (Eds.), *Review of inhalants.* NIDA Research Monograph No. 15. Washington, DC: National Institute on Drug Abuse.

Center for Prevention Research and Development. (2000). *Research-based approaches in the community domain.* Champaign, IL: University of Illinois,.

Centers for Disease Control and Prevention. (2009, September 9). The social-ecological model: A framework for prevention. Retrieved https://www.cdc.gov/violence prevention/publichealthissue/social-ecologicalmodel. html

Claire, J. (2013). Drug prevention programmes in schools: What is the evidence? London, UK: Mentor. Retrieved from https://hivhealthclearinghouse.unesco.org/library /documents/drug-prevention-programmes-schools-what -evidence

Clayton, R. R., Cattarello, R., Cay, L. E., & Walden, K. P. (1991). Persuasive communication and drug prevention:

An evaluation of the D.A.R.E. program. In L. Donohew, H. Sypepher, & W. Bukowski (Eds.), *Persuasive communication and drug abuse prevention* (pp. 83–107). Hillsdale, NJ: Erlbaum.

Cleveland, M. J., Collins, L. M., Lanza, S. T., Greenberg, M. T., & Feinberg, M. E. (2010, July). Does individual risk moderate the effect of contextual-level protective factors? A latent class analysis of substance use. *Journal of Prevention and Intervention in the Community, 38*, 213–228.

Cohen, A. Y. (1971, Spring). The journey beyond trips: Alternatives to drugs. *Journal of Psychedelic Drugs, 3*, 7–14.

Common Sense for Drug Policy. (2009, July 9). DARE admits failure. Retrieved from http://www.csdp.org/news/news/darerevised.htm.

Community Anti-Drug Coalition of America (CADCA). (2010). *Drug-free communities support program grantee roadmap to success: Training and technical assistance support system.* Alexandria, VA: Author.

Community Anti-Drug Coalition of America (CADCA). (2020). CADCA: Reducing drug use, one community at a time. Alexandria VA: Author. Retrieved from https://www.cadca.org/about-us

Drug Abuse Resistance Education (D.A.R.E.) (2016, October 22). Teaching students decision making for safe & healthy living. Los Angeles, CA: D.A.R.E America. Retrieved from http://www.dare.org/

Ennett, S. T., Tobler, N. S., Ringwalt, C. L., & Flewelling, R. L. (1994). How effective is drug abuse resistance education? A meta-analysis of Project D.A.R.E. outcome evaluations. *American Journal of Public Health, 84*, 1394–1401.

European Monitoring Centre ford Drugs and Drug Addiction. (2010, July 22). Step 2a: Models and theories. Lisbon, Portugal: Author.

Forman, S. G., & Linney, J. A. (1988). School-based prevention of adolescent substance abuse: Programs, implementation and future direction. *School Psychology Review, 17*, 550–558.

Feliz, J. (2010, October 7). The Partnership for a Drug-Free America changes name to The Partnership at Drugfree.org. New York, NY: Partnership to End Addiction. Retrieved from https://drugfree.org/newsroom/news-item/the-partnership-for-a-drug-free-america-changes-name-to-the-partnership-at-drugfree-org/

Franco, C. (2010, October 12). Drug courts: Background, effectiveness, and policy issues for Congress. Washington, DC: Congressional Research Service. Retrieved from http://www.fas.org/sgp/crs/misc/R41448.pdf

Goldkamp, J. (1993). *Justice and treatment innovation: The drug court movement.* Washington, DC: National Institute of Justice and the State Justice Institute.

Gonzalez, G. M., & Clement, V. V. (Eds.). (1994). *Preventing substance abuse.* Washington, DC: U.S. Department of Education.

Gopelrud, E. N. (Ed.). *Preventing adolescent drug use: From theory to practice.* OSAP Monograph No. 8, DHHS Pub. No. (ADM) 91–1725. Rockville, MD: Office of Substance Abuse Prevention.

Gordon, P. (1996a, July). The truth about D.A.R.E. *Buzz Magazine.*

Gordon, P. (1996b). Can Madison Avenue really save America by making illegal drugs totally uncool? *Buzz Magazine.* (August).

Hansen, W. B. (1997). A social ecology theory of alcohol and drug use prevention among college and university students. In *Designing Alcohol and Other Drug Prevention Programs in Higher Education.* Newton, MA: Higher Education Center for Alcohol and Other Drug Prevention, U.S. Department of Education.

Harm Reduction Coalition. (n.d.). Principles of harm reduction. Retrieved from http://harmreduction.org/about-us/principles-of-harm-reduction/

Health Foundation of Greater Cincinnati. (2010). *Supporting community-based substance abuse prevention.* Cincinnati, OH: Author. Retrieved from https://www.interactforhealth.org/docs/Supporting%20Community-Based%20Substance%20Abuse%20Prevention.pdf

Holstein, M. E., Cohen, W. E., & Steinbroner, P. (1995). *A matter of balance: Personal strategies for alcohol and other drugs.* Ashland, OR: CNS Productions.

Horowitz, H. L. (1987). *Campus life.* New York, NY: Knopf, 1987.

Jernigan, D., & O'Hara, J. (2004). Alcohol advertising and promotion. In R. J. Bonnie & M. E. O'Connell (Eds.), *Reducing underage drinking: A collective responsibility* (pp. 232–247). Washington, DC: National Academies Press.

King, R. S., & Pasquarella, J. (2009). *Drug courts: A review of the evidence.* Washington, DC: The Sentencing Project. Retrieved from http://www.sentencingproject.org/doc/dp_drugcourts.pdf

Kondrat, M. E. (2015, April 29). Person-in-environment. *Oxford Bibliographies.* Retrieved from https://www.oxfordbibliographies.com/view/document/obo-9780195389678/obo-9780195389678-0092.xml

Koss, M. P., Gidycz, C. A., & Wisniewski, R. (1987). The scope of rape: Incidence and prevalence of sexual aggression and victimization in a national sample of higher education students. *Journal of Consulting and Clinical Psychology, 34*, 186–196.

Larimer, M. E., Kilmer, J. R., & Lee, C. M. (2005, April). College student drug prevention: A review of individually oriented prevention strategies. *Journal of Drug Issues, 35*, 431–456.

Legal Action Center. (2016). Confronting an epidemic: The case for eliminating barriers to medication-assisted treatment of heroin and opioid addiction. New York, NY: Author.

Marlowe, D. B. (2010, December). *Research update on adult drug courts.* Alexandria, VA: National Association of Drug Court Professionals (NADCP). Retrieved from https://www.nadcp.org/wp-content/uploads/Research%20Update%20on%20Adult%20Drug%20Courts%20-%20NADCP_1.pdf

McIntyre, K., White, D., & Yoast, R. (1990). *Resilience among high-risk youth.* Madison, WI: University of Wisconsin.

Miller, D. W. (2001, October 19). D.A.R.E. reinvents itself— With help from its social-scientist critics. *Chronicle of Higher Education, 48,* A12–A14.

National Association of Drug Court Professionals (NADCP). (2011a). Drug courts work. Retrieved from http://www.nadcp.org/learn/drug-courts-work

National Association of Drug Court Professionals (NADCP). (2011b). What are drug courts? Retrieved from http://www.nadcp.org/learn/what-are-drug-courts

National Association of Student Personnel Administrators (NASPA)—Student Affairs Administrators in Higher Education. (2016a). Bacchus initiatives of NASPA: History. Retrieved from https://www.naspa.org/blog/what-is-peer-education-40-years-of-bacchus-a-history

National Association of Student Personnel Administrators (NASPA)—Student Affairs Administrators in Higher Education. (2016b). About NASPA: Advancing leadership, shaping change. Retrieved from https://www.naspa.org/

National Crime Prevention Centre. (2019). *School-based drug abuse prevention: Promising and successful programs.* Ottawa, Ontario, Canada: Author.

National Drug Court Resource Center (NDCRC). (2014, June 30). Drug Courts. Retrieved from https://www.ncjrs.gov/pdffiles1/nij/238527.pdf

National Drug Court Resource Center (NDCRC). (2020). What are drug courts? Wilmington, NC: UNCW Social Science Applied Research Center.

National Institute of Justice (NIJ). (2016, May 13). Overview of drug courts. Retrieved from http://www.nij.gov/topics/courts/drug-courts/Pages/welcome.aspx

National Institute on Drug Abuse (NIDA). (2002, February). Risk and protective factors in drug abuse prevention. *NIDA Notes.* Retrieved from https://archives.drugabuse.gov/news-events/nida-notes/2002/02/risk-protective-factors-in-drug-abuse-prevention

National Institute on Drug Abuse (NIDA). (2003, October). Preventing drug use among children and adolescents (In Brief). Bethesda, MD: Author. Retrieved from https:// www.drugabuse.gov/publications/preventing-drug-abuse-among-children-adolescents/chapter-1-risk-factors-protective-factors/what-are-risk-factors

National Institute on Drug Abuse (NIDA). (2007, March). *Drug abuse prevention: Drug abuse is a preventable behavior.* Bethesda, MD: Author.

National Institute on Drug Abuse (NIDA). (2014, March). Drug facts: Lessons from prevention research. Bethesda, MD: Author. Retrieved from https://www.drugabuse.gov/publications/drugfacts/lessons-prevention-research

National Institute on Drug Abuse (NIDA). (2016, March). Principles of substance abuse prevention for early childhood. Bethesda, MD: Author. Retrieved from https://www.drugabuse.gov/publications/principles-substance-abuse-prevention-early-childhood/chapter-1-why-early-childhood-important-to-substance-abuse-prevention

National Institute on Drug Abuse (NIDA). (2018, June). Understanding drug use and addiction. Bethesda, MD: Author. Retrieved from https://www.drugabuse.gov/publications/drugfacts/understanding-drug-use-addiction

National Institute on Drug Abuse (NIDA). (2020, February). Trends and statistics. Bethesda, MD: Author. Retrieved from https://www.drugabuse.gov/related-topics/trends-statistics

National Institutes of Health (NIH) & National Institute on Drug Abuse (NIDA). (1998). *Drug abuse and drug abuse research.* Washington, DC: U.S. Government Printing Office.

Norman, E. (1994). Personal factors related to substance misuse: Risk abatement and/or resiliency enhancement. In T. P. Gulotta, G. R. Adams, & R. Montemayor (Eds.), *Substance abuse in adolescence* (pp. 47–56). Thousand Oaks, CA: Sage Publications.

Office of Justice Programs. (2000, January 10). *Summary of drug court activity by state and county.* Washington, DC: U.S. Government Printing Office.

Office of National Drug Control Policy. (2007, February). National drug control strategy: The White House. Washington, DC: U.S. Government Printing Office, 2007.

Perkins, H. W. (1991). Confronting misperceptions of peer use norms among college students: An alternative approach for alcohol and other drug education programs. In *The higher education leaders/Peers network peer prevention program resource manual* (pp. 18–32). Washington, DC: U.S. Department of Education & Texas Christian University.

Perkins, H. W. (1997). College student misperceptions of alcohol and other drug norms among peers: Exploring causes, consequences, and implications for prevention programs. In *Designing alcohol and other drug prevention programs in higher education*. Washington, DC: U.S. Department of Education, Higher Education Center for Alcohol and Other Drug Prevention.

Perkins, H. W., & Berkowitz, A. D. (1986). Perceiving the community norms of alcohol use among students: Some research implications for campus alcohol education programming. *International Journal of the Addictions, 21*, 861–976.

Plant, M., Robertson, R., Plant, M., & Miller, P. (2011). *Drug nation: Patterns, problems, panics, and politics*. Oxford, UK: Oxford University Press.

ProCon.org. (2013, November 6). Is the D.A.R.E. program good for America's kids (K–12)? Retrieved from http://dare.procon.org/#Background

ProCon.org. (2014, February 4). Is the D.A.R.E. program good for America's kids (K–12)? Retrieved from http://dare.procon.org/

Robertson, E. B., David, S. L., Rao, S. A., & NIDA. (2003). *Preventing drug use among children and adolescents*, 2nd ed. Bethesda, MD: U.S. Department of Health and Human Services.

Rosenbaum, D. P., & Hanson, S. (1998, April 6). *Assessing the effects of school-based drug education; a six-year multilevel analysis of Project D.A.R.E.* Chicago, IL: University of Illinois at Chicago, Department of Criminal Justice and Center for Research in Law and Justice.

Ryan, B. E., Colthurst, T., & Segars, L. (1995). *College alcohol risk assessment guide*. San Diego, CA: UCSD Extension, University of California at San Diego.

Sherin, K. M., & Mahoney, B. (1996). *Treatment drug courts: Integrating substance abuse treatment with legal case processing*. Rockville, MD: U.S. Department of Health and Human Services.

Shiffman, S., & Wills, T. A. (Eds.). (1987). *Coping and substance abuse*. New York, NY: Academic Press.

Siegel, R. K. (2005). *Intoxication: The university drive for mind-altering substances*. Rochester, VT: Park Street Press.

Silver Gate Group & Robert Wood Johnson Foundation (2001). *Prevention 2000: Moving effective prevention programs into practice*. Princeton, NJ: Robert Wood Johnson Foundation.

Sloboda, Z., & David, S. L. (1999, April). *Preventing drug use among children and adolescents: A research-based guide*. Washington, DC: National Institute on Drug Abuse and National Institutes of Health.

Southwestern Illinois College. (n.d.). BACCHUS: A healthy lifestyles club for college students. Bellville, IL: Author. Retrieved from https://southwesternillinoiscollege bacchus.wordpress.com/

StateUniversity.com. (2011). Big business—Alcohol advertising and college sports. Retrieved from http://www.stateuniversity.com/blog/permalink/Alcohol-Advertising-and-College-Sports.html

Substance Abuse and Mental Health Services Administration (SAMHSA). (2019). *Key substance use and mental health indicators in the United States: Results from the 2018 National Survey on Drug Use and Health*. HHS Publication No. PEP19-5068, NSDUH Series H-54. Rockville, MD: Author.

Tatarsky, A. (2002). Harm reduction psychotherapy: A new treatment for drug and alcohol problems. New York, NY: Rowman & Littlefield.

Tinzmann, M. B., & Hixson, J. (2006). *What does research say about prevention?* Oak Brook, IL: North Central Regional Educational Laboratory.

United Nations Office on Drugs and Crime (UNODC). (2011). Preventing drug use among youth works. Retrieved from http://www.unodc.org/unodc/en/prevention/index.html

U.S. Department of Education. (1994). *Archived information: Current knowledge in prevention of alcohol and other drug abuse*, G. M. Gonzalez & V. V. Clement (Eds.). Washington, DC: Author.

U.S. Department of Education. (2008). *Alcohol and other drug prevention on college campuses: Model programs*. Washington, DC: Author.

U.S. Department of Health and Human Services, Office of Substance Abuse Prevention. (1989). Factors that influence alcohol and other drug use. In *Prevention Plus II: Tools for creating and sustaining drug-free communities*. DHHS Publication No. 89-1649. Rockville, MD: Author.

U.S. Government Accountability Office (GAO). (2003, January 15). *Youth illicit drug use prevention: D.A.R.E. long-term evaluation and federal efforts to identify effective programs*. GAO-03-172R. Washington, DC: Author.

Vogt, A. (2003, January 26). Now Many "Just Say No" to D.A.R.E. *Chicago Tribune*, pp. 1, 3.

Weil, A. (2004). *The natural mind: A revolutionary approach to the drug problem*. New York, NY: Houghton Mifflin.

Westermeyer, R. W. (n.d.). Reducing harm: A very good idea. Retrieved from http://www.fullspectrumrecovery.com/fullspec/images/stories/pdfs/reducing%20harm.pdf

Will, B. (2018, August 29). D.A.R.E. program is evolving. Grand Rapids, WI: WSAW-TV. Retrieved from https://www.wsaw.com/content/news/DARE-program-is-evolving-491995011.html

Wilson, M., & Wilson, S. (Eds.). (1975). *Drugs in American life*, Vol. 1. New York, NY: Wilson.

Wilson, R. W., & Kolander, C. A. (2011). *Drug abuse prevention: A school and community partnership*, 3rd ed. Burlington, MA: Jones & Bartlett Learning.

Zeese, K. B., & Lewin, P. M. (1998). *The effective drug control strategy*. Washington, DC: Network of Reform Group and the National Coalition for Effective Drug Policies. Retrieved from http://www.csdp.org/edcs/edc.htm

Zweig, J. M. (2011). Description of the drug court sites in the multi-site adult drug court evaluation. In S. B. Rossman, J. M. Zweig, D. Kralstein, K. Henry, P. M. Downey, & C. Lindquist (Eds.), *The multi-site adult drug court evaluation: The drug court experience* (pp. 8–23). Washington, DC: Urban Institute Justice Policy Center.

CHAPTER **18**

# Treating Drug Dependence

## Did You Know?

▶ A variety of approaches to drug addiction treatment exist, including behavioral and pharmacological therapies.

▶ No single treatment approach is appropriate for all individuals.

▶ Relapse rates for addiction resemble those of other chronic diseases such as diabetes, hypertension, and asthma.

▶ Comorbidity between drug addiction and other mental illnesses is common.

## Learning Objectives

**On completing this chapter, you should be able to:**

❭ Discuss assessment of addiction severity and readiness to change.

❭ List several principles that characterize effective drug treatment.

❭ Discuss the role of comorbidity in substance abuse and its treatment.

❭ Discuss pharmacological and behavioral strategies to treat addiction.

❭ Describe the Mental Health Parity and Addiction Equity Act.

❭ Discuss Screening, Brief Intervention, and Referral to Treatment (SBIRT).

# Treatment of Addiction

Individuals who are addicted to drugs come from all walks of life. Many suffer from occupational, social, psychiatric, or other medical problems that can make their addictions difficult to treat. Even in the absence of such complicating issues, the severity of addictions varies widely. Matching treatment with the needs of the client is essential. Further, it is valuable to intervene at the earliest possible stage of addiction with the least restrictive form of appropriate treatment. To accomplish this, it is important that treatment providers determine the severity of addiction as well as the readiness of an individual to change his or her behavior.

# Assessing Addiction Severity and Readiness to Change

Addiction severity can be determined in many ways, including the administration of standardized questionnaires. Of these, the Addiction Severity Index (ASI) is among the most widely used assessment instruments in the field of addiction (McLellan et al. 1980, 1985, 1992). The ASI is one of the most reliable and valid measurements of the magnitude and characteristics of client problems. It focuses on possible problems in six areas: medical status, employment and support, alcohol and drug use, legal status, family and social relationships, and psychiatric status. The ASI provides information that can be used to identify and prioritize which problem areas are most significant and require prompt attention.

When assessing and prioritizing problems, Maslow's hierarchy of needs is one model of individual development that is often considered. This theory postulates that individuals are motivated by unsatisfied needs and that lower fundamental needs must be met before higher needs can be satisfied. These primary needs include food, drink, warmth, sleep, and shelter. These can be extended in the case of substance abusers to problems such as (1) unidentified or inappropriately managed health problems, (2) medication-adherence issues (particularly in the presence of co-occurring mental or physical

health disorders), and (3) physical alterations because of drug or alcohol dependence (Stilen, Carise, Roget, & Wendler, 2007). Once these fundamental needs are addressed, a second level of needs involving security and safety can be addressed.

Simplistically, these include such issues as stability, order, law, and limits. Examples of common problem areas reflecting this level include inability for self-care, management of mental health issues, personal and public safety issues, and legal issues. If these needs are not met, individuals receiving substance abuse treatment cannot move to higher levels wherein love and belonging, self-esteem, and self-actualization (i.e., fulfilling personal potential) can be attained (Stilen et al. 2007).

As important as assessing addiction severity and prioritizing problem areas on which to focus is consideration of a person's readiness to change his or her abuse behavior. Pioneering work by DiClemente and Prochaska (1998) revealed that behavioral change is a many-stage process rather than a singular event. The stages described by DiClemente and Prochaska include the following:

- *Precontemplation*: An individual does not want to change or is not considering changing his or her behavior. The latter may be because he or she does not see a need for change.
- *Contemplation*: A person is considering changing his or her behavior.
- *Preparation*: A person is committed to a strategy for change.
- *Action*: A person is actively attempting to change.
- *Maintenance*: A person has changed his or her behavior. To complete the process of change, this behavior must become a part of his or her lifestyle.

Determining the stage of change at which an individual finds him- or herself can help providers select the best treatment plan to address a client's needs. This may help prevent the individual from refusing to accept all or parts of the treatment plan. Screening, Brief Intervention, and Referral to Treatment (SBIRT) can be an important first step towards identifying individuals who are in need of assistance (see "Here and Now: Screening, Brief Intervention, and Referral to Treatment (SBIRT)").

# HERE AND NOW

## Screening, Brief Intervention, and Referral to Treatment (SBIRT)

Screening, Brief Intervention, and Referral to Treatment (SBIRT) is an evidence-based practice used to identify, reduce, and prevent problematic use, abuse, and dependence on alcohol and illicit drugs. SBIRT arose as a consequence of an Institute of Medicine report, *Broadening the Base of Treatment for Alcohol Problems*, which recommended community-based screening for health risk behaviors. The screening can be conducted in any healthcare setting, including primary care centers, hospital emergency rooms, trauma centers, and other community settings. It can also be tailored for adolescents or adults. The overall goal of the SBIRT is to provide opportunities for early intervention with at-risk substance users before more severe consequences occur.

SBIRT consists of three main components.

1. *Screening*: A patient is assessed by a healthcare provider for risky substance use behaviors using standardized screening tools. The goal is to quickly assess the severity of substance use and identify the appropriate level of treatment.

2. *Brief Intervention*: A patient demonstrating risky substance use behaviors is engaged by a healthcare provider in short conversation and is provided feedback and advice. The focus is on increasing insight and awareness regarding substance use and motivation toward behavioral change.

3. *Referral to Treatment*: A patient is referred to brief therapy or additional treatment as appropriate.

Studies have demonstrated that SBIRT reduces healthcare costs, trauma, and the severity of drug and alcohol abuse.

Data from Institute of Medicine (IOM). (1990). *Broadening the base of treatment for alcohol problems*. Washington, DC: National Academies Press; Substance Abuse and Mental Health Services Administration (SAMHSA). (2011). *SBIRT: Screening, brief intervention and referral to treatment*. Rockville, MD: Author. Retrieved from http://www.integration.samhsa.gov/clinical-practice/SBIRT. Accessed December 24, 2019; Substance Abuse and Mental Health Services Administration (SAMHSA). (2017). *SBIRT screening, brief intervention and referral to treatment*. Rockville, MD: Author. Retrieved from http://www.samhsa.gov/sbirt; Substance Abuse and Mental Health Services Administration (SAMHSA). (n.d.). *SBIRT: Screening, brief intervention, and referral to treatment—Opportunities for implementation and points for consideration*. Rockville, MD: Author. Retrieved from http://www.integration.samhsa.gov/sbirt_issue_brief.pdf. Accessed December 24, 2019.

# Principles of Treatment

A variety of approaches to drug addiction treatment exist. Some include behavioral therapy such as counseling, psychotherapy, or cognitive therapy. Others include medications ranging from treatment medications (e.g., methadone, buprenorphine, nicotine patches, nicotine gum) to those intended to treat co-occurring mental disorders (e.g., antidepressants, mood stabilizers). The most successful drug abuse treatment programs typically provide a combination of therapies and other services to meet the needs of the individual abuser. They incorporate adequate assessment of treatment needs required not only as a direct consequence of the physiological and psychological effects of the drug but also from indirect problems such as the need for housing, legal and financial issues, poor education or vocational skills, or lack of family or childcare services. Such needs often are shaped by the abuser's gender, age, race, culture, and sexual orientation.

Because drug addiction is generally a chronic disorder characterized by occasional relapses, a one-time, short-term treatment is often inadequate. Further, many individuals who enter treatment drop out before receiving all of its benefits, reinforcing the fact that successful treatment often requires more than one treatment exposure. Of note, relapse rates for addiction resemble those of other chronic diseases such as asthma, diabetes, and hypertension (National Institute on Drug Abuse [NIDA], 2018b). **Figure 18.1** illustrates these statistics.

Research has shown that good outcomes are contingent on adequate duration of treatment. Generally, for outpatient or residential treatment, participation for fewer than 90 days is of limited effectiveness; treatments lasting significantly longer are needed (NIDA, 2018b). For methadone maintenance, 12 months of treatment often is the minimum needed, and some individuals who are

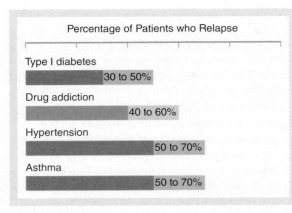

**FIGURE 18.1** Relapse rates for addiction resemble those of other chronic diseases such as asthma, diabetes, and hypertension.

National Institute on Drug Abuse (NIDA). (2018b). *Principles of drug addiction treatment* (3rd ed.). Washington, DC: National Institutes of Health.

addicted to opiates require extended treatment lasting several years (NIDA, 2018b).

To best target treatment for an individual, the type and goals of treatment must be determined. Consideration must be given to the fact that both largely depend on the view one holds of addiction. For example, if the disease model is applied to addiction, total abstinence is generally required because this model views drug abuse as a biological condition that is largely uncontrollable. On the other hand, if responsible drug use is the goal, then occasional and moderate drug use can be the intended end result.

Effective treatment allows addicts to stop abusing drugs, returns them to a drug-free state of existence, and transforms them into employable and productive members of society. Measures of effectiveness typically include assessing levels of family functioning, employability, criminal behavior, and medical condition.

As summarized in the following list, the National Institute on Drug Abuse has delineated 13 overarching principles that characterize effective addiction treatment (NIDA, 2018b):

1. *Addiction is a complex but treatable disease that affects brain function and behavior.* Drugs of abuse can alter brain function and structure, resulting in changes that persist long after drug use has ended. This may explain why drug abusers are at risk for relapse even after extended periods of abstinence and awareness of potentially destructive consequences.

2. *No single treatment is appropriate for all individuals.* Treatment settings and services must be matched to each person's particular needs.

3. *Treatment needs to be readily available.* Individuals who are addicted to drugs are often uncertain about whether to seek treatment. Hence, it is important that services be available as soon as an individual makes the decision to seek help. Treatment opportunities can be lost if such services are not immediately and readily accessible.

4. *Effective treatment attends to multiple needs of the individual, not just his or her drug use.* To be effective, treatment must address not only the individual's drug use but also any related medical, psychological, social, vocational, and legal problems. It is also important that an individual's age, ethnicity, gender, and culture be considered when implementing treatment.

5. *Remaining in treatment for an adequate period is critical for treatment effectiveness.* The appropriate duration of treatment depends on each person's individual problems and needs. As previously noted, research indicates that, for many, at least three months in treatment is needed.

6. *Behavioral therapies, including individual, family, or group counseling, are the most commonly used forms of drug abuse treatment.* Such therapies often have different emphases. These may involve improving problem-solving skills, providing incentives for abstinence, addressing motivation to change, building skills to resist drug use, and facilitating improved interpersonal relationships.

7. *Medications are an important element of treatment for many patients, especially when combined with counseling and other behavioral therapies.* Specific pharmacological therapies for treating substance abusers are discussed later in this chapter.

8. *An individual's treatment and services plan must be assessed continually and modified as necessary to ensure it meets his or her changing needs.* In addition to counseling, an individual may require various combinations of medical services, family therapy, vocational rehabilitation, or social and legal services.

9. *Many drug addicted individuals also have other mental disorders.* Because drug abuse and addiction often co-occur with other mental illnesses (see the discussion of comorbidity later in this chapter), patients presenting with one condition should be evaluated for any others. Treatment should address each identified issue, including the use of medications, if warranted.

10. *Medically assisted detoxification is only the first stage of addiction treatment and, by itself, does little to change long-term drug use.* Medical detoxification is the process of safely managing the acute physical symptoms of withdrawal associated with stopping drug use. It can be an important first step toward abstinence but alone is rarely sufficient to help individuals achieve long-term abstinence.

11. *Treatment does not need to be voluntary to be effective.* Sanctions or enticements in the family, criminal justice system, or employment settings can facilitate treatment entry and increase both retention rates and success of drug treatment interventions.

12. *Drug use during treatment must be monitored continuously because lapses during treatment do occur.* The knowledge that an individual's drug use is being monitored can be a powerful incentive to withstand urges to abuse drugs. Monitoring also provides an early indication of a return to drug use, signaling a possible need to adjust treatment plans.

13. *Treatment programs should test patients for the presence of HIV/AIDS, hepatitis B and C, tuberculosis, and other infectious diseases, as well as provide targeted risk-reduction counseling, linking patients to treatment if necessary.*

Many treatment programs apply one or more of these listed principles as part of their therapeutic strategy.

Of note, the age of the substance abuser is an important consideration when designing treatment. This includes both the age of first exposure to drugs and the age at which treatment is initiated. Research indicates that from birth through early adulthood the brain undergoes a prolonged process of development during which a behavioral shift occurs such that actions go from being more impulsive to more reflective and reasoned. Further, the brain areas most closely associated with judgment, decision making, and self-control undergo a period of rapid development during adolescence (NIDA, 2018b). Thus, adolescent drug abusers have unique needs that must be considered in developing a treatment approach to their addictions.

Gender-related considerations are also of importance in treating substance abuse. Treatment should attend not only to biological distinctions between genders but also to the social and environmental factors that can differentially affect motivations for drug use, effectiveness of and reasons for seeking treatment, environments where treatment is obtained, and consequences of not receiving treatment. For example, many life circumstances predominate in women as a group that may require specialized treatment approaches. These can, for example, include sexual and physical trauma followed by posttraumatic stress disorder (PTSD). Research indicates that these are more common in women than in men seeking treatment (NIDA, 2018b). Other factors that can be (although are not necessarily) unique to women include issues involving financial independence, pregnancy, and childcare. Each circumstance must be considered in developing a treatment plan.

Substance abusers involved with the criminal justice system are another population that often benefits from specialized treatment approaches. According to NIDA (2018b), combining criminal justice sanctions with substance abuse treatment can diminish both subsequent abuse and associated crimes. Initiating treatment in prison and continuing that same treatment on release also results in less drug use and less criminal behavior. Further, individuals under legal coercion tend to remain in treatment longer and do as well as or better than those who are not experiencing legal pressure (NIDA, 2018b).

Unfortunately, adequate treatment for criminal justice–involved individuals is often unavailable. Further, there are often few choices in the types of services provided. According to NIDA (2014), treatment that is of insufficient quality or not well suited to the needs of offenders may not yield significant reductions in drug use and recidivism. Untreated offenders are more likely than treated offenders to relapse to drug abuse and return to criminal behavior.

Therapeutic work environments that provide employment for abstinent drug-abusing individuals both improve life skills and promote a continued drug-free lifestyle. Further, some workplaces sponsor employee assistance programs that offer short-term assistance or counseling that links employees with substance abuse problems to local treatment resources.

Of note, several factors influence retention in treatment programs. These can include (1) individual motivation to change drug-using behavior, (2) degree of support from family and friends, and (3) pressure from employers, the criminal justice system, or extensions of the court (e.g., child protective services). It also is important for treatment providers to ensure a transition to continuing care or aftercare following a patient's completion of formal treatment (NIDA, 2018b).

## Comorbidity

Drug addiction is a complicated condition that often involves changes in the structure and function of specific parts of the brain. Such changes in regions of the brain affected by drug addiction can also occur in other mental illnesses such as anxiety, psychosis, and depression. Of note, overlapping factors, including genetic vulnerabilities, trauma, stress, or underlying brain abnormalities can contribute to both substance abuse disorders and other mental illnesses.

Comorbidity is a condition in which two or more illnesses occur in the same person, simultaneously or sequentially. This term also suggests interactions between the illnesses that affect the course and prognosis of both (NIDA, 2018a). The *Diagnostic and Statistical Manual of Mental Disorders* (DSM) is a widely used authority for diagnosing such mental health problems (see "Here and Now: Tools for Diagnosis").

Comorbidity between drug addiction and mental illnesses is common. Data indicate high co-occurrence of anxiety disorders (e.g., panic disorder, generalized anxiety disorder, and PTSD) with substance abuse disorders. Substance use disorders also occur with relatively high frequency with depression, bipolar disorder, psychotic illness and attention-deficit hyperactivity disorder. Patients with schizophrenia have higher rates of tobacco, alcohol, and drug use disorders than the general population (NIDA, 2018a).

Mental illnesses can sometimes lead to substance abuse and addiction in that individuals sometimes abuse drugs to self-medicate an underlying medical condition. However, the high incidence of comorbidity between substance abuse disorders and other mental illnesses does not mean that one necessarily caused the other. In fact, a causal relationship is difficult to establish for multiple reasons, including the fact that drugs of abuse can cause abusers to display one or more symptoms of another mental illness without actually having it. Further, some symptoms of either a substance abuse disorder or another mental illness may not be recognized until the disease has progressed considerably, and by then it often is difficult to retrospectively determine the precise onset of these disorders (for further discussion, see NIDA, 2018a).

Effective treatment of individuals with comorbid substance abuse and mental illnesses requires accurate diagnosis of both conditions. Individuals beginning treatment for substance abuse or addiction need to be screened for mental illnesses and vice versa. Accurate diagnosis may require monitoring after a period of abstinence in order to distinguish the effects of substance intoxication or withdrawal from the symptoms of comorbid mental disorders. According to NIDA (2018a), several fundamental barriers impede treatment of comorbid disorders. Among these, primary care physicians are the most common treatment providers for mental illness, whereas a mix of professionals with varying backgrounds

## HERE AND NOW

### Tools for Diagnosis

The *Diagnostic and Statistical Manual of Mental Disorders* (DSM) serves as a highly accepted and widely used authority for the diagnosis of psychiatric disorders. In May 2013, its fifth edition (DSM-V) was made available. Important changes from the previous manual include a revision of the chapter entitled "Substance-Related and Addictive Disorders." In particular, according to the American Psychiatric Association (APA 2013; the publisher of DSM-V), "substance use disorder in DSM-V combines the DSM-IV categories of substance abuse and substance dependence into a single disorder measured on a continuum from mild to severe." (APA 2013). Specific substances are described as separate use disorders (e.g., stimulant use disorder, alcohol use disorder, etc.), but "nearly all substances are diagnosed based on the same overarching criteria" (APA 2013).

One important distinguishing feature of DSM-V is its clarification of the definition of *dependence*. Many people confuse the terms *addiction* and *dependence* and fail to recognize that dependence is a normal response to a variety of drugs—not simply substances of abuse.

American Psychiatric Association. (2013). *Substance-related and addictive disorders.* Retrieved from http://www.dsm5.org/Documents/Substance%20 Use%20Disorder%20Fact%20Sheet.pdf

# HERE AND NOW
## Shared Pathways May Underlie Comorbidities Among Substance Abuse Disorders and Mental Illnesses

According to NIDA (2018a), three primary pathways can contribute to the co-morbidity between substance abuse disorders and mental illnesses. The first involves common risk factors. These include common genetic vulnerabilities, epigenetic factors (i.e., factors that are not dependent on gene sequences but rather are the process whereby genes are transcribed), brain regions, and environmental influences (e.g., stress, trauma). Self-medication (i.e., the use of addicting substances to temporarily alleviate symptoms of mental illness) may also contribute to co-morbidity. Finally, substance use can lead to changes in brain chemistry that resemble those in mental illnesses or "produce changes in brain structure and function that kindle an underlying predisposition to develop that mental illness."

NIDA. (2018). Why is there comorbidity between substance use disorders and mental illnesses? Retrieved from https://www.drugabuse.gov/publications/research-reports/common-comorbidities-substance-use-disorders/why-there-comorbidity-between-substance-use-disorders-mental-illnesses

and credentials provides substance abuse treatment. Often, neither background is broad enough to address the full range of problems presented by patients. In addition, a bias exists in some substance abuse treatment facilities against using any pharmacological intervention, including those necessary to treat serious mental illnesses such as depression. Many substance abuse treatment programs do not employ professionals who are qualified to prescribe, dispense, and monitor medications. Finally, many individuals needing treatment are in the criminal justice system, and adequate treatment services for both mental illness and drug use disorders can be largely lacking in these settings.

# Drug Addiction Treatment in the United States

According to the Substance Abuse and Mental Health Services Administration (SAMHSA, 2019), in 2018, an estimated 20.3 million persons ages 12 or older were classified with substance use disorder related to their use of alcohol or illicit drugs in the preceding year, including 14.8 million people who had an alcohol use disorder and 8.1 million people who had an illicit drug use disorder. This represents 7.8% of individuals age 12 or older. However, in 2018, only 3.7 million persons (1.4% of persons 12 or older) received treatment for a problem related to the use of alcohol or illicit drugs.

Based on SAMHSA data combined from 2010 to 2013, among individuals 12 or older who needed but did not receive illicit drug or alcohol use treatment, felt a need for treatment, and made an effort to receive treatment, the most common reported reason for not receiving treatment was a lack of health coverage and inability to afford the cost (37.3%). To address the issue of affordability, legislation such as the Mental Health Parity and Addiction Equity Act (MHPAEA) has been enacted (see "Here and Now: Insurance Coverage and Parity"). Other commonly reported reasons for not entering treatment included (1) a lack of readiness to stop using (24.5%), (2) a possible negative effect on the job (6.6%), (3) health insurance coverage but did not include treatment or did not cover cost (8.2%), (4) a lack of transportation or inconvenience (8.0%), and (5) not knowing where to go for treatment (9.0%) (SAMHSA, 2014).

As summarized by NIDA (2018b), the abuse of tobacco, alcohol, and illicit drugs costs the United States more than $600 billion annually in costs related to reduced work productivity, crime, and health care. Treatment can help reduce these costs. Research has demonstrated that treatment is far less expensive than simply incarcerating addicts. For example, the average cost per person for one full year of methadone maintenance treatment is approximately $4,700, whereas a full year of imprisonment costs approximately $24,000 (NIDA, 2018b).

Treatment has other economic benefits to society. For example, it has been estimated that every $1 invested in addiction treatment programs yields a return of between $4 and $7 in reduced drug-related crime, theft, and criminal justice costs. With healthcare savings included, total savings

# HERE AND NOW
## Insurance Coverage and Parity

In 2008, the Paul Wellstone and Pete Domenici Mental Health Parity and Addiction Equity Act (MHPAEA) was signed into law. The act requires health insurers and group health plans (those with more than 50 insured employees) to provide the same level of benefits for mental health or substance use treatment and services that the insurers provide for medical or surgical care.

Accordingly, financial requirements, factors such as copayments and the number of visits paid for by insurance must be comparable for mental health, substance abuse, and physical health services. This federal act requires that prior authorization requirements for mental health and substance abuse treatment must be comparable to or less restrictive than those for physical health services. According to the National Alliance on Mental Illness, "if a state has a stronger state parity law, then health insurance plans regulated in that state must follow those laws. For example, if state law requires plans to cover mental health conditions, then they must do so, even though federal parity makes inclusion of any mental health benefits optional."

Substance Abuse and Mental Health Services Administration (SAMHSA). (2016). Know your rights: Parity for mental health and substance use disorder treatment benefits. Retrieved from https://store.samhsa.gov/product/Know-Your-Rights-Parity-for-Mental-Health-and-Substance-Use-Disorder-Benefits/SMA16-4971. Accessed December 27, 2019; Centers for Medicare and Medicaid Services. (n.d.). The Mental Health Parity and Addiction Equity Act (MHPAEA). Baltimore, MD: Author. Retrieved from https://www.cms.gov/cciio/programs-and-initiatives/other-insurance-protections/mhpaea_factsheet. Accessed December 26, 2019; National Alliance on Mental Illness (NAMI). (n.d.). What is mental health parity? Arlington, VA: Author. Retrieved from https://www.nami.org/Your-Journey/Individuals-with-Mental-Illness/Understanding-Health-Insurance/What-is-Mental-Health-Parity. Accessed December 27, 2019.

can exceed costs by a ratio of 12:1. These savings do not include important benefits to the individual and society in the form of fewer interpersonal conflicts, improved workplace productivity, and reduced drug-related incidents among individuals who are treated successfully (NIDA, 2018b).

Several general therapeutic strategies for treatment have been developed. Some involve pharmacological interventions such as methadone maintenance or narcotic antagonist treatment. Other programs apply a drug-free approach. Programs can be short or long term and can be individualized or involve group participation. The following is an overview of various treatment approaches. Note that many treatment programs blend one or more of these approaches as part of their therapeutic strategy.

## ▪ Historical Approaches

Considerable effort has been expended to find treatments for substance abuse. Several approaches, or at least components of them, continue to be used today. These include those discussed in the following sections.

### ALCOHOLICS ANONYMOUS

Founded in the United States in the mid-1930s, Alcoholics Anonymous (AA) is now an international organization. The desire to stop drinking is the sole criterion required to join. The original founders of AA were strongly influenced by a religious movement known as the Oxford Group. AA outlines 12 successive measures, referred to as *steps*, that alcoholics should accomplish during the recovery process (Alcoholics Anonymous, 1952). These steps include admitting that the person addicted to alcohol has no power over the drug. He or she must also believe in a greater power that can help him or her overcome shortcomings. Individuals must make initial and ongoing assessments of their life and admit their wrongs. In addition, individuals must make amends to those whom they have adversely affected, except in situations where such actions could harm others.

AA has two types of meetings: open and closed. **Open meetings** are open to anyone who has an interest in attending and witnessing these meetings, and they last approximately 45 minutes to 1 hour. **Closed meetings** are for alcoholics who have a serious desire to completely stop drinking. These meetings are not open to viewers or "shoppers." At closed meetings, recovering alcoholics use testimonials to address how alcohol has diminished their quality of life.

## KEY TERMS

**open meetings**
alcoholics Anonymous meetings to which anyone having an interest in attending and witnessing is invited

**closed meetings**
alcoholics Anonymous meetings to which only alcoholics having a serious desire to completely stop drinking are invited

Some outgrowths of AA include Al-Anon, Adult Children of Alcoholics, and Alateen. These are parallel organizations supporting AA. Al-Anon is for spouses and other close relatives of alcoholics, and Alateen is exclusively for teenagers whose lives have been affected by someone else's alcoholism. Both relatives and teen members of alcoholic families learn means and methods for coping with destructive behaviors exhibited by alcoholic members.

## REHABILITATION PROGRAMS

The first rehabilitation programs grew out of the work that AA members did with other active alcoholics. The "twelth-stepping" program involves reaching out to others in need and attempting to draw them in. The movement began in the early days of AA when the organization's founder, Bill W., had alcoholics trying to stop drinking or "dry out" living at his house in Brooklyn. At that time, "[his] home was stuffed, from cellar to attic, with alcoholics in all stages of recovery" (Al-Anon, 1970). It was a natural transition to opening up "drying out houses" in the 1940s and 1950s.

Also during the 1950s, the **Minnesota model**, an inpatient rehabilitation model, was developed. It combined the AA philosophy with a multidisciplinary treatment team. The treatment plan used was based on assessment of the individual and prioritization of goals. This model, which borrows from social work practice, is still used in treatment programs. Because of the vagaries of insurance reimbursement in Minnesota, the program lasted 28 days because that was the length covered by insurance; therefore, alcoholism programs traditionally were roughly one month long.

## ▪ General Therapeutic Strategies

In addition to the approaches mentioned previously, there are numerous strategies to drug addiction treatment. Some are individualized and some are group based. Although not all treatment programs fit perfectly into any one of these categories, the following provides an overview of the general types of services available (NIDA, 1999, 2012, 2018b).

## MEDICAL DETOXIFICATION

As noted previously, medical detoxification is the process of safely managing the acute physical symptoms of withdrawal associated with stopping drug use, typically under the care of a physician. Medications including benzodiazepines and other sedatives are often used. Detoxification can be medically necessary because untreated withdrawal from some agents can be fatal—alcohol and barbiturates, for example. Although detoxification is sometimes referred to as a *distinct* treatment modality, it is more appropriately considered a precursor to treatment because it is designed to treat the acute physiological effects of stopping drug use. It is not designed to address the psychological, social, and behavioral problems associated with addiction; thus, it does not typically produce lasting behavioral changes. Detoxification is often followed and augmented by formal processes of assessment and referral to subsequent drug addiction treatment.

## SHORT-TERM RESIDENTIAL TREATMENT

Short-term residential programs were originally designed to treat alcoholism but have been used to treat other forms of addiction. These provide relatively brief treatment based on a modified 12-step approach. The original model consisted of a three- to six-week hospital-based, inpatient-treatment phase. This was followed by extended outpatient therapy and participation in a self-help group such as AA to reduce the risk of relapse once an individual leaves the residential setting.

## LONG-TERM RESIDENTIAL TREATMENT

Long-term residential treatment provides care 24 hours a day, generally in nonhospital settings. The **therapeutic community (TC)** is the most recognized residential treatment model. TCs focus on the "resocialization" of the individual and use a program's entire community (e.g., staff, other residents) as important treatment components. Treatment is highly structured and can be confrontational. It focuses on developing personal accountability and responsibility. Activities are designed to assist individuals in examining damaging self-concepts and beliefs and destructive patterns of behavior. An important goal is to implement new, more constructive ways to interact

## KEY TERMS

**Minnesota model**
a major model in the treatment of alcohol and drug abuse that involves a month-long stay in an inpatient rehabilitation facility, a multidisciplinary treatment team, systematic assessment, and a formal treatment plan with long- and short-term goals

**therapeutic community (TC)**
inpatient treatment that focuses on the "resocialization" of the individual and uses the program's entire community as important treatment components

with others. Planned lengths of stay in TCs are often between six and 12 months. TCs often offer comprehensive services, which can include employment training on site. Research indicates that TCs can be modified to treat individuals with special needs, including women, adolescents, persons with severe mental disorders, and individuals in the criminal justice system.

## OUTPATIENT TREATMENT PROGRAMS

The outpatient strategy varies in the intensity and forms of services offered. Such treatment often is more suitable for individuals who have extensive family or community support or those who are employed. The intensity of programs varies from those offering simply drug education to those employing higher levels comparable to residential programs in services and effectiveness. Group counseling often is emphasized.

## ▉ Behavioral Therapies

Several behavioral therapies have been successfully used to help engage individuals in treatment and increase the likelihood for successful outcomes. These are described briefly in **Table 18.1** (for additional discussion, see NIDA, 2018b).

## ▉ Pharmacological Strategies

Some treatment strategies employ pharmacological approaches to help patients with their addictions. These strategies are based on the properties of the drug to which they are addicted. Examples of these strategies follow.

## METHADONE

Treatment for opiate addicts is often conducted in specialized outpatient settings (e.g., methadone maintenance clinics) using methadone. Methadone is an opioid agonist (i.e., a drug that activates opioid receptors). It is a long-acting synthetic opiate medication administered orally for a sustained period at a dosage sufficient to prevent opiate withdrawal and decrease craving. Patients stabilized on adequate, sustained dosages of methadone can function normally. They can hold jobs, avoid the crime and violence of the street culture, and reduce their exposure to HIV by stopping or decreasing injection drug use and drug-related, high-risk sexual behavior.

© mangostock/ShutterStock, Inc.

A patient receives individual counseling in an alcoholism treatment center.

**TABLE 18.1** Behavioral Therapies Shown to Be Effective in Addressing Substance Abuse

| Therapy | Effective Targets | Description |
|---|---|---|
| Cognitive-behavioral therapy (CBT) | Alcohol, marijuana, cocaine, methamphetamine, nicotine | CBT is based on the theory that learning patterns play a critical role in the development of maladaptive behavioral patterns like substance abuse. A central element is anticipating likely problems and enhancing patients' self-control by helping them develop effective coping strategies. Techniques include exploring the positive and negative consequences of continued drug use, self-monitoring to recognize cravings early and identify situations that might put one at risk for use, and developing strategies for coping with cravings and avoiding those high-risk situations. |
| Contingency-management (CM) interventions and motivational incentives | Alcohol, stimulants, opioids, marijuana, nicotine | CM involves giving patients tangible rewards to reinforce positive behaviors such as abstinence. Rewards can include vouchers to be exchanged for goods or services that are consistent with a drug-free lifestyle or incentives consisting of chances to win prizes. The rewards increase in value with evidence of sustained abstinence (i.e., consecutive negative drug tests) but reset to the lowest value with any evidence of a drug use recurrence. |

| | | |
|---|---|---|
| Community reinforcement approach (CRA) plus vouchers | Alcohol, cocaine, opioids | CRA plus vouchers is an intensive 24-week outpatient therapy for treating people addicted to cocaine and alcohol. It uses a range of recreational, familial, social, and vocational reinforcers, along with material incentives, to make a lifestyle without drug use more rewarding than substance use. |
| Motivational enhancement therapy (MET) | Alcohol, marijuana, nicotine | MET is designed to help individuals resolve ambivalence about engaging in treatment and stopping drug use. The aim is to evoke rapid and internally motivated change rather than guiding the patient stepwise through the recovery process. MET consists of an initial assessment session that is followed by two to four individual treatment sessions. Motivational interviewing principles and coping strategies for high-risk situations are emphasized. |
| The matrix model | Stimulants | The model provides a framework wherein patients learn about issues critical to addiction and relapse and receive direction and support from a trained therapist. The therapist fosters a positive, encouraging relationship with the patient and uses that relationship to reinforce positive behavior change. Treatment materials draw heavily on tested treatment approaches and include elements of relapse prevention, family and group therapies, drug education, and self-help participation. |
| Twelve-step facilitation | Alcohol, stimulants, opioids | Twelve-step facilitation therapy is an active engagement strategy guided by three key ideas: (1) *acceptance*, which includes the realization that drug addiction is a chronic, progressive disease over which one has no control, that life has become unmanageable because of drugs, and that abstinence is the only alternative; (2) *surrender*, which involves giving oneself over to a higher power, accepting the fellowship and support structure of other recovering addicted individuals, and following the recovery activities laid out by the 12-step program; and (3) *active involvement* in 12-step meetings and related activities. |
| Family behavioral therapy (FBT) | | FBT is aimed at addressing not only substance use problems but also other co-occurring problems such as conduct disorders, child mistreatment, depression, family conflict, and unemployment. FBT utilizes contingency management as well as other behavioral strategies and involves the patient and at least one significant other. |

Data from National Institute on Drug Abuse (NIDA). (2018b). *Principles of drug addiction treatment* (3rd ed.). Washington, DC: National Institutes of Health. Retrieved from https://www.drugabuse.gov/publications/principles-drug-addiction-treatment-research-based-guide-third-edition/principles-effective-treatment

Patients stabilized on opiate agonists can engage more readily in counseling and other behavioral interventions essential to recovery and rehabilitation. According to NIDA (2018b), successful opioid agonist maintenance programs include individual or group counseling, as well as provision of or referral to other needed medical, psychological, and social services.

### NALOXONE AND NALTREXONE

An antagonist is a compound that suppresses the actions of a drug. Narcotic antagonists have properties that make them important tools in the clinical treatment of narcotic drug dependence (see "Here and Now: Expanded Options for Treatment of Heroin Addiction"). For instance, the short-acting opioid antagonist naloxone (Narcan) is often used in the emergency treatment of opioid overdoses.

Naltrexone is a long-acting synthetic opioid antagonist used as a treatment for opioid addiction. It is usually prescribed in outpatient medical settings, although treatment initiation often begins after medical detoxification in a residential setting. Individuals must be opioid-free for several days before taking naltrexone in order to avoid withdrawal symptoms. Naltrexone is taken orally for a sustained period and thus prevents all the effects of self-administered opioids. Naltrexone itself has neither subjective effects nor potential for abuse; however, patient noncompliance is a frequent problem, and thus many treatment providers have found naltrexone to be most appropriate for highly motivated,

# HERE AND NOW
## Expanded Options for Treatment of Heroin Addiction

Until 2000, opiate-dependence treatments such as methadone could be dispensed only in a limited number of clinics that specialize in addiction treatment. As a consequence of the Drug Addiction Treatment Act of 2000, the Food and Drug Administration (FDA) announced approval of Subutex and Suboxone tablets for the treatment of opiate dependence by specially trained physicians. Accordingly, the drugs can be prescribed in an office setting, and therefore are more accessible to patients needing treatment.

Subutex and Suboxone treat opiate addiction by preventing symptoms of withdrawal from heroin and other opiates. Subutex contains only buprenorphine (a partial opioid agonist) and is intended for use at the beginning of treatment for opioid abuse once the individual has undergone detoxification. Suboxone contains both buprenorphine and the opiate antagonist naloxone and is intended to be used in maintenance treatment of opiate addiction. Naloxone has limited effects if administered sublingually, but is effective as an antagonist if administered intravenously. It has been added to Suboxone to guard against intravenous abuse of buprenorphine by individuals who are physically dependent on opiates.

recently detoxified patients, such as professionals, parolees, and probationers, who desire total abstinence because of external circumstances. Of note, an extended-release preparation of naltrexone (Vivitrol) administered monthly by intramuscular injection has been approved by the FDA to treat alcoholism.

### BUPRENORPHINE

In 2000, Congress passed the Drug Addiction Treatment Act. This legislation allowed qualified physicians to prescribe specifically approved Schedule III, IV, and V medications for the treatment of opioid addiction in general medical settings (e.g., primary care offices). Such office-based treatment of opioid addiction is a cost-effective approach that increases the span of treatment and the options available to patients.

Buprenorphine is a **partial agonist** at opioid receptors—that is, a drug that can activate a receptor but is not able to elicit the maximum possible response that is produced by full agonists. It reduces or eliminates withdrawal symptoms associated with opioid dependence but generally does not produce the euphoria and sedation caused by other opioids. It is available in two formulations: Subutex, which contains only buprenorphine, and Suboxone, which contains both buprenorphine and naloxone.

### NICOTINE REPLACEMENT THERAPY

Nicotine was the first pharmacological agent approved by the FDA for use in smoking-cessation therapy. Nicotine replacement therapies—nicotine gum, transdermal patches, nasal sprays, and inhalers—are used to relieve withdrawal symptoms.

Other pharmacological therapies such as varenicline (Chantix) and bupropion (Zyban) are available by prescription to aid in smoking cessation.

### DISULFIRAM

Disulfiram (Antabuse) is a drug used to treat alcoholics. This drug causes nausea, vomiting, flushing, and anxiety if an individual consumes alcohol while taking the drug. Thus, this drug is perceived as a deterrent drug.

### ACAMPROSATE

Acamprosate acts on the glutamate and gamma-aminobutyric acid (GABA) neurotransmitter systems. It is used to treat symptoms of alcohol withdrawal because it purportedly reduces associated symptoms, such as anxiety, insomnia, restlessness, and dysphoria.

### TOPIRAMATE

Topiramate is sometimes used off-label to treat alcohol addiction. Its mechanism of action likely involves the glutamate and GABA neurotransmitter systems, although the precise mechanism of action is not known.

## KEY TERM

**partial agonist**
a drug that can activate a receptor but is not able to elicit the maximum possible response that is produced by a full agonist

# LEARNING PORTFOLIO

## Discussion Questions

1. Discuss the need to assess addiction severity and readiness to change.
2. List several principles that characterize effective addiction treatment.
3. Discuss the role of comorbidity in substance abuse and its treatment.
4. Describe Alcoholics Anonymous and its approach to assisting individuals addicted to alcohol.
5. Describe several therapeutic strategies to treat addiction.
6. Describe the therapeutic community approach to treating substance abuse.
7. Describe the Mental Health Parity and Addiction Equity Act.
8. Describe Screening, Brief Intervention, and Referral to Treatment (SBIRT).

## Key Terms

## Summary

1. Individuals who are addicted to drugs come from all walks of life. It is important that treatment providers determine the severity of a person's addiction as well as the readiness of that individual to change his or her behavior.
2. The process of determining addiction severity can be accomplished in many ways, including the administration of standardized questionnaires such as the Addiction Severity Index. The ASI provides information that can be used to identify and prioritize which problem domains are the most critical and require immediate attention.
3. Assessing a person's readiness to change his or her abuse behavior is important because this can help providers select the best treatment plan to address a client's needs. This may help prevent the individual who is receiving treatment from rejecting all or parts of the treatment plan.
4. Comorbidity is a condition in which two or more illnesses occur in the same person, simultaneously or sequentially. This term also suggests interactions between the illnesses that affect the course and prognosis of both.
5. Changes in the structure and function in regions of the brain affected by drug addiction can also occur in mental illnesses such as anxiety, psychosis, and depression. Overlapping factors, including genetic vulnerabilities, trauma, stress, and/or underlying brain abnormalities, can contribute to both substance abuse disorders and mental illnesses.

6. Effective treatment of individuals with comorbid substance abuse and mental illnesses requires accurate diagnosis of both conditions. However, several fundamental barriers can stand in the way of treating comorbid disorders.

7. One of the earliest real alcoholism recovery efforts was Alcoholics Anonymous. Programs modeled on AA, known as *12-step fellowships*, are major routes to recovery.

8. Numerous approaches to drug addiction treatment have been developed, including outpatient and residential treatment. Medical detoxification is not a treatment per se but rather a precursor to treatment.

9. Motivational enhancement therapy is a client-centered counseling approach for initiating behavior change by helping clients resolve their ambivalence about engaging in treatment and discontinuing drug use.

10. A major approach to heroin and other opiate addiction has involved the provision of methadone, a synthetic opiate.

# References

Al-Anon. *Al-Anon's favorite forum editorials.* New York, NY: Al-Anon Family Group Headquarters, 1970.

Alcoholics Anonymous. (1952). *The twelve steps of Alcoholics Anonymous.* New York, NY: Author. Retrieved from https://www.aa.org/assets/en_US/smf-121_en.pdf

Centers for Medicare and Medicaid Services. (n.d.). The Mental Health Parity and Addiction Equity Act (MHPAEA). Baltimore, MD: Author. Retrieved from https://www.cms.gov/cciio/programs-and-initiatives/other-insurance-protections/mhpaea_factsheet

DiClemente, C. C., & Prochaska, J. O. (1998). Toward a comprehensive, transtheoretical model of change. In W. R. Miller & N. Heather (Eds.), *Treating addictive behaviors: Processes of change.* New York, NY: Plenum Press.

Institute of Medicine (IOM). (1990). *Broadening the base of treatment for alcohol problems.* Washington, DC: National Academies Press.

McLellan, A. T., Kushner, H., Metzger, D., Peters, R., Smith, I., Grissom, G., Pettinati, H., & Argeriou, M. (1992). The fifth edition of the Addiction Severity Index. *Journal of Substance Abuse Treatment, 9,* 199–213.

McLellan, A. T., Luborsky, L., Cacciola, J., Griffith, J., Evans, F., Barr, H. L., & O'Brien, C. P. (1985). New data from the Addiction Severity Index: Reliability and validity in three centers. *Journal of Nervous and Mental Disease, 173,* 412–423.

McLellan, A. T., Luborsky, L., Woody, G. E., & O'Brien, C. P. (1980). An improved diagnostic evaluation instrument for substance abuse patients: The Addiction Severity Index. *Journal of Nervous and Mental Disease, 168,* 26–33.

National Alliance on Mental Illness (NAMI). (n.d.). What is mental health parity? Arlington, VA: Author. Retrieved from https://www.nami.org/Your-Journey/Individuals-with-Mental-Illness/Understanding-Health-Insurance/What-is-Mental-Health-Parity

National Institute on Drug Abuse (NIDA). (1999, October). *Principles of drug addiction treatment.* Pub. No. 99-4180. Washington, DC: National Institutes of Health.

National Institute on Drug Abuse (NIDA). (2012). *Principles of drug addiction treatment,* 2nd ed. NIH Publication No. 12–4180. Washington, DC: National Institutes of Health.

National Institute on Drug Abuse (NIDA). (2014, April). *Principles of drug abuse treatment for criminal justice populations.* Pub. No. 11-5316. Washington, DC: National Institutes of Health.

National Institute on Drug Abuse (NIDA). (2018a). Common comorbidities with substance abuse disorders. Washington, DC: National Institutes of Health, https://www.drugabuse.gov/publications/research-reports/common-comorbidities-substance-use-disorders/introduction

National Institute on Drug Abuse (NIDA). (2018b). *Principles of drug addiction treatment* (3rd ed.). Washington, DC: National Institutes of Health.

Stilen, P., Carise, D., Roget, N., & Wendler, A. (2007). *Treatment planning M.A.T.R.S. Utilizing the Addiction Severity Index (ASI) to make required data collection useful.* Kansas City, MO: Mid-America Addiction Technology Transfer Center in Residence at the University of Missouri–Kansas City.

Substance Abuse and Mental Health Services Administration (SAMHSA). (n.d.). *SBIRT: Screening, brief intervention, and referral to treatment—Opportunities for implementation and points for consideration.* Rockville, MD: Author. Retrieved from http://www.integration.samhsa.gov/sbirt_issue_brief.pdf

Substance Abuse and Mental Health Services Administration (SAMHSA). (2011). *SBIRT: Screening, brief intervention and referral to treatment.* Rockville, MD: Author. Retrieved from http://www.integration.samhsa.gov/clinical-practice/SBIRT

Substance Abuse and Mental Health Services Administration (SAMHSA). (2016). Know your rights: Parity for mental health and substance use disorder treatment benefits. Retrieved from https://store.samhsa.gov/product/Know-Your-Rights-Parity-for-Mental-Health-and-Substance-Use-Disorder-Benefits/SMA16-4971

Substance Abuse and Mental Health Services Administration (SAMHSA). (2017). *SBIRT screening, brief intervention and referral to treatment.* Rockville, MD: Author. Retrieved from http://www.samhsa.gov/sbirt

Substance Abuse and Mental Health Services Administration (SAMHSA). (2019). *Key substance use and mental health indicators in the United States: Results from the 2018 National Survey on Drug Use and Health.* (HHS Publication No. PEP19-5068, NSDUH Series H-54). Rockville, MD: Author.

© FOTOGRIN/Shutterstock.

## Drug Enforcement Administration

Because of the unique problems of drug abuse, in 1930 Congress authorized the establishment of the Bureau of Narcotics in the Treasury Department to administer the relevant laws. This agency remained in the Treasury Department until 1968, when it became part of a new group in the Justice Department, the Bureau of Narcotics and Dangerous Drugs. Harry Anslinger served as head of the bureau for more than 30 years—from its creation until his retirement in 1962. Anslinger was an agent during Prohibition, and later, as head of the bureau, he played an important role in getting marijuana outlawed by the federal government.

In 1973, the Bureau of Narcotics and Dangerous Drugs became the Drug Enforcement Administration (DEA) with the mission to enforce the laws of the United States that control and regulate drugs and substances with significant abuse potential. Today, the DEA is part of the Department of Justice, along with the Federal Bureau of Investigation, and is headed by an administrator selected by the president and confirmed by the Senate. The DEA has the responsibility of infiltrating and breaking up illegal drug traffic in the United States, as well as controlling the use of scheduled substances. It attempts to achieve its mission by investigating and prosecuting violators of drug laws at both the interstate and international levels. To achieve these objectives, the DEA and its agents identify and infiltrate drug gangs, manage national drug intelligence programs, and seize assets derived from the illegal drug trade. In 2019, the DEA employed 4,924 special agents and had 239 domestic offices and 91 foreign offices in 68 countries. It had an annual budget

of $3.1 billion to deal with illegal drug activity, a budget dwarfing the agency's initial budget of $73 million in 1974 (DEA, 2020). In 2020, the Acting Administrator of the DEA was Uttam Dhillon.

## The Substance Abuse and Mental Health Services Administration

With passage of the Alcohol, Drug Abuse, and Mental Health Administration Reorganization Act of 1992, the services and programs, but not the research, of the National Institute on Drug Abuse, the National Institute on Alcohol Abuse and Alcoholism, and the National Institute of Mental Health were incorporated into the newly created Substance Abuse and Mental Health Services Administration. This agency was given the lead responsibility for the prevention and treatment of addictive and mental health problems and disorders. Its overall mission is to reduce the incidence and prevalence of substance abuse and mental disorders by ensuring the best therapeutic use of scientific knowledge and improving access to high-quality, effective programs (Bush 1992).

## State Regulations

Questions regarding the applicability of state versus federal laws and the relative responsibilities of the respective regulatory agencies have been around for ages. In general, the U.S. form of government has allowed local control to take precedence over national control. Because of this historic attitude, states were the first to pass laws to regulate the abuse or misuse of drugs. Federal laws developed later after the federal government gained greater jurisdiction over the well-being and lives of U.S. citizens, and it became apparent that interstate trafficking and the national drug abuse problems it created could not be dealt with effectively on a state-by-state basis. Some early state laws banned the smoking of opium, regulated the sale of various psychoactive drug substances, and, in a few instances, set up treatment programs. However, these early legislative actions made no effort to *prevent* drug abuse. Drug abuse was controlled to a great extent by social pressure rather than by law. It was considered morally wrong to be an alcoholic or an addict to opium or some other drug.

The drug laws varied considerably from state to state in 1932, so the National Conference of Commissioners on Uniform State Laws set up the Uniform Narcotic Drug Act (UNDA), which was later adopted by nearly all states. The UNDA provided for the control of possession, use, and distribution of opiates and cocaine. In 1942, marijuana was included under this act because it was classified as a narcotic.

In 1967, the Food and Drug Administration (FDA) proposed the Model Drug Abuse Control Act and urged the states to adopt it on a uniform basis. This law extended controls over depressant, stimulant, and hallucinogenic drugs, similar to the 1965 federal law. Many states passed laws based on this model.

The federal Controlled Substances Act of 1970 prompted the National Conference of Commissioners to propose a new Uniform Controlled Substances Act (UCSA). The UCSA permits enactment of a single state law regulating the illicit possession, use, manufacture, and dispensing of controlled psychoactive substances. At this time, most states have enacted the UCSA or modifications of it.

Today, state law enforcement of drug statutes does not always reflect federal regulations, although, for the most part, the two statutory levels are not particularly contentious—despite some confusion. An example of where the two differ is marijuana, which has been approved for medicinal use in most states, is still considered to be a scheduled and restricted substance by federal statute. However, the federal position on marijuana is under considerable discussion and scrutiny at the congressional levels, with frequent hearings that have tried to reconcile the differences and attempt to address an apparent lack of research regarding potential medicinal use of marijuana and related substances. This discussion often becomes quite emotional with little science available to answer critical questions such as comparative therapeutic value relative to other FDA-approved drugs and potential short- and long-term side effects, especially in the developing brains of adolescents and those exposed to secondhand marijuana fumes. Despite such governmental efforts at both the state and federal levels, marijuana is still considered a Schedule I substance by federal regulatory agencies (Jaeger, 2020).

# References

Bush, G. (1992). Statement on signing the ADAMHA Reorganization Act. Retrieved from http://www.presidency .ucsb.edu/ws/index.php?pid=21218

Drug Enforcement Administration (DEA). (2020). Data and statistics. Retrieved from https://www.dea.gov/data-and -statistics

Jaeger, K. (2020). Congressional hearing exposes marijuana research limitations imposed by federal law. Marijuana Moment. Retrieved from https://www.marijuanamoment .net/watch-live-congressional-committee-holds-hearing -on-six-marijuana-bills/

# APPENDIX B

# Drugs of Use and Abuse

The following table provides detailed information about the drugs listed. Note that the heading *CSA Schedules* refers to categorization under the Controlled Substances Act (CSA). Roman numerals specify each schedule as a I, II, III, IV, or V drug.

The headings indicated in the first row describe the properties of the drugs listed in the corresponding column. *Substances* refer to specific drugs or the material in which the drug is found. *Products* refer to commercial names.

**TABLE 1** Dependence

| Drugs | CSA Schedules | Trade or Other Names | Medical Uses | Dependence | | |
|---|---|---|---|---|---|---|
| | | | | Physical | Psychological | Tolerance |
| **Narcotics** | | | | | | |
| Heroin | Substance I | Diamorphine, white horse, dope, smack, Skunk | None in U.S., analgesic, antitussive | High | High | Yes |
| Morphine | Substance II | MS-Contin, Roxanol, Oramorph SR, MSIR, God's drug, Mister Blue, morpho, unkie | Analgesic | High | High | Yes |
| Hydrocodone | Substance II, Product III, V | Hydrocodone with acetaminophen, Vicodin, Vicoprofen, Tussionex, Lortab | Analgesic, antitussive | High | High | Yes |
| Hydromorphone | Substance II | Dilaudid, little D, lords | Analgesic | High | High | Yes |
| Oxycodone | Substance II | Roxicet, oxycodone with acetaminophen, OxyContin, Percocet, Percodan Endocet | Analgesic | High | High | Yes |
| Codeine | Substance II, Product III, V | Acetaminophen, guaifenesin, or promethazine with codeine; Fiorinal, Fioricet, or Tylenol with codeine; coties; school boy; captain cody; | Analgesic, antitussive | Moderate | Moderate | Yes |
| Other narcotics | Substance II, III, IV | Fentanyl (Apache; China Girl; Foodfella) Demerol, methadone; Fizzies; Talwin, Paregoric, Buprenex, T. and Blue's, designer drugs (fentanyl derivatives) | Analgesic, antidiarrheal, antitussive | High–low | High–low | Yes |

| Durations (hours) | Usual Method | Possible Effects | Effects of Overdose | Withdrawal Syndrome |
|---|---|---|---|---|
| 3–4 | Injected, snorted, smoked | Euphoria, drowsiness, respiratory depression, constricted pupils, nausea | Slow and shallow breathing, clammy skin, convulsions, coma, possible death | Watery eyes, runny nose, yawning, loss of appetite, irritability, tremors, panic, cramps, nausea, chills, sweating |
| 3–12 | Oral, injected | | | |
| 3–6 | Oral | | | |
| 3–4 | Oral, injected | | | |
| 3–12 | Oral | | | |
| 3–4 | Oral, injected | | | |
| Variable | Oral, injected, snorted, smoked | | | |

| Drugs | CSA Schedules | Trade or Other Names | Medical Uses | Dependence | | |
|---|---|---|---|---|---|---|
| | | | | Physical | Psychological | Tolerance |
| **Depressants** | | | | | | |
| Gamma hydroxybutyric acid | Substance I, Product III | GHB, liquid Ecstasy, liquid X, sodium oxybate, Xytem | None in U.S., anesthetic | Moderate | Moderate | Yes |
| Benzodiazepines | Substance IV | Valium, Xanax, Halcion, Ativan, Restoril, Rohypnol, (roofies, R-2), Klonopin, downers, goof balls, sleeping pills, candy | Antianxiety, sedative, anticonvulsant, hypnotic, muscle relaxant | Moderate | Moderate | Yes |
| Other depressants | Substance I, II, III, IV | Ambien, Sonata, Meprobamate, chloral hydrate, barbiturates, methaqualone tranquilizers, muscle relaxants, sleeping pills | Antianxiety, sedative, hypnotic | Moderate | Moderate | Yes |
| **Stimulants** | | | | | | |
| Mephedrone | Substance I | Bath salts, ivory wave, others | None in the U.S. | Thought to be moderate | Thought to be high | Some |
| Methylone | Substance I | Bath salts, ivory wave, others | None in the U.S. | Likely | Likely high | Some |
| Cocaine | Substance II | Coke, flake, snow, crack, coca, blanca, perico, nieve, soda, bump, toot, C, candy, nose candy | Local anesthetic | Possible | High | Yes |
| Amphetamine/ methamphetamine | Substance II | Crank, ice, cristal, crystal meth, speed, Adderall, Dexedrine, Desoxyn, pep pills, bennies, uppers, truck drivers, dexies, black beauties, sparklers, beens | Attention deficit hyperactivity disorder, narcolepsy, weight control | Possible | High | Yes |

| Durations (hours) | Usual Method | Possible Effects | Effects of Overdose | Withdrawal Syndrome |
|---|---|---|---|---|
| 3–6 | Oral | Slurred speech disorientation, drunken behavior without odor of alcohol, impaired memory of events, interacts with alcohol | Shallow respiration, clammy skin, dilated pupils, weak and rapid pulse, coma, possible death | Anxiety, insomnia, tremors, delirium, convulsions, possible death |
| 1–8 | Oral, injected | | | |
| 2–6 | Oral | | | |
| –3 | Inhalation, injection | Euphoria, alertness, cardiovascular effects | Paranoia, hallucinations, cardiovascular effects, hyperthermia | Not known, but suspect some |
| –3 | Inhalation, injection | Euphoria, alertness, | Paranoia, cardiovascular effects | Not known, but suspect some |
| 1–2 | Snorted, smoked, injected | Increased alertness, excitation, euphoria, increased pulse rate and blood pressure, insomnia, loss of appetite | Agitation, increased body temperature, hallucinations, convulsions, possible death | Apathy, long periods of sleep, irritability, depression, disorientation |
| 2–4 | Oral, injected, smoked | | | |

| Drugs | CSA Schedules | Trade or Other Names | Medical Uses | Dependence | | Tolerance |
| --- | --- | --- | --- | --- | --- | --- |
| | | | | Physical | Psychological | |
| Methylphenidate | Substance II | Ritalin (illy's), Concerta, Focalin, Metadate, speed, meth, crystal, crank, go fast | Attention deficit hyperactivity disorder | Possible | High | Yes |
| Other stimulants | Substance III, IV | Adipex P, Ionamin Prelu-2, Didrex, Provigil | Vasoconstriction | Possible | Moderate | Yes |
| **Hallucinogens** | | | | | | |
| MDMA | Substance I | Ecstasy, XTC, Adam, MDA (love drug), MDEA (Eve), MBDB | None | None | Moderate | Yes |
| LSD | Substance I | Acid, microdot, sunshine, boomers, blue chairs, Loony Toons, pane, cubes | None | None | Unknown | Yes |
| Phencyclidine and analogs | Substance I, II, III | PCP, angel dust, hog, loveboat, ketamine (special K), PCE, PCPy, TCP, peace pill | Anesthetic (ketamine) | Possible | High | Yes |
| Other hallucinogens | Substance I | Psilocybin mushrooms, mescaline, peyote cactus, ayahausca, DMT, dextromethorphan (DXM), sacred mushrooms, magic mushrooms, mushrooms, ying yang, strawberry fields | None | None | None | Possible |
| **Cannabis** | | | | | | |
| Marijuana | Substance I | Pot, grass, *sinsemilla*, blunts, mota, yerba, grifa, 420, airhead (marijuana user), bud, catnip, reefer, roach, joint, weed, loco weed, Mary Jane | None for most states, although approved for medical purposes, such as pain, appetite, seizures etc., in some states | Likely, but minor | Moderate | Yes |
| JWH 018, 019, 073, 081, 122, 200, 203, 250, 398 | Substance I | Spice and related products | Marijuana-like effects | Marijuana-like | Marijuana-like | Likely |

| Durations (hours) | Usual Method | Possible Effects | Effects of Overdose | Withdrawal Syndrome |
|---|---|---|---|---|
| 2–4 | Oral, injected, smoked | | | |
| 2–4 | Oral | | | |
| 4–6 | Oral, snorted, smoked | Heightened senses, teeth grinding, dehydration | Increased body temperature, electrolyte imbalance, cardiac arrest | Muscle aches, drowsiness, depression, acne |
| 8–12 | Oral | Illusions and hallucinations, altered perception of time and distance | Longer, more intense trip episodes than other hallucinogens | None |
| 1–12 | Smoked, oral, injected, snorted | Unable to direct movement, feel pain, or remember | Drug-seeking behavior; DXM is not designated as a narcotic under CSA | |
| 4–8 | Oral | | | |
| 2–4 | Smoked, oral | Euphoria, relaxed inhibitions, increasing appetite, disorientation | Fatigue, paranoia, possible psychosis | Occasional reports of insomnia, hyperactivity, decreased appetite |
| Not known | Inhaled | Marijuana-like | Marijuana-like | Marijuana-like |

| Drugs | CSA Schedules | Trade or Other Names | Medical Uses | Dependence | | |
|---|---|---|---|---|---|---|
| | | | | Physical | Psychological | Tolerance |
| Tetrahydrocannabinol | Substance I, Product III | THC, Marinol | Antinauseant, appetite stimulant | Yes | Moderate | Yes |
| Hashish and hashish oil | Substance I | Hash, hash oil | None | Unknown | Moderate | Yes |
| **Anabolic Steroids** | | | | | | |
| Testosterone | Substance III | Depo Testosterone, Sustanon, sten, cypt | Hypogonadism | Unknown | Unknown | Unknown |
| Other anabolic steroids | Substance III | Parabolan, Winstrol, Equipose, Anadrol, Dianabol, Primabolin- Depo, D-Ball | Anemia, breast cancer | Unknown | Yes | Unknown |
| **Inhalants** | | | | | | |
| Amyl and butyl nitrate | | Pearls, poppers, rush, locker room | Angina (amyl) | Unknown | Unknown | No |
| Nitrous oxide | | Laughing gas, balloons, whippets | Anesthetic | Unknown | Low | No |
| Other inhalants | | Adhesives, spray paint hair spray, dry cleaning fluid, spot remover, lighter fluid, air blast, moon gas, sniffing, glue sniffing | None | Unknown | High | No |
| Alcohol | | Beer, wine, liquor | None | High | High | Yes |

| Durations (hours) | Usual Method | Possible Effects | Effects of Overdose | Withdrawal Syndrome |
|---|---|---|---|---|
| 2–4 | Smoked, oral | | | |
| 2–4 | Smoked, oral | | | |
| 14–28 days | Injected | Virilization, edema, testicular atrophy, gynecomastia, acne, aggressive behavior | Unknown | Possible depression |
| Variable | Oral, injected | | | |
| 1 | Inhaled | Flushing, hypotension, headache | Methemoglobinemia | Agitation |
| 0.5 | Inhaled | Impaired memory, slurred speech, drunken behavior, slow onset vitamin deficiency | Vomiting, respiratory depression, loss of consciousness, possible death | Trembling, anxiety, insomnia, vitamin deficiency, confusion, hallucinations, convulsions |
| 0.5–2 | Inhaled | | | |
| 1–3 | Oral | | | |

# Glossary

**acquaintance and date rape**   Unplanned and unwanted forced sexual attack from a friend or a date partner.

**acute**   Immediate or short-term effects after taking a single drug dose.

**acute alcohol withdrawal syndrome**   Symptoms that occur when an individual who is addicted to alcohol does not maintain his or her usual blood alcohol level.

**addiction**   Generally refers to the psychological attachment to a drug; addiction to "harder" drugs such as heroin results in both psychological and physical attachment to the chemical properties of the drug, with the resulting satisfaction (reward) derived from using the drug in question.

**addiction to pleasure theory**   Theory that assumes it is biologically normal to continue a pleasure stimulus once begun.

**addictive disorders**   *See* substance-induced disorders.

**additive interactions**   Effects created when drugs are similar and actions are added together.

**Adolescents Training and Learning to Avoid Steroids (ATLAS) program**   An anabolic abuse prevention educational program that empowers student athletes to make the right choices about steroid use.

**adulterated**   When contaminated substances are mixed in drugs to dilute them.

**affective education model**   *See* attitude change model.

**agonistic**   Type of substance that activates a receptor.

**alcohol abuse**   Uncontrollable drinking that leads to alcohol craving, loss of control, and physical dependence but with less prominent characteristics than found in alcoholism.

**alcohol dehydrogenase**   Principal enzyme that metabolizes ethanol.

**alcoholic cardiomyopathy**   Congestive heart failure resulting from the replacement of heart muscle with fat and fiber.

**alcoholic hepatitis**   Second stage of alcohol-induced liver disease in which chronic inflammation occurs; reversible if alcoholic consumption ceases.

**alcoholism**   A medical condition consisting of a physical and psychological addiction to ethanol (alcohol), a psychoactive substance.

**alcohol use disorder (AUD)**   A chronic relapsing brain disease characterized by an impaired ability to stop or control alcohol use despite adverse social, occupational, or health consequences. In the latest *Diagnostic Statistical Manual* (DSM-5), this disorder is further subdivided as mild, moderate, or severe.

**altered perceptions**   Changes in the interpretation of stimuli resulting from marijuana use.

**alternatives approach**   An approach emphasizing the exploration of positive alternatives to drug abuse based on replacing the pleasurable feelings gained from drug abuse with involvement in social and educational activities.

**amnesiac**   Causing the loss of memory.

**amotivational syndrome**   Controversial syndrome whose proponents claim that heavy marijuana use causes a lack of motivation and reduced productivity.

**anabolic steroids**   Compounds chemically similar to steroids that stimulate production of tissue mass.

**analgesics**   drugs that relieve pain without affecting consciousness

**analogs**   Drugs with similar structures.

**anandamide**   Naturally occurring fatty-acid neurotransmitter that selectively activates cannabinoid receptors.

**androgens**   Male sex hormones.

**anesthesia**   A state characterized by loss of sensation or consciousness.

**anesthetic**   Drug that blocks sensitivity to pain.

**angina pectoris**   Severe chest pain usually caused by a deficiency of blood to the heart muscle.

**anorexiants**   Drugs that suppress the activity of the brain's appetite center and cause reduced food intake.

**ANS**   *See* autonomic nervous system.

**antagonistic**   Type of substance that blocks a receptor.

**antagonistic interactions**   Effects created when drugs cancel one another.

**anticholinergic**   Agents that antagonize the effects of acetylcholine.

**antihistamines**   Drugs that often cause CNS depression and are used to treat allergies; often included in over-the-counter (OTC) sleep aids.

**antitussives**   Drugs that block the coughing reflex.

**antiretroviral therapy (ART)**   Refers to maintaining a regimen of taking a combination of several antiretroviral medicines to slow the rate at which HIV multiplies in the body.

**anxiolytic**   Drug that relieves anxiety.

**AOD**   Acronym for alcohol and other drugs.

**aphrodisiac**   Compound that is believed to cause sexual arousal.

**array**   Use of other drugs while taking anabolic steroids to avoid possible side effects.

**arrhythmia**   An irregular heartbeat.

**ART**   *See* antiretroviral therapy.

**ATLAS**   *See* Adolescents Training and Learning to Avoid Steroids program.

**ATOD**   Acronym for alcohol, tobacco, and other drugs.

**attitude change model**   Assumes that people use drugs because of lack of self-esteem; also known as the *affective education model*.

**AUD**   *See* alcohol use disorder.

**autonomic nervous system (ANS)**   Controls the unconscious functions of the body.

**awareness model**   *See* information-only model.

**axon**   Extension of the neuronal cell body along which electrochemical signals travel.

**BAC**   *See* blood alcohol concentration.

**BACCHUS Network**   Before 2014, a national and international association of college and university peer-education programs focused on alcohol abuse prevention and other related student health and safety issues. BACCHUS is an acronym for Boosting Alcohol Consciousness Concerning the Health of University Students.

**BACCHUS Initiatives of NASPA–Student Affairs Administrators in Higher Education**   Reformulated BACCHUS Network that is currently managed by the National Association of Student Personnel Administrators (NASPA) that continues to support higher education student leadership and peer education on health and safety issues.

**barbiturates**   Potent central nervous system (CNS) depressants; usually not preferred because of their narrow margin of safety.

**behavioral stereotypy**   Meaningless repetition of a single activity.

**behavioral tolerance**   Compensation for motor impairments through behavioral pattern modification by chronic alcohol users.

**benzodiazepines**   The most popular and safest CNS depressants in use today.

**beta-adrenergic stimulants**   Drugs that stimulate a subtype of adrenaline and noradrenaline receptors.

**binge**   Similar to a run but usually of shorter duration.

**binge alcohol users**   A pattern of drinking five or more drinks for men and four or more drinks for women on a single occasion such as at the same time or within two hours of each other on at least one day in the past 30 days; includes heavy use.

**binge drinking**   Consuming five or more alcohol drinks in a row on a single occasion.

**biotransformation**   Process of changing the chemical properties of a drug, usually by metabolism,

**blood alcohol concentration (BAC)**   Concentration of alcohol found in the blood, often expressed as a percentage.

**blood–brain barrier**   Selective filtering between the cerebral blood vessels and the brain.

**bootlegging**   Making, distributing, and selling alcoholic beverages during the Prohibition era.

**bronchodilators**   Drugs that widen the lungs' air passages.

**caffeinism**   Symptoms caused by taking high chronic doses of caffeine.

**cannabinoid system**   Biological target of tetrahydrocannabinol in marijuana.

***Cannabis indica***   Biological name of one of three major species of marijuana that originates from hash-producing countries (e.g., Afghanistan, Morocco, and Tibet); its effects include relaxation of the body, stress relief, and calmness and serenity; is known to cause a strong body high.

***Cannabis ruderalis***   Biological name of one of three major species of marijuana that is native to Asia and Central and Eastern Europe. This species has adapted to shorter growing seasons and the environments found in these three climates.

***Cannabis sativa***   Biological name of one of three major species of marijuana; originates from Colombia, Mexico, Thailand, and Southeast Asia; generally causes uplifting and largely psychological or mental energetic feelings, as well as providing pain relief for certain ailments.

**cannabis wax**   *See* marijuana wax.

**catatonia**   A condition of physical rigidity, excitement, and stupor.

**catecholamines**   Class of biochemical compounds including the transmitters norepinephrine, epinephrine, and dopamine.

**central nervous system (CNS)**   Part of the nervous system composed of the spinal cord and brain that is responsible for integrating sensory information and responding accordingly.

**central nervous system (CNS)**   One of the major divisions of the nervous system; composed of the brain and spinal cord.

**characterological model**   View of chemical dependency as a symptom of problems in the development or operation of the system of needs, motives, and attitudes within the individual; also known as the *personality predisposition model*.

**chewing tobacco**   Tobacco leaves shredded and twisted into strands for chewing purposes.

**chippers**   *See* floaters.

**chronic**   Long-term effects, usually after taking multiple drug doses.

**cirrhosis**   Scarring of the liver and formation of fibrous tissues; results from alcohol abuse; irreversible.

**closed meetings**   Alcoholics Anonymous meetings to which only alcoholics having a serious desire to completely stop drinking are invited.

**club drug**   Drug used at all-night raves, parties, dance clubs, and bars to enhance sensory experiences.

**CNS**   *See* central nervous system.

**cocaine babies**   Infants born to women who used cocaine during their pregnancies.

**codependency**   Behavior displayed by either addicted or nonaddicted family members (codependents) who identify with the alcohol addict and cover up the excessive drinking behavior, allowing it to continue and letting it affect the codependent's life.

**comorbidity**   Two or more disorders or illnesses occurring in the same person; they can occur simultaneously or one after the other; also implies interactions between the illnesses that can worsen the course of both.

**compulsive users**   Second category of drug users, typified by an insatiable attraction followed by a psychological dependence on drugs.

**congestion rebound**   Withdrawal from excessive use of a decongestant that results in congestion.

**congestive heart failure**   When the heart is unable to pump sufficient blood for the body's needs.

**control theory**   Theory that emphasizes that people left without bonds to other groups (peers, family, social groups) generally have a tendency to deviate from upheld values and attitudes.

**conventional behavior**   Behavior largely dictated by custom and tradition, which is often disrupted by the forces of rapid technological change.

**crack**   Already processed and inexpensive "freebased" cocaine ready for smoking.

**cross-dependence**   Dependence on a drug can be relieved by other similar drugs.

**cross-tolerance**   Development of tolerance to one drug causes tolerance to related drugs.

**cumulative effect**   Buildup of a drug in the body after multiple doses taken at short intervals.

**current drinkers**   At least one drink in the past 30 days; can include binge and heavy use.

**cycling**   Taking doses of steroid for a period of time, stopping for a time, and then restarting.

**D.A.R.E.**   *See* Drug Abuse Resistance Education.

**DEA**   *See* Drug Enforcement Administration.

**delirium tremens (DTs)**   The most severe, even life-threatening, form of alcohol withdrawal, involving hallucinations, delirium, and fever.

**demand reduction**   Attempts to decrease individuals' tendencies to use drugs, often aimed at youth, with emphasis on reformulating values and behaviors.

**dendrites**   Short branches of neurons that receive transmitter signals.

**dependence**   Physiological and psychological changes or adaptations that occur in response to the frequent administration of a drug.

**dependency phase**   Synonym for addiction.

**designer drugs**   New drugs that are developed by people intending to circumvent the illegality of a drug by modifying a drug into a new compound; Ecstasy is an example. Also known as *synthetic drugs* or *synthetic opioids*.

**detoxification**   Elimination of a toxic substance such as a drug and its effects from the body.

**diabetes mellitus**   Disease caused by elevated blood sugar from insufficient insulin.

**differential association**   Process by which individuals become socialized into the perceptions and values of a group.

**differential reinforcement**   Ratio between reinforcers, both favorable and unfavorable, for sustaining drug-use behavior.

**disease model**   Belief that people abuse alcohol because of some biologically caused condition.

**disinhibition**   Loss of conditioned reflexes because of depression of the brain's inhibitory centers.

**disinhibitor**   A psychoactive chemical that depresses thought and judgment functions in the cerebral cortex, which has the effect of allowing relatively unrestrained behavior (as in alcohol inebriation).

**distillation**   Heating fermented mixtures of cereal grains or fruits in a still to evaporate and be trapped as purified alcohol.

**diuretic**   Drug or substance that increases the production of urine.

**dopamine**   Neurotransmitter present in regions of the brain that regulate movement, emotion, cognition, motivation, and feelings of pleasure; it mediates the rewarding aspects of most drugs of abuse.

**doping**   The use of performance-enhancing drugs to increase athletic ability.

**dose–response**   Correlation between the amount of a drug given and its effects.

**"double wall" of encapsulation**   Adaptation to pain and avoidance of reality, in which the individual withdraws emotionally and further anesthetizes him- or herself by chemical means.

**drug**   Any substance that modifies (either by enhancing, inhibiting, or distorting) mind or body functioning.

**Drug Abuse Resistance Education (D.A.R.E.)** Drug-education program presented in elementary and junior high and middle schools nationwide by police officers.

**drug cartels** Large, highly sophisticated organizations composed of multiple drug-trafficking organizations (DTOs) and cells with specific assignments, such as drug transportation, security and enforcement, or money laundering.

**drug cells** Cells similar to terrorist cells and consisting of only three to five members to ensure operational security; members of adjacent drug cells usually do not know each other or the identity of their leadership.

**drug courts** Process that integrates substance-abuse treatment, incentives, and sanctions and places nonviolent, drug-involved defendants in judicially supervised rehabilitation programs.

**Drug Enforcement Administration (DEA)** The principal federal agency responsible for enforcing U.S. drug laws.

**drug interaction** When the presence of one drug alters the action of another drug.

**drugged driving** Operating a motor vehicle with a measurable quantity or quantities of a legal or an illegal drug in the driver's body, which most often results in impaired driving.

**drug prevention** Preventing or decreasing health problems, including social and personal problems, caused by drug dependency.

**drug testing** Urine, blood screening, or hair analysis used to identify those who may be using drugs.

**drug-trafficking organizations (DTOs)** Complex organizations with highly defined command-and-control structures that produce, transport, or distribute large quantities of one or more illicit drugs.

**drunken comportment** Behavior exhibited while under the direct influence of alcohol; determined by the norms and expectations of a particular culture.

**dry cultures** Cultures in which alcohol consumption is not as common during everyday activities (e.g., it is less frequently a part of meals) and access to alcohol is more restricted; abstinence is more common (e.g., Scandinavian countries, the United States, and Canada).

**DTOs** *See* drug-trafficking organizations.

**DTs** *See* delirium tremens.

**dual diagnosis** Individual who is simultaneously manifesting a mental health disorder(s) and addiction to drug use at the same time (e.g., a drug addict experiencing depression or anxiety).

**dysphoric** Characterized by unpleasant mental effects; the opposite of euphoric.

**EAP** *See* employee-assistance program.

**ecological model** Stresses that changes in the environment change people's attitudes about drugs; also known as the *person-in-environment model*.

**Ecstasy** *See* MDMA.

**edema** Swollen tissue because of an accumulation of fluid.

**electronic cigarettes (e-cigarettes)** Electronic nicotine-delivery systems; also called *vapes*, *e-hookahs*, *vape pens*, *tank systems*, *mods*, and *electronic nicotine delivery systems*.

**employee-assistance program (EAP)** Drug-assistance program for drug-dependent employees.

**enablers** Those close to the alcohol addict who deny or make excuses for enabling his or her excessive drinking.

**endocrine system** Relating to hormones, their functions, and sources.

**endorphins** Neurotransmitters that have narcotic-like effects.

**entactogen** A drug that enhances the sensation and pleasure of touching.

**environmental tobacco smoke** Term referring to secondhand smoke.

**equal-opportunity affliction** Refers to the use of drugs, stressing that drug use cuts across all members of society regardless of income, education, occupation, social class, or age.

**ergogenic** Drugs that enhance athletic performance.

**ergotism** Poisoning by toxic substances from the ergot fungus *Claviceps purpurea*.

**ethanol** The chemical and pharmacological term for drinking alcohol; the psychoactive ingredient in alcoholic beverages; often called *grain alcohol*.

**ethylene glycol** Alcohol used as antifreeze.

**euphorigenic** Having the ability to cause feelings of pleasure and well-being.

**experimenters** First category of drug users, typified as being in the initial stages of drug use; these people often use drugs for recreational purposes.

**expectorants** Substances that stimulate the secretion of mucus and diminish its viscosity.

**extreme binge drinking** The consumption of 10 or more alcoholic drinks in a row or 15 or more drinks in a row on a single occasion.

**FAS** *See* fetal alcohol syndrome.

**fear-based approach** *See* scare tactic approach.

**fermentation** Biochemical process through which yeast converts sugar to alcohol.

**fetal alcohol syndrome (FAS)** Condition affecting children born to alcohol-consuming mothers that is characterized by facial deformities, growth deficiency, and mental retardation.

**flashbacks** Recurrences of earlier drug-induced sensory experiences in the absence of the drug.

**floaters** Category of drug users; these users vacillate between the need for pleasure seeking and the desire to relieve moderate to serious psychological problems; this category of drug user has two major characteristics: (1) a general focus mostly on using other people's drugs (often without maintaining a personal supply of the drug) and (2) vacillation between the characteristics of chronic drug users and experimenter types; also known as *chippers*.

**freebasing** Conversion of cocaine into its alkaline form for smoking.

**frontal cortex**    Cortical region essential for information processing and decision making.

**gastritis**    Inflammation or irritation of the gut.

**gateway drugs**    Alcohol, tobacco, and marijuana—types of drugs that when used excessively may lead to using other and more addictive drugs such as cocaine, heroin, or crack.

**generational forgetting**    When knowledge of adverse drug consequences experienced by a particular generation or population is lost by the younger cohort.

**generic**    Official, nonpatented, nonproprietary name of a drug.

**genetic and biophysiological theories**    Explanations of addiction in terms of genetic brain dysfunction and biochemical patterns.

**genetics**    Study of cellular DNA and its functions.

**genogram**    A family therapy technique that records information about behavior and relationships on a type of family tree to elucidate persistent patterns of dysfunctional behavior.

**glaucoma**    Potentially blinding eye disease causing continual and increasing intraocular pressure.

**glia**    Supporting cells that are critical for protecting and providing sustenance to the neurons.

**goofballs**    Combination of potent stimulants and narcotics such as amphetamines and heroin

**HAART**    See highly active antiretroviral therapy.

**habituation**    Repeating certain patterns of behavior until they become established or habitual.

**half-life**    Time required for the body to eliminate or metabolize half of a drug dose.

**hallucinogens**    Substances that alter sensory processing in the brain, causing perceptual disturbances, changes in thought processing, and depersonalization.

**harm-reduction model**    Society-wide approach to drug use and abuse that focuses on reducing the harm experienced by the drug user or abuser as well as the harm to society.

**harm reduction-therapy (HRT)**    Nonjudgmental approach to helping people experiencing alcohol and drug problems to reduce the negative impact of substance use, abuse, or dependence in their lives.

**hashish**    Cannabis product made from the pure resin from the flowers of female plants with high amount of THC (the average THC content of all samples seized was 12.14% and often ranges from 7.03% [nondomestic] to 20.76%).

**heavy alcohol users**    Five or more drinks on the same occasion on each of five or more days in the past 30 days or consuming an average of more than one alcoholic beverage per day for women and an average of more than two alcoholic beverages per day for men and any drinking by pregnant women or underage youth.

**hepatotoxic effect**    Situation in which liver cells increase the production of fat, resulting in an enlarged liver.

**HGF**    See human growth factor.

**HGH**    See human growth hormone.

**high**    Condition lasting four to 16 hours after drug use; includes feelings of energy and power.

**highly active antiretroviral therapy (HAART)**    Maintaining a regimen of more recent types of medications to slow the rate at which HIV multiplies in the body.

**high-risk drug choices**    Developing values and attitudes that lead to using drugs both habitually and addictively.

**holistic self-awareness approach**    Emphasizes that nonmedical and often recreational drug use interferes with the healthy balance of mind, body, and spirit.

**homeostasis**    Maintenance of internal stability; often biochemical in nature.

**hormones**    Chemical messengers released into the blood by glands

**HRT**    See harm-reduction therapy.

**human growth factor (HGF)**    Natural hormone that stimulates normal growth.

**human growth hormone (HGH)**    Synthetic designer drug version of HGF; also referred to as simply GH (growth hormone).

**hyperglycemia**    Elevated blood sugar.

**hyperpyrexia**    Elevated body temperature.

**hypertension**    Elevated blood pressure.

**hypnotic**    CNS depressant used to induce drowsiness and encourage sleep.

**hypothyroidism**    When the thyroid gland does not produce sufficient hormone.

**hypoxia**    State of oxygen deficiency.

**ice**    Smokable form of methamphetamine.

**illicit drugs**    Illegal drugs such as marijuana, cocaine, and LSD.

**IM**    See intramuscular.

**increased use phase**    Taking increasing quantities of a drug.

**information-only**    Assumes that teaching about the harmful effects of drugs will change attitudes about use and abuse; also known as the awareness model.

**inoculation**    Method of abuse prevention that protects drug users by teaching them responsibility.

**insiders**    People on the inside; those who approve of or use drugs or both.

**insider's perspective**    Viewing a group or subculture from inside the group; seeing members as they perceive themselves.

**interdiction**    Policy of cutting off or destroying supplies of illicit drugs.

**intergang**    Between members of different gangs.

**intermediate clinical endpoint**    Measure of a therapeutic effect that is considered reasonably likely to predict the clinical benefit of a drug, such as an effect on irreversible morbidity and mortality.

**intragang**    Between members of the same gang.

**intramuscular (IM)**    Drug injection into a muscle.

**intravenous (IV)**    Drug injection into a vein.

**ischemia**    When tissue is deprived of sufficient blood and oxygen.

**isopropyl alcohol**    Rubbing alcohol; sometimes used as an antiseptic.

**IV**    *See* intravenous.

**jimsonweed**    A potent hallucinogenic plant.

**keratin layer**    Outermost protective layer of the skin.

**keratolytics**    Caustic agents that cause the keratin skin layer to peel.

**labeling theory**    Theory emphasizing that other people's perceptions directly influence one's self-image.

**licit drugs**    Legalized drugs such as coffee, alcohol, and tobacco.

**low-risk drug choices**    Developing values and attitudes that lead to controlling the use of alcohol and drugs.

**mainline**    To inject a drug of abuse intravenously.

**MAOI**    *See* monoamine oxidase inhibitor.

**margin of safety**    Range in dose between the amount of drug necessary to cause a therapeutic effect and that needed to create a toxic effect.

**marijuana wax**    Extremely potent cannabis spin-off made by using butane to extract the THC content, producing a "waxy" residue that is smoked or vaporized; has THC levels of approximately 90% and is highly hallucinogenic, often resulting in high levels of physical and mental impairment; also known as *cannabis wax.*

**Marinol**    FDA-approved synthesized THC in capsule form (dronabinol); primarily used to treat nausea and vomiting; often prescribed to people diagnosed with AIDS.

**master status**    Major status position in the eyes of others that clearly identifies an individual—for example, doctor, professor, alcoholic, heroin addict.

**MDMA**    A type of illicit drug known as Ecstasy or Molly that has stimulant and hallucinogenic properties; acronym for *methylenedioxymethamphetamine.*

**mead**    Alcoholic beverage made from fermented honey.

**medical marijuana**    Use of the THC in cannabis as a drug to calm or relieve symptoms of an illness.

**meditation**    State of consciousness in which there is a constant level of awareness focusing on one object—for example, yoga or Zen Buddhism.

**mental set**    The collection of psychological and environmental factors that influence an individual's response to drugs.

**metabolism**    Chemical alteration of drugs by body processes.

**metabolites**    Chemical products of metabolism.

**methyl alcohol**    Wood alcohol.

**Minnesota model**    A major model in the treatment of alcohol and drug abuse that involves a month-long stay in an inpatient rehabilitation facility, a multidisciplinary treatment team, systematic assessment, and a formal treatment plan with long- and short-term goals

**molecular biology**    Study of cellular functions and their regulation.

**Molly**    *See* MDMA.

**monoamine oxidase inhibitor (MAOI)**    Drug used to treat severe depression.

**moral model**    Belief that people abuse alcohol because they choose to do so.

**munchies**    Hunger experienced while under the effects of marijuana.

**muscarinic**    Receptor type activated by acetylcholine (ACh); usually inhibitory.

**muscle dysmorphia**    Behavioral syndrome that causes men to have a distorted image of their bodies, perceiving themselves as looking small and weak, even when they may be large and muscular; women with this condition think they look fat and flabby, even though they may actually be lean and muscular.

**mydriasis**    Pupil dilation.

**narcolepsy**    Condition that causes spontaneous and uncontrolled sleeping episodes.

**National Institute on Drug Abuse (NIDA)**    Principal federal agency responsible for directing research related to drug use and abuse.

**nervous system**    Relating to the brain, spinal cord, neurons, and their associated elements.

**neurons**    Specialized nerve cells that make up the nervous system and release neurotransmitters.

**neurotransmitters**    Chemical messengers released by nervous (nerve) cells for communication with other cells.

**nicotine**    Alkaloid derived from the tobacco plant.

**nicotinic**    Receptor type activated by acetylcholine (ACh); usually excitatory.

**NIDA**    *See* National Institute on Drug Abuse.

**nucleus accumbens**    Part of the CNS limbic system and a critical brain region for reward systems.

**open meetings**    Alcoholics Anonymous meetings to which anyone having an interest in attending and witnessing is invited.

**opiate receptors**    Receptors activated by opioid narcotic drugs such as heroin and morphine.

**opioid**    relating to the drugs that are derived from opium

**opioids**    Drugs derived from opium.

**oral fluids**    Oral fluid testing analyzes saliva samples for the presence of drugs of abuse and their metabolites.

**oral hypoglycemics**    Drugs taken by mouth to treat type 2 diabetes.

**OTC**    *See* over the counter.

**outsiders**    People on the outside; those who do not approve of or do not use drugs.

**outsider's perspective**    Viewing a group or subculture from outside the group and viewing the group and its members as an observer; looking "in" at the members.

**over the counter (OTC)**   Legalized drug sold without a prescription.

**paradoxical effects**   Unexpected effects.

**partial agonist**   A drug that can activate a receptor but is not able to elicit the maximum possible response that is produced by a full agonist.

**patent medicines**   The ingredients in these uncontrolled "medicines" were secret, often consisting of large amounts of colored water, alcohol, cocaine, or opiates.

**peptic ulcers**   Open sores that occur in the stomach or upper segment of the small intestine.

**performance enhancers**   Drugs taken to increase physical or mental endurance to embellish one's performance.

**peripheral nervous system (PNS)**   Includes the neurons outside the CNS.

**person-in-environment model**   *See* ecological model.

**personality disorders**   Broad category of psychiatric disorders, formerly called *character disorders*, that includes the antisocial personality disorder, borderline personality disorder, schizoid personality disorder, and others; these serious, ongoing impairments are difficult to treat.

**personality predisposition model**   *See* **characterological model**.

**pharmacokinetics**   The study of factors that influence the distribution and concentration of drugs in the body.

**phocomelia**   Birth defect; impaired development of the arms, legs, or both.

**placebo effects**   Effects caused by suggestion and psychological factors independent of the pharmacological activity of a drug.

**plateau effect**   Maximum drug effect regardless of dose.

**plateauing**   Developing tolerance to the effects of anabolic steroids.

**PNS**   *See* peripheral nervous system.

**polydrug use**   Concurrent use of multiple drugs.

**posttraumatic stress disorder (PTSD)**   A psychiatric syndrome in which an individual who has been exposed to a traumatic event or situation experiences persistent psychological stress that may manifest itself in a wide range of symptoms, including reexperiencing the trauma, numbing of general responsiveness, and hyperarousal.

**potency**   Amount of drug necessary to cause an effect.

**preoccupation phase**   Constant concern with the supply of the drug.

**precursor chemicals**   Chemicals used to produce a drug.

**primary deviance**   Any type of initial deviant behavior in which the perpetrator does not identify with the deviance.

**primary drug-prevention programs**   Drug-prevention programs with a broad range of activities aimed at reducing the risk of drug use among nonusers and ensuring continued nonuse and helping at-risk individuals avoid the development of addictive behaviors.

**primary prevention**   Preventing the use of any drug (total abstinence).

**prohibitionist philosophy**   Reducing or stopping unwanted drug use by legally banning and punishing drug use.

**proprietary**   Brand or trademark name that is registered with the U.S. Patent Office.

**proprietary medicine**   Pharmaceutical medicine that is protected from commercial competition because the ingredients or manufacturing method is kept secret or because it is protected by trademark or copyright.

**protease inhibitors**   Major breakthrough class of drugs used to treat HIV-infected individuals.

**protective factors**   Factors associated with preventing the potential for drug abuse such as self-control, parental support and parental supervision, academic competence, antidrug-use policies, and strong neighborhood attachment.

**pseudointoxicated**   Acting drunk even before alcohol has had a chance to cause its effects.

**psychedelics**   Substances that expand or heighten perception and consciousness.

**psychoactive drugs**   Drug compounds (substances) that affect the central nervous system and alter consciousness or perceptions.

**psychoactive effects**   How drug substances alter and affect the brain's mental functions.

**psychoanalysis**   Theory of personality and method of psychotherapy originated by Sigmund Freud and focused on unconscious forces and conflicts and a series of psychosexual stages.

**psychodrama**   Family therapy system developed by Jacques Moreno in which significant interpersonal and intrapersonal issues are enacted in a focused setting using dramatic techniques.

**psychological dependence**   Dependence that results because a drug produces pleasant mental effects.

**psychotherapeutic drugs**   Drugs that are used to treat mental disorders such as depression, schizophrenia, and manic–depressive disorders.

**psychotogenics**   Substances that initiate psychotic behavior.

**psychotomimetics**   Substances that cause psychosis-like symptoms.

**PTSD**   *See* posttraumatic stress disorder.

**pyramiding**   Slowly increasing the dose or frequency of steroid abuse, reaching a peak amount, and then gradually tapering off.

**rebound effect**   Form of withdrawal; paradoxical effects that occur when a drug has been eliminated from the body.

**receptors**   Special proteins in a membrane that are activated by natural substances or drugs to alter cell function.

**relapsing syndrome**   Returning to the use of alcohol after quitting.

**relief phase**    Satisfaction derived from escaping negative feelings by using a drug.

**REM sleep**    Restive phase of sleep associated with dreaming; REM stands for *rapid eye movement*.

**retrospective interpretation**    Social psychological process of redefining a person in light of a major status position— for example, homosexual, physician, professor, alcoholic, convicted felon, or mental patient.

**reverse tolerance**    Enhanced response to a given drug dose; opposite of tolerance.

**risk factors**    Factors associated with increased risk of drug use such as early aggressive behavior, lack of parental supervision, the lure of gang membership, drug availability, and poverty.

**Rohypnol**    So-called date-rape drug that is used by some people to commit sexual assault; the three most common date rape drugs are Rohypnol (flunitrazepam), GHB (gamma-hydroxybutyrate), and ketamine.

**role-playing**    Therapeutic technique in which group members play assigned parts to elicit emotional reactions.

**run**    Intense use of a stimulant, consisting of multiple administrations over a period of days.

**rush**    Initial pleasure after amphetamine use that includes racing heartbeat and elevated blood pressure.

**SC**    *See* subcutaneous.

**scare tactic approach**    Drug-prevention information based on emphasizing the extreme negative effects of drug use—scaring the audience of potential and current drug users and abusers into not using drugs; also known as the *fear-based approach*.

**secondary deviance**    Any type of deviant behavior in which the perpetrator identifies with the deviance.

**secondary drug-prevention programs**    Programs that consist of uncovering potentially harmful substance use before the onset of overt symptoms or problems or targeting newer drug users with a limited history of use; the main goal is to target at-risk groups, experimenters, and early-abuse populations.

**secondary prevention**    Preventing casual or recreational drug use from advancing to drug dependence.

**secondhand smoke**    Smoke released into the air from a lighted cigarette, cigar, or pipe tip and exhaled mainstream smoke.

**sedatives**    CNS depressants used to relieve anxiety, fear, and apprehension.

**self-medication**    Method of self-care in which an individual uses nonprescribed drugs to treat untreated and often undiagnosed medical ailments involving his or her psychological condition; self-prescribed drugs can include recreational drugs, psychoactive drugs, alcohol, and herbal products used to alleviate or diminish mental distress, stress and anxiety, mental illnesses, or psychological trauma.

**sensation-seeking individuals**    Types of people who characteristically are continually seeking new or novel thrills in their experiences.

**set and setting**    *Set* refers to the individual's expectation of what a drug will do to his or her personality; *setting* is the physical and social environments where the drug is consumed.

**side effects**    Unintended drug responses.

**sinsemilla**    Meaning "without seeds," this marijuana is made from the buds and flowering tops of female plants and is one of the most potent types.

**snuff**    Finely ground smokeless tobacco that can be moist or dry.

**snuff dipping**    Placing a pinch of tobacco between the gums and the cheek.

**social-ecological model**    Variant of the ecological or person-in-environment model that takes into account multiple factors regarding drug use and abuse and focuses on the complex interplay among individuals, relationships, communities, and societal factors.

**social influence theories**    Sociological theories that view a person's day-to-day social relations as a primary cause for drug use.

**social influences model**    Assumes that drug users lack resistance skills.

**social learning theory**    Theory that emphasizes how an individual learns patterns of behavior from the attitudes of others, society, and peers.

**social lubricant**    Belief that drinking (misconceived as safe) represses inhibitions, strengthens extroversion, and leads to increased sociability.

**socialization**    Growth and development process responsible for learning how to become a responsible, functioning human being.

**sociobiological changes**    Belief that biological forces (largely genes) have a direct influence on the root causes of social psychological behavior.

**speakeasies**    Small, often backroom bars where alcoholic beverages were illegally consumed and sold during the Prohibition era from 1920 to 1933 (in some states, Prohibition was longer than this period of time).

**speed**    Injectable methamphetamine used by drug addicts.

**speedballing**    Combining heroin and cocaine.

**speedballs**    Combinations of amphetamine or cocaine with an opioid narcotic, often heroin.

**SPF**    *See* sun protection factor number.

**spermatogenesis**    Biological development involving the production of mature sperm cells that occurs in the male gonad of a sexually reproducing organism (Biology Online, 2020).

**stacking**    Combining two or more different types of steroids.

**steroids**    Hormones related to the corticosteroids released from the adrenal cortex.

**structural analogs**    New molecular species created by modifying the basic molecular skeleton of a compound; structural analogs are structurally related to their parent compounds.

**structural influence theories**    Theories that view the structural organization of a society, peer group, or subculture as directly responsible for drug use.

**subculture** Subgroup within the population whose members share similar values and patterns of related behaviors that differ from other subcultures and the larger population.

**subculture theory** Explains drug use as a peer-generated activity.

**subcutaneous (SC)** Drug injection beneath the skin.

**subjective euphoric effects** Ongoing social and psychological experiences incurred while intoxicated with marijuana.

**substance-induced disorders** Type of substance-related disorder that involves problems caused by the direct effects of a substance such as intoxication, withdrawal, and other substance- or medication-induced mental disorders; also known as *addictive disorders*.

**substance-use disorder (SUD)** From the American Psychiatric Association's *Diagnostic and Statistical Manual of Mental Disorders*, fifth edition (DSM-5; 2013); term used by clinicians and psychiatrists for diagnosing mental disorders combining substance abuse and substance dependence into a single condition.

**sun protection factor (SPF) number** Designation that indicates a product's ability to screen ultraviolet rays.

**supply reduction** Drug-reduction policy aimed at reducing the supply of illegal drugs and controlling other therapeutic drugs.

**surrogate endpoint** Physical sign, laboratory measurement, radiographic image, or other measure that is expected to predict clinical benefit but is not itself a measure of clinical benefit.

**sweat (perspiration)** Used for drug testing; a skin patch absorb sweats for analysis for the presence of cocaine, marijuana, opiates, amphetamine, methamphetamine, or PCP.

**switching policy** FDA policy allowing the change of suitable prescription drugs to over-the-counter status.

**sympathomimetic** Agents that mimic the effects of norepinephrine or epinephrine.

**synapse** Site of communication between a message-sending neuron and its message-receiving target cell.

**synaptic cleft** Minute gap between the neuron and target cell, across which neurotransmitters travel.

**synergism** Ability of one drug to enhance the effect of another; also called *potentiation*.

**synesthesia** A subjective sensation or image of a sense other than the one being stimulated, such as an auditory sensation caused by a visual stimulus.

**synthetic drugs or synthetic opioids** *See* designer drugs.

**synthetic marijuana** Human-made mind-altering chemicals that are either sprayed on dried, shredded plant material so they can be smoked (herbal incense) or sold as liquids to be vaporized and inhaled in e-cigarettes and other devices (liquid incense); also known as *fake weed*.

**TC** *See* therapeutic community.

**teetotalers** Individuals who drink no alcoholic beverages whatsoever; a term in common usage in decades past; today, teetotalers are referred to as *abstainers*.

**teratogenic** Something that causes physical defects in a fetus.

**tertiary drug-prevention programs** Drug-prevention programs focusing on intervention and targeting chemically dependent individuals who need treatment; tertiary prevention involves treating the medical consequences of drug abuse and facilitating entry into treatment so further disability is minimized (basically the same as drug abuse treatment).

**tetrahydrocannabinol** Marijuana's main psychoactive ingredient.

**thalidomide** Sedative drug that, when used during pregnancy, can cause severe developmental damage to a fetus.

**The Onion Router** *See* Tor network.

**therapeutic community (TC)** Inpatient treatment that focuses on the "resocialization" of the individual and uses the program's entire community as important treatment components.

**threshold dose** Minimum drug dose necessary to cause an effect.

**tobacco chewing** Absorption of nicotine through the mucous lining of the mouth.

**tolerance** Changes in the body that decrease response to a drug even though the dose remains the same.

**Tor network** Browser used to access an online network that disguises the user's identity by moving the user's traffic across different Tor servers and encrypting the traffic so that it cannot be traced back to the user's location; also known as the Onion Router (Tor).

**toxicity** Capacity of one drug to damage or cause adverse effects in the body.

**tricyclic antidepressants** Most commonly used group of drugs to treat severe depression.

**tweaking** Repeated administration of methamphetamine to maintain a high.

**type 1 diabetes** Disease associated with complete loss of insulin-producing cells in the pancreas.

**type 2 diabetes** Disease usually associated with obesity; does not involve a loss of insulin-producing cells.

**uppers** CNS stimulants.

**vaping** The act of inhaling and exhaling drug-containing aerosol or vapor from tobacco or some forms of marijuana using electric devices such as electronic cigarettes (e-cigarettes).

**volatile** Readily evaporated at low temperatures.

**WADA** *See* World Anti-Doping Agency.

**Wernicke-Korsakoff's syndrome** Psychotic condition connected with heavy alcohol use and associated vitamin deficiencies.

**wet cultures** Cultures in which alcohol is integrated into daily life and activities (e.g., is consumed with meals) and is widely available and accessible (e.g., European countries bordering the Mediterranean have traditionally exemplified wet cultures).

**withdrawal** Unpleasant effects that occur when use of a drug is stopped.

**withdrawal phase**  Physical or psychological effects derived from not using a drug.

**withdrawal symptoms**  Psychological and physical symptoms that result when a drug is absent from the body; physical symptoms are generally present in cases of drug dependence to more addictive drugs such as heroin; physical and psychological symptoms of withdrawal include perspiration, nausea, boredom, anxiety, and muscle spasms.

**World Anti-Doping Agency (WADA)**  Organization lead a collaborative worldwide movement for doping-free sport.

**World Anti-Doping Code**  Core document providing a framework for harmonized antidoping policies, rules, and regulations within sport organizations and among public authorities.

**xanthines**  Family of drugs that includes caffeine.

# Index

Page numbers followed by *f* or *t* indicate material in figures or tables, respectively.